COMPACT

Classics®

YOUR PERSONAL PORTABLE LIBRARY

D0191795

VOLUME II

Compact Classics, Inc.
1993

COMPACT

Classics®

First Printing, October 1993
Second Printing, December 1993
Third Printing, August 1994

Lan C. England, Publisher
Stevens W. Anderson, Editor

Compact Classics, Inc.
P.O. Box 526145
Salt Lake City, Utah
84152-6145

ISBN 1-880184-11-7

Printed in the United States of America

COMPACT

Classics®

VOLUME II

■ **INTRODUCTION**: *Compact Classics II*

Here we go again. Volume II of *Compact Classics* places even more summarized classics at your fingertips. Concise, distilled, pure. Just like the first volume, Volume II is a must addition to any library. Available in its original seven-ring binder format, where pages can be removed and clipped into a 6 x 9 planning book for easy reading, anywhere, anytime. *Compact Classics* makes a perfect gift for that person who has, well, everything except the most complete compilation of important reading ever collected.

Volume II explores even broader horizons, ranging from philosophy and religion to more noteworthy quotes. It also includes an expanded section on great literature, the nucleus of good reading. You'll find children's and adolescent classics, more great business books, contemporary literature, poetry and drama. And, back by popular demand, even more *Trivia to Learn By*. In just minutes, you can be conversant on hundreds of subjects.

Invest in Yourself. Read even more *Classics*.

■ **INVITATION**: We still want to hear from you. **(See back page)**

Since *Compact Classics* is read by people around the world, our best suggestions for future inclusions come from *you*, the reader. If you have run across a particularly significant book, let us know about it. If we use your original suggestion in a future volume, we'll pay you for it. In the event that several people suggest the same title, we'll pay the first person who sent it in. So don't delay.

Compact Classics makes a wonderful gift for friends, family members, customers...for anyone! To order, call toll-free **1 800-755-9777**.

▬▬ INDEX: A Table of Contents

▬▬▬▬▬ LIBRARY #1: Drama Through the Ages ▬▬▬ 1

LIBRARY #3: Poets & Poetry   **233**

COMPACT

Classics®

LIBRARY #1: Drama Through The Ages

As you read the selections in this library, representing dominant epochs and genres in drama ranging from early Greek tragedy through the stark 20th-century surrealism of Ionesco, keep in mind the different cultures that have shaped and spawned them. You will come to appreciate even more keenly how different conditions of time and place inspire deeply divergent dramatic voices—and you may come to realize that there is no real difference at all; that the great heroine Antigone, forced to choose between the demands of society and her private loyalties, faces the same crucial dilemma as the very contemporary psychiatrist in "Equus"; and that perhaps the secret of all great drama through the ages lies in its ability both to reflect intricately and ultimately transcend the society that produces it. "The more the world changes, the more it stays the same."

THE ORESTEIA: AGAMEMNON

by
Aeschylus
(525-456 B.C.)

Type of work: Lyric Greek tragedy

Setting: Argos, Greek city in the north-east Peloponese; the Autumn of 1250 B.C.

Principal characters:

Agamemnon, King of Argos and victor of the Trojan War

Clytemnestra, Agamemnon's wife, Queen of Argos, and sister to Helen of Troy

Orestes, their son

Cassandra, daughter of Priam (the defeated King of Troy), priestess of Apollo, and captured mistress of Agamemnon

Aegisthus, cousin to Agamemnon and—in her husband's absence—Clytemnestra's lover

The Chorus, a group of elders who had remained in Argos, too old to fight in the Trojan War

Play Overview:

The Trojan War at last entered its tenth year, the year in which prophets had foretold that Troy would fall to Agamemnon and his Greek legion.

In the Greek city of Argos, Queen Clytemnestra had posted a watchman to look for the beacon-fire that would herald the long-awaited victory. Night after night, the watchman had perched on the palace rooftop, studying the drift of stars and brooding on the troubled fortunes of the House of Atreus. Among all the royal families of Greece, the House of Atreus had suffered the most. From its very beginnings, the family had lived under a curse which had moved generations of its descendants to commit unspeakable acts of savagery and violence.

Agamemnon's father, Atreus, seeking retribution on his brother Thyestes for having seduced his wife, had tricked him into attending a banquet feast featuring the flesh of Thyestes' own children. And even Iphigenia, Agamemnon's young daughter, had been sacrificed at the altar by her father as an oblation to obtain favorable sailing winds to Troy.

Now, these many years later, Clytemnestra remained bent on revenge against her husband for the death of her daughter. First, she had banished their only son, Orestes, forbidding him ever to return to Argos. She also took as her lover and co-conspirator Agamemnon's cousin Aegisthus, who, as the surviving son of Thyestes, had his own motives for revenge against Agamemnon.

One night just before dawn, the watchman at Argos saw the anticipated beacon-fire light the sky. He excitedly called from his post for Clytemnestra to "rise with instant shout and sing." Awakened, Clytemnestra did not sing.

In the streets of Argos a chorus of the city's old men, not yet having heard the news, were gathered near the palace to sing a lament for the ten years of death and destruction initiated by Helen's abduction. They also sang of Iphigenia's bloody sacrifice and of Clytemnestra's desire to avenge her daughter's death.

As the men sang, they caught sight of Clytemnestra outside the palace. Accompanied by her servants, she lighted altar fires and burned incense. Finally, one of the ancient men turned to Clytemnestra and asked, "Is it good and certain news you have, or is it only wished-for thinking with your sacrifice?"

Clytemnestra then related the blessed tidings; the beacon had signaled Argos' victory over Troy. To the old men, of course, she did not reveal that the beacon was also her sign to prepare to exact her revenge on their returning King.

At last a messenger appeared at the palace gates to announce that Agamemnon had just laid anchor in Argos. The news gladdened the chorus; but their melody was also filled with foreboding. Once again, their song took up the uneasy themes of Troy's destruction and the unending cycle of jealousy, savagery and violence passed down from generation to generation in the House of Atreus.

Agamemnon finally arrived in the city. Attired in his royal splendor, he drove his chariot to the palace gates. Behind him came a procession of wagons loaded with Trojan treasure, including his captive Trojan mistress, the princess Cassandra, the most prized treasure of all. "Welcome! I say on work well done," exclaimed one of the old men. For a moment, Agamemnon considered the group of ancients from his chariot, but failed to see the chorus' pleasure at his return was mixed with apprehension. When they hinted at the corruption that lay in wait for him within the palace, Agamemnon chose to focus instead on his own glory, on the "fat reek of wealth" and victory he had brought home.

Then Clytemnestra appeared at the palace gates to greet her husband. Concealing her treachery beneath a smile, she stroked Agamemnon's vanity by complaining how lonely and frightened she had been during her husband's long leave. Then hoping that Agamemnon would not see something amiss by Orestes' absence, the Queen quickly explained that their son's departure from Argos was to avoid possible danger caused by unrest among the people. Then she sought to coax her husband down from his chariot and into the sumptuous banquet that awaited him in the palace:

> And now, my lord, dear head, come down.
> Step from your car;
> But not upon our common earth:
> Not the foot, my king, that trod down Troy.

At first, Agamemnon was reluctant to step down upon the purple carpet Clytemnestra's servants had spread. Such a ritual welcome was reserved for the gods; to accept the honor would be sacrilege. Consumed, however, by his own ego—and his mind turned to "his choice flower," Cassandra, who still awaited his bidding in the chariot—he finally stepped down.

As Agamemnon, after embracing the ceremonial welcome, entered the palace, Clytemnestra followed closely behind, silently invoking Zeus' help in enacting her vengeance. However, her prayer was interrupted by the thought of Cassandra. Returning to the chariot, she addressed her rival. "Down from the car," Clytemnestra demanded. Then, with a threatening note in her voice, she warned, "From you I can expect only what is proper." Finally, losing patience with the proud and uncooperative mistress, Clytemnestra swept back into the palace.

Still standing silently in the wagon, Cassandra, a priestess of Apollo cursed with the gift of prophecy, understood all too well what she could expect from Clytemnestra. The chorus, pitying the beautiful mistress—who they likened to a "freshly captured animal"—tried to console her; with a song of compassion they gently tried to persuade Cassandra to come down from the chariot. And, as the hymn sprang from their lips, she began to speak as if in a trance. First she foretold that she would be sacrificed, then turned her attention to the horrible past of the House of Atreus:

Full of family butcheries:
Dangling with horrors;
Human slaughterhouse . . .

"I shall go, and do, and dare to die," she then pronounced, and then stepped down from the chariot.

The old men marvelled. By now they, too, perceived her impending fate, and watched in awe as she made her way to the palace gates. "How do you step with courage to the altar's stone?" they asked. Then, before entering, Cassandra turned to the elders and made a final appeal:

One more, one word—but not my dirge.
In the sun's last light I ask the sun:
"Let my slayers pay the price of me in blood—
A dying slave, poor easy prey."

As the palace gates closed behind the young prophetess, the chorus took up a lament—but they were interrupted a few moments later by the sound of a blood-chilling scream. "O-o! I am hit . . . mortally hit . . . within." One last wail sounded from the palace doors—and the old men recognized the voice of their King. Before they had time to act, however, the palace gates swung open. There, over the bloody corpses of Agamemnon and Cassandra, stood Clytemnestra, her hands and robes dripping with gore:

. . . I struck him twice,
And with a double groan
His limbs went loose, he fell.
I was on him with a third—"thanksgiving"—
stroke:
To Zeus of the world below, the keeper of the dead.
So he went down,
Life pumping out of him
With gurgling murderous spurts of blood
Which hit me with a black-ensanguined drizzle.
Oh it freshened me like drops from heaven . . . .

Suddenly, Aegisthus, who until then had kept himself hidden, strutted into view. "O sweet day of justice ushered in!" he cried, proclaiming

that his father, whom Agamemnon's father had served "the meat of [Thyestes'] own children," was finally avenged.

The gore and Aegisthus' gloating stunned the ancient ones. He would suffer "a rain of stones and curses from the people," they warned in verse. Aegisthus, though, would have none of it, and was about to order his guards to kill the elders, when Clytemnestra, her lust for revenge at last satiated, stepped between them. "Let us work no further evil," she coolly advised.

Aegisthus, momentarily calmed by Clytemnestra's words, promised the old men that their insolence would result very soon in a visit "full of vengeance." Unfazed by these threats, the chorus replied, "Not if fortune guides Orestes here and brings him home at last."

Their revenge on Agamemnon completed, Clytemnestra and Aegisthus began their reign in Argos—a reign darkened from the first, however, by the prophecy of Orestes' return.

Commentary:

Agamemnon, originally composed by Aeschylus (ES-chuh-luhs) as part of a tetralogy—the *Oresteia*—or cycle of four plays, and first performed for a competition in 458 B.C. at the festival of Dionysus, where it was awarded first prize. Only three of these plays—all of them tragedies—are still in existence: *Agamemnon, The Libation Bearers*, and *The Eumenides*. The fourth play, a comedy entitled *Proteus*, was lost. Presumably, it would have relieved the dramatic tension accumulated in the tragedies.

Agamemnon is, chronologically, the first of the plays. The theme of retribution, which the play enacts both in political and personal dimensions, is not simply a matter of right and wrong. Indeed, none of the principal characters acts solely from choice. Agamemnon's ten-year campaign against Troy, for instance, is waged not only to avenge Helen's abduction, but (on the larger stage where the gods act out their pleasures) to satisfy Zeus' desire to punish the House of Priam. In this sense, Agamemnon is merely an instrument through which Zeus and Athena play out their passions. The same may also be said of Clytemnestra and the murderous revenge she takes on her husband.

The *Oresteia*—named for Orestes, the banished son whose return is darkly prophesied at the end of *Agamemnon*—is considered the greatest lyric tragedy of all time. As the critic W.B. Stanford said, the golden age of Greece produced two enduring monuments: the Parthenon and the *Oresteia*. Enthusiasts have called the plays no less than a parable of human progress, a map of our psyche in its difficult passage from spiritual darkness to truth and light, from guilt to acceptance, from barbarism to civilization.

A key question introduced in "Agamemnon," then, is where will the cycle of darkness and vengeance lead? And, perhaps more importantly, how can this destruction be put to an end? This latter question, which touches on the very nature and significance of retribution and guilt, is elaborated and finally resolved as the other plays unfold.

ANTIGONE

by Sophocles
(c.496 - 406 B.C.)
translation by Paul Roche

Type of work: Poetic Greek tragedy

Setting: Thebes, a city of ancient Greece

Principal characters:

Antigone, daughter of Oedipus and sister of the dead Polyneices and Eteocles

Ismene, Antigone's sister

Creon, inexperienced, proud, and tyrannical king of Thebes

Haemon, son of Creon—and the betrothed of Antigone

Tiresias, a blind prophet

The Chorus, citizens of Thebes

Play Overview:

"What more, do you think, could Zeus require of us to load the curse that's on the House of Oedipus?" Antigone asks of her sister Ismene as the play opens. Those acquainted with the mythological history of The House of Oedipus would be hard-pressed to answer the daughter's question, for few family sagas have been as steeped in tragic events as theirs. For Oedipus and his offspring, misfortune seemed to be hereditary. As Ismene reminds Antigone:

Remember how our father died: hated, in disgrace, wrapped in horror of himself, his own hand stabbing out his sight. And how his mother-wife in one twisted off her earthly days with a cord. And thirdly how our two brothers in a single day each achieved for each a suicidal nemesis.

Among the family's tragedies, it was this last event which was now to lead to further tribulation for the surviving sisters.

Prior to the opening of this play, Oedipus' death had led his two sons, Polyneices and Eteocles, to battle for their father's Theban throne. Polyneices had joined forces with a neighboring city-state, Argos, to attack his native city of Thebes, leaving Eteocles and their uncle Creon—the regent since Oedipus' self-banishment—to defend the city. The brothers finally met in combat and slew one another. The Argive army then retreated in defeat, and victorious Thebes was left with Creon as its undisputed king.

Creon, exercising his newly acquired power, had proclaimed that his nephew Eteocles, who had died defending Thebes, would receive a heroic burial. Polyneices, however, who had died in an offensive against his own native city, would receive no burial at all; his body would be left to rot on the battlefield—the most ignominious end for any Greek. To ensure that this mandate be honored, Creon made it a crime against the state—punishable by death—to violate the edict by burying or in any other way honoring the corpse.

Yet, in prohibiting Polyneices' burial, Creon himself had transgressed a higher, more sacred law: in ancient Greece a corpse had to receive certain funeral rites in order to pass into Hades.

After hearing the news, Antigone led her sister Ismene beyond the city gates and informed her of Creon's decree—as well as of her grief stricken and angry intentions to defy it. Ismene pled with her sister to reconsider, or at least to maintain secrecy, but Antigone would not be swayed. She would not allow such a mandate to stand; she was determined to mourn her fallen brother as commanded by the gods. Polyneices' body must be buried in honor, and she would do the deed, fearing neither discovery nor punishment.

As the sisters turned for home, the Theban Chorus began its victory celebration: Now let us chase the memory far away of the wars that are past. Come call on the gods with song and dance all through the night.

Soon, however, a vexed Creon arrived on the scene to justify his harsh decree, saying, "you'll not catch me putting traitors up on a pedestal beside the loyal man. I'll honor him alone, alive or dead, who honors Thebes." No sooner had Creon spoken, however, than a sentry appeared to inform the king that someone—unknown and undetected by the guards posted near the body of Polyneices—had performed funeral rites upon the body—leaving it "not buried, [but] lightly veiled with ritual dust." Commanded, upon pain of death, to expose the perpetrator, the sentry soon returned—leading Antigone, who had defiantly gone back to the corpse to complete her lamentations.

"Guilty. I deny nothing," Antigone answered unflinchingly when questioned by Creon. " . . . So you chose flagrantly to disobey my law?" Creon asked. "Naturally!" replied Antigone, " . . . since Zeus never promulgated such a law. Nor will you find that Justice publishes such laws to man below. I never thought your edicts had such force they nullified the laws of heaven . . . " Antigone's refusal to repent of any wrong-doing angered Creon even more than her open disregard for his decree: "This girl, already versed in disrespect when she first disobeyed my law, now adds a second insult—vaunts it to my face." Even though Antigone was betrothed to his own son, Haemon, the King imperiously command that she must die. Disobedience—bad enough when practiced by a man—was, in this case, most intolerable to Creon, who certainly would not be "worsted by a woman."

Haemon then approached the King. Driven both by love for Antigone and the realization of his father's error, Haemon pled for leniency. He reminded Creon that the sympathy of the city was swelling towards Antigone. "Because no woman ever faced so unreasonable, so cruel a death for such a generous act . . .

`should not her name be writ in gold?' they say." But Creon remained firm; he would not give in to the clamor of the populace, nor to his son's brash defiance with the woman. The administration of punishment was a sovereign's right. To this Haemon replied, "What rights—when you trample on the rights of God?" Creon was outraged. "You shall not marry her alive!" he declared. The impassioned son rushed from the scene, leaving the father "raving" to his "chosen friends"—those who would never dare to contradict the King.

Meanwhile, Antigone was led to face her sentence—entombment, alive, in a "rock-hewn vault, with ritual food enough to clear the taint of murder from the City's name." As she was led to the tomb, Antigone retained her courage— even when Creon entered and demanded that her interment proceed without further delay:

> Seal up the tomb.
> Let her choose a death at leisure, or
> Perhaps an underground life forlorn.
> We wash our hands of this girl
> Except to take her from the light.

After Antigone was led away, the blind prophet Tiresias arrived with dire news that Creon's imperious edicts were wreaking havoc on the city: dogs and crows were now profaning the Thebes' alters with "carrion from the poor unburied son of Oedipus," voiding the prayers of the inhabitants. The prophet urged Creon to alter his edict, to remedy his blunders before it proved too late:

> To err is human, true,
> And only he is cursed who having sinned
> Will not repent, will not repair . . .

Then Tiresias chided his king that "where neither you nor gods above must meddle you have thrust your thumbs," and prophesied that "furies lie in wait for you, ready with the punishments you have engineered for others."

Even though Tiresias' past prophecies had always proven true and "never stirred the city to false alarm," Creon haughtily dismissed the trusted old counselor:

> Not even if Zeus's eagles come to fly away
> With carrion morsels to their master's throne
> Even such a threat of taint will not win his
> body burial.

But after the seer had departed, Creon reconsidered. It would be difficult for him to loosen his stance, he admitted, but "harder still to risk catastrophe through stubborn pride":

> How it goes against the grain
> To smother all one's heart's desire!
> I cannot fight with destiny.

Finally concluding that he had already lost his fight with destiny, Creon set off to undo his deeds—but too late. He had held onto his pride till the last; slow to smother his heart's desire, now Creon's heart was about to be smothered in grief.

After at last performing the burial rites for the remains of Polyneices, Creon hurried to the vault where Antigone had been entombed. There, inside the walled-up sepulcher, he found his son holding Antigone's lifeless body as it hung from a linen noose around her neck.

Crying and cursing his father, Haemon, sword in hand, lunged as if to impale Creon. But instead of striking his father, Haemon spat on him. Then he fell on his own sword, driving its blade clear through his body. The King's son, with Antigone's limp figure wrapped in his arms, then sank into death, " . . . corpse upon corpse . . ."

In the palace, meanwhile, Creon's wife, Eurydice, upon hearing the news of Haemon's death, had also taken her own life, cursing Creon in her last breath: "There at the altar, self-stabbed with a keen knife [she] invoked evil fortunes . . . upon the slayer of her son."

Alas, the tragic cycle of events which Creon's relentless pride had put into motion had come full circle. The King could now feel the reverence and bitter sadness Antigone had felt for her brother. Before being led out of the city to a self-imposed exile, Creon slumped in agony. The dead to be mourned were now his own . . . the rites of burial now his to perform.

Commentary:

Tragic drama originated in ancient Greece, and Sophocles was one of its most significant contributors. Chronologically, *Antigone* is the third work in "The Theban Trilogy," or "Oedipus Plays." While *Oedipus* may be considered the epitome of Greek tragic drama, *Antigone*, though smaller in scale, remains one of Sophocles' most revered and accessible works.

Ironically, it is Creon, not Antigone, who is the true protagonist in this play. It is he who propels the action along; it is he who holds power within his grasp; and it is he who possesses the "tragic flaw"—the three essential elements of the classic Greek "hero." Additionally, because Antigone's death is incongruous with the typical tragic ending—a tragic heroine rarely would be spared a lonely and ignominious destiny through suicide—she can better be seen as the principal external force leading to Creon's downfall.

Creon's tragic flaw—not unlike that of many contemporary leaders—is, of course, pride. While his reasons for not burying the fallen Polyneices at first may seem justifiable, in the end it is only arrogance that prevents him from carrying out the burial rites—and saving Antigone.

The extent to which pride governs Creon can finally be seen in his disregard of divine and natural law. The immortals of ancient Greece were notorious for their exacting revenge when offended. Only a foolishly smug and inexperienced mortal—like Creon—would dare risk provoking their wrath.

Such pride, the Chorus in "Antigone" concludes, does not go unpunished:

> Where wisdom is, there happiness will crown
> A piety that nothing will corrode.
> But high and mighty words and ways
> Are flogged to humbleness, till age,
> Beaten to its knees, at last is wise.

CYCLOPS

by
Euripides
(c. 479-406 B.C.)

Type of work: Satyr-play

Setting: Sicilian coast, c. 1100-1200 B.C.

Principal characters:

Cyclops, a huge one-eyed monster named Polyphemus

Silenus, a bald old man, enslaved by the Cyclops

Bacchus, the god of wine (also known as Dionysus)

Chorus of satyrs, attendants of Bacchus, who have some physical attributes of horses and goats

Odysseus, the mythical hero-king who fought at Troy

Play Overview:

In front of a cave near Mt. Etna, an elderly man named Silenus appeared dressed in a "filthy tunic." He carried with him the rake he used "to scour the cave" of the beastly Cyclops, who had enslaved Silenus and his companions the satyrs, taking them captive after their ship veered too close to shore. Now it fell upon poor Silenus to tend his new master's flock of sheep, clean his quarters, and prepare the "loathsome dinners" of the monstrous son of Poseidon.

How Silenus wished to serve Bacchus again instead of the "godless Cyclops"! In reality, though, the free-spirited Bacchus had played an unwitting hand in Silenus' awful fate: the great goddess Hera had planned to sell Bacchus, god of revelry and wine, to certain Lydian pirates who wanted him for their slave. Hearing of this, the faithful Silenus and crew of satyrs had set sail to warn their master. Ill-fatedly, the one-eyed, man-eating Cyclops had snatched them off their storm-tossed ship.

"No Bacchus here," one of the festivity-starved satyrs exclaimed, returning with the Cyclops' flock. Accompanied by his brother wood-land deities, he moved quickly as he herded the headstrong animals. Surveying the horizon, Silenus spotted something remarkable: "a Greek ship drawn up on the shore," and approaching the cave, the ship's crew, led by the famed Odysseus.

"We must have come to the city of Bacchus," said the captain to his seamen as he drew close enough to recognize the half-human, pointy-eared satyrs. "I am Odysseus of Ithaca," he greeted Silenus, "King of the Cephallenians." Silenus, assuming his usual fondness for merriment, mocked the hero. "I've heard of you. A glib sharper, Sisyphus's bastard." The mighty Odysseus retorted, "I am he. Keep your abuse to yourself." Then he explained that he had been returning from the Trojan War when his ship had been blown off course by "wind and storm." Where, he asked Silenus, had he landed? "No man inhabits here," old Silenus sighed in reply. A "Shepherd Cyclops" governed the island, a one-eyed beast who liked to "feast on human flesh."

At the mention of feasting, Odysseus, utterly famished after his ordeal at sea, ignored the intended warning and asked if the satyrs could get him something to eat in return for wine. The offer of wine delighted Silenus and his satyrs. He quickly ran into the cave to find Odysseus and his crew some food, returning loaded with wicker baskets of cheese and mutton. However, before he would give the provisions to Odysseus, he asked to test the wine-flask by taking a swig to seal their bargain.

But the thirsty Silenus was thwarted from drinking even a drop of his wine, which would have initiated a night of riotous celebration. At that moment, the Cyclops, wielding a monumental club, came into view. "Where can we run?" Odysseus asked. When Silenus instructed him to go into the cave, Odysseus bellowed, "Are you mad? Right into the trap?" Despite Silenus' assurances that there were safe "hiding-places" inside, Odysseus crowed, "Never!"; having withstood ten thousand Phrygians at Troy, rather than cower behind a rock, he would either die honorably or live gloriously.

Untroubled by such lofty ideals, Silenus and the satyrs scrambled into hiding. In terrible majesty, the Cyclops thundered with a gale-force voice, "Here. Here. What's going on? What's this uproar? Why this Bacchic hubbub? There's no Bacchus here, no bronze clackers or rattling castanets!"

Spotting the Greeks, the incredulous Cyclops roared, "Have pirates or thieves taken the country?" His face now pleasantly flushed with wine, Silenus crept out of the cave to speak to his master. This band of strangers had beaten him, he lied, because he would not let them "rob" the Cyclops. Hearing this, Odysseus also came out of hiding. "O noble son of the sea-god," he begged, "[don't] murder men who come to your cave as friends. . . . Shipwrecked men," he continued, were customarily "clothed and protected" by their hosts. Besides, Odysseus and his crew were valiant warriors who had "preserved" the temples of Cyclops's father, Poseidon. In typical sharp manner, Silenus interrupted Odysseus' grandiose speech: "A word of advice, Cyclops. If you eat all of his flesh and chew on his tongue, you'll become eloquent and very glib."

"I don't give a damn for my father's shrines," the Cyclops barked. "Why did you think I would?" Nor did the mighty and self-serving Cyclops fear "Zeus's thunder" or offer sacrifices to the gods. Why should he? He served "the greatest god of all": his own belly. He had no patience with "little laws—damn the lot of them!" He would "go right on indulging himself." And just now, as he marched his tasty morsel captives into his cave, he wanted to indulge himself by eating Odysseus.

A short while later, Odysseus escaped and stumbled back outside. "Zeus, how can I say what I saw in that cave?" he cried. Indeed, he had witnessed "unbelievable horrors." Cyclops had put "a cauldron of brass" over the fire; next, "this damned cook of Hades" had "slit the throat" of one of Odysseus' men, before bashing out the brains of another on a rock. Finally, the vile beast had hacked away at their flesh with a terrible cleaver and "put the pieces to roast on the coals."

In horror, quick-witted Odysseus had offered the Cyclops wine after he had finished his "awful meal" and "let out a staggering belch." The Cyclops had "drained it off in one gulp," thanking Odysseus for his generosity, exclaiming, "You are the best of guests!"

Taking advantage of the foolish monster's gleeful intoxication, Odysseus had quickly slipped out of the cave, whereupon an idea had occurred to him. "Listen to my plan," Odysseus told the satyrs, who eagerly awaited any chance for escape. Odysseus would continue to ply the gullible Cyclops with wine until he fell into a drunken sleep. Then he would sharpen the trunk of an olive tree with his sword and heat it in the Cyclops' own cooking fire. Once the tip caught fire, Odysseus would plunge the burning spear into the monster's eye. "May I lend a hand at this ritual?" one of the satyrs asked eagerly. "You must," Odysseus replied. "The brand is huge. You all must lift."

A moment later, the Cyclops reappeared at the entrance to his cave. "Mamama. Am I crammed with wine!" he slurred. "How I love the fun of a feast!" Then, turning to Odysseus, he said, "Here, here, my friend, hand me the flask."

Only too happy to oblige, Odysseus gave him more wine and, bolstering his stratagem, explained that he himself had "spent a lot of time" enjoying Bacchus' sweet refreshment. Surely, the god Bacchus was superior to all in "blessing the lives of men." "At least he makes very tasty belching," the monster allowed. Still, he wondered sluggishly, "How can a god bear to live in a flask?" Odysseus answered, "Wherever you put him, he's quite content. That's the kind of god he is: hurts no one." "I'm so drunk nothing could hurt me," the Cyclops said. Now, speaking in mock regard, Silenus urged the monster, "Lie down there; stretch yourself out on the ground." Cyclops eagerly complied.

As Cyclops situated himself into a heap near the mouth of the cave, he asked Odysseus his name. "Nobody is my name," Odysseus answered glibly. Then he asked, pointing out how he had thus far attended to the ogre's desire, "But how will you reward me?" "I will eat you last of all your crew," the Cyclops snapped back at him. Then guzzling a bit more wine, he exclaimed, "Mama. What a wizard the vine must be!"

Suddenly pulling himself to his feet, the Cyclops reached out and snatched up Silenus. "With him I'll sleep," he proclaimed. Startled, Silenus cried out as the lumbering monster dragged him into the cave, "I'm done for, children. Foul things await me."

"Rip out the eye of the Cyclops!" one of the satyrs bravely prodded Odysseus. Yet, when Odysseus told the flighty satyrs that it was time to begin their work, each on in turn back-stepped and cowered. "We're too far away to reach his eye," one said. "And just this moment we've gone lame," another interjected. "I knew from the first what sort you were," Odysseus sneered at them; "at least cheer on my men," he entreated the satyrs as he boldly stepped into the cave. Immediately the satyrs began a rallying dance, shouting wildly, "Go! Go! As hard as you can!"

"Owwww!" the wounded Cyclops' shriek drowned out their cheering. "My eye is scorched to ashes!" he cried as he came reeling blindly out of the cave, blood gushing from where his single eye once stared. "Nobody wounded me," the Cyclops howled. "Nobody blinded me."

"How could nobody make you blind?" the mischievous satyrs wondered.

"You mock me," the Cyclops uttered, groping on the ground in search of his attackers. "Where is nobody?" he demanded again. Just then Odysseus and his crew emerged from the cave. "Out of your reach," he mocked. "Looking after the safety of *Odysseus*," he said, too proud to refrain from revealing his true identity. "Have you changed your name?" the Cyclops asked skeptically. Odysseus, secure in the distance he kept from the sightless, raging beast, replied, "You have had to pay for your unholy meal."

"Ah! The old oracle has been fulfilled," the defeated Cyclops finally sighed. Indeed, the oracle had foretold that Odysseus would come from Troy and blind the Cyclops. But, the monster recalled loudly, this Odysseus would have to pay for his deed by roaming the seas for many years.

"Much I care!" Odysseus retorted. He would board his ship, sail for home, and take along the merry-making satyrs—who would henceforth serve only Bacchus.

Commentary:

"Cyclops" is one of Euripides's later plays, and was probably intended as the final piece in a quartet. The identities of the other three tragedies are not known, though translator William Arrowsmith believes that *Hecuba* may be among them. Beyond this uncertainty, it is agreed that "Cyclops" was intended as a "satyr-play." (In fact, it is the only surviving example of this genre.)

Always appearing after three tragedies in Greek drama, satyr-plays capped off a day's viewing in the Athenian theater. While little is known about the function of these tragi-comedies, invariably they included a chorus of fun-loving satyrs. Led by the elderly and jocose Silenus, the choral satyrs wore horses'—or occasionally goats'—ears and tails, and represented Dionysus (Bacchus), god of wine and revelry. Because satyr-plays depicted both carnal and spiritual aspects of existence, writers used techniques of both classical comedy and drama.

The ribaldry of the Cyclops and the cruelty and pride of Odysseus receive equal attention and carry equal weight in the play's dramatic structure. Presumably, both characters were equally capable of eliciting an emotional response from a classical Greek audience.

Today, perhaps, we tend to respond more forcefully to Odysseus' brutal gouging-out of the Cyclops' eye than we do to the Cyclops' outlandish buffoonery; whereas a classical audience may well have found more of note in the beast's swaggering taunts and drunkenness. Not only did he fall under the divine influence of Bacchus' intoxicating grapes, the Cyclops, in his own right, was revered in Greek myth as the child of both Earth and Heaven—and he, along with haughty Odysseus, perhaps are meant to tender tellingly modern characterizations of human nature.

THE TROJAN WOMEN

by
Euripides
(480-405 B.C.)

Type of work: Tragic drama

Setting: Troy, an ancient Phrygian city in north-west Asia Minor; c. 1250 B.C.

Principal characters:
   Poseidon, god of the sea
   Hecuba, the wife of Priam, slain King of Troy
   Paris, Hecuba and Priam's princely son
   Talthybius, a Greek messenger
   Cassandra, daughter of Hecuba and a priestess of Apollo
   Andromache, daughter-in-law to Hecuba
   Astyanax, Andromache's son
   Menelaus, a Greek king and pillager of Troy
   Helen, the wife of Menelaus, mistress of Paris, and the woman over whom the Trojan War was fought

Play Overview:

Before Prince Paris' birth, his mother, Hecuba, Queen of Troy, had a strange dream: she would give birth to a torch that someday would engulf Troy in flames. As a result, when Paris was born, Hecuba abandoned the newborn in the wilderness so that her dream foretelling the destruction of Troy would not prove prophetic. But a passing shepherd saved Paris and raised him as his son.

One day, many years later, three goddesses—Aphrodite, Athena, and Hera—appeared before young Paris, requesting that he judge which of them was most beautiful. When Paris chose Aphrodite, she promised to help him win Helen, the fairest woman in the world. But Helen was already married to Menelaus, King of Argos. This fact, however, did not stop Paris, as he pursued the lovely Helen, captured her, and carried her back to Troy. To exact revenge, the Greeks laid siege to the city.

For ten years the war dragged on. Finally, sequestering their best Greek soldiers inside a gigantic wooden horse set outside Troy—which the Trojans hauled inside the gates—the Greeks entered the city, ravaged "the gods' shrines" leaving the Trojan king, Priam, "dead upon the altar steps" of the blood-drenched temple, Priam's son dead at his side, and set Troy aflame, just as Hecuba had seen in her dream. Greece had claimed the victory.

Just before dawn, the sea god Poseidon appeared to Hecuba, who did not look up through her weeping. Poseidon also lamented Troy's desolation: "I built the towers of stone around this town of Troy, Apollo with me—and straight we raised them true by line and plummet—goodwill for them has never left my heart, My Trojans and their city." Then Poseidon corrected himself, for the city consisted of little more than smoke and ashes. He lamented the Trojan women taken to Greece as slaves, and acknowledged Hecuba's "many tears for many griefs." Her husband and all her sons, including Paris, had been killed in the siege; her daughter Cassandra, a priestess of Apollo, would be given to the great King

Agamemnon; and—as yet unknown to Hecuba—her daughter Polyxena now lay dead on the grave of Achilles, her Greek lover.

As he turned to leave, Athena, the goddess of war, stood by She had come to convince Poseidon to combine his might with hers in aid of the Trojans. Recalling her long animosity toward Troy and Paris—who had once proclaimed Aphrodite more beautiful than Athena—Poseidon marvelled, "What! Now—at last? Has that long hatred left you?"

Athena explained that one of the Greeks had desecrated the temple dedicated to her. With thoughts of revenge, she now revealed what she wanted from Poseidon:

> Your part, to make your sea-roads roar—
> wild waves and whirlwinds,
> while dead men choke the winding bay.

Poseidon agreed. Moments later, both were gone.

As dawn finally broke, Queen Hecuba slowly and painfully rose from her bed. Her thoughts again turned to her old age, her family's death, and her city's loss. "All was nothing—nothing, always," she said, overcome with bitterness. Who was to blame? Helen—"a thing of loathing, shame"—had precipitated all this misery. At her cries, the doors of the huts began to open and other women emerged to remind Hecuba that she was not alone in her grief; they also mourned their dead and feared their enslavement by the Greeks.

Suddenly a unit of Greek soldiers appeared. From among them stepped a messenger to address Hecuba. This soldier, Talthybius, had met her before, on those times when he had carried "messages to Troy from the Greek camp." The Greeks had indeed drawn lots for the Trojan women, and Hecuba' daughter Cassandra, once a priestess of Apollo, now belonged to Agamemnon. Hecuba was stunned. She could not believe it—her daughter served Apollo and would remain "a virgin, always." That, the messenger explained, was precisely the reason Agamemnon had chosen her. Andromache, Talthybius continued, the widow of her son Hector, had been selected by Achilles' son.

Finally the old Queen asked about her own fate. Whose slave would she become? "The King of Ithaca, Odysseus," the messenger replied. Then turning to the soldiers, Talthybius ordered them to bring Cassandra from her hut; she would be taken at once. Hecuba, however, blocked their path, vehemently affirming that Cassandra had gone mad.

Just then, Cassandra opened the door to her hut. She wore a garland in her hair and a priestess' dress. Holding a torch in her hand, she stepped into the morning light. "Fly, dancing feet," she said. "Oh, joy, oh, joy!" Then, seeing Hecuba there, she invited her, "Dance, Mother, come." Cassandra implored her mother not to grieve: the Trojans, not the Greeks, had earned the greater honor, for to die in defense of their own people was "to die well." What's more, her marriage to the Greek Agamemnon would "be bloodier than Helen's"; she would "lay his house as low" as he had theirs and "make him pay for all." Talthybius had heard enough. "Now you," he said angrily to Cassandra, "you know your mind is not quite right. Come with me to the ship now." At this, a command from an enemy, Cassandra addressed the Trojan dead. "You . . ." she said, "I shall come to you a victor."

As one chariot bore Cassandra away, another approached bearing Hecuba's daughter-in-law Andromache from Troy. Andromache stepped down from the chariot with her young son Astayanax and informed Hecuba that another of her daughters, Polyxena, was also dead. Even so, Andromache contended, Polyxena had more to celebrate than she. Hecuba, however, was unconvinced: Andromache at least still had a son at her side, one who might someday return in victory to rebuild Troy. "Death," Hecuba pronounced, "is empty—life has hope."

Soon, Talthybius returned with his soldiers. From the expression of anguish on his face, the women could see that something awful was about to happen. "I feel you [are] kind," Andromache told him. "But you have not got good news." For a long moment the Greek messenger could not bring himself to speak. "Your child," he finally gestured at her grandson, Astayanax, "must die. There, now you know."

"O God," Andromache wept. "There is no measure to my pain." Then Talthybius explained, as gently as he could, that Astayanax would be flung from a high wall of the city. At this, Andromache cradled the boy in her arms, moaning in deepest anguish. "Don't cling to him," Talthybius said. It would only make it worse. The Greeks would eventually become angry and deny Astayanax a proper burial.

Talthybius pried Astayanax from the grandmother's trembling arms and directed the soldiers to lead him away. A messenger, Talthybius reflected, "should be a man who feels no pity"— and he was not such a man. The soldiers led Andromache to the chariot and drove away. The women, looking on, dazed, were beyond even weeping.

Next, King Menelaus arrived on horseback. He had waged this war not for his wife, he proclaimed, but for the sake of her captor. Turning then to one of his soldiers, he ordered, pointing to Helen, "Seize her and drag her out by that long blood-drenched hair." Hearing this, the embittered Hecuba became ecstatic: "Kill her, Menelaus? You will? Oh, blessings on you."

When Helen appeared before Menelaus and the women of Troy, she was trembling slightly, but still beautiful, still radiant. "Am I to live or die?" she asked her husband. "Unanimous," he assured her: everyone wanted to see her die.

It was Paris and Aphrodite who were responsible for her abduction, Helen protested. "I lived a slave."

"No one with any sense will listen to you," Hecuba snapped, reminding her how she had been "mad with love" for Paris, and how she had demanded her "insolent way" for vanity's sake. "Kill her," Hecuba demanded of Menelaus.

Menelaus assured the old queen that he

would. When Helen, fearing for her life, insisted it "was the gods, not me," Menelaus would not listen. Instead, ordering his soldiers to escort her to the ship, he rode away.

Talthybius soon returned with the dead boy in his arms. Hecuba took her grandson and, holding him close and lifting his lifeless hands in her own, spoke softly over his body:

Dear hands, the same dear shape your father's
  had,
how loosely now you fall. And dear proud lips
forever closed. False words you spoke to me
when you would jump into my bed, call me
  sweet names
and tell me, Grandmother, when you are dead,
I'll cut off a lock of hair and lead my soldiers all
to ride out past your tomb.
Not you, but I, old, homeless, childless,
must lay you in your grave, so young,
so miserably dead.

The Trojan women gently took the child from Hecuba's arms and laid him on his father Hector's shield. Just as Andromache had requested before her ship set sail, the boy's body was covered with flowers and draped in linen. Then the women lifted the shield and carried the boy to his grave. Behind them, nothing was left of the beloved city Troy but dust and flames.

"Farewell, dear city," a woman said. "Farewell, my country, where once my children lived."

Commentary:

Edith Hamilton called "The Trojan Women" the "most savage piece of antiwar literature ever written." Indeed, few works approach the play's bitterly caustic condemnation of war.

"The Trojan Women" contains little dramatic action. Instead, the play broods lyrically on the emptiness of the Greek victory at Troy. The slaying of Astayanax, Hecuba's grandson, for example, dehumanizes Talthybius and his Greek conquerors more than it does the Trojans. Worse yet, Helen of Troy, the cause of the war, is condemned to die. Thus—with the exception of Helen—it is Troy's women, not Greece's men, who are the real victors, for they retain both their lives and their humanity. As Hecuba says, "Death is empty—life has hope."

Originally the third play of a tetralogy performed in a 415 B.C. competition in Athens, the production won second prize, an honor that belies the chilly reception Athenians gave it. Its performance came only a few months after the Greeks had committed atrocities against the inhabitants of Melos, a tiny island in the Aegean. Athens had invited Melos to join it in an alliance. When Melos declined, expressing its desire to remain neutral, Athens seized the island, systematically killed all its men, and enslaved its women and children. Paralleling the Melian atrocities, "The Trojan Women" no doubt touched a raw nerve.

Euripides depicts Troy's decimation with a graphic realism never before seen in Greek drama. Sophocles, Euripides' contemporary fellow playwright—and rival—reportedly evaluated the differences in their writing. He, Sophocles judged, showed men as they *ought to be*, while Euripides showed men as they *are*.

MEDEA

by
Euripides
(c. 479 - 406 B.C.)

Type of work: Lyric tragedy

Setting: Corinth; ancient Greece

Principal characters:
Medea, princess of Corinth
Jason, Medea's husband
Creon, King of Corinth
A chorus of Corinthian women, observers in the drama

Play Overview:

Prologue: Medea, a princess and a sorceress from the Black Sea kingdom of Colchis, fell in love with Jason of the Argonauts when he sailed to Colchis to retrieve the Golden Fleece from Medea's father, King Aeetes. Aeetes had agreed to surrender the fleece to Jason, on the condition that he perform a series of impossible feats. Abetted by Medea's sorcery, Jason successfully accomplished the tasks her father had set.

When Medea's father discovered he had been deceived, Medea also assisted Jason's escape, killing her brother and scattering his body parts in the sea to slow her father's pursuit. Such was her devotion to Jason.

In Iolchus, Jason's hereditary kingdom, Medea also helped him retaliate against his uncle Pelias, who had usurped Jason's right to his father's throne. Again through the use of sorcery, Medea persuaded Pelias' daughters to kill him. As a result, Medea and Jason were banished. Now, ten years later, living as exiles in Corinth with their two children, Medea heard that Jason had resolved to abandon her and the children in order to marry the daughter of Creon, King of Corinth.

Medea's nurse stood in front of their house, listening to Medea weep, and brooding on the devastation Jason's plans had caused. Not only would Medea and her children be abandoned by Jason, but they would also be banished from Corinth: Creon feared Medea would take revenge on his daughter if she stayed near.

As the nurse remembered the burden of betrayal, murder, and exile which Medea had borne for Jason, she became afraid. Medea, she knew, had a violent, passionate heart; she would not "put up with the treatment she [was] getting." What frightened the nurse even more, however, was the thought that Medea might harm her children: earlier she had seen Medea "blazing her eyes at them, as though she meant some mischief."

Meanwhile, a chorus of Corinthian women gathered outside Medea's house, hoping they might console her. But Medea's pain was beyond comfort, and as the chorus listened to her wail, they began to think that "this passion of hers moves her to something great."

Before long, Medea appeared and began a long, impassioned speech in which she reflected not only on her own grief, but on the grievous conditions of women throughout the world. "We women," she said, "are the most unfortunate creatures." Medea, however, had one burden the others did not: she had no escape, neither a family nor a home in which to take refuge from her sufferings. Because of this, she asked the women in the chorus for a "service".

> If I can find the means or devise any scheme
> To pay my husband back for what he has done to me—
> Him and his father-in-law and the girl who married him—
> Just to keep silent. For in other ways a woman
> Is full of fear, defenseless, dreads the sight of cold
> Steel; but, when once she is wronged in the matter of love,
> No other soul can behold so many thoughts of blood.

The chorus knew that Medea's grievance against Jason was justified, and agreed to remain silent about her desire for revenge. They kept this promise even when Creon arrived to see to it personally that Medea and her children were banished at once from Corinth. "I will not return home," he said, "until you are cast from the boundaries of my land."

Medea pleaded with Creon. Exile for her, she said, was of little concern; the banishment of her children, however, was most grievous. Jason, she informed Creon, had made no provision for the children. For their sake, she needed time to plan where they would go. "Allow me," she begged, "to remain here just for this one day."

Against his better judgment, Creon granted Medea's request, and left her to her preparations—which turned out to be murderous. With her extra day, she told the chorus, "I will make dead bodies of three of my enemies—father, the girl, and the husband."

When Jason arrived, he was angry at Medea. It was her violent temper that had been the cause of her banishment, he said. Her reaction to his plans to marry the princess had been unreasonable and provocative. If she could only see that his marriage served the "best and truest interest" of everyone concerned, he continued, then she would not now find herself in exile, and "life would have been good." As for now, Jason said, "I wish to help you and the children in every way, but you refuse what is good for you. Obstinately, you push away your friends. You are sure to suffer for it."

Medea was incensed by his words; she had never before heard such a self-justifying, specious argument. "Enjoy your wedding," she sneered. With the help of God, she told him, "you will make the kind of marriage that you will regret." At this, Jason left her, and the chorus lamented the suffering incurred "when love is in excess."

She would, she told the chorus, send her children to Jason's bride with a gift, "a finely woven dress and a golden diadem." When Jason's bride put on the dress, she would die from poison in the fabric. Then she unfolded the further gory details of her plan:

> I weep to think of what deed I have to do
> Next after that: for I shall kill my own children.

11

© 1993, Compact Classics, Inc.

> *My children, there is none who can give them*
safety,
> *When I have ruined the whole of Jason's house,*
> *I shall leave the land and flee from the murder of*
my
> *Dear children, and I shall have done a dreadful*
deed.

The chorus women were horrified to hear that Medea's vengeance included the murders of her own children. Can you, they asked Medea in unison, "have the heart to kill your own flesh and blood?"

"Yes," Medea replied, "for this is the best way to wound my husband."

Medea, setting her plan in motion, sent word to Jason that she wished to speak with him on an urgent matter. When Jason returned, she pretended to be contrite. She had gravely erred, she told him, but had "come to a better understanding now." Moreover, she wanted to make amends—to him, to his new bride, and to his father-in-law, Creon. She asked only two things: first, that Jason persuade his bride and father-in-law to permit her children to remain in Corinth; and second, as a demonstration of her good faith, that Jason take the children to the palace to convey a gift to his new bride.

Jason, moved by Medea's appeals, consented to fulfill her final requests. Then Medea called her children from the house:

> *Go children, go together to that rich palace,*
> *Be suppliants to the new wife of your father,*
> *My lady, beg her not to let you be banished.*
> *And give her this dress.*

After Jason and the children departed, Medea awaited the fulfillment of the first part of her scheme. Soon the children returned to her, along with news that their banishment had been lifted. Not long after, however, a messenger arrived from the palace, accusing Medea of having "done a dreadful thing," and telling her to flee at once. Jason's new bride, the messenger said, "is dead, only just now, and Creon dead, too, her father, by your poisons." Medea answered: "The finest words you have spoken. Now and hereafter, I shall count you among my benefactors and friends." Then she surprised the messenger even more by asking him to recount in detail how they had died: "You will delight me twice as much again if you say they died in agony."

The messenger related the entire horrifying story of how the princess' initial delight in the golden dress had gradually turned to terror, of how the poison had caused her flesh to drop away from her bones, and of how her father—seeing his daughter's corpse—had fallen on it and cried out, "O my poor child," before he himself succumbed to the poison.

When the account was finished, Medea turned to the chorus and said, "Women, my task is fixed: quickly as I may to kill my children, and start away from this land." Medea disappeared into the house, and a minute later the two children shrieked. At that moment, Jason returned—and to his horror, the chorus told him, "Your children are dead, and by their mother's own hand."

Jason began to pound on the house's bolted doors. Medea appeared on the balcony, standing in a chariot drawn by two winged dragons and holding the bodies of the two children. "Why do you batter these gates," she asked, "seeking the corpses and for me who did the deed?"

Medea and Jason began to quarrel and curse one another for the bitterness and pain each believed the other had caused. "I loved them, you did not," Medea accused. "You loved them, and killed them," Jason charged. "To make you feel pain," Medea justified.

Jason then begged Medea to let him "touch my boys' delicate flesh." But Medea refused. "I will not," she said. "Your words are wasted." She then flew away in her chariot, first to bury her children at Hera's temple, and then to Athens, where she would be safe. The chorus, stunned by the events they had witnessed, could only lament:

> *Many things the gods*
> *Achieve beyond our judgment. What we thought*
> *Is not confirmed and what we thought not god*
> *Contrives. And so it happens in this story.*

Commentary:

The puzzlingly cool reception afforded the *Medea* when it was first exhibited may be explained by its extraordinary raw power. Then, as now, the play seems to unsettle and subvert our notions of the family and, by extension, the community as a whole.

Other great tragedies, of course, accomplish similar moments of corrosion and pollution of familial bonds, Sophocles' *Oedipus Rex* and Shakespeare's *King Lear*, for instance. Unlike these great tragedies of family and state, however, Euripides' *Medea* offers its audience neither antidote nor consolation for the ruin of civilized life which the play unveils.

It is difficult to think of a more problematical character than Medea: on the one hand, she is a resourceful, loyal, and—because she is so clearly wronged by Jason—sympathetic character; on the other hand, she is—as the author of her children's murders—monstrously repugnant, the very embodiment of moral degeneracy. In violating the sacred maternal bond, she acts without regard to human nature. Because she represents a beyond-human passion, she is also beyond understanding.

Interestingly, the murders of Medea's children are not without precedent; indeed, she seems to have the uncanny ability to penetrate and pollute the very core of a family with murder. Earlier, she accomplishes the ruin of her father through the murder of her brother. Then, in Iolchus, she manages to induce the daughters of Pelias to murder their father. Finally, of course, by poisoning Creon's daughter, she causes the daughter to unintentionally poison her father. In each case, the bonds of a family are quite literally murdered from within.

Medea is also unsettling, powerful, and precarious because it tears apart the legend of the mythic, invincible hero. In the traditional myth, Jason is a character of heroic proportions, one who can accomplish impossible feats. Here, however, he is unmasked as a fraud, a "hero" who has accomplished nothing without the aid of Medea's sorcery.

If there is any attempt by Euripides to frame or interpret the dramatic course of action, it is in the enigmatic remarks of the chorus that close the play: "What we thought, is not confirmed, and what we thought not, god contrives . . ."

THE BIRDS

(from *The Comedies*)
by Aristophanes
(ca. 448-380 B.C.)

Type of work: Comedic lyrical social satire

Setting: A dramatic competition in Athens during the Second Peloponnesian War; 414 B.C.

Principal characters:
Pisthetaerus, an elderly Athenian
Euelpides, another old gentleman
Epops, King of the Birds, formerly a man
A Chorus of Birds

Play Overview:

Life in Athens during the last years of the fifth century B.C. had badly deteriorated. For one thing, there was the heavy burden of the fifteen-year-old Peloponnesian War that was still being waged against Sparta. Then, too, there were the costs of expanding the empire west into Sicily—and, there again, battling Sparta. Finally, and even more disheartening as the players on the skylit stage of *The Birds* irreverently attested to their Athenian audience—there was the prospect of enduring yet another tragedy by Euripides at this year's theater festival.

In such troubled times, it seemed that the only freedom to which an ordinary Athenian could look forward with any degree of certainty was the freedom to pay taxes. And if, in the middle of this sad state of affairs, you had found yourself on stage in this latest comedy from the pen of Aristophanes, taking the role of a disgruntled old man hounded by creditors and tax collectors, then the act of gathering your belongings and heading out of town would surely have seemed less a contrivance of comic desperation than an eminently reasonable response. Nor probably did it seem any less sensible to the audience living under these circumstances when you disclosed in the opening scenes that, before setting out for parts unknown, you had bought a crow and a magpie in the Athenian bird market, hoping that one bird or the other would guide you—by instinct you assumed—to Epops the Hoopoe, otherwise known as King of the Birds.

Epops had first been born not as a bird, but as a man; he had ruled in Greece as a king named Tereus. Long ago he had inexplicably mutated into a bird. Having traveled widely through the kingdoms of both men and birds, Epops, you might assume, should know of a place somewhere in the world where a poor refugee might settle down and live a life of comfort and ease.

Such was the plan that the two old gentlemen on stage, Euelpides and Pisthetaerus, had hatched. Now, with their meager belongings in tow, they found themselves facing the audience from the midst of a desolate mountain scene. They paused beneath a rocky crag, arguing between themselves and interpreting as best they could the squawks and caws of the two guide-birds which sat perched on their shoulders.

They had begun to lament their plan to escape Athens as an idea that was quite literally "for the birds," when the disturbance they were making brought Epops out from a rocky crag, having just awakened from a nap. It was molting season, and because he had lost so much of his plumage, to the startled Euelpides and Pisthetaerus

his aspect was sightly less than royal. Still, the travelers had come this far, they decided to explain their plight and ask if he could recommend a peaceful land beyond the reach of creditors where the worst they might suffer would be an invitation to dinner.

Epops made several suggestions, but all were rejected; none, it seemed, were ideally suited to the Athenians' paradisiacal fantasy. Finally, almost as an afterthought, the two humans asked Epops what life was like among the birds. Epops rehearsed the various advantages of birdhood—noting in particular that birds lived without need of money. Hearing this, Pisthetaerus suddenly had an idea. "You should build your own city-state in the clouds," he urged Epops. The birds, he enthused, could surround their city with huge walls and starve the gods themselves into submission "by preventing men's sacrifices from reaching heaven." Epops was intrigued by the notion. "By traps and nets and decoys," he added approvingly. "I've never heard a better idea!"

But such an ambitious proposition—one that would overthrow the whole established oligarchy of the gods—required approval of birds throughout the world. So Epops summoned the birds together in a chorus on stage in order that they might hear Pisthetaerus' plan.

The birds were naturally suspicious. Unlike Epops, none of them had ever been men. In fact, men had always been the enemies of birds: throughout history humans had captured them, killed them, eaten them. Thus, it was not, perhaps, unnatural, that the first act of the chorus was to form ranks and launch an assault on their human visitors.

After Euelpides and Pisthetaerus had endured much wing-beating and pecking from the birds, Epops finally rebuked his followers, reminding them that they had much to "learn from their enemies." Chastised, at least for the moment, the birds settled down to listen.

Pisthetaerus first rose to speak, presenting an eloquent argument. Hadn't the chorus read their Aesop? If so, they would know that birds were originally the masters of men. A remnant of the birds' primordial glory was even yet evident in man's lexicon: the owl, the eagle, the hawk, the dove, all were reverenced as symbols of courage, peace—the noblest ideals of humanity. Couldn't they see that if they built a walled city between heaven and earth, the birds could force both men and gods to once more worship them? They would be sovereign; the feathered tribes would reign! Point by persuasive point, Pisthetaerus laid out all the advantages of his plan. "I advise you," he forcefully concluded, "to create a city of birds."

"O reverend elder," the chorus of birds now intoned, "instead of our worst enemy you have become our dearest friend." Following much rejoicing, Euelpides and Pisthetaerus were led away to be honored with their own pairs of wings.

During this interlude, the chorus of birds—who were, after all, only actors in a comedy—took occasion to address the audience directly, entreating them to become citizens of their newly founded city. If the humans would agree to this treaty, the birds promised to control insect plagues and such, so that mankind would benefit; what's more, given wings, the humans, would not have to sit through another of Euripides' boring tragedies—they could simply fly home for a snack and be back in time for a comedy. If the human audience refused to pay homage, however, the siege of the birds would begin, and feathered battalions would be sent to pluck our the eyes of their cattle. In any case, the chorus concluded, the judges at the theater festival should definitely award first prize to their own most inspired drama.

The interlude ended, once more the birds assumed their stage roles, and the drama continued to unfold. Soon news came to Pisthetaerus that the building of the celestial city and all its fortifications had been completed. The question naturally arose as to what to call the new city. Pisthetaerus at first suggested "Sparta," but Euelpides objected that the name "Sparta" would even be an insult to his mattress. No, he insisted, such a lofty city required "something big, smacking of the clouds. A pinch of fluff and rare air. A swollen sound." Pisthetaerus thought a moment. "I've got it," he exclaimed. "Listen—CLOUDCUCKOOLAND!" Everyone agreed. "The perfect name," someone said. "And it's a big word too."

The problem was, however, that rumors of Cloudcuckooland-to-come had already spread to Athens. Pisthetaerus was at once besieged by a procession of the seediest characters from the noble city—each one seeking money by offering his corrupt services in the building of the project. There came an indigent poet offering to write celebratory verses; an itinerant prophet peddling a book of bogus oracles; a geometer putting in his bid to survey the new city; and an imperious Athenian legislator wishing to sell the city a huge volume of statutes and laws. In short, all of Athens seemed to be dreaming of feathers, a winged way of life, a life of ease. Among this clamoring crowd, the corrupt and self-serving soon found themselves unceremoniously either pummeled or expelled by Pisthetaerus himself. But Athenians who sued with a pure heart for the privileges of Cloudcuckooland, were given wings to soar aloft in their chosen professions: poets were empowered to gather inspiration for their works, and workmen to climb to the nethermost heights of their craft.

The gods, too, had by now received news of Cloudcuckooland and of the birds' fiat declaring themselves supreme rulers of the world. In fact, since communications between gods and man had been cut off and men were no longer making sacrificial offerings, the gods were growing very hungry. At first, Zeus dispatched Iris, goddess of the rainbow, who arrived on stage with her veils blowing in the wind by means of a stage crane. Pisthetaerus dismissed the gentle goddess so rudely, though, that Zeus next sent an Olympian delegation consisting of Poseidon, Triballus, and Heracles.

Now the idea behind this delegation—that more illustrious members of the pantheon were needed to obtain an audience with the now-winged Pisthetaerus—was sound enough. The constitution of the delegation, however, was another matter. Here, Zeus seemed to have seriously erred in that each member brought his own particular weakness to the table. Poseidon, for instance, was far too glum a god to possess any diplomatic talents. Triballus—being a Dorian god and speaking a barbarian tongue—could not make himself understood. And Heracles not only "burned less brightly" than other gods—he was, in fact, dim-witted—but he was also a renowned glutton—by this time a *hungry* glutton.

When the Olympian delegation arrived, Pisthetaerus was slicing pickles and his chef was preparing a barbecue— The chef was roasting three birds, Pisthetaerus explained—three "jail birds" who had been "sentenced to death for High Treason against the Sovereign Birds." Heracles licked his lips in anticipation, forgetting his diplomatic mission.

Needless to say, negotiations did not go well for the gods. First, they ceded their dominion over men to Pisthetaerus' birds and agreed to turn over Zeus's scepter. Then Pisthetaerus, still unsatisfied, laid down new terms: he would instruct the birds to end the gods' famine, he declared—and even invite them to dinner—but only if they also agreed to give him Basileia, Zeus' most beautiful wife. This was most unreasonable, Poseidon complained. "You won't have peace," he threatened as the Olympians rose to leave. "It's all the same to me," Pisthetaerus said nonchalantly. "O Chef," he called ignoring the gods, "make the gravy thick."

This last reference to the gravy was "more than Heracles could stand," and the envoys fell into a slavering quarrel. Finally—as the three of them sat down to dinner—Poseidon reluctantly agreed to all of Pisthetaerus' audacious demands. Then, in the distance, they heard the roll of Zeus' thunder. A bolt of lightning stuck the stage, Basileia was delivered before their eyes, and she and Pisthetaerus were promptly married.

Finally, Pisthetaerus, King of the Birds, extended one hand to Basileia—Zeus' scepter was clasped firmly in the other—and together they stepped into the stage crane's breeze, beating their wings. As the crane slowly lifted them up and offstage, the gods knelt in homage. And as the chorus of the birds exited the stage, they chanted "O greatest of gods!"

Commentary:

The Birds was first performed in competition at Athens' festival of Dionysus in 414 B.C. Despite the pleas of the chorus, the judges awarded it second, rather than first prize. Nonetheless, it may be Aristophanes' finest comedy, and certainly one of the masterpieces of Western literature. Indeed, it would be difficult to think of another work that can match The Birds for its rich mix of rollicking, absurd humor, self-conscious parody, and soaring lyricism.

The Birds is one of the first works of literature to treat the now familiar theme of Utopia. The ideal of Aristophanes' Utopia, however, is no real "ideal" at all. The ancient gods are starved out by the Cloudcuckoolanders, not from any pious intentions to establish a new haven for pure living or thinking, but in pursuit of the Ultimate Escape. Rather than a noble sanctuary, the city of the birds—and of frenzied, weak-willed, tax-evading humans—declares itself as the magical, flawed, tyrannical paradise of infamy.

In 405 B.C., Athens fell to Sparta. It marked not only the literary epitaph of Aristophanes, but also the end of Greece's golden age of drama.

THE LIFE OF KING HENRY V

by
William Shakespeare
(1564-1616)

Type of work: Historical drama

Setting: England and France; circa 1415

Principal characters:
 Henry V, King of England
 Archbishop of Canterbury, the King's advisor
 Charles VI, King of France
 Princess Katherine, Charles' daughter
 The Dauphin, Charles' son, the Crown Prince
 Pistol, a poor Englishman who goes to war
 Boy, an English child who accompanies Pistol
 Mountjoy, a French messenger

Story Overview:

In Shakespeare's two plays that make up *Henry IV*, a young Henry V underwent a profound metamorphosis. He had grown from a rakish prince who passed many idle hours at the Boar's Head Tavern into a shrewd young man. And as Henry V listened carefully to the advice of his dying father, Henry IV, to ward off domestic uprisings by encouraging "foreign quarrels," the prince took to heart his father's counsel: shortly after his father's death, the new monarch contemplated invading France.

Before undertaking his plans for war, young Henry inquired of the Archbishop of Canterbury as to whether he thought that an English monarch might "with right and conscience" lay claim to France. Having previously discussed with the Bishop of Ely how profitable such an invasion would be for the church, the Archbishop urged Henry to "invoke the warlike spirit" of his ancestors who had brought "defeat on the full power of France." After all, he assured the King, France belonged to Henry by ancient law; the French were merely preventing him from exercising his rightful rule over the country, "usurped from you and your progenitors."

Ironically, their conversation was interrupted by French messengers sent by the imperious Dauphin, heir to the French throne. The messengers informed Henry that their prince would never allow the English king to take possession of the French-governed dukedoms he had recently demanded:

Your Highness, lately sending into France,
Did claim some certain dukedoms, in the right
Of your great predecessor, King Edward the
 Third
In answer of which claim, the prince, our master
Says that you be advis'd: There's nought in
 France
That can be with a nimble [dance] won;
You cannot revel in dukedoms there.

As a gesture of utter disdain, the Dauphin had sent Henry, as a "tun of treasure," tennis balls. This insulting reminder of Henry's idle youth, however, only strengthened his resolve "to strike [the Dauphin's] father's crown into the hazard." Henry vowed to make "many a thousand widows weep" in France. Having been known as an irresponsible ne'er do-well in his youth, Henry chose to manifest and consolidate his power on the battlefield.

News of Henry's planned invasion quickly spread. In the midst of preparing his troops, Henry was outraged to discover that the French had hired three Englishmen to murder him. He condemned the three traitors—who once had been his trusted companions—to death, and took his early detection of the murder plot as a sign that fate was on his side. He reflected:

We doubt not of a fair and lucky war,
Since God so graciously hath brought to light,
This dangerous treason lurking in our way . . .

The French, meanwhile, debated the actual danger posed by Henry. Charles VI favored amassing "men of courage" to combat the English "with means defendant." His arrogant and incautious son, however, despised fearful displays of a country so "idly king'd" as England. Despite his countrymen's arguments to the contrary, the Dauphin persisted in thinking of Henry as no more than "a vain, giddy, shallow, humorous youth," wholly incapable of successfully waging war on France.

His sister, the Princess Katherine, however, was more pragmatic. Anticipating an English victory, she set out to learn as much English as she could. "De nail, de arm, de ilbow," she gaily recited.

Back in London, loyal Englishmen continued to respond to Henry's call to arms against France. Among them were a poor wayward boy and a man named Pistol. Pistol had recently attended to the ailing Sir John Falstaff in the Boar's Head Tavern. Falstaff had once been the British Crown Prince's drinking companion in the days before his ascension to the throne. After he gained the crown, however, Henry had denounced the old man, the rumor went, "killing his heart." Following Falstaff's death, Pistol had concluded that "men's faiths" were as fragile as "wafer cakes," and determined to enlist in the King's army "to suck" the spoils of war from France.

Accompanied by the young boy and some unscrupulous companions, Pistol joined the King's army. After they followed the King to Agincourt, however, Pistol and his cronies soon found themselves in a predicament. The King hung two of Pistol's friends for "filching" goods from French citizens, and before long, cowardly Pistol fled the battlefield. Only the wayward boy remained, to "seek some better service" for his King.

Henry's resolve soon surprised and impressed even his staunchest detractors. Rejecting Charles' peace offer of "Katherine his daughter" and a dowry of "some petty and unprofitable dukedoms," Henry seized the city of Harfleur, which fell easily to the English; the fortifications the Dauphin had promised had never materialized. Nevertheless, the French king sent his messenger, Mountjoy, to Henry to apprise him that his troops were of "too faint a number" to win all of France. Furthermore, Charles demanded a "ransom" and an act of contrition: he wanted to see the British monarch "kneeling" in deference to the French throne.

"Thou dost thy office fairly," Henry told Mountjoy. "My people are with sickness much enfeebled." However, Henry refused to give in to Charles' demands. His message to the French king was unwavering: "Yet, God before, tell him we will come on . . . "

Determined to press on to victory, Henry realized that he must first embolden his "weak and sickly guard." Thus, disguised as a Welshman in an old cloak, "walking from watch to watch, from tent to ten," he wandered about the camp, speaking of "fierceness," "obedience," and "conscience" to his unsuspecting soldiers. Unaware that they were in the presence of their monarch, the men listened as the cloaked stranger affirmed that the king's cause was "just and his quarrel honorable."

Inwardly, however, Henry harbored doubts about the justice of his cause. Was it worth the lives of his loyal subjects? "Every subject's duty is the King's," he reasoned, "but every subject's soul is his own." Bearing the responsibility of the lives of men was a "hard condition," he ruminated. "What infinite heart's ease must kings neglect, that private men enjoy!"

By daybreak, however, Henry roused his soldiers with a powerful call to arms. "This day is call'd the feast of Crispian," he began. "He that outlives this day, and comes home safe, will stand a tip-toe when this day is named." Each man would forever mark and would celebrate Saint Crispian's day:

Old men forget; yet all shall be forgot,
But he'll remember with advantages
What feasts he did that day: then shall our
names,
Familiar in his mouth, as household words,
Henry the King, Bedford and Essex,
Warwick and Talbot, Salisbury and
Gloucester,
Be in their flowing cups freshly remember'd.
This story shall the good man teach his son,
And Crispin Crispian shall ne'er go by,
From this day to the ending of the world,
But we in it shall be remembered . . .

The troops took their monarch's words to heart and battled for victory. Despite their meager numbers, they fought courageously on the fields of Agincourt. In the decisive moment of the conflict, Henry—grieving for the loss of two of his companions—ordered that "every soldier kill his prisoners"—an action that, ultimately, greatly strengthened the British position, giving Henry's army the battle.

Once again Mountjoy appeared and acknowledged England's victory: "The day is yours," he conceded. Then, with deference, he asked Henry's permission to bury the multitudes of French dead who lay on the fields. Now Henry gloated, exulting that "ten thousand

French" had died in the Battle of Agincourt while, miraculously, the English had lost fewer than thirty. Among those killed was the boy who had come to France with Pistol. Henry immediately called for the "holy rites" of funeral to be bestowed on the English dead.

Henry then set off for Charles' palace. When he arrived, he addressed the French king and his court magnanimously: "Peace to this meeting, wherefore we are met." He then proposed a truce, providing Charles would agree to England's demands. Sending his councilors off to attend to the particulars of the agreement, Henry announced that Katherine was his "capital demand" and that he wished to meet with her alone.

"O fair Katherine, if you love me soundly with your French heart," Henry told the beautiful French princess after the others had left the room, "I will be glad to hear you confess it brokenly with your English tongue."

After contemplating her position, the princess wondered aloud, "Is it possible dat I should love de enemy of France?" But Henry, as skilled in the art of persuasion as in war, assured his bride-to-be that he would henceforth be "the friend of France."

Commentary:

Probably written in 1599, The Life of Henry V was not an unqualified success. While one Elizabethan document noted that Henry "hath been sundry play'd," following a performance for the court of King James, the seventeenth-century critics largely ignored the play.

Henry V did not attract much critical attention until the early part of the 18th century, and even then the reviews were mixed. In 1817, for instance, the critic William Hazlitt wrote that Shakespeare's Henry "was a hero," but only in the sense that "he was ready to sacrifice his own life for the pleasure of destroying thousands of other lives." Hazlitt went on to call Shakespeare's Henry "a very amiable monster" who only served to evoke the audience's "romantic, heroic, patriotic and poetical delight" in the King's daring-do. For Hazlitt, Shakespeare's *Henry V* epitomized the awful results of brutality and immorality.

As numerous later critics have noted, however, the play is *about* war. Henry proved to be at his best when manifesting his unflinching patriotic zeal on the battlefield. More a warlord than a statesman, the historical Henry won popularity at home by becoming a hero. And by accrediting God for England's victory, he proved himself a good Christian and kept the favor of the church. In large measure, Shakespeare used the brutality of war to create a dramatic context in which to develop his protagonist. Were it not for Henry's singular responsibility for the bloodshed, the play would be devoid of drama. In Shakespeare's hands, Henry's character is a paradox, composed equally of recklessness and youthful exuberance, rooted in love of self and country. Amid the heroic glory, carefree individualism, and patriotic duty portrayed by Henry, Shakespeare vividly illustrates how much is sacrificed in the quest for greatness.

RICHARD II

by
William Shakespeare
(1564-1616)

Type of work: Historical tragedy

Setting: 14th-century England and Wales

Principal characters:
Richard II, King of England
Queen Isabel, Richard's wife
Henry Bolingbroke, his cousin (who later becomes King Henry IV)
Thomas Mawbray, Bolingbroke's enemy, Duke of Norfolk
The Earl of Northumberland, one of Bolingbroke's supporters
Duke of Aumerle, another of Richard's cousins, and a supporter
John of Gaunt, Richard's uncle, and Bolingbroke's father
The Duke of York, another of Richard's uncles, and Aumerle's father

Play Overview:

Early in his rule, Richard II had arranged for the murder of one of his uncles, the Duke of Gloucester—although it was not widely known that he had ordered his uncle's death. Richard II's cousin, Bolingbroke, blamed a man named Thomas Mawbray for planning the murder of the Duke and for swindling money from the military. Denouncing Bolingbroke as a liar, Mowbray vehemently denied these accusations.

The dispute between the two men had grown so ugly that King Richard found it necessary to intercede. Commanding Bolingbroke and Mawbray to appear before him, he listened to their venomous exchange and soon concluded that there was no recourse but to let "swords and lances" settle their grievances.

On the day Richard had appointed for the duel, he and his court assembled at Coventry. But combat was not in the cards. Richard surprised the crowd by declaring that such a rivalry could only lead to civil war. Instead of jousting, both of the men would be "banished," he declared-- Bolingbroke for six years, Mawbray forever. "A heavy sentence," Bolingbroke despaired; and Mawbray, despondent, said that he would henceforth "dwell in solemn shades of endless night." After warning the King to be wary of the lying Bolingbroke, Mawbray sorrowfully disappeared, and Bolingbroke prepared for his own departure. Before he went, however, he swore that wherever he might roam he would always "boast" that he was indeed "a true-born Englishman."

Not long after Bolingbroke left England, Richard relaxed at court with friends and another cousin, Aumerle. "What said our cousin when you parted with him?" Richard asked Aumerle. "'Farewell,'" Aumerle joked. Then Aumerle informed the King that he in fact felt nothing but disdain for Bolingbroke. Scorning his banished cousin as well, Richard poked fun at Bolingbroke's popular appeal:

> ... his courtship to the common people,
> How he did seem to dive into their hearts
> With humble and familiar courtesy,
> What reverence he did throw away on slaves . . .

One of Richard's friends then changed the subject. There was a much more pressing issue the King needed to confront: a rebellion in Ireland. "We will make for Ireland presently," Richard agreed. But, he wondered, how could he finance the journey? At that very moment, he received news that would provide him with the answer: his uncle Gaunt, the Duke of Lancaster—and the exiled Bolingbroke's father—was "grievous sick" and on the verge of death. This uncle's "coffers" would outfit soldiers for the "Irish wars," thought Richard.

Waiting for Richard to arrive at his side, the ailing Gaunt was attended by his brother the Duke of York. "Methinks I am a prophet new inspired," the dying man said, lamenting the divisions within his beloved England. Although York advised his brother not to waste his breath counseling their nephew Richard, Gaunt would not listen. And when Richard arrived, invoking the privilege of a dying man, Gaunt chastised the King for his royal extravagance that had nearly bankrupt England, and for the "flatterers" at court. Furious, Richard struck back at Gaunt as a "lunatic, lean-witted fool."

Shortly thereafter, Richard's uncle died. The King then revealed the true nature of his visit to Gaunt's house: to demand all the "plate, coin, revenues, and movables" of his uncle's estate. Horrified by Richard's callousness and greed, York pleaded with his nephew the King not to cause any more dissension within the family. But Richard dismissed his uncle's words; he was in need of Gaunt's estate to back his Irish wars. Then he added that he expected York to govern England while he was away. Before his nephew departed, York warned him that he would suffer for his selfishness, that "bad courses" could never "fall out good."

York's words proved prophetic. With Richard away in Ireland in company of Aumerle and others of his entourage, York soon found himself in the midst of a precarious situation: outraged by Richard's seizure of his father's estate, Bolingbroke had broken his exile, returned to England, and amassed a force of insurrectionists to retrieve it. Richard's wife was quite shaken by this news. "Uncle, for God's sake, speak comfortable words," she begged York. But York could not offer the Queen solace. "Comfort's in heaven, and we are on the earth," he regretfully advised.

Not long afterwards, York set off to meet Bolingbroke in Gloucestershire where his nephew had made camp. Though angered by what had happened, Bolingbroke felt no animosity towards York; he welcomed him warmly, calling him "gracious uncle."

York, on the other hand, did not regard his nephew entirely amiably; he reprimanded him, "Tut, tut! Grace me no grace, nor uncle me no uncle." Reminding his nephew that he had been banished by the "anointed king," York denounced Bolingbroke for his "gross rebellion and detested treason."

One of Bolingbroke's supporters, the Earl of Northumberland, intervened to plead with York. Could he not see that his nephew had been much abused by the King? Seeing some truth in these words, York began to relent. Still, his loyalties were divided between his two nephews. "I am neutral,"

York finally stated firmly. But no sooner had he uttered these words than he seemed to align himself with Bolingbroke, offering him and his rebels "shelter" and "repose" in a nearby castle.

A short while later, Richard left Ireland and arrived at Wales, delighted to be once more in his kingdom. He had learned of his cousin's insurrection, but he was not greatly concerned: Richard felt certain that "all the water in the rough rude sea" could not depose an "anointed king." His confidence was soon shaken, however, when he heard that York's Welsh troops—who had promised to support the King—had gone over to Bolingbroke. Richard became despondent by the news. "Comfort, my liege, remember who you are," Aumerle encouraged his cousin. Nonetheless, even as Richard 's mood started to improve, he was brought news just as disturbing: Bolingbroke had beheaded several of Richard's closest courtiers, and still Bolingbroke's influence among the commoners and royalty alike continued to grow. Richard despaired:

> Our hands, our lives, and all are Bolingbroke's,
> And nothing can we call our own but death
> And that small model of the barren earth
> Which serves as paste and cover to our bones.

Now destitute of both friendship and power, Richard sought refuge at Flint Castle, where he would simply "pine away." Troubled by the King's lack of confidence, Aumerle tried mightily to restore his spirits. But Richard would not listen to his cousin, warning him that "flatteries" did harm.

When Bolingbroke discovered that Richard had gone to Flint Castle, he sent the Earl of Northumberland there with word that Bolingbroke on "both his knees doth kiss King Richard's hand." But Northumberland did not kneel. Observing this offense, Richard—from a platform high on the castle—called down to Northumberland, berating him, "How dare thy joints forget" to show "duty to our presence?" The wily and cruel Northumberland, however, did not respond to the King's admonishment; he informed Richard that Bolingbroke only wanted to reclaim his rights, his "lineal royalties." If these rights were restored and his banishment overturned, Bolingbroke's insurrection would end. Immediately, Richard decreed that Bolingbroke's "demands" would "be accomplished without contradictions."

A moment later, however, Richard had misgivings. Turning to Aumerle, he wondered if he had not been too quick to "debase" himself. But just then Bolingbroke himself arrived, and Richard went down to the courtyard to meet his cousin. Watching his rival kneel before him, Richard chided, "Fair cousin, you debase your princely knee." Only then did Richard suddenly perceive that he had been tricked by Northumberland: Bolingbroke intended to steal his throne. "What you will have, I'll give, and willing too," Richard informed his cousin. But Bolingbroke and his followers seized Richard and spirited him back to London.

Although he was forced to hand his crown over to his cousin, Richard wavered. True, he had no choice in the matter—but who would he be if not the King? "I must nothing be," he mourned. Utterly defeated, Richard cried that he had nothing, not even the name he had received "at the font." Finally Bolingbroke, now the proclaimed King Henry IV, informed him that he was to be imprisoned in the Tower of London.

As Richard was being led to prison, Nurthumberland arrived to inform the deposed king that he was to be imprisoned in Pomfret Castle, instead of the Tower, and that his wife "must away to France." In agony, the former Queen begged Northumberland, "Banish us both, and send the King with me." But Northumberland ignored her. "One more adieu," Richard told his distraught wife as he was led toward Pomfret Castle, "the rest let sorrow say."

"Alack, poor Richard!" York's wife lamented when she heard of the his fate at Bolingbroke's hands. But her husband cautioned her that they all now had to pledge "lasting fealty to the new-made king." Moments later, however, their son Aumerle returned home and confessed of a plan that much alarmed his parents: Aumerle was part of a plot to murder Bolingbroke. Horrified, York denounced his son and rushed to the castle to warn his new King of the murderous plan. The Duchess and Aumerle followed quickly behind. Arriving at the castle, the Duchess begged, "Forever will I walk upon my knees," she promised, if only the King would forgive her son and spare his life. Henry IV astonished them all. "I will pardon him," he readily agreed, "as God shall pardon me." But, he informed them, the other conspirators would "not live within this world."

Soon afterward, the new monarch, uneasy in the thought that Richard could yet be restored to the throne, decided that the prisoner would have to die. Meanwhile, unaware of this edict, Richard agonized in his solitude at Pomfret Castle, passing the long hours questioning the nature of his own existence. Was he a "king"? Or was he a "beggar"? Or was he simply "nothing" at all? He concluded, "I wasted time, and now doth Time waste me."

One day when his jail keeper brought his meal, Richard asked him to taste the food as the keeper was "wont to do." The keeper refused. Right off suspecting treachery, Richard attacked the man, who screamed—which was all according to the new monarch's plan. Suddenly, hired murderers dashed into the room. Outwitting them, Richard grabbed one attacker's weapon and killed him. Then he felled another. But a third knight, the faithful Sir Exton, Henry's principal schemer in killing the deposed king, overtook Richard and delivered a mortal blow. Falling, Richard cried, "the king's blood stained the king's own land."

When Sir Exton returned with Richard's body, Henry banished the killer forever to hide his own treachery.

Proclaiming hatred for the "murderer," Henry insisted that he loved his poor dead cousin, and vowed to make a pilgrimage to the Holy Land—an atoning pilgrimage that would hopefully "wash the blood from his guilty hand."

Commentary:

Richard II was one of Shakespeare's most popular plays. In his time, he may have intended audiences to feel sympathy for Richard, since he believed his position to be "anointed" by God Himself. Bolingbroke, on the other hand, may evoke more sympathy from a contemporary audience, since his character reflects a will of the people.

Shakespeare's greatest strength was his ability to accurately portray on stage the turbulent, sometimes lethal, events that shaped English history.

RICHARD III

by
William Shakespeare
(1546-1616)

Type of work: Historical drama

Setting: 15th-century England (London, Salisbury, and Bosworth Field)

Principal characters:
Richard, Duke of Glouster, a treacherous, jealous, murderous aristocrat, and brother of King Edward IV
King Edward IV, King of England, Richard's elder brother
George, Duke of Clarence, Richard and Edward's youngest brother
Queen Elizabeth, Edward's wife
The Duchess of York, mother to Richard, George, and King Edward
Duke of Buckingham, a cousin to Richard
Queen Margaret, widow of King Henry VI, who was killed by Richard
Lady Anne, a widow whose husband and father-in-law were also killed by Richard.

Play Overview:

For having defeated them in battle—and to win back the throne—the sons of Richard II sought retribution against the family of Henry VI. Richard III, the most brutal of three brothers, murdered Henry's ailing son, stabbing him while the Queen looked on. Cursing them all, the Queen singled out the hunchbacked Richard III, calling him "the devil's butcher." In a frothing rage, Richard III sought out the king, whom he murdered on the spot. Richard's eldest brother, Edward, was then declared King of England. The stage for "Richard III had now been set."

Richard III stood on the streets of London, gloating about the victorious House of York. Though he had been instrumental in helping his brother to the throne, he now aspired it for himself. But his thoughts soon turned to his own deformity:

> *Cheated of feature by dissembling Nature,*
> *Deformed, unfinished, sent before my time*
> *Into this breathing world scarce half made*
> *up.*

Richard then took consolation in his own cleverness. In fact, he had just succeeded in pitting his brothers, King Edward and Clarence, against each other: Richard had tricked the King into believing there was a prophecy in which a kinsman, whose name began with the letter "G," would murder the King and win the throne. In response, King Edward had his brother, Clarence—whose given name was George—arrested.

In the midst of Richard's meditations, Clarence passed by, accompanied by an armed guard taking him to the Tower of London. Richard pretended to be shocked and outraged, and hinted that the King's wife or his mistress was responsible for Clarence's arrest. As soon as Clarence was out of sight, however, Richard, as deceitful in word as in deed, vowed to kill him, formulating how, for Richard's own political gain.

With the same thoughts for his brother, Edward, Richard formulated how God could, for Richard's own political gain, "take King Edward to his mercy." Besides the power it would bring, a position near—or on—the throne would make him a more attractive suitor for Lady Anne, one of the last remaining members of the once-powerful House of Lancaster—even though Richard had killed both her husband and her father-in-law.

A short while later, Richard spied Lady Anne as she followed the casket of her father-in-law, Henry VI, all the while cursing Richard for his crimes. When he approached, she lashed out at him spewing, "thou dreadful minister of hell."

But in an effort to deceive her, Richard then proclaimed his love for her—he had murdered her husband and father-in-law only to win for himself her "heavenly face." Feigning guilt, he even pronounced that he would lend her his "sharp-pointed sword" to kill him so that she might avenge the deaths. Not only did she refuse, she eventually agreed to wear Richard's ring. Before she departed, Anne told him how happy she was that he had "become so penitent."

Richard then decided to go to the palace to create trouble for Queen Elizabeth—Edward's wife—and her kinsmen. "A plague upon you all," he cried, accusing them in mock anger of imprisoning his brother Clarence. Meanwhile, the former Queen, Margaret—Lady Anne's mother-in-law—entered, whispering to herself loathing for Richard, the murderer of her husband and son. But Margaret finally could no longer bear to seethe quietly; she came forward and denounced all of them as "wrangling pirates" who had stolen her sovereignty. "Foul wrinkled witch," Richard hissed back at her. Thoroughly maddened by this insult, she cursed the House of York and predicted that Richard would bring ruin to all of them:

> *O but remember this another day,*
> *When he shall split thy very heart with sorrow,*
> *And say poor Margaret was a prophetess.*
> *Live each of you the subjects to his hate,*
> *And he to yours, and all of you to God's!*

Not long after, Richard met with two assassins, whom he hired to murder his brother Clarence. He instructed them to do the deed quickly, then sent them off.

When the murderers reached the Tower prison, they found Clarence sleeping. Earlier, however, Clarence had complained to his keeper about "fearful dreams of drowning." As if in fulfillment of prophecy, the murderers, after much arguing about the advisability of killing Clarence, first stabbed him, and then immersed him in a cask of wine.

Meanwhile, the gravely ill King Edward had called his own and his wife's families—including Richard—to his side and begged them to be "peaceful." Queen Elizabeth persuaded the king to pardon Clarence. But immediately Richard exclaimed, "But he, poor man, by your first order died." Edward grieved terribly at this news—little suspecting that Richard had been responsible for the death. Then Richard took his cousin, Buckingham, aside, and remarked how "guilty" of Clarence's execution the Queen's kinsmen appeared.

Fearing for the safety of her grandchildren, next in line for the throne, Edward's—and Richard's—mother, the Duchess of York, arranged to take Edward's sons to a sanctuary. Richard, however, persuaded the princes to go to the Tower, where, he said, they would be safer. Reluctantly, the princes left for the tower. They thought their grandmother and mother would join them later after arranging the coronation. But they would never see them again.

Still Richard was not satisfied: he had not yet gained public support. He conspired with Buckingham to spread lies about the legitimacy of the late King Edward. When the English citizenry rejected these rumors, Richard planned to feign reluctance to accept the throne. On the day of his coronation, he would stand between two priests with a prayerbook in his hand.

Once everyone had been assembled according to plan, Buckingham bade Richard to take control of the "kingly government." Richard declined, pretending to be a faithful supporter of the Crown Prince—who, for his "safety," was locked up in the Tower. The plan worked so well that before long the Mayor of London appealed to Richard, "Do, good my lord; the citizens entreat you." With false humility, Richard agreed to be king. And then with one last deception, he added, "Albeit against my conscience and my soul."

So, with Buckingham's help, he was crowned King Richard III. Buckingham, however, soon fell out of Richard's favor. One day referring to the young princes, Richard snarled, "I want the bastards dead." When Buckingham balked at the order, Richard became enraged—and quickly hired an assassin to smother the little princes in their sleep.

Word was sent to Anne that Richard demanded that she become Queen. Filled with trepidation, Anne went.

Not long after the princes were murdered, Richard decided to also kill his new wife, Anne. After the deed was done, he proclaimed that she had died of an illness—so that he could then pursue the beautiful Princess Elizabeth, Edward's daughter.

Queen Elizabeth, who still did not know the fate of her sons, was outraged when she found out Richard's intentions to marry her daughter. She claimed she would corrupt the young girl before she would let her marry Richard, but Richard was unfazed. So Elizabeth said she would consult with her daughter and would return with her decision.

Soon, the tide of fate gathered against Richard. Word was brought that the Earl of Richmond, a suitor of the throne, had gathered a naval fleet off the coast of Milford. At the Earl's side was Buckingham, Richard's defected accomplice. Another messenger brought news that revolts had sprung up in the realm, which angered Richard. He struck the messenger and told him to bring better news next time. The next messenger did in fact have better news: Buckingham had been captured in Salisbury, and was asking to see Richard. Denying his request, Richard ordered the execution of his old friend. "Wrong hath but wrong," he mused, penitently, "and blame the due of blame."

Soon, Richard made his way to Bosworth Field, where his forces would meet the Earl's. Settled into his tent the night before the battle, he found himself more down-hearted than usual. Finally, he fell asleep, but his dreams were haunted by the voices of his victims, who cheered on the Earl of Richmond.

The next day, Richard led his soldiers into battle. Before meeting his foe, Richard's horse was killed. Crying out, "A horse! My kingdom for a horse!" As Richard searched frantically for a mount, the Earl of Richmond fell upon him and killed him. The Earl proclaimed his intentions to marry Princess Elizabeth, and put the long war between the House of York and the House of Lancaster to rest. England would know peace at last.

Commentary:

This final work in the series of historical plays is quite devoid of typical prose and song.

Historically, Richard III he was the last English king of the House of York, whose death in 1483 led to the establishment—by Henry, Duke of Richmond—of today's Tudor monarchy. Richard III has been viewed more favorably by historians than by Shakespeare: he apparently was no more—or less—treacherous than others of his lineage.

Shakespeare created an unusually powerful, dramatic persona in the character of Richard, imbuing him with such a heinous nature that other characters in the tragedy refer to him, time and time again, as a "devil." His own mother eventually bewails her "accursed womb" for giving him life; and Richard himself confesses, "Alas, I rather hate myself ... I am a villain."

In spite of his evil character, Richard evokes surprising sympathy. This is perhaps due to his evolution—or devolution—from monster to mere mortal.

ANTONY AND CLEOPATRA

by
William Shakespeare
(1564 - 1616)

Type of work: Historic tragedy

Setting: Alexandria, Egypt and Rome, Italy (ca. 40-30 B.C.)

Principal characters:
  Antony, a leader of the Roman Triumvirate
  Cleopatra, a beautiful and clever Egyptian Queen
  Caesar and Lepidus, other Roman leaders of the Triumvirate
  Pompey, a powerful Roman rebel
  Octavia, Caesar's sister and Antony's second wife
  Enobarbus, Antony's wise friend and counsellor

Play Overview:

Antony first met Cleopatra when she was the mistress of Julius Caesar. Their affair began when Cleopatra—draped in gold and highly perfumed—sailed on a barge down the river Cydrus to meet Antony on matters of state. His passion for her intensified as the years passed—and frequently kept him from his duties in Rome. While Antony luxuriated in Alexandria with Cleopatra, Lepidus and Caesar, the other two members of the Roman Triumvirate, struggled with the threat of the insurrectionist Pompey, who continually pirated Roman fleets.

Attended by their friends and servants, Antony and Cleopatra enjoyed every sensual pleasure in the palace at Alexandria. Antony's friends, however, were troubled by his craving for the Egyptian Queen. One of his friends complained that Antony's doting surpassed "the measure" of good sense and that the mighty Roman leader had been reduced to "a strumpet's fool." But such thoughts certainly did not worry Cleopatra—who revelled in her lover's attentions—although she did have a concern of her own, namely, Antony's wife, Fulvia.

Finally, when jealousy overcame her, Cleopatra sought proof of Antony's love for her. One day when a messenger from Rome arrived, Cleopatra noticed the frown on Antony's face, an expression she attributed to a mysterious "Roman thought." After leaving Antony with the messenger, she commanded one of her attendants to summon Antony to her side. The moment he arrived, however, she feigned illness, hoping that he would dote on her. Antony did not oblige. Suspecting that it was Fulvia who preoccupied his mind, Cleopatra bristled with jealousy, saying, "hers you are."

Perhaps amused by her passionate outburst, Antony listened intently to his lover's tirade. Then he interrupted, informing her that he had to return to Rome, now besieged by Pompey's ships. Then he stunned Cleopatra with more interesting news: Fulvia was dead. Cleopatra's reaction to these tidings greatly surprised Antony; she explained haughtily that surely her own death would someday be "received" as Fulvia's had been—coldly. Antony comforted her, then took his leave, assuring her that his heart would "remain" with her.

When Antony arrived in Rome, he met with Lepidus and Caesar. Caesar had most strongly disapproved of Antony's sojourn in Alexandria, complaining to Lepidus that the general not only was in neglect of his stately duties, but "he fishes, drinks, and wastes" his time. But now confronted with the threat of Pompey's forces, Caesar ceased his murmuring; saving Rome was paramount, and they would have to consolidate their forces in order to win. Upon greeting Antony anew, however, he was unable to resist a brief chastisement, reminding Antony that he had reacted to his letters "with taunts" and that Fulvia and Antony's brother had conspired to overthrow Caesar. Antony insisted that he had no part in his family's conspiracies. Lepidus mediated, and Antony and Caesar reconciled their immediate differences.

At the suggestion of one of Caesar's friends, they cemented their alliance through marriage. Antony agreed to wed Caesar's sister, Octavia, after professing that he had become wise through from past mistakes and that in the future, in his devotion to Octavia, all would be "done by th' rule."

Antony's friend Enobarbus, however, doubted Antony's devotion to Octavia. As he conjured up in his mind her figure adorned in "cloth-of-gold-of-tissue" riding upon her gold-leafed barge, Enobarbus knew that Antony would never forsake the allure of the beautiful Egyptian Queen.

Back in Egypt, when Cleopatra received news of Antony's marriage, she became heart-broken and, characteristically, enraged. In fact, she first threatened to stab the messenger, then quickly reconsidered; she could make good use of the man. He would return to Rome and bring back to her a description of her new rival's "years," "her inclination," and "the color of her hair." Indeed, Cleopatra already sensed that Octavia presented little threat to her: where Antony preferred an untamed, garrulous woman, Octavia was a woman of most "holy, cold, and still conversation."

Elsewhere, Pompey, Rome's nemesis, also recognized that Octavia could not hold Antony. Summoned to Rome to effect a truce, the enemy general speculated that "first or last" Cleopatra's charms would again win Antony.

Before long Pompey's words proved true. On a state visit to Athens, Antony declared a separation from Octavia after learning that, in Antony's absence, her brother, Caesar, had broken the truce with Pompey. Next, Caesar had stripped Lepidus of his power and sentenced him to death. Vowing to "raise the preparation of a war on Caesar," Antony immediately sent Octavia back to Rome, while he set sail for Alexandria.

In her palace, Cleopatra had been greatly relieved to hear her messenger's depiction of Octavia: Antony's wife was rather short and "low-voiced." Cleopatra, thus, ridiculed her rival as "dull of tongue and dwarfish." Again confident of Antony's love, on his return to Alexandria she used her wiles to persuaded him to extend her sovereignty beyond Egypt into "lower Syria, Cyprus, Lydia," united her forces with Antony's in a war against Caesar, and insisted on being with Antony on the battlefield. Only Enobarbus dared caution that her presence in battle would take Antony's "heart," "brain," and "time" away from matters of war. But Cleopatra would not listen. Instead, she urged Antony to assemble his forces together with her own fleet to meet Caesar's troops at sea. Enobarbus candidly tried to dissuade Antony from waging a sea battle, for the army was trained for land warfare, but Antony also dismissed Enobarbus' advice.

In time, Antony and Cleopatra's forces clashed with Caesar's ships. In the midst of battle at Actium, however, Cleopatra changed her mind and commanded her ships to return to Alexandria. Antony panicked, "leaving the fight in height," and followed Cleopatra. Back in the palace, Antony brooded, dejected. The earth was "ashamed to bear" him, he concluded; he had "lost command." Even Cleopatra could not soften his sorrow. When she came to him, he wailed, "O, whither hast thou led me, Egypt?" She beseeched her lover's pardon, and he forgave her, saying, "Fall not a tear"; to him, each one of her tears was worth "all that is won and lost."

Soon, however, they comprehended the enormity of their defeat. Caesar, gloating in his victory, sent word that, in exchange for the "grizzled head" of Antony, he would give Cleopatra whatever she wished. Outraged, Antony challenged Caesar to meet him "sword against sword." But of course Caesar would never agree to a duel. By now desperate for some sort of victory, Antony wondered: Why not lead another army against Caesar? Elated by this new plan, he and Cleopatra celebrated—to feast and "mock the midnight bell."

When Antony awoke the next morning, his thoughts were already on battle, and he immediately began to put on his armor. When Cleopatra tried to help him, Antony told her happily that she was the "armorer" of his "heart." Then he kissed her and departed for his camp. There he heard troubling news: Enobarbus, his friend, his counsellor, had defected over to Caesar's camp. Within days, however, overcome with remorse for having deserted his friend, Enobarbus set off to find "some ditch wherein to die."

Antony never did learn of Enobarbus' death. Busy with the intricacies of warfare, Antony had another reason to despair. From his vantage point in Alexandria, he watched as the Egyptian fleets again turned and fled from the battle. "All is lost," he grieved. Then, convinced that Cleopatra was to blame, he raged, "The foul Egyptian hath betrayed me . . . Fortune and Antony part here."

Upon hearing that Antony considered her both a false lover and a false ally, Cleopatra, greatly saddened, longed to once more have him at her side. In a clever ploy to bring him there, she dispatched an attendant to tell Antony that she had died and that her body had been taken to her monument.

"All length is torture; since the torch is out," Antony cried out when he heard the news. Turning to one of his men, he commanded him to kill him with his sword. The soldier, though reluctant, finally lifted his sword and said, "Farewell, great chief." Antony bravely awaited death, but was stunned when the man instead thrust the sword into himself in order to "escape the sorrow" of witnessing his commander's death.

"Thou teachest me," Antony lamented. Then he fell on his own sword, but he did not die. "O dispatch me!" he called out. When Antony's men came running to his side, he pleaded with them to kill

him. But no one dared.

Soon, another of Cleopatra's attendants arrived, breathlessly explaining that news of Cleopatra's death had been a ploy. Mortally wounded, Antony said, "Bear me, good friends where Cleopatra bides." The Roman soldiers quickly conveyed Antony to Cleopatra's monument—which had been constructed to serve as her tomb. Embracing and kissing him, Cleopatra condemned her foolish actions. Antony, however, forgave her. Then, before waning into death, sought to comfort his beloved:

> The miserable change now at my end
> Lament nor sorrow at, but please your thoughts
> In feeding them with those my former fortunes,
> Wherein I lived the greatest prince o' the world .

Cleopatra, overcome with anguish, resolved to join him.

In Rome, Caesar, learning of Antony's death, did not rejoice; instead he mourned Antony as a "brother" and as a "mate in empire." Then he dispatched a messenger to invite Cleopatra to Rome, where he would treat her most "humble and kindly." Others had already unmasked Caesar's true intentions: she knew that he would make her his captive, parade her through the streets of Rome, and let her be "chastised by the sober eye" of her rival Octavia. Nevertheless, Cleopatra accepted the invitation.

Before Caesar and his men arrived to convey to Rome, however, Cleopatra arranged for a peasant to bring her a basket of figs. "Hast thou the pretty worm of Nilus there?" Cleopatra asked the man. He assured her he did. Among the figs, deadly asps slithered in the basket. Once Cleopatra had dismissed the man, she asked one of her attendants to dress her in her robe and crown. Putting an asp to her breast, Cleopatra then bade the serpent, "Be angry, dispatch," then, before dying, called out, "O Antony!"

When Caesar and his men entered the monument, they found the bodies of the Egyptian Queen and two of her attendants. "She shall be buried with her Antony," Caesar declared. Then he marvelled at the "pity" and the "glory" of Cleopatra and her beloved Antony.

Commentary:

"Antony and Cleopatra" depicts a world rife with opposing forces: honor clashing with dishonor, fidelity with promiscuity, domination with subjugation, trust with treachery. Overriding the character flaws, however, is one primary conflict between all that is "Roman" and all that is "Egyptian." "While there is one world in the play," critic Northrop Frye points out, "there are two aspects of it: the aspect of `law and order' represented by Rome and the aspect of sexual extravagance and license represented by Egypt."

Shakespeare uses a particularly clear-headed character, Enobarbus, to illuminate this conflict. An insignificant player in the drama, Enobarbus is free to speculate on the relative attributes of both nation-states. His primary role is simply to highlight the contrast between the intoxicating sensuality of Cleopatra's Egypt and the established mores of Antony's Rome—which Antony ultimately betrays to passion.

TROILUS AND CRESSIDA

by
William Shakespeare
(1564-1616)

Type of work: Tragic drama

Setting: Troy, an ancient Phrygian city in north-west Asia minor; c. 1250 B.C.

Principal characters:
> *Troilus*, a Prince of Troy
> *Cressida*, a Trojan maiden, second only in beauty to Helen
> *Pandarus*, Cressida's uncle, a disease-ridden Trojan lord
> *Hector*, a Prince of Troy, General of the Trojan army, and Troilus' eldest brother
> *Ulysses*, a Greek commander
> *Achilles*, Ajax and Diomedes, noble commanders of the Greek army, Achilles being the most skillful in battle

Play Overview:

It was the seventh year of the Trojan War. Helen, whose abduction from her husband Menelaus had caused the Greeks to lay siege to Troy, remained with her Trojan abductor Paris behind the city's walls. For the first time since the war began, Greeks and Trojans alike were questioning their motives and their resolve to fight.

The Greek army had fallen into chaos. Although in numbers they were superior to the Trojans, their morale had so deteriorated over the years that any possibility of victory now appeared to be extremely remote. As Ulysses, one of the Greek commanders, noted to King Agamemnon, they lacked unity and order. It was their own disarray that was defeating them. "Troy in our weakness stands, not in her strength."

Agamemnon quizzed the General as to how the Greeks might remedy the situation, and Ulysses replied quite simply: "Achilles." Achilles was the Greeks' champion warrior. The problem was, however, that he refused to fight. He was in love with the Trojan Princess Polyxena, and Polyxena's mother, Queen Hecuba, had made her daughter's suitor promise that he would not take part in the siege. Somehow, Ulysses concluded, Achilles and his Myrmidon soldiers must be humbled and roused to come to Greece's aid.

The Trojans, on the other hand, had begun to wonder aloud whether Helen merited their years of suffering. The Greeks had once more sent an emissary to Troy, asking King Priam to deliver Helen over to them and thus end the war. Priam was now seriously considering this possibility; even his eldest son, Prince Hector, was forced to admit that his sister-in-law Helen was "not worth what she doth cost—The keeping."

The young, idealistic Trojan Prince Troilus, however, vehemently disagreed. He contended that once a wife was taken she could not "honorably" be surrendered. But Troilus, as he argued with his father and brother returning Helen to the Greeks, was perhaps motivated by his own fortunes in love. His brother Paris, after all, had managed both to capture Helen in Argos and, against heavy odds, bring her back to Troy. Troilus, by

contrast, had fallen in love with the beautiful Cressida, a Trojan native. But in spite of the fact that Cressida was within arm's reach, Troilus had been unable to win her affections. Indeed, Cressida appeared to be wholly unaware of his existence.

Against this uncertain backdrop—the fortunes of love entangled with those of war—Cressida's uncle, the diseased and decrepit Pandarus, pleaded with Troilus not to lose hope. Troilus by now had grown impatient with Pandarus' attempts to bring him and Cressida together, and Pandarus took offense at this attitude, complaining of "small thanks for my labor." Nevertheless, he persisted, taking every opportunity to promote Troilus' interests with his niece. "[Have] you any eyes?" Pandarus asked Cressida, "Do you know what a man is? Is not birth, beauty, good shape, discourse, manhood, learning, gentleness, virtue, youth, liberality, and such like, the spice and salt that season a man?"

Cressida, for her part, pretended to be unmoved by her uncle's appeals—although, in fact, she held Troilus in some regard. She considered this feigned lack of interest to be a necessary tactic in love. A man's passions and desires could be more fully aroused, she had discovered, when she pretended to withhold her own. It was a simple but effective strategy. "Things won are done," she thought. "Men prize the thing ungained . . ."

This strategy, however, was neither unique to Cressida nor confined merely to games of love; variations of it were also applied to games of war. The Greeks' petition for Helen's release had been answered by a summons from Hector that each army's best soldier meet in single combat—a development that led back to the Greeks' quandary with Achilles, since Hector's challenge had clearly been intended for this heroic son of a goddess and a king.

After some debate, however, it was decided that Ajax—not Achilles—should meet Hector. "Ajax employed," reasoned Ulysses, "plucks down Achilles' plumes."

In Troy, meanwhile, Pandarus had at last succeeded in persuading Cressida to meet with Troilus. Troilus was ecstatic. "Expectation," he told Pandarus, "whirls me round. Th' imaginary relish is so sweet / That it enchants my sense." The night's tryst disappointed neither of the lovers. When morning finally broke, Cressida turned to Troilus and ruefully complained, "Night hath been too brief." The liaison was briefer, though, than even she could have imagined, for that very night Cressida's father—who years earlier had defected to the Greeks—had authored an agreement by which Cressida would be exchanged for a Trojan prisoner of war. This agreement of exchange was a *fait accompli*: the Greek commander Diomedes appeared at that moment to escort her to her father's tent. The distraught pair pledged their mutual love, and, as a token of enduring faithfulness, Troilus gave Cressida his sleeve and promised her that somehow, no matter what the dangers to him, he would visit her every night in the Greek encampment. Then Cressida was led off to her father.

By now, Achilles had heard of Hector's challenge—and that Agamemnon had selected Ajax for the match. He took this news as an insult; Ajax was a fool. "What, are [my] deeds forgot?" he asked Ulysses. Inwardly, Ulysses smiled. His strategy with Achilles—like Cressida's with Troilus—seemed to be working. His reply now pressed the ploy carefully home:

> Those scraps are good deeds past, which are
> devoured
> As fast as they are made, forgot as soon
> As done. Perseverance, dear my lord,
> Keeps honor bright. To have done, is to hang
> Quite out of fashion . . .

Much as he loathed it, that evening there was nothing Achilles could do but watch as the enemy armies assembled outside Troy for the match between their respective champions.

Hector, who had hoped to meet Achilles on the field, was greatly dismayed to find Ajax in his place: he had not expected that the Greeks would choose his own cousin as his foe. After parrying a few sword thrusts, he honorably declined to continue the match against the son of his mother's sister. The Greeks and Trojans, it was decided, would enjoy a brief respite and feast each other that night. Tomorrow the war would resume.

That night, Achilles invited Hector to his tent. He had finally given in to the calls to fight, and, as he told his friend Patroclus, this would be an opportunity to size up his foe. "I'll heat his blood with Greekish wine tonight," he said, "which with my scimitar I'll cool tomorrow."

Troilus also found in this unforeseen turn of events a wonderful opportunity: now he could see Cressida. But as he approached the tent of his beloved, he heard voices from within. It was Cressida and Diomedes, who, earlier that same morning, had introduced himself as her escort from Troy. Yet here he was in her tent, and here she was trying to persuade him not to leave, calling after him—in a plaintive voice—"Sweet honey Greek."

Cressida and Diomedes were having what appeared to be a lovers' quarrel—and the quarrel appeared to revolve around the sleeve Troilus had given her that morning as a pledge and token of his love. Cressida had obviously given the sleeve to Diomedes but now wanted it back. Diomedes refused, and was now demanding to know whose sleeve it was. "Tomorrow," Diomedes said, "I'll wear it on my helmet, and grieve his spirit that dares not challenge it."

Troilus was stunned by these words, utterly crushed by Cressida's fickle, duplicitous nature. This both was and was not his Cressida, he thought. Turning to Ulysses, he swore that the next day, when the Trojans again met the Greeks on the battlefield, he would have his revenge on Diomedes:

> Much as I do Cressid love,
> So much by weight hate I her Diomed;
> That sleeve is mine that he'll bear on his helmet;
> Were it a casque composed by Vulcan's skill,
> My sword should bite it.

As the next day's campaign wore to its close, the fighting—as usual during the last several years'

battles—yielded neither side the advantage. Troilus had found and fought Diomedes on the field, but, apart from Troilus' losing his horse, nothing conclusive had come of their confrontation.

Hector, who had been victorious all day, was preparing to retire from the field. He had just disarmed himself and turned toward Troy when Achilles reappeared. The two had met on the battlefield earlier that day. After parrying only a short time, though, Achilles had asked Hector's permission to withdraw; he was too tired, he said, to fight on. Now, however, presented with such an easy target, Achilles ordered his Myrmidon spearmen to kill Hector. He then tied the dead Hector to the tail of his horse and, in full view of the returning Trojans, dragged the dishonored body through the fields.

All of Troy was grief-stricken. All swore vengeance on the Greeks for the cowardly and treacherous act Achilles had committed. Troilus passed slowly through the gates of Troy, and, as he entered the city, heard Pandarus call out to him, "But hear you, hear you!" He looked up and called back to Pandarus, "Hence, broker, lackey! Ignominy and shame pursue thy life, and live aye thy name."

Commentary:

One of Shakespeare's most elusive and least performed works, "Troilus and Cressida" occupies a peculiar place in the Shakespearian canon: variously classified as a history, a comedy, and a tragedy, the play turns on an unusual, highly contrapuntal—and strangely frustrating—double plot. The first plot line concerns the Trojan War and revolves primarily around the characters of Hector and Achilles; the second is the love story involving Troilus and Cressida. What makes this double plot both intriguing and, finally, unsatisfying is that both sides of the story have what A.P. Rossiter calls a "false bottom"; that is, each plot line builds dramatic tension and rises to a climax, creating expectations which the play's action then refuses to fulfill.

The tension, for instance, that builds around the long anticipated combat scenes between the opposing champions Hector and Achilles is deflated not once, but twice. Similarly, the love story between Troilus and Cressida turns out to climax not in resolution, but instead in duplicity, deception and disillusionment. Even the dramatic tension that builds after Troilus and Diomedes pledge to take revenge on each other is deflated, neither fulfilling his pledge.

By the play's end, the Greeks have finally obtained an apparent advantage over Troy. It is, however, an ill-gotten advantage. Contrary to the tradition of the Homeric epic, Hector's death is achieved not through heroic combat but through a cowardly act of murder.

"Troilus and Cressida" is a brilliant play, characterized by its biting and caustic wit. Still, there are no heroes in this tragedy. Indeed, Shakespeare, perhaps anticipating the existentialist pessimism of the twentieth century on this Elizabethan drama, gives the last word to the sickly Pandarus, who turns to address the audience, first to bewail his own misfortunes, and second, in an unnerving gesture, "to bequeath you my diseases."

ALL'S WELL THAT ENDS WELL

by
William Shakespeare
(1564-1616)

Type of work: Dramatic comedy

Setting: Medieval France and Italy

Principal characters:
Bertram, a young aristocrat
The Countess of Rousillon, Bertram's mother
Helena, attendant to the Countess of Rousillon
Lafew, a French lord
The King of France
Diana, a beautiful young Florentine who befriends Helena

Play Overview:

Soon after the death of the Count of Rousillon, the Count's great friend--who also happened to be King of France--came down with a disease which the court physicians were unable to cure. Fearing that his own death was imminent, the childless King sent for his late friend's only child, Bertram, who was now his ward. The Countess of Rousillon was much aggrieved by her son's summons. "In delivering my son from me," she wailed, "I bury a second husband." But the French lord Lafew--who had come to take Bertram--reassured her that the King would conduct himself like a father toward her son.

A wise and kind-hearted woman, the Countess finally reconciled herself to her son's journey. Realizing the import of his bearing before the court, she composed herself to leave him with some motherly advice:

Be thou blessed, Bertram, and succeed thy
father
In manners as in shape! Thy blood and virtue
Contend for empire in thee, and thy goodness
Share with thy birthright! Love all, trust a few,
Do wrong to none . .

Though her son was very dear to her, the Countess also mourned aloud at how young he was--and how filled with vanity and self-importance. And as if to obligingly illustrate these unattractive aspects of his character, after bidding farewell to his mother, Bertram turned to her servant, Helena, and reminded the girl contemptuously that in his absence she had better pamper her mistress.

Unbeknownst to Bertram, however, Helena was in love with him and was very greatly saddened at his leaving. But Helena was a resourceful maid and she quickly devised a plan to follow Bertram to the king's court to win him for her husband. She would cure the King--with a secret prescription that her late father, a highly respected physician, had willed to her at his death.

"Why Helen, thou shalt have my leave and love," the Countess told the girl when she learned of the plan. And indeed the Countess did love Helena very much. "I am a mother to you," the warm-hearted woman rehearsed to her young attendant. Convinced of her patroness's trust and affection, Helena set off for court.

At first the King was reluctant to try Helena's remedy. But Helena persisted; if the cure failed, she proclaimed, "with vilest torture let my life be ended." Hearing these words, the King reconsidered. Would this "kind maid" truly offer her life to him if the prescription were inferior? Finally he told her, "I will try."

Clever girl that she was, Helena then asked the King what he proposed to give her in return, should the cure prove effective. Whatever she desired, replied the King. Helena responded that she wished to choose a husband from among the eligible bachelors at court. "My deed shall match thy deed," the King promised.

Helena's prescription did indeed cure the King. He was exuberant. Leading Helena in a spirited dance into the palace's Great Hall, he ordered Le Few to "Go, call before me all the lords in court." Then, with the court assembled, he turned to Helena:

Fair maid, send forth thine eye. This young
parcel
Of noble bachelors stand at my bestowing,
O'er whom both sovereign power and father's
voice
I have to use. They frank election make;
Thou has power to choose, and they have none
to forsake.

Helena did not single out Bertram immediately. She first approached various courtiers, both to test their obedience to the King's command and to build her confidence. "Sir, will you hear my suit?" she asked them one by one. Each assured her that he would. When at last, however, she dared to confess that her choice was Bertram, the young count protested. Incredulous at Bertram's reaction, the King addressed him: "Know'st thou not, Bertram, what she hath done for me?" Yes, Bertram knew--but even after the King had pointed out how "young, wise and fair" Helena was, he could not wipe away his "disdain" for her humble upbringing. Angry with Bertram's arrogance and impudence, the King chastened the lad:

. . . That is honor's scorn
Which challenges itself as honor's born
And is not like the sire. Honors thrive
When rather from our acts we them derive . . .

But Bertram still refused, objecting that he did not love Helena. To make the match sweeter to the headstrong young man, the King bestowed a rich dowry on Helena, equal to or greater than Bertram's own estate. Finally, seeing that he had no real choice in the matter, Bertram agreed, and he and Helena were wed.

But Bertram had resolved that he would never live with Helena; instead, he would go to war to fight on behalf of the Duke of Florence. That same day--with the help of his trusted, though unscrupulous, friend Parolles--Bertram composed a letter to his new bride explaining that he was going to war and charging her immediate departure from court. He would never think of Helena as his wife, Bertram informed her, unless she could fulfill two seemingly impossible conditions:

> When thou canst get the ring upon my finger, which never shall come off, and show me a child begotten of thy body that I am father to, then call me husband; but in such a "then" I write a "never" ...

Returning home to Rousillon, as Bertram had demanded, Helena found the Countess waiting to comfort her. The kind woman deplored her son's treatment of his new wife. But now Helena, still devoted to Bertram and certain that he would not return home to his mother from the battle if she remained there, decided to escape Rousillon for a time. Leaving the Countess a letter stating that she had gone on a religious pilgrimage, Helena set off for Italy.

On her way, Helena stopped in Florence, staying at the house of a widow and her lovely young daughter, Diana. The two of them, it appeared by their conversation, were acquainted with Bertram.

At first Helena did not reveal her true identity; she simply listened as the other women chatted. It turned out that Bertram had earlier pursued Diana, but that she had spurned him--and, so she had heard, recently married. Now, she could feel nothing but compassion for the poor lady who had married him, and contempt for his companion, the "vile rascal," Parolles.

Convinced that she was in sympathetic company, Helena finally revealed herself as Bertram's new bride. Would the mother and daughter give her "good aid"? she asked. Would they help her fulfill the terms of Bertram's letter? Indeed they would--particularly after Helena had presented them with a "purse of gold."

Diana found Bertram, advised him that she had reconsidered his proposition, and agreed to meet him in her chamber at midnight. But in exchange for her "chastity," she told him, he would have to agree to her terms: to trade his ring for hers and to refrain from speech in her bedroom. Bertram, overjoyed at the thought of lying with his lady, agreed. Unbeknownst to Bertram, however, as midnight approached, Helena took Diana's place in the dark room, and waited to exchange her ring for his.

Bertram was easily deceived; innocently, he spent the night with Helena. But still another deception awaited the susceptible Bertram: Helena had arranged to have news of her death reach her husband. And thus, believing her safely out of his way forever, Bertram at last returned home. The King, the Countess, and Lafew--whose daughter Bertram had now pledged to marry--were all assembled at Rousillon when he arrived. All mourned Helena; seeing her sorrow, even Bertram himself had a change of heart and professed his love for his departed wife. Moved by Bertram's declaration, the King forgave him of his harsh treatment of Helena:

> ... Our rash faults
> Make trivial price of serious things we have,
> Not knowing them, until we know their grave.
> Oft our displeasures, to ourself unjust,
> Destroy our friends and after weep their dust.

But no sooner had the King finished speaking than he noticed the ring on Bertram's finger--the very ring the King had once given to Helena as a gift. Translating this to mean that Helena's life had been "foully snatched," the King became infuriated.

Just then, in order to save Bertram's life, Diana burst into the room and recited the story of how she had arranged a darkened tryst with him where she had received his ring. "To prison with her!" ordered the King, bewildered and outraged.

And then, a moment later, Helena herself appeared. "Is't real that I see?" the King wondered aloud. For his part, Bertram immediately begged Helena's forgiveness. Helena, reminding Bertram of the terms of his letter, then pointed to the ring and revealed that she was expecting his child. "Will you be mine," she asked, "now you are doubly won?" And Bertram vowed that he truly would "love her dearly."

The King again pledged to pay Helena's dowry and, recalling all the troubles of the past, concluded that joy was very welcome indeed.

Commentary:

Throughout its history, "All's Well That Ends Well" has presented critics with problems of classification. In the strictest sense, the work is neither drama nor comedy; it seems to impart the kind of moral lesson that drama often presents, but also includes many farcical moments. "Dark Comedy," then, is the term most frequently used to categorize the play.

But what is the moral lesson portrayed, the reader may ask? First and foremost, "All's Well" emphasizes that virtue—not title, position or lineage—reaps the ultimate reward. Clearly, the plucky and persevering Helena's *virtue*—which the Countess praises early in the play and which the King recognizes as "wisdom" and "courage"—has won Bertram's affection by play's end. Not only has she demonstrated her steadfast loyalty to Bertram, but she has succeeded in outwitting him. Providing both the most dramatic and the most comic elements of the play, this devotion often takes a remarkably selfless form. Before leaving on her pilgrimage, for instance, she repents of her willfulness and sympathizes with Bertram:

> ... Poor Lord! Is't I
> That chase thee from thy country and expose
> Those tender limbs of thine to the event
> Of the none-sparing war?

Herein, Helena demonstrates her maturity. She—like the older characters, the King and the Countess—finds her dignity in caring for others, a virtue that has nothing to do with the circumstances of her birth. Life is *not*, after all, how all begins, but rather how "all ends" that matters.

A MIDSUMMER NIGHT'S DREAM

by
William Shakespeare
(1564-1616)

Type of work: Elizabethan comedic drama

Setting: Athens, in ancient Greece

Principal characters:
  Theseus, Duke of Athens
  Hermia and Lysander, lovers
  Demetrius, another of Hermia's wooers
  Helena, Hermia's friend, who is in love
    with Demetrius
  Oberon and Titania, the Fairy King and
    Queen
  Puck, Oberon's servant

Play Overview:

Theseus, Duke of Athens, impatiently anticipated his marriage to Hippolyta, Queen of the Amazons. His drifting thoughts were interrupted by the arrival of Egeus, an Athenian citizen, accompanied by his beautiful daughter Hermia and two young men. "Full of vexation come I," Egeus complained. He wanted his daughter to marry Demetrius, one of the young men who escorted him, but Hermia loved the other, Lysander. Complicating matters, both Lysander and Demetrius adored Hermia.

Theseus entreated Hermia to not be troublesome, and ordered her to comply with her father's wishes or else suffer, by Athenian law, one of two consequences: either death or life without a husband. Hermia, however, took matters into her own hands. She and Lysander, meeting in secret soon after, decided to flee to his aunt's house—which was outside the jurisdiction of Athenian law. Elated with their plan, they revealed it to Hermia's good friend Helena:

And in the wood, where often you and I
Upon faint primrose beds were wont to lie,
Emptying our bosoms of their counsel sweet,
There my Lysander and myself shall meet . . .

Helena listened thoughtfully. Hermia was truly her dearest friend, but she held Demetrius—Lysander's rival—in dearer esteem than any mere friendship. But no matter how hard she had tried, Helena had been unable to win his affections; Demetrius remained utterly smitten with Hermia.

Weighing Hermia's confidences, Helena decided that since she could not capture Demetrius for herself, she could at least please him by helping him win his chosen love. "I will go tell him of fair Hermia's flight," she resolved.

It was a glorious Midsummer's Eve when Hermia and Lysander met for their secret forest rendezvous. On that magical evening, however, the woods swarmed with many other presences. Demetrius had come in search of Hermia—and Helena had secretly followed Demetrius. A troupe of Athenian actors were also gathered among the trees to rehearse Pyramus and Thisby, a tragedy they hoped to perform at Theseus' wedding. And, finally, there was a group of fairies meeting in the woods to join in the revels

of Oberon, the Fairy King.

Oberon felt peevish that night. He and his Queen, Titania, were quarreling. Oberon wanted for his own Titania's pet protege, the Indian boy whom she always kept close by her side. Titania refused: the whole of Fairy Land would not be payment enough.

Now, Oberon intended to use his power as Fairy King to force Titania to comply. He directed his servant, Puck—who adored impish pranks—to find a "western flower" so that he could place the "juice of it on [the] sleeping eyelids" of his Queen. When she opened her eyes, Oberon merrily explained, she would fall in love with the first thing she gazed on—"be it on lion, bear, or wolf, or bull."

No sooner had Puck disappeared to find the wondrous flower, than Oberon spied Demetrius and Helena in a meadow. Clearly visible in the moonlight, Helena was chasing the callous young man. "I am sick when I do look on thee," Demetrius railed at poor Helena. The lovesick maid continued her pursuit: "I'll follow thee, and make a heaven of hell," she called after the fleeing youth. Oberon's heart went out to Helena. When Puck returned with the magical flower, the king instructed him to steal quietly near Demetrius while he slept and "anoint" his eyes with juice of the flower. When awakened, Demetrius would look upon Helena and love her.

Having sent Puck off on his mischievous errand, Oberon waited while Titania's attendants lulled their mistress to sleep; then he crept near with his magical potion and shook it gently onto the queen's dreamy eyelids. "Wake when some vile thing is near," Oberon gleefully instructed his wife.

Puck, meanwhile, searching the woods for his quarry, came across a young man in Athenian garments—Oberon's description of Demetrius—stretched out asleep on the ground beside a young woman. Puck sprinkled his potion on the Athenian's eyelids and sped away to meet Oberon. Puck, however, had blundered—the couple on the ground were Hermia and Lysander, not Helena and Demetrius.

When Lysander awoke, Helena, disheveled and breathless from chasing Demetrius, wandered into view. The magical juice worked all too well: Lysander fell instantly in love with Helena and denounced the "tedious minutes" he had passed with Hermia. Helena, dazed by Lysander's endearments, warily assumed that Lysander was mocking her. "O, that a lady of one man refused," she chastised him, "Should of another therefore be abused!" Then she stormed off—with Lysander, still under the spell, hurrying after her.

Hermia awoke moments later, distraught from a nightmare: "Methought a serpent [did] eat my heart away." Noticing Lysander's disappearance, she feared for his life and hurried off to look for him.

Not far away, meanwhile, the actors were about to begin the rehearsal of their play. "Speak, Pyramus, Thisby stand forth," intoned the director. But, while Bottom, the thespian playing the role of Pyramus, waited in a thicket for his entry, the ever-mischievous Puck slyly slipped an ass's head over his mask. When on cue Bottom stepped from the thicket, the huge mask so startled the other actors that they ran away. Bottom, unaware of his appearance, speculated that the company, as a joke, was trying to frighten him by leaving him alone in the woods. Thus, resolving to show no fear whatsoever, he ambled along the pathway, singing bravely.

Presently, back in Fairy Land, Titania opened her groggy eyes. "What angel wakes me from my flow'ry bed?" she asked. But it was no angel who stood before her: her gaze had alighted on none other than the actor, Bottom—looking very much like an ass. Overcome by this angelic beast, she instantly proclaimed her ardent love. Bottom, confused but pleased by this enchanting beauty's passionate confession, mused how "reason and love keep little company." Enraptured, Titania led the man with an ass's head away to her bower.

When Puck—who knew everything that went on in the woods—related to Oberon that Titania had become infatuated with a "monster," the Fairy King was elated. However, the arrival of Demetrius and Hermia, who were arguing about Lysander, interrupted his good mood. Hermia accused Demetrius of having murdered her lover in a jealous rage, and refused to believe Demetrius' denials. Hermia hastened off in alarm; Demetrius, frustrated, lay down and fell asleep. To set matters straight, Oberon sprinkled fairy juice on Demetrius' sleeping eyes, and sent Puck to make sure that Helena would be by his side when he awakened.

The plan worked. Seeing Helena, Demetrius raved, "O Helen, goddess, nymph, perfect, divine!" But at that moment, Lysander also reappeared to claim Helena as his own. Now Helena was even more bewildered than before: both men—these who had previously pursued only Hermia—fiercely proclaimed their devotion.

To confuse matters even further, Hermia suddenly stumbled onto the scene, looking on in puzzlement. How could her beloved Lysander suddenly claim to "hate" her and adore Helena? At last she turned her rage on Helena, her apparent supplanter. "You juggler! You canker blossom!" Hermia lashed out, as Lysander and Demetrius, meanwhile, continued hurling insults at one another.

Seeing what "knaveries" his servant had caused, Oberon once again sent Puck off to set matters straight. Puck managed, after some difficulty, to herd the four exhausted Athenians into a clearing. After Lysander fell asleep on the grass, he once again applied the juice to the eyes of a slumbering lover. "The man shall have his mare again," he whispered as he dashed away,

"and all shall be well."

Puck found Oberon sleeping at Titania's side. Her devotion to Bottom—that peculiar man with an ass's head—had rekindled Oberon's tenderness toward his Queen. When Titania awoke, the love spell was broken, and she promised to give her husband the Indian boy he had wanted for a courier. Oberon said:

Now thou and I are new in amity,
And will tomorrow midnight solemnly
Dance in Duke Theseus' house triumphantly,
And bless it to all fair prosperity.

Dawn lighted the sky. All had at last been set right. Lysander once more adored Hermia, and the "object and the pleasure" of Demetrius' eyes was Helena. The marriage became a triple wedding, and the actors assembled to perform their play. Just before they were to go on stage, Bottom appeared. He did not tell them about the wondrous "dream" he had witnessed the night before or how he had spent the night in the woods. How could he? "Man is but an ass," he mused, "if he go about to expound this dream." Perhaps, someday, he would commission the troupe's director to write a ballet about it: "It shall be called," he said to himself, "'Bottom's Dream,' because it hath no bottom."

The play began. The actors stumbled and botched the performance so completely that the tragedy became comedy—leaving the three married couples greatly amused. "This palpable-gross play hath well beguiled," Theseus told the actors. Then he turned to the other couples—and to his new wife—and said, "Sweet friends, to bed."

Everyone left the festivities, delighted. Oberon and Puck appeared—in fairy garb, of course—to celebrate the nuptial feast. Pleased to see such a joyous outcome, Oberon proclaimed that the "bride bed" of each couple would "blessed be" with happiness and children.

Commentary:

A Midsummer Night's Dream has been called Shakespeare's happiest work—and perhaps one of the happiest, most enchanting works ever written. The congenial confusion that results from the plot's comic convolutions serves not to obstruct romance, but to heighten anticipation of its impending pleasures.

For instance, Egeus' forbidding his daughter Hermia to marry Lysander—even going so far as to attach a penalty of death to his objections—is so utterly arbitrary that it seems impossible to imagine how his objections can *not* be overcome. The way in which Hermia and Helena triumph over the obstacles to their marriage desires serves to resolve the dramatic tension in a comic way.

The play evokes in us a nostalgia for a lost, but pagan, paradise. Unlike the familiar and darker pathos of the Biblical Eden, the paradise of "A Midsummer Night's Dream" is one in which the circumstances of our erotic birth are entirely happy, and its consequences are—as Oberon says at the play's end—entirely "blessed."

THE COMEDY OF ERRORS

by
William Shakespeare
(1564-1616)

Type of work: Farcical comedy

Setting: Ephesus, an ancient port city in Asia Minor

Principal characters:

Aegeon, a merchant of Syracuse
Aemilia, wife to Egeon and abbess at Ephesus
Antipholus of Syracuse and Antipholus of Ephesus, twin sons of Egeon and Aemilia
Dromio of Syracuse and Dromio of Ephesus, twin brothers and bondsmen to the two Antipholuses
Adriana, wife to Antipholus of Ephesus
Luciana, Adriana's sister
Solinus, Duke of Ephesus

Story Overview:

Aegeon arrived in Ephesus, after five years at sea, to find himself sentenced to death. As a result of recent animosity between Ephesus and Aegeon's native Syracuse, citizens of one city would be put to death if discovered in the other, unless a 1000-mark ransom was paid to buy his liberty. Since Aegeon could not afford the ransom, he was to be hanged at sunset.

Aegeon, sadly, did not dispute his sentence. Indeed, he welcomed it as a means "by the doom of death [to] end woes and all." When Solinus, the Duke of Ephesus, asked the merchant his motive for coming there, Aegeon replied:

> A heavier task could not have been impos'd
> Than I to speak my griefs unspeakable:
> Yet that the world may witness that my end
> Was wrought by nature, not by vile offense
> I'll utter what my sorrow gives me leave.

Aegeon then recounted the dismal, strange story behind his arrival in Ephesus.

Long ago in Syracuse, Aegeon had wed his beloved Aemilia. Six months later, he was forced to travel on business. Aemilia soon joined him, and while they were abroad, she bore fine twin sons, "the one so like the other as could not be distinguish'd." At "that very hour, and in the self-same inn," another woman also gave birth to identical twin sons. The parents of these twins, however, were exceedingly poor, so Aegeon bought their sons from them, intending to raise them as servants for his sons.

As the young family sailed home to Syracuse, a storm arose. The mother secured one of her infant sons and one of the infant servants to one end of the mast while Aegeon did likewise with the other son and servant at the other end. When the ship sank, the floating mast struck a rock, separating the family. Because of his wife's lesser weight, Aegeon explained, the part of the mast to which she clung "was carried with more speed before the wind." Aemilia's

helpless assembly of soggy boys was picked up by one ship, Aegeon's by another. Tragically, the ship that rescued Aegeon and his charges could not catch up to the vessel that had rescued Aemilia. The family seemed irrevocably severed, neither trio knowing the other's fate.

Aegeon returned to Syracuse with the two boys he had been spared, and raised them as best he could. Antipholus, however, "at eighteen years became inquisitive after his lost brother; and importun'd me that his attendant [named Dromio—so his case was like—might bear him company in the quest of him." Aegeon hesitantly complied; he desired to regain his lost son, but greatly feared losing the one that had been left to him. In the end, however, Antipholus and Dromio had set out to find their lost brothers. But as the months of their absence lengthened, Aegeon's anxiety grew, and at last he went sea on a search of his own, spending five years roaming through Greece and Asia. At last, as he returned to Syracuse in despair, Aegeon concluded, he had come to Ephesus, "hopeless to find, yet loath to leave unsought . . . any place that harbors men."

Meanwhile, Antipholus and Dromio had arrived in Ephesus the same day as Aegeon. Antipholus, however, forewarned of the fatal restriction upon travelers from Syracuse, knew he must not reveal his true identity or origins. Moreover, neither Aegeon nor his Syracusan son and servant knew that the lost twins they sought lived in Ephesus! Also grown to manhood, they likewise went by the names Antipholus and Dromio!

Now Ephesus was a legendary land of magic, and its inhabitants purportedly practiced sorcery. Thus, when Antipholus of Syracuse encountered strangers in Ephesus who called him by name and seemed to know him, he attributed it to enchantment. Of course, he was being mistaken for his twin, Antipholus of Ephesus. Even Adriana, the wife of Antipholus of Ephesus, and her sister, Luciana, mistook the Syracusan pair for their Ephesian counterparts. Upon meeting Antipholus of Syracuse in town, Adriana insisted he come home for dinner. The puzzled Syracusan wondered aloud, "What, was I married to her in my dream? Or sleep I now and think I hear all this? What error drives our ears and eyes amiss?" To Dromio of Syracuse the explanation seemed obvious, "We talk with goblins, owls, and sprites; If we obey them not, this will ensue: They'll suck our breath, or pinch us black and blue."

The Syracusans eventually went home with Adriana. Unfortunately, Antipholus fell madly in love with Adriana's sister, Luciana. When he confessed his adoration, however, she implored the "unfaithful husband" to remain true to his wife.

Throughout the day the twin Antipholuses continued to be mistaken for one another by people of the city. Yet, neither twin encountered the other, so each was left to speculate on the strange behavior of those around them. Antipholus of Syracuse prudently decided to flee the mystical city at the next possible opportunity. Antipholus of Ephesus, on the other hand, found the situation quite perplexing. He suddenly found himself greeted with allusions to earlier meetings of which he held no recollection; at dinnertime he found himself locked out of his house; at one point he was even arrested for not paying a debt that he had no memory of incurring. If this was a joke being perpetrated upon him, the Ephesian mused, it certainly was a most ingenious one!

The two Dromios felt equally bewildered. While on an errand for one Antipholus, either Dromio might be intercepted by the other Antipholus, who would demand the item that he had been sent to fetch—be it a loan of money, some repaired jewelry, a rope, or passage on a ship. Inevitably, the baffled servant would be reprimanded for disobedience or insolence—or worse still, robbery.

The chaos peaked when Adriana attempted to have Antipholus of Ephesus, her own husband, along with his attendant, restrained and treated for lunacy. Complaints had raged from all quarters regarding the pair's wild behavior, forcing Adriana to conclude they were mad. She ordered them both bound and taken home, in hopes that there they might be cured.

Shortly after the two protesting Ephesians had been taken away, the visiting pair of Syracusians appeared on the street, rapiers drawn, attempting to flee Ephesus. When Adriana saw them, she thought that her husband and servant had escaped. While she summoned help to recapture them, the Syracusians took refuge in the abbey. The abbess, Aemilia, granted them sanctuary and denied their pursuers admittance to retrieve them.

By now, sunset approached, and with it, the hour assigned for Aegeon to meet his death. Solinus accompanied him to the site of execution. As they neared the gallows, Adriana appeared and begged the Duke to intervene and persuade the abbess to release the man she presumed to be her husband. Before Solinus could speak with the abbess, Antipholus of Ephesus arrived on the scene, newly escaped from his captors and thoroughly enraged at the ill-treatment he had received from his wife. Solinus attempted to settle the dispute, but each of the witnesses gave a different account of what had occurred. Stymied, Solinus wondered, "Why, what a strange impeach is this! I think you all have drunk of Circe's cup."

At this point, Aegeon recognized his long-lost son. When the abbess emerged from the abbey with the pair from Syracuse, the day's mysterious and confusing proceedings became clear. The long search at last was over. Not only had sons, father, and two sets of twins miraculously been restored to each other, but a married pair were reunited. The honorable abbess herself was the lost Aemilia—Aegeon's still-faithful wife! Solinus spared Aegeon's life and allowed the divided family to reunite. Adriana reconciled with her true husband, which left the Syracusan Antipholus free to court Luciana.

And in the end, the two Dromios were still unable to distinguish between their masters, but it no longer mattered in the joy of reunion that swept over them all.

Commentary:

"The Comedy of Errors," unlike any other play Shakespeare wrote, contains no moralistic message, few memorable lines, and had little purpose other than entertaining its audience. Purely a farcial production, "The Comedy of Errors" is among Shakespeare's earliest works. We can detect elements that would reappear in his later works. Shakespeare returned to the motifs of identical twins and mistaken identity in "Twelfth Night." This plot device grants the audience a comedic advantage over the characters by letting them in on a secret of which the characters are ignorant and upon which the plot turns. The audience's knowledge of the reason for the "errors" of identity that launch the comedy offers them a privileged position from which it is comfortable to laugh, even as the characters fear for their sanity and safety.

Because the play stretches plausibility and believability to the extreme, critics characterize it as a farce, somewhat a blend of fantasy, improbability and slapstick. No explanation is attempted, for instance, as to how the twins might have been so completely identical, even in habits of grooming and dress. Again, the realm of comedy allows the audience to grant the playwright such license in exchange for laughter. Nevertheless, we feel secure that the family will be reunited and the father will be spared execution. Indeed, it is safe to laugh when we are certain there will be a happy ending. There is even a hint given that a wedding will soon take place between Antipholus of Syracuse and Luciana, a wedding being the standard conclusion of a comedic work.

Yet Shakespeare probes beyond mere farce in this comedy, exploring issues of a self that is left incomplete and isolated when deprived of its past and parentage. Thus, Antipholus of Syracuse pursues his lost kin with a yearning close to desperation:

I to the world am like a drop of water,
That in the ocean seeks another drop,
Who, falling there to find his fellow forth
Unseen, inquisitive, confounds himself.
So I, to find a mother and a brother,
In quest of them unhappy, ah, lose myself.

Only after finding his lost mother and brother is Antipholus able, as a whole being, to anticipate marriage and full adulthood.

THE TWO GENTLEMEN OF VERONA

by
William Shakespeare
(1564-1616)

Type of work: Romantic comedy

Setting: Italy

Principal characters:
Proteus, a young gentleman of Verona
Valentine, his companion
Speed, the go-between for Proteus
Julia, a young woman in love with Proteus
Silvia, a young woman of Milan with many
    suitors
The Duke of Milan, Silvia's aristocratic father
Thurio, a knight of Milan who hopes to
    marry Silvia
*Outlaws who live in exile in the forest near
    Milan*

Play Overview:

"Wilt thou be gone?" Proteus sadly asked his good friend Valentine. Although Valentine was indeed leaving for Milan, he had joyfully invited Proteus to accompany him. Proteus, however, had refused: he hoped to woo a girl in Verona named Julia.

Valentine considered his friend's pursuit of Julia to be foolish. "Love is your master," he scolded, "For he masters you." Would it not be infinitely more exciting to seek adventures abroad than to linger in Verona "sluggardized" by infatuation?

Proteus, however, was intent on romance. So, bidding his friend farewell, he wished Valentine success and happiness in his studies in Milan. Once the student had departed, Proteus was left to wait for a response to the message he had sent to Julia.

Ironically, the go-between was a man named Speed; but to eager young Proteus, Speed seemed very slow indeed. When the messenger finally appeared, Proteus breathlessly inquired, "Gav'st thou my letter to Julia?" Speed conceded that he had, but he was not immediately inclined to discuss the particulars of his meeting with the girl; he only wanted to discuss the tip he expected for his services. Poor, impatient Proteus filled the man's hand with money, only to receive unwelcome news: Speed perceived Julia to be "hard as steel" in regards to Proteus.

Privately, however, Julia had rhapsodized over the young man's letter. While she did not choose to make a public show of her affections, Julia was deeply disposed to love him. Secretly she kissed Proteus' words, and sent him a letter of her own.

When Proteus received Julia's letter, he was ecstatic to learn that she returned his love. But his joy soon turned to sorrow when his father demanded that Proteus go to Milan in order to gain experience through "travel in his youth." Meeting with Julia, Proteus promised to return to Verona as soon as possible. She slipped a ring on his finger and he promised to treasure it. In turn, he then gave Julia his ring, and bade her a wrenching farewell: "Alas, this parting strikes poor lovers dumb."

But even in his desolation, the heart-sick lover remained an obedient son. Proteus dutifully set off for Milan. At least, he reflected, he would now enjoy the companionship of Valentine.

The Valentine he found in Milan, however, bore little resemblance to the friend Proteus had known in Verona. The cocksure young man who once scorned the mystery of love had become the love-smitten "puppet" of an exquisite girl named Silvia. So obsessed was he with Silvia that he no longer had any inclination whatsoever to "discourse except it be of love."

Unfortunately for Valentine, Silvia's father, the Duke of Milan, still proposed that his daughter should marry Thurio, a noble-born but hopelessly shy and foolish knight. Recognizing Thurio as a fool, however, Valentine remained undaunted.

Meanwhile, Proteus himself had been quite charmed by Silvia on their first meeting. Thus he knew he had to praise the maid carefully, to avoid making his friend jealous. Was not Silvia "a heavenly saint"? asked Valentine. "No," Proteus finally answered. But she was, he allowed, "an earthly paragon." Disappointed with such a measured response, Valentine insisted that Proteus "Call her divine." But Proteus insisted, "I will not flatter her."

As soon as he was alone, however, Proteus could not refrain from admitting to himself that Silvia was in fact "fair." As it turned out, Proteus was fickle and easily infatuated. "The remembrance of my former love," he marvelled, "is by a newer object quite forgotten." Moreover, he had to admit that his loyalty to Valentine was now supplanted by his newly-found devotion to the "perfections" of Sylvia. And Proteus decided that he would use his "skill" to win the girl.

Proteus' skill, however, took the form of treachery. Knowing that Valentine and Silvia planned to elope, Proteus visited the Duke and lost no time in detailing their scheme:

> Know noble lord, they have devised a mean
> How he her chamber window will ascend
> And with a corded ladder fetch her down;
> For which the youthful lover now is gone. . .

Thanking Proteus for alerting him to his daughter's plan, the Duke promised that he would not reveal Proteus' betrayal.

Shortly after Proteus left, Valentine arrived. Forewarned, the Duke searched Valentine's cloak, finding a ladder and a love-letter written to Sylvia. "By heaven," the Duke exploded, "my wrath shall far exceed the love I ever bore my daughter. . . ." With that pronouncement, he banished Valentine from the city.

With Valentine out of the way, Proteus, of course, had yet another rival for Silvia's affection. Quickly he devised a plot to trick Thurio: First, he would lure the young nobleman to Silvia's house to sing her romantic, "wailful sonnets"; then, pretending to intervene on Thurio's behalf, Proteus would seize the occasion and proclaim his own love for Silvia. The poor cowardly knight—who was well aware that Silvia detested him—readily agreed to take Proteus by his side when he went to pay court at her window.

The two gentlemen met beneath Silvia's window, as planned. After Thurio had serenaded his lady with a flowery love song, he hurried away, leaving Proteus to plead his cause to Silvia. When Silvia appeared in her window, however, Proteus took credit for the serenade and declared his own love for her. Silvia, though, was not pleased; she denounced Proteus for his broken faith with Julia, and called him a "false, perjured, disloyal man!"

"I grant, sweet love, that I did love a lady," Proteus persisted, desperately trying to win her. "But she is dead." Unbeknownst to either Proteus or Silvia, this lie devastated someone else who happened to be listening—Julia herself, Proteus's abandoned lady. Driven by the "fire of love," she had journeyed to Milan to visit her betrothed. Since it was not considered proper for young ladies to travel alone, she had even gone so far as to dress as a page. Still disguised in this garb, she watched from the shadows in horror as Proteus wooed Silvia.

Causing Julia even more pain, Proteus—who thought she was a boy named Sebastian—soon asked her to be his page. Then, to her chagrin, he instructed her to take a ring to Silvia—the very same ring that Julia had given Proteus before he had left Verona.

Silvia, however, would not accept the ring. Instead, she expressed compassion for the poor girl Proteus had left behind. In truth, Silvia was still in love with Valentine, and set off on a journey that day at sunset to find him. As soon as she had reached the forest outside Milan, however, she was accosted by outlaws. "O Valentine," Silvia cried, "this I endure for thee!"

The Duke, meanwhile, had learned that his daughter had "fled unto that peasant Valentine." Accompanied by Thurio, Proteus, and Julia—still disguised as a boy— he left Milan to find her.

The outlaws were about to carry the abducted Silvia to their captain's cave when Proteus, who had rushed ahead of his companions, discovered her. Despite her circumstances, she was not relieved to see him. "I would have been a breakfast to the beast," she railed, "rather than have false Proteus rescue me." "I'll force thee to yield to my desire," he threatened.

Just at that moment, Valentine arrived. "Thou friend of an ill fashion!" he roared at Proteus. He then launched into a tirade, elaborating all of Proteus's wrong-doings. Proteus listened quietly to Valentine. His friend's words awakened his old loyalties. Surprising everyone, he repented. "My shame and guilt confound me," he said, confessing remorse at his own treacherous acts. For his part, Valentine generously forgave Proteus: "And once again I do receive thee honest."

Overcome with emotion, the page boy Julia swooned. When she awoke, she murmured, "my master charged me to deliver a ring to Madam Silvia, which of neglect was never done." Then she displayed the ring that Proteus had presented

to her in Verona. "Julia!" Proteus exclaimed, at last recognizing her.

Julia gently chided Proteus for his inconstancy and, for the second time that day, Proteus felt remorse. Taking Julia's hand, he said, "Bear witness heaven, I have my wish forever."

Meanwhile, nearby, the outlaws had captured the lagging Duke and Thurio. "A prize, a prize, a prize!" they shouted to their captain, rejoicing in their good fortune as they advanced toward the assembly. "Forbear, forbear I say," Valentine told the outlaws—finally revealing to his companions that he, in fact, was the outlaw captain. He explained that these were not wicked men, but simply "banished" citizens like himself. After listening carefully to Valentine, the Duke proclaimed, "Thou hast prevailed; I pardon them, and thee."

All was forgiven—even Thurio had a change of heart about Silvia. "Sir Valentine," he stated boldly, "I care not for her."

And joy reigned triumphant in the forest when the Duke announced that the two couples would marry on that very day—and celebrate their "good devotion" ever after.

Commentary:

Written in the 1590s, "The Two Gentlemen of Verona" may have been Shakespeare's first comedy. Though it normally appears in his chronologies after "As You Like It" and "Twelfth Night," many critics, noting shortcomings in the plot's structure, believe that "Two Gentlemen" precedes the other two comedies. In fact, it has been suggested that Shakespeare hurriedly wrote sections of the play in order to meet the deadline for a first performance.

While critics disagree about chronology, they tend to agree about the play's weaknesses. The final act is most frequently criticized: Proteus undergoes such a rapid and profound change in temperament that he seems to lose credibility as a character. One moment he denounces Valentine and is prepared to force himself on Valentine's fiance; the next he begs Valentine's forgiveness—then proclaims his devotion to Julia rather than to the avidly pursued Silvia. Although the name Proteus refers to a Greek sea-god who changes form, Shakespeare is nonetheless criticized for presenting his Proteus' chameleon nature only superficially—without motivation in the context of the play.

Whatever its shortcomings, "The Two Gentlemen of Verona" remains an important play. It is a seminal Shakespearean comedy that introduces themes and plot complications which resurface in later, more highly acclaimed works. It is, for instance, the first play to use the ring-exchange, which also figures prominently in "All's Well That Ends Well." Similarly, its use of the forest as a place of conflict resolution presages plays like "A Midsummer Night's Dream" and "As You Like It." "The Two Gentlemen of Verona" is also the first of the comedies to employ a female character disguised as a male. Thus, while "Two Gentlemen" is by no means Shakespeare's most successful comedy, it still offers a unique glimpse into his development as a master playwright.

THE WINTER'S TALE

by
William Shakespeare
(1564 - 1616)

Type of work: Tragicomic drama
Setting: Sicily and Bohemia, in the Golden Age
Principal characters:
Polixenes, King of Bohemia
Leontes, King of Sicily
Hermione, Leontes' wife, the Queen of Sicily
Paulina, her attendant
Camillo, Leontes' counsellor
Perdita, the daughter of Leontes and Hermione
Florizel, Polixenes' son

Play Overview:

For nine months Polixenes, King of Bohemia, had been a guest at the court of his childhood friend Leontes, the King of Sicily. The time had come, however, when Polixenes— "question'd by fears" of what may "breed upon our absence" in Bohemia—made arrangements to return to his own palace.

Leontes, greatly distressed by his friend's parting, pleaded with him to stay "one seven-night longer." Polixenes, however, was determined to depart the next day. "Press me not, I beseech you," he told Leontes.

Exasperated, Leontes turned to his wife Hermione. "Tongue-tied, our queen?" he said. "Speak you." Now Hermione, as it happened, was a woman of abundant charm and wit. Taking up her husband's cause, she cleverly argued that Polixenes could choose either to be her "prisoner" or her "guest."

"Your guest, then, madame," Polixenes finally relented. "Hermione, my dearest," Leontes said, complimenting his wife, "thou never spok'st to better purpose." Leontes had scarcely uttered these words, however, when a dark mood fell over him. Suddenly suspicious, he began to brood over the fact that Hermione had managed to persuade Polixenes to stay another week, whereas he had failed. Perhaps, Leontes thought, she and Polixenes had made a "cuckold" of him; indeed, perchance the baby Hermione now carried was not his own.

Leontes, now that his jealousy was aroused, could not rid himself of the thought that he had been "much deceived." Unable to bear his suspicions alone any longer, he called for his trusted counsellor Camillo. "How I am galled," Leontes raged, denouncing Hermione as "rank" and Polixenes as his "enemy." But Camillo, being most wise, tried to calm his lord. Leontes was imagining these things; his wife would never betray him for another. Leontes, however, could not be pacified—and ordered Camillo to "bespice a cup" of Polixenes' wine with enough poison to give his old friend "a lasting wink."

Camillo, wishing only to placate Leontes, agreed to carry out the plan and then left.

Shortly afterwards, he ran into Polixenes, who, having noted Leontes's disturbed countenance, pressed Camillo for an explanation, whereupon Camillo revealed Leontes' plan to poison him. Incredulous, Polixenes wondered aloud how such an infectious jealousy could take root in his friend Leontes. "I know not," Camillo answered, but one thing was certain: they should both make their escape to Bohemia that very night.

When Leontes learned the next day that Polixenes and Camillo had taken flight, he became further enraged. Venting his fury on Hermione, he publicly denounced her as "an adulteress," separated her from their young son Mamillus, and then imprisoned her.

Although many of the court protested Hermione's treatment, proclaiming her innocence, Leontes, now entirely mad, insisted that it was Polixenes who had made his wife pregnant—who had made her "swell thus."

Not long after her imprisonment, Hermione gave birth to a baby girl. Confident that Leontes would "soften at the sight of the child," Hermione's attendant Paulina brought the infant to the King. But Leontes' wrath only intensified. "Take up the bastard," he roared. "The bastard's brains with these my proper hands shall I dash out." Paulina, stunned by the King's reaction, shielded the infant from his wrath. Seeing that his servants were sympathetic toward the child, Leontes commanded Paulina's husband Antigonus to take it from the kingdom and abandon it in "some remote desert place" where "chance might nurse or end it." This Antigonus performed. Leontes then announced that the Delphic Oracle would be consulted to settle the matter of Hermione's guilt.

Aware that his palace lords were also sympathetic to Hermione, Leontes decided to grant her a public trial. Hermione, standing before the court, steadfastly maintained her innocence. Then, in the midst of the trial, messengers arrived with the Apollo's "seal'd-up oracle" from Delphi: everyone listened intently as its contents were read:

Hermione is chaste; Polixenes, blameless; Camillo, a true subject; Leontes, a jealous tyrant; his innocent babe, truly begotten; and the king shall live without an heir if that which is lost not be found.

"There is no truth at all i' the oracle," Leontes protested. Barely a moment later, however, he was brought news that his beloved son Mamillus had died. "Apollo is angry," the grief-stricken Leontes cried, suddenly aware that the oracle was indeed coming to pass.

Devastated by her son's death, Hermione collapsed. "The news is mortal to the queen," Paulina lamented, as Leontes mourned the tragic losses of both his son and his wife.

Sixteen years passed. During that time, the repentant Leontes had thought only of Mamillus, Hermione, and the lost "poor babe." But Perdita, as the child became known, had not in fact died. Forsaken by Antigonus on the coast of Bohemia with a bundle of gold and jewels, she had been found by a kindly shepherd and raised as his daughter. Now "grown in grace," the beautiful Perdita was being wooed by Florizel, the Prince of Bohemia and heir to its throne.

Florizel, who was Polixenes' only son, could think of nothing but "the celebration of that nuptial" which would unite him eternally to his beloved Perdita. As a result, he had recently neglected his duties at court, a point which had not escaped his father's notice. Moreover, although Polixenes had not met Perdita, he objected in principle to his son's courting a girl of humble origins. One night, to learn more about Perdita, he decided to pay the girl a visit.

Dressed in disguises, Polixenes and his trusted friend Camillo—who had settled in Bohemia after fleeing Leontes' services—arrived at the shepherd's cottage during sheep-shearing, an annual celebration. To his chagrin, Polixenes not only found Florizel there, but he also overheard him propose marriage to Perdita.

"Make your divorce, young sir," countered the angry Polixenes, removing his disguise. "For thee, fond boy," he continued, "we'll bar thee from succession." Florizel was angry but, at the same time, torn. He knew Polixenes would disown him if he wed lowly Perdita, and yet he could not forget her. Choosing to obey "fancy" instead of his father, Florizel decided to elope with Perdita and escape to a foreign country. Camillo, who was sympathetic to the pair, suggested they sail for Sicily. Once there, he advised them, Florizel could present himself to Leontes as an emissary from Bohemia, and, following Camillo's instructions to the letter, win Leontes' favor.

Meanwhile, Perdita's adopted father had decided that the only way he could escape Polixenes' ire was to tell him the story of how he had found Perdita and the gold. On his way to Polixenes' palace, however, the shepherd was waylaid by a rogue and taken aboard Florizel's ship.

When Florizel and Perdita arrived in Sicily, Leontes informed them they were as welcome at his court "as is the spring to the earth." Polixenes, though, who was yet determined to stop Florizel's marriage to Perdita, soon followed and denounced his son to Leontes and his court.

The shepherd, seizing Polixenes' arrival as a final opportunity to save himself, then related the story of Perdita's abandonment, and presented Polixenes and Leontes with his evidence—the bundled gold and jewels. The old kings were stunned; Leontes, overcome with joy, announced, "Our Perdita is found." And,

though this joy was compounded by his reunion with Polixenes and Camillo, he nonetheless lamented that Hermione was not there to share his happiness.

One day, Paulina, ever loyal to her mistress' memory, invited Leontes, his friends, and his new family to view a statue of the Queen. When she opened a curtain to reveal the life-like sculpture, Leontes marvelled at the "air that comes from her" and wondered aloud at what "fine chisel could ever yet cut breath."

No longer able to restrain himself, Leontes approached the statue to kiss its lips. Just then, Paulina mysteriously issued her command: "Music, activate her!" To everyone's surprise and delight, Hermione, who was "stone no more," descended from the pedestal.

"O! she's warm," Leontes cried out. After having lived in seclusion for so many years, dreaming only that Perdita might be found, Hermione now fell joyously into the arms of her long-lost daughter and her repentant husband.

Commentary:

The Winter's Tale was one of Shakespeare's late plays (approx. 1611). While he undoubtedly borrowed many elements of plot from Robert Greene's romance Pandosto: *The Triumph of Time* (1588), Shakespeare made several changes, including, most notably, the ultimate fate of Hermione.

The Winter's Tale has had an odd history in Shakespeare's canon. Frequently regarded as an imperfect work—a work marred by an uncharacteristically bleak and fanciful vision of nature and culture—the play now enjoys a reputation as being among Shakespeare's best and most imaginative works.

In part, the play's anomalous reputation can be explained by the fact that it represents a departure of sorts, both in terms of dramatic substance and techniques. Thus, for instance, although Shakespeare's work manifested a lifelong interest in mythology and folklore, *The Winter's Tale* takes that interest in a new direction, employing folkloric and mythological material in an episodic narrative that one critic has characterized as filled with "wild improbabilities" and "arbitrary symbolism."

Moreover, unlike many earlier works, this play brings these fantastic improbabilities to center stage and makes "fancy" its central theme. The effect is that both the drama and the narrative challenge our notions of nature and culture, particularly as these ideas relate to "generation." By drawing attention, then, to the "staged" or fictive elements of nature and culture, Shakespeare perhaps reminds us that generation—at least in the artistic sense of the word—is a process of constructing what is "natural" to us, or—as in the case of Perdita—recovering what is lost to us.

In this respect, *The Winter's Tale*—though it plays on traditional associations with a "sad tale"—may be one of Shakespeare's more benevolent visions of the fate of our nature and our culture.

THE BARBER OF SEVILLE

by
Gioacchino Rossini
(1792-1868)

Type of work. Comic opera

Setting: Seville, Spain; 17th century

Principal characters:
Count Almaviva, a young aristocrat
Figaro, a barber who comes to Almaviva's assistance
Rosina, the young woman Almaviva loves
Dr. Bartolo, Rosina's guardian
Don Basilio, Rosina's music teacher

Story Overview:

Before dawn on a square in Seville, a band of musicians hired by the dashing Count Almaviva gathered to play a serenade for the lovely Rosina. Almaviva himself stood nearby in the darkness gazing longingly at the closed window where he hoped his beloved would appear. Shortly, he began to sing of his adoration for her.

His heartfelt serenade, however, failed to rouse Rosina from her slumbers. "All my hopes are dashed to pieces!" Almaviva told his servant, who immediately gave the musicians a generous wage and asked them to leave.

Now standing alone on the square, Almaviva spotted Figaro, whom he had known in Madrid, holding a guitar. Singing a ballad, Figaro called himself the Barber of Seville—and "the most important man in town":

> There with my razor, ready I stand,
> Ready to tidy the frizziest whisker,
> I stand at attention, scissors in hand,
> Sometimes I cover matters romantic,
> Soothing a maiden, soothing a lover.
> Country and citified wish to be prettified . . .

Almaviva asked for Figaro's help in winning the enchanting young Rosina. "She is all I live for," he confessed. Suddenly, the window opened and Rosina herself emerged on the balcony with a letter in her hand. A moment later she was joined by her guardian, Dr. Bartolo, who insisted on knowing what was written on the paper. It was merely the words to an aria, Rosina averred; but then, as if by accident, she let the paper drop over the railing. Before Dr. Bartolo could rush down to retrieve it, Almaviva picked it up and read its contents: It beseeched whoever found it to help her escape from the despotic Bartolo; Rosina was being kept against her will by the tyrant. Hearing this, Figaro also denounced Bartolo. "An overbearing maniac," he groused. "He's quite determined that he'll marry her money."

Just then Dr. Bartolo walked out of his house, calling to Rosina that Don Basilio might soon appear. Basilio, Figaro explained to Almaviva, aside from being a matchmaker, a "truly clever swindler," and "a snake full of guile," was also Rosina's music instructor.

Now spotting Rosina behind the curtain, Figaro urged Almaviva to serenade her. Almaviva eagerly snatched up Figaro's guitar and voiced another love song, in which he called himself "Lindoro," a student; he did not want the girl to love him for his title or his money. But before Almaviva's serenade was finished, someone pulled Rosina away from the window.

Almaviva's worry for his beloved Rosina now turned to outrage. "How can I bear it!" he fumed. Musing over the situation, he turned to Figaro and promised him money if he could contrive a scheme to get him inside Dr. Bartolo's house. Figaro responded to Almaviva's proposition enthusiastically. "When I think of gold and silver, then at once my mind erupts like a volcano." Figaro suggested that the Count disguise himself as a commuting soldier and claim that, by military order, he was to be quartered in the house. Elated by the conspiracy, the two men initiated a joyous duet, Figaro delighting in the prospect of "pockets full of pay" and Almaviva thrilling in anticipation of a "paradise, full of milk and honey" with his beautiful Rosina.

Later that day, Rosina sat writing a love letter to her new suitor—and savior, she hoped— "Lindoro," when Figaro, having found a way into the house, crept past her bedroom. He hid himself, however, when Dr. Bartolo approached Rosina's room to announce that Don Basilio had arrived. Then, out of earshot of Rosina, the doctor warned Basilio of a certain Count Almaviva, who was said to be courting the girl. Don Basilio recommended that the easiest way to eliminate the Count would be slander:

> From the lips the innuendo
> starts another mad crescendo,
> slowly gathering its forces
> Far and wide the rumor courses,
> Till at last it shall resemble
> storms that make the forests tremble,
> When the lightning and the thunder
> lash in horror from on high

The doctor, however, preferred quick action. "I'll marry her tomorrow," he decided.

"The rascals," Figaro hissed, springing out from his hiding place after the two men had left the room. Immediately, he revealed to Rosina the doctor's plan to marry her. "The silly idiots!" she responded. "They'll have to deal with me!" Then she gave Figaro the letter she had penned to Lindoro. Figaro quickly took the letter and left.

A short while later, Almaviva—disguised as a drunken soldier—appeared at the doctor's door. "Howdy-do to you Dr. Barbaro," he greeted the doctor. "My name's Bartolo, you half wit," railed the doctor. Almaviva explained that he was to be quartered in the doctor's house; Bartolo, protesting, could nonetheless comply.

Meanwhile, Rosina entered the room. The young "soldier," at an opportune moment, managed to whisper to Rosina, "I'm Lindoro"—before Bartolo gruffly ordered Rosina back upstairs. Then Dr. Bartolo conveniently recalled that he was "exempt" from lodging soldiers. While Bartolo went to his desk to find the document to prove his claim, Almaviva slipped the departing Rosina the letter he had written her. Bartolo, spying the act, demanded to see the paper, but Rosina, having tucked the letter into her handkerchief, quickly substituted a laundry list in its place.

Later that day, Dr. Bartolo sat in his library. "The soldier, about whom I've inquired, is not known at all throughout the whole regiment," he ruminated suspiciously. Just then, a stranger walked into the library. Disguised now as a "music master," Almaviva introduced himself as "Don Alonso, a professor of music . . . and a pupil of Don Basilio [who is] stricken with fever." The young man said he would give Rosina her lesson that day. In an attempt to curry the doctor's favor, "Don Alonso" claimed he had intercepted a letter written by Rosina to Almaviva; the "music teacher" would use it to convince Rosina that Almaviva did not return her affection.

When Rosina entered the library, she immediately recognized the young music teacher as Lindoro. As Bartolo exited the room, she began her lesson by singing, in unison with Lindoro and in slightly disguised language, "In my heart sweet thoughts of love I cherish . . . "

Soon, the doctor re-entered the library, followed by Figaro, who insisted that Dr. Bartolo needed a shave. Giving in to the persistent barber, Bartolo handed Figaro his keys and sent him down the hall to fetch a towel. The moment Figaro was out of the room, however, he removed the key to Rosina's bedroom so that he and Almaviva could rescue her that night.

Then, with Dr. Bartolo settled into a chair, lathered up for his shave, Almaviva and Figaro's scheme nearly unraveled: Don Basilio himself unexpectedly arrived to give Rosina her lesson. Quick-witted Figaro hurried to meet him—and to feel his pulse. "It's a case of scarlet fever!" he announced in mock dread. Everyone immediately gasped. "Go to bed, oh won't you please!" they urged the startled Don Basilio. Beginning to believe he was, in fact, quite ill, Don Basilio returned home to attend to his "fevered brow."

Soon the doctor was situated back in his seat, ready for Figaro to recommence his work. As Figaro shaved him, however, Bartolo overheard "Don Alonso" and Rosina outlining her escape from the house that night. Now the deceivers were exposed! "I'll see you dead!" the doctor raged. "Just give me an ax!" In a fury, he chased the spurious Don Alonso and Figaro out of the house, and sent a servant to fetch Don Basilio.

When Don Basilio reappeared, he realized that the man posing as Don Alonso was in truth Count Almaviva. "Now that we know it," Dr. Bartolo sneered, "go summon my lawyer and see that he gets here quickly to arrange all the legal matters for my wedding." Ignoring the rain, which had begun to fall in torrents, Don Basilio hurried off to bring the lawyer.

The doctor then devised a plan to deceive Rosina into marrying him, and called her into the room. When she appeared, he showed her the letter she had written to her lover and told her that "Lindoro" only wanted to betray her to the Count. "This he left with his mistress just to amuse her!" the malevolent doctor said. Confused and in despair, Rosina declared a "vendetta" on Lindoro and agreed to marry Dr. Bartolo; she also conceded that "Lindoro" and Figaro were planning to come for her at midnight. "Lock yourself up in your room," the doctor commanded her. "I'll call the guards to help us."

At the stroke of midnight, Almaviva and Figaro used the stolen key to enter Rosina's bedroom window. " . . . you treacherous deceiver!" she railed when she saw Figaro. "You thought you could abduct me to sell to that devil Almaviva!" Taken aback at Rosina's rancor, Figaro earnestly asked, "What of this poor Lindoro? Do you love him?"

"Oh, yes!" she then admitted. "I love him dearly." Thrilled by her words, Almaviva knew his only hope now was to tell her the truth. He stepped out from the shadows and declared, "Though you call me Lindoro, I'm Almaviva."

"Now my darkness is turned to daylight," Rosina cried ecstatically. "All creation has smiled on me!" Figaro, moved by this joyful exchange, yet feared Dr. Bartolo's wrath, and beseeched the lovers to leave quickly. But, to everyone's dismay, the ladder they had used to reach Rosina's window had disappeared.

Suddenly, Don Basilio burst into the room, accompanied by a lawyer. Leaving the lawyer standing guard, Basilio went to summon the guards and Dr. Bartolo. Clever Almaviva seized the occasion and bribed the lawyer to wed him to his beloved Rosina. "Ah, what a blessed answer to my prayers," Rosina sighed following the hasty ceremony.

Too late, Dr. Bartolo returned with officers, demanding that they arrest Almaviva and Figaro at once. But to his amazement, he learned that Rosina and Almaviva had married. "What of her dowry?" the greedy doctor blurted out. "I'm not wealthy." But Almaviva's generosity suddenly softened him. "Keep it all for yourself," he told the doctor. Now the grateful Bartolo's countenance changed. "May heaven bless you always!" he exclaimed. The newlyweds exulted in response, "May smiling heaven send us bright skies forevermore!"

Commentary:

Gioacchino Rossini wrote *The Barber of Seville* when he was 24 years old. Commissioned in 1815 by Duke Francesco Sforza-Cesarini to compose a comic opera for a respected Spanish tenor, Rossini borrowed elements of plot from a trilogy consisting of *The Barber of Seville, The Marriage of Figaro*, and a third, lesser play by the eighteenth-century playwright Caron de Beaumarchais, *La Mere Coupable*. Beaumarchais' *Barber* had already been put into operatic form by Giovanni Paisiello, and Rossini also consulted this version before starting work on his own opera. Rossini was bitterly disappointed when his production opened to hisses and jeers. The audience—in deference to Paisiello—refused to listen to Rossini's version of the work.

Though Rossini's plot resembled Paisiello's, his music was distinctly his own, a fact that did not escape subsequent audiences, who took great pleasure in Rossini's more emotional production. "Rossini wrote [music] as an Italian speaks," music coach Maestro Ubaldo Gardini once stated, "full of warmth and enthusiasm, of joy and sorrow. He wrote for voices with a considerable range, and asked for exceptional flexibility rather than a mere display of virtuosity . . . " The vigor and emotional amplitude of Rossini's music was so strong that he received great acclaim from later masters, including Brahms, Beethoven, and Wagner.

THE MARRIAGE OF FIGARO

by
Wolfgang Amadeus Mozart
(1756-1791)

Type of work: Comic/farcical opera

Setting: A castle in seventeenth-century Seville, Spain

Principal characters:
- *Count and Countess Almaviva*, master and mistress of the castle
- *Figaro*, valet to Count Almaviva
- *Susanna*, maid to Countess Almaviva, and Figaro's fiancée
- *Cherubino*, Count Almaviva's wily page
- *Dr. Bartolo*, a physician of Seville
- *Marcellina*, Dr. Bartolo's housemaid
- *Don Basilio*, a music teacher
- *Antonio*, a gardener, uncle to Susanna
- *Barbarina*, Antonio's daughter

Commentary:

The Marriage of Figaro, an adaptation by Mozart and created as a sequel to Rossini's *The Barber of Seville*, is based on the comedy *La Folle Jouree*, or *The Marriage of Figaro* originally written by the Frenchman Caron de Beaumarchais. The opera was initially banned in Paris and Vienna because of its ridiculing jabs at the upper class, its confusing and masquerading plot and subplots, and its slap-stick temperament.

The principal themes of the opera are duty and love, the two conflicting forces most reflected in the characters of the aristocratic, unswerving Count Almaviva and the middle-class, more popular Figaro.

The farcical production is a brilliant spectacle. "I looked on with the greatest pleasure," Mozart wrote to a friend after attending the premier, "while all these people leapt around in sincere delight at the music of my Figaro . . . for here they talk about nothing but Figaro; nothing is played, sung, or whistled but Figaro: no opera draws the crowds but Figaro, always Figaro; it is certainly a great honor for me."

Story Overview:

Act I

In Figaro's apartment situated in Count Almaviva's palace near Seville, Figaro and Susanna prepared for their wedding, to be held later that day. Susanna wondered why Count Almaviva chose to give them the room which adjoined his own suite. The Count, she suspected, wished to take advantage of the situation and seduce her, even though, as of this, her wedding night, he would renounce his right to her. "I thought he had renounced his feudal right," Figaro said. "True," Susanna replied. "But Figaro's bride-to-be has caused him to repent of the renunciation."

Figaro was furious when he learned of Almaviva's intent to steal his fiancee and resolved that he would "play the tune if the Count wishes to dance." Then, much to Figaro's disgust, his ex-land-lady, Marcellina, appeared, along with her lawyer, ready to collect on a debt Figaro had never settled. This debt, "rashly contracted," was based on the understanding that if Figaro could not make good on his payment, he would marry Marcellina.

Susanna, annoyed to discover that the older Marcellina was in fact her rival, exchanged insults with the woman.

Realizing she was no match for Susanna's wit, Marcellina rushed furiously from the room, with Figaro following behind, trying to explain his situation.

Cherubino, Almaviva's page, now joined Susanna and lamented that the Count was very upset with him for his amorous behavior in respect to all the females in the castle. Then he confessed that his latest passion was for the Countess herself.

When, suddenly, they heard the Count approaching, Cherubino hid himself behind a chair; little could he afford to again be caught in a woman's room. Entering the room, Count Almaviva, thinking Susanna was alone, immediately began making advances toward her. But, alas, he too was interrupted in love-making, this time by the arrival of the music master, Don Basilio.

Hurriedly, the Count concealed himself behind the same chair as Cherubino—who, in turn, hastily crept around it and knelt on it, Susanna covering him with one of the Countess' dresses. Basilio, a man of many words—and also believing Susanna to be alone—gaily gossiped about silly Cherubino's rumored infatuation with the Countess. This so angered the Count that he rushed out of hiding—and, in so doing, pulled the dress off the chair to reveal a cringing Cherubino. Now aware that the youthful page had overheard his own indiscretions, the Count vented his anger by summarily dispatching Cherubino to join the army.

Figaro, re-entering the room, gave Cherubino some parting advice: as a true soldier he must give up his amorous exploits for the sterner duties of war; surely Cherubino would return a hero—assuming he came back alive, that is. Then, Figaro, Cherubino and Susanna marched off in mock-military style.

Act II

In the Countess' bedroom, Figaro and Susanna persuaded their mistress to teach her husband a lesson and put an end to his flirtatious behavior. They decided to have Basilio deliver a note to the Count hinting of an ongoing affair between the Countess and the page, while Susanna would arrange a romantic rendezvous with the Count. At the rendezvous, however, Cherubino the page, dressed as a woman, would take Susanna's place.

Summoning Cherubino—who had not yet departed for his post—they tried the disguise on him. Susanna then taught him on feminine manner-isms. After his lesson, Susanna retired for the evening, leaving Cherubino alone with the Countess. Just as Cherubino mustered enough courage to confess his love for her, the Count appeared. Amid much commotion, the Countess hid the page in her dressing room, where, fumbling around, he knocked over a stool. Hearing the stirrings from within, the Count's suspicions were instantly aroused, and he demanded to know whom she was hiding. The Countess refused to say, whereupon Almaviva compelled her to help him search for tools to break down the door.

Susanna, who had since returned to the room, took advantage of their absence to switch places with Cherubino, who promptly escaped through the window and set off for Seville. When the Count finally pried open the dressing room door, he and the Countess were both shocked to see standing before them an innocently smiling Susanna. The Countess then roundly upbraided her husband for his foolish suspicions.

Presently, Antonio the gardener entered, quite drunk, and carrying a broken flowerpot. For some time now the palace residents had been tossing a variety of rubbish out the windows into his flower beds, he complained. While this had been bad enough, now his limit had been reached: someone had just thrown down a man!

Figaro, having arrived to determine the source of the disturbance, tried to take the blame. But the Count became increasingly suspicious when Antonio held up the paper he had found in the garden: Cherubino's military commission. Figaro stammered, and finally professed that the page had left the charter with him, as it had not yet been stamped with the official seal. By now completely out of patience, the Count tore up the document.

Further complicating matters, Marcellina the landlady, Bartolo the physician, and Basilio the music teacher now entered the room to demand that Almaviva settle Marcellina's dispute with Figaro. The Count, suddenly seeing the opportunity to retaliate against Figaro and Susanna, promised to give the matter prompt consideration.

Act III

As planned, the Countess sent a forged love letter to her husband, arranging a secret rendezvous with Susanna. The Countess then readied herself to meet her husband, disguised as Susanna. In order to further fuel the deception, Susanna, meanwhile, approached Count Almaviva and lured him into professing his love for her.

However, the Count overheard Susanna whisper to Figaro something about the readiness of their plans. Now totally skeptical—not to mention outraged—he devised a plan of his own: he would avenge their duplicity by persuading Antonio, Susanna's uncle and guardian, to not allow her to marry Figaro because of his dubious parentage. The Count then tried to force Figaro to marry Marcellina—but the quick-thinking Figaro claimed that he could not marry without the consent of his parents; however, even though he had been stolen from his parents as a baby, he did have proof of his true identity: a birthmark upon his back.

When Figaro described the birthmark, Marcellina cried out in joy: she was his mother—and Dr. Bartolo, his father. Susanna entered and was momentarily shocked to see her betrothed in the arms of Marcellina, but became overjoyed when she, too, learned of Figaro's joyous discovery.

Barbarina, the gardener Antonio's daughter, now entered along with Cherubino, dressed in girl's clothes to conceal his presence from the Count. The Countess also entered, together with Susanna. As they walked, they discussed what should be said in the note to the Count, definitely fixing the time and place for the rendezvous. Finally, using a pin to seal the note, they penned their message, also stating that the pin was to be returned with the Count's reply.

The Count's spirits rose when, during the wedding dance later that evening, Susanna secretly slipped him the letter inviting him to step into the garden with her. Count Almaviva, anxious to open the letter, accidentally pricked his finger on the Countess' pin and dropped it. Obviously, Figaro thought to himself when he witnessed the act, Almaviva had received a note from another admirer—his very own bride-to-be.

Act IV

Barbarina lamented the loss of the Countess' pin as she entered the palace garden carrying a lantern. As Figaro and Marcellina also appeared, Barbarina explained to them that she was searching for the pin she was supposed to deliver to Susanna, along with a message from the Count. Figaro, now even more sure that his fiancee was wrapped up in an affair with the Count, rushed away furiously, swearing to avenge himself on all of womankind, and set out to seek Susanna.

Meanwhile, Susanna appeared in the darkened garden, disguised as the Countess. At the same time, the Countess, in an effort to expose her faithless husband, appeared masquerading as Susanna. Cherubino, seeing "Susanna," tried to steal a kiss from her. But just at that moment Count Almaviva turned up and rushed forward to embrace his "Susanna"—and Cherubino, still in the act of planting a kiss upon his beloved, kissed the Count instead. The Count immediately reached back to box the ears of the sassy Cherubino, but instead hit Figaro, who, by this time, had charged into the melee to defend his honor with Susanna. This gave Cherubino time to escape.

Now Figaro, when the real Susanna called after him, thought she was the Countess and, out of spite, wooed her tenderly. But this act only served to anger his Countess-disguised Susanna—who straightaway reached out and thumped him, revealing her true identity. Figaro happily accepted the blows, fully convinced that Susanna really loved him. They then embraced and forgave one another, passionately declaring their love.

The Count, however, now seeing his valet kneeling at his "wife's" feet and his own beloved "Susanna" having slipped away, became bathed in a fit of jealousy. Seizing the disloyal Figaro and vowing to expose the Countess' infidelity, Almaviva called for his servants to bring him a torch.

As the procession of lovers straggled out of the recesses of the flame-lit garden, Count Almaviva was about to discover how cleverly he had been fooled. There before him stood Susanna (in the Countess' clothing), his own wife (in Susanna's clothing), as well as Cherubino and Barbarina, who had also been awooing there. Being the fine gentleman that he was—and having been duped so completely—Count Almaviva gently begged his wife's forgiveness. Then, with the masquerading and adulterous confusion ended, the happy and properly assorted pairs made their way, arm in arm, to the chateau, there to witness "The Marriage of Figaro."

CARMEN

by
Georges Bizet
(1838-1875)

Type of work. Tragic opera

Setting: Seville, Spain; 1820s

Principal characters:
Micaela, a peasant girl
Zuniga, captain of the soldier "dragoons"
Don Jose, corporal of the dragoons
Carmen, a gypsy girl
Mercedes and Frasquita, Carmen's friends
Escamillo, a toreador
El Remendado and El Dancairo, smugglers

Story Overview:

Act I

At noon, the Seville town square was filled with people on their way to and from lunch. A group of dragoons (soldiers) stood singing a ballad to the passing throng, when they noticed Micaela in the crowd. One of the guards heard her ask for Don Jose, who would arrive with the changing of the guard.

Meanwhile, Zuniga, captain of the dragoons, queried Don Jose about the girls who worked at the cigarette factory. Don Jose denounced them as flirtatious and shallow, and claimed to pay no attention to them. He also confessed to Zuniga that he was in love with a peasant girl named Micaela.

When a bell rang, the girls from the factory strolled into the square, smoking and extolling the joys of smoke. Carmen, their overseer, came with them, and the soldiers and men of the village lustily greeted her. When the flocking soldiers asked her to chose a lover from among them, she took up a song—and sang of Don Jose, who stood nearby indifferently repairing his gun:

Gypsy love is a roving rapture,
A wanton bird that none can tame,
Not a bird for a fool to capture,
He plays a most elusive game.

Some pursue him with threats and curses
And some prefer a smoother plan,
Some may woo him with rhymes and verses,
give me a strong and silent man . . .

Then with a laugh, Carmen took a flower from her dress and threw it in Don Jose's face. As she ran away, he shouted after her, calling her a sorceress—even as he accepted the flower.

Later, while Don Jose stood guard in the square, Micaela brought a letter, some money, and a kiss to him from his mother. The letter forgave him for "his erring ways" and urged him to marry Micaela. After reminiscing with the girl about their small village and the memories they had shared there, Don Jose sent his love and a kiss with Micaela back to his mother. After she had left him to contemplate the letter, he sang of his desire to marry Micaela, and was about to throw Carmen's flower away, when excited voices burst from the factory: a riot had broken out. When Zuniga sent Don Jose to find out

what had happened, Don Jose returned with Carmen. She and another girl had been fighting. Before the guards were called to arrest the girls, Carmen had managed to wound the other girl with a knife, cutting a cross on her cheek. After the guards had tied Carmen's hands behind her back, the commander ordered Don Jose to watch over her.

The crowd slowly dispersed. Left alone with Don Jose, Carmen sang an enchanting invitation to her sentry:

There's a cafe in Seville,
Kept by my friend Lillas Pastia,
Where I dance a smooth Seguidilla
And drink Manzanilla.
I will soon be there with Lillas Pastia!

Still, I would be so very lonely,
Dancing would be a sad affair,
So, I will take my one and only
To come and sit beside me there!

Carmen's seductive singing persuaded Don Jose to release her so he could meet her at the cafe and watch her dance, and she immediately darted away. Don Jose's failure in his duty, however, earned him a demotion and two months in prison. When Carmen smuggled him a file to help him in his escape from his cell, he did not use it, feeling that such an escape would be dishonorable.

Act II

Two months later, at Lillas Pastia's tavern, gypsies, smugglers, and soldiers alike sat watching the gypsy girls dance. Carmen and her friends joined in with the riotous singing, and after awhile, Captain Zuniga invited three of them to leave with him when the tavern closed. The girls' refusal prompted Zuniga to taunt Carmen about loving a criminal; in his tirade, he also bragged that he knew about Don Jose's love for Carmen and his agreement to meet her upon his release—a release, he claimed, which had just occurred. Carmen simply laughed at the allegations.

Suddenly, outside the tavern, a crowd could be heard shouting praises for the toreador, Escamillo, who, in response, broke into song:

Toreador, be on your guard, Toreador,
Toreador!
Dark eyes that flash as brightly as a sword,
Promise you your reward,
And when you win the fight,
Toreador, you'll find your heart's delight!

Escamillo spied Carmen in the crowd and asked her if she could love him. She responded with passionate flirtations of her own as he strutted with his friends.

Soon, Frasquita, one of Carmen's associates from the factory, found El Dancairo, a known smuggler, sitting at a nearby table. Asking him about his plans for an upcoming raid, he replied that, if the women would consent to accompany them, his band would be even more successful. Carmen, who by then had joined Frasquita at El Dancairo's table, declined the invitation; she was in love and would rather occupy herself with the newly-released Don Jose. At the mention of the soldier's name, the smugglers eagerly sought Carmen's help in enticing Don Jose to join them in their raid.

Don Jose arrived soon thereafter. Pulling her flower from his coat, he boldly announced his love for Carmen:

I shall see the face of this woman,
She with her arts that are vile!
Who has shamed, with malice inhuman,
Him whom my love would never beguile.

Carmen began to dance for him, but when Don Jose heard the bugle sounding retreat, he told her he would have to leave. Carmen, angry, muttered that if he loved her, he would desert his post and live a life of freedom with her. Then, thinking to shame him into staying, she mocked him: certainly, he should "obey that call of duty," and "scamper back to his quarters."

Then Zuniga entered. Seeing Don Jose talking to Carmen, the captain of dragoons became overwhelmed with jealousy and challenged him to a fight. But the smugglers intervened, driving Zuniga from the tavern. After Zuniga had fled, Carmen asked Don Jose to join the smugglers. Realizing he had no other choice, Don Jose relented, thus resigning his military post indefinitely.

Act III

The raid had been a success, and the smugglers waited at a high meadow near the pass they planned to take as their escape route. Carmen and Don Jose quarreled, she inviting him to return home, as he clearly would never succeed as a smuggler. Frasquita and Mercedes idled away the time forecasting each other's fortunes with cards. Carmen, seeing the cards on their table, picked them up to determine what her fate would be. No matter how she dealt them, however, the cards predicted the same dire providence: death—first for her, then for Don Jose.

The smugglers left to seek a safe way through the pass just as Micaela appeared with a message for Don Jose. But before she could give it to him, Escamillo appeared, claiming to be looking for his love, a gypsy named Carmen. Now in a rage of jealousy, Don Jose drew his dagger to kill Escamillo, but Carmen interceded to stop the shedding of blood.

Micaela finally delivered her intended message to Don Jose: His mother was ill and wished to see him before she died. Ignoring Micaela, Don Jose brushed her aside to confront Carmen about Escamillo. In anger, he warned her that they would meet again. After a heated exchange, Don Jose went to see his mother.

Act IV

Some time later, at the square in Seville, the crowd at the bullfighting arena erupted in thunderous applause as Escamillo appeared with Carmen on his arm. She told him she had never loved anyone as she loved him, and they both vowed undying love. But Frasquita and Mercedes had warned her that Don Jose would be somewhere in the crowd. She scoffed at their warning, then reassured them she would speak with Don Jose before the bullfight.

After the multitude had entered the arena, Carmen and Don Jose found themselves alone on the plaza outside. Don Jose—the man she had destroyed—appeared distraught, a dramatic contrast to his triumphant rival Escamillo. They greeted each other curtly, then he broke down and pled for her forgiveness, imploring her to go away with him. She vigorously refused, saying that she was born free, and would also die free. Ruined, cheated, an outcast due to his love for Carmen, Don Jose, by now frantic, threatened her with harm.

In the arena, the crowd took up a shout as Escamillo entered the ring. Carmen tried to pass by the enraged Don Jose to enter, but he blocked her way, insisting on knowing if she truly loved the bullfighter. She replied, with biting scorn, that even in the face of death, she would admit that she did.

More cheers from the arena prompted Carmen to try to brush past Don Jose, but he caught her arm. He had not pawned his soul for her love, he screamed, only to be cast aside for another. Carmen, now maddened by Don Jose's obstinacy, screamed back at him; either let her go or kill her, she warned.

Cursing her as he pushed her away toward the arena, he vowed that she would be sorry for rejecting him. Before disappearing, Carmen turned, took from her finger the ring Don Jose had given her, and tossed it in his face.

Finally, the bullfight over, the crowd poured from the arena, shouting Escamillo's name and applauding his gallantry. All at once, Don Jose, brandishing a knife, rushed through the throng, seized Carmen, and stabbed her in the heart. In horror the crowd drew away. There knelt Don Jose, next to Carmen's limp body. In shame and anguish, he cried out that it was he who slew her—his own Carmen, the woman he adored.

Commentary:

Carmen premiered on March 3, 1875, just three months before the death of Georges Bizet. At the time, a rumor went around that Bizet had died of a broken heart because *Carmen* had failed during its first season at the Paris Opera Comique. In fact, Bizet was ill long before the opera opened, and died from the effects of overwork.

Carmen did not receive initial acclaim, perhaps due to its violence and its unsavory protagonist. But in nearly 125 years of subsequent showing, *Carmen,* as reviewer Ernest Newman relates, has assumed its place as a most brilliant work: "It is the most Mozartian opera since Mozart, the one in which enchanting musical invention goes hand in hand, almost without a break, with dramatic veracity and psychological characterization."

AIDA

by
Giuseppe Verdi
(1813-1901)

Type of work: Tragic opera

Setting: Ancient Egypt, around Memphis and Thebes

Principal characters:
The King of Egypt
Amneris, the King's daughter
Aida, Amneris' Ethiopian slave girl
Radames, Egyptian captain of the guard
Ramfis, high priest of Isis
Amonastro, King of Ethiopia, and Aida's father

Story Overview:

Act I

Ramfis, the high priest, stood in the great hall of the palace, speaking to the King's captain of the guard, Radames. The priest revealed that the Ethiopians were at that moment challenging Egypt in the Nile Valley and threatening the city of Thebes with a large army. The priest added that the goddess Isis had named the man who would lead the Egyptian army against the Ethiopians. He looked pointedly at Radames, then turned to report to the king.

Radames, in contemplation of Ramfis' revelation, exclaimed that he would finally realize his greatest ambition: to lead the Egyptian army to victory. He would then return triumphant to his beloved Aida, the slave of the king's daughter, Amneris. He sang of his love:

Heavenly Aida, fair as the sunrise,
Soft as the starlight touching a flower
Queen of my heart, oh reign there forever,
Filling with beauty my darkest hour.

Could we return to the land which bore you,
Where gentle breezes come drifting down;
I would enthrone you, lay all before you,
Give you the sunlight to be your crown.

When Radames had finished praising his beloved, Amneris appeared. Excitedly, he told her that he had at last achieved his life's ambition. Amneris, who was in love with the powerful captain of the guard, was dismayed that all he could think of was battle. She asked pointedly if "no other feeling touched his heart."

After Amneris left, Radames wondered if she had heard him proclaim his love for Aida. Amneris hadn't heard him—but she herself voiced her haunting suspicion that Aida was her rival.

Aida then entered Amneris' chambers, her head hung low. Amneris asked Aida why she seemed so sad, to which Aida answered that she was frightened by the prospect of war and that she was distressed by the danger facing the country. Amneris had no idea that Aida was speaking of Ethiopia, because the slave had carefully concealed her heritage. Amneris also had no idea that Aida was the daughter of Amonastro, the Ethiopian king.

Back in the palace hall, a messenger

reported that the Ethiopians had invaded Egypt and were now marching on Thebes. The messenger ended his report with the revelation that the Egyptian army was under the command of King Amonastro himself. When Aida heard her father's name, she cried out in fear and alarm.

The Egyptian king immediately announced that Radames would lead the army in defense of Thebes, and sent him to the temple of Vulcan to be vested with sacred armor.

Meanwhile, Aida agonized over her predicament. She could not bid Radames to return victorious without blaspheming her father, but neither could she pray for her father without betraying her love for Radames. Not knowing what else to do, she ran out of the hall.

Act II

As Amneris awaited the Egyptian army's return, her servants dressed her in festive garb for the victory celebration. Her slaves danced around her, singing of the delights that awaited the conquering Egyptian soldiers.

But when she saw Aida approaching, Amneris dismissed her other slaves. She resolved to force Aida into confessing her love for Radames. Knowing Aida was ignorant of which soldiers were returning and which had been killed, Amneris told Aida that Radames had been slain in combat.

As Amneris predicted, Aida swooned and fell into deep grief, betraying her feelings for the captain. Amneris derided her slave and told her how she had been trapped with the lie. Aida's mistress then revealed that Radames, in fact, was coming home with the army, alive. Overcome with joy, Aida shouted her thanks to the gods. But then Amneris challenged Aida to look upon her opponent—a daughter of the Pharaohs. Angered, Aida almost disclosed her own royal heritage, but then checked herself. Instead, she fell to her knees and begged Amneris' forbearance.

Amneris, pleased with Aida's submissive response, reminded Aida the proper role of the slave was to grovel in the dust, and this was how she commanded Aida to conduct herself at the festival. When they celebrated Egypt's victory over the invading Ethiopians, Amneris, on the other hand, noble daughter of the Pharaohs, would sit next to the king on his throne.

Outside, near the triumphal arch, a crowd gathered to pay their respects to the soldiers. The king entered as well and took his place on his canopied throne to await the return of Radames.

Radames finally rounded the corner in his chariot. He paused in front of the throne, and Amneris placed the victor's crown on his head. Behind Radames, the Ethiopian captives were chained together in a great procession. Aida, catching sight of her father among the captives and unable to contain herself, cried out. The crowd then looked on in disbelief as she embraced the prisoner, even as Amonastro whispered to Aida not to reveal his royal identity. Then, joined by Aida, he appealed to the Egyptian king, asking him to be merciful to the defeated.

Hearing this, the priests vehemently demanded that the king take revenge on the invading Ethiopians. But the people urged the king to hear the petitions of the conquered. Radames, admiring Aida's impassioned pleas, turned to the king and asked him to free the Ethiopian captives. Enraged, Amneris demanded her revenge on Radames—by killing the Ethiopians.

Ramfis finally interceded in the growing hostilities, suggesting that the king compromise by letting all the Ethiopians go free—except Aida's father. The king agreed and, having resolved the issue, told Radames that his reward for winning the battle would be Amneris' hand and the Egyptian throne. Radames and Aida looked toward each other in shock, while Amneris looked on in joy.

Act III

A distraught Aida walked down to the banks of the Nile and, with her face veiled, expressed her longing for her homeland:

Land of my youth, farewell,
Farewell forevermore!
O land of azure skies with fragrant warm
breeze,
Land of my childhood, bright happy days of
yore,
O smiling valleys, O laughing little rivers,
Land of my childhood, farewell forevermore!

Presently, still shackled in chains, Amonastro appeared and sternly reprimanded Aida for loving Radames, the conqueror of her people. He explained that the Ethiopians were poised to strike back, but they had to know the name of the pass through which the Egyptian army would march. Aida protested betraying Radames, but at her father's insistence, she eventually promised to obey. Hearing Radames approach, Amonastro hid behind some river grass.

Radames found Aida alone on the river bank, and swore that no matter what happened, it was she whom he loved. Aida asked Radames to flee with her to Ethiopia, to which he agreed. But, he explained, they would have to avoid the armies which were gathering again for battle. The only way to avoid them would be to go through the pass where the Egyptians waited in ambush. Aida asked Radames to name the pass, and he did.

As soon as Radames identified the site of the ambush, Amonastro sprang from the river grass and announced himself as King of the Ethiopians. Radames, now realizing that he had agreed to betray Egypt to run away with Aida, cried that he had become a traitor. Hearing his cries, Amneris and Ramfis, worshipping in the Temple of Isis nearby, rushed to his aid. As Amneris hurried from the temple, Amonastro lunged at her with a dagger. Radames restrained

him, but then let him go. Aida and her father disappeared into the night, while Radames, wailing in misery, surrendered himself to Ramfis.

Act IV

In the prison where Radames awaited his sentence from the priests, Amneris appeared, offering to save him if he would forsake Aida. Radames refused, and cursed Amneris for robbing him of his true love—perhaps even killing her. Amneris explained that only Amonastro had been caught and executed; Aida had escaped. Radames refused to accept mercy from Amneris; he simply and submissively proclaimed that he was ready to die:

Although I could defend myself,
Who would accept the reason,
That I would scorn to lend myself
To infamy or treason?
Although I revealed the sacred in word
unwisely spoken.
My faith is still unbroken, my honor still
remains.

The guards took Radames to the judgment hall, where the priests announced his sentence: he would be buried alive in a tomb under the altar in the Temple of Vulcan. Amneris raged at the priests, and as they took Radames to his fate, she screamed curses after them, but to no avail.

As the priests sealed the tomb, Radames lamented—not over his own death, but for the loss of his beloved Aida. But suddenly, Aida herself emerged from the shadows. She had foreseen his fate and had crept into the tomb to die with him. Radames, troubled that she, solely for love of him, was doomed, tried to remove the seal from the door to save her.   But it was too late. Aida died wrapped in Radames' arms—at the same instant that Amneris leapt to her death on the stones of the temple floor.

Commentary:

Verdi's *Aida* resounds of genius. In the staging of the opera, the final scene of Aida's death and Amneris' suicide are depicted simultaneously, using an ingenious divided set.

The story of Aida is based on a historical incident, the records of which were found by French archaeologist Auguste-Edouard Marriette while digging near Memphis.

Some historians have written that Verdi was commissioned by the Egyptian government to compose an opera for the debut performance of the Cairo theater, which opened in 1869. In fact, Verdi was not interested in writing an opera for the theater, but he was interested in writing an opera based on Marriette's discovery. When the opera was completed, the Egyptian government invited Verdi to bring it to Cairo. He accepted, and *Aida* became the first opera to be performed at the Cairo theater in 1871, two years after it opened. As if drawn to witness a portrayal of Amneris, one of their forerunning Egyptian sisters, the night of the premier three of the boxes on the first tier of the theater were filled with veiled women from the harem of Khedive.

LA BOHEME

by
Giacomo Puccini
(1858-1924)

Type of work: Tragic opera

Setting: Paris; 1830-31

Principal Characters:
Rodolfo, a Bohemian poet
Mimi, Rodolfo's lover
Marcello, a Bohemian painter
Musetta, Marcello's lover
Colline and Shaunard, respectively, a philosopher and a musician

Story Overview:

For the poet, Rodolfo, and his painter friend, Marcello, life was an affair of excess. As such, their material circumstances tended to fluctuate between the extremes of feast and famine: If a Bohemian had money, he spent it on himself and his friends, giving no thought to tomorrow; if he didn't, he simply suffered through the periods of poverty as best he could, surviving by his wits.

Christmas Eve in 1830 found Rodolfo and Marcello in rather desperate straits. In their unheated apartment, Marcello's hand were frozen. As he tried to work on a painting, he complained that his hands felt as if they had touched an iceberg. Rodolfo's spirits were not much brighter. He sat by a cold stove and gazed pensively out the window across the snow-covered rooftops of the city. He sighed, as he watched the smoke "lazily floating up from the stoves" all over Paris. "Love's a stove that squanders a lot of fuel," he mused.

They considered burning the painting to provide some warmth, but Rodolfo wouldn't hear of it. Instead, he offered up his five-act drama script to the flame: " . . . my drama shall give us warmth." Striking a flint to light his manuscript, Rodolfo said, "Let's begin with the first act."

The two friends warmed their hands before the burning manuscript. Soon, they were joined by a third friend, Colline, a philosopher who had spent the evening trying in vain to sell his books. "What fiery pages. Only the daring can dream such visions," Colline said, mocking Rodolfo's literary talents and warming his hands by the small flame. "Dreams that in bright flame soon disappear," they all said in unison, as the meager fire dwindled down, leaving the room cold again.

Later, yet another friend appeared at their door, Shaunard, a struggling musician, to their surprise entered the apartment loaded with firewood, cigars, food, wine, and a substantial amount of cash. He had just returned from an engagement for an eccentric who had hired him to perform a eulogy for his pet parrot, he explained—but his friends, seeing the stash of food and drink, were hardly interested in his story. Rejuvenated by this sudden shift of fortune, the Bohemian group decided to celebrate Christmas Eve at the famous and popular Cafe Momus. However, most unexpectedly, Benoit,

the landlord, appeared, asking for the long-overdue rent. When Marcello invited him to have a glass of wine with them, the landlord became drunk enough to brag about his marital infidelities. The quartet, in a mock display of sudden moral indignation, flung the dumbfounded landlord out of the apartment, without giving him another chance to ask for money. The friends then set out for the cafe, but Rodolfo stayed behind, explaining that he would join them later, as soon as he had finished writing an article for a magazine.

Rodolfo, however, was unable to write. "No inspiration!" he cursed. He laid his pen on the table and was about to give up when he heard a "timid knock at the door." There, pale and beautiful, was Mimi. Her candle had gone out and she was wondering if Rodolfo would kindly light it for her. For Rodolfo, the sight of her was "golden love awaking." Within a short time, his courage was such that he said to Mimi, "Your tiny hand is frozen! Let me warm it into life," and he took her hand into his own. Rodolfo then launched into the story of his life, concluding with the confession that "Bright eyes as yours, believe me, steal my priceless jewels in Fancy's storehouse cherished."

Mimi demurred to his advances at first, but admitted, "Sweet to my soul [is] the magic voice of love." Yet as Mimi stood there beside him like a vision "in the moonlight," Rodolfo knew that he had to convince her to partake of "love's eternal enchantment." Finally, she admitted that she, too, had fallen in love. Then, at his insistence, Mimi also told of her life's situation. She earned her livelihood by doing embroidery work. Her favorite subject was flowers, she professed; in fact, even during the winter, the small room where she stayed was filled with colorful embroidered flowers.

The new lovers now decided they would join Rodolfo's friends at the Cafe Momus. On the way, they mingled with the eclectic Paris crowd; at one shop Rodolfo stopped to buy Mimi a bonnet embroidered with roses. "The color," he said, "suits your complexion."

The pair found the others seated at a table outside the cafe, having already ordered a banquet to celebrate their good fortune. Everyone's spirits were buoyant, until Musetta appeared with Alcindoro, a rich old man and the latest in a series of "lovers without number." Although Marcello said that Musetta had "drained [his] heart of blood," he was still in love with her. And the fickle Musetta, as it turned out, had grown bored with Alcindoro. Now, seeing her former lover at the cafe, Musetta felt herself falling for Marcello all over again. Sending Alcindoro on an errand that would keep him occupied and away, Musetta threw her arms around Marcello. "Enchantress!" he exclaimed in response.

When the waiter finally brought their bill, the friends realized that their money was all spent, so Musetta ordered the waiter to put it on Alcindoro's tab. "Queen of our hearts," the friends cried, "the Latin Quarter hails its glorious queen!" Then, following a marching band down the street, they disappeared into the night.

Two months passed. Marcello and Musetta were still together, living in a tavern where they worked for room and board—she teaching singing, he painting murals. Rodolfo and Mimi, however, had quarreled and were on the verge of separating.

On a chilly February morning, Mimi appeared at the tavern looking for Marcello. At first, Marcello did not recognize her: she had grown ill, plagued by the effects of a persistent cough.

"Good Marcello!" she cried. "Help me!" She then explained that Rodolfo had become madly jealous and that even the smallest gesture or glance aroused his anger and suspicion. "And then at night," she continued, "I feel his eyes are watching, to spy upon my slumbers. . . . All is over," she sobbed. Marcello in fact already knew of their troubles because Rodolfo had spent the night at the tavern—and was there even now, sleeping.

Marcello warned Mimi that Rodolfo would awaken at any minute; not wishing to be seen, she slipped outside. Rodolfo did awaken, and immediately began complaining about Mimi's alleged flirtations. But Marcello was skeptical and thought something else was agitating his friend. "You are not sincere," he told Rodolfo. Rodolfo finally admitted that Marcello was right. The truth, he said, was that he feared "Mimi was slowly dying," and he was racked with guilt. He had nothing to offer her "but a squalid prison cell . . . no fire to warm her . . . only the cruel nightwind, [that] wails cold and cheerless."

Mimi, who had been hiding nearby, overheard Rodolfo and began to sob. Having betrayed herself, she stepped into view and Rodolfo tenderly embraced her. "Ah, Mimi!" he consoled. Then Rodolfo promised that they would remain "together till the spring returns." "Ah," she prayed, "that our winter might last forever!"

But while Mimi and Rodolfo managed to settle their differences at the inn, Marcello and Musetta parted company after an argument.

In the spring, both Rodolfo and Marcello were once again sharing their old apartment. Neither was able to work, and so to pass the time they tormented each other with stories about Mimi and Musetta, their lost lovers. Rodolfo told Marcello that he had recently seen Musetta and that she had talked with him "quite gaily," telling him that she was so luxuriously dressed, she no longer heard the voice of her heart from beneath all the satin and silk. Marcello answered that, likewise, he had run into Mimi and that she had also been dressed like a duchess, having accepted the kindnesses of a rich patron.

Weeks later, the two friends invited Colline and Shaunard to join them in a feast—actually a mock banquet featuring bread and a single herring. Their merriment continued until they heard a knock at the door. It was Musetta. "It's Mimi . . . " she said hoarsely. "It's Mimi . . . and [she] is ailing."

Mimi didn't have the strength to climb the stairs to the apartment, so Rodolfo and Marcello hurried down to carry her. Colline and Shaunard cleared a bed and Marcello and Rodolfo gently laid her in it. As Mimi slept comfortably, Musetta whispered to the others that Mimi, fearing that death was near, had abandoned her wealthy benefactor to return and die with her true love, Rodolfo.

Mimi gradually grew weaker. Musetta worriedly rushed out to pawn her earrings for money to hire a doctor. Colline also offered to sell his overcoat to buy medicine. After these two had left on their errands, Rodolfo and Mimi were finally alone. "My bonnet," she gestured to Rodolfo. "Do you remember how we met that evening . . . ? It was dark," Mimi went on, "and you took my hand so gently . . . "

Following several hours of reminiscing on the magic of the past, the pair's intimate moment was broken when Marcello and Musetta returned with news that a doctor was on his way. Mimi had a chill, and Musetta gave her a muff to warm her hands. "My hands," Mimi said drowsily, "are . . . much warmer; and . . . I'll sleep now." Musetta prepared the medicine and prayed to the Madonna for Mimi's recovery. When Colline returned, Shaunard had already detected Mimi's passing, but Rodolfo, filled with denial, would not believe what was already evident. He rushed to Mimi's bedside, lifted her in his arms, and cried her name. Finally realizing that she was indeed dead, he fell back onto the bed, and began to sob over her cold body.

Commentary:

The strength and uniqueness of *La Boheme* lies in its portrayal of Bohemian Paris. Rather than focusing on the characters, this opera brings to life an atmosphere of youth, for which it has been beloved ever since its creation.

La Boheme is the first of Puccini's "holy trinity" of operas that includes "Madame Butterfly" and "Tosca." It was first performed under the direction of Arturo Toscanini at the Teatro Regio in Turin, Italy on February 1, 1896. Despite the fact that it is now considered among Puccini's most perfect works, it received a lukewarm reception at its premiere.

The basic story of *La Boheme* had already been explored by one of Puccini's rivals, a composer who had developed a libretto based on a novel about Bohemian life in Paris. Puccini at first brushed the work aside, but his interest in the story was rekindled when he was sent an outline of the plot. Puccini collaborated with two other well-known poets, which angered his rival. However, Puccini was indifferent. "Let him compose. I will compose. The public will judge."

Puccini worked sporadically on *La Boheme* from 1892 until 1895. When he had finished drafting Mimi's death scene and the opera was completed, he wrote: "I had to get up and, standing in the middle of the study, alone in the silence of the night, I began to weep . . . It was as if I had seen my own child die."

MADAME BUTTERFLY

by
Giacomo Puccini
(1858-1924)

Type of work: Tragic Opera

Setting: Early 1900s; Nagasaki, Japan

Principal characters:
 Madame Butterfly (Cio-Cio-San), a young Japanese girl
 B.F. Pinkerton, an American naval officer
 Suzuki, Madame Butterfly's servant
 Sharpless, the U.S. Consul at Nagasaki
 Goro, a Japanese marriage broker
 Prince Yamadori, Butterfly's wealthy suitor

Story Overview:

Act I

Lieutenant Pinkerton, an American naval officer, decided to engage the services of Goro, a local marriage broker, to arrange a "marriage of convenience" between himself and Cio-Cio-San, a beautiful fifteen-year-old Japanese girl called "Butterfly" by her friends. Assured by the broker that the marriage would only be binding for as long as he consented to live with his "wife," Pinkerton entered into the arrangement with the assumption that he would eventually leave Butterfly behind, after which she would be free to marry whomever she wished. As part of the arrangement, Pinkerton leased a house, overlooking the harbor, to share with his bride.

Sharpless, the American Consul grew concerned when he heard of Pinkerton's arrangement. He had seen it happen before: a naval officer, simply looking for a little "comfort away from home," marries a local girl—such an arrangement always led to trouble. Sharpless walked up the hill to Pinkerton's new house and found the officer touring the grounds with Goro. Pulling Pinkerton aside, Sharpless warned that what may be a mere pastime for him most likely would be taken very seriously by the girl. The predominant Western philosophy in which the roving Yankee boldly ventures forth and expects the fairest of every land he visits to become his reward, did not apply in Japan, he explained. Japanese philosophy deemed that where love and honor are at stake, so is life itself.

Pinkerton shrugged off Sharpless' warning and invited the Consul to stay for a drink. Just then, Butterfly and her family arrived amidst a festive gathering of friends. As Butterfly approached the house, she sang:

This is one more step to climb.
One moment.
Across the earth and o'er the ocean,
Balmy breeze and scent of spring are blowing.
I am the happiest maiden, the happiest in Japan
In all the world!
I have obeyed the summons, the sweet summons of love,
Upon the threshold standing.
Ah, here the glory that life or death can offer
doth now await me.
Dear maidens, I hastened here at the call of my heart!

After the family had exchanged greetings with Pinkerton and Sharpless, the Consul spoke for a moment alone with Butterfly. She declared that she was deeply in love with Pinkerton, so much so that she had secretly gone to a Catholic mission and converted to Christianity, renouncing her own religion. Sharpless became more and more convinced that he had been right to warn Pinkerton—but Pinkerton stubbornly insisted on proceeding with the wedding.

The officials who would oversee the marriage arrived and the wedding began. The simple ceremony was then performed, and all the guests gathered to congratulate the couple. Seizing once more the opportunity, the Consul for the last time tried to convince Pinkerton that he had made a mistake. Unsuccessful, the Consul and the other officials soon left the celebration.

In honor of the newlyweds, the gathered guests sang to a Japanese God. In the midst of the merry-making, however, a strange figure dressed in flowing robes and ringing bells appeared, interrupting the revelry. The figure turned out to be Butterfly's uncle, a priest who had come to call down curses on Butterfly's head for turning her back on her religion. The priest turned to Butterfly's friends and family and called on them to also spurn her. Pinkerton, angered by the priest's rhetorical rantings, proclaimed the celebration over, and sent everyone home.

Momentarily saddened by the cursing she had borne, Butterfly's despair quickly gave way to childlike delight as Pinkerton filled her ears with words of love. However, after he likened her to a real butterfly, she became frantic with fear that she might receive the same treatment butterflies receive in America—to be caught and pinned on a board for display. But Pinkerton again assuaged her fears, and led his new bride into their home, to consummate their marriage.

Act II

Not long after the wedding, Pinkerton was called back to his naval duties, promising Butterfly that he would return "when the robins nest." But three years later, Butterfly—who had since given birth to Pinkerton's baby, a boy named Sorrow—still waited for his return.

Suzuki, Butterfly's faithful servant, prayed for Pinkerton's return. She offered the prayer for Butterfly's sake, because in her heart, Suzuki believed Pinkerton had simply deserted her mistress. But Butterfly herself remained hopeful, even chiding her servant for doubting that Pinkerton would return:

One fine day we'll notice
A thread of smoke arising on the sea
In the far horizon,
And then the ship appearing;
Then the trim white vessel
Glides into the harbor, thunders forth her can non,
See you? Now he is coming!

Butterfly further envisioned that when he did return, she would not go down to meet him, but would stand on the hill and wait for him to come to her. She sang:

> He will call, "Butterfly" from the distance.
> I without answering,
> Hold myself quietly concealed,
> A bit to tease him and a bit not to die
> At our first meeting . . .
> Banish your idle fears,
> For he will return, I know it!

Butterfly did not realize that, even as she sang, Pinkerton was in fact sailing back to Nagasaki—but without any intention of resuming relations with her. Before setting sail for Japan, Pinkerton had written Sharpless, asking him to inform Butterfly that he had married an American woman who would be joining him in Nagasaki.

Sharpless made an attempt to deliver the message, but when Butterfly saw the letter, she became overjoyed, thinking Pinkerton was returning to her. As Sharpless tried to explain the situation, Prince Yamadori arrived. Ever since Pinkerton's departure, Goro had been trying to match Butterfly with a new suitor. But the loyal Butterfly had only become offended, and had refused. As the money Pinkerton had left her dwindled down to nothing, however, Goro's persistence had increased; Prince Yamadori, the latest admirer Goro had sent, would make a perfect husband for Butterfly. Still, she insisted that she was married to Pinkerton.

Hearing this latest refusal and having been "made sport of" by Butterfly, Yamadori left the home, and Sharpless again tried to make Butterfly understand the truth. Frustrated by her enthusiastic interruptions, Sharpless asked her what she would do if, indeed, her husband never returned. Haltingly, she stammered that she could perhaps once more work as a geisha, or better, she could die. Filled with pity, Sharpless himself suggested that she marry Yamadori, but her abrupt reply was to bring in her baby and show him to the Consul. She explained that when Pinkerton heard that a fine son awaited him in Japan, he would hurry back. Then she sang to the baby:

> Do you hear, my sweet one,
> what that bad man had heart to fancy?
> That your mother should take you on her shoulder,
> And forth should wander in rain and tempest
> Through the town seeking to earn enough
> For food and clothing,
> And then before the kindly people
> To dance in measure to her song and cry out:
> "Oh listen, good people
> Listen for the love of all the eight hundred thousand gods
> And goddesses of Japan!

The Consul asked the child's name, and Butterfly answered that his name was "Sorrow"—at least until his father returned, at which time his name would change to "Joy."

Not having the heart to disillusion Butterfly, Sharpless departed.

After Sharpless left, Suzuki brought in Goro, the marriage broker. Again he tried to convince Butterfly of the hopelessness of her faith,

but his words only inflamed her.

All at once, a cannon salute echoed from the harbor, signalling the arrival of a magnificent man-o-war. Butterfly watched it steam into the harbor from the hilltop and recognized it as Pinkerton's ship, the *Abraham Lincoln*. Turning to Suzuki and Sharpless, she now chastised them for their doubts. They had been wrong; her husband had returned to her after all.

After decorating the house with cherry blossoms, Butterfly, Suzuki, and the baby sat down to await Pinkerton's arrival. Night fell, and Suzuki and the little boy drifted off to sleep. But Butterfly still waited, rigid and motionless, for the man who had forsaken her.

Act III

The morning broke, and Pinkerton, thinking of Butterfly, realized his conduct had been heartless and cruel. So, he persuaded Sharpless to walk up the hill with him to see her. Accompanied by his American wife, Pinkerton fell into a state of anguish as they approached the house.

Meanwhile, exhausted from a restless night, Butterfly had finally fallen into a deep sleep. Suzuki greeted the visitors, but, learning that the woman in the garden was Pinkerton's new wife, she begged them to take the child to America with them to rid Butterfly of the constant reminder of her beloved. Guilt-ridden, Pinkerton told Sharpless that he was unable to face Butterfly, and asked the Consul to settle the matter. Then he turned and headed back down the trail, leaving Sharpless alone on the hill.

Now roused out of her sleep, Butterfly appeared, radiant and hopeful. She expected to see her husband, but her hopes fell at the sight of Sharpless—and Pinkerton's new wife. Only now was the Consul finally able to convince her that her American officer would not return.

Butterfly graciously asked Sharpless to wish Pinkerton's American wife happiness; then she told him that Pinkerton could have their child, if he himself would come to retrieve his son. Finally, Sharpless left the sobbing Butterfly.

Butterfly, after bidding Suzuki to secure all the doors and windows, took her father's dagger from atop the shrine and read the inscription on the blade: "Death with honor is better than life with dishonor." Suzuki carried the boy into the room as Butterfly raised the dagger and placed it to her own chest. Momentarily distracted, she blindfolded the child and placed an American flag in his tiny hand, before again placing the dagger to her breast and plunging it deep into her body. Mortally wounded, Butterfly dragged herself to where the little boy was playing on the floor, gazing at him as her life slipped away. Just as Pinkerton entered to take the child, she took her last breath and closed her eyes.

Commentary:

Puccini's operas are characterized by strong images that create an atmosphere of time and place. *Madame Butterfly* is no exception. The scenes are lavishly staged, virtually taking the audience to a hilltop overlooking Nagasaki's beautiful harbor. *Madame Butterfly* was not an initial success, but over time, it has become a mainstay of any opera company's repertoire.

THE PIRATES OF PENZANCE

(or, "The Slave of Duty")
Book by Sir William Schwenck Gilbert (1836-1911)
Music by Sir Arthur Seymour Sullivan (1842-1900)

Type of work: Comic opera
Setting: A rocky sea-shore on the coast of Cornwall and Major General Stanley's estate
Principal characters:
   Frederick, a dutiful boy accidentally apprenticed to pirates
   Pirate King, leader of the pirate band
   Ruth, Frederick's dense nurse-maid
   Mabel, a beautiful young maiden loved by Frederick
   Major General Stanley, Mabel's father

Story Overview:

"When Fred'ric was a little lad he proved so brave and daring," that his father ordered his nursery maid, Ruth, to apprentice the boy to a ship's pilot. Unfortunately, Ruth was hard of hearing—and not very bright. Instead of taking the boy to a ship's pilot, she apprenticed him to a *pirate*. When Ruth realized the terrible mistake she had made, she was too frightened to return home to Frederick's father, so she stayed on with the pirates "as a kind of piratical maid-of-all-work." And once he found himself legally apprenticed to the Pirate King, Frederick considered it his duty to fulfill his indenture. Until he completed his term on his twenty-first birthday he worked studiously to be the best pirate possible.

But now as the pirates toasted the end of Frederick's apprenticeship thirteen years after his arrival, Frederick announced that he was leaving his criminal past. He explained to the pirates that he had only stayed with them out of a sense of duty; now that his duty was fulfilled, he was going to make amends to society by dedicating himself to their extermination.

The Pirate King agreed that extermination might be a solution to the pirates' dilemma; they could not make their piracy pay—and they didn't know why. Frederick replied that he *did* know why, "but alas I cannot tell you, it would not be right." "Why not, it's only 11:56," responded the Pirate King, "and you're one of us until the clock strikes twelve." Realizing he was still duty-bound, Frederick explained that the pirates were too tender hearted—they were not merciless enough; what's more, they studiously avoided attacking orphans. At this last accusation, the Pirate Lieutenant tried to excuse himself: "We're orphans ourselves, we know what it's like." "Yes, but it has got about," Frederick continued. "And what is the consequence? Everyone we capture says he's an orphan. The last three ships we took proved to be manned entirely by orphans. One would think that Great Britain's mercantile fleet was recruited solely from her orphan asylums. We know this is not the case." When queried as to whether he would have the pirates act totally *without* mercy, Frederick said, "Ah, why there's my problem. Til twelve o'clock I would, after twelve I wouldn't."

As Frederick prepared to leave, he voiced his concern over Ruth, who had won her "middle-aged way into [his] boyish heart." He felt it was his duty to marry the loyal woman, but, having been at sea since he was eight years old, and never having set eyes on another woman, he wondered if he would later learn to his disappointment that she was plain. After the pirates had assured Frederick that "there are the remains of a fine woman about Ruth," the youth promised that if Ruth was as fair of face as she hopefully claimed to be, he would marry her.

Finally, before leaving, Frederick called for the Pirate King to forsake his life of crime and return to civilization. The King refused, observing:
   . . . Oh, better far to live and die / under the brave black flag I fly, / than play a sanctimonious part, / with a pirate head and a pirate heart. / Away to the cheating world go you, / where pirates all are well-to-do; / but I'll be true to the song I sing, / and live and die a Pirate King. . . .

Frederick and Ruth then took leave of the pirates. Soon they came across Major General Stanley's beautiful young daughters. Clearly, Frederick quickly realized, as women went Ruth was plain:
   Fred: You told me you were fair as gold!
   Ruth: And, master, am I not so?
   Fred: And now I see you're plain and old.
   Ruth: I am sure I am not a jot so.
   Fred: Upon my innocence you play.
   Ruth: I'm not the one to plot so.
   Fred: Your face is lined, your hair is grey.
   Ruth: It's gradually got so.

Then, turning his back on the old nurse maid, Frederick approached Stanley's daughters with the tale of his sordid past, asking if there was not one of the girls who would obey the call of duty and help him reform by marrying him. While other sisters rejected Frederick, Mabel Stanley claimed that she would marry him as a matter of duty. Mabel's sisters, however, questioned her "sense of duty": "The question is, had [he] not been a thing of beauty, / would she be swayed by quite as keen a sense of duty?"

Now the pirates—who had followed Frederick and were lurking nearby—made a appearance. Their curiosity was also piqued by Stanley's lovely daughters. Frederick urged the girls to flee—but they were not fast enough. The pirates abducted them, with the intention of taking them in marriage. Mabel fiercely warned that she and her sisters were wards in Chancery and that their father was a Major General. At the mention of his name, the great Major General Stanley appeared in person, announcing himself as:
   The very model of a modern major general.
   I've information vegetable, animal, and mineral.
   I know the kings of England, and I quote the fights historical, from Marathon to Waterloo, in order categorical.

   I'm very well acquainted, too, with matters mathematical,
   I understand equations, both the simple and qua dratical.
   About binomial theorem I'm teeming with a lot o' news,
   with many cheerful facts about the square of the hypotenuse.

   For my military knowledge, though I'm plucky

and adventury,
has only been brought down to the beginning of
the century.
But still in matters vegetable, animal, and miner-
al,
I am the very model of a modern Major-
General.

When General Stanley learned that the pirates were about to marry his daughters against their will, he turned to the miscreants and recounted a sad story. He himself was an orphan, Stanley claimed, and the only things left to him in the world were his dear daughters. Hearing this, the kind-hearted pirates wept at the thought of splitting up an orphan's family, and immediately released the girls.

But while this genial lie saved the General's daughters, it also disturbed his sleep. He spent many hours in the family crypt, in torment of conscience, mourning his dishonor. Frederick tried to console the General by pointing out that if he had not spun the tale, the pirates surely would have taken his daughters to wife. But Stanley felt that he had shamed the dead ancestors upon whose tombs he wept. To this Frederick replied: "But you forgot, sir, you only bought the property a year ago, and the stucco in your baronial hall is scarcely dry." This made no difference to the general: "Frederick, in this chapel are ancestors; you cannot deny that. With the estate, I bought the chapel and its contents. I don't know whose ancestors they *were*, but I know whose ancestors they *are*, and I shudder to think that their descendant by purchase (if I may so describe myself) should have brought disgrace upon what, I have no doubt, was an unstained escutcheon." General Stanley was finally consoled when Frederick revealed that he was prepared to exterminate the pirates that very night, with the help of the local police—who were in fact quaking at the thought of battling blood-thirsty pirates.

A few hours before the attack was to begin, Ruth and the Pirate King approached Frederick, begging him to listen to them. Frederick had been the victim of a terrible paradox, they explained: he had been born on February 29. Therefore, if his life was counted by birthdays, he was only a little over five years old. Frederick found this amusing, but of no importance whatsoever—until someone pointed out that the terms of his indenture as a pirate did not expire until his "twenty-first birthday"—which would fall when he was 84. "We insist on nothing," Ruth added, well aware of Frederick's weakness. "We content ourselves with pointing out to you *your duty*." Against such an argument, Frederick's resistance broke: " . . . duty is before all—at any price I will do my duty." Once more a reluctant but dutiful pirate, Frederick revealed General Stanley's unatoned falsehood. "It breaks my heart to betray the honoured father of the girl I adore," he told the Pirate King, "but as your apprentice I have no alternative . . . General Stanley is no orphan!" At this, the King vowed to wreak vengeance fifty-fold on General Stanley.

Frederick bade farewell to his beloved Mabel, who pled with him to stay. "They have no claim!" she cried. "But Duty's name!" Frederick responded. "The thought my soul appalls, but when stern Duty calls, I must obey." In desperation, Mabel ran to inform the police of Frederick's return to piracy, and charged them to now do their duty and capture the dastardly pirates.

The police, hidden near General Stanley's estate, did not have long to wait. The pirates presently came up the road, singing just above a whisper: "Let's vary piracee with a little burglaree." General Stanley, awakened by their bungled march, emerged from the house. Then Stanley's daughters appeared, explaining the sounds they heard as the wind rustling through the trees, and wishing to find out why their father was out of bed on such an unsettled night. At that juncture the pirates came out of hiding and announced their intentions to kill the General and kidnap his daughters. Mabel begged Frederick to save her father. Frederick—still duty-bound—refused to intervene; but just as things looked truly sticky, the police leapt out of hiding and gave battle.

Unfortunately, the policemen were no match for the pirates, and were quickly disarmed. Once again, all appeared lost. "To gain a brief advantage you've contrived," the Police Sergeant announced boldly. "But your proud triumph will not be long lived." To this the pirates responded, "Don't say you're orphans for we know that game." But the policemen were unfazed. "On your allegiance," the sergeant answered, "we've a stronger claim . . . We charge you yield! We charge you yield in Queen Victoria's name!" The pirates surrendered themselves immediately, for, above all, they loved their Queen.

As the pirates were rounded up, Ruth stood to defend her long-time friends: "They are no members of the common throng; they are all noblemen, who have gone wrong." General Stanley, his own heart now softened, pardoned the pirates—and presented them with an unexpected gift: "Peers will be peers, and youth will have its fling. Resume your ranks and legislative duties, and take my daughters, all of whom are beauties."

This pronouncement left everyone happy: Mabel and Frederick were reunited, the former pirates and Stanley's daughters were wed—and the Sergeant of Police, having longingly eyed Ruth throughout the theatrical display, presented Ruth with a bouquet of flowers. General Stanley felt he had done very well:

My military knowledge, though I'm plucky and
adventury,
has only been brought down to the beginning of
the century. But still in getting off my daugh-
ters—eight or nine or ten in all,
I've shown myself the model of a modern Major-
General!

Commentary:

"The Pirates of Penzance" is unique among Gilbert and Sullivan's comic operas in that it was first staged, not in Britain, but in the United States, opening at New York's Fifth Avenue Theater on December 31, 1879.

Gilbert's story pokes fun at the Victorian sense of duty. Frederick, a virtual "slave of duty," ends up in a dutiful plot to kill the father of the girl he loves. At the same time, the cowardly policemen, though they sorrow for the criminals they are called upon to capture, actually play the heroes. Beneath the humor, however, runs a serious current, questioning blind obedience to any standard or ideal without consideration for human feelings or needs.

SAINT JOAN

by
George Bernard Shaw
(1856-1950)

Type of work: Historical and satirical drama

Setting: France; 1429 to 1456

Principal characters:
Joan of Arc, a young country girl
Captain Robert de Baudricourt, a military squire
Charles (later Charles VII), the eldest son ("Dauphin") of the King of France
The Archbishop of Rheims
Dunois, a young military commander from Orleans
The Earl of Warwick, an English aristocrat
The Inquisitor, a representative of the Church of England
Brother Martin Ladvenu, a young priest who tries to save Joan
A 20th-century messenger from the future

Play Overview:

[Throughout the Middle Ages, the English and French met frequently in territorial battles. During the fifteenth century, the English were intent on establishing their monarchy in France with the help of their French allies, the knights of Burgundy.]

Sunlight poured through the high window in the castle of Captain Robert de Baudricourt. Despite the beauty of the day, Robert was in an awful mood. His molting and scrawny hens would not produce eggs, and he scolded his steward, who—"scanty of flesh, scanty of hair"—appeared roughly as haggard as the hens. The poor servant explained to the Captain that the hens would not lay until Robert set his eyes on Joan of Arc, a young girl from the country who had a reputation for being either disastrously rash or else almost supernaturally courageous. For days now, Joan had petitioned to meet with Robert, but he had steadfastly refused to see her.

When the sly steward mentioned that perhaps Robert, appearing in all his military splendor, might throw some fright into proud Joan, the prospect pleased him so much that he finally agreed to receive the maid. But instead, Joan, dressed in full military uniform, overwhelmed the captain with her air of superiority; determined to go off to war and to fight like one of her male counterparts, Joan was imperious. "You are to give me a horse and armor and some soldiers," she announced, "and send me to the Dauphin [the heir to the French throne]"—these were God's instructions.

At first, Robert dismissed the young woman as "mad." Nonetheless, after learning that some of the local nobility supported Joan, he began to rethink her request. With some misgivings, he finally agreed to outfit her and dispatch her to the Dauphin. No sooner had the girl left than something of a miracle occurred: the hens began to lay a startling number of eggs. Flabbergasted, Robert exclaimed, "She did come from God."

Upon discovering that Robert had sent Joan to visit him, the Dauphin, Prince Charles, confided this news, with some sarcasm, to his castle's most exalted churchman: "What a pity, though you are an archbishop, saints and angels don't come to see you!" The Archbishop was not amused. Joan was "not a saint," he responded flatly, nor "even a respectable woman." After all, she dressed like a man and spoke out impertinently.

Not to be overruled by a spokesman of the Church, Charles decided to devise a test for Joan. He would seat a courtier in his place to receive her; would the divine power which she claimed as her inspiration help the young girl to discern that she was not, in fact, addressing the true heir to the throne?

Joan was not deceived. Glancing at the regally attired courtier, she said, "Thou canst not fool me. Where be the Dauphin?" Then, good naturedly, Joan chided the Prince himself: "It's no use, Charlie . . . thou must face what God puts on thee. If thou fail to be a king thou'lt be a beggar: what else art thou fit for?" Charles winced at the stinging truth of these words. "Oh do stop talking about God . . . " he quailed. Joan rebuked him, and prophesied of his—and France's—potential greatness:

I come from God to tell thee to kneel in the cathedral and solemnly give thy kingdom to Him for ever and ever, and become the greatest king in the world as His steward and His soldier and His servant. The very clay of France will become holy: her soldiers will become the soldiers of God. . . . The English will fall on their knees and beg thee let them return to their lawful homes in peace.

At these words, Charles' spirit soared. When he announced that Joan would lead the army at Orleans, the energized court erupted, "To Orleans!"

At her arrival on the battlefront, she scolded the young commander Dunois for gathering his troops "on the wrong side of the river"; the English and their Burgundian allies were camped on the opposite shore. Dunois defended his grounds for holding back: he was awaiting a change in the winds, awaiting God's sign. Joan corrected him: God was waiting for France to push the attack; the winds of victory were already with them. At that moment, the breeze shifted direction. Dunois knelt down in front of the woman whose presence seemed to have precipitated this miraculous altering of the elements. "God has spoken," he proclaimed.

Months later, in the English camp, the beaten soldiers were talking of "the Prince of Darkness" rather than of God. Joan's prowess in battle had caused the English and their allies to suffer many defeats—and they now damned her as a "heretic" whose head had been "turned" by her many victories. Two of her particularly vocal denouncers, the Earl of Warwick and the Bishop Cauchon, discussed the ramifications of the menace Joan presented. Warwick lamented that her power and heretical appeal could eventually overpower even the British aristocracy in a popular revolt; Cauchon condemned her as a threat to the Church, a woman who would eventually lead the world to "perish in a welter of war." The two men concurred: Joan would have to "die for the people."

Meanwhile, France's commoners had become fervent supporters of Joan. But Joan remained troubled as to why the aristocracy—courtiers, knights and churchmen alike—despised her. If not for the heavenly voices of St. Catherine, St. Margaret and St. Michael who directed her course, she thought to herself, she would "lose heart" and refuse to lead France into further battles.

The impatient attentions of the soldier-maiden once again turned to battle. She appealed to the French leaders to immediately storm the English lines; what was it that now stood in the way of an assault, she asked. "Oh don't let us have any more fighting," Charles moaned. The English had placed a high price on Joan's head, he added, and he could not afford to pay her ransom if she was apprehended. The Archbishop also criticized her "proud and disobedient" arrogance and warned that, if she was captured, she risked being burned at the stake.

To these earthly complaints, Joan's simple response was that she followed the dictates of her heavenly voices. Unconvinced and out of patience, the Archbishop finally resorted to threats: "If you put your private judgment above the instructions of your spiritual directors, the Church disowns you." Realizing that she had in essence been cast out by the nobility and the clergy, Joan once more affirmed her abiding faith in God: " . . . In His strength I will dare, and dare, and dare, until I die."

It was not long before Joan's faith was put to the ultimate test. Taken in battle by the enemy, she stood defiantly in the court of the Inquisition, accused of heresy. Even in the face of torture, Joan remained valiant. If her accusers tore her "limb from limb," she told the court, she would not give up her faith nor denounce her voices. When she scolded one of the Inquisitor priests for being a "rare noodle," the startled churchman reminded Joan that she was "in great peril." Then, in exasperation, he turned her over to a young priest named Ladvenu, who entreated her to forsake her voices and accept the dictates of the Church. Believing the young girl guilty only of ignorance, Ladvenu queried her as to why God would give her such "shameless advice" as to wear man's clothing. "If I were to dress as a woman," Joan responded, "[the soldiers] would think of me as a woman; and then what would become of me?" Ladvenu dismissed this as rustic logic at work, an example of a country girl's reasoning, as he argued before the court, neither the work of God or of the devil. But the court remained unconvinced—particularly inasmuch as this woman-soldier continued to answer their questions with scorn, unrepentant and unshaken in her impertinent faith.

Desperate to save Joan, Ladvenu nevertheless failed to impress upon her the gravity of her situation. At last he resigned himself to the girl's fate. "Are you prepared for a burning of a heretic this day?" he asked the executioner. At this, Joan finally cried out; alas, her voices had assured her that she would not, indeed, could not be burned. Now, suddenly she felt mocked by devils, tempted beyond her ability to withstand. "My faith is broken," she despaired, signing a recantation. But after placing her mark on the document, she listened in horror as the Inquisitor condemned her to "perpetual imprisonment." "Am I not to be set free?" Joan screamed. At once she seized the document and tore it up. Rather than live out her remaining days behind bars, she informed her accusers, she was prepared to die: "He wills that I go through the fire to His bosom . . . "

When the faggot was lit, even the hardened Inquisitors hesitated to witness the scene. Only Ladvenu could find the courage to approach the flames, holding high a cross so that Joan could see it as she gave up the ghost. Deeply moved by her whispered prayers and unshakable hope, Ladvenu proclaimed, "This is not the end for her, but the beginning."

Later, the executioner announced that no more would be heard from Joan of Arc. Her entire body had burned, he said—excepting the heart. "Hm!" Warwick remarked on hearing this declaration. "I wonder."

True to Warwick's musements, Joan's spirit returned to France: Twenty-five years after her execution, the Maid of Orleans arrived on a bolt of lightning in King Charles' bedroom. Terrified, the monarch took refuge under his sheets. "Easy, Charlie, easy," Joan comforted him good-naturedly. "Can't a poor burnt-up girl have a ghost?" Convinced that he must be dreaming, Charles relaxed and proceeded to recount the news of the kingdom since Joan's demise. But their pleasant chat was soon interrupted by a series of other spiritual guests—men who had either befriended or betrayed Joan during the course of her life. She greeted each warmly, laughing and joking. She even accepted Warwick's apology, breezily replying, "Oh, please don't mention it."

And then appeared the strangest visitor of all: a gentleman from A.D. 1920 who brought news that Joan, though it was a long time in coming, had been canonized. "Saint Joan!" the ghost enthused as the courtiers and churchmen knelt before her. "Should I rise from the dead, and come back to you a living woman?" Alarmed by such a thought, all the guests politely took their leave and disappeared. The old King, still believing himself caught up in a nightmarish comedy, finally stumbled groggily back bed, mumbling, "Poor Joan!"

Only Saint Joan remained outside the King's bedchamber. Bathed in heavenly light, she was left to wonder just when the world she cherished would finally welcome its saints.

Commentary:

George Bernard Shaw's Joan of Arc is a remarkably colloquial and robust saint, one who is unafraid to address aristocrats by their nicknames and dismiss her military superiors as "fatheads." In fact, as demonstrated by her preference to life over death and the enjoyment of fields and flowers over long hours of prayer, she is a saint who is every bit as swayed by earthly concerns as by heavenly ones.

From Shaw's point of view, it seems that it is Joan's playfulness and earthiness—her very humanity amid all her flaws and bluster—that lift her rashness into true courage—and that make her both venerable and vulnerable. "O God that madest this beautiful earth," Joan intones, as if to drive home this point, "when will it be ready to receive Thy saints? How long, O lord, how long?"

CYRANO DE BERGERAC

by
Edmond Rostand
(1868 - 1918)

Type of work: Romantic play

Setting: France; 1630's

Principal characters:

Cyrano de Bergerac, a romantic poet and swordsman

Roxane, Cyrano's beautiful cousin

Christian de Neuvillete, Roxane's lover

Comte de Guiche-married suitor of Roxane, Cyrano's enemy

Valvert, de Guiche's friend, and another enemy of Cyrano

Le Bret, Ragueneau and Ligniere, Cyrano's loyal friends

Commentary:

This famous play has several major themes, "loving devotion" and "honor" being the two most visible motifs. Cyrano's self- sacrificing, all-consuming love for Roxane dominates the action. Punctuating this near-worship—and adding comic relief—the honorable Cyrano both puts down slights against his appearance and vigorously defends others whom he feels have been wronged. In fact, Cyrano possesses all the most desirable romantic traits: he is a masterful poet, philosopher, swordsman and scientist.

Rostand's 1897 drama received immediate acclaim on its release, and since then it has been the source of inspiration for countless movies, plays and other stories. After almost a hundred years, the popularity of *Cyrano* has never waned.

Story Overview:

A boisterous crowd, eager for entertainment, throngs to the theater where a famous production is about to be enacted. Because of a personal grudge, however, Cyrano de Bergerac—a high-spirited young nobleman known everywhere by the jaunty white plumes in his hat and by his large nose—placed an informal ban on the drama's principle actor, Montfleury. A group of Cyrano's companions speculate as they wait for the play to begin: Will Cyrano appear to enforce his ban? Ragueneau, one of these companions, laughs as he describes his "wild swashbuckler" friend, and his "hat with three plumes, his cloak behind him over his long sword, cocked like a tail of a strutting Chanticleer, and to complete this Punchinello figure—such a nose! You can not possibly look on it without crying, `Oh no! Impossible! Exaggerated!'" "And God help the man who smiles," another adds grimly.

Then the young and handsome Christian spies Roxane entering the theater, and is immediately enamored with the beauty. Ligniere tells him all about the girl: "She is refined, intellectual, a cousin to Cyrano, rich enough, and orphan." However, there is an impediment to any would-be suitor: the Comte de Guiche, a wealthy and influential nobleman, loves Roxane. But de Guiche is also impeded: he is married to someone else.

Instead, de Guiche is attempting to arrange a marriage between Roxane and his fellow comte, Valvert, "a sad specimen . . . whom [de Guiche] can count upon to be obliging." Hearing that Roxane, even under pressure, has repeatedly refused Valvert's proposals, Christian expresses his eagerness to challenge the man to a duel.

On stage, meanwhile, the curtain rises and Montfleury steps out. Cyrano is nowhere to be seen—until suddenly a voice booms out: "Wretch . . . king of clowns, leave the stage at once." The startled crowd turns to see Cyrano, defiantly poised above them. Montfleury, frightened at the bristling Cyrano, exits at once. When the manager complains to Cyrano of the losses he will incur, the swordsman tosses a generously filled bag of gold onto the stage.

In the aftermath, Cyrano struts and proclaims: "Know that I glory in this nose of mine, for a great nose indicates a great man." When Valvert, who is also in the audience, mocks Cyrano's appearance, the two men draw their swords. "I'll compose a ballad while I fight you," Cyrano warns, "and at the end of the last line, thrust home." This he does, and Valvert falls, mortally wounded.

Later, Cyrano confesses to another companion, the sympathetic Le Bret, that he loves Roxane, and admits that the only thing in the world he fears is her ridicule; if he declares his love, she might laugh at his nose. Le Bret convinces Cyrano to disclose his feelings anyway.

Just then Roxane's maid approaches, asking that her mistress might have the pleasure of meeting with Cyrano the following day. Trembling with joy, hope—and disbelief—Cyrano accepts the invitation.

The next day Cyrano appears expectantly at the rendezvous. He soon learns, however, that Roxane has summoned him as a confidant. "I love someone in your regiment," she tells him. "He is proud, noble, brave, beautiful." The man in question, as it turns out, is Christian. Numbed, Cyrano still manages to rally from his broken heart and, out of honor and as a gesture of his love for Roxane, promises to protect the young cadet.

Later, back at the regiment, Christian makes an innocent—but obnoxious—quip about Cyrano's nose. Cyrano orders the other soldiers from the room, implying that he is about to kill the impetuous Christian for his effrontery. Instead, however, Cyrano, swallowing his outrage, reveals himself as Roxane's cousin and the envoy of her love for Christian. Delighted and flabbergasted, Christian sorrily admits that though he is brave with men, "with any woman [I am] paralyzed, speechless, dumb." "Come let us both win her together," suggests Cyrano. His plan is to write poetic love verses which Christian will send to the refined Roxane. Cyrano pours all his own ardor into these letters, dictated in Christian's behalf in response to Roxane's delicately penned love notes. After reading several of these stirring epistles, Roxane falls deeply in love with Christian.

Soon, de Guiche comes to call on Roxane. France is at war with Spain and he confides that, as commander of Cyrano's (and Christian's) musketeer unit, he plans to seek revenge on Cyrano for his braggadocio and personal slights. Alarmed, the wily Roxane flatters and teases the despised officer, then works her plan: "Will you order him into danger? He loves that. Leave him here with the cadets while all the regiment goes on to glory. That would torture him." With these words, she hopes not only to protect her cousin Cyrano, but to keep Christian safely at home where they can carry on their romance.

Immediately after de Guiche's departure, Cyrano stops by Roxane's home for a visit. She tells him of her delight with the sensitive love verses she has received, calling Christian a "master." Cyrano, blushing with pride at the knowledge that it is his own writing she truly loves, departs to brief Christian on the speeches the cadet will deliver to Roxane under her balcony—when he will finally meet her face to face. But Christian, by this time confident that he can impress his beloved, refuses Cyrano's help.

The two lovers meet at last. "Now tell me things," Roxane coaxes. "Speak to me about love." But Christian stammers awkwardly. "I love you," he finally blurts out. "I ask for cream," Roxane sneers, pushing him out the door, "you give me milk and water. That displeases me as much as if you had grown ugly."

Defeated, Christian again turns to Cyrano for help. In the dark of night they both return to Roxane's balcony, and Cyrano, in Christian's voice, offers tender speeches and responses to Roxane. Roxane, pleased that her lover has come to his senses, requests that Christian climb the balcony to kiss her. And Cyrano, watching from below, whispers to himself, "I have won what I have won. The feast of love and I am Lazarus. Kissing my words upon your lips . . . "

Meanwhile, de Guiche learns of Roxane's deception, and immediately orders the cadets to the front. Promising to protect Christian, Cyrano takes his leave with the cadet. Weeks pass; the starving and war-weary cadets press on in battle. Each morning Cyrano crosses through enemy lines to deliver Christian's letter—which he himself has written—to Roxane.

One day, de Guiche, still fuming at his betrayal, arrives in the cadet camp. By signaling with a subtle wave of his scarf, de Guiche will betray the weakly defended musketeers to a Spanish spy, and thus, under the guise of a surprise enemy ambush, wreak his final revenge on Cyrano and Christian.

Suddenly, Roxane also appears to deliver food to the starving soldiers. Turning to Christian, she expresses her true love for him: "I went mad with you. Think of the times you have written me. Forgive me for loving you only because you were beautiful. It is yourself I love now, your own self. I can love you if you were less charming . . . ugly even."

Crushed, Christian now realizes that it is not him but the soul of Cyrano whom Roxane truly loves. He returns to Cyrano and convinces him to expose the fraud. As the battle breaks out around them, Cyrano approached Roxane and inquires: "Could you love [the writer of these letters] if he were ugly, hideous, disfigured, grotesque?" Roxane answers boldly that she could. But just as Cyrano summons up the courage to confess his deception, Christian is carried into camp—mortally wounded by the battle's first volley. Stunned, Cyrano mutters, "All gone. I can not tell her now, ever." With his dying breath, Christian asks Cyrano if Roxane has learned the truth. Cyrano lies, saying Roxane indeed knows about the letters, but that she has chosen Christian as her beloved.

As Roxane weeps over her dead suitor, Cyrano mourns both the passing of his brave comrade and his own symbolic death as Roxane's lover. " . . . I am dead," he laments, "and my love mourns for me and does not know."

Roxane, her arms still carressing Christian's body, reaches into his coat and finds the last letter Cyrano has written. On it she sees Christian's blood—and the stain of a tear shed by Cyrano while he wrote it. This letter she keeps by her bosom from that day on.

Fifteen years have passed. Each week Cyrano visits Roxane in the convent where she had retired after Christian's death. But one day, Cyrano is late for his regular appointment. Eventually, word arrives that Cyrano has been ambushed by one of his powerful enemies; but this news is withheld from Roxane.

Though badly wounded, Cyrano finally staggers into the convent to keep his appointment with Roxane. When she asks in alarm about the blood stains on his garments, he reassures her, "It's nothing, just my old wound . . . " "We all have our old wounds," Roxane replies, motioning to her breast where the letter lies. "I carry mine here." Cyrano weakly asks if he can read the tattered letter. Then, in the growing darkness, he recites it word for word: "Farewell, Roxane. Death is near . . . "

Suddenly Roxane realizes the truth. "It was you!" she gasps. "And I might have known. Every time I heard you speak my name . . . the letters, the voice in the dark, and the soul. That was you." "The blood, however, was Christian's," Cyrano says quietly in defense of his fallen comrade. As death draws near, he confesses his love and gratitude: "I would not have known Womanhood and its sweetness but for you." Finally, in delirium, he rises and strikes out with his sword at imagined demons. "I recognize you know now," he calls out. "My old enemies . . . Lies! . . . Compromise! . . . Prejudice! . . . Cowardice! . . . Stupidity! . . . I know I can't defeat you all, I know that in the end you'll overwhelm me, but I'll still fight you as long as there's breath in my body! Yes, you've robbed me of everything: the laurels of glory, the roses of love! . . . "

Fallen, with Roxane bending to kiss his forehead, Cyrano closes his eyes and offers up to her his final words of loving rhyme: "When I go to meet God this evening . . . I'll still have one thing intact, without stain, something that I'll take with me unspotted from the world in spite of doom: The honor in my hat . . . my white plume."

A DOLL'S HOUSE

by
Henrik Ibsen
(1828-1906)

Type of work: Realistic drama

Setting: Norway; late nineteenth century

Principal characters:
  Torvald Helmer, a lawyer/bank employee
  Nora Helmer, his overly-coddled wife
  Kristine Linde, Nora's friend from her youth
  Krogstad, another lawyer who works in the same bank as Torvald
  Dr. Rank, the Helmers' close friend

Story Overview:

Act 1

On Christmas Eve, Torvald Helmer greeted his wife, Nora, as she returned from shopping: "So, little wastrel has been throwing money around again?" Smiling, Nora responded, "Oh but Torvald, this Christmas we can be a little extravagant, can't we?" After all, Torvald's bank promotion would finally give them a little extra money. Torvald laughed at his "irresponsible" wife, reminding her that he hadn't yet been promoted.

The conversation then drifted to that evening's Christmas tree-lighting party; Torvald proclaimed that Nora would not have to strain her "dear eyes" and "delicate little hands" making ornaments. Just then, the doorbell rang and Kristine Linde entered in her "travel dress."

"Kristine! It's you!" Nora exclaimed. The two friends quickly began chatting about the events of the past ten years. Nora shared the news about her husband's upcoming promotion in Mutual Bank's administration—a job that included "a big salary . . . all sorts of extras." Kristine sighed. Her own life, she admitted, could not have been more dismal. Her husband, whom she had never loved, had died three years ago without leaving her any money or children. After his death, she had worked various jobs while looking after her bedridden mother and two younger brothers. Then after her mother had died and her brothers had moved away, she felt not relief but "a great emptiness," without anyone "to live for any more." Now, after a period of bitter loneliness, she had come to Nora to see if Torvald could secure her an office job so that she might turn her life around.

Nora assured Kristine that both she and Torvald would help. "That's very good of you . . ." Kristine responded. "Especially since you've known so little trouble and hardship in your own life." Hearing this, Nora became infuriated. She and Torvald had struggled hard for what they had; he had worked odd jobs and had sewed and embroidered for neighbors. In fact, Torvald's long hours had once made him deathly ill. They had had to migrate to Italy to save his life. The move, however, had been expensive, and they had been forced to borrow the money from Nora's father, who had since died.

Calming herself, Nora felt compelled to reveal a secret that she had not entrusted to any one, including Torvald: "I've saved Torvald's life" Nora blurted out. She explained that although everyone believed her father had loaned them the money to travel to Italy, he had not. Rather, she had secretly borrowed the money, and had scrimped to repay the loan. "You know how men are," she rationalized. "Torvald would find it embarrassing and humiliating to learn that he owed me anything. It would upset our whole relationship." Someday, she would tell him; maybe "when I'm no longer young and pretty . . . when he no longer thinks it's fun when I dance for him and put on costumes and recite for him."

The doorbell rang again, interrupting their conversation. Mr. Krogstad, an long-time attorney friend of Kristine's—who, by demeanor and reputation, clearly could not be trusted—arrived to speak with Torvald.

Later, as Nora played with her children—her "sweet little doll babies"—Krogstad returned to the house to ask Nora's help in persuading Torvald to let him keep his "subordinate position in the bank." At first, Nora refused. Krogstad, however, threatened to reveal her secret: Nora had actually borrowed the money from him, after forging her father's signature on a bank note. Incriminatingly, the note had been dated three days after her father's death. What she had done constituted fraud. Krogstad himself, as he readily admitted, had committed a similar crime years ago, a because of it his reputation had been ruined. "If I'm going to be kicked out again," he warned, "you'll keep me company."

When Torvald returned home, Nora humbly asked him to let Krogstad keep his job. "Why, the man had forged signatures . . . " Torvald replied. "When a man lives inside such a circle of stinking lies, he brings infection into his own home and contaminates his whole family." Stricken by her husband's words, Nora suffered through Torvald's lingering lecture about how lying mothers corrupted their children.

Act 2

The next day—Christmas—Kristine arrived to find a troubled Nora sewing her dancing garb for the next evening's costume party. The two chatted as they worked together on the dress.

When Torvald came home, Nora once again begged him to let Krogstad keep his job, insisting that he listen to reason: "That man writes for the worst newspapers . . . There's no telling what he may do to you. I'm scared to death of him." No, Torvald answered. Everyone at the bank was already aware of Krogstad's imminent release; if Torvald changed his mind now, he would "look ridiculous." Furthermore, he had known Krogstad since his youth. "It's one of those imprudent relationships you get into when you're young that embarrass you for the rest of your life," he reflected. And when Nora persisted in arguing on Krogstad's behalf, an angry Torvald immediately posted Krogstad's dismissal letter, leaving his wife in a state of terror.

Later, Dr. Rank, a loving and trusted old family friend who was dying of tuberculosis, dropped by. "Chances are that within a month I'll be rotting in the cemetery," he told Nora. When he started "coming apart," he said, he would send the Helmers his card with a black cross marked on it to announce his death was near. Then, before leaving, Dr. Rank shocked Nora with a confession: "I have loved you as much as anybody . . . I'm at your service with my life and soul."

Shortly thereafter, Krogstad returned. He had been fired, and though Nora insisted that she had tried to prevent it, Krogstad fumed, "Even if you had the cash in your hand [to pay off your debt] right this minute, I wouldn't give you your note back." He then pulled out a letter addressed to her husband, which betrayed her secret. Nora begged him not to send it. "What do you want?" she asked in desperation. "I want to rehabilitate myself," Krogstad sneered as he walked to Torvald's post box and deposited the letter: "I want to get up in the world; and your husband is going to help me."

With nowhere else to turn, Nora confessed to Kristine that Krogstad had loaned her the money, and that she had forged the note. Kristine vowed to speak to Krogstad to prevent the letter from reaching Torvald. "There was a time," she concluded, "when [Krogstad] would have done anything for me."

That evening, Nora distracted Torvald from his mail by asking his help with her dance. But when Kristine returned, she conveyed bad news: Krogstad had left town until the following evening. Nora, however, spoke confidently: "I don't want you to try to stop anything. You see, it's a kind of ecstasy, too, this waiting for the wonderful."

Act 3

The following evening, Nora and Torvald attended the costume party while Kristine remained in their home to meet Krogstad. He and Kristine had once been lovers, but she had broken off the relationship to marry another man. "A heartless woman jilts a man when she gets a more attractive offer," was how Krogstad had characterized their break-up. But Kristine had felt justified in her actions: with a helpless mother and two siblings to care for, she had no choice but to marry a man with money.

Finally, Kristine unveiled her proposition: "Krogstad, how would it be if we two shipwrecked people got together? . . . You and I need one another." With a sudden change of heart, Krogstad suggested that he retrieve his letter. But Kristine discouraged it: "This miserable secret must come out in the open. Those two . . . simply can't continue with all this concealment and evasion."

Kristine was waiting when the Helmers returned from the party. How beautiful Nora had looked and how well she had danced the tarantella, an emotional Torvald announced. As he went to turn on the lights, Kristine told Nora that she had "nothing to fear from Krogstad," but that it was time to tell her husband everything. Then, embracing her friend, she said goodbye.

When Torvald returned to the front room, he continued flattering his "young, ravishing . . . most precious possession." Finally, he emptied the mail box. This time, Nora did not attempt to stop him. Among the letters was Dr. Rank's business card—a "black cross above the name . . . announcing his own death." Together they mourned the tragic fate of their dear, gentle companion; then, briefly kissing one another goodnight, they separated.

Coming across the letter from Krogstad, Torvald summoned Nora and began his accusations: she was "a hypocrite, a liar—oh worse! worse!—a criminal!" Making no effort to hide his displeasure, he railed that she had "ruined all [his] happiness"; he had been left "at the mercy of an unscrupulous man . . . all because of an irresponsible woman!"

Just then, the maid entered to deliver a letter to Nora. Still in a fit of rage, Torvald snatched it up to scrutinize it himself. As he read, a smile emerged on his scowling face. "I'm saved!" he exulted.

Krogstad had returned the forged note, which Torvald straightaway tossed into the stove to burn. But Nora looked on in dismay at the abrupt change in her husband's demeanor: an inflamed and raving lunatic had instantly been converted into an amiable, fawning harlequin. "I have forgiven you for everything," Torvald gushed. Indeed, he continued, he "wouldn't be a man if [he] didn't find [her] twice as attractive because of [her] womanly helplessness."

For Nora, however, Torvald's apology came too late; his self-centered, self-indulgent nature had been revealed to her. Finally she understood their relationship, his character, and the "great wrong" perpetrated upon her. Yet the real disappointment for Nora was Torvald's admission that he would give up his honor, to "appear" the gentleman, rather than stand up to Krogstad and stand by his wife. "Our home has never been more than a playroom," she sobbed. "I have been your doll wife here, just the way I used to be Daddy's doll child. And the children have been my dolls."

Nora concluded that the only way she could endure would be to leave Torvald and attend to her own "duties," beyond the scope of wife and mother. Torvald, of course, tried to dissuade her: "I'd gladly work nights and days for you, Nora— endure sorrow and want for your sake. But nobody sacrifices his *honor* for his love."

No, Nora would release Torvald from all responsibility and stand on her own. She slammed the door behind her as she went; it was the last she would see of her husband and children.

Commentary:

Many critics have interpreted "A Doll's House" as a feminist work. After all, Nora, a strong woman with a deep sense of commitment, is terrorized by her husband and by society—until Torvald's condescending character is unmasked.

Other critics have argued that the drama reflects the human condition in general. In other words, oppression, whether marital or social, relates to *personality* rather than to *gender*. Ibsen himself agreed with this later opinion. He was no "social philospher," he stated, nor did he compose the drama to "make propaganda," but to offer a "general . . . description of humanity."

Feminist issues, however, do indeed figure prominently in "A Doll's House." Even if Ibsen did not write as a social philosopher, he certainly did write during a period of great upheaval: a time in which the glaring spotlight of inequality was fully focused on women and their rights.

PYGMALION

by
Bernard Shaw
(1856-1950)

Type of work: Romantic comedy
Setting: London; early 1900's
Principal characters:
Henry Higgins, a bachelor and professor of phonetics
Colonel Pickering, an aristocratic student of Indian dialects
Eliza Doolittle, a flower girl
Alfred Doolittle, Eliza's father, a dustman (for American readers, that's a garbage collector)
Freddy Eynsford Hill, another young gentleman

Play Overview:

Professor Henry Higgins stood in his study, contentedly chatting with his new friend, Colonel Pickering. The two had met under the portico of St. Paul's church, where both were seeking shelter from an afternoon downpour. Higgins, after very vocally cataloging the city of origin of each passerby within hearing distance by his or her accent, had introduced himself to the mildly incredulous Pickering as a professor of phonetics. With pride and confidence, Higgins then pointed to a common street urchin, a flower girl, and promised—again in ringingly confident tones—that with three months of tutoring he could "pass the girl off as a duchess at an ambassador's garden party." A student of Indian dialects himself, Pickering had some doubts that such a feat could be achieved.

That evening, while discussing their common linguistic interests over wine and chocolates, the bachelors were interrupted in their reveries by the housekeeper, Mrs. Pearce, who announced that a young woman, Eliza Doolittle, wished to see the Professor. To the great surprise of both gentlemen, the flower girl from St. Paul's was then ushered into the study. Though dressed in her best hat and apron, the girl still appeared deplorably tacky and awkward standing in the magnificent home. And yet her eyes glimmered with a determination whose source was soon to be revealed. "I want to be a lady in a flower shop 'stead of selling at the corner of Tottenham Court Road," she said. "But they wont take me unless I talk more genteel. He said he could teach me. Well, here I am ready to pay him . . ."

Colonel Pickering quickly jumped at the challenge; here was a chance to discover the authenticity of his friend's self-assured pretensions. For the sake of a wager, Pickering promised to pay the expenses of the lessons if Higgins could pass the flower girl off as a "lady" at the ambassador's garden party. The deal was made. So excited were the two linguists over this new adventure that they hardly heard Mrs. Pearce's disapproving words: " . . . You can't take a girl up like that as if you were picking up a pebble on the beach." But, the plan was already set. The flower girl, Eliza, was rushed upstairs to take her first step towards refinement: a bath!

Meanwhile, below, as Colonel Pickering and Professor Higgins endured the screeching protests of a woman who had never before experienced a soaking, they received a second visitor: Eliza's father, Alfred, entered the study wearing an expression of wounded honor and stern resolution. The Welsh dustman first demanded to see his daughter. Higgins called for the freshly scoured Eliza. Upon seeing his daughter so primly scrubbed down and dressed up—and apparently still in possession of her womanly honor—Doolittle proceeded to explain that his given right as a father was simply to receive his due share of money for the loss of his daughter's earnings. "I'm one of the undeserving poor," he continued. " . . . Think of what that means to a man. It means that he's up agen middle class morality all the time . . . What is middle class morality? Just an excuse for never giving me anything."

After this eloquent oration, Higgins and Pickering were quite willing to give the man twenty pounds. Insisting on no more than five, however, Doolittle took his money and gave Eliza over to the care of Professor Higgins.

And so began the interminable lessons. Eliza, in her new clothes, spent most of each day seated uncomfortably in the study, while Higgins, striding restlessly about, forced her to speak into a laryngoscope, imitating the tones he produced on his tuning-forks. Had it not been for the gentle encouragement of her friend Colonel Pickering, even the plucky Eliza would soon have dashed back to home from which she had just escaped.

Higgins: Say your alphabet.
Eliza: I know my alphabet. Do you think I know nothing? I don't need to be taught like a child . . .
Higgins: Say A,B,C,D.
Eliza: (almost in tears): Ahyee, Beyee, Ceyee— . . .
Higgins: Put your tongue forward until it squeezes against the top of your lower teeth. Now say cup.
Eliza: C-c-c—I can't. C-cup.
Pickering: Good. Splendid, Miss Doolittle.

Such exercises went on for several months before Eliza finally made her first formal public appearance, at the home of Mrs. Higgins, Henry's mother. Mrs. Higgins had invited several guests to join her for tea. With Colonel Pickering by her side, Eliza made a stunning entrance, affecting the manners and refinements of a well-bred and debonair young sophisticate. It was only when she opened her mouth that this impression vanished. Not that Henry's careful tutoring had failed her—indeed, as far as it went, her mastery of the King's English was flawless: In clear, crisp, cool and artfully refined syllables, Eliza launched into a slang-studded, ungrammatical and graphically scandalous narrative on the murder of her alcoholic aunt. Some guests were shocked and offended; others were enraptured by this sophisticated new trend in speech. One particularly captivated admirer was a young gentleman by the name of Freddy Eynsford Hill.

Higgins, of course, was mortified by his protegee's debut. Lessons and training now continued to the point of exhaustion; Eliza's only relief came in her carefully structured practice excursions through various lesser social functions. To Higgins' surprise, his pupil proved to be quite talented musically. Returning home from a ball or concert, she was able to pick out pieces from the performance by ear on Higgins' piano. And in time, Eliza acclimated herself to her rarified linguistic settings, adopting the words and syntax proper to her teacher's elevated station. Finally, Higgins decided to try her out at an elegant garden party—the real moment of truth.

While Eliza prepared herself in the ladies' cloakroom for her grand entrance, Professor Higgins was approached by one of his former students, a whiskered Hungarian named Nepommuck, who introduced himself as the most gifted phoneticist on the continent, Nepommuck boasted that he could identify the origins of anyone in Europe simply through hearing his English. For Pickering and Higgins, Nepommuck naturally became the great test of their wager. If Eliza's accent deceived this man, Higgins' victory would be sweet indeed.

As the evening progressed, the hostess finally inquired about Miss Doolittle's mysterious background. With cool certainty, Nepommuck replied that Miss Doolittle, with whom he had been privileged to converse, was of royal Hungarian blood. "Only the Magyar races can produce that air of the divine right," he proclaimed, "those resolute eyes. She is a princess."

The bet was won—and gloriously. Pickering and Higgins arrived home in high spirits to celebrate the hard-earned victory. Elatedly congratulating each other on their splendid work, they hardly noticed the hurt and angry expression on Eliza's face. Only when the two bachelors were ready to retire for the night did Higgins even acknowledge his protegée's presence—asking if she had seen his slippers. Unable to control her fury any longer, Eliza threw the slippers at Higgins' feet.

Eliza: *Take your slippers; and may you never have a day's luck with them!*
Higgins: *What on earth—! . . . Anything wrong?*
Eliza: *Nothing wrong—with you. I've won your bet for you, haven't I? That's enough for you. I don't matter, I suppose . . .*
Higgins: *How dare you show your temper at me? Sit down and be quiet.*
Eliza: *What's to become of me? What's to become of me? . . . You don't care. I know you don't care. You wouldn't care if I was dead. I'm nothing to you—not so much as them slippers.*
Higgins: *Those slippers.*
Eliza: *Those slippers. I didn't think it made any difference now.*

That night, while the household slept, Eliza packed her bags. Shutting the front door behind her, she turned to walk away from her new life—forever—and there stood Freddy, waiting for another chance to meet his adored. Freddy smothered her with kisses, and Eliza, starved for comfort, responded.

The following morning, Higgins burst into his mother's drawing room explaining that Eliza had "bolted." He and Pickering had already set the police after her. When Higgins learned to his chagrin that Eliza was upstairs in his mother's own house, he wanted to rush up to see her, but his mother—wisely—told him to wait for Eliza to come down.

Finally Eliza appeared; behaving in a most proper and polite manner, she took a seat beside Colonel Pickering, overtly ignoring Higgins. She thanked Pickering for the kindness and respect he had shown her all the time they had been together; he had treated her like a lady, she remarked, and so she had stayed to learn how to speak and behave as a lady.

Events outside the house, however, soon left Eliza and Higgins alone together in the drawing room. Higgins tried to defend his own treatment of his pupil. His attitude towards Eliza was indeed different from Pickering's, he said, but equally as honorable. Then he added, "The great secret, Eliza, is not having bad manners or good manners . . . but having the same manners for all human souls . . . " For this very reason, he would "treat a duchess as if she were a flower girl."

Eliza refused to accept this. She would not return to her tutor's home. "I shall miss you, Eliza," confessed Higgins finally. "I have learnt something from your idiotic notions: I confess that humbly and gratefully. And I have grown accustomed to your voice and appearance. I like them, rather." From the sardonic professor, this was tantamount to a distraught declaration of love. But even these words did not suit Eliza. She was determined to establish her own new identity, and Henry would have to deal with her as his equal. Nothing less would do.

Eliza Doolittle stood, exited the drawing room, and walked into a new future. Eventually she married Freddy Eynsford Hill and, in an extension of her original plans, purchased a small flower shop for herself at the center of town. She always behaved as a loving, favorite daughter to Colonel Pickering; however, she never ceased nagging Henry Higgins—a habit established on the night she won his bet for him.

Commentary:

The title of the play refers to a story from Ovid's *Metamorphoses*. Pygmalion, a mythical sculptor, vowed never to marry, but to devote himself entirely to his art. The young man created a statue of a beautiful woman, whom he called Galatea, and fell in love with her. When the goddess Venus gave the statue life, Pygmalion and Galatea were soon married.

Likewise, Higgins' devotion to phonetics leaves little room for any other "distractions" in his life. Eliza, his student, is merely an object to be molded and changed by the power of his science. When this process is completed, however, Eliza proves to be much more than an object. And instead of marrying her "creator"—which, in truth, Higgins is not, since the essential Eliza changes only slightly from the moment when she first presents herself in Higgins' study until her grand entrance at the garden party—she demonstrates that she is, and has always been, a lady. Unable to gain Higgins' respect, however, as the true and determined lady that she is, Eliza finally forsakes the man she has striven so rigorously to please—and the man she could have so easily loved.

As Shaw perceptively and solemnly noted at the conclusion of the play: "Galatea never does quite like Pygmalion: his relation to her is too godlike to be altogether agreeable."

THE CRUCIBLE

by
Arthur Miller
(1915 -   )

Type of work: Historical drama

Setting: Salem, Massachusetts; spring of 1692

Principal characters:
John Proctor, a local farmer
Elizabeth Proctor, his "goodewife"
Abigail Williams, a girl of seventeen—the Proctors' former maidservant, John's former mistress, and leader of the "crying out" against witchcraft
Mary Warren, the Proctor's maid servant
Various town officials: the Reverend Parris, Abigail's uncle and a cold, strict village minister; the Reverend John Hale, a specialist in witchcraft and demonology; Judge Hawthorne, presiding magistrate over the Salem trials; and Deputy Governor Danforth, trial prosecutor

Commentary:

As Arthur Miller himself notes, this 1953 play is "more than a period piece." It was written partly in response to a similar but much more contemporary crisis: the anti-Communist hysteria which gripped America during the late forties and early fifties. Senator Joseph McCarthy accused the award-winning playwright of being a Communist sympathizer and called him before the House Un-American Activities Committee. Miller refused to cooperate, and as a result he was blacklisted. "The Crucible" was meant as a comment on this situation as much as on the actual historic events that underlie the drama.

Story Overview:

As the Reverend Samuel Parris prayed over his sick daughter, Betty, his niece Abigail entered with a younger girl, who offered news from the doctor. "He cannot discover no medicine for it . . . " the girl told him, " . . . he bid me tell you, that you might look to unnatural things for the cause of it." There were no "strange forces" to blame, Parris scoffed. But Abigail reported that she had heard rumors of witchcraft in town, and the village was in an uproar. In fact, the parlor was already filled with a crowd of fearful and suspicious neighbors. She offered to stay with Betty while her uncle went downstairs to speak with the curious crowd. " . . . What shall I say to them?" he snapped. "That my niece and my daughter I discovered dancing like heathens in the forest?" Yes, Abigail admitted to dancing naked with her cousins and others among the trees; but it had merely been "sport," she said.

The conversation was cut short as a member of the congregation, Mrs. Putnam, forced her way into the room shrieking that her own daughter, Ruth, was sick as well. Abigail, wishing to divert attention from her own misconduct, whispered in Parris' ear that not only she and Betty, but Ruth Putnam and Tituba, Parris'

black slave, had also been dancing, trying to conjure up the spirits of Mrs. Putnam's stillborn babies. Fear gripped Parris' heart; the rumors of witchcraft had been confirmed. But now, even as he accompanied the Putnams downstairs to lead the congregation in a psalm, upstairs, Abigail instructed each girl to give the same story: They had danced, Tituba had conjured Ruth Putnam's dead sisters, "and that is all." If they spoke another word of it, she threatened them with terrible reprisals: " . . . You know I can do it," she added. " . . . I can make you wish you had never seen the sun go down!"

Soon John Proctor, Abigail's former master—and lover—arrived at the house. Abigail sprang into his path. "You come five miles to see a silly girl fly? I know you better," she said. John admitted that he still felt softly for her, but vowed " . . . I will cut off my hand before I'll ever reach for you again, Abby." Embittered by this rebuff, Abigail brought John's wife into the fray. "She is blackening my name in the village!" Abigail fumed. Proctor seized the girl and shook her. "You'll speak nothin' of Elizabeth!" he screamed. Then he turned and fled.

Meanwhile, the Reverend Hale, an experienced demonologist, arrived at Betty's bedside with an armload of heavy books. He warned the gathering that they must beware of superstition. "The Devil is precise," he said; and if he found "no bruise of Hell upon her" they must look to other causes for her ailments. He then questioned Parris about the circumstances surrounding Betty's illness. As Parris described his discovery in the woods, Hale grasped Abigail's arm: "Abigail . . . your cousin is dying. Did you call the Devil last night?" Abigail, frightened, accused Tituba of the deed, and Hale turned on the terrified slave girl, who told him, "I do believe there be someone else witchin' these children . . . " Suddenly, Abigail, as though hypnotized, cried out, "I saw Bridget Bishop with the Devil!" Betty herself then rose from the bed, picking up the chant of accusations.

Eight days later, John Proctor returned late from the fields. Elizabeth greeted him with rabbit stew and news that their maid servant, Mary Warren, had gone to Salem that day to serve as an official of the court. There were now fourteen people in prison—and talk of hangings. Elizabeth asked her husband to go to Salem that night to convince the Judges that such charges of witchcraft were foolish. "I'll think on it," he replied hesitantly. Elizabeth, unable to hide her bitterness any longer, then accused him of protecting Abigail; after all, innocent people were suffering because of her foolish accusations. Perhaps because of his former lechery—maybe even a "promise made in bed"—he dreaded meeting Abigail in court.

As the Proctors argued, Mary Warren slipped in the door, exhausted from her day in court, handed Elizabeth a tiny rag doll she had made while sitting through the testimony, and confessed that Elizabeth's name had been brought up during the proceedings. Elizabeth turned to John in terror: "Go to Abigail . . . She wants me dead . . . she thinks to take my place."

Proctor, now in a bid to save his own wife from hanging, fetched his rifle; he was almost out the door when Reverend Hale appeared. The reverend warned that they must take every precaution to stay above reproach, including attending to their church duties. John assured the prosecutor that Abigail "had naught to do with witchcraft," a fact he was now willing to affirm in court.

Suddenly Giles Corey and Francis Nurse burst through the doorway with horrifying news: their wives had been taken. And a deputy appeared on their heels with a warrant for Elizabeth. As the deputy searched the house, he discovered the cloth doll Mary had given Elizabeth—and in its belly protruded a sewing needle. He divulged that Abigail had been stricken that very day with a strange and violent pain in the abdomen. Elizabeth agreed to be taken to jail, and instructed her husband to tell the children she had "gone to visit someone sick." Stunned, John weakly promised to rescue her, then immediately summoned Mary, insisting that she accompany him to testify that Abigail was lying; after all, Abigail had sat right beside her as she sewed the doll in the courtroom. Alarmed, Mary protested: "I cannot, she will turn on me." But Proctor convinced her that she would be safe.

The following day, Mary tearfully revealed to the assembled court that none of the girls had seen spirits in the forest; the fits and spells had been "only pretense." When Abigail was called to testify, she insisted Mary was lying. But Proctor and Hale both swore that it was Abigail who had led the other girls to dance naked in the woods. At this, Abigail became indignant, and prompted Judge Danforth to come to her defense. But even he could not decide who was telling the truth. Abigail then cast her eyes to the ceiling and, glancing about the air, murmured, "A wind, a cold wind has come." The other girls took up the chant, repeating everything Proctor screamed in his wife's defense. Proctor, trembling at the sight of his entire life collapsing around him, now broke down, and admitted to lechery with Abigail. Danforth and Hawthorne were shocked. Then Proctor, still speaking of Abigail, continued: "She thinks to dance on my wife's grave! And well she might, for I thought of her softly. God help me, I lusted . . . But it is a whore's vengeance, and you must see it . . . "

In order to confirm Proctor's story, Judge Danforth called for Elizabeth to be brought forward; her testimony would save her husband's life. His soul lifted by hope, John declared, "There are them that cannot sing, they that cannot weep—my wife, she cannot lie."

Elizabeth was first asked why Abigail had been dismissed from service. Not wanting to tarnish her husband's name, Elizabeth said she had

thought Abigail "fancied" John. Then Hale once again began to speak against Abigail, but as he did the girl began to wail, accusing Mary of witchcraft. By now hysterical, Mary tried to pass on the blame by accusing John Proctor of being a witch and forcing her to speak against Abigail. Danforth now demanded that John confess to lechery and renounce Hell. "God is dead!" Proctor screamed in fury and desperation. " . . . For them that quail to bring men out of ignorance, as I have quailed, and as you quail now when you know in all your black hearts that this be fraud—God damns our kind especially, and we will burn, we will burn together!"

By that Fall, townspeople filled the Salem jail. Cows and orphans wandered the countryside; people bickered over parcels of ground left behind by executed landholders. Hale and Parris sat together, counseling prisoners in their cells and trying to convince them to confess to witchcraft so their lives might be spared. Reverend Parris pled compellingly with Danforth and Hawthorne to pardon the remaining prisoners, since Abigail had vanished, along with thirty-one pounds from Parris' strongbox. The Judge and Governor brushed this possibility aside; with so many executions behind them, there was no way they could now grant pardons. Once more leading in Elizabeth Proctor—who had been saved from the gallows because she had been found to be pregnant—Hale urged her to convince her good husband to confess. Proctor was summoned. After weeks of torture, he appeared "another man, chained, bearded, filthy, his eyes misty as though webs had overgrown him."

John pled at his wife's feet for forgiveness. "John," she wept, "it come to naught that I should forgive you, if you'll not forgive yourself . . . I have sins of my own count. It needs a cold wife to prompt lechery . . . I am not your judge, I cannot be. Do as you will, do as you will!"

As the sun rose, the Judge and Governor entered the cell. Proctor lifelessly confessed to all counts of witchcraft. "Praise be to God," answered Danforth, eagerly drafting a confession to which Proctor could sign his name—a confession that also included a statement accusing many of John's neighbors of witchcraft. Seeing the names on the list, Proctor cried out, "I have three children—how may I teach them to walk like men in the world, and I sold my friends? . . . Beguile me not! I blacken all of them . . . the very day they hang for silence!" Then, still struggling whether to choose honor over death, Proctor finally signed the document—and then tore it up. "You have made your magic now," he told the Judge, "for now I do see a shred of goodness in John Proctor. Not enough to weave a banner with, but white enough to keep it from such dogs." Elizabeth, standing motionless, with tearstained face, ignored the Judge's pleas to change her husband's mind. "He have his goodness now," she said finally. "God forbid I take it from him!" Just then a burst of new sun poured in upon her face, softening the violent rattling of drumroll in the morning air.

DESIRE UNDER THE ELMS

by
Eugene O'Neill
(1888-1953)

Type of work: Drama

Setting: New England; 1850-51

Principal characters:
    Ephraim Cabot, patriarch of the Cabot family
    Eben Cabot, his youngest of three sons
    Abbie Putnam, Ephraim's third wife

Story Overview:

On an early New England morning in the spring of 1850, the seventy-five-year-old Ephraim Cabot, "all spick an' span" and "singin' a hymn," had simply hitched up his buggy and headed west for two months. Ephraim's sudden departure had mystified his sons: except for an infrequent trip into town, he had not set foot off his beloved farm in more than thirty years. The only thing he had bothered to say was, "Don't get no fool idee I'm dead. I've sworn t' live a hundred an' I'll do it, if on'y t' spite yer sinful greed. An' now I'm ridin' out t' learn God's message to' me in the spring, like the prophets done. An' yew get back t' yer plowin'.'"

Ephraim prided himself on being a hard man—"as hard as God," he liked to say. He believed it was his hardness that, by sweat and muscle, had transformed a rocky piece of ground into the finest farm in the county, a farm which, by universal acclaim, was not only productive but also "purty." His toughness, however, had also alienated his sons. In Ephraim's two month absence from the farm, that profound sense of alienation grew even more poisoned and vitriolic.

For the oldest sons, Simeon and Peter—from Ephraim's first wife—the farm promised nothing but a bitter existence. Their entire lives were devoted to piling "stones atop o' the ground—stones atop o' the stones—makin' stone walls—year atop o' year." For the youngest son, Eben—from Ephraim's second wife—the resentment against his father ran even deeper. The farm was a painful reminder that Ephraim had not only worked his mother into an early grave, but he had also stolen the farm from her and her family. The farm should have been Eben's by inheritance; instead, his father had usurped it as his own. Ephraim's, Simeon's, and Peter's claims on it were fraudulent, larcenous, and an insult to his mother's memory.

One evening, as Eben listened to his fatherless brothers dream about going west and striking it rich in California's gold rush, an idea entered his head—a way to rid himself of them and their claims on the farm. His mother, he remembered, had once shown him a secret hiding place beneath the kitchen floorboards. It was rumored that Ephraim kept his life's savings there—$600 in gold. Eben could pay Simeon and Peter $300 a piece—which would more than cover their expenses to California's gold fields—in exchange for written deeds to their "shares" in the farm.

The timing to execute his plan couldn't

have been more favorable. After a night in town, Eben returned home to his brothers with confirmed news that, according to the town preacher, their father had just been "hitched to a female 'bout thirty-five—an' purty . . . " His brother Peter's reaction was immediate: "Everythin'll go t' her now," he said, referring to the farm. Simeon agreed, and Eben's plan was set into motion. When he offered his brothers money for their shares—shares which now seemed to be worthless—they gladly accepted and promptly set off for California.

Nevertheless, Eben's problems were just beginning. When Ephraim returned home with his young new bride, Abbie Putnam, Eben realized that Abbie presented a more formidable obstacle than either of his brothers had posed. Indeed, the first thing that she said as she stepped from the buggy and gazed at the farm was, "It's purty—purty! I can't b'lieve it's r'ally mine." When Eben angrily contradicted her, insisting that the farm belonged to his mother and was now his alone, she laughed and replied, "Yewr'n? We'll see about that."

Abbie's presence complicated Eben's plans in yet another, surprising way: they were attracted to one another. From the moment the rivals had first met, a fire seemed to awaken in each a desire that could not be ignored. Abbie recognized it first. One Sunday afternoon as they stood talking beneath the two giant, brooding elms, she told Eben that, just like "them elums," they belonged to nature. Like nature and like the elms, there was something that grew and burned between them, deep inside—and it would continue to grow and burn until they were joined each to the other. "Nature'll beat ye," she warned Eben. "Ye might's well own up t' it . . . "

Eben felt troubled. At first he refused to admit that his rival was right. It was one of her tricks to steal the farm. "An' I'm onto ye," he accused her. "Ye hain't foolin' me a mite." But Eben's deep-seated desire for Abbie—which he confused with anger—did not dissolve or disappear anymore than did his genuine hatred for his father.

To complicate matters even more, Abbie gradually came to share Eben's hatred of Ephraim; her husband was either continuously chastising her, or ignoring her. This enmity finally inspired Ephraim's third wife to devise her own plan. One day, she suggested to Ephraim that they have a child together, an heir to the farm who, unlike Eben, would be as hard as Ephraim was. At the same time, however, she also wanted to possess Eben. To make her seduction more potent, she decided to play on Eben's hatred of his father by convincing him that, by making love to her, he would make a cuckold of his father.

One night, after her husband had retired for the evening in the barn, Abbie lured Eben down to his mother's parlor, a room that since her death had been a monument to her memory. There, after feverish, tormented whispering of their desires, they finally consummated their love.

For a long while afterwards, Eben was happy. It seemed to him that all his anger and rage—which, manifested as a ghost had for years pursued and haunted him like a fury—had miraculously disappeared. It was as if his thirst for retribution and vengeance against his father had been laid to rest the moment he had lain with his father's wife.

One spring night almost a year later, Ephraim had a party at his farmhouse to celebrate the birth of his son. Of course, every soul who attended knew that Eben was the child's true father. During the party, Eben, who couldn't stand "lettin' on what's mine's his'n," stepped outside to escape his father's oppressive but mistaken joy. Soon after, leaving behind the drinking and dancing, Ephraim followed to get a breath of fresh air. The two quickly fell into another of their bitter quarrels. Knowing his son's weakest point, Ephraim threatened that Eben would never have a share in the farm; the property, he said, would belong to his new son and to Abbie. What's more, he harshly revealed, the whole idea to have a baby had been Abbie's. "I wants Eben cut off," she had said, "so's this farm'll be mine when ye die!"

This disclosure mortified Eben. Later, Abbie tried to convince Eben he was wrong to believe his father—and wrong to believe that she didn't truly love him. Confused and maddened, Eben raged, "I wish [the baby] was never born! I wish he'd die this minit! I wish I'd never set eyes on him! It's him . . . that's changed everythin'!" Abbie tried again to appease Eben, promising that neither she nor their son would steal anything from him. "I'd kill him fust!" she vowed. "I do love ye! I'll prove t' ye! I'll prove I love ye better'n . . . everythin' else in the world!"

Early the next morning, before dawn, Abbie rose. In the kitchen downstairs, she found Eben, alone. Throwing her arms around his neck and kissing him, she began to cry hysterically. "I done it, Eben!" she confessed. "I told ye I'd do it! I've proved I love ye—better'n everythin'—so's you can't doubt me no more!" "What did ye do?" he asked nervously. "I—I killed him, Eben," she said. Yes, she had smothered their son.

Several silent moments passed. Eben was stunned. Had he heard right? When finally the horror of what she had done—supposedly for him—had sunk in, Eben stumbled from the house, shouting, "I'll deliver ye up t' the jedgment o' God an' the law!" After notifying the Sheriff of Abbie's deed, Eben's rage subsided, almost as quickly as it seized him. Now, as he limped home, he felt only love for her.

When he reached the house, he found her still in the kitchen; he broke down and began to sob. He loved her, he cried, and whether it was "prison r' death r' hell r' anythin'," that he would bear it along with her. Abbie tried to dissuade him, but Eben could no longer conceive of a life in which, together, they did not share a fate.

When the Sheriff came, Eben called out, "I lied this mornin', Jim, I helped her to do it. Ye kin take me, too." The sheriff somberly led Eben and Abbie out the back door to the gate that stretched under the weighty elm boughs. The sun was rising over the fields, and as the Sheriff took a last look at the farm, he said, "It's a jim-dandy farm, no denyin'. Wished I owned it!"

As providence would have it, Ephraim would have his farm, unchallenged, all to himself. And though he felt plagued by the prospect of more years of loneliness, he told himself that God, too, was lonesome, "hard n' lonesome," just like he was.

Commentary:

Desire Under the Elms, first released in 1924, scandalized its audiences. The play's unrelentingly dark vision of the American family, a vision of corrosive familial bonds articulated by greed, lust, Oedipal instincts, retribution, and murder, repulsed theatergoers. O'Neill, of course, did not introduce these themes into the theater; indeed, he largely borrowed them from classical Greek dramatists—Aeschylus, Sophocles, and Euripides. O'Neill, however, was among the first American playwrights to explore these tragic themes and to interpret them in an American context. Given the fact that this context was shaped by a Puritan heritage and sensibility, it is not surprising that *Desire Under the Elms* should have been viewed as shocking, sensationalistic, and immoral.

Consistent with classical dramatic tradition, O'Neill attempts to elaborate a genuinely tragic vision of the Cabot family—an "American house," as it were. For instance, like the great dramas profiling the Greek houses of Oedipus (*Cadmus*) and Orestes (*Atreus*), the Cabot family history is marked by father-son conflict of near mythical proportions. Ephraim and Eben are engaged in what amounts to a death struggle, with Eben having first defined this struggle in terms of the murder (by overwork) of his mother and the theft of his inheritance.

Over time, the boundaries of conflict expand to include Eben's stepmother Abbie Putnam. Subconsciously, perhaps, Abbie plays on Eben's Oedipal conflict with Ephraim, awakens his sexual desires, then seduces him in his birth mother's parlor. Abbie promises Eben, "I'll take yer Maw's place! I'll be everythin' she was t' ye!" Only after this seduction, after Eben has symbolically displaced his father, is he able to find retribution and lay to his mother's ghost to rest.

In keeping with the tragic Greek motif, the child of this "incestuous" union is damned even before birth. Despite Ephraim's supernatural and god-like vitality, everyone is aware—*except* Ephraim—that the child cannot be his. Abbie's murder of her son, then, only confirms what everyone else knows: that she and Eben have transgressed one of the most potent of sexual taboos.

Although "Desire Under the Elms" does not attain the tragic dimensions of its Greek antecedents, it touches upon their essential elements. O'Neill's mastery lies in his ability to transcribe these elements into a wonderfully disturbing tapestry that finds relevance in our modern Western culture.

EQUUS

by
Peter Shaffer
(1926 -   )

Type of work: Psychological drama

Setting: England; mid-1970s

Principal characters:
Martin Dysart, a middle-aged psychiatrist
Alan Strang, Dysart's seventeen-year-old very perceptive yet troubled patient
Frank and Dora Strang, Alan's father and mother
Jill Mason, Alan's friend

Play Overview:

[Audience Information: To heighten the intense psychological drama which impels "Equus," the stage set is quite stark: "A square of wood set on a circle of wood" is where the play's action takes place. The square of wood represents the boxing ring in which Alan's mental conflicts are acted out. On the outer edges of the circle surrounding the square, there are benches where the actors sit during the play, except when they speak their lines or contribute to the action. The Chorus engages in "humming, thumping, and stamping to announce the presence of Equus the God." Finally, actors dressed as horses appear wearing "hooves . . . metal horse-shoes . . . tracksuits of chestnut velvet [and masks of] silver wire and leather," beneath which—in order to emphasize the stylized and symbolic nature of these humanized horses—the actors' own heads are clearly visible.]

In the absolute darkness and silence onstage, a light illuminates Alan Strang and a horse named Nugget. The boy nestles up to the horse and, in return, the horse nuzzles the boy. Suddenly, a cigarette lighter flickers and a spotlight reveals the pensive figure of the psychiatrist, Martin Dysart, seated on a bench. Meditating on the scene in the square, Dysart marvels:

> . . . Of all nonsensical things—I keep thinking about the horse! Not the boy: the horse, and what it may be trying to do. I keep seeing that huge mouth kissing him with its chained mouth. Nudging through the metal some desire absolutely irrelevant to filling its belly or propagating its own kind. What desire could that be?

As Alan leads Nugget away, Dysart reveals that he is having serious doubts about his own professional and personal life. He's felt "all reigned up in old language and old assumptions, straining to jump clean-hoofed onto a whole new track of being." Ironically, his patient, Alan, has been the one who has forced Dysart to reevaluate the very quality and efficacy of his own life.

At first, Dysart felt reluctant to treat Alan. Already overworked, there were many other psychiatrists available to treat the boy. Dysart's friend, Hesther Salomon, however, pressed him to take the case. As a magistrate, Salomon knew that Dysart was the only psychiatrist compas-

sionate and open-minded enough to treat a boy who had committed an unspeakably abominable crime.

Dysart's interest had been immediately piqued. What had this boy done? "He blinded six horses with a metal spike," Hesther had said. Alan would be quite unlike any of Dysart's other patients, but the psychiatrist agreed to see him.

As soon as Alan checked into the hospital, Dysart met with him. Alan, however, rebuffed all of Dysart's initial overtures. No matter what he said, Alan responded by singing television jingles to block out the doctor's voice. For his part, Dysart had been utterly intrigued by this immensely strange and troubled boy.

In fact, Dysart experienced an unusually vivid dream. He dreamt that he was "a chief priest in Homeric Greece" assigned to sacrifice hundreds of children. One by one, two Greek servants threw the child victims across a stone and watched as Dysart disemboweled them. Dysart began to doubt that these butcheries were "doing any social good at all," so his servants snatched the knife out of his hand; Dysart knew that he would be the next victim.

Alan, too, suffered from nightmares. He repeatedly screamed the word "Ek" in his sleep. Interviewing Alan's parents, Dysart learned that the word *equus*—"horse" in Latin—fascinated the boy. In fact, horses had delighted Alan since childhood, and he kept a photograph of a horse in his bedroom: "A beautiful white one, looking over a gate." However, even though he worked in a stable, Alan did not like to ride horses.

Listening to the Strangs describe of their son, Dysart perceived that they had inculcated the boy with divergent views: his mother tended to be quite lenient, while his father imposed strict discipline. Frank Strang did not allow his son to watch television; he considered it a "dangerous drug," mentally fatal.

Equally dangerous, in Frank's opinion, was religion. He blamed the Bible for Alan's crime:

> A boy spends night after night having this stuff read into him: an innocent man tortured to death—thorns driven into his head—nails into his hands—a spear jammed through his ribs. It can mark anyone for life . . .

Furthermore, Mr. Strang continued, his zealot wife had instilled a religious obsession in their son. Religion, sex, and horses, he suggested, strangely intermingled in Alan's mind.

Frank went on to explain that, to replace a painting in Alan's bedroom of Christ's anguish at Calvary, he had bought his son the photograph of the horse. But once, he had seen Alan kneel in front of the photograph and had heard the boy say, "Behold—I give you Equus my only begotten son." Then Alan had threaded a piece of string in his mouth, like a bit of a horse, and begun to beat himself with a wooden coat hanger.

Discovering Alan's preoccupation with the anatomical nature of horses, Dysart decided to see whether this interest also extended to girls. Knowing that a girl named Jill Mason had worked in the stable with Alan, Dysart asked, "Did you have a date with her?" Alan unexpectedly exploded in a rage. Venting his anger, he began to query Dysart about his wife and his own sexuality.

Alan had struck a nerve: Dysart and his wife shared a childless and joyless marriage. To compound their unhappiness, Dysart's wife often ridiculed her husband's obsession with ancient Greek gods and "Geniuses of Place and Person." For his part, Dysart sneered at his wife's "antiseptic proficiency" and lack of curiosity about life. Sex played no part in their disagreeable relationship.

Noticing the sensitive and painful wound that was opened in Dysart when quizzed about his marriage, Alan later apologized for his stupid questions. Yet, the incident became the turning point in Alan's treatment. Little by little, the boy began to respond to Dysart's compassionate ministrations, and revealed that Equus—whom Alan worshiped as a god—wore chains in atonement "for the sins of the world." Speaking to Alan, Equus had once said, "I see you. I will save you." When Equus commanded Alan to mount the stable's horses, at night, naked, and with a stick in his mouth that he called the "Manbit," Alan did so, and rode them until he felt "Raw! Raw!"

Hearing this account, Dysart concluded that nighttime would be the best time to convince Alan to relate the story of what led up to the blinding. He offered Alan a "truth drug," in reality, nothing more than a placebo. Alan, believing in the power of the drug, answered truthfully when Dysart questioned him about Jill.

She had surprised the boy one afternoon by saying, "You've got super eyes," and proceeded to tell Alan that she had seen him staring into the horses' eyes. She wondered if he found them "sexy." Defensively, Alan blurted out, "Don't be daft!" The question, though, had unnerved him. Jill explained to him that girls often found horses sexy, then asked the nervous boy to take her out on a date that night. Hesitant at first, Alan finally agreed when Jill told him that she wanted to see a "skinflick."

Alan enjoyed the movie. While it was still in progress, though, he saw his father in the audience. Suddenly spotting Alan, Frank demanded that the boy leave. Alan stood up to him: he would not go home; he would see Jill safely back to her house.

Jill, however, was determined to take Alan to the stable where, she told him, they could cozily nestle in the straw. Unable to confess his concerns that the horses might witness them together, Alan finally acquiesced.

In the stable, Jill kissed him passionately. Then, hearing the stamping of hooves, Alan began to panic. Calming him, Jill proceeded to undress and watched as Alan silently removed his clothes, too. They lay down—but instead of Jill, Alan "felt Him" and "saw Him." It was Equus, and Alan was unable to respond in a romantic way.

"It's all right," Jill tried to comfort him. But Alan flew into a frenzy. "GET OUT," he screamed. Then he grabbed a pickaxe. Quickly dressing, the terrified girl tried once more to comfort Alan—but he just stood there "hissing."

"Equus the Kind . . . The Merciful . . . Forgive me!" Alan moaned. He saw Nugget's eyes roll. Then Nugget and the other horses approached, their hooves stamping angrily on the ground. "Thou—God—Seest—Nothing," Alan shrieked, as he stabbed toward Nugget, blinding him with the pick. And, one by one, he gouged out the eyes of five more horses.

"Find me! . . . KILL ME!" Alan screamed in remembrance, lying in Dr. Dysart's office. "Sssh," Dysart softly whispered, soothing the hysterical boy. "You'll never see him again, I promise." Covering Alan with a blanket, Dysart stayed with Alan until he fell asleep.

While Alan slept, Dysart despaired about his role as a mind doctor. "Passion," he lamented, "can be destroyed by a doctor. It cannot be created." Admitting that he, too, needed a "way of seeing in the dark," Dysart wondered aloud, "What dark is it?" The psychiatrist knew only that it "was not ordained by God" and that, for all time, he would feel the "sharp chain" in his own mouth.

Commentary:

"Equus" is a richly textured drama. Intermingling Classical Greek drama with the paradigms of modern Freudian theory, Shaffer explores the dark psyche of his disturbed young patient—and, at the same time, of Dysart's tormented mind. The dynamic tension between doctor and patient, mirror images of each other, is what makes the play so riveting. Each wants what the other possesses: Dysart longs for "passion," Alan seeks equilibrium. The psychiatrist, however, knows that attaining mental equilibrium exacts a price:

. . . I have honestly assisted children in this room. I have talked away terrors and relieved many agonies. But also—beyond question—I have cut from them parts of individuality repugnant to this God, in both his aspects. Parts sacred to rarer and more wonderful Gods.

This conflict between imposition of control, on the one hand, and a kind of rapture, on the other, centers on Classical Greek conceptions of Apollonian and Dionysiac elements of art. As the German philosopher Friedrich Nietzsch showed, the Apollonian element of art—and of life—is reasoned, orderly, full of light and predictability. The Dionysian, however, is irrational, chaotic, shadowed and random. In helping Alan to give up the dangerously Dionysiac aspect of his personality, Dysart hopes that the boy may eventually live "without pain." At the same time, however, he suspects that Alan will then be "a ghost," with neither the passion or will to celebrate life.

THE LESSON

by
Eugene Ionesco
(1912 -   )

Type of work: Absurdist drama

Setting: A tutor's sparsely furnished home, Europe; mid 20th century

Principal characters:
The Pupil, a "gay, dynamic" eighteen-year-old girl
The Professor, "a little old man with a little white beard"
The Maid, a middle-aged woman in a "peasant woman's cap"

Play Overview:

"Just a moment, I'm coming," the maid called upon hearing the doorbell ring. Rushing to the entryway, she wiped her hands on her apron and opened the door. The Professor's new pupil had arrived. "Good morning, Miss," the maid greeted the young girl at the door. Smiling shyly, the girl, who wore a gray, white-collared student's smock and carried a satchel under her arm, introduced herself.

"Sit down for a moment," the maid instructed her. "I'll tell him you're here." When the Professor entered, the girl rose to shake his hand. The old man, wearing a black skullcap and schoolmaster's coat, evidently found his student quite charming. "I am very sorry to have kept you waiting," he told her deferentially. Exceedingly polite, he apologized again and chatted casually with the fresh-faced girl. Then, quite hesitantly, he asked, "If you'll permit me, can you tell me, Paris is the capital city of . . . Miss?"

"France?" the girl guessed. "My congratulations," said the Professor in delighted tones. "You have your French geography at your fingertips." And when his new pupil confessed that she did not know all the "chief cities," he responded with sage sympathy: "We can't be sure of anything, young lady, in this world."

From time to time "lewd gleams" came into the professor's eyes as he studied his student, who, as it turned out, not only had trouble recalling the capitals of countries, but likewise the names of the seasons. With some prompting from her teacher, she was at last able to remember that, yes, "autumn" was a season. "You're intelligent," he praised her. "You seem to me to be well-informed, and you've a good memory."

"I have a great thirst for knowledge," the girl rhapsodized. In fact, she planned to take her "doctor's orals" in just three weeks' time. The professor congratulated her for her valor. Promising to prepare her as best he could, he added that they must get to work immediately. Arithmetic struck him as an appropriate subject to begin with; not only was it "more a method than a science," it was also therapeutic.

"You will do better not to start the young lady on arithmetic," the maid scolded, suddenly bursting into the room. "Arithmetic is tiring, exhausting." Irritated, the professor reminded the woman that he was the teacher and that he did not appreciate her advice. "She exaggerates," he complained when the maid had left the room. "She is always afraid that I'll tire myself." Then he began to drill the girl on addition. "Seven and one?" he asked her. "Eight," she responded. "And sometimes nine." "Perfect. Excellent," he gushed. "Magnificent . . . At addition you are a past master." When he began to quiz her on subtraction, however, she could not manage to subtract three from four. As hard as he tried, he could not make her understand the principle of subtraction. "No doubt, it is my fault," he said in disappointment. "I've not been sufficiently clear." Then, getting up from his chair, the Professor began to draw examples on an "imaginary blackboard with an imaginary piece of chalk" as he explained his theory of subtraction: "You always have a tendency to add. But one must be able to subtract too. It's not enough to integrate, you must also disintegrate. That's the way life is . . . "

"Yes, Professor," the girl agreed respectfully. Yet despite the many examples he gave—using sticks, noses, and fingers—she could not understand his strange theory of subtraction. Finally, in exasperation, he challenged her to multiply 3,755,998,251 by 5,162,303,508. To his astonishment, she answered correctly and with great alacrity. "Not being able to rely on my reasoning," the girl explained, "I've memorized all possible multiplications."

"I'm not happy with this," he chastised, "this won't do, not at all."

Suddenly he decided that it was time to switch to another subject. Just then, however, the maid again charged into the room and began pulling on the Professor's sleeve. "Go away," he erupted. "Let me be!" Then, refocusing his attention on his student, he promised to teach her the "elements of linguistics and comparative philology." But, hearing this, the maid once again intervened: "You mustn't do that! Philology leads to calamity."

"I'm an adult, Marie!" the Professor snapped; once more he sent his maid—this time with dismissive finality—from the room. Regaining his composure, he proclaimed that "in fifteen minutes' time" the girl would "acquire the fundamental principles of the linguistic and comparative philology of the neo-Spanish languages." At this, she clapped her hands in excitement. "Quiet!" the Professor bellowed; now the girl was beginning to annoy him.

After launching into a lengthy monologue about the neo-Spanish languages—which, he explained, included "Spanish, Latin, Italian, French, Portuguese, Romanian, Sardinian, or Sardanapalian," as well as "Turkish" and "jai alai"—he cautioned the girl that in speaking these languages the formation of sound was essential: to articulate correctly she must hold "her neck and chin very high" and rise up on the tips of her toes so as to "project the sounds very loudly . . . "

"I've got a toothache, Professor," the girl

abruptly complained. "That's not important," he pronounced, and went on to discuss the use of consonants in phrases. The girl, however, persisted in complaining about her tooth. "Let's go on," he insisted, moving to "suffixes," "prefixes," "terminators," and the "roots" of neo-Spanish words.

"Are the roots of words square?" his pupil suddenly wondered. "Square or cubed," he answered. Then, he explained that "one single notion is expressed by one and the same word . . . in all countries." Deciding it was time to test his pupil's abilities again, he asked, "How would you say, for example, in French: the roses of my grandmother are as yellow as my grandfather who was Asiatic?"

"My teeth ache, ache, ache," the girl protested. Nevertheless, he pressed her for an answer, demanding that she translate the phrase into Spanish, neo-Spanish, Romanian, and Sardanapalian. The girl strained to produce the answers that he wanted—but could only think of her aching mouth. "We're going to lose our temper," he threatened. "Son of a cocker spaniel! Listen to me!" Then, once again assuming his cool and precise professorial voice, he went on explaining "the different meanings" of the word "capital" in the various neo-Spanish languages.

"Oh dear! My teeth . . . " the student wailed. By now she had lost all of her initial enthusiasm. "Silence! Or I'll bash in your skull!" the Professor roared back. But now the girl was turning mean. "Just try to! Skulldugger!" she spat; whereupon the tutor grabbed her wrist and twisted it until she cried out. "No insolence, my pet, or you'll be sorry . . . " he thundered. Then, once more he returned to his abstruse theory of languages.

Finally, his poor student, fatigued but not yet completely resigned to her fate, moaned once more, "I've got a toothache." Now thoroughly enraged, the Professor shouted for the maid. "She doesn't understand anything, that girl," he railed when the woman appeared. "Don't get into such a state, sir," cautioned the maid. "You know where it will end."

"Stupid! stupid! stupid!" he exploded at the maid. "I called you to help me find the Spanish, neo-Spanish, Portuguese, French, Oriental, Romanian, Sardanapalian, Latin, and Spanish knives."

After declining with chilly dignity to defer to this rude address, the maid stalked from the room. But the Professor suddenly recalled that he had a knife in one of his drawers. With a new glint in his eye, he retrieved a large, gleaming carving knife, waved it in the air, and instructed his student to "pronounce the word knife in all the languages" of neo-Spanish.

"Oh no! I've had enough," cried the girl weakly as the knife was brandished in her face. "And besides I've got a toothache, my feet hurt me, I've got a headache." But now the teacher began circling her menacingly. "Repeat, repeat," he shouted. "Knife . . . knife . . . knife . . . " Terrorized, the girl inched toward the window.

"Pay attention," he brayed. "Don't break my window . . . the knife kills . . . " Then he attacked, stabbing her again and again until she fell to the chair.

"Oh, that's good, that does me good," muttered the Professor. But a moment later he cried out, "Oh! she is dead . . . dea-ead . . . " And then he called one final time for his maid.

"I made a mistake," the Professor blurted out when the maid reappeared. "And today makes the fortieth time!" she reprimanded him crossly. "You won't have any pupils left!" she added in exasperation.

Protesting that he was not to blame, the Professor denounced the girl; she had been a "disobedient" and "bad" student. "Liar," the maid hissed at him—and suddenly the professor lunged at the woman with his knife. The maid coolly wrestled the weapon from his grip, and slapped him until he fell to the floor. "I'm not one of your pupils, not me!" she yelled at the broken, sobbing man.

A moment later, however, she relented. "Ah, you're a good boy in spite of everything!" she consoled; she promised to help him bury the girl's body—as well as the bodies of his other thirty-nine victims. But the Professor, by now distressed, didn't know if that would be such a good idea. What if they were seen? After all, he reasoned, the sight of forty caskets might alarm people very much; it might positively set someone off! "Don't worry so much," the maid soothed. "People won't ask questions, they're used to it." Furthermore, she added, she would supply him with an armband "with an insignia, perhaps a Nazi swastika," to bolster his confidence.

"You're a good girl, Marie," he moaned. "Very loyal . . . " Then the doorbell rang and the maid bustled out of the room. A new pupil was at the door, ready to present herself for a lesson with the Professor.

Commentary:

The Lesson, Eugene Ionesco's second play, and opened to immediate critical acclaim. Ionesco was hailed as one of the foremost playwrights of absurdist drama, which delves into the irrationality that lies behind our attempts to understand the domestic human experience.

In *The Lesson,* Ionesco penetrates with his typically chilling blend of power and dark humor into the chaotic forces that live beneath the skin of the commonplace and the banal. Within the innocuous context of a tutorial, absurdity quickly manifests and magnifies itself: in the determination of the barely literate girl to pass a doctoral exam, in the professor's ludicrous theory of neo-Spanish languages, and—with grim and forceful finality—in the student's brutal murder. The Nazi armband the maid gives the professor—which symbolizes another "lesson" Ionesco's audiences were meant to receive—reminds us that ordinary citizens can, given sanction ("confidence," as the maid calls it), resort to evil and totally irrational acts. The most piously rationalized behavior often has little to do with reason—as the maid's remark that "arithmetic leads to philology, and philology leads to calamity" implies. The maid's statement is as true—and as *absurd*—as the brutality permeating daily life.

THE GLASS MENAGERIE

by
Tennessee Williams
(1914-1983)

Type of work: A "memory play" depicting the life of a poor and afflicted family

Setting: A big-city apartment; the 1930s

Principal characters:

Tom Wingfield, a young man who dreams of escape, adventure, and travel
Amanda Wingfield, Tom's idealistic and self-absorbed mother
Laura Wingfield, Tom's maimed sister, who has a limp in one leg and a tenuous grasp on reality
Jim O'Connor, Laura's gentleman caller

Commentary:

The Glass Menagerie is a "memory play," taking place neither in the present, nor in the past, but only in the mind of Tom Wingfield, the main character, as he recalls the events that led up to his leaving home. Tom both narrates the play and interrupts his narrative to offer his own interpretation of the events. A dimly lighted stage and constantly-playing background music give the play an impressionistic feel, which Williams felt would express "truth" better than would a "plastic" presentation.

Williams also asked that a screen be placed behind the action onto which images and words could be projected, giving the play more coherence and adding to its emotional force. Yet, this has never been done. However, much emotional effect *is* provided by the characters, especially Laura, who, as a fragile glass menagerie of her mother's making, finally entertains a gentlemen caller, who symbolizes "the long-delayed but always expected something that we live for."

Play Overview:

Scene 1

[The only entrance and exit to the apartment is the fire escape that opens onto an alley. The living room is furnished with Laura's collection of glass animals, an over-size photograph of their father who has long-since deserted the family, a *Gregg* shorthand diagram, and a typewriter.]

The scene begins with the Wingfield family sitting down for dinner. Amanda berates her son Tom for eating too quickly, and Tom angrily leaves the table to have a cigarette. Amanda, now alone with Laura, takes the opportunity to prompt her daughter to "stay pretty" for her "gentlemen callers." When Laura reminds her mother that she had never *had* any gentlemen callers, Amanda tells an oft-repeated story of her youth: "One Sunday afternoon in Blue Mountain—your mother received— *seventeen!*—gentlemen callers! Why, sometimes there weren't chairs enough to accommodate them all . . . "

Exasperated and depressed by hearing this worn-out narrative, Laura sighs that she isn't as popular as her mother had been and repeats that she does not expect to receive *any* gentlemen callers—not tonight, or any other night. In fact, Laura wails, she will probably end up an old maid.

Scene 2

Laura sits polishing her glass menagerie. When she hears her mother coming up the fire escape, she hurriedly puts away the animals and takes her place in front of the typewriter. Amanda enters the apartment, angry; she had stopped by Rubicam's Business College and discovered that Laura had dropped out after only two days. Everything is lost, she utters helplessly. What kind of a future can there be for Laura?

The girl protests her mother's scolding; she felt horrible at the college. On the very first day, she had been so frightened that she threw up. She couldn't go back, not after an episode like that!

Regaining some of her composure, Amanda announces that Laura will either work for a living or get married. With a deep sigh, Laura confides that indeed she had liked a boy once in high school. His name was Jim. He called her "Blue Roses" because of the time she'd had pleurisies and he had misheard her.

Scene 3

An argument between Tom and his mother breaks out, with Amanda accusing Tom of being selfish: he goes out drinking at night when he says he's going to the movies. Almost yelling, Tom reveals that he wants something more in life. He hates his job at the warehouse, and if he were in fact selfish he would have left home long ago. In his fury he calls Amanda an "ugly, babbling old witch." Hastily putting on his coat, Tom accidentally knocks over Laura's glass collection.

"My glass!—" Laura cried out like a wounded animal, "menagerie . . . " Tom picks up some of the pieces and stares at the shrieking Laura as if he wants to apologize—but he can't make himself do it.

Scene 4

Tom comes home drunk and noisily climbs up the dark fire escape. Looking for the door key, he removes movie ticket stubs and a bottle from his pocket. Finally he finds the key, but in his stupor he drops it through a crack in the landing. When Laura finally lets him in, Tom explains he feels like a magician he had once seen who had gotten himself out of a nailed coffin without taking one nail out. He wishes he could do the same to get around facing Laura—and his mom.

In the morning, Tom tries to make amends with Amanda. Gently he approaches her and says, "You say there's so much in your heart that you can't describe to me. That's true of me, too. There's so much in my heart that I can't describe to you!" He is a young man in search of adventure, travel, excitement, Tom announces. How much of that is he likely to find at a warehouse job? Somehow, he needs to escape.

Then Amanda confesses that she knows his secret: he has received a letter from the Merchant Marine and is getting ready to leave. She tells him to go ahead and abandon the family, but pleads with him to first find Laura a husband. Groaning, Tom heads off to work—after finally agreeing to invite someone at work home to meet Laura.

Scene 5

The scene begins with Tom advising Amanda that he has invited a "gentleman caller" over for dinner the very next day. Amanda explodes over the fact Tom should have given her more time; she needs to polish the silver, wash the curtains, and plan the dinner! Amanda then stops in her frenzied tracks to ask whether the gentleman caller drank—Laura's husband definitely must not be a drinker. Sarcastically, Tom replies, "Lots of fellows meet girls whom they don't marry!" But Amanda won't hear of it. "Oh, talk sensibly, Tom," she says. " . . . You are the only young man that I know of who ignores the fact that the future becomes the present, the present the past, and the past turns into everlasting regret if you don't plan for it!"

Later, Tom tries to make his mother face hard facts: Laura is crippled and "very different from the other girls . . . She lives in a world of her own, a world of little glass ornaments . . . She plays old phonograph records and—that's about all." Then he climbs down the fire escape and slips away to the movies.

Scene 6

Tom sits musing about his old high-school buddy, Jim. Jim had always conquered. He had starred in the school opera, captained the debate team, and served as class president. Now, six years later, Jim is stuck in a dead-end job just like Tom. But Jim likes Tom; every time they meet Tom comments on his high school successes. And Jim still calls Tom "Shakespeare," because he once caught Tom writing some mysterious bit of poetry.

Meanwhile, Amanda is frantically arranging Laura's dinner dress. Laura, her demeanor altered by the lacy dress, appears practically a new person. A "fragile, unearthly prettiness" has emerged, almost "like a piece of translucent glass touched by light, given a momentary radiance, not actual, not lasting." When she finishes fixing the dress, Amanda again rehearses the story about her marvelous youth and her many gentlemen callers. In her revelry, she offhandedly mentions the name of the gentleman caller Tom has invited home. Realizing that he is the same Jim from her days in high school, Laura immediately turns cold and gasps that she cannot bring herself to come to the dinner table.

Soon, Tom arrives home with Jim, and Amanda insists that Laura meet them at the door. Laura refuses and goes to listen to her Victrola instead. Once, after summoning her courage, Laura enters the living room and greets Jim, but after seeing that he does not recognize her, she scurries into another room.

Alone with Jim, Tom divulges his plans to run away to the Merchant Marines just as his father had done. In fact, using money reserved for the light bill, he had already paid his dues. Amanda enters the room, interrupting them, and once again she takes the part of a beautiful and vivacious young Southern belle; her enthusiasm for her memories makes her forget that this dinner is for Laura.

Amanda calls Laura to the table when the meal is ready. But when Laura surfaces, looking faint and lethargic, Amanda obliges her to go and sit on the couch.

Scene 7

Dinner ends—and Laura is still sitting on the couch. A soft lamp light amplifies her delicate beauty. Suddenly, all the lights go out. Amanda makes breezy excuses; then, giving Tom an accusing glance, escorts him into the kitchen so Jim and Laura can be alone together.

Jim enters the living room. Laura stiffens, breathless: this moment is to her "the climax of her secret life," the occasion for which she has dreamed. Laura can hardly speak, but manages to mention that she'd heard Jim sing in high school. She is "Blue Roses," she reminds him, referring to the nickname he had given her. Yes, he recalls. They had been in the same choir class—she always came in late, he grins. Laura glances down at her leg and awkwardly explains that she was unable to walk very fast.

Suddenly, Jim sits up and confidently diagnoses her problem as an inferiority complex; she needs to think of herself, not as "different," but as "unique." Gradually, she will conquer her fears and shyness. Was there was anything, he then asks, that particularly interests her? Laura turns to her glass collection and picks out a glass unicorn for him to hold. He admires it, then puts it back and asks if he can lead her in a dance. As Laura nervously places her hand in his, Jim coaxes her just to relax and move with him. Just as he says this, however, he bumps the table, causing the unicorn to fall, breaking off its horn. He apologizes. It is nothing, Laura assures him: "Now it is just like all the other horses."

At once Jim's voice grows soft, and he tells her that she is unique, and very pretty. "Somebody—ought to—*kiss* you, Laura!" he concludes. And then he places his lips on her's. Immediately afterward, he regrets his action. "I shouldn't have done that," he says. "I've—been going steady. . . . Being in love has made a new man out of me!" But Laura, a dazed smile on her face, is too enthralled to hear his apology. She swoons a bit, grabbing hold of the arm of the sofa.

Laura is speechless, and gives him the hornless unicorn as a souvenir. Then she kneels down beside her Victrola to wind it. Just then, Amanda enters carrying punch and cookies, and singing a song about lemonade. Bubbly as ever, she tells Jim he must come back and visit them often. But Jim mumbles that he is going steady and has to leave to pick up his girlfriend at the train station.

After Jim exits the apartment, Amanda turns to Tom. He should have known about Jim's romantic status. Then, as she starts in once more to condemn Tom's selfish, lazy manner, Tom lifts his glass, smashes it on the floor, and races out the door and down the fire escape.

Soon after that night, Tom loses his job for writing a poem on the back of a shoe box. Following in his "father's footsteps, attempting to find in motion what was lost in space," he joins the Merchant Marines and escapes his family. In the end, though, he cannot wipe the memories from his mind: "Oh, Laura, Laura. I tried to leave you behind me, but I am more faithful than I intended to be! I reach for a cigarette, I cross the street, I run into the movies or a bar, I buy a drink, I speak to the nearest stranger—anything that can blow your candles out!"

MURDER IN THE CATHEDRAL

by
T.S. Eliot
(1888-1965)

Type of work: Dramatic lyric tragedy

Setting: Canterbury, England; 1170

Principal characters:
Thomas Becket, Archbishop of Canterbury
A chorus of Canterbury women
Three Canterbury priests
Four knights of King Henry, Becket's rival

Play Overview:

It was December in the Year of Our Lord 1170, and a chorus of Canterbury women, "drawn by danger," proceeded toward the Cathedral. The precise nature of the danger that drew them they could not tell; they were only poor, simple, superstitious women. What possible calamity could be awaiting them at the Cathedral—the house of God Himself?

As they gathered outside the Cathedral, the women recited the litany of their sufferings under the turning wheels of political power. King Henry of Anjou and the English lords and barons were engaged in a struggle for power, and, as usual, it was the penniless who had suffered most. Indeed, their own beloved Archbishop, Thomas Becket, had unwittingly played a hand in their suffering by refusing to rescind his excommunications of the bishops who had crowned Henry the new King of England. Now, with the return of their Archbishop, yet unreconciled to Henry, they feared that they had been pulled to the center of the maelstrom; surely the King would see to it that Becket was punished. Yet, they concluded, there was nothing they could do but "wait and . . . witness."

A great uneasiness also rested upon the priests at the Cathedral of Canterbury, but their anxieties were focused on Becket's increasingly precarious position. In the Archbishop's absence, he had, according to rumor, compounded King Henry's troubles at home by implicating himself in intrigues with the Pope and with the King of France—both of whom Henry believed opposed his efforts to consolidate power and unify the state.

Just then a messenger arrived at the Cathedral. "I am here to inform you," he told the priests, that "the Archbishop is in England, and is close outside the city." One of the priests immediately inquired if Becket's exile was ended and if he and Henry were reconciled. The messenger replied that Becket was indeed returning to Canterbury with the full powers of his office restored; but as for his reconciliation with the King, the messenger said, "that is another matter."

The chorus of women, who had overheard the messenger, suddenly felt their intuition of impending peril confirmed. They reflected that their own "private terrors" and their own "secret fears" seemed little when compared to "the pattern of fate" into which they and everyone around them had now been drawn. "O Thomas, Archbishop, leave us, leave us," they cried. "Leave sullen Dover and set sail for France."

A priest was still chastising the women for their apprehensions when Becket himself arrived. "Peace. And let them be," the Archbishop commanded. "They speak better than they know, and beyond your understanding." Then he went on:
They know and do not know, what it is to act
and suffer.
They know and do not know, that action is suf-
fering,
And suffering action.

The priests apologized and withdrew to allow Becket to rest from his journey. As he lay in his chamber, a vision opened up to him in which the motivations for his return to England were tested by four tempters.

The first tempter came to remind Becket of the earthly pleasures he had known as "young Tom" in his lusty boyhood, and to persuade him to forget his quarrels with the King. It was far better, the tempter told him, to surrender his stern principles and return to the "gaiety" and "mirth and sportfulness" of his youth.

Becket dismissed this demon with the demurral that he had arrived "twenty years too late."

Then the second tempter appeared, reminding Becket of the secular power that he had once exercised as Chancellor. After all, Henry was only asking now that Becket unite his old duties with his present offices as Archbishop. "Real power," the tempter said, is "purchased at price of a certain submission." Becket again resisted; there was no way for him, as the mediator of God, to serve two masters. Henry bore only secular power; the Archbishop, spiritual power—he alone held the keys of both "heaven and hell."

The third tempter then came forward, claiming to be aligned with the antiroyalist baronial interests. If Becket would only realize that *no* reconciliation was possible with Henry and aid the barons in their plot to overthrow the King, the church could become "a new constellation" to the people of England. Becket, though truly tempted by this last offer, finally replied that he would not turn the church against the throne. "No one shall say," he concluded, "that I betrayed a king."

Now Becket was visited by a new apparition—and this fourth demon was not so easily dismissed as the previous three. "Seek the way of martyrdom," he urged. If Becket sacrificed himself on earth, he would be "high in heaven."

"No!" Becket answered. "Who are you, tempting me with my own desires? . . . To do the right thing for the wrong reason . . . Can I neither act nor suffer without perdition?" Echoing Becket's own words to the priests earlier that day, the fourth tempter replied:
You know and do not know, what it is to act
and suffer.
You know and do not know, that action is suf-
fering,
And suffering action.

Three weeks later, on Christmas morning, the Archbishop delivered his sermon in the Cathedral on the themes of martyrdom and spiritual peace. Martyrdom, he said, was a part of God's design to lead people back to the teachings of Christ. And spiritual peace was not a hostage to political strife or wars between nations; it was an inviolable gift from Christ. Then Becket closed his sermon with a farewell to his congregation. "I do not think," he told them, "I shall ever preach to you again . . . because it is possible that in a short time you shall have another martyr, and that one perhaps not the last."

The days passed while the chorus and the priests awaited and dreaded the fulfillment of Becket's martyrdom. Then, on the fourth day, four knights appeared. They had come, they said, as "Servants of the King" to discuss "urgent business" with Becket.

The Archbishop was summoned; calmly he entered the hall to hear an inventory of the King's grievances from the assembled knights. The King's authority, they told him, had been undermined by the actions of the Archbishop—in a display of rank ingratitude. It was only through King Henry, they reminded Becket, that he, a "tradesman's son" and a "backstairs brat that was born in Cheapside," had achieved any honor or power.

Becket denied these allegations, and argued that if the knights truly spoke for the King, their charges would have to be made in public. "Then in public," Becket said, "I will refute them."

The infuriated knights were about to assault the Archbishop when the priests intervened. Becket, the knights insisted, must rescind his previous excommunications. When Becket told them that it was not in his power to comply, the knights responded in bitter fury: "Priest, you have spoken in danger of your life." The knights on their next meeting, they warned, would come with sword in hand "for the King's justice."

"Now is too late / For action," mourned the chorus, and "too soon for contrition."

The priests, too, were distraught; they implored Becket to withdraw to the cloister, where he would be safe. Becket answered them with implacable calm:

All my life they have been coming, these feet.
All my life
I have waited. Death will come only when I am
worthy,
And if I am worthy, there is no danger.
I have therefore only to make perfect my will.

No sooner had the Archbishop finished speaking than the King's knights returned, pounding on the Cathedral doors. Despite the priests' protests, Becket instructed them to let them in.

Emboldened by liquor, the knights once again demanded that Becket absolve those bishops he had excommunicated, resign their powers, and renew his obedience to the King. Becket, again, refused: "Now to Almighty God . . . and to all the saints, I commend my cause and that of the church."

At these words, the four outraged and half-drunken knights drew their swords and summarily slaughtered the Archbishop.

"Clean the air!" cried the women of the chorus—the eternal witnesses of murder. The virtuous, saintly Archbishop was dead! "Clean the sky!

wash the wind! take stone from stone and wash them."

Then, as the clamor subsided, the knights turned to the audience to address them directly. One by one, they explained their reasons for striking down the recalcitrant Becket, secure in their belief that an English audience would, "in fair play," hear them out. First, the knights contended that they were entirely disinterested parties; in serving the King and the state, they had nothing to gain for themselves. Second, Becket had been the source of conflict between church and state; he had refused Henry's request to act as both Chancellor and Archbishop. Finally, it was clear that Becket had wished upon himself the role of martyr. Indeed, he had been heard years earlier, as he left for exile in France, to prophesy his own death. In this sense, the knights concluded, those assembled should judge Becket's death not as a murder but as "suicide while of unsound mind."

As the knights withdrew from the stage, they advised the audience to return to their homes and to do nothing to disrupt the peace and natural order that had now been restored. The priests were left alone on stage to contemplate the meaning of Becket's martyrdom. Surely, they judged, the church would be justified through his death:

For the Church is stronger for this action,
Triumphant in adversity. It is fortified
By persecution: supreme, so long as men will
die for it.

"We acknowledge ourselves," they concluded, "as type of the common man, of the men and women who shut the door and sit by the fire . . . who fear the injustice of men less than the justice of God . . . "

"Lord have mercy on us," they prayed. "Blessed Thomas, pray for us."

Commentary:

"Murder in the Cathedral" is one of the most powerful—and one of the most unusual—dramas to emerge from the modern theater. When it debuted at the Canterbury Festival in 1935, critics were immediately intrigued by the devices Eliot used to pull his audience directly into the play—not, in the modern sense, as lovers, drawn to dwell within the skins of the priests and the archbishop, but as a community of jurors, whose judgment on history will ultimately help them reshape the present and the future.

In order to engage his audience as actors, jurors, judges, and collaborators in the action, Eliot adapted many of the strikingly un-English and un-contemporary forms of classic Greek tragedy. The archaic and elegant poetry of the dialogue, and the stylized chorus of women who unroll the backdrops of the action for us, are both there, in part, precisely to remind us that this *is* a drama, a ritual enactment—and that we are here to take part in the ritual. It should come as no real surprise, then, when the King's knights finally turn to face us and plead their causes; when the priests deliver their final confession to us; or when we, the audience, are left to write the final scenes of the drama in our judgment and in our own communal future.

COMPACT

Classics®

LIBRARY #2: Literary Masterpieces

In this expansive literary mix, you will discover authors, ideas, and books that penetrate to the core of our shared human heritage. You will travel to the heart of light and darkness through these selections from classic worlds of mystery, mythology, war epics, love stories, Victorian novels, and science fiction/fantasy. Take a voyage *20,000 Leagues Under the Sea* in Jules Verne's intricate and elegant Victorian under-water frigate; savor the warm lessons learned by the kindergarten heroine in Beverly Cleary's *Ramona the Pest* and the married couples in Wallace Stegner's *Crossing to Safety*; walk with Toni Morrison's *Sula* through the luckless streets and the dead-end escape routes of an Ohio ghetto neighborhood, or enter into battle against the Devil's own nephew in C.S. Lewis' *Screwtape Letters*.

Wherever you choose to start, you will emerge from your travels into a world of expanded horizons and deeper perspectives. Enjoy the journey!

THE SHORT STORIES OF O. HENRY

(taken from *Best Stories of O. Henry*, by William Sydney Porter, Country Life Press, Garden City, N.J., 1945)

The Gift of the Magi

Mrs. James Dillingham Young, "Della" to her friends, had greatly scrimped on her spending—only to show that $1.87 saved. Not much to buy a present for her husband, she thought. And here it was, Christmas Eve. Della was thrifty with the twenty-dollars a week salary her husband received, but, at Christmas, a dollar went only so far. In fact, Della and her husband had but two possessions in which they felt pride: a gold watch James' father had given him, and Della's long chestnut-colored hair, which rippled across her back and fell below her knees.

Then it hit her. She would sell her hair to get money for the gift. Della remembered that she had once seen a sign that read: "Mm. Sofronie, Hair Goods of All Kinds." When Della arrived there, Madame Sofronie took one look at her tresses and said, "Twenty dollars."

"Give it to me quick," Della answered.

After it was over, Della spent the rest of the afternoon searching for the perfect gift: a handsome fob chain for Jim's gold watch. Jim would not be happy about the loss of her hair, but Della hoped the fine chain would replace displeasure with delight.

When Jim walked through the door that afternoon, he took one look at Della, and then turned silent. Hastily explaining that she had sold her hair to buy a present for him, Della was taken aback when Jim drew a package from his overcoat pocket and tossed it on the table. A haircut could not make him love her less, he said, "But if you'll unwrap that package you may see why you had me going a while at first."

It was the set of combs she had coveted for so long. She hugged them and promised her husband that her hair would grow quickly.

Then she gave Jim his present. Seeing the chain, he leaned back on the couch and smiled broadly. "I sold the watch to get the money to buy your combs," he confessed.

It is said the Magi, with their gifts of gold, frankincense, and myrrh, inaugurated gift-giving. "I have lamely related to you," concluded the storyteller, "the uneventful chronicle of two foolish children in a flat who most unwisely sacrificed for each other the greatest treasures of their house." But of all who give gifts, of all who receive gifts, these two were the wisest. They were the magi.

Mammon and the Archer

Robber baron Anthony Rockwall, unlike many of his neighbors in their Fifth Avenue mansions, appreciated that his son Richard, despite his enormous wealth, had grown up prudent and thrifty. Attentive to young Richard's needs, however, he could see that the boy pined for Miss Lantry, a wealthy young socialite. "She'll jump at you," he told his son, "you've got the money and the looks, and you're a decent boy."

"There are some things money can't accomplish," Richard gloomily replied. He then explained that Miss Lantry was sailing for Europe the next day, and he had made a date with her at 8:30 to see a play at Wallack's Theater. Richard calculated that he would only have a six- or eight-minute carriage ride to declare his love and to persuade Miss Lantry to marry him.

Richard arrived at Miss Lantry's at 8:32. He had just begun his rehearsed speech when he dropped the engagement ring—which had been his mother's wedding ring—from his vest pocket, and he had to scramble down from the carriage to retrieve it. However, only a block further down the street they were halted by a traffic jam. "I'm very sorry," Richard told Miss Lantry, "but they won't get this jumble loosened up in an hour. If I hadn't dropped the ring, we—"

"Let me see the ring," interrupted Miss Lantry. "I think theaters are stupid, anyway." The traffic jam, which lasted two hours, gave Richard the opportunity he needed to propose.

The next day, a man named Kelly called on the elder Rockwall to pick up a check. "I had to go a little above the estimate," Kelly apologized. "I got the express wagons and cabs mostly for $5; but the trucks and two-horse teams mostly raised me to $10 . . ." Then Rockwall, with a gleam in his eye, asked, "You didn't notice, anywhere in the tie-up, a kind of a fat boy without any clothes on shooting arrows around with a bow, did you?" No, Kelly hadn't. "If he was like you say, maybe the cops pinched him before I got there."

"I thought the little rascal wouldn't be on hand," chuckled Rockwall. "Good-by, Kelly."

A Retrieved Reformation

Jimmy Valentine, number 9762, served ten months of a four-year sentence before the governor finally paroled him. On the day before his release, the warden lectured Jimmy about going straight, but Jimmy paid no attention. After his release, he immediately retrieved his safe-cracking tools and, only a few weeks later, he was back to work.

Before long, two banks had been robbed. Strangely, however, the securities and silver had been left untouched in both banks—a fact the police found very interesting.

Finally, after a third bank had donated five thousand dollars, big-league detective Ben Price was called in. Ben, who had arrested Jimmy before, knew that these robberies bore Jimmy's trademark, and he patiently set out to catch him. "He'll do his bit next time," the detective vowed, "without any short-time or clemency foolishness."

In the meantime, Jimmy had traveled to Elmore, Arkansas to rob The Elmore Bank. Just as he entered the building to case the joint, however, he passed by a young woman who, after looking into her eyes, caused him to forget why he was there.

Jimmy decided to register at the Planter's Hotel as Ralph D. Spencer and look into the town's shoe-selling trade. He explained that he had come to town to open a shoe store.

A year later, Mr. Ralph D. Spencer's shoe store was prospering. Moreover, he was engaged to marry the young woman he had seen in the bank, Miss Annabel Adams, who happened to be the bank president's daughter. Wanting once and for all to leave his past behind him, Jimmy wrote a letter to his old associates, asking them to meet him in Little Rock where he would make them a present of his safe-cracking tools. He was in love, he explained, and he "wouldn't do another crooked thing for the whole world."

The following Monday, Detective Ben Price arrived in Elmore. "Going to marry the banker's daughter, are you Jimmy?" Price said softly to himself. "Well, I don't know!"

The morning of his trip to Little Rock, Jimmy breakfasted with the Adamses. Mr. Adams, who had just installed a new safe and vault at the bank, was eager to show it off to his family—including his future son-in-law. That morning Ben Price happened to wander into the bank at precisely the same moment to watch the proceedings. Suddenly, however, one of Annabel's sisters was accidentally locked in the safe. Mr. Adams tugged at the handle and groaned, "The door can't be opened. The time clock hasn't been wound nor the combination set." Without a second thought, Jimmy calmly opened his tool case, and, after a few minutes, the safe door swung open.   ·

Jimmy put on his coat and began to walk out of the bank. At the door, Ben Price blocked his path. "Hello, Ben!" Jimmy greeted the detective. "Well, let's go. I don't know that it makes much difference, now."

"Guess you're mistaken, Mr. Spencer," answered Ben. "Don't believe I recognize you. Your buggy's waiting for you, ain't it?" At that, Ben Price turned and strolled down the street.

The Duplicity of Hargraves

Major Pendleton Talbot and his daughter Lydia had just moved to an elite Washington boarding house so the Major could finish his book *Anecdotes and Reminisces of the Alabama Army, Bench, and Bar.* They were running low on money, but they hoped the book would be published soon.

Not long after they had moved into the boarding house, the Major and Lydia became close friends with Harry Hopkins Hargraves, a vaudeville and black-face actor. Hopkins, who was appearing in a local Civil War drama, was especially keen to hear the Major's tales of Southern life. Indeed, he seemed to absorb every detail as the Major read to him chapters from *Anecdotes.*

After four months in Washington, the Major and Lydia were broke. The publisher had informed the Major he would have to cut the book's length by half—and the Major had refused. On their way home from the publisher's, the Major and Lydia spent their last two dollars on theater tickets to see their friend Hargraves in his play "A Magnolia Flower."

As it turned out, Hargraves' character, Colonel Calhoun, was a rather vicious caricature of the Major. The audience loved the part, but the Major felt both humiliated and enraged. The next day, Hargraves offered the Major three hundred dollars as payment for the excellent character study, but the Major rejected it. That afternoon, Hargraves moved out of the boarding house.

A week later, an aged black man called on the Major and Lydia. Introducing himself as Uncle Mose, he explained that he had come to pay a debt he owed the Major. He explained that at the end of the Civil War, the Major's father had given Mose three mules and said if he ever came into money, to send him three hundred dollars. Now, Mose had come to make good that payment. The Major, touched by the old man's devotion and honesty, thanked Mose and accepted the money.

Another week passed, and Lydia received the following letter:

Dear Miss Talbot:

I thought you might be glad to learn of my good fortune. I have received and accepted an offer of two hundred dollars per week by a New York stock company to play Colonel Calhoun in "A Magnolia Flower."

There is something else I wanted you to know. I guess you'd better not tell Major Talbot. I was anxious to make him some amends for the great help he was to me in studying the part and for the bad humor he was in about it. He refused to let me, so I did it anyhow. I could easily spare the three hundred.

Sincerely yours,
H. Hopkins Hargraves.

P.S. How did I play Uncle Mose?"

Commentary:

The name O. Henry (1862 - 1910), William Sydney Porter's pseudonym, was taken from Orrin Henry, a guard in the Ohio Federal Penitentiary where, while a young man, Porter was imprisoned for bank fraud. Porter's time in prison was fruitful; it was there that he wrote his first short story, "A Retrieved Reformation," a story that perhaps best expresses his desire to go straight and become successful. Not only did this story become popular, but its dramatization as *Alias Jimmy Valentine* was the forerunner of a whole school of "cops-and-robbers" movies.

Almost all of Porter's stories effectively utilize a device some critics claim he invented: the surprise ending. "The Gift of the Magi" is perhaps Porter's most celebrated story, but New Yorkers especially enjoy "Mammon and the Archer"—it is, they feel, a most definitive characterization of their city. Indeed, "O. Henry" was a New York storyteller; nearly three quarters of his 600 hundred-plus stories are set in that city. In fact, when he died of tuberculosis at forty-eight, Porter's last words were, "Pull up the shades so I can see New York. I don't want to go home in the dark."

THE SHORT STORIES OF JOHN UPDIKE

Taken from *Trust Me,* a collection of works by John Updike (1932 -   ), New York: Alfred A. Knopf, 1987

Like Updike's novels, his short stories are generally set in the Northeast among financially comfortable people who find themselves in socially uncomfortable situations. The four stories below illustrate typical themes:

Trust Me

Harold was only three or four when, for the first and only time, he went swimming with his parents. "C'mon Hassy, jump," his father said. "It'll be all right. Jump right into my hands." Harold jumped—but his father failed to catch him. Slowly the little boy fell to the bottom of the pool. His father pulled Harold up, of course; but when he delivered the child to his waiting mother, she slapped her husband for being so careless. Harold always remembered that day, and he always felt somehow his mother had been angry at him, too. Despite the incident, he grew up trusting his dad; but alienated by his mother's cold, quick, humiliating tendencies.

During his divorce, Harold acquired a girlfriend, Priscilla, and introduced her to the joys of skiing. While Priscilla practiced her turns and snowplows on the baby slope, Harold conquered the steeper runs. When he swooped down on her as the afternoon drew to a close, Priscilla offered to show him her new prowess with the snowplow. "If you can snowplow here, you can come down from the top of mountain," Harold told her. Hesitantly, Priscilla agreed to make the try; but as the lift deposited them on the run's icy, wind-swept crest, she lost her nerve. "Just do your snowplow!" Harold encouraged. But, intimidated by the ice and height, she refused. In embarrassment, they walked down the mountainside. "You knew I wasn't ready for this," cried Priscilla. "Why did you bring me up here, why?" Harold stammered: "I thought you were. Ready. I wanted to show you the view." Doubtless, Harold's father had also wanted to show him the joys of the water.

Later, Harold attended a birthday party for his seventeen-year-old son Jimmy. After the party, Jimmy turned to his father and placed "a hash brownie" into his father's hand. "They won't do anything," Jimmy said reassuringly. Naturally, Harold became stoned on the train ride home. He barely made it to his home—after coaching himself through each step of the way. Sick and nauseated, Harold called Priscilla to ask if she could come over and help him. "I can't," Priscilla's voice snapped as she hung up the receiver. The click sounded like a loud slap—the same slap Harold had heard when he was a young boy at the swimming pool . . . "Except that his father had become his son, and his mother was his girlfriend. This much remained true: it had not been his fault, and in surviving he was somehow blamed."

As he waited for Priscilla to call back, Harold pulled out a dollar bill and stared at it, pondering the slogan over the ONE: "In God We Trust."

Still of Some Use

Though they had been divorced for quite some time, Foster came by to help his ex-wife clean out the house when she finally sold it. While working in the attic, he discovered dozens of old, board games. After determining they had no special value, he blithely launched them one by one out the attic window into the bed of his youngest son Tommy's truck parked below. He grew somewhat melancholy as he watched a game called "Drag Race!" spiral down into the truck. Suddenly, he realized why: as a father, Foster "had not played enough with these games. Now no one wanted to play."

A slamming door interrupted Foster's reflections. Ted, his ex-wife's new boyfriend, had come home, and Foster sensed it was time for him to leave. "By being on this forsaken property at all, Foster was in a sense on the wrong square"; he had broken the rules of the game. But as he was leaving, his ex-wife asked him to stop and have a talk with Tommy, who was taking the idea of moving away from the house he was raised in pretty hard. Foster tried to cheer his now-grown boy by describing what he might find at the dump when he went to unload the truck: " . . . I used to love it at the dump, all that old happiness heaped up, and the seagulls." Tommy was unconvinced. He begged his dad to ride along with him to the dump; the woman running it had yelled at him on his last trip, he said.

Seeing the sadness in Tommy's eyes, Foster relented. "O.K. You win. I'll come along. I'll protect you."

The time of playing games had ended. But, for this week, anyhow, Foster was still of some use.

Poker Night

The pain had grown too great, so he stopped at the doctor's office on his way to the poker game. The doctor mumbled a lot of energetic, hopeful things about surgery, chemotherapy and remission, but the patient, at least, knew he was going to die. He thought he knew, anyway. For the first few minutes he thought he knew. Later, filling the handful of prescriptions at the drugstore, he wondered if things might still turn out all right. He should tell Alma, his wife, he thought. But, as the old saying goes, bad news can wait; he'd break it to Alma after the poker game.

His game that night was about average; he finished up only five bucks in the hole. In fact, he only made two real mistakes. First, he chose to stay in the game with two pair because he doubted Jerry would be able to draw to a straight. Of course, Jerry *was* able to make the draw, and that was that.

His second mistake was folding on a full house—because too many pairs were already showing, he figured. But then Rick won that hand with an ace-high flush. Nevertheless, he felt a lot better after the game. He decided it must be due to the sense of camaraderie, of knowing that he and his poker buddies had grown old together. "We were all drawing near to death, and I guess that was the comfort of it, the rising up with them . . . But he never did get around to telling any of them what the doctor had said.

Alma was asleep when he got home; he woke her up and led her into the kitchen to deliver the news. She reacted appropriately— said and did all the right things. She cried, but not too much, came through with encouraging words about mysterious remissions, modern medicine, and taking it a day at a time. Despite her display of courage, though, he felt—almost saw—the wall that had suddenly sprung up between them. "You could see it in her face, her mind working. She was considering what she had been dealt; she was thinking how to play her cards."

Beautiful Husbands

Frankly, long before Spencer Ridgeway began having an affair with Dulcie Gunther, he admired her husband, Kirk. Kirk was everything that Spencer was not: a six-over golfer, tanned year-round, grey in just the right places, not balding, slender and athletic, urbane, handsome . . . in short, a beautiful husband.

At first, Spencer saw very little in Dulcie to warrant such a husband. But as he became better acquainted with Kirk's wife, her luster became apparent and Kirk himself slowly lost his "burnished patina." Spencer discovered that Kirk was actually brutal, rigid, vain, and utterly self-absorbed. Still, it took a long time for Spencer to purge Kirk from Dulcie's system. Finally, "the wraps of her first husband fell from her, so that Dulcie at last stood naked, fit to be loved." And Spencer *did* love her; soon afterward, they were married.

Some years later, at a barbecue following a women's golf tournament—which Dulcie's team had won—a sultry, athletic-looking woman approached Spencer, introduced herself as "Dierdre," and commented on what a great player Dulcie was. Just as she bustled off to find Ben, her husband, for introductions, Dulcie came up. "Isn't she great?" Dulcie smiled after Dierdre. "The Greenfields have just moved to town, and I've promised to have them over." Spencer could not see what was so great about Dierdre; but he reminded himself that, in the early years he had overlooked Dulcie's charms, too. Still, something sickly lurked in his stomach. "I don't want to meet new people," he told his wife.

When Ben and Dierdre finally walked towards them, something in Ben's approach reminded Spencer of Kirk. In his own way, Spencer thought, Ben was elegant, refined— another beautiful husband. Spencer felt his face go red, and protested softly: "I don't want to like him."

Commentary:

Many authors write stories about rich characters whose lives seem to fit their wealth: one jets to Monte Carlo to gamble away the night, another blackmails her sister-in-law, a third negotiates a multi-billion dollar deal to mine platinum in Mozambique. Readers may find such fictional cliches entertaining—but they also may have a difficult time suspending disbelief.

Not so with John Updike's fiction. He deals with the lives of the well-to-do caught up in quite human, believable situations. Harold, in "Trust Me," wrestles with both sides of the trust-betrayal coin. He wants to trust and be trusted, but somehow he is never quite able to leave the morass of his ambivalent early experience. In "Still of Some Use," Foster questions his worth and value in the aftermath of a seemingly friendly, affable divorce. The childhood gameboards and pieces he throws away perhaps represent his perception of a useless and failed life. In the game of life and love, he is not only finished, he has finished in last place. It could be argued that another interpretation of this story revolves around Foster not having played with *enough* of these games; that, in pursuit of wealth and appearances, he never truly "got into life"— and the joy and gamesmanship of life—in any meaningful measure.

Even the most arguably middle-class of Updike's characters, the anonymous poker player of "Poker Night," is financially secure; yet he faces the most trying of any personal crisis—his impending death from cancer. Again, he interprets his wife's reaction—and his own—as entirely too impassive. His life and death, he concludes, are only a passing speck both in the cosmos of the universe and in the relationship between him and his wife.

In a way, the characters in this 1987 collection of Updike's short fiction are almost too similar: professionals in their middle to late forties, almost always divorced or involved in affairs, whose children are typically in their late teens and early twenties. One wonders how Updike might portray a Southern dirt farmer or a young African American mother raising three kids in a Harlem ghetto.

Likely, this story collection was written with a singular theme in mind. Given the boundaries Updike set for himself in "Trust Me," he places highly credible, sometimes comic, always familiar characters in situations that seem to be both banally familiar and somehow banally tragic. He reminds us of our eternal fallibility—and the signs of our times; he shows us that even wealth and breeding insulate no one against the foibles of humanity—or against the angst of struggling through what Updike sees as an anchorless age, cut adrift from the historical, familial, religious, and community moorings which once made life purposeful and whole. Paradoxically, perhaps, John Updike, with all the subtlety and the sophisticated nuances of his prose and his perceptions, is writing to us more than anything else, as the Last New England Puritan.

THE SHORT STORIES OF KATHERINE MANSFIELD

(taken from *Collected Stories of Katherine Mansfield*, Constable Press, London, England, 1945)

The beauty in what is simple and imperfect deeply impressed Katherine Mansfield and actively shaped her fiction. Mansfield's characters are often found in situations where they must summon inner strength to confront cruelty and suffering in the world. The heroes of these stories emerge as humble people, often disdained by society, but always striving to understand the human predicament.

Her First Ball

Leila sat in the carriage with her Sheridan cousins, anticipating a very special evening. "Have you really never been to a ball before, Leila?" one of her cousins asked. "Our nearest neighbor was fifteen miles," Leila quietly replied. It was all so new to Leila—all the splendid flowers, the elegant clothes, the elaborately fashioned coiffures of the ladies.

When at last the cab pulled up in front of the hall, Laura Sheridan immediately led Leila to the ladies' room. Leila stared in wonder at the multitude of girls "tying ribbons again, tucking handkerchiefs down the fronts of their bodices, smoothing marble-white gloves."

"Ready, Leila?" Meg Sheridan asked as she guided Leila out the door, through the crowd, and onto the floor. Utterly dazzled, Leila experienced "a rush of joy so sweet that it was hard to bear alone." Various young men asked her to dance. In their arms, she quite "forgot to be shy." She floated across the dance floor "like a flower that is tossed into a pool." Once she paused to nibble on a sweet ice, but she had barely finished it when another partner approached to lead her back onto the dance floor.

Leila's new partner was shabbily dressed, "quite an old man—fat with a bald patch on his head." The man disconcerted her; he seemed somehow to have been waiting for her. He immediately guessed that Leila had never been to a ball before. "How did you know?" she inquired. Having attended dances for thirty years, the man explained, he simply knew. He then informed Leila that before long her "pretty arms" would turn into "short fat ones." What was worse, he matter-of-factly predicted, her heart would someday "ache, ache" because no one would desire her.

Startled, Leila laughed politely, but the man's words had certainly unnerved her. "Was this first ball only the beginning of her last ball after all?" she wondered. "Why didn't happiness last forever?" Leila told her partner that she no longer wanted to dance. She tried to maintain her composure, "but deep inside her a little girl threw a pinafore over her head and sobbed." She longed to be home, under the stars, with the familiar sound of baby owls in her ears.

But soon, obliged out of politeness to accept, she danced with another new partner. Swept up in the mood of the dance, Leila began to feel giddy again. "All became one beautiful flying wheel." And although the fat man now and again appeared in her gaze as she danced, Leila "didn't even recognize him . . ."

The Garden-Party

Gathered in their opulent home, the Sheridans prepared for an afternoon luncheon on the lawn. A band had been hired to play, catered waiters were coming to serve the food, and pots of pink lilies already adorned the walkways. The centerpiece of the party was to be a festive garden tent, which young Laura Sheridan would oversee.

Laura was reluctant at first to trust the workmen who had been hired to raise the tent. She tried to be severe with them, imitating the tone of her mother's voice. But to Laura's surprise and delight, the workmen's responses were friendly. "Why couldn't she have workmen for friends," she wondered, "rather than the silly boys she danced with and who came to Sunday night supper?"

Soon Laura's thoughts were diverted by the bustle inside the house. Summoned by her mother, Laura helped with her cousins' clothes, received the florist with his piles of canna lilies and the caterer with his array of cream puffs. As she bit into one of the sweet confections, Laura was stunned to hear the caterer say to the cook: "There's been a horrible accident. A man killed . . . " It was one of the workmen who lived in the little cottages near the Sheridan house. Thrown from his horse, he had died instantly, leaving behind a wife and five little children.

"Stop the garden party," Laura exclaimed. It would be heartless to continue in light of the tragedy. But Laura's sister retorted, "If you're going to stop a band playing every time someone has an accident, you'll lead a very strenuous life."

"It's only by accident we've heard of it," Mrs. Sheridan added. "If someone had died there normally—and I can't understand how they keep alive in those poky little holes—we should still be having our garden-party, shouldn't we?" And so, it was decided that the gala would go on as planned. Laura, her mother explained, simply could not "spoil everyone's enjoyment" for the sake of one dead man. Besides, Mrs. Sheridan had saved a special hat for Laura to wear—a hat "trimmed with gold daisies, and a long black velvet ribbon."

The guests arrived; the party was a perfect success. At the day's end, surveying all the leftover food, Mrs. Sheridan decided to fill a basket and send it with Laura to the "poor creature" whose husband had been killed.

As Laura walked down the road that led to the dank cottages, already she felt quite out of place; "her frock shone" and she still wore the daisy-trimmed hat.

When she arrived at the house, an old woman answered the door and invited her inside. In the kitchen, "with swollen eyes and swollen lips," the widow regarded her mutely. Then, to Laura's horror, the old woman motioned the girl into the room where the body lay. But the dead man looked unexpectedly peaceful. Laura studied him intently. "He was given up to his dream. What did garden-parties and baskets and lace frocks matter to him?" The man had found happiness.

On the road home, Laura met her brother. "Was it awful?" he asked. Laura surprised him: "It was simply marvelous," she told him. Then, "Isn't life . . . " she started to ask; but, inexplicably, she couldn't go on.

"Isn't it, darling?" her brother finished for her.

Miss Brill

Miss Brill was an old woman who relished life in all its endless variation. Every Sunday she would stroll to the Jardins Publiques to listen to the band, and, as a "connoisseur of people," to observe the young girls, the young soldiers, the peasant women—everyone and anyone who happened to wander into view.

One particular Sunday Miss Brill decided to wear her fur neckpiece to the park. "She had taken it out of its box that afternoon, shaken out the moth-powder, given it a good brush, and rubbed the life back into the dim little eyes." Draping it around her neck, she imagined it was a "little rogue biting its tail by her left ear."

This day was "brilliantly fine," and there were even more people in the park than usual. Taking her customary "special seat," she watched the children at play, although from time to time she glanced over at the older people, who, in contrast to the incandescent children, "looked as though they'd just come from dark little rooms or even—even cupboards."

Suddenly a young couple appeared and sat on the bench next to her. They were elegant and quite infatuated with one another.

"Not here, I can't," the girl said glancing at Miss Brill. "But why?" asked the boy. "Because of that stupid old thing at the end there. Why does she come here at all—who wants her? Why doesn't she keep her silly old mug at home?" The girl giggled: "It's her fu-fur which is so funny."

Usually Miss Brill bought a slice of cake before returning home from the park. This Sunday, however, she went directly back to her cupboard-like room. She took off her fur and put it back in the box. As she covered the box with the lid, Miss Brill thought she "heard something crying."

The Doll's House

Kezia Burnell liked to watch her sister Isabel hold "court" on the playground. Kezia and Isabel had become very popular with the other girls at school because they had received a marvelous gift: a beautifully crafted doll's house complete with wallpaper, red carpeting, tiny furniture, and, most enchanting of all, "an exquisite little amber lamp with a white globe."

The Burnells invited their schoolmates over to see their remarkable doll's house. First Isabel's favorite friends came; then, one by one or in small groups, the other girls visited. Before long, almost all of the girls at school had been selected by Isabel for a turn to view the beautiful display. There were, however, two girls who had been excluded: Lil and Else Kelvey, the daughters of a washerwoman mother and a convict father. Lil always wore a dress made from an old table-cloth, and her little sister Else, "a tiny wishbone of a child," invariably clung shyly

to Lil's skirts.

"Mother, can't I ask the Kelveys just once?" Kezia asked. "Certainly not, Kezia," her mother replied. And Kezia did not press the matter; the Kelveys were viewed with great disdain by all the other girls at school. A classmate had once taunted Lil by asking her if she was going to be a servant when she grew up. Kezia, however, did not enjoy tormenting the poor girls.

One day, swinging on the big white gates in front of her house, Kezia spotted the Kelvey sisters walking down the road. "You can come to see our doll's house if you want to," Kezia offered. Lil eyed Kezia uncertainly—until Else pulled on her sister's dress and searched her face with "big imploring eyes."

Kezia led the sisters to the courtyard where the doll's house stood. But just as Kezia began to point out the various rooms, her aunt appeared at the door. "How dare you ask the little Kelveys into the courtyard!" she demanded; and with that, she escorted the sisters off the property.

On the road beside the Burnells' house, the girls sat down on the ground. Else nestled close to Lil. Safe now—or at least safe from the Burnell sister's angry aunt—Else smiled and whispered, "I seen the little lamp."

Commentary:

In a letter to her brother-in-law, Katherine Mansfield (1888 - 1923) once wrote, "I can't help seeing all the evil and pain in the world. . . . There is cruelty for instance—cruelty to children—how are you going to explain that? and, as you say—the beauty—yes the beauty that lurks in ugliness . . . "

Thus, through Mansfield's compassionate eyes Lil and Else Kelvey emerge with remarkable grace and equanimity in "The Doll's House," calmly withstanding their neighbors' ridicule and disdain. Similarly, in "The Garden Party" sensitive Laura Sheridan rises beyond the barriers of both class—as the fashionable hat becomes an embarrassing indulgence in light of the tragedy—and the conventions of mourning. to perceive the nobility of the working man thrown from his horse: "He was wonderful," Laura tells herself. "Beautiful."

Likewise, the older man in "Her First Ball" represents Leila's surrender of her naivete'. Initially he horrifies the impressionable girl, but once she fathoms that eventually losing her youth is not a fate unique to her, but the fate of all humans, she fails to "recognize him again." And just as the strange man's behavior serves to illuminate Laura's perceptions, the tiny lamp in "The Doll's House" appears to embody hope, helping little Else keep her mind focused away from the cruelty that surrounds her.

The fur piece in "Miss Brill" is a reflection of the main character: somewhat old and dusty, but with shining eyes. After being ridiculed in the park, however, Miss Brill puts her beloved fur back in its box. And when she hears "something crying," it seems not to be her own weeping she hears, but the fur's. Miss Brill refuses to acknowledge her despair; like so many of Mansfield's characters, she retains her dignity in the face of even the most devastating pain.

THE SHORT STORIES OF NATHANIEL HAWTHORNE

(taken from *Complete Short Stories of Nathaniel Hawthorne*, Hanover House, Garden City, N.Y., 1959)

In a letter to Sophia, his wife, Hawthorne wrote, "Indeed, we are but shadows—we are not endowed with real life, and all that seems most real about us is but the thinnest substance of a dream—till the heart is touched." For Hawthorne, it is as if any individual is condemned to live a solitary life of dreams, locked away in his own narcissism until—or unless—he can become humanized, socialized.

Young Goodman Brown

Goodman was about to set out from his home in Salem on a night-long "journey" into the forest. His young wife, Faith, however, felt uneasy. Goodman gently assured her that if she said her prayers and went to bed at dusk, no harm would come to either of them.

As he walked the long gloomy path into the forest, however, Goodman thought how strangely Faith's anxious talk of dreams had touched the very purpose of his errand. He resolved then that after this one night of "demonic work," he would forever after "cling to [her] skirts and follow her to heaven"; he would no longer be tempted by sin. Reflecting how the forest now seemed dark enough to meet the devil himself, suddenly up ahead, Goodman spied a man seated at the foot of an old tree. "You are late, Goodman Brown," the man intoned. "Faith kept me back a while," Goodman answered.

Dusk was falling, and as the pair walked on into the deepest part of the forest, it became increasingly clear to Goodman that his "fellow-traveller" was no ordinary man. For one thing, he bore a striking resemblance to Goodman. For another, he carried a staff that seemed "to twist and wriggle itself like a living serpent." The pair walked on into the night, the man occasionally boasting of past exploits. Years earlier, he had joined Goodman's grandfather in lashing a Quaker woman through the streets of Salem; he had also helped Goodman's father "set fire to an Indian village, in King Philip's war." They too had often enjoyed similar midnight walks in the forest down this same path. Now, the man concluded, "I would fain be friends with you for their sake."

Goodman was perplexed. He had never before heard either his grandfather or father speak of these "dark matters." Moreover, he believed that if anyone in Salem had suspected that his family was party to such an unholy alliance, surely they would have long since been banished from New England. The man, however, assured Goodman that all New England was well acquainted with him, and that men great and small supported his "interests."

As the night drew on, Goodman became weary. Finally, the man paused and said, before vanishing into the forest, "Sit here and rest yourself a while; and when you feel like moving again, there is my staff to help you along."

Soon, a strange black cloud passed slowly overhead. Goodman thought he could detect within it the murmuring voices of his townspeople—and the voice of his young wife. "Faith!" he cried out in despair, and grabbed hold of the staff. Suddenly it seemed now as if he were flying along the forest path, following some fiendish course. Then he reached a clearing of burning trees where he could see a huge blazing rock that rose up like "an altar or a pulpit." The congregation was gathered around it, singing a hymn of familiar verses. Then a voice proclaimed, "Bring forth the converts!"

At this invitation, Goodman stepped out, and Deacon Gookin took him by the arm and "led him to the blazing rock." Goody Cloyse next escorted a second convert, "a veiled female," to Goodman's side.

"Welcome, my children," began the man who had earlier led Goodman there, "to the communion of your race." After preaching a long sermon on the dark mysteries of sin and on how the hearts of people communed by their mutual sympathies for sin, he turned to the converts and commanded, "And now, my children, look upon each other." Goodman did, and there—"by the blaze of hell-kindled torches"—he saw "his Faith." Now, the man said, they were fully undeceived; now they knew that virtue was a "dream" and that evil was the true "nature of mankind." As the congregation sang out a welcome hymn, Goodman turned to his wife and cried, "Faith! Faith!, look up to heaven, and resist the wicked one."

Then the vision ended, as quickly as it had come. Goodman awakened the next morning beside the huge rock, unable to remember whether or not his Faith had in the end resisted temptation. Indeed, he was not sure whether the events of the night were real or merely an awful dream. Though he was able to resume his life with Faith, he had been forever changed.

As the years progressed, Goodman became "a distrustful, if not a desperate man." When old age finally took him to the grave, neither his fellow townspeople nor his children and grandchildren could think of any hopeful inscription to put on his tombstone, "for his dying hour was gloom."

Rappaccini's Daughter

Giovanni Guasconti had just arrived in the southern Italian town of Padua to begin his University studies. He thought himself fortunate to have secured a room in such a curious and ancient palace. Giovanni's second-story window, however, opened onto an even greater curiosity below: a botanical garden attached to an opulent house. In the center of the garden stood the ruins of a marble fountain. He also was delighted to see a variety of flowering plants and shrubs. One shrub, in particular, caught his interest. Planted in a marble vase in the middle of the pool, it grew in a "profusion of purple blossoms, each of which had the lustre and richness of a gem."

While Giovanni sat at his window musing on the garden's wonders, he noticed "a tall, emaciated, sallow, and sickly-looking man, dressed in a scholar's garb of black" busily working below him. Giovanni could find nothing in the fellow's face that "expressed much warmth of heart," but there was something else that struck Giovanni as most odd: as the man pruned his shrubs, he wore thick gloves and a mask. Even this protection, however, was not sufficient when it came to tending the shrub with the luminous purple blossoms. When he approached this plant, he called for further assistance: "Beatrice! Beatrice!"

Beatrice, in all her radiant beauty, soon appeared in answer to this her father's calls, and Giovanni's sense of foreboding quickly dissipated as he watched Beatrice handle and inhale "the odor of several of the plants which her father had most sedulously avoided." In fact, Beatrice embraced the deadly plant and treated it as if it were her "sister," ministering to it with such tenderness that Giovanni "rubbed his eyes" in wonder. Somehow Beatrice and the flower "were different, and yet the same."

Later, when Giovanni ran into Dr. Baglioni, an old friend of his father, he learned that the strange gardener was Dr. Rappaccini, and that Beatrice was his only daughter. Dr. Baglioni also warned Giovanni that he must not become involved with Beatrice; Rappaccini's reputation, he said, had raised "certain grave objections as to his professional character." Moreover, Rappaccini was reputed to have cultivated "new varieties of poisons, more horribly deleterious than [those of] Nature." It was rumored that Beatrice herself had mastered her father's science.

In the days that followed, Giovanni's enchantment with Beatrice became mixed with the same alarm he had felt earlier about her father. One morning he had seen Beatrice pick "one of the richest blossoms of the shrub" and "fasten it to her bosom." Then, when a drop of dew fell from the flower onto a small lizard at her feet, the lizard immediately died. On the same morning, he had watched Beatrice gaze in delight at a butterfly in her garden. As soon, however, as it flew close to her, it fell dead at her feet as if her breath was fatal.

But these sinister sights did not deter Giovanni when one day his landlady offered to show him a secret passage that led into Rappaccini's garden. Nor did they prevent him from falling into an even deeper trance when Beatrice unexpectedly appeared. From that time forward, whether waking or sleeping, Giovanni could think of nothing but Beatrice—and "the flowers in Dr. Rappaccini's garden."

As their strange garden courtship blossomed, however, Giovanni seemed to be growing sick. Nevertheless, his rapture remained unbroken—until one day, as he reached to pick one of the purple blossoms she had promised him, Beatrice seized his hand and shouted, "Touch it not! . . . Not for thy life! It is fatal!"

The next morning when Giovanni awoke, he noticed a burning sensation in the hand Beatrice had touched. To his amazement, when he glanced down at it "there was now a purple print like that of four small fingers, and the likeness of a slender thumb upon his wrist."

Giovanni decided to test his theories about the Rappaccinis. In his room, he noticed a small spider fixed in its web. He knelt down to it, and, emitting "a deep, long breath," watched as the spider instantly died. Giovanni was horrified to think that his passion had been converted to poison, and that his own poisonous nature might

soon correspond to some "monstrosity" of his soul.

Tormented by these fears and by his feelings of rage toward Beatrice, Giovanni could do nothing but wander the streets of Padua. One day Dr. Baglioni saw the feverish Giovanni and guessed everything that had happened. Fortunately, he informed his young friend, there existed an antidote potent enough to render even "the most virulent poisons of the Borgias innocuous." Then he drew from his coat a silver vial and instructed Giovanni to give Beatrice one sip of the precious liquid, and "await the result."

Giovanni returned to his room, still confused. On the one hand, Beatrice was a monster, and "the only being whom [his] breath [would] not slay"; on the other, she was still the "heavenly angel" with whom he had fallen in love.

The next time he met Beatrice in the garden, Giovanni confronted her about the poisonous transformation he had undergone. Between fits of madness and compassion, he listened to Beatrice's tale of how her father had nourished her from infancy on poison, and how after these many years she had become immune to its effects. At this revelation, Giovanni produced the silver vial Dr. Baglioni had given him, and asked if they "should not quaff it together . . . and thus be purified from evil?"

"Give it to me!" Beatrice demanded, wanting to taste the antidote first in case it should cause an ill effect. Opening the vial, she tipped it to her mouth and drank. At the same moment, Dr. Rappaccini appeared in the garden—and by the look on his face, he had arrived too late: just as "poison had been [her] life, so the powerful antidote was [her] death." Beatrice grew faint. Gazing at her father, she said, "I would fain have been loved, not feared." Then she turned to Giovanni and, in her dying breath, sadly asked, "Oh, was there not, from the first, more poison in thy nature than in mine?"

Commentary:

Hawthorne (1804-1864) was not only a superb allegorist, but a supreme social realist as well. His vision of human nature, like that of most New England Puritans, was extremely dark: human nature is essentially corrupt, fallen, and stained by original sin. In "Young Goodman Brown," Goodman's rejection of Faith, the only one who could touch his heart, bring him inevitably toward his darker nature. If he had come to a recognition of his own grotesque, fallen condition, however, he may have been "touched"—and perhaps redeemed—by Faith and his Puritan community.

In "Rappaccini's Garden," Hawthorne examines how even "cultivated" forms of rejection, isolation and solitude can secrete a poison so potent that it becomes lethal to all who are forced to imbibe it. Like a reverse parable of the biblical Fall, "Rappaccini's Garden" presents an Eden whose charms are so fatal to Giovanni and Beatrice—Hawthorne's versions of Adam and Eve—that their salvation can only be purchased by escape, by expulsion from the garden. Salvation, then, requires the intercession of a community, of a social contract, of a "touch" that vitalizes rather than kills the heart.

THE SHORT STORIES OF GABRIEL GARCIA MARQUEZ

(taken from his *Collected Stories*)

Type of work: Magical realism

Settings: South American villages and towns

Commentary:

It is impossible to approximate here the sumptuous banquet of pleasures, delights, and bittersweet truths that await the reader of Gabriel Garcia Marquez; one must go directly to the stories to enjoy them fully. The inherent difficulties of representing his stories lie in the panoply of wonders and the extraordinary rich ness that characterize his narrative—a style dubbed by critics as "Magical Realism." Perhaps a brief discussion of this term might help to contextualize the three stories offered here—as well as to give readers a better sense of what they can expect as they enter for themselves into the many-layered worlds of this Nobel-Prize-winning writer.

Magical Realism is a slippery term; but essentially it refers to that quality of narrative that is achieved when the mundane is fused with the supernatural or mythic.

Several consequences arise from this unusual blend. For instance, linear time can no longer be adequately represented by simple narrative chronology. Instead, time becomes cyclical and differences between the natural and the supernatural collapse. In such a world, an angel can not only appear to the people of a village, but can also become an object of their derision. Similarly, a group of villagers can invest the corpse of a drowned man with the powers of a talisman, and then use their collective experience with the corpse to transform a shabby sprawl of shanties into a haven of unparalleled beauty.

And, of course, in one way or another, that is what we all do. Ultimately, this is the truth that empowers Garcia's fiction. Aware or unaware, we all "entertain angels"—and demons—throughout our daily rounds; the symbols of heaven, hell, and dreamtime haunt all our artifacts, all nature, all our transactions; and only through myth and magic do we weave meaning and coherence into life. It is Garcia's genius to bring this "spiritual" dimension of life into spatial existence—and to carry his readers into a world made whole, and holy, by the concretization of magic.

Big Mama's Funeral

A notoriously parsimonious, dictatorial, childless tyrant, Big Mama had exercised sole control over the town of Macondo for so long that everyone simply assumed she was immortal. But in her ninety-second year she became gravely ill.

The matriarch commanded her doctor to come immediately to her sickbed. Even though he was so old and wizened that he could only hobble with the support of two canes, the poor man had no choice but to comply: Big Mama had long ago banished all the other doctors from

Macondo.

Immediately the doctor perceived that the woman was dying, and so "applied bloated toads to the site of her pain, and leeches to her kidneys, until the early morning of that day when he had to face the dilemma of either hav ing her bled by the barber or exorcised by Father Anthony Isabel."

Finally, Big Mama's nephew went to summon the priest. In the presence of her heir nieces and nephews, Big Mama received the final benediction. Now, she decided, the time had come to read her will. In the suffocating heat of the afternoon, the assembled heirs listened while their aunt "raised herself up on her monumental buttocks" and enumerated her vast holdings of lands and monies. Then she turned to list her "immaterial possessions ": "The wealth of the subsoil, the territorial waters, the color of the flag, national sovereignty, the traditional parties, the rights of man, civil rights, the nation's leadership, the right of appeal, Congressional hearings, letters, of recommendation, historical records, free elections, beauty queens, transcendental speeches, huge demonstrations, distinguished young ladies." Finally, with the reading concluded, Big Mama "emitted a loud belch and expired."

The townspeople were utterly stunned by her death. Immediately they set about planning an extravagant funeral—which occasioned endless red tape. Certain issues, for instance, had to be settled: who would attend? Who would eulogize? How could Big Mama be aptly mythologized?

The days passed; "Big Mama's corpse, " . . . filled with bubbles in the harsh Macondo summer," awaited their decision."

But now, to further complicate matters, it was learned that the Pope himself had decided to attend the funeral. Accommodating the Supreme Pontiff and his retinue, of course, led to further delays—while, in the tropical heat, Big Mama's remains remained unburied.

In time, the arrangements fell into place and the great day of the funeral parade arrived. The townspeople watched in delight as the assembled dignitaries strolled by: in addition to the Supreme Pontiff, the President of the Republic, and other less important personages, a vast array of beauty queens appeared—including "the guava queen, the coconut queen, the kidney-bean queen, the 225 mile-long-string-of-iguana-eggs queen. . . . " The onlookers were so enthralled by the display that they failed to notice, until later, an even more spectacular scene: Big Mama's heirs had repaired to her former residence, where they had "dismantled the doors, pulled the nails out of the planks, and dug up the foundations to divide up the house." The only thing left for anyone to do in the face of this spectacle was to remember and recount the story of Big Mama's life and demise as a "lesson and example for future generations."

(The townsfolk in another story were also determined to keep the image of their colossus alive.)

The Handsomest Drowned Man in the World

Some children playing on the beach one day noticed a huge creature moving through the water toward shore. At first, the children thought it was a whale, but as it washed ashore they discovered that it was a man. The children were delighted; they played with the drowned man, covering and uncovering him with sand.

When the children's parents came upon the scene, they were aghast. Lying in the sand was a dead man, quite unlike any man they had ever beheld. With some effort, they managed to carry him to a nearby house where they proceeded to examine him: He was "taller than all the other men . . . there was barely enough room for him in the house . . . They thought that maybe the ability to keep on growing after death was part of the nature of certain drowned men. He had the smell of the sea about him and only his shape gave one to suppose that it was a corpse of a human being, because the skin was covered with a crust of mud and scales."

The women treated the dead man with great reverence. Not only did they clean him meticulously, but they also made clothes for him. Gradually, it occurred to them that this dead man had a supernatural quality, for "the wind had never been so steady or the sea so restless as on that night" when they laid him out. As a result, they decided to name him Esteban—after the famous Christian martyr.

All the fuss of the dead man, however, soon irritated the women's husbands, who sought to retrieve Esteban from their doting wives and toss him back into the sea. But the women had other ideas; they found Esteban very handsome and they hoped to keep him for a while longer.

Finally, though, it was decided that Esteban should be given a splendid funeral and burial. By now the men also had come to believe that Esteban was indeed extraordinary; they "fought for the privilege of carrying him on their shoulders along the steep escarpment by the cliffs." As they ascended, it occurred to everyone that—in contrast to the radiance of Esteban—their little village below looked rather shabby.

At that moment, they decided to refurbish their houses and their gardens, so that for all time people would wonder at the lovely village—and recognize it as Esteban's own.

(The villagers in this final tale received a visitor equally as strange as Esteban.)

A Very Old Man with Enormous Wings

One rainy day, a winged man fell into Pelayo's courtyard. The peculiar sight sent Pelayo running for his wife, Elisenda. Together they returned, cautiously approaching the strange figure, who they could see was "dressed like a ragpicker. There were only a few faded hairs left on his bald skull and very few teeth in his mouth, and his pitiful condition of a drenched great-grandfather had taken away any sense of grandeur he might have had. His huge buzzard wings, dirty and half-plucked, were forever entangled in the mud."

Pelayo and Elisenda asked a neighbor to come and have a look at the filthy creature. The neighbor lady had the answer: This was no mere man, but an angel who had come to take Pelayo and Elisenda's sick child. But the poor, bedraggled angel, declared the neighbor, was "so old that the rain [had] knocked him down," and he had fallen from the heavens into the mud.

Pelayo decided to house the angel in his chicken coop. Within a short time, although the angel remained weak and found himself sheltered in less than celestial circumstances, he managed to work a couple of miracles: the health of the couple's child improved, and the rain, which had been pouring down for days, finally stopped.

As the news of an angelic visitation spread, the townspeople crowded to Pelayo's house to see the "captive angel." Here the couple saw an opportunity, and began charging admission. Before long, they had acquired a small fortune, as people flocked from far and wide to witness the spectacle of an angel in a chicken coop.

The angel, however, adapted poorly to captivity. "Hens pecked at him," people plucked his wingfeathers for souvenirs, and some even hurled stones at him to see what he would do. Dejected, he had little appetite; he refused everything offered to him except for a little eggplant mush.

Soon, the novelty of a "haughty angel" was supplanted in the village by a more interesting attraction: "a woman who had been changed into a spider for disobeying her parents." The crowds ceased to come. But Pelayo and Elisenda did not worry. Using the money the angel had earned for them, they built a luxurious new home and bought fine new clothes. By and by, the angel became terribly neglected; soon he caught the chicken pox from Palayo and Elisenda's child, who regarded him as an immense toy.

One day, when the chicken coop caved in, there was no choice but to bring the angel inside for the winter. He was disoriented in his new surroundings, and as he lumbered about from room to room, Elisenda constantly complained about having to endure a "hell full of angels." Pelayo finally decided to move the angel to the shed. When the angel contracted a fever in the winter rains, they became convinced that he was going to die. Miraculously, however, the angel's wings suddenly began to sprout new feathers.

Then one day while Elisenda was preparing lunch by the kitchen window, she noticed that the angel was trying to fly. At first, he succeeded only in an "ungainly flapping," but soon, to Elisenda's astonishment and relief, he managed to get off the ground. As he ascended and eventually disappeared into heaven, she could not help but think that the fluttering angel reminded her of "a senile vulture."

THE SHORT STORIES OF EUDORA WELTY

(Taken from *Thirteen Stories by Eudora Welty* (1909-   ) Harcourt, Brace and Jovanovich, New York, N.Y., 1977)

The following four stories span twenty-five years of Eudora Welty's long career and illustrate the variety of themes with which her stories are weaved.

The Wide Net

William Wallace Jamieson's wife, Hazel, was pregnant. What that meant was that he could not get near her, even though the blessed day was yet six months away. Once, just to spite her, he stayed out all night carousing with his friend Virgil. The next morning he came home to an empty house—and to a letter from Hazel saying that she was going to drown herself in the Pearl River and that he would be sorry.

"Drown herself," Jamieson thought in puzzlement, "but she's in mortal fear of the water!" He rushed out the door to tell Virgil the news, and the two decided that they would have to drag the river. This meant they would need the wide net, so they headed up to Doc's house to borrow it. Along the way they recruited help: a bunch of the Doyles, the Malones, two of the tow-headed Rippen boys (whose own father had also drowned in the Pearl), and two young negroes, Sam and Robbie Bell.

The crew first followed the Old Natchez Trace downstream; then they began the slow ascent up the Pearl to the village. By noon, their net had snared a school of catfish and a baby alligator, but no Hazel, so they stopped and ate lunch and took a brief nap. But soon they were back out on the river. Late afternoon approached, and with it, the daily thunderstorm. The clouds were black and heavy, the wind shifted, and the thunder, when it came, shook the great magnolia tree under which the party had taken shelter. Then, two great bolts of lightning split trees on either side of the bank—and, as if the trees' deaths were some kind of cue, suddenly the storm was over. Returning to their task, the mud-caked crew soon finished dragging the river. But Hazel was still missing.

Jamieson, dazed, followed Doc back to his cabin. "Who says Hazel was to be caught?" Doc finally asked after a spell. "She wasn't in there. Girls don't like the water . . . Girls don't just haul off and go jumping in the river to get back at their husbands. They got other ways." Angry at being the object of Doc's humor, Jamieson thanked him for the use of the net and stalked away. Alone, he made his way to his own dwelling, not daring to think about the emptiness he felt inside. " . . . He had walked through the front room and through the kitchen when he heard his name called. After a moment, he smiled, as if no matter what he might have hoped for in his wildest heart, it was better than that to hear his name called out in the house." Hazel had been hiding in the house when her husband read the letter. As Doc had said, "they got other ways."

The Hitch-Hikers

The more someone talks, Tom Harris thought to himself, the more they are willing to say, and the more I am willing to listen.

As a traveling salesman peddling office supplies, Harris knew that listening was more important than talking—that is, if you wanted to make the sale. But just now, on the road to Dulcie, Mississippi, he was listening to one of the two hobo hitchhikers he had picked up droning on and on about music. Harris wished the tramp would stop talking and just start playing his guitar. But Sanford, the talkative one, contented himself with an occasional strum on the strings, while his companion, Sobby, fumed beside him in a silent rage.

When Harris pulled in at a roadside burger joint and bought a round of burgers and beer, the two hobos ploughed in as if they hadn't eaten all day—which they probably hadn't. Sobby was still drinking his beer when Harris pulled back onto the road. He had been hoping to reach Memphis that night. As time passed, however, he decided that it would be better to stop in Dulcie and take rooms.

At the Dulcie Hotel, Sanford and Sobby waited on the sidewalk while Harris went in. Mr. Gene, the proprietor, was still filling out the paperwork when his bellhop, Cato, burst in. "They was tryin' to take your car," Cato told Harris, "and down the street one of 'em like to bust the other one's head wide op'm with a bottle!" Harris rushed outside—to discover Sanford's bloody body slumped in the seat of his car. Fortunately, the man was not dead, and two bystanders had caught Sobby. After taking Sanford to the hospital and seeing Sobby carted off by the constable, Harris felt free to leave. He decided to drop in on a party hosted by Ruth, his girlfriend whenever he stayed over in Dulcie. But Ruth became jealous of other girls' attention to him at the party, and Harris, feeling hassled, soon left. The earlier violence, the rain, and Ruth's jealousy could have spoiled his evening, "but it was too like other evenings; this town was too like other towns for him to feel either good or bad."

Then, as Harris sat looking out into the night, a woman's voice interrupted his reverie. He accompanied this stranger to an all-night cafe, only to find out she was not quite a stranger. He had seen her earlier at the party, it turned out, but had not remembered her. —And he had seen her before that, too. They were old lovers, she reminded him, from his days on the coast.

Still, as daybreak neared, their conversation died, and Harris and the woman said their farewells.

Meanwhile, back at the hotel, Harris was told that Sanford had died during the night, and Sobby was being held for murder. Asked to confess, all Sobby could say was "I done it, sure." Then he added his motive for the fatal beating: "He was uppity . . . . He bragged. He carried a guitar around. It was his notion to run off with the car."

The next day, as Harris prepared to continue on down the highway, a little negro boy approached him and asked, "Does you want the box?" "The what?" asked Harris. "The po' kilt man's gittar. Even the policemans didn't want it."

"No," Harris replied, placing the instrument into the boy's outstreached hands.

Why I Live at the P.O.

Sister's family had turned against her.

It all started when Sister's sister, Stella-Rondo, left her husband, Mr. Whitaker, and returned unexpectedly—and without explanation—to China Grove with a tow-headed two-year-old named Shirley-T. Stella insisted that Shirley-T was adopted, but Sister was sure that Stella had given birth to her and was too proud to admit it. Stella, angered by this accusation, thought she'd "fix" Sister by telling Papa-Daddy, their grandfather, that Sister thought he ought to cut his beard. Proud as he was of his beard—never once trimmed since he was a young man—Papa-Daddy took offense at Sister and refused to have anything more to do with her—except to fuss at her.

Her taste for revenge not yet satisfied, Stella next told Uncle Rondo that Sister had said he looked ridiculous in his flesh-colored kimono. Sister's protests that she had said no such thing fell on deaf ears. Of course, Uncle Rondo *did* look ridiculous, but such a judgment from his favorite niece was too much to bear, and he, like Papa-Daddy, took to antagonizing Sister at every opportunity. Finally, even Mama took up against Sister.

Feeling "put upon," Sister eventually moved out, taking with her every gift she had given her family and making sure nothing she felt she owned was left behind: "The thermometer and the Hawaiian ukulele were certainly mine, and I stood on the stepladder and got all my watermelon-rind preserves and every fruit and vegetable I'd put up, every jar." Since Sister was also China Grove's postmaster, she announced that she would exercise her prerogative to live at the post office; that way, the only time any of her family would ever see her was when they came to get their mail. The consensual response of the family was that, in order to avoid Sister altogether, they would prefer not to get or send any more mail.

Five days later, neither side had made a gesture of compromise. "If Stella-Rondo should come to me this minute, on bended knees," remarked Sister, "and *attempt* to explain the incidents of her life with Mr. Whitaker, I'd simply put my fingers in both ears and refuse to listen."

Livvie

Livvie was only sixteen years old when she married Solomon, already an old man. "He asked her, if she was choosing winter, would she pine for spring, and she said, 'No indeed'" So Solomon carried his bride up the Natchez Trace deep into bayou country.

Nine years went by, and Solomon got so old he gave out and spent entire days sleeping in his bed. Livvie knew he would die soon, and wondered what she would do after he did. Her whole world had been her husband; she never even saw anybody else, except Solomon's field hands, and she only saw them from a distance; Solomon had forbidden her to wander far from home.

Then one day, as spring was about to burst upon the bayou, Livvie's life changed. After all those nine long solitary years, a traveling makeup saleswoman, Miss Baby Marie, knocked at her door. Livvie had no money, so she could not buy anything; but Miss Marie let her try out a lipstick anyway. After Miss Marie had gone, Livvie, feeling extra pretty, walked down the Old Natchez Trace, where she saw a man—besides Solomon, the first she had seen close up since she was married—walking along that ancient highway. The man sauntered over and introduced himself as Cash. Then, without invitation, he walked her home. Seized by a notion, Livvie suddenly turned on him, placed her arms around his waist, and kissed him. And in that very moment, she could sense that Solomon's death was near. She broke from Cash and ran toward the house. But moments later Cash caught up with her and ran alongside.

Solomon awoke to the sight of Livvie and Cash standing before his bed. "So here come the young man Livvie wait for," he said weakly. Livvie, torn by guilt, began to sob, repeating Solomon's name. But the dying man spoke again: "God forgive Solomon for carrying away too young girl for wife and keeping her away from her people and from all the young people would clamor for her back." Then he reached out his hand, gave Livvie his silver watch, leaned back, and died.

Cash took Livvie's hand and led her out of Solomon's bedroom to the front door of the house. Just then a bird broke into full song and Cash took Livvie in his arms. In the yard, a young peach tree was shining in the bursting light of spring.

Commentary:

As these four stories illustrate, Eudora Welty's writing has none of the exotic and flamboyant in it. She reserves her interests to the ordinary: angry women hoodwinking their husbands, the murder of one tramp by another, a family fight, and mismatched couples.

Welty's settings are similarly realistic. The Natchez Trace, a storied old animal trail first utilized by the Indians and later adopted by European settlers, figures prominently in her fiction; she is its storyteller. The Trace leads William Wallace Jamieson and company down to the Pearl in search of his wife's body, and Solomon takes young Livvie up the road to his bayou castle—only to lose his young bride to still another man wandering up the Trace.

Welty's characters also resonate with believability, as she paints them in various shades of gray. Tom Harris, the office-supplies salesman, is both rootless and empty of permanent commitment and, at the same time, generous and giving. Sister, in "Why I Live at the P.O.," is a paranoiac in a family of paranoiacs; but this does not prevent her from seeing what to do, nor does it prevent the reader from enjoying the story's humor. Likewise, Livvie is able to "choose the winter" without "pining for spring," but greets spring readily when it comes.

Welty's stories, settings and characters are genuine; and her inspired, down-to-earth writing brings them all together into four true dimensions of life.

THE LION, THE WITCH, AND THE WARDROBE

First of *The Chronicles of Narnia* series
C.S. Lewis
(1898—1963)

Type of work: Children's fantasy and religious allegory

Principal characters:

Lucy, "a very truthful girl"

Edmund and Susan, her brother and sister

Peter, another brother, the eldest and bravest of the four

Aslan, Narnia's majestic ruler

The White Witch, an evil enchantress who has cast a spell on Narnia

Story Overview:

One rainy day, in a large house in the heart of the English countryside, Lucy Pevensie entered the enchanted world of Narnia through a magical wardrobe. The four Pevensie children had been visiting the Professor in his old house to escape the bombs of World War II that were devastating London. Like all children, they were curious, and had decided to explore the many rooms of the house. Lucy, the youngest, had come across the wardrobe at the end of a long, bare room. Oddly enough, she couldn't feel the back of the wardrobe with her hands. Somewhere in the distance a dim light glowed. As she followed the light, the fur coats in the wardrobe slowly turned to trees.

The light turned out to be an ordinary lamppost. However, Lucy discovered the land of Narnia was anything *but* ordinary when she spied a faun, half-man and half-goat, hurry past carrying books and parcels. He invited Lucy to tea, and she accepted. They had such a pleasant time—until the faun, reluctantly explained that he was under orders to turn any children appearing in Narnia over to the White Witch. Sensing Lucy was a good person, though, he helped her return.

At last Lucy found herself safe in the spare room. Though it seemed as if she had been gone for a dreadfully long time, no one had even missed her. Furthermore, they didn't believe her story.

During a game of hide and seek on another rainy day, Lucy and Edmund both hid inside the wardrobe, and suddenly they both found themselves in Narnia. Lucy started off to visit her friend, Mr. Tumnus, leaving Edmund behind. As he surveyed the area, Edmund came face to face with the White Witch. Knowing a child's weakness, she fed him the sweetest and best candy in the world, Turkish Delight. Edmund ate and ate. The more he devoured, however, the more he wanted to eat; in this manner, she persuaded him to reveal much about his brother and sisters. She seemed particularly interested in knowing that there were four children in all. When the Turkish Delight was finally gone, Edmund greedily asked for more. But all the Witch gave him was a sweet smile—and the command that he must bring his brother and sisters to her castle between the two hills on the Western horizon. Only then could he have more; in fact, he could have as much as he wanted.

Later, as was bound to happen, all the children found themselves in Narnia via the wardrobe in the spare room. At once, Peter lashed out at Edmund for his nastiness to Lucy. After this unpleasant scene, Lucy suggested they all go and see her friend, Mr. Tumnus. But as they reached the mouth of the faun's cave, they came upon a horrible display of destruction. Mr. Tumnus' door had been ripped off its hinges and the contents of the cave were strewn about and broken. There was no sight of the dear faun, but there was a note left behind stating that Mr. Tumnus, guilty of high treason against the Queen of Narnia, had been arrested, taken before the Queen, and turned to stone. The note was signed by Fenris Ulf, a huge and terrifying wolf, and Captain of the Secret Police.

Lucy could not bear to think of her good friend standing as a cold, lifeless statue in the palace of the White Witch. There was only one thing to do: the faun had saved her life, now she must save his. Susan and Peter were ready to join her, but Edmund had no intention of doing any such thing; his thoughts were only of Turkish Delight. Still, he decided to tag along; it would be difficult finding the White Witch all by himself.

The children encountered a beaver who had been expecting them. He told them how they might find the faun, and about a legend of four children who would sit on the Four Thrones, ending the reign of the White Witch.

"And another thing," he added, "Aslan is on the move." Never had the children felt so much power and dignity at the sound of a name, and they eagerly listened to Mr. Beaver recite another old prophecy about the great lion Aslan: "Wrong will be right, when Aslan comes in sight, at the sound of his roar, sorrows will be no more, when he bares his teeth, winter meets its death and when he shakes his mane, we shall have spring again."

"Ooh!" said Susan, "Is he safe? I feel quite nervous about meeting a lion." "Safe?" said Mr. Beaver. "Who said anything about safe? 'Course he isn't safe. But he's good. He's the King, I tell you. Word has been sent that you are to meet him, tomorrow if you can, at the Stone Table."

For hours the children and Mr. Beaver discussed Aslan, and their plans to rescue the faun. Suddenly, they noticed that there was one less person at the table. Edmund was gone! Mr. Beaver said he had seen treachery in Edmund's eyes from the start; surely he had eaten of the White Witch's Turkish Delight, and was under her spell. "We've not a moment to lose," the beaver cried. "The White Witch will be here as soon as she gets word from Edmund and will try to cut us off from the Stone Table."

Meanwhile, Edmund had indeed located the Witch and had told her everything he knew about his siblings, Mr. and Mrs. Beaver, and Aslan. At once she dispatched Fenris Ulf, along with his best deputy, to storm the party at the home of the beavers. In the meantime, she planned to hinder them from reaching the Stone Table. Taking Edmund along for the ride, she and her dwarves headed out in her sled, pulled by reindeer with bells attached to their harness.

Peter, Susan, Lucy, and the beavers had already snatched up a few belongings and were traveling along the frozen river bed that led to the Stone Table. They pressed forward through the intricate patterns of shadow, snow, and ice shining in the moonlight, hoping the falling snow would cover their tracks and mask their scent from the Witch's ferocious wolves. When Lucy finally could go no further, they sought shelter in a secluded cave. There, in cave's safety and warmth, they slept, but were soon suddenly roused by the sound of bells rending the stillness of the night. They all held their breath in fear, thinking the Witch had detected them. What joy, what relief, to find that it was only Father Christmas! This meant that the Witch's spell was breaking! Calling the children "Sons of Adam and Daughters of Eve," Father Christmas presented each of them with a special present: Peter was given a sword and shield; Susan, a quiver and bow, along with a horn that would always summon help; and then he placed in Lucy's hand a shining diamond vial containing an elixir that would miraculously heal any wounds.

The snow began to melt, which slowed the witch's sled. The children were able to reach Aslan and the Stone Table in safety.

Beholding Aslan in all his glory, the children were at first afraid to approach the great lion. After some nervous discussion, the duty of addressing Aslan fell to the eldest of the Sons of Adam, Peter. He drew his sword, raised it to a salute, and said, "We have come—Aslan." Aslan's regal, yet gentle, voice boomed in reply. "Welcome, Peter, Son of Adam." Surrounded by a half-circle of centaurs and leopards, and a host of other good creatures nearby, he had prepared a festival of music and delicious food.

Aslan then sent forth his swiftest centaurs to recapture Edmund, which they succeeded in doing. But the White Witch was by no means content to lose the kingdom of Narnia without a fight. That night she visited Aslan under the white flag of truce to play her final, most sinister hand. First, she demanded the death of Edmund, according to the laws of the "Deep Magic Since the Dawn of Time." This Deep Magic declared that every traitor belonged to her as lawful prey; for every treachery committed, she had a right to kill, to exact her justice.

Some of Aslan's followers gasped in disbelief; others challenged the Witch to try taking Edmund from them. Susan, utterly horrified, turned to Aslan for guidance: "Isn't there something you can do to work against the Deep Magic?" "Work against the Emperor's magic?" he replied, with something of a frown on his face. Then Aslan gave out a stern warning: "Fall back, all of you, and I will talk to the Witch alone." Minutes later, he returned to announce that the Witch had consented to renounce her claim on Edmund's life. This news brought great relief and cheer.

Lucy and Susan found themselves unable to sleep that night, worrying and wondering. In the morning, they decided to go to Aslan. At first they couldn't find him; then Susan pointed toward the trees at the edge of their camp. A lion with his head bowed low was trudging, slowly, heavily, toward the Hill of the Stone Table. When he spied them, the great lion turned and said, "Oh, children, children, why are you following me?" Lucy responded in earnest: "We couldn't sleep. Please, may we come with you—wherever you are going?" Seeing the love in the children's eyes, Aslan could not rebuke them: "I should be glad of company tonight. Yes, you may come but you must promise to stop when I tell you, and after that leave me to go on

alone." The girls promised. They walked on through the darkness, stroking the glorious fur of Aslan's golden mane to comfort him. Then it was time for him to proceed alone.

But Lucy and Susan just couldn't return to camp; something awful was about to happen. Hiding in the bushes, they witnessed the saddest, most horrible scene of their entire lives. Aslan made his way to the Stone Table where the Witch and all her evil army were waiting. Revelling, mocking voices filled the air as the White Witch tied Aslan to the table and plunged her sharpened knife into his side. Lucy and Susan buried their faces in their hands, unable to watch. When it was over, the Witch and her host of evil demons scuttled off to find the four children, and to kill those who had been faithful to Aslan.

Lucy and Susan went to the great lion, whose massive body lay slain on the table. They put their arms around him and wept at his side all that night—until a faint light began to appear on the eastern edge of the sky, and they turned to leave. Then they heard a great cracking sound coming from behind them. They turned to see the table, split into two huge pieces, and Aslan's body, gone. "Who's done it?" cried Susan. "What does it mean? Is it more magic?"

"Yes!" announced a great voice. "It is more magic." Aslan, in all his majesty, then appeared, alive again, his mane glistening in the dawning sun. There was "Deeper Magic from Before the Dawn of Time," he explained, of which the White Witch had no knowledge. "When a willing victim who had committed no treachery was killed in a traitor's stead, the table would crack and Death itself would start working backward."

The children rode swiftly on Aslan's back to the Witch's castle to set the stone captives free. What a joy it was for Lucy and Mr. Tumnus to be together again! They lost not a moment in celebrating as they all ran to battle against the White Witch and her foul army. They arrived just in time to relieve Peter's weary forces and save Narnia. Edmund, sorry for the trouble he had caused, had fought most bravely and had managed to destroy the Witch's powerful wand; but he had been wounded severely. Lucy administered the elixir from the diamond vial and healed him, while Aslan exterminated the wicked White Witch once and for all.

The children ruled Narnia for many years until the day they came across a rusted lamppost in the forest. In the next moment, they appeared in the professor's bedroom, the very moment they had first stepped into the wardrobe.

Commentary:

Before becoming a Christian, C.S. Lewis was a devout atheist for nearly his entire adult life. From the time of his conversion, however, his writings express great faith. His defense of Christianity rests on what he considered the indisputable fact of the resurrection of Christ. Thus, in the first book of the Chronicles of Narnia, *The Lion, the Witch, and the Wardrobe*, he has retold this story using a poignant and beautiful allegory, one that is as meaningful as it is obvious.

THE HOBBIT

by
J.R.R. Tolkien
(1892 - 1973)

Type of work. Fantasy adventure

Setting: Middle Earth; whenever

Principle characters:
Bilbo Baggins, a hobbit
Gandalf, a wizard
Thorin Oakenshield, leader of the dwarf party
Elrond, leader of the elves
Gollum, a small lake dweller
Bard, Lake Town's mayor
Smaug, a terrible dragon

Story Overview:

Bilbo Baggins, a diminutive, hairy-footed hobbit, was perfectly content to live in his comfortable little hole in the hillside in the quiet village of Hobbiton, had not Gandalf the Wizard come into his life. Gandalf wanted Bilbo to join him and a party of 13 dwarves on a great adventure. Bilbo's hesitance was noticed by Gandalf, but not by the dwarf band, led by Thorin Oakenshield.

Thorin explained that he was the dwarf grandson of Thror, King under the Mountain. A fierce dragon named Smaug had driven the dwarves from their homeland. Now the dwarves aimed to travel to Lonely Mountain, kill Smaug, and reclaim the mountain's treasures. Bilbo would serve as the mission's burglar even though, as he contended, he knew nothing about burgling.

The party set off in grand style, traveling as best they could the paths dictated by the ancient dwarf maps. One evening, they noticed a campfire in the distance. Bilbo was sent to investigate—and was immediately captured by trolls. One by one, the dwarves followed after him, until they had all fallen into the trolls' trap. The trolls argued about whether to eat their captives now, or wait until later. Gandalf, aware of the troll's slow wit and love of arguing, cleverly prolonged the discussion until daylight, at which time the trolls turned into stone. Rescued from the trolls, the party searched for the treasure the trolls were sure to keep, and found in the lair some food, coins, and swords. The swords would be particularly useful, as they had no other means of defense. Even tiny Bilbo found a knife, although to him it seemed to be the size of a sword.

The adventurers next made their way to the valley city of Rivendell, where Elrond ruled the land of the elves. A hardy meal and lively conversation ensued. During the chat, Bilbo brought up the topic of runes and maps, and asked Elrond to interpret the writings on the dwarf maps. Elrond, examining the maps, explained that they gave a clue to a secret entrance to Lonely Mountain. The object of the clue would become apparent later.

The treacherous Misty Mountains lay in the path of the party. Scaling these could take days. After a long day's excursion up the trails, the band sought shelter in a snug, dry cave.

During the night, however, goblins entered through secret entrances and stole the party's horses. The dwarves, and a reluctant Bilbo, managed to capture the small band of goblins and bring them before their goblin king. The thieves had nothing personal against the dwarves, they explained in their defense; they only wanted the horses. But then the goblin king spied the writing on the troll-sword which Thorin carried: "Orchrist, the Goblin-cleaver," it read in ancient goblin language. At once, the displeased king ordered the whole lot of dwarves killed. But Gandalf came to their rescue—at the last possible moment, as was the habit of wizards. He conjured up a strong wind to blow out the goblins' torches; he then used his sword to kill the goblin king.

Bilbo and the dwarves fled for their lives down the dimly-lighted passageways. During the escape, the unfortunate Bilbo was knocked unconscious and became separated from the rest of the party.

When he came to, Bilbo wandered for hours in the dark mountain corridors. Cold, tired and hungry, he needed to find the way out. As he traveled, he came across a small ring. It must be a goblin ring, he decided—and put the trinket into his pocket. He soon happened upon a cold, underground lake. Gollum, a small, slimy lake dweller who feasted on fish and ill-fated goblins who got lost in the tunnels (not unlike Bilbo), suddenly appeared. Gollum hungrily eyed Bilbo; surely the hobbit would make a tasty treat. But Bilbo was not about to let this happen. Following a brief exchange, they came up with a compromise: Bilbo would submit himself to a game of riddles that would give the winner his wish—either freedom from the tunnels, or a nice dinner. Each took his turn posing a riddle that the other subsequently guessed correctly. Bilbo finally got the best of Gollum at the modest riddle, "What have I got in my pocket?" Gollum, stumped, attempted to stall by mentioning a "birthday present" he had for Bilbo, which he immediately went to find. Returning, Gollum soon guessed that the object in Bilbo's pocket was a ring, for it was none other than the thing for which Gollum had been hunting.

Suddenly, Gollum began chasing Bilbo, but Bilbo was already well out in front, running through the tunnels. Unexplainably, Bilbo put on the ring—and was astonished to see Gollum run right past him. Following his assailant, hoping to find an exit, Gollum's own mutterings revealed the secret of the ring: it made its wearer invisible. Bilbo merely had to follow Gollum through the tunnels that led to the surface.

Bilbo presently rejoined the party of dwarves, but kept the ring a secret as he told what had happened. The travelers moved on through the forest toward Lonely Mountain. By and by they were surrounded by vicious wolves. The only place of escape was up into the trees, a place that seemed safe enough—until the trees began to burn. Fearing for their lives, the adventurers again looked to Gandalf to rescue them, but even he could not come up with a solution. This time, their deliverance would come from a different source: eagles. Long ago, Gandalf had rescued and nursed to health the king of the eagles. Now this king had decided to return the favor by having his eagles carry the party to safety.

Another near-fatal adventure ensued as the company made its way through the gloomy forest of Mirkwood. They traveled without Gandalf these days, as he was attending to other matters. Day after day they walked, never seeing the direct sunlight. Then they awoke one morning to find themselves covered with spider webs. Bilbo, by donning his magic ring, escaped from the webs and freed the others. As they ran to safety, Bilbo used his ring again, along with his sword, to slay many of the hungry beasts. He was so impressed with himself that he named his sword "Sting," after its ability to kill spiders.

When Bilbo returned to the others, he found that they had been captured by wood-elves. Bilbo, still unseen, followed silently and watched as his friends were put in jail. It took weeks for Bilbo to devise with a strategy to free the dwarves. It seems that after finishing a barrel of wine, the wood-elves floated the empty barrel back down the river to the humans who produced it. Bilbo freed his dwarf friends, smuggled them to the dock, and secreted them in the empty barrels. One by one he sent them all down the river, hopping on the last barrel himself.

The humans of Lake Town were surprised to find dwarves in the barrels, but when the dwarves explained the situation, all was well. Lake Town lay in the shadow of Lonely Mountain—and the dwarves were pleased that their journey was nearing its end. They traveled the rest of the way to the mountain and began looking for the secret passageway. Bilbo remembered the clues given by Elrond the elf king, and found the camouflaged door that led to the passage opening.

Now came Bilbo's opportunity to be a burglar. The dwarves sent him to steal a piece of treasure. This he did, though awed by the sight of the magnificent and deadly Smaug, still in the castle after all of these years. Smaug could smell Bilbo, but of course could not see him. The hobbit noticed a spot on Smaug where the armor protecting him had fallen away. This spot was near a vital organ, and Bilbo saw this as perhaps Smaug's only weakness in battle. A small bird had followed Bilbo into the cavern, and he made sure he pointed out the weakness to the bird.

As Bilbo left with his small piece of stolen treasure, Smaug became enraged, and vowed revenge against the people of Lake Town. He immediately took to the air, breathing fire on the town and burning down several buildings. Meanwhile, the bird carried his valuable information to Bard, mayor of the town. Bard, an expert marksman, drew his surest arrow and, aiming carefully, brought down the evil Smaug, dead.

After many days of uncertainty as to Smaug's demise, the dwarves entered the mountain. Ecstatic at roaming the halls of their ancestors' castle, carved into the mountainside, they assumed their mission was complete and reveled in their good-fortune. A while later, however, Bard appeared at the castle gates asking for a share of the treasure to rebuild the town; it was he who had exterminated the dragon, and certainly Lake Town had sustained much damage. The stubborn dwarf king refused to share the hoard, claiming birthright inheritance to the whole of it. But Bard, equally as stubborn, vowed to fight for what he felt was his fair share. The matter became more complicated with the arrival of an army of wood-elves, who also demanded a portion of the riches.

On the morning of the great battle between the three armies, Gandalf suddenly appeared to announce that an even greater danger approached: the goblins, teamed up with a vicious pack of wolves, were now bent on revenge against the dwarves who had murdered their king. Threatened by a common enemy, the three armies quickly settled their differences and joined forces to fight the goblin swarm. The pitched battle proved to be long-lasting, the goblin forces appearing to gain ground on the battlefield. Then yet another army appeared, that of the eagles. Together with their new allies, the dwarf, human, and wood-elf troops emerged victorious.

Victory, however, was not secured without sacrifice. Thorin Oakenshield, the new King under the Mountain, lay mortally wounded. Before dying a noble death, he patched up whatever differences he had with his former enemies, and bid Bilbo a fond farewell.

The dwarves set up a new kingdom in the mountain, summoning all their scattered relatives to join them. The men of Lake Town, who had fought valiantly, gained more than enough treasure to rebuild their city, and the elves shared in the prize as well.

As for Bilbo, he took but two small bags of treasure, enough to last him a lifetime in his humble mien, but he carried with him a wealth of memories of this, his greatest adventure.

Commentary:

The Hobbit, published in 1937, was only the beginning of the adventures in Middle Earth. J.R.R. Tolkien followed up this story with his *The Lord of the Rings* trilogy (1954-55) and *The Simarillion* (1977). In the subsequent stories, Bilbo passes the ring down to his nephew, Frodo, who strikes out on many adventures, and also running into Gollum, as had his Uncle Bilbo.

Part of what Tolkien wished to depict in *The Hobbit* were the class divisions so prevalent in his time, symbolized by the new, hostile, warring races of creatures that he imagined.

In addition to its being a fanciful adventure novel, *The Hobbit* can also be read as a coming-of-age book. Bilbo, although mature in years, still needs to learn more about his true self, the one that savors adventure. Here, Bilbo tests himself, discovers his gift for helping others, and gradually becomes a better, more caring person as a result of his enlarged understanding.

MATILDA

by Roald Dahl, Viking Kestrel, New York, N.Y., 1988

Type of work: Children's fiction

Setting: A modern-day English village

Principal characters:

Matilda Wormwood, an extremely intelligent little girl

Mr. and Mrs. Wormwood, Matilda's insensitive, selfish parents

Miss Honey, Matilda's gentle teacher

Miss Trunchbull, head teacher at Matilda's school, a harsh and ruthless woman

Story Overview:

Matilda Wormwood, a remarkably bright little girl, had taught herself to read by age three; by the age of four she had pored dozens of times over the only book to be found at her parents' house, *Easy Cooking*. Now Matilda was hankering after something to challenge her advanced faculties. So while her mother was out playing bridge all day and her used-car-salesman father was at work, Matilda walked to the public library and read books all afternoon.

After she had polished off all the children's books in the library, she moved on to the adult books, beginning with *Great Expectations* by Charles Dickens. At that point a revolution occurred in Matilda's life: Mrs. Phelps, the librarian, informed her that she could check out the books and take them home. So Matilda started going to the library once a week to return her books and check more out. She spent her days reading, alone in her room with a cup of hot chocolate—but in her mind she was worlds away, sharing in the adventures of her books. "She went on olden-day sailing ships with Joseph Conrad. She went to Africa with Ernest Hemingway and to India with Rudyard Kipling. She travelled all over the world while sitting in her little room in an English village."

Matilda's parents "were both so wormless and so wrapped up in their own silly little lives" that they failed to notice anything unusual about Matilda. In fact, they both saw Matilda "as nothing more than a scab," and "looked forward enormously to the time when they could pick their little daughter off and flick her away, preferably into the next county or even further than that."

Mr. Wormwood, Matilda's father, was a dishonest character, a "small ratty man whose front teeth stuck out underneath a thin ratty moustache." He liked to wear loud checked jackets and yellow or green ties. He completely ignored Matilda and only addressed her brother, Michael, to whom he passed on the unsavory secrets of his trade—including tactics such as stuffing gear boxes with sawdust to eliminate rattling noises, and rolling back odometers to reduce the mileage on the cars he sold.

Mrs. Wormwood was large and platinum-haired, "except where you could see the mousy-brown bits growing out from the roots." Exhausting her days playing bingo and her evenings watching soap operas, she believed that girls should not be intellectual "blue-stockings" but should work single-heartedly at making themselves attractive so they could obtain a wealthy husband.

Matilda soon became tired of being treated like a dolt. Her frustration at her family's small-mindedness grew and grew, until she resolved to use the only weapon she had: her extraordinary brain. And Matilda also decided to get even with her parents for all their ignorance and little meannesses.

The first punishment Matilda devised was placing Superglue in her father's favorite pork-pie hat, the one he thought made him look especially rakish and daring. The next time he dressed up and went out in public, Mr. Wormwood discovered that he couldn't remove his hat without removing his scalp—and the hat stayed on his head until Mrs. Wormwood finally cut the thing off and shaved her husband's hair down to the skin in the place where the hat band had been.

Then one day Matilda's father came home from work in a horrible mood. When he saw Matilda absorbed in a book, unfazed by the ever-blaring telly, he was infuriated; what business did Matilda have "getting pleasure from something that was beyond his reach"? Out of pure spite, he grabbed the library book out of her hands and ripped it up. Matilda was horrified. But instead of crying, she cooked up another punishment for her father. The next day she borrowed the talking parrot that belonged to her friend Fred, and stuffed it, cage and all, up the chimney. When the parrot started talking, she convinced her family it was a ghost. Matilda was vindicated when she saw her parents fleeing in terror from the house and the unearthly voice of her "ghost."

Matilda was already five-and-a-half years old before she started school—because her parents didn't pay attention to such things. Her teacher was Miss Jennifer Honey, "a mild and quiet person who never raised her voice and was seldom seen to smile, but there is no doubt she possessed that rare gift for being adored by every small child in her care." Miss Honey was so excited by Matilda's elevated abilities with reading and manipulating numbers that she went straight to the Headmistress to recommend that Matilda be moved up to a higher grade.

Now the Headmistress, Miss Trunchbull, was quite the opposite of Miss Honey: a "gigantic holy terror, a fierce tyrannical monster who frightened the life out of pupils and teachers alike . . . She had an obstinate chin, a cruel mouth and small arrogant eyes." Miss Trunchbull hated children, especially small ones; her ambition was to set up a school without any children in it at all. Of course, she did not believe Matilda had any unusual gifts. She told Miss Honey flatly that no child, not even Matilda, would be allowed to move up and disrupt the order in her school.

So, Miss Honey began borrowing books from the upper-level teachers and leaving Matilda to study on her own while the other students in the class practiced multiplication and spelling. Miss Honey also went to have a chat with Matilda's parents. When she arrived at the Wormwood residence, soon after Matilda had gone to bed, Mr. and Mrs. Wormwood met her with irritable expressions; because of her visit they had been obliged to turn off the telly. Like Miss Trunchbull, they didn't believe Matilda had any special abilities, and furthermore, they didn't see any reason for her to develop her intellect at all. Mrs. Wormwood decreed that Matilda should concentrate on her looks; after all, she wouldn't catch a husband by "multiplying figures at him." For his part, Mr. Wormwood believed all a university education would do for Matilda would be to teach her bad habits.

So Matilda stayed in the lowest level at school and continued studying upper-level lessons, all the while trying to stay out of the way of Miss Trunchbull, who did horrible things to children. A former Olympic hammer-thrower, one day the Headmistress had actually launched a little girl into the air by her pigtails (Miss Trunchbull did not like pigtails); on another day she made a little boy eat an entire chocolate cake by himself for stealing a piece of the cake from her private hoard—which he managed to do (though with great difficulty) much to Miss Trunchbull's displeasure.

On still another day, when Miss Trunchbull came into Matilda's class to teach, she hoisted one boy up by his hair for missing a multiplication question, and held up another by his ears for misspelling a word. When Miss Trunchbull found a newt in her water jug (placed there before class by a mischievous little girl), she blamed it on Matilda and, screaming and ranting, threatened to expel her. This made Matilda extremely angry—so angry that something suddenly burst inside her and she started to feel a strange new power radiating from within her. "Little flashes of lightning seemed to be flashing out of her eyes . . . as though vast energy was building up somewhere inside them." It was almost as though "millions of tiny little invisible arms with hands on them were shooting out of her eyes towards the glass she was staring at." And Matilda, with her mind-power, knocked the glass with the newt in it right over into Miss Trunchbull's lap!

After class, Matilda told Miss Honey about her curious and miraculous new power. Miss Honey invited Matilda home for tea to talk about what had happened.

Miss Honey lived in an ancient cottage with no running water, no stove, no refrigerator, and no bed. While she and Matilda sipped their tea, the teacher revealed an astonishing secret to Matilda: Miss Honey's mother had died when she was very young and her father had brought her aunt to live with them to care for his little girl. Her aunt was a horrible person, and before too long, she murdered Miss Honey's father and made it look like a suicide (or so Miss Honey suspected). Miss Honey's father's will was lost, and, on his death, her aunt took possession of everything. This aunt had turned Miss Honey into a virtual slave; she had such a hold on the girl that she could make her do anything. She even made Miss Honey sign over most of her wages. The only way Miss Honey could free herself from her aunt was to rent that little hovel; it was all she could afford. So she lived very poorly, but she didn't have to live with her aunt anymore—although she was forced to see her at work every day. Yes—the horrible aunt was, in fact, Miss Trunchbull.

When Matilda heard this awful story, she immediately set about to find a way to remedy the situation. The next time Miss Trunchbull came to teach Miss Honey's class, Matilda was ready. Using her amazing new power, she made a piece of chalk write, all by itself, on the board. The message on the board said "Agatha, this is Magnus. Give my Jenny back her house, give my Jenny her wages, then get out of here. If you don't, I will come and get you like you got me. I am watching you, Agatha." (Miss Honey's first name was Jenny, Miss Trunchbull's first name was Agatha, and Magnus was Jenny's father.)

As she read this message, Miss Trunchbull fainted flat on the floor of the classroom. When she came to, she fled the room—and the town. Thereafter, Magnus Honey's will was found, Miss Honey got her house, her wages, and her father's bank account back, a new head teacher was appointed at school, and Matilda was moved up to the top class. Miss Honey was extremely grateful to Matilda and they became close friends, having tea together every day after school at Miss Honey's house. However, Matilda lost her extraordinary power to move things with her mind. Miss Honey thought that perhaps it was because she was challenged enough in the higher classes that her brain didn't have to exercise in other ways—like working wonders.

One day when Matilda came home from Miss Honey's house, she found her family frantically packing; her father informed her that they were moving to Spain, permanently. Matilda raced as fast as she could back to Miss Honey and explained that her father was a crook who sold stolen cars—and it was likely he had finally been caught. Terrified of being carried off to Spain by her parents, she begged Miss Honey to let her stay with her. Quickly they dashed back to Matilda's house.

Mr. and Mrs. Wormwood readily agreed to let Matilda stay; they hardly gave it much thought. As they drove off, they didn't even look back at their daughter. Clasped deep in the loving embrace of Miss Honey, Matilda very happily watched them go.

Commentary:

Matilda is a modern-day fairy tale—but with a few twists. It has all the elements: the heroine (Matilda), the wicked parents (Mr. and Mrs. Wormwood), the wicked witch (Miss Trunchbull), and the fairy godmother (Miss Honey). But instead of using magic or beauty, this heroine uses her brains to bring about a happy ending. And instead of the fairy godmother saving her, this heroine ends up saving the fairy godmother from the wicked witch. This fairy tale is also distinct in the lively wit and sense of humor that run through it—something more fairy tales could use.

Dahl treats his heroine—and children generally—with great respect. Matilda is a brilliant and clever little person who is only hindered by the ignorant adults in her life. Dahl has crafted a story that applauds the wisdom of young children and pricks the conceit of adults who think they know everything. Matilda, in her fairy tale, changes her life for the better by sheer determination, grit, imagination—and a little bit of magic.

STONE FOX

by John Reynolds Gardner (illustrated by Marcia Sewall), Thomas Y. Crowell, New York, N.Y., 1980

Type of work: Dramatic children's literature

Setting: Rural Wyoming, near the city of Jackson; late 1800s

Principal characters:
    Willy, a polite and resolute young ten-year-old boy
    Grandfather, Willy's grandfather, a potato farmer
    Searchlight, Willy's large dog
    Stone Fox, a renowned and reclusive Indian sled racer

Story Overview:

Willy was living with his grandfather on a potato farm in Wyoming. The work was hard, but it was fun to be with Grandfather. Sometimes he would play tricks—like the time he dressed up as a scarecrow and spooked Willy out in the fields.

But one day Grandfather wouldn't get out of bed. He just lay there, sadly staring at the ceiling in gloomy silence. And this time, he was not playing. Willy ran out of the house. "Come on, Searchlight!" he called to the immense, sleepy black dog with the silver-dollar-sized white spot gracing her forehead. Searchlight was a ten-year-old mutt—in fact, born the same day as Willy.

Willy and Searchlight ran the mile down the road to Doc Smith's log cabin. "Doc Smith," called out the boy, "Come quick!" "What seems to be the matter, Willy?" asked the doctor. Willy, distressed, answered, "Grandfather won't answer me." He saw the doctor's tanned, wrinkled brow wrinkle even more deeply beneath her shock of snow white hair. Quickly he helped her hitch up her horse to the wagon, and together they rode back to the farm with Searchlight running on ahead. When they got there, they found that Grandfather hadn't moved.

Using just about everything in her little black bag, Doc Smith completed her examination. Medically, Grandfather was as healthy as an ox, she explained, but, for whatever reason, he had given up on life. It happened sometimes, she said. It was a sickness that started in the mind, and then spread to the body. It looked like Grandfather just didn't want to live anymore. Of course, he could go to live with the other sick folks at an old folks' home, Doc Smith suggested. No, Willy insisted. "I'll find out what's wrong and make it better. You'll see, I'll make Grandfather want to live again."

The harvest was just weeks away. There was a lot of work to be done, but Willy was sure that if the harvest was a good one, Grandfather would get well. "Gonna be our best crop ever, Willy," Grandfather had told him. Only one thing remained: the boy had to go into nearby Jackson and rent a horse to pull the plow. From under the floorboards in a corner of the bedroom, Willy withdrew the strong box where Grandfather kept his money. But it was empty! So this was why Grandfather was so discouraged; no wonder he had taken ill.

Willy knew that he had to do something—and soon. The harvest couldn't wait; every day of delay would only increase the danger of losing all the crops to an early freeze. He decided that if he

had to, he would dig up the potatoes with his own hands.

And then Searchlight solved the problem. She walked up to the plow and stood in front of it. In her mouth was the harness she wore during the winter when she pulled the snow sled. "Digging up a field is not the same as riding over snow," Willy told her in an effort to talk her out of it. But the dog wouldn't move; Searchlight had also made up her mind.

It took Willy and the enormous dog ten days to finish plowing up all the potatoes—but they *did* it! Either the dirt was softer than Willy had remembered, or Searchlight was stronger, because she actually seemed to enjoy the task. "We made it, Grandfather," Willy said as tears of happiness rolled down his cheeks. "See?" Willy held up two handfuls of money, earned from his sold crop. "You can stop worrying. You can get better now." But Grandfather merely placed his hand on the bedcover, palm down. Willy and Grandfather had worked out some hand signals during the last few weeks. Palm down meant "no." Evidently, it was not the crop Grandfather had been worried about. It was something else. But what?

Time passed, and soon the winter snows spread over Wyoming. But little Willy was ready; he had stocked enough wood and food to last them until spring.

After breakfast each morning, Willy would hitch up Searchlight to the old wooden sled that Grandfather had bought from the Indians, hop aboard, and ride behind Searchlight for five miles across the countryside to the schoolhouse on the outskirts of town. Through the long hours of classtime, Searchlight waited patiently by the sled. If there were no errands to run after school, Willy and Searchlight would race up and down Jackson's Main Street, kicking up a stream of snowdust behind them. Then, each day at a little before six, Willy positioned his sled in front of the old church and waited, his eyes glued on the big clock that loomed high overhead. At the first stroke of six, Searchlight would lunge forward with such force that Willy was almost thrown from the sled. "Go, Searchlight! Go!" he yelled. And did Searchlight go! She had run this nighttime race a hundred times before, and she knew the exact location of every fallen tree and hidden gully. Little Willy sucked in the cold air and felt the sting of the wind against his face. It was a race all right; a race they always won.

One winter night when Willy and Searchlight reached Grandfather's farmhouse, they found a horse tied up outside and a man standing on the front porch. The man demanded to speak with Grandfather. Little Willy tried to explain that Grandfather was ill and couldn't speak, but that didn't stop the man from barging in anyway. He was a government official from the State of Wyoming, he said, and Grandfather owed the state five hundred dollars in back taxes. If he didn't pay, the farm would be taken away and sold.

Willy now understood the real reason why Grandfather had become sick. If only he could figure out a way to pay the taxes on the farm, maybe

Grandfather would get better. But where was a ten-year-old boy going to get five hundred dollars?

Willy found his answer on a poster in the general store the next day. Every February, Jackson sponsored the National Dogsled Races. Some of the finest dog teams in the country came. It was an open race; any number of dogs could be entered. And, as if in answer to prayer, the cash prize for the winner this year just happened to be five hundred dollars.

Willy entered the race. He could hardly contain his excitement. The first five miles of the route lay along the same terrain he traveled every day; he could sled it with his eyes closed. And the last five miles led back into Jackson along South Road, which was mostly straight and flat.

But word soon spread around town that the legendary mountain man "Stone Fox" had entered the race. Stories about the awesome Indian quickly followed: no white man had ever heard Stone Fox speak; because of the treatment his people had received at the hands of the pale-skinned invaders, he refused to acknowledge them. His peaceful tribe, the Shoshone, Willy learned, had been forced to move from Utah and resettle with another tribe called the Arapaho in Wyoming. Now, Stone Fox was using the money he won from racing to buy back the land his tribe had given up—and he had never yet lost a dogsled race.

Each day during the next week, boy and dog scouted out every inch of the ten-mile track that awaited them. Willy didn't waste his time worrying. He had made up his mind to win and nothing was going to stop him; not even Stone Fox.

As Willy and Searchlight returned home on the night before the race, Willy heard the sound of barking dogs coming from the old deserted barn near the schoolhouse. Curious, he squeaked the barn door open. There, on a bed of straw in a corner of the barn, lay five beautiful Samoyeds. And standing beside them, tall and mute in the darkness, was Stone Fox. "I'm going to race against you," Willy said after a moment. "I know you wanna win, but I wanna win, too. I gotta win. If I don't, they're going to take away our farm . . . . So I'll win." Stone fox remained motionless, and silent. Willy backed over to the barn door. "I'm sorry we can't both win," he said as he turned into the night.

The old church clock showed just a few minutes before ten as the nine dogsledders lined up across Main Street the next morning, with Stone Fox in the middle and Willy right beside him. All the adult contestants were experienced mountain men with superb teams. Still, bets were running as high as a hundred to one for Stone Fox. Not one cent had been bet on little Willy and Searchlight. "Morning, Mr. Stone Fox," Willy said to his towering companion. But Stone Fox's face was frozen like ice as he kept his cold gaze out on the track.

All at once, the watching crowd fell silent as the mayor stepped out into the street, raised a pistol into the air, and fired. The race had begun! Searchlight sprang forward with such force that Willy could barely hang on. In what seemed like only seconds, the dog and boy had shot down Main Street, turned onto North Road, and were gone, well ahead of the others. In fact, Stone Fox started out dead last, chugging so slowly down Main Street that everyone was sure something must be wrong.

The course was full of dangerous twists and turns, but with only one dog and a small sled to manage, Willy didn't have to slow down like the other racers. With each turn, he pulled farther and farther ahead. At the end of the first five miles, little Willy was so far out in front that he couldn't see anyone behind him. He knew, however, that the five miles returning into town would not be as easy; with the trail growing straighter and flatter, the other racers were sure to narrow the gap.

Doc Smith's house flew by on the right; Grandfather's farm was coming up next. As they passed the farm, Willy noticed someone in the window—someone with a full beard. It was Grandfather! He was sitting up in bed, waving Willy on. Tears of joy rolled down the boy's face. Everything was going to be all right.

But now Stone Fox was finally making his move. One by one he began to pass the other sledders as though they were standing still. Soon, his five Samoyeds were nose and nose with Searchlight.

As the finish line came within sight, Searchlight poured on the steam. The sled seemed almost to fly off the ground. Stone Fox was left behind—though not by much. "Go, Searchlight! Go!" Willy cried out above the roaring crowd that lined the home stretch.

And then it happened. "She was a hundred feet from the finish line when her heart burst." She slumped, suddenly lifeless, into the snow, just ten feet from the finish line.

"The crowd became deathly silent." Then, all eyes turned to Stone Fox as he brought his sled up alongside little Willy—and stopped, looking down at his young challenger as he cradled Searchlight's limp body in his arms. "Is she dead, Mr. Stone Fox?" Willy asked, looking up at him. Putting one massive hand on the dog's stilled chest, Stone Fox simply looked at little Willy, "and the boy understood."

Slowly the Indian rose. "With the heel of his moccasin Stone Fox drew a long line in the snow. Then he walked back over to his sled and pulled out his rifle." As the other racers began to appear, Stone Fox fired his rifle into the air, bringing the sleds to a stop. "Anyone crosses this line—I shoot," he proclaimed, finally breaking his silence. Then Stone Fox nodded to the boy. "The town looked on in silence as little Willy, carrying Searchlight, walked the last ten feet . . . across the finish line."

Commentary:

Stone Fox, written a hundred years after the events it depicts, is based on a Rocky Mountain legend the author heard told over a cup of coffee at a cafe in Idaho Falls. Although the characters are fictitious, the tragic ending to the story, the tale of a dog giving its last breath in service to its master, is reported to have actually occurred.

As a true Western fable, as a universal epic of youthful grit and enterprise, as an unforgettable account of the matchless bond between boy and dog, and as a ennobling portrayal of the mysterious Shoshone Stone Fox, John Reynolds' book has already emerged as a classic work of children's literature.

CHARLOTTE'S WEB

by E.B. White, Harper and Row, New York, N.Y., 1952

Type of work: Humanistic children's classic

Setting: A midwest country farm; early- to mid-twentieth century

Principal characters:

Fern Arable, an imaginative, conscientious eight-year-old farm girl

Wilbur, a small, lovable pig

Charlotte, a large, intellectual, congenial spider

Templeton, a gluttonous, lazy yet clever rat

Story Overview:

Fern watched one morning as her father left the house with an ax in hand. The evening before, a new litter of pigs had been born, and one of them was a runt—a small weakling piglet who could never mean anything to the farm but trouble. But now Fern tearfully pled for him to spare the animal. "... It's unfair," she cried. "The pig couldn't help being born small, could it? If I had been very small at birth, would you have killed me?"

Somehow, her father was touched by Fern's earnestness and agreed to let the girl take care of the pig. She named him Wilbur; lovingly she feed him from a bottle and strolled him around with her dolls. Each morning he would walk her to the bus stop for school. Life seemed flawless.

When Wilbur was five weeks old, Mr. Arable, however, decided that he had become too big for Fern to take care of. They arranged to sell him to Fern's uncle and aunt, Homer and Edith Zuckerman, and Fern visited him almost everyday.

But Fern was not able to come every single afternoon, and one day Wilbur admitted that he desperately needed a friend. Yet, when he appealed to the other farm animals, they all refused. The goose couldn't move from the eggs she was sitting on; the lamb cruelly informed Wilbur that "pigs mean less than nothing to me"; and even Templeton, the fat, self-indulged, grumpy rat declined to frolic, skip, or jump with Wilbur, who threw himself down in the manure and sobbed.

That night Wilbur heard a tiny voice. "Do you want a friend, Wilbur?" it said. "I'll be a friend to you. . . . I like you." Wilbur spun around to see who was speaking, but could see no one. The voice instructed him to go to sleep; in the morning, it would reveal its source.

Sure enough, at daybreak, Wilbur's new friend introduced herself. "Salutations!" said a large gray spider hanging from the top of a big web stretched across the corner of the doorway above Wilbur's pen. "My name is Charlotte. Charlotte A. Cavatica. But just call me Charlotte." At first Wilbur was a bit reluctant to make fast friends with the spider, but agreed after getting better acquainted with Charlotte and discovering that her bug-eating proclivities were instinctive habits of survival.

Summer arrived, and Wilbur began to grow bigger and bigger. Life was good again—until one hot afternoon when the nosey old sheep informed Wilbur that Farmer Zuckerman had hatched a conspiracy to fatten him up so they could kill him come Christmas time. "They're going to turn you into smoked bacon and ham," said the sheep. At that Wilbur burst into tears and began to race around. "I don't want to die!" he yelled. "Save me!" Then Charlotte spoke up; soothingly she promised Wilbur that somehow she would find a way to spare him this terrible fate.

Day after day Charlotte waited for an idea to come to her—and finally it came: "Why how perfectly simple! The way to save Wilbur's life is to play a trick on Zuckerman. If I can fool a bug, I can surely fool a man. People are not as smart as bugs."

Charlotte worked throughout most of that night. The next morning, Lurvy, the farm's hired hand, noticed a delicately woven spider web in the corner, each thin strand decorated with tiny beads of water from the morning dew. Then he saw something in the center of the web—a message clearly woven in block letters. "SOME PIG," it read. Lurvy's initial reaction, of course, was that he was seeing things. He took a closer look. Then, somewhat dazed, he walked back down to the house to get Mr. Zuckerman.

"There can be no mistake about it," Zuckerman exclaimed when he saw the web. "A miracle has happened . . . right on our farm, and we have no ordinary pig." Word of the wondrous event quickly spread, and people came from miles around to witness the mystical message. Mrs. Zuckerman was the only one to wonder if the spider who had written the message might not be even more extraordinary than the pig.

A few days later, Charlotte called a meeting for all the animals. Its purpose was to gather suggestions for a new message to weave into her web. Finally, the goose nominated the word "Terrific," and everyone agreed to it—everyone, that is, except Wilbur. "I'm not terrific," he said bluntly. Charlotte, however, replied, "That doesn't make a particle of difference. Not a particle. People believe almost anything they see in print." So that evening, Charlotte started work on her second web. By morning, the word TERRIFIC was neatly woven into the web above Wilbur's door. Once again, Mr. Zuckerman called it a miracle, and soon people who had first journeyed to see "SOME PIG" returned to read that the pig was also "TERRIFIC." Now arrangements were made to have a large crate built with gold letters on the side saying "Zuckerman's Famous Pig." In September, Wilbur would journey to the County Fair.

Meanwhile, Charlotte was laboring to come up with another word to add to Wilbur's miracle. She had struck a deal with Templeton, informing him that since the pig's food was Templeton's chief source of supply Wilbur's destiny and his own were closely linked. Templeton agreed to look for magazines and other sources of words in the dump, which he often frequented. After several ventures, he finally came back with a piece of cardboard in his teeth from an old package of soap flakes; "With New Radiant Action," it read. After watching Wilbur run around and do a back flip with a half twist, Charlotte decided that Wilbur was indeed "RADIANT," and her evening's activities were cut out for her.

On the opening day of the fair, everyone rose bright and early. Mrs. Zuckerman gave Wilbur a buttermilk bath, leaving his skin with the luster of pure white silk. Just before Wilbur was to be loaded into the crate, Charlotte, who had planned to stay home and weave her egg sac, announced that she had decided to go with him after all. When he learned what sort of left-over late-night feasts a rat might encounter at a fair, Templeton also vaulted into the crate. "It's hard to believe he was the runt of the litter," said Mr. Arable as Wilbur himself was loaded in. "You'll get some extra good ham and bacon, Homer, when it comes time to kill that pig." Clearly, making good at the fair was Wilbur's one hope.

When they arrived at the fair, Charlotte climbed to a post under the roof of the new pig pen. She noticed another pig on the other side of Wilbur and lowered herself down to get a closer look. This pig, a brooding, enormous animal, much bigger than Wilbur, told Charlotte that she could call him "Uncle." Throughout the day, Wilbur heard people making favorable remarks about Uncle's prodigious size.

In the meantime, Charlotte was not feeling well. "Bring me . . . a word!" she told Templeton that evening. "I shall be writing tonight for the last time." Templeton soon appeared with a newspaper clipping between his teeth. The last word Charlotte would weave for Wilbur was "HUMBLE."

The next morning, Wilbur awoke to find a weaker and somewhat shrunken Charlotte huddled overhead, with a curious object attached next to her on the ceiling. It was her egg sac. Wilbur noticed that the spider seemed downhearted. "I just don't have much pep any more," she said. "I guess I feel sad because I won't ever see my children."

Before long, the crowds had arrived at the fairgrounds for another day of games, rides, and contests. At Wilbur's pen, "everyone rejoiced to see that the miracle of the web had once again been repeated. Wilbur gazed up lovingly into their faces. He looked very humble and very grateful. Fern winked at Charlotte."

Suddenly, Avery called everyone's attention to the blue ribbon hanging from the pen next door. Uncle had already won first prize. The onlookers were deeply disappointed—until an announcement came over the loudspeaker. Mr. Zuckerman was to report to the judges' booth immediately: a special award was about to be presented. The announcer dramatically recounted the repeated miracle of the web. "Whence came this mysterious writing?" he asked, as Charlotte listened over the loudspeaker. "Not from the spider, we can rest assured of that. Spiders are very clever at weaving their webs, but needless to say spiders cannot write."

At the judges' booth, Mr. Zuckerman was handed twenty-five dollars and a medal to hang around Wilbur's neck. Both the Zuckermans and the Arables were pleased.

Back in the pen, Wilbur and Charlotte, finally alone, conversed. "Why did you do all this for me?" Wilbur asked. "I don't deserve it. I've never done anything for you." Charlotte, in her customary, loving manner, replied, "You have been my friend . . ."

". . . But you have saved me, Charlotte," said Wilbur in awe, "and I would gladly give my life for you—I really would." Charlotte then announced that she would not be returning with him to the barn. She was too weak; in a day or two she would be dead. Hearing this, Wilbur threw himself down in agony and sobbed. Then an idea struck him: if Charlotte couldn't make it back, at least he could take her children with him. He shook the sleepy Templeton—still suffering the effects of an all-night eating spree—and pleaded with him to fetch the egg sac. Of course Templeton was in no hurry to do anyone a favor—until Wilbur promised him that he would always get first pickings at the trough. Satisfied, Templeton climbed up and snipped the threads with his sharp ugly teeth and dropped the sac in front of Wilbur, who gently lapped it up and positioned it on top of his tongue; Charlotte had said the egg sac was strong and waterproof. Just as the pig was being shoved into the crate, he looked up and gave Charlotte a wink—"and she knew her children were safe." Smiling, the spider summoned all her strength to wave one of her front legs at her friend.

The next day, all alone, Charlotte died.

Wilbur watched over the egg sac through the winter. Finally, one fine spring day, hundreds of tiny spiders emerged from the sac, waving their forelegs at him. For several days they crawled around the farm, carrying their tiny draglines behind them. Then, on a warm, slightly windy day, the spiders climbed to the top of the fence and let their spinnerets form balloons. "Good-bye!" they called to Wilbur as they drifted out of sight.

Wilbur was frantic. "Come back, children!" he cried. One tiny spider turned to explain: "This is our moment for setting forth. . . . We are going out in the world to make webs for ourselves."

That afternoon, Wilbur sat staring at the dreary doorway where Charlotte's web used to be. Suddenly he heard a voice. "Salutations!" it said. There on top of the doorway were three small webs—three of Charlotte's daughters had decided to stay.

Mr. Zuckerman took very good care of Wilbur for the rest of his days. Nobody ever forgot the miracle of the web—and Wilbur never forgot Charlotte.

Commentary:

Charlotte's Web not only examines the miracle of nature through a child's imagination, it also symbolically and gracefully portrays the natural cycle of life itself. It's a book about beginnings and endings, losses and gains, childhood wishes, new friendships, and birth and death. The references to the endless succession of the seasons—especially summer passing into fall—mirror those events that children find most significant: the loss of a friend, the death of a pet—all signs pointing to an end of childhood and a journey into the ongoing, infinite cycles of adulthood.

MRS. FRISBY AND THE RATS OF NIMH

by Robert C. O'Brien, Atheneum, New York, N.Y., 1971

Type of work: Children's fantasy

Setting: A farm near the Thorn Mountains

Principal characters:

Mrs. Frisby, a loving mouse-mother of four

The Fitzgibbons, a human family of farmers

A number of animal characters: Jeremy, a friendly crow; Dragon, the Fitzgibbons' cat; Mr. Ages, a wise, kind, elderly white mouse; Nicodemus, leader of the Rats of NIMH, and the brave rat, Jonathan

Story Overview:

Mrs. Frisby lived alone with her four children in their cinderblock winter home, sunk deep into the Fitzgibbon's garden after the previous spring's planting. Her husband Jonathan had died the summer before. Widowed, Mrs. Frisby struggled on her own each day to find food for her family.

Before winter ended, her son Timothy had become ill. Throughout this particular February morning he had worsened; by now, he was delirious with fever. "Timothy must have medicine," his anxious mother decided, and she set out to consult Mr. Ages, the white mouse who had helped out when, as a baby, Timothy had been bitten by a spider.

The journey across the farmyard was always perilous. To avoid the chance of running into Dragon, the Fitzgibbons' wily cat, Mrs. Frisby took a long, circuitous route, reaching Mr. Ages home late in the day. Mr. Ages cordially invited Mrs. Frisby in and asked her to explain Timothy's symptoms. "He has pneumonia," concluded Mr. Ages. "I have some medicine that will help him. But the most important thing is to keep him warm. And he must stay in bed."

By the time Mrs. Frisby thanked Mr. Ages and rushed out with the precious medicine, it was close to sundown, so she decided to cut across the yard. Hurrying on her way, however, she came across a terrified crow who had entangled himself in a snarl of string that was caught in the fence. She could not leave him to the cat, she decided, so she stopped to free him—just in time. The crow, Jeremy, fluttered away from a pouncing Dragon, with Mrs. Frisby clinging to his back. "If the time ever comes when I can help you," said the grateful Jeremy as he dropped Mrs. Frisby at her home, "I hope you will ask me."

Just a few days later, Mrs. Frisby's worst nightmare became a reality: On a foraging trip, she overheard the Fitzgibbon family discussing spring planting plans to plow up their garden, including Mrs. Frisby's cinderblock home. Mrs. Frisby was beside herself; Timothy was still not well enough to travel! Waylaying Jeremy the crow, she asked if he knew of any solution. "I don't know . . . " he answered. "I'm sorry." But he flew her to a wise old owl in the middle of the forest, who he hoped could help her.

The pair arrived just at dusk, an owl's best time for thinking. The owl invited them into his nest. Though nervous—for owls are known to eat mice!—Mrs. Frisby, reassured by Jeremy, entered the nest. After the owl had heard the details of her situation, he at first concluded that he could not help her; when he learned that she was the widow of the distinguished Jonathan Frisby, however, his tone changed. "You must visit the rats," he told her mysteriously. "The rats on Mr. Fitzgibbon's farm are not like the rest of us . . . Go there." He then said that at the main entrance to the rats' home, under the rosebush, she must ask Justin the sentry for a rat named Nicodemus.

The next morning, Mrs. Frisby left to see the rats. The rosebush was an enormous tangle, and she had a hard time finding a way in, until she noticed a spot where the thorns had been worn off. She pushed at this spot and a door opened to a fascinating, well-built, beautiful landscape. But, Mrs. Frisby stopped in her tracks, for the huge and menacing sentry on duty was not Justin, but Brutus, and he chased the terrified mouse away. But, luckily, Mrs. Frisby fled straight into the path of her friend Mr. Ages, who was hobbling through the rosebush on an injured ankle.

Mr. Ages escorted her back to the entrance, where Justin had now joined Brutus to confront the mice. When Mr. Ages introduced Mrs. Frisby to Justin as the widow of Jonathan, she was conducted, with great respect, to meet Nicodemus.

Confused and overawed by the plush, electrically lighted rooms and corridors around her, Mrs. Frisby was left to wait for a while in the library. She sat down to practice her reading; Jonathan had taught her a little bit about books. Presently Nicodemus appeared. "Now," he said, "what is it that we can do to help you?" After hearing her predicament, Nicodemus and his advisers devised a plan for moving Mrs. Frisby's cinderblock, as the owl had proposed, to the lee side of a large rock where the plow would not touch it. The job would be hazardous, though, he warned, because of Dragon. The rats normally drugged the cat's food when they needed to work. But the hole into the kitchen near Dragon's food dish was too small for them to fit through, so Mr. Ages had been administering the drug for them; that was how he had injured his ankle on the previous night.

" . . . If you will give me the powder and show me the way, I will put it in Dragon's bowl," volunteered Mrs. Frisby bravely. Nicodemus demurred; he finally divulged that Mrs. Frisby's husband had been killed in an encounter with Dragon while attempting just that very feat. This news came as a shock to Mrs. Frisby. She had never known how her husband died—only that one night he had not returned home. She shuddered, but for the sake of Timothy she was determined to go through with the mission.

With this decided, Justin left to retrieve the sleeping powder for Dragon while Nicodemus sat down with Mrs. Frisby to tell her the story of the rats of NIMH, and of how they came to know and revere her husband.

Years before, Nicodemus had been an ordinary young sewer rat. He had led a simple life—until the day he was captured in the marketplace and carted off by humans to a tall building called the National Institute of Mental Health (NIMH). There, the animals were placed into individual cages, to be tested, poked, prodded, and injected by Dr. Shultz and his research assistants. The injections, as they slowly learned, were part of an experiment to increase the animals' intelligence; and it worked beyond the wildest dreams of the human researcher. Over time, the rats developed many refined skills, among them, the ability to read. Years later, they finally devised a plan for escaping. On the night of their perilous exodus they had been heroically aided by a white mouse from an adjacent cabinet—Jonathan Frisby.

Life became most interesting for the liberated rodents. One day they broke into a vacant estate; for eight months they camped there, reading everything they could get their paws on. Later, they happened upon a dead tinker. They put his small tools and electric motors to good use, creating an elaborate and technically advanced network of caves and tunnels under the Fitzgibbons' fields.

Life was luxurious now for the triumphant rats, but Nicodemus was uneasy. He feared that ease and complacency would ultimately lead to the demise of the rat civilization. He especially disliked the fact that, in order to procure food and materials, they were obliged to steal from the Fitzgibbons.

Finally, Nicodemus had hit upon a solution: the rats would teach themselves how to farm. They had scouted out a piece of ground, Thorn Valley, to cultivate and were prepared to migrate there, where they could live in austere but productive independence. However, as the departure date drew nearer, several of the rats defected.

Nicodemus paused in his story; by now it was time for Mrs. Frisby to tranquilize Dragon. With Justin and Mr. Ages she crept up to the house, slipped through the hole in the wall, dashed out, and dumped the prescribed powder into the dish of cat food. Before she was able to escape, however, she was snatched up—and caged—by a gleeful little Billy Fitzgibbon.

While the family dined, Mrs. Frisby listened intently from her cage to Mr. Fitzgibbon's tale of a strange occurrence he had heard about earlier that day. It seems that six or seven rats had been electrocuted at the hardware store a few days before in an attempt to steal a motor. Now the exterminators had been called in. Mrs. Frisby then heard the farmer say something about a squad of men from the Public Health office who, fearing an outbreak of rabies, had offered to remove the Fitzgibbon's rats as well.

Exterminators! Mrs. Frisby must warn the rats! She tried urgently, again and again, to lift her cage door, but she was not strong enough. All at once, Justin appeared, carrying tools to free her. Once outside, Mrs. Frisby quickly recounted all that she had heard. Then, with Justin, she hurried off to supervise the rats as they moved her cinderblock home. It was a perilous project, and Mrs. Frisby feared for Timothy's life, but the rats managed to move the house—and Timothy—to a safe location.

The next morning, Brutus appeared at the Frisby home and asked if Mrs. Frisby would come to meet with Nicodemus. There, she repeated once more what she had heard the previous evening. Immediately, Nicodemus began drawing up plans to save his rats and cover their tracks as they escaped. He was quite sure that the electrocuted rats were the defectors from his colony, and that the "Public Health Office" was more concerned with eradicating all possible traces of the secret NIMH experiments than with rabies.

To quell suspicion, it was decided that the rats must leave behind an illusion of normalcy when they evacuated the rat hole. They would methodically destroy all signs of intelligent civilization; then they would dig a false back door. After the evacuation, ten rats would be left behind as a rear guard.

The next day, Mrs. Frisby watched from her vantage point on an old hickory tree as the white "Public Health" truck rolled into the Fitzgibbons' driveway. The exterminators, seeing nothing amiss, inserted a long hose into the rat hole and placed a cage over the phony exit. Then they began to pump cyanide into the hole. Back in the blackberry bramble, at the real exit, Mrs. Frisby counted seven guard rats exiting. Only seven—not the original ten.

Then the guard rats began to dart around back and forth in and out of the trees. The exterminators were convinced that they had chased many dozens of rats out of their fully inhabited nest. As they were carrying out these diversionary tactics, Mrs. Frisby suddenly noticed an eighth rat, unseen by the men, stumble out of the hole. At the edge of the woods, he collapsed. Meanwhile, the disgruntled exterminators finally unearthed only two dead rats. But which two rats? Justin? Nicodemus? Mrs. Frisby couldn't tell; the men were blocking her view. Carefully, Mrs. Frisby climbed down the tree and ran to the fallen eighth rat. It was Brutus—and he was alive! As he revived under Mr. Ages' ministrations, he recounted how he had stumbled over another rat as he ran to escape the cyanide. Then, in the darkness, an unseen third rat had helped him struggle out to fresh air. Then, "when we got near the end . . . he gave me one last shove toward it, and then he turned back." This hero—Jonathan—had died trying to save one last fallen comrade.

And so the rats of NIMH departed; and Mrs. Frisby returned to her newly resettled home. Later in the spring, when it was sufficiently warm, she moved her family to a summer residence by the river. That first night there, she told her children the story of Jonathan and the Rats of NIMH, and about their courageous father.

Commentary:

Mrs. Frisby and the Rats of NIMH can be read and enjoyed as an adventure story, as a mystery, as a science fiction fantasy, as a protest against man's cruelty to animals—and as a telling satire against the "rat race" that so many people follow today. First published in 1971, the story has won many prestigious awards, and remains a favorite among children—and their parents.

RAMONA THE PEST

by Beverly Cleary, W. Morrow, New York, N.Y., 1968

Type of work: Humorous juvenile fiction

Setting: An elementary school somewhere in the U.S.

Principal characters:

Ramona Quimby, an imaginative, spunky kindergartner

Beezus, her know-it-all older sister

Mrs. Quimby, their mother

Howie Kemp, Ramona's annoying young neighbor—and sometime friend

Miss Binney, Ramona and Howie's kindergarten teacher

Story Overview:

"I'm not a pest," Ramona Quimby declared. "Then stop acting like a pest," replied her sister, Beezus.

It was Ramona Quimby's first day of school and, as a brand new kindergartner, she felt too grown up to tag along with her older sister. She was also reluctant to walk with her neighbor, Howie Kemp. Howie was a solid-looking boy who "never got excited" about anything. Ramona resented having to get along with Howie just as much as she resented having to "get along" with her. But they had no choice; their mothers were friends. And just now, Ramona saw Mrs. Kemp coming up the walk, with Howie and his baby sister in tow. If Ramona had to wait for them, she was afraid she would be late—and on her very first day of Kindergarten! But Ramona once again had no choice in the matter; she and her mother ended up walking with the Kemps.

After yelling and complaining all along the way that she would be late, Ramona finally made it to school—on time. Her Kindergarten teacher introduced herself as Miss Binney. "Sit here for the present," she told Ramona with a smile. Ramona sat—and her imagination ran wild with anticipation about what the "present" could be. Miss Binney must love her *best* to promise her a present! She decided she would sit *extra* still, just to be absolutely sure of receiving the gift.

As Ramona sat, she gazed over at a big girl named Susan. Ramona thought about how fun it would be to *boing* Susan's long, springy, beautiful, old-fashioned curls; but then she remembered: to get her present, she must stay in her seat.

Ramona's daydreams were interrupted when the teacher began leading the class in a new song. "Oh say can you see . . . " the song began. Ramona was confused at first about the next phrase—something to do with the "dawnzer lee light"; she finally decided that a "dawnzer" must be a special name for a lamp. Miss Binney told Ramona to stand up when she sang the "dawnzer" song, but Ramona didn't move. She knew the teacher must be testing her to see if she could really sit still for the *present*, so even when the class started playing some games, Ramona stayed put. Finally Miss Binney asked Ramona why she wasn't participating. "You told

me to sit here for the present, and I have been sitting here ever since school started," Ramona said. The teacher reddened. Then she gently explained that what she had meant was to sit still "for now." Ramona was crushed.

When the day finally came to an end, Ramona decided that her first day in Kindergarten had not turned out quite as she had wanted. But then she remembered the next day promised a new adventure: Show and Tell.

After hours of looking for something to take for Show and Tell, Ramona concluded that her doll, Chevrolet, would do. The next morning she walked outside with her Mom—and Chevrolet—to meet the Kemps. Howie had not brought anything for Show and Tell, so Ramona's mother told her to run inside and get something for him. Ramona raced in and grabbed the first toy she could find: a beat-up bunny that the cat had adopted as a "practice gopher."

At school, Ramona volunteered to be the first one up for Show and Tell. She proudly held up her doll. "I named her after my aunt's car," she said. When the class began to laugh, Ramona flushed in embarrassment. But Miss Binney said she thought Chevrolet was a lovely name. Then she called on Howie to show what he had brought. Reluctantly, he held up the bunny. The teacher told the class that the bunny's worn out condition meant that it must have received lots of love. Fascinated, Ramona thought of how the cat gripped the bunny between its teeth and battered it with its claws. Miss Binney then tied a big red ribbon around the bunny's neck.

When Howie and Ramona got home from school that day, they fought over who would keep the ribbon. Eventually they arrived at a settlement: Howie could have the ribbon if he would remove a wheel from Ramona's tricycle making it into a "bicycle"—a contraption that did indeed scoot along the ground quite well as long as Ramona remembered to lean to one side to keep the axle without a wheel from scraping the ground.

Every day at school Ramona worked on her biggest challenge: how to get Davy, the only boy in short pants, to kiss her. One day while she was routinely chasing Davy around the playground, she grabbed him by the shirt so hard that his buttons popped off. Davy avoided Ramona as much as possible from then on. This made Ramona sad—but not sad enough to stop chasing him.

Ramona's second goal in Kindergarten was to learn how to read and write. She soon learned to print all the letters in her name, and she was especially intrigued by the tail on the letter "Q," which was the first letter in her last name. She started off drawing her Q's to look like two cats, with ears and whiskers to match the tails—but she quickly erased them so Miss Binney would not be disappointed.

On the first rainy morning of the school

year, Ramona was in a bad mood. "No! I don't want to be sensible," she shouted. She refused to wear Howie's used rain boots. The tops were no longer shiny! But her mother insisted, and finally Ramona put on the brown boots and headed for Kindergarten. Sure enough, some of the boys teased her for wearing boys' boots. She hung her head—and suddenly noticed a worm wriggling in a puddle. An idea popped into Ramona's head. She picked up the worm and twisted it around her finger. "It's my engagement ring," she declared. "Who are you engaged to?" asked Ann. "I haven't decided," said Ramona.

When Ramona got home from school that afternoon, her mother told her they were going shopping for new shoes. And at the store, the shoe salesman, who knew little girls, convinced her mother that Ramona also needed a new pair of shiny red boots. Ramona "left the store so filled with joy she set her balloon free" and watched it sail triumphantly into the sky.

On her way to school the next morning, Ramona spied a big puddle of mud. Traipsing into the middle of it, she thought, would be a perfect way to try out her new boots. "Look at my elephant feet!" she called happily—only to discover that both her feet were suddenly stuck fast in the mud. Suddenly, the bell sounded for school; Ramona began to cry. Soon, Miss Binney appeared and asked Henry Huggins, the crosswalk guard, to help Ramona out of the puddle. Henry was not at all excited about this, but, stepping into the muddy water, he plucked Ramona right out of her boots and carried her to the sidewalk. Ramona cried even harder; she wanted her boots. Finally Henry consented to go back into the puddle to retrieve them. Ramona thanked the crossing guard. Then she slid a worm she had found onto her finger and said, "I'm going to marry you, Henry Huggins."

For Halloween, Ramona decided that she wanted to be the baddest witch in the world. Her mother went shopping and bought her the scariest mask Ramona had ever seen. In fact, Ramona even scared herself the first time she faced her new hooked nose and ominous teeth in the mirror before the Halloween parade. She began chasing all her classmates around the playground. "Yah! Yah!" she shrieked. "I'm the baddest witch in the world!"

Then, as Ramona giggled and screamed, she caught sight of Susan, dressed up in an apron and pantalettes like an old-fashioned girl. This time, the temptation was too strong. "I'm the baddest witch in the world!" yelled Ramona as she boinged one of Susan's curls. Susan turned and ran crying to Miss Binney; but she couldn't tell the teacher which witch on the playground had boinged her. At first Ramona was happy; but then a new thought crossed her mind: If Susan didn't know who she was, maybe no one else would know who she was in the Halloween parade—Ramona ran to the classroom and made herself a sign to carry. "Ramona Quimby," it said—and the "Q" had ears and whiskers to match the tail.

Ramona soon passed through two other firsts: her first loose tooth and her first day of walking to school by herself. Her mother had told her to leave at quarter after eight. Now

Ramona was smart enough to know that since a quarter was worth twenty-five cents, she would have to leave for school at exactly 8:25. But as she started on her way, Ramona became confused. The sidewalks were empty; no one else was walking to school. Somehow, even though she had followed her mother's instructions so carefully, she was late! But when the panicked Ramona finally raced up to the classroom door, Miss Binney was not cross. "Next time try to walk a little faster," she told Ramona with a smile.

All through the day, as Miss Binney taught the lessons, Ramona wiggled her loose tooth. When it finally came out, everyone except Susan admired the bloody hole in her mouth, and Miss Binney agreed to keep the tooth for her until after school. But Ramona was indignant at Susan's slight. She once again boinged Susan's hair during recess. "Do you think you can stop pulling Susan's hair?" asked Miss Binney. Ramona thought for a moment. Susan had tattled on her all year long; Susan always acted big. "No," Ramona told Miss Binney honestly. "I can't." Miss Binney looked surprised; but she sent Ramona home until she could refrain from pulling Susan's curls. "Ramona is a Kindergarten dropout!" gloated Beezus when she heard Ramona's report. But Ramona had another explanation for not attending school: "Miss Binney . . . doesn't want me."

One night while Beezus was reading, her mother told her to use more light. "Why don't *you* turn on the dawnzer," suggested Ramona. Her family looked puzzled. "What's a dawnzer?" asked her father. "A lamp," replied Ramona importantly. "It gives a lee light." After a moment of silence, Beezus suddenly erupted. "She—she means `The Star-Spangled Banner . . . '" gasped Ramona's big sister between snorts of laughter. Ramona ran to her room—and kicked the wall again and again with her new shoes as loud as she could.

A few days later, Howie came to deliver a letter to Ramona from Miss Binney. "Dear Ramona Q.," read the letter—and the "Q" had cat whiskers and ears to match the tail, just like Ramona's Q's—"I am sorry I forgot to give you your tooth, but the tooth fairy will understand. When are you coming back to Kindergarten?" And suddenly "Ramona did not care if the tooth fairy understood . . . Miss Binney understood and nothing else mattered."

"Tomorrow," announced Ramona Quimby joyfully, "I'm going back to Kindergarten!"

Commentary:

Beverly Cleary has written many children's books, and is a winner of the prestigious Laura Ingalls Wilder Award for books considered to have had a lasting impact on children's literature. Cleary has a way of writing that makes *any* reader young at heart. It is easy to relate to Ramona's character. As children, we all wanted to be bigger. Life was just not fair for little kids. But life *was* full of great adventures, perversely magical misunderstandings, and even more magical awakenings. As one critic aptly put it for all of us: "Ramona's adventures ring as true as the recess bell."

A DAY NO PIGS WOULD DIE

by Robert Newton Peck, Knopf, New York, N.Y., 1972

Type of work: Coming-of-age novel

Setting: A Shaker farm in Learning, Vermont; mid 1900s

Principal characters:
Robert Peck, a twelve-year-old boy
Haven Peck, Robert's father, a farmer and hog slaughterer
Lucy Peck, Robert's mother

Story Overview:

One April day during recess Robert Peck stormed out of the schoolyard and headed for a ridge near his farm. Spotting a stone, he picked it up and threw it hard, wishing he were aiming at the hateful classmate who had ridiculed him for being a Shaker. Someday, he was going to make that boy "bleed like a stuck pig," he pledged.

But just then a mournful noise interrupted Robert's fantasies of revenge. Turning around, he saw the Tanner's cow, Apron, "pumping up and down" in a bid to give birth to a calf. The head had already emerged and the calf had begun to bawl, a sound that sent Robert scrambling to Apron's side. He chased the cow through a patch of pricklers, all the while trying to get a grip on the shricking calf. "Calf," he said, "you stay up ma's hindside and you're about to choke." Finally, he removed his pants and managed to tie one of the legs around the calf's head. At last, the calf was delivered.

Then, suddenly, swaying "like she was dizzy or sick," Apron fell to one side and stopped breathing. Robert quickly opened the cow's mouth and slid his hand down her throat, where he felt an object "about apple-sized." At that point, the cow rose and lunged forward, biting him over and over again. His hand closed tight around the obstruction, he tugged unflinchingly; he had just felt the object yield when the cow gave him a frantic kick and he passed out. As he regained consciousness, Robert looked down to see the object he had pulled from Apron's throat; he was flabbergasted to find that he was holding onto a goiter.

As he walked home, the bites on Robert's arm hurt him terribly; but he "never let out a whimper"—not even while his mother stitched up his wounds. Tucked in his bed after she had finished, he delighted in his father's attention. Mr. Peck gave his son "two beads of spruce gum . . . rich and full of sappy juices," and then he bent over the boy to pull "the crazy quilt" around him. From the smell of his father's hands, Robert knew that he had been killing pigs that day. The boy, however, did not mind; it was a "smell like hard work."

The next day Robert discovered that his own hard work had won him an unexpected gift. To express his gratitude for Apron's deliverance, Mr. Tanner presented the boy with a little piglet that kicked and squealed in his arms. Robert's father wasn't certain his son should accept the offering since "it's not the Shaker Way to take frills for being neighborly." When the man insisted that the pig be received as a belated birthday gift to Robert, however, Mr. Peck relented. Robert was so excited that, just like the small pig, he himself "gave a squeal." To the boy, this little bright-eyed female seemed beautiful. "Clean white all over, with just enough pink to be sweet as candy," she was the very first thing that Robert "had ever really wanted, and owned." He named her Pinky.

Pinky followed Robert everywhere and nuzzled his boots like a cat. At his side while he worked or caught frogs, she liked to "slobber" all over him; and whenever she happened to wander away, she would run back to him like a "Fallen Angel." Even when his Aunt Matty sat him down to start tutoring him in English, Pinky was by his side. "Next time," said his aunt, "I'll teach the pig."

The Shaker Laws that set him and his family so stringently apart from their neighbors made Pinky even dearer to Robert. The Laws did not allow him to dress up or to attend baseball games on Sunday, as all his friends did; in fact, from Robert's point of view, the Laws seemed to require a life made up almost entirely of "dirt and work."

Of course, Robert's father saw the situation differently. "We live the Book of Shaker," he said. "We are not worldly people, and we suffer the less for not paining with worldly wants and wishes. I am not heartsick, because I am rich and they are poor."

His father's words confounded Robert; actually, adults in general often confounded him. One night in the midst of a thunder storm, for instance, Mrs. Hillman "from up the road" appeared, lantern in hand, at the Pecks' door, distraughtly announcing that her husband had gone to "rile" a grave. When Robert arrived with his father and Mrs. Hillman at the cemetery, they found Mr. Hillman digging up the grave of his illegitimate baby daughter, whose mother had "hung herself" after drowning the baby. Mr. Hillman was now determined to rebury the baby on "Hillman land." He would not disturb the mother's remains, he explained, but that baby girl was a Hillman, his own "soul and dust," and with the Hillmans her dust was bound to rest. Mr. Peck didn't raise his gun to threaten his neighbor. Instead, he invited him home for breakfast. Silently, Robert and his father then watched together as Mr. Hillman freed his daughter's casket from the sodden ground and tied it securely to his wagon.

This was the first of several experiences Robert was to have with death that year. Shortly after the confrontation at the cemetery, the Pecks were visited by a neighbor named Ira Long who wanted to "weasel" his dog

Hussy In order to train the dog to keep weasels away from his chickens, Mr. Long's idea was to place her in a barrel along with a weasel that Mr. Peck had captured. After this encounter the dog was quite sure to "hate weasels until her last breath." Robert observed how upset and shaky the "sweet little dog" became as Ira Long arranged her in the barrel. A moment later, Mr. Peck emptied the sack containing the weasel into the barrel, and Robert pressed down hard on the lid, which, with all the "scratching and chasing and biting" going on inside, was not an easy job. Although he had assumed the fight would prove to be "a real excitement," the whole thing suddenly struck Robert as cruel and "senseless"; suddenly he "felt the shame of being a part of it."

Abruptly, the furor in the barrel came to an end. Then, as the lid was removed, Hussy started to cry. She had killed the weasel—all that remained were "small pieces of fur, bones, and bloody meat." But when "Ira reached down to lift her out of the barrel . . . one of her front paws was chewed up so bad . . . it was nothing but a raw stump."

"Kill her," Robert cried. "She's dying." After Hussy had been delivered from her misery, the boy walked outside, dug a hole in the ground, and buried her under the timothy grass near an apple tree. "Hussy," he said after he had prayed over her, "you got more spunk in you than a lot of us menfolk have brains."

A few months later Robert was made to confront yet another death—one that caused him considerably more pain than Hussy's had. Pinky—who had won "FIRST PRIZE FOR BEST BEHAVED PIG" at the fair—turned out to be barren. After she had been bred twice without success, Pinky was deemed by Mr. Peck to be a luxury they could no longer afford; she just "ate too much to be kept as a pet." Finally, one dark day in December, the butcher said simply, "Rob, let's get it done."

Robert's father took his "sticking knife"— a short, blunt instrument with a curved blade—into the shed where Pinky was kept. Carrying the "spine saw," Robert followed after him and found the animal "curled up warm in the clean straw." Wrapping his arms around her big white neck, "smelling her good solid smell" for the last time, he squeezed his eyes shut, to keep the tears from falling.

"Help me, boy," his father said. "It's time." With every ounce of courage he could muster, Robert let go of Pinky and moved out of his father's way. Then with eyes again tightly closed, he heard his father strike her head with a crowbar. At that moment, he hated his father "for every pig he ever killed in his lifetime . . ."

Even though Pinky was still "moving, breathing" as she was dragged onto the snowy ground of the shed, Mr. Peck got right to work. Holding onto her feet to keep her from kicking, Robert watched, speechless, as his father methodically proceeded to butcher his pig. "Oh, Papa. My heart's broken," he finally began

to cry. "So is mine," his father confessed, stroking his son's face with his finger to brush away the tears. "But I'm thankful you're a man." Then Robert "kissed his hand again and again, with all its stink and fatty slime of dead pork." And, looking up, for the first time in his life he saw tears in his father's eyes.

Still later that year, Robert had one final death to face. When the first cold days had blown into Vermont that fall, his father had told the boy that this would be his "last winter." Robert had not been able to accept these words as fact, yet as winter came and went he found himself more and more apprehensive. Then one morning in May, Robert was unable to raise his silent father from bed. "I'll do the chores," Robert said quietly. " . . . You just rest." Somehow, though, in some part of him, instinctively he already knew that his father was dead.

At the funeral, Robert delivered a brief eulogy. In the hours since his father's death, he had been gratified to see the great reverence the community had shown for this stern and gentle man. Mr. Peck's neighbors and fellow butchers had come from all over the countryside to pay their respects. "There would be no work on this day," the butcher's son concluded. Surely, this was "a day no pigs would die."

Robert himself had dug a grave in the orchard where his father was laid to rest. That night Robert returned to the plot.

"There was no gravestone, no marker," in accordance with the Shaker Laws. "Goodnight, Papa," Robert said. "We had thirteen good years."

Commentary:

According to its author, Robert Peck, *A Day No Pigs Would Die* is a semi-autobiographical work. Like the main character who shares his name, the writer, born in 1928, grew up on a farm in Vermont where his father made a living butchering pigs.

To highlight the novel's theme of discovery, Peck has situated his characters in an isolated township, where, over the course of a year, Robert leaves his boyhood behind him and acquires some of the wisdom—and much of the heartbreak—of manhood. This maturity, as Robert's father sees it, entails "just doing what's got to be done." By the time Robert loses his father, he has also learned how to forgive—and even how to respect what previously has filled him with loathing. Just before Mr. Peck dies, his hated butchering tools suddenly take on a special beauty for his son: *I looked at all the handles of his tools. It was real beautiful the way they was gilded by work.*

And ultimately it is this bittersweet blend of grief, resolution, and mellowing forgiveness that will send Robert along the road to a manhood capable both of absorbing his father's rich commitment to authentic work and plainspoken, valiant acceptance, and of magnifying this legacy with new depths of awareness and compassion.

THE WITCH OF BLACKBIRD POND

by Elizabeth George Speare, Houghton Mifflin, Boston, Mass., 1958

Type of work: Juvenile historical adventure

Setting: Connecticut; 1687

Principal characters:

Katherine (Kit) Tyler, a displaced, free-thinking young woman

Nathaniel (Nat) Eaton, a handsome and roguish young seaman

John Holbrook, a somber theological student

William Ashby, the son of a wealthy landowner

Judith Wood, Kit's beautiful cousin

Mercy Wood, Kit's patient, crippled cousin

Matthew Wood, the strict Puritan patriarch of the Wood Family

Hannah Tupper, a lonely Quaker woman— the witch of Blackbird Pond

Commentary:

This work by Elizabeth Speare won a Newberry Award for the most distinguished children's book of 1959. The novel paints an accurate and colorful picture of the religious fervor that prevailed in 17th-century New England. Although they themselves were dissenters from the Church of England, the Puritans, ironically, did not readily allow others the same privilege, often persecuting or casting out Quakers for their beliefs.

With its skillful weaving of history, adventure, and romance, *Blackbird Pond* proffers a far-reaching message. The story's heroine is an open-minded, intellectual young woman who finds herself trapped in a closed society. Her rebellion against bigotry makes for reading that is at once captivating and thought-provoking.

Story Overview:

When Prudence Cruff dropped her doll overboard, Kit immediately "plunged headlong over the side" into the water. "She had the doll in her hand before her numbed mind realized that there had been a second splash." She glanced quickly around to see Nathaniel, the captain's son, swimming clumsily toward her. Kit laughed, with smooth, vigorous strokes she glided back to the ship, leaving Nat to paddle behind her. Back on board, the other passengers stared at her as if "she had sprouted a tail and fins right before their eyes." Only after Kit returned the little girl's precious toy did she realize the source of their suspicious, almost hostile expressions: How was it, that a young woman knew how to swim like that? their eyes asked silently. The only two faces in which she could find comfort were those of a young man in a black hat, whose lips twisted upward in a half-suppressed smile, and Prudence Cruff, who clutched her rescued doll and stared at Kit in adoration.

Two hours later, dressed in the green silk brought with her from her old home on a beautiful turquoise bay on Barbados, Kit glanced up to see the same half-smiling young man she had noticed earlier. He introduced himself as John Holbrook. Kit soon learned that John, like herself, was en route to Wethersfield, the home of Kit's stalwart Puritan aunt and uncle. "I trust you will be a surprise to the good people of Wethersfield," he said sarcastically. "What will they make of you, I wonder?"

Just then, Nat arrived to announce that Kit was to dine that evening with Goodwife Cruff and her family. Making a face, Kit complained that the woman would curdle her food. Nat chuckled and answered, "Tis certain she expects you will curdle hers. She has been insisting to my father that you are a witch. She says no respectable woman could keep afloat in the water like that." The "water trial" was one certain way to discern a true witch; an innocent person would sink like a stone.

In the nine days it took to complete the journey up the Connecticut River to Wethersfield, Kit observed her fellow travelers: Prudence Cruff, a miserable little wraith, seemed never to have been fed properly; Goodwife Cruff, the child's mother, was obviously a selfish and suspicious woman; and the child's father appeared for the most part spineless, although on occasion he secretly managed to slip the girl some food from his plate. And Nat Eaton was an aloof sort, busy with his rigging chores. Only John Holbrook seemed to remember that Kit even existed.

Kit and John had time to learn more about each other. John was entering theological school. Kit had been raised in Barbados by her grandfather, who had recently died, leaving her with large debts. After selling everything to meet the payments, she had bought passage to Connecticut, hoping to live with her aunt. However, when she showed up unannounced on the Wood family doorstep in Wethersfield, her aunt and uncle were surprised indeed.

Kit soon discovered that things were quite different in Wethersfield. Her Uncle Matthew, a strict Puritan, seized her seven trunks of silk dresses ad accessories and refused to allow her to unpack them. She had to borrow some drab "suitable" clothing from her cousins.

Kit found that work in the religious household was never-ending. On the day of her arrival, she carded wool with her crippled cousin Mercy, then went to stirring soap alongside her pretty cousin Judith. In carding, however, she was slow; and stirring soap made her arms tired; so Judith had to stir it herself. Later, the family found an easier job for Kit: making corn pudding—which she also ruined.

On Sunday, Kit declined to attend Meeting. She and her grandfather only went to Christmas Mass, she explained. Uncle Matthew, however, replied that she was now a member of *his* household and she would "attend Meeting like a God-fearing woman." Still, Kit managed to steal out of church to see the town, and what she saw left her aghast: a row of frame houses huddled around a small clearing, a meeting house next to a pillory, a whipping post, and stocks.

After dinner that evening, Matthew announced that William Ashby had asked permission to pay his respects to Kit. Judith, who had assumed William Ashby was interested in her, was momentarily stunned. However, she tossed her head and informed her sisters that she had changed her mind and was determined instead to marry John Holbrook. Thereafter, on Saturday evenings, William would visit Kit. He turned out be less than interesting, so Kit was thankful when John Holbrook and the family would also join them

One June morning on their way to weed the onion plot, the cousins passed the Great Meadow, "a great level sea of green, broken here and there by a solitary graceful elm." Kit felt an immense sensation of freedom there. Further on, she noticed a little house nestled in a swampy area near Blackbird Pond. Judith told her that it belonged to Hannah Tupper—a widow, who was also said to be a witch; no one ever went near her house.

At home that evening, the girls found Mercy brimming with excitement: the schoolmaster-reverend had recommended that Kit and Mercy be hired to teach school that summer. The duties involved little more than teaching the children the alphabet and how to read and write their names, but the girls welcomed the opportunity.

Over the days that followed, Mercy patiently endured teaching from the beginning readers. But, before long, Kit began making up her own verses and narratives and also had the children act out Bible stories. Unfortunately, during one of these Biblical dramatizations, the schoolmaster walked into the room. Considering such charades blasphemous, he sent the children home. Kit too fled and ran toward the Great Meadow, where she dropped into the grass, sobbing. After a few minutes, sensing that she was not alone, Kit looked up to see someone staring at her. An old woman "with short-cropped white hair and faded, almost colorless eyes set deep in an incredibly wrinkled face," quietly assured Kit that providence had sent her there; the Great Meadow always provided a cure when a heart was troubled. Suddenly, Kit realized she was gazing into the face of Hannah Tupper—the witch!

Hannah invited Kit to her home to eat and tidy herself. Kit readily accepted. Other than a cat, Hannah lived alone. She did mention occasional visits from a seafaring friend, and Kit could just imagine a white-haired, weather-beaten man "coming shyly to the door with his small treasures from some distant shore." Upon hearing a little about the old woman's life, Kit felt comfortable sharing some of her own history. And within a short hour, Hannah—though hardly saying a word—had given Kit strength to do what she needed to do.

Later, back home, Kit reported that she had apologized to the schoolmaster, begged his forgiveness, and had been granted a second chance. She also mentioned her visit with Hannah Tupper. Aunt Rachel promptly warned her that the woman was dangerous. Besides, Hannah was a Quaker, and "quakers cause trouble wherever they go." In that moment, Kit made up her mind: she would not obey her aunt and uncle; she had found a place of freedom and peace, and nothing would keep her from going back to see the avowed witch.

Two weeks passed before Kit found time to strike out toward the Great Meadow. As Kit sat beside Hannah, a shadow suddenly fell across the doorway, and there stood Nat Eaton before them. So Nat was Hannah's seafaring friend! Apparently, years ago, Hannah and Nat had also met up in the Great Meadow, and Nat had been coming ever since to do odd jobs for the widow.

Summer wore on. Kit grew restless in her teaching duties. She wished she could be more like Mercy, always patient and loving with the children. Mulling this over one day, Kit noticed a

small figure darting away from the door. Investigating, she found little Prudence Cruff hiding behind a tree. The girl hesitantly divulged that her mother had forbidden her any association with Kit; but Prudence came anyway and listened to Kit's lessons from the doorway.

After that, Kit secretly arranged to teach Prudence at the home of Hannah Tupper. At first the girl was afraid of the "witch," but soon she learned to love Hannah as much as Kit and Nat did. Prudence was a quick learner, and Kit gave her eager pupil a copy book in which Prudence was to practice copying her name.

One September day as Kit was returning from Hannah's, she met John on the road. He gravely warned her against keeping Hannah's company, and then turned his attention to Mercy. Kit was elated; everyone had assumed it was Judith who had held his interests.

Meanwhile, political controversy was taking hold of the town. Some of the citizens supported King Charles' charter; others opposed it. Mischief abounded, most of it the work of young radical seamen—including Nat. In time, Nat was apprehended, put in the stocks, and banished from the community.

A short while later, a "mysterious fever" struck the town. Rumors quickly spread: The witch had caused this epidemic! Kit hurried to the widow's cottage—barely before a mob arrived to burn the house to the ground—and hid Hannah in the swamp. Then spying the *Dolphin*, Nat's father's ship, anchored nearby, she swam out and enlisted help to bring the old woman to safety.

This was just the beginning of Kit's troubles. The next morning, Kit, too, was arrested. Goodwife Cruff had found Prudence's copy book in which she had practiced writing her name. Since Goodwife was convinced the child was stupid, she surmised that Kit had placed a curse on her child.

The trial convened the next day. Witnesses came forth one after another with all manner of claims against Kit. At the height of the hearing, however, Nat and Prudence entered the courtroom to offer their testimonies. The magistrate took the child on his lap and asked her to read from the Bible; then he requested that she write her name. To her father's amazement, Prudence performed perfectly. At once, Cruff turned in anger on his wife—and dropped the charges of witchcraft against Kit. But Nat, still banished from the community, once again left town—for good, Kit thought regretfully.

On the day of the first Autumn snowfall, William came to visit Kit. Before he left, the two reconciled, awkwardly agreeing that they were terribly mismatched. Then as Winter came and went, Judith and William saw more and more of each other.

In April, two marriages were announced: John to Mercy, and Judith to William. Kit silently made her own plans; she would return to Barbados as soon as warmer weather came. But on the second day of May, a trim little sailing vessel arrived at the wharf. As Kit watched, a seaman stood up: it was Nat.

This new ship—named the *Witch*—was his own, he announced. And when Kit asked if she could tour the craft, Nat smiled and replied, "When I take you on board the *Witch*, it's going to be for keeps."

SING DOWN THE MOON

by Scott O'Dell, Dell Publishing Co., New York, N.Y., 1970

Type of Work: Young adult historical novel

Setting: Northeastern Arizona and New Mexico; the 1860s

Principal characters:
Bright Morning, a fourteen-year-old Navaho girl
Tall Boy, a young Navaho warrior
Various members of Bright Morning's family and tribe

Story Overview:

The first day of Spring, "the day the waters came," had finally arrived, and Bright Morning's mother would once more allow her to tend the sheep. Not since she had deserted the flock during a thunderstorm the previous year had Bright Morning been entrusted to herd the sheep up the canyon.

The girl reached the fields of Canyon de Chelly early, well before her friends White Deer and Running Bird came with their flocks. The others, seeing Bright Morning among the sheep, teased her about the young warrior Tall Boy, whose parents wanted her as their daughter-in-law. Healthy and industrious, still Bright Morning was not as pretty as the other girls in the village, and many of the villagers thought Tall Boy's parents only had an eye for her family's sheep. Bright Morning ignored their taunts, simply pointing out to White Deer, "Three of your sheep have strayed," and to Running Bird, "One of yours is eating poison weed."

The next day the young warriors of the village went out on a raiding party against the Ute tribe, long-time enemies of the Navaho. Tall Boy—a name he himself assumed after tracking and killing a brown bear—proudly led the way on his white pony. Bright Morning's mother, detesting the haughtiness of his ways, said, "I hope that he does not kill another bear. If he does he will call himself Very Tall Boy and we will have much trouble with him." As Tall Boy crossed the river, he turned and raised his hand to Bright Morning. She waved back, wishing "for his sake . . . he would kill another bear."

While the three girls grazed their flocks later that day, Running Bird watched as a line of ten mounted white soldiers moved towards the village. The Navahos called them "Long Knives" for the bayonets on the end of their rifles. Arriving amongst the small gathering of hogans, one of the Long Knives disappeared into the dwelling of Old Bear. A long time passed before the Long Knife emerged from the hogan and rode away with his companions. Word quickly spread that the Long Knives had come to threaten them with destruction if the peace was not kept; if the warring continued, they "would come back and burn the houses and kill everyone in the village." Bright Morning hoped the soldiers would never hear about Tall Boy's latest raid on the Utes.

As she tended her flock early the next day, Bright Morning gazed contentedly at the ten sheep her mother had given her and dreamed of how the sheep might multiply. Caught up in her happy daydream, she did not notice the approach of two horsemen until her black dog began barking at them. Too late she comprehended that the men were Spanish slave hunters. The Spaniards closed in and easily caught Bright Morning and Running Bird. "We will not harm you," one of the Spaniards, an ugly scar on his cheek, said. "You will like the place you are going. Do not try to flee."

For four days the slavers and their captives rode, traveling at night and sleeping during the day. On the fourth night, the small band approached the dim lights of a town, obviously a white man's village. There the Spaniards separated, each taking one of the girls with him.

Bright Morning was taken to the last house on the street and sold to a young Spanish woman who already had another Indian girl-slave, Rosita. Rosita appeared happy; she smiled and talked cheerfully with Bright Morning as the woman and slaver haggled over price. Bright Morning, however, resolved never to smile or work cheerfully while in this place.

Three days later, the Senora of the house bought Bright Morning two dresses and a pair of red shoes. Staring at the strange apparel, Bright Morning vowed not to wear them for long; as soon as she could find where Running Bird had been taken, they "would steal away and take the road to home."

The next day Bright Morning met a Nez Perce girl at the market. This girl whispered, "There is a baile (dance) at your house tonight. My Senora is sending me to help you get the house ready . . . Your friend lives in the second house near the market. My name is Nehana." At the baile that night, Nehana sidled over to Bright Morning. "In ten days, at the church," she whispered. Then, in an instant, she turned and vanished. Bright Morning hardly slept that night.

On the tenth day, Bright Morning appeared at the church as planned—accompanied by the Senora and Rosita. Catching Bright Morning's eye as they passed, all Nehana could do was hold up one finger. Bright Morning knew that the signal meant to meet her there the following night.

After supper the next evening, Bright Morning feigned sickness and went up to her room. She quickly packed some supplies and clambered down the wall to the street below. Nehana and Running Bird were waiting for her at the church. Taking three horses, the girls rode away towards Canyon de Chelly.

Halfway home, two horsemen stepped out of the trees and shouted a single word in Navaho. Bright Morning responded, recognizing Tall Boy's voice. Tall Boy was shocked to see her, but with no time to speak, began leading them back home. Hours later, however, three Spaniards caught up with them, demanding the return of their horses. Tall Boy remained silent. When one of the Spaniards made a move for his rifle, Tall Boy rammed him through with his lance. The other Spaniards ran to the trees, but one turned and fired his pistol, hitting Tall Boy in the arm. The Navahos bolted away from the scene and soon found themselves back in Canyon de Chelly. Tall Boy's right arm, however, would never serve him again.

The next winter, three Long Knives entered the village and posted a message on a tree. "People of the Navaho Tribe are commanded to take their goods and leave Canyon de Chelly," it read.

Two days later a large group of Long Knives was seen approaching. The villagers hastily gathered food and blankets and, sweeping away their tracks behind them, headed into the canyons nearby. The soldiers entered the village and set up camp. The next morning, the villagers awoke to a staggering sight: their hogans were being burned to the ground. "They have learned we are camped here," Bright Morning's father lamented. "They do not want to climb to attack us. It is easier to wait there by the river until we starve."

Over the next weeks, Old Bear and others died of cold and hunger. Finally, Bright Morning's father ruled that the villagers must go down. Tall Boy made a lance that he could throw with one hand; though ashamed of his useless arm, he was still a warrior. He would stand and fight.

When the haggard tribe, consisting of some two dozen men, women and children, reached the canyon floor, the soldiers rode by, unaware of the Navahos' presence. Tall Boy hurled his lance, but his crooked left arm could not send it straight; it missed its mark, landing at the Long Knives' feet. Tall Boy fell back into the arms of his tribe, no longer a warrior, but a "boy," crushed and beaten, who flees for his life." The soldiers quickly surrounded the band and herded them south. "Like sheep before the shepherd, we went without a sound."

Soon they met up with other refugees; it seemed as if the whole Indian nation was being driven south. Bright Morning's father asked a Long Knife where they were going. Pointing southward, the soldier simply said, "Fort Sumner."

Life was miserable on the trail towards the fort. Tall Boy said nothing as he trudged along, wearing the same, steady, humiliated scowl he had taken on after his failed attack. His people were being herded like animals—and he could do nothing for them. Bright Morning's father tried to cheer the family, saying, "The soldiers tell me we are going to a place of running water and deep grass. Cast your eyes around; you will see many people sitting beside their fires. They are hungry but not starving. They are unhappy, yet they are alive." But Bright Morning's mother responded, "We are walking to our deaths. The old die now. The young die later. But we all die."

The old and sick perished rapidly. "In the daytime flocks of buzzards followed us and at dusk coyotes sat on the hills and howled." Spring arrived before the survivors reached Fort Sumner, a garrison situated in the middle of Bosque Redondo—"Round Forest"—a gray, forsaken "flat bottomland covered with brush." Bosque Redondo was a place of sorrow. The mixed and sometimes hostile Indian tribes were almost entirely dependent on the white soldiers. The women could no longer feed their children, relying on rations of flour brought by the Long Knives. The men, no longer brave warriors, grew idle, talking only of how the white man had driven them into the desert either to watch them die or to kill them outright.

Amid the hardships, Tall Boy once more joined with the tribe in its customary, day-to-day living. Finally accepted by Bright Morning's mother, the two young Navahos married in the fall and moved into their own hut nearby.

The next winter was difficult, and Bright Morning witnessed the famine and death of many of her people. She would soon give birth, but her child would not be born in Bosque Redondo, she decreed.

Bright Morning began to tell Tall Boy of her nightly dreams, dreams of Canyon de Chelly, of her sheep wandering, unattended. She must return there, she insisted. At first, Tall Boy grew irritated at her foolish talk; what she was suggesting was futile. But he soon was to decide differently.

While gathering firewood far out in the desert, an Apache warrior accused Tall Boy of stealing wood from Apache lands. With his one good arm Tall Boy struck down his attacker. Later that night two soldiers came and took him to the fort prison. Not until spring had come did Tall Boy appear, quietly entering the hut. "We go now," he said to Bright Morning; the guards soon would discover his absence. Gathering the blankets and food that Bright Morning had prepared in anticipation of such an escape, they rode for six nights, hiding during the day. Bright Morning bravely bore their son during their journey.

Finally, Tall Boy pointed out the tall mountains of Canyon de Chelly, teasing Bright Morning that he had returned only because he was tired of hearing about sheep. "If there is one left it will be shaggy like a buffalo," he prophesied, "and so wild you will have to catch it with a trap." But as they neared the mouth of the canyon, Bright Morning spied a shaggy ewe followed a small lamb. Before moving away, both ewe and lamb allowed Bright Morning and her newborn son to pet them. Then, as Tall Boy readied a cave suitable for shelter, he waved her home. Yes, turning from the sheep that would forever be hers, Bright Morning knew she was finally home.

Commentary:

Scott O'Dell's *Sing Down the Moon* portrays a small segment of Navaho Indian life in the 1860s, as seen through the eyes of a youthful Navaho girl. The story focuses particularly on a tragic event in American history, the "Long Walk," the forced migration of Navahos from their original homelands onto desert reservations. The United States Army under Kit Carson drove the Navaho nation 300 miles to Fort Sumner and held them there until 1868. Told in a stark, spontaneous vernacular, *Sing Down the Moon* captures the harsh reality of the journey, and the conspicuous change that came upon the oppressed Navaho nation.

ZEELY

by Virginia Hamilton, Collier Books, New York, N.Y., 1967

Type of work: Coming-of-age novel

Setting: Rural Ohio, mid-20th century

Principal characters:

Elizabeth Perry, a girl who reinvents herself as "Geeder"

John Perry, her brother, whom she renames "Toeboy"

Uncle Ross, their uncle, a farm owner

Nat Tayber, Uncle Ross' hog-raising tenant farmer

Zeely Tayber, Tayber's hauntingly beautiful daughter

Story Overview:

"Aren't train stations grand?" Elizabeth Perry exclaimed as she studied the graceful pillars and the immense, elegant windows of the depot. But a moment later the inventive eleven-year-old was jerked from her reverie as their train pulled into the station. Her parents reminded John to obey his older sister, then they ushered the two children aboard the train.

Elizabeth would miss her parents for the next few months, but she did not mind saying good-bye; she and John were off on a great adventure. They would spend the entire summer on their Uncle Ross's farm. It wasn't the farm—which she barely remembered—that excited Elizabeth so much; it was the fact that she would be doing something different. The city where she lived had begun to weary her.

Suddenly, a marvelous idea occurred to her: she and John would change their names for the summer. "From now on," she announced in her usual bossy way, "you are to call yourself Toeboy—understand?" This struck Elizabeth as the perfect name for John since he loved to go barefoot on the farm. She then decreed that she would be known as "Geeder." Horses answered to "Gee," she explained, and, as she boasted to her brother, "I bet I can call a mare to me even better than Uncle Ross!"

The next morning, Uncle Ross met them at the station, as planned. "I'm Toeboy!" his nephew called out to him. "And I'm Geeder," his niece shouted. "New names for a new summer," Uncle Ross grinned. "I like that!" He was such a warm-hearted man that the children immediately felt comfortable with him, even though it had been a long time since they had seen him.

Geeder and Toeboy spent part of that first day re-exploring the farmhouse, with its old-fashioned pump-room, well stocked pantry, and lovely parlor, where photographs of their ancestors adorned the walls. Later, they ambled around the farm, reacquainting themselves with the sycamore bordered pond, marvelling over the tenant farmer's "prize razorback hogs," and discovering a nearby road that led into town. Geeder decided to rename the town "Crystal." "If you stand on the road," she explained condescendingly, "you can probably see the beginning, the middle, and the end of it, just the way you can see through a piece of glass." But what, she wondered, could she name the road? "Leadback Road!" she determined after a moment, because

the road would always lead them back to the farm. "Crystal has a crack in it, Toeboy," she envisaged, "and the crack is Leadback Road!"

That night, Geeder and Toeboy camped out under the stars on the farmhouse lawn. Toeboy had arranged his sheets "beneath a sprawling lilac bush," but now he wanted to move next to his sister, whose improvised bed lay closer to the road. "Just better stay where you are," Geeder warned. "Late at night in the country, night travellers walk along dark roads." "What kind of things are they?" Toeboy wondered nervously. After some consideration, he decided to stay safe under the lilacs. Delighted to have spooked her little brother, Geeder drowsily searched the sky for comets.

She was just drifting into sleep, when she suddenly roused with a start: "Something tall and white was moving down the road." Whatever it was, it seemed to be headless and armless—and "moving with it was something that squeaked ominously." Finally the figure passed by, out of sight, and Geeder fell back into a fitful sleep.

Shortly after they woke up on the lawn the next morning, Geeder and Toeboy had their first glimpse of their uncle's tenant farmer—Nat Tayber. Actually, the image of Mr. Tayber didn't make much of an impression on them; it was impossible to focus on anything but the girl who walked with him—his teenage daughter Zeely.

"Zeely Tayber was more than six and a half feet tall, thin and deeply dark as a pole of Ceylon ebony. She wore a long smock that reached her ankles. Her arms, hands, and feet were bare, and her thin, oblong head didn't seem to fit quite right on her shoulders." Transfixed, Geeder stared in wonder at Zeely's high cheekbones and mysterious eyes. "The face was the most beautiful she'd ever seen."

The next morning, Uncle Ross offered little to satisfy their curiosity about the Taybers. "Mr. Tayber and his daughter live to themselves," he said simply. "They stay aloof from the whole town."

Now Geeder's fascination with Zeely intensified. Why didn't the beautiful young woman have friends? Why was she so quiet? Why didn't her father's hogs bother her? As the days passed, Geeder's thoughts turned more and more to Zeely. Toeboy befriended some neighborhood children, but Geeder avoided them, preferring to go off by herself and fantasize about the enigmatic girl.

One day when she and Toeboy were supposed to be piling up old magazines for Uncle Ross, Geeder—distracted as usual—sat down and began leafing through one of them. "I knew it all the time! I knew it!" she suddenly burst out: she had found a picture of a queen of the Watusi tribe who looked exactly like Zeely. "There isn't any doubt that Zeely's a queen," she announced. "The picture is proof." Uncle Ross tried gently to correct her. "You may have discovered the people Zeely is descended from," he said, "but I can't see that that's going to make her a queen." But Geeder knew otherwise: Zeely was unquestionably a queen.

How Geeder wished she could look like Zeely! However, no matter how hard she tried, she could not elongate her neck and arms, nor grow taller. She could adorn herself with exotic beads, though, and, on the night of the harvest bonfire, that's just what she did.

"You can take turns wearing my necklaces," she told the other girls gathered around the bonfire. Then she began to talk about Zeely; solemnly she proclaimed her to be a Watusi queen. For a while the children listened, but then they got up and started to dance. Without saying good-bye, Geeder took back her necklaces and left. Well, she reminded herself, at least she could look forward to seeing Zeely the next day while the Taybers moved their hogs to Red Barn, a livestock "clearing house."

That night, once again Geeder and Toeboy slept out under the stars. As Toeboy, still half watching for night travelers, tossed and turned on the ground, a white, regally graceful shape drifted quietly through the shadows down Leadback Road. Toeboy, dumfounded, looked on as his sister slept.

When they woke up the next morning, Geeder waved off her brother's attempts to talk. "Toeboy, it's begun!" she cut him off. Nat Tayber had come into view, prodding his hogs with a pole. Far behind them, Zeely gracefully moved in the morning mist, wearing her long, white smock and carrying a pail of feed for the animals. They were on their way to Red Barn. As the brother and sister ran to catch up with the Taybers, Toeboy finally managed to tell Geeder he'd seen Zeely walking alone the night before. "That wasn't Zeely Tayber," Geeder exclaimed. "That was a night traveller!" Frightened, the boy lagged behind as they continued on down the road.

"I don't *like* it here," Toeboy said when they entered town, "and I don't want to see those animals hurt." Indeed, Nat Tayber was beating the hogs fiercely with his poles. "Zeely won't let them get hurt," said Geeder calmly. Suddenly, however, an enormous sow fell, frothing and grunting as though injured. When she saw Nat Tayber approaching the sow with his stick poised, Geeder raced straight into the line of hogs toward Zeely—"who moved to shield Geeder from the hogs." Breathlessly Geeder explained that the sow was hurt. At this, Zeely walked quickly over to her father and wrestled the pole from his hand, then tended to the wounded sow. Squatting down beside her, Geeder held the feed pail for the older girl. Their work done, silently, Zeely got up and headed toward Red Barn. "I helped her," Geeder thought excitedly on the way back to the farm. "I knew she'd want me to."

A few days later, Zeely came to the farm to tell Uncle Ross she wanted to talk to Geeder in the nearby catalpa forest. Filled with a mixture of dread and delirious excitement, Geeder waited among the trees to see "Miss Zeely" again.

At last Zeely approached. "Please follow me," she told Geeder, leading her through the maze of trees. The girls stopped in a clearing and sat down. For awhile, they talked casually. Geeder was stunned to learn that Zeely had come from Canada. Then, abruptly, Zeely revealed that she knew Geeder had said she was a queen.

Embarrassed, Geeder cried out, "I didn't mean anything bad!"

"You are very much like I was at your age," Zeely smiled. She, too, had made up stories and avoided other children. To please her shy daughter, Zeely's mother had made the Watusi robes she now wore. But then the unthinkable had happened: Zeely's beloved mother died. Just before her death, however, she had told her daughter a wonderful story about "a young woman who waited for a message" to "tell her who she was and what she was to do."

Listening to the tale, Geeder was confused at first. But then Zeely continued with another revelation: she did not particularly like being so tall or so "different," she said; nor did she enjoy always smelling of hogs. Over the years, however, she had made peace with herself. "I stopped making up tales a long time ago," she said, "and now I am myself."

"Myself," Geeder repeated. Stroking the girl's hair, Zeely told her, "You have a fine way of dreaming."

That night Geeder came down to dinner wearing a "nice" dress, one that, as Geeder, she had never worn; only Elizabeth wore that dress. As they ate, she relived her meeting with Zeely for Toeboy and Uncle Ross. "There's not another thing in the world Zeely Tayber could be but a queen," Geeder concluded: not a queen with "kingdoms and servants," but rather a "queen when you think how Miss Zeely is." When they had finished dinner, Geeder went back upstairs and gazed at the sky. Yes, Zeely had been the night traveller. Looking at the evening star, Geeder imagined that it was Zeely, and that it would always be there in the sky. Geeder was hungry—had Uncle Ross saved her a sweet potato?

Commentary:

Virginia Hamilton, born in 1936, has published numerous fictional and non-fictional works since her first book, Zeely. She says, however, that she retains a "special feeling" for Zeely, which has drawn on so many of the author's own interests and experiences. Springing out of an abiding curiosity about her own African-American heritage and about African history in general, the novel emphasizes the imaginative power of storytelling which has played such a vital role in defining ethnicity both in Africa and America.

Hamilton credits the oral tradition as an impetus for her own writing: "I am a teller of tales," she states, "in part, because of the informal way I learned from Mother and her relatives for passing the time . . . and for putting their own flesh and blood in the proper perspective."

Similarly, both Geeder and Zeely use tales. As a child, Geeder, however, starts out by creating tales that distance herself from the reality of her own being. In contrast, the very wise Zeely comes to recognize that the true power of imagination resides in its ability to expand true character and nobility. With great compassion for her young friend, Zeely encourages Geeder to rediscover and embrace Elizabeth, whom Geeder—through her insight and inventiveness—has helped to come of age.

SOUNDER

by William H. Armstrong (illustrated by James Barkley), Harper & Row, New York, N.Y., 1969

Type of work: Juvenile humanistic classic

Setting: 19th-century American South

Principal characters:
Sounder, a loyal coon dog
Boy, a determined, dignified black boy, the oldest of three siblings
Father, a quiet, powerful man, Sounder's master
Mother, a stern, hardworking, nurturing woman

Story Overview:

The boy stood on the porch with his father gazing out on the cold October night. The only light came from their own cabin. The white man who owned the fields sprinkled the negroes' cabins far apart, "like flyspecks on a whitewashed ceiling."

The boy didn't go to school anymore. After walking eight miles every morning and night in the cold, he had become sick and had to give it up. But at least he had Sounder, the faithful coon hound.

The old dog's ability to hunt was very valuable to the family. However, it was the dog's voice that was truly priceless. A stranger hearing his bark might have thought it sounded like the bark of six dogs in one place, but neighbors knew it was Sounder.

The hunting was bad that year, and the family often went hungry. Each evening, the boy sat up with his mother for a while, trying to ease the loneliness that set in at night when his father was gone. He was never afraid when his father was there.

Besides having to endure the feelings of isolation, the boy wished he could learn to read. He knew if he had a book he could teach himself—and that with a book he wouldn't feel so lonesome.

One morning, the boy awoke to the deliciously rare scent of sausage and ham. His mother was humming to herself, something she only did when she was worried, like when she was rocking a sick child.

After the third night of feasting, the boy stood at the door and watched as the sheriff and his two deputies approached the cabin. There were two things he could smell a mile away, the sheriff sneered: "One's a ham cookin' and the other's a thievin' nigger." The lawmen clicked a pair of handcuffs on the father's wrists.

Sounder, sensing trouble, sprang toward the cabin. The boy held the dog back while the deputies brought his father out. When the sheriff ordered one of them to "chain him up," the boy thought he was talking about the dog—until he saw one of the men snap a set of manacles onto his father's wrists. As the wagon started down the road, the boy lost his grip on the dog, and Sounder darted away, devoutly chasing after his master. One of the deputies, seeing the dog sprinting toward them, leveled his

shotgun at the dog. He fired and Sounder fell to the ground in a limp mass. The boy, as much as he wanted to cry, left the hound there and began gathering wood as his mother had asked. Suddenly, a loud yelp came from the road and the boy jumped to his feet, racing toward the noise. Sounder was trying to get up, but kept falling. "The blast had torn off the whole side of his head and shoulder." The badly injured dog finally made it to the porch and crawled underneath. His mother called the boy. "Come in, child. He is only dying," she explained carefully. "Creatures like to die alone. They like to crawl away where nobody can find them . . . He didn't want to be shot down like a dog in the road. Some creatures are like people," she said.

At home, the boy sat in quiet dejection by his mother and listened for a sound—any sign of life—under the porch. After awhile, the boy went outside and put his own supper in Sounder's dish and slid it under the house.

The next morning, the boy's mother struck out for town to sell walnut kernels. As she began walking down the road, the boy heard her humming a familiar melody:

You gotta walk that lonesome valley,
you gotta walk it by yourself,
Ain't nobody else gonna walk it for you.

When she was out of sight, the boy went outside to dig a grave for his beloved Sounder. "He felt like crying, but he didn't. Crying would only bother him. He would have his hands full . . . carrying Sounder's body. His nose would start dripping and be powerful troublesome because he wouldn't have a free hand to wipe it."

The boy crawled under the porch, but he couldn't find the dog. He scanned the property, traipsing as far away from the house and his younger siblings as he dared, tears streaking down his dusty face. Still, Sounder was nowhere to be seen.

Late that evening, his mother arrived home; she had taken the ham back to the owner.

When the boy reported that he couldn't locate Sounder under the porch, his mother suggested that the dog had gone into the forest to heal. In the forest, she explained, he could chew on oak leaves to draw out the poisons of infection.

But after several weeks had passed and the boy still hadn't found Sounder, his mother took him aside and explained that he had just learned an important lesson of life: "Some people is born to keep, some is born to lose. We was born to lose, I reckon."

On Christmas day, the boy set out for town with a cake for his father. When he reached the jail, a red-faced guard let him in, but demanded to see inside the box. Picking up the cake, the guard crumbled it onto the floor, saying he was just looking for a hacksaw or a file. Instantly, the boy felt an uncontrollable hatred for the man. How he wished he could see the guard chained up, like a bull he had once seen, shackled so a doctor could vaccinate him; when the needle had barely pierced the bull's neck, it had lunged forward and choked itself to death. The boy could just imagine the cruel guard crumpling to the floor in just such a bloody heap.

Making his way down the echoing hall to his father's cell, the boy once more rehearsed what he was going to say. His mother had carefully coached him to act "perkish" so he wouldn't "grieve" his father. But when he entered the cell and handed over the crumbled cake, the boy could only ramble on about Sounder; and, before he knew it, visiting time was over. He *had* grieved his father after all. When he returned home, he told his mother that his father had asked not to send him to visit anymore.

The next morning, the boy awoke to a familiar whine coming from outside the cabin door. He ran to open it, and "there on the cabin porch, on three legs, stood the living skeleton of what had once been a mighty coon hound." One eye was gone and one ear was just a stub; he couldn't support his weight on his one shoulder, so, when he moved at all, he limped on three legs. He didn't bark anymore, he just whined—but he was alive!

Then his mother came home one day with the awful news that her husband had been sentenced to hard labor. She didn't even know where he had been sent. The boy was getting old enough now to journey away from home, she said sadly. His mission would be to call on every prison work-site he found, and ask about his father.

The boy set out, searching. The days stretched into months, and the months into years. After every journey, the boy would return home with the sad news that his father was nowhere to be found. On one of his journey's however, the boy found a tattered book in a trash can. The kindly local school teacher invited the boy to stay in his cabin while the boy attended school, in exchange for help with the chores.

When the boy returned home to tell his mother, she thought this bit of fortune might be a sign and encouraged him to go. The boy left, taking only his tattered book.

In the summers, the boy would return home to do his father's work in the fields so the cabin rent could be paid. Frequently, after he finished his work, the boy would read to his brothers and sister.

One blistering August afternoon, the boy and his mother, sitting on the porch, spotted a figure on the road coming slowly toward them. Suddenly, Sounder tore off down the road at coon hunting speed, faster than he had moved in years; and he barked, his familiar vigorous bark that echoed across the hills. The dog's master, such as he was, had come home. Half

his body had been paralyzed by a dynamite blast, he dragged his bent leg behind him, and his arm dangled at his side. His mouth was even disfigured. He had been told that he was going to die, but he swore he would return home first.

Life didn't change much after that. For the remainder of the summer the boy continued helping his father, then he went back to school. In October, he returned again for a few days to prepare the farm for winter.

During this visit, his father was unusually spirited, and one night he took Sounder off into the woods to hunt. Limping beside one other headed into the pine woods, they looked as identical as a man and dog could look. And as they went, Mother "took up her singing where she had left off":

. . . Ain't nobody else gonna walk it for you,
You gotta walk it by yourself.

As dawn approached, Sounder returned, alone, scratching at the door. Following the dog's lead, the boy was brought to the foot of a tree. There his father sat, motionless; he could not be awakened.

The boy returned to the cabin with the news. After a long silence, his mother finally spoke. "When life is so tiresome," she sighed, "there ain't no peace like the greatest peace— the peace of the Lord's hand holding you."

Before the boy departed for school again, he dug a hole next to his father's grave for Sounder. "It'll be ready if the ground freezes," he had said. "He'll be gone before I come home again."

"And the boy was right. Two weeks before he came home for Christmas, Sounder crawled under the cabin and died." Somehow, the boy was glad. He had read in the book with the torn cover the thought, "Only the unwise think that what has changed is dead." Now, he understood what it meant.

Years later, walking the earth as a man, it would all sweep back over him, again and again, like an echo on the wind . . . A harvest moon would cast shadows forever of a man walking upright, his dog bouncing after him. And the quiet of the night would fill and echo again with the deep voice of Sounder, the great coon dog."

Commentary:

Sounder is a poignant tale of understated significance. The characters' namelessness brilliantly lends itself to sharpen the focus on details. Names are unimportant in the plot; without them—and without diminishing the dignity or individuality of each person—the story has a universal appeal.

The work is both poignant and understated. Amid the near-encyclopedic background of prejudice and oppression, we witness a wonderful, contrasting portrayal of a man and his dog, each mirroring the other's pain. Caught in the middle of this drama is a boy, whose life quickly unfolds in a bittersweet mix of misery, hatred, growth, love, and acceptance.

THE SHORT STORIES OF BRETE HARTE

(taken from *The Short Stories of Brete Harte*, The Modern Library, New York, N.Y., 1947)

Through his string of gamblers, prostitutes, miners, outlaws, and other Old West eccentrics, Brete Harte (1836 - 1902) presents a realistic glimpse into the hardened and often bizarre characters that went west hoping to line their pockets with gold.

The Luck of Roaring Camp

Men by the thousands migrated to the isolated mining camps of the California Sierras in the 1850s to escape their pasts or seek their fortunes in gold. One such camp—named for its inhabitants' unruly behavior—was called Roaring Camp. Roaring Camp also included two female residents: one, an ass named Jinny, the other, Cherokee Sal, a pregnant prostitute.

By and by, Sal went into labor, and all the men—either because any one of them could have fathered the child or because a birth had never occurred in camp—gathered outside her cabin. One of the men, a "prominent citizen" called Kentuck, nominated Stumpy to assist Sal in birthing the child. Stumpy's "qualification" was that he was a notorious bigamist; he had more "experience" in esoteric matters like women giving birth. So Stumpy went into the cabin as rest of the camp "sat down outside," awaiting "the issue."

While they waited, the men placed bets on the child's gender, its complexion, and even whether mother and child would survive the birth. Before long they heard a "sharp, querulous cry," and it seemed that all "Nature had stopped to listen." Their joy was dampened, however, by the news that Sal had died.

Sadness gave way to confusion: What would they do with the orphaned boy? After much debate, the men decided that the he should be raised in Roaring Camp rather than sent to a "respectable" town, and that another woman like Sal—the only kind of woman likely to accept an invitation to the camp—should definitely not be invited to mother the child. Finally they decided that Stumpy should assume responsibility for the infant's care.

No one was certain whether it was Stumpy's practiced hand at raising children or the ass's milk, but, alas, the boy "thrived." When he was a month old, someone suggested he should be named and christened. John Oakhurst, an itinerant gambler, remarked that the child "had brought 'the luck' to Roaring Camp." This notion greatly appealed to the men, and so they christened the babe "Thomas Luck," variously calling him "Tommy Luck," "Tommy," or simply "The Luck."

The Luck's influence on Roaring Camp was immediate and profound. Within a year, the camp had earned a singular reputation throughout the Sierras. One of the stage coach drivers boasted that the men in Roaring Camp grew flowers around their houses and bathed twice a day. "But," the driver cautioned, "they're mighty rough on strangers, and they worship an Ingin baby."

The camp's prosperity multiplied, the men claimed, because The Luck was with them. On fine summer days, Stumpy would bring Tommy to the gulch where the men panned for gold and lay him

on a blanket spread over pine boughs. Sometimes, the men brought "him a cluster of wild honeysuckles, azaleas, or painted blossoms of Las Mariposas." It seemed in that summer idyll of 1850 that all of nature was The Luck's "nurse and playfellow."

In contrast, however, the winter of 1851 was terribly unkind to Roaring Camp. That spring, when the winter snowpack finally began to melt, the Sierras flooded and the gulch was quickly "transformed into a tumultuous water course." One night, the water overflowed the banks and nearly all of Roaring Camp was swept away.

The next morning, it was discovered that Stumpy's cabin was gone, Stumpy had drowned, and The Luck of Roaring Camp had disappeared. Later that day, Kentuck trod into camp, The Luck of Roaring Camp dead in his arms. Referring to the tiny figure, Kentuck said, "he's a takin' me with him. Tell the boys I've got The Luck with me now."

The Outcasts of Poker Flat

From the very moment Mr. John Oakhurst of stepped into the street that morning, he knew that something in Poker Flat's "moral atmosphere" felt palpably different. "I reckon they're after somebody," Mr. Oakhurst guessed, and "likely it's me."

Oakhurst's gambler's instincts were right on both accounts. Poker Flat, maturing and developing respectable middle-class overtones, had formed a vigilante committee to rid itself of morally "objectionable characters." And Oakhurst, it turned out, was high on the committee's list, as were two prostitutes, the Duchess and Mother Shipton, and a known drunk and suspected thief named Uncle Billy. The vigilante committee escorted Oakhurst and his fellow reprobates to the edge of town and ordered them, "at the peril of their lives," not to return.

The nearest settlement—a mining camp called Sandy Bar—lay "a day's severe travel" over the mountains. Sandy Bar had not yet undergone the "regenerating influences" of Poker Flat, so the exiles decided to travel there. By midday, however, the Duchess tired and told her companions that she would go no farther that day. Oakhurst objected: they had completed "scarcely half the journey." Moreover, winter was fast approaching, and they were not properly provisioned with food and fuel; they should not be delayed by bad weather.

But Oakhurst's arguments had no effect on the others. Their supply of liquor seemed sufficient, and they expected an easy journey to Sandy Bar the next day.

Before long, everyone but Oakhurst was drunk. Gazing at his "recumbent fellow exiles," he felt, for the first time in his gambling career, oppressed by "his pariah trade." The sounds of an approaching rider interrupted his gloomy ruminations. It was Tom Simson, an "innocent" from Sandy Bar who several months earlier had lost forty dollars to Oakhurst in a poker game. Afterward, Oakhurst had taken Tom aside, advised the young man that he was a lousy gambler, and returned his money. Since that day, Simson had become Oakhurst's "devoted slave."

Tom, it turned out, was running away from

Sandy Bar toward Poker Flat. He had eloped with Piney Woods, "a stout, comely damsel of fifteen." Concerned for the couple's safety, Oakhurst tried to persuade them not to delay their journey. He and his companions, he warned Tom, had neither supplies "nor means of making camp." Tom replied that he had enough provisions for everyone and had seen a ruined cabin that the group could repair with pine boughs for protection from the elements. The women could stay inside and the men could bed down outside. Despite Oakhurst's protests, the camp of outcasts gained two more members.

Awakening before dawn the next day, Oakhurst discovered that snow had fallen during the night—and that Uncle Billy had slipped away with Tom's mules and most of the food. Only enough remained to last, maybe, ten days.

The storm continued, and for the next week the group's meager rations continued to dwindle. They passed their time with accordion music and recitations from the *Iliad*. Mother Shipton was the first to die; she had starved herself and given nearly all her rations to Piney. "Give 'em to the child," Mother Shipton told Oakhurst just before she drifted off.

After Mother Shipton's burial, Oakhurst suggested to Tom that the only way to save Piney was to summon help from Poker Flat. There was, Oakhurst said, only "one chance in a hundred" Tom would succeed. Tom agreed to go, and after he and Piney "parted with a long embrace," he set out. Oakhurst intended to accompany Tom as far as the canyon and then return to stay with the two women.

Night came and went, but Oakhurst did not reappear. When the Duchess noticed a few days' worth of firewood "piled beside the hut," she knew that Oakhurst deliberately did not return, in order to spare the little food that remained.

The storm grew worse. The second night after the men left, wind blew the pine boughs off the roof and snow cascaded into the cabin. The next morning, the women "found themselves unable to feed the fire." The Duchess desperately asked Piney if she could pray; when Piney replied she could not, the Duchess cradled Piney's head on her shoulder, and the two of them fell asleep.

Two days later, the rescue party from Poker Flat reached the cabin. The Duchess and Piney were "still locked in each other's arms." Not far from the cabin, the rescuers found Oakhurst seated beneath a large tree, "a bullet in his heart" and a Derringer in his hand. Stuck to the tree above his head with a Bowie knife, they found a note written on the two of clubs. "Beneath this tree lies the body of John Oakhurst," it read, "who struck a streak of bad luck on the 23d of November 1850, and handed in his checks on the 7th of December, 1850."

An Ingenue of the Sierras

Before the stage had crossed Galloper's Ridge, Yuba Bill, riding shotgun, put out the coach's sidelights. He had heard that the Ramon Martinez gang would be lying in wait. If the stage could make it over Galloper's without being seen, they would be safe.

The coach passed silently on, beyond the brush where Bill had expected the gang and presumably out of danger. Bill still felt troubled; and before the coach made its next rest stop, he learned from a muleskinner that the coach had been clearly visible as it passed over Galloper's Ridge. It seems one of the passengers, the muleskinner continued, had hung a white handkerchief out the window, which was clearly visible in the moonlight.

There was only one passenger aboard the stage that neither Bill nor the driver knew: a girl whom Judge Thompson—another passenger—had befriended on the trip. She seemed like a "prairie blossom," the Judge said, as "simple and guileless as a child." Bill, however, was dubious, and decided to speak with her himself.

He found his opportunity when he saw one of the station helpers roughly handle the girl's trunk. "Look out, will yer!" Bill cried, grabbing the trunk from the man. But in his rush to help, Bill dropped the trunk and the lid sprang open. Inside, Bill caught sight of a large "quantity of white lace-edged feminine apparel, of an apparently superior quality."

Bill apologized to the girl and promised that the stage company would replace her trunk. During their conversation, she admitted that her real name, listed on the manifesto as Miss Mullins, was actually Miss Hemmings. She traveled incognito, she explained, because her father—the notorious miser Eli Hemmings—forbade her to marry her sweetheart, Charley Byng, a poor debt collector. She had signaled Charley with her handkerchief when the stage crossed Galloper's Ridge.

"What firm does he collect for?" the Judge asked. Miss Hemmings answered that it was a Spanish firm called Ramon Martinez! Bill took the Judge aside to discuss the matter privately. A talk with Charley Byng was in order, they determined. If Charley assured them that he would renounce the Martinez gang, then they would help the young couple get married and see them off to Sacramento where they might begin a new life.

Byng's "criminal antecedents" were soon forgotten and the couple was married, and everyone drank a toast to their happiness before putting them on the Sacramento stage. Yuba Bill felt a special sense of "satisfaction." His enthusiasm was soon stifled, however, when he learned that he had been duped by that ingenue Miss Hemmings—and her *husband* "Charley Byng."

Martinez, it turned out, had "lately been robbing ordinary passengers' trunks." One trunk that he had stolen contained, like Miss Hemmings' trunk, "a lot o' woman's wedding things." Moreover, Eli Hemmings was a "confirmed old bachelor" who had never had a daughter. Finally, the man calling himself "Charley Byng" fit the description of Ramon Martinez to a tee.

Bill felt momentarily depressed. Then "a gleam of mirth came into his gloomy eyes" and he laughed. "But I got even after all!" he grinned. Martinez was now "tied up to that lying little she-devil," Bill gloated, "hard and fast!"

Commentary:

Except among aficionados of "Western" writers, Brete Harte's literary production has been largely ignored and forgotten by twentieth-century readers. Regardless of whether we read Harte's stories for their literary value or for their historical interest, his work rewards our curiosity and is deserving of our attention.

THE OX-BOW INCIDENT

by
William Van Tilburg Clark
(1889-1971)

Type of work. Western fiction and social drama

Setting: Bridger's Wells; 1885

Principal characters:
Art Croft, a free-lance ranch hand
Gil Carter, Art's cowboy partner
Jeff Farnley, a hand working on the vast Harley Drew ranch
Major Tetley, a powerful rancher
Gerald, Tetley's sensitive son
Arthur Davies, a sensible old storekeeper

Story Overview:

It was early afternoon when ranch hands Art Croft and Gil Carter descended the last mountain pass and gazed across the valley to the little frontier town of Bridger's Wells. The spring roundup had not worked out all the tension of their long, cooped-up winter months, and as the two cowboys approached Canby's Saloon, they looked forward to whiskey, cards—and maybe some female companionship.

At first, the banter at Canby's was light and easy-going. As the afternoon progressed, however, and other riders and ranch hands filtered into the saloon, Croft and Gil began to hear stories of cattle rustlers plaguing the valley's ranchers. Croft and Gil grew quiet and concerned; as newcomers, they had not yet earned the town's complete trust. Suspicious glances from several men at the bar deepened their uneasy feelings.

After some whiskey-drinking, a game of poker soon erupted into a fight over Gil's unusual run of good luck. Gil and Croft were standing at a side-entry to the barroom deciding on the best way to appease the aggrieved parties, when a rider abruptly galloped up to the saloon with news that rustlers had stolen some of Harley Drew's cattle—and murdered one of Drew's hands, Larry Kinkaid.

The messenger had scarcely finished speaking when Farnley, Kinkaid's best friend and one of Drew's best ranch hands, left the saloon and mounted his horse, intent on riding off to find and lynch the murderer. Someone else suggested forming a posse; but Arthur Davies, the town's old storekeeper, and Reverend Osgood, the Baptist preacher, intervened. They urged Farnley and the others to leave things in the hands of the sheriff and Judge Tyler, and to let the law take its course.

Farnley would not be swayed; but the others, faced with the possible prospect of hunting down and hanging some of their own townsmen, were hesitant at first to join him. Then one man in the crowd broke the impasse. Judge Tyler's justice was too slow, he complained. At his rousing demand to "Stretch the bastards," everyone—including Croft and Gil—gave their approval to appoint a lynching posse.

A number of men went home to get guns, provisions, ropes, and horses. Only a few stayed at Canby's, where Davies and Osgood again tried to convince them that lynching was tantamount to murder. The law, however slow, he insisted, expressed the conscience of society, and to disregard it was to disregard conscience. Croft could see that Davies had a point, and finally he agreed to accompany Davies' young assistant, Joyce, to summon Judge Tyler.

Before long, a heavy wind and a damp chill blew hard to the east, promising a late snowstorm. This seemed to temper the mob's enthusiasm.

Meanwhile, when Croft and Joyce arrived at the Judge's house, they found him talking with Deputy Mapes, the acting sheriff while Sheriff Risley was out of town. He would meet with the posse, he said; he wanted the murderer captured and brought in for trial, not lynched. But Mapes, eager to use his temporary power, stepped in to announce he intended to deputize the whole group and take over leadership, whether the Judge liked it or not. While the two argued, Croft and Joyce returned to the saloon.

Back at the saloon, the crowd had swelled to some twenty men, but they still seemed lukewarm about their task. Then, as the men milled about, Ma Grier, the owner of the town boardinghouse, approached. Ma was a strong, aggressive woman—more comfortable on a horse than in petticoats. Her appearance cheered the men; here, finally, was a leader to head them up. Then the rumor circulated that Major Tetley, an ex-Confederate calvary officer and a powerful man in Bridger's Wells, was also on his way. "I knew," Croft later recalled, "if Tetley came he'd take over." Something about Tetley's demeanor commanded respect and obedience; the posse, thought Croft, would do Tetley's bidding.

Finally, Judge Tyler arrived. But the Judge's long-winded warnings to bring the murderer back alive only primed the crowd further for a lynching. "It's all been said for you, Tyler," bellowed the town bum, his courage bolstered by ample quantities of whiskey. "All we want's your blessing." However, the Judge's questioning of Greene, the rider who had brought news of the murder, revealed something new: Greene had not actually *seen* Kinkaid's body; he had heard the news from someone else and then ridden straight to town. Again, enthusiasm among the assembled men began to waver.

Within minutes, however, Major Tetley made his appearance—with news that one of his ranch hands had seen three strangers driving forty head of Drew's cattle up Bridger's Pass on the west end of the valley. Again the mood shifted. The men were fortified; the raiding murderers were not anyone they knew. Over Tyler's continued objections, Mapes deputized the posse, and the group set out after their quarry.

As the company ascended the pass, night fell, bringing with it the snowstorm that had threatened earlier. Blinded by the storm, the men heard a stagecoach approaching from the opposite direction. As they rode up to stop the coach and get information, the shotgun rider, thinking the posse was a gang of robbers, fired. Croft, shot in the shoulder, soon grew weak and dizzy from loss of blood, but he refused to return to town; and news from the stagecoach's driver reinforced his determination. Just over the crest of the mountain, the driver had seen two, possibly three men sitting around a campfire in a small draw. The posse hurried on, everyone taking sips of whiskey to ward off the cold and feed their courage. Midnight approached.

Suddenly, during a brief lull in the storm, several of the riders spotted a campfire. From the Ox-Bow, a mountain valley at the top of the pass, they could hear the mooing of cattle. Tetley and his posse had soon surrounded the three sleeping figures at the campfire and disarmed them.

Tetley directed the interrogation. Donald Martin, a dark-complected young man, insisted there was some mistake; he had bought the cattle earlier from Harley Drew, but Drew had not yet given him a bill of sale. What's more, he claimed he and his family had just moved into a neighboring town, Pike's Hole.

Martin's companions, a Mexican called Juan Martinez and a feeble-minded older cow-puncher, Alva Hardwick, confirmed his story, but the posse remained unmoved. Growing more and more desperate, Martin finally demanded that he and his associates be taken to Pike's Hole where his story could be verified, or back to Bridger's Wells for trial. "I won't talk without a proper hearing," he said. "Suit yourself, son," Tetley responded. "This is all the hearing you're likely to get short of the last judgement."

Of all those in the posse, only Arthur Davies and Tetley's youngest son Gerald believed Martin. Among the others, any lingering doubts were removed when Kinkaid's pearl-handled revolver was found in Martinez's belongings. Goaded on by Mapes and Farnley, the posse determined that the three would be hanged at daylight.

That night, Martin was permitted to write a last letter to his wife; he gave it to Davies to deliver.

As dawn approached, Davies made one final plea for the lives of the captives. When the decision was put to a vote, however, only three men—including Gerald—stood with Davies. The prisoners would hang.

Tetley directed the lynching—as he had the "trial"—and appointed two of the mob, Ma Grier and Farnley, to whip the horses out from under the condemned men. As the third executioner he chose Gerald—here was a task that might finally make a man of the boy.

At Tetley's gunshot, Ma and Farnley whipped their horses sharply; both the Mexican and the old man died instantly. But Gerald did not cut Martin's horse; instead he let it walk slowly out from under the rider. When Martin began to squirm and kick, Farnley had to finish the job with a bullet. Embarrassed by the bungled execution, Tetley struck his son with the butt of his pistol. Then the posse pulled out of the Ox-Bow, driving the cattle ahead of them.

Sheriff Risley was first to ride up to meet them—closely followed by Judge Tyler, Harley Drew—and another familiar rider. "Jesus," Gil exclaimed, "it's Kinkaid!" And there, sure enough, sat Larry Kinkaid, head bandaged, but very much alive!

"I knew it didn't feel right. I knew we should wait," muttered Gil. "Everybody would hang it on Tetley now," Croft mused to himself. But Risley made no charges of murder. Instead he asked for ten volunteers to resume the search for the real rustlers. Everyone who could ride volunteered. Except for a few.

While Croft recuperated from his wound in a room above the saloon, and Gil steeped his conscience in whiskey, young Gerald Tetley went quietly home and hanged himself in his father's barn. And later, when he learned of his son's suicide, Major Tetley threw himself on his cavalry sword.

Davies, the storekeeper, meanwhile, wondered uneasily to the convalescing Croft if he could have spoken up more forcefully to prevent the lynching. "None of us would have stood there and seen them hang if we'd known," moaned Croft, half conscious. "But that was just the point," Davies lamented. "Nobody had known *anything* for sure. And yet, nobody had found the courage to confront Tetley. Everyone was guilty—but no one was guilty.

Gil, drunk but steady, came up to escort his wounded friend down to the bar for a couple of drinks. "I'll be glad to get out of here," Gil muttered, as the two returned to their room above the saloon.

Commentary:

Although *The Ox-Bow Incident* is written with all the trappings of a classic Western, there are no white and black hats in Clark's riveting psychological study—no good guy leading a blazing shootout against the bad guy and then, when the smoke clears, riding off into the sunset. Instead, the first-person narrative draws us directly into the experience of the mob-posse as their emotions shift from doubt, anger and stubbornness through pity and revulsion, and then, in the final scenes, to fear, remorse, and denial.

"The book was written in 1937 and `38," Clark later explained. " . . . it was a kind of American Nazism that I was talking about . . . that ever-present element in any society which can always be led . . . to use authoritarian methods to oppose authoritarian methods . . . What I wanted to say was, it can happen here . . . "

And, indeed, we leave the book convinced that an "Ox-bow Incident" could and *can* happen here; it can happen anyplace where anger and outrage prevail over reason and law.

DEATH COMES FOR THE ARCHBISHOP

by
Willa Cather
(1876 - 1947)

Type of work: Historical/religious fiction

Setting: Southwestern United States; late 1800s

Principal characters:
Father Jean Latour, a Catholic missionary and Vicar Apostolic of New Mexico
Father Joseph Vaillant, his friend and fellow priest

Commentary:

Willa Cather's sensitive and poignant chronicle of the missionary labors of two priests blends the beautiful landscape of the southwest with the historical careers of these two men. Eking out a meager existence, they become one with the land and varied cultures of the region. The novel is filled with folkloric miracles, rituals, and legends, the mainstays of peasant culture.

The challenges Latour and Vaillant face are tough. They contend with both heat and desert isolation and discover along the way a singular dedication to God and an abiding joy in the poor Mexican and Indian people they serve. Lengthy digressions into theology sometimes weaken plot development, but Cather's descriptive skills vividly evoke the spirit and beauty of the Old West.

Story Overview:

Father Latour plodded through the bleak red hillocks that marched on towards the horizon, each a seeming replica of the other. The oppressive heat and the lack of food weakened him. He paused to reflect on what had brought him to this desolate region.

A year ago he had been sent to assume the New Mexican bishopric, along with Father Vaillant, a compatriot French-Catholic priest and long-time friend. Now, returning to Santa Fe from Mexico City, where he had gone to obtain papers documenting his priesthood authority, he had become lost in the maze of red hills, grey cedar trees and mule paths that zigzagged across the main trail.

Ahead Latour spied a gaunt cedar, split in the center to form a cross. He knelt by the tree and prayed for deliverance. As he resumed his journey across the parched sand, his mare, stumbling under his weight, suddenly became attentive. Her nostrils flared and she trotted vigorously forward. A stream of blue water suddenly appeared, flowing undisturbed through the yellow and red of the desert. Along its banks were lush green trees, and —in answer to his prayer— a small village.

The overjoyed villagers, who had not seen a priest for years, welcomed and revived Latour. Aptly, they called their community Hidden Water. On the following day, the priest performed long-overdue marriages and baptisms before continuing along the trail to Santa Fe.

Home at last, the enormity of Latour's assignment overwhelmed him: build churches throughout the Southwest; preach the word of God in the scattered Mexican and Navajo villages; bring order to an untamed land. Addressing Vaillant, he said, "I wish I knew how far this is. Does anyone know the extent of this Diocese or of this territory?" Vaillant answered, "For the present Santa Fe is the diocese. Establish order at home. That is far enough."

Latour and Vaillant discussed rumors of a recent miracle. A local farmer had beheld a vision of the Virgin Mary, who bade him to gather wild roses in his ragged mantle. Then he asked him to tell his priests that a church and shrine must be built on the spot where the roses had been plucked. The village priests had doubted the man's story; nevertheless, when he opened his mantle to pour out a stream of roses, they beheld a beautiful image of Mary painted on the tattered material. "Doctrine is well enough for the wise," Vaillant noted, "but a miracle is something we can hold in our hands and love." Latour added, "Where there is great love there are always miracles . . . "

The self-absorbed prelates who had preceded Latour and Vaillant had built up magnificent churches and assumed lavish lifestyles, exacting a high toll on the people. Through their loving and unselfish ministry, however, the two new priests quickly won the love of their parishioners. Of the two, Latour was the more astute, studious, and meditative. Vaillant, in contrast, was a country-born paysan, simple and homely. A wart graced his nose, straw-colored hair poked raggedly from his head, and he suffered frequently from ill health. Yet, his fervor for the gospel knew no bounds; in his pure crusade to serve God's children, he quickly adapted himself to the rigors and customs of his office. Still, both priests—not out of self-indulgence but out of necessity—became beggars for the cause, because Rome lent them no financial support.

Father Vaillant was particularly adept at financial maneuverings. During one stay in Albuquerque to perform marriages and baptisms, Vaillant was entertained by a wealthy rancher named Lujon. Forbearing a direct request for money, Vaillant eyed two beige mules and asked Lujon for one of them. The following day, as he prepared to depart, he told Lujon, "I could not go about on a mule like this while the Bishop rides a common hack." At this, the rancher offered him a fine horse, but Vaillant demurred: "I will raise the price of marriages until I can afford both mules," he hinted. Then he suggested, "If I were a rich ranchero like you, I would do a splendid thing. I would furnish the two mounts that are to carry the word of God about this heathen country. Every time you think of these mules, you will feel pride in your good deed." Unable to argue, the rancher wistfully acquiesced, and Vaillant returned with two choice mules, Contento and Angelica. The animals served Vaillant and the Bishop well and faithfully for many years.

Everywhere they went, adoration greeted the two priests. Women kissed the Bishop's Episcopal ring and townsfolk decorated their streets with colorful streamers whenever the churchmen visited. Latour "had already learned that with these people religion was necessarily theatrical." Even death was viewed as "a dramatic climax, when the soul passed in full consciousness through a lowly door to an unimaginable scene." In fact, when a death was imminent, it was the neighbors' custom to gather to watch the process, and to capture the last words of the dying. To the neat, convent-trained Latour, these practices seemed excessive; to the passionate Vaillant they were part and parcel of the culture introduced by the first monks who had entered the area with Coronado's Spanish conquistadors over three hundred years earlier.

After subduing the stigma caused by the excesses of past prelates, Latour next confronted the diocese's old order, an order headed by the veteran priest Antonio Jose Martinez. Martinez ignored the orthodox practices of celibacy and abstinence from gluttony; in short, he abused the people's trust in him as a religious leader. Changing this order would not prove to be an easy matter, as the Bishop discovered when he rode into Taos to investigate the situation. "I shall reform these practices as rapidly as possible," Latour warned Martinez. "I hope it will be but a short time until there is not a priest left who does not keep all of his vows." Martinez answered scornfully, "It will keep you busy Bishop. Rome has no authority here . . . I will organize my own church. I will have the people. You are among barbarous people my Frenchman . . . " Martinez's prophecies proved self-fulfilling. He soon apostatized and formed his own sect, taking many of the old flock with him. Taos' remaining Indians and Mexicans were left confused, often attending both churches. The schism did not heal until Martinez's death.

Latour was repeatedly discouraged by the desecrations that went on in his parishes. "One night, his prayers were empty words that brought him no refreshment. His soul had become a barren field. His work seemed superficial. His diocese was still a heathen country. The Indians travelled their road of fear and darkness. The Mexicans were children who played with their religion." But in spite of the sluggishness of the work, Latour and Vaillant gained the trust of the many peons who had previously been mistreated.

Latour knew they must find a way to proselytize the outer fringes of the diocese, but did not want to sever himself from Vaillant. One day, Vaillant, himself filled with the desire to spread the gospel, said, "I must hunt for utterly lost Catholics who have never seen a priest. They are full of faith and have nothing to feed on but the most mistaken superstition. They remember their prayers all wrong." With great misgivings, Latour dispatched Vaillant to the Arizona district, where his ministrations proved very successful. Vaillant had a way with the peons; he conformed to their ways. "To communicate with peons, he was quite willing to speak like a peon."

After Vaillant opened the Arizona territory, he was recalled to head the Colorado sector, an area populated by gold-hungry prospectors. Vaillant was reluctant to go, but "it was the discipline of his life to break ties; to say farewell and move on into the unknown." Vaillant, however, accustomed to the charity of the Mexican, Navajo and Hopi peoples, was now exposed to hardened and greedy white settlers who were there for one reason only: to make a profit. In order to procure supplies and materials for his parish, Vaillant traveled south. As usual, the poverty-stricken peasants, who loved him, opened wide their hearts and their purses.

Years passed. Vaillant, now Bishop of Colorado, returned to Santa Fe to attend Bishop Latour's ordination as Archbishop. As the two old friends conversed after the ceremonies, Latour confessed his admiration of Vaillant. "You are a better man than I," he said. "You have been a great harvester of souls, without pride, without shame. I have always been a little cold. If hereafter we have stars in our crowns, yours will be a constellation." The devoted priests again went their separate ways, in the service of God and man. In this life, they never were to meet again.

Before he died, Archbishop Latour was obsessed by one great ambition: to leave a permanent mark of his religion on the landscape. It was time to construct a Romanesque cathedral in Santa Fe. To do this required a great amount of money, but Latour felt the exorbitant costs were justifiable. Over his last years, offerings poured in from adobe-dwelling peasants and wealthy ranchers alike. When the church was completed, Latour had a fine orchard and garden carved into its landscape, which he enjoyed for his remaining days. Although he had always pictured himself as retiring to live out his last days in his own green gardens of France, now, as the end drew near, he found that he could not leave the land where he had given his all.

Latour had witnessed many changes in the American West: the conquering of the Navajos and Apaches; the advent of the railroad; the mass farming of the western plains; the sacrifice of many missionaries. Greater than these, Latour remarked, "I have lived to see two great wrongs righted. I have seen the end of black slavery and I have seen the Navajos restored to their own country."

On this day, as Latour lay on his deathbed, the church and yard were filled with parishioners, who had come to pray for him. Many of his final thoughts turned to Vaillant and himself in their youth. He recalled with a smile that Vaillant, who had died some years earlier, had at first been unwilling to come to America and join the order.

Finally, in the hush of twilight, the Cathedral bell tolled, and the villagers fell to their knees in homage to the great man who had served them so well. Death had come for their beloved Archbishop.

SHANE

by
Jack Schaefer
(1907 - 1991)

Type of work: Classic Western novel

Setting: Wyoming; 1889

Principal characters:
> *Joe Starrett*, a cowpuncher turned farmer
> *Marian Starrett*, his wife
> *Bob Starrett*, their young son, and narrator of the story
> *Shane*, an honorable but mysterious drifter
> *Fletcher*, a powerful and pushy cattle rancher

Story Overview:

Shane rode into our valley in the summer of '89. When he stopped to ask for water, I could tell there was something different about him. I guess Father could too, because he asked the stranger to stay for dinner, and then for the night. After I was in bed that night, I heard Father and Mother discussing Shane, who was sleeping in the barn. Mother was worried; she thought Shane was a dangerous man—and Father agreed. "But not to us, my dear," he added quietly.

Next morning we had rain, so Father persuaded Shane to stay over another day. Father seemed to see something in Shane that he liked and trusted. After the storm, Father showed Shane all around the farm, including the big burl oak stump that he had been working to uproot for some time. (Whenever Father was upset, we would hear him chopping at the roots of that hard old stump.)

Later that day, a peddler named Ledyard came by with a cultivator that Father had been wanting. When Ledyard asked $110 for it, Shane spoke up to say he had seen one like it in Cheyenne for $60. At this, Ledyard flushed; he asked Father if he trusted this tramp and his opinions. When Father replied that he would trust Shane any day, Ledyard started in on the drifter, calling him names. Then suddenly, in mid-sentence, he stopped and turned a deathly pale. I glanced back at Shane; he stood staring quietly at Ledyard, his hands clenched at his sides and a dangerous, ice-cold look in his eye. Ledyard quickly dickered a deal with Father and rode off.

Afterward, Shane disappeared, but we soon heard chopping coming form the direction of the old stump. Father told Shane he didn't need to do that, but Shane only replied, "A man has to pay his debts." I started to object that Shane didn't owe us anything for meals and bed, but Father stopped me. "He doesn't mean meals," he said. Then Father got another axe and started hacking away at a root on the opposite side.

The two of them worked on those roots all day. Finally, at just about dusk, they got them all cut. Then, their backs straining, they eased the giant stump out of the hole. A pleased look passed between them. Suddenly, Mother screamed and ran toward the house—her apple pie was burning!

While the menfolk and I ate dinner, Mother bustled around working on another pie. When the pie was finally baked and served, Father remarked on how good it tasted, and Shane, between bites, also mumbled out a compliment: It was the best tree root he had ever eaten, he said. After a pause,

they all burst out laughing, Mother included. Maybe my *parents* understood Shane, but I sure didn't.

Next morning, Father flat out asked Shane if he was on the run from anything. "Not in the way you mean," Shane replied. Satisfied with the answer, Father invited our new friend to stay and help get the farm ready for winter. We had tried to hire help from time to time, but every one of our men had been run off by cowhands from the Fletcher ranch. Strangely, it wasn't until Father described how Fletcher was trying to ruin the farmers in our valley to provide his cattle more rangeland, that Shane decided to stay. But the powerful cattleman was off on business; for the time being, anyway, the family wouldn't have to fret about Fletcher.

Shane pitched right in; he was plenty rugged and willing, though not much for farming. Once I asked Father if he could beat Shane in a fight. His reply revealed the depth of the respect that, in just a few weeks, had been cultivated between the two men. "If I had to, I might do it," replied Father. "But, by Godfrey, I'd hate to try it. Some men just plain have dynamite in them, and he's one. I'll tell you though, I've never met a man I'd rather have more on my side in any kind of trouble."

That summer was the best summer of my life. Between Father, Shane and me, we extended the corral, enlarged the herd, cut and stacked the hay, and got lots of other things done. Something troubled me, though: Shane never carried a gun. This was rare in our times, and it seemed even more amazing when, one day, I found his obviously well-cared-for pistol stowed with his other goods in the barn.

On one occasion, Shane saw me playing with an old broken six-shooter. He stopped to give me some pointers on how to use it. Then he added, "Listen, Bob. A gun is just a tool. No better and no worse than any other tool—a shovel or an axe or a saddle or a stove or anything. Think of it that way. A gun is as good—and as bad—as the man who carries it. Remember that."

When summer ended, Fletcher returned to the valley, a sizeable cattle contract in his pocket, and demanded that his herds get the run of the valley. He offered to pay the farmers for any improvements they had put in, but he wanted them off the land. The farmers met to discuss the situation. Father pointed out that Fletcher's next move would likely be to try to run Shane off.

Over the next weeks, Shane was challenged to fight several times by Fletcher's main hired hand, Chris. Amid taunts, he refused all dares—until one day he turned around and pummeled the bully into submission.

For a time again we had peace in the valley. But one day, in town to help pick up supplies, I watched five of Fletcher's men enter the saloon behind Shane and light into him with their fists. Shane knocked two of them down, but then the other three piled on and held him while Morgan, the biggest of the bunch, lit into him, one blow after another. All of a sudden Father burst into the saloon, Mother close behind. With a look of contempt in his eye, Father picked up the man holding Shane's left arm and threw him clear across the room. Then, while Shane turned his fury on the other cowboy who had been holding him, Father went after Morgan, knocking him down. He was going to do more, but Shane stopped him—Morgan was his, he said. Father ordered Mother and me to leave, but Mother firmly replied that Shane was family—and we were staying.

Even though Morgan was much bigger than Shane, Shane beat him badly. After the fight, several of the farmers offered to pay for the damages to the saloon. It looked like maybe they were beginning to believe that times might be changing, and that maybe Fletcher couldn't drive them from the land after all.

Back at home, Mother doctored Shane's and ather's wounds. "Did ever a woman have two such men?" Her pride was obvious—but there was something more than that in back of her words.

After that, thing were quiet again for a while—but not peaceful. Shane and Father kept their eyes and ears open, waiting for more trouble. First we heard that Fletcher was back in town, along with a gunman named Stark Wilson. And later that very day came the news that Wilson had picked a gunfight with one of the farmers and killed him.

The panicked farmers held another meeting at our house. Shane assured them that none of them had anything to worry about; Fletcher's next move would be against one man only—that was Joe Starret, the strongest farmer in the valley . . . my Father.

Shane was right. Not long after that meeting, Fletcher rode up to our farmhouse with Wilson and two other men. He started right off with an offer to buy the farm; Father and Shane could even stay on as ranch hands, he said. Father refused. Then Fletcher offered even more money—and ordered Father to come into town that night to bring him an answer. Before the men left, Wilson managed to throw an insult at Mother, and both Father and Shane started forward in anger. But Mother diffused the trouble. "Both of you would have acted like fools just because he said that about me," she chided. "I'll have you two know that if it's got to be done, I can take as much as you can."

Father was convinced that his answer to Fletcher—"No deal"—would inevitably lead to a gunfight. All day, we sat and brooded. Finally Father broke the silence. He expected to be shot, he told us matter-of-factly, but he still thought he could survive long enough to kill Wilson. Then, glancing over at Shane, he added, "It helps a man to know that if anything happens to him, his family will be in better hands than his own."

Shane responded to this by jumping up and striding to the barn. "Shane's got his gun!" I shouted as I saw him walking back. But Father was against anything like that; he appreciated the gesture, but it was his fight, he said, not Shane's. Besides, Shane obviously had some old conflicts of his own to resolve. Shane didn't argue. He just drew his gun, struck Father over the head with it, watched him fall, and then walked away to go out and saddle up his horse. Without hesitation, I started out ahead of Shane on foot, racing towards town, anxious to see him in action.

As Shane entered the saloon, he took in the scene. There was Wilson, but Fletcher was missing. Leveling his words at Wilson, Shane made it clear that the gunfighter would have to face him, not Father. Wilson drew for his gun. Shane fired, shattering Wilson's shoulder with a slug; but Wilson snatched the six-shooter into his other hand and raised it again, trying to squeeze the trigger—and Shane struck him dead with a second shot.

Then a third shot range out—and I noticed a bloodstain begin to spread on Shane's stomach. Suddenly, he spun and fired once more—this time at Fletcher, who had been hiding on the balcony. Fletcher toppled over the rail onto the floor below.

"I expect that finishes it," Shane declared, reloading his gun, rubbing hand across his wound, and heading for his horse. Then it dawned on me: Shane was leaving! I ran after him, an ache greater than I could bear welling up inside me. As I hid my face in his horse's flank, he said, "A man is what he is, Bob, and there's no breaking the mold. I tried that and I've lost. But I reckon it was in the cards from the moment I saw a freckled kid on a rail up the road there and a real man behind him, the kind that could back him . . . " Then he tenderly added, "Go home to your mother and father. Grow up straight and strong and take care of them . . . There's only one more thing that I can do for them." With that, he rode away.

At home, Father was clearly expecting to hear that Shane was dead. But even after learning that Shane had left town alive, all that night Father fretted. In the morning, he announced that we would have to move; he just couldn't stand staying on there with memories of Shane. But Mother pointed out that the memories were all good ones, and that if we moved we would be giving up everything Shane had fought for. Then she challenged Father to pull out even one of the corral posts that Shane had set. Of course, he couldn't—and a new look of understanding and hope crossed his face. "He's all around us and in us, and he always will be . . . " Mother said. "We have roots here we can never tear loose."

Commentary:

Shane, first published in 1949, serves up many of the classic ingredients of a vintage Western: the lone white hat stoically facing off against black-hat bullies at the appointed shootout; the triumph of law and order; family solidarity over rampant, uncaring individuals; and the laconic hero riding off from the land he has tamed into the sunset—still alone and untamed himself.

But *Shane* is an unusual Western in that the story focuses on people rather than action. Shane, Mother, Father . . . they call up refreshing reminders of a romantic, bygone era. And because they are never painted larger than life, Schaefer's heroes remain *real* heroes. They face a hard future with courage and the willingness to sacrifice. They are people who feel passions, but control them; people who consider relationships—friendships as well as the bonds between a husband and wife—as sacred; people who live by their personal code, even when they see that no happy endings are guaranteed.

Schaefer's writing is quiet and understated—and as powerful and full of integrity as the characters he portrays.

DRUMS ALONG THE MOHAWK

by
Walter Edmonds
(1903-)

Type of work: Early-American historical fiction

Setting: Upper New York Mohawk Valley; 1775-1783

Principal characters:
Gil Martin, a young settler
Lana Martin, Gil's wife
Blue Back, a Mohawk Indian scout

Story Overview:

Gil Martin, a handsome young colonist, married pretty Lana Borst on July 10, 1776. Lana's mother, in tears, made wedding gifts of the family Bible and a peacock feather. Gil had been torn between accepting from his parents a cow or a clock, and finally decided on the cow; it would be of greatest use in the Mohawk Valley wilderness of upstate New York, where he intended to take his new bride.

Gil and Lana left immediately after the wedding, and stopped for the night at a small tavern. The innkeeper rented them the top room, and Gil tipped him to keep other lodgers from dividing it with them.

The talk in the taproom that night turned toward the Colonists' struggle for independence. "The trouble with the American Army," said a one-eyed loyalist named Caldwell, "is your Continental Congress." John Adams and the other delegates were "scum," Caldwell concluded before departing the inn. Gil asked Lana if she feared the hostile country into which they were headed, and the war that had just begun. As she climbed the stairs to their honeymoon room, glowing with pride and happiness, she answered, "Not of Indians."

The next day, Gil and Lana reached German Flats, the Mohawk Valley settlement. Their cabin was located on the outskirts of the settlement, and Lana, upon first inspection of the dreary structure, told herself, "You mustn't start crying." But eventually she grew to love the small shanty, because so much of herself and her work was in it.

The war soon reached the outskirts of German Flats. Certainly the Indians and their Tory warlords would not attack until sometime next years, Captain Demooth assured the settlers. Nonetheless, a militia would have to be formed. So, on muster day, nearly all the able-bodied men in the settlement turned out to report. As he walked along, Gil passed a few Indians sitting on John Wolfe's porch. Wolfe, he knew, was an ardent loyalist.

After drinking a few beers apiece, the newly-assembled militia marched over to Wolfe's store to have a better look at the Indians. Discussing Wolfe's political views along the way, when they reached his place the angry, drunken recruits pillaged the store. In the midst of the plundering, Gil spied Caldwell's eye patch hanging in an upper loft, and "Wolfe" was immediately arrested on suspicion of housing spies. When he did not deny the charge, he was

sent to prison.

Demooth was to be proven wrong about timing of the Indian raids. While Gil was holding a ground-clearing party with his neighbors, Blue Back, an Indian scout, rode up to warn them that a party of Senecas and Tories, led by Caldwell, was advancing toward them. The colonists quickly packed their valuables and abandoned their houses for the stockade.

In the ensuing raid, Caldwell's band burned the houses and the crops, and killed Lana and Gil's cow. The rough ride to the stockade in the wagon proved to be too much for Gil's pregnant wife; Lana lost their first child while huddled in the fort. Even Lana's prized peacock feather was stolen in the invasion (in fact, Blue Back had pilfered it). Lana now fell into a deep depression. She refused food, she also refused Gil's company, preferring to be alone. Finally he broke down and confessed to Lana, "You're like a dead person. As if I'd killed you." Over the next months Lana obeyed her husband's wishes and tried to salvage their relationship, but her heart was not in it; severed by fear and uncertainty, the closeness they once enjoyed had become a distant memory.

Finally, the united Indian chieftains met to decide whether they would support the British or the Colonists. After the council had dispersed, an Oneida chief came to the settlement to announce, "Our counsel fire is extinguished and can no longer burn." The five tribes—Mohawk, Cayuga, Oneida, Onandaga, and Seneca—would choose sides as they pleased. The Senecas and Mohawks were allied with the British, and the venomous tone of this council meant that they would soon be on the warpath in earnest.

Gil and Lana were soon presented with the opportunity to work for a widow, Mrs. McKlennar. While interviewing them, the irascible old woman freely admitted, "I've got a long nose and I poke it where I like. You may think I'm a nuisance." Nevertheless, Mrs. McKlennar became a much-needed source of financial support.

The militia was called up soon after accounts that Joseph Brant, a Mohawk Chief, had amassed a party of six hundred warriors near the settlement. Joe Boleo, another scout, brought news of an additional 1400 hostiles, including Tories, marching to merge with the Mohawks.

The total colonial militia from all the surrounding counties numbered only eight hundred men. Unfortunately, the army, pushed forward by an overconfident officer named Colonel Cox, marched right into an ambush. Only two hundred and fifty Colonists—including Gil, who was wounded in the arm—survived. Nonetheless, they had succeeded in driving the enemy from the area.

The Colonial army wondered what would happen next. Then Joe Boleo, who knew the

Indian mind, prophesied, "If [the Indians] hadn't been whipped so bad they might wait to come along with the next army. But the way it is they won't wait. They'll want to get their face back. They'll be after scalps. They won't care whose." Indeed, Joe's prediction was accurate. Small bands of Tory-led Senecas struck in a series of "lightning raids." A runner from a neighboring town arrived to report: "They burnt every house and barn in town. There ain't a thing left."

Captain Demooth now petitioned General Washington to send regular troops. Washington replied, "Let them take care of themselves like the other frontiers." But New York's problem was different than that of most settlements: John Butler's Rangers, a Tory band, was about to move south and unite with the hostile Indian nations. Against these combined forces, the small settlement was defenseless. The men were shot and scalped; women were raped, then scalped alive. By the time any sort of militia could be mustered, the attackers would slip away into the woods.

Joseph Brant, the Mohawk chief, soon raised an army of Indians and Tories. Caldwell, with a detachment of 350 men, then made his way to German Flats. When Adam Helmer, a strongly built, blonde sentry saw the advancing Mohawk scouts, he decided to try to outrun them. He shot the vanguard in the chest and bolted from his spot like an animal, outrunning his pursuers to the fort.

Helmer entered the fort near nightfall and warned Colonel Bellinger, who fired the cannon—the signal to seek shelter in the fort. As the last of the settlers straggled to the blockade in the darkness, over their shoulders they could see their homes torched by the invaders. The whole valley was lighted up as the enemy sacked the homes and burned the barns and crops the settlers had worked so hard to raise. Though infuriated, the outnumbered farmers could do nothing more than watch as their possessions were reduced to charred rubble.

Weeks later, Gil and Lana joined with the others in replanting and rebuilding—only to have raiders return once more to loot and burn. Only Mrs. McKlennar's stone house was left intact. Over the next several years, the hardy farmers survived bitter winters and severe flooding, poor crops and very little food. During this time, Lana gave birth to two healthy and hungry boys. Due to Mrs. McKlennar's generosity, the Martins fared better than most.

Eventually, the colonial militia marched north and attacked the Onondagas, who had raided them constantly. They were able to reach the Indian village to burn it, but did not know that Blue Back had warned the inhabitants, and they escaped. The strike, however, only served to bring more vengeful assaults on the colonial settlements.

During one of these counterattacks, a mixture of sixty Indians and Tories descended on the fort at German Flats. With only five men and twenty-seven women and children inside the fort, Mrs. McKlennar came up with a plan to protect themselves. "There's fifteen grown women here," she declared. "We'll rig up to look like men." Her ruse worked. The Indians made no more than a half-hearted effort to attack the fort, then ran off.

When the settlers emerged from the fort, Mrs. McKlennar swore she would not leave her house again. "I'd rather lose my scalp," she vowed, "than to go through this again." But soon a company of Tories and their Indian allies once more entered the valley. Two drunken, torch-bearing Indians broke into McKlennar's house. "What do you mean coming into my house," she snarled. The incredulous Indians informed her that they had set fire to her house. "If I'm to get out of this house," she screamed indignantly, "you'll have to move my bed out for me." The Indians, cowed by the provoked woman, lifted her bed—with her in it—and carried it outside while the house burned around them. Then she bade them be off, and they loped off with remorse etched on their faces.

By and by, Colonel Willet reached the Mohawk Valley to lead an expedition against the marauding Butler's Rangers. Gil was recruited as a lead scout, along with Adam Helmer, Joe Boleo, and a young newlywed, John Weaver.

The Colonials fought like lions; Butler's army was eventually beaten, and the German Flats militia was sent to finish them off. During the snowy trek north, however, a group of Butler's advance Highlander scouts ambushed the scouting party. As they fought back, John Weaver received the first fatal bullet from the retreating Highlanders. The militia pursued the fleeing Tory force, slaughtering them in large numbers. John Butler himself was killed, and the survivors dropped their weapons and fled north. In all the fighting, John Weaver was the only Colonial casualty.

Colonel Willet's campaign was to be the last. With word arriving that General Washington had defeated Cornwallis in Virginia, hostile forays became smaller and less frequent.

The settlers cautiously rebuilt. Gil and Lana returned to Deerfield and constructed a new cabin on their piece of scorched land.

Then one day, Blue Back came out of the woods, walked up to Gil, and gave him the peacock feather he had stolen long ago. Lana nearly fainted when she saw it. "We've got the children. We've got each other," she said to her husband. "No one can take those things away. Not any more."

Commentary:

Because he incorporated into his work many characters that actually lived during the period, Edmonds' novel is authoritative and authentic. His story deals harshly with the loyalist sympathizers, who bitterly opposed the American colonist's struggle for freedom, but Edmonds' treatment of the Colonists is equally harsh. The Colonists—though often depicted as persevering, hardy, virtuous settlers who survive against all odds—also waged war with and stole from their neighbors, as was the case with John Wolfe in the novel. Edmonds' vivid depiction of warring "savages" and the frequent feuds and struggles for control of the Mohawk Valley are informative and colorful slices of Americana.

TWENTY-THOUSAND LEAGUES UNDER THE SEA

by
Jules Verne
(1828 - 1905)

Type of work: Science fiction/adventure

Setting: Under the ocean; 1866

Principal characters:

Professor Pierre Aronnax, a French oceanic scientist

Ned Land, Aronnax's Canadian harpooner friend

Captain Nemo, captain of the *Nautilus*

Story Overview:

During the late years of the nineteenth century, the world was rocked by reports of a strange and gigantic sea creature that traveled the open seas, attacking and sinking ships. It appeared to be 150 feet long and moved at amazing speeds—much faster than modern vessels. Professor Aronnax, a marine-life researcher for the Museum of Paris, theorized that the creature was a huge narwhal, native to waters so deep that it had to be much larger and stronger than an average sea-going mammal. At any rate, whatever the monster was, it commanded sufficient force to punch holes in the sides of even the strongest cast iron ships, sending them to the ocean floor.

On the high seas, Captain Farragut, chief officer of the *Abraham Lincoln*, ordered his crew to track the menace and destroy it. Professor Aronnax had been requested to accompany them in order to identify the mysterious monster.

After a lengthy search, Farragut finally sighted his deadly quarry. All day long the creature led the steamer through a taunting game of tag; at night it lay as a sinister shadow on the surface, a phosphorous light emitting from its bulk. Finally, the command was given and the ship steamed toward its target. When they were almost upon the monster, Ned Land, the ship's expert harpooner, thrust his weapon directly into it; to his horror, the harpoon barely made a dent. Suddenly, breaking on the steamer's deck came a rushing torrent that washed the professor, his servant, Conseil, and the harpooner Ned, overboard. As they floundered half conscious in the dark swells, they caught their last glimpse of the frigate, a crippled and shadowy hulk torn asunder, stern to rudder.

The abandoned group was ready to give up, until they felt something firm under their feet and found themselves standing on the creature itself—a beast made of sheet iron! In short order, a hatch opened; eight men appeared and politely guided the three survivors into the interior of the metal monster.

The castaways were given clothing and a meal, which consisted of various seafood selections. Finally, the commander of the mysterious vessel appeared. Tall and imposing, Captain Nemo introduced his crew. Then, with an air of troubled annoyance, he accused Aronnax and his companions of conspiring to destroy his submarine, the *Nautilus*. "I am not what you call a civilized man!" Nemo warned his new prisoners. "I have done with society entirely. I do not obey its laws and I desire you never to allude to them before me again."

With the exception of a few occasions when they were ordered to retire to their cabins, Aronnax, Ned and Conseil were given free run of Captain Nemo's intricately appointed submarine—but they were denied permission ever to leave the *Nautilus*. "In retaining you," Nemo told them, "it is not you that I guard but myself. I am nothing to you but Captain Nemo and you are nothing to me but passengers of the *Nautilus*."

Professor Aronnax was immediately intrigued by his jailer-host and plied him with questions. During one conversation at the dinnertable, Nemo eloquently proclaimed his passion for the ocean depths: "The sea does not belong to despots. Upon its surface men can still exercise unjust laws, fight, tear one another to pieces and be carried away with terrestrial horrors. But at thirty feet below its level, their reign ceases. There I recognize no masters. There I am free!"

Aronnax was also captivated by Nemo's magnificent craft. A tour of the submarine revealed lavish furnishings, European art, and a vast library of twelve thousand volumes. The many complex devices and inventions that sustained the vessel as a splendidly intricate and self-sufficient organism were no less remarkable. Besides possessing the equipment to net its own food from the sea and to store the oxygen which allowed it to remain submerged for days at a time, the submarine was powered entirely by electricity—generated from refined sodium, an extract of sea water. Shaped like a 232-foot long cigar with armor plating, the *Nautilus* was capable of speeds up to fifty miles an hour; its high-intensity lamp could shine half a mile into the darkest depths. Nemo had avoided detection in the building of this huge vessel by obtaining each part from a different corner of the world and then assembling the craft on a deserted island. Clearly, Captain Nemo was a man of enormous wealth—and perverse genius.

But Nemo's submarine held one treasure that the marine biologist considered most wonderful of all: in the forward room, two metal panels slid apart to reveal a great port-window display view of the underwater panorama. The beautiful and vast array of exotic fish drew gasps from the newcomers to the *Nautilus*. "Ah, I understand the life of this man," Aronnax marvelled. "He has made a world apart for himself in which he treasures all its greatest wonders."

After several days of enjoying the library and museum, Aronnax received an invitation from Nemo to accompany him on a walk—a walk on the sea floor. During their excursion, they explored Crespo, an underwater forest. Aronnax, far from feeling imprisoned, was more than content to remain on this marvelous submarine. Ned Land, however, did not share this love of the depths. One day, when the *Nautilus* ran aground on an island near Borneo, he begged permission to go ashore to hunt for game and to feel solid earth beneath his feet one last time. Nemo granted Ned and his companions a brief leave.

The next day, island natives attacked the hunters, forcing them to again seek refuge aboard the *Nautilus*. When Aronnax informed Nemo that the island was inhabited by savages, the captain replied caustically: "Savages! Where are there not any? Besides are they worse than others, these whom you call savages?"

While Nemo waited for the high tide to carry his submarine from its sandy perch, the natives surrounded it and tried to board the craft. But when they grasped the handrails, a paralyzing "thunder bolt" of electricity threw them off and sent them fleeing back to their dugouts.

The *Nautilus* resumed its voyage; and Dr. Aronnax continued his daily log, noting every new wonder he saw. The port window revealed a whole world of exotic living marvels; creatures of every size, shape, and color inhabited the depths.

Then one day, Nemo announced, without explanation, that the professor and his companions would be confined for a time to their rooms. Locked within, they were fed a delicious dinner— food that turned out to be tainted with drugs. When Aronnax awoke, he realized that the sub had been in some kind of battle; but only later did he discover what had happened.

Some days following, when they reached the coast of Ceylon, Nemo suggested the group go on a shark-hunting expedition—without guns. "Do not mountaineers attack the bear with a dagger in their hand," Nemo reasoned, "and is not steel surer than lead?" On their hunt the adventurers encountered a huge oyster, which Nemo pried open, revealing a pearl the size of a coconut. Eventually, they came upon another hunter—an Indian skin diver, searching for pearls. Then, from the rocks where they had hidden themselves to observe the diver, they watched in horror as a large shark swam menacingly closer. As man and shark met and grappled, the shark struck the diver with its tail, knocking him senseless. Armed with only a knife, Nemo intervened. The shark turned on the captain, and he stabbed at it desperately, again and again, but soon the powerful jaws of the predator held him pinned him to the ocean floor with the intent of snapping him in two. At that last, desperate moment, Ned rose from hiding and swiftly plunged his harpoon deep into the heart of the enraged beast.

When the little group gratefully reached the surface, Nemo gave the Indian diver a bag of valuable pearls. "That Indian is an inhabitant of an oppressed country," he explained cryptically, "and I am still to my last breath one of them!"

Not until the expedition had returned to the *Nautilus* did Nemo thanked Ned. Ned's stinging reply was terse: "I owed you that."

After a harrowing voyage to the Antarctic— in which the *Nautilus* was nearly crushed by icebergs and run aground by strong ocean currents— the submarine made its way to the Mediterranean by way of a secret passage under the Isthmus of Suez, anchoring near the site of a shipwreck. It was here that Aronnax finally learned the source of Nemo's fortune: the captain had been plundering the treasures of sunken ships. And what was to be the destiny of all this treasure? Nemo's nebulous reply was, "Do you think these riches are lost because I gather them? Do you think I am ignorant that there are suffering beings and oppressed races on the earth? Do you not understand?"

Once again the *Nautilus* resumed its journey. On one occasion the vessel was attacked by a huge

school of octopus. Surfacing, the crew—including Ned and the professor—struggled to the deck armed with axes. As Ned struck savagely with his harpoon at the invaders, he was knocked to the deck. Then, just as one of the monsters was about to sink its sharp beak into Ned's body, Nemo emerged from behind and clubbed it, allowing Ned to escape and plunge his harpoon through its heart. Now he had settled his score with Land. Nevertheless, one of the *Nautilus'* crew had been killed, and Nemo could not hide the tears that sprang from his eyes and rushed down his cheeks.

The restive Ned finally convinced Aronnax to petition once more for their release. Aronnax confronted Nemo. "You impose actual slavery upon us," he charged. But Nemo coldly refused the request, an act that made even Aronnax determined to escape at the earliest opportunity.

One day, an approaching vessel fired off several volleys at the *Nautilus*. Furious, Nemo laid plans to counterattack. He retreated and hid from the hostile ship for a day; then, once the enemy's guard was down, he turned and sped back towards it, ramming it and passing completely through its hull. Below deck, the professor could only gaze helplessly through the window, appalled at the fate of the unfortunate crew. And the sight of the struggling, drowning men was too much for even Nemo to bear. When the professor saw him again, Nemo was weeping in his own cabin, kneeling, his arms outstretched towards a picture of his family, murmuring in despair. "Almighty God, enough! enough!"

The desperate men now resolved to leave the *Nautilus* and the ominously unpredictable fits of its captain by any means possible. Jumping on a side boat, they fought to cut the riggings. Just then the submarine began to dive, and at once their small craft was wrenched from its moorings by the submerging craft's whirlpool. Somehow, through some miracle, Aronnax and his companions awoke on dry land. To the end of their lives they were left to ponder the fate of the *Nautilus*—the vessel which had unfolded to them the ocean's magical secrets— and which had left them to ponder forever the ineffable veils that shrouded all the secrets of the enigmatic Captain Nemo.

Commentary:

Published in 1870, **20,000 Leagues Under the Sea** introduces the *Nautilus*, the spiritual forerunner of our modern nuclear submarines. In fact, though most of the myriad inventions described in Nemo's delicately detailed underwater microcosm have long been surpassed by reality, Verne's uncanny speculations also include some technological embellishments that modern science has yet to achieve.

Verne fills his work with the most intricate observations. He identifies thousands of species of marine life—using Latin names familiar only to the most experienced marine biologist. The author himself had a deep love for the sea, and ran away from home at an early age to enlist on a three-masted ship as a cabin boy—only to be retrieved by anxious parents. In a later work, **Mysterious Island,** Verne unravels many mysteries about the fate of the *Nautilus* and the secrets of its charismatic captain that are left so intriguingly—and so maddeningly—unanswered in **20,000 Leagues Under the Sea.**

TREASURE ISLAND

by
Robert Louis Stevenson
(1850 - 1894)

Type of work: Adventure fiction

Setting: England, the Hispaniola, and Treasure Island; 1700's

Principal characters:
Jim Hawkins, an enterprising young lad
Billy Bones, a pirate captain
Doctor Livesey, Jim's benefactor
Squire Trelawney, an experienced seaman and friend to Doctor Livesey
Long John Silver, a one-legged buccaneer
Ben Gunn, a marooned sailor

Story Overview:

Jim Hawkins was startled one day when a gnarled, filthy old seaman with "a saber cut across one cheek," demanded room and board at the inn kept by his parents, the Admiral Benbow. And after taking up residence, Captain Billy Bones, as he called himself, lived up admirably to his colorful appearance. He cursed loudly, drank copious amounts of rum, and told harrowing tales of murder and other dark deeds at sea. Bones was especially fond of one particular ditty:

"Fifteen men on a dead man's chest—
Yo ho and a bottle of rum!
Drink and the devil had done with the rest—
Yo ho ho and a bottle of rum!"

The old buccaneer was a true seadog. He bullied Jim's parents—who feared to ask for his rent—and alternately terrified and entertained the townsfolk. Everyone held him in awe, except Dr. Livesey, whose refined manners and powdered hair marked him as one of the town gentry.

One evening when the gentleman doctor came to visit Jim's ailing father, Bones, drunk and in a rage, as usual, pulled a knife to Livesey's throat. Unperturbed, the doctor ordered him to put down the knife and, invoking his powers as a magistrate, threatened that he would have Bones "hunted down," "routed out" and hanged if he did not obey. Bones retreated, "grumbling like a beaten dog." The doctor also warned Bones that if he did not cease his heavy consumption of rum, he would soon be dead—but the surly seaman ignored the advice.

Then one day "a pale tallowy creature wanting two fingers of his left hand" came to the inn asking for Bones. He collared young Jim and hid with him behind the parlor door, waiting for the Captain's return. When Bones entered the room, the stranger stepped forth and revealed himself. "Black Dog!" gasped the Captain. And Jim was summarily banished from the room as the two old seamates started a spirited argument. As the argument finally erupted into blows, Black Dog, wounded, scurried from the inn, leaving Captain Bones behind him to fall "full length upon the floor" in a swoon.

Now bedridden, Bones grew weaker and weaker. Semi-delirious, he rambled to Jim about escaping from a mysterious curse involving some-

thing called "the black spot." Jim found out more about this one day when a blind beggar approached the inn, tapping with his cane. This old codger grabbed the terrified lad by his shirt, and forced him to lead the way to the Captain, whom he confronted with a piece of blackened parchment inscribed with the message, "You have till ten tonight." Reading these words, Bones fell back—dead. He had been summoned to his doom by the Black Spot.

That evening Jim and his newly widowed mother opened the Captain's sea chest and rifled it in a search for the back rent that Bones owed. Among other trifles, they found a bag of assorted coins and a canvas package. Just then they heard the tapping of the beggar's cane outside. Together, they snatched up the coins and the packet and stole out of the inn. Hidden close to a low ridge, Jim watched a motley group of cursing buccaneers assail the inn. Among them was the blind beggar, Pew. Suddenly, a group of revenue officers galloped up and the men scattered. In the confusion, blind Pew darted out in the street and was trampled to death under the horses.

After the furor had died down, Jim took the canvas package to be opened by the trusted Dr. Livesey and his friend Squire Trelawney. When it was discovered to contain the map of an island, with a detailed account of buried treasure, excitement rippled through the room. Trelawney decided to outfit a ship and recover the lost treasure; Jim was invited to come along as cabin boy.

In addition to Dr. Livesey, Trelawney enlisted the aid of a Bristol innkeeper named Long John Silver. When Trelawney told the peg-legged salt that he needed a crew, Silver was more than willing to comply. Long John gathered a rough-looking gang though experienced gang, and signed himself on as cook. For captain, Trelawney chose a sharp-spoken man named Smollet. Finally, all was readied; the ship Hispaniola set sail.

Jim, assigned as Silver's mate, took an immediate liking to the garrulous old man. He was especially enamored of the sailor's parrot, Cap'n Flint, who repeatedly shrieked "Pieces of Eight, Pieces of Eight," and "would swear straight on, passing belief for wickedness."

One night, looking for a forbidden apple, Jim climbed into the fruit barrel. When he heard men approaching, he stayed put; the crewmen were speaking in hushed tones about taking over the ship. Suddenly a cry of "Land Ho" diverted their attention. Jim scrambled out of the barrel and raced to warn the Dr. Livesey, Smollet, and Trelawney. Apparently there were only seven trusted men on board. The rest, recruited by Silver, were nothing more than pirates. The doctor listened gravely and then decided to use Jim as a spy. The men are not shy with him and Jim is a noticing lad."

Meanwhile, Treasure island had indeed been spotted. Captain Smollet allowed Silver to take a landing party ashore, reasoning that if he prevented their going the men would mutiny on the spot. And at the last minute, Jim, full of his own plans, hopped aboard a skiff. When the boat reached shore, he ran and hid in the overgrowth. From this vantage point, he observed the mutinous crew—and was repulsed at seeing Silver impale an honest sailor with a well-aimed fling of his sharpened crutch.

The frightened boy retreated into the jungle—only to find himself face to face with the most ragged, bedraggled looking man he had ever seen. "I'm poor Ben Gunn I am," the weathered hermit told him, "and I haven't spoke with a Christian these three years."

Gunn, as it ensued, had been marooned after leading a party in a futile search for treasure buried years earlier by a certain Captain Flint. Flint had gone ashore with six men to bury the booty; he had returned to his ship alone. And among the guard crew awaiting him on board were Gunn, Billy Bones—and Long John Silver. Flint had kept his silence with them all.

Meanwhile, Dr. Livesey had decided to move the honest sailors left in his charge from the ship to the remains of an old fort he had discovered on the island. However, when Livesey's overloaded skiff began to go down, the pirates looking on from shipboard overpowered their guard and fired the ship's cannon at the sinking craft. Livesey's men finally reached shore and took refuge in the fort. Soon Silver approached, under a flag of truce. In return for their treasure map, he offered, he would leave Smollet's party alive. "Refuse that," he bellowed, "and you've seen the last of me but musket balls." Smollet response was an offer to "clap you all in irons and take you home to a fair trial in England." "Before an hour's out," Silver cursed, "I'll stove in your blockhouse like a rum puncheon. Them that die'll be the lucky ones!" And, true to his word, when the hour was up Silver sent a group of pirates over the walls of the blockade. But after a bloody melee, the remaining pirates decided they had had enough and bolted back over the wall.

Within the fort, Captain Smollet had been wounded, and only four of his faithful men were left to fight. While the pirates recouped, Livesey went out to seek Ben Gunn, and Jim also struck out into the jungle. There he stumbled upon Gunn's homemade boat and paddled out to the *Hispaniola,* which he found guarded by only two pirates, both drunk and fighting. Silently, Jim set to work cutting the anchor. When the obviously untended ship began drifting erratically, Jim decided to board it.

On deck, one of the pirates lay dead; the other was wounded in the leg. "I've come aboard to take possession of this ship," Jim announced, giving the man a drink and tending to his wound. But suddenly the pirate rose up and came at the lad with a knife. Jim seized the mainmast rope and began to climb for his life, with the pirate close behind. Finally, just ahead of the pirate, he reached the crow's nest and cocked his twin pistols. "One more step, Mr. Hands," Jim smiled, "and I'll blow your brains out!" The pirate smiled back and pretended to surrender; but as soon as Jim relaxed a bit, he flung his knife. The blade grazed the boy's shoulder, pinning him to the mast. But Jim had not

yet lost his spirit. Firing the pistols, Jim toppled the pirate into the sea.

In the dark of night, the boy returned to shore. Creeping toward the fort, he saw too late that it had been taken by the pirates. Awakened by the parrot's warning squawk, the pirates seized the boy before he knew what was happening.

Jim found the pirate group in a nasty mood. Though they had spared Livesey so that he might dress their wounds, they had already served Silver with the "Black Spot" of Death.???why?and were about to kill Jim as well—but Silver, as usual, held an ace. "I'll save your life—you save Long John from swinging," he whispered to Jim—and turned to display the missing treasure map before the mutineers. The Black Spot was retracted; once again the pirates rallied around Silver.

Pretending allegiance to the pirates, Jim set out with them. But when they came across a pile of human bones arranged to point out the way, the group was struck with fear. That fear rose to a fever pitch when they heard the voice of Ben Gunn, hidden in the brush, singing life into the sleeping bones with the words to "Fifteen Men." Still, the pirates pressed on, trembling. At last they came to the spot . . . only to discover a gaping hole in the ground. The treasure had been stolen!

Just then, shots rang out—and two pirates fell dead. Doctor Livesey quickly grabbed Silver and Jim and raced for cover. This, Livesey realized, was the work of the sly hermit Gunn. In fact, Gunn had long since removed the treasure and hidden it in a well-provisioned cave. And, when the group returned, Trelawney was waiting at the cave's entrance when the group returned. "You're a prodigious villain and imposter, sir," Trelawney spat at Silver. Undaunted, Silver replied, "Thank you kindly sir."

The five survivors, with Silver in tow, loaded the hoard of gold and coins into the *Hispaniola* and set sail. The three surviving pirates were left marooned—and very drunk—on the island, along with necessary supplies. When they came upon another island, Silver convinced Gunn to help him launch a boat over the side, and the resourceful pirate—crafty to the end—escaped with a bag of gold. "I think we were all pleased to be so cheaply quit of him," Jim wrote.

At last, the remaining men reached Bristol. There they divided the spoils. Jim surmised that Silver had returned to his long-suffering wife to live out his life in comfort, for, as he observed, "his chances for comfort in another world" were small indeed. And from then on Jim and his mother lived comfortably. Jim confessed, however, that in his worst nightmares thereafter he would awaken "with the sharp voice of Captain Flint ringing in [his] ears, `Pieces of eight, pieces of eight!'"

Commentary:

Stevenson traveled abroad much of his early life; thus, the heroes gracing the pages of his novels are often after his own image: brave young seafarers. He produced *Treasure Island* after being hounded by his young stepson to write "something really interesting." The suspense and lively action of the novel has enthralled readers old and young alike for over a century.

SENSE AND SENSIBILITY

by
Jane Austen
(1775 - 1817)

Type of work: Classical Romance

Setting: Sussex and Devonshire, England; late 18th century

Principal characters:
  Elinor Dashwood, a practical, sensible young woman
  Marianne Dashwood, her emotional younger sister
  Mrs. Dashwood, their mother
  Mrs. Jennings, Mrs. Dashwood's good-humored, gossipy friend
  Edward Ferrars, a shy gentleman whom Elinor loves
  Mrs. Ferrars, Edward's domineering mother
  Mr. Willoughby, a charming fortune-hunter whom Marianne loves
  Lucy Steele, a gentle young woman in love with Edward
  Colonel Brandon, a middle-aged man who loves Marianne

Commentary:

Sense and Sensibility is the story of two sisters, one practical, calm, and sensible; the other exactly the opposite, constantly living on an emotional roller coaster, possessing little sense but a great deal of "sensibility"—what current American usage would term "sensitivity." As the work unfolds, the author shows a clear preference and admiration of sense over sensibility. The novel is also a love story. Each sister seeks after unrequited love, and, after much disappointment, is finally rewarded.

In this novel, as in her other works, Jane Austen paints a vivid and witty picture of the life and manners of upper- and middle-class English society at the end of the eighteenth century. Her heroines are intelligent, spirited young ladies, forced by the era in which they live to wait for fortune or love to come their way, rather than pursuing it themselves.

Story Overview:

"Good heavens!" Marianne Dashwood exclaimed, "he is there—he is there— Oh! why does he not look at me? Why cannot I speak to him?" Marianne sat in "an agony of impatience" staring at Mr. Willoughby. When at last he turned around, Marianne greeted him in affectionate tones. She held out her hand to him, but Willoughby spoke only to Elinor, and never even glanced at Marianne.

The next morning the girls were breakfasting with their hostess, Mrs. Jennings, when a letter from Willoughby was delivered to Marianne. He had never meant for her to love him, he wrote, for his affections were engaged elsewhere. Deeply hurt, Marianne ran from the room. Mrs. Jennings remarked to Elinor that she had never seen a girl so desperately in love. When she asked when Willoughby and Marianne were to be married, Elinor replied that no engagement had ever been mentioned, and excused herself to look after Marianne. Elinor found her sister stretched out on the bed, choked with grief. Elinor read the letter and grew increasingly angry toward Willoughby. This letter was so cruel!

The next morning, Mrs. Jennings reported that Willoughby was soon to be married. Marianne, totally distraught and heartbroken, could not be comforted. Her health started to decline.

Meanwhile, Elinor also suffered from love-sickness. Lucy Steele had taken her into her confidence and related that she was secretly engaged to a young man of some means Edward Ferrars. But because his mother expected him to "marry well," it had to be kept confidential. Elinor, however, herself felt strongly attracted to Ferrars. Lucy's further revelation that they had been engaged for four years stunned Elinor; Edward had never even mentioned Lucy's name. Lucy chattered on and on about her fears of meeting his mother, Mrs. Ferrars, a harsh woman who certainly would refuse to consent to their wedding.

Lucy also mentioned a ring which Edward wore, a lock of her hair enclosed in its center. She had seen the ring, responded Elinor calmly, but her voice "concealed an emotion and distress beyond anything she had ever felt before." Certainly she had seen the ring—and believed its lock of hair to be her own. Inwardly she was "mortified, shocked, confounded." But Elinor, unlike her more sentimental sister, suffered in silence, and never told anyone of the conversation or showed any difference in demeanor.

When he heard that Marianne was ill, Colonel Brandon came to visit. The women had been introduced to him at their mother's home in Barton Park, and he had immediately fallen in love with Marianne. She, though, had shown only mild interest in the thirty-five-year-old man. Though worried about her health, he was elated that she would not marry Willoughby after all.

Brandon now shared with Elinor a secret he had faithfully kept to himself: As a younger man he had been in love with a woman named Eliza, who had been forced to marry his brother. The brother later abandoned Eliza and her child while Brandon served in the East Indies. After his return, Brandon found Eliza and her daughter. Eliza subsequent death had left Brandon the girl's guardian. Years later, the girl ran away with none other than Mr. Willoughby, who later abandoned her and never returned. When Elinor relayed this story to her sister, Marianne refused to believe it. And her health continued to grow steadily worse.

Meanwhile, Elinor learned that Mr. Edward Ferrars was to be married to a Miss Morton, the only daughter of a rich lord. One day Elinor and Marianne's brother invited them to attend a dinner party at his home; Lucy Steele and Mrs. Ferrars also attended. Guessing that Elinor was in love with Edward, and wanting to put the girl in her place, Mrs. Ferrars snubbed her. Mrs. Ferrars was, after all, "not a woman of many words . . . and of the few syllables that did escape her, not one fell to the share of Miss Dashwood, whom she eyed with the spirited determination of disliking her at all events." Simultaneously, Mrs. Ferrars extolled Lucy's virtues. But Mrs. Ferrar's plan failed. The only difficult thing for Elinor was watching Lucy and Edward together. She suffered in silence, though it was almost more than she could bear.

Mrs. Ferrar's treatment of Elinor greatly displeased Marianne; she could not stand seeing Elinor slighted in the smallest point. "Her spirits were quite overcome, and hiding her face on Elinor's shoulders, she burst into tears."

Some time later, Lucy's sister accidentally revealed the secret about Lucy and Edward. Edward's mother immediately fell into violent hysterics. Even Elinor would be a better match for Edward than Lucy, she screamed as she disowned Edward and gave his birthright to his brother, Robert.

Now Edward had no chance of marrying anyone; he had no inheritance and no income, nor had he ever learned even the rudiments of a profession. So, he sought to acquire a position in the Church. It turned out that Colonel Brandon, a man of considerable connections and entitlements, was able to have Edward hired on as minister of the local parish. Colonel Brandon asked Elinor to tender the offer to Edward. Elinor thought it ironic that "the preferment, which only two days before she had considered as hopeless for Edward, was already provided to enable him to marry; and she, of all people in the world, was fixed on to bestow it!"

As the months passed, Marianne sank deeper in despair. She learned that Willoughby had wed and that his wife had delivered a baby, and became so ill that death was imminent.

One night, her pulse weakened; in delirium, she spoke wildly and cried for her mother. Elinor, about to send a messenger to ask their mother to come at once, was surprised when Colonel Brandon stopped by. He quickly took in the situation and personally set off to escort Mrs. Dashwood to Marianne's bedside.

About noon the next day, Marianne began to show signs of improvement. The doctor arrived and declared her out of danger. Then, just as the clock struck eight, Elinor heard a carriage driving up to the house. She rushed down the stairs and into the drawing room, expecting to see her mother. Instead, she saw Willoughby! He begged Elinor to give him just ten minutes to explain his actions. Her curiosity piqued, she sat down to hear his story.

His fortune had never been large, Willoughby began, and thus he had always intended to marry a woman of means. Despite himself, he had fallen in love with Marianne. But greed—and his unwillingness to be embarrassed by cutting off his earlier engagement—got the better of him, and he renounced Marianne. In fact, his wealthy fiancee had dictated the heartbreaking letter he had sent to Marianne. Moreover, he had never really loved his fiancee. When he heard that Marianne was deathly ill, and haunted by the fact that he had treated her shamefully, he could not let her die "thinking him the greatest villain upon earth, scorning and hating him in her last moments," and resolved to come and beg her forgiveness. With Elinor's assurance that her sister had already forgiven him, pitied him, and wished him well, Willoughby took his leave.

Mrs. Dashwood soon arrived and took over the recuperation of her daughter. Later, Elinor told them both of Willoughby's story; as Elinor had predicted, both readily forgave him. Marianne steadily improved. In time she was taking short strolls in the garden, happy to be in the company of the good and gentle Colonel Brandon. Soon after that, the two announced plans to be married.

Weeks passed with no word of Lucy or Edward—until one day a servant returned from the city with news that Mr. Ferrars and Miss Steele had married. Before tipping his hat and leaving, however, the messenger added that Miss Steele—now Mrs. Ferrars—had inquired after Elinor and Marianne and indicated that she and her husband would be sure to call on the sisters.

One day not long after, Elinor sat with her mother and sister, when a figure of a man on horseback drew her eyes to the window. He stopped at her gate. It was Edward! He entered the room, and after a minute of embarrassed silence, Mrs. Dashwood asked after Mrs. Ferrars' health. Edward answered that his mother was very well. Another awkward pause followed, whereupon Elinor asked if *his* "Mrs. Ferrars" was at Longstable, Edward's home.

"No, my mother is in town," answered Edward innocently.

"I meant," said Elinor, exasperatedly taking up some work from the table, "to inquire after Mrs. *Edward* Ferrars."

She dared not look up. Edward colored, seemingly perplexed. "Perhaps you mean—my brother—you mean Mrs.—Mrs. *Robert* Ferrars," he ventured after some hesitation. "Perhaps you do not know—you may not have heard that my brother is lately married to—to the youngest—to Miss Lucy Steele"; after Edward's inheritance had been cut off, he explained, it seems Lucy's affections had gone over to Robert.

Hearing this most wonderful news, Elinor ran from the room, tears of joy streaming down her face. Edward followed after her, declaring his love.

A ROOM WITH A VIEW

by
E.M. Forster
(1879 - 1970)

Type of work: Victorian novel

Setting: An English pension in Florence, Italy, and a countryside manor in England; nineteenth century

Principal characters:

Lucy Honeychurch, a young Englishwoman of well-to-do family

Miss Bartlett (Charlotte), Lucy's old-maid cousin

George Emerson, a quiet young man of questionable social status

Cecil Vyse, Lucy's suitor, an erudite young man without a vocation

Mr. Beebe, a Protestant clergyman from Lucy's parish

Story Overview:

As the chaperone and moral guardian of Lucy Honeychurch, Miss Charlotte Bartlett was naturally suspicious when a Mr. Emerson and his son George offered to exchange rooms in the Italian hotel where they were all staying so that the women might have a view of the River Arno. But Mr. Beebe, the respected rector of her local parish in England, convinced Miss Bartlett that the offer was indeed well-meant. Speaking on behalf of Miss Bartlett, Mr. Beebe then arranged for the exchange of rooms. Nevertheless, Miss Bartlett remained offended at Mr. Emerson's lack of decorum; in fact, she disliked the Emersons altogether.

Though he was clearly lacking in tact and social grace, Lucy herself saw Mr. Emerson as a kind and generous man. She was most perplexed, however, by his son's lack of vigor. She could not understand how George, a young man well imbued with the gifts of health and education, could be so sour, on the few occasions when they had been obliged to converse with one another, all George could do was complain that "the universe doesn't fit."

Once settled in the Bertolini Pension in Florence, Lucy and Miss Bartlett discovered they had few interests in common. Less wealthy than her young cousin, Miss Bartlett had been assigned to accompany Lucy only because of the generosity of Lucy's mother. Now enraptured with the Italian sites, Miss Bartlett's fancy was to go out with her new novelist friend, Miss Lavish, leaving Lucy behind either to play the piano—an enterprise that brought her much peace and relieved the youthful passions that seemed to be bottled up inside her—or else to tour Florence alone or with other guests of the pension. On one such excursion to the Piazza Signoris, Lucy was shopping through an art display when she encountered two men bickering about a debt. Suddenly, one of the men reached out and struck the other violently on the chest. The injured man leaned toward Lucy as if to speak, but only a spate of blood emerged from his mouth. Just before Lucy fainted, she caught sight of George Emerson.

George revived Lucy and escorted her back to the pension. There, among other congenial acts, he disposed of some unhappily blood-spattered paintings that Lucy had bought in the piazza. Now Lucy saw for the first time that George Emerson was trustworthy, intelligent, and kind.

One day, Lucy, Miss Bartlett, and several other pensioners accepted an invitation from Mr. Beebe to spend a day in the country. When they reached their destination—a meadow with a view of Florence and the Val d'Arno—the group broke up. Leaving Miss Lavish and Miss Bartlett alone to their gossip, Lucy, seeking out Mr. Beebe, wandered back to the carriage and asked the driver in her broken Italian where she could find the "buoni uomini," or the good man. The driver led her to a small, violet-covered terrace hidden amongst the trees, which opened onto a vista of unmatched beauty. Standing there on the terrace with her was indeed a "good man"—but not the clergyman she had expected. It was George Emerson, who turned quickly toward her and gave her a kiss—a most deplorable act, which did not go unnoticed by Miss Bartlett, who stood off at a distance.

Back at the pension, Lucy felt confused. After dinner, she decided to talk with George and ask him not to divulge their kiss. Miss Bartlett, fearing that Lucy's mother would find her an unsuitable chaperone, also determined that the brief encounter should be forgotten. The next morning, Lucy and Miss Bartlett decided to take the train to Rome, where they would briefly stay with the Vyses, old friends of the family, before returning home to England.

Six months later, Lucy was back at Windy Corners, her home outside of London. After receiving three other offers, she had finally accepted a marriage proposal from Cecil Vyse, who, in terms of money and position, was superior to Lucy and the Honeychurches. Mrs. Honeychurch was greatly pleased by the news; Freddy, Lucy's younger brother, was not.

Cecil, a tall, Medieval-looking sort of man, had all the proud appearance of a Gothic statue. But though he was educated and well trained in social etiquette, at times he behaved quite rudely in public. He admittedly had no profession. "It is another example of my decadence," he explained. "My attitude—quite an indefensible one—is that as long as I am no trouble to any one I have a right to do as I like."

One afternoon as they walked in the woods, Cecil asked Lucy if he could kiss her. She quickly assented. The kiss, however, was passionless, and though Lucy and Cecil had both looked forward to their impending marriage, they now had mutual doubts.

Meanwhile, another complication had developed. Sir Harry Otway, a neighbor of the Honeychurches, was looking for new tenants for a country house he owned which was known as Cissie Villa. Cecil, who did not like Sir Harry, recommended as a joke that he rent the villa to a couple of working-class men Cecil had met at the National Gallery in London. Sir Harry, however, took him seriously, and promptly arranged to rent Cissie Villa to the two men.

Lucy was furious. Not only was Cecil's joke in poor taste, but, since she had hoped that two of her friends might rent the villa, the joke was also at her expense. Then, to complicate matters even further, Lucy discovered that the men to whom the villa had been rented were none other than Mr. Emerson and his son George. Lucy was horrified. Freddy, on the other hand, was delighted; in George, he saw a rival suitor for Lucy.

Not long after, Lucy received a letter from Miss Bartlett stating that she had heard the Emersons had rented Cissie Villa. Miss Bartlett went on to advise Lucy that she tell her mother about her dalliance with George in Florence. Lucy, however, felt that too much time had passed; she could not possibly confide in her mother now.

A few days after the arrival of Miss Bartlett's letter, Freddy announced that he wanted to invite George Emerson over for a Sunday-afternoon tennis match with Lucy's fiance. Lucy tried to dissuade her brother, but to no avail.

Sunday, the scheduled tennis day, arrived. Cecil begged out of the first doubles match, which meant that Lucy had to take his place. While she, George Emerson, Miss Bartlett, and Freddy played, Cecil relaxed at courtside reading a new novel written by none other than Miss Bartlett's Florentine friend, Miss Lavish. When the match was over and everyone had gathered round to chat, Cecil began to read aloud a choice passage from Miss Lavish's novel, something about "a view." Lucy was stunned. As she listened to a detailed description of the moment when George had kissed her on the terrace outside Florence, she realized that Miss Bartlett had violated her vow of confidence. Changing the subject, Lucy suggested that they go in to tea. But still she could not avoid the inevitable. Cecil, returning to the tennis courts to retrieve the book, left Lucy and George alone for a moment; and George kissed Lucy for the second time.

Lucy, denying her feelings, finally decided to confront George with his offense, who answered that he did not believe Lucy should marry Cecil. "He is the sort who are all right so long as they keep to *things* . . . but kill when they come to *people*," he declared. "He should know no one intimately, least of all a woman." Then George unashamedly professed his love for Lucy—a better love, he said, than she would find anywhere.

Although she said nothing at the time, Lucy realized that George was right about Cecil. Shortly afterwards, she broke off her engagement.

Due to the tangled changes of events, Lucy now felt that she needed to get away for a while. Earlier, two friends had written to invite her to vacation with them in Greece, and, with her mother's permission, Lucy made arrangements to go. Just days before the trip, she stopped by the church to pick up Miss Bartlett, who had been visiting Mr. Beebe's mother. While Lucy waited for the church service to end, she was led into Mr. Beebe's study. George's father, Mr. Emerson, was also there, sitting by the fire. Unaware that she had already broken off her engagement with Cecil, Mr. Emerson—unable and unwilling to hide his feelings any longer—begged Lucy to reconsider her forthcoming marriage. She should put trust in love, he said, not in decorum. He was sorry, he added, that George had made advances while she was betrothed, but

"love is so seldom answered by love"—as it *had* so obviously been answered between Lucy and George. Upon hearing Mr. Emerson's strange yet candid plea, Lucy saw at last "the whole of everything at once."

Back at the Bertolini Pension in Florence, the room that had been Mr. Emerson's and George's—the room with the view—was now occupied by the married couple. The Honeychurches, however, were not there to wish the newlyweds well; they had not yet forgiven Lucy's "deception." For his part, George remained optimistic. "If we act the truth," he said, "the people who really love us are sure to come back to us in the long-run."

Commentary:

Two prominent Victorian themes—the rigid differentiations between gender roles and class status—make up this novel's interweaving narrative. The goal and the challenge of the typical young middle-class Victorian woman was to marry "well"—to carve out a secure life for herself within her male-dominated society. Miss Bartlett, for instance, says at one point, "It was not that ladies were inferior to men; it was that they were different. Their mission was to inspire others to achievement rather than to achieve themselves." Similarly, Cecil's attitudes mirror the conventional Victorian notion of womanhood. When, for example, Lucy embraces him, he thinks, "At last she longed for attention, as a woman should, and looked up to him because he was a man"; and, later, when their first kiss holds none of the romantic mystery he expects, he recasts the scene to his own liking: "He . . . took her in his arms; she rebuked him, permitted him, and revered him ever after for his manliness." Unquestionably, a feminist—or non-feminist, for that matter—of today would find "Medieval" Cecil's perspective wearisome—as did Forster himself.

Throughout the novel, social status and money are of the utmost importance. At the Bertolini Pension, Miss Bartlett sizes up which of the other boarders she can mingle with according to these criteria. Likewise, when Lucy's mother evaluates her daughter's match with Cecil, she over-zealously reports, " . . . He's good, he's clever, he's rich, he's well connected . . . I'll say it again if you like: he's well connected."

If E.M. Forster had a knack for enlivening the Victorian period, even while he smiles—sometimes caustically—at many of its institutions, perhaps it has something to do with the fact that it was his own; *he* lived it. His intimate descriptions of the clothing and physical surroundings of the time sets the stage for the development of his plots, and his unerring ear for contemporary dialogue and his well-drawn characters apply the finishing touches.

But underneath the layers of genteel satire and Forster's lavish attention to the trappings of Victorianism, sounds a voice of authentic protest. Throughout *A Room With a View* he earnestly—even grimly—nurtures the liberation of the individual human heart from the life-stifling corsets of convention. Perhaps today he would still be sounding his strong, subtle call to freedom—not from the strait-laced profiles of Victorianism, but from the sometimes even more sterile mores of office and marketplace relationships—in a timeless fight of the self against the world.

THE SEA-WOLF

by
Jack London
(1876 - 1916)

Type of work: Romantic adventure

Setting: A seal-schooner on the Pacific Ocean; late nineteenth century

Principal characters:
  Humphrey Van Weyden, a young bachelor and literary critic
  Wolf Larsen, Captain of the *Ghost*
  Maud Brewster, a delightful authoress

Story Overview:

Humphrey Van Weyden, young literary critic and aristocrat, had no idea what adventures awaited him as he boarded the *Martinez* ferryboat, heading from Sansalito to San Francisco. The foggy, dream-like night held no portent of danger, until the ferry collided with a passing cruiser and began to sink. To the sound of sirens and screaming women, Humphrey plunged overboard into the murky water.

Hours later, he awoke to find himself alone and afloat in the vastness of the sea. Losing consciousness to the lulling rhythms of the water, the young gentleman was nearly dead by the time he was spotted and pulled aboard the *Ghost*, a seal-hunting boat on its way to Japan.

Humphrey's reception on the *Ghost* was anything but sympathetic. The shipmates showed scant concern for the well-being of the frail shipwreck victim who lay before them. They seemed more interested in the events taking place on deck. Wolf Larsen, the ship's captain, was pacing the length of the hatchway, watching as one of his sailors died.

Even in his weakened state, Humphrey was impressed by the apparent strength of the infamous Captain Wolf "Sea Wolf" Larsen. Within the body of solid muscle and deliberate motion, Humphrey saw an even "greater strength that lurked within, that lay dormant and no more than stirred from time to time, but which might arouse, at any moment, terrible and compelling, like the rage of a lion or the wrath of a storm."

When the dying sailor's muscles finally relaxed into lifelessness, Wolf Larsen angrily cursed his name for perishing at the beginning of the voyage and leaving his crew short-handed. After a hasty burial, the disgruntled captain swung around to face Humphrey. Here was a man to replace the unfortunate sailor. Stripped of his fine attire, Humphrey, now christened "Hump," had no choice but to join the captain's crew as a lowly cabin-boy.

"What do you do for a living?" Wolf Larsen finally asked his new guest. "I—I am a gentleman . . . " Humphrey replied uncertainly. "You stand on dead men's legs," the captain shot back savagely. "You've never had any of your own. You couldn't walk alone between two sunrises and hustle the meat for your belly for three meals. Let me see your hand . . . Dead men's hands have kept it soft. Good for little else than dishwashing and scullion work."

Thus began Humphrey's evolution from scholarly aristocrat to fighting sailor. With a glint in his eye, Wolf Larsen foretold such a transformation when he assigned Humphrey his new post: "And mind you, it's for your own soul's sake. It will be the making of you. You might learn in time to stand on your own legs and perhaps to toddle along a bit."

The end was apparent—but slow was the process. Humphrey's first nights on the *Ghost* were punctuated by fear. Placed in servitude to the cook, Mr. Mugridge, "Hump" suffered much abuse. "Cooky" was a malicious, fainthearted cockney who thrived on the weakness of others to gain his own sense of power and superiority. Hump was his inescapable target.

When first threatened by Cooky, Humphrey bolted. Though mocked and disgraced for his flight, he knew that, far from being a fighter, his only strength came from rational formulas and moral arguments—now, worthless instruments.

Several days later, the struggle for domination continued. Cooky spent hours sharpening a galley knife as he watched Hump from a corner in the kitchen. Sailors quickly spread the word: "Cooky's sharpening his knife for Hump." His life threatened, Hump—who all his life had been called "Sissy" Van Weyden—had no choice but to stand up to the bully. Stealing a knife and whetting it in view of Cooky, he confronted his opponent squarely in the face. The show-down ended in Cooky's backing-down. "Yer not 'arf bad, 'Ump!" Mr. Mugridge exclaimed afterward. "You've got spunk, as you Yanks s'y, an' I like yer in a w'y. So come on an shyke." Having survived to this point, Humphrey soon became chief of the kitchen and was called with respect *Mr. Van Weyden*.

As Cooky challenged Humphrey's physical strength and courage, Wolf Larsen challenged Humphrey's mind and ideals. His own kind of intellectual, Larsen was eager for a peer he could convert to his own harsh philosophy. He often called Humphrey to his cabin to engage in long-winded debates. These encounters revealed to Humphrey a mind twisted until there no longer was room for a ray of hope, but fashioned by the brutality and beastliness of men in a fight for conquest and glory. "I believe that life is a mess . . . " Wolf Larsen declared at one such meeting. "The big eat the little that they may continue to move, the strong eat the weak that they may retain their strength. The lucky eat the most and move the longest, that is all . . . " But Humphrey retorted with the zeal of idealism: "They have dreams, radiant, flashing dreams—"

"Of grub," Wolf concluded brusquely. "Life? Bah! It has no value. Of cheap things it is the cheapest . . . Where there is room for one life, she sows a thousand lives, and it's life eats life till the strongest and most piggish life is left." It was this attitude that, to Humphrey, made Wolf Larsen most enigmatic and dangerous.

But Wolf's danger was not only found in words. All the crew feared the brutality of their captain. When plans for a mutiny led by a man named Johnson were unveiled, an unbridled rage was loosed in Wolf Larsen. However, even after seriously wounding Johnson with the mere slap of his hand, the terrible words of a mutinous follower rang out, "God damn your soul to hell, Wolf Larsen

... you coward, you murderer, you pig!"

Then it was that Wolf's fury became madness. And yet, through it all, the captain stood motionless, lost in a great curiosity. He saw the epithet as proof of his philosophy: The ship captain's role was to destroy the weak.

A bloody brawl erupted. Humphrey stood aside, watching the crew's savage attacks with a sickened sense of nightmare: "All my days had been passed in comparative ignorance of the animality of man . . . And it seemed to me that my innocence of the realities of life had been complete indeed. I laughed bitterly to myself, and seemed to find in Wolf Larsen's forbidding philosophy a more adequate explanation of life than I found in my own."

Soon, Humphrey could no longer withstand the pull of Wolf's harsh philosophy so graphically lived out in that show of force. Hump became immersed in Johnson's plans for escape, and even contemplated a murderous plot against his captain.

Meanwhile, as the *Ghost* approached the rocky islands of Japan, fog, gales, and typhoons slowed the progress of the ship. One day a small boat was found drifting at sea; inside it sat four men and a woman, all grateful to be rescued. As may be imagined, a woman on deck roused the passions of the crew of the *Ghost*, Humphrey in particular. Here was a lady, refined and educated in the same society he once enjoyed. Wolf Larsen, on the other hand, approached the woman as he would any other aristocrat: "I suppose you're like Mr. Van Weyden there, accustomed to having things done for you. Well, I think doing a few things for yourself will hardly dislocate your joints."

As he listened to the woman defend herself as a writer and journalist, Humphrey suddenly recognized her as the famous critic Maud Brewster. Both, it seems, had read the other's writings and essays with equal interest and appreciation. An immediate bond was established between the two—a bond which excluded Wolf and his pack of ignorant sailors.

Maud joined Humphrey in his search for an opportunity to escape. A victory celebration over the defeat of an attacking ship provided such a moment. Wolf Larsen's spirits were high as he came on deck to discuss philosophy with the intellectual members of his crew. Maud took the lead, describing the nature of the soul, and the victory of good over evil. As always, Wolf Larsen rejected such a viewpoint. "Bosh and nonsense!" he exclaimed impatiently. "It is the desire that decides." The dialogue continued late into the night, until Humphrey gradually drifted into sleep.

Humphrey awoke to find Maud grappling overpowered in Wolf Larsen's arms. Filled with rage, the young gentleman sprang with his knife, leaving a deep gash in Wolf's shoulder. The captain soon lost consciousness from pain and loss of blood. Losing no time, Maud and Humphrey clambered into a boat at the side of the schooner and sailed away from the *Ghost*—and all it embodied.

The voyage was difficult for the two escapees. And yet, there existed a peace and comradeship between them that made bearable the storms, fog, cold nights and long hours of toil.

The small craft finally washed onto an uninhabited island. Winter was setting in, food and provisions were scarce; the need for survival was strong in the minds of both. What's more, the travelers knew that their rickety boat could take them no farther, and so the island, they knew, would be their home for a time.

Weeks passed. Then one morning Humphrey and Maud stood stunned and exuberant at finding the *Ghost* silently rising before them, apparently vacant and deserted, anchored on shore. Humphrey jumped aboard, only to run nearly head on into the staring eyes of Wolf Larsen. Humphrey raised his gun to shoot, but could not bring himself to pull the trigger. Then, after a brief exchange, Wolf Larsen sat down on a stool and slept.

It was soon learned that Wolf Larsen had been blinded and was suffering from a grave and painful illness. The captain spent days in his cabin, moaning. His body gradually deteriorated until he was bedridden and dumb. Remaining skeptical and invincible to the end, the dying man's last word was in reply to a question about immortality: "B-O-S-H."

After Wolf's death, Maud and Humphrey boarded the *Ghost*, a new life ahead of them. As the boat sailed back toward familiar scenes and people, the couple looked forward to a world in which they would never be separated.

Commentary:

Before writing *The Sea Wolf,* Jack London penned a letter to a friend in 1903: "I am on the track of a sea story . . . which shall have adventure, storm, struggle, tragedy, and love . . . My idea is to take a cultured, refined, supercivilized man and woman, (whom the subtleties of artificial, civilized life have blinded to the real facts of life), and throw them into a primitive sea-environment where all is stress and struggle . . . and make this man and woman rise to the situation and come out of it with flying colors."

The Sea Wolf, undeniably, embodies an exploration of how a civilized man faces up to a brutal society. As a literary critic, Humphrey is accustomed to using reason alone as his means of survival. Aboard Wolf Larsen's ship, however, he is suddenly forced to join a larger conflict in which untamed competition is the rule. It is within this environment, however, that Humphrey is endowed with even greater moral integrity, courage and sensitivity. Both he and Maud rise above the philosophies of Wolf Larsen to continue on their quest of a humane and civilized world.

Yet, the enigma and strength of Wolf Larsen remain with the reader long after the two lovers sail into the sunset. One wonders to what extent the Sea Wolf's philosophy is an accurate portrayal of humanity. Who, in fact, "won" the argument over idealism and realism, peace and struggle? In simple equations, Humphrey and Maud are the only survivors in the struggle and, thus, the conquerors. And yet, London himself, refusing to accept the finality of the death of the "Sea Wolf," argues that, even today, his presence and philosophy is alive and well:

Somewhere within that tomb of the flesh still dwelt the soul of the man. Walled by the living clay, that fierce intelligence we had known burned on; but it burned in silence and darkness. And it was disembodied. To that intelligence there could be no objective knowledge of a body. It knew no body . . . It knew only itself and the vastness and profundity of the quiet and the dark.

THE SHORT STORIES OF SHIRLEY JACKSON

(taken from *The Magic of Shirley Jackson*, Farrar, Straus and Giroux, New York, N.Y., 1966)

In her short fiction, as in her novels, Shirley Jackson often creates singularly alienated characters who are unable to contend with the pressures of modern life. At times, their sense of unreality verges on the insufferable. Indeed, as Jackson's husband noted after her death, her "powerful visions of suffering and inhumanity" imbued her fiction with a uniquely satiric perspective on human nature.

The Lottery

It was June 27th, the day of the village's annual lottery. The children assembled ran ahead of their parents, laughing and rolling in the dust, collecting small, rounded stones. Their pile of rocks in a corner of the town square was soon fairly big. The fathers stood in groups talking about farms, crops, tractors, and the weather. Their wives exchanged bits of gossip and tried to control their children. A carnival atmosphere prevailed as everyone waited for the lottery to begin.

The lottery's original paraphernalia was lost long ago, but the black box they used now predated Old Man Warner, the oldest man in town. Most of the primal ritual had been lost as well. About all that remained of the formal ceremony was that Mr. Summers, who conducted the lottery, exchanged a few words with everyone who drew a number. He had set the old box on a three-legged stool in the center of the square and had made sure that someone would draw for the young and the sickly.

This year Tessie Hutchinson was the last to arrive. "Thought my old man was out back stacking wood," she explained, "and then I looked out the window and the kids was gone, and then I remembered it was the twenty-seventh and came a-running."

Now Summers reminded people of the rules, even though most everyone had heard them so many times before. "Keep the paper folded in your hand without looking at it," he instructed them, "until everyone has had a turn." The crowd had grown quiet. Then as he read off the list in alphabetical order and each individual came forward to take his slip of paper, quiet conversations began.

"They do say," Mr. Adams told Old Man Warner, who had participated in the lottery seventy-seven times, "that over in the north village they're talking of giving up the lottery." "Pack of young fools," the octogenarian snorted. "There's *always* been a lottery. Bad enough to see young Joe Summers up there joking with everybody," Mrs. Adams added that some places had already quit the lottery. Warner replied caustically, "Nothing but trouble in that. Pack of young fools."

After the last name was called, it became apparent that the Hutchinson family had drawn the black dot. "It wasn't fair!" Mrs. Hutchinson shouted; Summers had not given her husband enough time to pick. But a voice piped up from the back, "All of us took the same chance . . . be a good sport, Tessie." The Hutchinson's slips of paper were collected, put back in the box, and stirred. The three children, their father, and finally their mother drew their slips. Tessie drew the black mark

"All right, folks," Mr. Summers said officially, "Let's finish quickly." The villagers had forgotten parts of the ritual and had lost the original black box, but they still remembered how to use the stones. Someone even remembered to thrust a few pebbles into the hands of little Davy Hutchinson. "It isn't fair," Mrs. Hutchinson cried out in vain, standing in the center of a space the crowd had created as it drew back from her. Then a stone struck the side of her head. "Come on, come on, everyone," Old Man Warner said.

"It isn't fair, it isn't right!" Mrs. Hutchinson screamed, " . . . and then they were upon her."

The Daemon Lover

Since one-thirty in the morning, when Jamie left, she had not slept well. Finally rising, the future Mrs. James Harris found it difficult to get going: she spent almost a full hour drinking her morning coffee. Today was her wedding day and she could not decide what to wear. Along about eleven, she showered, pulled her nightshirt back on, then heated up more coffee and smoked another cigarette while she sat by the window waiting for Jamie to return.

She woke with a start. It was almost one. Now, she really had to rush, but managed to dress and put her makeup on in less than half an hour. Growing hungry, she left Jamie a note on the door and went down to the drugstore to eat. When she dashed back, she found the apartment *still* empty. She would have to go find him.

Strangely enough, she did not find Jamie's name on the building register where he said he lived, and the apartment supervisor didn't recognize his name. The supervisor, however, told her that a stranger had watched an apartment for some tenants in the building, and suggested she try them. But Jamie was not there either; the couple had not seen him when they returned from their trip that morning.

The future Mrs. Harris began to grow frantic, and walked up the street, asking the news dealer, the druggist, and the florist if they had seen "a rather tall man in blue suit carrying a bunch of flowers pass this way this morning." Everyone had seen someone matching this rather vague description, and directed her to various locales.

Eventually, she wound up on a street lined with nondescript row houses. "I seen him. He went in there," a boy answered, pointing to the house next door. "Top floor. I followed him till he give the quarter. Way to the top . . . " Then he asked her, "You gonna divorce him?"

The future Mrs. James Harris went to the top of the house, where she found two doors. Behind the first door she discovered an empty little attic room with bare floorboards. Behind the second, she heard low voices and laughter. She could not bring herself, however, to knock on that door. But she would later return often to that door; in fact, she came "every day for the first week. She came on her way to work, in the mornings; in the evenings, on her way to dinner alone, but no matter how often or how firmly she knocked, no one ever came to the door."

My Life With R.H. Macy

"The first thing they did was segregate me from the only person in the place I had even a speaking acquaintance with," the woman began. Thereafter, her life at R.H. Macy's department store had grown steadily worse. Some beautiful young woman—invariably named "Miss Cooper"—would meet her, then another Miss Cooper would say, "13-3138 here belongs with you," and then off she and Miss Cooper would go.

They handed her a big book with pads of little sheets that read, in order, "Comp. keep for ref. cust. d.a. no. or c.t. no. salesbook no. salescheck no. coerce no. dept. date M." Then still another Miss Cooper came and discussed the salesbooks with all the clerks. Number 13-3138 listened for a while, then Miss Cooper asked them to write on the little sheets. "I copied from the girl next to me," admitted 13-3138. "That was training."

Later, 13-3138 was given her locker number—1733—her time clock number—712—her cash-box number—1336—her cash-register number—253—her cash-register-drawer letter—K—her cash-register-drawer-key number—872—and her department number—13. "And that was my first day," she recounted.

The next day she was on the floor—an official sales clerk. However, on her first sale, the customer gave 13-3138 a D.A. number that threw her off. In the end, she had to ring up the sale as a "No Sale," and then made the mistake of tearing up the duplicate triplicate sales ticket she had filled out.

Near the end of her second day she had slipped and torn her panty hose. Macy's would replace them for her, but when one of the Miss Coopers handed her some paperwork with the numbers "13-3138" where her name should have been, she walked out.

"So far," she concluded, "I haven't been back to Macy's for my third day . . . I wrote Macy's a long letter, and I signed it with all my numbers added together and divided by 11,700, which is the number of employees in Macy's. I wonder if they miss me."

Colloquy

"What seems to be the trouble?" the doctor asked Mrs. Arnold. "Doctor," she replied, "how do people tell if they're going crazy?"

The doctor looked up, and she added with no little exasperation, "I hadn't meant to say it like that. It's hard enough to explain anyway, without making it so dramatic." The doctor's suggestion that insanity was a complicated illness only aggravated Mrs. Arnold's frustration. Taking a different tack, the doctor asked her to tell him about it.

"When I was a little girl," she began . . . then she stopped herself, asked him if, back then, there used to be words like "psychosomatic medicine," "international cartels," or "bureaucratic centralization." "What," she wanted to know, "do they mean?" The doctor started to explain about international crises and the disintegration of cultural patterns, but Mrs. Arnold cut him off in mid-sentence. Her husband, she said, tears trickling from her eyes, had come home from work one day grumbling that his news dealer had not saved him a copy of the *Times;* then her husband had rambled on about social planning at the local level, surtaxes on net income, geopolitical concepts, and deflationary inflation. "He really said deflationary inflation," she wailed.

The doctor tried to calm her, explaining that "in a disoriented world like ours today, alienation from reality frequently—" but she interrupted him again. Repeating his words—*disorientation, alienation, reality*—Mrs. Arnold stood up. Before the doctor could stop her, she opened his office door. "Reality," she said as she closed the door behind her.

Commentary:

Shirley Jackson (1919 - 1965) is probably best known for *"The Lottery,"* which has been reprinted in nearly every high school and university reader in modern American literature. Following its release, it was banned in South Africa; at least *they,* Jackson noted with pride, understood the significance and vitality behind the story. A chilling tale, it depicts people blinded and desensitized by their unquestioning adherence to tradition.

Similarly, the future Mrs. Harris in *"The Daemon Lover"* is dehumanized: deceived and exploited by her fiancee. James Harris manipulates his way into her heart—and bed—only to disappear on the morning of their wedding. As a result, she becomes obsessed with him, even though she can only participate in his life from behind a closed door.

"My Life With R.H. Macy," on the other hand, is a playfully entertaining story of a young female department store clerk who refuses to be reduced to a collection of numbers. Equally amusing and poignant is *"The Colloquy,"* a tale of one woman's dissociation and alienation from a world that, since her childhood, has changed dramatically.

It is impossible to avoid feeling empathy for her character's plights. Indeed, whether Jackson's stories humor us, intrigue us, or shock us, these sensitive and honest explorations *move* us in one direction or another.

THE SHORT STORIES OF JAMES BALDWIN

(taken from *Going to Meet the Man,* Dial Press, New York, N.Y., 1965)

James Baldwin (1927 - 1984) published his first collection, *Going to Meet the Man,* in 1965. Thus, these raw, searing portrayals of the inhumanity experienced by African-Americans emerged at a time when profound racial upheaval was spreading throughout America—and not just at the South's lunch counters.

The Rockpile

To children, the rockpile was like a magnet; they made it a part of all their games. But Roy's mother, Elizabeth, fearing her son's safety, would not allow him to play at the rockpile. Today, though, he got his older brother John to promise not to tell, then climbed down from his upper window while his mother's back was turned. Soon enough, the game on the rockpile turned into a fight and Roy got hit over the eye with a tin can. Bleeding and crying all at once, he was brought inside and laid on the couch. Sister McCandless helped Elizabeth clean and bandage the cut, which, despite Roy's noisy tears, was just a shallow scratch.

Just then, Roy's father, Gabriel, came home. Seeing Roy's bandages, Gabriel made sure he was all right, then turned angrily on John, as if the older boy were responsible for Roy's disobedience. Now John often took the brunt of his Gabriel's anger, since he was not real family, but, as Elizabeth put it, "nameless, a stranger, living, unalterable testimony to his mother's days in sin." Gabriel demanded an immediate answer: "How come you didn't tell your mother . . . ?" Goaded by John's silence, Gabriel threatened a beating.

Elizabeth interceded. "Ain't a soul to blame for Roy's lying up there now but you . . . you because you done spoiled him so that he thinks he can do just anything and get away with it." For an instant, Gabriel looked at Elizabeth with pure hatred, then realized his wife, his helpmeet, was talking sense. Seeing her husband's mood change, Elizabeth ordered John to get his father's lunch box off the floor. Then, her back to the room as she listened to "the scrape and jangle of the lunch box" being picked up, she winced as John bent "his dark head near the toe of his father's heavy shoe."

The Man Child

Eric, son of a son of a son of a farmer, knew he was late, and shuffled along quickly since he did not want to be in the fields after dark. As he walked, he thought about things in the way only an eight-year-old can, filled with ideas and losing track of time. His dad would be at the tavern with his pal Jamie; only his mom would be home. Eric was an only child, though he had a baby sister in the graveyard. After her last miscarriage, his mom had changed, forever drained by the experience.

Thinking of his baby sister's loss made Eric remember Jamie's birthday party. Eric's father and Jamie had grown up together, gone to war together, survived together—and, since the miscarriage, drank together. His dad had also bought Jamie's farm after Jamie had lost his wife, and lost everything. Childless, Jamie had now become a member of Eric's family. He did not seem to resent his position, but Eric noticed that Jamie did not talk enough for anyone to know how he felt or what he thought.

Spying his home in the distance, Eric remembered the day his dad had walked with him across all their land and told him that, when he died, Eric would own it, even the part of it that had once belonged to Jamie. Eric had felt proud then, and ever after, when he explored the neighborhood, Eric tried to carry himself like a landowner. When Eric reached the porch, his mother fussed at him for being late, then made him go around to the pump to wash up.

While Eric scrubbed his face and hands, Jamie appeared suddenly, startling Eric. "Come on, little fellow," Jamie urged, "we got something in the barn to show you." Eric went along, thinking an overdue cow was about to calf. They were already in the barn, the door closed, before Eric realized there were no cows inside. "Where's my Papa?" Eric asked. Then Jamie moved toward Eric and clamped his hand around the boy's throat, cutting off the scream. In a flash of intuition, Eric snorted, "Why do you hate my father?" But then he realized it wasn't his dad that Jamie hated, it was him, the one who would one day inherit the land—Jamie's land. "Jamie, you can have the land," Eric whispered desperately. "I don't want the land," Jamie replied, squeezing harder. "This land will belong to no one." When Eric heard his mother calling him he wanted to answer her so badly—but at that moment Eric's breath went out of him and he fell face down on the barn floor, his head flopping unnaturally on a broken neck.

Jamie, on his way out of town, strolled past the music-filled tavern where Eric's dad was seated. Even when the music had long faded out behind him, Jamie whistled the song he had heard.

Come Out the Wilderness

Ruth Bowman hated the white man she lived with. Even though she could not imagine herself with any other man, she hated him. Paul stayed out all night with his artist friend, never bothered to call her to tell her he would be late, then waited to come home until after she left for work. What's more, Paul was going to leave her—she saw it in his eyes—not for another woman, but simply because he was ready to go. She told herself that Paul would not treat her this way if she was white. Once, during an argument, she screamed at him, "We're not down on a plantation, you're not the master's son, and I'm not the black girl you can just sleep with when you want to and kick about as you please!" Now he was going to leave her—and she could not forgive him.

Earlier, Ruth had, in the words of the old slave spiritual, "come out the wilderness," and left her rural southern roots for New York. It seemed to have helped, because she worked for a progressive insurance company that would hire Negroes. In fact, her boss, Mr. Davis, also a black man, just today had pulled her out of the steno pool and promoted her to be his personal secretary. But she still felt dirty. As she waited for Paul's call, Ruth remembered the first time she had felt filthy. Her brother had discovered her and some farm boy lying in the barn and, jumping to the obvious conclusion, had attacked both of them. When her father had separated the three, her brother gave her a venomous look, saying, "You dirty . . . you dirty . . . you black and dirty—" Ruth ran away; nothing, she felt, would ever make her clean again. A few years later, she ran farther away, to New York. And it had not made her clean, coming out of that wilderness.

After work, Ruth went to a bar frequented by theater people, hoping to brace herself against Paul's inevitable announcement. There she saw an actor that reminded her of a white boy she had met soon after coming to the city. Their eyes met briefly; then he looked up and away. The actor's up-and-away glance and the pain in his eyes told her that "in spite of everything, his color, his power or his coming fame, he was lost. He did not know what had happened to his life. And never would." It was the same with all the white boys Ruth had known. Pain drove them into her arms, then drove them away again. "The sons of the masters were roaming the world, looking for arms to hold them. And the arms that might have held them—could not forgive." *Her* arms could simply not forgive.

A sob escaped Ruth's lips, and the waitress stared at her sharply. Ruth hurried out, an early evening mist mingling with her tears. She walked briskly, tears—and mist—streaking down her face, hoping to hide the fact that she did not know where she was going.

Going to Meet the Man

He was angry because he could not perform; he had been working too hard, that was all, his wife had assured him. Neither could he drive "over there" to get some nigger girl to help him out—not anymore. Times were changing. The niggers had lost their sense of place, and that made him even angrier.

A sudden grating of tires on the gravel road outside started the dogs barking. He reached spontaneously for his pistol, then let it slide back into the holster as the sound receded in the distance.

At work, the niggers had lined up to register to vote, and despite all the intimidation, they would not stop singing and would not disperse. Going to jail and getting beat did not change their minds, either. He had beaten one of the boys almost to death. How much longer could he take hearing them sing? As a deputy sheriff, everyday he had to listen to them, arrest

them, beat them—then turn around to hear all over again their damned singing.

"I stepped in the river at Jordan"; where had he heard that song? It was on his way to a picnic. Early one morning, his parents had taken him to a picnic his father had promised he would never forget. The drive to Harkness had seemed to last forever, and a big crowd was already gathered by the time they arrived. Then he saw him: a huge black man chained to a tree in the center of the crowd. A fire roared nearby. Perched on his daddy's shoulders, he had watched the silver knife slash away the prisoner's manhood . . . watched kerosene splash over the black man's body . . . watched as flames engulfed him . . . and smelled the sickening odor of something both sweet and rotten.

Now, as he lay in bed, he thought of the boy he had beaten, of the black man in the fire—and something between a laugh and a howl bubbled up out of his soul. He grabbed his wife. "Come on sugar, I'm going to do you like a nigger," he screamed at her, "just like a nigger, come on sugar, and love me just like you'd love a nigger." But before he was through, he heard the sound of tires on the gravel road, which started the dogs to barking again.

Commentary:

Two of Baldwin's stories deal with a subject that has long been taboo: interracial relations between the sexes. In "Going to Meet the Man," he explores the link between the sexual exploitation of black women and the twisted character of the oppressor. Baldwin's conclusion is chilling, as the deputy psychologically associates lynching, castration, and sexual desire. The association of sexuality and violence is heightened by his demand that his wife submit in the way that black women had previously been forced to.

Approaching the subject from a different angle, Ruth's anger at white men stems from her sense of being filthy; the sexual exploitation of Black women slaves by white plantation owners prevents her from accepting her own sexuality.

John, in "The Rockpile," though indirectly, is also a victim of sexual exploitation. Born to an unwed mother, he must endure the stigma of *legal* illegitimacy—something still taken seriously in 1965—which translates in the eyes of others into *moral* illegitimacy, making him a legitimate target of physical abuse.

Baldwin perhaps seeks to juxtapose Eric's brutal murder in "The Man Child" with the sexual brutality of "Going to Meet the Man," suggesting that the two situations are morally equivalent. In contrast, many of Baldwin's later works seek to accentuate the great caring and tenderness that prevail in Black culture; but, as he explains, these come only after offering up a glimpse of the prolonged dehumanization Blacks have suffered. And though we may someday overcome the ugly effects of slavery, the past will not easily be forgotten.

THE SHORT STORIES OF ANTON PAVLOVITCH CHEKHOV

(taken from *Anton Chekhov's Short Stories*, Norton Publishing, New York, N.Y., 1979)

Anton Chekhov (1860-1904) is one of the greatest Russian storytellers. His broad spectrum of fiction explores many themes and tones. Some are touching tales of love and affection, while others evoke a subtle sense of comic genius. Chekhov's abilities as a storyteller cut across genres and styles. For the literary world, his death from tuberculosis at age forty-four was a "literal" tragedy—a pun Chekhov likely would have approved of.

The Dependents

Mihail Petrovitch Zotov, a solitary seventy-year-old, awoke before dawn, roused by the cold and his aching extremities. Annoyed because he was out of tea—and because it was too late to go back to sleep—Zotov said his prayers and hobbled out to sit on the porch to await the sunrise. Lyska, a dog as old and frail as Zotov himself, limped toward her master, her tail wagging. "Be off! The plague take you!" he screamed. The dog slunk off to the other end of the porch and lay down.

As the sun turned the sky deep purple, then violet, then red, and finally orange, Zotov directed his gaze toward the barn. He watched with unalloyed hatred as a pinch-bellied, spindly-legged, grey-haired horse—again as decrepit as Lyska and Zotov himself—emerged from its ramshackle home. "Plague take you," Zotov repeated. "Shall I ever see the last of you, you jail-bird Pharaohs! . . . I wager you want your breakfast! he jeered. He had no food for himself, much less his dependents.

As the morning wore on, Zotov's anger welled up like an infected boil, until it burst out like an explosion. His bellowing eventually drove his beasts to the gate of his property, where they stood, dolefully watching as he went to his neighbor to beg tea for himself, oats for the horse, and scraps for the dog. "Take them to Ignat the slaughterer," said Mark Ivanitch. "You live like a beggar and keep animals!" After a few glasses of vodka at the local tavern, Zotov, drunk, resolved to leave his farm and go to live with his great-niece, Glasha. Returning to his home, he bundled up a few belongings, ignored Lyska and the horse, and started out on the ten-mile walk.

Zotov was not yet a mile into the county when he heard steps behind him. Turning, he saw the animals quietly plodding after him. Their refusal to go back, despite his harsh encouragements to do so, weakened Zotov's resolve. He could not appear at Glasha's residence with these pathetic creatures tailing him, but he also lacked the heart to leave them to die of hunger. "Hadn't I really better take them to Ignat?" Zotov asked himself rhetorically.

Later, the old man remembered only a few of the events at the slaughterhouse. Ignat had kept him waiting two hours, forcing him to swim in the sickening smell of hides, cabbage, and death. He remembered the horse put into a

stand, hearing two thuds followed by a dog's bark, a yelp, and a third dull thud. "Further, Zotov remembers that in his drunken foolishness, seeing the two corpses, he went up to the stand, and put his own forehead ready for a blow. And all that day his eyes were dimmed by a haze, and he could not see his own fingers."

The Student

Making his way home from hunting, Ivan Velikopolsky, a sacristan's son and student at the clerical academy, followed the stream's path through the forest. A cold, bitter wind blew through the trees. Since it was Good Friday, Ivan's thoughts were dark and brooding. Just such a wind as this, thought Ivan, had blown in the time of Rurik, of Ivan the Terrible, of Peter—and the same poverty, hunger, darkness, and feeling of oppression Russia knew now had always existed, and would always exist; the passage of a thousand years would make life no better. Suddenly, Ivan did not want to return home.

He stopped by a large campfire. The woman there recognized him at once and welcomed him. They talked. Warming himself by the fire, Ivan remembered that Peter, in the night Jesus betrayed, had denied his Master three times while warming himself by just such a fire. Reminded of the tale, Ivan recounted it to the woman. When he finished, the woman cried great tears of grief. Ivan quickly bade his farewells and hastened to return to the warmth of his own home.

As he walked on in the darkness, Ivan thought that since the old woman had wept, she must have had an empathetic heart toward Peter the night before the Crucifixion; she must have had some taste for bitterness. But Peter's denial had occurred some 1900 years—yet it still had some relation to the present, to the woman, to his desolate village, to himself . . . to all people. Somehow, this thought stirred joy in his soul.

"The past," he pondered, "is linked with the present by an unbroken chain of events flowing one out of another." It was a comforting, beautiful thought, one that gave him a definite place and purpose in the world. Life suddenly seemed full of lofty meaning—and he became eager to get home.

Volodya

Volodya, a shy, pale, sickly-looking lad of seventeen, was troubled. First, he was about to fail his mathematics exam tomorrow, which meant he would be expelled from the academy. Second, his and his mother's presence at the Shumihin's country villa constantly mortified him, for he knew the Shumihins looked upon him and his *maman* as poor relations who must be tolerated. Third, Volodya was in love with Anna Fyodorovna, a married woman of thirty. Yet to love a married woman felt disagreeable. "It's not love," he decided, "It is only a little intrigue . . . Yes, an intrigue . . . " Still, when

Anna had discovered him in the arbor and openly flirted with him, he had put his arm around her waist and told her he loved her. She did not actually resist so much as insist she had things to do, he recalled later, so that meant he could approach her again, he supposed—when the time was right.

Passing through the house at a later time, Volodya heard Anna recounting the story of his approach to her lady friends—including *maman*—over tea. "They talked aloud in cold blood," Volodya writhed in shamed agony as he slunk away, "and *maman* laughed! . . . *Maman!* My God, why didst Thou give me such a mother?" From that moment on, Volodya hated his mother.

Later that night, though, when Volodya entered his room seeking medicine for Madame Shumihin, she again flirted with him, and he again attempted amorous advances that she did not actively resist. Again, though, the timing was wrong.

Now Volodya resolved to make one last attempt to seduce Anna. He deliberately missed his train back to school and schemed in his mind to meet her alone in the garden—only to have his plans destroyed when her husband returned from town for his weekly visit. Crushed, Volodya's only wish was to escape, to lengthen himself from Anna Fyodorovna. He and *maman* took the afternoon train back to their village. Yet Volodya's depression worsened on the train and he quarrelled with his mother over the Shumihin's treatment of her. *Maman* would not hear it, however, and dismissed her son's ill mood.

Back at Lady Petrovna's boarding house, their home, Volodya became despondent. After a second quarrel with his mother, this time over her aristocratic pretensions and the fact that *maman* had run through two fortunes—her own and her dead husband's—Volodya secreted himself away in one of the boarding house's vacant rooms, hoping to avoid the sight, even the thought of the woman he hated. What a world; what a cruel world. Finding a revolver, he put its muzzle in his mouth and squeezed the trigger; nothing happened. He fumbled around with the unfamiliar weapon, felt something else projecting from its rear, pushed it forward, then put the barrel back into his mouth. Once more he pressed trigger. A terrible force hit the back of his head, and he fell face down on the table before him. The next thing Volodya knew, he felt his father suddenly seize him with both hands, and they fell headlong into a very deep, dark pit. "Then everything . . . blurred and vanished."

A Slander

Sergey Kapitonitch Ahineev, the writing master, presided over all the details of his daughter's wedding to a teacher of geography and history. The festivities went off well and the guests were talkative. Near midnight, when it was time for supper, Ahineev went into the kitchen to check on the meal. He spoke to the cook. "Show me the sturgeon, Marfa." She lifted the newspaper and Ahineev gazed and gasped. The fish was huge, masked in jelly, and decorated with capers, olives, and carrots. Bending down, Ahineev smacked his lips in pleasure. "Ah-ah, the sound of a passionate kiss," came an inquisitive voice from the hall. " . . . Who is it you're kissing out there, little Marfa?" Then assistant usher Vankin barged into the kitchen and Sergey Kapitonitch politely introduced himself. But Sergey's protest that he was not kissing Marfa appeared to fall on deaf ears as Vankin turned and left.

After discussing the rest of Marfa's preparations, Sergey went into the drawing room. There he saw Vankin laughing and joking with the inspector's sister-in-law. "Talking about me!" Sergey thought. "I must do something to prevent his being believed!"

Sergey spent the next half hour mingling with his guests. His conversation centered around one variation or another of a common theme. "We were talking of Vankin," he would say. "Queer fish, he is. He went into the kitchen, saw me beside Marfa, and began inventing all sorts of silly stories. `Why are you kissing?' says he. He must have had a drop too much. `And I'd rather kiss a turkeycock than Marfa,' I said. `And I've a wife of my own, you fool,' said I. He did amuse me!" Sergey was so relieved by his guests reaction to his defense that he drank four glasses too many. He slept that night like an innocent babe—and thought no more of the sturgeon incident.

But, alas, an evil tongue did its work, and Sergey's efforts ultimately failed. Only a week later, the headmaster of Sergey's academy took the writing-master aside and explained that while he, the headmaster, could hardly govern about what his teachers did on their own time, Sergey must be more discreet about his relationship with the cook. "Live with her, kiss her . . . as you please," he warned, "but don't let it be so public, please. I entreat you! Don't forget that you're a schoolmaster." Ahineev, mortified, straightway felt cold and faint. At supper that night, he only picked at his food. "Why aren't you gobbling up your food as usual?" asked his wife naively. Then, "Brooding over your amours. Pining for your slut of a Marfa?" she abruptly scolded as she slapped him.

Sergey quickly stormed to Vankin's home. "Why did you set this slander going about me?" Sergey asked accusingly. But Vankin only stared at Sergey blankly, as if not understanding a single word his accuser had spoken. "What slander?" the startled man finally said. "God blast me! Strike me blind and lay me out, if I said a single word about you! May I be left without house or home, may I be stricken with worse than cholera!" Vankin's sincerity convinced Sergey. Clearly, it was not the assistant usher who midwifed the slander. "But who, then, who? Who, then?" Sergey wondered. "Who then? we, too, ask the reader."

ANIMAL FARM

by
George Orwell
(1903 - 1950)

Type of work: Allegorical political satire

Setting: The Manor Farm (represents Russia during and after the Communist Revolution)

Principal characters:
Old Major (*i.e. Karl Marx*), an ancient and venerated boar
Snowball (*i.e. Trotsky*), a young porcine intellectual
Napoleon (*i.e. Stalin*), an unscrupulous, aggressively fierce young pig
Boxer (*i.e. the Russian worker*), a huge, hardworking male horse
Mollie (*the Russian bourgeois capitalist*), a frivolous mare
Moses (*i.e. organized religion*), a tame raven
Squealer (*i.e. Russia's propaganda machine*), a young pig and fluent orator
Various dogs (*i.e. Stalin's secret police*), men (Capitalist enemies) sheep, hens and other animals (those who follow)
Farmer Jones (*i.e. Czar Nicholas*)
Frederick (*i.e. Germany*)
Pilkington (*i.e. England*)

Commentary:

George Orwell, a dedicated British Socialist, wrote this classic 1945 fable in embittered protest against what he saw as the perversion of socialism by post-Revolutionary communism in the U.S.S.R. Rather than highlighting factual incidents from the grim cauldron of horrors that had boiled to a climax under the Stalinist regime, Orwell chose to focus an allegorical mirror on the brutal dynamics that blazed beneath the action. And within this mirror, the pigs and sheep and horses of *Animal Farm* move as vivid and grisly reflections of the historical figures and factions they represent.

But Orwell's book mirrors more than the evils of Soviet Communism. Read closely, it is also an impassioned indictment of Capitalism. And read more closely still, *Animal Farm* reflects the haunted and ironic image of the dark gulf which the author sees opening—perhaps inevitably—between the two eternal poles of idealism and expediency; between all noble ends and their self-betraying necessary means. This little "fairy story," as Orwell calls it, is in the end an angry, eloquent and almost despairing protest against the tragic potential for tyranny in *all* social institutions—including even language itself—over those very ideals and hopes for human transcendence that they are supposed to nurture and to serve.

Story Overview:

One day on the Manor Farm, the Old Major, a venerable eleven-year-old boar known as Old Major gathered the animals together. "Now comrades," he said, "What is the nature of this life of ours? Let us face it: our lives are miserable, laborious and short." He went on to detail Farmer Jones' cruel exploitation as he butchered the animals and plundered the products of their labor. "Is it not crystal clear then, comrades," concluded Old Major, "that all the evils of this life spring from the tyranny of human beings? Only get rid of Man and the produce of labor would be our own. All men are

enemies. All animals are friends."

At this passionate invocation of a world ruled by those whose lives and labor made it fruitful—the animals themselves—everyone broke into a rousing anthem until the disturbance was silenced—for the time being—by a round of shot fired above them by Farmer Jones.

Three days later, Old Major died, and the other pigs—generally recognized as the cleverest of the animals on the farm—began to expound his teachings on "Animalism." Napoleon and Snowball, pre-eminent among the younger pigs, led the discussions, which centered on open rebellion. At first the other animals objected: some were swayed by thoughts of food or loyalty; others, like Mollie, the carthorse—who loved the ribbons that Farmer Jones tied in her hair—actually enjoyed the frills that man provided. The pigs were angered by the apathy that greeted their call to battle. They were equally exasperated by the raven, Moses, who squawked of forbearance, and of a better life "in heaven" after death. Napoleon "had to argue very hard to persuade [the animals] there was no such place." Finally, however, he convinced the group to accept Animalism.

Meanwhile, Farmer Jones, "fallen on evil days," began to neglect the animals. One day he failed to feed them altogether, and they broke into the stalls to get at the food. When Jones and his farmhands burst into the barn, whips ready, the enraged animals attacked the men and drove them completely off the farm. The animals were left victorious—and alone.

In their initial elation, the animals burned all the farm implements, along with any other items that smacked of man— including Mollie's ribbons. Then they warily entered the farmhouse—where, to their utter disgust, they found Mollie, trying on a fine ribbon. Seeing how weak and capricious even an animal could be, they agreed that in their new order no animal would inhabit the house, put on clothes, or in any other way imitate humans.

As the first order of business, Snowball removed the Manor Farm sign from the front gate and replaced it with a sign reading "Animal Farm." Then, in great white letters, on the barn wall the pigs painted the Seven Commandments of Animalism:

1. Whatever goes on two legs is an enemy.

2. Whatever goes on four legs, or has wings, is a friend.

3. No animal shall wear clothes.

4. No animal shall sleep in a bed.

5. No animal shall drink alcohol.

6. No animal shall kill another animal.

7. All animals are equal.

Just then, the unmilked cows "set up a loud lowing" of complaint. The pigs, whose forehooves made "good milkers," soon filled many buckets from the cows' swollen udders; but they left the apportionment of the milk until later, after "more important work" in the fields. "When the animals came back in the evening, it was noticed that the milk had disappeared."

Later, when the pigs also appropriated the windfallen apples, they explained that "day and night we are watching over your welfare. It is for *your* sake that we drink that milk and eat those apples." Napoleon and Snowball now organized committees to put the others to work—though, as managers, they themselves participated in none of the actual labor. But the animals were given all the hay they could eat, and gradually they accepted the pigs' dominance.

Meanwhile, Farmer Jones had spread the news of the uprising to his neighbors, Pilkington and Frederick. Frightened by the thought that their own animals might revolt, they agreed to form a contingent of men to launch a counterattack on Jones' farm.

A fierce battle ensued. The animals, led by Snowball, once again drove the humans from the farm. Snowball was wounded in the engagement, and several animals were killed, but the survivors were elated by their successful defense. Afterward, Mollie, discouraged by the dearth of ribbons in her life, left the farm never to return.

Now Snowball and Napoleon began to compete for leadership. Their struggle culminated at a meeting where the animals were to vote on Snowball's plan for a windmill he had designed to supply electricity to the farm, thus easing the animals' burden. Napoleon appeared at the meeting with a contingent of sheep which he had trained to interrupt Snowball's speech, repeatedly bleating out the Animal Farm slogan, "Four legs good, two legs bad"—until no animal could remember what was being said. Then, just before the vote was called, Napoleon summoned a pack of ferocious dogs, who chased Snowball from the farm. After this display, the animals dared not question Napoleon's will; nor did they fail to note that the dogs he always kept around "wagged their tails to him as other dogs did to Mr. Jones."

Even after Napoleon's brainwashing sessions, when some of the animals came forward, fervently confessing their allegiances to Snowball, they were immediately torn apart by Napoleon's dogs—who then set them to building the windmill, which he had once opposed. But it was the workhorse Boxer, in his simple-minded faithfulness, who truly inspired the animals. When Boxer promised that "I will work harder," and agreed that "Napoleon is always right," any objections to the project were silenced.

The building of the windmill began. The pigs, as usual, did no actual work. While they supervised, Boxer wore himself out hauling huge stones from the quarry. Napoleon then determined that certain "materials" would be needed to finish the mill and decreed that he must bend the "two legs bad" rule—the First Commandment of Animalism—and deal with a man who could make their purchases. The animals were also placed on rations in order that their "surplus" food could be sold to purchase the needed materials. When the hens were told they had to give up their eggs, they put up a brief and futile resistance in which nine hens were killed. The shocked animals consulted the list of commandments; they concluded that they must have had remembered the sixth incorrectly, for it now read "No animal shall kill another animal *without cause.*"

Soon "Comrade Napoleon" had persuaded Pilkington and Frederick to buy wood from Animal Farm. "Napoleon had forced Frederick to raise his price by twelve pounds"; but Frederick, in turn, swindled Napoleon by paying for the wood with false notes. Enraged and humiliated, Napoleon now prepared for a follow-up attack from Frederick, It came the next morning. Frederick's men managed to destroy the newly finished windmill, but once again were finally driven off by the angry animals. The pigs watched the battle from the safety of the farmhouse—and, later, got uproariously drunk on Farmer Jones' whiskey.

Before long, Napoleon had moved into Farmer Jones' house, sleeping in his bed and soon drinking all his liquor. And when the animals again went to look at the Seven Commandments, they found written, "No animal shall sleep in a bed *without sheets*" and "No animal shall drink alcohol *to excess.*"

Through the never-ending exhortations of Squealer, the animals began to reconstruct the windmill and to accept even smaller rations. Squealer even convinced them—almost—that they had never been happier or better fed. And their "readjustment" hardships were forgotten under endless processions and marches celebrating their victory over Frederick—and honoring their benefactor and greatest hero of all, Napoleon.

As the windmill neared completion, old Boxer was approaching his retirement. One day, as he hauled a great load of stone, the faithful old workhorse collapsed, and Napoleon arranged for a cart to take him "to the hospital." But when the already uneasy animals gathered to wave goodbye to their friend, they were told what was written on the "hospital" van's side: "Alfred Simmons, Horse Slaughterer and Glue Boiler." As they called out to warn Boxer, he tried to escape, but he was too feeble to kick his way out. The next day Squealer assured everyone that he himself had been there at the hospital when Boxer died; the doctor, he said, had just bought the cart from the horse slaughterer. Relieved and chastened, the animals returned to their duties.

Finally, the windmill was rebuilt. But rather than supplying power to the farm, it was used to grind corn—which was then sold for a profit. The suffering animals worked by now out of habit, still under the dim illusion that it was they who ran the farm. "None of the old dreams had been abandoned."

Then one day their illusions were shattered. Napoleon and his charges appeared in the yard, dressed in Jones' clothes and striding on two legs instead of four. In his hoof Napoleon clasped a whip—while the sheep bleated, "Four legs good, two legs better." Indeed, the last Commandment of Animalism had been altered to read, "All animals are equal *but some animals are more equal than others.*"

Later that day, Jones' neighbors arrived in their carts to be entertained. The animals gathered around while Pilkington toasted Napoleon for his successful management tactics, tidy profits and his "discipline" of the animals. "If you have your lower animals to contend with," pronounced the human farmer, emptying his mug, "we have our lower classes." In pride, Napoleon announced that the name of "Animal Farm" would revert to "Manor Farm"—and, in the end, the animals could not distinguish which of the guests were men and which were pigs.

THE RED BADGE OF COURAGE

by
Stephen Crane
(1871 - 1900)

Type of work. Personal episodic war novel

Setting: American Civil War

Principal characters:
Henry Fielding, a sensitive, inexperienced youth
Jim Conklin, a gangly young soldier
Wilson, a boisterous recruit

Story Overview:

Private Henry Fleming, like many young men his age, had ached to go to war. He had dreamed of engaging in acts of heroism, detailed campaigns against the enemy, and the noble discipline of army life. The frequent newspaper write-ups of the brave battles against "Johnny Reb" only served to heighten his vivid imagination.

Henry's mother opposed the war—and the kind of men who fought in it—and resisted his clamoring zeal to join up. "Henry," she warned, "don't you be a fool." Then she hid her face and wept.

Henry enlisted the very next day. Expecting a tear-fraught scene when he confronted his mother again, he was oddly disappointed to hear her stoical response: "The Lord's will be done . . . Watch out and take good care of yourself. Don't go a-thinkin' you can lick the whole rebel army at the start. Yeh must never do no shirkin' on my account. If yeh have to be kilt or do a mean thing, don't think of anything 'cept what's right."

After impatiently enduring this oration, the youth had hastily departed, leaving his mother sobbing over her peeled potatoes. But once on the road, he felt a pang of guilt and, turning a last time toward home before trudging off to the brigade, he bowed his head.

Henry's romantic illusions of war were quickly shattered. The drudgery of camp life, endless drills and—most maddening of all—the long days of doing nothing, soon took their toll. After a while, "he had grown to regard himself merely a part of a vast blue demonstration." His mess-mates argued and fidgeted, impatient for a taste of battle. Various theories of how they would enter the fighting were invented and wagered on, the foremost being that they would outflank the enemy and attack them from the rear.

Amid these speculations, Henry struggled with a problem he felt exclusively his own: would he stand bravely when faced with enemy fire, or would he run? He was consumed by the question, and could find no one with whom to share his fears. Try as he might, he could not convince himself of his courage—and the twinkling lights of the enemy campfires across the valley did nothing to ease his mind.

The brigade was divided into two groups: seasoned soldiers and raw recruits. The veterans generally scorned the younger men, referring to them as "fresh fish." The new recruits in turn boasted of their superior knowledge compared to that of their "mindless" commanders.

One day Henry chanced to hear two of his companions, Conklin and Wilson, as they agreed vehemently over the rumor of a planned disencampment. The tall, thin Conklin claimed to have overheard that the troops were in for a long march. The loud and boisterous Wilson, on the other hand, was skeptical. The next day, much to Wilson's delight, the brigade stayed put, and, hounded by his scoffing comrade, Conklin was forced to defend his honor with his fists.

One gray morning, however, the rumor became truth: the brigade was mustered and ordered to move out. Entering a deep forest near a battle site, he heard the popping of muskets sound in the distance. Henry's valor was about to be tested.

The Union soldiers approached the field of battle, a plot of ground surrounded on all sides by trees. Wilson, in premonition of his own death, turned over to Henry a packet of personal letters. Suddenly, fear rose up in Henry's throat; everything around him appeared ominous, threatening.

Skirmishers led the brigade into the fray. Then, just as the men were about to rise up in an all-out charge, a companion brigade raced past them in frenzied, full retreat—despite the shouted orders from their officers to turn and fight. But now, witnessing the charging rebel soldiers, Henry's own fear was swept aside. He fired his musket, and suddenly his ears were filled with the roaring of gunfire. It sounded like "a firework that once ignited, proceeds superior to circumstances until its blazing vitality fades." Filled with the rage of battle and choking on the thick smoke of the fusillade, he reloaded his musket and fired mechanically into the noise and dust.

Finding themselves alive after this first assault, Henry and his comrades relaxed a little—only to confront another bitter attack launched by the persistent Rebels. Now, one by one, weary soldiers around him dropped their muskets and ran wild-eyed toward the rear. Seeing his companions in retreat, Henry also threw down his weapon and joined the blind panic. He passed a tattered regiment hastening to the front and thought them fools. They were mindless puppets, "sacrificed to the war god."

Henry slunk through the woods until he came upon a general surrounded by his orderlies. Here he discovered that the regiment he had previously termed "fools" had come to the rescue of his brigade, turning back the advancing Confederate forces. The battle had been won; but Henry had retreated in shame—and suddenly he felt himself cheated. A surge of remorse swept over and through him. He tried to justify his cowardice—he was, after all, only one small part of a large army. And, like a frightened squirrel, he had merely followed his instinct to escape danger, so that he could return and fight again. Still, he avoided rejoining to his brigade.

Henry continued to work his way through the woods, the sounds of warfare fading away behind him. In a clearing, he came across the corpse of a dead soldier, with ants swarming over its greying skin. Shivering at the sight, Henry turned and ran back toward the battle-ground, where he joined a tattered column of wounded soldiers staggering away from the front lines. Now awash in grief, he "wished he too had a wound, a red badge of courage."

Henry was horrified by the sight of one gaunt, pitiful, dazed and ashen-faced refugee in the crowd. Drawing nearer, he discovered that the soldier was Jim Conklin, trudging along stiffly, a bloody wound slashing down the side of his body as if it had been inflicted by wolves. Henry, trying his best to sooth his dazed comrade, followed along till, at last, Conklin swayed to the side of the road, his limbs jerking, pain contorting his features. Then he fell to the ground, a smile twisting his face into a death mask.

Once more Henry fled. He wandered about in the confusion of the back lines while, all about him, columns of soldiers marched to their various destinations. He wished he could be counted among the dead. He envied them. They were heroes, he, a deserter and a coward.

As Henry neared the front lines once more, a swarm of blue-coated soldiers suddenly emerged from the crest of a hill, running in his direction and followed by the roar of gunfire. When Henry tried to question one of the panic-stricken fugitives, the enraged soldier swung a musket and struck him in the head.

Stunned, he was helped back to his regiment. Wilson, the same private who had earlier turned over his packet of letters to Henry, was waiting among the group; but he was a changed man: no longer a swaggering braggart, but helpful, quiet and sensible. Now, as Henry's wound was washed, his shame vanished. In returning the letters to his comrade, he actually felt superior to Wilson who, after retreating from the noble death that he had foreordained for himself, no longer seemed the virile hero he had claimed to be.

Following a day's rest, the regiment was moved to a wooded area where they prepared for battle. But this time when the shots were fired, Henry held his position doggedly. With an intense hatred towards his enemy, he fired into the air and swore like a madman, much to the delight of his lieutenant. When the battle had ended and the enemy troops had dispersed, Henry, in his frenzy, actually had to be restrained from further fire. He was a hero; and his regiment was chosen to lead the next charge—a battle most of the soldiers would not survive.

On command, the Union troops moved forward, with men falling in grotesque, twisted shapes all around. The standard bearer dropped, and Henry snatched up the flag from the dead man's hands to take up the charge. With his

wounded lieutenant, he moved among the men, cursing and cajoling them to fight. It seemed as though the whole field of battle revolved around their small group, as though they alone poured a wilting fire into the Rebels' retreating ranks.

Just then the general rode up, rebuking the regiment's colonel for retreating under fire. "Mud-diggers," he called the men, a term they hotly resented. Once more the regiment was called upon to advance and retake a coveted position by a fence. The enemy returned the charge, pelting the bluecoats with demoralizing fire. Unfaltering, Henry pressed onward, shouting encouragement to the troops. When they saw they were about to be overtaken, the Rebel forces retreated, leaving only a few stubborn greycoats gathered around their flag. The Union ranks stopped short of this salient line and fired a volley into the group. With that, the Rebel flag fell into their hands, along with four prisoners. The battle had been won.

But once the smoke cleared a bit, the regiment beheld another advancing group of Confederates. Again the men positioned themselves and began to fire, bravely beating back the enemy in a cloud of smoke and whining musket balls. By degrees, the field grew quieter, till at last the firing ceased and the triumphant regiment was ordered to fall back.

As the blue-clad survivors made their painful, slow way across the silent battlefield, time stood still. The whole action seemed now to have lasted only a brief moment. Henry had fought with valor. Many had witnessed his note-worthy deeds on this second day of battle, and he flushed with pride upon hearing the regimental officers' commendations of his courageous flagbearer.

Then, suddenly, Henry's pride was assailed by the memory of his cowardice on the first day. His earlier act of desertion overshadowed and dulled his later acts of heroism. True, no one had seen him bolt in fear, but "for a moment he blushed and the light of his soul flickered with shame."

It was only with time that Henry came to understand: his first fears had stemmed from inexperience. Now he had faced the enemy—and himself. He knew now the true measure of his courage. "He had rid himself of the great sickness of battle. The sultry nightmare was in the past." No longer a boy, he was a veteran, a man.

Commentary:

Stephen Crane's colorful imagery and animation place him among the great realist writers of his day. Focusing on one soldier's inner struggles, his personal victories and defeats, rather than on the more obvious collective conflicts of war, his novel serves as an effective tool to convey the true impacts of battle. Henry was impelled to fight first by the vision of glory, then, in turns, by fear, bloodlust, vanity, and, finally, and finally, by a soldier's well-earned pride.

Authentic to the last detail, this work, a precursor to modern war fiction, reveals the vividness of battle and blends it with symbolism and feeling.

SULA

by Toni Morrison, Knopf and Random House, New York, N.Y., 1973

Type of work: Rural African-American cultural novel

Setting: The Bottom, a black neighborhood in the hills above the city of Medallion, Ohio; 1919 through 1965

Principal characters:
Sula, a fiercely independent young girl
Nel, her loyal best friend
Hannah, Sula's mother
Eva, Sula's grandmother, the matriarch of a ramshackle establishment

Commentary:

Pulitzer-Prize-winning Toni Morrison's *Sula* resonates with the subtexts of black culture: its vernacular, its pathos, and its passion. "The Bottom" can be seen as a representation of the paradox faced by individuals who try to rise above the barriers of race and class. Those, like Sula, who attempt to escape the despair and cultural chaos that billow through both the individual lives of poverty-stricken black Americans, have their spirits crushed, while those, like Nel, who acquiesce to the conditions, are slowly crippled *by* the culture. There is always a sense of frustration and provocation. Action doesn't seem to lead anywhere but back to "the Bottom." Her characters are constantly faced with picking the best among bad choices. But the worst choice of all, Morrison seems to be saying, is to do nothing, "to watch" while a little boy drowns or a woman is engulfed in flames, to passively look on as life—no better today than it was tomorrow—passes by.

Story Overview:

In 1919, the toll of World War I was conspicuous in the Bottom, a black neighborhood of Medallion, Ohio. One war victim was Shadrack, a shell-shocked young man who, every January 3rd after that year, had celebrated his own "National Suicide Day," walking through the Bottom down Carpenter's Road "with a cowbell and a hangman's rope calling the people together, [telling] them that this was their only chance to kill themselves or each other."

In November, 1920, ten-year-old Nel Wright traveled with her mother to visit New Orleans. The trip was more than an awakening for Nel—it was a jolt. She and her mother were isolated in a "colored" train car and made to use "colored" toilet facilities. "It was on the train . . . that she resolved to be on her guard—always."

Soon after her return from New Orleans, Nel befriended a neighbor girl named Sula. The friendship was scorned by Nel's fastidious mother. But Nel "preferred Sula's woolly house . . . where Sula's mother, Hannah, never scolded or gave directions" to her own well-ordered home.

Sula lived in the ramshackle rooming house kept by her crippled and solitary old grandmother, Eva. Once, Eva had been a stable and sociable married woman. But when her husband, BoyBoy, walked off and left her penniless with three children, she grew desperate; finally

one day she had walked over to the track and stuck her leg under a train. The insurance money she collected had fed the children. Then, just a few years later, BoyBoy had returned to Eva's door—with another woman in tow. Eva took his visit hard. Soon afterwards she "began her retreat to her bedroom." So, under Eva's "distant eye," her children had grown up. Eventually her middle child, Pearl, had married and moved away; then Hannah, widowed when Sula was three years old, moved back with her mother. Plum, the boychild, went to war in 1917 and returned in 1920 to his bedroom, a daydreaming drug addict.

One night about a year after his homecoming, Eva had struggled on her one leg down to Plum's bedroom—the same room where she had cradled him as a newborn in her arms. Finding Plum, as usual, immersed in his fantasy world, she doused him with the contents of the can she carried. Then, while Plum looked on in a stupor, Eva struck a match and lit his kerosene-soaked body. "Quickly, as the whoosh of flames engulfed him, she closed the door and made her slow and painful journey back to the top of the house."

As Nel and Sula turned twelve, both their friendship and their sense of sexuality deepened. The twenty-one-year-old Ajax's comment of "pig meat" when they passed him on the way to the ice cream parlor actually delighted and excited them. Days later, however, Sula overheard something that hurt her—her own mother's comment to a neighbor lady: " . . . I love Sula," said Hannah quietly, "I just don't like her."

During this turbulent passage, Nel and Sula were bonded forever by a searing coming-of-age experience. They were playing together in the woods one day when Chicken Little, a small neighborhood boy, showed up. The girls hung a tire swing from a tree limb over and pushed Chicken Little back and forth across the gulf. Sula, though, in trying to grab the boy, lost her grip, sending him fluttering into the current. While the two girls sat, dumb, silent, motionless, "the water darkened and closed . . . over the place where Chicken Little sank." Suddenly, Sula was pierced by the conviction that Shadrack, who lived just through the woods, must have seen what had happened. Swallowing her panic, she ran to his house and casually asked if he had seen anything. "Always," came Shadrack's cryptic one-word reply.

Eventually a bargeman found Chicken Little's crumpled body lying somewhere downriver. Nel and Sula attended the funeral—but neither girl ever told what had happened.

One day during the next year, Hannah turned to the aging Eva and asked offhandedly, "Mamma, did you ever love us?" Eva responded with an offended litany of the hardships she had suffered for her children. Then, in the same casual voice, Hannah continued: "What'd you kill Plum for, Mamma?" At this, Eva recounted the dreams she'd had that Plum would try to crawl back into her womb. " . . . I had to keep him out so I just thought of a way he could die like a man not all scrunched up inside my womb, but like a man."

The following day as Eva gazed out the window, she noticed Hannah lighting a yard fire. Then she glanced out again—and Hannah was burning. "The flames . . . were licking the blue cotton dress, making her dance." With all the energy in her being, Eva lifted herself onto her good leg and hurled herself reeling out the second-floor window. But Eva didn't reach her daughter in time; Hannah died on the way to the hospital. Eva recovered from her own injuries that day—but she never would forget the disturbing memory of "Sula standing on the back porch just looking" at her burning mother, not doing anything to save her.

In 1927, Sula's friend Nel married Jude, a capable man, full of dreams, but thwarted in his hopes to get on a road-building crew. It was "rage and a determination to take on a man's role anyhow that made him press Nel about settling down . . . " Sula was elated about Nel's wedding—and about her own plans to leave Medallion to see what the world offered. Neither girl realized that it would be ten years before they'd see each other again.

When Sula returned to Medallion in 1937, she came strutting home dressed like a movie star. But "Eva looked at Sula pretty much the same way she had looked at BoyBoy that time when he returned after he'd left her . . . " When Eva warned that God would punish Sula, Sula angrily shot back, "Which God? The one watched you burn Plum?" Eva immediately answered, "Don't talk to me about no burning. You watched your own mamma." But in the end, Sula won the battle; a few months later she had Eva put in a rest home.

Nel was overjoyed by Sula's return; the friend "who made her laugh, who made her see old things with new eyes, in whose presence she felt clever, gentle and a little raunchy." But both women had changed; they had grown up—and grown apart. When Nel questioned Sula's decision to put Eva in a home, Sula defended herself warmly. Eva, after all, was dangerous; she had murdered Plum.

The fatal blow to the friendship, however, came when Nel walked in on Sula—in the arms of Jude. At the same moment, Nel had lost both her husband and her best friend. Even two years later, the people of the Bottom still gossiped about the way Sula had lured away Nel's husband. In short, Sula was now regarded as an evil force, and any death or other unfortunate event was linked to her. At twenty-nine, she found herself a reject, a pariah. At first, the attentions of Ajax, the Bottom's own Don Juan, reanimated Sula. Ajax was fascinated by her independent air. But soon enough he recognized the signs that Sula would, "like all of her sisters before her, put to him the death-knell question, 'Where you been?'"

Although she was only thirty, Sula's health was dealt a deathly blow by Ajax's departure. Nel, hearing this, came to visit "her enemy." Spiritually abandoned by Hannah—the mother who had withered under the same soul-deep abandonment from her own mother—Sula had felt ever since she was ten years old that the only person she could count on was Nel: Nel, her best friend; Nel, her accomplice in the death of Chicken Little.

Sula was surly. "You think I don't know what your life is like because I ain't living it?" she asked as she downed her pain medication. "I know what every colored woman in this country is doing . . . Dying. Just like me." When Nel asked why Sula had stolen her husband, she responded, that she hadn't loved loved him— "He just filled up the space." "I was good to you, Sula," Nel pled. "Why don't that matter?" Sula answered wearily: "Being good to somebody is just like being mean to somebody. Risky. You don't get nothing for it."

As Nel left, Sula drifted off under the medication, mumbling about how she had "stood there watching her burn and was thrilled. I wanted her to keep on jerking like that, to keep on dancing." Then all at once Sula realized that her own body wasn't breathing; and the last thought that came into her head was, "It didn't even hurt. Wait'll I tell Nel."

With Sula's burial, people in the Bottom felt "a brighter day was dawning." There were hopeful signs that a tunnel would be built, and Negro workers would be hired to build it. Instead, a late-autumn ice storm froze everything and locked the Bottom in the grip of cold. Finally, with the coming of the new year, 1941, the cold broke. As January 3 rolled around, the sun shone brightly, and Shadrack reluctantly embarked on his usual solitary National Suicide Day parade.

This National Suicide Day, however, was different. For once, the Bottom's residents joined in. First one or two, then more, until a sizable crowd paraded down the street. Then, at the mouth of the new tunnel—which, it turned out, blacks had been excluded from working on—the procession turned into a riot. "Old and young, women and children, lame and hearty, they killed as best they could" at the tunnel "they were forbidden to build." When the thawed earth finally gave way and the tunnel collapsed, "a lot of them died there."

One day in 1965, twenty-four years after the collapse of the tunnel, Nel headed through the familiar streets of the Bottom to pay a visit to Eva at the Home for the Aged. "Tell me how you killed that little boy," was Eva's first request. Nel insisted that it was Sula who had been pushing the swing. "You. Sula. What's the difference?" Eva told her. "You was there. You watched, didn't you? Me, I never would've watched."

Nel left the old folks' home summoning up a long-buried memory of the quandary they had dealt with: Why hadn't they tried to rescue Chicken Little? Why didn't they ever tell anyone? But it wouldn't have done any good, Nel thought. "I did not watch it," she finally said under her breath, "I just saw it."

Then, wandering down by the cemetery and recalling her friend Sula's lonely death, she paused at the grave site. In a burst of transcendence, Nel fathomed how much she really loved Sula.

OLIVER TWIST

by
Charles Dickens
(1812-1870)

Type of work: Social fiction

Setting: Victorian London and vicinity

Principal characters:

Oliver Twist, an orphan
Agnes Fleming, Oliver's mother
Mr. Bumble, a fat workhouse beadle
Mrs. Corney, workhouse matron
Mr. and Mrs. Sowerberry, the unpleasant undertaker and his wife
The Dodger, Bates, Crackit, Fagin, Sikes, and Nancy, thieves
Monks, Oliver's half brother
Mr. Brownlow, a kind, wealthy old man
Rose Maylie, Agnes Fleming's sister
Mrs. Maylie, Rose's adoptive aunt

Commentary:

This first novel by Dickens treats the criminal and aristocrat positions in English society, while accurately portraying the divisions within both. His often sardonic, ruthless descriptions of the corrupt institutions designed to help society, characterize, in vivid twists of irony, the blackness of life for the poor of his time.

Story Overview:

Oliver Twist was born in the workhouse, where his mother was brought after she was found her lying in the street, sick and racked with the pangs of childbirth. When the baby had been delivered, the mother gasped, "Let me see the child and die." The surgeon and the drunken nurse in attendance held out the newborn before her eyes, whereupon she "gazed around wildly, shuddered, fell back and died."

For the next nine years, Oliver was entrusted to the care of Mrs. Corney, the matron entrusted with the workhouse's orphaned children. Mrs. Corney spent most of the weekly seven pence allotted to each orphan for her own means, starving the little ones in her care.

One day it was decreed that Oliver was old enough to be returned to the main workhouse with the older children and adults. The workhouse beadle, Mr. Bumble, brought him to the board of trustees, who declared that the boy was to be taught a decent trade: picking oakum.

In the workhouse, the emaciated youngsters, fed barely three meals of watery gruel a day, had developed a system of picking straws to determine upon whom the unlucky task of asking for more food would fall. One day soon after his arrival, Oliver drew the lot. When he had finished his bowl of gruel and asked for more, the master's mouth dropped in astonishment. It was the height of disrespect for a new boy to demand such privileges.

The indignant trustees tossed the miserable wretch into a cell and posted a bill for his sale: for five pounds any tradesman could buy him. Oliver was soon purchased by Mr. Sowerberry, an undertaker.

On his first night's stay at the mortuary, Oliver was fed scraps from the dog ration and consigned to his berth among the coffins in a dismal storage room. Nor was this treatment ameliorated during the following days and nights. Then, one day, another servant tried to incite Oliver to anger by insulting his dead mother. Oliver, goaded to violence, immediately "felled him to the ground," after which he was soundly beaten by the Sowerberry's and sent to his room.

Before dawn the next day, Oliver furtively packed his few belongings and fled. Begging for food along his way, the weary orphan trudged for seven days until he reached the village of Barnet, near London. There he was befriended by a shabbily dressed young thief who called himself "the artful Dodger." Promising Oliver the chance for friends and a roof over his head, the "Dodger" brought him to Fagin the Jew, Dodger's new employer.

Fagin, a loathsome and depraved criminal, supervised a lively gang of youthful thieves. Soon Oliver was initiated, with the help of the Dodger, another young adventurer named Charley Bates, and Fagin himself, into the sly and delicate art of picking pockets. The lessons were taught in such an amusing manner that Oliver was unaware that was he was doing was illegal. The whole procedure was played out as a game, like touch tag or drop the handkerchief.

But when Bates and the Dodger took Oliver on his first caper where they attempted to steal the handkerchief of a passing gentleman, Oliver watched bewildered as his companions took quietly to their heels. Suddenly realizing that he was implicated in some sort of crime, he froze. When he finally came to his senses and turned to run, the Dodger and Bates, trying to blend in with the crowd, joined in the chase and called for him to halt. Finally, Oliver was struck down by the mob and taken summarily to court. Reeling from pain and illness, the boy fainted.

Fortunately, a witness to the crime was able to clear Oliver of wrongdoing. Mr. Brownlow, the gentleman whose handkerchief had triggered the drama, dropped his charges and took pity on the haggard waif. He brought Oliver home with him where a maid nursed the surprisingly pleasant mannered boy back to health. And now, for the first time in his life, Oliver experienced the reality of love. He thrived under the Brownlows' affection.

As time progressed, Mr. Brownlow noticed more and more the striking resemblance between Oliver and the face in a portrait of Agnes Fleming, a family friend, which hung in the Brownlow parlor.

Meanwhile, Nancy, one of Fagin's thieves, had been coerced to spy on Oliver. One day, while Brownlow was on an errand, Nancy abetted by another member of the band accosted Oliver in the street and kidnapped him. But after they took him back to Fagin's, Nancy regretted the act and secretly vowed to help the boy. Late one night, she overheard a man named Monks plot with Fagin to destroy Oliver with a life of crime.

Back at the workhouse, meanwhile, after all these years, new developments were unfolding. Mrs. Corney, the children's matron, had been privy to the dying words of the nurse who tended Oliver's mother during childbirth. The impoverished nurse had confessed to stealing and pawning a locket from the dying woman. Mrs Corney had retrieved the locket from the pawn shop and had kept it hidden all these years.

During these years, Bumble, the workhouse beadle, sensing that Mrs. Corney was actually quite wealthy, had courted and married her. One day, Bumble was approached by a stranger named Monks—one of Fagin's lackeys—who paid the beadle for information about Oliver. Again sensing a profit could be had, Bumble implied that his wife might have further information to share. Later, the Bumbles secretly met with Monks and sold him the locket, pledging that they would preserve silence. With a leer, Monks then turned to open a trap door—and dropped the locket into the river below.

Bumble also answered an advertisement posted by Brownlow inquiring about the whereabouts of Oliver. He told Brownlow that Oliver had mercilessly beaten a workhouse servant and had bolted for no apparent reason. This destroyed Brownlow's esteem for Oliver. Shaken by this news, with his esteem for Oliver destroyed, Brownlow left town.

Back in the London slums, Fagin held the kidnapped Oliver prisoner until he decided the time was ripe to involve him in a robbery. This act would reintroduce Oliver to the criminal world, forever dooming him to a life on the street.

And so it was orchestrated: Two thieves, Sikes and Crackit, took Oliver along to help them break into a house. Sikes successfully forced Oliver through a small window—but the servants heard the ruckus, appeared with a gun, and shot the trapped and terrified intruder. Reaching in through the narrow opening, Sikes grabbed Oliver and carried him off into the darkness. But Crackit persuaded Sikes to abandon the now unconscious boy, who they threw in a ditch.

When he regained his senses, Oliver, his mangled arm dripping with blood, hobbled weakly to the first house he saw—the same house he had just burgled. Mrs. Maylie, its owner, with her niece, Rose, took mercy on the wounded lad. She sent for the officers, who listened attentively to Oliver's story. Afterwards, exhausted, the young burglar fell into a long, deep sleep.

Like the Brownlows, the Maylies found themselves strangely taken by their inadvertent guest. In the Maylies' country retreat, Oliver was carefully nursed back to health. Having suffered pain and abuse in the bleak city, the boy basked in the joy of his new surroundings, but he never forgot the earlier kindnesses of the Brownlows. His one great regret was that he could not renew his bonds with them; Mr. Brownlow, he discovered, had left London.

One day, Oliver was delivering a letter when—by chance—he ran into Monks. Cursing Oliver, Monks fell to the ground in an epileptic fit. The man's strange behavior deeply disturbed the boy.

Later, back in the city, Nancy overheard Fagin and Monks planning to recapture Oliver. At the risk of her own life, she drugged her paramour Sikes and stole off to reveal the plot to Oliver's protectress, Rose Maylie.

On a trip to the city, meanwhile, Oliver finally caught a glimpse of Mr. Brownlow, who had just returned to London. Overjoyed, he confided this good news to Rose, who, in turn, traveled to Brownlow's house to apprise him of all that had happened. She recounted her conversation with Nancy, and warned him of the scheme to kidnap Oliver. When she told Brownlow that Oliver himself was in the coach, Brownlow "hurried out of the room, down the stairs, up the coach steps, and into the coach without another word." The reunion was a joyous one; Brownlow "laughed and wept upon [Oliver's] neck in turns."

By this time, Fagin was beginning to suspect Nancy's duplicity; he had the young woman followed wherever she went. According to a previous arrangement, Nancy met Brownlow at a spot on the London Bridge, where she told Brownlow how he could find Monks. Fagin's spy hurried back with this information.

Upon hearing the news, Fagin decided to let Sikes take care of Nancy. When Fagin told Sikes of Nancy's treachery, the thief was enraged. Bursting into the room where his mistress was sleeping, he confronted her, shouting, "You were watched tonight and every word you said was heard!" Then he threw her to the floor and he clubbed her to death.

In another part of London, Mr. Brownlow had trapped Monks and brought him to his house, where Monks made a startling revelation: His real name was Edward Leeford. His father, Edwin, had separated from Edward's mother and married Agnes Fleming—the mother of Oliver Twist. Not long after his second marriage, Edwin died in Rome, but he had left a large inheritance to his sons, Edward and Oliver. Edward had hoped to destroy Oliver in order to claim the entire inheritance for himself.

The workhouse Bumbles—the only survivors who knew of Edward's secret—were then brought in for questioning. Mr. Bumble, so declared Mr. Brownlow, would never again occupy the high, "parochial office" to which he was accustomed.

Following Nancy's murder, the police moved in and captured Fagin and most of his den of thieves. The other few, Sikes included, were eventually apprehended by a mob of townspeople, but Sikes, desperately trying to escape the mob, slipped and tumbled to his death from a rooftop.

Fagin was tried and found guilty of robbery and complicity to murder, much to the joy of the townsfolk. Harrowed up by his crimes and imprisoned at Newgate to await hanging, Fagin gibbered madly in his cell. Oliver and Brownlow visited the prisoner to determine the whereabouts of certain documents he kept in his possession. After revealing whereabouts of the documents, he was led away to meet his fate on the gallows.

In spite of his half-brother's diabolic schemes against him, Oliver split the inheritance with Monks.

THE HUNCHBACK OF NOTRE DAME

by
Victor Hugo
(1802 - 1885)

Type of work: Gothic Romance

Setting: Paris, France; 1842

Principal characters:
Quasimodo, the grotesque hunchbacked bell-ringer of Notre Dame
Esmerelda, a beautiful sixteen-year-old gypsy girl
Pierre Gringoire, a poet and writer
Claude Frollo, an archdeacon who desires Esmerelda for his own

Story Overview:

It was the Festival of Fools day in Paris. A boisterous crowd had gathered to witness the performance of a play written by the Pierre Gringoire—and to choose the Prince of Fools, the title bestowed on the ugliest person in all Paris. Several acts into the play, however, the Parisians grew restless and demanded that the "Prince of Fools" be elected immediately.

To Gringoire's consternation, the crowd turned its attention from his production to the contest. After several hideous contestants had shown their faces, one particularly grotesque figure appeared before the judges. His huge head was "covered with red bristles [and] between his shoulders rose an enormous hump." This candidate had a forked chin and lip from which protruded a tusk, and one eye was covered by a wart. In spite of his deformities, however, he was strong and agile. This hideous creature was unanimously acclaimed Prince of Fools.

"It's Quasimodo," the crowd roared, "the bell ringer of Notre Dame." Placing a jester's hat on his head, a miter in his hand, and a robe on his rounded back, they paraded him through the streets of the city, singing and playing instruments. Quasimodo was overcome; this was the first time he had ever felt "the gratification of self-love." Deaf from long years of ringing Notre Dame's massive bells, he grinned in dignified muteness at the spectacle around him.

The procession paused when the crowd reached a spot where a trained goat, danced gracefully to the enchanting sounds of a beautiful young gypsy girl's tambourine. The girl was named Esmerelda. Suddenly, Frollo barged through the crowd, snatched the scepter from Quasimodo's hand, and ripped off the hat and robe. The gathering stood aghast at the Archdeacon's harsh treatment—yet they knew Quasimodo would submit himself to the master who, many years earlier, had taken in a deformed, unwanted baby left in the foundling box at the gates of the cathedral.

Later that night, Gringoire, now destitute and forced to walk Paris' cold streets, watched in horror as two men—one of them hooded—abducted the beautiful dancer Esmerelda. Gringoire called for the guard and drew closer to the scene, and saw that the hooded man's partner was none other than Quasimodo, who,

on orders from the other, struck Gringoire to the ground. Phoebus, the captain of the guard, appeared and commanded the two men to free Esmerelda In the ensuing melee, Quasimodo's accomplice released Esmerelda and escaped. Esmerelda, moved by Phoebus' bravery, immediately fell in love with him.

Gringoire soon ran into a band of thieves and beggars, who threatened to hang him unless one of their women agreed to marry him. Just as the noose was lowered about his neck, Esmerelda stepped forward and volunteered herself. The couple was married, but Gringoire did not enjoy a wedding night—Esmerelda now loved Phoebus; she had rescued the poet merely out of pity.

Meanwhile, Quasimodo, for his part in Esmerelda's attempted kidnapping, was sentenced to a flogging in the marketplace and a one-hour public humiliation on the revolving pillory. Bleeding and exhausted, he was soon overcome by thirst and pled for water. His plea, however, was greeted with scorn by the throng, who hurled stones and insults at him. But once more, just as she had with Gringoire, Esmerelda appeared. The derisive crowd parted, and she ascended the pillory and placed a water flask to Quasimodo's swollen lips. "A big tear was seen to trickle slowly down his deformed face . . . perhaps the first that he had shed since he arrived at manhood." Quasimodo spied Frollo in the distance, which mitigated Esmerelda's kindness; secretly, the Archdeacon had become infatuated with her and wanted her for himself. To Quasimodo, all but this curious and enchanting girl had turned away from him.

Over time, Esmerelda's love for Phoebus turned more fiery; she even trained her goat to spell out Phoebus' name with alphabet blocks—an act many considered irrefutable evidence that she was a sorceress. At the same time, Frollo became more jealous of Esmerelda's attraction to Phoebus. One day, learning that the pair planned a rendezvous, he followed them to the prescribed spot and watched from a hiding place. When he saw Phoebus kiss Esmerelda, the priest, overcome by envy, leapt out and plunged his dagger into the captain's breast. Stunned, Esmerelda pulled the dagger from Phoebus' body, and then, as the assailant fled, she fainted.

When Esmerelda was found with the knife in her hand, she was arrested for murdering Phoebus. Frollo decided that if he could not have her for himself, he would rather see her hang for murder and witchcraft. His confederates brutally tortured Esmerelda, extracting a confession that she had used sorcery to murder Phoebus. The judge's sentence was three-fold: "to pay an indemnity, to do penance before the grand porch of Notre Dame, and to be taken with her goat to be hanged."

While Esmerelda awaited execution, Frollo appeared at her cell door and confessed that it was he who had killed her lover. He tried to strike a deal: in return for her love, he would spare her life. Horrified, the girl cried, "Begone monster! Leave me to die! Nothing shall bring us together, not even hell itself."

Unknown to Esmerelda, Phoebus had not died from his wound. On the day of the execution, he and his new fiance gazed on at the court proceedings. Soon to be married, did not come forward. Esmerelda, however, caught sight of him, but unfortunately too late: her doom was sealed; there would be no rescue.

Frollo came to give Esmerelda last rites and once more to offer himself to her; once more she refused him. Taken to the town square, the hangman was just about to place the noose around Esmerelda's neck, when Quasimodo vaulted up on the scaffold, scooped the girl into his arms, and carried her into the cathedral shouting, "Sanctuary, Sanctuary!" Safe within Notre Dame's walls and high atop the bell towers, the hideous hunchback held the girl aloft for the delighted crowd to see.

After Esmerelda had rejected him, Frollo hurriedly left the proceedings, missing the girl's rescue. He wandered the streets of Paris and reflected on "the folly of eternal vows" and "the vanity of chastity." Later, when he returned to his room in the cathedral, he looked out at the spires of Notre Dame, and there beheld a spectacle that made him shudder. "Twas she herself, pale . . . sad . . . she was free. She was dead." The sight of her "ghost" chilled his blood.

In the meantime, Quasimodo brought Esmerelda food and blankets. "In the day time you shall stay here," he explained, motioning to the locked doors. "At night you walk about all over the church. But stir not a step out of it either by night or by day, or they will catch you and kill you and it will be the death of me." Esmerelda, at first frightened by her rescuer's appearance, was joy-struck when she found that he had saved her goat as well.

"Never till now was I aware how hideous I am," Quasimodo said, gazing upon the lovely girl. "When I compare myself with you, I cannot help pitying myself, poor unhappy monster that I am." When Esmerelda asked him why he had risked his life to save her, he replied, "You have forgotten a wretch who attempted to carry you off, a wretch to whom the very next day, you brought relief on the ignominious pillory. A draught of water and a look of pity are more than I can repay with my life." Then, giving her a whistle that would warn him if anyone came to abduct her, he departed.

Although Quasimodo loved Esmerelda, he also knew that she still loved Phoebus. A few weeks later, he stole into the night to bring Phoebus for her. But the captain, still overcome by guilt, refused to come: "Tell her I am going to be married, and that she may go to the devil." When the sensitive hunchback returned to the bell towers, he did not have the heart to tell Esmerelda the truth; he simply had not been able to find Phoebus, he reported

Archdeacon Frollo had since learned that he had not seen the Esmerelda's ghost and that she was, in fact, in the cathedral. He secured a key to her room and tried to force himself upon her. As repulsed and terrified as ever, Esmerelda blew the whistle. Quasimodo suddenly sprang from the darkness and, not recognizing his guardian, attacked him. But when he heard Frollo's voice, the devoted creature groveled at the feet of his master and said: "Kill me first and do what you please afterward." It was only the girl, now armed with a sword—and Quasimodo's presence—who prevented the priest from any further mischief. Frollo slunk away, still vowing that if he could not have her, no one would.

Frollo, still determined to have Esmerelda, now concocted a scheme to free her from Quasimodo and to win her love. He enlisted the aid of Gringoire (whose purpose was to obtain the trick goat with which he could make money) and his band of robbers, who, blind to the priest's deadly intention, were happy to come to Esmerelda's aid, since she was an outcast like themselves. Gringoire's band would attack the cathedral—claiming that the sanctuary had been rescinded—creating a diversion that would allow Frollo to spirit Esmerelda away.

Quasimodo, however, met the robbers with a hail of beams and stones, and with a rain of molten lead. This defense gave the king's guards time to gather at the cathedral and rout the attackers on the steps of the church. Frollo's plan, however, was successful. As the siege raged on outside, he slipped into the cathedral's upper chambers and abducted Esmerelda and turned her over to the authorities.

Now, perched atop a spire, Frollo watched the hangman position the noose around Esmerelda's neck. Behind him, Quasimodo also watched the tragic proceedings, a silent rage fomenting in his heart. When the execution order was given and Esmerelda met her fate, Quasimodo suddenly lunged at Frollo, sending him plummeting to his death. Shifting his gaze from the fallen figure in the street to the lifeless gypsy girl swinging at the end of the noose, the hunchback breathed a pathetic sigh: "There is all I ever loved."

Quasimodo disappeared, never to be heard from again. But in the open grave of criminals outside the city, two skeletons lay locked in embrace: one horribly misshapen, the other small and delicate.

Commentary:

As an example of the Romantic movement, Hugo's monumental novel, rich in human emotion and filled with a wide range of characters, is somewhat atypical. How the loving and the innocent survive—and, many times, die—in the corrupt world in which they find themselves is a touching spectacle. We recognize the contrast between the hunchback's noble character and the twisted, disfigured soul of the staid Archdeacon Frollo.

The book's theme, then, is that it is society rather than human nature that binds and fetters people, and that, though imperfect, we truly are created in the image of God. And, as Quasimodo and Esmerelda show us, only through human kindness and acceptance can we transcend physical limitations and achieve spiritual reunion with God.

THE AGE OF INNOCENCE
by Edith Wharton
(1862-1937)

Type of work: Novel of social conflict

Setting: An upper-middle class district of New York City in the 1870s

Principal characters:
Newland Archer, a young man torn between convention and defiance
May Welland, his socially conventional fiancee
Ellen Olenska, May's cousin, a non-conformist, and Newland's true love
Mrs. Manson Mingott, May and Ellen's grandmother, matriarch of New York society
Julius Beaufort, a scandalous womanizer
Mr. and Mrs. van der Luyden, a socially influential couple, capable of making or breaking any reputation

Story Overview:

New York society at its finest; "an exceptionally brilliant audience" was attending the opera that night. There in the box where the affluent and influential Mingott family posed, Newland Archer had just arrived fashionably late. "Poor" Countess Ellen Olenska, a cousin to Newland's new fiancee, May Welland, was being slated as the black sheep of the Mingott clan due to her "scandalous" breakup with her European husband. Ellen even failed to appear later that evening at the party given by the renowned womanizer Julius Beaufort, where May and Newland formally announced their engagement; she claimed that she could find nothing "appropriate" to wear.

Later that week, as the informed gossip Sullerton Jackson dined at the Archer home, the conversation turned to Ellen and how she had escaped Europe and the brute hands of her husband, the count—with the aid of a secretary. Newland daringly responded that he thought "women should be free . . . as free as we are." Then, seeing Jackson's shocked expression, he hastily added that society, of course, would never allow women to obtain such freedom.

A few days later, the Mingotts sent out invitations to a dinner in honor of the "Countess Olenska." All the invitees declined, however, with the exception of Jackson and Beaufort. When Newland learned of this cruelty, he convinced his reluctant mother to help Ellen. His mother, in turn, appealed to the van der Luydens, one of the few claimants to "real aristocracy" in New York society, who invited Ellen to attend a reception at their home to meet the Duke of Austrey, an unusual privilege indeed.

At the reception, Ellen "broke etiquette" by leaving the Duke in mid-sentence to take a seat next to her cousin's fiance, Newland. At the end of the evening, Ellen informed Newland that she would meet with him the next afternoon at 5:30. He was surprised, as they had not previously discussed any such meeting. Nonetheless, he arrived at Ellen's house on time, with only a tinge of regret for not having discussed his whereabouts with May—who might show up there at any

moment herself. Ensconced in the parlor, Ellen told Newland that he and Beaufort were the only two friends in which she could confide; all the others only wanted to exchange pleasantries. "Does no one want to know the truth here Mr Archer?" she pleaded. "The real loneliness is living among all those kind people who only ask one to pretend."

The following day, as Newland and May sat discussing their engagement, he suddenly realized with disappointment that they were merely reciting the "proper" catechisms to each other. "We are . . . " he thought to himself, "as paper dolls cut out of the same folded paper."

When Newland returned home that evening, he learned that Ellen had attended a social gathering with Beaufort. The van der Luydens disapproved of their protégée socializing with such a "commoner," and fled to her rescue by tutoring her in the potential consequences of this social blunder. Newland was later severely disappointed to find that Ellen herself had acted as a "paper-doll cutout" by appropriately sending an elaborate thank you note to the van der Luydens.

Two weeks later, Newland was approached by the head of his law office and asked to take on the countess' divorce. He had just begun to erase Ellen's image from his mind; yet, since both the Mingotts and the Wellands had commissioned him for the case, he was bound to take it. Later, Newland was asked by members of Ellen's family to urge the countess to drop the proceedings, as it would be scandalous to have an "unpleasant" divorce hanging over their heads. Newland dutifully undertook this mission also, and Ellen sadly thanked him for his advice.

Several days passed, and Ellen and Beaufort continued to see one another. It almost as if the vulgar, philandering Beaufort had charmed Ellen against her will. Now when Ellen wrote to Newland to request that they meet again, Newland packed his bags and joined May's family in St. Augustine. There, in fear of succumbing to his desire for Ellen, he tried to talk May into moving up their wedding date. His fiancee refused; she had to respect her parents' request that she observe a long engagement. Upon his return home, Newland asked Mrs. Mingott to appeal to May's parents to move the date up. She agreed.

Newland finally visited Ellen, who now was staying at her aunt's house, and confessed his love for her; if she would accept his marriage proposal, he would break his engagement with May in order to marry Ellen. Ellen reminded him, of course, that he himself had made that impossible by convincing her to drop her divorce proceedings. What's more, just days previous she had received a letter from her husband begging her to return home.

At that instant—in the cruelty of timing—a telegraph arrived from May: she had accepted Newland's request to move the wedding plans forward.

Exactly one month later, they were wed. Newland's mind was barely present during the ceremony. Afterward, as the couple prepared to take their leave, May, oblivious to her groom's far-away thoughts, excitedly turned to him. " . . . It's just our luck," she chattered, "the wonderful luck we're always going to have together."

The newlyweds traveled to London, where they were introduced at a dinner party to a poor, learned Frenchman. Newland found M. Revere's intellectual and moral liberty refreshing; May saw the Frenchman as "dreadfully boring."

In time, Newland began accepting his marriage as an "inevitable sort of business." Back in New York, he again happened upon M. Rivere and learned that he was in fact the secretary who had helped Ellen escape from her husband. He had just been dispatched from London to offer Ellen a generous financial payment if she would return to the count. However, he begged Newland not to allow her to accept this offer; he knew the situation, and feared for Ellen's safety if she returned. Newland immediately set up a "business trip" to Washington—where Ellen now lived in self-imposed exile—in order to offer his advice.

Ellen, however, who had fallen out of grace with her family after refusing her husband's first bid for reconciliation, was soon summoned home to New York when Grandmother Mingott suffered a stroke. Since Ellen would be coming to him, Newland abruptly canceled his "business trip." Instead, he went to pick Ellen up when her ferry arrived.

On their way home, Newland acknowledged that each time he was in Ellen's presence—even the very first time they met—he knew that he loved her. No, Ellen insisted, it could never be. With tears running down his cheeks, Newland stopped the carriage, got out, and walked the rest of the way home. That night, he opened the bedroom window; the room was stuffy. May warned that he could "catch his death." In fact, Newland felt like he already had.

A week after Ellen's arrival in New York, Mrs. Mingott confided in Newland that she had invited Ellen to remain in her home, despite the fact the family wanted her cut off; and now she needed his assistance in fighting the family on Ellen's behalf. He agreed. Lastly, Mrs. Mingott admitted that she knew of their situation and thought that he and Ellen should have married.

When Newland went to find Ellen, he found her again breaking a "cardinal rule": paying a call on the now-disgraced and bankrupt Beauforts. As they talked, Ellen told Newland she was considering returning to her husband after all rather than stay and "destroy the lives of the very people who helped me remake mine." They agreed to meet again two days later.

Later that evening, May arrived home and unexpectedly announced that she had judged Ellen too harshly. Yet, Newland observed, in her very next breath this forgiving creature was criticizing Ellen's social error in visiting the Beauforts.

The next evening, Newland decided to appeal to May for his freedom. He had barely mentioned Ellen's name, when May raised her hand to stop him. It didn't matter anymore, she declared; it was over. She would divorce him properly and without making a scene. Now it was Ellen's turn. After all, she had recently been granted independence from her husband and was soon to return to Europe.

May generously organized a farewell dinner for Ellen, a "tribal rally against a kinswomen who was about to be eliminated from the tribe." Everyone attended. But as Newland gazed on the guests' faces, he suddenly became aware that everyone there—including his wife—thought of him and Ellen as lovers.

After the party had ended, May told Newland that she was pregnant. Furthermore, she had confided this possibility to Ellen on the evening of their conversation. " . . . And you see," May finished victoriously, "I was right." Newland's fate *had* been determined.

Twenty-six years later, Newland sat reflecting on the past. He had been blessed with two sons and a daughter, and was universally regarded as a fine citizen and a faithful husband. May had passed away, heroically sacrificing her life to bring their last child into the world. Newland truly mourned her passing.

Now he was travelling to Paris with his oldest son, Dallas, who had recently become engaged to Fanny Beaufort. Upon their arrival, Dallas announced his plan to stop off and see Ellen Olenska. "After all," Dallas said, "Isn't she the one you could have chucked everything for but didn't?"

Evidently, on her death-bed, May told Dallas that his father had sacrificed the thing he most wanted when she asked him to. Newland admitted that his wife had never actually *asked* him to give up Ellen—or anything else. Dallas broke in, "I forgot . . . you never told each other anything. You just sat and watched each other, and guessed at what was going on underneath. A deaf and dumb asylum . . . "

When they neared Ellen's home, Newland settled down on a bench, then directed his son to go on ahead; he needed some time to think before going in. After all these years, it seemed he was finally free to pursue his true love. Yet, as he sat there and imagined the scene of their reconciliation, he decided it was more real to him there in his heart than if he were to actually go inside. Getting to his feet, Newland started back toward the hotel.

Commentary:

The Age of Innocence is a brilliant portrayal of the struggle between individual aspiration and social entrapment. Wharton's characters exist in a society where creativity and imagination are stifled within the narrow confines of a concrete frame, constricted by the conventional and unimaginative.

May and Ellen represent two opposing views: the ritualistic social tribe on one hand, and the free latitude of personal identity on the other. Ironically, it is Newland's inattention to the very social system in which he is trapped that finally decides his fate for him. He falls victim to his own ignorance of the conspiracy that is fashioned throughout his life to pigeonhole him into a societal and familial niche of expectations. It is not until Ellen's farewell dinner that it finally dawns on him "in a vast flash of many broken gleams" that, with Ellen's departure, his life of confinement has just begun: " . . . By means as yet unknown to him, the separation between himself and his partner of guilt [Ellen], had been achieved."

THE SHORT STORIES OF MARK TWAIN

(taken from *The Complete Short Stories of Mark Twain*, Doubleday and Company, New York, N.Y., 1985)

Before he began writing novels and short stories, Mark Twain (the pseudonym of Samuel Langhorn Clemens; 1835-1910) earned his living as a journalist. As a result, his short stories usually read more like slightly improbable newspaper stories than pure invention. These four stories, written between 1865 and 1897, represent a stylistic and chronological cross-section of Twain's best fiction.

The Notorious Jumping Frog of Calaveras County

"In compliance with the request of a friend of mine," Twain begins, "I called on good-natured, garrulous old Simon Wheeler, and inquired after my friend's friend, Leonidas W. Smiley." But the request for this favor was actually a ruse; in truth, Leonidas W. Smiley never existed. Rather, his friend had known "that if I asked old Wheeler about [Leonidas Smiley], it would remind him of his infamous *Jim* Smiley, and he would go to work and bore me to death with some exasperating reminiscence as long and as tedious as it should be useless to me. If that was the design, it succeeded."

This "infamous *Jim* Smiley," it turned out, was a gambler of almost supernatural repute. He would bet on absolutely anything, take any side of the bet. He'd would wager, for example, on a cock-fight, a cat-fight, a dog-fight, or even on which of two birds would fly off a fence first.

Smiley often bet—and always won—on his bullfrog, Daniel Webster. One day, Smiley bet a newcomer forty dollars that Daniel could jump farther than any frog in Calaveras County. "Well," said the man, "I'm only a stranger here, and I ain't got no frog; but if I had a frog, I'd bet you." Obligingly, Smiley went to catch him a frog in a nearby swamp; while he was gone, however, the stranger poured a hefty quantity of quail-shot down Daniel Webster's throat.

When Smiley returned with a freshly-caught frog in hand, the contest began. Counting three, Smiley yelled "Git!" and "the new frog hopped off lively." Meanwhile, "Dan'l give a heave," Wheeler recalled, "and hysted up his shoulders—so—like a Frenchman, but it warn't no use—he couldn't budge; he was planted as solid as a church." The stranger gladly took Smiley's money. As he walked away he turned and said over his shoulder, "I don't see no p'ints about that frog that's any better'n any other frog." A few moments later, when Daniel belched out a handful of quail-shot, Smiley figured out what had happened. "He took out after that feller," Wheeler continued, "but he never ketched him. And—"

At this point Wheeler heard his name called and stopped in mid-sentence to go answer the summons. When he returned, he started in on another tale, one about Smiley's one-eyed yellow cow. But, Twain said, "Lacking both time and inclination, I did not wait to hear about the afflicted cow, but took my leave."

The Story of the Bad Little Boy

"Once there was a bad little boy named Jim—though, if you will notice, you will find that bad little boys are nearly always called James in your Sunday-school books." But things went differently for this bad little boy from the way they usually go in Sunday-school books. Jim did not have a pious mother who was dying of consumption or destined to go to her grave from anxiety over her little Jim's welfare. In fact, "She said if he were to break his neck it wouldn't be much loss."

Once, when Jim stole the key to the pantry and ate his mother's jam, then put tar in the jar so she would not notice, "a terrible feeling didn't come over him, and something didn't seem to whisper to him 'Is it right to disobey my mother?' . . . and then he didn't kneel down alone and promise never to be wicked any more." No, Jim ate that jam, put the tar in the jar, and laughed.

On another occasion, Jim stole the teacher's penknife. Afraid he would get caught with it, he slipped the knife in George Wilson's hat—poor George Wilson, "the moral boy, the good little boy of the village, who always obeyed his mother, and never told an untruth . . ." When the knife slipped out of George's hat and he was about to get whipped for stealing, no one appeared to make Jim into an honest, God-fearing, upstanding, moral young man. The episode ended with a pointed, but very un-Sunday-school-like, moral: " . . . and so the model boy George got thrashed."

No, "this Jim bore a charmed life." Nothing bad ever happened to him . . . He . . . did not get sick or bitten by a dog when he ate too many of a farmer's stolen apples, and did not shoot off three or four fingers when he stole his father's gun and went hunting on the Sabbath." On the contrary, Jim grew up, married, raised a big family, and got wealthy through all manner of cheating and dishonest, unscrupulous means. "And now he is the infernalest wickedest scoundrel in his native village—and is universally respected, and belongs to the legislature. So you see, there never was a bad James in the Sunday-school books that had such a streak of luck as this sinful Jim with the charmed life."

Is He Living or Is He Dead?

Twain spent the month of March, 1892 at a posh hotel on the French Riviera, and there he became acquainted with a gentleman whom he gave the anonymous name of "Smith." During breakfast one morning, Smith pointed out an old, wealthy silk dealer, Theophile Magnan, from Lyon. "I supposed," Twain said, "that Smith would now proceed to justify the large interest which he had shown in Monsieur Magnan; but instead he dropped into a brown study . . . for some minutes." At last Smith returned recounting the fairy tale about the little boy who owned a beautiful songbird, which he loved very much but often neglected. Presently the bird died. Smith added, "it isn't children only who starve poets to death and then spend enough on their funerals and monuments to have kept them alive and made them easy and comfortable."

The conversation now turned into a story. As a young man, Smith reminisced, he, along with three of his friends, had spent several years trying to earn a living as artists. Despite the obvious merit of their work, no one bought their paintings. One of the group, Carl, finally hit upon a plan to improve their condition: One of the four would have to die in order to gain recognition for his work. It was a law, Carl explained, "that the merit of *every* great unknown and neglected artist must and will be recognized, and his pictures climb to high prices, after his death." So lots were drawn and one of the young painters, Francois Millet, was elected to fill this role. The other three would travel around France, pretending to be Millet's students, alluding to his reputation as a master and dropping casual, ominous remarks about his "impending death." At the appropriate time, Millet would indeed "die," a wax dummy would be buried, and the four friends would split their earnings from Millet's enormous stock of paintings and sketches.

The plan worked magnificently. They all became quite rich. "Yes, we same old four," Smith concluded, "who had lovingly shared privation together . . . carried the cof—" "Which four?" Twain broke in. "*We* four—for Millet helped to carry his own coffin. In disguise, you know. Disguised as a relative—distant relative." After the burial, the four conspirators did not even know how to begin to spend all the money they had made.

"It is a wonderful history, perfectly wonderful!" Twain exclaimed. "Whatever became of Millet?" Smith replied: "Do you remember the man I called your attention to in the dining room today? *That was Francois Millet* . . . Yes. For once they didn't starve a genius to death . . . *This* songbird was not allowed to pipe out its years unheard and then be paid with the cold pomp of a big funeral. We looked out for that."

A Story Without an End

One of the ways he had found to pass the time during a recent cruise, Twain related, was by completing incomplete stories. After dinner, someone would tell a story, but leave off the ending. Each member of the group then made up his own ending, to everyone's delight.

One story, however, defied the most ambitious and persistent efforts to arrive at a suitable ending—because the original version had no ending. The fellow who told it had begun reading it twenty-five years earlier but had been forced to leave it unfinished when the train on which he was riding suddenly derailed. The story follows:

John Brown, a good-hearted, bashful, and upright Presbyterian living in Missouri, longed to marry the modest, sweet, and beautiful Miss Mary Brown. Mary's mother, who opposed the match, seemed to be wavering, so John resolved to make an ardent attempt to win her over to his cause. Donning his best white suit, complete with matching white hat, and renting the most ornate carriage and livery in town—which included an elaborately stitched lap-robe—he drove out to the Brown farm.

As he rode along, a gust of wind blew his hat off his head and across a mud-filled ditch. In order to present himself properly, John would have to recapture the hat, but he did not want to risk soiling his suit. So, looking far down the road in either direction, he doffed his clothes, set them on the carriage, crossed the ditch, and retrieved his hat. Just as John ran for the carriage, however, the horses began easing down the road. He finally caught the carriage and mounted the seat. Quickly he slipped on his shirt and threw the lap-robe across his legs and lower torso, hoping to find a secluded spot in which to finish dressing.

At last he turned into a narrow, tree-covered trail—and immediately froze. Standing before him were Mary Brown, her mother, and two impeccably respectable friends of the Browns, Mrs. Taylor and her daughter. Wrapping the lap-robe tighter around his nude lower body, John looked on in speechless shock. The Browns and the Taylors, it seemed, had gone to help a family whose house had burned down, and in the aftermath of the fire, they had found themselves without a conveyance to return home. John Brown's arrival seemed a godsend, but, since his carriage was only a two-seater, the women spent considerable time discussing how to get all four of them back to the Brown's farm, all the while largely ignoring John. For his part, he said nothing and did not stir from his seat.

At length, the older women decided that Mary should ride with John back to the farm, fetch their wagon, then return to pick them up. Just then, Mrs. Taylor told her daughter, "The evening chill will be coming on pretty soon, and those poor old burnt-out people will need some kind of covering. Take the lap-robe with you, dear." The young woman stepped to the buggy and put out her hand to take John's lap-robe—

Thus ended the tale. Twain's companions never were able to come up with a satisfactory ending. Everyone sought a happy finale, certainly, but how to arrive at it perplexed them. At three in the morning, the group gave up and went to bed.

"Meantime," Twain concluded, "Mary was still reaching for the lap-robe. We gave it up, and decided to let her continue to reach. It is the reader's privilege to determine for himself how the thing came out."

THE SHORT STORIES OF O. HENRY

(taken from *The Best of O. Henry*, Running Press Book Publishers, Philadelphia, Pennsylvania, 1978)

O. Henry's stories are jammed with an anecdotal flavor that makes him one of the most loved short fiction writers.

The Ransom of Red Chief

The kidnapping thing sounded like a perfect plan to Bill and Sam; later, Bill would call it a "temporary mental apparition."

They picked a ten-year-old boy named Johnny Dorset, the son of a man so rich they figured they could get two thousand dollars from him. Guiding their buggy past the Dorset house under the cover of night, they offered Johnny some candy. Instead of taking the bait, the kid hit Bill in the face with a rock. Finally, Bill and Sam got control of the boy and brought him to a cave outside of town. The kid said, "Ha! cursed paleface, do you dare to enter the camp of Red Chief, the terror of the plains?"

Hey, this was all right, they figured. The kid was playing Indians. Bill was designated as his white captive "to be scalped at daybreak," and Sam was supposed to be "Snake-eye, the Spy," who would be "broiled at the stake." Both kidnappers grinned; the kid would be back home soon, and they'd have their money in hand.

All through dinner Red Chief talked up a storm, every so often letting out a war whoop. This, he said, was the most fun he'd ever had.

In the morning Sam was awakened by Bill's screaming. "Red Chief was sitting on Bill's chest, with one hand twined in Bill's hair . . . industriously and realistically trying to take Bill's scalp." By the time Sam managed to wrest the knife away, "Bill's spirit was broken." Every time Red Chief let out one of his blood-curdling war whoops, Bill cowered in terror.

Sam left the cave to see if anyone was searching for Red Chief; to his surprise, the town was as calm as could be. But when Sam returned to the cave, Red Chief was threatening to smash Bill with a rock and had already dropped a hot potato down his back. While Sam and Bill sat wondering why nobody was out combing the area for the boy, Red Chief got out a slingshot and hit Bill with a stone.

Finally Sam grabbed the boy, shook him, and threatened to send him home. Taking this threat seriously, Red Chief promised to behave—if he could play Black Scout with Bill, and ride him to the stockade. With this agreed, Sam left Bill to entertain Red Chief and hurried off to deliver the ransom note. While he was gone, Bill, thoroughly shaken by Red Chief's whippings as he was ridden to the stockade, tried to send the kid home. But Red Chief wouldn't go.

That night, when Sam went to fetch the ransom money, all he found was a note, written by the kid's father:

I think you are a little high in your demands, and I hereby make you a counter-proposition . . . You bring Johnny home and pay me two hundred and fifty dollars in cash, and I agree to take him off your hands. You had better come at night, for the neighbors believe he is lost, and I couldn't be responsible for what they would do to anybody they saw bringing him back.

Sam and Bill—especially Bill—knew when they were beaten. They took Red Chief home, paid the ransom, and begged Mr. Dorset to hold him for ten minutes. By then, said Bill, "I shall . . . be legging it trippingly for the Canadian border."

"And as dark as it was," Sam related, "and as fat as Bill was, and as good a runner as I am, he was a good mile and a half out of Summit before I could catch up with him."

A Harlem Tragedy

Mame Cassidy unveiled her black eye and cut lip to her friend Maggie Fink. "Ain't it a beaut?" she asked.

Mrs. Fink was envious. Her husband, after all, *never* hit her; all he did was come home from work and read the paper. Once a week, however, Mrs. Cassidy's husband would get rip-roaring drunk and beat up his wife; then for the rest of the week he was just as sweet as candy. "This eye," said Mrs. Cassidy proudly, "is good for theater tickets and a silk shirt waist at the very least."

Mrs. Fink pretended to be shocked. "Why, ain't I alive?" Mrs. Cassidy replied, "And didn't I marry him? Jack comes in tanked up; and I'm here, ain't I? Who else has he got a right to beat?"

Just then Mr. Cassidy burst in, clutching tickets to the circus and a silk shirt waist. Maggie Fink promptly excused herself, went upstairs to her apartment, and cried. Why didn't her husband hit her? Didn't he care about her?

The next day was Labor Day, and the Cassidys danced through it like a whirlwind; circus, picnicking in the park—they did the lot. The Finks, meanwhile, hung around the house. Mrs. Fink did the wash while she watched Mr. Fink reading his newspaper. "He reposed in the state of matrimony like a lump of unblended suet in a pudding." Finally, Mrs. Fink had had enough. She decided to show Mrs. Cassidy that her husband could be a man and beat her, too. Suddenly she turned on Mr. Fink like a tornado. "You lazy loafer!" she cried shilly, "must I work my arms off washing and toiling for the ugly likes of you? Are you a man or are you a kitchen hound?"

Utterly taken aback by her indignity, Mr. Fink dropped his paper. Good! Mrs. Fink stepped forward and punched him in the face. He sprang to his feet, and she hit him again, eagerly awaiting the return blows.

Returning from their day's activities, Mr. and Mrs. Cassidy heard the ruckus upstairs. Breathlessly, Mame ran to meet Maggie Fink to find out if Mr. Fink had hit her: "Oh, Maggie, did he? Oh, did he?"

But Mrs. Fink, peering out from a tear-streaked face, "its velvety, pink-and-white, becomingly freckled surface . . . unscratched, unbruised, unmarred by the the recreant fist of Mr. Fink, could only sob. "He-he never touched me, and—he's—oh, Lord—he's washin' the clothes—he's washin' the clothes!"

One Thousand Dollars

Lawyer Tolman handed young Gillian one thousand dollars, an inheritance from his rich uncle. The money, however, carried with it one stipulation: that Gillian give the lawyer a complete accounting of how he spent it. Gillian laughed, amused, and remarked that he had no idea what to do with it. One thousand dollars was an awkward sum. Anything more, he thought—or anything less—would be easier to spend.

Gillian went to talk to a friend, Old Bryson. The joke, he said, was that his uncle, Septimas Gillian, was worth a half-a-million, and had left it all to a cure—a "microbe!" His uncle had willed a major part of his wealth to the man who found the cure, and another share to the hospital he had stayed in. Three other inheritors—Septimas' butler, his housekeeper, and Miss Hayden, his ward—had each received ten dollars. And that was the extent of the bequest.

Finally Gillian turned to ask Bryson what his advice would be; what should Gillian do with the thousand dollars? Bryson replied that a thousand dollars could buy a lot of things: a house, milk for one hundred babies for three months, an education—it could even rent Madison Square Garden for a night. Or, he added, it could be used to purchase a sheep ranch and a diamond pendant for Miss Lauriere, a friend of Bryson's.

Gillian warmed to this latter idea. However, when they went to break the news to Miss Lauriere, she told Bryson that she'd prefer a diamond necklace—for two thousand dollars.

Gillian decided it was time to leave Bryson and Miss Lauriere, so he hopped into a cab and asked the driver what he would do if he had a thousand dollars. Open a saloon, the driver said. Then seeing a blind man selling pencils on a corner, Gillian jumped out of the cab and posed the same question to him. The blind man reached into his pocket and withdrew, to Gillian's astonishment, his own hefty bank balance—$1,785.

Returning to the cab, Gillian next went to the house of his late uncle. There he found Miss Miriam Hayden, his uncle's ward, writing letters in the library, looking small and beautiful. He handed the money over to her, saying there had been an attachment to the will stating that she should have it. Then he added, "I suppose, of course, that you know I love you."

As she always had, Miss Hayden refused his advances. So Gillian, leaving the money on the desk, borrowed a pencil from her and wrote a note for the lawyers:

Paid by the black sheep, Robert Gillian, $1,000

on the account of eternal happiness, owed by heaven to the best and dearest woman on earth.

He returned to the law office; he had spent the money, he advised Tolman, handing him the envelope containing the note. Then Tolman called his partner into the office and together they opened another envelope and read its contents.

Apparently, Tolman explained, there had been a codicil to the will, saying that Gillian would receive an additional $50,000 dollars if he had spent the original one thousand either philanthropically or intelligently. But if he had used the money disreputably, as he had done so many times in the past, the money would go to Miriam Hayden.

Tolman reached for the envelope, but Gillian was quicker. He grabbed it, smiled, and explained that he'd lost the money at the races. The two lawyers frowned as he left the office, "whistling gayly in the hallway as he waited for the elevator."

Commentary

O. Henry (1862 - 1910), by birth William Sydney Porter, wrote most of his short stories between 1900 and 1910, producing in all about 600 pieces. The stories are extremely well-liked, partly because of their anecdotal, witty feel and their trademark "end twists," and partly because they inevitably plant a seed of redemption in otherwise wicked characters.

Examples of both elements abound; O. Henry is the master of the surprise ending *and* of the likeable-though-idiosyncratic character. The bungling, almost uncle-like kidnappers in "The Ransom of Red Chief" wind up *paying* to have the handful-of-kid taken *off* their hands. In the unique story "A Harlem Tragedy," by parodying both the perpetrators and the victims of domestic violence and finishing off with a bizarre reversal of the male/female roles, O. Henry teaches lessons he could teach in no other way: perhaps spouses ought to gladden one another out of *love* rather than *guilt* . . . maybe— even in these more liberated, sensitive times— we should ponder how we interact within our families to see if we are *truly* liberated and sensitive. And, lastly, O. Henry places a thousand dollars into *your* hands and asks, in a roundabout way, what *you'd* do with it. By using young Gillian as his cross-section sample, O. Henry shows that if an irresponsible, free-wheeling person can choose to do the right thing—and be blessed for it in the end—that each of us, through our individual choices, has a chance for salvation.

O. Henry's own life, however, unlike the lives of his characters, was marked by tragedy. In 1898 his wife died and he began a three-year prison term for embezzlement. Then he himself died in 1910 at the early age of 47. However, his life, like his stories, ended with a certain "twist" to it: O. Henry's funeral was accidentally scheduled at the same time as a wedding—which began the moment the coffin was carried out of the chapel.

THE DEVIL'S DICTIONARY

(originally published in 1906 under the title: *The Cynic's Word Book*)
by Ambrose Bierce, Dover Publications, New York, N.Y., 1958

Dictionary, *n.* A malevolent literary device for cramping the growth of a language and making it hard and inelastic.

The *Devil's Dictionary* began as part of a weekly newspaper in 1881, and continued as such until 1906. This dictionary by Ambrose Bierce (1842-1913) is a generous mixture of satire and truth. A celebrated American cynic and humorist, Bierce assembles herein his most shrewd and pointed observations regarding politics, philosophy, business, religion, and the general state of mankind. Bierce's observations cut to the quick of the human condition. Although written nearly one hundred years ago, Bierce's commentary is just as applicable today as it was in his time. If brevity is the soul of wit, these gems of cynical wisdom are as insightful a collection as anyone would hope to find.

Politics

Abdication, *n.* An act whereby a sovereign attests his sense of the high temperature of the throne.

Poor Isabella's dead, whose abdication,
Set all tongues wagging in the Spanish nation.
For that performance 'twere unfair to scold her,
She wisely left a throne too hot to hold her.
To History she'll be no royal riddle —
Merely a plain parched pea that jumped the griddle.

       - *G. J.*

Battle, *n.* A method of untying with the teeth a political knot that would not yield to the tongue.

Boundary, *n.* In political geography, an imaginary line between two nations, separating the imaginary rights of one from the imaginary rights of the other.

Cannon, *n.* An instrument employed in the rectification of national boundaries.

Conservative, *n.* A statesman who is enamored of existing evils, as distinguished from the Liberal, who wishes to replace them with others.

Diplomacy, *n.* The patriotic art of lying for one's country.

Insurrection, *n.* An unsuccessful revolution. Disaffection's failure to substitute misrule for bad government.

Senate, *n.* A body of elderly gentlemen charged with high duties and misdemeanors.

Philosophy and Science

Cartesian, *adj.* Relating to Descartes, a famous philosopher, author of the celebrated dictum, *Cogito ergo sum*—whereby he was pleased to suppose that he demonstrate the reality of human existence. The dictum might be improved, however, thus: *Cogito cogito ergo cogito sum*—"I think that I think, therefore I think that I am"; as close an approach to certainty as any philosopher has yet made.

Gravitation, *n.* The tendencies of all bodies to approach one another with a strength proportioned to the quantity of matter they contained — the quantity of matter they contained being ascertained by the strength of their ten-

dency to approach one another. This is a lovely and edifying illustration of how science, having made A the proof of B, makes B the proof of A.

Esoteric, *adj.* Very particularly abstruse and consummately occult. The ancient philosophers were of two kinds—*exoteric*, those that the philosophers themselves could understand, and *esoteric*, those that nobody could understand. It is the latter that have most profoundly affected modern thought and found greatest acceptance in our time.

Newtonian, *adj.* Pertaining to a philosophy of the universe, invented by Newton, who discovered that an apple will fall to the ground, but was unable to say why. His successors and disciples have advanced so far as to be able to say when.

Optimism, *n.* The doctrine, or belief that everything is beautiful, including what is ugly, everything is good, especially the bad, and everything right that is wrong ... Being a blind faith, it is inaccessible to the light of disproof—an intellectual disorder, yielding to no treatment but death. It is hereditary, but fortunately not contagious.

Truth, *n.* An ingenious compound of desirability and appearance. Discovery of truth is the sole purpose of philosophy, which is the most ancient occupation of the human mind and has a fair prospect of existing with increased activity to the end of time.

Religion

Clergyman, *n.* A man who undertakes the management of our spiritual affairs as a method of bettering his temporal ones.

Deluge, *n.* A notable first experiment in baptism which washed away the sins (and sinners) of the world.

Heaven, *n* A place where the wicked cease in troubling you with talk of their personal affairs, and the good listen with attention while you expound your own.

Sacred, *adj.* Dedicated to some religious purpose; having divine character; inspiring solemn thoughts or emotions; as, the Dalai Lama of Tibet; The Moogum of M'bwango; The temple of Apes in Ceylon; the Cow in India; the Crocodile, the Cat and the Onion of ancient Egypt; the Mufti of Moosh; the hair of the dog that bit Noah, etc.

Scriptures, *n.* The sacred books of our holy religion, as distinguished from the false and profane writings on which all other faiths are based.

Unction, *n.* An oiling or greasing. The rite of extreme unction consists in touching with oil consecrated by a bishop several parts of the body of one engaged in dying. Marbury relates that after the rite had been administered to a certain wicked English nobleman it was discovered that the oil had not been properly consecrated and no other could be obtained. When informed of this the sick man said in anger,

"Then I'll be damned if I die!" "My son," said the priest, "that is what we fear."

The Self-Centered Man

Absurdity, *n.* A statement of belief manifestly inconsistent with one's own opinion.

Bigot, *n.* One who is obstinately and zealously attached to an opinion that you do not entertain.

Calamity, *n.* A more than commonly plain and unmistakable reminder that the affairs of this life are not of our own ordering. Calamities are of two kinds: misfortune to ourselves, and good fortune to others.

Egotist, *n.* A person of low taste, more interested in himself than in me.

Happiness, *n.* An agreeable sensation arising from the contemplation of the misery of another.

Hypocrite, *n.* One who, professing virtues that he does not respect, secures the advantage of seeming to be what he despises.

Self-evident, *adj.* Evident to one's self and to nobody else.

Selfish, *adj.* Devoid of consideration for the selfishness of others.

The Rich

Abasement, *n.* A decent and customary mental attitude in the presence of wealth and power.

Impunity, *n.* Wealth.

Nobleman, *n.* Nature's provision for wealthy American maids ambitious to incur social distinction and suffer high life.

Rich, *adj.* Holding in trust and subject to an accounting the property of the indolent, the incompetent, the unthrifty, the envious, and the luckless. That is the view that pervades the underworld, where the Brotherhood of Man finds its most logical development and candid advocacy. To denizens of the midworld the word means good and wise.

The Battle of the Sexes

Bride, *n.* A woman with a fine prospect of happiness behind her.

Female, *n.* One of the opposing, or unfair, sex.

Helpmate, *n.* A wife, or bitter half.

Male, *n.* A member of the unconsidered, or negligible sex. The male of the human race is commonly known (to the female) as Mere Man. The genus has two varieties: good providers and bad providers.

Miss, *n.* A title with which we brand unmarried women to indicate that they are in the market. Miss, Missis (Mrs.), and Mister (Mr.) are the three most distinctly disagreeable words in the language, in sound and sense. Two are corruptions of Mistress, the other of Master. In the general abolition of social titles in this our country they miraculously escaped to plague us. If we must have them let us be consistent and give one to the unmarried man. I venture to suggest Mush, abbreviated to Mh.

Weaknesses, *n. pl.* Certain primal powers of Tyrant Woman wherewith she holds dominion over the male of her species, binding him to the service of her will and paralyzing his rebellious energies.

Literature

Blank-verse, *n.* Unrhymed iambic pentameters— the most difficult kind of English verse to write acceptably; a kind, therefore, much affected by those who cannot acceptably write any kind.

Humanity, *n.* The human race, collectively, exclusive of the anthropoid poets.

Imagination, *n.* A warehouse of facts, with poet and liar in joint ownership.

Novel, *n.* A short story padded. A species of composition bearing the same relation to literature that the panorama bears to art . . . The art of writing novels, such as it was, is long dead . . . Peace to its ashes . . .

Type, *n.* Pestilent bits of metal suspected of destroying civilization and enlightenment, despite their obvious agency in this incomparable dictionary.

Everyday Life

Auctioneer, *n.* The man who proclaims with a hammer that he has picked your pocket with his tongue.

Beg, *v.* To ask for something with an earnestness proportioned to the belief that it will not be given.

Commendation, *n.* The tribute we pay to achievements that resemble, but do not equal, our own.

Dentist, *n.* A prestidigitator who, putting metal into your mouth, pulls coins out of your pocket.

Fib, *n.* A lie that has not cut its teeth. An habitual liar's closest approach to truth: the perigee of his eccentric orbit.

Homicide, *n.* The slaying of one human being by another. There are four kinds of homicide: felonious, excusable, justifiable, and praiseworthy, but it makes no great difference to the person slain whether he fell by one kind or another— the classification is for advantage of the lawyers.

Interpreter, *n.* One who enables two persons of different languages to understand each other by repeating to each what it would have been to the interpreter's advantage for the other to have said.

Technicality, *n.* In an English court a man named Home was tried for slander in having accused a neighbor of murder. His exact words were: "Sir Thomas Hold hath taken a cleaver and stricken his cook upon the head, so that one side of the head fell upon one shoulder and the other side upon the other shoulder." The defendant was acquitted by instruction of the court, the learned judges holding that the words did not charge murder, for they did not affirm the death of the cook, that being only an inference.

Zeal, *n.* A certain nervous disorder afflicting the young and inexperienced. A passion that goeth before a sprawl.

A soldier, a journalist, and a brazenly honest author, Ambrose Bierce mysteriously disappeared in 1913 at the age of 71. Having travelled to Mexico as an observer to Pancho Villa's revolutionary army, Bierce's last bit of correspondence contained this characteristic line: "If you hear of my being stood up against a Mexican stone wall and shot to rags, please know that I think it a pretty good way to depart this life."

THE SCREWTAPE LETTERS

by
C. S. Lewis
(1898 - 1963)

Type of work: Fictional correspondence

Setting: Written from Hell and Earth

Commentary:

Nearly everyone has at one time or another offered the phrase "The devil made me do it" as an excuse for their actions. But wouldn't it be intriguing to know exactly how this happens—how the devil really makes us do it? For the reader who wishes to gain delightful and provocative insights into the process of temptation, C.S. Lewis' *The Screwtape Letters* is the place to begin. Since its first serialized appearance during World War II in the now extinct *The Guardian* magazine, *The Screwtape Letters* has become one of Lewis' most enduring classics.

The book is written as a series of letters from a high-level senior devil to his nephew-apprentice, outlining the manner in which humankind may most effectively be tempted. Though the work is filled with masterful quips and observations about human nature, Lewis experienced dissatisfaction during the writing. "Though I had never written anything more easily," he recalled, "I never wrote with less enjoyment. The work into which I had to project myself while I spoke through Screwtape was all dust, grit, thirst and itch. Every trace of beauty, freshness, and geniality had to be excluded. It almost smothered me before I was done. It would have smothered my readers if I had prolonged it."

A firm believer in God and goodness, Lewis no doubt pushed the limits of the "devil's advocate" role in creating this tale. However difficult the book was for Lewis to write, though, the reader is rewarded with an account that is simultaneously hilarious and thought provoking.

Description of Characters:

Screwtape: A high-level demon well versed in the fine art of winning souls for Satan, "Our Father Below"

Wormwood: Screwtape's nephew, a lower-caste apprentice devil who has just been assigned his first "patient"

The Patient: Wormwood's target, a man in his mid 30's and a recent convert to Christianity

Preface:

Devils thrive on feasts of human souls; by absorbing human will into their own beings, they increase their own "selfhood." Satan's "war aim" is to draw "all other beings into himself," Screwtape explains. In the final analysis, it comes down to a war between freedom and slavery; a battle waged by immortals for human wills. And mankind is given the ultimate choice: either to become one with God, or to end up a tasty morsel—literal "soul food"—of the devils.

A devil's task is to "gradually undermine his patient's faith and prevent him from the formation of virtues," effectively removing him from heaven's reach. Screwtape's letters to his nephew-apprentice, Wormwood, outline what the aspiring young demon must do to succeed. We are then made privy to both the triumphs and setbacks that Wormwood experiences with his patient.

We first encounter the patient—often referred to as "the disgusting little vermin"—as the initial euphoria of his recent spiritual conversion is fading; and we watch closely as Wormwood and Screwtape go to work on his soul.

Overview:

The tactics and tidbits of advice offered in Screwtape's letters revolve around several major themes . . .

False Humility. One of the most effective methods used for worming into a human soul is to instill into his mind a sense of false humility. This false humility may be gradually inculcated, through a variety of means. Screwtape first discusses prayer, noting that when their patient gets on his knees to confess his sins he is merely engaging in "parrot talk." In reality, the man believes that by virtue of his conversion, he has already run up a favorable balance on God's ledger. Therefore, by inducing him to feign humility through regular prayer, the devils may begin to capture his soul.

Another extremely effective ploy is to catch the patient during a time when he is feeling truly contrite and poor in spirit, then using that genuine humility to make him feel *proud* of how humble he is! "If the patient can say `By jove! I'm being humble,'" Screwtape writes, "almost immediately his pride—pride at his own humility—will appear."

As another route to spiritual pride, Wormwood is encouraged to induce within his patient the idea that as a devout Christian he is better than non-believers. Ironically, gloats Uncle Screwtape, once a man truly believes that he is heaven-bound, he is on the road to hell. Pride creeps in, turning his interests ever more to the things of the world. Before long, he will be critical of his friends, the books he reads, his home, and all possessions; indeed, each of them will appear earthly, shallow. Soon he will neglect his religious studies, his prayers and his love of others, the very things that would send his soul heavenward.

Screwtape continually advises Wormwood to push his patient toward worldliness. "You should always try to make the patient abandon the people or food or books he really likes in favour of the `best' people, the `right' food, the `important' books." This strategy is crucial to the demonic cause. "The man who truly and disinterestedly enjoys any one thing in the world, for its own sake, and without caring twopence what other people say about it, is by that very fact fore-armed against some of our subtlest modes of attack . . . . I have known a human defended from strong temptations to social ambition by a still stronger taste for tripe and onions."

The Road to Hell Is Paved With *Good Intentions:* A favorite gimmick used by the devils to drag their victims down is best described as "the road to hell is paved with good intentions." While the human spirit is often directed towards spiritual ideals, the physical body can easily be distracted by worthy—although worldly—pleasures which keep a man from progressing towards heaven, which is precisely the Tempter's plan.

Humans seem to undulate from one extreme to the other. This undulation is based on the human tendency to concentrate on the trivial, while ignoring the very things that would guide his soul to heaven. Thus, friendly conversation and restful moments in front of the fireplace can be the Devil's workshop. And, after a while, " . . . you no longer need a good book . . . to keep him from his prayers or his work or his sleep; a column of advertisements in yesterday's paper will do." In the same manner, keeping an individual concentrating on the trivial will keep him from influencing his society for good. "Certainly we do not want men to allow their Christianity to flow over into their political life, for the establishment of anything like a really just society would be a major disaster."

Screwtape points out that human mood and existence is marked by a series of "troughs and peaks." He therefore encourages Wormwood to labor over his patient's soul while he is in one of the troughs, because at that point it is easiest to undermine his faith and reliance on "the Enemy" (God).

Undermine Reliance On *One* Church: One of Screwtape's most interesting (and uproarious) comments hits upon an extremely effective principle in weakening human faith: that of undermining reliance on one church. "If you can't cure a man of churchgoing," he instructs, "make him a connoisseur of churches; a man who is continually looking for the church that `suits' him . . . In fact, he may reach the point that since he did not find a church which suited him in all his travels, then church must not be for him altogether. The search for churches makes man a critic of that which he should be a pupil."

Linked to being a "church connoisseur" is the practice of individuals in one church criticizing the beliefs of rival congregations, effectively undermining the faith and effectiveness of the Christian community as a whole. Screwtape advises that such a situation is to be encouraged. "The real fun is working up hatred between those who say `mass' and those who say `holy communion' . . . All the purely indifferent things—candles and clothes and what not—are an admirable ground for our activities."

The Creation of the *Historical Jesus:* One of the most subtle methods the devils use is that of creating a "historical Jesus." Screwtape outlines four ways in which the historical Jesus works to Hell's advantage: First, the historical Jesus can be stretched into any shape and used to promote any ideal, good or bad; thus, "Jesus" has been the battle cry for a multitude of humanitarian, liberal, catastrophic, revolutionary, and Marxian causes. The advantages of the historical Jesus are numer-

ous. First, it distracts men's minds from who Jesus really is and what he really did. It grants him the image a mere "teacher," one in the mold of the other great moral—and mortal—teachers. Hence, the historical Jesus dilutes the usefulness of his instruction, and the fundamental meaning of Christianity becomes vague.

Another aim of the historical Jesus, Screwtape writes, "is to destroy the devotional life. For the real presence of the Enemy [God], otherwise experienced by men in prayer and sacrament, we substitute a merely probable, remote, shadowy, and uncouth figure, one who spoke a strange language and died a long time ago." Jesus becomes a "myth," and humans have a difficult time taking myths seriously.

Lastly, Screwtape argues that "few individuals are really brought into the Enemy's camp by the historical study of the biography of Jesus, simply as biography." True conversion to Christianity is a *spiritual* occurrence; it is *not* based on the historicity of Jesus' life. Therefore, as long as study of the historical Jesus prevents a man from experiencing the spiritual side of Christianity, it is to be encouraged.

A *Gradual* Descent to Hell: Once individuals have acquired the requisite characteristics—false humility, has become a connoisseur of churches, and believes in the historical Jesus—they are well on their way to hell. Screwtape cautions Wormwood, however, against hoping for too much success too soon, advising him that the best manner in which to bring souls to hell is a slow and evolving one. "Indeed, the safest road to Hell is the gradual one," he writes. " . . . the gentle slope, soft underfoot, without sudden turnings, without milestones, without signposts." If the patient allows Wormwood to "benumb his heart," "distract his purpose," and think of himself as a Christian though his "spiritual state is much the same as it was . . . "—which he will out of his half-conscious reluctance to face his blaring guilt head-on—his ongoing pride and arrogance will seal his fate. The time will come, soon enough, for him to live out eternity with Father Below—and another soul will be lost, forever.

Wormwood's initial work brings about his patient's submissive regression. But, alas, spared by an untimely death of a relative, he repents—and Wormwood's efforts appear to have been in vain.

In the final chapter, Wormwood asks his Uncle Screwtape whether he still loves him in spite of his failure. Screwtape's reply is swift: "I think they will give you to me now; or a bit of you. Love you? Why, yes. As dainty a morsel as ever I grew fat on." This last letter is appropriately signed, "Your increasingly and ravenously affectionate uncle, SCREWTAPE."

And, so it seems, Hell, a literal eat-or-be-eaten world, is denied the damnation of one human soul; and Screwtape is allowed the subsequent consumption of lowly Wormwood.

Finally, Lewis reminds us of Martin Luther's apt remark:

> The best way to drive out the devil, if he will not yield to texts of Scripture, is to jeer and flout him, for he cannot bear scorn.

LIFE WITH FATHER

by
Clarence Day
(1874 - 1935)

Type of work: Autobiographical comedy

Setting: New York City; 1880's

Principal characters:
Clarence Day, the irascible and amusing Father
Vinnie, his lovingly determined wife
Clarence Jr., their observant young son

Commentary:

By the end of Clarence Day's book, one sees that in spite of Father's gruffness and surface stubbornness, he is all bark and no bite. Indeed, he truly loves his family, and although measured by modern standards, he may seem authoritarian and abrasive, his lovingly determined Victorian wife is every inch a match for him as they strike the vibrant balance that shapes the upbringing of their four sons. This nostalgic tale is filled with a menagerie of emotions: amusing quips, hard language, painful experiences and loving relationships.

Day's warm and amusing anecdotal portrait of his boyhood family and their boisterous but affectionate interactions in late 19th-century New York, provides an enlightening glimpse into the mores of a bygone era.

Story Overview:

Occasionally, on Saturday mornings, he would take his young namesake, Clarence Jr., soberly combed, shod, and suited for business, to help out at the office—running errands and filling ink wells. And after office duties one memorable Saturday, father and son took in lunch at Delmonico's, followed by a chocolate eclair and a Wild West show. On the way home, Clarence Jr. announced that he wanted to be a cowboy. Father, who always dressed immaculately, chuckled that cowboys lived wild, "slummy" lives—Clarence could not grow up to be a cowboy. "Put your cap on straight" he added, "I am trying to bring you up to be a civilized man." Clarence did not agree. "What with fingernails, improving books, dancing school, and sermons on Sunday, the few chocolate eclairs that a civilized man got to eat were not worth it."

⋄ ♦ ⋄

Father strongly disapproved of fat on his body, and chose horseback riding as his route to fitness. He bought a spirited horse named Rob Roy and, true to form, "expected him to do what he was told. Rob Roy never looked upon the transaction in this way." When the stubborn animal rebelled, Father gave him the whip, the horse reared defiantly and stamped the ground, refusing to obey. Man and horse "both perspired so freely that between them they must have lost gallons." In the end, Father lost the battle and sold the horse, exchanging him for Brownie, a spiritless, "philosophical" old cart horse.

One day Mother expressed her wish that everyone in the family should take up riding. Father became angry. " . . . if he had foreseen that we all would be wanting to ride, just because he, a hard working man got a little relief in that way, he would have gone without the relief . . . He would sell out." But then he went out and bought another, faster horse for himself. Dependable old Brownie was turned over to his sons.

⋄ ♦ ⋄

Father had no patience with sickness, and actually defied disease. "If the damn germs want to have a try at me," he challenged, "bring 'em on." He had even less patience with someone else's sickness—especially Mother's. When Mother became ill, Father felt "lost" and fretful. "He pished and pooed and muttered that it was silly . . . a sign of weak character." To Father's chagrin, however, "Every time he tried to strengthen Mother's character in this respect . . . she seemed to resent it."

When Father turned seventy four and contracted pneumonia, his first real ailment, at first he refused to believe that it was anything but a cold. Finally the doctor convinced him he was in trouble. From behind his bedroom door he began to bellow and curse God: "Have mercy! I say have mercy, damn it!"

Though he could not bear complaints of pain from others, Father suffered boisterously with his own occasional headaches. He let everyone know that he was suffering dreadfully. "The severity of a headache could be judged by the volume of sound he put forth," Clarence writes. "His idea seemed to be to show the headache he was just as strong as it was, and stronger."

⋄ ♦ ⋄

Father had a strong penchant for ice. But when the family moved into a home in the country, ice was at times difficult to come by. One hot day, the ice man didn't come at all. Father, livid, drove the cart into town and bought two ice chests and a large cake of ice from a butcher. Returning home, he then called the ice man and demanded he make a special delivery, threatening and cursing. Satisfied when he finally had his two chests filled with ice, he told Clarence, "King Solomon had the right idea about these things. `Whatsoever thy hand findeth to do, do thy damnedest.'"

⋄ ♦ ⋄

One day the family cook suddenly quit and walked out. Since Mother had no experience in the kitchen, Father took it upon himself to find another cook. He stormed into one agency, loudly announcing that he had no time for "fol-de-rol." "Where do you keep 'em?" he bellowed. Seeing the clerk's startled expression, he roared out once more. Then he marched past her into the room where a group of women waited to be interviewed for various positions and impulsively picked out Margaret, "a little woman with honest gray eyes"—who wasn't even applying as a cook. Nevertheless, flattered at being chosen out of a roomful of applicants by such a "masterful gentleman," Margaret took the job. And, as it turned out, she became a good cook, staying on with the family for twenty-six years.

When the family moved to their summer home in the country, however, Margaret usually stayed behind to watch the city house. A succession of cooks came and went in rapid order; Father unnerved every one of them. At breakfast one day with a new cook he raged to Mother, "Slop! Does she call this confounded mess coffee? I swear I can't imagine how she concocts such monstrosities!" Then—while heartily devouring his breakfast—he droned on about how the whole meal had been ruined.

After a full supper at which he ate every morsel, Father would also roar and sigh, "Starved!" or "Poisoned!" When Mother laughed at his antics, he would complain over her laughter: "I am a sick man and nobody in this house [cares]!" Finally he sent for Margaret, who, looking "strangely swollen and bulky," secreted him pans of food under her clothing. When Mother joked that Margaret would surely go to heaven for her actions, Father shot back that just as surely he'd find Margaret there so she could cook for him. "You'd be very fortunate, Clare," replied Mother, "to get to the same part as Margaret." Father scowled: "Hah! I'll make a devil of a row if I don't."

❖ ♦ ❖

In his unending quest to create a family of musicians, Father decided that Clarence should take up the violin—despite the fact that the boy was tone deaf. For several months Clarence tortured his neighbors, his family, and his music teacher with horrendous "cry-like-a-baby" sawings. Presently, unable to bear any more, Mother intervened. "This awful nightmare can not go on," she bawled. Father pooh-poohed her, but she replied, "You're downtown. You don't have to hear it." Clarence was finally spared when the family moved and his younger brother became the chosen artist—"led away and imprisoned in the front basement"—to study the violin.

❖ ♦ ❖

Mother and Father were always at odds when it came to the monthly budget. Mother had no use for bookkeeping and refused to keep records of her expenditures. Father, frustrated, never knew what to expect from one month to the next. Mother insisted that it wasn't her fault; the high bills didn't necessarily mean she was extravagant. "Well, it certainly means you've spent a devil of a lot of money," Father told her.

One month when he found that the bills were lower than usual, he cited this as evidence that Mother could in fact spend less when she put her mind to it. Mother agreed—but in her next breath she told Father that now he ought to "give her the difference." After a half-hearted defense, Father found himself unable to counter this tactic. He gave in.

❖ ♦ ❖

It was Mother who taught the growing children to fear God. Daily she studied the Bible with them, and particularly urged them to memorize the 23rd Psalm. Clarence responded half-heartedly; he could not imagine his Father "being comforted by the Lord's rod and staff, or allowing anyone whatsoever to lead him to a pasture and get him to lie down somewhere in it." As a result, Clarence's memorizing and Bible study sufferred greatly.

❖ ♦ ❖

Fifteen years after the telephone came into common usage, Father—fighting every bit of the way—finally relented and had one installed. A typical telephone conversation with Father was something to behold: "Speak up, speak up, damn it!" he would shout at the reciever, getting red in the face. "Who is it? Who are you? I can't hear a word you are saying. I can't hear a damn word, I tell you!" Mother, in her attempts to wrest the phone from him, brought on more roars into the receiver, "I will not give you this telephone. Will you let me alone? I am trying to find out who the devil this person is. Halloa! I say halloa there, do you hear me? . . . What's that? Oh it's you Mrs. Nichols. Wait a moment." Then he'd hand the phone to Mother.

❖ ♦ ❖

Mother loved to entertain, but here again she met stiff resistance from Father. His philosophy concerning guests was that New York was full of hotels "designed for the one special purpose of housing these nuisances. If they got tired of hotels . . . they should be put aboard the next train at once, and shipped to some large empty desert. If they wanted to roam . . . keep 'em roaming."

Whenever he was pressed by Mother to help entertain guests, Father pouted: "I am not a Swiss courier. I do not intend to hold a perpetual Mardi Gras to please gaping villagers." But Mother usually managed, after energetic meneuvers, acquienscence form Father; and when the guests arrived, he was invariably a gracious host. In everything, Father seemed to enjoy initial resistance; he was at his best in the middle of a fray. But when he finally submitted—to entertaining, or to go out, or to making a trip or summering in the country—he and Mother had a grand time.

❖ ♦ ❖

All his life, Father spoke freely on any subject—and when he disapproved of manners or ideas he considered substandard, his response was immediate and forceful. When Mother, for instance, had the audacity to offer a favorable opinion of President Harrison, Father retorted, "What do you know about it? The President is a nincompoop . . . "

At the age of seventy, Father was as ornery as ever. "I won't have anything to do with this blood pressure," he objected when a nurse came to take his. "Everyone has blood pressure, Mr. Day," soothed the nurse. "A lot of them have," rejoined Father, "but I haven't. I won't." Submitting at last, he learned that his pressure was high. "Pooh!" he snorted, "What of it? All poppycock."

❖ ♦ ❖

One warm summer afternoon Mother took Father to the family cemetery plot to help raise a sunken gravestone. Father balked: "I don't care how much it's settled. I don't want to be buried with that infernal crowd anyhow." To resolve this new-found dilemma, he decided to buy a new gravesite far away from his family, "one on the corner where I can get out!"

Mother stared at Father in disbelief: "I almost believe," she said finally, betraying a measure of admiration, "he could do it."

by
Clarence Day
(1874 - 1935)

Type of work: Autobiographical comedy

Setting: New York City; 1860 to 1929

Principal characters:
Father (Clare Day), a stern, opinionated and amusing businessman
Mother (Vinnie Day), his doughty yet loving wife
Clarence Jr., their stubborn son

Commentary:

Life with Mother carries the same marvelously funny, simple, earthy tone as *Life With Father,* but, taken more from Mother's perspective, is possibly a more empathetic glimpse at the Day family. It does, however, include almost as many vignettes starring Father as it does Mother.

This account spans a great deal more of the Day family history, continuing right up to Mother's death. Since Mother and Father were always inseparable, their conversations and interactions in this volume are numerous. The author probably intended that these new episodes focus on Mother as a personality in her own right; to allow the reader a fuller view of her distinct and colorful character. Even in those preliberation days before and during the battles for women's suffrage, Mother did more than hold her own against the bellowing of Father—she made the Day home civilized.

Story Overview:

Time never mellowed either Father Day's determined nature or Mother's determination to make him see the error of his ways. Their son Clarence, now grown up, captured a typical sortie between his parents in an article he wrote about Father's unorthodox dog-training methods:

"Good Jackie," said Father. As the dog was frightened of his gruff manner and shrank from him, Father would command angrily, "Come here, sir." The dog, ever more frightened, tried to escape.

Mother intervened, "I wish you'd let Jackie alone. He doesn't know what you want of him."

"Pooh! Of course he does," declared Father and dragged the new dog out from under the sofa. "Sit UP," Father demanded, "Sit UP, sir."

"Oh please don't. How can you expect the poor thing to sit up when he doesn't know a word you're saying," Mother wailed.

"Will you let me alone?" shouted Father, and turned again to the cowed Jackie.

"I'll not stay here and see that dog frightened to death," Mother replied and went to the door.

"Frightened! What nonsense. I know dogs. They all like me."

Mother opened the door and the dog scurried through the exit in spite of Father's attempt to grab it.

He shouted, "Confound it! Now see what you've done! You've spoiled my whole plan." Mother objected, "You could never . . . "

Father shouted "I COULD!" But I can't do a thing if I'm interfered with. JACKIE! JACKIE! Come here sir!"

When Mother read Clarence's article, she triumphantly showed it to Father. "I hope you'll behave yourself after this," he responded, still not seeing her point. "That's how you kept interfering with my training of that dog."

❖ ◆ ❖

Years earlier, Father had met Mother on a sea voyage. He was twenty-five, she only seventeen; but even in those first days of their courtship he could be slightly irritating. When Father approved of a particular dish at the ship's dining table, he would accost the steward and loudly demand, "Here, bring that back I want some more—that is good!" Embarrassed and flustered, Mother would remind him that "There are other people here besides you."

Mother had grown up in an affluent family. Luckily for loyal readers of the Day family chronicles, when she reached her twentieth year, her brother, the sole surviving heir, fell on hard times and lost his fortune. Until then, Father's attempts at courtship had been sporadic; not an upper-crust type, he objected to marrying a girl with expensive tastes. When Mother's family, however, were notified of the impending financial failure, they advised her to invite Father to their home in Ohio. Father, accustomed to the luxuries of the big city, was appalled at the small Ohio town. To him, true to his blunt and vocal temperament, he complained that Painesville was nothing more than a "damned hole." Eager to leave, he finally asked Mother outright to marry him, grumbling that "he should think she'd want to get out of there too." With all his abrasiveness, Mother found something solid and authentic in Father which she missed in her more polished suitors; and she consented. They married in June, 1873.

❖ ◆ ❖

Mother set out with the task of raising a family. She was always a loyal and protective guardian to her four lively sons. Whenever an outraged neighbor complained of her boys' pranks or rough games, she would respond briskly that the offended party was "just talking nonsense." Then "she would rush to our defense, stun the enemy, and hurry straight out."

When disciplinary matters came to Father's attention, however, Mother's attempts to assuage him were about as effective as a whisper in a gale. Once when Clarence struggled to tell Father that a mishap of his had occurred "accidentally," Father shouted, "Of course it was 'by accident' but it's your business to see that accidents of this sort don't happen. And a spanking will probably assist you to bear that in mind." Mother at once piped in with, "Oh not this time, Clare. Clarence didn't really mean to knock off the cabman's hat with his little snowball." But Father had been riding in the besieged coach that day. I know boys," he declared as he led Clarence away for punishment.

⋄ ♦ ⋄

Father was a great proponent of foreign languages and tried with his usual methodical vigor to introduce his sons to the "civilized enlightenments" of German. Clarence, however, could never make it past the pronunciation of the word "Ich." Then one winter Mother hired a German tutor—not for Clarence, but for herself. Although she really did not want to learn German, after an elderly and impoverished fraulein offered her lessons, she decided that she would surprise Father. Mother was quickly disillusioned, however. She had apparently expected "the German language to behave like a gentleman and not be too hard on a busy woman who had several small boys to take care of, and who was studying it out of pure kindness, merely to help poor Fraulein." When, instead, she found herself exasperated beyond patience, she finally prevailed on Father himself to finish the lessons—and, to her disappointment, Father did very well.

⋄ ♦ ⋄

Although the onset of the Eighties ushered in the flowering of the women's emancipation movement, Mother was never a proponent. The underlying feeling among Mother's circle of high-spirited Victorian ladies was that a woman had no need of "equality"; instead she had certain "prerogatives" which God and nature had given her. Mother had no very clear idea what a woman's "prerogatives" were; but whatever they were she thought she might need them and her feelings about them were vigorous. Father was adamantly bewildered by all this; "He professed never to have heard of the most ordinary feminine privileges."

⋄ ♦ ⋄

Though he lavished Mother with jewels during their marriage, she lamented that she had never received an engagement ring from Father. Now Mother's allies warned her that "Any man who had successfully evaded one duty would naturally suppose he could keep on evading for life"; and soon Mother began to demand an engagement ring. Father passed this off as ridiculous.

Then Mother found out from Grandma that before he had met her Father had been engaged to a certain Bessie Skinner. Mother inquired as to why they had broken off the engagement and Grandma told her that, being cousins, they were always arguing, so "Bessie up and returned that ring to Clare." At this revelation, Mother shrieked, "WHAT? He gave that woman a RING? Whatever became of it?" Father probably still had it, she was told. Mother raced home and burst through the door. "Clare, why did you never give me that ring?"

Father found the ring—a modest little token purchased during his impetuous youth—and sheepishly surrendered it to Mother, who "clutched it victoriously." Mother then pilfered Father's cufflinks, had the pearls removed, and, along with the two small diamonds from Bessie's ring, had a new ring made. Father did not recognize the new setting and, frowning, muttered something about "more extravagance." To this Mother replied, "What I'd really like now would be a nice diamond necklace."

⋄ ♦ ⋄

When Mother took sick, Father was at a loss. "Dear Vinnie," he would repeat helplessly over and over, while patting her hand. "Stop it Clare! That's enough!" she would snap. During one convalescence, Mother finally hit on a way to put Father's solicitude to work; she asked him to attend a tea party for her and bring her back some cheerful tidbits of gossip—along with "some of those nice little sandwiches Mrs. Nichols has. Bring some in your pocket." At the party, however, Father saw that sneaking the tea sandwiches into his pocket would involve stealth and furtiveness; he could not bring himself to do it. When he returned home and went to sit down, Mother first gushed, "Don't sit on my sandwiches . . . " Then, observing his silence: "Oh Clare, didn't you bring even one?" "It was impractical," he offered. "In short, there was no way to do it."

"You will never do anything that you think isn't suitable," Mother said irritably. "Why of course I won't," he frowned. "Why should I?" "Not even for me?" countered Mother. "Oh, damn," said Father. "Oh, damnation!"

⋄ ♦ ⋄

Mother was one woman who kept up with fashion trends, which in the Eighties happened to be rubber trees and pug dogs. Notwithstanding, when Mother suggested the family buy a pug, Father growled: "I must positively decline to begin domesticating monstrosities." He added that he "doubted whether pugs were dogs anyhow." At last Mother settled for a porcelain statue of a pug dog and tied a ribbon around its neck to add to its realism.

⋄ ♦ ⋄

As she grew older, Mother hankered for an apartment. Father, of course, would hear nothing of it. She first tried reason to persuade him: "You'd be a lot more comfortable in an apartment." But, to Father, an apartment wasn't a real home. "If you buy it," Mother countered, "then it's your home just like a house." In disgust—and putting yet another matter to rest—Father replied, "It's a hole in the air just the same."

When Father died in the family home, Mother finally did move to an apartment, furnished to suit her varied tastes. There she lived and entertained, surrounded still by many of her beloved friends and furnishings from an age gone by, and, with undiminished zest, making them all vitally at home in the new age. She died quietly, at home—just two days after hosting a particularly vibrant party—in January, 1929.

THE SHORT STORIES OF EDGAR ALLAN POE

(taken from The Tell-Tale Heart and Other Writings)

Scholars disagree about whether Edgar Allan Poe (1809-1849) invented the modern short story, but it is certain that economic need impelled him to write the tales that have tingled spines for over 150 years. Poe preferred poetry, but his short stories are what he is remembered for.

The Tell-Tale Heart

He had loved the old man with whom he lived—but had hated the old man's eye. "Whenever it fell upon me," he related, "my blood ran cold." The young man *must* be freed from that infernal eye! And so, he at last determined that the old one must die.

Each night at midnight the soon-to-be murderer slowly opened the old man's bedroom door. Cunningly, he cracked open the lantern so that only a single ray shone on the old man's face. For seven nights, however, the lantern disclosed both eyes shut—and thus the evil deed could not be done. For "it was not," thought the schemer, "the old man who vexed me, but his Evil Eye."

On the eighth night, as the door opened, the old man awoke—his cursed vulture eye leering into the blackness—and asked, "Who's there?" The murderer spoke not a word. Several long, silent minutes passed before the older man let out a veritable moan of terror. Then, he opened his lantern. The light fell immediately on the old man's fogged blue eye. Then began the horrid sound; the old man's heartbeat grew louder and louder and louder, until the murderer actually feared that its beating would wake the neighbors. Enraged by this thought . . . by the Eye . . . and by the concussions emanating from the dark room, the murderer fell upon his screaming victim, dragged the heavy bed on top of him, and waited for the heartbeat to stop. When at length it ceased, he dismembered the corpse and buried it beneath the planked floor.

The body was barely interred when three officers from the local constabulary knocked at the door, summoned by a neighbor who had heard the old man's death scream. At first, their conversation was light and amiable; the murderer, confident that his deed was hidden, explained that the scream had been his own, caused by a nightmare. Yet, as the constables tarried, the young man thought he could once again hear the old man's heart begin to beat. Faint at first, the sound grew in intensity, until the killer was convinced that the constables must be able to hear it as well! Still, the officers smiled and talked in pleas-

antries. Finally, the murderer could no longer stand the sound, the tension. "Villains!" he cried, "dissemble no more! I admit the deed!—tear up the planks!—here, here!—it is the beating of his hideous heart!"

The Pit and the Pendulum

The Spanish inquisitors announced the sentence: death. Upon hearing this, the prisoner fainted—only to awaken later in a pitch-black dungeon. Frantically, he groped along the floor and walls of his prison, probing its dimensions. Would his imminent doom be a slow and drawn out process, he wondered, or would death come quickly? At last exhausted by his own frenzy, he fell asleep.

Again he awoke, this time to find food and water at his side. The room was still dark; he ate. Then he began to grope exploringly around his prison. Suddenly he slipped and fell to the floor at the edge of a seemingly bottomless pit. All his terror was reawakened. As he realized the death he had just avoided, once again he fainted. When he awoke, again he found fresh food and water at his side. He drank the water in one drought and immediately fell back into a drugged sleep.

Stirring a fourth time, he found himself bound by cords to a wooden beam in the now-lighted torture chamber. One arm had been left free to allow him to eat from a bowl of salted meat at his side. Looking about the room, he first noted its rounded iron walls—and then the large pendulum that swung back and forth high above him. Slowly he began to realize that, with each swing, the pendulum was inching down toward him. As it came closer, the manner of his death became apparent; the pendulum bob had been honed into a razor-sharp blade that would slowly eat into his chest and slice him in half.

Days passed—perhaps weeks—and the pendulum steadily descended. Rats, emboldened by the prisoner's immobility, constantly snatched tidbits of meat from his bowl and nipped at his fingers, then scurried back into the pit below him.

As the blade drew within three inches of his chest, the prisoner began to alternate between calm acceptance, panicked desperation and raving insanity. Then, suddenly, a spark of hope took hold. The rats, he thought—which had eaten all but a single morsel from his bowl—could also eat through the rope! He grabbed the last bit of salted meat and rubbed it onto one strand of the cord which bound him. Temporarily frightened by the sudden motion, the animals drew back for a moment; but scores of rats soon issued from the pit and assaulted his bonds—even as the blade made its first contact with his robe. On the third pass, the nerves of his chest seemed to sing as the blade cut lightly into his flesh.

Not any too soon, the taut rope grew slack, and the prisoner scrambled off the beam onto the floor, careful to avoid the pit a second time. But he had not time to exult; without warning, the iron plates that walled his round prison suddenly began to glow with heat. Then the grating sound of iron being dragged across stone assaulted his ears, and he realized the iron walls, now pressing themselves tightly together, would soon force him into the pit. Ever closer crept the walls, sealing his doom. "Anything but the pit!" he whispered as he tottered on its brink. And then he started to fall—just as the walls began to retreat and trumpets sounded! In an instant, "an outstretched arm caught my own as I fell, fainting, into the abyss. It was that of General Lasalle. The French army had entered Toledo. The Inquisition was in the hands of its enemies."

The Cask of Amontillado

Montressor vowed to avenge the insults of the haughty Fortunato in such a manner that Fortunato would know vengeance was being exacted. He soon hit upon the perfect vehicle for his purposes: his enemy's love of fine wine. Happening "by chance" upon Fortunato during Carnival, Montressor lured him into the catacombs beneath the ancestral Montressor home with the promise of testing a cask of Amontillado, a very rare—and expensive—Italian wine. The foul air of the catacombs, which held the remains of preceding generations of Montressors, aggravated Fortunato's cough. Despite Montressor's many unctuous suggestions that they turn back, however, his guest insisted that they continue. Fortunato gratefully accepted the draughts of wine offered by his host to fortify himself against the fetid air.

At last they reached their goal. Montressor motioned his unwitting companion toward a niche at the far end of a crypt, next to which sat a pile of bones. This niche, Montressor indicated, held the coveted cask of Amontillado. Fortunato greedily pushed through the dark entryway—as Montressor had anticipated he would—only to bump against a solid granite wall. Torpid with drink and stunned by the shock of his collision, Fortunato was unable to resist as Montressor quickly clapped shackles around his ankles. Still bewildered, the chained man said nothing as Montressor produced stones, mortar and a trowel from beneath the pile of bones and proceeded to wall up the entrance.

Finally, as his tormentor finished the seventh tier, Fortunato, sobering up, began to scream. Montressor taunted him, answering shriek for shriek to demonstrate no one could hear the hysterical cries. At this, Fortunato grew quiet; and Montressor continued his grisly labors. Then, when his pompous victim's tomb lacked but one stone, he was startled by a sudden laugh from Fortunato. "A very good joke indeed," the prisoner said uncertainly. "An excellent jest. We will have many a rich laugh about it at the palazzo—he! he! he!—over our wine." In answer Montressor merrily cried out, "The Amontillado!" Then he forced the last stone into position and mortared it in place.

Before beginning his ascent, Montressor re-erected the rampart of bones on the wall. "For the half of a century no mortal has disturbed them. *In pace requiescat* [rest in peace]!"

Commentary:

The stories presented here are vintage Poe— characterized by grotesque invention and forceful plot construction. Whether writing about guilt and insanity ("The Tell-Tale Heart"—1843), cruelty and torture ("The Pit and the Pendulum"—1842), or cold-blooded vengeance ("The Cask of Amontillado"—1846), Poe leaves the reader enthralled from page to page with uncertainty about what will happen next. *After* finishing the story, however, and upon reflection, the reader inevitably says, "Well, of course, how else could it have happened?"

Indeed, Poe's greatest gift to literature was his ability to "haunt" his readers; to manipulate their psychological state as he portrays that of his characters. Consider, for example, "The Pit and the Pendulum": The reader first feels a rush of relief at having avoided falling into the pit, followed by mounting desperation as the pendulum swings ever closer, then stomach-wrenching revulsion as rats swarm the prisoner's body, and, finally, gasping relief when the condemned man is, at the very last second, rescued.

As the first—and perhaps still the foremost—master of literary suspense, Poe lives on through his skillful "novellas" and the evocative imagery of his poetry.

THE SHORT STORIES OF EDITH WHARTON

(taken from *The Ghost Stories of Edith Wharton*, Scribner, New York, N.Y., 1973)

Asked if she believed in ghosts, Edith Wharton answered: "No, I don't believe in ghosts, but I'm afraid of them." She explained this seeming paradox in her preface: "It is in the warm darkness . . . far below our conscious reason that the faculty dwells with which we apprehend the ghosts we may not be endowed with the gift of seeing." The person who hears a ghost story, she felt, employs a conscious act of imagination, or "believing," to perceive the supernatural.

Pomegranate Seed

Charlotte Ashby bounded apprehensively up to her doorstep. Would she find a letter waiting for her today? Since the letters had started coming, she had not been able to enter the house without first checking that one was there. Seven had come so far, each "a square graying envelope with 'Kenneth Ashby, Esquire,' written on it in bold but faint characters," obviously the handwriting of a woman. When her husband saw them a disturbing change would come over him. He would gaze at Charlotte with "the look of a man who had been so far away from ordinary events that when he returns to familiar things they seem strange." Each time he would take the letter upstairs to his room, where he would remain for several hours.

Charlotte wondered if the letters were being sent by one of her husband's old girl-friends. But that hardly seemed possible; all of his friends told her that he had never so much as looked at another woman since his first marriage, to Elsie Corder, who had died and left him a widower, until the letters. Charlotte and Kenneth's own marriage had been filled with joy. The letters had built up a silence between them; somehow, the terrible secret hidden within them had created an ever-widening rift.

Now, Charlotte opened the door and saw the letter. This time she simply had to do something, she thought. She waited in the library and watched as her husband came home, slowly opened the letter, and read. As he did, his face turned an ashen grey. Then he kissed it and began to put into his pocket.

Charlotte confronted him. She saw him kiss the letter; how many more times would these letters push him into a state of misery. But her questions only made him angry, and, saying the letter was business, stalked up to his bedroom. After an hour, however, he returned, a tired-looking man. "There it is," she thought, "He knows what's in the letter and has fought his battle out again, whatever it is . . . while I'm still in darkness."

After dinner, Charlotte suggested they go away on holiday. Kenneth refused vehemently. "Don't ask me," he said. "I can't leave—I can't!" Charlotte replied, "Is it because she's forbidden you that you won't go away with me?" At this, Kenneth's wept, and Charlotte tried once more to get through to him. It hurt her to see how much

he suffered when he opened the letters. Finally, clinging to her tightly as though frightened, he relented: "Of course we'll go away together."

When Charlotte awoke the following morning, Kenneth had already left the house. He had left a message with the maid that, tomorrow, he would be ready to sail. Charlotte was overjoyed; she had won! She was stronger than this other woman. Kenneth was hers! She spent the morning packing and, at noon, called his office to find out where they were going. The secretary informed her that Mr. Ashby had gone out of town. Charlotte hung up the phone, dismayed.

Kenneth didn't come home at five o'clock, as normal. At seven his office called to say he had still not returned. At her wit's end, Charlotte went to her mother-in-law's house; perhaps he was there. But he was not. Charlotte and Mrs. Ashby walked home together, hoping he would have arrived home by then. Instead, they found another letter in the box. Mrs. Ashby picked it up, her hands shaking. She sat down in a chair and told Charlotte to open it.

Charlotte opened the letter, but the writing was so faint she couldn't read it. She handed it to her mother-in-law, and asked, "Whose handwriting is it?" Mrs. Ashby was unable to answer. "I can't—I can't," she gasped. Then her anxious eyes traveled to the picture of Kenneth's dead wife Elsie. Charlotte knew, then, who sent the letters. She and Mrs. Ashby called the police—they had to find Kenneth—that is, if they thought it would do any good.

The Eyes

Andrew Culwin "sat back in his armchair, listening and blinking through the smoke circles with the cheerful tolerance of a wise old idol," while his guests in the library exchanged ghost stories. Finally it was his turn, though he was such a sensible man no one expected him to know anything of the supernatural.

As a young man, Mr. Culwin met a cousin, Alice Nowell. Though she was "neither beautiful nor intelligent," nevertheless he felt some affection for her. He had "handled it rather rashly, and put it out of joint." But when he decided to leave for Europe, Alice kissed him so sweetly that he, feeling guilty, promised to take her abroad.

That night, however, he was awakened by a pair of eyes. The eyes were hideously old, with sunken orbits and "red-lined lids." They held an "expression of vicious security," seeming "to belong to a man who had done a lot of harm in his life, but had always kept just inside the danger line." The eyes glowered at him all night long, and in the morning, he fled to England, abandoning poor Alice.

The eyes didn't reappear for a long time. Alice, to his surprise, sent a letter introducing her kind-hearted cousin Gilbert Noyes, who wanted to be a writer. Culwin took him on to soothe his guilt over Alice, but it soon became apparent that Noyes was an idiot and simply could not write.

After several months, Culwin just could not bring himself to fire Noyes.

By and by, the eyes returned to haunt Culwin. "There they hung in the darkness, their swollen lids dropped across the little watery bulbs rolling loose in the orbits . . . They were eyes which had grown hideous gradually, which had built up their baseness . . . bit by bit, out of a series of turpitudes slowly accumulated through the industrious years."

All the while, Culwin continued to encourage Noyes, and the eyes continued to torment him. Finally Culwin could stand Noyes' foolishness no longer, and blurted out the heavy-handed news: his writing was no good. Noyes left in dejection, eventually to take an office job, vegetate, and marry "drearily" in China. After that the eyes left Culwin for good.

"Put two and two together if you can," he said, finishing the story. "For my part, I haven't found the link." One of the guests, who had barely heard the end of the story, sat staring in horror at Culwin's reflection in the mirror. When Culwin turned, "he and the image in the glass confronted each other with a glare of slowly gathering hate." Those terrible eyes, and his own eyes, were the same.

The Triumph of Night

Faxon stood at the train station in the freezing blast of snow. The sleigh from Weymore was scheduled to arrive soon, but it was obvious it wouldn't come. It probably wasn't his hostess' fault; likely, she had told the butler to pick him up and on such a cold night he had conveniently forgotten.

Presently, however, a sleigh drove up to meet him. A man named Frank Rainer, nephew to the famous philanthropist, John Lavington, emerged. Rainer and Faxon, both young men, hit it off immediately. Rainer enthusiastically invited his chilled acquaintance to stay with him for the night at his residence in Overdale. Faxon agreed eagerly.

Faxon's face, though etched with fatigue, was a ruddy, healthy color, but his hands were ash grey. Rainer, for his part, reported that he had tuberculosis, but his uncle, "luckily," hadn't sent him off to Arizona or New Mexico to recuperate. A new doctor had assured him that the present climate wouldn't impair him, as long as he kept his dancing and dining out to a minimum. "All the same," said Faxon, with an outpouring of brotherly love, "you ought to be careful."

After picking up two other men from the train station, a Mr. Grisben and a Mr. Balch, they returned to Overdale. Rainer sent Faxon upstairs to refresh himself while he attended to some business.

When Faxon went about looking for the dining room, making a wrong turn he entered the study. There sat Rainer, Mr. Balch, Mr. Grisben, and Mr. Lavington, finishing up Rainer's will. Another figure, resembling Mr. Lavington in almost every respect, stood behind the philanthropist, staring at the old man with malice and hostility. Faxon agreed to sign the will as a witness, and, to his relief, when he next

looked up, the hateful figure was gone.

At dinner, Mr. Grisben kindly told Frank Rainer that he didn't look at all well, and that he ought to have gone off to a more balmy climate. "You look like the day after an earthquake," he exclaimed. Suddenly, the menacing figure reappeared behind Mr. Lavington's chair. But Mr. Grisben, also gazing at Lavington, gave no sign of seeing the figure. Once more, Faxon tore his eyes from the figure and stared at the table.

"I won't look up," Faxon thought, "I swear I won't!" But then he looked up. The figure was still there, now glaring angrily at Rainer. Suddenly, Faxon's "last link with safety snapped," and he ran outside into the snow.

Why could only he see the figure? Why had he, the stranger, been singled out for the vision? His chill, his weariness, must have deluded his senses, he thought. Or, perhaps—perhaps his driftlessness, the fact that he had no private life, had made him sensitive to another world? No, better to think of himself as ill, deluded, than as a victim of such terrible warnings.

Rainer chased after Faxon to bring him back to the house. But as they walked back, Faxon became more and more convinced that "he was the instrument singled out to warn and save; and here he was, irresistibly, driven, dragging the victim back to his doom!" Then Rainer "swerved, drooped on Faxon's arm, and seemed to sink into nothing at his feet." All at once Faxon stared down at his hands—they were blood-red!

With Rainer dead, Faxon never made it to Weymore to visit his hostess. Instead he returned East to stay with a friend and recuperate from the trauma. Months later, he began to feel better and he started reading through old newspapers. He discovered that because of a crash in Wall Street and the recent failure of one of Lavington's companies, Lavington was ruined.

"Faxon stood up with a cry. That was it, then—that was what the warning meant! And if he had not fled from it, dashed wildly away from it into the night . . . the powers of darkness might not have prevailed . . . The powers of pity had singled him out to warn and save, and he had closed his ears to their call, and washed his hands of it, and fled. Washed his hands of it!"

Commentary:

This collection of stories by Edith Wharton (1862 - 1937) is not entirely representative of the rest of Wharton's work. Her novels (*The House of Mirth, Summer* . . .) published just after the turn of the century depict women who, forced to assume only certain narrow roles dictated by society, are compelled to choose paths that lead to desperate unhappiness and self-destruction.

Ghost Stories, different from her other fiction, has a relevancy all its own. Full of secret passageways, archaic mansions, terrible secrets, and vengeful spirits, the stories in this volume bring us back to the times when, as children, we found ourselves awakened in the dark of our bedroom or when unknown sounds in the night made our hair stand on end. We peek between the fingers of our shivering hands and behold an "other-world," one plagued by witches, demons, and above all, ghosts.

DR. JEKYLL AND MR. HYDE

by
Robert Louis Stevenson
(1850 - 1894)

Type of work: Psychological thriller

Setting: London, England; nineteenth century

Principal characters:

Dr. Jekyll, a noble and prominent London physician

Mr. Hyde, his fiendish alter ego

Mr. Utterson, Jekyll's lawyer and close friend

Dr. Lanyon, Jekyll's professional associate

Commentary:

Ironically, Robert Louis Stevenson, in his last years, disparaged the revision of *Dr. Jekyll and Mr. Hyde* that was finally published in 1886, after his wife complained that the first version "did not contain enough moral message." That lost first writing may indeed have drawn an even deeper and more authentic psychological portrait than the thriller which has become by far Stevenson's best-known work.

But today, more than a century after their conception, Jekyll and Hyde seem almost eerily prophetic When Jekyll notes in his journal that his "bad" nature flourished in spite of, but precisely *because* of his efforts to repress it; when he contends that "man will ultimately be known for a mere polity of multifarious, incongruous, and independent denizens," he presages our concerns with both multiple personalities and the "depth of self" that modern psychologists talk about. *Jekyll and Hyde* remains a classic, an ageless portrait of a tormented human soul.

Story Overview:

Mr. Utterson, a highly respected attorney, was strolling with his friend, Mr. Enfield, through the dark, misty streets of London. They were discussing an incident that had horrified Enfield: he had witnessed the brutal trampling of an eight-year-old girl by a mysterious little man, who then "left her screaming on the ground." Enfield, along with members of the girl's family, had chased the attacker and demanded that he make reparations. The villain led them to a decrepit cellar door in an otherwise blank brick facade and turned over to the parents a note for ninety pounds which was signed by Dr. Jekyll, an eminent physician. The only thing that Enfield could report about this "damned Juggernaut" after describing his general "air of deformity," was his name: "It was a man of the name of Hyde."

Utterson was singularly disturbed. His client and friend—the very Dr. Jekyll who signed Mr. Hyde's note—had entrusted Utterson with his will. And in this will, Jekyll had bequeathed his entire estate to a certain Edward Hyde in the event that he, Jekyll, should disappear for a period of three months. Utterson could not understand why a man of such stature and prominence would associate with a man of such terrible disposition. Was it blackmail? At first "I thought it was madness," Utterson mused, " . . . Now I begin to fear it is dis-

grace."

Seeking to delve further into this mystery, the lawyer called on Dr. Lanyon, one of Jekyll's longtime professional associates. Lanyon had little information; Dr. Jekyll, he explained, had embarked years earlier on a series of chemical experiments that had distanced him from the rest of the medical community.

Utterson was intrigued by now with this forbidding stranger. "If he be Mr. Hyde," he resolved, "I shall be Mr. Seek." And one night, hiding near the door of Jekyll's residence, Utterson heard footsteps. As the smallish man locked the door, Utterson stepped forward, introduced himself as a friend of Jekyll's, and demanded an explanation. Hyde, "pale and dwarfish . . . gave an impression of deformity without nameable malformation, he had a displeasing smile . . . and spoke in a husky, whispering, and somewhat broken voice. He seemed hardly human." The two men stared icily at one another. Then, following a brief but hostile exchange, Hyde rushed back into the house and slammed the door.

Utterson was now even more anxious to confront his friend, fearing that Jekyll was hiding a terrible secret. After many calls, the lawyer finally found Jekyll at home, serenely seated in his living room. "You know," Utterson began, "that will of yours—I never approved of it," then revealed his distaste for young Hyde, of whom, he said, he had learned "abominable" things. Jekyll simply replied that Utterson must trust him and fulfill the will as written. Utterson acquiesced. Then, to reassure the doubtful lawyer, Jekyll added, " . . . the moment I choose, I can be rid of Mr. Hyde."

A month later, an old gentleman was found cruelly murdered. A maid had recognized Mr. Hyde as the culprit who " . . . with apelike fury . . . [hailed] down a storm of blows under which the bones were audibly shattered." The police, having found a letter addressed to Utterson in the dead man's possession, called on the lawyer to identify the body. Utterson reluctantly obliged—he recognized the dead man's mangled corpse as that of Sir Danvers Carew, a distinguished client—and he also admitted to knowing the murderer. When he took the police to Hyde's residence in the slums of Soho, however, they found the residence empty.

Angered, Utterson again called on Jekyll and demanded pointblank whether the pale and dejected doctor had been "mad enough to hide this fellow." Jekyll sobbed that he had learned his lesson: "I swear to God I will never set eyes on him again . . . I am done with him in this world . . . "

Time passed. Much to Utterson's relief, Hyde seemed to have vanished from the earth, and Jekyll's demeanor was improved. Once quite a solitary man, he now came out of seclusion to associate freely with his friends, just as he had before.

But bliss was short-lived. One night, Dr. Lanyon summoned Utterson to his home. The usually robust doctor had totally changed. A death-warrant etched his face. A "terror of mind" had apparently sent the dying Lanyon into sudden shock. In his last act, Lanyon turned over a sealed envelope to Mr. Utterson with the instructions to open it if Dr. Jekyll died or disappeared. Troubled by it all, Utterson again called on Jekyll, only to discover that the doctor now refused to see anyone.

A short time later, Utterson was visited during the night by Jekyll's frightened young servant, Poole, who insisted the lawyer follow him to his master's home. There he found that Jekyll had locked himself in his cellar laboratory many days earlier, his only subsequent communications consisting of hoarse and desperate demands for a certain "medicine," accompanied by angry notes of instruction to the pharmacist, whose concoctions he berated as "impure." Poole had caught one fleeting glimpse of a masked "monkey" figure, however; "and if that was my master, why did he cry out like a rat, and run from me?" Fearing the worst, Poole and Utterson axed down the door. But it was too late. Hyde's body lay contorted on the floor, a vial of poison clenched in his hand, his facial muscles still twitching. Jekyll was nowhere to be found. A search of the room revealed a lengthy journal, along with a note from Jekyll asking Utterson to read both the journal and the packet from Lanyon.

As Utterson read, in disbelief and horror, the mystery slowly unfolded. Lanyon's note told of a letter he had received from Mr. Jekyll, asking him to come to Jekyll's home, force open the desk, and remove a drawer containing several vials of chemicals. It also said that a man would come for the drawer later that night. At midnight, Hyde had appeared at Lanyon's door. When Lanyon gave him the drawer, Hyde had asked for a glass, mixed the chemicals, and challenged Lanyon to observe "a new province of power." Then, after reminding Lanyon of his oath of silence as a doctor, Hyde swallowed the potion—and before the physician's gaze, was transformed into Dr. Jekyll!

"My life is shaken to its roots; sleep has left me," he wrote. "I feel that my days are numbered and that I must die." Unable to unburden himself because of his oath, Lanyon had left only the letter he had written as a testimony of these events.

Utterson then turned to Jekyll's journal: His life's experiences, he stated, had drawn him "steadily closer to that truth by whose partial discovery I have been doomed to such a dreadful shipwreck, that man is not truly one, but truly two."

As a youth, he had felt no conflict between good and evil. "Indeed, the worst of my faults was a certain impatient gaiety . . . " But his "imperious desire" to portray himself as a lofty and dignified gentleman had led to a widening and deepening schism between his noble, daylight "public" self and the "lower elements of my soul." Finally he could no longer resist his one "beloved daydream": To liberate his two selves from each other.

After long experimentation, he concocted a drug that "controlled and shook the very fortress of identity," and allowed "the unjust [to] go his way, delivered from . . . aspirations and remorse," while "the just [walked] steadfastly . . . on his upward path."

Recognizing the struggle that raged within him, Jekyll had fought to repress his less developed evil personality. Each time he drank the potion, however, "I felt younger, happier in body, I was conscious of a heady recklessness. I knew myself to be tenfold more wicked, sold a slave to my original evil, and the thought braced and delighted me like wine."

The doctor had taken every precaution to separate the public identities of Jekyll and Hyde. He rented a room in Soho which he frequented as Hyde, and drew up a will to ensure that if Hyde somehow took final control, he would be cared for.

Over time, the urge to transform himself into the evil Hyde grew stronger and stronger. For a while the repentant Jekyll succeeded in repressing his wicked and bold alter ego. But "I began to be tortured with throes and longings, as of Hyde struggling after freedom; and at last in an hour of moral weakness, I swallowed the transforming draught," and Hyde's pent up energies exploded in rage against the unfortunate Sir Danvers: "I mauled the unresisting body, tasting delight from every blow, my lust of evil gratified and stimulated." Fearing capture and punishment, Hyde transported his possessions from his room in Soho to Jekyll's house—where he drank the potion's antidote.

This time, Jekyll wrote, he had firmly resolved to bury the incarnation of Hyde once and for all. Devastated by the ruthless act, he sought penance and solace by returning to his former friends and associates. But his new life came to an abrupt end in the park one day when Jekyll—even without taking the drug—suddenly found himself transformed into Hyde. "Now I was the common quarry of mankind . . . a known murderer." Fearing the gallows and unable to return to the lab, Hyde had penned the letter to Lanyon under the signature of "Dr. Jekyll."

In full view of the mortally terrified Lanyon, the potion had once again restored Hyde to his better self. But from then on Jekyll's mind and body were captive to Mr. Hyde. Whenever Jekyll became sick or tired, Hyde gained control. The end neared as his original supply of the formula dwindled and he tried to replenish it; but he found the essential catalytic salt no longer sparked the final chemical reaction. Locked in his laboratory, Mr. Hyde was trapped. Finally, swallowing the last dose of his formula, Dr. Jekyll made his final journal entry. Then, in his last besieged moments, helplessly overcome by Hyde, he gulped down poison, and lay twitching on the floor when Poole and Utterson axed down the door.

Jekyll's final journal entry read,

I am finishing this statement under the last of the old powders. The doom that is closing in on us has already crushed him. I bring the life of that unhappy Jekyll to an end.

DRACULA

by
Bram Stoker
(1847-1912)

Type of work: Horror novel

Setting: Eastern Europe and England; late 1890s

Principal characters:

Lucy Westenra, a young upper-class woman

Mina Murray, Lucy's friend

Jonathon Harker, a lawyer, and Mina's fiance

Arthur Holmwood, the only son of Lord Godalming and heir to that title

John Seward, a doctor and insane-asylum keeper

Quincey Morris, an American friend of both Arthur and Dr. Seward

Dr. Van Helsing, a Dutch doctor and Dr. Seward's former professor

Count Dracula, a Transylvanian noble

Story Overview:

Though the Eastern European countryside was lush and verdant, lawyer Jonathon Harker felt uneasy. As he traveled to resolve a problem with a client's estate, he had met with several warnings to, frankly, stay away from his destination: the castle of Count Dracula, a Transylvanian noble. Others had even gone so far as to slip him a clove of garlic, or a small crucifix—talismans, they said, to ward off evil.

Jonathon himself had dismissed these admonitions as nothing more than rampant superstition. But as he neared the castle, the sky let loose a torrential downpour. The Count's gaunt coachman appeared and offered Jonathon a ride to the castle. He accepted gratefully, but the warnings echoed in his mind as the coach was followed closely by an eerie blue flame—and a pack of howling wolves.

Jonathon's discomfort grew the moment he was introduced to Count Dracula. His host possessed a strong face—"aquiline, with high bridge of the thin nose and peculiarly arched nostrils . . . The mouth . . . under the heavy moustache, was fixed and rather cruel-looking, with peculiarly sharp white teeth; these protruded over the lips, whose remarkable ruddiness showed astonishing vitality in a man of his years . . ."

The Count was as cultured and polite as any noble person, but Jonathon couldn't quite shake the vague impressions of strangeness—impressions that were reinforced when Jonathon noticed that when the Count passed in front of a mirror, no reflection passed with him. Gradually, unease swelled to a dull, aching, fear.

Later, Jonathon awoke to the sounds of scraping and scratching. Taking a candle into the hall, Jonathon gasped when he saw Dracula climbing down a wall—headfirst. In horror, he watched the Count scale the wall, then disappear into the shadows. Choking back a scream, Jonathon ran down the hall, desperate to escape the madness that surrounded him.

The first room he encountered happened to be the Count's. A breeze whispered the curtains covering a small window on the far wall, indicating it was open. Jonathon quickly climbed through the window—only to find himself in an even stranger place. He stood in the freshly dug and furrowed courtyard of a small, ruined church; Jonathon could see the crumbling walls in the weird half-light that filtered down from overhead. He became aware of coffin-shaped boxes, filled with rich black earth from the church's cemetery. Each was stamped with a shipping label.

Jonathon troll-walked between the rows of boxes, his eyes darting furtively left and right. He froze in his tracks when he saw what appeared to be a body lying in one of the boxes. Jonathon's breath caught in his throat when he realized the body was that of the Count. The unnaturally pale Dracula was lying perfectly still, his sightless eyes staring into eternity. Jonathon cracked the corpse on its head with a shovel he found nearby, then sprinted away from the castle.

Meanwhile, back in England, Jonathon's fiancee took a trip to the seaside town of Whitby to celebrate the engagement of her friend, Lucy. While she was there, a Russian freighter crashed into the Whitby pier during a furious storm. Dockworkers reported seeing a large dog jump from the ship during the accident. The only crewmember found on board was the captain—dead. The ship's log told of disappearing crewmen, and an unnamed horror that drove the captain to tie himself to the ship's wheel, clutching a rosary to ward off the evil. The cargo manifest listed 50 boxes of earth, which had been picked up and spirited away by a Whitby businessman.

A couple of days later, Mina awoke to find that Lucy had wandered off during the night, apparently sleepwalking. Mina found Lucy in a church's cemetery, a dark figure with a white face and red eyes hovered over the hypnotized girl. As Mina approached, the specter disappeared, and Lucy fell over as if in a coma.

A few days later, Lucy had regained her strength, and Mina received word from Jonathon that he had been ill and was recovering in a Buda-Pesth hospital. Mina immediately made plans to join him there, where they were married right in the hospital room.

When Lucy moved back to her family's home in London, she relapsed into her illness, and her fiance, Arthur Holmwood, asked Dr. Seward, the director of a local asylum—and Lucy's former suitor—to attend to her. After examining the girl, a mystified Seward called in his former professor, Dr. Van Helsing, for another opinion. It was obvious Lucy had lost a lot of blood, but transfusions had little effect. In fact, Lucy's condition worsened until she was barely clinging to life. Arthur and his friend, Quincey Morris, both donated blood, but Lucy died the next day.

Alarmed at the symptoms Lucy presented, Dr. Van Helsing forbade Arthur from kissing her as she lay dying, and after she was dead, the doctor laid a cross and a clove of garlic on her body. Lucy was buried in the family crypt.

Later, Dr. Van Helsing contacted Mina to find out if she could shed any more light on the mystery of Lucy's death. Mina presented the doctor with her diary, which recounted the peculiar scene in the cemetery. She also gave him a copy of Jonathon's diary, which detailed his own harrowing experience in the Count's castle.

With solid evidence that Dracula was indeed a vampire, and fearing that Lucy also had been made into an immortal monster, the doctor, along with Quincey and Arthur, raced to her tomb, but found it empty. Seemingly out of thin air, a hideous—yet frighteningly sensuous—creature appeared before them: Lucy. "The sweetness was turned to adamantine, heartless cruelty, and the purity to voluptuous wantonness . . . the lips were crimson with fresh blood." The men lured what had been Lucy into the vault, sealing the tomb with crumbs of Host—sacramental wafers. The next day, they returned and destroyd the creature. After filling her mouth with garlic, they vowed to hunt down the evil that had corrupted young Lucy.

The three friends joined with Seward, Jonathon, and Mina for their quest. Putting together all the information they had between them, they learned that vampires could appear in any form, but could only change at sunrise, sunset, noon, or midnight. They also realized the earth-filled boxes had been delivered to the house next door to the asylum. The hunters resolved to find the Count's boxes and sterilize them with the Host so he could not find refuge there. Suspecting that Dracula would be looking for Jonathon and Mina, they told the couple to stay under cover. Mina, they said, was "too precious . . . to have such risk."

Leaving Jonathon and Mina behind, the others explored the house next door. There they found thousands of rats scurrying between boxes of soil, all amid a stench "as though corruption had become corrupt itself." Realizing the vampire was close—and that Mina and Jonathon were alone—the men rushed to their room, only to find the Count forcing Mina to drink his blood from an open vein in his chest, while Jonathon lay in a stupor. Brandishing a sacred wafer, they advanced on the vampire, who, sickened by the relic, vanished in cloud of smoke.

Van Helsing approached Mina and touched her forehead with the Host; it burned a scar into her flesh. Realizing she had become unclean, the crusaders vowed to kill Dracula before Mina became like him. If they failed, they also vowed to drive a stake through Mina's heart rather than let her turn into a blood-seeking monster.

Van Helsing hypnotized Mina, and through her unholy spiritual tie with Dracula, was able to learn that the vampire was aboard a ship. The destination, however, eluded the doctor, although he knew it was somewhere in Europe. The crusaders paired off, planning to hunt the entire continent until they found him. Van Helsing and Mina volunteered to travel to Transylvania in case Dracula had returned to his homeland. The others agreed to meet them there if their own searches proved unfruitful.

Mina, however, began to grow more vampire-like with each passing day: she slept all day, refusing to eat, and was terrorized by the Holy Host that Van Helsing used to protect her. One night, as they neared the castle, Mina was visited by three ghostly personages—Dracula's brides. Calling in haunting, chanting voices, they begged Mina, as their "sister", to join them. Van Helsing chased them away, but could not drive their deadly, alluring voices from his mind.

The next day, trudging through the gravelike stillness of a heavy snowfall, Mina and the doctor reached the castle. Immediately, they encountered the three brides, lying in their tombs. Even in stasis, the brides evoked smoldering seduction. Van Helsing found himself being drawn in by their awesome power, but at the last minute, he drove a stake through each of their hearts, saving himself.

Hearing a commotion outside, Mina and Van Helsing noticed a small band of gypsies hurriedly carting a coffin-shaped box toward the castle. As the noisy group approached, Van Helsing saw four figures rushing through the snow trying to catch up to the gypsy band. Gradually, the doctor recognized the figures as Seward, Jonathon and the others. He would later learn that they had been following the gypsies—Dracula's disciples—since they offloaded the vampire's coffin from the ship. They hoped to intercept them before they reached the castle to prevent Dracula from being able to awake at sunset.

Outside the castle gates, the four crusaders caught up with the gypsies. In the short battle that followed, Quincey was mortally wounded, but they were successful in prying open the coffin's lid.

Just as the sun shed its final rays, Jonathon sheared through Dracula's throat with a great knife as, concurrently, Quincey plunged his knife into the Count's heart. Dracula's face, in the brief moment before it, along with his body, dissolved into dust, took on an expression of utter peace. Then, as Quincey faded into death, he gazed into Mina's eyes, her forehead now completely cleansed of Dracula's mark.

Commentary:

Bram Stoker's *Dracula* is a story that has meaning on several levels. On a superficial plane, the novel is a good, scary yarn about vampires and evil monsters. On another, it is a typical Christian allegory of good against evil. On still another, Stoker's views come across as perhaps ahead of their time. The author seems to be saying that men spend their entire lives seeking unrepressed sexuality from liberated females, but when it happens, they are afraid of it. They then seek to control it which results in its repression, which ultimately and inevitably ends in female oppression. *Dracula* is smooth, eerie reading. It also is great, if subtle, cannon fodder for the feminist movement.

MURDER ON THE ORIENT EXPRESS

(American title: *Murder in the Calais Coach*)
by Agatha Christie
(1891 - 1975)

Type of work: Murder mystery

Setting: Aboard the famous *Orient Express*, snowbound in Yugoslavia; the early 1930's

Principal characters:

Inspector Hercule Poirot, a brilliant Belgian sleuth

A convoluted string of household servants, train employees, and regional and foreign travelers, each coming into play as eager solvers of—and suspects in—the murder on the *Orient Express*

Commentary:

Dame Agatha Christie, author of over sixty popular books, is the most renowned of all detective/murder mystery novelists. For years, readers have enjoyed following her myriad clues until, always in the final pages, the guilty culprit was exposed. Christie's most famous and loveable personality was the Belgian detective Hercule Poirot, who starred in her stories from 1920 until her death in 1975.

Murder on the Orient Express is perhaps Christie's most popular murder mystery. Nearly all the action takes place on this celebrated and glamorous international express train. Any of the characters, it seems, could be guilty of the crime. Even Mother Nature, by sending a most inopportune snowstorm, makes her way into the story line.

In writing *Murder on the Orient Express*, Christie was influenced by two primary interests: One was her fascination with the *Orient Express*. "When I had travelled to France or Spain or Italy, the *Orient Express* had often been standing at Calais, and I had longed to climb up into it," she wrote in her autobiography. The second influence was the tragic Lindbergh baby kidnapping. In 1927 Charles Lindbergh made the first solo flight across the Atlantic; some five years later, his infant son was mysteriously kidnapped and killed. The first interest provided the setting for the story; the second, a startling twist to the plot.

Story Overview:

Inspector Hercule Poirot was returning from Syria to Europe on the *Orient Express*, little knowing that he would soon be using his deductive instincts to solve a murder on that very train. Poirot's fellow travelers were a colorful and international assortment of characters. There were princesses, a lady's maid, a Russian, several Americans, a Hungarian count and countess, Frenchmen, Englishmen, and for good measure, an Italian, a Swede, and a German. To make the journey even more interesting, nearly every ethnic group represented held the others in disdain. As the conductor noted, traveling is a most bizarre phenomenon—on a train, total strangers live together in intimacy for a few days or weeks, then part, perhaps never to meet again.

Poirot came to know a little bit about the other travelers on the train:

M. Ratchett — An American businessman who is more malevolent than benevolent.

Mary Debenham — An English governess whose

manner is as calm and unruffled as her coiffure.

Colonel Arbuthnot — His French is limited, but he displays an adroit verbal defense in an argument with Poirot.

Antonio Foscarelli — Information gushes out of this swarthy Italian like the blood from the victim.

Edward Henry Masterman — A spare, neat, haughty British valet.

Cyrus Hardman — An American traveling salesman who knows more than he tells and tells more than he knows.

Princess Dragomiroff — A frail, unbecoming Russian *grande dame* whose immense pearls are as improbable as what comes out of her mouth.

Greta Ohlsson — A Swedish-trained nurse with a sheep-like face.

Mrs. Hubbard — The stereotypical American matron: she never stops talking, but her actions definitely speak louder than her words. She is also the mother of a child kidnap/murder victim.

Hildegarde Schmidt — Princess Dragomiroff's cook and maid; Poirot senses she is deeply involved in something surreptitious.

Count Andrenyi — A Hungarian diplomat more attached to the Hungarian Embassy than it is to him.

Countess Andrenyi — The Count's slight yet powerful wife; the youngest, prettiest sojourner.

On the long journey, the train's passengers had sat side by side, calmly chatting in the dining room, with the exception of the boisterous American matron, Mrs. Hubbard, whose anecdotes bored everyone within hearing. Finally, weary of her discourse, the handsome Hungarian couple, Count and Countess Andrenyi, quickly fled the dining car; the others soon followed. Slow to take a hint, Mrs. Hubbard stalked after the crowd, leaving Inspector Poirot alone with the American businessman, Mr. Ratchett, and his efficient and multilingual secretary, Hector MacQueen.

Ratchett, a prime example of the "Ugly American," immediately cornered Poirot to complain of the many enemies he had garnered over the years—enemies fierce enough to kill him, he professed—and offered Poirot a sizeable sum of money if he would help protect him. Poirot was politely hesitant: "My client_le, Monsieur, is limited nowadays. I undertake very few cases." Ratchett, however, was not about to give in. "Why, naturally, I understand that," he retorted. "But this, Mr. Poirot, means big money . . . Big money."

At this, Poirot gazed at the man thoughtfully for some minutes, his face completely expressionless. An offer of $20,000 for a couple days' work did not interest him, however, if the work—or his client—was not to his liking. "You do not understand, Monsieur," he replied. "I have been very fortunate in my profession. I have made enough money to satisfy both my needs and my caprices. I take now only such cases as—interest me . . . I regret, Monsieur, that I cannot oblige you." But the

American still would not bend. "What's wrong with my proposition?" he asked, insulted. Poirot rose. "If you will forgive me for being personal—I do not like your face, M. Ratchett," he said, and left the restaurant car.

Poirot never regretted his decision. Sadly, Ratchett did not live long enough to regret anything.

At precisely twenty-three minutes to one in the morning, Poirot was roused by a cry. He peeked out of his compartment. Hearing only the normal banter of the conductor and M. Ratchett issuing from Ratchett's compartment, Poirot dozed off. Moments later, Mrs. Hubbard flew through the aisle insisting that a man was in her compartment; a search turned up nothing but a conductor's suit button.

After falling asleep once more, Poirot heard something heavy collapse with a thud against his door. Springing up, he saw nothing in the hall but a woman wrapped in a scarlet kimono. Poirot decided that he was just suffering from nerves, and he slept again until morning. Awakening, Poirot found that, during the night, the train had come to a standstill in Yugoslavia, its progress blocked by a drifting snowstorm.

Soon, Ratchett was found in his compartment, dead. At least a dozen knife wounds penetrated his body—some delivered with great force, others consisting of little more than scratches. All were delivered seemingly haphazardly and at random.

Detective Poirot's old friend, Mr. Bouc, director of the *Compagnie Internationale des Wagons Lits*, came to Poirot to beseech him to track down the killer. "Come, my friend," said M. Bouc. "You comprehend what I am about to ask of you. I know your powers. Take command of this investigation. No, no, do not refuse . . . By the time the Yugoslavian police arrive, how simple if we can present them with the solution! You solve the mystery! We say, `A murder has occurred—*this* is the criminal!'"

Poirot agreed to M. Bouc's request, and accepted the commission. To him, an unsolved crime was somewhat of a gift.

The "little grey cells of the mind" went quickly to work. The investigating physician, Dr. Constantine, reported that Ratchett died around 1 a.m.; yet the train had been bogged down in snow since 12:30, and there were no footprints in the fresh-fallen snow leading to or from the tracks. Clearly, the murderer was still on the train, which reduced the list of suspects to little more than a dozen perfectly respectable-looking individuals. It was a case tailor-made for Poirot's logical mind.

A tour of Ratchett's compartment turned up many clues, none of which escaped Poirot's notice. Several wounds on the corpse were deep, yet the edges did not gape and had not bled—suggesting that at least several blows were delivered to an already dead man. Also, some of the knife blows had undoubtedly been thrust by a right-handed person, while others had been delivered by someone using the left hand. Exasperated, Poirot cried, "The matter clears itself up wonderfully! The murderer was a man of great strength—he was feeble—it was a woman—it was a right-handed person—it was a left-handed person. Ah!"

As Poirot investigated further, he found several more clues. A sniff of an empty glass showed that the victim was drugged into sleep (the work of Ratchett's valet perhaps?); the burnt matches found on the floor, along with a pipe cleaner, were unlike those found in Ratchett's pocket (possibly dropped by the only pipe-smoker on board, Colonel Arbuthnot?); a lady's handkerchief embroidered with the initial H lay on the ground (so, the killer could be either Mrs. Hubbard or Hildegarde Schmidt, maid to the frail Princess Dragomiroff); the dented watch in Ratchett's pocket pointed precisely to 1:15. Indeed, thought Poirot, the profusion of clues seemed too convenient; they could very well be "red herrings" left by a clever killer.

The clue which interested Poirot the most was a charred fragment of paper, on which he was able to make out only a few words: "—member little Daisy Armstrong" Ah! Poirot remembered the case vividly. Little Daisy Armstrong had been kidnapped and killed years ago, by a man named Cassetti, and American. Clearly, Cassetti had been masquerading as Ratchett. In other words, Ratchett, the victim in this case, was a killer. But who then, out of a sense of justice or vengeance, murdered the killer?

As the hours passed, the train director became even more anxious to solve the case, and suggested the dirty deed be pinned on the only Italian on board: Antonio Foscarelli. " . . . Italians use the knife!" the director pointed out. Fortunately for Antonio, Poirot possessed no such prejudices. " . . . This is a crime very carefully planned and staged . . . " the Inspector conjectured. "It is not—how shall I express it—a *Latin* crime. It is a crime that traces of a cool, resourceful, deliberate brain—I think an Anglo-Saxon brain."

In the final analysis, Poirot's "little grey cells" again came through, and he solved the mystery . . .

"There are two possible solutions to the crime," Poirot told the assembled passengers. "I shall put them both before you . . . to judge which solution is the right one."

The first of Poirot's theories involved the *timing* of the crime. The victim's watch showed he was killed at 1:15. However, the train had crossed a dateline in its journey, and if Ratchett had omitted adjusting his watch back an hour as he should have done, he could have actually been stabbed at *12:15*. This would mean the murderer could have abandoned the train to flee into the wilderness *prior* to the storm's arrival.

As for his second theory, Poirot postulated that many, if not all, of the suspects on the train had struck a blow to M. Ratchett. With the *multitude of clues*—the different types of wounds and the great number of objects found at the scene—it was entirely possible that *all* the train occupants were guilty—and equally possible that they were *not* guilty. Even if a single assailant—either the aforementioned killer or one of the travelers—struck the *first* blow, Poirot concluded, there was no way of knowing who struck the *fatal* blow.

Poirot then asked M. Bouc and Dr. Constantine to judge which of the explanations was the correct one. Both agreed. "The first theory you put forward was the correct one . . . " M. Bouc answered. "I suggest that that is the solution we offer to the Yugoslavian police when they arrive."

"Then," said Poirot, "having placed my solution before you, I have the honour to retire from the case . . . "

THE SHORT STORIES OF RAY BRADBURY

(Taken from *The Stories of Ray Bradbury*, Random House, New York, N.Y., 1965)

Ray Bradbury (1920 -   ) is well-known for his eerie, macabre novels (*Something Wicked This Way Comes*) as well as for his science fiction thrillers (*Fahrenheit 451*). Bradbury, however, is also a skillful story teller, as these three examples illustrate.

The Rocket Man

Neither Doug nor his mother could sleep. Doug's father would soon arrive for his quarterly visit, and earlier that evening Doug's mother had asked him to convince his father to stay home this time. Doug had answered he would try. "But," he cautioned his mother, "it won't do any good."

Later that night, as they lay awake in their beds, they could feel the air grow hot and see the walls brighten for an instant— and they knew *his* rocket had passed over their house. Since, however, it was clear neither one would sleep, they got up and ran through their checklist again.

The next day Doug's father arrived. It was the typical four-day visit, and, as always, Doug and his father discussed everything except his being a Rocket Man. Doug's mother, though, seemed hardly to notice his father. For his part, the Rocket Man did the best he could to feel at home on earth; he even avoided looking at the sky. After a couple of days, however, he could no longer resist the temptation, and he began to gaze longingly at the stars. They would lose him again, Doug's mother knew, just as they had before.

On the last day of his visit, the Rocket Man turned to Doug, said, "Don't ever be a Rocket Man." Doug was surprised. "I mean it," his father continued, "because when you're out there you want to be here and when you're here you want to be out there." Always the sky was there to remind him. Doug replied that he had often thought of being a Rocket Man. His father, however, who seemed not to have heard him, continued, "I *try* to stay here . . . Promise me you won't be like me," he begged. "Okay," Doug finally agreed.

The next evening, Doug asked his mother why she treated his father so coldly in one moment and, in the next, spoiled him. "When he went off into space ten years ago," she began, "I said to myself, 'He's dead. Or as good as dead. So think of him dead. And when he comes back, three or four times a year, it's not him at all, it's only a pleasant little memory." But at other times, she admitted, she could not help herself; she could not deny her deeper feelings. "What if he died on Jupiter or Saturn or Neptune? On those nights when those planets were high in the sky, we wouldn't want to have anything to do with the stars."

The next day Doug and his mother received news that the Rocket Man's ship had fallen into the sun. Huge and merciless, the sun now seemed like something that Doug and his mother could not escape. For a long time afterwards, Doug's mother would sleep through the day. They would eat breakfast at midnight, lunch at three, and dinner at six in the morning. The only time they ever went out was "when it was raining and there was no sun."

The Veldt

Lydia Hadley had anxiously asked her husband George to take a "look at the nursery." Something had unsettled her, and as they opened the door and walked into the room, a three-dimensional African veldt, or "electronic babysitter," appeared before them. George, although he thought the experience a little too realistic, could find nothing wrong with it—not until the veldt's odorophonics blew the scent of lions, dust, and fresh blood across the landscape and, in the distance, he could see lions feeding on something. "Did you hear that scream?" Lydia asked uneasily.

Although the Hadleys had nothing to fear, when the lions suddenly charged them they nonetheless ran quickly out of the room. "It's too real," Lydia protested. When the door suddenly shook, as if something had banged against it from the other side, George agreed to lock the nursery for a few days.

That night, however, their children, Wendy and Peter, managed to break into the nursery. George and Lydia lay in bed and listened to vaguely human screams — and to the roar of lions. "They sound familiar," Lydia said uneasily, referring to the screams. That night, with the smell of cats in the air, George and Lydia tossed and turned in their bed.

A few weeks later, the psychologist David McClean, after a brief visit to the nursery, advised George and Lydia "to have the whole damn room torn down and your children brought to me every day during the next year for treatment." The veldt, he informed them, was making their children hostile.

When the children heard that George intended to shut the nursery down, Peter wailed at the ceiling, "Don't let Father kill everything." Then, turning to his father, he shouted, "I wish you were dead!" The tantrums continued, and Lydia finally prevailed upon George to switch the nursery back on—just for awhile, just to pacify the children while they packed for a trip to Iowa.

Before they were finished packing, however, George and Lydia heard the children cry out to them, "Daddy, Mommy, come quick—!" They ran down the hall and into the nursery. The veldt was empty, except for the lions, and Peter and Wendy were nowhere in sight. "Peter? Wendy?" George called out. The door slammed, and clutching at the door handle, George could not open it. "Why they've locked it from outside!" George said. They heard Peter's voice outside. "Don't let them switch off the nursery and the house," he was saying. Then they heard the lions, and as they turned, they saw the beasts edging slowly toward them, crouched, their tails stiff. George and Lydia screamed, and as they did, they suddenly "realized why those other screams had sounded familiar."

The Best of All Possible Worlds

Two neighbors, an older and a younger man, were watching another man follow an attractive woman off the train. "Idiot!" said the older man. "I followed her off the train once myself," said the younger man. The older man snorted, "I, too, five years ago." For a time, the two complained about relationships between men and women. Then the older man said, "I have known only one man who came close to having the very best of all possible worlds." Seeing his younger friend's obvious interest in hearing his account, the older man obliged.

About a year ago at a party in New York, he began, he had met a recently married fellow named Smith. Smith's wife was so gorgeous and intelligent that the older man had to exercise considerable restraint to keep his hands off her. A few weeks later, Smith invited the older man to spend the weekend in the country, where he was introduced to Mrs. Smith. This Mrs. Smith, however, was a dark and tawny woman, while the Mrs. Smith he had seen in the city was blonde and pale. "He'd married again, eh?" asked the younger man. "Hardly," the older man replied. Smith was simply married to two different women.

A few weeks later in New York, he saw Smith again and, congratulated him on his new wife. Then he learned that the two wives were actually the same woman! Apparently, Smith, who had a penchant for other women, had married an actress. When she saw that her husband became bored with her, she would change herself into a different woman, so altering her appearance, speech and mannerisms that Smith was able both to "stray" and to remain faithful at the same time.

When the tale ended, the young man swallowed and remarked, "Your friend Smith solved his problem, all right."

"I have a friend, too," the younger then said. "His situation was similar, but—different. Shall I call him Quillian?" The older man consented to hear the story, but added, "Yes, but hurry. I get off soon."

One night, the younger man related, he had seen Quillian sitting at a bar with a beautiful redhead. A week later, he had run into Quillian again, only this time with a dumpy-looking woman who seemed content merely to walk along and hold Quillian's hand. "Ha," the younger man said, "here's his poor little parsnip wife who loves the earth he treads, while other nights he's out winding up that incredible robot redhead."

A month later, he had bumped into Quillian again. "Oh God," Quillian had pleaded, "don't tell on me! My wife must never know!" Just then, someone called Quillian's name. Looking up, the younger man said, he saw the dumpy-looking woman. Clearly, the beautiful redhead was Quillian's wife, and the dumpy one was his mistress. "He too," the young man concluded, "had, if you think about it, the best of all possible worlds."

The train rumbled to a stop and the men got off at the station. Shaking hands, each man looked toward the other's car. A beautiful woman sat in each. "I wonder," thought the older man, "if that woman there is . . . "

"I wonder," thought the younger man, "if that lady in his car could be . . . " The neighbors got into their cars and drove off into the December snow.

Commentary:

Bradbury's short stories often explore unexpected narrative corners of science fiction. In "The Rocket Man," for instance, he addresses a frequently overlooked element of space drama: the lives and concerns of the families astronauts leave behind. By contrast, Bradbury seems to fall back on cliches in "The Veldt" to narrate a tale of technology gone wrong. Symbolically, at least, the story seems to question the wisdom of entrusting the care of our children to technological progress. Readers may even find in the nursery-veldt a rather sinister parallel to the pernicious effects of television today.

"The Best of All Possible Worlds" is a very un-Bradburyesque story, lacking all the elements of the macabre or science-fiction. Instead, Bradbury explores an age-old myth: that the grass is always greener on the other side. We meet two men, each with "friends" who have achieved ideal relationships with women. At the end, we are left to wonder if the stories these two men tell are actually about themselves. In any event, we must conclude that Quillian and Smith seem, in their way of thinking, at least, to have found "the best of all possible worlds."

THE WAR OF THE WORLDS

by
H. G. Wells
(1866 - 1949)

Type of work: Early science fiction

Setting: England; late 1800's to early 1900's

Principal characters:
The narrator, a philosopher and writer
Dr. Ogilvy, an astrologist and scientist
An artilleryman
A clergyman
Multiple Martian invaders

Story Overview:

"No one would have believed that his world was being watched keenly and closely by intelligences greater than man's and yet as mortal as his own. Early in the twentieth century came the great disillusionment."

In 1894, the first of many strange sightings on the planet Mars took place. As an observer, I could make out tiny pinpoints of light leaving its surface, as though "flaming gases rushed out of a gun."

I watched the bursts of light from Dr. Ogilvy's observatory. The astrologist speculated that these were merely gaseous disturbances. "The chances of anything man-like on Mars are a million to one," he said. But the flames were sighted ten nights in a row. Fair England could not suspect that the bursts of light signaled the launching of an invasion—an attack that would prepare the way for Mars' colonization of the warm, green planet Earth.

"Then came the night of the falling star." The meteor left a green streak in the sky, and, in the morning, Ogilvy excitedly went to investigate. The strange object had fallen near some the sand pits adjoining his suburban neighborhood, the force of the impact creating a massive crater. A scaly, crusted cylinder about thirty yards in diameter had struck the earth. "The Thing itself lay almost entirely buried in sand," still hot from its entry through the atmosphere. Ogilvy could hear perplexing hammering noises coming from inside.

Just then the top portion of the cylinder began to flake off and turn slowly as if unscrewed from within. "Good heavens!" Ogilvy cried out. "There's a man in it! Half roasted to death! Trying to escape!" At that moment he connected the sightings on Mars with the Thing that lay before him now, and ran off toward Woking, a nearby village. Everyone he tried to warn thought him quite insane. He finally captured the attention of a journalist and the two of them returned to the cylinder.

By eight o'clock a large and curious crowd had gathered—including myself. The top of the cylinder had ceased to rotate, and many speculated that the rotation was automatic. Suddenly the top began to rotate again. When the object's end fell off, "a big grayish bulk the size of a bear" rose slowly out of the cylinder. The creature appeared a glistening leather lump, with two enormous dark eyes and a toothless mouth with a pointed upper lip bordered by ugly-looking tentacles. All at once "the monster toppled over the brim of the cylinder and [fell] into the pit," apparently weighed down by Earth's greater gravitational pull. This creature was followed by others, who immediately set about digging a moat around their craft.

The panic-stricken crowd fled. I confess, I too was "a battleground of fear and curiosity," torn between the desire to return and the desire to flee. I circled the pit, which by now was a tangle of tentacles. Then I saw a rod that held a revolving disk emerge from the Martian and rise to the level of the ground. The jostling crowd presently returned to gawk at the strange sight, followed by a small bunch of soldiers who approached the pit waving a white flag. Suddenly, the monster emitted a flash of light, accompanied by three puffs of greenish smoke and a faint hissing sound; and, to my horror, each soldier had instantly become a pillar of fire. The Martian at once unleashed its deadly heat ray on the crowd, then turned it on the town, indiscriminately burning houses and trees. Ogilvy and about forty others were killed. The war of the worlds had begun.

Terror-filled survivors streamed out of Woking and past surrounding villages whose inhabitants were not yet aware of the deadly visitors. Before long, army soldiers and artillery surrounded the area. All the while, the aliens were busy building a structure inside the pit. Then, just after midnight, a second cylinder hit the ground to the northwest of town.

When evening fell the next day, the Martian machine—which now resembled a tall, glittering metal milking stool, opened fire, leveling a college adjacent to my house. Cable-like tentacles hung from the lower part of the machine's hood. Inside the hood at the top a Martian controlled the destructive machine. The alien hooted "Aloo" as it advanced, wreaking death in its path. It grasped people with the cables and crushed them against trees and walls.

Soon, there were three such death machines in the vicinity, each guided by a tentacled Martian warrior-pilot perched high on the tripod of his metallic beast. I managed to gather a few precious possessions, then rented a carriage and traveled with my wife in haste to Leatherhead, a village twelve miles away. But consumed with curiosity concerning the Martians' destructive mission, I left my wife in care of a cousin and returned to Woking. By now the entire town and its neighboring communities had been attacked.

I set out at dawn the next morning. The countryside was alive with alien machines striding through dense clouds of deadly green smoke. I cautiously made my way back to my house, which I found as yet unburned, though all around were the flaming remains of what had once been a peaceful town. Stunned at the sight of the many charred and crushed bodies littering the yard outside, I happened upon an artilleryman—one of the few who had survived the first attack. He shared with me his philosophy of survival: the strong would go into hiding in London's sewers, he surmised, from where they would mount a resistance by stealing alien machines and fighting back; in this new world order, survival of the fittest would be the password. In the middle of his account, an alien tripod, sending houses up in flame as it went, advanced toward us. We, along with several other neighbors, fled.

Instantly, I yearned to retrieve my wife and leave the country. I felt the invaders would destroy all of England.

A group of us headed across a bridge spanning the Thames River. All at once, five machines appeared on the horizon, approaching at about thirty miles an hour. A hidden gun battery opened fire on the advancing machines. "Get under water," I remember crying as we dived into the water. At the same time, a machine was struck by the artillery shells. It fell into the water along with us, its damaged heat ray firing wildly in all directions, then striking the water. Instantly, the river heated to a boil. Badly scalded, I nevertheless struggled to shore and watched the remaining Martians carry off their fallen companion.

Seeing my path to Leatherhead blocked, I headed towards my brother's home in London, taking shelter in houses along the way, and next fell in with a curate who suggested the attack was a punishment from God. "All the work," he raved, "all the Sunday Schools—What [have we] done?" I finally calmed the hysterical priest sufficiently to convince him to follow me to London.

Meanwhile, news of the attack flashed over radios nationwide. "The Martians are able to discharge enormous clouds of a black and poisonous vapor by means of rockets," the authorities solemnly announced. "They have smothered our batteries and are advancing slowly towards London, destroying everything in their path." Bedlam erupted as six million frantic civilians savagely fought their way out of London. My brother got caught up in the human flood that struggled to escape their doomed city. Fights erupted everywhere; the byways were ungovernable as men and women turned wild with frenzy.

From launchers that now swung from their cable-like tentacles, the aliens fired gas-filled canisters that did not explode but emitted huge volumes of a heavy, dark, poisonous smoke that coiled upwards, then sank and spread itself over the countryside.

My brother, meanwhile, along with a host of other civilians, made his way to the coast to be picked up by a battleship. Three Martian machines waded into the water to intercept them—only to be met by the ironclad *Thunder Child*. The Martians retreated a few paces when the ship entered the fray, then turned their heat rays on it. Severely crippled, the ship opened fire, felling one Martian. Then it turned its guns on another, which fired back. This time the *Thunder Child* exploded in a fireball, taking with its Martian attacker.

All the while my curate friend and I were trapped in a deserted cellar. A cylinder had fallen nearby, throwing earth up around the cellar doors. From our imprisoned vantage point, we were able to observe the Martians close up. Lacking both stomach and legs, our outer space invaders appeared all head. "They did not eat. Instead they took fresh living blood and injected it into their veins," blood extracted from captured men they scooped up in their machines.

Alone and in constant danger, we survived by eating food hidden in a pantry. But as time passed, it became apparent that the priest was going insane. "I have been still too long," he raved one day. "Woe unto the inhabitants of the earth!" I pled for him to remain still, but he ignored me and set off towards the aliens. Grabbing a meat cleaver, I struck him with the flat of the blade, killing him in the process. The aliens detected the noise, and I was forced to hide in a coal bin as tentacles explored the cellar and removed the curate's still-warm corpse.

When I emerged from my hiding place several days later, the aliens were gone; all was still. Arriving in London, I found the poison blanketing the ground in powdery black sheets. The vast city was deserted, except for dogs and a drunken man, lying in the gutter. I encountered the wreckage of a Martian machine that looked as if it had veered out of control and hit a building; another machine, its hood open, stood motionless on the outskirts of the abandoned city. "A multitude of black birds was circling and clustering around the hood. Out of the hood hung lank shreds of brown at which the hungry birds tore."

I made my way to one of the Martian earthenwork laboratories. Peering cautiously into the darkness, I saw their ugly bodies stretched out in a row. "They were dead, slain by the putrefactive and disease bacteria against which their systems were unprepared. Slain by the humblest thing that God in His wisdom had put upon this earth."

Relieved, I returned to my home, knowing that London would be rebuilt . . . the world was now safe. Striding from room to room, I heard my wife's voice, and joyfully ran to her side.

Commentary:

This science fiction classic still ranks among the genre's historical best. Though the modern reader will find *War of the Worlds* to be rather unsophisticated and tame when compared with today's more technical movie/novel portrayals, the novel became so popular in its day that Orson Wells aired it on the radio. Due to Wells' convincing narrative style, the story stirred up a panic, even though Wells continually assured his audience that this was purely a work of fiction.

THE INVISIBLE MAN

by
H. G. Wells
(1866-1946)

Type of work: Science fiction

Setting: England; late nineteenth century

Principal characters:
The Stranger, (Griffin) the invisible man
Mrs. Hall, landlady of the Coach and Horses Inn
Mr. Marvel, a tramp forced into a partnership with Griffin
Dr. Kemp, Griffin's last confidant
Colonel Adye, head of the police in Port Burdock

Story Overview:

It was early in February when the stranger came to the village of Iping and entered the Coach and Horses Inn. Brushing the snow from his coat, he demanded a fire and a room. Mrs. Hall, the proprietress, offered to take his coat, hat and muffler into the kitchen to dry, but he refused; instead, to Mrs. Hall's dismay, he stood there, dripping all over her rug. After she had served him lunch, the stranger curtly dismissed Mrs. Hall without introducing himself. But even under all his heavy trappings, she had still managed to discern that his entire face was swathed with bandages.

That afternoon, Teddy Henfrey dropped by to fix the clock in the parlor. Noticing the bundled figure seated nearby, Henfrey took his time with the job—he hoped to find out more about this peculiar fellow. When he tried to speak with the stranger, however, he was told to stop delaying, finish his job, and get out.

Baggage, along with some chemical equipment, arrived from Bramblehurst railway station the next day. As Mr. Hall and the driver carried in the luggage, the stranger came out to check their progress. Suddenly, the driver's dog viciously attacked him, ripping holes in his glove and trousers. The stranger fled to his room. Mr. Hall followed to see if he was all right, but was met with a rebuff.

Later, Mr. Hall reported to his wife that when he glanced at the hole in the trousers, all he had seen inside was blackness. The Halls concluded that the stranger must be a half-breed, whose skin, like that of a horse or a cow, had come out in splotches of color, and that out of embarrassment, he tried to hide it. This rumor quickly circulated in Iping, along with other theories: perhaps the stranger was a criminal hiding from the law, or maybe just a harmless lunatic. The reclusive visitor did nothing to contradict any of these conjectures.

That spring, Mr. Cuss, the town's physician, heard of the stranger's bandaged face and of the hundreds of bottles that he reportedly kept at the Coach and Horses. His professional curiosity aroused, the doctor found an excuse to barge in as the stranger worked over some documents in Mrs. Hall's parlor. As he entered, the bandaged figure quickly slid his hands into his pockets. Mr. Cuss began to question him about his activities, but just

then a draft blew one of the papers into the lighted fireplace, and, without thinking, the stranger sprang to retrieve it. To the doctor's amazement, the stranger's coat sleeve stayed stiff, though nothing appeared to fill it. Then, with an invisible hand, the stranger turned and pinched the doctor's nose—and invited him to leave. Mr. Cuss immediately staggered out of the inn and started home.

Early one morning the vicar and his wife were awakened by odd sounds coming from the room below. Hearing the chink of money, they rushed down the stairs to stop the thief. To their astonishment, however, the room was completely empty—and their money had disappeared.

That same morning, back at the Coach and Horses, the Halls noticed the stranger's door ajar. The room was apparently empty, but his clothes lay piled on the bed. Suddenly the clothes and other objects in the room flew toward them, seemingly of their own accord. They fled the room, just as the door slammed and locked behind them. The Halls pronounced their experience a sure sign of witchcraft.

When the stranger rang for breakfast the next morning, Mrs. Hall refused to answer. Word of the robbery at the vicarage had spread throughout the village, and the Halls felt certain that their visitor had been the culprit. At midday, Mrs. Hall confronted their still bandaged guest, demanding to know the meaning behind the eerie events in his room. In angry response, he jerked off his hat, glasses, false nose, and the bandages covering his face—and there was nothing there, nothing at all to be seen but the empty air!

At once, everyone in the Coach and Horses fled in terror out the door. Taking advantage of the situation, the stranger scooped up some cheese and bread from the kitchen and returned to his room. And when the sheriff, accompanied by a small mob, arrived soon afterward to make an arrest for the vicarage robbery, the invisible lodger merely stripped off his clothes and left the inn, unseen.

Outside town, the Invisible Man ran into a tramp, Mr. Marvel, whom he coerced into becoming his accomplice. Accompanying his invisible master back into town, Marvel made his way to the Coach and Horses and opened the parlor door so that it would not seem to be opening by itself. Inside, the Invisible Man found his room occupied by the vicar he had robbed that morning—and by Mister Cuss. Forcing their faces down onto the table, he warned them to do exactly as he said or he would kill them. A few minutes later, with the men's clothes and his own three diaries wrapped in a table cloth, the Invisible Man leaped from the window. He handed his bundle to Mr. Marvel, who darted away up the lane.

The streets filled with people intent on catching Mr. Marvel, but the Invisible Man routed the pursuers and rampaged his way through town, breaking windows and cutting the main telegraph line. Even with the wires down, however, news of the Invisible Man and his destructive swath soon stretched over the countryside.

Meanwhile, the desperate Mr. Marvel tried to give his master the slip, but the Invisible Man caught him and warned that if he ever tried to escape again, he would be killed. The pair then proceeded to Port Stowe, where the Invisible Man stole what money he could and deposited it in Mr. Marvel's pockets.

But in the next town, Port Burdock, Mr. Marvel made another escape. Fleeing into a pub called the Jolly Cricketers, he barred the door behind him, and begged for help. But suddenly, the Invisible Man, who had slipped in through a back door, rushed across the room to attack Marvel. The men in the pub came running to Marvel's aid, however, and one managed to shoot the Invisible Man in the arm.

Weakened by his wound, the Invisible Man gave up his pursuit and sought refuge for the night in a nearby house. By chance, the dwelling he chose belonged to a Doctor Kemp; by and by the doctor noticed a trail of dried blood leading from the door to his bedroom. At the end of the trail, Kemp found himself confronting the newly bandaged arm of the Invisible Man. Then, to his further amazement he heard himself hailed by name. Recognizing Kemp as an old schoolfellow from years back, the fugitive introduced himself as "Griffin" and tried to help Kemp recall his visible appearance as a six-foot-tall albino with a pink and white face and red eyes. He had won the school medal for chemistry, he reminded Kemp.

Kemp provided his old schoolmate with a nightshirt and food, and offered to let him stay in his room while he slept downstairs. Only after he found himself alone once again, evicted from his own bed by a man he could not see, was the doctor struck by the strangeness of the situation. "Am I dreaming? Has the world gone mad—or have I?" he laughingly asked himself, testing the locked door. "Barred out of my own bedroom, by a flagrant absurdity!"

That night the doctor worriedly paced the floor. After reading the newspaper accounts of Griffin's crime sprees, he had concluded that the man sheltered under his roof was rapidly turning into a crazed killer. Finally, Kemp decided to send for Colonel Adye, the trusted chief of the Port Burdock police force. The next morning, when Kemp awoke, Kemp set out to detain him until Colonel Adye could come to make the arrest. He encouraged his guest to explain how he had become invisible. Griffin obliged.

In his early twenties, Griffin had abandoned the study of medicine and gone into physics. The properties of light particularly fascinated him. He soon came to realize that the secret to rendering an object invisible lay in lowering its refractive index to that of air. Griffin knew that the one intractable barrier to total invisibility in a normal human body was the pigments; but it dawned on him that as an albino, lacking pigment, he himself was an ideal subject for an experiment.

A lack of money was the only thing that stood in the way of Griffin realizing his dream of proving invisibility's power. Craving this power, he stole the necessary funds from his father.

Within a few months, however, the old man, disgraced and ruined by debt, had shot himself; but Griffin by then was far too absorbed in his experiments to waste many regrets on the death.

The first subject of Griffin's final experiment was a white cat. Unfortunately, during the procedure, the cat yowled and protested until the landlord became convinced that his tenant was vivisecting the animal. By the time his landlord arrived to evict him, however, Griffin had already turned the process on himself—and, as a parting shot, had set the apartment ablaze.

Soon Griffin realized that when rain, snow or fog settled on his body, it made his outline discernable. Even the London air covered him with dirt and delineated his figure. So, after pilfering some clothing and a mask from a local theatrical costume shop, he had moved to the country, settling in Iping, where the newspaper accounts began.

Kemp had successfully kept Griffin talking about his past until Colonel Adye arrived with the police. But when Griffin heard the men advancing up the stairs, he ducked past them. Out of frustration, anger, and his desperation to elude entrapment, the escaping fugitive wound up breaking a child's ankle and killing a man.

The next day, Kemp received a note from Griffin proclaiming himself the ruler of Port Burdock and giving himself the titles "Death" and "Terror." The note ended with a vow that Griffin would kill Kemp that same day. Although the police immediately put a guard on the house, Griffin was still able to slip past and enter. Minutes later, Kemp burst through the door screaming that he was being chased by the Invisible Man. As Griffin finally caught up to the doctor and dragged him to the ground, the curious mob who had taken up a vigil at the residence joined in the fray, piled on top of the assailant, and, despite his invisibility, beat him to death. And as Kemp stood and looked down on the body of his erstwhile friend, it slowly regained its natural dimensions and visibly pale hues.

Commentary:

In his book *The Invisible Man,* H.G. Wells created a story that has more meaning to denizens of the late twentieth century than to his audience of the nineteenth. His plot revolves around a genius who uses his knowledge and skills to establish an advantage over others. In the process, however, Griffin only succeeds in pitting himself against the moral necessities of a civilized culture. Luckily, he is prevented from ushering in the reign of terror that he envisions.

What were Griffin's incipient motives for wanting to become invisible? Did the guilt ensuing from his complicity in his father's death push Griffin over the edge into a full-scale life of crime? Are there tenable comparisons between the ethical implications of Griffin's experience and that of some scientific laboratory experiments being conducted today? These questions—and others that can be extracted from Wells' classic novel and the films that followed—are at the root of the work of the enduring appeal of this work. *The Invisible Man* will undoubtedly reach through the twenty-first century as an object of compelling and continual interest.

THE CAVES OF STEEL

by Isaac Asimov, Ballantine Books, New York, N.Y., 1953

Type of work: Science fiction/murder mystery

Setting: New York City of the future

Principal characters:

Elijah "Lije" Baley, a New York police detective

Jezebel "Jesse" Baley, his wife

Bentley Baley, their son

R. Daneel Olivaw, a robot detective

Julius Enderby, Police Commissioner of New York

Story Overview:

New York had become one of 800 gigantic cities, each a self-contained self-sufficient steel "cave" supplying the wants and needs of twenty million people. Before retreating to their caves of steel, however, the citizens of Earth had colonized thirty worlds in space. "Spacers" were the representatives of the colonists, who had returned to earth to open up the isolated planet to space.

The Spacer community had brought with them robots to take care of their every need. After a short war between Earth natives and the Spacer citizenry, robots, under Spacer direction, began to be introduced to the Earth culture, displacing many workers and resulting in numerous anti-robot riots.

One day, New York detective Lije Baley was called into the office of Police Commissioner Julius Enderby, who informed the detective that he had been assigned to work with a Spacer to solve a murder in Spacetown, a Spacer enclave on the edge of New York. Promised a promotion and the additional living space and privacy that went along with it, Detective Baley agreed to the assignment. The catch was that his Spacer partner would be a robot. This angered Baley. Working with a machine was a demeaning proposition; furthermore, if the robot turned out to be a better detective than Baley, he knew he could lose his job.

In Spacetown, Baley discovered that his new partner, R (for "Robot") Daneel Olivaw was an advanced model, designed to look completely human. Ironically, Daneel had been made in the exact image of his creator, Dr. Sarton, the robotics engineer whose mysterious murder the robot was now helping Baley investigate. Baley also learned something else: experts concluded after analyzing the brain waves of all the Spacers in the enclave that none of them was capable of murder. The Spacers believed that the crime had been committed by an Earthman—and Spacer security checks at the gate to Spacetown showed that the only Earthman who had entered the area during the crucial period was Baley's boss, Commissioner Enderby.

Enderby had been scheduled for an appointment with Sarton just before he was killed. Enderby's brain wave analysis, however, showed that, like the Spacers in the enclave, he was incapable of murder. (In fact, Enderby had been so upset upon hearing of Sarton's death that he had dropped and broken his old-fashioned

spectacles.) Clearly, the Spacers had concluded, another Earthman must have somehow entered Spacetown and committed the murder. However, this reasoning left Baley unconvinced.

While returning to Baley's small apartment, the two policemen stopped to quell an anti-robot riot. Daneel threatened the rioters with a blaster, and they dispersed. But Daneel's actions troubled Baley; he knew that robotic systems were governed by programmed laws—and the first law prohibited the harming of humans.

Later that week, Baley's wife, Jesse, related to her husband the spreading rumors that a robot had entered the city and was staying in the apartment of a policemen. She was frightened, she admitted. She did not want to become embroiled in an anti-robot riot.

The next day Baley met with Daneel and Dr. Fastolfe, the Spacer liaison; Enderby also participated in the meeting by video. Baley stated flatly that he had solved the case. No actual murder had taken place, he said. The creator had simply destroyed his robot, he theorized; Dr. Sarton was now masquerading as Daneel. Baley concluded that Sarton must have been involved in an elaborate scheme to provide the Spacers with an excuse to invade Earth and take control, and offered the reasoning for his theory. First, the "robot" looked too real; secondly, he had pulled a gun on humans—a highly uncharacteristic act; and, lastly, the robot frequented men's rooms. Fastolfe intervened abruptly at these assertions and pointed out that in breaking up the riot, the robot's gun was not fired, and that rest-room visits were made only to allow Daneel time to phone his supervisor. What's more, examinations had ascertained that Daneel was in fact a robot.

Baley was eventually convinced by Fastolfe's confident assurances—but still not entirely. Though he feared the Spacers might have been upset by his accusations, they were not. Instead, they insisted that Enderby keep such an original thinker on the case. After the meeting, Dr. Fastolfe explained to Baley that some of the Spacers were concerned about the future of mankind. They saw City culture as a bomb about to explode, because population growth demanded more resources than were available. On the other hand, Spacer culture had become too stable and frozen for growth and development to occur. The enlightened Spacers wanted to force the City dwellers to leave their hives and move out into space once more to revitalize the colonies. Baley contemplated these ideas; but he was still more interested in solving the murder case.

Meanwhile, Daneel now focused his attention on the group of Earthmen who had caused the earlier riot, postulating that Sarton's murderer would be found among them. Apparently, many of the members of the group were Medievalists—political archconservatives who yearned to return to the no-robot "good old days."

Later, while Baley ate—and Daneel sat—at a community kitchen, the robot pointed out that they were being watched. As they left, they saw that they were being followed, but Baley managed to lose the pursuers during a chase over the moving sidewalks. Daneel identified two of the men as participants in the riot. Fearing that they were in danger, Baley and Daneel soon took an apartment away from Lige's family. A short while later, Baley's adolescent son, Bentley, showed up at the apartment—at his mother's request—to check on his father's safety. Bentley had obtained the new address from his father's office.

At the office the next day, Baley, along with Dr. Gerrigel, a robotics specialist, confronted Daneel. Still suspicious about Daneel's actions at the riot, Baley had asked the expert to verify that no one had tampered with the robot's "First Law." Dr. Gerrigel's tests confirmed that all of the robot's mechanisms were intact. Daneel pointed out that his gun was fake anyway. With his final doubts answered, Baley was forced to consider the idea that an Earthman had indeed committed the murder.

Now it was Daneel's turn to confide that he believed Baley's own wife was involved in the anti-robot conspiracy. How was it, he argued, that Jesse had known he was a robot? Daneel also pointed out that she had sent their son into a supposedly dangerous situation. She would never have done this—unless she knew when and where the riots were going to take place.

Then, as Baley launched into a loyal defense of his wife, Jesse herself arrived at the office and tearfully confessed her involvement with the Medievalists. One day after she and Baley had had an argument, she had looked up an old acquaintance and joined the group in an attempt to "stop the robot invasion." She had done some spying for them, but nothing more serious. Now, disturbed and disillusioned by the Medievalists' tactics, she feared for her husband's life.

Jesse was able to identify one of the Medievalist conspirators, Francis Clousarr. After the detectives arrested Clousarr, Baley questioned him about his motives. Clousarr, it turned out, felt threatened by robots; he not only despised their patronizing manner, but also begrudged their superior abilities. Baley defended humanity: "We can't ever build a robot that will be . . . a human being . . . . We can't create a robot with a sense of beauty or a sense of ethics or a sense of religion. We can't . . . as long as we don't understand what makes our own brains tick. We're forever teetering on the brink of the unknowable."

Daneel then called the office and discovered that the robot office boy, R. Sammy, had been deliberately deactivated—"killed," as Daneel referred to it. Enderby ushered Baley into another office, where he was closely questioned. Suddenly it dawned on Baley that *he* was being framed for the destruction of the office robot. He appealed to Daneel to help him, but Daneel then disclosed that he was being taken off the case. His assignment to Baley had concealed a special agenda, revealed the robot: To prove the compatibility between humans and robots. This he had accomplished. The urgent concern of the Spacers, as Baley knew, was to go back into space and recolonize. This time, the humans would recolo-nize space in partnership with robots. This had been their secret agenda in assigning Daneel to work with Baley.

Before Daneel returned to Spacetown, Lige asked him for one last favor: the use of his logical mind for a few hours. After this final consultation, Baley and Daneel confronted Enderby with a stark accusation: He was the only person "who could have deactivated R. Sammy. Enderby retaliated with another attempt to blame Baley. At this, Baley drew his blaster and repeated the accusation, affirming that the Medievalists could not have known that the robot had come to earth with someone knowing it. And the Commissioner was one of the very few who knew of Daneel's presence in the City. Baley also charged that Enderby had informed the Medievalists when they had moved to the apartment, using Jesse as a tool. And the only plausible motive for the destruction of the office robot was to cover up the Commissioner's own involvement in the murder of Dr. Sarton. Enderby had given the office robot a blaster to carry across the open space while they were being admitted into Spacetown. Once Enderby and R. Sammy had been admitted to the Spacer enclave, Enderby had taken the gun from the robot and killed Sarton with it.

Daneel reminded Baley that brain-wave analysis had already shown Enderby was not capable of murder. But Baley was not swayed. From enlarged pictures of the murder site, he pointed out pieces of Enderby's broken spectacles caught in the door track of the murder scene—a place Enderby said he had never been. Then he charged his boss with entering Spacetown as an agent of the Medievalists to destroy the Spacers' new state-of-the-art robot, Daneel. Nervous, he had dropped and broken his glasses. Without the spectacles he had mistaken Dr. Sarton himself for the robot double that the eminent Spacer had designed. And thus Sarton had been murdered by Enderby in R. Daneel's stead.

At this point, Commissioner Enderby broke down and confessed. When the Spacers heard the story, they assured him they would not prosecute; since Enderby had assumed he was shooting a robot, the murder had been accidental. In return for this leniency, however, the Spacers demanded Enderby's cooperation in putting men in space again. Enderby heartily agreed.

Commentary:

Caves of Steel is both a classic science fiction and a classic detective story. Asimov (1920 - 1992), who published many books in both areas, successfully blends both genres in this novel.

As a science fiction novel, *Caves* extends some current trends out into the future and asks, "What if?" Asimov's extensions and conclusions are both reasonable and insightful. On the other hand, Asimov was aware that in most science-fiction mysteries some new invention or discovery helped in solving the mystery. Asimov wanted his mystery to "not cheat the reader"; to allow the detectives to sort through motives and follow clues and false trails until they solved the case by way of analysis and thought. The long publishing history of this book shows how successful his efforts were.

DUNE

by Frank Herbert, Chilton Book, New York, N.Y., 1965

Type of work: Science fiction

Setting: The desert planet Arrakis
(also known as Dune), A.D. 10,190

Principal characters:
Leto Atreides, Duke of Caladan and Arrakis
Jessica Atreides, Leto's concubine
Paul Atreides, Duke Leto and Jessica's only son
Baron Vladimir Harkonnen, enemy of the Atreides family
The Padishah Emperor, a wicked ally of the Harkonnens

Commentary:

In *Dune*, Frank Herbert invents an entirely new and complex society, and introduces a domain whose power is wielded by three factions: a Space Guild with a monopoly on interplanetary travel, the Bene Gesserit religious school, and the Padishah Emperor.

The story of *Dune* can be read on many levels: as the adventures of a young boy called upon to vanquish his enemies; as the struggles of a man to control his own destiny; and as the dilemma of a prophet fighting against his role as the "messiah" of an oppressed people while trying to prevent a universal "holy war."

Story Overview:

For twenty generations, the noble Atreides family—Duke Leto Atreides, his concubine Jessica, and their son Paul—had ruled the watery, tropical world of Caladan. Now they were leaving their home-world to govern the sparsely settled desert planet of Arrakis. Arrakis, desolate as it might be, was considered one of the richest bases in the universe—for the prized spice Melange was found only in its deserts. Melange was valued for two remarkable properties: it extended its users' lives and it gave them a limited ability to look into the future. Without the spice, the Space Guild navigators would be working blind; they would have no way to foresee the paths of safest passage for their ships, and travel between the stars would become impossible. Members of the Bene Gesserit, a highly esteemed and powerful religious sect, also used the spice for the prevuisionary powers it conferred—and also as a way to detect whether or not others were telling the truth.

The Duke's son, Paul, was a remarkable young man haunted by dreams of the future—dreams that usually came true. While he slept, he often found himself in a mystical cavern on a desert planet, where he foresaw two approaching events: he would meet a woman who would captivate him, and he would meet the Reverend Mother of the Bene Gesserit.

One part of this vision soon became reality. As Paul awoke one morning, his mother, Jessica—a lapsed member of the Bene Gesserit—introduced him to the Reverend Mother. And, just as he had dreamed she would, the Reverend Mother detected Paul's potential to become the Kwisatz Haderach, "one who can be many places at once," a Bene Gesserit who would be able to see the future in its

vast entirety. Sadly, the Reverend Mother contemplated the small chance Paul had of surviving to reach that potential. "We may be able to salvage you," she told him. "Doubtful, but possible. But for your father, nothing."

The popular House of Atreides had for generations been enmeshed in a feud with the great and powerful House of Harkonnen. And Paul's father, Duke Leto Atreides, had recently acquired an even greater enemy: the Padishah Emperor, who had allied himself with Harkonnen to defeat the Duke. The Harkonnens were known throughout the universe for their merciless enslavement of those occupying their planets. Atreides, on the other hand, was renowned for his fairness, loyalty and justice. But now that the Duke's army had grown to rival the Padishah Emperor's fanatical Sardaukar forces, the Emperor saw in Atreides a threat to his own power; thus he had united with the Harkonnens to destroy the House of Atreides.

On their planet Caladan, however, the Duke and his family were safe; a piece of bait was needed to lure them out into a trap. And that baited trap was the planet Arrakis. Arrakis was a Harkonnen world. As part of the plot, the Emperor turned over the valuable planet to the Atreides in a feigned gesture of honor and good will. "There it is . . . the biggest mantrap in all history," the Harkonnen leader chuckled in his basso voice. "And the Duke's headed into its jaws. Is it not a magnificent thing that I, the Baron Vladimir Harkonnen, do?" As the Duke, Paul and Jessica traveled to their new home, however, they were not entirely naive. They knew that the planet was filled with Harkonnen spies bent on their destruction.

Arriving on Arrakis, Paul, to his astonishment, was greeted by worshipful shouts of "Mahdi!" Local legend had long foretold that a savior would come, "the child of a Bene Gesserit, to lead them to true freedom." Paul was the chosen one.

Soon after their arrival, Duke Atreides began building up the defenses of his new planet. "Our supremacy on Caladan," he declared, "depended on sea and air power. Here, we must develop something I choose to call *desert* power."

Within days, Duke Leto uncovered a Harkonnen ploy to expose Jessica, his faithful mistress, as a traitor. The Duke realized that something must be done. He advised Paul of a plan: he would pretend to suspect Jessica as a spy. "The Harkonnens think to trick me by making me distrust your mother," he told Paul. "They don't know that I'd sooner distrust myself . . . If anything should happen to me, you can tell her the truth—that I never doubted her, not for the smallest instant. I should want her to know this."

Leto Atreides noticed one important factor that Baron Vladimir Harkonnen had missed: Harkonnen had not bothered to take a census of the Fremen desert dwellers. He dismissed the whole tribe as a negligible band of scavengers. But Duke Leto could see in the Fremen the power of numbers and knowhow; and far from being simple outcasts,

© 1993, Compact Classics, Inc.

177

the Fremen were a complex, warrior society. Most important of all, the Fremen hated Harkonnen as much as Duke Leto did. The Duke sensed that if he could recruit a sizeable Fremen force to add to his own army, he could defend Arrakis against the power-hungry Baron.

Meanwhile, Paul had been greatly transformed by his stay on Arrakis. Melange was mixed into everything that he ate and drank, and slowly he found himself able to divine whether someone was telling the truth or not, just as a Bene Gesserit "truthsayer" could. Paul's mind began to catch glimpses of future events, even when he was awake. He knew intuitively the customs of the Fremen and was able to use the right words when speaking with them. The Fremen often were forced to put on complicated garments known as stillsuits to reclaim the moisture their bodies lost in the desert heat; and Paul, though he had never before seen one, felt totally at home when he first donned one of these water-conserving suits. Paul's every act convinced the Fremen that he was indeed the "voice from the outer world" come to lead them to vengeance and freedom.

In the meantime, for Paul's father, time was running out. Though Duke Leto had expected—and received—an initial rash of small raids, sabotage and assassination attempts from the Harkonnens and the Emperor, he had underestimated how much his enemies wanted him destroyed. Before Leto's defense preparations were complete, Baron Harkonnen launched a full-scale invasion. Not only did the Harkonnens attack with a mercenary army, but the Emperor sent legions of his elite Sardaukar, dressed in Harkonnen uniforms. And even as this overwhelming horde struck at the Atreides forces, the Duke was being betrayed by an undercover agent, the Atreides family doctor, who delivered up the unsuspecting Duke Leto to Baron Harkonnen. The triumphant Baron, his enemy in hand, wasted no time in striking down his rival.

But the traitorous doctor had only acted in an attempt to save his own wife, a Harkonnen hostage. Despite his treachery, he arranged for Jessica and Paul to hide among the Fremen. Soon, however, Imperial Sardaukar troops discovered where Paul and Jessica were hidden, and attacked their protectors. In the confusion of battle, Paul and Jessica made an air escape out over the desert—only to find themselves caught in one of Arrakis' massive, 800-kilometer-per-hour sandstorms. The Harkonnen troops, seeing the loss of their own pursuing spaceships, assumed that Paul and Jessica had also perished in the storm. But the Bene Gesserit had a saying: "Do not count a human dead until you've seen his body. And even then you can make a mistake." Paul safely crashlanded the craft. When a nearby band of Fremen tried to capture the two Caladanians for the precious water in their bodies, Jessica used her Bene Gesserit training to defeat the chieftain, and then convince him to let them live in peace with the Fremen tribe. Because of her ties to Bene Gesserit, Jessica was soon accepted as a Reverend Mother and Paul, anoint by the Fremen as "Paul Muad'Dib," officially became the "Voice from the Outer World."

One member of this Fremen warrior band was Chani. Seeing her elfin face for the first time, Paul knew at once that this was the girl he had always loved! "The familiarity of that face, the features out of numberless visions in his earliest prescience, shocked Paul to stillness . . . "

Like Paul's father and mother, Paul and Chani began their life together without taking marriage vows; it would not do for Duke Paul Atreides to marry the lowly girl. Instead, decreed Jessica, Paul eventually must marry a noblewoman whose offspring could help him regain Arrakis from the Harkonnen. Paul was their one remaining hope.

Now, living with Chani and the Fremen in the desert meant that Paul's food had an increased dosage of Melange in it—a concentration that greatly heightened Paul's prescience. And Paul could see a troubled future, filled with a terrible purpose. "He sensed it . . . Somewhere ahead of him on this path, the fanatic hordes cut their gory path across the universe in his name. The green and black Atreides banner would become a symbol of terror. Wild legions would charge into battle screaming their war cry: `Muad'Dib!'"

As this horrible apocalyptic vision engulfed him, suddenly "he felt a new sense of wonder at the limits of his gift. It was as though he rode within the wave of time . . . and all around him the . . . waves lifted and fell, revealing and then hiding what they bore on their surface. Through it all, the wild holy war still loomed ahead of him, the violence and the slaughter." *"It must not be,"* he thought. *"I cannot let it happen."*

But almost immediately, the prophecy began to fulfill itself. Harkonnen soldiers had now begun killing the Fremen for sport, and the Fremen rallied behind Paul Muad'Dib and his army. Paul, seeing himself placed at the center of destiny, "walking a thin wire of peace with a measure of happiness, Chani at his side," found himself propelled ever closer to a showdown with the Baron Harkonnen and the Emperor, and the start of the bloody jihad that he so wished to avoid.

The guerrilla war began. Streams of Fremen came to follow Muad'Dib against their Harkonnen oppressors. The desert-bred warriors proved to be more adept fighters than the Emperor's fanatical Sardaukar, and, finally, the Fremen victories forced the Emperor and Baron Harkonnen to visit Arrakis personally—joined by their entire armies—to crush the rebellion.

Instead, Paul's legions of Fremen entirely struck down the Sardaukar and Harkonnen armies. And, with Paul's military victory and his complete control of Arrakis, still the only source of Melange, Paul Atreides, Muad'Dib, forced the Emperor to accept peace on his own terms: Paul would marry the Emperor's daughter and rule the empire as Regent. In this way only he could be certain that the holy war would not spread from Arrakis to other planets. But Paul would keep Chani as his beloved one, though married to another in name. At this declaration, "a bitter laugh escaped Jessica." Turning to Chani, she said, "Think on it, Chani: that princess will have the name, yet she'll live as less than a concubine—never to know a moment of tenderness from the man to whom she's bound. While we, Chani, who carry the name concubine—history will call us wives."

FAHRENHEIT 451

by Ray Bradbury, Simon & Schuster, New York, N.Y., 1967

Type of Work: Science fiction

Setting: A city in the future

Principal characters:

Guy Montag, a book-burner fireman

Mildred, his wife

Captain Beatty, Montag's supervisor

Faber, an old man—an advocate of books

Story Overview:

Returning home from work early one morning, Guy Montag saw a young woman walking toward him. Drawing nearer, he realized that it was his new teenage neighbor, Clarisse, so he stopped and introduced himself. Catching the scent of kerosene on him, she said, "And you must be—the fireman." Something in her voice troubled Montag. But fireman was a perfectly good profession; both his father and grandfather had been firemen. After all, burning forbidden books and the homes of those who harbored them was a civic service.

"Is it true," Clarisse asked, "that long ago firemen put fires out instead of going to start them?" No, Guy answered. Then she stared at the "451" stitched on his char-colored sleeve. 451: the temperature at which books burn.

Clarisse was a strange girl, Guy decided. She admitted to rarely watching the 3-D television "parlor walls." And she asked unexpected questions. "Are you happy?" she shot at Guy as he turned to take his leave.

When he entered his darkened bedroom, Guy sensed something wrong. Then he stumbled over a pill bottle—and realized that Mildred, his wife, had overdosed on sleeping pills. He called for help, then watched as the arriving technicians inserted big snake like tubes into her body to pump her stomach. The technicians assured him that this was a routine situation, one they handled many times each night.

In the morning Mildred remember nothing that had happened. As usual, her only desire was to sit in the middle of the living room with its three "parlor walls," seashell earphones plastered to her ears, and live out the painless fantasies of plot-less soap operas. It seemed that her only ambition was to be able to afford a fourth parlor wall—*then* her life would be complete.

As the days passed, Guy often caught glimpses of Clarisse—usually doing something very strange, such as tasting the rain.

At work, meanwhile, Guy stayed increasingly clear of the Mechanical Hound. This robot hunter could be calibrated to discern the scent of any person, then chase them down and rip them to shreds. For some reason the hound kept sniffing at the nervous Montag and extending its silver sensor needle. When he complained to Captain Beatty about the hound, Beatty only laughed.

Then one day while they were playing cards at the firehouse, the firemen heard a squadron of planes flying overhead. They were greatly surprised by the subsequent news report that another war was imminent.

One night a tip came in that books were hidden in the attic of a nearby house. And sure enough, when the firemen sped to the address and chopped their way into the attic, they found it stacked with books and magazines. While Guy stood by the staircase with the woman whose home they had invaded, the other firemen started to throw books down from the attic. Suddenly Guy had a strange urge. Without thinking, he reached down and picked up one of the books. "His hand had done it all, his hand, with a brain of its own, with a conscience and a curiosity in each trembling finger, had turned thief. Now it pressed the book back under his arm, pressed it tight to a sweating armpit . . . with a magician's flourish!"

Guy was shocked by what he had done. He joined the other firemen as they doused the pile of books with kerosene and prepared to ignite the house. However, the woman planted herself on the front porch in an astonishing act of defiance, then calmly struck a match and set herself aflame. Along with her belongings, she was soon reduced to ashes.

At home that night, Guy hid the filched book under his pillow. Visions of the woman on the porch of the burning house flooded his head. He tried to talk to Mildred about his uneasiness, but she had long since been conditioned to stay in the safe world of her parlor wall melodramas; she was not programmed to face or share real-life sensitivities and feelings. At one point she did casually remark, however, that the girl next door—Clarisse—had been run over and killed several days earlier.

Guy awoke the next morning with chills and a fever. He asked Mildred to call his work and report that he was sick, but she resisted. Again he tried to explain how he had felt about watching a woman burn up with her books, but Mildred was not interested. Then, in the middle of their argument, Captain Beatty drove up to the Montag house.

After the amenities, Beatty asked Guy how he felt. Suddenly Guy was puzzled—how did the Captain already know he was sick? "Every fireman, sooner or later, hits this," Beatty explained, launching into an obviously canned lecture on the history of books and firemen. Guy's thoughts rushed to the stolen book he had hidden under his pillow.

Beatty's account revealed that Clarisse had been right: once upon a time firemen had made their living by putting fires out. In those days, *most* people read books; and for years book-burning—by anyone—had actually been a criminal offense. But with the advent of television, people came more and more to look for vivid images and simple plots in their reading rather than anything that required thought, feeling, or sustained focus. Soon, books became more and more subordinate to television. Over time an unwritten rule evolved that no book should provoke or offend *anyone*—and more and more writings were censured on the ground that they might "disturb" readers. Authors, "full of evil thoughts," locked up their typewriters. "It didn't come from the government down. There was no dictum, no declaration, no censorship to start with, no! Technology, mass exploitation and minority pressure carried the trick . . . "

After Beatty left, something snapped inside of Guy. Taking Mildred by the hand—and, at the same time, taking a figurative leap of faith—he removed the ventilator cover to reveal a whole cache of books. Then, all day long he forced her to sit and listen to him read. He read on, until she broke away—again to watch her walls.

Now Guy thought back a man named Faber whom he had once talked with in the park. He was sure that the old man had a book of poems in his pocket, but for some reason he never did report him. He had kept Faber's name and address in his file, though. So now, confused and distressed, Guy went to see this "man of books." After re-introducing himself, he asked Faber how many copies of the Bible he estimated were left in the world—how many copies of Shakespeare, of Plato. "None!" Faber shot back. "You know as well as I do!" Then Guy pulled out a copy of the Bible that he had pilfered from a book-burning. Faber was puzzled. Why, truly, had this man come to him? "Nobody listens any more," Guy answered. " . . . I want you to teach me to understand what I read."

Just why *were* books important, Guy now asked in humility. Books, Faber explained, "show the pores in the face of life. The comfortable people only want wax-moon faces, poreless, hairless, expressionless. The good writers touch life often, the mediocre ones run a quick hand over her. The bad ones rape her and leave her for the flies."

After discussing various possible strategies to turn their society around, Faber, as Guy was about to leave, gave him a communications "seashell" so they could talk privately together and tune in on each other's conversations.

When he got home, Guy found his wife and her friends, as usual, watching the walls. Disgusted, he switched off the walls and tried to strike up a conversation with the women. Exasperated by their shallow responses, he impulsively produced a book and started to read to his wife's frightened guests—even as he heard Faber scream one word into his ear: "Don't!"

Finally compelled to declare his newfound love of books, Guy one day marched into the fire station and handed Beatty a book. Predictably, Beatty began to lecture Guy on the dangers of reading, but their discussion was abruptly interrupted by the alarm bell, and both firemen jumped into the fire engine. To Guy's astonishment, the engine came to a halt at his own house! As Mildred raced down the steps with a suitcase toward a taxi, the firemen chopped open the door, tore apart his books, and set the building ablaze. Had Mildred been the one to turn him in, Guy asked Beatty. Indeed, Mildred *had* tried to report him—but her friends had beat her to it.

Suddenly Faber's voice was roaring in Guy's ear: "Get out of there!" Before Guy could react, Beatty's fist had knocked the shell out of his ear. Then, putting the shell to his own ear, Beatty promised that he would trace the communication and apprehend Guy's accomplice. "No!" Guy screamed, pulling the safety catch off his flame thrower and aiming the weapon at the Captain. But Beatty only mocked him, daring him. Now with nothing to lose, Guy discharged the full force of the fire on Beatty screaming, "We never burned *right!*" Then he turned the flamethrower on the attacking Mechanical Hound that had just rounded the corner.

With great effort Guy made his way to Faber's house and warned him. Realizing that a new Mechanical Hound must already have been brought in to trail him, Guy then fled to a fellow fireman's house. Hoping to lead the hound on a false scent, he bathed and doused himself in alcohol. Then he ran on until he finally collapsed, exhausted, on a river bank—just as the pursuing hound crossed to his side of the river.

Not far off, Guy now saw a fire—not a book-burning fire, but a warming fire with men gathered around it. When he had dragged himself into their circle, the men assured him that he was safe; they had been following the news and knew who he was. Applying to his body a chemical designed to alter his scent, the approaching Mechanical Hound started off in the wrong direction, probably to kill some poor innocent on the street.

The men introduced themselves as rebels who had fled from society's life-stifling constrictions. Now, as fugitives, they had developed techniques to help themselves recall any book they had ever read, keeping the knowledge safe within their memories until the world came to its senses. The runaways anticipated that this great awakening could only come through some disastrous upheaval—and even as they were talking, bombs began to drop on the city across the river. The war had begun.

Watching as his native city was destroyed before his eyes, Guy worried only briefly about Mildred. He could not mourn deeply, he acknowledged; he and his wife had never touched each other's lives. He hoped, however, that Faber had made it to safety before the bombs fell.

Suddenly Guy remembered some verses from Ecclesiastes: *To everything there is a season . . . * Then a verse from Revelations materialized in his head: *And on either side of the river there was a tree of life . . . And the leaves of the tree were for the healing of the nations.*

Commentary:

Fahrenheit 451, like most good science fiction, is a cautionary tale. Ironically, Bradbury noted in 1972 that he had been asked to revise some of his books in order to give them a more feminist and minority-oriented tone. In effect, he was being asked to censor his own book about censorship! Since then, the trends toward "no-thought" reading and "politically correct" writing have certainly not abated; even now, some forty years after its first publication, *Fahrenheit 451* is an important and timely warning.

THE SHORT STORIES OF JOYCE CAROL OATES

(taken from *The Assignation: Stories by Joyce Carol Oates,* Ecco Press, New York, N.Y., 1988)

Joyce Carol Oates manipulates her characters, *subjectively* focusing on the mundane facets of their lives. Indeed, objectively, we find little of note in their circumstances; only as we are led to penetrate their thoughts and memories do we find the conflicts and pervasive sense of emptiness that make us appreciate their private dramas.

Photographer's Model

She was only nine or ten when her Uncle Billy started taking pictures of her and showing them off in his filling station. He posed her in jeans, playsuits, bathing suits—what have you—but never anything crude. There were a few nudes, but he decided not to send them out.

Whatever Billy got paid, he gave half to her. "Billy split it all with me," she said, "which isn't what they usually do, photographers. Some of them are such bastards."

The first time she pulled on black, textured stockings and looked at herself, she was shocked. She knew, then, that she had it. While her face was not unlike the faces of other women, she had the legs; she had the perfect legs. She had made a lot of money since that time. No, the hot lights did not bother her, except when she had to work with another model.

Her father said it was the devil's work, but since she had broken off contact with her parents years ago, what he said didn't matter. Her only regret was leaving Uncle Billy. She had just left, without telling him, because she knew she could earn much more in New York. He had been angry; they didn't speak to one another for years. She had missed Billy, especially since he was the only one, besides herself, who felt proud of her. "Billy would just look at me smiling his big funny smile like we put over something on somebody," she recalled. "He'd say, Jesus, kid, you got it all now, don't you?" Finally, they reconciled. Now he was dead, and she still missed him. Big-time contracts kept rolling in—but big-time photographers could be real bastards.

The Heartland

The young woman had driven a thousand miles to see her parents. But, reaching their Midwestern home, she decided her coming had been a mistake; her visit was intrusive, awkwardly timed. When she had called to tell them she was driving out, she had heard the television blaring in the background, and her mother, rather than turning the volume down, had hurried through the conversation.

Now in their home, the *apparently un-prodigal* daughter caught snatches of her parents' hushed conferrals—as if, somehow, they meant for her to hear. "There's no getting out of this is there," they said, and "Why did she come when nobody invited her?"

Dinnertime conversation, under these conditions, was coerced, lackluster; yet the daughter noticed that her father, always the family's brooder, laughed and smiled much more than she remembered. His voice, too, seemed a pitch or two higher. After dinner, the three watched television over butterscotch-ripple ice cream and Oreo cookies. Then, suddenly, it was 11:00. Bedtime. Her parents' crude innuendoes and flirtatious banter were new to the young woman—and shocking; somehow, despite the contrary evidence of her birth, she had always seen them before as asexual beings.

After kissing and hugging them goodnight, she closed the door of her bedroom and lay down. From her parents' room came the sounds of lovemaking, punctuated by voices and laughter. Were the sounds real? Or did they just have the television set in their bedroom turned on?

The Assignation

Some sort of noise—probably the television next door—awakened her from her heavy daytime sleep. Before she had a real name, her parents used to call her "Baby." Now Baby moved slowly, deliberately about her apartment, taking swigs from a can of beer, preparing herself for her shower. She loved to virtually scald herself in the tub. She had lain down earlier to put her thoughts in order about last night and the "maybe" to come. Both had seemed equally vague and shadowy—as if she were staring into the dark, seeing nothing. It was like that in the shower, too: "Eyes shut, not seeing the tile with its arabesques of cracks and fractures, the inside of the shower stall splotched with grime, not seeing and not wanting to see, that would only break the mood."

She dried off and dressed slowly, unconsciously, with the absent-mindedness born of habit and repetition. Looking at herself in the mirror, she was not plagued with questions like Is this me? or, Am I inside? What she saw was what she was.

She began to feel excited about the night to come, about what might happen, about what would not happen, about what would almost happen but would by merest chance or happenstance be deflected. "You have to take your chances," Baby thought. "Can't just bury your head in the sand for Christ's sake."

Dressed, Baby finished her beer, smoked another cigarette, then drank a cup of coffee over the sink, too restless to sit down. Finally, turning on a light by the front door, she stepped out, locked the door behind her, and stopped for a few contemplative moments on the stoop, peering into the night.

Eventually, I was there, waiting for her in the darkness.

Adulteress

The woman was in love with two men at once: her husband and her lover. She had taken up with her lover only because she missed the early years of her marriage; she had forgotten why she was in love with her husband. They had never had children. Originally the baby had been delayed until after a trip to Europe. After the vacation, though, the baby was simply "put off."

Sleeping with two men left her breathless, lightheaded, with a touch of altitude sickness; a soft sensation of panic, dread.

Her lover and her husband knew each other on a casual basis. Occasionally the three had dinner or drinks together. Once, when they met at a hotel lounge, she watched her lover as he refused to look at her. Instead, he scrutinized her husband, intently, rigidly, as though he wanted to say something but had been struck mute. Unable to bear the sense of her lover's rejection, she excused herself to the bathroom.

She was not drunk or hysterical; she nevertheless splashed cold water on her wrists and blotted her face and neck with damp paper towels. At that very moment, she was sure, her lover was telling her husband that he adored her and wanted to marry her, that he hated deception, wanted to behave responsibly, honorably, but that he was in love and found it necessary to . . .

Suddenly a drunken older woman staggered into the room. The woman was still pretty; she carried off her white pantsuit better than most women her age. All at once she turned and began to vomit.

When the younger woman returned from the bathroom, her husband and her lover seemed to have been waiting for her. She had been gone ten, maybe fifteen minutes. What *had* they been talking about, she wondered. However, the two men merely smiled and asked if she would like another bottle of champagne. Why *had* she been gone so long? inquired her husband. "There was a sick woman in the ladies' room," she said. "I couldn't just leave her."

The Stadium

Traveling in Europe, the man, no longer young but not yet old, began feeling his soul drain from him, drop by precious drop. Now, at the summer solstice, he found himself in a land where the sun barely set and the night was strangely illuminated. He woke often at night, his hair damp and pressed to his forehead; but, after spending a lifetime turning fear into a sort of art, he did not feel frightened by his mortality.

One morning, standing at his hotel window, he drew a breath and trembled with what felt like bliss. Later that morning, he would be giving a lecture to several hundred people at the university, and he would have to dress the part. But at the moment he had on his old sweats and running shoes, and was making his way to the public stadium he had seen the day before. He was going to run.

The fresh air slammed into his lungs; the seats of the stadium towered above him; the cinder track, really only a mile long, reached far out of sight, a huge, swollen oval. He wondered for a moment why he had come; but the time had passed to wonder. So he began to run. He heard at his back a low, murmuring sound, the quiet drone of a crowd; he listened to the speaker system humming, heard the cinders crunching beneath his shoes. The little thought, when it came to him, dawned calmly: "Here are fine-ground bones, preceding yours." Still he ran; a tiny figure, dwarfed by the stadium, he ran. Just ran.

Commentary:

This collection of Joyce Carol Oates' short stories illustrates the gritty, existential quality of her prose. Ms. Oates' works do not pretend to moralize; rather, they tell a simple story that spotlights her understanding of the individual experience of "being"—of just how it feels to exist inside one's own skin. No central philosophical insights emerge from these stories, except possibly that unvarnished existence itself is a complex and variegated experience well worthy of portrayal, without glamorous overlays of fiction.

In several of Oates' passages we encounter statements that might pass for existential credos. The young woman in **"The Assignation,"** for example, does not trouble herself with thoughts of "Is this me?" and "Am I inside?"—she simple *is*. The only time really present to her is today; yesterday and tomorrow barely matter. Similarly, the runner in **"The Stadium"** has come to a ripened age, a moment where he feels his mortality. Sensing that an illness has entered into his race of life—a malady that will eventually overtake him—he nevertheless confronts it all unafraid, the ominous approach of death failing to intimidate him. He simply continues to run.

And in **"Adulteress,"** the woman seems to at once hate her duplicitous life and to cling to it. Thus, she dreads losing it—hoping the dream-like trance will never end—yet she also yearns to "behave responsibly," remove deception, conduct herself "honorably"—characteristics she secretly also wishes her lover could be endowed with. Ultimately, she exists and operates in ways that even she herself cannot explain.

Thus, Oates fuses the objective and subjective aspects of our lives into a whole, and shows us this aggregate, one slice at a time.

THE SHORT STORIES OF JOHN CHEEVER

(taken from *The Stories of John Cheever,* Ballantine Books, New York, N.Y., 1982)

John Cheever writes insightfully about the travails of suburbanite upper-middle-class men and women. Cheever's characters typically respond to the disastrous circumstances of their lives by developing unusual obsessions to keep their pain from overwhelming them. As smart and innovative as these characters usually are, they find themselves overwhelmed by their own inventions—and whimsy swells into fantasy and drifts out of control.

The Chimera

They were at their wit's end. With "three beautiful children" to consider, however, the two had long ago decided to endure their miserable marriage. But the situation seemed to tax the couple more with each passing day.

"You've ruined my life, that's what you've done," Zena railed. After all she'd had important ambitions that she'd put aside for the sake of her marriage. "I might have climbed the Matterhorn," her husband shot back. He, too, had certainly made sacrifices. Wasn't he the one who cooked most of their dinners—on a charcoal grill? And just recently he had brought her in a particularly nice breakfast on a tray: "two hard-boiled eggs, a piece of Danish, and a Coca-Cola spiked with gin." But what was his wife's shrewish reaction? At the sight of him, she had burst into tears. "I cannot any longer endure being served breakfast in bed by a hairy man in his underwear," she'd sobbed.

And it was not just his wife's endless complaining that blackened his life; it was the whole grim landscape of his marriage—utterly barren of tenderness, love and good cheer.

So, understandably, he found himself very pleasantly surprised one evening when a desirable woman floated into his arms while he stood barbecuing in his own back yard. She was, it was true, simply an "idle reverie," but she was undeniably lovely, with her dark, fragrant hair and olive-colored skin. Her name, as it turned out, was Olga, and she revealed with a smile that she had just arrived from California, where she had left her husband. For a "sweet hour," Olga lingered—and then, as abruptly as she had come, she disappeared.

Try as he might, he could not summon Olga back to his side. Finally one night as he read in the bathroom (Zena would simply not tolerate a light on in either the kitchen or the bathroom while she slept) Olga materialized. Perched on the edge of the bathtub, she confessed that she needed a job. "I'll look around and see if I can find something," he promised.

Suddenly Zena's voice roared from the bedroom, "You're talking to yourself," she scolded; then, sporting "bellicose hair curlers," she burst into the bathroom to fumble in the medicine cabinet for a sleeping pill.

A few nights later, Olga appeared again. True to his word, he reported, he had found her a job as a receptionist. She was delighted. In a festive mood, she invited him up to her furnished room. But, with great regret, he declined. The fact was, he had just discovered a note from one of his children: "Dere Daddy," it read in childlike innocence, "do not leave us."

Even though, as he often reminded himself, Olga was only a "fiction," he found he could not summon her at will. A week passed before she appeared again. But this time she returned to him drunk and whimpering. Holding her, he learned that she had visited a few bars with a man at her office, who had first "seduced" her—and then fired her. Too distraught to stay, she again vanished from his arms.

Although she had promised to return the following evening, Olga failed to show. It wasn't until days later that she finally came walking—or rather staggering—through the yard to his porch, haggard and dishevelled. Nevertheless, he couldn't wait to hold her and to hear what had happened during her absence.

Olga admitted that her seducer had come back to her and they had thrown a raucous party. The landlady had complained, and the police had arrived to cart Olga off to jail. After spending three days in the Women's House of Detention, she had decided to return to her husband in California, for good.

But "you can't go," he howled. "If you go it will only prove that even the most transparent inventions of my imagination are subject to lust and age."

"Stop talking to yourself," his wife shouted at him. And at that moment a new thought occurred to him: By leaving, wasn't Olga simply making room inside his life for a multitude of women of every conceivable description? Now he could begin to invent in earnest.

(Like Zena's husband, the businessman in the following tale was faced with a woman scorned—his mother.)

The Angel of the Bridge

His mother liked to figure skate—just as she had in her youth—"dressed like a hat-check girl" in a "red velvet costume," with a "red ribbon in her white hair." The elderly woman was an old-fashioned New Englander who missed "the vanishing and provincial world of her youth." But her son was a respected businessman. For obvious reasons, he scrupulously avoided her at the rink.

Nor did the son sympathize with his mother's fear of flying. Once when he had taken her to the airport in Newark, she had been seized by a panic attack. "I want to go home!" she'd blurted out. "If I have to die suddenly, I don't want to die in a flying machine."

But although she had raised him in the same small town that had shaped her, this younger son of hers had no fear of planes; he was delighted by the "incandescence of high altitudes."

His older brother was not so fortunate, however. Arriving at the apartment building for a dinner appointment one evening, he phoned from the lobby and asked the businessman to come and meet him downstairs. That was when the businessman learned that his brother was terrified of elevators. "What are you afraid of?" he asked incredulously. "I'm afraid the building will fall down," his trembling brother revealed.

Although he also felt rather bad to see his older brother so "humiliated—crushed," the businessman could not help but laugh. Later he told his wife about his brother's phobia, and the couple agreed that it was unfortunate—but also "terribly funny."

A few weeks later, they were also captured by the sadness of the situation when his brother's company moved to a new office on the fifty-second floor of a skyscraper; the brother was forced to resign. It took him quite awhile to find another position, with a firm located safely on the third floor.

Once he had settled into his new job, the brother invited the businessman and his family to dinner at his New Jersey home. They enjoyed themselves, but on the way home, while crossing the George Washington Bridge, the businessman experienced a most unsettling sensation: a strong gust of wind struck the car and he imagined that he could feel the bridge swing; he was certain that it would literally split in two.

The following day he found that he was paralyzed by the thought of crossing another bridge. He consulted his family doctor; when that didn't help, he saw a psychiatrist, who suggested "full analysis." The businessman, however, decided simply to "muddle through" on his own. Determined not to be crippled by fear, he set out in his car to cross the Triborough Bridge. But anxiety seized him again; this time he "nearly lost consciousness" on the bridge.

That same day he flew to California on business. After nightfall, he gazed thoughtfully for awhile at the neon signs of San Francisco. At last he determined that his phobia was an expression of his "clumsily concealed horror of what is becoming of the world." This insight implanted in him a modicum of peace—but later he found that he still could not bring himself to cross the Bay Bridge.

When he returned from California, his daughter asked him to drive her back to college in New Jersey. Gripped by terror, he managed to pilot them across the George Washington Bridge. But he could not bring himself to face the same route again. On his return trip to the city, he opted to drive out of his way to cross the Tappan Zee Bridge, which was "more securely fastened to its shores." As he approached the Tappan Zee, though, his panic grew worse than ever. Surely his life was over. He stopped the car.

"I didn't think anyone would pick me up on the bridge," said the girl as she climbed into his car. She was hitchhiking into the city, as it turned out, where she sang in coffeehouses. He turned the key in the ignition, and all at once she launched into a medley of old folk songs. Before long the girl had sung them across the bridge—which now struck him as a wonderful "and even beautiful construction."

The businessman drove on towards home. All around him the night was engulfed in peace. He decided henceforth to avoid using the George Washington Bridge, so as not to push his luck with his new-found ease in crossing bridges.

Commentary:

John Cheever (1912-1982) wrote and published some two hundred stories during his lifetime. An American master of the genre, Cheever often focuses his stories on urban professionals whose struggles he imbued with mythic proportions. In their scrupulously manicured backyards or spacious co-op apartments, his white-collar heroes and heroines forge their routes through a distinctly contemporary chaos—as harrowing at times as Ulysses' adventures in *The Odyssey*. It is not surprising, then, that many of his characters turn to the past to try to find answers to their calamitous lives.

Thus, for instance, Zena's husband conjures up his "chimera"—a fantasy creature from Greek mythology—to withstand the desolation of his marriage. And even more tellingly, the businessman in "The Angel of the Bridge" explains his phobia as a longing for the past: "It was at the arc of a bridge that I became aware suddenly of the depth and bitterness of my feelings about modern life, and of the profoundness of my yearning for a more vivid, simple, and peaceable world."

Ironically, with these words, the businessman has just come full circle to arrive at the same longing for the past that motivated his mother and his older brother—to his impatience and embarrassment. It is the absence of the observable past, in fact, which seems to torment so many of Cheever's characters. Tucked away in suburbs or skyscrapers, ostensibly to discover more fulfilling lives, instead they encounter a profound emptiness and alienation into which, in hopes of mitigating their misery, they invite their chimeras, phantom lovers, and songs of the past. Thus lodged in their fanciful yet seemingly safe havens, they entertain all the hungry little pets of their own imagination that will ultimately eat them whole.

THE SHORT STORIES OF FLANNERY O'CONNOR

(taken from *Collected Stories of Flannery O'Connor,* Viking Press, New York, N.Y., 1988)

Flannery O'Connor (1925 - 1964) is an enigma; her singular vision of human nature, as embodied in these three stories, has long baffled and delighted readers. This contradictory response may in part be explained by her uncanny ability to take elements of the grotesque, the spiritual, and the comic, and distill them into moments of extraordinary epiphany and revelation.

A Good Man Is Hard to Find

A family in Georgia sat arguing about their vacation. Everyone wanted to go to Florida — except for Grandmother, who yearned to visit relatives in Tennessee. The old woman, in an effort to sway her son, Bailey, read aloud a newspaper article about how that "The Misfit" had escaped from prison and was on his way to Florida. But Bailey, his wife, and their children John Wesley and June Star, had no intention of changing their minds. "Tennessee is just a hillbilly dumping ground, and Georgia is a lousy state too," grumbled John Wesley.

The next day while on their way to Florida, they stopped at a barbecue restaurant owned by a round man named Red Sammy Butts. Over lunch, Grandmother brought up the subject of The Misfit, and Red Sammy said he would not be surprised if the escapee robbed his restaurant. The world was full of riff-raff, concluded Red Sammy shaking his head. "A good man is hard to find."

When they got back in the car, an idea occurred to Grandmother: why not take a little side road here to visit an old plantation she had seen once in her youth? Appealing to the children, she went on about a treasure said to be hidden in the house, even hinting something about a secret panel. (She did not mention that the house was in Tennessee.)

Sick and tired of the pandemonium the excited children were causing in the back seat, Bailey gave in. But as he maneuvered over the rutted dirt road indicated by his mother, suddenly he lost control of the car and it turned over in a ditch.

They found themselves on a stretch of road surrounded by dark woods. Everyone seemed to be okay, except Grandmother, who limped out from under the dashboard. Soon, a car approached and stopped. The three men inside just sat there staring at the family. Finally, after several minutes had gone by, the bespectacled, scholarly-looking driver got out. He and his two sidekicks were holding guns. It was then that Grandmother knew she was staring into the face of The Misfit.

To make matters even worse, the children spoke to the criminal in the most impudent manner. "Children make me nervous," The Misfit intoned. That set the old woman off; she began to cry, pleading for her life. Then she decided it might be more effective to flatter him: "I know you're a good man. You don't look a bit like you have common blood. I know you must come from nice people." The Misfit replied, "God never made a finer woman than my mother, and my daddy's heart was pure gold." Then he instructed his sidekicks to take Bailey and John Wesley into the woods. Two shots rang out. "Pray, pray," Grandmother said—but The Misfit went on talking about himself and his family.

Before long, The Misfit ordered Bailey's wife, June Star, and the baby into the woods; more shots sounded. "Jesus," the old woman wailed, "You've got good blood. I know you wouldn't shoot a lady. I know you come from nice people . . . " But her words fell on deaf ears. "You're one of my babies," she gasped in sudden understanding. And The Misfit leveled his gun and fired at her, "three times through the chest."

Coldly, he turned to one of his sidekicks and commanded him to get rid of the body. "She would have been a good woman," he explained dispassionately, "if it had been somebody there to shoot her every minute of her life."

The Life You Save May Be Your Own

His name was Tom T. Shiftlet, and one day at sunset he ambled into Lucynell Crater's front yard. She and her daughter, another Lucynell, had been rocking on their front porch. Immediately the younger Lucynell "began to stamp and point and make excited speechless sounds." Mrs. Crater noted that the man coming toward them carried a tin toolbox in his right hand, and his left arm was partially missing.

Introducing himself, Shiftlet assured the women that he was possessed of "a moral character" and asked about the old rusted car beneath the tree. "There ain't a broken thing on this plantation that I couldn't fix for you," he announced, "one-arm jackleg or not." Mrs. Crater asked if Mr. Shiftlet was a married man. "Lady," he told her, "where would you find an innocent girl today? I wouldn't have any of this trash I could just pick up." Pleased with this response, Mrs. Crater began to praise her "sweet" and "smart" and tidy daughter. She "wouldn't give her up for a casket full of jewels," the elder Lucynell declared. In truth, she was quite eager for Lucynell to marry so that there would be a man on the property.

Now the junior Lucynell appeared much younger than her thirty years. What's more, Mrs. Crater emphasized, "she can't sass you back or use foul language." And this was true; her daughter was a deaf-mute.

Shiftlet decided to stay on awhile. At night he slept in the back seat of the car, and by day he went about his chores. In his spare time, he even began to teach Lucynell a few words. Of course, Mrs. Crater, "ravenous for a son-in-law," was delighted.

One day Mrs. Crater took it upon herself to propose to the man. "Saturday," she told Mr. Shiftlet, "you and her and me can drive into town and get married." The crafty Mr. Shiftlet immediately protested that he had no money and that he wanted to take a bride "to a hotel and giver something good to eat." Negotiations began and Mr. Shiftlet finally convinced Mrs. Crater to give him money for a hotel.

The following Saturday they did drive into town, and Mr. Shiftlet and Lucynell were wed. "You got a prize!" Mrs. Crater enthused to the bridegroom. But Mr. Shiftlet did not seem to notice. He quickly drove Mrs. Crater, who had begun to cry, back to her house and deposited her there.

Then he sped away with Lucynell at his side.

After a while, Shiftlet surmised from Lucynell's fidgeting that she was hungry, and pulled into a diner. When they sat down, Lucynell immediately put her head on the counter and fell asleep. "She looks like an angel of Gawd," the waiter said as he brought her plate of ham and grits. But Mr. Shiftlet looked straight at the boy; Lucynell was only a hitchhiker, he lied. Then he jumped to his feet, stalked out of the diner, started the car and sped away.

From time to time, Mr. Shiftlet noticed signs along the road: "Drive carefully. The life you save may be your own." Though he had Mrs. Crater's money and her car, Mr. Shiftlet felt glum. Maybe some company would improve his spirits. Before long, he stopped for a hitchhiker—a young boy who had absolutely nothing to say. "I got the best old mother in the world," Mr. Shiftlet suddenly confided to the silent boy. "I never rued a day in my life like the one I rued when I left that old mother of mine." Then Mr. Shiftlet pulled to the side of the road and started to cry. "He took her from heaven and giver to me and I left her."

"You go to the devil!" the boy burst out unexpectedly, leaping out of the car. Shocked, Mr. Shiftlet drove on in a daze. "Oh Lord!" he exclaimed. "Break forth and wash the slime from this earth." Then he accelerated and sped on to Mobile.

Greenleaf

Mrs. May was fond of talking. She was not, however, particularly fond of listening. Recently it had come to her attention that her worker, Mr. Greenleaf, lacked initiative. What's more, Mrs. May simply could not abide Mrs. Greenleaf, a "large and loose" woman who engaged in "prayer healing." They were folk who "lived . . . off the fat she had struggled to put into the land." For fifteen years, Mrs. May had endured the Greenleafs, but now her patience was wearing thin.

The final straw came late one moonlit night when a bull wandered into the yard while Mrs. May slept. She found her dream invaded by odd chewing noises: " . . . Whatever it was had been eating as long as she had the place and had eaten everything from the beginning of her fence line up to the house and now was eating the house and calmly with the same steady rhythm would continue . . . eating her and the boys, and then on, eating everything but the Greenleafs, and on and on, until nothing was left but the Greenleafs on a little island all their own in the middle of what had been her place."

Waking up to the spectacle of a bull munching beneath her window, Mrs. May reluctantly prepared to go retrieve Mr. Greenleaf. "If it was my boys they would have got thet bull up theirself," is what he'd likely say, and Mrs. May hated to hear about Mr. Greenleaf's twin sons, O.T. and E.T., who had done rather well and married French girls. In contrast, her own two sons were a disappointment; Mrs. May knew that they would never treat Mr. Greenleaf with an "iron hand." Without their help, Mrs. May had to confront Mr. Greenleaf herself. She knew the bull belonged to his sons, and she wanted it penned at once. But Greenleaf complained that the bull would just break out again. Now Mrs. May was furious. She got into her car

and drove off to the twins' house. When she found that neither of the twins were at home, she vented her rage on one of their workers: "You can tell Mr. O.T. and Mr. E.T. if they don't come get him today, I'm going to have their daddy shoot him the first thing in the morning." The next morning, the twins did not appear.

That night, at dinner, Mrs. May whined, "I'm the victim. I've always been the victim." "Pass the butter to the victim," one of her sons said dryly.

Mrs. May spent that night once more haunted by the sounds of a bull chewing. In the morning she found Mr. Greenleaf in the barn. "Go get your gun," she told him. "Ain't nobody ast me to shoot my own boys' bull!" he protested, but he obeyed, and they drove around Mrs. May's property searching for the bull. At last they sighted the animal in some woods. While Mrs. May waited, Greenleaf walked out to dispose of it. After awhile, she stepped out of the car. Finally, growing more and more impatient, she reached in the car window and blew the horn.

Moments later the bull appeared. "Here he is, Mr. Greenleaf," Mrs. May called. Suddenly, the bull turned and charged: "One of his horns sank until it pierced her heart and the other curved around her side and held her in an unbreakable grip." Mr. Greenleaf rushed out of the woods and fired four rounds into the bull's eyes—but it was too late. Mrs. May had abided the circumstances of her life; now she was called to abide those of another—for the treeline, she saw, was now "a dark wound in a world that was nothing but sky"; a darkness that opened into a world of "unbearable light."

Commentary:

Flannery O'Connor's stories, which first appeared in the late 1940s, employ a paradoxical sense of fate. Thus, for instance, in "A Good Man Is Hard to Find" we realize by story's end that, in a grotesque parody of redemption, the grandmother's fate is to meet The Misfit and to be "saved" by his murdering her. It is only in that moment, when her death warrant is sealed, that the mysteries of faith and redemption are revealed in the old woman's recognition that The Misfit is her kindred, "one of my babies." The irony of The Misfit's final remark is that it represents quite literally the truth of the woman's character.

There are skewed epiphanies in the other two stories presented here. In "The Life You Save May Be Your Own," Mr. Shiftlet's revelation comes in the form of an apocalypse; the moral stain and corruption of human nature will be purged only when the Lord, as he says, designs to "break forth and wash the slime from the earth." In "Greenleaf," Mrs. May's death invokes yet another apocalyptic vision. After the bull has buried its horn in her heart, she discovers—as one "whose sight has been suddenly restored"—that the world is "a dark wound" which opens onto a vista of "unbearable light."

As one can see by these works, an O'Connor epiphany—Christian though it may be—does not abide easily within the traditions of faith. The grotesque and comic aspects of these revelatory moments unsettle rather than reassure our sensibility. Yet it is precisely this ofttimes disturbing quality that makes O'Connor's vision of human nature so fresh and new.

THE SUN ALSO RISES

by
Ernest Hemingway
(1899-1961)

Type of work: Symbolic social commentary

Setting: Western Europe, 1920's

Principal characters:

Jake Barnes, an American newsman living in Paris (the novel's narrator)

Robert Cohn, a well-to-do Jewish American also living in Paris

Brett Ashley, a highly sensuous Englishwoman

Mike Campbell, Ashley's fiance, a bullying Scotsman

Pedro Romero, a promising young Spanish bullfighter

Montoya, a Pamplona hotel owner and a close friend of Barnes

Story Overview:

"The sun also ariseth," says the preacher in Ecclesiastes, "And the sun goeth down and hasteth to his place where he arose . . . I considered all the living which walk under the sun . . . There is no end of all the people, even of all that have been before them. [And] . . . that which is crooked cannot be made straight . . ."

Robert Cohn suffered insult after insult because he was a Jew, and took up boxing in college so he could defend himself. He became such a good boxer that, at the expense of a permanently flattened nose, he even won a middleweight title. In spite of this, Cohn remained essentially a naive and idealistic intellectual, interpreting his own life through the books he read— through the smoked glass of other people's experiences.

Cohn's mistress, encouraging him to write a novel and imbibe the glamour of living abroad, had convinced him to go with her to Paris, where Cohn met Jake Barnes. Barnes, an American newsman living on assignment in France, was flawed by a disfigurement even more central than Cohn's Jewishness: during World War I he had been wounded in combat and left impotent.

Cohn's Paris novel did indeed get written— and published; and, from then on, though he lived mainly on an allowance from his wealthy mother, he passed himself off as a writer. Barnes, the working journalist, however, remained skeptical.

Paris was exciting in the twenties. Barnes and Cohn were part of the elite cafe crowd. They and their friends, including titled Europeans as well as luminous literati and "sportsmen," Bohemian hangers-on, and rich expatriates, from everywhere, spent their evenings mingling, trysting, and drinking at all-night clubs and bistros. One night, Barnes ran into an all-too-well-remembered old friend—Lady Brett Ashley. Jealousy flooded his soul the moment he noticed Brett— at the center, as usual, of a group of young men. "Brett was damned good-looking. She wore a slipover jersey sweater and a tweed skirt . . . She was built with curves like the hull of a racing yacht, and you missed none of it with that wool jersey." Swallowing his emotions, Barnes coolly chatted with Brett, introduced her to Cohn, then invited her to take a taxi ride around the city.

In the dark, quiet taxi, Barnes once again relived his memories of the time he had spent in the English hospital recovering from his war wounds. Brett—Lady Ashley—had been his army nurse; they had grown intensely close. But Brett's sensual nature and Barnes' impotence soon turned the relationship into a hell of frustration. Now the old heartaches, the unfulfilled desires, once again resurfaced.

"Don't touch me," she said. "Please don't touch me."

"What's the matter?"

"I can't stand it . . . "

"Don't you love me?"

"Love you? I simply turn all to jelly when you touch me."

"Isn't there anything we can do about it? . . . "

"I don't know," she said. "I don't want to go through that hell again."

The exchange wore on—staccato and awkwardly impassioned.

Not long after this, Cohn spoke with Barnes about his own increasing interest in Lady Ashley. "She's a remarkably attractive woman," said Cohn. "I don't know how to describe the quality. I suppose it's breeding." Barnes answered laconically: "You sound as though you liked her pretty well." "I do," admitted Cohn. "I shouldn't wonder if I were in love with her."

Barnes explained to Cohn that Brett was already engaged—on the rather freewheeling terms that were common among their circle—to a Scotsman named Mike Campbell. At this, Cohn dreamily responded that he didn't feel Brett would go through with the marriage. "I don't believe she would marry anybody she didn't love." Cohn was acting like a prep-schooler, Barnes groused. But in private moments, Barnes pondered his own chaotic feelings.

I lay awake thinking and my mind jumping around. Then I couldn't keep away from it, and I started to think about Brett and all the rest of it went away . . . Then all of a sudden I started to cry. Then after awhile it was better and I lay in bed and listened to the heavy trams go by . . .

During the next few weeks, Barnes and Brett continued to meet sporadically, and the tension between them continued to grow. Finally, Brett took a trip to San Sebastian. She simply couldn't stand being near him in Paris any longer, she told Barnes—but she also assured him that she would eventually come back. Coincidentally, Cohn left the city at the same time—to collect himself and gather material for his second novel, he explained.

In Brett and Cohn's absence, Barnes planned a trip with Bill Gorton, a writer-friend who was visiting Europe. They would fish in the Pyrenees, then, in June, attend the fiesta in Pamplona. A few weeks later, Cohn contacted Barnes from Biarritz and said he would like to travel with them to Spain. Barnes acceded. Then, before leaving, he unexpectedly ran into Brett, newly returned from San Sebastian. When she found out that Barnes was leaving for the fiesta, she remarked that she—and her fiance—would like to accompany him. Barnes—cool and generous as ever—agreed to let them come along. However, when Brett learned that Cohn was going too, she seemed inexplicably concerned. "Won't it be hard on Robert to have me there?" she asked. "I don't think so," Barnes curtly answered. "Why should it?" Ashley's reply—equally as curt—was the bombshell he had half-consciously both dreaded and expected: "Who do you think I was with in San Sebastian?"

In spite of this brief impasse, the group met and traveled together to Spain. The affair at Pamplona was splendid. Any time not spent dancing or sleeping was spent drinking or watching the bull fights. Barnes remarked on the seamless days and nights in a world that seemed suspended outside of time: "It was as if nothing you did had any consequences."

But, early on in the trip, a few consequences did begin to make themselves felt. Mike Campbell, drunk more often than not, began bullying the "tagalong intellectual," Robert Cohn. "What if Brett did sleep with you?" he sneered. "She's slept with lots of better people than you . . . Tell me, Robert, why do you follow Brett around like a poor bloody steer? Don't you know you're not wanted?" Brett interrupted her fiance. "I say, Michael, you might not be such a bloody ass." Then, laughing off the incident, she chided, "But you put it so badly." Finally she turned to Barnes and added, "I'm not saying he's not right, you know . . ."

At the fiesta, Barnes' Spanish friend Montoya introduced him to a promising young matador named Pedro Romero. Romero was extraordinarily good-looking, and, at 19, had already become a master torero. Montoya considered Barnes to be a true connoisseur of bull-fighting, a rare trait among non-Spanish aficionados. He felt that he could trust Barnes to help protect Romero from corrupting influences that could deflect the pure, unadulterated spiritual energy which made up the essence of a great matador.

Barnes and his friends thrilled as they watched Romero in the ring. He moved with liquid grace, never resorting to gimmickry in order to make the sport appear more dangerous than it was. The young man was almost hypnotic in his performance. And, predictably, not only the bull, but Lady Ashley too fell under his spell.

A couple of days after the opening of the fiesta, Brett asked Barnes to introduce her to Romero. Barnes hesitated, then acquiesced, even though he also knew that he was betraying Montoya by bringing about circumstances that would almost certainly corrupt the young matador.

As Barnes had foreseen, a torrid affair soon developed between the young bullfighter and Brett. The other members of the group each reacted differently to this turn of events: Cohn went into a jealous fit; Mike became loud and abusive; and Barnes himself went on a drinking binge, seeking refuge both from jealousy and from a perverse, half-formed and half-explained sense of guilt. By fiesta's end, Mike had stomped off back home to Scotland, Cohn had flown to Paris, Barnes was still wallowing in liquor—and Romero and Brett had disappeared.

Now Barnes and Gorton returned together to France. After parting ways in Biarritz, Barnes traveled on by himself to San Sebastian, where he set out to place his life in order once again. He pondered that in life—even life during the dreamtime of the festival at Pamplona—there are, in truth, always consequences.

A few days later, when the telegram from Brett arrived at his hotel, he was not surprised. "Am rather in trouble," read her message.

As Barnes went to sign his return telegram, he found himself safe behind the usual mask of detachment; he berated himself for his foolish sentiments: "Send a girl off with one man. Introduce her to another to go off with him. Now go and bring her back. And sign the wire with love. That was it all right."

Barnes found Brett at a hotel. Just the day before, she had ordered Romero to leave. Romero had insisted that she let her hair grow out, act more "womanly," and let him care for her; and Brett, in turn, had confronted Romero with the reality of her independence, demanding that he behave less like a child and more like a man. She and Romero would have destroyed each other, she finally concluded: he wanted a worshipper and a dream; she wanted to be worshipped—and to be free.

Brett decided, in the end, to go back to Mike. But not before she and Barnes had a few drinks, enjoyed a nice dinner, toured Madrid—and shared one, last, tearful conversation.

. . . I could feel her crying. Shaking and crying. She wouldn't look up. I put my arms around her . . .

"Oh, Jake, we could have had such a damned good time together."

Ahead was a mounted policeman in khaki directing traffic. He raised his baton. The car slowed suddenly pressing Brett against me.

"Yes," I said. "Isn't it pretty to think so?"

Commentary:

"An absorbing, beautifully written and tenderly absurd, heart-breaking narrative . . ." *The New York Times* announced when *The Sun Also Rises* first appeared. " . . . A gripping story, told in lean, hard athletic prose . . . filled with that organic action which gives a compelling picture of character."

On one level, Hemingway's novel is a tale about unattainable love; on another level, it carries a theme of betrayal and infidelity. Written from Jake Barnes' point of view, from a newsman's perspective, the book is, in essence, a confession. Unable to consummate his love for Brett, Barnes introduces her first to Cohn—the intellectual—and then to Romero—the unadulterated, unworldly warrior—both of whom become surrogates for two different faces of himself. His motives are compulsive, and at first obscure; he acts at the expense of his friendship with Cohn and Montoya, and at the cost of his reputation as a man of honor in Pamplona. Throughout the novel, as Barnes lives out his life as a kind of genial stoic, wryly and heroically resigned to the wayward inflictions of fate and human perversity, the storyline eventually unmasks him as a human being caught in the same web of love, exploitation and betrayal as the rest of the protagonists. If Barnes had finished telling the story without finally acknowledging his own complicity in Brett's betrayals—and his own betrayals of Brett—the novel would have been little more than the memoirs of an eventful holiday spree. But at the end, Barnes resigns himself to his situation—not to a "perceived inadequacy," as today's therapeutic voices might soothe, but to a real and crucial incapacity. With ironic dignity he accepts both his own guilt and his own helplessness, and thus resumes the heroic pathos-filled role he was meant to play all along.

CRIME AND PUNISHMENT

by
Fedor Dostoevski
(1821 - 1881)

Type of work: Psychological fiction

Setting: Mid-nineteenth-century
St. Petersburg, Russia

Principal characters:
Raskolnikov, an impoverished, hand-
some, intelligent young student
Dounia, his sister
Svidrigailov, an abusive man, Dounia's
former employer
Sonia, a prostitute
Razumihin, Raskolnikov's friend
Porfiry, inspector of police

Commentary:

Dostoevski's novel deals with two major
themes: that of suffering for our sins, the kind
of suffering that leads to confession and
redemption; and the Ideal of the "extraordinary man." The work's main character,
Raskolnikov, is a sensitive student who, driven by poverty and intellectual pride, believes
he is above both moral and social laws. Torn
between his "extraordinary man" theory and
the mores that govern common men,
Raskolnikov alternately shifts in personality
back and forth between his intellect, compassion, and guilt. By suffering, he is ultimately
punished—and thus redeemed.

Story Overview:

Owing back rent on his cramped and
squalid room, Raskolnikov quietly slipped
past the landlady's door and exited the building. "With sinking heart and nervous tremor,"
he counted the steps to Alyona the pawnbroker's apartment. As a result of his destitute
condition, Raskolnikov dreamed of committing the perfect crime: to rob and murder
Alyona.

Stepping inside the shop, he pawned his
watch with her and carefully observed where
she kept the keys and money. His plan would
work, he knew it would. Upon leaving the
shop, however, his mind took a turn: "How
loathsome it all is!" he uttered. " . . . can I, can
I possibly . . . no, it's rubbish. How can such
an atrocious thing come into my head? Yes,
filthy above all . . . loathsome." But soon he
was able to convince himself that Alyona was
a blight on society, while he, an extraordinary
man, deserved more. Besides, he told himself,
he would use the money to help others, and
so his "one tiny crime would be wiped out by
thousands of good deeds."

Perhaps some of the money could be
used to help his sister Dounia. Earlier, he had
received a letter from his mother telling him
that his sister was engaged to Luzhin, who
had offered to marry Dounia without a
dowry. Raskolnikov was suspicious of the
arrangement from the beginning; surely

Luzhin intended to gain control over her, in
essence, buying his sister like a common prostitute. The situation reminded him of his
friend, Sonia, who, to support her family,
worked as a prostitute, selling herself to a
man she did not love.

Determined to follow through with his
plan, Raskolnikov hurried to Alyona's flat.
Once there, he watched nervously while the
old woman fumbled with the package he had
brought. Then, suddenly he struck her repeatedly with the blunt end of an axe. After gathering up all the money, keys and trinkets he
could find, he emerged from the bedroom—to
find Lizaveta, the woman's sister, staring in
horror at Alyona's body. Rushing at her,
Raskolnikov again raised his axe and opened
her skull with its sharp edge. After wiping the
blood from the axe and his hands,
Raskolnikov returned to his room. It was
there that weakness and "fear gained more
mastery over him"—and he slunk into a corner, ashamed of his fear. After all, his theory
of the extraordinary man condoned violence.

When the police knocked at his door to
collect on his back rent, Raskolnikov thought
they had come to arrest him for the murder.
For a moment, he contemplated confessing to
the murders then and there. Instead, as he listened to the police discuss the gory details at
the murder scene, he fainted—an act that
surely would make him a prime suspect.

Raskolnikov soon learned that two
painters had been arrested for the killings.
After hiding the stolen jewelry in the park, he
returned to his room, where he remained for
four days, feverish and deeply depressed.
During this time, Raskolnikov received several visits from his friend Razumihin, as well as
from the police and his family. When his
mother, Dounia, and Dounia's fiancee Luzhin
came to see him, he flew into a rage, bitterly
denouncing Luzhin and refusing to approve
the marriage of his sister to a "beggar" who
sought "complete control over her."

Raskolnikov, for the most part, only
wanted to be left alone, but he also felt a
strong compulsion to return to the scene of
the crime. Giving in to this urge, he met the
painters there and told them he would confess all. On the way to the police station, however, he witnessed an accident in which
Sonia's drunken father was run down and
killed by a cart. Immediately, he lost his
nerve.

It wasn't until several days after the
murders that chief inspector Porfiry began his
investigation. He wanted to interview all of
Alyona's clients. At the same time,
Raskolnikov, who was plagued by nightmares, once more walked to precinct head-

quarters to confess his guilt. Seeing the man's strangely tortured behavior and hearing his theory that, for a man of "lofty" genius like himself the end justified the means, Porfiry eyed Raskolnikov with great interest. The theory both intrigued and baffled the inspector, especially since Raskolnikov had secured an alibi for his whereabouts on the day of the murder.

The next day, Svidrigailov, who had formerly employed Dounia as a governess, arrived in St. Petersburg to see Dounia. The man reported that his deceased wife had left him a three-thousand-ruble inheritance, and he wanted Dounia to have it as a way to expiate his sins against her. Since, in the interim, Dounia had rejected Luzhin and turned her affections to Raskolnikov's friend Razumihin, Raskolnikov refused to permit Dounia to meet with Svidrigailov.

Meanwhile, Raskolnikov visited Sonia's house to scold her for being a prostitute. Sonia, a devout girl, explained that she had only stooped to the profession to support her family after her father had wasted all their money on liquor. Raskolnikov, suddenly frightened by his own atheistic views—and much impressed with Sonia's simple faith—now begged the sympathetic girl to read the Biblical account of the raising of Lazarus. After she did so, he dropped to the ground, kissed her foot, and cried, "I did not bow to you, I bowed to all the suffering of humanity." Then with eyes "glittering as though he were mad," he said, "I've come to you, we are both accursed, let us go our way together."

Feeling a deep love for Sonia, and now seeing their friendship was cemented for all time, he promised to tell her who had killed the pawnbroker and her sister. Raskolnikov then proceeded to confess. Svidrigailov, however, who rented the adjoining room, heard everything—and he looked forward with interest to learning more.

Now Raskolnikov, whose conscience increasingly tormented him, again met with Porfiry. The policeman intimated that he already knew Raskolnikov was the murderer, and he was about to "surprise" the student when they were interrupted by a painter who confessed to the murder.

Over the next few days, Raskolnikov began to see Sonia as his savior, who would resurrect his dead soul by acting as his confessor. He went to Sonia's flat and—with Svidrigailov's ear again pressed to her door—admitted to the killings. When Sonia asked why he had done it, his theory of the extraordinary man failed him. Instantly, he understood that in killing the two women he had destroyed himself; he keenly felt his guilt, for he had not murdered for money, nor to prove that he was superior to other men. Now it seemed as if everyone knew the truth about the murders—Sonia, Porfiry . . . and Svidrigailov.

Porfiry again brought Raskolnikov to the station. The painter, he informed Raskolnikov, had made a false confession as a way to suffer, and thus atone, for his own sins. Conceding that he admired the young intellectual, Porfiry accused Raskolnikov of being the murderer, and promised him a lesser sentence if he would plead insanity. He, being a patient man, would wait for Raskolnikov's complete confession.

On his way home, Raskolnikov met Svidrigailov, who again told Raskolnikov that he desired his sister. Raskolnikov coldly warned him that he would kill him if he did not leave Dounia alone. Aware now that Svidrigailov had overheard his admission of guilt, Raskolnikov reminded Svidrigailov that he was capable of carrying out his threat.

In the meantime, Svidrigailov managed to lure Dounia to his room. There, he informed her that her brother was a murderer and offered to protect him in exchange for her love. Dounia, however, did not believe him. Infuriated by her refusal to see the truth and craving to have her, Svidrigailov tried to rape her. "It is very hard to prove assault," he laughed. Breaking away from his grasp, Dounia withdrew a revolver from her pocket and fired, grazing her attacker's head.

Now convinced that Dounia would never return his love, Svidrigailov decided to give Sonia the 3000 rubles instead. Then, he went home, put the barrel of a revolver against his right temple, and pulled the trigger.

Dounia confronted Raskolnikov about the murders. She had come believe, she said, he was "a contemptible person, and ready to face suffering" for his crime. Raskolnikov, however, denied his guilt. Instead, he retorted angrily, "Crime? What crime? I killed a vile noxious insect, a pawnbroker." Eventually, Sonia, after pledging her undying devotion to him, managed to persuade him to turn himself in and begin to do penance for his sins.

On his way to the police station, Raskolnikov, now at peace, dropped to his knees at a crossroads and kissed the earth "with bliss and rapture"—finally, he was carrying his own cross back to God. When passersby mocked him, he almost lost his resolve. But, seeing Sonia in the distance, her protective gaze giving him strength, he walked into the station and announced, "It was I killed the old pawnbroker woman and her sister."

Judged temporarily insane, Raskolnikov was sentenced to serve eight years in a Siberian labor camp, indeed a light penalty for such a terrible crime. Two months after the trial, Dounia and Razumihin were married. For her part, Sonia followed Raskolnikov to Siberia to support him and aid in his recovery, staying in a nearby village. In Raskolnikov's suffering, Sonia witnessed "his gradual regeneration, his initiation into a new unknown life."

THE CATCHER IN THE RYE

by J.D. Salinger, Bantam Books, Inc., New York, N.Y., 1945

Type of work: Psychological journey

Setting: New York City; the near future, 1949-1950

Principal characters:
Holden Caulfield, a disturbed and sensitive adolescent
Phoebe Caulfield, his ten-year-old younger sister
Sally Hayes, his girlfriend

Story Overview:

Unlike his high-school classmates, who were already dreaming of solid careers as businessmen and professionals, Holden Caulfield had turned his soul loose to wander through quiet lands of its own. "You know that song," he would say, "'If a body catch a body comin' through the rye'? . . . I keep picturing all these little kids playing some game in this big field of rye and all. Thousands of little kids, and nobody's around—nobody big, I mean—except me. And I'm standing on the edge of some crazy cliff. What I have to do, I have to catch everybody if they start to go over the cliff—I mean if they're running and they don't look where they're going I have to come out from somewhere and catch them. That's all I'd do all day. I'd just be the catcher in the rye and all. I know it's crazy, but that's the only thing I'd really like to be. I know it's crazy." Crazy, indeed: Holden was telling his story from behind the walls of a mental hospital.

In December of 1949, Holden was expelled from the Pencey Prep School for Boys. He had failed four out of his five classes, and he refused to apply himself at all to his studies. This was the fourth academy Holden had flunked out of. On the eve of his departure, Holden went to see his history teacher, Mr. Spencer, who had asked him to stop in for goodbyes. He found Mr. Spencer smelling of Vicks Nose Drops, and wearing a ratty bathrobe that opened to reveal his "bumpy old chest." Almost immediately the old man launched into a farewell lecture. "Life is a game, boy," he declared. "Life is a game that one plays according to the rules." Yes, Holden was failing in school—and in life, said Mr. Spencer—because he didn't play according to the rules.

After suffering through this visit, Holden returned to his dormitory. His roommate, Stradlater, who was prepping himself for a date, asked him for a last favor: could he come up with a descriptive essay about a "house" or a "room" for Stradlater's English assignment? Holden agreed; but after Stradlater left, he couldn't think of any house or room to write about—so he scrawled some lines about his brother's baseball mitt.

My brother Allie had this left-handed fielder's mitt. He was left-handed. The thing that was descriptive about it, though, was that he had poems written all over the fingers and the pocket and everywhere. In green ink. He wrote them on it so that he'd have something to read when he was in the field and

nobody was up at bat. He's dead now. He got leukemia and died when we were up in Maine, on July 18, 1946.

When Stradlater returned from his date and read Holden's essay, he went crazy. "For Chrissake, Holden," he shouted. "This is about a goddam baseball glove . . . You don't do one damn thing the way you're supposed to . . ."

This was the second verbal assault Holden had endured that night; he struck out at Stradlater with his fist. But when the much stronger Stradlater responded, Holden was left beaten. Humiliated, his nose bleeding, he gathered his things and ventured into the December night.

Since Holden had not yet told his parents about his expulsion, he was not expected home for Christmas vacation until Wednesday. So he took a train to the west side of New York and checked into the Edmont Hotel. On his way up in the elevator, he was informed by the attendant—who doubled as a pimp—that for only five dollars he could arrange to have a girl sent to his room. Feeling as if he were in some remote, lonesome country, Holden acquiesced. When the prostitute appeared, however, he changed his mind. He handed her the $5.00 and sent her away. But a few minutes later the girl showed up at his door again, with her pimp in tow. The pimp demanded another $5.00. When Holden refused to pay any more, the pimp barged into the room and pummeled him. Afterward, Holden climbed into bed and pondered awhile: "I felt like jumping out the window. I probably would've done it, too, if I'd been sure somebody'd cover me up as soon as I landed. I didn't want a bunch of stupid rubbernecks looking at me when I was all gory." Then after a few more dead-sober thoughts about this, Holden turned over to plan what he would do for the next few days.

The following morning, Holden checked out of the Edmont and called his girl, Sally Hayes, to ask her if she wanted to see a movie. O.K., said Sally, she would meet him later that afternoon.

After that, he wandered absently through the streets. Suddenly he heard a child singing. "If a body catch a body coming through the rye," crooned the little boy. And at that moment, at that very instant, Holden felt happy. The song reminded him of his mission, of what he had always wanted to be: the catcher in the rye.

Stepping cheerfully, Holden proceeded down the street to a museum, one he hadn't been to since he was a young child. There, standing once more in front of the familiar glass cases, the pleasant musty odor returning to his lungs, he noticed that everything was positioned exactly the way he remembered it. In all those years, nothing had changed. The best thing about a museum was that it always stayed the same, he thought: "Certain things they should stay the way they are. You ought to be able to stick them in one of those big glass cases and just leave them alone. I know that's impossible, but it's too bad anyway."

Reluctantly, Holden exited the museum.

After the movie that afternoon, Sally and Holden went ice skating. As he gazed out over the rink, Holden couldn't help but think how phony everyone was. Sally, the movie actors, the theatergoers, the skaters, all the students at his four schools—they were nothing but phonies. Practically the only people who weren't phony, he concluded, were himself, his ten-year-old sister, Phoebe, and his dead brother Allie. He had let himself flunk out of school. It was all a fraud; he refused to live by Mr. Spencer's rules. After all, the rules must be phony, too.

But when Holden tried to share this news with Sally, she was bewildered. They argued. Finally Holden rushed out of the ice rink, leaving Sally behind, crying. He meandered for awhile; then he found a bar and got drunk.

Towards the end of the evening, still at the bar, he staggered into the men's room and initiated an argument with a stranger. The man punched him until he passed out and hit the floor. When he came to, he felt an overwhelming urge to see his little sister. Not wanting his parents to know he was home already—that he'd been kicked out of his fourth school—he took a cab to his family's apartment building and crept through the dark toward Phoebe's bedroom.

When he woke her up, Phoebe was overjoyed to see Holden. Their parents weren't home, she said; they wouldn't be returning until late that night. "Daddy's going to kill you," the girl erupted when Holden told her that he'd been expelled. No, that would never happen, Holden said, because he was going to move West and live in a cabin all by himself. He had only come home to say good-bye to Phoebe. But Phoebe finally made her brother promise to stay in New York, at least until Friday, so he could see her school play. Finally, with $8.65 borrowed out of his sister's Christmas gift fund, Holden made his way out of the apartment.

Unable to find a room for the night, Holden showed up at the home of one of his old teachers, Mr. Antolini. Mr. Antolini seemed happy to see him, and invited him to stay the night. But then, as they drank coffee together, Antolini started in just like Mr. Spencer before him, with a lecture. Holden was "headed for a big fall," he warned. Then, in a kinder voice, he advised: "You'll find that you're not the first person who was ever confused and frightened and even sickened by human behavior. You're by no means alone on that score, you'll be excited and stimulated to know. Many, many men have been just as troubled morally and spiritually as you are right now. Happily, some of them kept records of their troubles. You'll learn from them—if you want. Just as someday, if you have something to offer, someone will learn something from you."

Holden had suddenly grown very tired; could he go to sleep now? Bedded down on Antolini's couch, Holden nodded off quickly. But he did not sleep long. He was awakened by a hand stroking his head. There, sitting next to him on the floor was his teacher: Mr. Antolini was apparently making a pass. Holden got up

and bolted out of the house; for the rest of the night he sat up in a bus station.

In the morning Holden walked to Phoebe's school and asked an office attendant to deliver a note to her explaining that he couldn't wait until Friday to move West after all. He was leaving today, and he wanted Phoebe to meet him in front of the museum during her lunch time to say good-bye.

When his sister showed up at the museum—twenty minutes late—she was carrying a suitcase. "I'm going with you," she announced firmly. "No, you're not," retorted Holden. Finally, after a tearful argument, brother and sister decided to spend the rest of the day in the park. Holden could not keep his eyes off Phoebe. He loved her. How idyllic, how perfect, how beautiful she was, riding around and around in the park on the carousel.

When D.B., Holden's older brother, came to visit him in the mental hospital, he asked Holden what he thought about all the stuff that had happened. Holden didn't know how to respond. "If you want to know the truth," he said after a minute's thought, "I don't know what I think about it."

For over six months the puzzle of Holden's life had remained unresolved. Every now and then there was talk of his being reinstated in school. The question was, could he apply himself? Could he survive? Could he catch himself? No one seemed to know; no one seemed to understand. Even Holden himself just didn't understand.

Commentary:

Almost everyone who has weathered adolescence can, to some extent, relate to Holden Caulfield. Though the particulars of Holden's life are unique, his experience is universal. "Many, many men have been just as troubled morally and spiritually as you are right now," says Mr. Antolini. "You'll learn from them . . . Just as someday, if you have something to offer, someone will learn something from you."

Holden, however, does not want to teach anybody anything. Instead, he wants to prevent people from having to suffer the way he has. Though he has failed in salvaging his own life, he nevertheless yearns to be the Catcher in the Rye, the savior who can keep innocent, playful children from falling off the cliff of adolescence, who can keep their lives as pure and unchanged as a museum exhibit. But heroic as these intentions are, Holden has burdened himself with an impossible responsibility. Eventually, every child must fall off the cliff; and there is no catcher in the rye.

Holden will never be able to prevent the moment in childhood—and the inevitable moments throughout life—when anyone who ventures out to play in the rye field finds himself suddenly staring through an unmasked sky at the gray gods below. But perhaps—as Mr. Antolini suggests just before he himself snatches away Holden's last slice of ground—perhaps in telling his story, Holden will be able to teach somebody else something useful about the encounter.

THE AWAKENING

by
Kate Chopin
(1850 - 1904)

Type of work: Psychological passage

Setting: The New Orleans French Quarter and the Gulf Islands; early 1900s

Principal characters:
Edna Pontellier, a young married woman with two small children
Leonce Pontellier, Edna's husband, a Creole businessman
Robert Lebrun, an entertaining young bachelor
Adele Ratignolle, Edna's graceful, motherly friend
Mademoiselle Reisz, a temperamental little woman, another of Edna's confidants, and a brilliant pianist
Alcee Arobin, a suave playboy
Dr. Mandelet, the Pontelliers' semi-retired physician friend

Story Overview:

The Pontelliers vacationed with their children at the Lebrun estate on Grand Isle, a favorite destination among the upper-class Creole community. After his reading of the paper was interrupted by the constant screeching of Madame Lebrun's parrot, Leonce Pontellier decided to take a walk. Outside, he encountered his strikingly attractive wife Edna, and her friend Robert Lebrun, both fresh from swimming in the Gulf.

Robert's mother owned the Lebrun resort, and every summer, Robert would choose one of the female guests for his special attentions, to help her "feel waited on" during her stay. This summer, Robert had focused on Edna. They enjoyed swimming together, and Edna had come to discover that the sea led her to "wander in the abysses of solitude," where she could reflect on her "position in the universe." These feelings set off a chain of events that would soon change Edna forever.

One afternoon Edna sat on the beach with her friend Adele Ratignolle, a matronly Creole, and shared with Adele some of her past romances. A series of distant infatuations had preceded her marriage to Leonce. Leonce's absolute devotion to her, she mused—along with her family's disapproval of his Catholic upbringing—had been her main motives for marrying him. But now she confessed to a certain, unexplained restlessness.

Later in the day, Adele asked Robert to stay away from Edna, fearing that in her state of discontent, Edna might take his flirtations seriously.

A few evenings later, Robert suggested that the guests take a swim. Edna, typically afraid to be alone in the water, ventured far out, until it seemed that she had come to a point "where no woman had swum before." But when she returned to shore to tell her husband about her daring act, he condescendingly replied that he had been watching her the whole time; she really wasn't that far out. Edna, perturbed by this slight, returned to her cottage—followed closely by Robert. After sitting a while in silence together on the porch, Robert left. It was then that Edna recognized her latent feelings of desire for him.

The next morning, Robert and Edna, along with several other guests, traveled across the bay to a neighboring island. There, they attended Mass at a quaint little Gothic chapel. During the service, a feeling of stifling oppression overtook Edna. Hurrying outside to gain her composure, she found herself followed by Robert. Together they strolled to a nearby cottage, where Edna calmed herself, finally falling into restful sleep. When she awoke, Robert was sitting outside under an orange tree. "How many years have I slept?" asked Edna, joining him. "The whole island seems changed." Robert grinned and told her she had slept precisely one hundred years, but that he had remained there the whole time to guard her slumber.

As they sailed back to Grand Isle, Edna realized that this summer had been different from any other in her life. She—her entire inner self—was changing. She was at last awakening to a sense of her own individuality.

As the guests assembled for dinner one evening, Robert abruptly announced that he was leaving for Mexico the next morning—"to meet a friend," he claimed. But then glancing over at Edna's saddened face, he knew that she could see through his excuse—his feelings for Edna had grown beyond friendship, and he was leaving out of a sense of propriety.

As the end of summer approached, the Pontelliers returned to their home on Esplanade Street, an exclusive section of the New Orleans French Quarter. Though Mr. Pontellier was in many ways an attentive husband, he was also deeply disturbed when Edna didn't "keep up appearances." One Tuesday, the day when the Pontelliers normally received visitors, Edna disappeared without telling a soul where she was going. Then, when she eventually returned, she was unrepentant, which doubly annoyed Leonce.

As the days passed, Edna spent more and more time alone. She wandered, allowing her whimsical moods to overtake her, tired of the day-to-day expectations placed on her. One day, in her melancholy, she decided to visit Mademoiselle Reisz, who had been a guest at Grand Isle that summer. Mademoiselle Reisz had enthralled the resort's guests with her beautiful piano melodies. Now she played again for the pensive and brooding Edna, but the music only intensified Edna's melancholy.

Meanwhile, Leonce visited Dr. Mandelet, a semi-retired physician and friend of the family, to inquire if it was possible that Edna's mind had become slightly unbalanced. He told the Doctor that not only had his wife completely abandoned her own reception day, but she had forgone many other domestic responsibilities—and now she even refused to attend her sister's wedding. Dr. Mandelet assured Edna's husband that the one thing women could be counted on was moodiness; and, besides, Edna's female sensibilities had always been exaggerated. Leonce must patiently wait for her to pass through this rebellious phase.

On the eve of Leonce's departure for a business trip, Dr. Mandelet dined with the Pontelliers. While he noticed some subtle changes in Edna, she did not appear to be nearly as unbalanced as Leonce had implied. In fact, the doctor saw a rather enchanting transformation; Edna had changed from a listless young wife tied down to society's conventions into a woman radiating with life and self-awareness.

The next day, Leonce left on his business trip. Edna's children had gone with their grandmother to visit her farm, leaving their mother alone. Instead of feeling bereft, however, Edna found the solitude refreshing.

A few days later, Alcee Arobin, a suave, fashionable man about town, and his middle-aged admirer, Mrs. Highcamp, came to invite Edna to the races. Edna had met Alcee previously at her father's stables. Following an uninteresting dinner with the Highcamps, Alcee took Edna home. He would not leave until she promised to attend the races with him again. It was not Edna's person that initially excited Alcee's interest, however; rather it was her passion for sport—her knowledge of horses was better than most men's.

As time progressed, Edna increasingly sought Mademoiselle Reisz's company in an attempt to quiet her own inner turmoil. During one visit, Edna confided that she was planning to move into a four-bedroom cottage around the corner from her husband's home. She must live in her own house, she contended; she had taken up a resolve never to belong to anyone other than herself. When Mademoiselle told her that Robert was coming into the city soon, Edna confessed her love for Lebrun. Her sympathetic friend could only warn in metaphor: "The bird that would soar above the plain of tradition and prejudice must have strong wings."

Edna transfered to her new home only those possessions which she had acquired apart from her husband's resources. Then she set out to host a dinner to celebrate her new-found freedom, inviting a select group: the Highcamps, Madame Lebrun and her son, Victor, the Ratignolles, and Alcee—who had quickly gained Edna's confidence and familiarity. The breathtaking spread of food, on a table covered in pale yellow satin, lace, fine crystal and yellow roses, was matched in majesty only by Edna herself, radiant in her gold satin gown and sparkling diamonds. Today was her twenty-ninth birthday.

While the evening was alive with laughter, Edna could not help feeling despondent—her beloved Robert was not among them. After the other guests had departed, Alcee remained. And, though he meant nothing to her, his gentle caresses soon acted as a narcotic.

Edna often frequented a lush garden cafe in the suburbs. Late one afternoon as she was eating a light meal and paging through a book, Edna glanced up—and there stood Robert Lebrun. Both were a bit shocked at meeting so unexpectedly, but Edna managed to persuade Robert to join her. Why had he been avoiding her, she asked innocently—and cruelly, for she knew the reasons. Still, Robert accompanied Edna home. As he sat in a chair by the window, Edna leaned over and kissed him. He followed her lead, drawing her close and holding her hand in his. In Mexico, where he had gone to escape her presence, he admitted that he had dreamed of her becoming his wife. "Your wife!" Edna blurted out, breaking from his embrace in shock and disappointment. Then, suddenly, it dawned on her. Robert was no different than all the rest. He was no "free spirit"! He was as tied to convention as Leonce. She would never be herself; Leonce, Robert, family obligations, social duties . . . they would all somehow see to that.

Just then Adele's maid arrived with a message begging Edna to come quickly. Weeks before, Edna had promised that she would stay with Adele during the birth of her baby. Before leaving, Edna pled with Robert to wait for her. Then he kissed her with great passion.

Although Edna stood valiantly by Adele's side for as long as she could bear it, the birth process sickened her, and eventually she was forced to return home. But when she arrived, all she found was a note from Robert: "Goodbye, because I love you."

With no place else to go, Edna returned to the Lebrun's Grand Isle resort. As she walked toward the sea, now chilled by late-season weather, her mind was on her children. She removed her swimsuit as she entered the water, standing under the lowering sun like a newborn creature. The water was cold and deep, but she reached out with long, sweeping stokes. "The touch of the sea is sensuous, enfolding the body in its soft, close embrace." Robert did not understand. Perhaps Dr. Mandelet would have . . . but it was too late.

The shore was far behind her now, and she did not look back. Awake to reality, she now only wanted to drift into slumber. At last she would find her freedom.

Commentary:

At the age of twenty, Kate O'Flaherty moved from St. Louis to New Orleans to marry Oscar Chopin, a French Creole. After the failure of his cotton business, followed by his death in 1884, she was left alone to raise her children and forge a literary career.

The Awakening was Chopin's major work but, because of its sexual and feminist overtones, it was not accepted by the literary community until fifty years after its publication. Today it is viewed as an important piece of regional American fiction.

Edna had married into a social structure that valued strictly defined roles. Her husband was the provider, the community icon who possessed much property, including a devoted wife and two children.

The sea is a symbol of freedom from this proprietorship. It is in the sea where Edna's sensuousness is first awakened and where she initially asserts her independence. And since she was introduced to the sea by Robert Lebrun, she associates him with her struggle for freedom. However, when Robert proposes marriage, Edna cannot understand how the man who guided her toward autonomy now wishes to keep her in bondage.

As Edna strives toward becoming an individual by breaking social conventions, she still finds herself bound by familial obligations. She attempts to integrate her "awakening" into her life, but fails. Rather than revert to the oppressive world from which she has escaped, however, she again seeks the sea—and with it the ultimate liberation.

THE SHORT STORIES OF ISAK DINESEN

(taken from *Seven Gothic Tales*, H. Smith and R. Haas Publishers, New York, N.Y., 1961)

Dinesen's romantic-satirical short stories, usually set in 19th-century Denmark and France, deal primarily with the aristocracy from which Baroness Karen Blixen (Dinesen's real name) had sprung. But her fictional bluebloods--perhaps because they are drawn from her own intimate background--are no glittering celebrities, inevitably they prove to be austere, fully grounded people with more than their share of psychological hang-ups.

The Deluge at Norderney

While vacationing at Norderney, Denmark, a coastal spa, a group of Northern Europe's most privileged and colorful citizens suffered a calamity. "The sea broke the dikes in two places and washed through them," and the vacationers suddenly found themselves surrounded by salt water. The waters rose swiftly, and soon they feared for their lives.

Among the stranded group was the eccentric Miss Malin Nat-og-Dag. Although an old lady of the strictest virtue, she believed herself to be "one of the great female sinners of her time." This elderly virgin was accompanied by her beautiful sixteen-year-old goddaughter, the Countess Calypso, and by Jonathan Maersk, a quiet young gentleman who had sought a cure for melancholia at the spa.

Much to everyone's relief, they were soon rescued--and their rescuer, who appeared in a small boat with his head bandaged from an injury incurred in an earlier rescue--was none other than Cardinal Hamilcar, a man renowned throughout the Continent for his noble blood and "visionary gift." In fact, many people believed the Cardinal to be a genuine guardian angel.

But no sooner had this paragon snatched the three genteel holiday makers from the jaws of death than the group confronted yet another casualty of the flood's devastation: a family trapped in a hayloft. Generously, the Cardinal and his companions--knowing the boat could not bear the weight of additional passengers--exchanged places with the exhausted family members--even as the flood waters continued to rise around them.

Lighting a lantern in a corner of the dark loft, the four began to review their lives. The Cardinal started off, pondering that, perhaps because of his own privileged childhood, he often thought the Lord visited men with disaster so that they might be humble in His presence. For her part, Miss Malin explained that she had once considered being a nun--but as a Protestant, she could only content herself with the pious delusion that she had committed adultery with a multitude of young men. Indeed, she "carried the weight" of her imagined sins "like an athlete."

Finally, young Jonathan entered the conversation. As a child he had revelled in nature, but by and by he had forsaken the countryside for Copenhagen, where he had become the protege of an illustrious Count. He had felt honored by this arrangement--until, to his astonishment, he learned that the Count was actually his own father! Immediately, his admiration and gratitude were washed away in a flood of resentment and criticism. He began to disdain the Count as "a man of fashion" whom God could not tolerate. Finally, to free himself from the Count's attentions, he had fled to Norderney for the salt water, which he was certain was "the cure for everything."

"I want you for Calypso," Miss Malin unexpectedly announced. Her unfortunate goddaughter had been raised by an uncle, also a count, who "disliked and mistrusted everything female." Filling his house with "lovely young boys," the Count had ensured that his niece had learned to despise everything feminine. So deep was the girl's disparagement of her own sex that she had almost been driven to cut off her hair and breasts. Instead, she had happened upon a painting of nymphs, and showcases filled with her great-grandmother's magnificent clothing. Suddenly she saw her femininity as a wondrous gift. Forsaking her uncle's home, she had gone to live with Miss Malin.

"I should not have minded dying to serve this lady," Jonathan said after hearing the story. Giving the couple his blessing, the Cardinal proceeded to marry Calypso and Jonathan right there in the hay loft, whereupon the exhausted newlyweds fell fast asleep.

The Cardinal now declared that it was time to remove his bandages. "But will it not hurt you?" Miss Malin asked. Indeed it would not, he said, because the stains on the cloth were not actually from his own blood: he had killed another man with a beam; couldn't Miss Malin "recognize the blue blood of Cardinal Hamilcar" on the bandages? Dazed by the revelation, Miss Malin demanded, "Who are you?" The man confessed that he had been the Cardinal's servant. But in killing his master, he had transformed himself into a hero who had saved the lives of others.

After hearing this account, the eccentric old woman stoically turned to him and said, "Kiss me"--and the impostor took her in his arms. As "they felt the heavy boards gently rocking, floating upon the waters," the dawn broke--and the water continued to rise.

The Old Chevalier

As a young man in Paris, Baron Von Brackel had fallen under the spell of a beautiful married woman with "an unrivaled energy." Unluckily for the Baron, however, most of her energy was funnelled into tormenting young men, frequently inflicting upon the Baron outbursts of jealousy and rage.

Interestingly, these feral displays of jealousy came in direct response to the Baron's admiration for the woman's husband, "as if she herself had been a young man who envied him his triumphs." She stole young men's hearts "to pile up more conquests than the man with whom she was in love." Finally, after hearing more of the Baron's praise of her husband than she could tolerate, she had poisoned the Baron's coffee. But before ingesting much of the deadly liquid, he had recognized the "mortal, insipid taste" and dropped the cup. Regaining his composure after a few moments, he had marched out of her life.

In utter despair, the young Baron now sat down on a bench along the avenue near the woman's house. The rain fell in torrents, but he was too numb to mind. After awhile, he noticed the approach of a drunken young girl with "radiant eyes like stars" and wearing "a black hat with ostrich feathers drooping sadly" in the downpour. When he got up and started walking toward home, the girl followed him.

The Baron invited the girl, who called herself Nathalie, to join him for champagne. Sitting by a roaring fire in his apartment, she drank avidly, still soaking wet in her black attire. "You must take off your clothes and get warm," her host insisted, and he lost no time in helping to free the acquiescent Nathalie of her bedraggled garments. He stared in wonder at her nakedness: "All her body shone in the light, delicately rounded and smooth as marble. One straight line ran through it from neck to ankle, as though the heaven aspiring column of a young tree." Delighted by Nathalie's "wild spirit," the young Baron spent the evening with his companion, drinking, dining, and playing the guitar. He rejoiced in discovering a new love; never before had he experienced such a "feeling of freedom and security." After a night of exquisite pleasures, the Baron fell asleep.

Hours later, he awoke with a start. Nathalie stood before him, again dressed in her shabby black dress. "And you will give me twenty francs, will you not?" she demanded. Dazed to discover that their night of love had been nothing more than business, he handed her the money. After bestowing on him "an encouraging, consoling glance such as a sister might give a brother," Nathalie disappeared. All at once, the Baron experienced a "sensation of suffocation...of being buried alive." He dressed hurriedly and rushed out to the street. There was no trace of the girl. Afterward, he thought regularly of Nathalie--and feared for her.

Fifteen years later, Baron Von Brackel found himself struck with the strange sensation that, soon, he would meet again with Nathalie. Visiting an artist's studio one day, the Baron spotted the "skull of a young woman," a skull possessing "a rare beauty." Taking it in his hands, he marvelled at how "pure" and "safe" the bone felt--and had the eerie sensation of being transported back to that rainy night so many years before. But to the Baron's disappointment, the artist claimed to know nothing whatsoever about the history of the wondrously beautiful skull.

The Supper at Elsinore

One day, two old women returned to their childhood home. As girls, Eliza and Fanny De Coninck had been lovely, pampered belles. However, they had rejected all their numerous suitors; each paled in comparison to their younger brother, Morten, the object of their awe.

Lacking the general "fineness of feature" of his sisters, Morten nonetheless possessed one remarkable asset: an "extraordinarily noble and serene forehead" which drew the admiration of the citizens of Elsinore as if it had been "the diamond tiara of an emperor, or the halo of a saint."

During the Napoleonic Wars, Morten's uncle had outfitted him with a boat so that the young man could sail off to assist the Emperor's cause. To no one's surprise, Morten had returned a hero, after which he decided that he had "gathered his laurels and could now marry and settle down..." After choosing a bride, he left Eliza and Fanny to oversee the details of the nuptials.

But on the day of the wedding, Morten disappeared. His sisters suffered horribly; enduring a "fatal melancholy," they lived ever since only for news of Morten. Rumors abounded: Morten was said to have gone to America to fight, to have settled in the Antilles as a "slave owner," to have become a pirate. To escape the worst of the gossip, the sisters moved to Copenhagen. But, understandably, when they had learned from their old housekeeper, Madam Baek, of Morten's return to Elsinore, they left Copenhagen at once.

Madam Baek had warned them that there was a slight problem: Morten was no longer a man, but a ghost. Still, the sisters set off; now, arriving at their childhood home, they were filled with nostalgia, entering the dining room and taking their places at the table as if they were children waiting for their brother to come home after a day at play.

Morten finally did appear. They found it rather unsettling to note that he had not aged as much as they had and that he wore shabby clothes. "All in all," though, they found their bother's countenance "as quiet, considerate, and dignified as it had always been."

"Good evening, little sisters," he greeted them warmly. "I come from hell." The sisters, still undaunted, informed Morten that because of the bad name he had given the De Coninck family, they had been left "old maids." To this, he boasted breezily, "I had five wives." Furthermore, he said, he had become a pirate-- and a pirate without regrets. Eliza felt gratified to learn that Morten had named his ship, *La Belle Eliza*, after her. Yes, he had relished his life as a buccaneer, but it had not ended well: he had been hanged in Havana.

Suddenly the clock began to strike twelve; it was midnight. Morten vanished. "Brother! Stay! Listen!" Fanny cried. "Take me with you!" But, he did not return. Smiling and motionless, her sister sat, still marvelling over *La Belle Eliza*.

Commentary:

Many of Dinesen's stories pivot around the theme of purity: virginal "maiden ladies" tormented by their imagined sins or spiritually tethered to their imagined ideals; other characters only able to feel "pure" and "safe" when the object of their desire is lifeless and no longer threatening. Perhaps the heart of Dinesen's message is that we are all sullied in one way or another by those undeviating characteristics that make up humankind's flawed legacy.

THE SHORT STORIES OF ISAAC BASHEVIS SINGER

(taken from *A Crown of Feathers and Other Stories*, Farrar, Straus and Giroux, New York, N.Y., 1973)

In the introduction to his stories, Isaac Bashevis Singer—referring to Polish-Jew victims of the Holocaust—writes, "The vandals who murdered millions of these people have destroyed a treasure, an individuality that no literature dare try to bring back." Any attempt to restore time-honored Yiddish folkloric traditions, Singer implies, would not only be an impossible task, but, in a strictly moral sense, it would be a profanation as well: it would be tantamount to denying, to desecrating the memory, the history, and the culture of a people who, having been systematically exterminated, are now permanently and forever lost to us.

A Crown of Feathers

Akhsa, who had been orphaned at birth and raised by her grandparents, was now faced with the consequences of rejecting the match that had been chosen for her. Not long after her grandmother's death, Akhsa's grandfather had arranged her marriage to a Talmudic scholar named Zemach. On the day of the wedding, however, Akhsa had refused to go through with it, shaming both her grandfather and her prospective groom. Mortified by her disobedience, Akhsa's grandfather soon died, and once again she was left alone.

One night, while she lay on her bed mourning and wondering what she would now do with her life, her grandfather's ghost appeared to her, asking that she to redeem herself and marry Zemach. But to complicate matters, the ghost of Akhsa's grandmother also appeared; the grandmother, however, had come to tell Akhsa that she should follow her heart—and, moreover, that she should abandon Judaism and become a Christian.

Confused, Akhsa wrestled with the uncertainty of which spirit was telling the truth. As a sign, Akhsa's grandmother told her that when she awoke the next morning she would find a crown of feathers inside her pillow. And when Akhsa went to look, the crown was there, just as her grandmother had said it would be. The next day, she renounced Judaism and converted to Christianity.

When the period of mourning her grandfather's death was over, Akhsa decided to marry a much older nobleman. It was, unfortunately, a horrible match. Soon after their wedding her husband began to drink heavily and carouse with peasant women.

Then Akhsa's husband died. Once again she was left alone; and once again, as she wondered what she should do next, the ghost of her grandfather appeared. "Find the man you shamed," he told her. "Become a Jewish daughter."

This time she obeyed the ghost. After a three-month search, she found Zemach in the village of Izbica. At first, Zemach scorned Akhsa, refusing even to look at her. But the village elders and teachers, moved by Akhsa's new humility, persuaded Zemach to relent and marry her.

Her marriage to Zemach was no easier than her first. Zemach's sense of guilt required that they expiate their sins: he saw to it that he and his wife fasted and endured much hardship. One summer afternoon, after a day-long fast, Akhsa walked down to the river to gather sorrel leaves for their evening meal. Sitting down to rest, she fell asleep. When she awoke, night had fallen, and, peering into the darkness, she could see that her grandfather's ghost had come again. "My daughter," he said, "your ordeal is over. We are waiting for you—I, Grandmother, all who love you. Holy angels will come to meet you." She returned home exhausted and confused, and when Zemach began to berate her for being late, she collapsed on the floor.

Because Akhsa was dying, Zemach went to find a doctor. While he was gone, she drowsed, hoping to see a sign, hoping that now "the pure truth [would be] revealed." When she awoke, she cut open her pillow, and inside she found a crown of feathers. Braided into it were the four letters of God's name—Yud, Hai, Vov, Hai. "Is *this* crown more of a revelation than the other?" Akhsa wondered. She received no answer, however, and at dawn she died.

The women of the Burial Society were curious as to why Akhsa had cut open her pillow. "[If] there is such a thing as truth," one of them mused, "it is as intricate and hidden as a crown of feathers."

The Son from America

Berl and Berlcha lived a modest life in the tiny village of Lentshin, Poland. Years earlier, their son Samuel had gone to America, and for a long time he had been sending his parents monthly money orders. Three times a year, then, Berl and Berlcha would walk to Zakroczym and cash the money orders—but they never seemed to spend the money. Why should they? They had a half acre of ground, a goat, and some chickens that "provided most of their needs"; and what Berlcha earned selling chickens and eggs gave them enough to buy the flour for their bread.

One Friday morning, while Berlcha was kneading dough for the Sabbath loaves, a young nobleman appeared at the door. "Mother, it's me, your son Samuel—Sam," the nobleman said. Apparently, Samuel had sent a cable to tel them he was coming, but his parents had not yet received it. He hugged Berlcha and kissed her on both cheeks, and when Berl entered, he greeted his father the same way. Neighbors who heard the good news came to welcome Samuel home and to help his parents prepare for the Sabbath.

Following Sabbath services in the synagogue, Samuel, who could not see any material difference that his money had made in his parents' lives, turned to his father. "Why didn't you spend it?" he asked. "On what?" Berl replied simply. "Thank God, we have everything."

The next night, Samuel walked through the little village, fingering the checkbook and the letters of credit he had in his jacket pocket. He had come home with charity in his heart; he had brought much of his own money, as well as funds from the Lentshin Society of New York, which had organized a ball to benefit the village. But Lentshin did not need *this* charity. At home, Berlcha sang a rhyme her grandmother had taught her: "Thy holy sheep / In mercy keep / In Torah and good deeds; / Provide for all their needs, / Shoes, clothes, and bread / And the Messiah's tread."

The Cabalist of East Broadway

A young writer—as he strolled through the streets of his old New York neighborhood—reflected on how everything had changed. The only constants he could see were the Yiddish newspaper, which was still published on East Broadway, and Joel Yabloner, who remained just as toothless, ragged, and disheveled as he had always been. Yabloner was a curious case. Although he had written extensively on Jewish mysticism and translated several important works, his labors seemed not to have made a difference in his life: he had remained a poor scholar.

Years passed, and the next time the young man saw Yabloner, they were both in Tel Aviv. Yabloner, now fresh-faced, with a new set of teeth and dressed immaculately, was giving a lecture on the *Cabala*. In the years since he had emigrated to Israel, he had somehow made good.

After the lecture, the writer asked Yabloner why he had not emigrated sooner. Yabloner's answer was as oblique and mysterious as the *Cabala* itself: "Man," he said, "does not live according to reason."

Several more years passed. One day, after delivering a manuscript to the East Broadway Yiddish newspaper, the writer happened to stop in at the old neighborhood cafeteria; and there—looking once again emaciated, wrinkled, shabby, and toothless—sat Joel Yabloner. Something in the old man's face told him that Yabloner did not want to be disturbed.

Then, just a few weeks later, the writer saw Yabloner's name in the obituaries. Wondering what had happened, he remembered Yabloner's last words to him in Tel Aviv: "Man does not live according to reason."

Grandfather and Grandson

Reb Mordecai Meir, a pious Hasidic Jew, had essentially divorced himself from the world. With the exception of his sick wife, he did not associate with women; he did not read the Yiddish newspapers; and though he owned a small shop, he had long left the care of it to others—he could not even have said just what it sold. Moreover, even though he had lived his entire life in Warsaw, he would have been hard pressed to find his way around the city. In short, Reb Meir's entire day was taken up entirely with study, prayer, and worship. Meir was convinced that "At every turn the Evil Spirit lay in wait,"

and "there was only one sure way to defeat him: with Torah, prayer, Hasidism."

Understandably, Meir was irritated when his grandson, Fulie, came to live with him. Fulie was an "enlightened" Jew, which is to say he had rejected Hasidism. To Reb Meir, his grandson was a Jew in name only. Fulie was a radical; he talked only of the Capitalist oppressors, the revolt of the proletariat, and religion as the opiate of the masses. Meir thought Fulie's talk of ushering in a worker's paradise was misguided. "Except the Lord build a house," he said, "they labor in vain that build it."

Yet Fulie *was* his grandson, and it would have been a sin to turn him away. Moreover, at first Meir thought he might hope to win Fulie back to Hasidic ways. It soon became clear, however, that this would never happen.

One night, Fulie interrupted Reb Meir during midnight prayers. Meir tried to explain to his grandson that he was praying for the Messiah's coming, but Fulie only scoffed at him. "If he hasn't yet come," he flatly asked, "why should he come now?" Then Fulie came to the point. "There will be a big demonstration tomorrow," he said, and "if something should happen to me, I want you to give this envelope to a girl by the name of Nekhama Katz."

All through the next day, Meir heard cries and gunshots from the square where the rebels were demonstrating—and he prayed even more fervently for the imminent arrival of the Messiah. When strangers brought Fulie's body back that evening, he was saddened but not surprised. Meir did not notice that Nekhama Katz never came for her letter. A few hours later, however, the police did come. The old man pointed to the corpse, but the police turned away and began to search the apartment. They found Fulie's letter, and as they read it, occasionally they glanced over at Meir.

When the police finally arrested Meir, he did not ask why. Once in the carriage, he began to confess his sins, but one of the policemen interrupted him: "Hey you, Jew, old dog, who are you talking to, your God?" Meir, since he spoke neither Polish nor Russian, did not understand what he was asked. He answered with the only Gentile words he knew. "Yes, I am Jew. I pray God."

Commentary:

The work of Isaac Bashevis Singer (1904 - 1991) is characterized by its passionate celebration of Jewish culture and faith. Akhsa, beset by guilt and demons of her own making, never loses her will to live. Similarly, when Reb Mordecai Meir is drawn into the maelstrom created by the political upheavals around him, he, too, confronts and embraces his uncertain fate, bearing witness with the only non-Hebrew words he knows.

Perhaps, in part, it is Singer's ardent commitment to truth—and to faith that endures in the face of horrible truths—that has earned his work such international acclaim. As a token of his contributions to the literary arts, Singer was awarded the Nobel Prize for Literature in 1970.

THE SHORT STORIES OF HEINRICH BOLL

(taken from *18 Stories*, translated by Leila Vennewitz, McGraw-Hill, New, York, N.Y., 1966)

Heinrich Boll (1917 - 1985) is a major figure of post-World War II literature, winning the Nobel Prize in 1972 for his contributions to the renewal of German literature after the near-destruction of the culture under Hitler and fascism. Boll's fiction takes a friendly but uncompromising look at post-war Germany. As the following three stories illustrate, his chief themes are modern-day humanity's dehumanization and the omnipresence of conflict.

Like a Bad Dream

The young man and his wife, Bertha, waited anxiously for the Zumpens to arrive for dinner. This would be an important dinner for the young contractor; he had married into the excavating business, and Mr. Zumpen was head of a city council that awarded contracts for large housing projects. Tomorrow's awarding of an excavation contract could mean upwards of 20,000 marks for the young couple. Bertha's father had persuaded Zumpen to attend the dinner, but the contractor would have to do the rest by himself.

The dinner itself went very well. Cognacs and cigars lubricated the after-dinner conversation, but, inevitably, silence fell after the four exhausted their repertoire of pleasantries. Before he knew it, the young contractor had let slip by his opportunity to discuss the contract. The Zumpen's bid their hosts farewell and departed. "Why," Bertha asked softly, "didn't you mention the contract to him?" Her husband shrugged his shoulders. "I didn't know how to bring the conversation round to it," he answered weakly.

Though it was already ten-thirty at night, Bertha insisted they go over to the Zumpen's: "There's 20,000 marks involved."

Mrs. Zumpen did not look the least surprised when the couple appeared at the door. Her husband had gone out, she explained, but she invited them in. Then she handed the young man a file marked *Contracts*. When the contractor opened the file, there sat his bid, right on top of the stack, with the words "Lowest Bid" pencilled across it in red. Mrs. Zumpen smiled, offered them drinks, then proposed a toast. The young man watched in disbelief as Mrs. Zumpen allowed Bertha to raise his price per square foot by fifteen pfennigs, an additional profit of 4,500 marks—and still leaving him the lowest bidder.

Then Bertha turned to her husband and said, "Get out your check book and write a check for three thousand marks; it must be a cash check and endorsed by you . . . When the contract is awarded, there will be an advance, and then it will be covered." The couple drove home, Bertha happy, her husband, bewildered, shocked, appalled. "I suppose the check was for Zumpen," he muttered. "Of course," Bertha answered.

Later that evening, Zumpen called. Bertha had accidentally raised the price by twenty-five, not fifteen, pfennigs. The young man blurted out unthinkingly that it had not been a mistake, so he and Zumpen negotiated an additional kickback of 750 marks. "It's like a bad dream," he thought, as he drove alone to Zumpen's house to deliver a second check. Bertha did not meet him when he returned. "I knew what she was thinking," he remembered, "she was thinking: he has to get over it, and I have to leave him alone; this is something he has to understand. But I never did understand. It is beyond understanding."

Action Will be Taken: An Action-Packed Story

"Probably one of the strangest interludes in my life," the young clerk recounted, "was the time I spent as an employee in Alfred Wunsiedel's factory." The clerk, generally loath to work, now and then found that financial necessity propelled him into activity. Just such a situation forced him to take a position at Wunsiedel's as a phone attendant. During a pre-employment test, one question asked: "How many telephones can you handle at one time?" He had answered without hesitation, "When there are only seven telephones, I get impatient; there have to be nine before I feel I am working to capacity." He got the job.

Even with nine telephones, however, the clerk felt under-utilized. Eventually, thirteen phones sat on his desk. When one rang, he would pick it up and shout, "Take immediate action!" or "Do something!" or "We must have some action!" or "Action will be taken!" or "Action has been taken!" or "Action should be taken!" This was in deference to his employer; indeed, Wunsiedel himself seemed obsessed with action. Each morning, entering the plant, the factory owner would greet his employees with, "Let's have some action!" The standard reply, of course, was "Action will be taken!"

One Tuesday morning as the young man was working busily at his phones, Wunsiedel rushed into his office and said, "Let's have some action." This time, however, something in Wunsiedel's face caused the clerk to hesitate. "Answer! Answer, you know the rules!" Wunsiedel shouted. "Action will be taken," the young man uttered halfheartedly—and then there really *was* some action. Wunsiedel dropped to the floor, rolling over on his side to block the doorway. The man was dead! The clerk rushed over to his superior's desk and said, "We've had some action!"

At Wunsiedel's memorial service, the funeral director offered the distraught clerk a job as a professional mourner, which suited perfectly his propensity to inactivity. Afterward, he took to visiting Wunsiedel's grave, "for after all I owe it to him that I discovered my true vocation."

"It was not until much later," the young

man said, "that I realized I had never bothered to find out what was being produced in Wunsiedel's factory. I expect it was soap."

The Adventure

Fink walked into the church and, without looking at the names, pushed one of the buttons under the sign that read "Confessional Bell." He dipped his finger in a pink plaster basin-full of water, crossed himself, then knelt down in the center nave to pray and wait for the priest to enter the confessional to hear his confession.

Actually, Fink only tried to pray. Over his folded hands he kept glancing toward the confessional booths so as not to miss the priest—and to survey the repairs being made in the war-ravaged church: scaffolding here and there; jagged, pock-marked walls; the front entrance blocked up with stones; and a double row of plaster saints all missing their heads, casualties of war. Their truncated, motionless figures seemed to hold out their hands to him in supplication.

As if in answer to the mutilated saints, Fink tried to summon remorsefulness and contrition, but his sin, his "adventure," had already begun to acquire the luster and patina of a recollection. Spasmodic prayer suddenly mingled with recurring memories, and the omnipresent desire to get all of it over and done with and get out of the church and away from this bombed-out town. It hardly seemed like a sin anyway. It had been as automatic as going to confession; he merely followed the rules of the game, almost out of a sense of propriety or politeness. Fink had, it was true, felt disgusted even before it happened, but persuaded himself it was simply a mechanical act dictated by instinct, by nature. Nevertheless, afterward, he felt as though an arrow had struck him "unerringly in that invisible something for which he could find no other name than soul," and, at that moment, he knew he must seek forgiveness.

Now, just as Fink began to grow impatient, the priest approached from the sacristy and entered the confessional. Fink followed. The ritual preliminaries completed, sweat began pouring down his face. "I have committed adultery," he stammered.

"Once," Fink sighed at the priest's question of how many times.

"Today," he answered when asked how long ago—although the act already seemed as though it had occurred in the distant past. Now Fink's mind took over. A salesman of pre-fabricated homes, Fink knew that it would be difficult to avoid seeing the woman again, since she had ordered a home. No, he did not love her, Fink spoke truthfully. No, he did not wish to see her again, he lied in his next breath.

Now the priest spoke. "Think of the Bible message," he counseled. "If thy left hand offend thee, cut it off. Accept the possibility of material loss." As the priest ran through the commandments, Fink stopped the priest on "Thou shalt not lie." He had to confess: "The houses, our houses are not quite the way they look in the catalogue—I mean, they—people are often disappointed when they actually see them . . . " Hearing this, the priest failed to suppress an "Aha." He cleared his throat, then told Fink, "Now we will take it all together and fervently beseech Our Lord Jesus Christ to obtain our forgiveness." After a prayer and a few long moments more, the priest looked at Fink through the screen, pronounced the *Absolvo te*, and said, "Praise be to Jesus Christ."

"For ever and ever Amen," Fink answered.

It was over; it seemed as though hours had elapsed. Fink, stiff from kneeling and wet with perspiration, again tried to pray, but the flicker of candles in front of the altar of the Mother of God cast a gigantic, outlandishly detailed silhouette of an old woman onto the front wall. Fink noted the single hairs protruding from the woman's forehead and their hard, black shadow on the wall; her small childlike nose; her lips moving silently in prayer: "a fleeting memorial, towering above the truncated plaster figures and seeming to grow out beyond the edge of the roof."

Commentary:

Both the young excavation contractor in "Like a Bad Dream" and Fink, the guilty adulterer in "The Adventure," emerge dazed and dehumanized. Neither Bertha, the contractor's wife, nor the Zumpens consider bribery in the least morally objectionable; still, the contractor feels he is caught up in a genuine "bad dream." Fink, though rationalizing his committing adultery as "merely following the rules of the game," is also fascinated by the true devotion of his shadowy fellow worshipper. To him the act of adultery itself had been mechanical, instinctual. Now, his confessional and prayers had been the same, devoid of passion. It is as though he is asking, "Where is the tenderness and sensuality that ought to accompany both my physical and spiritual self?"

The young clerk in "Action Will Be Taken," along with his co-workers and employer, are reduced to robots, mechanically flinging action-related phrases into the phone or at each other, although the clerk never even bothered to learn what it was the factory produced. Boll perhaps uses this story to teach that each of us should be truly in tune with our lives and goals, and try to resolve those moral, inner conflicts that so easily dehumanize and defeat us.

Most of Boll's stories are set against war or post-war backdrops, testimony to the dynamic standing World War II played in Germany's history. Boll's place in German literature is as a scribe, to record thoughts and feelings of those recovering from the psychological turmoil of war, in order to remind a generation having been born since 1945 that, for them, the war is a living memory, not mere history.

EXODUS

by
Leon Uris
(1924 -   )

Type of work: Historical fiction

Setting: Palestine and Europe in the 1930s and 40s

Principal characters:

Kitty Fremont, an anti-Semitic American nurse

Mark Parker, an American news correspondent

Ari Ben Canaan, a Jewish underground fighter

Karen Hansen Clement, a young Jewish refugee girl

Commentary:

In *Exodus*, Leon Uris not only tells the story of two seemingly distinct human beings—a Christian and a Jew, who ultimately find they are very much alike—but also presents an inspired account of the tragic and courageous history of the Jewish people. Uris' dynamic characters bring to life the story of an exiled people seeking a home, a nation in which they can peacefully observe their faith. It is also the story of how that people rediscovered themselves in the ashes of the Holocaust.

Story Overview:

After serving as a news correspondent during World War II and the Nuremberg War Crimes Trials, Mark Parker came to Cyprus for a much-needed vacation. He also took the opportunity to visit his best friend's widow, before going to Palestine to cover the creation of a Jewish state there.

Kitty Fremont had married Mark's friend before the war, but her husband had been killed on Guadalcanal. Shortly thereafter, their only daughter died of polio. Kitty had spent the rest of the war as a nurse, working with injured children. She now worked for the United Nations establishing orphanages for the young survivors of the war. "There's going to be a war, Kitty," Parker warned her. " . . . Some people are out to resurrect a nation that has been dead for two thousand years. Nothing like that has ever happened before. What's more, I think they're going to do it. It's these same Jews you don't like."

As Mark and Kitty ate at an outdoor restaurant one night, Mark's eyes widened as he recognized the man who was approaching their table. Ari Ben Canaan was a leader in the illegal movement to smuggle Jews into Palestine against the will of British authorities. Ari disclosed to Mark that he had devised a way to free three hundred refugee children from the detention camps the British ran on the island of Cyprus. These camps held Jews who the British had caught trying to enter Palestine. Ben Canaan's strategy was not just to transport the children to Palestine, but to do it in such a way as to make world opinion turn against the British. Ari wanted Mark to write the story of the escape for the world's newspapers.

Ari also wanted Kitty's help. She had been offered a job working in those Cyprus detention camps, but turned it down when she learned she would be aiding Jewish children. Ari entreated her

at least to visit the camps before refusing the job. As an American, Kitty could more easily pass messages and documents in and out and help to prepare for the escape. Ari appealed to Kitty's "American conscience"; it was her duty to aid in the deliverance of the children.

After Ari left, Kitty told Mark, "Well . . . I'll say one thing. This Ben Canaan doesn't act like any Jew I've ever met. You know what I mean. You don't particularly think of them in a capacity like his . . . fighters . . . things of that sort."

Ari's appeal worked: Kitty's conscience drove her to visit the detention camps before refusing to help. Kitty had boasted to Ari that she was accustomed to "blotting up bodies off the receiving room floor" of Cook County Hospital, and so the camps would not impress her. But she was wrong. The plight of the camp's residents and workers stunned her. She was appalled by how much the British-run settlements resembled German concentration camps. Indeed, many of the Jews held here were wartime survivors of the Nazi death camps.

Ari gave her a tour of the cramped quarters and introduced her to many of the residents. "I'd like to show you another old man here," he said, sidling over to a withered skeleton-like figure. "He took the bones of his grandchildren out of a crematorium in Buchenwald and carted them off in a wheelbarrow. Tell me, Mrs. Fremont, did you see one better than that at the Cook County Hospital?" Still, Kitty was determined to decline the task—until, leaving the children's compound, she heard the sound of laughter for the first time. The happy giggles emanated from Karen Hansen Clement, a young girl that very much reminded Kitty of her late daughter.

Karen was the only one of her family who had been smuggled out of Germany before the war began. In Denmark, she became Karen Hansen. During the German occupation, the Danes protected the Jews, and Karen survived. But, when the war ended, she left Denmark to find her family. "Karen rued the day she had opened that secret door marked Jew, for behind it lay death." As she wandered Europe, confirming the death of relative after relative and of so many other neighbors, friends, Jews, Karen Hansen Clement sank deep in melancholy.

Then, arriving in the camps, there was a turning point in her life. The children flocked to her. "She seemed to know instinctively how to dry a runny nose, kiss a wounded finger, or soothe a tear, and she could tell stories and sing at the piano in many languages. She plunged into her work with the younger children with a fervor that helped her forget a little of the pain within her . . ."

Kitty quickly realized that she saw in Karen a replacement for her own daughter. She immediately agreed to help these would-be-Jewish citizens so that she could stay near Karen, and ultimately convince the girl to return to the United States with her.

As the arrangements for the escape were put in place, the British somehow detected that something was amiss. British authorities threatened to crack down on the refugees, but reconsidered when they realized who these people were: graduates of concentration camps would not be easily intimidated.

With Mark and Kitty's help, the plan came off without incident. Three hundred children were smuggled out of the camp and placed aboard the ship *Exodus*. But, as it turned out, Ari's scheme called for more than just the mere freeing of the children. He had Mark alert the British of the breakout; within minutes, a destroyer had been dispatched to head off the *Exodus*. Within an hour, the harbor was encircled by British vessels, tanks and armed soldiers, all facing the children of the *Exodus*. Ari quickly informed the British that there were explosives on the ship, and that it would be sunk if they tried to board her.

As intended, Ari had created an awkward situation. In the eyes of the world, the British appeared to be ogres who would risk the deaths of children rather than give them safe passage to Palestine. The children of the *Exodus* then launched a hunger strike, heaping even more pressure on the British. As each child fainted from starvation, they were carefully brought out onto the deck where reporters could see them.

The hunger strike, however, was more than Mark had expected from Ari. "You ghoul . . . you stinking ghoul," Mark snarled. Ari deflected Mark's criticism. "Call me what you want, Parker," he responded. " . . . We've had the hell knocked out of us for two thousand years. This is one fight we're going to win . . . Six million Jews died in gas chambers not knowing why they died . . . If three hundred of us on the *Exodus* die we will certainly know why. The world will know too."

World opinion turned more and more against the British. After the children threatened to commit suicide if they were refused passage to Palestine, the British government agreed to release the *Exodus*.

Kitty, in order to stay close to Karen, accompanied the ship to Palestine. There, she accepted a job at the Gan Dafna youth settlement, where Karen had been assigned, showering the disturbed children with the love and warmth they so desperately needed. Patience, skill and love were the remedies for these children's lamentable pasts.

The settlement was named after Ari Ben Canaan's childhood sweetheart. Arabs killed Dafna before the war, but Ari refused to show his anger. Instead, he overcame this tragedy "by deepening his determination not to be thrown from the land. Ari Ben Canaan was all soldier."

Kitty, meanwhile, continued in her efforts to convince Karen to return to America with her before the threatened war with the Arabs started, but found herself drawn more and more to the Jewish people, particularly to Ari Ben Canaan. On one occasion Ari took Kitty on an outing with a military unit of young Jews. Kitty was stunned at what she saw: "What kind of army was this? What kind of army without uniform or rank? What kind of army where the women fought alongside their men with rifle and bayonet? Who were these young lions of Judea? She looked at the face of Ari Ben Canaan and a chill passed through her body." Then she realized that this was an army of ancient

Hebrews, the Army of Israel, of God himself! Dan, Reuben, Samson, Deborah Judah: The names of immortal warriors spun through Kitty's mind.

It became clear that Kitty was falling in love with the land of Palestine, and with Ari Ben Canaan as well. Still, she was frightened. She had to leave them both, take Karen, and return to America before it was too late. "Then it came to her that she had been fleeing from this very feeling she had for him, this new desire for Ari which could lead her to stay in Palestine." She would not lose another person she cared for. But, if Ari showed "the slightest signs of really caring she might not have the strength . . . " But "Kitty wanted more than what Ari could give her, she wanted a man who could show emotion, one that could cry."

Kitty stayed; even after the war for Israel's independence began, she and Karen stayed. On paper, it seemed impossible that the Jews could survive the Arabs' onslaught. They were outnumbered in soldiers forty to one, in population a hundred to one, and in equipment a thousand to one. Nevertheless, they were prepared to lose every man, woman, and child to preserve their land. The Arabs were not willing to pay so high a price. "Call it divine intervention, if you will, or maybe . . . let us say that the Jews have too many Ari Ben Canaans. . . . And the hundred other settlements . . . who fought for days without food and water, the new immigrants who rushed to the battle lines, the ingenuity employed in place of guns, the raw courage which made extraordinary heroism a commonplace—all these stopped the Arabs." The Arabs could not overcome the heritage or the will of a people who had fought for their freedom under King David. They received "strength and faith from an unseen source." They stopped the Arabs.

With victory in hand, other Jews came to Israel. " . . . Some walked through burning deserts. Some flew on the rickety craft of the airlift. Some came in jam-packed holds of cattle freighters. Some came in deluxe liners. They came from seventy-four nations. The dispersed, the exiles, the unwanted came to that one little corner of the earth where the word Jew was not a slander."

Victory exacted a price, however. One of the last to die was Karen. Kitty, once more grieving a loved one's death, now saw that Ari could take no more. Weeping bitterly, he poured out the "bottomless" grief and rage of a lifetime: "All my life . . . I have watched them kill everyone I love . . . they are all gone now . . . all of them. . . . I have died with them. I have died a thousand times. I am empty inside . . . . . . Why must we send children to live in these places? This precious girl . . . this angel . . . *why* did they have to kill her too? . . . Why must we fight for the right to live, over and over, each time the sun rises? . . . Why don't they let us alone? *Why don't they let us live!*"

As if this had broken a logjam, Ari was finally able to acknowledge his need for Kitty, who promised to stay with him. She joined Ari's surviving family in the Passover Seder meal. Ari solemnly spoke:

Why is this night different from all other nights of the year? This is different because we celebrate the most important moment in the history of our people. On this night we celebrate their going forth in triumph from slavery into freedom.

THE FOUNTAINHEAD

by Ayn Rand, The Bobbs-Merrill Company, Inc., New York, N.Y., 1943

Type of work: Philosophical romantic fiction

Setting: Near-future America

Principal characters:
The Individualist
  Howard Roark, a gifted architect and rebel
The Collectivists
  Peter Keating, a second-rate, people-pleasing architect
  Gail Wynand, a power-seeking newspaper owner
  Ellsworth Toohey, Roark's nemesis, an architectural critic for Wynand newspapers
The Heroine
  Dominique Francon, an idealist, hardened by contempt

Story Overview:

"The lake lay far below him." Standing naked at the edge of the cliff, Howard Roark—hair the color or ripe orange rind, gray eyes that were cold and steady, and a contemptuous mouth, shut tight like that of an executioner or a saint—laughed.

Roark had just been expelled from the Stanton Institute of Technology Architectural School. His offense: refusing to fit into the philosophical scheme of mediocrity. Roark, like his buildings, was an original; he believed that "a building is alive, like a man. Its integrity is to follow its own truth, its one single theme, and to serve its own single purpose." And in this philosophy, he refused to make concessions or to compromise his standards in order to gain the community's stamp of approval. Nor did he allow the Dean to give him a second chance. Roark passionately insisted that buildings should be erected, not as a testimony to historic culture, but in fulfillment of their own unique purposes. A building's form, he argued, "must follow its function . . . the structure of a building is the key to its beauty, [and] new methods of construction demand new forms . . ."

Unlike Roark, Peter Keating was an incurable people-pleaser, driven by the desire to feel superior. He ingratiated others with his good looks, effortless popularity, and by transforming himself into whatever other people wanted. Among Keating's manipulations was the proposal of marriage to his boss' exquisitely beautiful daughter, Dominique Francon. Consequently, he advanced rapidly in the prestigious architectural firm of Francon & Heyer.

While Keating climbed the career ladder, Roark stubbornly took the path of greatest resistance, fighting the establishment, refusing to take much-needed commissions whenever he felt his principles were violated. Keating—with hardly a principle to be violated—was out to ruin anyone he had to get to the top—including Howard Roark. In fact, Keating had hired Roark in an effort to disguise his own incompetence, but Roark was later fired by Guy Francon due to his unwillingness to compromise. Before the left, however, Roark had designed the structural frame of the very building that later brought Keating to his pinnacle of success. It was said he had designed the "most beautiful skyscraper on earth."

Though Roark was in desperate need, he refused Keating's offer to accept a share of the prize money. He had merely done Keating a favor and wanted no payment or acknowledgment for a design that had been violated with renaissance trappings.

Soon, Roark received a long-awaited call from the Manhattan Bank Company. The bank's board praised his plan to construct a fifty-story building in the center of Manhattan and offered Roark the commission—"on one minor condition." What seemed inconsequential to the board was "only a matter of a slight alteration in the facade"; Roark's building was to include a "simplified Doric portico in front, a cornice on top, and [Roark's] ornament was [to be] replaced by a stylized Greek ornament." Roark, again, refused to bend.

Two days later, Roark left for Connecticut to work in a granite quarry. There, he spotted Dominique Francon, who had retreated to her father's colonial mansion for the summer. There sprouted an instant love-hate attraction between Roark and Dominique.

The quarry belonged to Dominique's father, and she enjoyed the feeling of power she had over the workers, including Roark. She arranged for Roark to come to her mansion to fix her fireplace; he sent another worker instead. Later, she confronted Roark: "Why didn't you come to set the marble?" He answered, "I didn't think it would make any difference to you who came. Or did it, Miss Francon?" Soon after, however, it was Roark who appeared in her bedroom to demand submission. His boldness provoked a passionate response, but it was a fierce rather than a tender passion, " . . . the act of a master taking shameful, contemptuous possession of her was the kind of rapture she had wanted."

Only a week later, Roark received word that his architectural services were needed at another project, and he departed. Dominique was left alone, with her pain—and her desire.

Meanwhile, Ellsworth M. Toohey was busy with his newspaper column, *"One Small Voice."* In it he praised Keating's Cosmo-Slotnick Building:

There is no personality stamped upon that building—and in this, my friends, lies the greatness of the personality. It is the greatness of a selfless young spirit that assimilates all things and returns them to the world from which they came . . . . Thus a single man comes to represent, not a lone freak, but the multitude of all men together . . .

In New York, back at her job on the newspaper, Dominique caught a glimpse of the publicized drawing of the Enright House. Toohey's comment was, "As independent as an insult, isn't it?" But Dominique, unaware that Howard Roark was the house's architect, did not share the same opinion: "You know, Ellsworth, I think the man who designed this should have committed suicide. A man who can conceive a thing as beautiful as this should never allow it to be erected."

Roark and Dominique were later formally introduced at a party. Of course, Dominique gave no hint that she already knew him. Roark was comfortable, self-possessed and appropriately polite. Upon leaving she turned to the hostess and confessed, " . . . He is the most revolting person I've ever met." However, Toohey, who had refused an introduction to Roark, overheard Dominique's subsequent self-betraying comment that "he's terribly good-looking."

In fact, Toohey embarked on a mission, in alliance with Dominique, to destroy Roark. She could not stand to see him survive, nor flourish, for surely the public's indignation would bring his self-governing spirit to ruin. Toohey, for his part, could not bear to see an independent soul rise above the mass to greatness, and Roark epitomized independence. Toohey shared Keating's theory on how to get ahead, advice Keating again gave Roark at the party: "It's a secret, Howard. A rare one. I'll give it to you free of charge with my compliments: always be what people want you to be. Then you've got them where you want them. I'm giving it free because you'll never make use of it."

Dominique's obsession to shatter Roark conflicted with her lust for him. Cooperating with Toohey in an all-out campaign to crush Roark, after each success preventing him from winning a commission, she would sleep with him. Then, inexplicably, one day she up and married Peter Keating, a "third-rate architect and a man who represented all she deplored in humankind.

Toohey anonymously arranged a commission for Roark to design the Stoddard Temple of the Human Spirit, hoping to use the commission as an opportunity to condemn Roark's work. During the construction, Mr. Hopton Stoddard would be taking a world tour of the holy shrines of all faiths. The celebrated opening, a highly publicized event, was organized to coincide with Stoddard's return. Dominique herself posed for the central statue.

The plan went as outlined. The community responded with outrage at the public display. When the suit was brought against Roark, Dominique testified for the prosecution. Between the lines, however, her testimony subtly glorified the independent soul.

Gail Wynand, the publisher of Toohey's newspaper, had been out of town during this crusade against individualism. Early on, Wynand had risen from the wretched "Hell's Kitchen" by dreaming dreams filled with truth and beauty. However, finally succumbing to the reality, disillusionment, and cynicism of newspaper reporting, he slowly changed his focus to the attainment of power. And his vehicle was the *Banner,* a scandalous weekly tabloid; and, yes, it did buy him a great deal of power.

After a while, Dominique's marriage to Peter Keating ended; just as he had bought power, Wynand "bought" Dominique for the sum of $250,000, plus commission, to design an important building. Bit by bit, even though the marriage began as an expression of self-loathing, Dominique grew to care for Gail Wynand. Wynand also gradually began construct a new view of life, a life with higher ideals. And, one day seeking out someone to draw up his and Dominique's new residence, he befriended and commissioned a talented architect: Howard Roark.

Roark, meanwhile, had allowed Keating to again take advantage of his talent, and designed a huge low-income housing project called Cortlandt Homes. The only condition he placed on Keating was that Cortlandt be built in exact accordance with Roark's design. However, when construction was nearly completed, Roark discovered design changes had been made—"mutilations," he called them—and he had no choice but to demolish the structure. Roark took the media rap. Finally, Dominique and Toohey's mission had been accomplished.

But Wynand immediately set out to defend Roark, publishing a number of convincing stories. But his valiant attempts proved futile. Swimming against the rugged opposition of Ellsworth Toohey, Wynand found himself astonishingly powerless. He was forced to capitulate—at the expense of his own, newly discovered integrity. Wynand fired Toohey, but Toohey, in turn, took most of the writing staff with him.

Within a week, Wynand had closed the *Banner;* he also divorced Dominique, who had finally seen the error in her ways. Then, finally giving in to her true, unadulterated feelings, at last she became Mrs. Howard Roark.

When his trial came to an end, Roark was exonerated. Afterwards, Gail Wynand presented his ex-wife's new husband with a contract to erect the tallest skyscraper in New York, the Wynand Building. "Build it," he told Roark, "as a monument to that spirit which is yours . . . and could have been mine."

Commentary:

A large, extremely complex novel that took Ayn Rand (1905 - 1982) five years to write, *The Fountainhead's* theme deals with the heavily philosophical battle between individualism and collectivism. In her work, Rand's partiality to the former—the personal, inward motivator over the political or societal outward motivator—is clear and unmistakable.

Keating symbolizes the collectivist, one who places societal interests above self-excellence. Collectivists tend to look into other's eyes in order to determine what they believe.

Roark, on the other hand, represents the individualist, one whose convictions, values and purposes are drawn from his own mind. Individualists live in accordance with their own, pure goals. Initiative, creativity, independent thinking, these characteristics color the individualist, who, according to Rand, is the force that truly furthers the destiny of mankind. Her belief that " . . . to hold an unchanging youth is to reach, at the end, the vision with which one started," is one Roark exemplifies. His victory at the end of the novel validates his life—and Rand's individualist philosophy.

GETTING USED TO DYING

by Zhang Xianliang, Harper Collins, New York, N.Y., 1989

Type of work: Autobiographical novel

Setting: America and Europe; 1987-88
(looking back on experiences in China throughout the years of the narrator's life—1936 onward)

Principal character:
The protagonist/narrator, an unnamed Chinese writer

Commentary:

In *Getting Used to Dying,* the narrator travels from China to San Francisco to New York, and finally to Paris. Along the way, he reminisces upon his life inside China, interweaving events of the past with the present, and with fantasies of "what could have been." He fills these disjointed remembrances with imagery and metaphor, conveying his deepest, most powerful sentiments directly to the mind of the reader. Observations that might to us seem common and mundane, are significant to the author; in contrast, what to us might seem large-scale happenings barely receive mention. Indeed, it is from the seemingly trivial that the author presents a powerful portrait of his fatalistic worldview.

In this potent narrative, Zhang Xianliang attempts to reveal the conceptions that pass through the minds of most modern-day Chinese intellectuals. The protagonist's personality is split: one side embraces the passionate, creative Chinese writer; the other embodies the criticized, punished, and "reformed" labor camp prisoner, devoid of love, empathy, and courage. *Getting Used to Dying,* like most epic-proportion works, is a unique chronicle that must be read in its original form to be fully appreciated.

With the tightening of censorship that followed the incident in Tiananmen Square in 1989, the Chinese government banned *Getting Used to Dying* and placed Zhang under investigation.

Story Overview:

In 1959, while working in the labor camps of the northeastern Chinese province of Ningxia, I made an aborted attempt at suicide by hanging. I could not go through with it. Despite my suffering, something within me chose life over death. I returned to my cell, bitter with myself for being too cowardly to take my own life. "But dying is not so simple," I later pondered. "We normally achieve it only once in a lifetime."

This incident became a "rehearsal for dying," the first of many that would play over and over in my mind. I witnessed unreal scenes in which I suffered "intellectual death" at the hands of the oppressive Chinese government, my strong, outspoken presence as a detractor of the government giving way to "cowardice and indecision."

In 1987, almost thirty years later, under the sponsorship—and tight control—of the Chinese government, I embarked upon a speak-ing tour of the Western nations, beginning with a journey by air to San Francisco. The following sketches represent the breadth of my journey, drawing on memories, events, hopes and fears both past and present.

Jing Hui's House, San Francisco

Upon arriving in San Francisco, I proceeded to the house of Jing Hui, where I was greeted warmly. Jing Hui still had the dog that I remembered from the last time we had met, a dog named "Freedom." The carefree use of the name struck me as terribly ironic. In China, the word *freedom* "struck terror in the hearts of some Chinese, so that even today one does not dare say it out loud." In America, as a dog's name, the word became trivialized; even the dog was "more adornment than dog." Freedom had a different meaning in America than it did in China.

Even though Jing Hui was a kind host, she was away nearly all of the time I stayed with her. But everything in her house shocked me, trumpeting over and over the differences between China and the West. Whereas in China we feel the daily struggle to live, our spirits intact, it seemed to me that Americans went about their daily business in a sort of naive bliss. The commercials I saw on television seemed pointless. Even the ashtrays in Jing Hui's house "elegantly announced that they were not for actual use."

Jing Hui's absence, aside from leaving me much time for my musings, also made time for old longings; I yearned to see someone from my past. A, an old lover I once knew in China, lived here. I recalled that in my first years as a prisoner in the labor reform camps, all us prisoners had watched propaganda films featuring A in the starring role, sometimes as "the valiant leader of a women's guerilla attachment, sometimes a lady doctor whose 'class alignment' was absolutely pure." Back then, I imagined stealing her love as a form of "retaliation" against the system she represented.

Later, after meeting A in person and becoming romantically involved with her, I paradoxically imagined that I had actually joined the side I had bitterly hated previously; that day "I took her kiss to be my real rehabilitation."

Alone now at Jing Hui's house, I called A on the telephone. By her brief, strained stammerings, however, I could tell that she was with another man. Disappointed, I was left to myself for the night, with my memory of her as my only company.

New York

I moved on to New York, where I was greeted by C, a Taiwanese volunteer that had been charged with my care during that part of my tour. C brought a fresh sense of adventure to replace the disappointment I felt at not meeting A in San Francisco. She was a woman who secretly hoped to find in me a release from the burdens of strict formality that her learned sophistication had placed upon her. I was happy to provide her with that release.

After speaking at a writer's convention, C and I went to dinner, then to her apartment for the night. While C slept, I lay awake, gazing at a bouquet of China Pinks. The pirouetting, blood-red flowers drew me back in time, back to China and a singular, defining moment in my life . . .

Ningxia, China, 1970

After being arrested and re-sentenced to the labor camps in Ningxia, I was selected to join a group of convicts in a mass execution. We were brought into town on a tractor. Along the way, I spoke freely and lightheartedly with one of the State soldiers. When this, my new comrade, asked if I was not afraid to die, I replied cheerfully: Was it not true that Chairman Mao himself had instructed us long ago not to fear death? If I were to fear death, I would not be a good soldier for Chairman Mao! How ironic my words seemed. Even here, on the way to the execution ground, I had become a comrade of the revolutionaries. I was an intellectual; it was my "most appropriate" duty to die.

From town, all of us were loaded onto a truck and taken to the Central Meeting Ground, located on the edge of town at the site of a former graveyard. A crowd had gathered, and while we stood in line, a shot rang out, and then another, and another. The shots came faster and louder down the line of prisoners "like a string of firecrackers." Within minutes, I was one of only a handful of prisoners left standing. They had not meant for me to die; instead, my presence there was as an observer—a grand scare tactic. The Chinese government often endeavored to intimidate prisoners like myself who had appealed our criminal convictions.

Although no real bullet ever struck my body, a psychological bullet became firmly lodged inside my mind. Memories of this incident and the fear imposed by the omnipresent Chinese government would haunt me for the rest of my life.

Ningxia, China, 1960

The labor reform camps were sites of paradox, where bizarre events often took on the normal impression of everyday occurrences. Once, while I was serving time for writing "reactionary" poetry and fiction, I found myself, along with several other prisoners, assigned to the fields—not to dig potatoes or other crops, but to dig human bones. Still, to the labor reform convicts, "like harvesting crops, it was nothing more than another sort of physical labor."

At the time, the families of prisoners who had died in the camp were pressing the Chinese government. "Our relatives have died," the families were saying, "and their belongings may have been lost . . . *but what about their bones?*" The camp administrators had to come up with the human skeletons necessary to satisfy the families involved in the suit. In order to meet their demands, each litigant would be presented with a complete skeleton in a plastic sack.

Of course, since the camp's burial ground was filled with shallow, unmarked graves, identification of individual skeletons would be impossible. But the administrators said that made no difference; the important thing was to make sure the skeleton was intact. If anyone received a skeleton with a finger or toe bone missing, that person might report to Beijing that the convicts had been tortured before being executed.

Each prisoner had to dig up ten skeletons a day or go without food. Ironically, I had to dig up skeletons, or else I myself would become one. At the time, I took no special thought toward any deeper meaning that this unconventional chore might have held. "I had no interest in philosophizing. All I wanted to do was fill my quota."

New York, with A

As it turned out, a second opportunity to see A presented itself in New York. Somehow she tracked me down and called me on the telephone; her voice quivered with worry. Back in China, I was being censured again, she said. She would be in New York the next day on business, and she would meet me there.

The next night, we sat at a table in a Chinese restaurant. She had brought several newspapers with her that recited the Chinese government's new criticisms of my writings. We were less alarmed about the criticism than we were the possibility that this new wave of ideological "purism" might set China in motion for another political storm.

For a writer to be criticized in China was serious business. It meant that my writings were considered unlawful, dangerous—and that a punishment would follow. I didn't know what to do next, but A believed that my safest course of action would be to go into hiding. The American government would offer political asylum on the basis that I would face persecution if I returned to China. I thought about the consequences of such a move. My fear was not that I might be caught, but rather what the Chinese would think of me if I was never to return.

Finally, after much thought, I decided that I must return to China. Much of my life had been spent in labor reform camps, being rehabilitated by the Chinese government. I still owed them a hole in my head—and they owed me the bullet that I never received. "Only when that debt is settled will I be at peace. I must go back to get that bullet that belongs to me!" All those years of reform had imbued me with a deep sense of duty toward my country. While at odds with my role as an outspoken critic of China, this strange sense of duty was nevertheless strong. I could never lead a normal life outside of China; for too long I had been criminally disloyal to my country. Only by returning there to face justice—and death—would I truly find peace.

ALL QUIET ON THE WESTERN FRONT

by
Erich Maria Remarque
(1898 - 1970)

Type of work: Fictional study of social and wartime sentiments

Setting: World War I's famous Western Front

Principal characters:
Paul Baumer (narrator), a German infantry-man
Stanislaus Katezinsky (Kat), Paul's older friend and fellow soldier
Kropp, Tjaden, Haie, Muller, Kemmerich, other German soldiers

Commentary:

Remarque's unique novel of World War I trench warfare not only catalogues the grim realities of war but poignantly describes the spiritual and physical destruction of the youth who are sacrificed in the struggle.

Before he was twenty years old, Remarque had fought on the Western Front; and his graphic accounts of death, misery and the loss of personal ideals ring oppressively true. Undoubtedly, he left this work on the "war to end all wars" as a testament and a warning to the future; but World War I, was we well know, did not end war. It did usher in a century of deepening disillusionment and spiritual rootlessness that remains part of our legacy even in the technological Promised land of the nineties.

Because Remarque opposed the Nazi regime and wrote against the party, he was eventually deported from Germany. He came to America, where he became a citizen in 1947.

Story Overview:

Paul's unit rested not far from the front lines. Half of the unit had been destroyed in an English artillery barrage—leaving twice as much food for the survivors. And Kat, the forty-year-old man fighting alongside seven young kids just out of school, always had an uncanny way of dispensing provisions. No one had to ask where the double rations of food and cigarettes came from.

" . . . It would not be such a bad war if only one could get a little more sleep," Kat complained after the meal. Indeed, sleep had come with difficulty during the first weeks at the front.

Kantorek, Paul's old school teacher, had propped up the war as a glorious event; "Iron Youth" sent to repel the foe! "Naturally we couldn't blame Kantorek for this . . . " Paul reasoned. "There were thousands of Kantoreks, all of whom were convinced that they were acting for the best—in a way that cost them nothing. That is why they let us down so badly."

In due time, faced with the true effects of war, even the teacher's wisdom had vanished. What's more, their commander, Corporal Himmelstoss, had ordered them to carry out punishing and cruel drills. They hated him, and could no longer trust authority figures in general, thinking themselves more experienced. "We were all at once terribly alone, and alone we must see it through."

The men went to visit a member of their unit, Kemmerich, who had been wounded in the thigh and now lay in a field hospital. The man's foot had been amputated, but crazed with gangrene and fever, he did not know this. "He it is still and yet it is not he any longer," Paul thought when he saw his friend. "His features have become more uncertain and faint and his voice sounds like ashes." Kropp attempted to comfort the delirious soldier: "Now you will be going home soon. You would have had to wait at least three or four months for your leave"; and Muller brought him his possessions. Among the articles were a fine pair of leather boots. Muller tried to negotiate for the boots, but Kemmerich was unwilling to part with them. Once outside, Muller—carrying the boots—told the group that Kemmerich was "done for."

On the way back to the barracks they discussed how the fighting could be ended. Kropp joked that his idea would do the job: give all the generals and ministers clubs and let them personally fight it out in an arena. "That would be much simpler and just than this arrangement where the wrong people do the fighting."

Meanwhile, Himmelstoss was making their lives miserable—especially that of Tjaden, who had a bladder disorder and wet his bed every night. Himmelstoss tried to correct this by placing another man who had the same problem over Tjaden's bunk, then, each night, reversing the men's position. One evening, finding the corporal drunk, the men crept up behind him and threw a sheet over his head. Using a whip, each man—Tjaden in particular—satisfied his bitter anger by taking a turn in the thrashing.

Soon after, Himmelstoss was openly reprimanded for his harsh mistreatment. The men thereafter took bold pleasure in jeering and insulting their leader.

Finally, they shipped out to the front.

To me the front is like a mysterious whirlpool Though I am in water far away from its center, I feel the whirl of the vortex sucking me slowly, irresistibly, inescapably into itself. We march up, moody or good tempered soldiers—we reach the zone where the front begins and become on the instant human animals.

The unit was hit with heavy bombardment: men, crying out in unabashed fear, crouched inside trenches and shell craters; the screaming of a thousand wounded horses filled the air; gas fumes choked the soldiers—and those lucky enough to have gas masks waited in fearful silence, wondering if they were airtight. Straightway, the unit found cover was in a graveyard, only to have shells coffins and corpses unearthed all around them when the shells pounded down.

Finally the gas dispersed and the shelling ceased. Kat and Paul prepared to perform a mercy killing on a young soldier with mortal wounds to the stomach and hip. "Young innocents," Kat murmured before firing the bullet.

Later, back at the barracks, the young men

began discussing what they'd do once the war ended. Most planned on returning to mundane, ordinary jobs; and Paul, drafted right out of school, had no idea what he would do with his life. Oddly, though, it seemed no one could remember even the most humorous high school prank they had pulled. "The war has ruined us for everything," Albert said. Paul agreed:

We are youth no longer. We don't want to take the world by storm. We are fleeing. We fly from ourselves. From our life. We are cut off from activity, from striving, from progress. We believe in such things no longer, we believe in the war.

As they marched to the next offensive, the company passed stacks of coffins. Each man knew that one of the coffins was meant for him: "The front is a cage in which we must await fearfully whatever may happen"— one continual round of shelling, gas—and rats. In an effort to relieve their boredom, the men took sport in killing the bold, hungry rats, which had grown huge from feeding on dead bodies. Presently, the rum and cheese rations improved—sure signs of an impending battle. Then the attack came. "We have become like wild beasts," Paul explained. "We do not fight, we defend ourselves against annihilation." Men blown apart, decapitated, and other horrible scenes flashed across their eyes. Still they advanced, scurrying over mangled corpses, fighting on instinct, killing mechanically, without feeling.

The French having been driven back, the German company also fell back to the original front lines, gathering up any food they could find along the way. Of the some two hundred men, only thirty-two remained.

With the battle over, Paul had time to reflect again.

Here in the trenches, [memories] are completely lost to us. We are dead and they stand remote on the horizon. We could never regain the old intimacy with those scenes. We are forlorn like children and experienced like old men. I believe we are lost.

The remnants of the company rested and found company with some French girls across the river. Swimming to the other side, the soldiers entertained themselves, bribing the girls with gifts of bread and sausage. Paul was soon after given a two-week leave. He felt odd about returning home, his companions still at the front.

As the train neared his father's home, the scenes became more familiar, bringing back childhood memories. The sound of his sister's voice made him break down and cry. "I try to make myself laugh or speak but no word comes, so I stand on the steps, miserable, helpless, paralyzed, and against my will the tears run down my cheeks."

Paul found that the war had changed him so much that he scarcely knew how to behave. "Was it very bad out there, Paul?" his mother questioned. He wanted to cry out, "Mother, you could never realize it," but lied instead, saying, "No, Mother, not so very. There are always lots of us together so it isn't so bad."

News came that his mother had cancer. With this sad revelation—and the stream of questions asked about the war . . . questions Paul could not

somehow answer—a strange and lon[e] suddenly fell over him. He felt awkwa[rd] civilian clothes, and his thoughts continua[lly] dered to the front:

Leave is a pause that only makes everythi[ng] it much worse. I was a soldier, and now I am no[thing] but an agony for myself, for my mother, for everyth[ing] that is so comfortless and without end.

Before returning to the front, Paul paid a visit to Kemmerich's mother. In order to spare her the details of his long period of suffering, he lied, telling her her son had been killed instantly.

"This is where I belong," Paul blurted out in emotion upon reuniting with his comrades, most of them still alive.

Paul's unit was called into action again. In the ensuing battle, Paul was separated from his group. Panicking and caught in a hail of machine-gun fire, he crawled into a hole and buried himself in the mud to avoid detection. When a French soldier landed there too, Paul frantically stabbed him. At first appalled at the brutality and horror of his deed, Paul shrank from the wounded man. When he overcame his terror, he was filled with remorse and relieved the suffering of the soldier during his last hours. Never having before killed a man face to face, his conscience burned in torment; "Every gasp lays my heart bare." When the soldier finally died, Paul addressed the corpse, promising the man he would write a letter to his wife. Paul finally recovered his senses and crawled back towards his lines. There Kat found him, still in agony over what he had done, and the older veteran assured his weeping comrade that he had committed no crime.

The war dragged on. Dysentery, disease and death dogged the soldiers constantly. One day, while guarding a supply dump, both Paul and Albert were wounded. Paul's leg healed and soon he began hobbling around the hospital; but Albert's leg had to be amputated. Unable to bear his friend's jealous gaze, Paul returned home for a short while to his mother and sister.

Again in a trench on the front lines, Kat was wounded in the knee with shrapnel and Paul carried him to the rear. When he reached his destination, Kat was dead; he had bled to death, a tiny piece of shrapnel having pierced his head. Grieving and demoralized, Paul affirmed:

I am twenty years old: yet I know nothing of life but despair, death, fear, and fatuous superficiality cast over an abyss of sorrow. I see how peoples are set against one another and unknowingly, foolishly, obediently, innocently slay one another. Our knowledge of life is limited to death. What shall come out of us?

Paul was alone. His comrades, one by one, had been killed. Even more than their physical death, Paul shuddered at how they had been spiritually murdered.

Rumors circulated that the end of the war was near, but they only served to madden the already disillusioned, weary soldiers, many of whom now stood on the front lines supported by wooden legs.

[Paul] fell in October 1918, on a day that was so quiet and still on the whole front, that the army report confined itself to the single sentence: All quiet on the Western Front.

JURASSIC PARK

by Michael Crichton, Knopf, New York, N.Y., 1990

Type of work: Science fiction/adventure novel

Setting: Isla Nublar, off the coast of Costa Rica; August 1989

Principal characters:

Dr. Alan Grant, a noted paleontologist

Ellie Sattler, Dr. Grant's assistant, a graduate student in paleobotany

Dr. Ian Malcolm, a mathematician specializing in chaos theory

John Hammond, an eccentric billionaire, founder of InGen and creator of Jurassic Park

Gennaro, legal consultant for InGen

Dennis Nedry, designer of Jurassic Park's computer system—and a spy for InGen's rival

Muldoon, a former big game hunter, now Jurassic Park's game warden

Story Overview:

Just as Dr. Alan Grant had uncovered another fossilized velociraptor skeleton in the Montana Badlands, he was interrupted by a phone call from John Hammond, one his wealthy sponsors. Hammond insisted that Grant and his assistant, Dr. Ellie Sattler, fly down to Hammond's private island near Costa Rica for a consultation. "Quite apart from his curiosity about the island in Costa Rica, Grant understood that if John Hammond asked for his help, he would give it. That was how patronage worked," Grant's irritation at the interruption was soothed, however, by the promise of $60,000 for a weekend of work.

Aboard Hammond's private jet, Grant and Ellie met Gennaro, a lawyer for InGen, Hammond's company, and Ian Malcolm, a mathematician specializing in the field of chaos theory, the supposition that large natural systems are inherently unpredictable. According to Malcolm, Hammond's mysterious island project was doomed to fail; it was a chaotic situation, highly unpredictable. Hammond hoped to prove him wrong and set the minds of his investors at ease with this on-site inspection.

Isla Nublar was a volcanic, mist-covered, rainforested seamount rising from the ocean. From the helipad where they landed, Grant and the others gazed across the island. "To the south, rising above the palm trees, Grant saw a single trunk with no leaves at all, just a big curving stump. Then the stump moved and twisted around to face the new arrivals. Grant realized he was not seeing a tree at all. He was looking at the graceful, curving neck of an enormous creature, rising fifty feet into the air. He was looking at a dinosaur."

Gennaro led his guests into the compound. Over a path that led down to some large white buildings, a sign read "WELCOME TO JURASSIC PARK." Gennaro explained why the group had been invited: "As you realize by now, this is an island in which genetically engineered dinosaurs have been allowed to move in a natural park-like setting . . . The attraction isn't open to tourists yet, but it will be in a year. Now, my question to you is a simple one. Is this island safe?"

Hammond, of course, was already convinced of the island's safety, so much so that he'd flown his grandchildren, Tim and Alexis, down to spend the weekend with the others. Tim was an 11-year-old dinosaur nut who was thrilled that a scientist like Dr. Grant was on the island. Eight-year-old Alexis, on the other hand, would have rather spent her vacation playing baseball.

The group's tour began with the control room, from which the entire park was monitored and operated. Then they moved on to the lab where an engineer explained how dinosaur DNA was extracted from ancient blood-sucking insects trapped in amber. The DNA was analyzed, then used to clone a complete animal. According to Hammond's scientists, the dinosaurs could only be reproduced in the laboratory. All the dinosaurs were females and they had also been engineered so they could not survive without lysine, a critical amino acid, which the handlers fed the dinosaurs with their daily meals. The scientists assured the visitors that the island was secure.

However, Grant was troubled by what he saw. "He didn't like the idea of dinosaurs being used for an amusement park." He especially didn't like the idea of Hammond reproducing velociraptors, a breed of dinosaur he had studied extensively. They were intelligent—and dangerous—pack hunters. Even secure on the island, they had to be confined behind high-voltage electric fences.

The guests continued on in electric Land Cruisers that followed buried cables in the road. They moved across the island, passing through fenced enclosures containing various species of dinosaurs, including an ailing stegosaurus. Leaving their vehicles for a closer look at this animal, Malcolm explained the problem as he saw it. "The stego is a hundred million years old. It isn't adapted to our world. The air, the solar radiation, the land, the insects, the sounds, the vegetation—everything is different." While probing for a possible source of the stego's illness, Grant found a bit of a velociraptor eggshell, which led him to believe the dinosaurs were indeed breeding, despite Hammond's assurances.

With a storm rolling in, Grant, Malcolm, the kids, and members of the park's staff started back to the visitor's center while Ellie and Gennaro stayed with the park veterinarian. Suddenly, the power went out, stopping the cars.

Back in the control room, the computers had gone down, and system analyst Dennis Nedry was nowhere in sight. As it turned out, Nedry had been hired by InGen's competitors to steal a set of dinosaur embryos. After shutting off the power and disabling the security systems—including the electric fences around the dinosaur paddocks—he hurriedly helped himself to samples of frozen dinosaur embryos, then went to the basement and commandeered a Jeep. "Three minutes to the east dock. Three minutes from there back to the control room"—and he would be a rich man. Except for one thing: he became disoriented in the storm. Stopping to gain his bearings, he noticed a smallish dinosaur running nearby. Then "Nedry felt something smack wetly against his chest. He looked down and saw a dripping glob of foam. . . . He felt sudden excruciating pain in his eyes. Spit. The dinosaur had spit in his eyes." Blinded, he was easy prey for the hungry carnivores.

When Ellie and the vet finally returned to the visitor's center, Muldoon immediately borrowed their Jeep and went looking for the others. To his horror, Muldoon found that the fence around the T-rex enclosure had been flattened and that the Land Cruisers had been wrecked. Cries of pain led him to Malcolm, who had suffered deep lacerations on his legs. But Grant and the kids were missing.

It wasn't until morning that Arnold, the chief engineer, was able to restore the power.

Meanwhile, the T-rex, by now hunting its prey, had trapped Grant and the children under a waterfall—which they quickly determined was man-made. A door at the back of the wall offered a means of escape, but only Grant was able to get through before the big dinosaur reached through the waterfall and blocked Tim and Alexis from reaching the door.

On the other side of the door, Grant found a long tunnel that led out of the park toward the other side of the island, a Jeep—and a baby velociraptor. Grant's worst fears were realized—the raptors were breeding, and they were no longer contained in the park.

Tim and Alexis eventually succeeded in entering the door, and were relieved to find Grant waiting for them. Taking the Jeep back to the visitor's center, they learned that the power had failed again and the center had been reduced to a shambles by the scavenging dinosaurs.

Meanwhile, at the visitor's center, Hammond and Ellie tended to Malcolm. In shocked dismay, they watched as several velociraptors climbed on the roof and started biting through the bars that covered the skylight in Malcolm's room. Grant, contacting the others by radio, learned that someone would have to go outside the fence surrounding the center to the maintenance shed to restart the generators. Grant quickly formed a plan.

While Grant sprinted to the shed, Ellie emerged from the center to distract the raptors that were on the other side of the fence. As she approached them, the wiry dinosaurs lunged again and again at the fence, until Ellie realized that they were the ones doing the distracting. Ellie pivoted just in time to see the velociraptors that had been on the roof pouncing to the ground, ready to attack. With nowhere else to go, Ellie scrambled for the gate and ran for the maintenance shed.

Grant was able to turn on the power, and he and Ellie, eluding dinosaurs as they went, made their way back to the visitor's center. Outside the control, however, stood one of the predators. "The velociraptor was six feet tall and powerfully built . . . The raptor was alert; as it came forward, it looked from side to side, moving its head with abrupt, bird-like jerks . . . a gigantic, silent bird of prey." Soon this menacing creature was joined by the rest of its pack.

Grant gradually lured the beasts into the laboratory. Injecting a number of unhatched eggs with highly toxic chemicals, he rolled them toward the raptors. As he had anticipated, they ate the eggs—dying within seconds.

While Grant was in the lab with the dinosaurs, Ellie and the kids scrambled into the control room to reset the security systems. Just as the velociraptors above Malcolm's room chewed through the last bit of steel protecting the glass, 10,000 volts of electricity coursed through the bars, killing them instantly.

After everyone was reunited, Grant told the others of his discovery under the waterfall. In order to confirm his suspicions, he convinced Ellie, Genarro, and the kids to ride with him through the tunnel to the other side of the island to see if there was a raptor nest.

To their horror, at the end of the tunnel Grant and Ellie found a colony of velociraptors living in the damp concrete caverns. Because of a genetic flaw unforseen by the park's engineers, the raptors had been breeding for quite some time.

All at once, the raptors turned and ran from the tunnel through a large vent that opened onto the beach. Fascinated, Grant and Ellie watched as they lined up like a small reptile army. Slowly, it dawned on Grant that the dinosaurs had left the tunnel to watch a ship pass. " . . . They want to migrate," Ellie whispered.

Suddenly, a low-flying Costa Rican National Guard helicopter appeared on the horizon, sending the dinosaurs scrambling for shelter. Grant and the others just stood and waited.

Transported back to Jurassic Park to pick up the others, they learned that, while they had been investigating the tunnel, Malcolm had died of his injuries; Hammond had also been killed by some scavenging dinosaurs after he fell into a nearby ravine. As the helicopter winged toward Costa Rica, Grant turned in time to witness another helicopter annihilate the island with rockets and missiles.

The Jurassic Park survivors were put up in a nice hotel—and were politely informed that, except for Tim and Alexis, they would not yet be permitted to leave the country. It seemed some unknown animals were moving inland, migrating in a straight line from the coast into the mountains and jungles. And, even stranger, these animals ate only foods rich in lysine.

Grant knew he wouldn't be returning to the United States.

Commentary:

Although *Jurassic Park* is, at its core, a stirring, non-stop action-adventure story, the novel is also a thought-provoking, cautionary tale about a danger that seems all too viable.

The work addresses a number of important questions, mostly through the voice of Ian Malcolm. Malcolm questions everything that happens on Isla Nublar, harshly attacking the motive behind the genetic creation of the dinosaurs. He straightforwardly wonders if we *should* do something merely because we *can* do it.

Malcolm's chaos theories point out how futile it is for humanity to control nature, or even attempt to control nature—a theory proved in the novel by the uncontrollability of the dinosaurs. In the end he notes that progress is like death; one can never see the other side until after the fact.

PATRIOT GAMES

by Tom Clancy, G. P. Putnam's Sons, New York, N.Y., 1987

Type of work: Action adventure novel

Setting: Contemporary London and Annapolis, Maryland areas.

Principal characters:
Jack Ryan, a Naval Academy history teacher and ex-U.S. Marine
Cathy Ryan, Jack's wife, an eye surgeon
The Prince of Wales, heir to the British throne
Sean Miller, an Irish terrorism strategist

Story Overview:

Jack Ryan had come to London on a working vacation. But shortly after meeting his wife, Cathy, and daughter, Sally, in a park, he heard a grenade explode, and immediately forced them both to the ground. On the road bordering the park, Jack saw two men firing automatic weapons into an explosion-damaged limousine. He managed to work his way closer to the action without being seen and tackled the gunman at the rear of the car. Then, using the gunman's own weapon, Jack shot him in the hip and immobilized him. The other gunman, before jumping in a black sedan, turned and fired, just as Jack shot back. Jack felt the bullet hit his left shoulder, and collapsed before he could fire a second shot.

When he woke up in the hospital, Jack learned that the limousine had been carrying the Prince of Wales, heir to the British throne, and his family. Jack's prompt action had thwarted the assassination attempt of the Irish terrorists. As a reward, the Queen wanted to knight Jack, inviting him, Cathy and Sally to be her guests at Buckingham Palace.

Soon after Jack was released from the hospital—and given a hero's reception by the press—Cathy told him that she was expecting their second child.

Later, Jack testified at the trial of Sean Miller, the gunman he had wounded. All during the trial—and afterward—Jack was shaken by Miller's icy, inhuman stare. Although he was fiercely cross-examined by Miller's attorney, Jack's testimony proved to be fatal to the defense, and Miller was convicted. Soon after the trial, Jack and his family returned home to Maryland.

Meanwhile, British officials and the head agent of London's division of the FBI grew increasingly concerned: Somehow the terrorists were receiving inside information about the Prince's schedule. The government forces launched an extensive investigation.

Back in America, Washington's CIA officials had been impressed both by Jack's heroism and the writing he had done for a CIA cover agency. They wanted to recruit him, but decided to proceed slowly.

Then an unexpected and frightening thing happened: Sean Miller escaped from captivity when terrorists—acting once again on inside information—attacked his prison convoy. British intelligence officials noted that this particular group behaved quite differently from other terrorist organizations. In fact, the only "rule" they had not broken—yet—was carrying out a terrorist operation on American soil. Worried that the organization's tactics might be changing, the FBI agent in London alerted Jack that he could be in danger. Jack asked the CIA for all the details they could give him about the terrorists, and the agency complied with his request.

As the FBI had suspected, Miller's intent was to kill Jack. He and a team of assassins flew to the United States and immediately began stalking the Ryan family. Miller noticed that although Cathy varied her routes, she always picked up Sally from day care at the same time every day. He also noted that Jack left the Naval Academy after work from a particular gate. Accordingly, the terrorists drew up their plans.

One day, as Cathy left the day care center, a van slipped in beside her. In a rush to make up time on the way home, Cathy slipped her Porsche into the fast lane. When Cathy was about halfway home, two highway patrol cars took up the chase—only then noticing the van tailing her. Suddenly, a machine gun blast sprayed the speeding Porsche. One police car followed the van and the other stopped to assist Cathy and Sally, who had crashed into a concrete railing. The terrorists escaped pursuit by pulling into a crowded mall and abandoning the van.

When Jack got to the hospital, he found that Cathy had suffered only minor injuries, but Sally's condition was critical. Then when he discovered that his wife's arm injury had not in fact been caused by a bullet, he realized with horror that Miller had targeted his whole family.

Immediately, Jack reported to the CIA and offered his services to help stop the terrorists. With Sally now home recuperating from her wounds, Jack pondered what to do next. "You couldn't let your life be dominated by fear, but you couldn't ever let yourself lapse into a feeling of security," he reasoned. " . . . He wanted to lash out, if not at them, then at destiny . . . He could fight back . . . by joining the team full time. He would not be the master of his fate, but at least he could play a part."

British agents eventually exposed the source of their intelligence leak: a highly-placed agent who was privy to all the Prince's travel plans—including an unpublicized dinner visit to the Ryans' residence later that week.

In the meantime, Jack's research had uncovered an isolated desert camp in Libya at which the Irish terrorists trained prior to each attack. Satellite observations now showed that the training camp was deserted; another operation was about to be launched. U.S. and British security forces responded by setting up a manned safety net around Jack's home. They were unaware, however, that a terrorist, disguised as a power-line technician, had already made his way inside the net.

Though the Prince and Princess had been warned of the possible dangers involved in proceeding with the dinner party, they nonetheless insisted on attending. Masses of security personnel patrolled the grounds.

Acting on an anonymous tip, police were sent to a house on the other side of town, where they found a cache of weapons and explosives. Noticing an unidentified van pull out of the garage, they began pursuing it—playing right into the terrorists' hands.

Next, a power-company truck loaded with terrorists approached the grounds. Before reaching the security checkpoints, some of the armed band were let off. Then, when the truck reached the roadblock, the rear doors opened and men carrying automatic weapons opened fire on the security forces. The other terrorists, having since made their way through the woods, simultaneously ambushed the blockade, killing most of the guards. One survivor was able to send out a radio message calling for help, but a storm had grounded all aircraft so the bulk of the rescue forces would have to travel by car. One helicopter, however, made a desperate attempt to land, managing to unload some federal agents before it was shot down.

One side of the Ryans' property was bordered by a cliff that dropped straight into the ocean. Because of the treacherous terrain, security on this side was light, allowing Sean Miller and two of his henchmen to arrive by boat at the base of the cliff.

Meanwhile, inside the house, Jack and his guests heard the shots. But before they could do anything, Miller and his companions stormed in on them. After tying up the captives, Miller went outside to issue further instructions to his attack team.

While all of this was going on, Robby, a friend of Jack's, was in a bathroom at the far end of the house, quite unaware of the terrorists' entry. Fortunately, the terrorists were also oblivious to Robby's presence. As Robby returned to the main part of the house, he heard one of the terrorists cursing his wife. Fortunately, Robby quickly put the pieces together and kept hidden. Since he had not been seen, he retreated to find Jack's guns and ammunition. Then, prepared and armed, he crept within sight of the gunmen. When one of the terrorists viciously slapped his wife, Robby rose and emptied a shotgun blast into him. The sound was disguised by a thunderclap, and Robby managed to unload on a second terrorist before he realized what was happening. Even though their hands were tied, Jack and the Prince tripped up the third terrorist and kept him from getting to his gun. Following several intense moments of struggle, Robby finally ended up holding the shotgun to the head of the third gunman.

At gunpoint, the terrorist revealed that

Miller's boats were still moored at the base of the cliff. Jack's party made their way quietly to the bluff and down the ladder, where two boats were tied. Taking careful aim, Jack shot one of the terrorist guards. Another then turned and shot wildly, killing one of Jack's group. Nonetheless, they managed to get the boat started, and quickly sped away. Several terrorists, including Miller, scrambled down the cliff in pursuit and followed after them in a boat. Federal agents, watching the scene unfold, were finally able to dispatch another helicopter, but, unable to distinguish Ryan's boat from the terrorist boat, the government marksmen held their fire.

Jack and the Prince raced up the bay to Annapolis, protected by the wind and waves from terrorist gunfire. When they reached the Naval Academy dock, they enlisted help from Navy and Marine security personnel. As the terrorists neared the dock, they opened fire, but Navy security teams returned the fire and forced the terrorists away from shore.

With the Prince and the women safely ashore, Jack, using his CIA authority, commandeered a Navy patrol boat to pursue the terrorists. Presently, other federal agents radioed for the Coast Guard to join in the chase.

Jack soon realized that the terrorists, in the hope of gaining sanctuary, had boarded a foreign-registered ship. However, the Coast Guard had ruined this plan by forcing the vessel into the harbor.

State Police began boarding the ship, rounding up panic-stricken terrorists as they went—but Miller was not among them. Searching more meticulously, Jack finally found Miller and forced him out of hiding. At last, as Jack and the elusive and menacing terrorist faced one another, eye to eye, Miller backed down. In Jack's face Miller "saw . . . a look he had always reserved for his own use": *"I am Death," Ryan's face told him. "I have come for you . . . "* [And] *for the first time in his life, Sean Miller knew fear.*

Jack grappled with his rage, coming very near to killing Miller—but at the last minute he regained control of himself.

After the remaining terrorists were taken into custody, Jack rushed to the Base Hospital in time to help Cathy through the last stages of labor. As he welcomed his new little son into the world, he was glad that the baby's father was not a murderer.

Commentary:

Patriot Games offers a look at the forces which influenced Jack Ryan to be the kind of CIA officer he was in other best-selling Tom Clancy novels such as *The Hunt for Red October*. Less technical in nature and more people-oriented than the earlier Clancy works, *Patriot Games* is therefore more accessible and interesting to those readers not particularly enamored by the equipment and technology of war. While the orientation has changed, the tension and excitement for which Clancy is famous has not.

THE STAND

by Stephen King, Doubleday, Garden City, N.Y., 1978

Type of work: Contemporary symbolic horror

Setting: Boulder, Colorado and Las Vegas, Nevada; June 1990 through January 1991

Principal characters:

Mother Abigail, a 108-year-old prophetic black woman

Randall Flagg, the "Dark Man"

Stuart Redman, a survivor of the "Superflu"

An assembly of other survivors of earth's tragic environmental disaster

Story Overview:

The government's "Project Blue" had developed a fatal "Superflu" virus that, like a nuclear weapon, had the capability of bringing an entire population to its knees. Resembling the AIDS virus, it could constantly alter its blueprint and eventually wear the body out. Following an accident involving germ warfare agents, one infected worker had escaped to become the human host for this deadly virus. Highly contagious, the virus quickly spread, nearly wiping out earth's human population—reducing the human race to a plodding assortment of cynics. What route could they take now? Who would lead them on this newly brutal and baffling planet?

Stuart Redman had been on shift at the Texaco station in Arnette, Texas, when a blue Chevy with California plates recklessly swerved into a gas pump. Coughing up thick mucus, the driver died within minutes. Soon, everyone in Arnette was sick, except Stu; seemingly resistant to the virus, he was taken to the Plague Center in Stovington, Vermont. His immunity to the fatal virus was inexplicable.

Finally freed from investigative probings by the scientists, Stu met up with sociology professor Glen Bateman, who told him of a recurring nightmare he was having of a faceless "Dark Man" with red eyes. That night, Stu too dreamed of the same terrifying Dark Man.

Meanwhile, down in Shoyo, Arkansas, Superflu survivor Nick Andros dreamt of an elderly black woman in Nebraska named Mother Abigail, who invited him and his friends to come to her. The dream impressed Nick so much that he and his two friends—a guileless, semi retarded man named Tom Cullen and a disorganized but resourceful man named Ralph Brentner—set off immediately.

When they arrived, Mother Abigail greeted Nick by name and appointed him "leader." She instructed Nick and Ralph to move to Boulder, Colorado, to prepare a place where she and her righteous followers could assemble. Ralph, she knew, was the kind of man who couldn't fill out a job application without having it look like it had been through a Hamilton-Beach blender, but when the fabric of the world began to tear open, would say, "Let's slap a little epoxy in there and see if that'll hold her"; more often than not, it did.

In the meantime, Stu and Glen made their way toward Nebraska in company of two survivors from Maine, Harold and Fran—Harold, all along the route, chewing on PayDay candy bars

while jealously guarding Fran from Stu's advances.

Elsewhere, in Phoenix, Arizona, Lloyd Henreid sat in his prison cell, starving. It had been days since his last meal—a rat. He salivated unconsciously, staring at the teeth marks in his cellmate's leg. Suddenly, Randall Flagg, the immortal "Dark Man," appeared in his cell, promising Lloyd his freedom one condition that he become Flagg's loyal servant. "You and I, Lloyd," the enigmatic Flagg glowered, "we're going to go far. It's a good time for people like us."

Flagg, "reborn" when the Superflu hit, was "a lonely lunatic cell looking for a mate to set up house for a malignant tumor . . ." He was also a powerfully demonic man who felt a transfiguration coming on. "He could taste it, a sooty hot taste that came from everywhere, as if God was planning a cook-out and all of civilization was going to be the barbecue."

Flagg also needed "Trash." At nine years of age, Donald Merwin Elbert had begun lighting fires in people's trash cans; ever since then, his fires had gotten bigger and bigger. The angry explosions had become his lifeblood. The "Trash Can Man" had come there, his final destination, for the Great Burning—the one the Dark Man had promised him. After Lloyd's warm handshake, Trash, for the first time in his life, felt like he belonged. But the very next day, Trash learned that it could be cold in hell. For his initiation, he had to drive the crude nails into the hands and feet of the first crucifixion victim.

Larry Underwood was the last member of the group to arrive in Boulder, having followed Harold's trail of PayDay wrappers all the way from Maine. Along the road he had met Nadine Cross, a school teacher. Nadine was the only one who didn't admit to having dreams. But she was lying: she had dreamed about Randall Flagg—who now called her to come to Las Vegas. To her, Flagg was her savior, "the dark man, the Walkin' Dude . . ."

After Mother Abigail greeted Larry, she turned to Nadine. "Something about the woman made [Abigail] feel grave-cold. He's here, she thought. He's come in the shape of this woman . . ."

The following day, Larry walked over to Harold's to thank him for the trail of candy wrappers Harold had left for him to follow. He was surprised to find a smiling, broad-shouldered boy who looked like he hadn't eaten a PayDay for a month. When Harold left the room momentarily to fix them a drink, Larry noticed a loose stone that sat over the hearth. Removing the stone, he saw that a ledger was hidden inside the crevice. He replaced the stone and waited for his drink.

When Larry left Harold's place, he noticed the shades were pulled down throughout the entire house. In Boulder, he reflected, only the houses of the dead had their shades drawn. "When they got sick, they had drawn their curtains . . . and died in privacy, like any animal in its last extremity prefers to do. The living—maybe in subconscious acknowledgement of that fact of death—threw their shutters and their curtains wide."

The "Free-Zone Committee" was established

to provide structure in the new society. Committee members included Abigail, Stu, Fran, Larry, Nick, Glen and Ralph. Along with discussing matters such as how to deal with power outages and how to improve housing, it was decided that three non-committee survivors would be sent to act as spies in Flagg's Las Vegas camp. Judge Ferris, a clever 70-year-old man, Dayna Jurgens, a dauntless woman self-trained in the art of weaponry, and simple-minded Tom Cullen were selected for this mission. However, when the committee went to gain Abigail's approval, she was missing. She had felt her sin, "the one she thought of as the mother of sin, pride," and set out on a pilgrimage to purge herself of sin, to seek God—and she would return only if it were His will. Harold volunteered to serve on the search committee—but he had already heard, and decided to follow, the alluring voice of Flagg. Along with Nadine, he would have his revenge on the Free-Zone Committee.

Several months later, Tom returned, alone, from his Las Vegas spy mission; the others had been killed. Apparently, Flagg's mysterious "third eye" wasn't able to track Tom's movements; his uncomplicated mind and heart were too childlike and pure.

That afternoon, Fran and Larry decided to see what Harold's ledger contained. They wondered: What side was he on? Had he gone over to Flagg's camp? Looking through the ledger, the scrawls seemed to be those of a profoundly disturbed mind. The first sentence read: "My great pleasure this delightful post-Apocalypse summer will be to kill [Stu], and just maybe I will kill [Nadine], too."

Later that evening, Harold and Nadine looked on as the committee members filed into Ralph's home. Harold held the signaling device: ". . . His thumb rested lightly on the send button. He would depress it and blow them all to hell . . . " It was Fran's instinct that warned her to get everyone out of the house. But for Nick, it was too late: Harold pushed the button.

At that moment, Mother Abigail suddenly reappeared, very near death, to strengthen the committee for one final crusade: to destroy the Dark Prince. Stu, Larry, Glen and Ralph, weaponless, left on their mission that very night.

Nadine, convinced that Harold was a traitor, that he had gone over to the wrong side, determined to make him pay. As they biked along the highway, he flipped over the side of a guard rail and broke his leg. Nadine refused to rescue him: ". . . Someone who would betray one side would probably betray the other . . . " Harold, left for dead, held a gun to his head and pulled the trigger.

Nadine continued on alone through the cold desert. Suddenly she could feel Flagg's cold dark presence. "She felt his baking heat. He radiated it, like a well-stoked brick oven. His smooth timeless hands slipped around hers . . . and then closed over them tight like handcuffs." In a flash, she felt repulsed by his presence. In less than an hour, she would be catatonic—and pregnant; later she would jump off a balcony to her death.

Flagg camped in the desert that night, his dreams filled with the coming of his followers. He couldn't believe they were coming to him of their own choice, "wrapped in righteousness like a clutch of missionaries approaching the combat's village."

But, in the end, only three survived the journey. Stu had fallen into a ravine and shattered his leg, and the others had gone on without him. Before long, Flagg's men captured them and placed them in separate jail cells. Within twenty-four hours, Glen was staring Flagg in the eyes, laughing. "Oh pardon me . . . " said Glen. "It's just that we were all so frightened . . . We made such a business of you . . . I'm laughing as much for our own foolishness as for your incredible lack of substance . . . " Glen laughed and laughed—until his entire face was blown off, and he could laugh no more.

During the night, Larry made peace with himself; he knew he was going to die a martyr's death. "If there's a God—and now I believe there must be—that's his will," he concluded. " . . . Somehow all of this will end as a result of our dying."

The captives were placed in two cages attached to a flat bed. It was Ralph who understood the implications of the machinery. "Larry," he said in a dry voice, "They're going to pull us to pieces!" Suddenly, the mood of the gathered crowd changed. Unexpectedly, one man cried out, "This ain't right! You know it ain't . . . This ain't how Americans act . . . listening to some murderin' freak in cowboy boots . . . " All at once, sensing his power waning, Flagg began reacting to another, more ravaging and unknown terror.

Trash, it turned out, had "thrown dirt into the foolproof machinery of the Dark Man's conquest." Trash, a gruesome display of the last stages of radiation sickness, parted the crowd riding a dirty electric cart—and dragging an A-Bomb behind him. Larry felt a sense of relief wash over him as the "silent white light filled the world," a "holy fire" sent to consume the righteous and the unrighteous alike in nuclear holocaust.

One year later, the citizens of Boulder were revelling once more in the pleasures of good health, electricity and television. Fran and Stu were in the process of planning their next project—to rebuild Maine.

And halfway around the world, on a primitive Pacific Island, a man named Russell Faraday introduced himself to a native tribe; he had come on a mission, he announced. The islanders reverently knelt at the Dark Man's feet, worshipping him, loving him. Truly, "life was such a wheel that no man could stand upon it for long. And it always, at the end, came round to the same place again."

Commentary:

The Stand portrays the cardinal struggle between good and evil in a post-Apocalyptic world where the few survivors must quickly choose a side before it is chosen for them. Abigail's community is left with the difficult responsibility of choice, while Flagg's sinister society mirrors Nazi Germany during the reign of Hitler, where individuals mechanically follow orders without questioning the cause—or the effect. When the world comes to this point, one of the book's characters says, "someone has to take a stand."

DINNER AT THE HOMESICK RESTAURANT

by Anne Tyler, Knopf (dist. by Random House), New York, N.Y., 1982

Type of work: Contemporary novel

Setting: 1940s to 1980s; Baltimore and other Eastern U.S. cities

Principal characters:
Pearl Tull, a single parent
Beck Tull, her estranged husband
Cody Tull, their eldest son
Ezra Tull, their second son, and framer of The Homesick Restaurant
Jenny Tull, their daughter and youngest child
Josiah Payson, Ezra's slightly retarded boyhood friend

Story Overview:

As Pearl Tull lay dying, she tried to tell her son, Ezra, that he "should have got an extra." She meant an extra mother— in the same way she had chosen to have extra children after her first child, Cody, almost died. But after having two more, Pearl realized that having an extra child was not as simple as she had supposed, for she could not bear the idea of giving up either Ezra, "so sweet and clumsy it could break your heart," or Jenny, who was "such fun to dress and give different hair styles." Losing any of her children would be heartbreaking.

Pearl had married Beck Tull at the age of thirty, narrowly averting the tragic status of spinsterhood. "Auntie Pearl," besieged with requests to baby-sit, assaulted with pitying looks . . . that was not her idea of a life. Beck Tull was younger—twenty-four—lean, rangy, wavy black hair and eyes a brilliant shade of blue. Some people thought he was "a little extreme." But she agreed to marry him anyway.

Beck's job as a salesman with the Tanner Corporation kept the family on the move. Somehow, promises of a richer territory or a promotion never materialized. Beck always said it wasn't his fault, "I'm surrounded by ill-wishers," he claimed, but Pearl wasn't convinced. She grew increasingly ill-tempered.

One Sunday evening, Beck informed Pearl that he didn't want to stay married. He had been transferred again, to Norfolk; this time "he thought it best if he went alone." From then on he occasionally sent money and always updated Pearl on his continually changing address, but Pearl never shared the letters with the children.

Cody, the oldest child, was a troublemaker who was always jealous of the attention bestowed upon his fair-haired, younger brother, Ezra. So, he devised elaborate schemes to make Ezra appear the rebel. Once he arranged empty beer bottles, a crumpled pack of Camels and a box of pretzels around Ezra while he was sleeping and took photographs that Pearl later discovered when she picked up the roll of developed film. Another time, Cody removed the mattress supports of Ezra's bed and placed pornographic magazines underneath. When Ezra sat down, the bed collapsed under his weight, and Pearl arrived to find a dazed Ezra

surrounded by photos of women in "garter belts and black lace brassieres . . . " Despite his jealousy, however, Cody retained a wistful desire to be as good and considerate as Ezra.

Jenny, the studious youngest child, was deeply affected by her mother's violent rages. Later, when Ezra was drafted into the army, Jenny agreed to keep in touch with Mrs. Scarlatti, the owner of a restaurant where Ezra worked. She also promised to visit Josiah Payson, Ezra's semi-retarded friend who "jibbered and jabbered" when he was teased or made to feel uncomfortable. Mrs. Scarlatti, "a white-faced woman in a stark black knife of a dress . . . [her] black hair was swept completely to the right, like one of those extreme *Vogue* magazine models," intimidated Jenny. However, Jenny found the child-like Josiah charming; his face lit up with happiness when Jenny told him that she was Ezra's sister. He explained that he wanted to work for Ezra when he returned from the army. Ezra dreamt of someday buying Mrs. Scarlatti's restaurant, Josiah said, and converting it into a place where people could "come just like to a family dinner . . . he'll cook them one thing special each day and dish it out on their plates and everything will be solid and wholesome, really homelike."

One day, Josiah invited Jenny to dinner at his home. There, Jenny felt she was in the middle of some fairy tale, "where the humble widow, honest and warm-hearted, lives in a cottage with her son." In this safe setting, "everything else— the cold dark of the streets, the picture of her own bustling mother—seemed brittle by comparison, lacking the smoothly rounded completeness of Josiah's life." When Josiah stumbled close to her after walking her home, and enveloped her in his arms, she overcame her surprise, and kissed him back, longing to savor his simplicity. Suddenly Jenny's mother shattered the quiet by barging in on the couple, striking Jenny and calling her a piece of trash for taking part in such "anomalistic love." Josiah, confused by the vehemence he witnessed, rushed down the porch steps and disappeared.

After Ezra returned home from the war, Mrs. Scarlatti became ill and was hospitalized. With Mrs. Scarlatti indisposed, Ezra took the liberty of altering the restaurant. First, he added a garlic soup Mrs. Scarlatti had previously deemed "too hearty" for the fine, formal nature of the restaurant. Eventually, Ezra replaced the stuffy wait staff with warm-hearted women, and scrapped the menus in favor of the specials being listed on a blackboard. Ezra "grew feverish with new ideas, and woke in the night longing to share them with someone. . . . He'd cook what people felt homesick for—tacos like those from vendors' carts in California . . . that vinegary North Carolina barbecue . . . "

When Mrs. Scarlatti recovered and visited the restaurant, however, the changes shocked her. She told Ezra to change the sign: "It's not

Mrs. Scarlatti's anymore." Truly, Ezra had renamed it "The Homesick Restaurant." Some nights he offered only one entree; sometimes four or five selections. "But still you might not get what you asked for. `The Smithfield ham,' you'd say, and up would come the okra stew. `With that cough of yours, I know this will suit you better,' Ezra would explain."

Jenny, meanwhile, became a pediatrician. After her second divorce, she happened upon a bear of a man, a single parent of six children and was immediately drawn to them; she could fill some void in their life. Eventually they were married.

When Slevin, the eldest son of Jenny's husband, stole Pearl's vacuum, Pearl suggested, "I wonder if he's asking for some psychological help in some way." But Slevin explained that he just "needed to borrow" the vacuum cleaner for a spell. "For what?" Jenny asked. "For . . . I don't know," Slevin reluctantly replied. "Just for . . . See, there it was in the pantry. It was exactly like my mother's. Just exactly. You know how you never think about a thing, or realize you remember it, and then all at once something will bring it back? . . . It had that same clothy smell, just like my mother's . . . so I wanted to take it home. But once I got it here, well, it didn't work out. It's like I had lost the connection. It wasn't the same after all."

Even into adulthood, Cody, who had become a businessman, continued to resent Ezra. When Ezra decided to marry a woman named Ruth, Cody resolutely sought to woo her to be his wife instead. Ruth, at first put off by the antics of this sophisticated, sleek executive, eventually succumbed to Cody's attentions, and they married.

Ezra, embittered and broken-hearted by Ruth's double dealing, devoted all his attention to the restaurant. He repeatedly tried to gather his family together for a "big family meal, one that would last all the way through dessert." But each time the family came, someone became insulted or hysterical and marched off in a huff, and Ezra's visions for a real "family supper" disintegrated. However, on the occasion of Pearl's death, a meal—at The Homesick Restaurant— was planned after the funeral.

Before the service, Ezra reluctantly told Jenny, Cody and their families that he had invited their father, Beck. "It wasn't *my* idea," Ezra explained. "It was Mother's. She talked about it when she got so sick."

The funeral began; Beck appeared. A man with a tight-skinned face and "an elaborate plume of silver hair," he was "like a child presenting some accomplishment." He seemed pleased to discover his children grown—"Look at you!" he said. "Both my sons are bigger than I am." But the reception he was given mystified him. Cody acted as though his father had been absent for a day rather than thirty-five years; Jenny, for her part, appeared distant and distracted; Ezra—only Ezra—remained his characteristically kind, genuine self, and calmly invited his father to join them for lunch.

At the restaurant, Beck was quite taken by the size of the gathering. " . . . It looks like this is one of those great big, jolly, noisy, rambling . . . why, *families!* . . . like something on T.V. Lots of cousins and uncles, jokes, reunions . . . " Cody, awakened to the reality of the situation, suddenly interrupted, "It's not really that way at all . . . it's not the way it appears . . . not more than two or three of these kids are even related to you . . . as for me, well, I haven't been with these people in years . . . you think we're some jolly, situation-comedy family when we're in particles, torn apart, torn all over the place, and our mother was a witch . . . a raving, shrieking, unpredictable witch . . . "

Stunned silence greeted his tirade. "She wasn't *always* angry," Ezra finally said with aplomb, setting the gathering somewhat back on kilter.

But before long, Beck slipped away, unnoticed. It was shortly after Cody had related the story of an associate who had found out unexpectedly that he had fathered a daughter some time before. The girl's mother had told Cody's associate that, since he had never been there, he was only the girl's father by biological fact.

When Ezra discovered Beck had left, he urged the family to go after their father. But no one moved. "Please! . . . " he begged. "For once, I want this family to finish a meal together." Finally they agreed and spread out into the city, searching for a man with flowing silver hair—a man they hardly knew.

It was Cody who found Beck as he was looking for the Trailways bus station. "How could you just leave us . . . dump us on our mother's mercy?" he asked. Beck explained, weakly, that Pearl "just used up his good points." Every week, arriving home, he was made to feel unappreciated; he somehow muddled everything up; he "just couldn't seem to make anyone happy." In spite of how Pearl had treated him, he had always wanted to share his happy experiences with her, even long after he had abandoned her. Cody, in agony for something to say to break the tension, happened to glance down the street and see his family rounding the corner. "They've found us," Cody said. "Let's go finish our dinner."

Commentary:

Dinner at the Homesick Restaurant subtly addresses the difficulty of creating and maintaining family relationships. This enigma—what constitutes "family," and by what mysterious means is it fashioned?—spirals throughout the novel. Before Pearl marries Buck, she wonders if she has missed out on learning some secret, one that was common knowledge for other girls; likewise, Ezra constantly frets about his ability to "connect" with people, and so goes out of his way to establish ties through his restaurant.

The Homesick Restaurant is an aptly-named novel. In an almost kaleidoscopic, mythical way, Anne Tyler creates a nostalgic yearning for "home"—a safe haven where warm ties bind and "family" is treasured.

CROSSING TO SAFETY

by Wallace Stegner, Random House, New York, N.Y., 1987

Type of work: Contemporary novel

Setting: Battell Pond, Vermont, 1972, and flashbacks to as far back as 1937

Principal characters:
Larry Morgan, a writer and the story's narrator
Sally Morgan, his wife
Sid and Charity Lang, friends of the Morgans

Story Overview:

There was no sense of disorientation when I awoke in the cottage. We had made so many good memories there over the years that there was a sense of peace— of returning home. I left Sally asleep and went for a walk over the old, familiar paths. Returning, I helped Sally into her braces.

As we took a bite to eat, Charity's daughter, Hallie, stopped by to invite us to the Big House for brunch and a picnic birthday celebration for her mother. I wondered if Charity would be up to it, as sick as she was. But Hallie assured me that the picnic had been Charity's idea—and we all knew how successful it would be if we opposed it. So, while Sally napped, I sat on the porch and reminisced: "It was no effort. Everything compelled it."

In 1937, with the Depression in full swing, I was lucky to get a job at all, so we were content with the one-year fill-in contract in Madison, Wisconsin. Teaching English classes also would give me time to write.

I got home from the university one day the next week and found Sally talking to Charity Lang, the wife of another young professor. As far as I could see, except for the fact that both Sally and Charity were pregnant and were due to deliver at about the same time, we had nothing in common with the well-to-do Langs; but in spite of this we liked Charity, and she seemed to like us. We were agreeably surprised to find through our association, that we hit it off quite well with Sid and Charity.

That was a very busy year for me. Almost every minute not spent teaching or correcting papers was occupied writing in the furnace room. We were thrilled when the short story I had written during the week before school started was accepted by a publisher. The extra money was critically needed.

About the only times I saw Sally was during meals. I was thankful that Charity was able to spend so much time with her. Their friendship—indeed, our four-way friendship—seemed to deepen each day of the fall and winter.

On the same day we went to see Charity and the new baby in the hospital, big news came in the mail. Harcourt Brace and Company had accepted my novel. Ecstatic, we called Sid and some other friends to come over, and we had a party. After a while, Sally felt tired—but since she was due to give birth at any time, this didn't seem out of the ordinary. I put her to bed. When the party finally broke up, I found Sally crying as she struggled to change the bedding. She had wet the bed, she said; but I knew better, and Sid and I rushed her to the hospital. After what seemed like days, the doctor gave up trying to get the baby to present properly and just kind of snatched her out. Yes, it was a her, and she had lots of bruises and a broken arm, but she was essentially healthy.

All the young instructors spent that year agonizing over whether they would be kept on by the university. I had been hired as a temporary, with no promise at all of being allowed to stay, but still I hoped, along with the rest.

Sid himself wanted to be a poet, but Charity was convinced that poetry wouldn't get him a permanent position. She made him agree not to write any more poems, at least until he got some tenure. She saw what his potential was, and was determined to see him rise to a rank that would ensure him the prestige he deserved.

One day in late March, Sid came to my office to see if I had heard . . . The university's decision was etched in the distress on his face. "Don't tell me they didn't up you," I moaned. "They didn't up me, no," he replied. "But they didn't down me either. Renewed instructorship, three more years after next year." All at once I felt hollow inside. Sid's distress was for me; the Department of English had "x-ed me out." Quite a few others besides me had also been released. This hurt Sid. He was no happier than I was to think that he had been preferred over his friends—some of whom he generously thought of as his betters.

Later, Sid came to my office to announce that we both needed a change; we needed to get out into the beautiful early spring weather. He suggested that we get the babies a sitter, rent a boat, and take the girls sailing. I finally relented.

At the beginning it was a wonderful sail. But when we were well out into the lake a sudden storm came up. I wanted to lower the sail, but Charity vetoed the move. I think Sid agreed with me, but he had no choice in the matter; Charity had overruled him before he had even spoken. We continued sailing, with me bailing as fast as I could, but the boat took on more and more water. I passed out the life preservers, but almost before we knew it we found ourselves in the water, clinging to the overturned boat. We floated in the freezing water for what seemed like hours, but was probably only ten or twelve minutes, before a rescue boat fished us out of the lake.

Sid and Charity visited us later, Charity babbling about how awful they felt to have nearly drowned us, especially after what the English department had done. Even though I was in the process of sending out application letters, the university had left its decision until so late that I knew I would have trouble finding another position.

Now Sid and Charity tendered their offer: Sally and the baby could come and stay the summer with them on their lake-side property in Vermont; after my two-month teaching stint was over, I could join them there. Meanwhile, in order to save on rent, I could mind their house in Madison while I taught summer school. We couldn't do anything but agree to the arrangement.

Two months later, I arrived in Vermont. The lake, Battell Pond, and the surrounding countryside were stunning. I could see that the respite had helped Sally. After a few days I was into the customary routine: resting, eating, talking, walking. It was a magnificently relaxing time for me, even though I was still writing every spare minute.

We did have one dinner party at the lake—which I later realized had been set up for my benefit. A publisher, a relative of Charity's, had been invited—and had been encouraged to read my novel before he came. He agreed that the book was good and offered me some part-time work in Boston, with the chance for a full-time position as an editor.

We all decided to end the summer with a cross-country hike. On the morning we were to head out, Charity insisted that we had forgotten to pack the tea. Sid disagreed, but, as usual, Charity got her way and Sally retrieved another box from the house. That evening after we had made camp, while the women were out exploring, Sid took the extra package of tea and quietly tossed it into the fire. I didn't understand either of the Langs, nor could I see how they survived living together; but, by some miracle, they managed.

A few days into the trip, Charity decreed that we should follow the compass cross-country until we found a trail or a road. Sid suggested that we follow a creek bed where the walking was much easier. Predictably, we ended up following Charity's compass. Then, one more day to go in our hike, Sally suddenly came down with a high fever and painfully swollen joints. When she got worse, Sid rode a mule to the nearest village to summon a doctor.

Sally had polio. Both legs and part of one arm were paralyzed. But she remained determined to walk again—and eventually, she did, with the aid of braces and crutches. In the meantime, our baby, Lang—named in honor of Sid and Charity—had gone back to Madison with the Langs, who insisted on paying our bills. Luckily I got the editing job in Boston and continued to write. Eventually we moved back to the Southwest, a climate that was easier for Sally to cope with.

Meanwhile, Sid and Charity had built a new, larger home in Madison, because Charity was just sure Sid was due for a promotion and tenure—and, even when she was proven wrong, Charity was always right. As fate would have it, Sid got a release instead of a promotion, and the Langs went back to Battell Pond for a while. Meanwhile, I had developed some good contacts and I was able to help Sid get a position at Dartmouth College. At last we were able to repay Sid and Charity for our medical bills.

Now, many years later, here we all were, back at Battell Pond. Charity was suffering from inoperable cancer and would soon die. When we went up to see her, we expected to greet an ashen and haggard woman. Instead we found her still apparently brimming with energy. " . . . She [was] not going to be shushed, not even by cancer."

As we talked, it was evident that Charity had made peace with herself about dying. "Dying's an important event," she insisted. "You can't rehearse for it. All you can do is try to prepare yourself and others. You can try to do it right."

Later, as Sid and I drove around together making arrangements for the picnic, Sid unburdened himself. Unlike his wife, he was still at war with the inevitable. Not only did he fear for his own loss, and for Charity, but he was annoyed that she was trying to manage her death in the way that her life now refused to be managed. She was even still managing his life; she had given him a list of several "suitable" women for him to court after her death.

As we returned to the house, Sally came out to meet us. Charity had taken a turn for the worse and wouldn't be able to go along on the picnic after all. Still, she wanted the rest of the family, including Sid and me, to follow through with the plans while Sally and a few of the women took her to the hospital; she did not want Sid to suffer with her—or to see her die.

Reluctantly, Sid agreed to his wife's wishes. Again, Charity got her way. Or almost. That afternoon, Sid disappeared. The family went ahead with the picnic while I stayed behind to look for him. Finally, about the time the family was returning, Sid came out of the woods. Whether he had been writing poetry, hiking his own route, or simply clearing his mind, for once he had got his own way: he had mourned Charity to suit himself, not her.

Commentary:

In this novel, the Pulitzer Prize-winning Stegner explores the complex connections within marriages and between married couples. Larry and Sally have cultivated one type of relationship; Sid and Charity have cultivated quite another. Sid understands that a dominant mother and a dependent father have shaped his wife's expectations—and Charity can't change, while Sid decides that he can—and he does.

Larry and Sally are a more "traditional" couple. They struggle against economic and physical hardship, but their love—together with Sid and Charity's support—carries them through. Each couple possesses qualities that help nourish the other couple, a bridge of friendship in times of need that lets them cross to safety.

Stegner avoids the usual stereotypes and trite developments. For instance, as opposed to conventional modern "soap opera" plots, each husband stays at arm's length from the other's wife, taking care to avoid a too-intense relationship. There are no affairs, no compromising situations, no shouting, and no explicit "soap-box statements." There is only a quiet, compassionate story of caring and understanding.

THE BONFIRE OF THE VANITIES

by Tom Wolfe, Farrar, Straus Books, New York, N.Y., 1987

Type of work: Satiric novel

Setting: New York City; 1980s

Principal characters:
Sherman McCoy, a wealthy bond trader
Judy McCoy, Sherman's socialite wife
Maria Ruskin, Sherman's married mistress
Henry Lamb, a congenial black youth from the South Bronx
Freddy Button, a high-society lawyer
Thomas Killian, a hard-boiled criminal lawyer

Commentary:

The Bonfire of the Vanities is Tom Wolfe's first novel. Best known as a journalist, Wolfe (1931 -) has been widely regarded for the publication of his acclaimed account of astronauts and test pilots, *The Right Stuff*. Both as a journalist and a novelist, he claims to be influenced by the "analytical insights of the best essays and scholarly writing, and the deep factual reporting of hard reporting."

Critics have likened Wolfe's *The Bonfire of the Vanities* to the works of Thackeray and Dickens, among others, despite his occasionally overpowering prose and stilted dialects.

Actually, some of his preoccupations with dialect, characterization, and modes of reporting in general—the very elements for which he has been most criticized—lend an unusual authority and texture to his writing. As critic Terrence Rafferty writes, its appeal largely "derives from the fact that Tom Wolfe is an absolute master of the world of appearances; he understands every nuance of how people see themselves, and each other. He's so good at picking up modes of social perception that he often gives the impression that nothing else matters."

Indeed, in *The Bonfire of the Vanities*, these "modes of social perception" create an astonishingly intricate portrait of a city and its widely divergent inhabitants.

Story Overview:

Sherman McCoy, who liked to think of himself as "Master of the Universe," was a Yale man with an imposing chin. He had a six-year-old daughter named Campbell and a wife named Judy who was "forty years old . . . No getting around it . . . Today good-looking . . . Tomorrow they'll be talking about what a handsome woman she is . . . Not her fault . . . But not mine either," Sherman had concluded.

But Judy was only a part of Sherman's problem. Adding to his general dissatisfaction was the fact that he considered himself to be "still in the season of the rising sap." Sherman was a bond trader who earned $980,000 a year at the prestigious firm of Pierce & Pierce. Nonetheless, he couldn't shake the feeling that he "must deserve more, from time to time, when the spirit moved him."

Recently the spirit had moved him to keep company with Maria Ruskin, a stunning brunette, who—in addition to being married to someone else—"walked with a nose-up sprocket-hipped model-girl gait." And it was Maria who irrevocably altered Sherman's life one night. After picking her up at the airport in his flashy Mercedes roadster, Sherman took a wrong turn off the highway and became lost in the South Bronx.

"Look over there," Maria said, surveying the urban wasteland of "asphalt, concrete, and cinders" just beyond the window of the Mercedes. "It says the George Washington Bridge . . . it's civilization! Let's get outta here!"

"Okay, okay, I see it," Sherman said, pulling onto the ramp. But a tire was blocking the road. He got out of the car to move it, conscious not to scuff his "$650 New and Lingwood shoes." All at once Maria shouted out in alarm: "Sherman!" Two black youths were approaching him on the ramp. "Yo!" one of them called out. "Need some help?"

Sherman panicked. "Do something! Act!" he thought to himself. Shoving the tire at one of the youths, Sherman skidded back to the car, suddenly oblivious to the cost of his shoes. "Get in!" Maria screamed. Sherman slid into the car, which Maria—now in the driver's seat—put into gear. The thinner of the boys stood directly in front of the car. "Look out!" Sherman warned—but Maria drove right into the boy; there was "a terrific jolt" as she sped away.

"Just take it easy," Sherman told her. "We're okay now, we're okay." When they managed to find the expressway back to Manhattan, Sherman caressed Maria's neck and thought, "I saved her! I am her protector!" Once they had pulled onto Maria's street, Sherman, after inspecting his fender, was quite relieved to find that there was no dent. Although Sherman and Maria discussed notifying the police, they decided against it. If someone should ever ask them about the incident, they would merely explain that they had been attacked by the youths and had fought their way out. Pleased with themselves, the two went up to Maria's apartment for a night of "Pure Bliss!" Once again, Sherman was "Master of the Universe"—and now he was also "King of the Jungle."

Meanwhile, as Sherman was prowling the bedroom jungle, Henry Lamb, the youth struck by the departing Mercedes, lay comatose in a hospital bed. Before lapsing into unconsciousness, however, Henry had provided the police with a description of the car and a partial license number. The assistant district attorney immediately began investigating the case, as did Reverend Reginald Bacon, a black activist and self-proclaimed "street socialist," and finally, the case was taken up by Peter Fallow, a reporter for a local tabloid.

Picking up a copy of the paper, Sherman despaired: while his identity as the owner of the car that had struck Henry Lamb was as yet unknown, he might later be identified. With a curious mix of fascination and dread, Sherman began religiously to follow the story in the news.

As the days passed, the doctors at Lincoln Hospital termed the coma "probably irreversible" and classified Lamb's condition as grave. As his chances for recovery worsened, the case quickly became a populist cause. Lamb was described as a respectful young man and an exemplary student.

Reverend Reginald Bacon, chairman of the Harlem-based All People's Solidarity, called this "the same old story. Human life, if it's a black life or a Hispanic life, is not worth much to the power structure. If this had been a *white* honor student struck down on Park Avenue by a black driver, they wouldn't be trifling with statistics and legal trifles . . ."

A terrifying thought came into Sherman's head as he read the latest article: the two youths were simply "well-meaning boys who wanted to help . . . " No matter how hard he tried, Sherman could not get Henry Lamb out of his mind; he was unable to concentrate on his work. Instead, Sherman continually went out to get a shoe shine or to hide in the men's room at Pierce & Pierce, so he could pore over each new article.

One column especially tormented him: the report described Lamb's South Bronx neighborhood as "seething" and "up in arms" over the authorities' reluctance to pursue the case aggressively. Sherman feared that the proverbial noose had begun to tighten around him. In near hysteria, he decided to consult his lawyer, Freddy Button.

When Sherman finished relating the story, Freddy urged him to consult with a criminal lawyer at "Dershkin, Bellavit, Fishbein & Schlossel." To Sherman, this "torrent of syllables was like a bad smell." Puffing on a never-ending chain of cigarettes, Freddy went on to describe criminal lawyers as "crude, coarse, sleazy, unappetizing—you can't even imagine what they're like." But despite these characteristics, Freddy added, criminal attorneys "know how to make deals." Freddy recommended a lawyer named Thomas Killian. Sherman accepted the advice with some skepticism, but eventually contacted Killian.

"Assuming Lamb don't die," Killian said, "there's reckless endangerment." He listed a few other scenarios, but to Sherman each sounded as bad as the others. To his great relief, Killian advised him not to turn himself into the police.

A few days later, however, Sherman received an urgent phone call from Killian, whose numbing words paralyzed his client: "They're gonna place you under arrest." Apparently Lamb's companion the night of the accident heard the woman in the Mercedes say the name "Shuhman," and the youth had later identified a photograph of Sherman as that of the man present at the scene of the crime. Killian, however, told him not to worry; he might go to jail for a short stay, but soon he'd be "outta there. Ba-bing."

After long deliberation, Sherman decided to tell his wife the truth about the incident. But to spare Judy complete devastation, he would say that he had had a "brief flirtation" with Maria, but no affair. "Oh, I don't know what you did with your Maria Ruskin, and I don't care," Judy said calmly when he admitted to his Bronx catastrophe. "That's the least of it, but I don't think you understand that." Not knowing what else to say, Sherman went up to his daughter's bedroom. "They're saying I hit a boy with my car and hurt him badly," Sherman told little Campbell, who, perched on one of her "miniature boudoir chairs" was busily writing a book about a koala bear. "I didn't do any such thing

but there are bad people who are saying that . . . but all you have to know is, it isn't true."

"Does that mean you'll be famous?" Campbell asked innocently. "Will you be in history, Daddy?" Then when she told her father that she loved him, Sherman began to weep.

The dreadful words "I'm going to jail" haunted Sherman all that night. At 7:15 the next morning, Killian appeared to escort his client to the car where two detectives awaited him. To Sherman's disgust, one of them addressed him by his first name. Sherman suddenly felt like "a servant . . . a slave . . . a prisoner."

Finally, they arrived at the Bronx precinct. In the pouring rain, the detectives led Sherman, handcuffed, through a throng of reporters and angry protesters, who shouted curses and insults at him. Sherman felt "dead, so dead he couldn't even die." Entering the jail, he was searched, fingerprinted, and photographed before being taken to his cell.

Before long, however, Sherman was placed in front of a judge, who released him on a $100,000 bail. Shouts filled the courtroom: "You gonna get what Henry Lamb got . . . Say your prayers, Park Avenue!" Sherman knew only that he was free again. His life, though, as he soon found out, had irreversibly changed. He received death threats; the press hounded him; his family life disintegrated; and, worst of all, he was "hemorrhaging money" and perilously close to financial ruin.

Months later, when the trial finally began, Sherman suffered yet another devastating blow: Maria Ruskin—the one person whose testimony might free him—testified against him. Lying to defend herself against prosecution, she claimed that Sherman had been driving when Henry Lamb was struck. Moreover, she said that Sherman had seemed to take a singular pride in the incident, calling it "a fight in the jungle." Sherman was quickly indicted on charges of reckless endangerment.

To Sherman's astonishment and relief, however, the judge—suspecting "tainted testimony" on the part of Maria Ruskin—dismissed the indictment. Leaving the courtroom, Sherman had to ride the judge's elevator downstairs to escape the frenzied mob protesting the ruling.

Subsequently, as an article released by *The New York Times* revealed, Henry Lamb died from the head injuries sustained as a result of being struck by Sherman's automobile. Once again Sherman was taken to "the Bronx Central Booking Facility," where he told a reporter, "I now dress for jail, even though I haven't been convicted of any crime."

At his arraignment, Sherman pleaded "Absolutely innocent," and then insisted on defending himself during his upcoming trial. As a newspaper column described the prisoner's predicament, in addition to being "estranged" from his wife and devoid of cash, Killian, who had recently moved into a "stately Georgian structure," had refused to continue defending the newly impoverished Sherman McCoy. But despite all of his tribulations, Sherman was seen—"dressed in open-necked sportshirt, khaki pants, and hiking shoes"—raising his hand during the arraignment "in a clenched-fist salute."

THE FIRM

by John Grisham, Dell Publishing, New York, N.Y., 1991

Type of work: Legal thriller

Setting: Memphis, Tennessee and various other cities; 1990s

Principal characters:
Mitch McDeere, a brilliant graduate of Harvard law school
Abby, Mitch's wife
Tarrance, an FBI agent
Ray McDeere, Mitch's brother, serving time in prison for murder
Various members—living and dead—of the law firm Bendini, Lambert, and Locke

Story Overview:

"With forty-one lawyers, the firm was the fourth largest in Memphis. Its members did not advertise or seek publicity. They were clannish and did not fraternize with other lawyers. Their wives played tennis and bridge and shopped among themselves. Bendini, Lambert and Locke was a family, of sorts."

The newest member of the firm's family was Mitch McDeere. Recruited, like all the firm's members, fresh from law school, the firm made him an offer he couldn't refuse: a starting salary of $80,000 a year, plus bonuses; a low-interest mortgage on a home; a new BMW; and the guarantee of a partnership at a young age. He was the only man they wanted, they told him. He would fit right in. And he could not refuse.

Mitch and his wife, Abby, immediately sold their old Mazda hatchback, rented a U-Haul, and moved to Memphis. Upon their arrival, a new home awaited them and a black BMW 318i sat glistening in the carport. The home's yard would be re-done to their specifications and an interior decorator would be around within the week. "Mitchell Y. McDeere, 25 years old and one week out of law school, had arrived."

That first night, Mitch and Abby accepted a dinner date with Lamar Quin, an associate member of the firm, and his wife, Kay. When they got to the Quin home, however, they found Kay crying and Lamar sitting in the back yard, oblivious to the fact that he was being soaked by a lawn sprinkler. Mitch learned that two members of the firm, Hodge and Kozinski, had been killed in an explosion on a boat near Grand Cayman Island earlier that day. Lamar had been close to both of them. "Four days later, on what should have been his first day behind his new desk, Mitch and his lovely wife joined the other thirty-nine members of the firm, and their lovely wives, as they paid their last respects."

The morning after the funerals, Mitch was introduced to Avery Tolar, the partner who was to be his mentor. Tolar seemed to take great delight in breaking the firm's strict rules against drinking and philandering. "We have too many rules," he protested. Still, Tolar was very good at what he did—and Mitch decided he would also be one of the best. He immersed himself in the Capps file, a major case with which Tolar need-

ed help; he arrived early for work and left late; industrious to the point of obsession, he billed the clients for more hours of work than any other new lawyer in the history of the firm.

On the first Monday in August, at a special ceremony in one of the libraries of the Bendini Building, the firm's executives unveiled commemorative portraits of Hodge and Kozinski. To Mitch's surprise, three other portraits also graced the wall. Those three, Mitch discovered, had met similar tragic deaths. "Five dead lawyers in twenty years. It was a dangerous place to work," he mused.

But there wasn't much time for musing. Now, as the date for the bar exams approached, Mitch turned his thoughts to other matters. He hadn't been studying like he should; he was worried that he might become the first member of the firm to flunk the exams. However, when the results came back, he found he had scored the highest marks of the year. The firm instantly gave him a raise and a bonus—and added his name to the top of the firm's letterhead. His good life had become even better.

A week later, Mitch was approached by a man who identified himself as Special Agent Tarrance, FBI. Tarrance revealed little about his investigation, but cautioned Mitch not to trust anyone in the firm. The deaths of Hodge and Kozinski were not accidental, Tarrance warned. Frightened, Mitch approached his superiors, who scoffed at the rumors. He shouldn't fret, they said; the FBI and the IRS often harassed the firm.

But Mitch did fret. The next time he visited his brother Ray, who was serving a lengthy prison term for murder, Mitch asked him where he could get some help. Ray referred him to Eddie Lomax, an ex-cop and ex-con, now a private investigator. Mitch went to Lomax and asked him to look into the deaths of the three firm members who had died before Hodge and Kozinski.

Mitch's long hours and suspicions were quickly taking their toll, and one day Tolar suggested that Mitch accompany him on a business trip to Grand Cayman for a little R and R. On his first night there, Mitch met an exotic and beautiful woman on the beach. Though his instincts told him to run, he gave in to temptation—and the drinks he'd had at the bar—certain that no one would ever know.

The next day, Mitch drove to the local library to conduct his own inquiry into the deaths of Hodge and Kozinski. While there, he realized that he was being followed. Evading his pursuer, he left the library and sought out Abanks, the owner of the boat on which Hodge and Kozinski had died. He asked Abanks a few questions—and received fewer answers.

Later, back in Memphis, Lomax's research had turned up suspicious holes in the deaths of all the firm's deceased. Mitch now knew he was in real trouble. "Since the Caymans, he had known someone was following, watching, listening. For the past month, he had spoken carefully on the phone, had caught himself watching the rear-view mirror, had even chosen his words around the house. Someone was watching, and listening, he was sure."

The day after Christmas, Lomax's secretary, Tammy, sobbing and terrified, called Mitch on the phone to tell him that Lomax had been found dead, shot three times in the back of the head.

Agent Tarrance and the FBI made contact with Mitch again, and explained to him that Bendini, Lambert and Locke was, in fact, a branch of a large, illegal business owned by the Morolto Mafia crime family of Chicago. Joining the firm was like marrying into a Mafia family; there was no way out. The five dead members were killed when they tried to resign. The Feds, in order to bust the firm, wanted Mitch's help, and he agreed.

Mitch apprised Abby of the situation; they both felt frightened, and unsure of what to do next. To make matters worse, a man named DeVasher, the firm's alleged head of security, approached Mitch with some incriminating photographs of Mitch and the girl on the beach. Smiling, he warned Mitch that if he had one more little chat with Tarrance, the photos would be mailed to Abby. Mitch could just imagine where the photos had been—probably passed around the senior partners' fifth-floor dining room. He hoped they'd enjoyed them, Mitch thought. "They'd better enjoy the remaining few months of their bright and rich and happy legal careers."

With the help of Tammy, secretary to the late Eddie Lomax, Mitch began removing files from the Bendini Building, photocopying them, and returning them before anyone missed them. The Feds wanted all the evidence necessary to indict all the members of the firm and expose the Morolto family; they wanted all the players laid out on a silver platter. In return, Mitch insisted on a payment of two million dollars and a parole for his brother Ray. He knew he had the Feds over a barrel and he wasn't willing to play games with them. "I'll dictate the terms of transfer [of the money] and it'll be done exactly as I say," he told Tarrance. "It's my neck on the line from now on, boys, so I call the shots."

In his short time at the firm, Mitch had learned some valuable lessons. And since he didn't trust the government's ability to protect him, he began to secretly fashion his own plans.

After weeks of painstaking work, Mitch was nearly ready to hand over his copied documents—all 10,000 of them—more than enough for the FBI to obtain a search warrant for the Bendini Building. But the exchange never occurred. Tarrance, distress in his voice, risked calling Mitch at the office: the Mob had a mole inside the FBI, he warned, and they were on to Mitch. Mitch hung up the phone, walked out of the Bendini Building, and began to run for his life.

According to plan, he met Abby and his brother Ray in Florida. "We can't go back," he told them. "We either disappear or we're dead." Both the Feds and the Mob were after them now,

but Mitch had sketched out his moves carefully. Using his stolen knowledge to transfer ten million dollars of the firm's own money into his personal numbered account, he laid low. He set aside some of the money for his mother and deposited some more into Abby's parents' account. Back in Memphis, all the senior partners had skipped town.

Holed up in a sleazy motel, Mitch commenced videotaping a deposition in which he explained each of the documents he had copied, describing how the Morolto family operated within the firm to launder money. Of course, the deposition was inadmissable at trial, "but it would serve its purpose. Tarrance and his buddies could show the tapes to a grand jury and indict at least thirty lawyers from the Bendini firm. He could show the tapes to a federal magistrate and get his search warrants. Mitch had held to his end of the bargain."

One night, Mitch, Abby, and Ray left the hotel one by one and made their way down the beach to a pier. One of DeVasher's assassins spotted them, but Ray knocked him flat and then strangled the unconscious man. They waited in the darkness as an hour passed. Then a black rubber boat appeared, piloted by Abanks, the Caymanian divemaster. They quickly boarded and headed for open water.

Before disappearing herself, Tammy made one last telephone call to let Tarrance know where he could find the videotapes and documents. Then she told him goodbye.

Somewhere in the islands, Mitch and Abby lived out their lives. Though they dwelt in fear and uncertainty, they had escaped with their lives and eight million dollars. And they still had each other.

Commentary:

John Grisham was himself trained as a lawyer. His writing style reads much like a legal brief, plain and straightforward, with little in the way of flowery narrative. The style is well-suited to the genre, however, and is almost brutally effective in scenes such as the one in which Eddie Lomax is assassinated. Indeed, the very sparseness of the narration makes that scene all the more chilling, much more hair-raising than if it had been explicitly described.

The Firm represents one of the most popular literary genres of the early 1990s: the legal thriller. This genre, focusing on lawyers and their professional encounters with the underworld, is a perfect format for exploring the darker side of human nature. For example, the novel closely explores the dangers of greed. It is Mitch's greed and his hunger for quick success that first involve him in his troubles; and it is only through his own resourcefulness that he survives. Apparently, Grisham suggests, true life and happiness are far from being mere functions of money.

However, it is to Grisham's credit that very few of his characters are simplistic, two-dimensional metaphors for avarice; in fact, to varying degrees at least, all *The Firm's* characters are sympathetic, even those who want Mitch silenced.

BLACK ELK SPEAKS

by Nick Black Elk, as told through John G. Neihardt (Flaming Rainbow), University of Nebraska Press, Lincoln, Nebraska, 1961

Type of work: Historical biography

Setting: The Great Plains of the United States

Commentary:

John Neihardt (1881 - 1973) suggests in the Introduction to this biography that the way Black Elk (1863 - 1950) will help restore his nation's hoop to wholeness is through this book and the sacred knowledge it contains. Indeed, the work has not only become a modern religious/cultural classic, but has also served as a valuable source of information for young Native Americans searching for their roots.

Overview:

Black Elk, Holy Man of the Oglala Sioux, filled his sacred pipe with tobacco made from the bark of the red willow. Four ribbons hung from the stem, representing the four quarters of the universe: black for the west, "where the thunder beings live to send us rain"; white for the north and its "great white cleansing wind"; red for the east, where light and the morning star come forth "to give men wisdom"; and yellow for the south, which brings the winds of summer, and "the power to grow." Beneath the ribbons was an eagle feather, symbolizing the four powers working as one. As the old medicine man held the sacred pipe, he told the story of how this holy emblem had first come to his people.

Long ago, two Oglala scouts were out searching for bison, when ahead of them they saw a beautiful woman, dressed all in white buckskin. The first scout raced after her, hoping to catch her for his own, but a white cloud overcame and surrounded him. And when the cloud blew away, he was nothing but "a skeleton covered with worms." The woman told the second scout to return to his camp. There he was to tell the people that she would soon appear among them, "and that a big tepee shall be built for me in the center of the nation." So the people heard the words of the scout and built a lodge for the woman.

Soon the woman came to her tepee, singing, "A voice I am sending as I walk. In a sacred manner I am walking." And as she chanted her song, a sweet-smelling cloud emanated from her mouth. Then she gave the holy pipe to the chief of the village. It was carved with a bison calf on one side to suggest "the earth that bears and feeds us." Hanging from the stem were twelve eagle feathers to represent twelve moons (months) of the year. "With this," the woman told the chief, "You shall multiply and be a good nation. Nothing but good shall come from it. Only the hands of the good shall take care of it, and the bad shall not even see it." Then, leaving the tepee, she once more took up her song. As the people watched her go, suddenly "was a white bison galloping away and snorting."

Black Elk lit the pipe, then offered it to the four powers that are one power: "Grandfather, Great Spirit, you have been always, and before you no one has been. There is no one to pray to but you. . . . Everything has been made by you . . . the voice I have sent is weak, yet with earnestness I have sent it. Hear me!" After these words, cradling the sacred pipe, he began to tell of his long life: "I am a Lakota of the Oglala band. My father's name was Black Elk, and his father before him bore the name, and the father of his father, so that I am the fourth to bear it."

He continued with his narrative. His mother, White-Cow-Sees, gave birth to him in "the winter when the four Crows were killed" (1863) during "the Moon of the Popping Trees" (December). The boy's first memory was of his father, who broke a leg during "The Battle of the Hundred Slain." At the time, three-year-old Black Elk had not yet seen the "wasichus" (white men) who fought on the other side of this battle. He remembered, though, that "everyone was saying that the wasichus were coming, and that they were going to take our country and rub us all out and that we should all have to die fighting." As it turned out, it was the wasichus who lost the Battle of the Hundred Slain, but as Black Elk grew older, he saw "others and others without number"—wasichus who had "found much of the yellow metal that they worship and that makes them crazy." These men wished to seize the land. They sought to build a road "to the place where the yellow metal was," but the tribes knew it would frighten the bison away, and "let other wasichus come in like a river." And so the wars with the wasichus continued.

It was the summer after this early Battle of the Hundred Slain when Black Elk first "heard the voices." One day during May—"the Moon when the Ponies Shed"—as the boy played alone in a field, he heard someone calling to him, but there was no one there. After this the voices called to him several other times, but each time he heard them he would run away. So the frightened boy was able to escape these voices; but during the next summer while he was out on horseback he received a vision that he could not ignore. As he rode past a tree, a kingbird spoke to him from its perch on a limb. "Listen!" it said. "A voice is calling to you!" Then, from the clouds came two warriors singing a sacred song: Behold, a sacred voice is calling you; all over the sky, a sacred voice is calling." Arriving home, he did not impart this vision to anyone, but from that day on he thought about it often.

Then, during his ninth summer, the voices reached out again. "It is time," they said. "Now they are calling you." Again Black Elk tried to escape the voices, but this time he became sick. Unable to walk, the boy lay in his family's tepee, watching the sky. Now the two Indian braves he had seen the year earlier in the sky appeared again in the clouds, bearing long spears with "jagged lightning" flashing from their tips. The warriors drew closer, and urged Black Elk to follow them. All at once, a tiny cloud swooped down from the sky and picked him up, so that he might follow the thunder beings above the clouds. Then from the west came a herd of "twelve black horses . . . with necklaces of bison hoofs." From the north came twelve white horses and twelve white geese; from the east came twelve sorrel horses "with necklaces of elk's teeth . . . eyes that glimmered like the daybreak star, and manes of morning light"; and from the south came twelve buckskins, "with horns upon their heads, and manes and tails that grew like trees and grasses." The sky was filled with "horses, horses everywhere . . . dancing round." Then the thunder beings led the boy to a tepee with a rainbow for a door. Inside the tepee sat six old men. "Your grandfathers all over the world . . . have called you here to teach you," said the first old man. He gave Black Elk a wooden cup filled with water, and "in the water was the sky." This water had "the power to make live." Next, he handed the boy a bow, "the power to destroy." Pointing to himself, the old man said, "Look close at him who is your spirit now, for you are his body and his name is Eagle Wing Stretches." As he spoke, he rose to his feet and became a thin, sickly black horse.

The second old man, the Grandfather of the North, now handed the boy an herb. "Take this and hurry," he commanded, pointing towards the horse. The boy fed the herb to the animal; instantly it grew fat and happy. This herb, the Grandfather told Black Elk, contained the power of "the white cleansing wind." And as he spoke, he stood and became a white goose.

The third Grandfather then gave him a pipe "which had a spotted eagle feather outstretched upon the stem." This, he said, would grant the boy the power to heal. He pointed to a man who was "bright red all over, the color of good and of plenty." As Black Elk watched, the red man lay down and rolled on the ground; then he rose from the ground as a bison and galloped towards the sorrel horses of the east.

The fourth Grandfather showed Black Elk two roads that ran across the Earth, one black, one red. The red road was the good road; the black road signaled war, famine, and poverty of spirit. The Grandfather warned that soon the Indian Nation would be walking the black road.

The fifth Grandfather, "the oldest of all," became a spotted eagle, and hovered over Black Elk. "All of the wings of the air shall come to you," he said. "You shall go across the earth with my power."

When the sixth Grandfather spoke, Black Elk saw that he too was old, but not agelessly old like the others; instead he was old "more as men are old." Then this last Grandfather began to grow backwards in age, until he became a boy, and Black Elk saw that the Grandfather was himself. Each grandfather had now given him all he needed to restore "the center of the nation's hoop to make it live."

When Black Elk awoke, inside his body once more, he was told he had been ill for twelve days, and that during this time, Whirlwind Chaser, the medicine man, had witnessed light traveling all through his body. Still, the boy did not speak of his twelve-day vision. But from that time on, he felt happy when storms came, "as if someone were coming to visit."

Then, at the age of sixteen, Black Elk experienced a terrible foreboding, having "not yet done anything that the Grandfathers wanted me to do." Now he trembled in fear when clouds and thunder beings called after him: "Behold your Grandfathers! Make haste . . . it is time, it is time!" Finally, growing weaker, he went to Black Road, a medicine man, for help. Upon hearing of Black Elk's vision, the old man told him: "Ah, you must do your duty and perform [enact] this vision for your people on earth."

So with the help of Black Road, Black Elk fasted and purified himself in the sweat lodge, preparing himself to perform the Horse Dance so the tribe might also witness and share his vision. Next, the tribe gathered the needed ceremonial elements: " . . . four black horses; four white horses; four sorrels; four buckskins; four of the most beautiful maidens; and six very old men to represent the grandfathers.

The day of the dance, lightning streaks were painted on the horses, and Black Elk himself was painted "red all over, with lightning on my limbs." The maidens dressed themselves in scarlet buckskin and put on wreaths of sage. The Grandfathers painted a circle on the ground; inside they placed the gifts of the cup, the bow, the herb, the pipe, the flowering stick, a white goose wing, and a hoop. Then the ceremonial procession danced around the circle, intoning a sacred song.

When the Horse Dance was ended, Black Elk was no longer tired and sick; in fact, it was after this dance that his infirm tribespeople began to come to him for purifications and healings.

Black Elk's most powerful curative tool was the "four-rayed herb" he had seen in his vision. The healer also used sacred rituals: the heyoka ceremony, where everything was performed backwards, and the elk ceremony, which invoked "the source of life and the mystery of growing." But still Black Elk remained sad: Though he could help men, women and children as become well, he was helpless—he could not revive his nation as a whole. As a tribe, the Oglala Sioux were slowly consumed by the wasichus; his people were walking the black road.

Still, it was not until late in 1890 that his hopes were finally killed. That year, during December—Black Elk's birth month, the Moon of the Popping Trees—the Oglala holy man witnessed the aftermath of one of the bloodiest clashes in history between native American peoples and the United States government: the Battle at Wounded Knee. "I did not know how much was ended," he said quietly. "I can still see the butchered women and children lying heaped and scattered all along the crooked gulch . . . and I can see that something else died there in the bloody mud . . . a people's dream died there. And it was a beautiful dream."

Tears streamed down the old man's face as he raised a prayer to the Grandfathers in the rainbow tepee: "In sorrow I am sending a feeble voice, O six Powers of the World. Hear me in my sorrow, for I may never call again. O make my people live!"

THE TALE OF GENJI

by Lady Murasaki Shikibu, translated by Arthur Waley, Houghton Mifflin Company, Boston and New York, 1925

Commentary:

The Tale of Genji is an account of life among the rich and powerful in ancient Japanese society. Rather than leaving readers with a "message" or moral, this archaic novel recounting the romantic adventures of the fair prince Genji, son of the Emperor and his concubine, Kiritsubo, imparts a feeling and an image—conveying the essence of Japan's so-called "Golden Age."

The language of the book is detached and formal, with much the flavor of a carefully narrated fairy tale from the West. Behind its refined tone, however, surge the political, social and sexual practices of the Japanese court of over 800 years ago. As a snapshot glimpse into ancient Japanese culture—courtly traditions and romantic customs coupled with intrigue, clandestine affairs, and mildly erotic poetic exchanges—the work portrays, as few other books have, the psyche of an entire people.

Genji's sexual manipulation of women, who, due to class or gender restrictions, are fundamentally powerless—and the maneuverings these women are forced to resort to in order to endure the selfishness of their commanding male counterparts—can be quite startling at times. The author, Murasaki, apparently finds nothing wrong with this, commenting that at Genji's age, "it was inevitable that he should cause a certain amount of suffering." Also, many of the obsessions, that Genji and his associates have with appearances and "saving face"—whether the "face" pertains to rank, power, art, clothing, writing style, or indirect poetic forms of speech—survive to this day, in one form or another, in modern-day Japan.

And perhaps there is a message after all. After squandering his energies by seizing every opportunity to seduce young women, regardless of their social or marital status, and then neglecting them to the extreme, Prince Genji pays a tragic price for his dalliances. Tutored by death, Genji finally comes to an understanding of true love and true life.

Story Overview:

Although the offspring of one of the Emperor's subordinate concubines, young Genji, with his fair looks and gracious manner, was a favorite of the royal court. Presently, however, after being cruelly taunted by the ladies of the court led by Kokiden, the Emperor's legitimate wife and mother of the heir apparent, his concubine mother grew sick and eventually died.

Young Genji soon became enamored of Fujitsubo, one of the Emperor's young consorts. She reminded Genji, in both appearance and manner, of his departed mother. "And so, young though he was, fleeting beauty took its hold upon his thoughts; he felt his first clear predilection." Fujitsubo quickly became the first of Genji's many illicit liaisons.

Shortly after Genji underwent the ritual hair cutting and changing of robes that signified his initiation into manhood, his beauty so impressed the Minister of the Left that, seeking out the Emperor, the Minister arranged a wedding between his only daughter, Aoi, and Prince Genji. As the wedding proceeded, when Genji drank from the ceremonial Love Cup, his father, the Emperor, bound the young bride and groom together with a purple band and recited a poetic prayer, pleading that "the purple fillet might symbolize the union of their two houses; and . . . nothing should sever this union save the fading of the purple band." Then he performed the Grand Obeisance, presenting the couple with "horses from the Royal Stables and the hawks from the Royal Falconry . . . Gifts of every kind were showered upon them . . and boxes of cake and presents lay about so thick that one could scarcely move."

Although Princess Aoi was quite beautiful, being both somewhat shy and four years Genji's senior, she treated him with a certain aloofness. Unaffected by her coolness, Genji went about his business as a young prince.

One night Genji sought shelter at the home of his friend Ki no Kami, who had been charged with watching over his young stepmother, Utsusemi. As darkness fell, Genji wasted no time in finding the room in which Utsusemi was staying. Entering the room, he found couched in a seat facing away from the door, a small woman, "who, to Genji's slight embarrassment, on hearing his approach pushed aside the cloak which covered her, thinking that he was the maid for whom she had sent." Unfazed, Genji carefully employed his powers of persuasion on her. "Why do you treat me so unkindly?" he asked, after repeatedly suffering her rebukes. "I think that Fate meant us to meet. It is harsh that you should shrink from me as though the World and you had never met."

Hearing Genji's compassionate words, Utsusemi lamented how fate had chained her to an undesirable husband. Then warning Genji to *"tell none that you have seen my room,"* she surrendered to the many tender comforts that he offered her. In the morning, Genji departed for the palace. Later, he tried again to meet with Utsusemi, but was rebuffed. During one attempt, he crept into Utsusemi's room, only to find that she had fled his approach, leaving another woman in her bed. In order to save face, Genji explained to this woman that it was she he had come to visit, and "they were soon getting on very well together."

But not all of Genji's affairs were so frivolous and painless. While visiting his ailing foster-mother, Genji became taken with a pale-faced woman, Yugao, whom he had caught sight of as she peered out from the doorway of a run-down tenement. After inviting her to join him, Genji took her to an abandoned, dilapidated villa in the country, where at last he removed the cloth mask that he had worn in her presence until that moment in order to conceal his identity. Again, Genji's amazing looks served him well; "the beauty of his uncovered face, suddenly revealed to her in this black wilderness of dereliction and decay, surpassed all loveliness that she had ever dreamed of or imagined." But as the couple lay together in the darkness, a ghost appeared and chided Genji for trifling with a member of the lower classes. And afterwards, the young woman began to suffer terrible nightmares. Hour by hour she grew paler, and eventually she succumbed from her unconquerable fright. Genji transported Yugao's lifeless body to a secluded mountain monastery, where, in secret, he performed the obligatory funeral rites. Following this incident, he became increasingly despondent over his loss, until, coming across a hermit-priest, he was cured of his depression.

While he lingered in the mountains, Genji came across the spectacle of a beautiful and delightful young child. Learning that this girl, Murasaki, was the product of a union between the priest's niece and the brother of Genji's old flame, Fujitsubo, and observing the resemblance of the child to Fujitsubo— and to his own dead mother—Genji offered to adopt her. His offer was continually rebuffed—until the day when the child's caretaker, an ailing sister of the hermit-priest, finally died. Genji then took the thin, grief-stricken child and presented her at the palace, where she soon became the subject of much gossip by the ladies of the court, who did not realize that she was not of age to be the object of Genji's next romance. "Aoi was cold and sullen as ever." Genji, for his part, was unconcerned by the talk. "Let them draw their own conclusions. That did not matter.. Now indeed [the girl] had `a new father' of whom she was growing every day more fond. When he came back from anywhere she was the first to meet him, and then wonderful games and conversations began, she sitting all the while on his lap without the least shyness or restraint."

While he pursued his attempts to formally adopt Murasaki, Genji also resumed his ardent visits to Fujitsubo. This eventually resulted in the birth of a child—a child whose great beauty and striking resemblance to Genji did not go unnoticed by members of the court. Most gossipers, however, supposed that this remarkable similarity must be due to a shared father—the Emperor.

And so, though Murasaki had brought a glimmer of earnestness into his life, all the while Genji continued his affairs; he preyed upon women—until at last he was dramatically awakened to the depths where his pas-

sions had carried him. Lady Aoi, nearing childbirth, became deathly ill, possessed by an incurable ailment. "Constantly . . . she would break out into fits of sobbing so violent that her breath was stopped . . . " Seeing her in such a condition, for the first time Genji became greatly alarmed; suddenly he realized his love for her. "After all, she was his wife; moreover, despite all the difficulties that had risen between them, he cared for her very much indeed." He took his wife's hand and gazed at her, and through his tears "he saw that there was no longer in her eyes the wounded scorn that he had come to know so well, but a look of forbearance and tender concern." The tears flooded down Aoi's cheeks. "I did not think that you would come," she said tenderly. "I have waited for you till all my soul is burnt with longing." Then, "Aoi suddenly started up and bore a child."

"For the moment all was gladness and rejoicing." But despite the "constant rituals of exorcism and divination . . . performed under [Genji's] direction," Aoi's condition worsened. Genji, Aoi's father, as well as his father, the ex-Emperor (for he had since given up the throne to the heir apparent) each lingered in great dismay by her bedside. Genji gazed as his new-found love: "Her hair, every ringlet still in its right place, was spread out over the pillow. Never before had her marvelous beauty so strangely impressed him. Was it conceivable that year after year he should have allowed such a woman to continue in estrangement from him? . . . "

After lying in a trance-like state for several days, Princess Aoi at last slipped away from life. All Japan mourned to have lost "one who was so young and so strong."

Genji was much affected by his wife's death. He mourned bitterly at never having fully won nor savored Aoi's affections, and harshly chastised himself for having neglected so fair a princess. The poem he had sent to Aoi before her death now became his lament:

The fault is mine and the regret,
if careless as the peasant girl
who stoops too low amid the sprouting rice
I soiled my sleeve in love's dark road.

"Life," he concluded, " . . . was not long enough for diversions and experiments; henceforward he would concentrate."

And concentrate he did. With his attentions firmly fixed on Murasaki, he raised the child as his own. And, by and by, although still young and very innocent, she grew "into as handsome a girl as you could wish to see . . . Nor was she any longer at an age when it was impossible for him to become her lover."

Eventually, after many days and nights of courting her, the night came when Genji did not leave Murasaki's room. The next morning, Genji ordered the symbolic wedding cakes to be brought; "Genji's strange patronage of [his] young mistress had at last culminated in a definite act of betrothal."

WAR AND PEACE

by
Leo Tolstoy
(1828 - 1910)

Type of work: Epic and romantic Russian novel

Setting: Russia; the Napoleonic Era

Principal characters:
Prince Andrey Bolkonsky, a cynical, intellectual soldier-prince
Pierre Bezuhov, a sensitive nobleman and seeker of truth
Natasha Rostov, Pierre's beautiful and well-to-do lover
Nikolay Rostov, a soldier, Natasha's older brother
Sonya, a relative of the Rostovs who falls in love with Nikolay
Anatole Kuragin, a womanizing, high-ranking officer

Commentary:

Tolstoy's purpose in writing his 1600-page *War and Peace* was to present a historical account of the French invasion of Russia and also to provide himself a forum for his own intellectual and spiritual insights and theories. He accomplishes this through the characters' searches for identity as well as in the volume's two extensive epilogues.

Tolstoy fought in the Crimean War, adding to the realism of his accounts of the Napoleonic struggle. Soon after, he experienced a religious conversion, gave up all his material wealth, and lived out his remaining days in the simple life of a peasant.

This work, written in 1869, has been termed an epic because it portrays history as cyclical. To Tolstoy, every human being holds great influence over others. And even as the novel draws to a close, the births and lives of the second generation begin their ever-more influential, historical journeys along the never-ending river of life.

Story Overview:

During a magnificent dance held in St. Petersburg, Pierre and Prince Andrey, close friends, sat to one side discussing the rise of Napoleon, who had singlehandedly saved his country from inner destruction. But now the same Frenchman waged war against Russia, and everyone held differing viewpoints on how best to defend their motherland. "To help England and Austria against the greatest man in the world is not right," Pierre, the boorish idealist said; to which the realist Andrey replied, "If no one fought except on his own conviction, there would be no wars. I am going because the life I am living here does not suit me." Indeed, Andrey had experienced the misfortune of marrying a society woman whose only interest lay in the numerous soirees among the elite. His fondest wish was to escape his pregnant wife by leaving Russia and going to war.

At the battle of Austerlitz Andrey had been assigned adjutant to general Kutuzov. Nikolay, another young soldier, had declined a position in the rear, choosing instead to fight with the front-line "Hussars," or Russian Cavalry. Both men, spurred on by pride, were filled with the foolish notions of glory—but were quickly disillusioned when they took part in a battle and saw the first-hand horrors of war. Nikolay's steed was shot from under him and he retreated from the advancing French troops. Andrey was wounded in a desperate charge. As he lay there gazing up at the sky among the masses of dead and wounded soldiers, Napoleon and his victorious generals approached nearby. The Emperor himself glanced half-heartedly at Andrey and, thinking he was dead, almost passed by—when he thought he saw the young officer move. Napoleon had Andrey picked up and cared for, and later asked him, "And how do you feel, mon brave?" As the rest of the Russian army retreated, Andrey could not answer.

Pierre, meanwhile, having inherited a fortune, married a beautiful but disloyal woman whose only interest was retaining her name through social climbing. At dinner, a former gambling friend, Dolohov, insulted Pierre. Incensed at this—and more so at the rumor that Dolohov had had an affair with his wife—Pierre challenged the more experienced man to a duel, and though he had hardly ever fired a gun, Pierre managed to wound Dolohov. He then left town, alone, and joined the brotherhood of Freemasons, a religious order founded to care for the needy and lift the lower classes. He had finally found people who shared his ideals.

Soon thereafter, Andrey returned from the war to find his estranged wife about to give birth. Andrey looked helplessly on at the frightened, accusing, deathlike face of his wife, who seemed to blame him for her pain. When she died right after the birth, Andrey, haunted by her ordeal, fell into a deep and cynical depression. Austerlitz . . . his wife . . . he no longer could summon the lofty ideals he once knew.

Pierre, once more in company of his friend, noticed that Andrey seemed to have lost his zeal for life. Pierre spoke to him about Freemasonry and the good it could do, but Andrey spurned such philosophical drivel. "What error can there be," Pierre replied, "in wishing to do good? . . . There is a future life. The Some One is God."

"It's true. I believe it," Andrey finally affirmed, and began to think that, yes, perhaps he could remove himself from life's "abyss." The despair that tortured him gradually began to fade.

The handsome Nikolay, Andrey's army mate, had also returned from Austerlitz, resigned to marry his cousin Sonya, a girl completely devoted to him but whom he did not love in return. The now-healed rascal Dolohov tried to woo her, but she rejected him in favor of Nikolay. Dolohov, in revenge, challenged Nikolay to a game of cards, and won 43,000 rubles. The embarrassed young man quickly borrowed money from his father, paid Dolohov, and returned to the war.

In 1809, Napoleon and Alexander, Czar of

Russia, signed a never-honored peace treaty. Each chose at random one soldier from each of their ranks to receive the Legion of Honor. Nikolay marvelled that an officer rather than a man of real courage was recognized: "Our business is to do our duty. To fight and not to think. That is all."

Andrey found himself suddenly attracted to a long-time acquaintance, Natasha, Nikolay's younger sister. Immediately the seeds of renewal planted by Pierre sprang forth in love. He forgot his dead wife and began to think of marriage. However, Natasha's quarrelsome old father, considering her too inexperienced to run a household, refused to allow Natasha to marry until a year had elapsed. Andrey, dejected, left Moscow to work for the government. During this time, the handsome yet disreputable Anatole Kuragin, who had left his first wife, spied Natasha and determined to make her his own. With her fiance gone, Natasha was weakened and almost ran away with the insistent high-ranking officer. Pierre confronted Anatole and stood up for his absent friend. Anatole soon left for Petersburg, but when Andrey learned of the near-marriage, he rejected Natasha and pursued Anatole for revenge.

About this time, Pierre himself became disillusioned; he had found many of the masons to be corrupt and concerned only with themselves and with their own status and wealth, at the expense of the truly needy. "The Order should be preparing men of virtue, punishing vice and folly, patronizing talent, and raising men from the dust and attaching them to the Brotherhood," he argued. The Freemason members—who had in fact inducted Pierre into the order solely for his wealth—did not approve of his rhetoric, and Pierre left the Order, never to return.

Pierre, alone, was sensitive to heartbroken Natasha, and soon found rebirth in his relationship with the woman. Natasha, who still pined over the loss of her beloved Andrey, tried but failed to take her own life. As she recovered, Pierre tenderly cared for her needs. But because of his friendship with Andrey and being such a short time since Andrey and Natasha had been lovers, he could not bring himself to proclaim his affection. In despair, he also departed Moscow.

The war of 1812 ensued, and Nikolay and Andrey enlisted as before. Again Nikolay found his way to the front lines, but this time he felt mortal. Still full of courage, he led a charge. When he hesitated killing a French soldier, he was awarded a medal for bringing him back a prisoner. Confused, he thought, "So that's all there is in what is called heroism! And did I do it for my country's sake? Why should I kill him? And they have given me St. George's Cross. I can't make it out at all."

The night before the battle, Andrey paced the floor out of the bitterness he harbored over Anatole robbing him of Natasha. It was killing him, knowing that Anatole was alive and happy while he, unfulfilled, wallowed in sadness. Then Andrey, meeting up again with Pierre, at first assumed Pierre represented the Freemasons, and treated him with hostility, but soon realized Pierre was there as a friend, bringing news of his family. Later, Pierre asked Andrey to define his idea of success in war. Andrey answered: "Success never depends on position, equipment or numbers, but on the feeling that is in me and in each soldier. A battle is won by those who firmly resolve to win it!"

The sun rose, the battle commenced, and Andrey stood in his ranks as the field jumped to life around him. A grenade landed nearby and everyone around scrambled for cover. But Andrey froze, staring at the bomb, his mind suddenly alive to his existence: " . . . I do not wish to die. I love life." Just then the bomb exploded, throwing Andrey to the ground, gravely wounded. Though he was taken to be nursed by his precious Natasha, he soon died, after declaring his love.

In the subsequent Battle of Borodine the Russians lost half their regiments. They brought the French to a temporary stand-still outside of Moscow, however, giving its citizens time to escape. Nevertheless, with Moscow abandoned, the French soldiers moved in and began burning the deserted houses. In the melee of events, Pierre saved the life of a French officer; later, the officer in turn saved Pierre from a French firing squad after he was captured as a prisoner of war. Arrested for alleged "incendiary activity," he in fact had remained behind with thoughts of assassinating Napoleon. While in prison, Pierre became acquainted with another prisoner who taught him patience, acceptance, appreciation, and love, even for those who persecuted him. Amid his privations, he regained faith, "not faith in any kind of rule, words or ideas, but faith in an ever-living ever manifest God."

Despite the French occupation of Moscow, the Russian soldiers remained in good spirits. Ironically, Napoleon's troops suffered low morale. The Russians had burned everything on the road to Moscow, ensuring that the French would find nothing along their route of retreat. After looting and burning much of the city, the soldiers, inadequately supplied, began their demoralizing march home. The struggle to survive, Cossack skirmishers, the bitterly harsh winter, and the lack of food all but destroyed Napoleon's Grand Army.

Pierre was eventually rescued during a raid by Russian troops, and returned to Moscow. His imprisonment had changed him much. "Now a smile at the joy of life played about his lips and sympathy for others shone in his eyes." He had lost his entire fortune but proclaimed, "By being ruined I have become richer." With his little remaining money, he helped rebuild Moscow, which rapidly sprang back to life. He later met up with Natasha, who told him of Andrey's death. Pierre sought to comfort the grieving woman, and gradually their love for each other rekindled. Natasha proved to be an excellent wife to Pierre: "she let her love for her husband and children overflow all bounds." Four children and eight years of devotion was a fulfillment of all their dreams.

Nikolay also returned from war, married Marya, Andrey's sister, and they adopted Andrey's son. Sonya never married. Rejected after having waited faithfully for eight years, she nonetheless remained with Nikolay, content to be his servant.

BILLY BUDD

by
Herman Melville
(1819-1891)

Type of work: Allegoric tragedy

Setting: H.M.S. *Indomitable;* 1797

Principal characters:
Billy Budd, a cheerfully innocent young foretopman in the British fleet
Captain Vere, captain of the *Indomitable*
John Claggart, the ship's vile master-of-arms

Story Overview:

Billy Budd knew nothing of his parents, only that he had been found in Bristol in a silk-lined basket. "Yes Billy Budd was a foundling, a presumable by-blow, and, evidently, no ignoble one." It was apparent to any onlooker that this large, healthy, jubilant young man was of a better class than the sailors who surrounded him on the *Rights-of-Man.*

This obvious nobility was what caught Lieutenant Ratcliffe's attention when he boarded the *Rights-of-Man* with the assignment to impress part of her crew into service on Captain Vere's H.M.S. *Indomitable.* Billy Budd was chosen as the only crew member to be drafted into His Majesty's service.

The captain of the *Rights-of-Man* protested the Lieutenant's decision. Billy Budd, he said, was his best man, "the jewel of 'em." The captain spoke on: "Before I shipped that young fellow, my forecastle was a rat-pit of quarrels .... But Billy came; and it was like a Catholic priest striking peace in an Irish shindy. Not that he preached to them or said or did anything in particular; but a virtue went out of him, sugaring the sour ones."

Still, the officer could not persuade the lieutenant to reconsider, and soon Billy Budd found himself on one of the *Indomitable's* transfer boats.

Billy, only twenty-one, was not in the least self-conscious. "Billy in many respects was little more than a sort of upright barbarian, much . . . as Adam presumably might have been ere the urbane serpent wriggled himself into his company." And though this Edenic innocence was crowned by a halo of virginal illiteracy, the young man could sing to touch the heart of a prince. It was as if his angelic voice were but the expression of the harmony within him. Despite all this, when Billy had strong "heart-feelings" he developed a pronounced stutter; when deeply pressed he was even rendered speechless.

The crew of the *Indomitable* took the same liking to Billy as the *Rights-of-Man* crew had. Soon, Captain Vere, commander of the *Indomitable,* considered giving Billy—or "Baby Budd, the Handsome Sailor" as the lad came to be called—a promotion.

But one of the ship's petty officers, John Claggart, master-at-arms, was at odds with Budd. Claggart functioned as "a sort of chief of police charged among other matters with the duty of preserving order on the populous lower gun decks." A tall personage of about thirty-five years, he "looked like a man of high quality, social and moral." Inwardly, however, Claggart was a schemer, shrewd and deceitful, who secretly resented Billy. John Claggart had not learned his guiles in any earthly school; he had been born evil—in the same way that Billy had been born innocent and filled with kindness.

After young Billy was brought on board the *Indomitable*—especially after witnessing his first "gangway-punishment," a brutal flogging—he had "resolved that never through remissness would he . . . do or omit aught that might merit even verbal reproof." Yet for even the most petty offenses he found John Claggart's underlings besetting him with caustic chastisement.

Budd went to the experienced and wise old Danskar mainmastman for counsel—the very crewman who had lovingly nicknamed him *Baby.* "The salt seer attentively listened, accompanying the foretopman's recital with queer twitching of his small ferret eyes . . . ." Then the old man spoke: "Baby Budd, [the master-of-arms] is down on you."

Soon after this warning, Billy accidentally spilled some soup on the gun deck—a not-too-uncommon mishap at sea—just as Claggart chanced to walk by. The master-of-arms did not betray even a hint of hostility or a clue that anything was amiss. In truth, though, John Claggart, in his festering hatred of the lad, felt sure that the spilled soup was an open show of Billy's contempt for him. His dislike of Billy, "like a subterranean fire, was eating its way deeper and deeper in him."

Some few nights after the spilled-soup incident, Billy was approached by an ally of Claggart's who offered to pay him for his support in some nebulous scheme—perhaps a mutiny. Disgusted at the offer, Billy broke in: "I don't know what you are d-d-driving at, or what you mean, but you had better g-g-go where you belong! If you d-don't start, I'll t-t-toss you back over the r-rail!"

Shortly thereafter, however, Claggart went privately to Captain Vere and hinted to him that a mutiny was brewing. In his silvery, low, serpent-like voice, he implied that William Budd was behind the plot. Captain Vere was astonished. "There is a yardarm-end for the false witness," he warned Claggart. Undaunted, Claggart assured the Captain that he would soon have proof of Budd's false character.

Captain Vere summoned Billy Budd to his cabin. As Billy stood before him, with Claggart in attendance, Vere saw once again in Budd the very innocence of Adam before the fall. Then he turned to Claggart and commanded him to repeat his accusation. Billy was so repulsed by

© 1993, Compact Classics, Inc.

the falseness which then spewed out of Claggart's mouth, that he was rendered speechless. Captain Vere put his hand on Billy's shoulder and told him to take his time. But a helpless, hopeless feeling welled up in the young man's breast; his face took on "an expression which was as a crucifixion to behold. The next instant, quick as the flame from a discharged cannon at night, his right arm shot out, and Claggart dropped to the deck."

Minutes later, the ship's surgeon pronounced Claggart dead. Captain Vere's mind instantly turned to the Biblical story of Ananias, whom God had struck down for lying. "It is the divine judgment . . . " he cried. "Look! Struck dead by an angel of God! Yet the angel must hang!"

Hang an angel of God? The crewmen stood aghast. Was Captain Vere responding with a martinet's devotion to official statute, or had the turn of events somehow driven him to madness? "Who in the rainbow can draw the line where the violet tint ends and the orange tint begins? Distinctly we see the difference of the colors, but where exactly does the one first blendingly enter into the other?" Captain Vere summarily called for a drumhead court composed of the first lieutenant, the captain of marines, and the sailing master.

The court convened in Captain Vere's cabin, where the crime had taken place. As the sole witness, Vere was first to present his testimony. The jury then asked Billy if the testimony was true. "Captain Vere tells the truth," Billy confirmed. "It is just as Captain Vere says, but it is not as the master-at-arms said . . . He foully lied in my face and in presence of my captain, and I had to say something, and I could only say it with a blow, God help me!"

Billy was ushered outside and the court was left to make a decision. In their love for the innocent young sailor, however, they could only remain silent. At last Captain Vere broke the eerie hush: "However pitilessly the law may operate in any instances, we nevertheless adhere to it and administer it . . . Let not warm hearts betray heads that should be cool." To the simple minds of the ship's crew, the Captain explained, it would appear that Billy Budd had committed homicide "in a flagrant act of mutiny." If he was not punished accordingly, his acquittal could encourage the men to rise in brazen rebellion. With this, reluctantly, the court declared Billy guilty—and sentenced him to be hanged from the yardarm in the early morning watch.

Captain Vere informed Billy of the verdict. Later that night the ship's chaplain paid the young prisoner a visit and tried to awaken him to both the reality of his imminent death and the hope of salvation through his Savior. But the chaplain's efforts fell on the condemned man "like a gift placed in the palm of an outreached hand upon which the fingers do not close." Finally, he withdrew, reasoning that, come Judgement Day, Billy's childlike innocence would serve him better than religion.

The next morning, the crew assembled for the hanging. " . . . None spake but in whisper, and few spake at all." The final preparations were made, and before them stood Billy, the humiliating hemp about his neck. His last words, " . . . wholly unobstructed in the utterance, were these—'God bless Captain Vere!' . . . with one voice from alow and aloft came a resonant sympathetic echo—'God bless Captain Vere!' And yet at that instant Billy alone must have been in their hearts, even as he was in their eyes."

With the signal given, "the vapory fleece" shot downward "with a soft glory as of the fleece of the Lamb of God." As the body was pulled aloft by the rope around its neck, the dawn broke, casting a majestic shade of rose-colored light on the ascending figure. To the wonder of all, Billy never struggled in death. It was as if his inner peace had at last somehow overcome his body and, in that moment, was gone.

As the *Indomitable* sailed on, it entered into combat with the French ship *Athée* (*"Atheist"*). In the midst of the fighting Captain Vere was mortally wounded by a musket ball. Before his death, he was heard to murmur the words, "Billy Budd, Billy Budd."

The *Indomitable* emerged from her engagement victorious. Weeks later, an article appeared in a naval chronicle describing how John Claggart had uncovered an evil plot aboard the *Indomitable*, headed by one William Budd. Confronted by his perfidy, Budd had drawn a knife and stabbed Claggart in the heart. For the world at large, this was the final notice of Billy Budd. The incident—like Billy—was dead.

A ballad, however—"Billy in the Darbies"—was circulated among the working classes in memory of the poor "Handsome Sailor." And sailors, for years to come, kept track of the spar from which Billy had been hanged, reverencing it even as the Cross.

Commentary:

Herman Melville's final work—left unfinished at his death—*Billy Budd* is a unique treatise on the conflict of joy and innocence versus bitterness and guile. Billy Budd is the personification of mankind's joy, peace, and general goodness. Throughout the work Melville compares Billy to Adam, Christ, Joseph, and other messengers—and martyrs—of peace.

On the other hand, Billy's nemesis, John Claggart, was a serpent among men, born with an evil guile and the need to destroy peace and happiness. This is Melville's bleak and austerely hopeful commentary on mankind: that Claggart-like men have existed throughout history, and forever will be born, to breed hate, false accusations and betrayal; that beings born in purity—the true "elect"—will inevitably serve both as scapegoats and beacons of illumination in this world; and that both the good and the evil among us will live out their ordained destinies—either damned on earth to the hell of their own tormented souls, or taken up to heaven as spirits eternally triumphant, saved in the midst of darkness by their inner, innocent light.

THE DIARY OF A YOUNG GIRL

by
Anne Frank
(1929 - 1945)

Type of work: Historical autobiography

Setting: Amsterdam, Netherlands; 1942-44

Principal characters:
Anne, a young Jewish girl
Margot, her older sister
Mummy, their mother
Daddy or "Pim," their father
Mr. and Mrs. Van Daan, other residents of the Secret Annex
Peter Van Daan, their son
Mr. Dussel, another resident
Various office employee "protectors"

Diary Overview:

Although she had a loving family and many good friends, Anne Frank didn't feel she could quite trust any of them with her deepest feelings. So, when she received a diary for her birthday on June 12th, 1942, she was delighted. She wrote:

I hope I shall be able to confide in you completely . . . and I hope that you will be a great support and comfort to me . In order to enhance in my mind's eye the picture of the friend for whom I have waited so long, I don't want to set down a series of bald facts in a diary like most people do, but I want this diary itself to be my friend, and I shall call my friend Kitty.

In 1933, Anne's family had emigrated from Germany to Amsterdam, Holland, where her father opened up a food business. Life had been relatively routine and peaceful— until the arrival of the Germans in 1940. Anne complained to "Kitty" about the new anti-Jewish decrees:

Jews must wear a yellow star, Jews must hand in their bicycles, Jews are banned from trains and are forbidden to drive. Jews are only allowed to do their shopping between three and five o'clock and then only in shops which bear the placard "Jewish shop" . . . Swimming baths, tennis courts, hockey fields, and other sports grounds are all prohibited to them. Jews may not visit Christians. Jews must go to Jewish schools, and many more restrictions of a similar kind.

But even though, as a Jew, her freedom was strictly limited, Anne found life bearable, even enjoyable. She shared schoolgirl adventures with friends—and boyfriends. "As soon as a boy asks if he may bicycle home with me and we get into conversation," she told Kitty, "nine out of ten times I can be sure that he will fall head over heels in love . . ."

Then, in July of 1942, Anne's schoolgirl life was suddenly disrupted forever, when her older sister Margot received a call-up notice for deportation from the Gestapo. Immediately the Frank family made arrangements to go into hiding. Fortunately, they had been putting away necessities for many months in preparation for this eventuality. Their hiding place was to be in a "Secret Annex" on the second and third floors of Mr. Frank's office building. The entrance to their quarters was hidden by a moveable cupboard. A courageous group of Mr. Frank's non-Jewish employees now became the family's protectors and their link with the outside world, supplying them with food and with news about the war.

A week after the Franks moved into the Annex they were joined by a Mr. and Mrs. Van Daan and their son Peter. From then on, the two families shared meals and lived "like one large family." Anne first described Peter to Kitty as a "rather soft, shy, gawky youth; can't expect much from his company." And she soon came to totally dislike Mrs. Van Daan, whom she saw as a selfish and short-tempered woman.

To make matters worse, Anne was not getting along at all well with her mother or her sister, whose natures seemed "completely strange" to her. Anne loved and adored her father, however.

The young residents were supplied with schoolbooks so they could keep up with their studies. Anne studied French and shorthand; she loved history but hated algebra. She read anything she could get her hands on—that her parents deemed suitable—and she also spent her time tracing back family trees and working on her collection of pictures of film stars.

The weeks droned on. The Annex's occupants remained caged together in their cramped quarters; they dared not even make any noise during the day, lest people in the warehouse next door hear them and suspect their presence. Occasionally they heard news of the outside world from their protectors. A few months after they had gone into hiding, Anne wrote:

Our many Jewish friends are being taken away by the dozen. These people are treated by the Gestapo without a shred of decency, being loaded into cattle trucks and sent to Westerbork, the big Jewish camp in Drente . . . Prominent citizens—innocent people—are thrown into prison to await their fate. If the saboteur can't be traced, the Gestapo simply puts about five hostages against the wall. Announcements of their deaths appear in the papers frequently. These outrages are described as "fatal accidents."

In November, about four months after the Franks and Van Daans had taken refuge in the Annex, they decided to take in an eighth person, Albert Dussel, a dentist. Dussel brought them even more sobering accounts of events in the outside world. Jews were continually being rounded up by the Germans, he said. No one was spared—not the elderly, the sick, not expectant mothers, or even newborn babies.

After a short time, Dussel became annoyingly patronizing. In her diary, Anne referred to him as "a stodgy, old-fashioned disciplinarian, and preacher of long, drawn-out sermons on manners." Since Anne had to share her bedroom with him, she often received the "benefit" of his advice and experience.

In her confidences to Kitty, Anne frequently described the nightly air raid attacks and the less than adequate and spoiled food they were forced to eat. Yet even amid the squalor and harshness, "I usually come to the conclusion that it is a paradise compared with how other Jews who are not in hiding must be living."

The daily routine in the Annex continued, punctuated occasionally by the drama of air raids and by the inevitable squabbles and misunderstandings among the eight tired internees. Soon the Franks marked the first anniversary of their life in the Annex. On St. Nicholas' Day, inasmuch as they had no gifts to exchange, Anne and her father wrote a poem to present to each person.

Now Anne was fourteen years old. Even with Kitty at hand, she longed for someone to talk to, someone who could truly understand and respond to her. "Somehow or other," she wrote finally, "I took it into my head to choose Peter." She began making visits to Peter's room, where she helped him do crossword puzzles.

Meanwhile, however, the quarrels between the Franks and the Van Daans intensified, and Anne sometimes wished that the Franks hadn't consented to the Van Daans' coming. "I think it's all to the good to have learned a bit about human beings," she wrote, "but now I think I've learned enough." But, as she also reflected:

The war goes on just the same, whether or not we choose to quarrel . . . and so we should try to make the best of our stay here . . . Now I'm preaching, but I also believe that if I stay here for very long I shall grow into a dried-up old beanstalk. And I did so want to grow into a real young woman!

Throughout their stay, the residents looked on their protectors with great admiration and gratitude. "They have pulled us through up to now and we hope they will bring us safely to dry land . . . never have we heard one word of the burden which we certainly must be to them."

One night, after an argument with Dussel, Peter went to Anne for solace. He told her how much he admired her for always speaking her mind. Anne was surprised and glad to have finally found a sympathetic ear. A few days later she wrote, "Don't think I'm in love, because I'm not, but I do have the feeling all the time that something fine can grow up between us, something that gives confidence and friendship."

Within a few weeks, Anne began to waver from this noble platonic position: "Kitty, I'm just like someone in love, who can only talk about her darling. And Peter really is a darling."

In one entry Anne reflected on how she had changed, since the start of her ordeal, from "a terrible flirt, coquettish and amusing," to a much more serious person:

Then I think about "the good" of going into hiding, of my health and with my whole being of the "dearness" of Peter, of that which is still embryonic and impressionable and which we neither of us dare to name or touch, of that which will come sometime; love, the future, happiness and . . . the world, nature, beauty and all, all that is exquisite and fine.

Outside, the war raged on, as did Anne's vivid descriptions:

On Sunday . . . planes dropped half a million kilos of bombs . . . how the houses trembled like a wisp of grass in the wind . . . Who knows how many epidemics now rage . . . People have to line up for vegetables and all kinds of other things . . . Doctors are unable to visit the sick, because if they turn their backs on their cars for a moment, they are stolen . . . Morale among the population can't be good, the weekly rations are not enough to last for two days. The invasion is a long time coming . . .

Several times the Annex residents expressed the fear that the Nazis had uncovered their hiding place and would come for them. " . . . We are Jews in chains," Anne penned, "chained to one spot, without any rights . . . [But] surely the time will come when we are people again, and not just Jews."

On June 6th the Allied invasion of occupied Europe finally began; and by the end of the month, as Anne noted, the tide was beginning to turn in favor of the Allies.

Cherbourg, Vitebsk, and Sloben fell today. Lots of prisoners and booty . . . In the three weeks since D-day not a day has gone by without rain and gales, both here and in France, but a bit of bad luck didn't prevent the English and Americans from showing their enormous strength, and how!

Anne's last diary entry was written on August 1, 1944. Three days later, the Gestapo raided the Secret Annex and arrested the residents and their protectors. All the Jews were sent to German and Dutch concentration camps.

In March 1945, just two months before the liberation of Holland, Anne died of typhus and starvation in the camp at Bergen-Belsen. By that time, her mother, the Van Daans, and Dr. Dussel, had all perished. Her sister Margot, the only member of her family who had not eventually been separated from her after their arrest, had died in the same camp just a few days earlier.

Anne, dressed in rags, with her large eyes staring out of an emaciated face, "was not informed of her sister's death," a survivor recalled, "but after a few days she sensed it, and soon afterwards she died, peacefully, feeling that nothing bad was happening to her."

Commentary:

As Anne Frank confided to her diary, her dream was to someday become an author or journalist. And even if she didn't write well enough for others, she added, she wanted to leave some record, some expression of herself: "I want to go on living even after my death! And therefore I am grateful to God for giving me this gift, this possibility of developing myself and of writing, of expressing all that is in me."

Her diary, dumped from a briefcase onto the floor of the Annex by German officers on the day of the arrest, was originally circulated as a memorial to the Frank family. It was first published in Holland in 1947; eventually it was translated into more than 17 languages; in the 1950's, it was adapted as an internationally acclaimed play and, later, a movie.

In raiding the Annex, the Nazi soldiers were instructed to leave behind no record of their mission; in this, they failed. An accurate, literate commentary on the socio-political climate of the time had been preserved through the hopes, dreams and writings of a remarkable young girl.

COMPACT

Classics®

LIBRARY #3: Poets & Poetry

In these brief overviews you will get acquainted—or reacquainted—with some of the essential voices in English-language poetry over the past four and a half centuries. You will be invited into the life, times, and works of diverse poets such as Shakespeare, Rudyard Kipling, Dorothy Parker, and Jack Prelutski, "thought musicians" who serve both as representatives of their eras and genres and as the individual creators of individual poems. And surely you will find no form of discourse within the realm of language that is quite so individual as a poem.

Good poetry distills and clarifies a writer's deepest engagements with life, offering up to the reader a rare "elixir" of words and emotions. Let the poems in this library sink into you one by one: the sensual rhythms of Lord Byron, the bleak and powerful imagery of Eliot, the bright, pungent darts of Dickinson, and the sharp but subtle barbs of Nash. Accept, and savor, these "music-of-the-soul" offerings.

Section B: Mid- and Late-Nineteenth-century Lyricists ————

Section C: Twentieth-century Verse: Master Poets ————

Section D: A Modern Mix: Today's Favorites ————

WILLIAM SHAKESPEARE

(1564-1616)

It wasn't until the age of 27—middle-aged by that era's standard—that Shakespeare began to write poetry. His often much younger contemporaries, however, agreed that he was the epitome of the master wordsmith. Time has validated that opinion—and even enhanced it.

Very little is known of Shakespeare's early life; in fact, even his later years—aside from a bit here and a piece there—are riddled with uncertainties about his personal and professional life. (For a more complete sketch of his life and legacy, please consult the Biographies Library in Volume I of *Compact Classics / The Bathroom Book*.)

Shakespeare is best-known for his highly poetic plays (for play overviews, please refer to the Literary Classics or Drama sections found in both volumes of *Compact Classics / The Bathroom Book*). Herein, however, we will focus on his superb sonnets.

Many themes are apparent in Shakespeare's poetic body of work; some are lighthearted pieces, some consist of sincere communications, and others contain serious commentary. In all of the poetry, however, there breathes a surplus of power.

This following light verse was apparently written to mock a love sonnet written by an associate to his fair lady love:

Sonnet CXX

My mistress' eyes are nothing like the sun;
Coral is far more red than her lips' red:
If snow be white, why then her breasts are dun;
If hairs be wires, black wires grow on her head.
I have seen roses demask'd, red and white,
But no such roses see I in her cheeks;
And in some perfumes is there more delight
Than in the breath that from my mistress reeks.
I love to hear her speak, yet well I know
That music hath a far more pleasing sound.
I grant I never saw a goddess go,
My mistress, when she walks, treads on the ground:
And yet, by heaven, I think my love as rare
As any she belied with false compare.

A warning against deceivers is sounded in Shakespeare's earliest-known poem, *A Lover's Complaint*:

For further I could say "This man's untrue,"
And knew the patterns of his foul beguiling;
Heard where his plants in others' orchards grew
Saw how deceits were gilded in his smiling;
Knew vows were ever brokers to defiling . . .

Over time, some critics have come to the conclusion that Shakespeare's sonnets are autobiographical in nature, writings through which he could relay his perceptions and experiences. Other critics, however, assert that the sonnets are mere figments of Shakespeare's fertile imagination.

The first 126 sonnets are dedicated to a young friend of Shakespeare's, while the rest appear to be written to a "dark lady" who steals both his own heart and that of his young friend. The poet imagines that the Dark Lady holds some sort of strange power over him, but he feels helpless to do anything about it:

Sonnet CLII

In loving thee thou know'st I am forsworn,
But thou art twice forsworn, to love me swearing;
In act thy bed-vow broke, and new faith torn
In vowing new hate after new love bearing.
But why of two oaths' breach do I accuse thee,

When I break twenty? I am perjur'd most;
For all my vows are oaths but to misuse thee,
And all my honest faith in thee is lost;
For I have sworn deep oaths of thy deep kindness,
Oaths of thy love, thy truth, thy constancy;
And, to enlighten thee, gave eyes to blindness,
Or made them swear against the thing they see;
For I have sworn thee fair - more perjur'd I,
To swear against the truth so foul a lie!

Shakespeare understood the power of time—in the world and in the lives of people. The words, meter and rhyme all work together in this sonnet to accomplish his purpose.

Sonnet LXIV

When I have seen by Time's fell hand defaced
The rich-proud cost of outworn buried age;
When sometime lofty towers I see down-razed,
And brass eternal slave to mortal rage;
When I have seen the hungry ocean gain
Advantage on the kingdom of the shore,
And the firm soil win of the watery main,
Increasing store with loss and loss with store;
When I have seen such interchange of state,
Or state itself confounded to decay;
Ruin hath taught me thus to ruminate,
That Time will come and take my love away.
This thought is as a death, which cannot choose
But weep to have that which it fears to lose.

As powerful as time is, the poet obviously believed that love could persist through time.

SONNET XXX

When to the sessions of sweet silent thought

I summon up remembrance of things past,
I sigh the lack of many a thing I sought,
And with old woes new wail my dear time's
    waste:
Then can I drown an eye, unused to flow,
For precious friends hid in death's dateless
    night,
And weep afresh love's long since cancell'd woe,
And moan the expense of many a vanish'd
    sight;
Then can I grieve at grievances foregone,
And heavily from woe to woe tell o'er
The sad account of fore-bemoaned moan,
Which I new pay as if not paid before,
  But if the while I think on thee, dear friend,
  All losses are restored and sorrows end.

Other sonnets speak of the power of love to outlast time. This one is among the most popular:

SONNETS CXVI

Let me not to the marriage of true minds
Admit impediments, Love is not love
Which alters when it alteration finds
Or bends with the remover to remove:
O, no! it is an ever-fixed mark,
That looks on tempests and is never shaken;
It is the star to every wandering bark,
Whose worth's unknown, although his height be
    taken.
Love's not Time's fool, though rosy lips and
    cheeks
Within his bending sickle's compass come;
Love alters not with his brief hours and weeks,
But bears it out even to the edge of doom.
  If this be error and upon me proved,
  I never writ, nor no man ever loved.

Occasional despair flows through the sonnets. Shakespeare mourns disappointments, dissatisfactions, losses, the death of friends. Yet in each case, before the piece ends, his beloved Dark Lady reassures him and rejuvenates him. For a time, a new theme emerged: not only does love conquer time, it conquers all.

Sonnet XXIX

When in disgrace with Fortune and men's eyes,
I all alone beweep my outcast state,
And trouble deaf heaven with my bootless cries,
And look upon myself and curse my fate,
Wishing me like to one more rich in hope,
Featured like him, like him with friends pos-
    sessed,
Desiring this man's art, and that man's scope,
With what I most enjoy contented least;
Yet in these thoughts myself almost despising,
Haply I think on thee, and then my state,
Like to the lark at break of day arising
From sullen earth, sings hymns at heaven's
    gate;
  For thy sweet love rememb'red such wealth

brings,
  That then I scorn to change my state with
    kings.

Shakespeare's The Rape of Lucrece is based on a historical tale of a Roman emperor's son who is entranced by the great virtue of a married noblewoman. Unable to assail that virtue, the son finally rapes his paradigm. Afterward, as she mourns the act, we hear another description of the power of time.

Time's glory is to calm contending kings,
To unmask falsehood, and bring truth to light,
To stamp the seal of time in aged things,
To wake the morn, and sentinel the night,
To wrong the wronger till he render right;
  To ruinate proud buildings with thy hours
  And smear with dust their glitt'ring tow'rs...

Why work'st thou mischief in thy pilgrimage,
Unless thou could return to make amends?
One poor retiring minute in an age
Would purchase thee a thousand friends,
Lending him wit that to bad debtors lends:
O, this dread night, wouldst thou one hour
    come back
I could prevent this storm, and shun thy wrack!

Shakespeare's plays frequently portrayed how mankind's sexual appetites and lust for power or position lead to fatal mistakes that destroy lives. In his poetry, these same deadly motivations are in force.

So that in venturing ill we leave to be
The things we are for that which we expect;
And this ambitious foul infirmity,
In having much, torments us with defect
Of that we have; so then we do neglect
  The things we have; and, all for want of wit,
  Make something nothing by augmenting it.

The reader can feel Lucrece's terror as she tries to save herself by reasoning with an unreasonable man:

She conjures him by high almighty Jove,
By knighthood, gentry, and sweet friendship's
    oath,
By her untimely tears, her husband's love,
By holy human law, and common troth,
By heaven and earth, and all the power of both,
  That to his borrow'd bed he make retire,
  And stoop to honour, not to foul desire.

'My husband is thy friend, for his sake spare
    me;
Thyself art mighty, for thine own sake leave me;
Myself a weakling, do not then ensnare me;
Thou look'st not like deceit, do not deceive me;
My sights, like whirlwinds, labour hence to
    heave thee.
If ever man were moved with woman's moans,
Be moved with my tears, my sighs, my groans.

JOHN DONNE

(1572-1631)

"No man is an island; every man is . . . part of the main."

John Donne penned these lines during a life spent struggling to be part of a society which spurned him.

Born in 1572 to a middle-class English family, Donne first studied at Oxford, then at a philosophy workshop called Lincoln's Inn, and finally enlisted in the military and took part in naval raids on Spain. Electing to elope with the daughter of one of his wealthy sponsors landed him in prison for a short time. A fanatic concerning social status, his greatest desire was to be recognized as a "man of breeding." Accomplishing this feat, however, was difficult in Elizabethan England, as Catholics were unmercifully persecuted by members of the Anglican Church—including the Queen herself. Despite the fact that he was sponsored by many wealthy and influential patrons, Donne failed to acquire the entitled rank of a well-bred individual.

Sometime in his early twenties, Donne renounced the Catholic Church. His reasons are unclear, but his desire to gain social favor played a major part in his decision. Knowing he would always be a second-class citizen as a Catholic, Donne simply refused to be a part of in any religious rites. His poetry from this point on takes on a ferocious, raging tone in which he rails against God, Satan, death, life . . . virtually anything that held religious overtones. Remaining a deeply spiritual person in spite of his public outcries of rebellion, Donne privately felt he had damned his soul by renouncing his church.

In 1615, perhaps out of guilt—but more likely due to his continuing quest for social acceptance—Donne joined the Anglican ministry, enticed by Elizabeth's successor, King James I. The king promised to a good salary, thus the poet lived out his life in relative comfort.

Virtually all of Donne's known poetry was written before 1615. His recorded sermons, however, resound with the same vigor—and anger—as his poetry. His works are characterized by robust, direct language. In spite of archaic spellings, the images created are instantly accessible to the modern reader. Many of the poems begin with a strong directive phrase; others open with an unflinching question that demands an immediate answer. Donne's inner turmoil—and perhaps his ego—gave him an urgency to write about subjects such as God and death—topics his contemporaries often either ignored or treated very lightly. In *Holy Sonnet #10* he not only addresses these themes, he attacks them with relish.

Death be not proud, though some have called thee
Mighty and dreadfull, for, thou art not soe,
For, those, whom thou think'st, thou dost over-throw,
Die not, poore death, nor yet canst thou kill mee;
From rest and sleepe, which but thy pictures bee,
Much pleasure, then from thee, much more must flow,
And soonest our best men with thee do goe,
Rest of their bones and soules deliverie.
Thou are slave to Fate, chance, kings, and desperate men,
And dost with poyson, warre, and sicknesse dwell,
And poppie, or charmes can make us sleepe as well,
And better then they stroake; why swell'st thou then?

One short sleepe past, wee wake eternally,
And death shall be no more, Death thou shalt die.

Donne's work can be a kind of cathartic experience for those who are reluctant to confront God on His own terms. The following lines from *Holy Sonnet #14* well illustrate his near-blasphemous rantings.

Batter my heart, three person'd God; for, you
As yet but knocke, breathe, shine, and seeke to mend;
That I may rise, and stand, o'erthrow mee, 'and bend
Your force, to breake, blowe, burn and make me new.
I like an usurpt towne, to'another due,
Labour to'admit you, but Oh, to no end,
Reason your viceroy in mee, mee should defend,
But is captiv'd, and proves weake or untrue.
Yet dearely' I love you, and would be lov'd faine,
But am betroth'd unto your enemie,
Divorce mee, 'untie, or breake that knot againe,
Take mee to you, imprison mee, for I
Except you'enthrall mee, never shall be free,
Nor ever chaste, except you ravish mee.

Holy Sonnets reflect a tortured mind that operates somewhere between self-loathing, anger, and humble supplication.

Holy Sonnets #163 and #164 most graphically depict this juxtaposition.

Holy Sonnet #163

Oh my blacke Soule! now thou art summoned
By sicknesse, death's herald, and champion;
Thou art like a pilgrim, which abroad hat done
Treason, and durst not turne to whence hee is
*   fled,*
Or like a thiefe, which till death's doome be
*   read,*
Wisheth himselfe deliverd from prison;
But damn'd and hal'd to execution,
Wisheth that still he might be imprisoned;
Yet grace, if thou repent, thou canst not lacke;
But who shall give thee that grace to beginne?
Oh make they selfe with holy mourning blacke,
And red with blushing, as thou art with sinne;
Or wash thee in Christ's blood, which hath this
*   might*
That being red, it dyes red soules to white.

Holy Sonnet #164

As due by many titles I resigne
My selfe to thee, o God, first I was made
By thee, and for thee, and when I was decay'd
Thy blood bought that, the which before was
*   thine,*
I am thy sone, made with thy selfe to shine,
Thy servant, whose paines thou hast still repaid,
Thy sheepe, thine image, and till I betray'd
My selfe, a temple of thy Spirit divine;
Why doth the devill then usurpe in mee?
Why doth he steale, nay ravish that's thy right?
Except thou rise and for thine owne worke fight,
Oh I shall soone despaire, when I doe see
That thou lov'st mankind well, yet wilt not
*   chuse me.*
And Satan hates mee, yet is loth to lose mee.

Though his poetry was greatly influenced by the turbulent religious temperament of the time, Donne did not limit himself to strictly religious themes. He explored other genres, including satire and romance. His romantic poetry is fraught with changing voices, sometimes opening with bold statements and closing with pitiful, meaningless maxims. *Woman's Constancy* echoes with a sense of hopelessness, perhaps born out of the feeling that if he could not love himself, no one else possibly could either.

Now thou hast lov'd me one whole day,
To morrow when thou leav'st, what wilt thou
*   say?*
Wilt thou then Antedate some new made vow?
*   Or say that now*
We are not just those persons, which we were?
Or, that oathes made in reverentiall fear
Of Love, and his wrath, any may forsweare?
Or, as true deaths, true maryages, untie,

So lovers contracts, images of those,
Binde but till sleep, deaths image, them
*   unloose?*
*   Or, your owne end to Justifie,*
For having purpos'd change, and falsehood; you
Can have no way but falsehood to be true?
Vaine lunatique, against these scapes I could
*   Dispute, and conquer, if I would,*
*   Which I abstaine to doe,*
For by to morrow, I may thinke so too.

In this same poem, another theme common to Donne's work is addressed: a fascination with changability and transmutability, a fixation conceivably rising from his own betrayal of the religion of his youth.

In counterpoint, Donne's work also seems to reflect a need to belong, to be an integral part of the proverbial "big picture." This idea is poignantly illustrated by Donne's most famous work, *No Man Is An Island*:

No man is an island,
entire of itself;
every man is a piece of the continent,
a part of the main.
If a clod be washed away by the sea,
Europe is the less,
as well as if a promontory were,
as well as if a manor of thy friend's
or of thine own were:
any man's death diminishes me,
because I am involved in mankind,
and therefore never send to know
for whom the bell tolls;
it tolls for thee.

WILLIAM BLAKE

(1757-1827)

William Blake was born in London in 1757 to a middle-class family. Educated at home by his mother, who shielded her sensitive child against the severe schools of the day, Blake demonstrated an early and active imagination, as well as a talent for seeing visions, which he first expressed in drawings. His father, recognizing his artistic talent, sent him away to drawing school at the age of ten.

Later, Blake was apprenticed to an engraver. When, at age 21, his apprenticeship ended, he began accepting commissions, all the while studying painting at the Royal Academy. In 1782 Blake married Catherine Battersea; a year later he printed his first poems, *Poetical Sketches*. Then in 1787 he published *Songs of Innocence*, a highly innovative creation not only in its language but also in its presentation. The poems were engraved in an ornate calligraphic style which became Blake's trademark.

Inspired by the storming of the Bastille in 1789, Blake next wrote *The Marriage of Heaven and Hell*. Then, as if to forecast the success of the French Revolution, he wrote and engraved the poem *America*. To give voice to his disillusionment with the "French Reign of Terror," Blake also penned *Songs of Innocence and Experience*. On the 12th of August, 1827, Blake died, still poor, yet hard at work on his last project, an illustration of Dante's *Divine Comedy*.

In *Songs of Innocence* Blake first expresses some of his deepest thoughts about mankind and God. He vigorously celebrates the spirit of innocence—not only the natural state of childhood, but also the condition of simplicity and unrestrained love to which the mature soul aspires. The verses are simple, appealing to both children and adults. But the clarity and innocence are often deceiving. Beneath the rhythms—often borrowed from nursery rhymes—is a deeper significance hidden in certain symbols. In *The Lamb*, for instance, the lamb represents Jesus, the Lamb of God. Likewise, the themes of shepherds and their flocks represent serenity, while the peaceful pastures symbolize a state of innocence or eternity.

The Lamb

Little Lamb, who made thee?
Dost thou know who made thee?
Gave thee life, and bid thee feed,
By the stream and o'er the mead;
Gave thee clothing and delight,
Softest clothing, wooly, bright;
Gave thee such a tender voice,
Making all the vales rejoice?
Little Lamb, who made thee?
Dost thou know who made thee?

Little Lamb, I'll tell thee,
Little Lamb, I'll tell thee:
He is called by thy name,
For he calls himself a Lamb.
He is meek, and He is mild;
He became a little child.

I a child, and thou a lamb,
We are called by His name.
Little Lamb, God bless thee!
Little Lamb, God bless thee!

Holy Thursday describes an annual service at St. Paul's Cathedral on Ascension Day. The boys from the charity schools—orphanages—of London march to the church to give thanks for their blessings. The "beadles" spoken of are the parish officers who supervise them.

Holy Thursday

'Twas on a Holy Thursday, their innocent faces clean,
The children walking two and two, in red and blue and green,
Grey-headed beadles walk'd before, with wands as white as snow,
Till into the high dome of Paul's they like Thames' waters flow.

O what a multitude they seem'd, these flowers of London town!
Seated in companies they sit with radiance all their own.
The hum of the multitudes was there, but multitudes of lambs,
Thousands of little boys and girls raising their innocent hands.

Now like a mighty winds they raise to Heaven the voice of song,
Or like harmonious thundering the seats of Heaven among
Beneath them sit the aged men, wise guardians of the poor;
Then cherish pity, lest you drive an angel from your door.

Five years later, Blake's verse had kept its simplicity, yet had taken on an entirely different mood. In *Songs of Experience*, "experience" denotes a world of disillusionment in which innocence is dashed by harsh reality. In order to emphasize this contrast, he composes many of the *Songs of Experience* as ironic counterparts or parodies of the earlier poems. *The Tyger* is, for example, an ironic counterpart to *The Lamb*, the "tyger" representing God's righteous anger.

The Tyger

Tyger! Tyger! burning bright
In the forests of the night
What immortal hand or eye
Could frame thy fearful symmetry?

In what distant deeps or skies
Burnt the fire of thine eyes?
On what wings dare he aspire?
What the hand dare seize the fire?

And what shoulder, and what art,
Could twist the sinews of they heart?
And when thy heart began to beat,
What dread hand? and what dread feet?

What the hammer? what the chain?

In what furnace was thy brain?
What the anvil? what dead grasp
Dare its deadly terrors clasp?

When the stars threw down their spears
And water'd heaven with their tears,
Did he smile his work to see?
Did he who made the Lamb make thee?

Tyger! Tyger! burning bright
In the forests of the night,
What immortal hand or eye
Dare frame thy fearful symmetry?

Between his *Songs of Innocence* and *Songs of Experience*, Blake wrote and engraved *The Marriage of Heaven and Hell*, a collection of verse, proverbs, and prose allegory inspired by the new age of political freedom which Blake felt was dawning on Europe. The book consists of four parts, *The Argument, The Voice of the Devil, A Memorable Fancy*, and the *Proverbs of Hell. The Argument* is free-verse piece touching upon the perversion of paradise by ecclesiastical and political tyranny. In its commentary, Blake sets forth his philosophy on good and evil. Good is associated with passivity and conventional wisdom; evil with creativity and genius. In Blake's scheme, Devils are poets and Hell is the realm of truth. Angels, on the other hand, are the souls of those pious souls who blindly and hypocritically follow the laws of conventional morality.

The Argument
Rintah roars & shakes his fires in the burden'd air;
Hungry clouds swag on the deep.

Once meek, and in a perilous path,
The just man kept his course along
The vale of death.
Roses are planted where thorns grow,
And on the barren heath
Sing the honey bees.

Then the perilous path was planted,
And a river and a spring
On every cliff and tomb,
And on the bleached bones
Red clay brought forth;

Till the villain left the paths of ease,
To walk in perilous paths, and drive
The just man into barren climes.

Now the sneaking serpent walks
In mild humility,
And the just man rages in the wilds
Where lions roar.

Rintah roars & shakes his fires in the burden'd air;
Hungry clouds swag on the deep.

America was also inspired by Europe's new-found liberty. America had won its revolutionary war. France, recently having won its own emancipation from monarchism, was embarking on what appeared to be a majestic project of renewal. Blake saw the current events unfolding around him as all part of spiritual awakening—a struggle towards spiritual freedom. To prophesy the struggle's success, *America* was set against the backdrop of the American Revolution. Here, "Albion" refers to England, against which Washington and other American patriots had fought.

Passage from America: A Prophecy
The Guardian Prince of Albion burns his nightly tent:
Sullen fires across the Atlantic glow to America's shore,
Piercing the souls of warlike man who rise in silent night.
Washington, Franklin, Paine & Warren, Gates, Hancock & Green
Meet on the coast glowing with blood from Albion's fiery Prince.

Washington spoke: "Friends of America! look over the Atlantic sea;
A bended bow is lifted in heaven, & a heavy iron chain
Descends, link by link, from Albion's cliffs across the sea, to bind
Brothers & sons of America, till our faces pale and yellow,
Heads deprest, voices weak, eyes downcast, hands work-bruis'd,
Feet bleeding on the sultry sands, and the furrow of the whip
Descend to generations that in future times forget."

The strong voice ceas'd, for a terrible blast swept over the heaving sea:
The eastern could rent: on his cliffs stood Albion's wrathful Prince,
A dragon form, clashing his scales: at midnight he arose,
And flamed red meteors round the land of Albion beneath;
His voice, his locks, his awful shoulders, and his glowing eyes
Appear to the Americans upon the cloudy night.

Solemn heave the Atlantic waves beneath the gloomy nations,
Swelling, belching from its deeps red clouds and raging fires.
Albion is sick, America faints! enrag'd the Zenith grew.
As human blood shooting its veins all round the orbed heaven,
Red rose the clouds from the Atlantic in vast wheels of blood,
And in the red clouds rose a Wonder oe'r the Atlantic sea;
Intense! naked! a Human fire, fierce glowing, as the wedge
Of iron heated in the furnace; his terrible limbs were fire
With myriads of cloudy terrors; banners dark & towers
Surrounded; heat but not light went thro' the murky atmosphere.

The King of England looking westwards trembles at the vision . . .

GEORGE GORDON (LORD) BYRON

(1788-1824)

When George was born in 1788, he was given the last name of Gordon, taken from his mother's side of the family. At age ten, however, he inherited the title of "Lord" Byron from a great uncle on his father's side. After his father deserted the family, Byron moved to Scotland with his mother. He was first educated at Aberdeen, then Harrow, then Trinity College, Cambridge. Though he never earned a degree, he did earn a reputation for wild and reckless living.

Shortly after forsaking college, he and a friend toured Europe for two years, spending time in Portugal, Spain and Greece. The first two cantos of *Childe Harold's Pilgrimage* and *Oriental Tales* were inspired by his feelings during his travels. These poems became immediately successful.

Back home in England, Byron married and had a child. However, after only one year together, the couple separated. As one historian observed, "Byron was wild and his wife was a prude, and nothing else needs to be said."

After the divorce, rumors spread that Byron had entered into an incestuous relationship with his half-sister, Augusta. When Augusta did in fact have a baby, Byron, though he never admitted the child was his, was forced to move to Switzerland to escape the stinging criticism.

Apparently, these personal trials aroused Byron's poetic muse. During this time, Byron wrote *Parisina, Hebrew Melodies, The Prisoner of Chillon*, Canto III of *Childe Harold's Pilgrimage*, and *Manfred*. He later toured Italy, where he completed Canto IV of *Childe Harold, Beppo* and *Don Juan.*

In 1823, Byron returned to Greece, which by then was embroiled in revolution. He quickly took up the cause, spent vast amounts of money supporting it, and was even made an officer in the rebellion. But bad weather and over-exposure caused him to become critically ill, a sickness that led to his death in 1824. The Greeks, who considered him a national hero, gave him every honor accorded one of their own fallen comrades in arms.

Critics have never been kind to Byron's work. He has been accused of everything ranging from fostering moral corruption to perpetrating crimes against the English language—and he has also been described as a poet in search of a style. Most likely, Byron found his voice with *Beppo* and *Don Juan.* Had he lived longer, his work may have become more stable.

Byron often writes of loss. loss of love, of home, of honor, of everything humanity holds dear. This began with *Childe Harold*. Although he insisted that he did *not* represent Harold, that Harold was a fictitious character created to link all the pieces of the "Pilgrimage," still it is easy to feel Byron's sense of loss in Harold's reveries. The image of even his dog forgetting him is strangely poignant.

Childe Harold's Pilgrimage— Canto The First

For who would trust the seeming sighs
  Of wife or paramour?
Fresh feres will dry the bright blue eyes
  We late saw streaming o'er.
For pleasures past I do not grieve,
  Nor perils gathering near;
My greatest grief is that I leave
  No thing that claims a tear.

And now I'm in the world alone,
  Upon the wide, wide sea;
But why should I for others groan,
  When none will sigh for me?
Perchance my dog will whine in vain,
  Till fed by stranger hands;
But long ere I come back again
  He'd tear me where he stands.

Critics have termed the *Childe Harold* cantos as an exploration in "the agony of humanity." That agony, and Byron's lifelong search for love and honor, are a significant part of *Don Juan*:

Canto The Seventh

O Love! O Glory! what are ye who fly
  Around us ever, rarely to alight?
There's not a meteor in the polar sky
  Of such transcendent and more fleeting flight.
Chill, and chain'd to cold earth, we lift on high
  Our eyes in search of either lovely light;
A thousand and a thousand colours they
Assume, then leave us on our freezing way.

In spite of his own personal immorality, Byron clearly espoused a broadened, universal morality, and mourned its frequent absence in mankind. In Canto I of *Don Juan*, he criticizes war by way of his description of a battlefield:

Three hosts combine to offer sacrifice;
Three tongues prefer strange orisons on high;
Three gaudy standards flout the pale blue skies;
The shouts are France, Spain, Albion, Victory!

The foe, the victim, and the fond ally
That fights for all, but ever fights in vain,
Are met-as if at home they could not die-
To feed the crow, on Talavera's plain,
And fertilize the field that each pretends to gain.

For whatever virtues he lacked, honesty was one of his redeeming characteristics. Byron never lied to himself about his morality. His feelings about his unfeigned nature are apparent in *Childe Harold*:

If my fame should be, as my fortunes are,
Of hasty growth and blight, and dull Oblivion bar

My name from out the temple where the dead
Are honour'd by the nations let it be,
And light the laurels on a loftier head!
And be the Spartan's epitaph on me,
"Sparta hath many a worthier son than he."
Meantime I seek no sympathies, nor need;
The thorns which I have reap'd are of the tree
I planted,-they have torn me-and I bleed:

I should have known what fruit would spring from
  such a seed.

Clearly Byron recognized that he was the source of his own problems. *Epistle to Augusta* emphasizes this even more:

I have been cunning in mine overthrow,
The careful pilot of my proper woe.

Mine were my faults, and mine be their reward.
My whole life was a contest, since the day
That gave me being, gave me that which marr'd
The gift,-a fate, or will, that walk'd astray.

Many critics believe Byron's many dalliances with satire to be among his best work. They certainly was among the most popular, though some attributed this popularity to the public's appetite for gossip about the literary coterie. When one of his works was criticized, Byron wrote the following:

To A Knot Of Ungenerous Critics

Rail on, Rail on, ye heartless Crew!
My strains were never meant for you;
Remorseless Rancour still reveal,
And damn the verse you cannot feel.
Invoke those kindred passions' aid,
Whose baleful stings your breasts pervade;
Crush, if you can, the hopes of youth,
Trampling regardless on the Truth.
Truth's Records you consult in vain,
She will not blast her native strain;
She will assist her votary's cause,
His will at least be her applause,

English Bards And Scotch Reviewers is a collection of satire inaugurated early in Byron's career and completed after some criticism of his poetry. Unlike his attacks on critics in general, here he skewered his contemporaries on an individual basis. The following was directed toward a now-obscure acquaintance, Viscount Strangford:

For thee, translator of the tinsel song,
To whom such glittering ornaments belong,
Hibernian Strangford! with thine eyes of blue,
And boasted locks of red or auburn hue,
Whose plaintive strain each love-sick miss admires,
And o'er harmonious fustian half expires,
Learn, if thou canst, to yield thine author's sense,
Nor vend thy sonnets on a false pretence.
Think'st thou to gain thy verse a higher place,
By dressing Camoens in a suit of lace?
Mend, Strangford! mend thy morals and thy taste;
Be warm, but pure; be amorous, but be chaste:
Cease to deceive; thy pilfer'd harp restore,
Nor teach the Lusian bard to copy Moore.

Byron's satire was not limited to specific poetry. He was not above taking what we now call a "cheap shot" on almost any occasion. For example, many of Coleridge's readers share Byron's plea:

And Coleridge, too, has lately taken wing,
But like a hawk encumbered with his hood,—
Explaining metaphysics to the nation—
I wish he would explain his Explanation.

Childe Harold's Pilgrimage, a fine example of Byron's descriptive verse, was not all written

or published simultaneously. The first two Cantos were published together early in Byron's career; the third and fourth were published separately late in his short life.

Canto The Second

He that has sail'd upon the dark blue sea
Has view'd at times . . . a full fair sight
When the fresh breeze is fair as breeze may be,
The white sail set, the gallant frigate tight;
Masts, spires, and strand retiring to the right,
The glorious main expanding o'er the bow,
The convoy spread like wild swans in their flight,
The dullest sailor wearing bravely now,
So gaily curl the waves before each dashing prow.

Byron's love affair with Greece and its revolution provided the force behind *The Giaour*:

Clime of the unforgotten brave!
Whose land from plain to mountain-cave
Was Freedom's home or Glory's grave!
Shrine of the mighty! can it be,
That this is all remains of thee?
Approach, thou craven crouching slave;
Say, is not this Thermopylae?
These waters blue that round you lave,
Oh, servile offspring of the free-
Pronounce what sea, what shore is this?
The gulf, the rock of Salamis!
These scenes, their story not unknown,
Arise and make again your own;
Snatch from the ashes of your sires
The embers of their former fires;
And he who in the strife expires
Will add to theirs a name of fear
That Tyranny shall quake to hear,
And leave his sons a hope, a fame,
They too will rather die than shame;
For Freedom's battle and once begun,
Bequeath'd by bleeding sire to son,
Though baffled oft is ever won
Bear witness, Greece, thy living page
Attest it many a deathless age!

Perhaps Byron's greatest descriptive piece was written about himself and his feelings. Reverting to *Childe Harold* (Canto III), we see the feeling of the creator as he views his own, enigmatic nature:

He, who grown aged in this world of woe,
In deeds, not years, piercing the depth
  of life,
So that no wonder waits him; nor below
Can love, or sorrow, fame, ambition, strife,
Cut to his heart again with the keen knife
Of silent, sharp endurance: he can tell
Why thought seeks refuge in lone caves, yet rife
With airy images, and shapes which dwell
Still unimpair'd, though old, in the soul's haunted
  cell.

'T is to create, and in creating live
A being more intense, that we endow
With form our fancy, gaining as we give
The life we image, even as I do now.
What am I? Nothing: but not so are thou,
Invisible but gazing, as I glow
Mix'd with thy spirit, blended with thy birth,
And feeling still with thee in my crush'd
  feelings' dearth.

PERCY BYSSHE SHELLEY

(1792-1822)

O wild West Wind, thou breath of Autumn's
being,
Thou from whose unseen presence the leaves of
the dead
Are driven, like ghosts from an enchanter flee-
ing . . .

. . . Be thou, Spirit fierce,
My spirit! Be thou me, impetuous one!

Drive my dead thoughts over the universe
Like withered leaves to quicken a new birth!
And like the incantations of this verse,

Scatter, as from an unextinguished hearth
Ashes and sparks, my words among mankind!
Be through my lips to unawakened Earth

The trumpet of a prophecy! O Wind,
If Winter comes, can Spring be far behind?

    Ode to the West Wind, the best known of Shelley's shorter poems, expresses the prophetic role the poet saw himself playing. His political ideas were tinged with a poetic quality, and his poetry was infused with politics.

    Percy Bysshe Shelley fueled his work with philosophy and politics, a radical departure from the poetry of his day. Born in Sussex, England, he was schooled at Eton and Oxford. He was expelled from Oxford, however, for publishing an inflammatory pamphlet, "The Necessity of Atheism." After leaving school, he involved himself in several political causes in Ireland and England.

    In an effort to elude his creditors and escape the antagonism of his critics, Shelley left for Italy with his second wife, wandering the countryside with a colorful group of English expatriates. It was during these bohemian ramblings that most of his best poetic work was done, including *Prometheus Unbound, Ode to the West Wind, the Cenci, Adonais,* and, what proved to be his last, unfinished work, *The Triumph of Life.* At age 29, Shelley drowned at sea while sailing to Lerici from Leghorn.

    Critic T. S. Eliot—who openly derided Shelley's views—admitted that, void of those revolutionary shades, his poetry would have been nothing more than a "wax effigy"—a metaphor taken directly from one of Shelley's own works, *In Defense of Poetry.*

    Queen Mab; A Philosophical Poem, Shelley's earliest serious effort, marked the first time the poet had in any degree succeeded in fusing his artistic and political concerns. Savaged by critics who thought

the poem to be simply a vehicle for his views, its chief value is its interesting handling of themes and motifs that received fuller treatment in later, more mature works.

. . . Now stands adorning
This lovely earth with taintless body and mind;
Blest form his birth with all bland impulses,
Which gently in his noble being wake
All kindly passions and all pure desires

All things are recreated and the flame
Of consentaneous love inspires all life.

    After *Queen Mab,* Shelley took to composing poems commemorating political injustices and furthering the cause of reform both in England and on the continent: *The Masque of Anarchy* inspired by the St. Peter's Field Massacre; *Ode Written in October 1819* and *Ode to Liberty*—whose stimulus was the Spanish revolution; *Ode to Naples*—written on the occasion of the war of the kingdom of Naples against Austrian domination; *Hellas*—treating the Greek struggle for liberation from the Turkish empire; and the two major poems *The Revolt of Islam* and *Prometheus Unbound*—both springing from signs of revolution that Shelley felt were manifesting themselves throughout the world.

    More than any poet before him, Shelley defined poetry in a social sense. His notions of the role of poetry as an instrument for social and moral reform are superbly set forth in his *Defense of Poetry,* written in 1820 in response to an essay challenging poets to leave civic matters to reasoners and merchants. Easily Shelley's most famous and frequently quoted prose work, in it he explained that, of all the factors giving rise to the birth of civilization, art and drama played the biggest part.

    Shelley applied this innovative theory to his own verse-making. He deemed it his poetic vocation to awaken the whole of Europe, a continent spellbound by superstition and tyranny.

    This idea of change—of the inescapable certainty of the nature of change, not only in the seasons, but also in governments and laws—Shelley also treats in his brilliant *Ozymandias.* In all worldly rulers he sees the interceding hand of certain fate.

I met a traveller from an antique land
Who said: Two vast and trunkless legs of stone
Stand in the desert. Near them, on the sand,

Half sunk, a shattered visage lies, whose frown,
And wrinkled lip, and sneer of cold command,
Tell that its sculptor well those passions read
Which yet survive, stamped on these lifeless
  things,
The hand that mocked them, and the heart that
  fed;
And on the pedestal these words appear:
"My name is Ozymandias, king of kings:
Look on my works, ye Mighty, and despair!"
Nothing beside remains. Round the decay
Of that colossal wreck, boundless and bare,
The lone and level sands stretch far away.

Of all the Romantic poets, it was Shelley who most consistently maintained a devotion to political activism. As a result, he incurred the fear and loathing of the conservative establishment. On Shelley's death, one review declared, "Shelley, the writer of some infidel poetry has drowned . . . now he knows whether there be a God or no."

While it is true that in many of Shelley's works politics overshadows the poetry, the most successful of his poems are less explicitly political. Instead, bipartisan issues are stripped bare and treated separately from other contemporary affairs. Thus they become integrated as part of his overall poetical vision.

Such is the case with *Prometheus Unbound*, Shelley's best long poem, in which he translates his revolutionary ideas into a universal and mythological language. Composed in 1818 in the ruins of the Baths of Caracalla in Rome, *Prometheus Unbound* is an unstageable drama based on Aeschylus' Greek tragedy *Prometheus Bound*. Where the Greek playwright used strong images of mythical beings to propel his story, Shelley takes those same images and converts the play into a socio-political allegory.

He gave man speech and speech created thought,
Which is the measure of the universe;
And science struck the thrones of Earth and
  heaven
Which shook but did not fall; and the harmo-
  nious mind
Poured forth in all-prophetic song,
And music lifted up the listening spirit
Until it walked, exempt from mortal care
Godlike o'er the clear billows of sweet sound.

JOHN KEATS

(1795 - 1821)

"If poetry can't come as naturally as leaves to a tree, it shouldn't come at all."

Naturally, the words came easily to John Keats, who wrote some of the finest lyrics in the English language. Although raised in an orphanage, by age 16 he had completed a prose translation of Virgil's *Aeneid*. A year later, he turned to verse. He studied for a career in medicine, but by his twenty-first year he had determined to devote his full talents to literature.

Though his early poems were popular with the public, they were not critically acclaimed. In a letter to his friend, James A. Hessey, he wrote: "Praise or blame has but a momentary effect on the man whose love of beauty in the abstract makes him a severe critic on his own Works. My own domestic criticism has given me pain without comparison . . . "

Keats founded his poetry on myths and fables, structuring verse around ideas such as beauty and truth. He once wrote in a letter that imagination, in its purity, finds sublime beauty and sublime truth. "I am certain of nothing but the holiness of the Heart's affections," he said, "and the truth of Imagination—What the imagination seizes as Beauty must be truth."

Most famous for his Odes, Keats' prime subject matter was nature, in keeping with the Romantic temperament of the time. The Ode is a form in which each stanza plays a particular role. The first stanza presents an idea, the second contradicts it, and the third reconciles the two opposing ideas.

On a walking tour in the Scottish Highlands, Keats came down with the chills and a sore throat. The illness turned out to be tuberculosis, which claimed his life at the age of 25. Even during his short life, "death"—especially premature death—weighed heavily on the poet's mind. In *When I Have Fears*, Keats presages his early demise, a loss that would come, he speculated, before his pen had "gleaned my teeming brain . . . "

ODE TO A NIGHTINGALE

I.

My heart aches, and a drowsy numbness pains
My sense, as though of hemlock I had drunk,
Or emptied some dull opiate to the drains
One minute past, and Lethe-wards had sunk:
'Tis not through envy of thy happy lot,
But being too happy in thine happiness,
That though, light-winged Dryad of the trees,
In some melodious plot
Of beechen green, and shadows numberless,
Singest of summer in full-throated ease.

II.

O, for a draught of vintage! that hath been
Cooled a long age in the deep-delved earth,
Tasting of Flora and the country green,
Dance, and provencal song and sunburnt
mirth!
O, for a beaker full of the warm South,
Full of the true, the blushful Hippocrene,
With beaded bubbles winking at the brim,
And purple-stained mouth;
That I might drink and leave the world unseen,
And with thee fade away into the forest dim:

III.

Fade far away, dissolve, and quite forget
What thou among the leaves hast never
known,
The weariness, the fever and the fret
Here, where men sit and hear each other groan;
Where palsy shakes a few, sad, last gray hairs
Where youth grows pale, and specter-thin, and
dies;
Where but to think is to be full of sorrow
And leaden-eyed despairs,
Where Beauty cannot keep her lustrous eyes,
Or new Love pine at them beyond tomorrow.

Keats was famous for his device of mixing the senses, often dizzying the reader in the process. Reveling in wine, a bird's song, and, finally, forgetfulness as the pleasure of youth fades away, the poem's speaker finds that escape is impossible—and his thoughts turn inward, back into a world where suffering, death, and fleeting youth still haunt the recesses of his mind.

Ode on Melancholy was written in the same pattern. Here, Keats' admonishes the reader to embrace sadness and avoid escape, to take joy in the emotions of the present, whether good or bad.

ODE ON MELANCHOLY

I.

No, no go not to Lethe, neither twist
Wolfbane, tight-rooted, for its poisonous wine;
Nor suffer thy pale forehead to be kissed
By nightshade, ruby grape of Proserpine;
Make not your rosary of yew-berries,
Nor let the beetle, nor the death-moth be
Your mournful Psyche, nor the downy owl
A partner in your sorrow's mysteries;
For shade to shade will come too drowsily
And drown the wakeful anguish of the soul.

II.

But when the melancholy fit shall fall
Sudden from heaven like a weeping cloud,
That fosters the droop-headed flowers all,
And hides the green hill in April shroud
Then glut thy sorrow on a morning rose,
Or on the rainbow of the salt, sand-wave,
Or on the wealth of the globed peonies;
Or if thy mistress some rich anger shows,

Emprison her soft hand and let her rave,
  And feed deep upon her peerless eyes.

III.

She dwells with Beauty — Beauty that must
  die;
And Joy, whose hand is ever at his lips
Bidding adieu; and aching Pleasure nigh
  Turning to poison while the bee-mouth sips:
Ay, in the very temple Delight
  Veiled Melancholy has her sov'reign shrine,
    Though seen of none save him whose strenu-
    ous tongue
Can burst Joy's grape against his palate fine;
  His soul shall taste the sadness of her might,
    And be among her cloudy trophies hung.

The next two odes are perhaps Keats' finest and best-known works. He died within a year of completing these poems, having created living works that assured his own immortality.

AUTUMN

Season of mists and mellow fruitfulness!
  Close bosom-friend of the maturing sun;
Conspiring with him how to load and bless
  With fruit the vines that round the thatch-
  eves;
To bend with apples the moss'd cottage-trees,
  And fill all fruit with ripeness to the core
    To swell the gourd, and plump the hazel
    shells
  With a sweet kernel; to set budding more,
And still more, later flowers for the bees,
Until they think warm days will never cease
  For summer has o'er-brimm'd their clammy
  cells.

Who hath not seen the oft amid thy store?
  Sometimes whoever seeks abroad may find
  Thee sitting careless on a granary floor,
  Thy hair soft-lifted by the winnowing wind,
Or on a half-reap'd furrow sound asleep,
  Drowsed with fume of poppies, while thy hook
    Spares the next swath and all its twined flow-
    ers;
And sometimes like a gleaner though dost keep
  Steady thy laden head across a brook;
Or by a cider-press with patient look
    Thou watchest the last oozings hours by
    hours.

Where are the songs of Spring? Ay, where are
  they?
  Think not of them, Thou hast thy music too,
While barred clouds bloom the soft-dying day,
  And touch the stubble-plains with rosy hue;
Then is a wailful choir the small gnats mourn
  Among the river shallows, borne aloft
  Or sinking as the light wind lives or dies;
And full-grown lambs loud bleat from hilly
  bourn;
  Hedge-crickets sing; and now with treble soft
  The redbreast whistles from a garden-croft;
    And gathering swallows twitter in the skies.

Ode on a Grecian Urn explores the concept that, through art a singular fleeting moment can be preserved for eternity.

ODE ON A GRECIAN URN

I.

Thou still unravished bride of quietness,
  Thou foster-child of silence and slow time,
Sylvan historian, who canst thus express
  A flowery tale more sweetly than our rhyme:
What leaf-fringed legend haunts about thy
  shape
  Of deities or mortals, or of both,
    In Tempe or the dales of Arcady?
What men or gods are these? What maidens
  loath?
  What mad pursuit? What struggle to escape?
    What pipes and timbrels? What wild ecstasy?

II.

Heard melodies are sweet, but those unheard
  Are sweeter; therefore, ye soft pipes, slow on;
Not to the sensual ear, but, more endeared,
  Pipe to the spirit ditties of no tone;
Fair youth beneath the trees, thou canst not
  leave
  Thy song, nor ever can those trees be bear;
    Bold Lover, never, never canst thou kiss
Though winning near the goal — yet, do not
  grieve
  She cannot fade, though thou hast not thy bliss
    Forever wilt thou love, and she be fair!

III.

Ah, happy, happy boughs! that cannot shed
  Your leaves nor ever bid the Spring adieu;
And, happy melodist, unwearied,
  For ever piping songs for ever new;
More happy love! more happy, happy love!
  For ever warm and still to be enjoyed.
  For ever panting, and for ever young;
All breathing human passion for above,
  That leaves a heart high sorrowful and cloyed,
    A burning forehead, and a parching tongue.

IV.

Who are these coming to the sacrifice?
  To what green altar, O mysterious priest,
Leadest thou that heifer lowing at the skies,
    And all her silken flanks with garlands
    dressed?
What little town by river or sea shore,
  Or mountain-built with peaceful citadel.
    Is emptied of this folk, this pious morn?
And, little town, thy streets for evermore
  Will silent be; and not a soul to tell
    Why thou art desolate, can e'er return.

V.

O Attic shape! Fair attitude! With breed
  Of marble man and maidens overwrought,
With forest branches and the trodden weed;
  Thou, silent form, dost tease us out of thought
As doth eternity: Cold Pastoral!
  When old age shall this generation waste,
    Thou shalt remain, in midst of other woe
Than ours, a friend to man, to whom thou
  say'st,
  Beauty is truth, truth beauty — that is all
    Ye know on earth and all ye need to know.

ELIZABETH BARRETT BROWNING

(1806-1861)

"All the life and strength which are in me," wrote Elizabeth Barrett Browning in 1840, "seem to have passed into my poetry." To her, life was poetry. She wrote her first poem, a birthday ode to her mother, when she was only eight years old. She received such praise for this piece, that it became a common practice for her to write birthday odes for the members of her family. When Elizabeth was fourteen, her father, Edward Barrett, published fifty copies of her epic poem *The Battle of Marathon*. Following its publication, poetry was to be her life's work.

Browning spent considerable time reading, writing, and studying, often being tutored alongside her brother Edward, whom she lovingly called "Bro." During her childhood, she was exceptionally close to her ten younger brothers and sisters. Browning found as much joy in boisterous outdoor activities with her siblings as she did in writing. Her childhood was both active and happy; she excelled physically as well as mentally. However, at age fifteen, her young life took a drastic turn: she contracted measles. Shortly thereafter, she began suffering from another, undiagnosed disease. As was common in her day, she was sent away from home, spending nearly a year at the Gloucester Spa receiving treatment for a spine complaint.

After months isolated and in bed, upon returning home Browning was weak and depressed. The melancholy was deepened by the fact that Bro had been sent to a boarding school while she was away. Browning missed the companionship of her brother, but also despaired the fact that, while his education would continue, hers would not. More and more troubled about being denied further training simply on the basis of gender—her whole world thus altered—poetry took on a greater significance; it became her source of being.

In 1828 Browning's mother died unexpectedly, causing her to retreat even more deeply into herself and her poetry. She isolated herself from her family and friends and clung desperately to her religious faith.

Four years after his wife's death, Mr. Barrett moved his family to London. Unfortunately, the climate there had an ill effect on Browning's health. She nearly died of a lung hemorrhage in 1838. Bro accompanied her to Torquay, Australia to recover, and it was there that she suffered the most devastating tragedy in her life—the drowning of her beloved Bro. Browning spent the following three months grieving in a darkened room, unable to speak or write.

Finally she returned to London, where she again began to write, soon publishing vast amounts of poetry. In 1845, correspondence with the young poet Robert Browning commenced. After five months of exchanging letters, the two poets met. Sixteen months later, they married secretly and moved to Italy. While there, her career as a poet flourished as she expanded her poetic repertoire and took up writing about political and social issues.

At the beginning of her marriage, Browning enjoyed a reprieve from her physical ailments. For the first time in a very long time, she was healthy and happy. In 1849 she gave birth to a son. Then, in 1850, she suffered a miscarriage—her fourth in all—and her ailments returned. For eleven years her health deteriorated, until, in 1861, Elizabeth Barrett Browning died, cradled in the arms of her husband.

How Do I Love Thee?
Let Me Count The Ways

How do I love thee? Let me count the ways.
I love thee to the depth and breadth and height
My soul can reach, when feeling out of sight
For the ends of Being and ideal Grace.
I love thee to the level of everyday's
Most quiet need, by sun and candlelight.
I love thee freely, as men strive for Right;
I love thee purely, as they turn from Praise.
I love thee with the passion put to use
In my old griefs, and with my childhood's faith.
I love thee with a love I seemed to lose
With my lost saints,—I love thee with the breath,
Smiles, tears, of all my life! —and, if God choose,
I shall but love thee better after death.

Perhaps the most famous of Elizabeth Barrett Browning's poems, *How Do I Love Thee? Let Me Count the Ways* is part of a large collection of love poems titled *Sonnets from the Portuguese* written for Robert Browning. In this collection, she explores the emotional depths and complexities of this, her most intimate bond. She was quoted as saying that a poet's primary responsibility is "to tell the truth." In *Sonnets from the Portuguese*, the truth is openly declared, revealing her many-faceted relationship with Browning. The result is a wide range of poems, each possessing a profound beauty and truth.

Sonnets from the Portuguese X

Yet, love, mere love, is beautiful indeed
And worthy of acceptation. Fire is bright,
Let temple burn, or flux. An equal light
Leaps in the flame from cedar-plank or weed.
And love is fire. And when I say at need
I love thee ... mark! ... I love thee—in thy sight
I stand transfigured, glorified aright,
With conscience of the new rays that proceed
Out of my face toward thine. There's nothing low
In love, when love the lowest: meanest creatures

Who love God, God accepts while loving so.
And what I feel, across the inferior features
Of what I am, doth flash itself, and show
How that great work of Love enhances Nature's.

Sonnets from the Portuguese XIV

If thou must love me, let it be for naught
Except for love's sake only. Do not say
'I love her for her smile . . . her look . . . her way
Of speaking gently . . . for a trick of thought
That falls in well with mine, and . . . brought
A sense of pleasant ease on such a day—
For these things in themselves, Beloved, may
Be changed, or change for thee,—and love, so
    wrought
May be unwrought so. Neither love me for
Thine own dear pity's wiping my cheeks dry,—
A creature might forget to weep, who bore
Thy comfort long, and lose thy love thereby!
But love me for love's sake, that evermore
Thou may'st love on, through love's eternity.

Sonnets from the Portuguese XXXVIII

First time he kissed me, he but only kissed
The fingers of this hand wherewith I write;
And ever since, it grew more clean and white,..
Slow to world-greetings, quick with its 'Oh, list,'
When the angels speak. A ring of amethyst
I could not wear here, plainer to my sight,
Than that first kiss. The second passed in height
The first, and sought the forehead, and half missed,
Half falling on the hair. O beyond meed!
That was the chrism of love, which love's own
    crown
With sanctifying sweetness, did precede.
The third upon my lips was folded down
In perfect, purple state; since when, indeed,
I have been proud and said, `My love, my own.'

Browning also shared a deep relationship with God. Much of her poetry, especially
her early poetry, is profoundly religious:

From A Sabbath Morning at Sea

And though this sabbath comes to me
Without the stolid minister
Or chanting congregation,
God's spirit brings communion, He
Who brooded soft on waters drear,
Creator on creation.

Himself, I think, shall draw me higher,
Where keep the saints with harp and song
An endless sabbath morning,
And on that sea commixed with fire
Oft drop their eyelids, raised too long
To the full Godhead's burning.

From De Profundis

I praise Thee while my days go on;
I love Thee while my days go on:
Through dark and dearth, through fire and frost,
With emptied arms and treasure lost,
I thank Thee while my days go on.

And having in Thy life-depth thrown
Being and suffering (which are one),
As a child drops his pebble small

Down some deep well, and hears it fall
Smiling—so I. THY DAYS GO ON.

As Browning matured in her versemak-
ing, she experimented with different themes.
She began to view her poetry as a weapon
with which to combat social and political
wrongs. In one of her most poignant poems
The Cry of the Children, the exploitation of children in the labor force is lamented:

From The Cry of the Children

Do you question the young children in the sorrow
Why their tears are falling so?
The old man may weep for his tomorrow
Which is lost in Long Ago;
The old tree is leafless in the forest,
The old year is ending in the frost,
The old wound, if stricken, is the sorest,
The old hope is hardest to be lost.
But the young, young children, O my brothers,
Do you ask them why they stand
Weeping sore before the bosoms of their mothers,
In our happy Fatherland?

`For oh,' say the children, 'we are weary,
And we cannot run or leap;
If we cared for any meadows, it were merely
To drop down in them and sleep.
Our knees tremble sorely in the stooping,
We fall upon our faces, trying to go;
And, underneath our heavy eyelids drooping,
The reddest flower would look as pale as snow;
For, all day, we drive the wheels of iron
In the factories, round and round.

Personal and political, passionate and
objective, lyrical and declamatory, Browning's
epic poem Aurora Leigh, published in 1856,
was the pinnacle of her poetic achievements.

From Aurora Leigh

With quiet indignation I broke in,
`You misconceive the question like a man,
Who sees a woman as the complement
Of his sex merely. You forget too much
That every creature, female as the male,
Stands single in responsible act and thought
As also in birth and death. Whoever says
To a loyal woman, "Love and work with me,"
Will get fair answers if the work and love,
Being good themselves, are good for her—the best
She was born for. Women of softer mood,
Surprised by men when scarcely awake to life,
Will sometimes only hear the first word, love,
And catch up with it any kind of work,
Indifferent, so that dear love go with it.
I do not blame such women, though, for love,
They pick much oakum; earth's fanatics make
Too frequently heaven's saints. But me your work
Is not the best for,—nor your love the best,
Nor able to commend the kind of work
For love's sake merely.'

HENRY WADSWORTH LONGFELLOW

(1807-1882)

All are architects of Fate,
　Working in these walls of Time;
Some with massive deeds and great,
　Some with ornaments of rhyme.

Nothing useless is, or low;
　Each thing in its place is best;
And what seems but idle show
　Strengthens and supports the rest.

Thus begins Longfellow's poem *The Builders*, a work which reflects both his personal moral philosophy and that of the time in which he lived.

The only American honored in the Poet's Corner of Westminster Abbey, England, this professor published twelve books, in addition to writing several textbooks and much poetry. During his lifetime, his verse was translated into many languages, making him one of the most celebrated voices of the Western world.

In the seacoast town of Portland, Maine, Henry Wadsworth was born in 1807 to the eminent Longfellow family. He showed a zest for learning and, unlike many of his fellow poets, enjoyed a happy childhood. Attending Bowdoin college, he was offered a professorship of modern languages, subsequently traveling in Europe for a time to prepare himself to teach and to write grammar textbooks.

Longfellow soon married and began a career at Harvard University. Thereafter, his young wife died. Longfellow's second marriage brought him six children and eighteen years of relatively blissful family life. At the height of his success and fame, personal tragedy struck once more, with the death of his wife. Amid rewarding literary praise, he spent the remainder of his life alone.

In 1839, shortly after becoming a Harvard professor, Longfellow published *Voices of the Night*. One poem in this collection, *Psalm of Life*, became particularly popular and served as a springboard for his career in poetry.

The Victorian age was known for its sentimentality. Longfellow also expounded on the prevalent philosophies of the day; literally thousands were writing poetry on similar themes. What set him apart, however, was his superior writing skills and the pathos that he managed to infuse in his verse.

The poem which first brought Longfellow fame has remained popular. *A Psalm of Life* is a clear example of the author's moral philosophy: the individual can make a difference; therefore, each *should* each do all that he or she *can* do.

A Psalm of Life
(What The Young Man Said To The Psalmist)

Tell me not, in mournful numbers,
　Life is but an empty dream!—
For the soul is dead that slumbers,
　And things are not what they seem.

Life is real! Life is earnest!
　And the grave is not its goal;
Dust thou art, to dust returnest,
　Was not spoken of the soul.

Not enjoyment, and not sorrow,
　Is our destined end or way;
But to act, that each to-morrow
　Find us farther than to-day.

Art is long, and Time is fleeting
　And our hearts, though stout and brave,
Still, like muffled drums, are beating
　Funeral marches to the grave.

In the world's broad field of battle,
　In the bivouac of Life,
Be not like dumb, driven cattle!
　Be a hero in the strife!

Trust no Future, howe'er pleasant!
　Let the dead Past bury its dead!
Act,-act in the living Present!
　Heart within, and God o'erhead!

Lives of great men all remind us
　We can make our lives sublime,
And, departing, leave behind us
　Footprints on the sands of time;

Footprints, that perhaps another,
　Sailing o'er life's solemn main,
A forlorn and shipwrecked brother,
　Seeing, shall take heart again.

Let us, then, be up and doing,
　With a heart for any fate;
Still achieving, still pursuing,
　Learn to labor and to wait.

Longfellow's storytelling talents and his interest in history came to the fore much later with the publication of *Evangeline*, *The Song of Hiawatha*, and *The Courtship of Miles Standish*. This latter piece differs from his others in that it is a story rather than a poem, drawing heavily from an old pilgrim's tale.

The following selection from *The Courtship of Miles Standish* accentuates Longfellow's sensitivity toward women, a unique characteristic during his time.

" . . . That is the way with you men; you don't
　understand us, you cannot.
When you have made up your minds, after thinking
　of this one and that one,
Choosing, selecting, rejecting, comparing one with
　another,
Then you make known your desire, with abrupt and
　sudden avowal,
And are offended and hurt, and indignant perhaps,
　that a woman
Does not respond at once to a love that she never
　suspected . . . "

"No!" interrupted the maiden, with answer prompt
　and decisive;
"No; you were angry with me, for speaking so
　frankly and freely.

It was wrong, I acknowledge; for it is the fate of a
   woman
Long to be patient and silent, to wait like a ghost
   that is speechless,
Till some questioning voice dissolves the spell of its
   silence.
Hence is the inner life of so many suffering women
Sunless and silent and deep, like subterranean rivers
Running through caverns of darkness, unheard,
   unseen, and unfruitful,
Chafing their channels of stone, with endless and
   profitless murmurs . . . "

"When from the depths of my heart, in pain and
   with secret misgiving,
Frankly I speak to you, asking for sympathy only
   and kindness,
Straightway you take up my words, that are plain
   and direct and in earnest,
Turn them away from their meaning, and answer
   with flattering phrases.
This is not right, is not just, is not true to the best
   that is in you;
For I know and esteem you, and feel that your
   nature is noble,
Lifting mine up to a higher, a more ethereal level.
Therefore I value your friendship, and feel it perhaps
   the more keenly
If you say aught that implies I am only as one
   among many,
If you make use of those common and complimentary phrases
Most men think so fine, in dealing and speaking
   with women,
But which women reject as insipid, if not as insulting."

   Hiawatha resulted from Longfellow's sur-
rendering his professorship to write full-time.
He completed this poem, along with several
lesser ones, within a year after leaving the university. In spite of some criticism, this poem
was well received by the masses, much more so
than the poet had expected. Public readings of
it began almost immediately.
   Here, rhyme yields to rhythm and purpose. Even read silently, the poem pulses with
the cadence of a chant.

The Song Of Hiawatha
Should you ask me, whence these stories?
Whence these legends and traditions,
With the odors of the forest,
With the dew and damp of meadows,
With the curling smoke of wigwams,
With the rushing of great rivers,
With their frequent repetitions,
And their wild reverberations,
As of thunder in the mountains? . . .

I repeat them as I heard them
From the lips of Nawadaha,
The musician, the sweet singer.

O my children! my poor children!
Listen to the words of wisdom,
Listen to the words of warning,
From the lips of the Great Spirit,
From the Master of Life, who made you!

"I have given you lands to hunt in,
I have given you streams to fish in,
I have given you bear and bison,
I have given you roe and reindeer,
I have given you brant and beaver,
Filled the marshes full of wild-foul,
Filled the rivers full of fishes;
Why then are you not contented?
Why then will you hunt each other?
 "I am weary of your quarrels,
Weary of your wars and bloodshed,
Weary of your prayers for vengeance,
Of your wranglings and dissensions;
All your strength is in your union,
All your danger is in discord;
Therefore be at peace henceforward,
And as brothers live together."

   In 1861, Longfellow's second wife died in
a tragic fire. Trying to save her the poet was
severely burned. His way of dealing with grief
was to retreat; not much of his feelings about
that death or about the ongoing Civil War were
reflected in his ensuing writings. "With me," he
once said, "all deep feelings are silent ones."
Only a quote from Tennyson that begins, "Sleep
sweetly tender heart, in peace," grace the blank
pages of his journal during this time, belying
his inner grief. Finally, eighteen years later, he
came to grips with the death, writing The Cross
of Snow.

The Cross of Snow
In the long sleepless watches of the night,
A gentle face—the face of one long dead—
Looks at me from the wall, where round its head
The night-lamp casts a halo of pale light.
Here in this room she died; and soul more white
Never through martyrdom of fire was led
To its repose; nor can in books be read
The legend of a life more benedight.
There is a mountain in the distant West
That, sun-defying, in its deep ravines
Displays a cross of snow upon its side.
Such is the cross I wear upon my breast
These eighteen years, through all the changing
   scenes
And seasons, changeless since the day she died.

   The success of Longfellow's works hinge
on his moral impulse, his storytelling skill, and
his understanding of a human interest in history. Their charm also rests in the poet's ability to
convey a sense of serenity and peace, even in
disquieting times. In The Day is Done the healing power of poetry is invoked to salve the
troubled heart:

 . . . Then read from the treasure volume
   The poem of thy choice,
And lend to the rhyme of the poet
   The beauty of thy voice.

And the night shall be filled with music,
   And the cares, that infest the day,
Shall fold their tents, like the Arabs,
   And as silently steal away.

EDGAR ALLAN POE

(1809-1849)

Alone

From childhood's hour I have not been
As others were—I have not seen
As others saw—I could not bring
My passions from a common spring—
From the same source I have not taken
My sorrow—I could not awaken
My heart to joy at the same tone—
And all I lov'd—I lov'd alone—
Then—in my childhood—in the dawn
Of a most stormy life—was drawn
From ev'ry depth of good and ill
The mystery which binds me still—
From the torrent, or the fountain—
From the red cliff of the mountain—
From the sun that 'round me roll'd
In its autumn tint of gold—
From the lightning in the sky
As it pass'd me flying by—
From the thunder, and the storm—
And the cloud that took the form
(When the rest of Heaven was blue)
Of a demon in my view.

One of America's greatest poets, short-story writers, and literary critics, Edgar Allan Poe's writing—regardless of genre—possessed a haunting quality. At first he was lauded only for his romantic lyric poems, horror fiction, and clever detective stories. Since World War I, however, his symbolic verses and tales have also been appreciated.

Edgar Poe was born in Boston, Massachusetts. Deserted by his father, and his mother taken in death, the two-year-old was put in the foster home of Mr. and Mrs. John Allan, from whom he took his middle name.

Although the Allan's never formally adopted Edgar, they gave him some monetary support and encouraged him to study law, which he did, attending school in London and at the University of Virginia. He proved to be an excellent student. However, in an effort to win money for books and clothing, he turned to gambling, soon became consumed in debt, and eventually withdrew from school. To appease his foster father, Poe enlisted in the army and later entered the U.S. Military Academy. But determined to follow a literary career, the young man finally broke regulations, forcing his dismissal from the Academy. He thereafter lived with his aunt, marrying her daughter, and supported them all on the receipts from his written publications.

While editing and writing articles for several literary magazines, Poe wrote and published his first volume, *Tamerlane and Other Poems*, then *Al Aaraaf, Tamerlane and Minor Poems*. Even as one of the most successful and respected writers around, still he was underpaid, and his family often went without food.

Poe's works are often shrouded in mystery. And, like his poetry, much of his later life as well as his death remain a mystery. Although some details about his later years are recorded, they seem to have been marked by tragedy.

Poe's love verse was written in a form called acrostic poetry, in which the left edge of the poem spells out a name or a word.

An Acrostic

Elizabeth it is in vain you say
"Love not"—thou sayest it in so sweet a way:
In vain those words from thee or L.E.L.
Zantippe's talents had enforced so well;
Ah! if that language from thy heart arise,
Breathe it less gently forth—and veil thine eyes.
Endymion, recollect, when Luna tried
To cure his love—was cured of all beside—
His folly—pride—and passion—for he died.

In *Annabel Lee*, simple rhymes and charming images heighten the work's underlying eeriness.

Annabel Lee

It was many and many a year ago,
In a kingdom by the sea,
That a maiden there lived whom you may know
By the name of Annabel Lee;—
And this maiden she lived with no other thought
Than to love and be loved by me . . .

. . . And this was the reason that, long ago,
In this kingdom by the sea,
A wind blew out of a cloud, chilling
My beautiful Annabel Lee;
So that her high-born kinsmen came
And bore her away from me,
To shut her up in a sepulchre,
In this kingdom by the sea.

The angels, not half so happy in heaven,
Went envying her and me—
Yes!—that was the reason (as all men know,
In this kingdom by the sea)
That the wind came out of the cloud by night,
Chilling and killing my Annabel Lee.

But our love it was stronger by far than the love
Of those who were older than we—
Of many far wiser than we—
And neither the angels in Heaven above,
Nor the demons down under the sea,
Can ever dissever my soul from the soul
Of the beautiful Annabel Lee;—

For the moon never beams, without bringing me dreams
Of the beautiful Annabel Lee;
And the stars never rise; but I feel the bright eyes
Of the beautiful Annabel Lee:—
And so, all the night-tide, I lie down by the side
Of my darling—my darling—my life and my bride,
In the sepulchre there by the sea—
In her tomb by the sounding sea.

Poe's most famous work, *The Raven*, is a obsessively haunting piece. The visiting bird's only word is "Nevermore," a simple lament that finally emerges as a disturbing answer to each of the questions the narrator poses—questions directed both to the raven, and to himself.

The Raven

Once upon a midnight dreary, while I pondered, weak
and weary,
Over many a quaint and curious volume of forgotten
lore—
While I nodded, nearly napping, suddenly there came a
tapping,
As of some one gently rapping, rapping at my chamber

251

© 1993, Compact Classics, Inc.

door.
'Tis some visitor,' I muttered, 'tapping at my chamber door—

Only this and nothing more.'

Ah, distinctly I remember it was in the bleak December,
And each separate dying ember wrought its ghost upon the floor.
Eagerly I wished the morrow;—vainly I had sought to borrow
From my books surcease of sorrow—sorrow for the lost Lenore—
For the rare and radiant maiden whom the angels name Lenore—

Nameless here for evermore.

And the silken sad uncertain rustling of each purple curtain
Thrilled me—filled me with fantastic terrors never felt before;
So that now, to still the beating of my heart, I stood repeating:
'Tis some visitor entreating entrance at my chamber door—
Some late visitor entreating entrance at my chamber door;

This it is and nothing more.'

. . . Open here I flung the shutter, when, with many a flirt and flutter,
In there stepped a stately Raven of the saintly days of yore.
Not the least obeisance made he; not a minute stopped or stayed he,
But, with mien of lord or lady, perched above my chamber door—
Perched upon a bust of Pallas just above my chamber door—

Perched, and sat, and nothing more.

Then this ebony bird beguiling my sad fancy into smiling,
By the grave and stern decorum of the countenance it wore,
'Though thy crest be shorn and shaven, thou,' I said, 'art sure no craven,
Ghastly grim and ancient Raven wandering from the Nightly shore—
Tell me what thy lordly name is on the Night's Plutonian shore!'

Quoth the Raven, 'Nevermore.'

Much I marvelled this ungainly fowl to hear discourse so plainly,
Though its answer little meaning—little relevancy bore . . .

. . . Bird or beast upon the sculptured bust above his chamber door,

With such name as 'Nevermore.'

But the Raven, sitting lonely on that placid bust, spoke only
That one word, as if his soul in that one word he did outpour.
Nothing farther then he uttered; not a feather then he fluttered—
Till I scarcely more than muttered: 'Other friends have flown before—
On the morrow he will leave me as my Hopes have flown before.'

Then the bird said, 'Nevermore.'

Startled at the stillness broken by reply so aptly spoken
'Doubtless,' said I, 'what it utters is tis only stock and store,
Caught from some unhappy master whom unmerciful Disaster
Followed fast and followed faster till his songs one burden bore—
Till the dirges of his Hope that melancholy burden bore

Of "Never—nevermore."'

But the Raven still beguiling all my sad soul into smiling,
Straight I wheeled a cushioned seat in front of bird and bust and door;
Then, upon the velvet sinking, I betook myself to linking
Fancy unto fancy, thinking what this ominous bird of yore
What this grim, ungainly, ghastly, gaunt, and ominous bird of yore

Meant in croaking 'Nevermore . . . '

. . . Then, methought, the air grew denser, perfumed from an unseen censer
Swung by Seraphim whose foot-falls tinkled on the tufted floor.
'Wretch,' I cried, 'they God hath lent thee—by these angels he hath sent thee
Respite—respite and nepenthe from they memories of Lenore!
Quaff, oh quaff this kind nepenthe and forget this lost Lenore!'

Quoth the Raven, 'Nevermore.'

. . . 'Prophet!' said I, 'thing of evil!—prophet still, if bird or devil!
By that heaven that bends above us—by that God we both adore—
Tell this soul with sorrow laden if, within the distant Aidenn,
It shall clasp a sainted maiden whom the angels name Lenore—
Clasp a rare and radiant maiden whom the angels name Lenore.'

Quoth the Raven, 'Nevermore.'

'Be that word our sign of parting, bird or fiend!' I shrieked, upstarting—
'Get thee back into the tempest and the Night's Plutonian shore!
Leave no black plume as a token of that lie thy soul hath spoken!
Leave my loneliness unbroken!—quit the bust above my door!
Take thy beak from out my heart, and take thy form from off my door!'

Quoth the Raven, 'Nevermore.'

And the Raven, never flitting, still is sitting, still is sitting
On the pallid bust of Pallas just above my chamber door;
And his eyes have all the seeming of a demon's that is dreaming,
And the lamp-light o'er him streaming throws his shadow on the floor;
And my soul from out that shadow that lies floating on the floor

Shall be lifted—nevermore!

ALFRED, LORD TENNYSON

(1809-1892)

Ring Out Wild Bells

Ring out, wild bells, to the wild sky,
The flying cloud, the frosty light;
The year is dying in the night;
Ring out, wild bells, and let him die.

Ring out the old, ring in the new;
Ring, happy bells, across the snow;
The year is going, let him go;
Ring out the false, ring in the true . . .

Ring out false pride in place and blood,
The civic slander and the spite;
Ring in the love of truth and right,
Ring in the common love of good.

Alfred, Lord Tennyson's poetry truly *did* ring out a new message of truth and human love. As one of the supreme craftsmen of the English language and chosen as Britain's national poet, he was blessed with a remarkable range of literary talent. What's more, he was highly dedicated to refining his art.

Alfred Tennyson was born in Somersby, Lincolnshire. After just a few years in school, his father became dissatisfied with the quality of his children's schooling and brought them home to be educated.

In 1827, Alfred and his brother Charles published *Poems by Two Brothers*, which also included poems by another brother, Frederick. That same year, Alfred went to Cambridge University, where he met Arthur Hallam. The two men became devoted friends. Hallam was Tennyson's biggest fan, and enthusiastically encouraged his writing. In 1830, after Tennyson published *Poems, Chiefly Lyrical*, Hallam penned and published a critical essay praising the book. Tennyson, though reluctant to continue writing, nevertheless yielded to Hallam's persuasiveness, publishing *Poems* in 1832.

In the fall of 1833, Hallam died unexpectedly; Tennyson was overcome with grief. For the next year and a half, he struggled with depression, *In Memoriam*, a lengthy, philosophic masterpiece made up of 133 individual poems, being one of his few creations during this period. As time went on, Tennyson's friends urged him to publish again. Among this cadre of supporters were John Stuart Mills, Ralph Waldo Emerson, and Henry Longfellow. The poet refused to publish his work, but he did pick up his pen and resume his career.

Finally, economic pressures forced Tennyson to publish again in 1842. Another edition of *Poems* was published, then came his *The Princess*. Tennyson married in 1850 and thereafter avoided public life. In that same year, he finally published *In Memoriam*, though anonymously.

The critics liked this book—and the public loved it. By the end of the year, it had sold 60,000 copies, and Queen Victoria offered the 41-year-old Tennyson the position of poet laureate of England, vacant since the death of Wordsworth.

Living in his country homes, the poet turned out inspiring and creative works. Having long considered an Arthurian epic, in 1859 Tennyson published the first version of *Idylls of the King*. He continued to add pieces to it throughout his long life.

As the years passed, he produced six more volumes of poetry and became the first poet presented with a peerage, becoming Lord Tennyson nine years before his death in 1892.

His body was buried in the Poets' Corner of Westminster Abbey.

In a long struggle to deal with the death of his good friend, Tennyson's *In Memoriam* alternates between utter despair and hopeful abandon.

But I remained, whose hopes were dim,
Whose life, whose thoughts were little worth
To wander on a darkened earth,
Where all things round me breathed of him . . .

Whatever way my days decline,
I felt and feel, though left alone,
His being working in mine own,
The footsteps of his life in mine . . .

In words, like weeds, I'll wrap me o'er,
Like coarsest clothes against the cold;
But that large grief which these enfold
Is given in outline and no more . . .

The following lines from *The Princess* ring with tenderness, and are believed to have been written several years after Tennyson's first son was delivered stillborn.

As thro' the land at eve we went,
And pluck'd the ripen'd ears,
We fell out, my wife and I,
O, we fell out, I know not why,
And kiss'd again with tears.

And blessings on the falling out
That all the more endears,
When we fall out with those we love
And kiss again with tears!

For when we came where lies the child
We lost in other years,
There above the little grave,
O, there above the little grave,
We kiss'd again with tears.

Though all of Tennyson's poems are lyrical in nature, some are more musical than others, such as this beautiful lullaby from *The Princess*:

Sweet and low, sweet and low,
Wind of the western sea,
Low, low, breathe and blow,
Wind of the western sea!
Over the rolling water go,
Come from the dying moon, and blow,
Blow him again to me;
While my little one, while my pretty one, sleeps.

Sleep and rest, sleep and rest,
Father will come to thee soon;
Rest, rest, on mother's breast,
Father will come to thee soon;
Silver sails all out of the west

Under the silver moon:
Sleep, my little one, sleep, my pretty one, sleep.

While these lines have their own rhythm and melody, the loneliness of the mother waiting for her husband to come home is still readily apparent.

Tennyson's most exquisite images came from nature. *The Brook* was first published in

Maud and Other Poems:

I come from haunts of coot and hern;
  I make a sudden sally
And sparkle out among the fern,
  To bicker down a valley.

By thirty hills I hurry down,
  Or slip between the ridges,
By twenty thorps, a little town,
  And half a hundred bridges.

I murmur under moon and stars
  In brambly wildernesses;
I linger by my shingly bars;
  I loiter round my cresses;

And out again I curve and flow
  To join the brimming river,
For men may come and men may go,
  But I go on forever.

The following images are also from *The Princess:*

The splendor falls on castle walls
  And snowy summits old in story:
The long light shakes across the lakes,
  And the wild cataract leaps in glory.
Blow, bugle, blow, set the wild echoes flying,
Blow, bugle; answer, echoes, dying, dying, dying.

O hark! O hear! how thin and clear,
  And thinner, clearer, farther going!
O sweet and far, from cliff and scar,
  The horns of Elfland faintly blowing!
Blow, let us hear the purple glens replying:
Blow, bugle; answer, echoes, dying, dying, dying.

One of the earliest examples of the poet's remarkable story-telling skill is *The Lady of Shalott.*

. . . Lying, robed in snowy white
That loosely fell to left and right—
The leaves upon her falling light—
Thro' the noises of the night
  She floated down to Camelot;
And as the boat-head wound along
The willowy hills and fields among,
They heard her singing her last song,
  The Lady of Shalott.

The Charge of the Light Brigade is a Tennyson classic.

Half a league, half a league,
Half a league onward,
All in the valley of Death
  Rode the six hundred.
'Forward the Light Brigade!
Charge the guns!' he said.
Into the valley of Death
  Rode the six hundred.

'Forward the Light Brigade!'
Was there a man dismay'd?

Not tho' the soldier know
  Someone had blunder'd.
Theirs not to make reply,
Theirs not to reason why,
Theirs but to do or die.
Into the valley of Death
  Rode the six hundred.

Cannon to the right of them,
Cannon to the left of them,
Cannon in front of them
  Volley'd and thunder'd;
Storm'd at with shot and shell,
Boldly they rode and well,
Into the jaws of Death
Into the mouth of hell
  Rode the six hundred.

Flash'd all their sabres bare,
Flash'd as they turn'd in air
Sabring the gunners there,
Charging an army, while
  All the world wonder'd.
Plunged in the battery-smoke
Right thro' the line they broke;
Cossack and Russian
Reel'd from the sabre-stroke
  Shattered and sunder'd.
Then they rode back, but not,
  Not the six hundred.

Cannon to the right of them,
Cannon to the left of them,
Cannon behind them
  Volley'd and thunder'd;
Storm'd at twith shot and shell,
While horse and hero fell,
They that had fought so well
Came thro' the jaws of Death
Back from the mouth of hell,
All that was left of them,
  Left of six hundred.

When can their glory fade?
O the wild charge they made!
  All the world wonder'd.
Honor the charge they made!
Honor the Light Brigade,
  Noble six hundred!

At age 81, just three years before his death, Tennyson picked up an old envelope and wrote *Crossing the Bar* across the back of it.

Sunset and evening star,
  And one clear call for me!
And may there be no moaning of the bar,
  When I put out to sea,

But such a tide as moving seems asleep,
  Too full for sound and foam.
When that which drew from out the boundless deep
  Turns again home.

Twilight and evening bell,
  And after that the dark!
And may there be no sadness of farewell,
  When I embark;

For though from out our bourne of Time and Place
  The flood may bear me far,
I hope to see my Pilot face to face
  When I have crossed the bar.

WALT WHITMAN

(1819-1892)

"I hear America singing, the varied carols I hear . . .
. . . Singing with open mouths their strong melodious songs."

The poetic tradition in America was strongly influenced by Walt Whitman. Many succeeding poets (Carl Sandburg, Hart Crane, Henry Miller, and Allen Ginsberg, among others) sensed the great contribution and influence this literary figure had on their work.

Whitman's poetry broke with tradition of stanzaic patterns and measured lines, which brought a certain sense of freedom and naturalness to his lines.

The second son of a carpenter/contractor, Whitman was reared by semiliterate parents in a rural village on Long Island, New York. The political atmosphere in the home was liberal???, shaped by the teachings of Quakerism. But the youth read with captivated diligence the few nineteenth-century novels he could procure, the "classics" of European literature, and The Bible.

After probing into several different professions, Whitman finally settled down to teach in the village schoolhouse. Finding he had many talents in journalism, at the age of 22 he ventured to Manhattan, eventually becoming a journeyman printer.

Whitman soon mastered the newspaper trade and contributed many short stories and essays to a local paper. Later, as editor of The Brooklyn Daily Eagle, he penned many lyrical poems, most of them political in orientation. However, after two years he was dismissed for his radical views. After work as editor of a New Orleans newspaper, Whitman opened up his own printing and stationery store and began writing his greatest poetry.

Leaves of Grass was published in 1855, the title springing from a biblical allusion to the nature of humanity. Few copies of the first edition sold, yet, over time, it became a classic. One's Self I Sing is the first inscription and entry in the volume. In it, Whitman revealed a spiritual connection he felt between the human soul and the world at-large.

One's-Self I sing, a simple separate person,
Yet utter the word Democratic, the word En-
 Masse.

Of physiology from top to toe I sing,
Not physiognomy alone nor brain alone is worthy
 for the Muse,
I say the Form complete is worthier far,
The Female equally with the Male I sing.

Of life immense in passion, pulse, and power,
Cheerful, for freest action form'd under the laws
 divine,
The Modern Man I sing.

In "I Hear America Singing," Whitman celebrated the common, everyday laborer: the man or woman, mother or father who is often overlooked and taken for granted. The songs these strong Americans sing are hopeful manifestations of free enterprise and the "American Dream."

I hear America singing, the varied carols I
 hear,
Those of mechanics, each one singing his as it
 should be blithe
 and strong,
The carpenter measures his as he measures his
 plank or beam,
The mason singing his as he makes ready for
 work, or leaves
 off work,
The boatman singing what belongs to him in
 his boat, the
 deckhand singing on the steamboat deck,
The shoemaker singing as he sits on his bench
, the hatter
 singing as he stands,
The wood-cutter's song, the ploughboy's on
 his way in the
 morning, or at noon intermission or at sun
 down,
The delicious singing of the mother, or of the
 young wife at
 work, or of the girl sewing or washing,
Each singing what belongs to him or her and
 to none else,
The day what belongs to the day—at night the
 party of young
 fellows, robust, friendly,
Singing with open mouths their strong melodi
 ous songs.

Combining romantic love and animal instinct with very real life-bearing situations, O Me! O Life! contemplates the struggle and spiritual emptiness of modern times. The optimistic conclusions that are finally drawn, however, are characteristic redeeming features of much of Whitman's lyrical poetry.

O me! O life! of the questions of these recur
 ring,
Of the endless trains of the faithless, of cities
 fill'd with the
 foolish,
Of myself forever reproaching myself, (for who
 more foolish
 than I, and who more faithless?)
Of eyes that vainly crave the light, of the
 objects mean, of the
 struggle ever renew'd,
Of the poor results of all, of the plodding and
 sordid crowds
 I see around me,
Of the empty and useless years of the rest, with
 the rest me
 intertwined,
The question, O me! so sad, recurring   Wha
t good amid these,
O me, O life?

Answer.

That you are here—that life exists and identi
ty,
That the powerful play goes on, and you may
   contribute a verse.

Along with the other sides of life,
Whitman celebrated sexuality, and sought to
expose societal repression.

The Dalliance of the Eagles

Skirting the river road, (my forenoon walk, my
   rest,)
Skyward in air a sudden muffled sound, the dalliance of the eagles,
The rushing amorous contact high in space together,
The clinching interlocking claws, a living, fierce,
   gyrating wheel,
Four beating wings, two beaks, a swirling mass
   tight grappling,
In tumbling turning clustering loops, straight
   downward falling,
Till o'er the river pois'd, the twain yet one, a
   moment's lull,
A motionless still balance in the air, then parting,
   talons loosing,
Upward again on slow-firm pinions slanting, their
   separate
 diverse flight,
She hers, he his, pursuing.

To A Stranger

Passing stranger! you do not know how longingly
   I look upon
   you,
You must be he I was seeking, or she I was seeking,
   (it comes to me as of a dream,)
I have somewhere surely lived a life of joy with
   you,
All is recall'd as we flit by each other, fluid, affectionate,
   chaste, matured,
You grew up with me, were a boy with me or a girl
   with me,
I ate with you and slept with you, your body has
   become not
   yours only nor left my body mine only,
You give me the pleasure of your eyes, face, flesh,
   as we
   pass, you take of my beard, breast, hands, in
   return,
I am not to speak to you, I am to think of you when
   I sit
   alone or wake at night alone,
I am to wait, I do not doubt I am to meet you
   again,
I am to see to it that I do not lose you.

Whitman was a great admirer of
Abraham Lincoln, the man and his mission.
Furthermore, Lincoln was a recognizable figure who reflected the poet's own democratic
ideas. *O Captain! My Captain!* is a dedication
to the president, a captain guiding his ship
through troubled waters.

O Captain! My Captain!

O Captain! my Captain! our fearful trip is done,
The ship has weather'd every rack, the prize we

sought is won,
The port is near, the bells I hear, the people all
   exulting,
While follow eyes the steady keel, the vessel grim
   and daring;
     But O heart! heart! heart!
      O the bleeding drops of red,
       Where on the deck my captain lies,
       Fallen cold and dead.

O Captain! my Captain! rise up and hear the bells;
Rise up—for you the flag is flung—for you the
   bugle trills,
For you bouquets and ribbon'd wreaths—for you
   the shores
   a-crowding,
For you they call, the swaying mass, their eager
   faces turning;
     Here captain! dear father!
      This arm beneath your head!
       It is some dream that on the deck,
       You've fallen cold and dead.

My captain does not answer, his lips are pale and
   still,
My father does not feel my arm, he has no pulse
   nor will,
The ship is anchor'd safe and sound, its voyage
   closed and done,
From fearful trip the victor ship comes in with
   object won;
     Exult O shores, and ring O bells!
      But I with mournful tread,
       Walk the deck my Captain lies,
       Fallen cold and dead.

This Dust Was Once the Man

This dust was once the man,
Gentle, plain, just and resolute, under whose cautious hand,
Against the foulest crime in history known in any
   land or
   age,
Was saved the Union of these States.

Just as he was aware of the historical
significance that Lincoln played in the rescu-
ing and restoration of a nation, Whitman, as a
poet, was conscious of his own labors toward
discovery and innovation. Looking back at
Whitman's life as a whole, *Full of Life Now* renders a fitting self-portrait.

Full of Life Now

Full of life now, compact, visible,
I, forty years old the eighty-third year of the
   States,
To one a century hence or any number of centuries
   hence,
To you yet unborn these, seeking you.

When you read these I that was visible am become
   invisible,
Now it is you, compact, visible, realizing my
   poems, seeking me,
Fancying how happy you were if I could be with
   you and become
   your comrade;
Be it as if I were with you. (Be not too certain but I
   am now
   with you.)

EMILY DICKINSON

(1830-1886)

This is my letter to the world,
That never wrote to me,—
The simple news that Nature told,
With tender majesty.

Her message is committed
To hands I cannot see;
For love of her, sweet countrymen,
Judge tenderly of me!

These lines from *My Letter to the World* are but a few from one of the 1,700 poems written, while in seclusion, by Emily Dickinson. Only ten of her poems were published during her lifetime—and those without her consent—while her first volume of poetry became public four years after her death.

Dickinson was born in 1830 in Amherst, Massachusetts, and spent her life there. Her father, although an austere man, once was said to have rang the bells of the Baptist Church just so everyone in the village would come outdoors to see the sunset.

Dickinson studied at Amherst Academy—a Puritan stronghold. At age seventeen, her year at Mount Holyoke seminary was the only time she spent away from her parents' home. Upon her return, little by little she withdrew from the affairs of the community. Her sometime brooding poetry indicates that, at this point, she could only write while observing the world from a distance.

Dickinson's writing career began at school sometime before 1858. Her work was not meant for publication, but written as additions to letters—they almost comprising poems in their own right, filled with rhyme, rhythm and of riddle-like phrases.

Friends and editors pleaded with her to publish her works, but these well-meaning associates succeeded in getting only a fraction into print.

In 1874, Dickinson's father died, and, eight years later, her mother died. From then on, her only real contact with the world was with and through her sister, Lavinia, who was later responsible for bringing Dickinson's works into publication.

Manifesting a New England point of view, one of tradition, self-discipline, and austerity, Dickinson wrote sparse verse. Symbols of nature—such as sunlight, birds, and mushrooms—were worthy of poetry, as well as were the classic topics of life, love and death.

Dickinson recognized what to her was an obvious overlap between religion and nature, writing in an 1856 letter: " . . . all have gone to church . . . and I have come out in the new grass to listen to the anthems."

The following poem about nature also carries religious overtones—as well as references to death.

There's a certain slant of light,
On winter afternoons,

That oppresses, like the weight
Of cathedral tunes.

Heavenly hurt it gives us;
We can find no scar,
But internal difference
Where the meanings are.

None may teach it anything
'Tis the seal, despair,—
An imperial affliction
Sent us of the air.

When it comes, the landscape listens,
Shadows hold their breath;
When it goes, 'tis like the distance
On the look of death.

Dickinson detected the beauty in nature even when it was gloomy and depressing outside:

The sky is low, the clouds are mean,
A travelling flake of snow
Across a barn or through a rut
Debates if it will go.

A narrow wind complains all day
How someone treated him;
Nature, like us, is sometimes caught
Without her diadem.

Contrast this more mellow, somber tone with the exultation in the following verses, where the first stanza's deliberate break in rhyming patterns is then reinstated in the subsequent stanzas. After Dickinson's death, publishers often had to choose from among several renditions of a line or stanza she had tried—none of which were crossed out. In this case two versions of the first stanza exist, neither of which are rhymed.

I taste a liquor never brewed
From tankards scooped in pearl;
Not all the vats upon the Rhine
Yield such an alcohol!

Inebriate of air am I,
And debauchee of dew,
Reeling through endless summer days
From inns of molten blue.

When landlords turn the drunken bee
Out of the foxglove's door,
When butterflies renounce their drams,
I shall but drink the more!

Till seraphs swing their snowy hats,
And saints to windows run,
To see the little tippler
Leaning against the sun!

If Dickinson's religion was personal, it was also certain and unwavering:

I never saw a moor,
I never saw the sea;
Yet know I how the heather looks,
And what a wave must be.

I never spoke with God,

Nor visited in heaven;
Yet certain am I of the spot
As if the chart were given.

The Puritan outlook—embracing a belief that true worship requires a special kind of behavior—was also evident in Dickinson's work.

Triumph may be of several kinds.
There's triumph in the room
When that old imperator, Death,
By faith is overcome.

There's triumph of the finer mind
When truth, affronted long,
Advances calm to her supreme,
Her God her only throng.

A triumph when temptation's bribe
Is slowly handed back,
One eye upon the heaven renounced
And one upon the rack.

Severer triumph, by himself
Experienced, who can pass
Acquitted from that naked bar,
Jehovah's countenance!

Emily Dickinson wrote many poems about death, but did not approach it with the preoccupation other poets often reserved for the subject.

Afraid? Of whom am I afraid?
Not death; for who is he?
The porter of my father's lodge
As much abasheth me . . . .

Although her verse is brief, the imagery is strong and vivid. The words, rhymes and rhythms combine to generate deep impact.

I felt a funeral in my brain,
    And mourners, to and fro,
Kept treading, treading, till it seemed
    That sense was breaking through.

And when they all were seated,
    A service like a drum
Kept beating, beating, till I thought
    My mind was going numb.

And then I heard them lift a box,
    And creak across my soul
With those same boots of lead, again,
    Then space began to toll

As all the heavens were a bell,
    And Being but an ear,
And I and silence some strange race,
    Wrecked, solitary, here.

A collection of Dickinson's poems makes it clear that at one time she was deeply in love with someone. Apparently, that love not returned or fulfilled, prompted some powerful poems:

Rearrange a wife's affection?
When they dislocate my brain,
Amputate my freckled bosom,
Make me bearded like a man!

Blush, my spirit, in thy fastness,
Blush, my unacknowledged clay,
Seven years of troth have taught thee

More than wifehood ever may!
Love that never leaped its socket,
Trust entrenched in narrow pain,
Constancy through fire awarded,
Anguish bare of anodyne,

Burden borne so far triumphant
None suspect me of the crown,
For I wear the thorns till sunset,
Then my diadem put on.

Big my secret, but it's bandaged,
It will never get away
Till the day its weary keeper
Leads it through the grave to thee.

Words and phrases like "entrenched," "none suspect," and "secret," suggest that Dickinson's sweetheart was never even aware of her feelings.

Modern advocates of the women's movement have come to view Emily Dickinson as one of the earliest examples of feminism. Even in her isolation, she was a sharp observer of life and the human race.

Success is counted sweetest
By those who ne'er succeed.
To comprehend a nectar
Requires sorest need . . . .

To fight aloud is very brave,
But gallanter, I know,
Who charge within the bosom,
The cavalry of woe . . . .

Dickinson's seclusion may have intensified her understanding of human emotions:

What fortitude the soul contains
That it can so endure
The accent of a coming foot,
The opening of a door!

Dickinson recognized both the joys and the terrors of the quiet, introspective life:

One need not be a chamber to be haunted,
One need not be a house;
The brain has corridors surpassing
Material place.

Far safer, of a midnight meeting
External ghost,
Than an interior confronting
That whiter host.

Far safer through an Abbey gallop,
The stones achase,
Than, moonless, one's own self encounter
In lonesome place.

By her own standard, Dickinson's life and poetry were great successes. Her epitaph might well have read:

If I can stop one heart from breaking
I shall not live in vain:
If I can ease one life the aching,
Or cool one pain,
Or help one fainting robin
Unto his nest again,
I shall not live in vain.

CHRISTINA ROSSETTI

(1830-1894)

Rigidity, structure, conformity, and propriety . . . these defined the Victorian world into which Christina Rossetti was born. Strict moral values and social etiquette—especially for women—were the rule. Just as the close-fitting and suffocating corset restricted a woman's body in the name of fashion, so the social rules and mores inhibited a woman's spirit in the name of propriety. Despite such constraint, Rossetti found her voice, and became one of the outstanding female poets of the nineteenth century.

Born into a literary family, Rossetti and her siblings were versed in the classics. The children lived in an austere home; aside from reading and writing, they had little else to occupy their time. As they matured, all of the Rossetti children developed into notable writers.

Only 17, Christina was first in her family to publish poetry. Titled **Verses,** this work was intensely religious, reflecting the influence the Bible played in her life. Rossetti was also profoundly affected by St. Augustine's **Confessions** and a Kempis' **The Imitation of Christ.** Much of her work resonates with religious themes.

A Victorian woman was faced with three choices: marriage, sisterhood, or spinsterhood. Rossetti, having declined two marriage proposals and refusing to join the All Saints' Sisterhood, was consigned the latter of the three choices, and her poetry reflects the pain of an isolated existence. Writing about the anguish born of unfulfilled love, to Rossetti, death loomed the most palatable escape. The poetess died from cancer in 1894.

The most famous of Rossetti's poems is *Goblin Market,* first published in 1862. On the surface, the poem appears to be a simple nursery rhyme-like story about two sisters. On a deeper level, it is a poetic essay on repressed female sexuality.

Goblin Market

Morning and evening
Maids heard the goblins cry:
"Come buy our orchard fruits,
Come buy, come buy:
Apples and quinces,
Lemons and oranges . . . "

Evening by evening
Among the brookside rushes,
Laura bowed her head to hear,
Lizzie veiled her blushes:
Crouching close together

In the cooling weather,
With clasping arms and cautioning lips,
With tingling cheeks and fingertips.
"Lie close," Laura said,
Pricking up her golden head:
"We must not look at goblin men,
We must not buy their fruits:
Who knows upon what soil they fed
Their hungry thirsty roots?"
"Come buy," call the goblins
Hobbling down the glen.
"Oh" cried Lizzie, "Laura, Laura,
You should not peep at goblin men."
Lizzie covered up her eyes,
Covered close lest they should look;
Laura reared her glossy head,
And whispered like the restless brook:
"Look, Lizzie, look, Lizzie,
Down the glen tramp little men."

As the poem proceeds, both girls know that they should avoid the goblin men, yet hearing them is inevitable, and, eventually, Laura succumbs to their call, exchanging a lock of her hair—a symbol of her virginity—for the sweet fruit they offer. Upon partaking of the goblins' fruit, Laura is no longer able to hear their customary cry of "Come buy, come buy." Longing for the sweet fruit, she goes out in a vain search for the goblin market. Pining for the forbidden fruit, Laura becomes sick to the point of death. Lizzie, however, having resisted the goblins' call, bravely ventures to the goblin market to purchase fruit for her sister. The goblin men, however, will not allow her to take fruit for someone else. They try to force her to eat the fruit, but she fiercely resists, returning home with her clothes tattered, her body bruised, and her face covered with the juice of the enslaving fruit. When Laura sees what Lizzie has done, she rushes to her and kisses away the juice—which is no longer sweet, but bitter. But, finally, the fruit's bitterness, combined with the love of her sister, redeems Laura from her ruin.

Although "Goblin Market" cheerfully concludes with a "Love conquers all" message, the vast majority of Rossetti's poetry is not nearly so optimistic. Throughout her life, she struggled between striving for sacred love or secular love, believing that she could only have one or the other. She found neither; her desire for an intimate union through marriage remained unfulfilled, as did her desire to join herself with God. As a result, a preoccupation with death began to pervade the work.

Her early poetry voices a need to have a deep and meaningful relationship with God, as the final stanza of *A Christmas Carol* reveals:

What can I give Him,
Poor as I am?
If I were a shepherd
I would bring a lamb,
If I were a Wise Man
I would do my part,—
Yet what I can I give Him,
Give my heart.

Mary Magdalene is also an expression of religious longings:

She came in deep repentance,
And knelt down at his feet
Who can change the sorrow into joy,
The bitter into sweet.

She had cast away her jewels
And her rich attire,
And her breast was filled with a holy shame,
And her heart with a holy fire.

Her tears were more precious
Than her precious pearls—
Her tears that fell upon His feet
As she wiped them with her curls.

Her youth and her beauty
Were budding to their prime;
But she wept for the great transgression,
The sin of other time.

Trembling betwixt hope and fear,
She sought the King of Heaven,
Forsook the evil of her ways,
Loved much, and was forgiven.

Disappointed by her religion, Rossetti hungered for an intimate earthly relationship. *L.E.L.* sums up her empty, romantic yearnings of spinsterhood:

Downstairs I laugh, I sport and jest with all;
But in my solitary room above
I turn my face in silence to the wall;
My heart is breaking for a little love.
Though winter frosts are done,
And birds pair every one,
And leaves peep out, for springtide is begun.

I feel no spring, while spring is well-nigh
    blown,
I find no nest, while nests are in the grove:
Woe's me for mine own heart that dwells alone,
My heart that breaketh for a little love.
While golden in the sun
Rivulets rise and run,
While lilies bud, for springtide is begun.

All love, are loved, save only I; their hearts

Beat warm with love and joy, beat full thereof:
They cannot guess, who play the pleasant parts,
My heart is breaking for a little love.
While bee-hives wake and whir,
And rabbit thins his fur,
In living spring that sets the world astir.

I deck myself with silks and jewelry,
I plume myself like any mated dove:
The praise my rustling show, and never see
My heart is breaking for a little love.
While sprouts green lavender
With rosemary and myrrh
For in quick spring the sap is all astir.

Perhaps some saints in glory guess the truth,
Perhaps some angels read it as they move,
And cry one to another full of ruth,
"Her heart is breaking for a little love."
Though other things have birth,
And leap and sing for mirth,
When springtime wakes and clothes and feeds
    the earth.

Yet saith a saint, "Take patience for the scythe";
Yet saith an angel: "Wait, and thou shalt prove
True best is last, true life is born of death,
O thou, heart-broken for a little love.
Then love shall fill the girth,
And love make fat thy dearth,
When new spring builds new heaven and clean
    new earth."

Lonely and insecure, Rossetti longed for the solace of death. Lines from *Looking Forward* reveal a last hope for happiness.

Sleep, let me sleep, for I am sick of care;
Sleep, let me sleep, for my pain wearies me.
Shut out the light; thicken the heavy air
With drowsy incense; let a distant stream
Of music lull me, languid as a dream,
Soft as the whisper of a summer sea.

Her finest poem, *Three Stages*, lends a vivid impression of the heartache Rossetti felt.

The fruitless thought of what I might have been,
Haunting me ever, will not let me rest.
A cold North wind has withered all my green,
My sun is in the West.

But, where my palace stood, with the same stone
I will uprear a shady hermitage:
And there my spirit shall keep house alone,
Accomplishing its age.

There other garden-beds shall lie around,
Full of sweet-briar and incense-bearing thyme:
There will I sit, and listen for the sound
Of the last lingering chime.

RUDYARD KIPLING

(1865-1936)

Oh, East is East, and West is West
And never the twain shall meet,
Till Earth and Sky stand presently
At God's great Judgement Seat;
But there is neither East nor West,
Border, nor Breed, nor Birth,
When two strong men stand face to face,
Though they come from the ends of the earth!

These first two lines of *The Ballad of East and West* are often quoted out of context, evidencing how Rudyard Kipling's extraordinary skill sometimes over shadowed his message. The final lines of the stanza reverse the meaning of this poem.

Born in Bombay, India, to ordinary English middle-class parents, Kipling's life was far from ordinary. He spent the first years of his life in relative comfort, attended to by Indian servants. When Rudyard was six, his parents returned to England to see to the boy's education, and he and his sister were placed in the care of a couple who ran a boarding house. Kipling became a voracious reader, but the master of the house disapproved of the activity, and soon Kipling's book were seized; the young poet, it is believe, was subsequently tormented—and possibly tortured—while in this home. When his mother learned of these conditions, she immediately returned to England and placed her son in a reputable boarding school.

At age 17, Kipling was hired to write for a newspaper in India. There was able to spend time with his family, yet the experiences of his childhood held strong sway on his work.

Kipling spent seven years writing poetry and articles for various papers in India. He published poetry (*Departmental Ditties*) and short stories (*Plain Tales from the Hills*), both of which became popular books in India and in Europe.

In time, Kipling returned to England to live. Soon, he married—and, for him, life had finally blessed him with bliss. While honeymooning in America, however, Kipling's bank failed, stranding the couple. With the help of relatives, they found a place to live, and Kipling resumed his writing. During this time, he published two books of verse, *Barrack Room Ballads* and *Seven Seas*. He also completed *The Jungle Book* and its sequel.

After four years in America, the Kiplings returned to England. There they lived quietly and happily, a good life interrupted only by the tragic death of their oldest daughter.

Captains Courageous and *Kim* were soon published, followed by the Just So stories. In 1907, Kipling became the first Englishman to win the Nobel Prize for literature. As he grew into middle-age, he became an activist, involving himself in such events as the Boer War and World War I. His son, John, entered World War I and was soon reported as missing in action, presumed dead. This new tragedy devastated the family. After the war, Kipling withdrew from public view, and his writing took a more mellow, less strident tone.

Critics of the day generally rated him highly as a writer, and not so highly as a poet. In addition to his anti-imperialist views, he tended to rely heavily on rhyme and meter—all during a time when imperialism was in vogue and Romantic

poets were turning to free-verse and other experimental forms. Finally, his poetry became popular with the masses. Most critics, however, continued to think of good poetry as *unpopular*, thus Kipling's "popular" poems couldn't be "good" poems.

Kipling is regarded a true "poet of the people." *Barrack Room Ballads* includes some of the best examples of "people poetry," such as *Danny Deever*, *Mandalay*, and *Gunga Din*. Danny Deever describes the execution of a soldier from the viewpoint of other soldiers, concluding with:

"What's that so black against the sun?" said Files-on-Parade.
"It's Danny fightin' hard for life," the Colour-Sergeant said.
"What's that that whimpers over 'ead?" said Files-on-Parade.
"It's Danny's soul that's passing now," the Colour-Sergeant said.

Mandalay, on the other hand, is a love story, a rhythmic masterpiece that embraces the classic line, "I've a neater, sweeter maiden in a cleaner, greener land":

. . . By the old Moulmein Pagoda, lookin' lazy at the sea,
There's a Burma girl a-settin', and I know she thinks o' me;
For the wind is in the palm-trees, and the temple-bells they say:
"Come you back, you British soldier; come you back to Mandalay!"
Come you back to Mandalay,
Where the old Flotilla lay:
Can't you 'ear their paddles chunkin' from Rangoon to Mandalay?
On the road to Mandalay,
Where the flyin'-fishes play,
An' the dawn comes up like thunder outer China 'crost the Bay!

Gunga Din was sometimes criticized among elitist reviewers not only for its rhyme scheme but for its explicit moral message.

I shan't forgit the night
When I dropped be'ind the fight
With a bullet where my belt-plate should 'a' been.
I was chokin' mad with thirst,
An' the man that spied me first
Was our good old grinnin', gruntin' Gunga Din.

'E lifted up my 'ead,
An' he plugged me where I bled,
An' 'e guv me 'arf-a-pint o' water green
It was crawlin' and it stunk,
But of all the drinks I've drunk,
I'm gratefullest to one from Gunga Din.

You Lazarushian-leather Gunga Din! . . .
Though I've belted you and flayed you,
By the livin' Gawd that made you,
You're a better man than I am, Gunga Din!

With the death of his son, who was missing in action, Kipling's dramatic poetry takes a totally different turn. In *A Nativity* his words clearly and consistently return to his son's well-being:

A Nativity
The Babe was laid in the Manger

Between the gentle kine—
All safe from cold and danger—
"But it was not so with mine,
          (With mine! With mine!)
"Is it well with the child, is it well?"
The waiting mother prayed.
"For I know not how he fell,
And I know not where he is laid."

... "My child died in the dark.
Is it well with the child, is it well?
There was none to tend him or mark,
And I know not how he fell."

... "But I know for Whom he fell"—
The steadfast mother smiled,
"Is it well with the child—is it well?
It is well—it is well with the child!"

Examples abound of Kipling's light verse in **Barracks Room Ballads** and **Seven Seas**. Unique in its lack of military overtones is the piece *When Earth's Last Picture Is Painted*:

When Earth's last picture is painted
and the tubes are twisted and dried,
When the oldest colours have faded,
and the youngest critic has died,
We shall rest, and, faith, we shall need it—
lie down for an aeon or two,
Till the Master of All Good Workmen
shall put us to work anew.
And those that were good shall be happy:
they shall sit in a golden chair;
They shall splash at a ten-league canvas
with brushes of comets' hair.
They shall find real saints to draw from—
Magdalene, Peter, and Paul;
They shall work for an age at a sitting
and never be tired at all!
And only The Master shall praise us,
and only The Master shall blame;
And no one shall work for money,
and no one shall work for fame,
But each for the joy of the working,
and each, in his separate star,
Shall draw the Thing as he sees It
for the God of Things as They are!

Even Kipling's light verse could have a sting.:

The Old Men

This is our lot if we live so long and labour unto the
end—
That we outlive the impatient years and the much too
patient friend:
And because we know we have breath in our mouth and
think we have thoughts in our head,
We shall assume that we are alive, whereas we are really
dead.

Perhaps another reason the critics so disparaged Kipling's poems was they carried such moralistic messages. Indeed, Kipling's moralizing could penetrate to the heart of the blameworthy. *The Mary Gloster* is a prime example.

. And they asked me how I did it, and I gave 'em the
Scripture text,
"You keep your light so shining a little in front o' the
next!"
They copied all they could follow, but they couldn't copy
my mind,
And I left 'em sweating and stealing a year and a half
behind.

... Harrer an' Trinity College! I ought to ha' sent you
to sea—
But I stood you an education, an' what have you done
for me?
The things I knew was proper you wouldn't thank me to
give,
And the things I knew was rotten you said was the way
to live.

Because Kipling wrote about men of action, he was much loved by the common English soldiers and sailors. Often he wrote about them for a reason, as seen in *The Last of the Light Brigade*:

The Last of the Light Brigade

There were thirty million English who talked of
England's might,
There were twenty broken troopers who lacked a bed for
the night,
They had neither food nor money, they had neither ser-
vice nor trade;
They were only shiftless soldiers, the last of the Light
Brigade.

They felt that life was fleeting; they knew not that art
was long,
That though they were dying of famine, they lived in
deathless song.
They asked for a little money to keep the wolf from the
door;
And the thirty million English sent twenty pounds and
four!

... O thirty million English that babble of England's
might,
Behold there are twenty heroes who lack their food tonight;
Our children's children are lisping to "honour the
charge they made—"
And we leave to the streets and the workhouse the charge
of the Light Brigade!

Another popular poem—though rejected by the critics, perhaps for being "too neatly tied up"— is *If*.

If you can keep your head when all about you
  Are losing theirs and blaming it on you,
If you can trust yourself when all men doubt you,
  But make allowance for their doubting too;
If you can wait and not be tired by waiting,
  Or being lied about, don't deal in lies,
Or being hated, don't give way to hating,
  And yet don't look too good, nor talk too wise:
... Yours is the Earth and everything that's in it,
  And—which is more—you'll be a Man, my son!

The Children's Song spotlights both Kipling's own attitude toward the critics and his own personal moral code:

Teach us to look in all our ends
On Thee for judge, and not our friends;
That we, with Thee, may walk uncowed
By fear or favour of the crowd.

Teach us the Strength that cannot seek,
By deed or thought, to hurt the weak;
That, under Thee, we may possess
Man's strength to comfort man's distress.

Teach us Delight in simple things,
And Mirth that has no bitter springs;
Forgiveness free of evil done,
And Love to all men 'neath the sun!

W. B. YEATS

(1865 - 1939)

One of the greatest poets of the twentieth century, William Butler Yeats directed the themes of his works on art, Irish nationalism, and the supernatural. Also a dramatist, he authored twenty-six plays. Among his many accomplishments, Yeats won the Noble Prize for Literature in 1923.

Born in Dublin, Ireland, Yeats spent his childhood in London and western Ireland, and grew up promoting the cause of the Irish. He co-founded the Irish Literary Theatre to support nationalism and encourage the writing and producing of plays about the Irish way of life. Unlike most poets, his verse improved as he grew older. In the last ten years of his life he produced his best work.

Collected Poems, published in 1950, contains most of his verse. He later wrote "A Vision," a guide to his theories which serves quite useful in interpreting and understanding some of his more difficult poems.

Yeats' politics are most pronounced in the work, *Easter, 1916.* Here, Yeats recounts the events of the Irish rebellion, provides the reader with a list of the central figures in that revolt, and extols the rebels' courage in the face of insurmountable odds. He loved these revolutionaries, the heroic founders of the Irish Republic.

Easter, 1916

I have met them at close of day
Coming with vivid faces
From counter or desk among grey
Eighteenth-century houses.
I have passed with a nod of the head
Or polite meaningless words,
Or have lingered awhile and said
Polite meaningless words,
And thought before I had done
Of a mocking tale or a gibe
To please a companion
Around the fire at the club,
Being certain that they and I
But lived where motley is worn:
All changed, changed utterly:
A terrible beauty is born.

That woman's days were spent
In ignorant good-will,
Her nights in argument
Until her voice grew shrill.
What voice more sweet than hers
When, young and beautiful,
She rode to harriers?
This man had kept a school
And rode our winged horse;
This other his helper and friend

Was coming into his force;
He might have won fame in the end
So sensitive his nature seemed,
So daring and sweet his thought.
This other man I had dreamed
A drunken, vain glorious lout.
He had done most bitter wrong
To some who are near to my heart,
Yet I number him in the song;
He, too, has been changed in his turn,
Transformed utterly:
A terrible beauty is born.

Hearts with one purpose alone
Through summer and winter seem
Enchanted to a stone
To trouble the living stream.
The horse that comes from the road,
The rider, the birds that range
From cloud to tumbling cloud,
Minute by minute they change;
A shadow of cloud on the stream
Changes minute by minute;
A horse-hoof slides on the brim,
And a horse splashes within it;
The long-legged moor hens dive,
And hens to moor-cocks call;
Minute by minute they live:
The stone's in the midst of all.

Too long a sacrifice
Can make a stone of the heart.
O when may it suffice?
That is Heaven's part, our part
To murmur name upon name,
As a mother names her child
When sleep at last has come
On limbs that had run wild.
What is needless death after all?
For England may keep faith
For all that is done and said.
We know their dream; enough
To know they dreamed and are dead;
And what if excess of love
Bewildered them till they died?
I write it out in a verse—
MacDonagh and MacBride
And Connolly and Pearse
Now and in time to be,
Wherever green is worn,
Are changed, changed utterly:
A terrible beauty is born.
September 25, 1916

Formulating his own theories about the nature of time and history, Yeats' ideas are in part derived from his notions of spirituality. He viewed history as a being "gyre," a symbolic whirlpool or eddy in which time is tossed and spun around, finally to disappear in the bottomless void. The complicated scheme of his poetry separates time into a series of "gyres" marking the various eras through which civilization has passed.

To Yeats, the "gyre" is an important element signaling the end of the Christian epoch and the coming of Armageddon. The "rough beast" is a sphinx-like image of the coming catastrophe which is let loose by a world where the "centre cannot hold," and extreme anarchy reigns. He also uses a spiritual symbol—the "soul of the world"—to express the concept of apocalypse.

The Second Coming

Turning and turning in the widening gyre
The falcon cannot hear the falconer;
Things fall apart; the centre cannot hold;
Mere anarchy is loosed upon the world,
The blood-dimmed tide is loosed, and everywhere
The ceremony of innocence is drowned;
The best lack all conviction, while the worst
Are full of passionate intensity.

Surely some revelation is at hand;
Surely the Second Coming is at hand.
The Second Coming! Hardly are those words out
When a vast image out of Spiritus Mundi
Troubles my sight: somewhere in sands of the desert
A shape with lion body and the head of a man,
A gaze blank and pitiless as the sun,
Is moving its slow thighs, while all about it
Reel shadows of the indignant desert birds.
The darkness drops again; but now I know

That twenty centuries of stony sleep
Were vexed to nightmare by a rocking cradle,
And what rough beast, its hour come around at last,
Slouches toward Bethlehem to be born?

A rewritten "Leda" legend from Greek mythology, the following sonnet, *Leda and the Swan*, relates how Zeus transformed himself into a swan in order to seduce Leda. In this poem, Yeats touches on eroticism; but as more than a mere tale of seduction, he poses questions about sharing in intimate relations with a deity, alluding to the immaculate conception of Christ. Hence, both knowledge and power combine to bring the opposites of love and war, life and death into the world.

Leda and the Swan

A sudden blow: the great wings beating still
Above the staggering girl, her thighs caressed
By the dark webs, her nape caught in his bill,
He holds her helpless breast upon his breast.

How can those terrified vague fingers push
The feathered glory from her loosening thighs?
And how can body, laid in that white rush,

But feel the strange heart beating where it lies?

A shudder in the loins engenders there
The broken wall, the burning roof and tower
And Agamemnon dead.
Being so caught up,
So mastered by the brute blood of the air,
Did she put on his knowledge with his power
Before the indifferent beak could let her drop?

The elements which set *Leda* apart as such a powerful work were Yeats' supreme sense of diction, rhythm and metrics. The lines of the verse almost sing with a music-like cadence.

In *Sailing to Byzantium*, the narrator leaves the natural world to sail over the seas, coming to rest at a far-off region of the mind. As the mind's journey over territory and time ends, the poet becomes a prophet, all-knowing, all-wise, and timeless—much in the same way Yeats himself tried to span history with his literary efforts.

Sailing to Byzantium

I
That is no country for old men. The young
In one another's arms, birds in the trees,
—Those dying generations—at their song,
The salmon-falls, the mackerel-crowded seas,
Fish, flesh, or fowl, commend all summer long
Whatever is begotten, born, and dies.
Caught in that sensual music all neglect
Monuments of unageing intellect.

II
An aged man is but a paltry thing,
A tattered coat upon a stick, unless
Soul clap its hands and sing, and louder sing
For every tatter in its mortal dress,
Nor is there singing school but studying
Monuments of its own magnificence;
And therefore I have sailed the seas and come
To the holy city of Byzantium.

III
O sages standing in God's holy fire
As in the gold mosaic of a wall,
Come from the holy fire, perne in a gyre,
And be the singing-masters of my soul.
Consume my heart away; sick with desire
And fastened to a dying animal
It knows not what it is; and gathers me
Into the artifice of eternity.

IV
Once out of nature I shall never take
My bodily form from any natural thing,
But such a form as Grecian goldsmiths make
Of hammered gold and gold enamelling
To keep a drowsy Emperor awake;
Or set upon a golden bough to sing
To lords and ladies of Byzantium
Of what is past, or passing, or to come.

ROBERT FROST

(1874- 1963)

The Road Not Taken

Two roads diverged in a yellow wood,
And sorry I could not travel both
And be one traveler, long I stood
And looked down one as far as I could
To where it bent in the undergrowth;

Then took the other, as just as fair,
And having perhaps the better claim,
Because it was grassy and wanted wear;
Though as for that the passing there
Had worn them really about the same,

And both that morning equally lay
In leaves no step had trodden black.
Oh, I kept the first for another day!
Yet knowing how way leads on to way,
I doubted if I should ever come back.

I shall be telling this with a sigh
Somewhere ages and ages hence:
Two roads diverged in a wood , and I—
I took the one less traveled by,
And that has made all the difference.

Like his poem, Robert Lee Frost has made all the difference in American poetry. A four-time Pulitzer Prize winner, Frost was so an expert that many of his earlier poems are as splendidly composed as his later works. Finding inspiration in the landscapes, folkways, and simple speech mannerisms of New England, Frost's works have been much lauded and loved for their incisive simplicity.

The Road Not Taken exemplifies Frost's straightforward style and depth. Though not always understood simply, his effects are dependent on a certain slyness for which the reader needs to be prepared. During a lecture, Frost explained that this poem was not meant to be an allegory or metaphor of some sort, but simply an account of a time he and a friend took a walk in the woods. Coming to a fork in the road, each decided to take a different road—and eventually they ended up in the same place. The difference between the roads was a matter of opinion, the poet pointed out, not a matter of greatness.

The work of Frost is direct and graceful; its language is unadorned. Of course—as is the case with most great poetry—a measure of ambiguity leaves room for interpretation. He employed traditional meters and rhyme schemes in his writing as well as a definite narrative which gave subtly and power. One supposed the last line of Stopping By Woods on a Snowy Evening ("... miles to go before I sleep") was an ref-

erence to approaching death, or some sort of disguised death-wish. To these interpretations, Frost replied, "No, it means to get the hell out of there."

Frost's father passed away soon after Robert's birth in California, whereupon his mother moved the family to New England. There, Frost briefly attended Dartmouth College, worked on a country paper, and then turned to teaching school. He also studied at Harvard for two years, but concluded that formal study was not his style. While later in life Frost accepted invitations to lecture at several universities, he spent most of his time farming a few acres of ground in New England.

However, it was in England that Frost's brilliant career was born. His first two volumes of verse were published there and, after receiving critical acclaim, were also published in the United States.

While Frost often turned his attentions to serious themes and ideas, he did not hesitate to apply humor to the most horrible condition. In the following two works—both touching on the theme of the final apocalypse—Frost's wit is apparent.

Fire and Ice

Some say the world will end in fire,
Some say in ice.
From what I've tasted of desire
I hold with those who favor fire.
But it had to perish twice,
I think I know enough of hate
To say that for destruction ice
Is also great
And would suffice.

U.S. 1946 King's X

Having invented a new Holocaust,
And been the first with it to win a war,
How they make haste to cry with fingers
    crossed,
King's X — no fairs to use it any more!

In the Mending Wall, Frost again turns to humor to undermine the solemn question of how it is that any of us can get along, save for the walls which keep us apart. In this verse, the narrator and his neighbor perform the simple chore of repairing a stone wall. The narrator cannot see the sense in it, but his neighbor is firm in his belief that "good fences make good neighbors."

The Mending Wall

Something there is that doesn't love a wall,

That sends the frozen-ground-swell under it,
And spills the upper boulders in the sun;
And makes gaps even two can pass abreast.
The work of hunters is another thing:
I have come after them and made repair
Where they have left not one stone on a stone,
But they would have the rabbit out of hiding,
To please the yelping dogs. The gaps I mean,
No one has seen them made or heard them made,
But at spring mending-time we find them there.
I let my neighbor know beyond the hill:
And on a day we meet to walk the line
And set the wall between us once again.
We keep the wall between us as we go.
To each the boulders that have fallen to each.
And some are loaves and some so nearly balls
We have to use a spell to make the balance:
`Stay where you are until our backs are turned!'
We wear our fingers rough with handling them.
Oh, just another kind of out-door game,
One on a side. It comes to little more:
There where it is we do not need the wall:
He is all pine and I am apple orchard.
My apple trees will never get across
And eat the cones under his pines, I tell him.
He only says, `Good fences make good neigh-
    bors.'
Spring is the mischief in me, and I wonder
If I could put a notion in his head:
`Why do they make good neighbors? Isn't it
Where there are cows? But here there are no
    cows.
Before I built a wall I'd ask to know
What I was walling in or walling out,
And to whom I was like to give offence.
Something there is that doesn't love a wall,
That wants it down. I could say `Elves' to him,
But it's not elves exactly, and I'd rather
He said it for himself. I see him there
Bringing a stone grasped firmly by the top
In each hand, like an old-stone savage armed.
He moves in darkness as it seems to me,
Not of woods only and the shade of trees.
He will not go behind his father's saying,
And he likes having thought of it so well
He says again, `Good fences make good neigh-
    bors.'

Stopping by Woods on a Snowy Evening
is one of Frost's most puzzling works.
Though speculation abounds as to its interpretation, the author maintained a stubborn
silence about the poem's possibilities.

Stopping By Woods on a Snowy Evening

Whose woods these are I think I know.
His house is in the village, though;
He will not see me stopping here
To watch his woods fill up with snow.

My little horse must think it queer

To stop without a farmhouse hear
Between the woods and frozen lake
The darkest evening of the year.
He gives his harness bells a shake
To ask if there is some mistake.
The only other sound's the sweep
Of easy wind and downy flake.

The woods are lovely, dark and deep,
But I have promises to keep,
And miles to go before I sleep,
And miles to go before I sleep.

Frost, especially at the height of his
career, held public readings where his magnificent voice kept listeners spellbound. His
oratory powers were showcased at John F.
Kennedy's Inauguration, where the poet
delivered the Inaugural Poem, "The Gift
Outright," to a nationwide audience. Here
he speaks sensitively yet with perspective
of an American historical dilemma.

The Gift Outright

The land was ours before we were the land's.
She was our land more than a hundred years
Before we were her people. She was ours
In Massachusetts, in Virginia,
But we were England's, still colonials,
Possessing what we still were unpossessed buy,
Possessed by what we now no more possessed.
Something we were withholding made us weak
Until we found out that it was ourselves
We were withholding from our land of living,
And forwith found salvation in surrender.
Such as we were we gave ourselves outright
(The deed of gift was many deeds of war)
To the land vaguely realizing westward,
But still unstoried, artless, unenhanced,
Such as she was, such as she would become.

JAMES JOYCE

(1882-1941)

First and foremost known as a writer of prose (his fiction and short story collections are masterpieces) the poetry of James Joyce is no less skillfully executed. In fact, his poetic offerings best reveal the true identity of the writer. Simple and direct, the work mirrors the inner-reflections of a genius.

James Joyce, born in Dublin, Ireland, was educated at Jesuit schools and earned a degree in modern languages at University College Dublin. His ambitions were to be a writer and to study medicine. He gave up the second dream to teach English in Yugoslavia, during which time he published his poems in a small volume titled *Chamber Music.* Joyce lived most of his married life in Paris, France and Zurich, Switzerland. Through the years, he published a number of prose works and another collection of verse called *Pomes Penyeach.*

The success of Joyce's poetry rests in its clear, "musical" language. Almost totally lacking in complexity, many critics have been led to regard them instead as lyrics. In part, they *are* lyrics. Joyce was an excellent singer and loved music, and his *Chamber Music* collection was regarded as, apart from poetry, a suite of songs arranged "approximately allegretto, andante, cantabile, mosso." Indeed, it was his hope that the poems would eventually be set to music.

I

Strings of the Earth and air
  Make music sweet;
Strings by the river where
  The willows meet.

There's music along the river
  For Love wanders there,
Pale flowers on his mantle,
  Dark leaves on his hair.

All softly playing,
  With head to the music bent,
And fingers straying
  Upon an instrument.

Poem *XII*, from *Chamber Music,* was brought to life one night when a lady friend remarked that the moon "looked tearful." Joyce, never one to perpetuate a cliche, disagreed. He said the moon looked like "the chubby hooded face of some jolly fat [monk]."

XII

What counsel has the hooded moon
  Put in thy heart, my shyly sweet,

Of love in ancient plenilune,
  Glory and stars beneath his feet-
A sage that is but kith and kin
  With the comedian Capuchin?

Believe me rather that am wise
  In disregard of the divine,
A glory kindles in those eyes,
  Trembles to starlight, Mine, O Mine!
No more be tears in moon or mist
  For thee, sweet sentimentalist.

Though his poems were simple and direct, Joyce wielded a varied form, capable of exploring the entire spectrum of human events, from love to war.

XXXVI

I hear an army charging upon the land,
  And the thunder of horses plunging, foam about
their knees:
  Arrogant, in black armour, behind them stand,
Disdaining the reins, with fluttering whips, the charioteers.

They cry unto the night their battle-name:
  I moan in sleep when I fear their whirling laughter.
  They cleave the gloom of dreams, a blinding flame,
Clanging, clanging upon the heart as upon an anvil.

They come shaking in triumph their long, green hair:
  They come out of the sea and run shouting by the shore.
My heart, have you no wisdom thus to despair?
  My love, my love, my love, why have you left me alone?

In order to perfect his writing skills, Joyce took to using devices such as abstraction and imagery to develop new themes. One outstanding thematic poem is *Ecce Puer,* written as a dual piece, both to commemorate the near-concurrent death of his father and birth of his grandson.

Ecce Puer

Of the dark past
A child is born
With joy and grief
My heart is torn

Calm in his cradle
The living lies.
May love and mercy
Unclose his eyes!

Young life is breathed
On the glass;
The world that was not

Comes to pass.

A child is sleeping:
An old man gone.
O, father forsaken,
Forgive your son

Poems from *Chamber Music* clearly demonstrate Joyce's haunting love affair with romantic imagery and simple emotion.

XIV

My dove, my beautiful one,
Arise, arise!
The night-dew lies
Upon my lips and eyes,

The odorous winds are weaving
A music of sighs:
Arise Arise
My dove, my beautiful one!

I wait by the cedar tree,
My sister, my love,
White breast of the dove,
My breast shall be your bed.

The pale dew lies
Like a veil on my head.
My fair one, my fair dove,
Arise, arise!

As if not content to allow the thought to finish, he picks up where he left off in *XV*.

XV

From dewy dreams, my soul, arise,
From love's deep slumber and from death,
For lo! the trees are full of sighs
Whose leaves the morn admonisheth,

Eastward the gradual dawn prevails
Where softly-burning fires appear.
Making to tremble all those veils
Of grey and golden gossamer.

While sweetly, gently, secretly,
The flowery bells of morn are stirred
And the wide choirs of faery
Begin (innumerous!) to be heard.

Perhaps Joyce's lyrical sense is best illustrated in poem *XVI*.

XVI

O cool is the valley now,
And there, love, will we go
For many a choir is singing now
Where Love did sometime go.
And hear you not the thrushes calling,
Calling us away?
O cool and pleasant is the valley
And there, love, will we stay.

WILLIAM CARLOS WILLIAMS

(1883-1963)

This Is Just To Say

I have eaten
the plums
that were in
the icebox

and which
you were probably
saving
for breakfast

Forgive me
they were delicious
so sweet
and so cold.

In his poetry, William Carlos Williams created an American voice. Rather than staying within
the formal conventions of most previous traditions,
he chose to express American English in the
rhythm of American speech, on "a measure of the
ear." His style was new—and, at times, was criticized as insubstantial.

On one occasion, during a television interview with Williams, it was pointed out that one of
Williams' poems, containing lines such as "2 par-
tridges/2 mallard ducks/a Dungeness crab" was
nothing more than "a fashionable grocery list."
Williams readily admitted that it was in fact a grocery list. "But is it poetry?" he was then asked.
Williams' response was classic—and classically
stated his overall philosophy toward writing: " . . .
In prose, an English word means what it says. In
poetry, you're listening to two things . . . you're listening to the sense, the common sense of what it
says. But it says more. That is the difficulty." The
lines of his verse, he went on to explain, when studied for their rhythmic qualities, form a "jagged pattern." He considered this pattern as the soul of his
poetry; the words and the meaning—if there was
one—was secondary.

Williams was born to immigrant parents in
Rutherford, New Jersey to immigrant parents,
where he remained virtually the entire 80 years of
his life. Unlike many writers of his day who travelled to Europe, he chose to live in and focus upon
American society. Known widely in his time as the
"doctor-poet," as a practicing medical doctor he
produced the bulk of his work at the busy height of
his career.

A clear example of his approach to poetry is
Le Medecin Malgre Lui, published in 1915.

Oh I suppose I should
wash the walls of my office
polish the rust from
my instruments and keep them
definitely in order
build shelves in the laboratory
empty out the old stains
clean the bottles
and refill them,
buy another lens, put
my journals on edge instead of letting them lie flat
in heaps—then begin
ten years back and
gradually
read them to date
cataloguing important
articles for ready reference.

I suppose I should
read the new books.
If to this I added
a bill at the tailor's
and at the cleaner's
grew a decent beard
and cultivated a look
of importance—
ho can tell? I might be
a credit to my Lady Happiness
and never think anything
but a white thought!

Williams advocated using speech unencumbered by special significance or meaning. A man
"makes a poem," he once said, and the reader
should be able to read it. He felt that a poet's duty
was "to lift by use of his imagination and the language he hears, the material conditions and
appearances of his environment to the sphere of the
intelligence where they will have new currency . . . "

Experimenting with natural speech, Williams
adapted his work to a variety of speakers whose
voices reflected different emotions. The Widow's
Lament in Springtime takes this route.

Sorrow is my own yard
where the new grass
flames as it has flamed
often before but not
with the cold fire
that closes round me this year.
Thirty-five years
I lived with my husband.
The plumtree is white today
With masses of flowers.
Masses of flowers
load the cherry branches
and color some bushes
yellow and some red
but the grief in my heart is stronger than they
for though they were my joy
formerly, today I notice them
and turned away forgetting.
Today my son told me
that in the meadows,
at the edge of the heavy woods
in the distance, he saw
trees of white flowers.
I feel that I would like to go there
and fall into those flowers
and sink into the marsh near them.

New directions in poetry were opened
through Williams' use of unadorned images. The
Red Wheelbarrow uses very simple language to portray its message.

The Red Wheelbarrow

so much depends
upon

a red wheel
barrow

glazed with rain
water

beside the white
chickens.

In this poem, the wheelbarrow, the rain and

the chickens are not presented as symbols representing larger ideas. They are, according to Williams, intended to express their own importance within the context of the poem—"no ideas but in things."

This simple use of "things" also appears in Poem.

Poem

As the cat
climbed over
the top of

the jamcloset
first the right forefoot

carefully
then the hind
stepped down

into the pit of
the empty
flowerpot

Symbolism, however, did become a part of Williams' later works. In his epic poem *Patterson*, he relies on abstraction as well as concrete images to support his notions.

a bud forever green,
tight-curled, upon the pavement, perfect
in juice and substance but divorced, divorced
from its fellow, fallen low—

Divorce is
the sign of knowledge in our time,
divorce! divorce!

In *Asphodel, That Greeny Flower*, the concept of image is put in perspective.

Are facts not flowers
and flowers facts

or poems flowers
or all words of the imagination
interchangeable?

To Williams, everything can be conceived in the imagination; thus, objects, ideas, facts, images, etc. are all interchangeable.

As a physician, Williams maintained a close and continuous contact with humanity. He saw patients daily, a practice which found voice in his poetry:

A Cold Front.

This woman with a dead face
has seven foster children
and a new baby of her own in
spite of that. She wants pills

for an abortion and says
um hum, in reply to me . . .

. . . She looks at me with her mouth
open and blinks her expressionless
carved eyes, like a cat
on a limb too tired to go higher

from its tormentors . . .

The *Old Men* is another piece which reflects Williams' acute, clinical ability to observe.

Old men who have studied
every leg show
in the city . . .

Old men cut from touch
by the perfumed music—
polished or fleeced skulls

that stand before
the whole theater
in silent attitudes
of attention—

. . . Solitary old men for whom
we find no excuses—
I bow my head in shame
for those who malign you.
Old men
the peaceful beer of impotence
be yours!

In *The Poor*, the idea of scrutinizing people themselves is combined with detailed descriptions of their surroundings.

It's the anarchy of poverty
delights me, the old
yellow wooden house indented
among the new brick tenements

Of a cast iron balcony
with panels showing oak branches
in full leaf. It fits
the dress of the children

reflecting every stage and
custom of necessity—
Chimneys, roofs fences of
wood and metal in an unfenced

age and enclosing next to
nothing at all: the old man
in a sweater and soft black
hat who sweeps the sidewalk—

his own ten feet of it
in a wind that fitfully
turning his corner has
overwhelmed the entire city

For Williams, the theory of a poem did not sprang from the ethereal, abstract heights, but from the factual, down-to-earth depths. *To a Dog Injured in the Street* demonstrates Williams' ability to develop generalizations from isolated events.

It is myself
not the poor beast lying there
yelping with pain
that brings me to myself with a start—
as at the explosion
of a bomb, a bomb that has laid
all the world to waste.
I can do nothing
but sing about it . . .
I remember Norma
our English setter of my childhood
her silky ears
and expressive eyes . . .
I remember also a dead rabbit
lying helplessly
on the outspread palm
of a hunter's hand . . .

William Carlos Williams was known as a "poet's poet" for much of his career—he was hardly recognized outside of literary circles. In 1946, although by then he had published well over a dozen books of poetry, the American public could no longer ignore him. Williams enjoyed increasing respect from then until his death in 1963, when, posthumously, he was awarded the Pulitzer Prize and the Gold Medal for Poetry.

EZRA POUND

(1885-1972)

Salutation

O generation of the thoroughly smug and thoroughly uncomfortable
I have seen fishermen picnicking in the sun,
I have seen them with untidy families,
I have seen their smiles full of teeth and heard ungainly laughter.
And I am happier than you are.
And they were happier than I am;
And the fish swim in the lake and do not even own
clothing.

For Ezra Pound, happiness could be found in the simple life a fishermen, not among the "exquisite and excessive" people who stroll through their lives afraid to be spoken to, yet wanting to speak. He held a vigorous affinity for the working class— and an equally vigorous distrust of the middle and upper classes.

Leaving his home town of Haley, Idaho, Pound attended Hamilton College and the University of Pennsylvania, where, in 1906, he received his M.A. in romance languages. Traveling to Europe, he became a willing American expatriate living in London, Paris and Rome. A member of the Lost Generation, a group of American writers living abroad that also included Gertrude Stein and Ernest Hemingway, Pound exerted a strong influence over modern literature through his associations with other great writers.

After living in some of the major cities of Europe, Pound, fully enamored with the Fascist politics of Mussolini, finally settled in Rapallo, Italy, doing radio broadcasts from the 1930s through the Second World War. After the Allied forces captured Italy, Pound was imprisoned and tried for treason. Eventually he was found insane and locked up for thirteen years in St. Elizabeth's Hospital. It was only through the tireless efforts of such friends as T.S. Eliot and Archibald MacLeish that Pound was freed and permitted to return to Italy.

As a poet, Pound often employed what he called "masks" in his work, even titling one of his collections Personae, a reference to his technique of assuming a personality that was not his own. Likewise, in the Odyssey Pound assumes the voice of an ancient Greek to hide the source of his political denunciations.

In Hugh Selwyn Mauberley, the poet reveals via the life of the title character a living symbol of his age. Pound's own frustration with society was evident. He repeatedly denounces war and poverty. His jour-

nalist, near-autobiographic voice tends to weave a realistic fabric of the world during the Twentieth Century's early decades.

Hugh Selwyn Mauberley

I

For three years, out of key with his time,
He strove to resuscitate the dead art
Of poetry; to maintain "The sublime"
In the old sense. Wrong from the start—

No hardly, but, seeing he had been born
In a half-savage country, out of date;
Bent resolutely on wringing lilies out of acorns . . .

Caught in the unstopped ear;
Giving the rocks small lee-way
The chopped seas held him, therefore, that year.

His true Penelope was Flaubert,
He fished by obstinate isles;
Observed the elegance of Circe's hair
Rather than mottoes on sun-dials.

Unaffected by "the march of events,"
He passed from men's memory in l'an trentiesme
De son eage ; the cast presents
No adjunct to the Muse's diadem.

II

The age demanded an image
Of its accelerated grimace,
Something for the modern stage,
Not, at any rate, an Attic grace;

Not, not certainly, the obscure reveries
Of the inward gaze;
Better mendacities
Than the classics in paraphrase!

The "age demanded" chiefly a mould in plaster,
Made with no loss of time,
A prose kinema, not, assuredly, alabaster
Or the "sculpture" of rhyme . . .

V

There died a myriad,
And of the best, among them,
For an old bitch gone in the teeth,
For a botched civilization,

Charm, smiling at the good mouth,
Quick eyes gone under earth's lid,

For two gross of broken statues,
For a few thousand battered books.

Pound frequently wrestles with forces and attitudes antithetical to art and the artist. Phrases such as "I never mentioned a man but with the view/ Of selling my own works," and "Don't kick against the pricks,/ Accept opinion" can be found in his poetry,

271

© 1993, Compact Classics, Inc.

satirical attacks against those who write for money rather than love.

In the following work, he speaks as a young Chinese woman, many miles distant and many years away.

The River Merchant's Wife: A Letter

While my hair was still cut straight across my
  forehead
I played about the front gate, pulling flowers.
You came by on bamboo stilts, playing horse,
You walked about my seat, playing with blue
  plums.
And we went on living in the village of Chokan:
Two small people, without dislike or suspicion.

At fourteen I married My Lord you.
I never laughed, being bashful.
Lowering my head, I looked at the wall.
Called to a thousand times, I never looked back.

At fifteen I stopped scowling,
I desired my dust to be mingled with yours
Forever and forever and forever.
Why should I climb the look out?

At sixteen you departed,
You went into far Ku-to-yen, by the river of
  swirling
        eddies,
And you have been gone five months.
The monkeys make sorrowful noise overhead.

You dragged your feet when you went out.
By the gate now, the moss is grown, the differ-
  ent mosses,
Too deep to clear them away!
The leaves fall early this autumn, in wind.
The paired butterflies are already yellow with
  August
Over the grass in the West garden;
They hurt me. I grow older.
If you are coming down through the narrows of
  the river

      Kiang,
Please let me know beforehand,
And I will come out to meet you

      As far as Cho-fu-Sa.

Borrowing and translating from literature, Pound never hesitated to use a line from another piece of writing or mix an allusion with another one to create a new idea or image. He was well versed in diverse poetic styles and genres, from ancient Chinese verse to medieval French poetry.

Pound simplified his work with haiku-like brevity. The first draft of *In a Station of the Metro*, for instance, was almost thirty lines long. Paring it down until he reached the perfect metaphor, the perfect feeling, Pound creates juxtaposition of emotion to image.

In a Station of the Metro

The apparition
Of these faces in the crowd;
Petals on a wet, black bough.

So read many of his stylized pieces:

Alba

As cool as the pale wet leaves
  of lily-of-the-valley
She lay beside me in the dawn.

This final sonnet was one of Pound's earlier works, reflecting a strict adherence to rhyme and meter. Pound later forsook this style as his confidence in his own abilities grew. Still, the marvelous and vibrant imagery and word-choice so evident in this piece, leave no doubt as to how far Pound would go with his poetry.

A Virginal

No, No! Go from me. I have left her lately.
I will not spoil my sheath with lesser bright-
  ness,For my surrounding air has a new
  lightness;
Slight are her arms, yet they have bound my
  straitly
And left me cloaked as with a gauze of ether;
As with sweet leaves; as with a subtle clearness.
Oh, I have picked up magic in her nearness
To sheathe me half in half the things that
  sheathe her.
No, No! Go from me. I have still the flavor,
Soft as spring wind that's come with birchen
  bowers.
Green come the shoots, aye April in the branch-
  es,
As winter's wound with her sleight hand she
  staunches,
Hath of the trees a likeness of the savor:
As white their bark, so white this lady's hours.

MARIANNE MOORE

(1887-1972)

"Observer" is an appropriate title for a book of Marianne Moore's poetry. She wrote about nature, animals, and birds as well as human nature—verbally freezing them for the reader to study.

Moore was born in Kirkwood, Missouri and educated in the Metzger schools, where she studied art and drawing. She maintained an interest in drawing throughout her life. It was during her academic training that Moore began writing poetry. Her first works were printed in the Bryn Mawr literary and alumni magazines.

After graduation, Moore taught at the U.S. Industrial Indian School in Carlisle, where one of her students was Jim Thorpe, the Olympic gold medalist. Continuing to write poetry, Moore remained unrecognized until, during a stint in England, her first book, *Poems,* was published. *Observations* was published in America three years later, receiving the Dial Award.

By 1935, *Selected Poems* brought Moore a wider audience range, and her later *Collected Poems* won the Bollingen Prize. For her work, she has received the National Book Award and the Pulitzer Prize. Other achievements include the National Institute of Arts and Letters Gold Medal for Poetry, the Poetry Society of America's Gold Medal for Distinguished Achievement, and the National Medal for Literature.

What Are Years?

What is our innocence,
what is our guilt? All are
    naked, none is safe. And whence
is courage: the unanswered question,
the resolute doubt,—
dumbly calling, deafly listening—that
in misfortune, even death,
    encourages other
    and in its defeat, stirs

the soul to be strong? He
sees deep and is glad, who
accedes to mortality
and in his imprisonment rises
upon himself as
the sea in a chasm, struggling to be
free and unable to be,
    in its surrendering
    finds its continuing.

So he who strongly feels,
behaves. The very bird,
    grown taller as he sings, steels
his form straight up. Though he is captive,
his mighty singing
says, satisfaction is a lowly
thing, how pure a thing is joy.
    This is mortality,
    this is eternity.

From the music of Brahms to the music of birds, Moore's language carries a musical sense. She had a knack for putting down onto paper the things that she saw.

Propriety

in some such word
    as the chord
    Brahms had heard
    from a bird,
sung down near the root of the throat;
it's the little downy woodpecker
    spiraling a tree—
    up up up like mercury;

a not long
sparrow-song
    of hayseed
    magnitude—
a tuned reticence with rigor
from strength at the source. Propriety is
    Bach's Solfegietto—
    harmonica and basso.

The fish-spine
on firs, on
    somber trees
    by the sea's
walls of wave-worn rock—have it; and
a moonbow and Bach's cheerful firmness
    in a minor key.
    It's an owl-and-a-pussy-

both-content
agreement.
    Come, come. It's
    mixed with wits'
it's not a graceful sadness. It's
resistance with bent head, like foxtail
    millet's. Brahms and Bach,
    no; Bach and Brahms. To thank Bach

for his
first, is wrong.
    Pardon me;
    both are the
unintentional pansy-face
uncursed by self-inspection; blackened
    because born that way.

Keeping Their World Large

All too literally, their flesh and their spirit are our
    shield.

New York Times, June 7, 1944

    I should like to see that country's tiles, bed-
    rooms,
stone patios
    and ancient wells: Rinaldo
Caramonica's the cobbler's, Frank Sblendorio's
    and Dominick Angelastro's country—
    the grocer's, the iceman's, the dancer's—the
    beautiful Miss Damiano's; wisdom's

and all angels' Italy, this Christmas Day

273

© 1993, Compact Classics, Inc.

this Christmas year.
A noiseless piano, an innocent war, the
heart that can act against itself.
Here,
each unlike and all alike, could
so many—stumbling, falling, multiplied
till bodies lay as ground to walk on—

"If Christ and the apostles died in vain,
I'll die in vain with them"
against this way of victory.
That forest of white crosses!
My eyes won't close to it.

All laid like animals for sacrifice—
like Isaac on the mount,
were their own sacrifice.

Marching to death, marching to life?
"Keeping their world large,"
whose spirits and whose bodies
all too literally were our shield,
are still our shield.

They fought the enemy,
we fight fat living and self-pity.
Shine, o shine,
unfalsifying sun, on this sick scene.

Nevertheless

you've seen a strawberry
that's had a struggle; yet
was, where the fragments met,

a hedgehog or a star-
fish for the multitude
of seeds. What better food

than apple-seeds—the fruit
within the fruit—locked in
like counter-curved twin

hazel-nuts? Frost that kills
the little rubber-plant-
leaves of kok-saghyz-stalks, can't

harm the roots; they still grow
in frozen ground. Once where
there was a prickly-pear-

leaf clinging to barbed wire,
a root shot down to grow
in earth two feet below;

as carrots form mandrakes
or a ram's-horn root some-
times. Victory won't come

to me unless I go
to it; a grape-tendril
ties a knot in knots till

knotted thirty times,—so
the bound twig that's under-
gone and over-gone, can't stir.

The weak overcomes its
menace, the strong over-
comes itself. What is there

like fortitude! What sap
went through that little thread
to make the cherry red!

The process of creative expression—in particular, that of master musicians, artists, and of course, writers—intrigued the poet.

The Paper Nautilus

For authorities whose hopes
are shaped by mercenaries?
Writers entrapped by
teatime fame and by
commuters' comforts? Not for these
the paper nautilus
constructs her thin glass shell.

Giving her perishable
souvenir of hope, a dull
white outside and smooth-
edged inner surface
glossy as the sea, the watchful
maker of it guards it
day and night; she scarcely

eats until the eggs are hatched.
Buried eight-fold in her eight
arms, for she is in
a sense a devil-
fish, her glass ram'shorn-cradled freight
is hid but is not crushed;
as Hercules, bitten

by a crab loyal to the hydra,
was hindered to succeed,
the intensively
watched eggs coming from
the shell free it when they are freed,—
leaving its wasp-nest flaws
of white on white, and close-

laid Ionic chiton-folds
like the lines in the mane of
a Parthenon horse,
round which the arms had
wound themselves as if they knew love
is the only fortress
strong enough to trust to.

Moore attempted to give permanence to temporal things, using language and a sharp eye to capture a "verbal photograph" for the reader to contemplate.

Silence

My father used to say,
"Superior people never make long visits,
have to be shown Longfellow's grave
or the glass flower at Harvard.
Self-reliant like the cat—
that takes its prey to privacy,
the mouse's limp tail hanging like a shoelace from
its mouth—
they sometimes enjoy solitude,
and can be robbed of speech
by speech which has delighted them.
The deepest feeling always shows itself in silence;
not in silence, but restraint."
Nor was he insincere in saying, "Make my house
your inn."
Inns are not residences.

T. S. ELIOT

(1888 - 1965)

Burnt Norton

Time present and time past
Are both perhaps present in time future,
And time future contained in time past.
If all time is eternally present
All time is unredeemable.
What might have been is an abstraction
Remaining a perpetual possibility
Only in a world of speculation.
What might have been and what has been
Point to one end, which is always present.
Footfalls echo in the memory
Down the passage which we did not take
Towards the door we never opened . . . .

Though Thomas Stearns Eliot published only a few of his poems, his influence on twentieth-century verse has been vast and profound. He struggled against the artistic temperament of Victorian England in an effort to find a new way of illustrating the world. Most of his work is a curious mix of opposites: dark and light, hope and despairing, hate and love.

Eliot was the grandson of a Unitarian minister. In St. Louis, Missouri, Eliot studied in private schools, then left for Harvard where he received his M.A. degree. Traveling to Europe, England became his adopted homeland, where he converted to the Anglican Church. He found work with Faber and Faber Publishing, eventually becoming its director.

That poetry required "hard labour" for both writer and reader was Eliot's thinking, and poetry should not be limited to common language—like an advertising jingle.

On occasion, Eliot would speak with a different voice, simply for effect. In the following poem, the speaker addresses the listener like a Biblical prophet.

Gerontion

Here I am, an old man in a dry month,
Being read to by a boy waiting for rain.
I was neither at the hot gates
Nor fought in the warm rain
Nor knee deep in the salt marsh, heaving a cut-
*   lass,*
Bitten by flies, fought.
My house is a decayed house . . . .

Signs are taken for wonders. "We would see a
*   sign!"*
The word within a word, unable to speak a word
Swaddled with darkness. In the juvescence of
*   the year*
Came Christ the tiger

In depraved May, dogwood and chestnut, flow-
*   ering judas,*

To be eaten, to be divided, to be drunk
Among whispers . . . .
After such knowledge, what forgiveness? Think
*   now*
History has much cunning passages, contrived
*   corridors*
And issues, deceives with whispering ambitions
Guides us by vanities. Think now
She gives when our attention is distracted
And what she gives, gives with such supple con-
*   fusions*
That the giving famishes the craving. Gives too
*   late*
What's not believed in, or if still believed
In memory only, reconsidered passion . . . .

Unnatural vices
Are fathered by our heroism. Virtues
Are forced upon us by our impudent crimes . . .

And an old man driven by the Trades
To a sleepy corner.

Tenants of the house,
Thoughts of a dry brain in a dry season

In *The Love Song of J. Alfred Prufrock*, Eliot assumes the voice of an old man. The narrator, however, is actually a young man imagining himself in old age, lamenting a past lived without risk or passion. After inviting the reader through "certain half-deserted streets,/ The muttering retreats/ Of restless nights in one-night cheap hotels . . " the poem turns to a central concern:

. . . And indeed there will be time
For the yellow smoke that slides along the street,
Rubbing its back upon the window panes;
There will be time, there will be time
To prepare a face to meet the faces that you
*   meet;*
There will be time to murder and create,
And time for all the works and days of hands
That lift and drop a question on your plate;
Time for you and time for me,
And time for a hundred indecisions,
And for a hundred visions and revisions,
Before the taking of toast and tea.

In the room the women come and go
Talking of Michelangelo.

And indeed there will be time
To wonder 'Do I dare?' And, 'Do I dare?'
Time to turn back and descend the stair,
With a bald spot in the middle of my hair . . . .
Do I dare
Disturb the universe?

The narrator continues, sorrowing, "I have measured out my life with coffee spoons," and "No! I am not Prince Hamlet,

275

© 1993, Compact Classics, Inc.

nor was meant to be."

I grow old . . . I grow old . . .
I shall wear the bottoms of my trousers rolled.
Shall I part my hair behind? Do I dare to eat a
*   peach?*
I shall white flannel trousers and walk . . . .
I have heard the mermaids singing, each to each.
I do not think that they will sing to me.
I have seen them riding seaward on the waves
Combing the white hair of the waves blown back
When the wind blows the water white and
*   black.*
We have lingered in the chambers of the sea
By sea-girls wreathed with seaweed red and
*   brown*
Til human voices wake us, and we drown.

Distressed by the apparent shallowness of life and the lack of God and meaning in modern times, the poet turned his pen to this disheartening theme again and again. In *The Wasteland*, Eliot focused his poetic powers, enormous knowledge, and great imagination to create what some consider his greatest work.

The Wasteland
I. The Burial of the Dead

April is the cruelest month, breeding
Lilacs out of the dead land, mixing
Memory and desire, stirring
Dull roots with spring rain.
Winter kept us warm, covering
Earth in forgetful snow, feeding
A little life with dried tubers . . . .

What are the roots that clutch, what branches
*   grow*
Out of this stony rubbish? Son of Man,
You cannot say, or guess, for you know only
A heap of broken images, where the sun beats,
And the dead tree gives no shelter, the cricket no
*   relief*
And the dry stone no sound of water . . . .
And I will show you something different from
*   either*
Your shadow at morning striding behind you
Or your shadow at evening rising to meet you;
I will show you fear in a handful of dust.

Eliot's work next focused on his fleeting memories. In the *Unreal City* his thoughts turn to the bleak streets of London:

. . . Under the brown fog of a winter dawn,
A crowd flowed over London Bridge, so many,
I had not thought death had undone so many.
Sighs, short and infrequent, were exhaled,
And each man fixed his eyes before his feet . . .

There in the crowded byways, overheard conversations show loss of communication and sordidness; families and friends elicit a sense of separateness; humanity is wrenched apart, to exist in wretched, lonely hovels. Rats dot the landscape. Then enters Tiresias—a seer who is both male and female—who proceeds to foretell the future stark lives of Londoners, destined to naught amid "oil and tar" riding the surface of a river's water and the merchandising of everything and everyone.

My friend, blood shaking my heart
The awful daring of a moment's surrender
Which an age of prudence can never retract
By this, and this only, we have existed
Which is not to be found in our obituaries
Or in memories draped by the beneficent spider
Or under seals broken by the lean solicitor
In our empty rooms . . .
. . . I have heard the key
Turn in the door once and turn once only
We think of the key, each in his prison
Thinking of the key, each confirms a prison . . .

DOROTHY PARKER
(1893-1967)

"It was quite a childhood: a terrifying father hammering her wrists; a rather lunatic stepmother hammering at her mind; a sister and a brother too remote in age for any communion; the servants put out of reach by social convention . . . She hated being a Jew and began to think that her mother had deserted her by dying. She began to hate herself." So a childhood friend describes the adolescent life of Dorothy Parker. From the time she was born until the day she died, it was an anguished and lonely existence.

Her mother, Eliza Marston Rothschild, died shortly after Dorothy's birth. Subsequently, she was raised by her Jewish father, whom she feared, and her devoutly Catholic stepmother, whom she hated.

Complicated by the fact that she, a Jewish girl, was sent to the Catholic school at the Blessed Sacrament Convent, Dorothy was troubled and unable to assimilate. Eventually, she was expelled for insisting that the Immaculate Conception was really spontaneous combustion. Sent to Miss Dana's private boarding school, Dorothy received an intensely traditional education. Though the social rules were excessively strict, the academic atmosphere was exceptionally fertile, and the poet within her began to unfold.

Following her graduation, Parker held a series of writing jobs for various magazines. While employed by *Vogue* and *Vanity Fair*, her caustic and impeccable wit became well-known, and eventually her literary trademark. Monthly morticians' journals were frequent sources of inspiration for the titles of her poems, stories, and books.

Despite the severe bitterness that dominates her writing, there was a more caring side. Compassion found expression through social activism. Being no stranger to pain and suffering, Parker was quick to take up the causes of others. In 1927 she marched against the execution of Sacco and Vanzetti; later, she helped to found the Anti-Nazi League. During the McCarthy era, Parker was blacklisted by the California State Senate Committee on Un-American activities because of her financial contributions to learning centers in communist countries. She appeared before the New York State joint legislative committee in 1955 and pled the Fifth Amendment.

When Parker died of a heart attack at age 73, she left the bulk of her estate to the Reverend Martin Luther King Jr. She had never met him, yet admired him greatly and wanted to aid his cause.

It is not surprising that Parker left her estate to a stranger rather than to a loved one; her personal life was turbulent and sad. Commenting on Parker's final years, one of her friends wrote: "Her captains and kings had long departed. I saw her . . . before she died . . . and she said, in effect, that all those she loved were dead, and that she, herself, had been dead for a long time." The combination of a painful life mixed with a droll, sardonic wit, resulted in a truly unique poetic voice.

Drawing on her own traumatic relationships with men, Parker's chosen poetic theme was often love—or rather, failed love:

Unfortunate Coincidence

By the time you swear you're his
Shivering and sighing,
And he vows his passion is
Infinite, undying—
Lady, make a note of this:
One of you is lying.

As in *Unfortunate Coincidence*, Parker's poems tend to follow the conventional rules of rhyme and rhythm. The fact that she adheres to such conventional rules makes her piercing wit all the more effective. The musical quality of her language lulls the reader along, then strikes with venomous sarcasm and cynicism:

Indian Summer

In youth, it was a way I had
To do my best to please,
And change, with every passing lad,
To suit his theories.

But now I know the things I know,
And do the things I do;
And if you do not like me so,
To hell, my love, with you!

Godspeed

Oh, seek, my love, your newer way;
I'll not be left in sorrow.
So long as I have yesterday,
Go take your damned tomorrow!

Experience

Some men break your heart in two,
Some men fawn and flatter you,
Some men never look at you;
And that cleans up the matter.

General Review of the Sex Situation

Woman wants monogamy;
Man delights in novelty.

Love is woman's moon and sun;
Man has other forms of fun.
Woman lives but in her lord;
Count to ten, and man is bored.
With this the gist and sum of it,
What earthly good can come of it?

Love Song
. . . My love runs by like a day in June,
And he makes no friends of sorrows.
He'll tread his galloping rigadoon
In the pathway of the morrows.
He'll live his days where the sunbeams start,
Nor could storm or wind uproot him.
My own dear love, he is all my heart—
And I wish somebody'd shoot him.

Men
They hail you as their morning star
Because you are the way you are.
If you return the sentiment,
They'll try to make you different;
And once they have you, safe and sound,
They want to change you all around.
Your moods and ways they put a curse on;
They'd make of you another person.
They cannot let you go your gait;
They influence and educate.
They'd alter all that they admired.
They make me sick, they make me tired.

News Item
Men seldom make passes
At girls who wear glasses.

Symptom Recital
I do not like my state of mind;
I'm bitter, querulous, unkind.
I hate my legs, I hate my hands,
I do not yearn for lovelier lands.
I dread the dawns's recurrent light;
I hate to go to bed at night.
I snoot at simple, earnest folk.
I cannot take the gentlest joke.
I find no peace in paint or type.
My world is but a lot of tripe.
I'm disillusioned, empty-breasted.
For what I think, I'd be arrested.
I am sick, I am not well.
My quondam dreams are shot to hell.
My soul is crushed, my spirit sore;
I do not like me any more.
I cavil, quarrel, grumble, grouse.
I ponder on the narrow house.
I shudder at the thought of men . . .
I'm due to fall in love again.

The topic of life itself is treated skepti-cally by Parker. Aside from failed love, the single most prominent theme in her poetry is death:

The Flaw in Paganism
Drink and dance and laugh and lie,
Love, the reeling midnight through,
For tomorrow we shall die!
(But, alas, we never do.)

Cherry White
I never see that prettiest thing—
A cherry bough gone white with Spring—
But what I think, "How gay 'twould be
To hang me from a flowering tree."

Coda
There's little in taking or giving,
There's little in water or wine;
This living, this living, this living
Was never a project of mine.
Oh, hard is the struggle, and sparse is
The gain of the one at the top,
For art is a form of catharsis,
And love is a permanent flop,
And work is the province of cattle,
And rest's for a clam in a shell,
So I'm thinking of throwing the battle—
Would you kindly direct me to hell?

"The Small Hours"
No more my little song comes back;
And now of nights I lay
My head on down, to watch the black
And wait the unfailing gray.

Oh, sad are winter nights, and slow;
And sad's a song that's dumb;
And sad it is to lie and know
Another dawn will come.

Epitaph
The first time I died, I walked my ways;
I followed the file of limping days.

I held me tall, with my head flung up,
But dared not look on the new moon's cup.

I dared not look on the sweet young rain,
And between my ribs was a gleaming pain.

The next time I died, they laid me deep.
They spoke worn words to hallow my sleep.

They tossed me petals, they wreathed me fern,
They weighted me down with marble urn.

And I lie here warm, and I lie here dry,
And watch the worms slip by, slip by.

Resume
Razors pain you;
Rivers are damp;
Acids stain you;
And drugs cause cramp.
Guns aren't lawful;
Nooses give;
Gas smells awful;
You might as well live.

Using her wit as a defense against her pained existence, Parker's naked honesty redefined poetic expression. It was life from a different angle, a contrary and bitter viewpoint. As she often said, in more than sarcastic tones: "You might as well live."

OGDEN NASH

(1902 - 1971)

Arthur

There was an old man from Calcutta,
Who coated his tonsils with butta,
Thus converting his snore
From a thunderous roar
To a soft, oleaginous mutta.

Widely known as a writer of light, humorous, and satirical poetry, Ogden Nash was appreciated and imitated by both his peers and rivals. And even since his death, his reputation has continued to grow.

Nash is famous for combining wit and imagination with memorable rhyme. He began his career, however, writing serious poetry—sonnets and other works concerning "beauty, truth, and pain." But this early phase did not last long. "I had better laugh at myself before anyone laughs at me," he once said. Not long after, he started writing his characteristic brand of poetry dealing with the minor idiocies of humanity.

After first publishing his poems in *The New Yorker* magazine, Nash's first book, **Hard Lines,** met with immediate success. It introduced a variety of themes that Nash would continue to explore. Other books of poetry included **Many Long Years Ago** (1945), **You Can't Get There From Here** (1957), **The Old Dog Barks Backwards** (published after his death, 1972), and **I Wouldn't Have Missed It** (1975).

Nash's biting commentaries on society marked the beginning of his satirical verse, and announced his two major themes: the countless problems of the contemporary city and the futility of the human quest for meaning. In fact, though whimsical in nature, his poetry cuts to the heart of deep human issues; it ridicules what he considered foolish behavior—including his own.

The poem *More About People,* for example, reflects on the inexplicable correlation between work and survival.

When people aren't asking questions
They're making suggestions
And when they're not doing one of those
They're either looking over your shoulder or stepping on
   your toes
And then as if that weren't enough to annoy you
They employ you
Anybody at leisure
Incurs everybody's displeasure
It seems to be very irking
To people at work to see other people not working
So they tell you that work is wonderful medicine
Just look at Firestone and Ford and Edison
And they lecture you till they're out of breath or something
And then if you don't succumb they starve you to death
   or something
All of which results in a nasty quirk
That if you don't want to work you have to work to earn
   enough money so that you won't have to work

Nash was unconcerned about meter in his poetry; nor did he worry that the lines of his poems were unequal in length. He often stretched sentences over several lines to produce eye-opening and comical rhymes, as can be seen in *The Terrible People:*

People who have what they want are very
   fond of telling people who haven't what
   they want that they really don't want it,
And I wish I could afford to gather all
   such people into a gloomy castle on
   the Danube and hire half a dozen
   capable Draculas to haunt it

The complications of modern American life and the idiosyncracies of city living were, to Nash, food for thought, as is evident in the poem, *I WILL ARISE AND GO NOW,* written in 1949.

In far Tibet
There live a lama,
He got no poppa,
He got no momma . . .

He got no soap,
He got no opera,
He don't know Geritol
From copra,

Got no opinions
Controversial,
He never hear
TV commercial . . .

He use no lotions
For allurance,
He got no car
And no insurance.

No Alsop warnings,
No Reston rumor
For this self-centered
Nonconsumer.

Indeed, the
Ignorant Have-Not
Don't even know
What he ain't got.

If you will mind
The box-tops, comma,
I think I'll go
And join that lama.

This same urban theme can also be seen in City Greenery:

If you should happen after dark
To find yourself in Central Park,
Ignore the paths that beckon you
And hurry, hurry to the zoo,
And creep into the tigers lair.
Frankly, you'll be safer there.

Nash drew much inspiration from the animal world. His writing often showed great esteem for these souls, God's creatures.

Abasbenadhem

. . . The finest of the human race
Are bad in figure worse in face.
Yet just because they have two legs
And come from storks instead of eggs
They count the spacious firmament
As something to be charged and sent

Though man created cross-town traffic,
The Daily Mirror, News and Graphic,
The pastoral flight and fighting pastor,
And Queen Marie and Lady Astor,

He hails himself with drum and fife
And bullies lower forms of life.

Not that I think that much depends
On how we treat our feathered friends,
Or hold the wrinkled elephant
A nobler creature than my aunt.
It's simply that I'm sure I can
Get on without my fellow man.

The Turtle
The turtle lives twixt plated decks
Which practically conceal its sex.
I think it clever of the turtle
In such a fix to be so fertile.

The Mules
In a world of mules
There are no rules

The poet loved to play with language, pushing puns, often grouping combinations of strange words, cleverly comparing apparently unrelated objects, inventing words, or misspelling real words to maintain his rhyme and create a carefully planned effect:

Reflection of the Fallibility of Nemesis
He who is ridden by a conscience
Worries about a lot of nonscience;
He without benefit of scruples
His fun and income soon quadruples.

After the birth of his first child, Nash dealt in verse with the subject of parenthood.

Don't Cry Darling, It's Blood Alright
Whenever poets want to give you the idea that something is
particularly meek and mild,
They compare it to a child.
Thereby proving that though poets with poetry may be rife
They don't know the facts of life.
If of compassion you desire either a tittle or a jot,
Don't try to get it from a tot . . .
. . . Therefore I say unto you, all you poets who are so crazy about meek and mild little children and their angelic air,
If you are sincere and really want to please them, why, just go out
and get yourself devoured by a bear.

My Daddy
I have a funny daddy
Who goes in and out with me,
And everything that baby does
My daddy's sure to see,
And everything that baby says,
My daddy's sure to tell
You must have read my daddy's verse.
I hope he fries in hell.

In the following pieces, Nash focuses on age and death. Still he manages to maintain a certain element of comedy to prevent the works from crossing into the morbid:

The Middle
When I remember bygone days
I think how evening follows morn;
So many I loved were not yet dead,
So many I love were not yet born

Crossing the Border
Senescence begins

And middle age ends
The day your descendants
Outnumber your friends.

Old Men
People expect old men to die,
They do not really mourn old men.
Old men are different. People look
At them with eyes that wonder when
. . . People watch with unshocked eyes;
But the old men know when an old man dies.

Nash, the master humorist, in the poem Pastoral explores a rural scene, getting right to the heart of the situation.

Pastoral
Two cows
In a marsh
Mildly munching
Fodder harsh.
Cow's mother,
Cow's daughter
Mildly edging
Brackish water.
Mildly munching
Wile heron,
Brackish minded,
Waits like Charon.
Two cows,
Mildly mooing;
No bull;
Nothing doing.

Although Nash kept a very loose sense of rhythm and meter, he was extremely adept at limerick-style ditties.

Samson Agonistes
I test my bath before I sit,
And I'm always moved to wonderment
That what chills the finger not a bit
Is so frigid upon the fundament.

Limerick One
An elderly bride of Port Jervis
Was quite understandably nervis,
Since her apple-cheeked groom,
With three wives in the tomb,
Kept insuring her during the service.

Benjamin
There was a brave girl of Connecticut
Who flagged the express with her pecticut
Which critics defined
As presence of mind,
But deplorable absence of ecticut.

The Termite
Some primal termite knocked on wood
And tasted it, and found it good,
And that is why your Cousin May
Fell through the parlor floor today.

The Parsnip
The parsnip, children, I repeat,
Is simply an anemic beet.
Some people call the parsnip edible;
Myself I find this claim incredible.

The Octopus
Tell me, O Octopus, I begs,
Is those things arms, or is they legs?
I marvel at thee, Octopus;
If I were thou, I'd call me Us.

DYLAN THOMAS

(1914-1953)

*. . . He's a stranger, outside the season's
    humours,
Moves, among men caught by the sun,
With heart unlocked upon the gigantic earth.
He alone is free, and, free, moans to the sky.
. . . Even among his own kind he is lost,
Is love a shadow on the wall,
Among all living men is a sad ghost.
He is not a man's or woman's man,
Leper among a clean people
Walks with the hills for company,
And has the mad trees' talk by heart . . .*

So begins a semi-biographical work of
poetry by Dylan Thomas, *Poet: 1935*.
Obscure, cryptic, difficult to follow, nevertheless the potency emanating from his
works radiates with energy. Although his
poetry was veiled in riddle, Thomas himself was open, easy going, and well liked.

Thomas was born in Wales, son of an
English teacher who had poetic aspirations
himself. Though the youth's academic
career was unremarkable, he did excel in
English. He began entering poetry con-
tests—which he often won—in *The Sunday
Referee*, a local newspaper. From 1934-1936,
Thomas published two books: *Eighteen
Poems* and *Twenty-Five Poems*.

A third book, *The Map of Love*, containing prose pieces as well as verse, was
published in 1939. His last English volume
of new verse was *Death and Entrances*,
published in 1946, and yet another antholo-
gy, *Collected Poems 1934-1952*, was in print
before Thomas' exhausting American tour
during which he became critically ill. On
November 9, 1953, he succumbed to a high
fever.

Thomas' death was greatly mourned;
the critics felt Thomas was just hitting his
stride both as a poet and writer. Over the
years hence, his work has traveled the spectrum between critical acclaim and derision.
In recent years, his poetry has enjoyed
renewed interest, with Thomas himself
becoming a sort university English department "icon."

Most of Thomas' poetry is traditional
in nature, focusing on birth, death, love,
sex, and religion. Intermingling of these
disparate themes, however, is his true hall-
mark. *Written for a Personal Epitaph*, published at age 16, shows the poet's intuitive
skill in blending themes—as well as an
early preoccupation with death:

*Feeding the worm
Who do I blame
Because laid down
At last by time,
Here under the earth with girl and thief,*

*Who do I blame?
Mother I blame
Whose loving crime
Moulded my form
Within her womb,
Who gave me life and then the grave,
Mother I blame.
Here is her labour's end,
Dead limb and mind,
All love and sweat
Gone now to rot.
I am man's reply to every question,
His aim and destination.*

Not easily deciphered by the casual
reader, his works are often compared to
"puzzles" and "forbidding cliffs." His
images are vivid, but not always easy to
categorize. *Epitaph* demonstrates this early
tendency toward abstraction, but his work
just a few years later had become more
complex, more imaginative, as represented
by the following piece, *The Force That
Through the Green Fuse Drives the Flower*.
Apparently, Thomas considered both his
own life and that of the world as linked in
fate and controlled by the same forces.

*The force that through the green fuse drives the
    flower
Drives my green age; that blasts the roots of
    trees
Is my destroyer.
And I am dumb to tell the crooked rose
My youth is bent by the same wintry fever . . . .*

By his early 20s, with the publication
of *Twenty-Five Poems*, Thomas' verses had
become extremely difficult to interpret. Its
density was deliberate, as he compacted as
many images as he could into a small space.
Critic Edith Sitwell, trying to analyze his
writing, claimed that his density was
"largely the result of the intense concentration of each phrase, packed with meaning,
of the fusion (not confusion) of two profound thoughts." (*Sunday Times, September
1936.*)

Typical of that fused density are the
ten sonnets included in *Altarwise By Owl-
light*.

VIII

*This was the crucifixion on the mountain,
Times nerve in vinegar, the gallow grave
As tarred with blood as the bright thorns I wept;
The world's my wound, God's Mary in her
    grief,
Bent like three trees and bird-papped through
    her shift,
With pins for tear drops is the long wound's
    woman.
This was the sky, Jack Christ, each minstrel*

angle
Drove in the heaven-driven of the nails
Till the three-colored rainbow from my nipples
From pole to pole leapt round the snail-waked
world.
I by the tree of thieves, all glory's sawbones,
Unsex the skeleton this mountain minute,
And by this blowcock witness of the sun
Suffer the heaven's children through my heart-
beat.

Some of Thomas' symbology is clear in this sonnet, while some is left undeciphered. Easily evident are the references to the mountain, vinegar, thorns, Mary, and the tree of thieves. Other allusions are left for readers to interpret for themselves. For his part, Thomas never supplied interpretations, insisting that the *images* were the all-important element. His feelings about those who attempt to decipher mean are clear in these lines:

To Others Than You
Friend by enemy I call you out.

You with a bad coin in your socket,
You my friend there with a winning air
Who palmed the lie on me when you looked
Brassily at my shyest secret . . .
. . . I never thought to utter or think
While you displaced a truth in the air,

That though I love them for their faults
As much as for their good,
My friends were enemies on stilts:

With their heads in a cunning cloud.

Twenty-Five Poems marked a transition in Thomas' style and subject matter. Rather than follow the literary trends of his day, he decided to return to more simplistic themes and language. This poem reflects his decision.

I HAVE LONGED TO MOVE AWAY
I have longed to move away
From the hissing of the spent lie
And the old terrors' continual cry
Growing more terrible as the day
Goes over the hill into the deep sea;
I have longed to move away
From the repetition of salutes,
From there are ghosts in the air
And ghostly echoes on paper,
And the thunder of calls and notes.

I have longed to move away but am afraid;
Some life, yet unspent, might explode
Out of the old lie burning on the ground,
And crackling into the air leave me half-
blind . . .

After the Funeral is also less complex, typical of the new direction Thomas had taken.

AFTER THE FUNERAL
(In memory of Ann Jones)
. . . I know her scrubbed and humble sour hands
Lies with religion in their cramp, her threadbare
Whisper in a damp word, her wits drilled hol-
low,
Her fist of a face clenched on a round pain;
And sculptured Ann is seventy years of
stone . . . .

In his best-known poem, written in homage to his dying father, Thomas disciplined himself in both form and word, demonstrating that, far from stemming from a lack of skill, his customary free-flowing style was deliberate.

Do Not Go Gently Into That Goodnight
Do not go gentle into that good night,
Old age should burn and rave at close of day;
Rage, rage against the dying of the light.

Though wise men at their end know dark is
right,
Because their words had forked no lightning
they
Do not go gentle into that good night.

Good men, the last wave by, crying how bright
Their frail deeds might have danced in a green
bay,
Rage, rage against the dying of the light.

Wild men who caught and sang the sun in
flight,
And learn, too late, they grieved it on its way,
Do not go gentle into that good night.

Grave men, near death, who see with blinding
sight
Blind eyes could blaze like meteors and be gay,
Rage, rage against the dying of the light.

And you, my father, there on the sad height,
Curse,bless, me now with your fierce tears, I
pray.
Do not go gentle into that good night.
Rage, rage against the dying of the light.

Finally, Thomas' talent is displayed in rare form in *The Conversation of Prayer*. (Here the hidden rhymes have been highlighted to show that they indeed exist.) As the images—that of a boy going downstairs to pray and an old man going upstairs to comfort his dying wife—cross, so do the rhymes.

THE CONVERSATION OF PRAYER
The conversation of **prayers** about to be **said**
By the child going to **bed** and the man on the
stairs
Who climbs to his dying **love** in her high **room,**
The one not caring to **whom** in his sleep he will
move
And the other full of fears that she will be
dead . . .

SYLVIA PLATH

(1932-1963)

POPPIES IN OCTOBER

Even the sun-clouds this morning cannot manage
such skirts.
Nor the woman in the ambulance
Whose red heart blooms through her coat so
astoundingly—

A gift, a love gift
Utterly unasked for
By a sky

Palely and flamily
Igniting its carbon monoxides, by eyes
Dulled to a halt under bowlers.

O my God, what am I
That these late mouths should cry open
In a forest of frost, in a dawn of cornflowers.

Sylvia Plath was born in Boston, Massachusetts. When she was eight, her English professor father died—a loss from which she would never recover.

Just a few months after her father's death, Plath published her first poem in the *Boston Traveller*. She attended Smith College and Newnham College on scholarship, and entered several writing contests, all of which she won. While at Newnham, she met another poet named Ted Hughes, whom she married. After receiving her masters degree, Plath returned to Smith, where she taught English until moving to England some years later.

Plath's first poems, it seemed, were churned out tediously, nursed by the thesaurus and the dictionary. Plath became known for her ruthless perceptions of her own work—if she didn't like a word or a line in a poem, she scrapped the entire piece. She studied different styles in an effort to find one that would fully express the anguish she felt. In fact, critics say Plath didn't truly find her own voice until after her second child was born in 1962.

Some critics have suggested that Plath's creativity stemmed from her self-destructiveness. Even as an infant she possessed this tendency. On one occasion when the little one-year-old was sitting on the beach, she immediately crawled toward the ocean, unafraid, not stopping at the water's edge. Plath's mother had to rush into the crashing waves to drag her petulant child out of the water.

At 19, Plath attempted suicide. Not unexpectedly, her poetry in the preceding months had become rife with symbols of death. Her husband, writing later, confessed that by then Plath's "poetry and death became inseparable." Still, her suffering, likely originating with the death of her father, proved to be a powerful creative impetus.

Plath explored other voices in addition to poetry. She published a radio play, a children's book, a collection of short stories, and a novel titled *The Bell Jar*, written under the pseudonym Victoria Lucas.

Soon after separating from her husband and giving birth to her second child, the breadth and depth of Plath's poetry both accelerated and expanded; gone were the plodding forays into the thesaurus and the dictionary. *The Bell Jar* was published just one month before Plath's death. After the publication of her novel, she turned to writing poetry even more frantically than before, sometimes drafting three or four complete works a day.

Sylvia Plath once claimed, "Dying is an art . . . I do it exceptionally well." On February 11, 1963, she took her own life.

Ironically, Plath felt an almost pathological aversion to desecration of plant and animals, or to ruin of any type, for that matter. In particular, she considered the Holocaust one of humanity's greatest insults. Using the disturbing metaphors of a Nazi death camp, she lashed out in bitterness and anger at her father's death. *Daddy* is thought to be a thinly-veiled, allegoric look into Plath's own life and death (though, of course, many of the lines are figurative).

Daddy

You do not do, you do not do
Any more, black shoe
In which I have lived like a foot
For thirty years, poor and white,
Barely daring to breathe or Achoo.

Daddy, I have had to kill you.
You died before I had time—
Marble-heavy, a bag full of God,
Ghastly statue with one grey toe
Big as a Frisco seal

And a head in the freakish Atlantic
Where it pours bean green over blue
In the waters off beautiful Nauset.
I used to pray to recover you.
Ach, du.

In the German tongue, in the Polish town
Scraped flat by the roller
Of wars, wars, wars.
But the name of the town is common.
My Polack friend

Says there are a dozen or two.
So I never could tell where you
Put your foot, your root,
I never could talk to you.
The tongue stuck in my jaw.

It stuck in a barb wire snare.
Ich, ich, ich, ich,
I could hardly speak.
I thought every German was you.
And the language obscene

An engine, an engine
Chuffing me off like a Jew.
A Jew to Dachau, Auschwitz, Belsen.
I began to talk like a Jew.
I think I may well be a Jew.

The snows of the Tyrol, the clear beer of Vienna
Are not very pure or true.
With my gypsy ancestress and my weird luck

And my Taroc pack and my Taroc pack
I may be a bit of a Jew.

I have always been scared of you
With your Luftwaffe, your gobbledygoo.
And your neat moustache.
And your Aryan eye, bright blue.
Panzer-man, panzer-man, O You—

Not God but a swastika
So black no sky could squeak through.
Every woman adores a Fascist,
The boot in the face, the brute
Brute heart of a brute like you . . .

. . . If I've killed one man, I've killed two—
The vampire who said he was you
And drank my blood for a year,
Seven years, if you want to know.
Daddy, you can lie back now.

There's a stake in your fat black heart
And the villagers never liked you.
They are dancing and stamping on you.
They always knew it was you.
Daddy, daddy, you bastard, I'm through.

In *Lady Lazarus*, Plath exclaims, "I have
done it again. One year in every ten I manage
it." Apparently referring to her previous suicide attempt, these lines became ironically
prophetic.

Lady Lazarus
I have done it again.
One year in every ten
I manage it—

A sort of walking miracle, my skin
Bright as a Nazi lampshade,
My right foot

A paperweight,
My face a featureless, fine
Jew linen.

Peel off the napkin
O my enemy.
Do I terrify?—

The nose, the eye pits, the full set of teeth?
The sour breath
Will vanish in a day.

Soon, soon the flesh
The grave cave ate will be
At home on me

And I a smiling woman.
I am only thirty.
And like the cat I have nine times to die.

This is Number Three.
What a trash
To annihilate each decade.

What a million filaments.
The peanut-crunching crowd
Shoves in to see

Them unwrap me hand and foot—
The big strip tease.
Gentleman, ladies,

These are my hands,
My knees.
I may be skin and bone,

Nevertheless, I am the same, identical woman.
The first time it happened I was ten.
It was an accident.

The second time I meant
To last it out and not come back at all.
I rocked shut

As a seashell.
They had to call and call
And pick the worms off me like sticky pearls.

Dying
Is an art, like everything else.
I do it exceptionally well . . .

In the poet's most hopeful moments, she
shows a strong and sensitive attention to
beauty—rather like an anaesthesia for the pain
that haunted her. In *Black Rook in Rainy
Weather*, she hopes for a piecing together of
lovely, inspiring moments to defend and
shield herself against despair. Painful as her
story is, her moments of celebration are rare—
but momentous.

Black Rook in Rainy Weather
On the stiff twig up there
Hunches a wet black rook
Arranging and rearranging its feathers in the rain.
I do not expect miracle
Or an accident

To set the sight on fire
In my eye, nor seek
Any more in the desultory weather some design,
But let spotted leaves fall as they fall,
Without ceremony, or portent

Although, I admit, I desire,
Occasionally, some backtalk
From the mute sky, I can't honestly complain:
A certain minor light may still
Leap incandescent

Out of kitchen table or chair
As if a celestial burning took
Possession of the most obtuse objects now and
    then—
Thus hallowing an interval Otherwise inconse-
    quent

By bestowing largesse, honor,
One might say love. At any rate, I now walk
Wary (for it could happen
Even in this dull, ruinous landscape); skeptical,
Yet politic; ignorant

Of whatever angel may choose to flare
Suddenly at my elbow. I only know that a rook
Ordering its black feathers can so shine
As to seize my senses, haul
My eyelids up, and grant

A brief respite from fear
Of total neutrality. With luck
Trekking stubborn through this season
Of fatigue, I shall
Patch together a content

Of sorts. Miracles occur,
If you care to call those spasmodic
Tricks of radiance miracles. The wait's begun
    again,
The long wait for the angel,
For that rare, random descent.

SHEL SILVERSTEIN

(1932-   )

"I want to go everywhere, look at and listen to everything. You can go crazy with some of the wonderful stuff there is in life."

Shel Silverstein collects his "stuff of life" in the form of highly imaginative poetry and distorted line drawings.

Born in Chicago, Illinois, in 1932, Silverstein began drawing and writing at around age 14 He admits: " . . . I couldn't play ball, I couldn't dance. Luckily, the girls didn't want me." Since those early years, he has established himself as a journalist, a composer, a playwright, a cartoonist, a lyricist, and a folksinger—and appeared in a 1971 movie. Even in the 1950s as a U.S. Army private in Korea and Japan, Silverstein served as a cartoonist for the Pacific edition of the *Stars and Stripes*, the American military newspaper.

Silverstein, a former ad-copy writer, never set out to be a writer of children's verse until a friend urged him to visit Ursula Nordstrom, a children's book editor. Nordstrom, after much persuasion, finally convinced Silverstein that he could write for children. Ever since, he has produced books and poems that resonate with energy, attracting large followings of both juvenile and adult readers.

Silverstein's *The Giving Tree* was published in 1964, becoming his best-known work. However, most of his poetry is found in two larger works titled *The Light In the Attic* and *Where the Sidewalk Ends*.

Astute observation of children and adults interacting with other children and adults mixed with advice, both good and bad, are Silverstein's trademarks.

Listen to the MUSTN'TS

Listen to the MUSTNTS, child,
Listen to the DON'TS
Listen to the SHOULDN'TS
The IMPOSSIBLES, the WON'TS
Listen to the NEVER HAVES
Then listen close to me—
Anything can happen, child
ANYTHING can be.

In *Hector the Collector*, Silverstein parodies the things people value most. Hector is very much surprised that what to him is a treasure is not appreciated by others:

Hector the Collector
Collected bits of string,
Collected dolls with broken heads
And rusty bells that would not ring.
Pieces out of picture puzzles,
Bent-up nails and ice-cream sticks,
Twists of wires, worn-out tires,
Paper bags and broken bricks.
Old chipped vases, half shoelaces,

Gatlin' guns that wouldn't shoot,
Leaky boats that wouldn't float
And stopped-up horns that wouldn't toot.
Butter knives that had no handles,
Copper keys that fit no locks,
Rings that were too small for fingers,
Dried-up leaves and patched-up socks.
Worn-out belts that had no buckles,
'Lectric trains that had no tracks,
Airplane models, broken bottles,
Three-legged chairs and cups with cracks.
Hector the Collector
Loved these things with all his soul—
Loved them more than shining diamonds,
Loved them more than glistenin' gold.
Hector called to all the people,
"Come and share my treasure trunk!"
And all the silly sightless people
Came and looked . . . and called it junk.

Another poem that raises doubts about the value of things is *Ol' Man Simon*.

Ol' man Simon, planted a diamond,
Grew hisself a garden the likes of none.
Sprouts all growin', comin' up glowin',
Fruit of jewels all shinin' in the sun.
Colors of the rainbow,
See the sun and rain grow
Sapphires and rubies of ivory vines,
Grapes of jade, just
Ripenin' in the shade, just
Ready for the squeezin' into green jade wine.
Pure gold corn there,
Blowin' in the warm air,
Ol' crow nibblin' on the amnythyst [sic] seeds.
In between the diamonds, ol' man Simon
Crawl about pullin' out platinum weeds.
Pink pearl berries,
All you can carry,
Put 'em in a bushel and
Haul 'em into town.
Up in the tree there's
Opal nuts and gold pears—
Hurry quick, grab a stick
And shake some down.
Take a silver tater,
Emerald tomater,
Fresh plump coral melons
Hangin' in reach.
Ol' man Simon,
Diggin' in his diamonds,
Stops and rests and dreams about
One . . . real . . . peach.

The theme of frugality bordering on stinginess appears in a sad-silly poem called *Lester*, in which the character is given a magic wish by the goblin in the banyan tree. Lester, a clever lad, wishes for two more wishes, turning his one into three. The wishing for more wishes goes on and on, until Lester has "Five billion, seven million, eighteen thousand thirty-four" wishes. He then spreads them on the ground and dances around them, all the while wishing for more, and more, and more. Silverstein then concludes with the moral of his story:

. . . While other people smiled and cried
And loved and reached and touched and felt.
Lester sat amid his wealth
Stacked mountain-high like stacks of gold,
sat and counted—and grew old.

Lester died, and when he was found with his zil-
lions of wishes it was discovered that not one
was missing.
In a world of apples and kisses and shoes
He wasted his wishes on wishing.

Silverstein's commentary on what is of true worth carries over into a sly little poem that parody's children's fears. In it, he paints the imagined fears as absurd, and therefore, manageable.

THE GOOGIES ARE COMING

The googies are coming, the old people say,
To buy little children and take them away.
Fifty cents for fat ones,
Twenty cents for lean ones,
Fifteen cents for clean ones,
A nickel each for mean ones.

The googies are coming, and maybe tonight,
To buy little children and lock them up tight.
Eighty cents for husky ones,
Quarter for the weak ones,
Penny each for noisy ones,
A dollar for the meek ones.

Forty cents for happy ones,
Eleven cents for sad ones.
And, kiddies, when they come to buy,
It won't do any good to cry.
But—just between yourself and I—
They never buy the bad ones!

The poem *Ma and God* sets up an amusing conflict between the two supreme beings in any child's life, and then specu-lates on who is really the higher authority:

God gave us fingers — Ma says, "Use your
fork."
God gave us voices — Ma says, "Don't
scream."
Ma says eat broccoli, cereal and carrots.
But God have us tasteys for maple ice cream.

God gave us fingers — Ma says, "Use your
hanky."
God gave us puddles — Ma says, "Don't
splash."
Ma says, "Be quiet, your father is sleeping."
But God gave us garbage can covers to crash.

God gave us fingers — Ma says, "Put your
gloves on."
God gave us raindrops — Ma says, "Don't get
wet."

Ma says be careful, and don't get too near to
Those strange lovely dogs that God gave us to
pet.
God gave us fingers — Ma says, "Go wash
'em."
But God gave us coal bins and nice dirty bodies.
And I ain't too smart, but there's one thing for
certain —
Either Ma's wrong or else God is.

In *How Not To Dry the Dishes* Silverstein offers practical advice to any child wishing to escape the duty and drudgery of dishwashing:

If you have to dry the dishes
(Such an awful, boring chore)
If you have to dry the dishes
('Stead of going to the store)
If you have to dry the dishes
And you drop one of the floor
Maybe they won't let you
Dry the dishes anymore.

But Silverstein's poetry is not all naughtiness and dubious advice. Much of his work takes on a more whimsical, funny style. *Me-Stew* and *Moon-Catchin' Net* are two of many pieces that capture his knack for fanciful whimsy—a knack that charac-terizes the true genius of Shel Silverstein.

Me-Stew

I have nothing to put in my stew, you see,
Not a bone or a bean or a black-eyed pea,
So I'll just climb in the pot to see
It I can make a stew out of me.
I'll put in some pepper and salt and I'll sit
In the bubbling water—I won't scream a bit.
I'll sing while I simmer, I'll smile while I'm
stewing,
I'll taste myself often to see how I'm doing.
I'll stir me around with this big wooden spoon
And serve myself up at a quarter to noon.
So bring out your stew bowls,
You gobblers and snackers.
Farewell—and I hope you enjoy me with crack-
ers!

Moon-Catchin' Net

I've made me a moon-catchin' net,
And I'm goin' huntin' tonight,
I'll run along swingin' it over my head,
and grab for that big ball of light.

So tomorrow just look at the sky,
And if there's no moon you can bet
I've found what I sought and I finally caught
The moon in my moon-catchin' net.

But if the moon's still shinin' there
Look close underneath and you'll get
A clear look at me in the sky swingin' free
With a star in my moon-catchin' net.

JACK PRELUTSKY

(1940-   )

The Ways of Living Things

There is wonder past all wonder
in the ways of living things,
in a worm's intrepid wriggling,
in the song a blackbird sings,
In the grandeur of an eagle
and the fury of a shark,
in the calmness of a tortoise
on a meadow in the dark,
... In a fish's joyful splashing,
in a snake that makes no sound,
in the smallest salamander
there is wonder to be found.

One of Jack Prelutsky's most serious poems, "The Ways of Living Things" is long on humor and vivid imagery that bring to life the real and imaginary animals that stride across the landscape of his work.

Born in Brooklyn, New York, to an electrician father and a housewife mother, Prelutsky was a brilliant and precocious child, yet restless and nonconforming in school. However undisciplined his behavior, he did exhibit one glorious talent: an exceptional singing voice. By age ten, he sang regularly at weddings and other occasions. Later, he attended a music-oriented high school in New York.

Prelutsky's path to fame as an opera singer came to an end after he heard the great Italian tenor, Luciano Pavarotti. Knowing he could never sing like that, he moved on to other endeavors. From one occupation to the next, he spent much of his time traveling and playing the guitar.

Feeling that his life was meant to be spent in the arts but not content being a folk singer, Prelutsky ventured into drawing, spending an entire six months creating imaginary animals and writing short poems for each. At the urging of a friend, Prelutsky submitted his work for publication and was informed that his poetry had potential in the poetry, but not his drawings. Thus encouraged, Prelutsky set out to create poems that would peak children's interest. Foregoing the trend to write "deep" and "meaningful" verse, he focused on nonsense lines laced with colorful imagery.

Prelutsky's work resonates within a child's imagination. Designed to be read out loud, some of the poems contain tongue twisters. Thus, as a child moves through a poem, here and there he learns something new about words, nature, dinosaurs—or himself.

Prelutsky's amusing poems often play to the natural curiosity children have about animals.

Alligators Are Unfriendly

Alligators are unfriendly,
they are easily upset,
I suspect that I would never
care to have one for a pet.
I know they do not bellow,
and I think they do not shed,
but I'd probably be nervous
if I had one in my bed.

Alligators are not clever,
they are something of a bore,
they can't heel or catch a Frisbee,
they don't greet you at the door,
for their courtesy is lacking,
and their tempers are not sweet,
they won't even fetch your slippers
... though they just might eat your feet.

Animals—both real and imaginary—that might be unfamiliar to children are described in ways that create vivid mental pictures.

The Yak

Yickity-yackity, yickity-yak,
the yak has a scriffily, scraffily back;
some yaks are brown yaks and some yaks are black,
yickity yackity, yickity-yak.

Sniggildy-snaggildy, sniggildy-snag,
the yak is all covered with shiggildy-shag;
he walks with a ziggildy-zaggildy-zag,
sniggildy-snaggildy, sniggildy-snag ...

Help

Can anybody tell me, please,
a bit about the thing
with seven legs and furry knees,
four noses and a wing?

Oh what has prickles on its chin,
what's yellow, green and blue,
and what has soft and slimy skin?
Oh tell me, tell me, do.

And tell me, what has polka dots
on every other ear,
what ties its tail in twenty knots,
what weeps a purple tear?

Oh what is growling long and low
and please, has it been fed?
I think I'd really better know ...
it's sitting on my head.

Prelutsky sometimes concludes his poems with a punch line or otherwise unexpected surprise.

The Sheriff of Rottenshot

The sheriff of Rottenshot, Jogalong Jim,
wore a one-gallon hat with a ten-gallon brim.

© 1993, Compact Classics, Inc.

287

He was short in the saddle and slow on the
    draw,
but he was the sheriff, his word was the law.

Jogalong Jim didn't know how to fight,
his boots were too big and his britches too tight,
he wasn't too bright and he wasn't too brave,
and he needed a haircut, a bath and a shave.

His rifle was rusty and couldn't shoot straight,
his bony old pong groaned under his weight.
The sheriff of Rottenshot, Jogalong Jim,
was lucky that nobody lived there but him.

The thought of eating strange things
can be extremely funny to children.

Twickham Tweer

Shed a tear for Twickham Tweer
who ate uncommon meals,
who often peeled bananas
and then only ate the peels,
who emptied jars of marmalade
and only ate the jars,
and only ate the wrappers
from his chocolate candy bars.

Though he sometimes cooked a chicken,
Twickham only ate the bones,
he discarded scoops of ice cream
though he always ate the cones,
he'd boil a small potato
but he'd only eat the skin,
and pass up canned asparagus
to gobble down the tin,

He daily dined on apple cores
and bags of peanut shells,
on cottage cheese containers,
cellophane from caramels.
Poor Twickham Tweer passed on last year,
that odd and novel man,
when he fried an egg one morning
and then ate the frying pan.

Nigel Gline

When Nigel Gline sat down to dine,
he yawned, "This meal's a bore!
It's nothing more than what I've had
a thousand times before.
I'm through with cheese and chocolate,
I'm done with beans and beef,
I'd like a tasty tree instead."
So Nigel ate a leaf.

He liked that leaf, and swallowed more,
then nibbled on a twig,
that hardly seemed to be enough,
his appetite was big,
the twigs were so delicious
that he started on a limb,
soon every branch upon that tree
had vanished into him.

"It's time to try the trunk!" he said,
and ate it on the spot,
the bark was easy to digest,

the knots, of course, were not.
Now Nigel Gline declines to dine,
deep roots grow from his toes,
and birds nest in the leafy boughs
that stem from Nigel's nose.

Prelutsky overstates problems that
most children face such as the stress of
homework and the trauma of moving, col-
oring them with humor. Through exaggeration and fantasy, he helps children deal sensibly with their very real concerns.

A Remarkable Adventure

I was at my bedroom table
with a notebook open wide,
when a giant anaconda
started winding up my side,
I was filled with apprehension
and retreated down the stairs,
to be greeted at the bottom
by a dozen grizzly bears.

We tumultuously tussled
till I managed to get free,
then I saw, with trepidation,
there were tigers after me,
I could feel them growing closer,
I was quivering with fear,
then I blundered into quicksand
and began to disappear.

I was rescued by an eagle
that descended from the skies
to embrace me with its talons,
to my terror and surprise,
but that raptor lost its purchase
when a blizzard made me sneeze,
and it dropped me in a thicket
where I battered both my knees.

I was suddenly surrounded
by a troop of savage trolls,
who maliciously informed me
they would toast me over coals,
I was lucky to elude them
when they briefly looked away—
that's the reason why my homework
isn't here with me today.

We Moved About a Week Ago

We moved about a week ago,
it's nice here, I suppose,
the trouble is, I miss my friends,
like Beth, who bopped my nose,
and Jess, who liked to wrestle
and dump me in the dirt,
and Liz, who found a garter snake
and put it down my shirt.
    . . . the more I think about them,
the more it makes me sad,
I hope I make some friends here
as great as those I had.

LARRY LEVIS

(1946-)

The voice in the poetry of Larry Levis is often alone, watching, contemplating both the rough and the tender edges between people. His work addresses the music, cities, and personalities that inhabit realms. These "rough and tender" poems touch upon both human connection and separation. Often referring to people's "souvenirs"—personal symbols, objects and places by which people interact with other people during the course of their lives.

Born in Fresno, California, Levis' academic career centered on English and writing, culminating with a PhD in Modern Letters from the University of Iowa. Having authored five books of poetry and one collection of short stories, Levis' first publication, *The Wrecking Crew*, won many honors, including the United States Award of the International Poetry Forum. *The Afterlife* won the Lamont Award of the American Academy of Poets in 1976. *The Dollmaker's Ghost* won the Open Competition of the National Poetry Series. The fourth collection, Winter Stars, was published in the Pitt Poetry Series in 1985. Other awards include three fellowships in poetry from the National Endowment for the Arts, a Fulbright and a Guggenheim Fellowship.

From a single scene and a nondescript group of characters, Levis reaches out and grabs his reader's entire being. A poem—such as *Decrescendo*—may begin with the story of a nameless group of musicians in a nameless bar on no one particular night, but then it becomes larger, pulling the whole world, bit by bit, it seems, into the emotional landscape.

Decrescendo

If there is only one world, it is this one.

In my neighborhood, the ruby-helmeted woodpecker's line
Is all spondees, & totally formal as it tattoos
Its instinct & solitude into a high sycamore which keeps

Revising autumn until I look out, &
Something final will be there: a branch in winter—not
Even a self-portrait. Just a thing.

Still, it is strange to live alone, to feel something
Rise up, out of the body, against all that is,
By law, falling & turning into the pointless beauty

Of calendars. Think of the one in the office closed
For forty-three summers in a novel by Faulkner, think
Of unlocking it, of ducking your head slightly
And going in. It is all pungent, & lost. Or

It is all like the doomed singers, Cooke & Redding,
Who raised their voices against the horns
Implacable decrescendos, & knew exactly what they

Were doing, & what they were doing was dangerous.

The man on sax & the other on piano never had to argue
Their point, for their point was time itself; & all
That one wished to say, even to close friends,
One said beside that window: The trees turn; a woman
Passing on the street below turns up her collar against
The cold; & if the music ends, the needle on the phono-

graph
Scrapes like someone raking leaves, briefly, across
A sidewalk, & no one alone is, particularly, special.

That is what musicians are for, to remind us of this, unless

Those singers die, one shot in a motel room
By a woman who made a mistake; & one dead
In a plane crash, an accident.

Which left a man on sax & another on piano
With no one to back up, &, hearing the news,
One sat with his horn in a basement in Palo Alto,
Letting its violence go all the way up, &
Annoying the neighbors until the police came,
And arresting him—who had, in fact, tears
In his eyes. And the other, a white studio
Musician from L. A., who went home & tried

To cleave the keyboard with his hands until
They bled, & his friends came, & called his wife,
And someone went out for bandages & more bour-
bon—

Hoping to fix up, a little, this world.

One of Levis' strengths is his ability to perceive—and define—the spaces between people. He might use the distance between lovers, for example, to define the characters' relationship; the love—or lack of love—between father and son can also be given a spacial correlation. " ... We do *not* choose, & do not fall apart. But we are apart," reads a line in the poem *Oklahoma*.

"Distance" and "detachment," implies Levis, are not synonyms. Neither is aloneness synonymous with loneliness: sometimes, being alone makes us lonely. Sometimes, however, the bliss of solitude, especially after daily confronting a collective mass of humanity, is the most potent elixir of the soul.

Oklahoma

Often, I used to say: I am this dust; or, I am this wind.
And young, I would accept that. The truth is, it was never the case.
I have seen enough dust & wind by now to know
I am a little breath that always goes the distance
Longing requires, & to know even this will fail
The truth is, dear friends, we fall apart;
And for mysterious reasons, not entirely clear to us,
We choose to live alone. The truth is,

We do not choose, & do not fall apart. But are apart.
She

Dresses in the dark of a New Year, &, if she had been born a
Catholic,
She might cross herself. But she is not a Catholic.
To clothe the temple of the soul, & that music
When the last bell on the toe of the dancer stops,
She puts on a gray silk dress, a fur coat.

It is snowing in Iowa City.

In the Old World, there was always another season.
The unpicked fruit about to fall. Nursing,
The painful suckling of infants by new mothers,

© 1993, Compact Classics, Inc.

And an unchecked laughter from the workingmen's bar
Among long closed streets of wharves & warehouses
With a quiet as old as habit, or the worn sky

Over all the sleeping Bibles. I suppose was simply

Smug, & male.

❖ ♦ ❖

I rise, & put on my precisely faded jeans, a black
   Hawaiian shirt
With ridiculous light yellow roses; & sharp-toed
Cowboy boots.
     Style, after all, is a kind of humor,
Something truly beneath contempt.

Even here, on the Southern Plains, in Oklahoma City.

Though something, beneath the armor we put on,
Is always missing, the trouble with this wind
Is that it drives the land away: These raw cuts
In the red dirt of the roadside almost speak for them-
   selves.
Are they painful? They look as if they once were.
Someday, see for yourself, & take care when you
Do so. Look closely, but take care.
And put your arms around each other's waists so you
   don't
Slip through to anything truer
Than you meant to be.

The earth, for example, has often been a lie,

And the wind its rumor.

Together once, they drove all
The better people away.

    There emerges an urban flavor in some of
the poems, bleak yet beautiful images of gritty
people bustling about—and accomplishing little.

My Story in a Late Style of Fire
Whenever I listen to Billie Holiday, I am reminded
That I, too, was once banished from New York City.
Not because of drugs or because I was interesting
   enough
For any wan, overworked patrolman to worry about—
His expression usually a great, gauzy spiderweb of
   bewilderment
Over his face—I was banished from New York City by
   a woman.
Sometimes, after we had stopped laughing, I would look
At her & see a cold note of sorrow or puzzlement go
Over her face as if someone else were there, behind it,
Not laughing at all. We were, I think, "in love." No,
   I'm sure.
If my house burned down tomorrow morning, & if I &
   my wife
And son stood looking on at the flames, & if, then,
Someone stepped out of the crowd of bystanders
And said to me: "Didn't you once know . . . ?" No.
   But if
One of the flames, rising up in the Scherzo of fire,
   turned
All the windows blank with light, & if that flame could
   speak,
And if it said to me: "You loved her, didn't you?" I'd
   answer,
Hands in my pockets, "Yes." And then I'd let fire &
   misfortune
Overwhelm my life . . .
   . . . That morning, when she asked me to leave, wear-
ing only
That apricot tinted, fraying chemise, I wanted to stay.
But I also wanted to go, to lose her suddenly, almost
For no reason, & certainly without any explanation.
I remember looking down at a pair of singular tracks
Made in a light snow the night before, at how they were
Gradually effacing themselves beneath the tires
Of the morning traffic, & thinking that my only other
   choice
Was fire, ashes, abandonment, solitude. All of which
   happened
Anyway, & soon after, & by divorce. I know this isn't
   much.
But I wanted to explain this life to you, even if
I had to become, over the years, someone else to do it.
You have to think of me what you think of me. I had
To live my life, even its late, florid style. Before
You judge this, think of her. Then think of fire,
Its laughter, the music of splintering beams & glass,
The flames reaching through the second story of a
   house
Almost as if to—mistakenly—rescue someone who
Left you years ago. It is so American, fire. So like us.
Its desolation. And its eventual, brief triumph.

    Memories are held as much in places and
objects as they are in people's hearts and minds. In
the previous poem, the flame spoke to the writer,
drawing out of his inner self an honest answer, a
guileless response that a mere person could not
elicit.
    In the following poem, the waves too hold
memories and questions, but they will not release
their historical recollections nor seek answers to
their doubts concerning human existence.

Late Semptember in Ulcinj
—for Colleen McElroy

Birth & Death own the little walled cottages;
Since one's illiterate, the other always speechless,
There's no real way of meeting either.
And what did you come here for if not to hear
Finality in the soft click of a latch,
Or in the long thou of the empty wavebreak?
The rocks glistening for a second after it
Would find it strange that they meant anything.
And the gull's cry, & the sore screech of a winch
On a fishing boat a hundred yards offshore,
Are the poor speech of everything there is,
An unregretting blossoming & humming.

You walked beside the ancient, mottled walls,
Listening, it seemed then, to nothing.
And it's only later you remember, if at all,
The clattering of dishes, the fading dawn & cat
   calls,
Sausages the color of overcast skies on a grill,
And a group of soldiers marching on the square,
Repeating the routine motions of some drill,
And someone lost, someone muttering to herself,
The cafe's emptier than abandoned puzzles . . .

The sea wall overlooked the rocks, the choppy
   water,
Four teenagers playing solemnly with a knife
Whose falling shadow told each one of a fortune,
And a woman reading something on the beach
Who yawned, stretched, & seemed to fall asleep.
It was the custom to wear nothing there,
Where the wave sprawl on the rock cannot
   remember.

COMPACT

Classics®

LIBRARY #4: World Religions

The selections in this library address the crucial questions that life poses to every member of the human family: What is my destiny? Who or what is God—the Supreme Being—and what does this God ask of me? How can I unite with my God?

In almost all of today's living religions, East and West, the directions these questions have taken are marked by the emergence of great leaders or prophets who have infused a transcendent vision into the traditions that shaped them. Our first library section, "Living World Religions—Origins and Doctrines," will introduce you to these leaders and their visions, and to the movements and precepts that emerged from them. The second and third sections, which spotlight the world's great religious texts, will introduce you to the actual voices of Jesus, Mohammed, Confucius, and the Buddha, and of Augustine, Luther, Calvin and other great disciples and pioneers.

Of course—and regrettably—these sections are not, in any sense, to be considered as complete or as categorically accurate. We have tried to offer as much information as can be coherently organized within the space available. Wherever possible, summaries have been read and edited by knowledgeable, ranking clerics from each of the groups represented; however, some beliefs and emphases within a sect will obviously differ from congregation to congregation and even from individual to individual. Also, we regret that space compels us to limit our scope here to movements claiming approximately one million or more adherents.

Here, then, is a sampler and a silhouette of the living, time-honored faiths that have shaped the heart of our world.

Section A: Living World Religions - Origins & Doctrines——— 293 to 318

Section B: Middle-Eastern/Eastern Works ———————————

Section C: Judeo-Christian Works ———————————

Virtually every religion contributes to the world's overall spiritual landscape. Since hundreds of thousands of distinctly different methods of worship exist around the world, it would be difficult, if not impossible, to document every single religious movement and its doctrine. Therefore, the following section only includes those churches that claim at least 1 million adherents worldwide.

The information in the following sections was compiled from many different sources and represents a generalized outline of each religion's tenets. They do not take into account the differences of opinion that may arise within various congregations. Also, these treatments are not intended to provide an in-depth doctrinal analysis of the world's major religions. They are simply introductions to what many people around the world believe.

❖ ◆ ❖

Seventh-day Adventist

The term "adventist" has been used to denote those movements whose doctrines are founded on the second coming, or advent, of Christ. The adventist movement originated in early nineteenth century discussions concerning this event. At that time, several prominent scholars from the Church of England, as well as other European theologians, concluded that the second advent of Christ was near.

In America, a similar movement sprang into existence. A major group, comprising members from many different religions, was led by a farmer named William Miller. Through his own scriptural interpretations, Miller predicted that Christ would appear in 1844. When 1844 came and went without Jesus' return, the movement lost momentum and eventually dwindled in numbers until only a small group remained.

Undeterred, this group maintained that Biblical prophecies about Jesus' return could be correctly interpreted and claimed an accurate prediction could be made. Thus, still convinced that Christ would soon return, they continued to research the Bible hoping to better understand prophecies concerning the advent of Christ. After much deliberation, this group came to the conclusion that the world must be warned *before* Christ could ever come again. From this movement grew the Seventh-day Adventist church.

Currently, the Seventh-day Adventist religion claims more than 3.5 million adherents. The church also supports close to 40,000 full-time missionaries outside America. Many of these workers are health-care providers in a world-wide chain of Seventh-day Adventist hospitals and clinics.

Seventh-day Adventist Fundamentals

A distinctive and fundamental Seventh-day Adventist doctrine holds that the Sabbath actually falls on Saturday, not Sunday. Seventh Day Adventists borrowed this doctrine—known as the Sabbath Truth—from the Seventh-day Baptists. The foundation of this doctrine comes from Orthodox Judaism—Jesus' religion—which has always observed the Sabbath on Saturday. Also, since Christians assert that Christ rose on the first day of the week, which was a Sunday, Saturday must be the Seventh Day—the Sabbath.

Since adventists are fundamentally Christian in their beliefs and practices, they observe common Christian conventions such as Baptism, the Holy Trinity and the Virgin Birth. They baptize by immersion, claiming to follow the example of Christ in the New Testament. Seventh-day Adventists believe that the doctrine of the Virgin Birth is essential to fundamental Christian belief, saying that without it, Christ could not have assumed the qualities of God while in the form of a man.

The Trinity, according to Seventh-day Adventists, is comprised of "three persons in one God." These three personages are God the Father, the Son and the Holy Spirit. The key to salvation rests in having faith in the atoning sacrifice of Jesus Christ. They believe Christ is the King of Kings, the Lord of Lords, and the one who will eventually rule the earth.

Seventh-day Adventists do not share the common belief that a person's spirit enters heaven or hell immediately upon death. Instead, they maintain that the dead "sleep" until the return of Jesus Christ, when all souls will be resurrected and judged according to their faith.

Adventists believe salvation comes by grace alone. Therefore, all must acquire faith in Jesus Christ. Good works, penance or wealth are not guarantors of achieving salvation—faith alone will save man.

Though all will be saved by their faith and not by their works, Seventh-day Adventists believe that good works are a manifestation of an individual's faith. The Bible outlines 10 very specific commandments as well as provides several exhortations uttered by Christ himself. Not simply a matter of obligation or responsibility, keeping these commandments exemplifies an individual's love for Christ. Like Jesus said, "If ye love me, keep my commandments" (John, 14:15).

- Seventh-day Adventists closely follow the teachings of Paul who wrote that the body is a "temple of the Holy Spirit." As such, the body must not be defiled by alcohol, tobacco or other harmful substances.

- Adventists believe Christ's return will be heralded by tremendous political and religious events that will involve the earth's entire population.

- The Seventh-day Adventist religion maintains it is founded not on "new doctrines," but on "old truths." Adventists claim these "old truths" were obscured by pagan traditions.

- Early adventists made a practice of predicting the date of Christ's return. The Seventh-day Adventist church, however, does not. Although Christ's return is imminent, as signaled by the fulfilling of prophecy, no one knows when that event will take place.

◇ ◆ ◇

Anglican (Church of England and Episcopalian)

Note: The Church of England and the Episcopal Church are simply two denominations of the same doctrinal and historic tradition. For this reason, both are included under this heading.

The Church of England and the Episcopal Church are two denominations with virtually the same doctrinal tradition. In America and Scotland the Church of England is known as the Episcopal Church; it functions as an autonomous branch of the Anglican Communion. In most places, members of the Church of England, including Episcopalians, are called Anglicans.

The Anglican church formally originated in 1532 when King Henry VIII severed England's ties with Rome and declared himself Supreme Head of the Church in England. However, this does mark the beginning of the Anglican Church as much as it marks the culmination of centuries of reform.

As early as the mid-1300's, John Wycliffe—an English religious scholar—denounced the office of the Pope on the grounds that papal authority had no scriptural precedent. Furthermore, Wycliffe taught that the Bible should be considered the single source of doctrine—a source to which no ecclesiastical authority could add.

Then, at the beginning of the 16th century, Thomas Cramner, the archbishop of Canterbury, introduced a reformed liturgy written in common language. This work, called *The Book of Common Prayer*, provides the foundation for Anglican doctrine.

Cramner also introduced a new edition of the Bible, which he and a corroborator, William Tyndale, had translated. Cramner also issued a series of 42 "Articles of Religion" which outlined the doctrine of the reformed church. All of these actions helped bring about the establishment of the Anglican church.

Several different movements in Europe had already begun to question Papal authority, but these groups were inhibited by powerful church and state ties between the Roman Catholic Church and various European governments. While King Henry was not, technically, the founder of the Anglican Church—there was no central founder—he should be given credit for providing the necessary freedom under which the Reformation could flourish in England.

In 1537, King Henry ordered the Tyndale Bible—also known as Cramner's Great Bible—placed in all the churches of his kingdom. But, facing pressure from hard-line Catholics who found common access to scripture objectionable, he soon reversed this order. He also issued the Six Articles Act in which he reaffirmed Catholic belief. From the start, Henry's intention was to establish a Catholic Church in England that was independent from Rome and its papal authority.

Henry's separation from the Roman Catholic Church culminated with Pope Leo refusing to grant him a divorce from his wife Catherine of Aragon when she remained childless. The Pope refused on the grounds that the king sought the annulment in order to marry another woman. In 1532, King Henry became infuriated with the church and used this as an excuse to part ways with the pontiff. He renounced the pope and declared himself Supreme Head of the Church in England. He then annulled his union with Catherine and promptly married Anne Boleyn. However, Catherine's daughter Mary, a loyal Catholic, was deeply embittered by Henry's actions; after Henry's death, she forcibly reintroduced Catholicism to England. In 1553, she married a Spanish prince and punished those who would not renounce their Reformist beliefs. In her zeal, she ordered the execution of many Anglicans, including Thomas Cramner. True to his reputation as a waffler, Cramner renounced his beliefs during his trial. But, after he was sentenced to death anyway, he immediately reversed his testimony and died at the stake as a martyr for the Anglican cause. The bloody reign of Mary ended just five years after it began when Mary's successor, Elizabeth, reintroduced Anglicanism to England in 1558.

By that time, however, the Anglican

Church was facing pressure on two fronts: the Roman Catholic Church was in a state of self-reformation following the Council of Trent, causing dissatisfied Anglicans to take a closer look at Catholicism and, within the Anglican Church, as well as other Protestant movements, the Puritans were pushing for a revised service book that more resembled the ascetic teachings of John Calvin. The Puritans also favored the elimination of the episcopacy—the ranks of bishops that governed the Anglican church. Eventually, the *Book of Common Prayer* was prohibited and the episcopacy was eliminated as England became a commonwealth. But when monarchy was restored in 1660, the previous organization of the Anglican Church was also restored.

It is important to note that Henry VIII is not the founder of the Anglican church. His renunciation of the Roman Catholic Church's centralized power was simply a catalyst for putting to end the unrest that had been building in England as English Catholics became increasingly uneasy with Pope Leo's arbitrary usurpations of authority.

In the 1570's, the Anglican Church spread to America, primarily through English explorers who almost exclusively possessed Anglican chaplains. These chaplains baptized Native Americans as well as colonists in Virginia. The church quickly spread, especially in the South, in spite of the fact that ministers had to travel back to England for ordination. Kings Chapel in Boston (now a Unitarian edifice) was the first Episcopal church in New England.

The Anglican Communion is a group of 25 Anglican Churches, of which there are close to 70 million members. Membership in the Church of England is estimated between 1.5 and 1.7 million.

Anglican Fundamentals

Anglican and Catholic ideas about God closely correspond to each other. That is, the manner in which God chooses to reveal himself is the nature of God. Anglicans believe God is Creative Reality (God the Father), Expressive Act (God the Son) and Responsive Power (God the Holy Spirit). This doctrine is defined in the *Book of Common Prayer*, the basis for Anglican belief. This work contains the abridged and revised liturgies from old Roman Catholic service books that were circulated in the early 1500's.

Anglicans believe that Jesus Christ is "truly God, and truly man, united in one person." His mortal manifestation was accomplished for the salvation of mankind through the crucifixion, and through the proclamation of discipleship by baptism. Christ also instituted the sacraments which Anglicans hold to be sacred: Baptism, Confirmation, Communion, Marriage and Holy Unction. Anglicans reaffirm their faith through the Apostle's Creed and the Nicean Creed—both of which are statements of belief in God. These two creeds also illustrate the Catholic origins of the Anglican Church, since they are fundamental credos of the Roman Catholic church.

Since the *Book of Common Prayer* makes provisions for the private confession of sins to a priest, many Anglicans follow this practice and are granted absolution by their confessor. Unlike the Roman Catholic church, however, this is entirely optional. Confession, both private and general, are considered to be "means of grace," though one is not "better" than the other. Absolution can be granted through regular church services as well.

Beliefs about heaven and hell generally follow Catholic teachings. Anglicans consider heaven a condition where those who have lived a life of "perfect service to God" have the chance to revel in His spirit. Conversely, hell corresponds to a state of alienation from God. Those who possess the potential for goodness spend time in a purifying state before they are admitted into the presence of God's spirit. Though this parallels Catholic doctrine, the term "Purgatory" is not used in Anglican teaching.

Anglicans consider salvation as the "health and wholeness" of life. Only God can grant deliverance from earthly encumbrances such as selfishness and arrogance. Resurrection signifies a union of one's "whole" personality—not with a physical body but with a spiritual body, which is defined as an "instrument of self-expression."

Each Anglican congregation is administered by a Bishop who oversees the administrative and theological needs of the church. The Anglican Communion is governed by a House of Bishops, made up of area Bishops who are elected to represent the various Anglican dioceses and a House of Deputies, comprised of electees who are made up of ministers and other officials of non-Bishop status. Together, these two Houses are referred to as the Episcopate.

Fast Facts

• The term, "episcopal" comes from the Greek word *episkopos*, which means "overseer" (or bishop).

• Episcopalians believe in the principles of confession and absolution, but private confessions are not required of members. The church grants forgiveness of sins during a regular worship service.

• Unlike other Protestant groups, there are several communities of Episcopalian monks and nuns around the world.

- Episcopalian clergy are allowed to marry if they choose.

- By retaining Catholic doctrine almost in its entirety while rejecting papal authority, Anglicans are uniquely Catholic *and* Protestant.

⋄ ♦ ⋄

Baptists

The Baptist movement is thought to have originated from two different Protestant groups of the early 1600s—the Separationists and the Puritans. John Smyth, a preacher from the Church of England, founded what has become the Baptist church after renouncing the episcopacy in favor of a more individualized form of worship. He and his followers formed the first recorded Baptist congregation in 1609.

Baptist Fundamentals

Baptists traditionally avoid interpreting the "essence" of God. They generally recognize the Trinity as a manifestation of God in three separate personages: God the Father, Jesus Christ and The Holy Ghost. The physical nature of these personages remains less important than how they function. Baptist's can simply accept them without predicting their form.

The Baptist religion is not as much a "church" as it is a denominational movement. While the term "church" is used for convention, it refers to any Baptist congregation that has adapted the fundamental doctrines of baptism by immersion and preaches faith in Jesus Christ as its central tenet. Any group of believers can form their own congregation, which then becomes an entity unto itself. Although denominated Baptists, they are not subject to any authority higher than that found within the congregation itself.

Understandably, doctrine about specific issues varies widely from congregation to congregation. The common thread shared among Baptists entails a public confession of Christian faith as manifested through baptism by immersion. Christ reigns as the central figure in Baptist theocracy and is considered the only accepted authority when it comes to religious questions.

Sacraments are not generally practiced among Baptists, though the first Sunday of every month is set aside for a communion service. The bread and cup the members partake of during this service are symbolic in that they serve as memorial icons to the Last Supper. The spiritual meaning derived from the service is completely up to the individual and is not dictated by the officiating clergy.

The ultimate goal for Baptists is achieving salvation. Salvation, however, is a subjective term and means different things to different people. Baptist doctrine emphasizes this individual outlook. It is not up to the church to provide salvation, it is up to the individual to secure his own. Generally, this is accomplished by becoming a true believer in Christ.

Since it is not the church's obligation to intervene in this process, confession of sin is a matter between the individual and God. Salvation will be granted to those who can give evidence of having lived a Christian life, through faith in Christ and the good works that result from that faith.

Fast Facts

- With 26 million members, the Baptist church is the largest Protestant movement in the United States.

- The largest national population of Baptists outside the U. S. is located in the former Soviet Union, with more than 550,000 members.

- The largest Baptist group in the world is the Southern Baptist Convention—including more than 34,000 churches and their 11 million members.

⋄ ♦ ⋄

Buddhism

Note: Buddhism comprises literally hundreds of schools of doctrine and discipline. These beliefs are not always complimentary and are occasionally even contradictory. For this reason, this treatment only deals with those beliefs most generally accepted by Buddhist schools.

Buddhism was founded in the fifth century B.C. by Siddhartha Gautama, a mystic who forsook Hindu philosophy in favor of seeking "Truth." Born into a powerful ruling family in northeastern India, Gautama enjoyed many privileges while growing up. He married very young and became a father, but a seer had predicted that Gautama's future held two possibilities: he would either become a world ruler or a homeless wanderer. The seer predicted the boy would become a wanderer if he saw, either together or separately, an old man, a diseased man, a corpse and a well-dressed monk.

A wealthy and powerful man who wanted his son to follow after him, Gautama's father unsuccessfully prevented him from seeing these things. While such sights might be considered unpleasant or useless, Gautama learned important lessons from all of these signs. From the first three spectacles he learned the relative insignificance of worldly things, and the fourth sign showed Gautama how to successfully renunciate his current life. So, at age 29, Gautama gave up his family life, as well as the prestige and wealth that went along with it, and set out in search of Truth.

He studied early Hindu philosophy but was ultimately dissatisfied with its beliefs and practices, though his objections are not clearly documented. Then, while meditating one day under a bo-tree after a long fast, Gautama found himself tempted by every earthly pleasure imaginable. After successfully warding off these temptations, he was shown all his previous lives; then he was shown the present condition of the universe. Finally, he was made to understand the entire chain of causes and effects (karma). Through these experiences and visions, Gautama finally came to understand Truth. In this way Gautama became the Buddha, or "Enlightened One."

For the next 45 years, the Buddha traveled extensively, spreading his particular message of salvation.

Today, Buddhism has evolved into several branches, each a result of local and regional influences. Of these branches, the two largest are Theravada (orthodox) Buddhism and Mahayana Buddhism. Theravada is practiced in most South-East Asian countries, with the exception of Viet Nam, which practices mainly Mahayana Buddhism. Mahayana Buddhism is practiced in Tibet, Mongolia, China, Japan and Korea. Mahayana—meaning "large vehicle"—can accommodate many different beliefs. Because of this accommodation, Mahayana Buddhism is further subdivided into smaller groups.

Of the 250 million Buddhists around the world, only 500,000 live outside Asia.

Buddhist Fundamentals

The Buddha translated his enlightenment into four great, or Noble, Truths. These are:

- *All life is suffering—there are more tears in the world than water in the ocean.*
- *Suffering results from desire, the will to live and attachment to this world.*
- *Suffering can be overcome through the elimination of desire.*
- *Desire can be eliminated through meditation and the attainment of wisdom.*

Supplementary to the Four Noble Truths is the Eightfold Path—a series of steps by which desire can be eliminated:

1. The Right View—understanding the Four Noble Truths.

2. The Right Thought—having generally positive thoughts about people and all forms of life.

3. The Right Speech—avoiding bitter or unkind words.

4. The Right Action—acting without violence or vanity

5. The Right Work—employment that causes no harm to others.

6. The Right Effort—using time wisely in ways that are self-improving and productive.

7. The Right Mindfulness—becoming self-aware and compassionate.

8. The Right Concentration—meditation, intensely focusing on a single point in order to clear the mind.

Buddha called his teachings the *dharma*, or spiritual law. The *dharma* teaches that once the desire for earthly possessions—including life itself—is eliminated, the believer can then reach Nirvana, which means "extinguished." Though the Buddha himself never attempted to explain the nature of Nirvana, many of those who have followed him have. Some believe Nirvana is not so much a physical place as a state of mind achieved through intense meditation. Those who believe Nirvana is an actual place concede that one does nothing in Nirvana but meditate. But no matter what people believe about Nirvana, it represents an escape from the Wheel of Life—a doctrine the Buddha borrowed from Hinduism. The Buddha did reject, though, the Hindu belief that the soul is reunited with Brahman (the Creator) after escaping the Wheel of Life. He neither believed in Brahman, nor the human soul.

Buddha accepted the Hindu doctrine of *karma*—the accumulation of positive or negative effects from actions performed during one's life—but he was still convinced that ultimate salvation came from *within* the individual, not from his or her actions. Although Buddha ultimately diminished the central role that karma played in Hinduism, he did indicate that certain rules, or guidelines, would have to be enacted to make sure that his followers were of pure mind and heart. He called these guidelines the 10 Precepts. The first five apply to all Buddhists:

1. Abstinence from destroying life.

2. Abstinence from stealing.

3. Abstinence from impurity.

4. Abstinence from lying.

5. Abstinence from strong and intoxicating drinks, which cause stupidity.

The next three Precepts apply to monks and some pious laypeople:

6. Abstinence from eating after noon and other forbidden times.

7. Abstinence from dancing, singing and seeing spectacles.

8. Abstinence from ornaments (that are worn), scents and finery.

The next two Precepts apply only to monks:

9. Abstinence from large beds.

10. Abstinence from accepting gold or silver (money).

These constitute the 10 most widely practiced precepts among Buddhists. Different Buddhist sects have other precepts as well. In Thailand, there are 227 Precepts; in China, there are 250.

Among his followers, Buddha established a *sangha*—a community of monks. But unlike Hindu practice, Buddha felt that admittance to the religious order depended not so much on the person's social or economic status, but on the person's spiritual status. Thus, the only people not allowed to join the order were "troublemakers"—including criminals of all kinds. Buddha also excluded people with no hands or feet. While Buddhist scripture fails to explain why, scholars think that a person with no hands or feet wouldn't have been able to travel or care for themselves, as the early monks did. For a long time women were also excluded from this order but near the end of Buddha's life he relented and admitted a number of nuns into the *sangha*. This monastic order, though somewhat changed over time, is still practiced in Theravada Buddhism, the orthodox sect.

Like many religious leaders, Buddha illustrated his teachings with stories. These stories, called the Jataka Tales, recount specific incidents in Buddha's more than 1,000 lifetimes. Like the parables of Christianity, the Jataka Tales are an important element of Buddhist teaching. Each story illustrates a Buddhist moral or belief.

Fast Facts

• The Buddhist temple Angkor Wat is one of the wonders of the world.

• Mahayana Buddhism believes that the Buddha was a god. There have been and will be other Buddhas, but there will only be one called The Buddha.

• Theravada Buddhism teaches that there are no gods.

• Zen Buddhism teaches that meditation is the only way to salvation. From Zen come the famous "Unanswerable Questions," such as: "What is the sound of one hand clapping?"

• Tantric Buddhism teaches that magical effects can be achieved by repeating a mantra, or series of meaningless symbols. A mantra is "fitted" to an individual only after he or she has studied with a teacher.

• Pure Land Buddhism teaches that the faithful will go to a paradise after they die where "the trees are covered with flowers and glow like lamps, gold and jewels abound . . . lovely girls . . . charm the faithful." All of these ideas are radical departures from Bhuddist orthodoxy.

❖ ♦ ❖

Catholic/ Eastern Orthodox

The Catholic religion is the largest of all Christian movements. Estimates of actual numbers vary, but it is generally thought that there are as many as 650 million Catholics world-wide. Nearly two thirds of all Christianity is Catholic. The origin of the Catholic church dates to the year 33 A.D., when Christ founded the Christian Church. Catholics believe their church connects directly back to the original Christian church through the Apostle Paul—who founded the Christian church in Rome.

In 1054, the Catholic Church separated into Western and Eastern factions with headquarters in Rome and Constantinople. Ecclesiastical pressures had been mounting for some time; the Eastern Church recognized the four Patriarchs as the leaders of the church, while the church in the west recognized the Pope as the leader. As the conflict between the two movements escalated, the church in the east began exercising more and more independence from the church in the west. Eventually, the great Schism occurred and the two movements became entirely separate entities: the Roman Catholic Church and the Eastern or Greek Orthodox Church.

While some theocratic differences exist between these two churches, they derive their basic doctrinal tenets from the same ecumenical councils, of which the last was held in the year 787, when the churches were still united.

Catholic Fundamentals

As instituted by Christ in the New Testament, Catholics believe Baptism is a necessary prerequisite for salvation. To ensure that a person will not die "in his sins" without being baptized, Catholics baptize infants. Catholics also practice six other sacraments:

Eucharist- Also known as Holy Communion. A priest consecrates bread and wine after which they literally become the body and blood of Christ (transubstantiation). At the high point of the Mass they are served to the congregation.

Confirmation- This signifies the completion of a member's initiation into Catholicism, which begins at Baptism. During the ceremony, the person is anointed with consecrated oil (or chrism), which signifies the power of the Holy Spirit.

Penance- Penance brings about the forgiveness of sins through steps the sinner takes to reconcile him or herself before God. Normally, a member confesses his or her wrongdoings privately to a priest, who absolves the sins. The priest then outlines a course of action through which the member can be forgiven.

Unction- This sacrament is performed by a priest who anoints an ill person with consecrated oil, thereby forgiving the sick person of his or her sins as well as conferring a state of grace.

Marriage- Marriage is performed by a priest who unites a couple after they have recited vows of matrimony. The church does not recognize civil divorces but church-granted divorces can be obtained under special circumstances.

Holy Orders- In this ceremony spiritual authority to administer the sacraments is conferred to an ordained priest by a bishop.

The Roman Catholic Church is administered by a hierarchy of bishops, archbishops, cardinals and a Pope. Non-Catholics commonly make the assumption that Catholics believe the Pope can do no wrong. But, in actuality, the Doctrine of Infallibility simply refers to the fact that the pope cannot lead the church into doctrinal error as long he is acting in his papal capacity. The pope, like any member of the Catholic Church, is subject to temptation and regularly attends confession.

Concerning the Trinity, Catholics believe God, Jesus Christ and the Holy Ghost are one in substance, yet three in person. Catholics believe God can be everywhere at once. Neither Catholic authorities nor scholars attempt to endow God with physical attributes, although Catholics recognize that Jesus Christ took on a physical body during His life on earth.

Catholics believe that all are born with sin, since we are all descendants of Adam—who fell from the grace of God through disobedience. They believe this "original sin" can only be cleansed through Baptism. Sins committed by the individual are confessed to a priest. If the situation warrants, the good works of Saints can be transferred to the individual, relieving at least some of the burden of repentance.

After this life, Catholics believe spirits go to one of three places. The first is heaven, a paradisiacal place where God resides, reserved for those who have been baptized, repented of their sins and lived a life of good works. The second is purgatory, an intermediate state where a soul is sent who is not yet pure enough for heaven. This place is only reserved for those who have not died in a state of serious sin. In purga-

tory, souls wait to be purged of their sins and prepare for heaven. The last place a soul might go to is hell, where the unrepentant will spend eternity. Hell, like heaven and purgatory, is as much a state of being as an actual place. In hell, the soul is tormented by the presence of evil and great pain.

It should be noted that the Eastern Orthodoxy does not embrace the doctrine of purgatory.

Fast Facts

- Children who die before Baptism are placed in a state of "limbo"—a state of natural and eternal happiness. Children in this state do not suffer, even from a sense of loss.

- Catholicism uses symbols, such as the cross, representations of saints and other sacred objects to enhance meaning and teach truth. Catholics do not worship these objects, however.

- Catholic priests are allowed to participate in interreligious prayer services, or in the worship services of other faiths as long as they do not perform a specific role in the service, such as reading scriptures or preaching.

- Holy water is regarded as a symbol of spiritual purification. It is occasionally sprinkled on buildings or vehicles in an effort to drive away the forces of Satan. The water itself has no power, but is used in conjunction with prayer.

- *Catholic* literally means "universal."

❖ ◆ ❖

Church of Christ, Scientist (Christian Scientists)

The Christian Scientist movement originated in 1866 under the direction of Mary Baker Eddy in Lynn, Massachusetts. After suffering a severe injury, Eddy claimed to have recovered almost instantly after reading a Biblical passage which describes Jesus' healing a man stricken with palsy. From this experience sprang Eddy's conviction that salvation lies in the concept of "divine metaphysics"—the term Eddy used to define Christian Science. She recorded this event, as well as other insights, in a book called *Science and Health with Key to the Scriptures.*

As with many religious leaders, Mrs. Eddy's original intention was not to form a new sect. She wanted her insights to contribute to *all* religions. Meeting stiff resistance from the organized churches of her time, Eddy resorted to teaching anyone who would listen to the concepts she had discovered. The movement spread quickly because of its simple message of faith and healing.

The Church of Christ, Scientist makes no estimate of its membership. However, independent studies indicate that there are roughly 600,000 fully admitted Christian Scientists around the world. Ironically, the number of those who follow Christian Scientist teachings but have not been granted full membership in the church appears to be greater than the number of those who have been admitted.

Christian Scientist Fundamentals

The Christian Science movement is based on the principle that both matter and evil are unreal. The only reality for a Christian Scientist is God and that which they consider good. They describe God as a "Mind," or more simply, "Good." God's Son, Jesus Christ, showed the way of salvation not by atoning for man's sinful state but by providing a means by which man can be *healed* from his sinful state. Once Christ overcame sin, sickness and death, those things ceased to exist for Him. This is the example Christian Scientists seek to follow in their own beliefs and actions.

One of the most important elements of Christian Science doctrine centers around physical and spiritual healing. Reliance upon this principle—when practiced by someone who has been properly accredited by church authority—sometimes precludes the acceptance of modern medical treatment. Christian Scientists believe that since sin and sickness are not real, the belief in them is potentially punishable by God. This explains why believers occasionally die before being healed.

Christian Science meetings are identical all over the world. Two elected readers read passages selected from the Bible to the congregation. Readings are also taken from Christian Science texts such as *Science and Health*. These readings are supplemented by individual and group study during the week. They hold a meeting during the week where members have the chance to relate their testimonies of healing.

The Christian Science church is governed by a Board of Directors. Local churches are also governed by their own Board of Directors. Each local church has its own constitution, which names the leaders of that congregation, but the *Church Manual* dictates the nature of these constitutions, ensuring that they are all identical in policy. The Board of Directors is responsible for all of the church's activities, including publication of their widely-circulated periodicals— the *Christian Science Journal* and the *Christian Science Monitor*.

Fast Facts

- The Christian Science Church is financed almost exclusively by voluntary donations.

- There are more than 3,000 Christian Science Churches worldwide.

- Christian Scientists are often mistakenly perceived as "faith healers," but Christian Science doctrine stresses that healing is a result of *understanding* divine law, not believing in something not known.

❖ ◆ ❖

United Church of Christ

The United Church of Christ is actually made up of four distinct denominations: the Congregational Church, the Christian Church, the Evangelical Synod and the Reformed Church. The Congregational Church and the Christian Church merged in 1931, and the Evangelical Synod and Reformed Church merged in the early 1940's. In 1957, the two groups joined together. In next few years, the United Church of Christ drafted two important theological treatises—the first in 1959, which outlined the creed of the United Church of Christ; the second in 1961, which became the church's constitution.

Though the United Church of Christ's doctrine is deeply rooted in four different religious traditions, it follows a generally Protestant theme. As of 1989, worldwide membership of the United Church of Christ stood at 3.5 million.

United Church of Christ Fundamentals

On July 8, 1959, representatives from the two groups of churches that made up the United Church of Christ adopted a Statement of Faith which has become the church's creed. This statement of faith outlines a deep belief in God the Eternal Spirit and The Lord Jesus Christ. Further, it outlines God's mission as one of "calling worlds into being," creating man and "seeking to save all people from aimlessness and sin."

They believe God appeared as Jesus Christ to reconcile the world, and in conquering death and sin, provided a means for salvation. Therefore, they acknowledge Jesus Christ as the sole head of the church.

As with other Protestant movements, the United Church of Christ recognizes two sacraments as essential to worshipping God. The first of these, Baptism, is extremely critical since Christ Himself established the way to salvation through baptism. When infants are presented for Baptism, they are sprinkled with Holy Water, signifying the purification of Christ. The second sacrament, Holy Communion, is important because, according to scripture, it is the only other sacrament in which Christ himself participated. Through Holy

Communion members of the United Church of Christ become intimately aware of their Savior and His presence in their lives. Like other Protestant religions, the United Church of Christ does not perpetuate the doctrine that Christ is *physically* present in the bread and wine. Instead, they claim He is spiritually present during the ceremony as the elements of the sacrament are passed to the gathered worshippers.

Also in keeping with traditional Protestant beliefs, the United Church of Christ does not teach that heaven and hell are actual places in the universe. Members make up their own minds about the nature of heaven and hell through scriptural precedent, though most believe that heaven and hell are states of mind. They also believe that judgement belongs to God and man cannot escape that judgement.

Fast Facts
- The United Church of Christ is organized through local associations which belong to larger conferences. Every two years, the church holds a General Synod, which is attended by conference representatives.
- They consider the Bible to be the Word of God and assert that it serves as an inspiration for the United Church of Christ's work. Members are not charged, however, to believe literally in scriptural texts.
- No liturgical style has been adapted by the church. The development of a format for worship is seen as an ongoing effort.
- The United Church of Christ belongs to the World Council of Churches, an ecumenical association that encourages dialogue between religious movements.
- The church teaches that God seeks to bind in covenant all faithful people, no matter what their age, race or religion.

✧ ◆ ✧

Confucianism

Many scholars don't consider Confucianism so much a religion as it is a system of ethics developed to address the needs of humans as they live their lives in the present. It can be argued that Confucianism doesn't answer traditional theological questions such as those concerning the origin and destiny of humanity. Still, Confucianism's fundamental teachings can be traced to ancient Chinese beliefs, including those that concern Heaven and its host of gods and spirits. This religion was so fully integrated into Chinese society that the government itself employed "specialists" to advise them on how to proceed.

Confucius, born Kong Qiu, is thought to have lived in the 5th century B.C. Not much is known of his early life, and much that has been written about him is more or less conjecture. The *Annals of Confucius*, compiled by his disciples shortly after his death, provides one of the more reliable sources of his sayings and teachings.

Confucius was educated as a public servant and rose to become the keeper of public lands. Though he aspired to hold a high position in the government, it is thought that he made his reputation as a teacher rather than as a politician. Confucius trained others for government service and was known as one of the few teachers who would accept students from all walks of life, rather than just from the well paying rich.

Confucius spent his life studying and teaching; eventually he became recognized as one of China's eminent scholars. At age 54, he took it upon himself to travel from state to state offering advice and teachings to those who would listen. He was likely supported by the rulers of the various states, who at that time found it fashionable to surround themselves with men of academic achievement.

During his travels, he gained a small number of followers who would eventually carry on his teachings. Three years before his death, Confucius returned to his home state of Lu, where he studied quietly until his death.

Various descriptions of Confucius describe him as an individual of extraordinary charisma. Accounts claim that Confucius was nearly six feet tall—a phenomenal height for a man in China at that time—thus explaining descriptions of him as a giant (though some scholars believe that the term "giant" is used figuratively as well as literally).

Since Confucianism is more a philosophy than a religion, there have been few attempts to account for its membership. However, Asian history demonstrates that Confucianism has had a profound effect on the lives of nearly 25% of the world's population over the last 2000 years. Today, it is thought that Confucians number around 300 million.

Confucian Fundamentals
Though it cannot be said that Confucius was the founder of a specific religion, it is quite clear that he was a deeply spiritual individual. He accepted the doctrine of the day, though with a healthy dose of skepticism in regards to the magic and superstition that pervaded ancient Chinese belief. Primarily, Confucius was a scholar who thought all religion sought the same things: well-being, happiness and harmony. He taught that these goals could be achieved through the careful observance of

certain guidelines rather than through elaborate rituals.

Confucius founded his teachings on some of the religious classics of his time, including *The Odes, The Historical Documents, The Book of Rites, a Book of Divination, and The Spring and Autumn Classic*. Though these works existed before Confucius, his use of them resulted in them being called *The Confucian Canon*. He was selective in the references he made to these works, careful to cite only those passages that conformed to his evolving beliefs.

One of these beliefs was that true wisdom and saintliness—the objective of religion—cannot be fully achieved by mere mortals. Confucius addressed this by providing people with an *attainable* ideal, one that centered around nobility of character. In fact, he called this ideal *Jun-zi*—the Chinese word for "noble." For Confucius, nobility wasn't dependent on privileged social status, but on the cultivation of moral qualities. Thus, anyone can become a *Jun-zi*, as long as their commitment is constant and continually developing.

The moral qualities Confucius insisted his followers assume were:

• Loyalty to one's inner-self.
• Consideration towards others.
• Moderation in all things.
• A cultured manner.
• Meticulous observation of the rites and ceremonies that pertain to human behavior.

Confucius taught that true happiness and harmony come from the observation of certain guidelines by which relationships should be managed. This concept was outlined in his *Five Forms of Human Relationship*, which, in essence, taught that relationships exist on different levels, and that courtesy, reverence and the correct form of social interaction would result in social harmony. Perhaps the most famous of Confucius' sayings—commonly known as the Golden Rule—specifically relates to this principle: *"We should do our best to treat others as we wish to be treated"* (Mencius 7a:4).

Though Confucianism holds no doctrine of an afterlife, archaeologists have discovered that early Confucians almost universally believed in some sort of existence after death. The Confucianist view of God can best be described as agnostic since Confucius accepted the existence of a supreme being—but he did not require such a belief of his followers. The orthodox Chinese religion of his day described Heaven as a supreme cosmic spiritual power. Confucius promoted traditional worship as a sacred duty.

Confucius' disciples compiled a series of four books, together called *The Analects*, which further explained his philosophies. The first of these works includes a treatment of Confucius' principle of "The Right Way," a concept that social stability comes from following the way of the ancient rulers who governed through the use of moral sensibility, not fear. Thus, people can govern themselves. The second book expounds upon Confucius' strong feelings about education and its foundation. The third book deals with Confucian sayings and aphorisms, which explain how relationships should be governed. The fourth book is an extension of Confucius' teachings, written by Mencius, one of his disciples.

Fast Facts

• Confucians believe that through education individuals can overcome human weakness.

• A large temple erected in honor of Confucius at the place of his death—now in the Shandong province—has become a place of pilgrimage.

• During the Han dynasty, Confucianism was declared the state cult of China.

• Although Confucianism was eventually replaced by Communism in China, an effort has recently been made to conserve the great intellectual and cultural heritage of Confucianism.

✧ ◆ ✧

Christian Church (Disciples Of Christ)

The Christian Church (Disciples of Christ) began as two separate groups—Christians and Disciples. The Christians were founded by Barton W. Stone, a former Presbyterian from Kentucky. Stone was convinced that Christians should unite on the basis of their faith in Christ. He was deeply opposed to what he termed the "divisive doctrine of denominationalism." He believed that all people who claimed to be Christians should, in theory, believe the same things.

The Disciples originated in Pennsylvania under the leadership of Alexander and Thomas Campbell. In the early 1800's, Thomas Campbell preached to his congregation about the virtues of having closer relations with all Christian churches. His son Alexander joined him in 1810 and began to lay down the formative theology for the Disciple movement. The Campbells toyed with the idea of calling their organization "Christian," but felt the term was too pretentious. Instead, they called themselves Disciples. Because of their similar beliefs and relative close proximity, the Christians and the Disciples joined forces in 1832, officially becoming the Christian Church (Disciples of Christ).

The Disciples of Christ comprise one of the largest truly "American" churches. Today, there are nearly 1.5 million Disciples.

Disciples of Christ Fundamentals

While the concept of Christian unity is fundamental to Disciple of Christ belief, this idea is not expressed as a doctrine so much as an objective. In fact, the Disciples of Christ claim no doctrine other than a profound belief in Jesus Christ. Since religious creeds and dogma represent a "rightness of belief," they are inherently divisive, because every congregation claims a tradition that is unique to itself. Barton Stone was famous for his quote, "Deeds are more important than creeds."

Any matter that divides Christianity is considered objectionable by Disciples. Therefore, individuals are encouraged to make choices about particular beliefs for themselves.

Membership in the church is attained by confessing faith in Jesus Christ through a simple statement of that fact. Members are then baptized in the manner that Christ himself was baptized—by immersion. Only those who are old enough to understand the meaning of their confession of faith in Christ are baptized. Baptism, as instituted in the New Testament, is an act of surrender to God; it is symbolic of the birth, death and resurrection of Jesus Christ.

While Disciples are baptized in the name of The Father, The Son and The Holy Spirit, they spend little time speculating about the nature of the Trinity. Issues such as original sin and predestination are relatively unimportant to Disciples. Instead, Disciples focus their attention on expanding Christian thought through unity. The nature of Heaven and Hell, like the nature of God, is not considered as important as faith in Jesus Christ.

Disciples generally believe people are sinful by nature and that they can only be redeemed through faith in Jesus Christ. They believe that God, being a rational and loving entity, has provided a means by which all can attain salvation. Walter Scott, a founding member of the Disciples of Christ, outlined a five-fold plan for salvation that includes faith, repentance, baptism, newness of life and the gift of the Holy Spirit.

Originally, the church was established as a congregational organization where local churches were bound together in a kind of loose association. Because this association did not provide for a churchwide representative voice, the government of the church was restructured in 1968. Under this new organization, a 3-level church government was put in place.

The basic unit of the Disciples' church remains the local congregation. Each congregation elects its own representatives from its own body and ministerial ranks. Each congregation, however, establishes its own organization and is autonomous in handling its affairs.

Fast Facts

- Disciples have no church authority that determines doctrine.

- The official name of the church is Christian Church (Disciples of Christ).

- Butler University, Drake University and Texas Christian University are three of the more than 30 institutions of higher learning associated with the church.

⤣ ✦ ◊

Episcopalian (see Anglican)

◊ ✦ ◊

Hindu

With a history that dates back at least 3000 years, the Hindu religion is one of the oldest faiths in the world. It is also one of the largest, with close to 650 million adherents.

The term "Hindu" was first coined by Europeans in an effort to describe the Indian way of life. Hindus themselves have no word that denotes their religion, but as a matter of clarity, they often refer to their belief as *sanatana dharma*—meaning "eternal order" or "eternal law." Hinduism is actually a catch-all term that is applied to a variety of different religions that share essential characteristics.

The origins of Hinduism have long ago been lost, but it is thought that the faith never had a single founder, nor did it ever have a central core of doctrine. Instead, the Hindu religion has evolved more as a way of life than as a theocratic orthodoxy.

In the past, the Western study of Hinduism was more or less relegated to the sacred Sanskrit texts—the Upanishads—works written by Brahman scholars some 1500 years B.C. Sanskrit, an ancient language resembling the classic languages of Europe, was introduced to the Harappa (early Indian) culture by Aryan invaders. They also brought sacrificial cults which the Harappa civilization adapted as its own. These cults were ruled by gods of nature and natural forces. Those who associated themselves with these cults were called "Brahmans," after the god, Brahma (the Creator). The Brahmans were highly ascetic and spent many isolated hours in meditation. Today, most of the Brahman gods have been forgotten but a few are still honored.

Though these are the earliest examples of Hindu philosophy and theology, the Hindu movement didn't really begin until Brahman tradition began to be challenged. From these dissenters came two of India's greatest religious icons: Vardhamana Mahavira, founder of the Jainist movement, and Siddharta Gautama, founder of the Buddhist movement. More importantly, however, the Brahman society—an elite class of scholars and philosophers—began to lose its power. Only then did Brahman philosophy begin to filter downward and non-Aryan traditions began to assimilate into Indian culture.

Over time, public sacrifices became private rituals and the rising Hindu movement became one of personal devotion. This led to the creation of the *sutras*—a collection of statements which provides the main philosophies of Hinduism. The two epic Hindu works, *Mahabharata* and *Ramayana,* which also came from this transition, detail much of the mythology upon which Hindu belief is based.

Hindu Fundamentals

One distinguishing characteristic of Hinduism is its diverse, sometimes contradictory beliefs. These differences come about through the localized adaptation of Hindu principles. Still, all of Hinduism shares some essential characteristics.

The first doctrine, *samsara* (reincarnation) teaches that life moves in an endlessly repetitive, circular motion. For Hindus, life begins with birth, moves through to death and eventually reaches rebirth. After death, humans can be reborn into either a higher or a lower form of life depending upon their *karma*—the effect of one's actions, which can be either positive or negative. The accumulation of good *karma* brings about one's birth into a higher life later. Conversely, negative *karma* causes one to be born into a lower life.

Hindus have a generally pessimistic view of this life cycle since it is, in essence, a trap from which escape is difficult. The ultimate goal, then, is to gain release from *samsara.* However, endless and diverse theories abound as to how this release can be achieved. The two most popular beliefs, though, are that this release either comes from a vast knowledge, or an intense devotion to a personal god. One or the other of these will result in *moshka* the ultimate liberation from the life cycle.

Another basic Hindu belief is the doctrine of the universal Self and the Ultimate Reality. For the Hindu, the Ultimate Reality is the source of all that exists. Eventually, all that exists will return to that source. The Ultimate Reality was never created, nor will

it ever be destroyed. It is infinite and all-embracing. Ultimate Reality is in all things and it is the true Self of all living things.

Since Hinduism is as much a social order as it is a religious one, a system of four different castes has evolved in India. The Brahmans constitute the highest caste and are considered the most pure of all Hindus. The lowest caste—the Shudras—is characterized by physical and spiritual impurity. In the two middle-castes—the Kshatriyas and the Vaishyas—the distinctions are less clear. Within each caste are thousands of subgroups which are determined by geographic and linguistic boundaries. These subgroups are called classes, which are simply local or regional methods for determining social status. There are no clear-cut guidelines for determining class mobility but status can be enhanced by owning land or holding a position of authority. While the Brahman caste is always considered the highest, it is not always the most powerful. In some villages, the middle castes own the most land or the most authoritative positions.

Hindus can be further divided into three broad categories according to their principle deity. Most worship Vishnu—the controller of human fate—and are called are called Vaishnavas. The Shaivites worship Shiva—the god of destruction and the source of good and evil. The Shaktas worship Shakti—Shiva's female counterpart. While the god Brahma has a central place in Hindu mythology, he is not important in worship and there are very few temples dedicated to him.

Fast Facts

• Yoga is one of six systems in Hindu philosophy.

• When a Hindu dies, the body is cremated and the ashes are thrown into a sacred river such as the Ganges.

• Hindus worship by bringing gifts to a shrine dedicated to their god, then walk around the edifice, keeping it on their right.

• Marriage dates are fixed by astrological calculation; the ceremony is solemnized with the bridegroom leading the bride around a sacrificial fire in seven steps.

❖ ◆ ❖

Islam

Islam originated in the small Saudi Arabian town of Mecca, which had become a commercial center for trading between the Indian Ocean and the Mediterranean countries. At the center of town was an ancient and sacred religious object called the Ka'ba. The significance of the Ka'ba varied with the different groups that annually came to worship in its presence. During the time of pilgrimage, fighting was not allowed within the environs of Mecca, so trade fairs and huge commercial markets sprang up during the time of the pilgrimage since people could come and mingle with their enemies without fear of attack.

This led to great wealth and prosperity among the Meccan traders but it also led to a decline in religious belief since the tradesmen grew convinced that they could manipulate events through their wealth and business expertise. The prevailing moral temperament shifted from the spiritual traditions of the nomads to a "money-buys-all" mentality.

Muhammad ibn Abd Allah, the founder of Islam, was born in the midst of this increasing social and religious friction. His father died before his birth and his mother died shortly thereafter, so he was raised by his grandfather. Unable to engage in trade while a minor, he was hired by a wealthy widow to manage her merchandise on a trading trip to Damascus. The widow was so impressed by Muhammad that she offered to marry him. Though she was nearly 40 at the time, (and he was much younger) they had several sons and daughters, though only the daughters survived.

His marriage granted him the right to become a full fledged tradesman and allowed him to experience first-hand the growing unrest in Mecca. Muhammad, described as an introspective individual, made a habit of retreating to a cave outside the town every summer to meditate for a month. During one of these meditations, Allah called Muhammad to be a prophet. At this time he received the first of many spiritual messages he was to carry to the citizens of Mecca. As he continued to receive such messages, he was instructed to carry them to people everywhere. Generally, these messages were comprised of short passages of instruction or inspiration. Muhammad collected some of these passages into chapters; the rest were compiled after his death. These passages became the Qur'an (Koran)—the fundamental scriptural work of Islamic faith.

Muslims (his followers) describe Muhammad as an intellectually gifted individual. The evidence of this was his ability to turn, in a short time, a small group of followers into a powerful religious and political community. Muhammad also became a great military leader by defeating the powerful Persian and Iraqi armies, which gave him control of the entire Arabian Peninsula.

Muslims endowed Muhammad with other traits such as compassion and integrity; he quickly became the model for Muslim behavior. Muslims elevated him to infallible status, believing he was incapable of error in any way. Stories of his activities and teachings were circulated by his followers. These stories came to be called the *Hadith*—the rough equivalent of Christianity's parables.

With more than 540 million members, Islam is one of the world's largest religious movements.

Fundamentals of Islam

The word "Islam" means surrender, referring to the surrender to God. Islam teaches that God is omnipotent and that humans are but slaves before Him. Therefore, everything a person does must conform to God's will; God will make manifest His will to those who truly seek it.

The revelation of God's will is not so much a function of theology in Islam as it is the knowledge of "revealed law." The Qur'an is made up of a series of guidelines that all Muslims are exhorted to apply to their lives. However, Muhammad's compilation of messages were only adequate for the early stages of Islamic belief. As the empire of Islam grew in power and size, it was necessary to seek the will of God from the perspective of the community, which often faced problems vastly different than those addressed by the Qur'an alone. Local Muslim leaders would meet in the town mosque, or church, and study how to best apply Qur'anic instruction; if no solution seemed appropriate, pre-Islamic customs or local customs would be applied.

This adaptation led to the differing branches of Islam, of which there are two main divisions and several subdivisions. These two divisions are Sunni and Shi'a. The majority (90%) of Muslims belong to the Sunni group. Primarily, these two branches differ only in leadership and organization. Doctrinally, they are similar.

Islam is founded on Five Pillars. These outline the beliefs and practices mentioned in the Qur'an that are to be obeyed by all Muslims. They are:

1. Belief in One God.

2. Belief in Angels.

3. Belief in many prophets, but only one message.

4. Belief in Judgement.

5. Belief in the knowledge of God.

Islam worship is based on the Five Pillars of Observance. These include:

1. *Shahada* (the creed)—"There is no God but Allah and Muhammad is His prophet."

2. *Salat* (prayer)—Facing Mecca, the five compulsory daily prayers are said at dawn, at noon, afternoon, sunset and nightfall.

3. *Zakat* (charity)—Giving 2.5% of one's

income and the value of some properties. This is considered an obligation as well as an act of worship.

4. *Siyam* (fasting)—Fasting is an opportunity to practice restraint.

5. *Hajj* (pilgrimage)—It is the obligation for all Muslims to make the journey to Mecca at least once in their lifetime. Only those who are too ill or impoverished are excused.

Islamic religious life is centered around the *Shari'ah*—an Arabic term meaning "holy law." This law applies not only to the rituals and practices of worshipping Muslims but to the management of community affairs and social customs. To Muslims, the sense of community is not limited strictly to a set of geographical boundaries, but reflects more a religious association. The Qur'an uses the term community to describe the associations of all religions, including Christianity and Judaism.

Fast Facts

- Islam uses a lunar calendar instead of a solar calendar. It is divided into twelve months but has 11 fewer days than the calendar used in the West.

- Each month has some religious significance. The two most well known months are Ramadan, the month of fasting, and Dhu al-Hijjah, the month when Muslims make their pilgrimage.

- During the month of Ramadan, practicing Muslims don't eat between sunrise and sunset. Some of the less-devout interpret this to mean a person can feast between sunset and sunrise. Pious Muslims, however, look down on this practice.

- In Islamic mosques, a small niche is carved in the wall that faces Mecca. This serves to orient worshippers to the proper direction while praying.

- The Saudi Arabian government provides for the security, housing and food for the more than 2 million Muslim pilgrims that make the journey to Mecca every year.

- Islam has 99 names for God, most of which refer to one of His attributes.

- Muslims regard Muhammad as a prophet and the Father of Islam, but they do not claim he was a god.

- The Dome of the Rock, a mosque in Jerusalem, is purported to be the spot from which Muhammad ascended into heaven at the end of his life.

- Contrary to popular Western belief, Islam is not a harsh or angry movement. Anti-Western sentiments generally belong to Muslim extremists who do not represent the mainstream views of Islam.

❖ ◆ ❖

Jehovah's Witness

The Jehovah's Witness movement has been recognized as a legal entity since 1884, when the Watch Tower Bible and Tract Society was established by Charles Taze Russell and his associates. Russell was a leader of a group of Christians who came to refer to themselves as Witnesses—following the Biblical prophet Isaiah's reference to Christ's followers as witnesses of Jehovah. The term witness is also used in the book of Acts referring to Christ's admonition to be "witnesses of me . . . unto the uttermost parts of the earth." In simple terms, Jehovah's Witnesses try to carry out this commandment by proclaiming the word of Christ to all people. In doing so, they witness of the divinity of Christ and his teachings.

As of 1988, Jehovah's Witnesses numbered around 1.8 million world-wide.

Jehovah's Witness Fundamentals

The most fundamental doctrine for Jehovah's Witnesses centers around their conviction that Jehovah is the one and only God. This claim has been continually challenged by Satan and eventually resulted in his being cast out of heaven in 1914—an event marked by great turmoil on earth.

Christ—who is not the same person as Jehovah—is now present on earth, though he is invisible to human eyes. Though he cannot be seen, his presence can be verified by a careful study of world events since 1914, events which fulfill prophecies of Matthew.

Jehovah's Witnesses believe that Jehovah has outlined clear guidelines for human behavior and interaction. Adherence to these guidelines is often the source of persecution and misunderstanding. For example, Jehovah's Witnesses take very literally the scripture, Leviticus 17:10, which forbids the ingestion of blood. They see no difference between eating or drinking blood and having blood fed intravenously. In emergencies, Jehovah's Witnesses will accept plasma, but in the end would rather die than incur the wrath of God.

Another point of doctrine over which Jehovah's Witnesses are misunderstood is their refusal to salute the flag. This is not so much an indication of a lack of patriotism so much as it is a refusal to worship graven images. Flags are symbols of earthly sovereignty and should never be placed in a position higher than God's. Tied to this is the Jehovah's Witness' refusal to serve in a military capacity. They believe all wars arise because of worldly conflict, not divine retribution. Jehovah's Witnesses assert that if a war is ever sanctioned by God, they will be the first to enlist. But such an event has not happened.

Jehovah's Witnesses believe that only 144,000 people will be able to live in the actual presence of God. This is often misunderstood to mean that only 144,000 people will be saved. In fact, the rest of the faithful will have the chance to live on earth, which will be transformed into a paradise where humans will no longer know pain, sorrow, misery or strife. Geographical boundaries will then cease to exist, as will all political divisions. When this occurs, at the resurrection, the graves will yield up all the dead, who, having proved themselves obedient to God, will live on the paradise earth.

Jehovah God is the creator of the world and all that resides thereon, including the human race. God has given the world the Bible, which contains His Word. This Word details all that is necessary to be able to live again in His presence. In the median of time, God provided a Savior—Christ Jesus—who furthered the idea of becoming Witnesses for God by commanding His apostles to take the Word of God to the four corners of the world.

Jehovah's Witnesses have one mission: to testify of Jehovah. His Word cannot be fulfilled without this Witness.

Witnesses are governed by God, and only by God. As such, Witnesses submits themselves to no one else. This does not mean that Witnesses grant no authority to governments; following laws is necessary to avoid chaos and anarchy. However, these laws must be in accordance with God's laws, or they cannot be just.

Jehovah's Witnesses believe that hell is represented by the grave itself, not by some dark and fiery place to which the damned are condemned. Hell is a place of rest and hope. Heaven, on the other hand is comprised of the spirits that have inherited the Kingdom of God—these will number 144,000. There is no intermediate state mentioned in the Bible, so Jehovah's Witnesses do not accept the doctrine of purgatory, which is nothing more than a human invention.

Fast Facts
* Jehovah's Witnesses consider active prosylitization essential to their religion. Members are encouraged to contact people anywhere and everywhere.

* In some countries where a period of military service is mandatory, devout Jehovah's Witnesses spend the length of their tour in prison.

* Witnesses believe Christ was crucified by being nailed to a thick pole rather than to a cross.

* Only those who have been called to the ranks of the 144,000 can partake of the sacramental bread and water. Those callings are not issued by church authority but directly from Jehovah to the individual.

❖ ◆ ❖

Judaism

While generally regarded as a religion, Judaism is more accurately described as a religious way of life, rather than a specific set of doctrines. Defining what a Jew is depends on the application of the definition. For example, a cultural definition includes any person who considers Jewish traditions and literature as his or her own. But, in a practical sense, a Jew is simply a person who thinks of himself or herself as a Jew. And, because of immigration laws, the nation of Israel defines Jews as persons born of a Jewish mother and who have not embraced another religion.

Jewish Fundamentals

Much of what Jews believe is found in the Talmud, the chief scriptural work of Judaism. The Talmud is organized into 63 "orders," each containing ancient legal and theological writings. All Jewish law originates in the Talmud.

The Torah (the law)—the first five books of the Old Testament (Genesis-Deuteronomy)—also contains sacred writings. However, the Torah itself—a hand-printed scroll of these texts—is housed in the Ark of each Synagogue and is considered the most sacred object of Jewish worship.

The Jewish prayerbook, which identifies the three essential elements of Jewish faith:

Love of Learning- For thousands of years, Jews have had a compulsory education system and consider education not just a privilege but a responsibility. Even the poor are educated in Jewish communities. In ancient times, Jewish children were taught to associate learning with sweetness by being fed honey cakes baked in the shape of alphabet letters.

The Worship of God- Among Jews, it is generally understood that the best way to worship God is to emulate those qualities that are Godlike. These include mercy, justice, compassion and tolerance. An observant Jew tries to adapt these qualities as his or her own. The prayerbook stresses that worshipping God should be founded on love, not fear.

Good Works- Jews believe that, being Jews, they have certain obligations to their fellowmen. This means providing for those who cannot provide for themselves and performing other good works. It is not enough, however, simply to do good works out of a sense of obligation. Truly good deeds only come from the heart.

Jews recognize God as the Creator of the world and believe that God is the father of all people, that he is all-powerful, all-knowing and merciful as well. The phrase, "The God of Abraham, Isaac, and Jacob" refers to the fact that God and his will, never changes. It means there is only one God, and He is not only the God of the prophets, but of all people.

To the Jew, the essence of God is knowledge. This does not refer to arcane knowledge about a myriad of subjects but a knowledge of the truth, the law, and traditions. Knowledge is so important to Jews that Jewish faith is based on a hierarchy of teachers—the word "rabbi" literally means teacher. Jewish faith describes God as a purely spiritual being who takes on absolutely no physical human attributes.

Jews maintain that one of the greatest gifts of God is the knowledge that people are made—in a spiritual sense—in His image. The interpretation of this phrase is that men and women on earth are all God's children. As such, there can be no intermediary between people and God; an individual's salvation must be worked out by that individual.

Jews don't believe that people are inherently evil because of the fall of Adam; rather, each is judged according to his own works. Also, physical appetites are not in and of themselves sinful, simply because God himself created them.

Fast Facts

- Of the 14 million Jews around the world, only four million live in Israel. The largest population of Jews—six million—is in North America.
- The "Kosher" laws outline dietary habits and are contained in the book of Leviticus.
- Jews consider the home to be a more sacred place of worship than the synagogue. The family is the essential unit of Judaism.
- There are three branches of Judaism: Orthodox, Conservative and Reform. Their differences are founded in traditions, not necessarily doctrines.

❖ ◆ ❖

Lutherans

Lutheran Church was founded on October 31, 1517—the date Martin Luther parted ways with the Roman Catholic church. Luther's main complaint was the sale of indulgences—certificates written by the church which were said to reduce the amount of time a soul would stay in purgatory after death. Though his original intention was not to separate from the Church, his criticisms and teachings quickly led him into disfavor with Catholic church authorities. In light of these criticisms, Martin Luther became the original Protestant.

Luther also felt that liturgical music should be accessible to the congregation and not just be limited to a church-appointed choir or chorus. For the first time religious congregations found themselves participating in the ceremonies with song. Without this shift in religious aesthetics, the world may never have known the second-most famous Lutheran—Johann Sebastian Bach.

Around the world, close to 80 million people claim to be Lutherans, although an exact count is impossible, since individual Lutheran congregations use different means to account for adherents.

Lutheran Fundamentals

The Lutheran church claims no doctrines other than those that pertain to Christian belief as explained in the New Testament. They consider God as the Creator and believe He has given people the capacity to recognize and choose between right and wrong. Much Lutheran doctrine finds its roots in the Roman Catholic church but even in those cases where certain ideas may be similar, Martin Luther established an interpretation of those ideas that is uniquely Lutheran.

For example, Luther adapted only two of the seven sacraments practiced by the Roman Catholic church. One of these is the Holy Communion, a ritual Lutherans recognize as an encounter between the worshipper and the Lord rather than merely a symbolic gesture. Lutherans do not believe that a physical change takes place in the sacramental bread and wine, but rather that the Lord is present during the ceremony itself. The second sacrament practiced by Lutherans is Baptism; through it, Lutherans believe the worshipper is born into the Kingdom of God and becomes an heir to salvation.

Penance is unnecessary since God has promised forgiveness to those who ask for it. Since the Holy Unction, while well-founded in Christian theology, has no scriptural precedent it is considered unnecessary as well. The other three sacraments, confirmation, marriage and ordination, are simply rites to which no divine grace is attached.

In keeping with orthodox Christian tradition, Lutherans accept the doctrine of the Holy Trinity. For Lutherans, the Trinity is made up of God the Father, God the Son and God the Holy Ghost. These distinct personalities make up one God. Lutherans accept this definition on faith alone. The fact that God is three distinct personalities, or that He manifested himself in the form of Man is what is important, not *how* these feats are accomplished.

Lutherans believe the God is the embodiment of Truth and that all truth emanates from this one source. As such, Lutherans believe that theirs is the only true church. This is not to say that other churches do not contain the truth, however.

The goal for the human race, again in keeping with traditional Christian belief, is to achieve salvation—existence with God. This will happen only after people have learned to be completely obedient to His Will and His Word. This will not happen gradually, but will be the result of the fulfillment of God's purpose, which lies beyond the limits of present life.

Salvation is a gift from God, one that people cannot work for, but like any other gift, can only be wished for. Recognition of the human condition and its inherent weaknesses is the first step in allowing God to grant this gift of faith. Trying to save ourselves is pointless, as Luther himself discovered. Only after allowing God to save him, through his faith in Christ, was Luther able to reconcile the fact that as a member of the human race, he could still be saved through the grace of God.

Fast Facts
• J.S. Bach, a Lutheran organist, was fired from several congregations for embellishing hymns too much.
• Lutheran congregations do not always worship in the same way. Some parishes practice elaborate liturgies and others hold simple services consisting of a short sermon and a hymn.
• Martin Luther believed that enforced celibacy was wrong. He himself married a nun who had converted to the Lutheran church. Some people claim Luther left the Catholic church in order to marry but in fact he married eight years after his departure.

❖ ◆ ❖

Methodists

The Methodist Church was founded by John Wesley in England during the spring of 1738. Wesley was educated at Oxford University and had been ordained to the Anglican priesthood. The Anglican church at that time was rife with rules and rituals in which Wesley tried in vain to find religious satisfaction. During a prayer meeting one day, Wesley realized that peace cannot be found in ritual but in faith. This realization became the basic tenet of Wesley's belief.

Wesley took it upon himself to preach this idea to those the Anglican church had been unable to reach. His simple message appealed to a great number of people and Wesley organized them into societies within the Anglican church. He exhorted these societies to pray together and help one another to work out their own salvation.

Though his intention was not to form a new church, the Anglican diocese Wesley belonged to refused to ordain ministers to preside over the new societies and refused to allow their places of meeting to be consecrated. In response, Wesley took it upon himself to ordain ministers and consecrate the meeting places.

The term "Methodist" was first used by members of the Oxford University student body in reference to members of the "Holy Club"—a society formed by young John Wesley and his brother Charles in 1729. This group followed a proscribed daily schedule of visiting the sick, conducting schools, and praying. Because of this rigid schedule, members of the Holy Club were sometimes called, often derisively, "Methodists." Since Wesley demanded that his followers participate in religious observances and conduct themselves according to certain guidelines, the Methodist name quickly became associated with the entire movement.

Around the world there are an estimated 18 million Methodists. Outside America, the trend has been for traditional Methodist communities to either merge with Christian churches within that country or become autonomous groups that share Methodist beliefs without being recognized Methodist congregations.

Methodist Fundamentals

Methodists recognize God's form as that of a Trinity. It is important to think of God as a Creator, a Savior and a Divine Presence.

Like other Protestant groups, Methodists only recognize two sacraments: Baptism and Holy Communion. According to scripture, Jesus participated personally in only these two sacraments. For Methodists Baptism is a manifestation of faith in God's mercy and symbolizes a rebirth into a spiritual way of life. Holy Communion represents redemption through the death of Jesus Christ and symbolizes the Christian love that ought to prevail among those professing to be Christians.

While Methodists only recognize these two ordinances as sacraments, they also recognize marriage and confirmation as ordinances.

According to Methodist tradition, God is directly accessible to those who seek him; no intermediary is needed to intercede in the process of salvation. Occasionally, members of the clergy will counsel individuals about revising their actions or their thoughts. But Methodists generally accept the traditional Protestant concept of an "individual priesthood of all believers." They feel the nature of God bestows grace upon his children in the form of healings and reconciliations. This was revealed to humanity through the life of Jesus Christ.

They believe that humans are the children of God, and that they are placed on earth to learn meaningful lessons that will aid them in acquiring faith in the mercy of God.

Methodist perceptions of heaven and hell are difficult to summarize because no specific doctrine is shared by all Methodists. In general, however, Methodists reject the notion that heaven and hell are physical places complete with their respective attributes of golden streets and fiery lakes and brimstone. Instead, Methodists believe that heaven is a state of mind and spirit where individuals can freely associate with God. Hell, conversely, is a state of mind and spirit where no such association can take place. The doctrine of Purgatory is not accepted by Methodists since they believe that God's punishment is redemptive, not punitive in nature.

The United Methodist Church, the main American body of the Methodist Church, is governed by a Council of Bishops who are elected during jurisdictional conferences of ministers and laymen. Each bishop oversees an Area and parish ministers are appointed by the presiding bishop of the Area. A General Conference takes place every four years, during which legislative matters are discussed at length. General Conferences are composed of clergy and laity in equal numbers. A Judicial Council is also called by the General Conference to oversee matters of church law.

Fast Facts

• Methodist doctrine is founded upon three sources: the Bible, the *Book of Hymns* and the *Book of Discipline.*

• The Methodist church belongs to the World Council of Churches and actively participates in consultations on religious unity.

• Methodists believe the scriptures are one of four sources of Christian theology. The other three are tradition, experience and reason.

❖ ♦ ❖

Mormon (Latter-day Saints)

Although better known as the "Mormon" church, the official name is The Church of Jesus Christ of Latter Day Saints. As the name implies, the LDS church is fundamentally a Christian church, though some mistake it as a cult.

The LDS church was founded in New York by Joseph Smith on April 6, 1830. Mormons believe that the LDS church is the modern restoration of the church Jesus Christ organized in ancient Jerusalem. Not long after Christ's crucifixion, the gospel was taken from the earth, as those who had the authority to officiate in church ordinances died or were killed. Joseph Smith, in an effort to determine which church was "the true church," restored this early Christian church under the direction of the Lord.

Perhaps the most significant aspect of the LDS church is the Book of Mormon—a scriptural work that documents Jesus Christ's visiting people living in the Americas after his resurrection. LDS members believe this work was translated by Joseph Smith from ancient records found on a hillside in New York.

With close to 9 million members, the LDS faith is one of the fastest growing religions in the world. A large part of this expansion is due to a massive effort on the part of full-time missionaries who are called to seek out and teach people about the Mormon church. Ordained missionaries currently number around 50,000, most of whom are young men and women between the ages of 19 and 23. There are more than 300 LDS missions around the world.

Mormon Fundamentals

Mormons believe that four basic principles are the keys to exaltation (salvation). These are faith in the Lord Jesus Christ, repentance, baptism by immersion, and the gift of the Holy Ghost. Accomplished in this order, each step leads to the next.

Mormons do not baptize infants, but they do baptize children who are eight years old or older; children at least eight years of age are capable of understanding the significance of baptism, while infants are not.

The foundation of the LDS church is what Mormons call the Priesthood, defined as the authority given to perform ordinances in Christ's name. While the LDS church shares many doctrinal similarities with other Christian churches, Mormons stress the importance of authentic priesthood authority. Mormon priesthood holders trace their line of authority to Jesus Christ—who restored this authority to Joseph Smith. Ordinances such as baptism and marriage are performed with this authority.

Mormons believe that God is a physical being and cite biblical references which explain that we are created in God's image. The Trinity, or Godhead, is comprised of God the Father, Jesus Christ and The Holy Ghost. They consider all three as separate, distinct persons, though they are "one in purpose."

The purpose of God is the exaltation of His children. He has outlined a specific plan which includes a period of mortal existence on earth, for which they will be held accountable. The central figure in this plan is Jesus Christ, who, through his example and teachings, provided a model for behavior, and through his sacrifice and resurrection, overcame the obstacles—sin and death—that keep people from the presence of God.

Mormons view God as the literal Father of the spiritual self. His purpose is the exaltation of his children, which is simply the chance to live in God's presence after this life. This reward is reserved for those who have completed certain ordinances within the church and who have lived their lives in accordance with Christ's teachings.

Mormon's believe that since God is, in effect, the father of all individuals, people can develop a personal relationship with Him. They feel that God communicates with those who seek him in prayer—in much the same way a father communicates with a child who is seeking guidance.

To Mormons, all people are the children of God. They believe that people are sent to the earth to be tested; here, people prove to themselves and to God whether or not they are worthy to live eternally with God. While this may seem harsh, Mormons believe that God communicates with people here on this earth and that those who truly seek to do good will receive the guidance they need. They define human purpose as the pursuit of joy, which can be achieved through obedience and faithful adherence to gospel principles.

According to Mormon doctrine, people will be judged solely on the basis of their own actions and not be held accountable for anyone else's transgressions, including Adam's disobedience.

Mormons believe that man is eternal in nature; they claim that people existed as spirits before the creation of the world and that they will exist in a perfected state after the resurrection.

The LDS church is governed by a prophet and 12 apostles. It's organization is patterned after the apostle Paul's description in the New Testament of Christ's church.

Fast Facts
• Though the church at one time did endorse polygamy, few members ever actually engaged in the practice, and those that did generally did so in order to care for women whose husbands or fathers had been killed through persecution or the hardships of migrating to the west. Modern polygamist groups are not members of the Mormon church.

• Mormon temples differ from meetinghouses in that temples are places where necessary ordinances are performed by priesthood holders for both the living and the dead. These ordinances include baptism, confirmation and marriage. All of these—even marriage—are considered eternal in nature.

• All young men deemed worthy by church authorities are ordained to the priesthood at age 12. Mormons believe that the priesthood is not a function of spiritual achievement but a means by which God's will can be enacted by men.

• Mormon meetings are characterized by speakers called from the general congregation to expound on gospel principles. Children as young as eight can be called to speak

• Mormons follow a code of health which prohibits the use of alcohol and tobacco, as well as beverages containing stimulants, such as coffee and tea.

• The Mormon Church is headquartered in Salt Lake City, Utah, which was settled in 1847.

✧ ◆ ✧

Presbyterians
Presbyterians think of themselves as belonging to a particular form of religious government rather than a particular form of worship. Though the term Presbyterian refers directly to this government, the Presbyterian movement is Protestant in nature. Presbyterian principles are founded on the teachings of John Calvin, who, at age 24, parted ways with the Catholic church for various reasons. Calvin advocated establishing a church government that emulated the church of the first century A.D. This government is founded on a hierarchy made up of two classes of elders: teaching elders—ordained ministers and pastors who teach; and ruling elders—persons elected to fill administrative roles within the church.

Though John Calvin is considered one of the primary instigators of the Presbyterian movement, John Knox, a British religious dissenter, is credited with establishing the Presbyterian church in Scotland, the acknowledged center of Presbyterianism.

Though difficult to estimate, it is thought that there are close to 22 million Presbyterians around the world.

Presbyterian Fundamentals

The Presbyterian interpretation of God does not differ from the vast majority of Protestant movements. They believe the Trinity to be three manifestations of one God. God's will is for individuals to seek a direct, personal relationship with Him. In the Presbyterian church ministers and pastors are teachers; they do not act as intermediaries. God grants forgiveness and salvation to individuals who have established a personal relationship with Him.

Central to Presbyterian doctrine is the belief that Jesus Christ is the Son of God and that he became mortal in order to accomplish certain tasks necessary for our salvation.

Presbyterians accept God's nature by faith even if they don't fully understand it.

The concept of having a personal relationship with God is one of the main points upon which John Calvin disagreed with the Church of Rome. He taught that salvation was rooted in seeking "to know God," not in ritual and dogma. In keeping with this notion, as well as their belief about the nature of God Himself, Presbyterians do not employ a confessional in the sense that other Christian churches do. Instead, confession is made directly to God. On occasion, the penitent will ask a pastor or minister to listen to his or her confession, but the church leader acts in no way as an intermediary.

Baptism is considered an important element of faithful Presbyterian worship, although Presbyterians don't consider the sacrament of Baptism necessary to salvation. Baptism itself is an outward manifestation of a worshipper's inner commitment to the Lord.

Presbyterians believe that heaven and hell are states of mind more than physical places. Presbyterians reject the descriptions of heaven having streets of gold and hell filled with fire and brimstone. These images are rooted in an earthly, material perspective. Salvation is determined by God alone, and not by some human achievement. Therefore, salvation does not come from good works but rather results from an increased personal knowledge of God.

Fast Facts

- Early Presbyterians came from a Puritanical background that prohibited the use of symbols in worship. Since then, Presbyterians have incorporated elaborate Gothic architecture into their edifices.

- The Presbyterian church is credited with raising the standard of literacy in Scotland—and other areas—by encouraging its members to read and study the Bible and other religious texts.

- Four courts govern the Presbyterian church. From lowest to highest, these are: the Session, the Presbytery, the Synod and the General Assembly. The General Assembly oversees the entire church.

❖ ◆ ❖

Shinto

Shinto, as a movement, does not have a clear historical background. It is thought that Shinto belief was first introduced to the Ainu, Japan's indigenous people, by invaders from North-East Asia. The new settlers brought with them a rich tradition of legends and myths that helped shape this new religion. Eventually, the warring tribes and clans were brought under central control, forming the nation of Japan—and its religion.

Since Shinto comes from a variety of different traditions it has no single founder. Instead, Shinto is an evolution of primitive religions that were heavily dependent on rites and ceremonies. By the fourth century A.D., this conglomeration of movements fused into one and since the fourth century A.D., the Shinto religion has remained virtually unchanged.

Shinto is considered the state religion of Japan and is practiced by some 60 million people.

Shinto Fundamentals

In its earliest form, the Shinto religion was intensely focused on the powers of nature—a carry-over from the initial invaders of the Japanese islands. The worship of natural forces was presided over by an order of priests who could divine the will of the gods through elaborate ceremonies.

Early worshippers experienced a strong aversion to things that were impure or caused impurity. Death was one of the most potent forms of this pollution. When someone died, family members would immediately bury the body, then would wash themselves with water. In many cases, the home would be abandoned and rebuilt somewhere else. When clan chieftains—and later emperors—died, the entire city would be evacuated and relocated somewhere else.

By the fourth century A.D., the religion had come to be called Shinto, taken from the Chinese word *shin dao*, which means "way of the gods." Shinto teaches that the Japanese islands were specially created by the gods and that the emperor and his people were descendants of these deities.

Shinto has reinforced its inherent doctrinal lapses with threads of cultural and social tradition. Political and social ceremonies—while they have no theological basis—are still considered Shinto rites simply because Shinto has come to reflect the entire society of Japan. Its fundamental teaching is that Japan is "the source of all other countries" and "in all matters it excels all the others."

As a polytheistic religion, much of Shinto's belief rests in the worship of various gods, and in the recitation of colorful myths and legends surrounding these gods. Shinto worshippers have shrine in their homes dedicated to one or more of these gods, at which all members of the family enact on a daily basis a short, but solemn, ceremony. During this ritual, small gifts of rice, salt or water are left at the shrine. On special days, the gifts may take the form of fruit or other foods. It is believed that the gods control all aspects of life and making offerings to them ensures that the gods will favor the worshipper. The faithful worshipper who heeds the will of the gods will be greatly rewarded, both in this life and the next.

Each town has its own shrine, characterized by an unpainted wooden structure and sacred symbols. The shrine consists of a sacred enclosure with an opening on one side that leads to the outer shrine. A short passage connects the outer shrine with another sacred enclosure, in which the "treasure" of the shrine rests. This "treasure," is usually nothing of monetary value—a piece of glass or a pebble—but it represents the invisible presence of whatever god to which the shrine belongs.

In the Eighth century A.D., a Shinto priest founded a sect called the Shingon Buddhists. His teachings led to the formation of the Ryobu Shinto sect in the 12th century, which eventually became the dominant form of Shinto. Since its roots were deeply entrenched in Buddhist belief, the two religions became entwined. Joint sanctuaries sprang up which were overseen by both Buddhist and Shinto monks. Buddhist rites were performed at Shinto shrines and an amalgamated priesthood was formed to interpret the doctrines of the two movements. Though the two religions in effect joined efforts, they never became fused into one. Today, many Japanese practice both religions. In some cases, a Japanese couple may marry in a Shinto ceremony, but then observe Buddhist tradition at funerals and memorial services. Since both Buddhists and the Shinto are relatively tolerant of diverse theological viewpoints, the two religions have existed peacefully together for a millennium.

Fast Facts
- Shinto recognizes more than 800 gods and spirits.

- Of the 800 gods and spirits recognized by the Shinto religion, more than 200 have shrines dedicated to them.
- The Konko-Kyo sect teaches that there is only One True God.
- One of the most popular Shinto gods is Hachiman, the protector of human life.

❖ ◆ ❖

Unitarian Universalists

In 1961, two religious traditions—the Unitarian and the Universalist—merged to form one denomination. The Unitarians and Universalists had long shared similar views, as well as similar histories, so their union was almost inevitable.

The Unitarian movement owes its origins to several early "freethinkers," some of whom actually died for their Unitarian beliefs. One such example is that of Michael Servetus, a man who rebelled against the strict Calvinist regime in Geneva during the 1500's. He was burned at the stake in 1533 for professing that worship was a matter of personal choice. Unitarians also consider King John Sigismund of Transylvania to be an integral part of the foundation of the Unitarian church. In 1568, King John issued an edict supporting religious freedom which allowed his subjects to worship differently than their king without placing their loyalty under suspicion.

From Eastern Europe, Unitarianism spread to England. John Priestly, an English religious refugee, brought Unitarian ideas to America. In 1785, Boston's King's Chapel became the first Unitarian chapel in the United States.

Universalists also came out of the Calvinist movement in Europe. Because they did not seek to acquire existing church buildings and properties, Universalism was considered more a philosophy than a religion. Some early Universalists still maintained membership in the Calvinist church. The first Universalist church, however, was formed in 1779 by John Murray in Gloucester, Massachusetts.

During the nineteenth century missionaries spread Universalist ideas throughout America.

Today, there are more than 4500 Unitarian congregations in the world. Membership is estimated at close to 1 million, but there maybe more since many people may not realize they are Unitarians. Since Unitarianism is more a philosophy than a denomination, anybody who accepts fundamental Unitarian beliefs is considered to be Unitarian. These fundamentals include: a belief in the value of all persons, a conviction that everyone has the right to believe whatever they choose, a belief that religious ideas must be tested by personal experience, a desire to acquire truth wherever it may be found, and respect for the teachings of *all* great religions while still exercising personal judgement.

Unitarian Fundamentals

The term "Unitarian" was first applied during the sixteenth century to those who rejected the notion that God exists as a Trinity. A Unitarian believes God is God and Christ was an "inspired" individual who should not be equated with God. God is not three persons in one, neither is He three separate persons. God's presence is manifest by His own spirit and not by another being such as the Holy Ghost.

Universalists believe that God is a God of love, and therefore cannot limit salvation to a few "elect" individuals. Salvation is a gift for all men regardless of their sins or lack of faith.

Unitarian Universalists address God more often in meditation than they do in traditional prayer. Communication with God is not so much an attempt to influence Him for favors or "blessings" as it is a time to express feelings, to verbalize concerns and to outline hopes and aspirations. Unitarian Universalists place less emphasis on who is listening to these meditations than on the vocalization process itself.

Unitarian Universalist congregations are made up of agnostics, pantheists, nature worshippers, even atheists. No special meaning can be attached to the proclamation "I believe in God," since the word "God" has so many connotations. People must decide what, or who, God is for themselves.

Of Jesus Christ, Unitarian Universalists admire his example of ethical leadership. They accept his teachings and his example of how people should treat one another. Unitarian Universalists don't accept Jesus as the final religious authority any more than they would accept Buddha or Mohammed. But Unitarian Universalists do consider themselves to be Christians if only because the movement grew out of Christian roots. Unitarian Universalists are not strictly limited to Christian tradition in their beliefs, however.

Though Universalists and Unitarians come from religions that focused on different central doctrines—the idea that God is a unified being and the belief that salvation is achievable by all humans—their theology arrives at the same conclusion: human beings are not separate from God but are *manifestations* of Him.

Unitarian Universalists have a strong belief in the worth of all human beings. Without making suppositions about an afterlife, they believe that this life is a time to learn valuable lessons. These lessons are learned as people fill their social obligations to create a just and peaceful society. A strong sense of personal liberty is fundamental to finding and living a meaningful life. When individual freedom is curtailed, people end up living the lives of others and don't discover what valuable lessons await them.

Fast Facts

- The Unitarian Church works with the National Council of Churches of Christ to promote religious unity but the church has not been allowed to join the council because of its broad and non-traditional view of Christ's mission and role.

- Unitarians reject the traditional Christian notions of a virgin birth and resurrection. They see these as anachronistic ideas that have no scientific or historical foundation.

- They believe heaven and hell are merely imaginary places. One Unitarian said, "Our task is not to get men into Heaven; it is to get Heaven into men."

THE KORAN

This is no invented tale, but a confirmation of previous scriptures, and explanation of all things, a guide and a blessing to true believers. (12:111)

Islam is the most wide-spread religion on Earth. In the centuries immediately following the life of the prophet Mohammed (c. 570 - 632), the force of Islam expanded throughout the Middle East and Africa, Spain, and parts of southeastern Europe. Mohammed preached that there is but one God (*Allah*), and that he, Mohammed, was God's messenger. Those who believe in Allah, and accept Mohammed as His prophet, are called *Moslems* (or *Muslims*), meaning *ones who submit to God*.

The central Islamic canon is the *Koran* ("Qur'an," meaning *recitation*), said to be the actual word of God as revealed to Mohammed by the angel Gabriel. Parts of the *Koran* resemble the Bible, the Apocrypha, and the Talmud, including many stories that appear in the Old Testament. It also contains stories about Abraham, Moses, Jesus, and other of Mohammed's prophet-predecessors. These tales and teachings were first memorized or written, then compiled to form the holy book. The text is divided into seven chapters, and sixty-six sections called *suras*.

Mohammed lived in poverty his entire life, and, though he spoke for Allah, he did not make vast claims to power: *"I do not tell you that God's treasures are with me; I do not know what is hidden, nor do I tell you that I am an angel. I only follow what is revealed to me."* (VI:50)

Many favors, however, were granted unto him by Allah through Gabriel: *We chose you as Our apostle . . . We lifted up your heart, removed your burden and gave you high renown; We found you orphaned and gave you shelter. We found you wandering and gave you guidance . . .* (XLVIII:2) Mohammed, as God's messenger, was guarded against hypocrites; his enemies were laid low. (III:47, VIII:30). Far more than a mere poet or soothsayer, he held the high calling of receiving and dispensing the word of Allah (see I XVIII:2, LXIX:41-42)

Text Overview:
God and Humanity

Moslems have numerous titles for Allah: Master of the worlds; Forgiving and compassionate; Lord of the day of judgment; Creator, preserver and destroyer; The first and the last; Grievous tormentor of the wicked . . . According to the suras, Allah, in his infinite power, created the universe in six days, or six thousand-year periods (XXII:46). Allah is the one and only creator. *If you ask them who it is that has created the heavens and the earth and subjected the sun and the moon, they will say: "Allah." How then can [unbelievers] turn away from Him?* (XXIX: 61) Allah is "Eternal, absolute, He does not beget, nor is begotten, and there is none like Him." (CXII:1)

Allah gave creation to the seven heavens and stacked them one above the other, placing Mankind as the noblest creature on earth. (XL:59) [Allah] molded

man into a most noble image and in the end [He] shall reduce him to the lowest of the low, except the believers who do good works. (XCV:5)

Throughout history, God has given mankind the holy books—the *Koran*—and sent His prophets—Muhammad being the last of these—to teach people their duty to God and humanity.

The *Koran* teaches that Allah is just and merciful; He boldly asks believers to do good works, repent, and purify themselves so that they may receive Paradise after death (CIII:3). The faithful shall reap great rewards, but the unfaithful will incur the wrath of God on the Day of Judgment, also known as the Overwhelming Event. *On the Day of the Overwhelming Event, the earth will be laid low by an apocalyptic blaze: On that day there shall be downcast faces, of men broken and worn out, burnt by a scorching fire . . .* (XCI:1)

For the faithful, however, . . . *there shall be radiant faces, of men well-pleased with their labors, in a lofty garden. There they shall hear no idle talk. A gushing fountain shall be there, and raised couches and goblets placed before them; silken cushions ranged in order and carpets richly spread. (LXXXVI-II:1)* Faithfulness is the key to salvation. The *Koran* suggests that man is capable of exhibiting varying degrees of faith (*iman*) and unbelief (*kufr*); the faithful will warrant glory on the Day of Judgment, while the unbeliever will experience perdition.

One who truly possesses faith recognizes the signs of Allah in everything on earth: "In the heavens and the earth are signs for those who believe." (XLV:2) These signs, called *ayat*—including such things as human love and kindness, diversity of language and color, and lightning and rain—enable the faithful to "see" God, even though "the vision of Man does not apprehend Him" (VI:103), surely, Allah is too great to be fully perceived by humans. Not only do believers perceive the signs of God in the world, they also proclaim Allah as the one and only God and recognize that "the only true faith in Allah's sight is Islam." (III:19) Indeed, *Moslems are those who, at the mere mention of God, Feel a tremor in their hearts, and when they hear His signs recited find their faith strengthened and put their trust in their Lord; who establish regular prayers and distribute alms from the gifts [God] has given them for sustenance. (VIII:2-3)* Further, all good actions and the avoidance of evil are characteristic of the faithful. *True believers are those that have faith in Allah and his apostle (Mohammed), and never doubt, and who fight for His Cause with their wealth and persons. (XLIX: 14)*

The greatest privilege of the believer is that he or she will meet God in the Hereafter: *Do good works and fear Allah. Bear in mind that you shall meet Him. (II: 223)* The unbeliever, in contrast, is characterized by ingratitude (*kufr*): *[Allah] grants all that you ask Him. If you reckoned up Allah's favors you could not count them. Truly man is unjust and ungrateful. (XIV:37)*

Unbelievers show their *kufr* by their disbelief in the signs of God: *O people of the Book, why do you disbelieve in the signs of God when you yourself bear witness to them?* (III:63) In addition, unbelievers are conceited, corrupt, insubordinate, and unjust. They refuse to accept guidance, and they return to unbelief after being converted.

The greatest of sins, according to the *Koran*, is that of polytheism (belief in or worship of more than one god). Polytheists worship empty idols, Mohammed insists, and thus have no power; "Let them not approach the Sacred Mosque." (IX: 28) All sinners may be pardoned except polytheists, who have no chance of forgiveness in this world or the next. As the verses state: *Allah will not forgive idolatry. He will forgive whom He will all other sins. He that serves other gods besides Allah has strayed far from the truth.* (IV:116)

Virtue and Justice

Moslems are enjoined to help anyone who petitions them for help, and not to judge another's motives. God himself will judge the dishonest petitioner and reward the giver both in this life and the world to come.

The *Koran* teaches believers to honor parents, show kindness to slaves, care for the orphaned and widowed, and exhibit charity to the poor. Faith, kindness, honesty, patience, industry, and courage are emphasized as characteristics of the believer.

The *Koran* forbids stealing, lying, adultery, and murder; punishment for such crimes is based on the Old Testament law of retaliation: "an eye for an eye and a tooth for a tooth." For instance, killing is punished by death, unless the death is accidental, in which case "blood money" should be paid to the dead person's relatives.

It could be interpreted in some verses that unbelievers are to be put to death if they do not embrace Islam. These verses, espousing the highest commandment of *Jihad*, or "Holy War," were given for the purpose of spreading Islam throughout the world (not unlike the often brutal Christian Crusades): *The unbelievers follow falsehood while the faithful follow the truth. . . . When you meet the unbelievers strike off their heads, and when you have laid them low, bind them firmly.* (XLVII:3-4)

Those who fight and die in Allah's name, the *Koran* reads, will meet Him in the great Hereafter. Thus, it is a great privilege to die for Allah's sake, and those who fall on the battlefield in the course of Holy War become martyrs, *. . . for those who are slain in the cause of Allah, He will not allow their works to perish . . . He will admit them to the Paradise He has made known to them. . . . [They] shall be forgiven their sins and admitted to gardens watered by running streams . . .* (XLVII: 5 and III:194)

The Koran prescribes prayer, fasting, pilgrimage and purity as necessary elements of the faithful life. The steadfast Moslem prays at regular intervals throughout the day (early morning, middle afternoon, late afternoon, dusk, and nighttime), glorifying Allah, begging forgiveness and mercy, and praising his oneness. When praying, Moslems are urged to *stand up with all*

devotion before Allah. When you are exposed to danger pray while riding or on foot; and when you are restored to safety remember Allah, as He has taught you what you did not know.* (2:239)

Fasting is required during the whole month of Ramadan, the ninth month in the Islamic year and the period during which Mohammed received the verses. During this time, believers refrain from food or drink from dawn to sunset each day.

Pilgrimage (*Haji*), as commanded by the Koran, entails donning the pilgrim's simple garb and journeying to the city of Mecca (located in Saudi Arabia) to circle the Ka'aba. The Ka'aba, or House of Ka'aba, is a sacred shrine believed to have been built by Abraham and Ismael: *[Allah] enjoined Abraham and Ismael to sanctify Our House for those who walk round it, who meditate in it and who kneel and prostrate themselves.* (II:119)

All able-bodied Moslems are enjoined to make this pilgrimage at least once. Less important pilgrimages may be made to the sacred hills of Safa, Marwa, and Arafat, as well as the Sacred Monument, where an animal sacrifice should be offered.

Life and Death

Life is a period of testing and preparation. According to the *Koran*, the angels in heaven record a person's good and bad deeds, a heavenly journal to be used by Allah in the final judgment. After death—the gate to eternal life—everyone will receive the record of his or her deeds on earth. The good, who will go to heaven, will receive their record with the right hand, while the wicked, who will be consigned to hell, will receive it with the left.

The *Koran* places great emphasis on purity in both the physical and spiritual sense, for "Allah loves those who purify themselves." (IX:105) Through purity, one is blessed: *Blessed is the man who has kept [his soul] pure, and ruined he that has corrupted it!* (XCI:9)

Purity not only involves good works, but the uttering of kind, wise words: *Do you not see how Allah compares a good word to a good tree? Its root is firm and its branches are in the sky; it yields its fruit in every season by Allah's leaves. Allah gives parables to men so that they may take heed. But an evil word is like an evil tree torn out of the earth and shorn of its roots.* (XIV:24)

Impurity is the absence of virtue and piety. The impure are Godless, sinful, and wicked: *Allah will separate the wicked from the just. He will heap the wicked one upon another and then cast them into Hell.* (VIII:37)

The *Koran* outlines the promising fate of the Islamic faith, and the steps which lead toward true belief. Allah, like the Judeo-Christian God, is seen as at once merciful and unmerciful; kind and revengeful; loving and reproachful.

Due to the recent resurgence of fundamentalism in certain Islamic sects, there is a danger of stereotyping *all* Moslems as violent, religious zealots. By studying the *Koran*, Western cultures can overcome their prejudices, and learn more about a remarkable and fascinating set of spiritual beliefs.

BHAGAVAD-GITA

As translated from the Sanskrit by Sir Edwin Arnold

The *Bhagavad-gita*, meaning literally "The Song of the Blessed One," was incorporated into an Indian epic called the *Mahabarata* in about 200 B.C.E. The 700 "shlokas" (verses) of the *Bhagavad-gita* make up only a fraction of the *Mahabarata*, which encompasses some 100,000 verses. In the 8th century, the great philosopher-saint Shri Shankaracharya decided that the *Bhagavad-gita* was, in itself, an important work, and that it should stand alone. Since that time, it has been published on its own and is now much more widely read than the Mahabarata.

The text, in many respects, contains an inspiring story, and, inasmuch as there are many translations and interpretations, Sir Edwin Arnold is to be praised for his beautiful and poetic translation from the original Sanskrit, a formidable task. More than any other piece of Indian literature, its eighteen chapters give us a relatively succinct, clearly defined explanation of the Hindu, or *Vedic* faith, a set of religious ideals which have had profound influence on India's traditional social structure. And, in spite of the fact that some critics view the Hindu faith as a kind of religious justification for India's stratified caste system, it should be emphasized that its true religious sentiments are both genuine and penetrating.

Perhaps one of the most difficult Hindu concepts for a westerner to come to terms with is the notion of *detachment*, i.e., denying and ultimately liberating oneself from one's passions and desires. After all, many in Western society are taught to affirm their emotions and eagerly pursue their various desires, not to deny them. However, one must be patient with this characteristic Hindu perspective and try to fully understand it before prematurely dismissing it as extreme.

The main text of the *Bhagavad-gita* is an eighteen-chapter dialogue between Arjuna, a warrior-prince, and Krisna, who is an earthly incarnation of the solar deity Vishnu. The setting of the story is a battlefield where two clans, the Pandavas (the clan portrayed as being virtuous and just) and the Kauravas, are poised to fight. The leaders of each clan are cousins, and many of the other warriors are relatives opposing one another. Arjuna, a troubled human hero and leader of the Pandavas, has been reluctantly forced to engage in righteous battle against his own kinsmen. Krisna, disguised as a charioteer, attends Arjuna in order to bolster his faltering will with wise discourse.

In the opening chapter we find Arjuna and Krisna mounted on a chariot, prepared to give the fighting orders. Before he begins, Arjuna requests that they visit the front lines to survey the scene. Upon doing so, Arjuna is suddenly distraught at the sight of so many

kin about to slaughter each other, and questions the purpose of such a battle:

> Krisna! As I behold, come here to shed
> Their common blood, yon concourse of our kin
> My members fail, my tongue dries in my mouth
> A shudder thrills my body, and my hair bristles with horror
> The life within me seems to swim and faint;
> Nothing do I foresee save woe and wail.

Arjuna continues in this vein for some time, and his passionate exhortation for peace concludes the first chapter. Krisna vehemently chastises Arjuna for his sentiment, and submits that the proper thing for Arjuna to do is to go into battle dutifully. The remainder of the story consists of Krisna teaching and Arjuna questioning. Indeed, it takes a considerable amount of convincing for Krisna to finally persuade Arjuna that he must fight.

To Krisna, however, the battle is merely an archetype; his overall philosophy touches upon the virtuous life. Periodically, God comes to earth to put virtue back in her rightful place, says Krisna. God incarnates himself in an earthly shape, or emanation, called an *avatara*. Krisna himself is an avatara of God.

Interestingly, Hindus ultimately believe in one God, although they worship a number of deities, considering them aspects of an all-encompassing God. Humans, too, can be considered manifestations of God in that the spark of divinity breathes in every human.

In the *Bhagavad-gita* we see Krisna, God incarnate, coming to the aid of noble Arjuna, who, as an advanced soul, represents the side of virtue in a battle which ends up annihilating nearly all of its participants. The text as a whole—and specifically the teachings of Krisna—is an excellent profile of Hindu thought. Fundamental ideas of the faith are put forth in the context of Arjuna's inner crisis. Central to the story are the ideas of *reincarnation, karma*, the *caste system*, the *unity of opposites*, and *right action*.

The notion of reincarnation is somewhat familiar to most Western readers. Hindus believe that when people die, they are reborn on Earth again and again—until they learn the correct life path and attain *Nirvana*, a state of eternal bliss. The earthly world is an illusion—or what Hindus call "Maya"—and its complexities and impediments essentially a test to be overcome. A soul can never die, but takes on many different forms in its ascent towards—or descent from—the unity of God.

Karma is the law governing action and the consequences thereof. A life of virtue will lead one toward a more favorable earthly existence in the next life. Conversely, every sin committed in this life will return as an added hurdle in the next.

Closely tied to the ideas of reincarnation and karma is the *caste system*, in which Indian society is partitioned into four strata: the *Brahman*, or priestly class; the *ksatriya*, or warrior class; the *vaishya*, or merchant class; and the *shudras*, the working class and untouchables. Hindus believe that, warranted by his actions in previous lives, a person merits membership in the caste to which he belongs. For society to function properly, each class must fulfill a specific duty. Traditionally the Brahman constitute the religious and political power of India, the ksatriyas make up the military, the vaishya are concerned with trade, and the shudras are laborers. To follow through with one's duty is of the utmost importance. As Krisna says, "To die performing duty is no ill, but one who seeks other roads shall wander still." One must accept the role he or she is born to play, and willingly act out the assigned tasks. No earthly role is necessarily more important than any other because all duties carry equal weight and every soul on earth is compelled to perform them all in a succession of lifetimes:

> Thy task prescribed with spirit unattached
> gladly perform
> Since in performance of plain duty man
> Mounts to his highest bliss.
> By works alone Janak and ancient saints
> reached blessedness.

Krisna beseeches Arjuna to follow through with his war; not only does he represent the cause of virtue and his opponents that of moral decay, but, as a ksatriya, it is his blessed duty to go to war. "Fight! Vanquish foes and doubts, dear hero!" Krisna urges him. "Slay what haunts thee in fond shapes, and would betray." He says further that one should maintain a detached attitude toward one's duty, while still performing it uprightly. That which is called *right action* is "wrought without attachment, passionlessly, for duty, not for love, nor hate, nor gain." The dictates of "Tyaga" pronounce that one should not be concerned with the *fruit* of one's acts, because if a person is focused on the end, or motivated by some sort of emotion or passion, then *the act itself* will be sullied and impure. It is pointless for Arjuna to be distraught about going into battle, Krisna declares; it is out of right action, his unshakable duty, to do so. And since souls are immortal, it is foolish for Arjuna to think he will truly "destroy" any of his foes:

> Thou grievest where no grief should be!
> Thou speak'st words lacking in wisdom!
> For the wise in heart
> Mourn not for those that live, nor those that
> die.
> Nor I, nor thou, nor any one of these
> Ever was not, nor ever will not be
> For ever and ever afterwards.
> All that doth live, lives always! . . .
> As there come infancy and youth and age,
> So come there raisings-up and layings-down

> Of other and other life abodes,
> Which the wise know, and fear not.

Because of the immortality of souls, joy and sorrow, as well as other dichotomous passions, are, ultimately, irrelevant concepts:

> The soul which is not moved,
> The soul that with a strong and constant
> calm
> Takes sorrow and joy indifferently,
> Lives in the life undying! That which is
> Can never cease to be; that which is not
> Will not exist. To see this truth of both
> Is theirs who part essence from accident,
> Substance from shadow.

In this illustration, the earthly world is the shadow and the substance is the divine. Hence, we should realize that the events of this world, both positive and negative, are illusory, transitory, and insignificant. Furthermore, argues Krisna, sensory experience should be disregarded as much as possible. Sensory experience (all feelings and ideas acquired by way of the senses) leads to attraction, which in turn leads to desire. Desire gives birth to passion, recklessness, and ultimately, the undoing of purpose, mind, and man. In short, desire is the root cause of man's suffering.

The perfect man is one who has transcended the temporal world and sees beyond the bounds of opposites, perceiving instead a *unity of opposites*. "If a man sees everywhere—taught by his own similitude, one life, one essence in the evil and the good, hold him a yogi—yea, [he is] well-perfected." He is one who has "true knowledge," that is, one who sees a single "changeless life in all the lives, and in the separate, one inseparable." The enlightened soul is one who has renounced the world: "That is the true renouncer, firm and fixed, who—seeking naught, rejecting naught—dwells proof against the opposites."

Krisna tells Arjuna that on his path toward perfection he must beware of three things in particular, obsessions which he calls the doors of hell: *lust, wrath,* and *avarice.* Man will never advance unless he places himself beyond these doors and holds no importance in his own ego.

After much deliberation, Arjuna finally comes to acknowledge that Krisna does in fact represent God's true word, grants that what he has taught is true, and pledges that he will willingly obey:

> Trouble and ignorance are gone! The light
> Hath come unto me, by thy favour, Lord!
> Now I am fixed! My doubt is fled away!
> According to thy word, so will I do!

The ***Bhagavad-gita*** ends at this juncture. According to Hindu legend, in the ensuing battle all but a handful of warriors are slaughtered. Arjuna's Pandavas, with a few more survivors than the Kauravas, are declared the victors—and virtue is returned to her throne in India.

THE VEDAS

Authors: Numerous and unknown
Composed:1500-1000 B.C.

Introduction:

"Hinduism" designates the traditional social and religious structure of the Indian people. In India this religious complex is called "the eternal religion," as, for centuries, it has incorporated many aspects of truth and enlightenment for the Indian people. It is an ever-changing religion which, over the ages, has been influenced by Buddhism, Islam, Christianity, Jainism and Zoroastrianism.

Because of this inclusive nature, Hinduism has many sacred texts, composed by a vast number of people, most of whom are unknown. The oldest collection of such texts is known as the "Vedas." Orthodox Hindus ascribe superhuman origins and divine authority to this assembly of writings.

There are, in fact, various narratives delineating the origins of the *Vedas*, but all of the traditional accounts agree that the knowledge of the *Vedas* was revealed to "seers" during states of deep contemplation. In Sanskrit the word "veda" means "knowledge" or "sacred teaching." The *Vedas* are also referred to as "shruti," meaning "that which was revealed."

The *Vedas* is composed of an enormous complex of scriptures, approximately six times the size of the Bible in length. They originated from the Vedic Indians, who settled on the banks of the Indus river during the period in which the oldest texts were composed. According to rough estimates—the only estimates available—this was around 1500 to 1000 BCE.

The Vedic Indians were divided into numerous small tribes, who supported a closed caste-like group of priestly nobility. Although writing as we know it had not yet been developed as an art form, the priestly schools perfected an extraordinary power of memory. The *Vedas* survived through oral transmission for centuries, before being recorded in written form.

Text Summary:

The *Vedas* are divided into four parts:

1. the **Rigveda**—the Veda of poetry;
2. the **Samaveda**—the Veda of songs;
3. the **Yajuveda**—the Veda of sacrificial texts;
4. the **Atharvaveda**—the Veda of Atharvan, a priest of the "mystical fire ceremony.

The four Vedas initially served the chief priests as manuals for the correct application of hymns and rituals used in sacrificial practices. To perform a complete sacrifice, four different priests were needed:

(1) The *hotar* ("caller"), who, using the poetry of the Rigveda, recited hymns inviting the gods to partake of the sacrificial offering.

(2) The *udagatar* ("singer"), who, employing the Samaveda, accompanied his preparations and offerings with singing.

(3) The *adhvaryu* ("general priest"), who, borrowing from the holy Yajuveda, carried out the sacred rite and thereby murmured the appropriate verses and formulas (yajus)

(4) The *high priest*, whose duty it was to supervise and direct the sacrifice as a whole. He was, however, not particularly connected to the Atharvaveda in any way.

The sacrificial offering often incorporated the drinking of *Soma*, an intoxicating plant juice which was both an offering for the gods, and a drink of immortality. Soma also was worshiped as a Vedic god.

The *Rigveda* is the oldest and most extensive of the four Vedic texts. Composed of upwards of 1,000 hymns, it is considered the cornerstone of the other Vedas. Some of its hymns deal with subjects such as the nature of God, as this one titled "To the Unknown God":

In the beginning there arose the Golden Child. As soon as born, he alone was the lord of all that is He established the earth and this heaven: Who is the God to whom we shall offer sacrifice?

He who gives breath, he who gives strength, whose command all the bright gods revere, whose shadow is immortality, whose shadow is death:—Who is the God to whom we shall offer sacrifice?

He who through whose might became the sole king of the breathing and twinkling world, who governs all this, man and beast:—Who is the God to whom we shall offer sacrifice? . . .

. . . He who by his might looked even over the waters which held the power and generated the sacrifice, he who alone is God above all gods:—Who is the God to whom we shall offer sacrifice?

May he not hurt us, he who is the begetter of the earth, or he, the righteous, who begat the heaven; he who also begat the bright and mighty waters:—Who is the God to whom we shall offer sacrifice?

Pragapati, no other than thou embraces all these created things. May that be ours which we desire when sacrificing to thee: may we be lords of wealth!

The hymns of the *Rigveda* are often embroidered with poetic imagery. They were composed specifically to praise the gods. The bards who authored the verses were not interested in explaining the god about which they spoke, but rather to celebrate him; they took little interest in the human listener, but rather in the god himself.

The bards even competed to produce the most flattering poems possible about each particular god. Hence, there is not one highest god, but a long series of gods, each of which is variously called "very great," "the greatest," "very shining," "very mighty," "beautiful to look at," and "very generous to the pious." Many of the gods are said to exterminate all enemies and rule all of heaven and earth. Superlatives abound with no restraint.

One noble circle of gods is the "Maruts" or "storm gods," who are frequently and eloquently petitioned for assistance:

Come hither, Maruts, on your chariots charged with lightning, resounding with beautiful songs, stored with spears, and winged with horses! Fly to us like birds, with your best food, you mighty ones! . . . He who holds the axe is brilliant like gold . . . On your bodies there are daggers for beauty; may they stir up our minds as they stir up the forests . . . Ye brilliant Maruts, welcoming these prayers, be mindful of these my rites . . . bring offspring for ourselves with food. May we have an invigorating autumn, with quickening rain.

Many of the poems are beautifully artistic, and a whole series are disguised in veiled language, born in the closed circles of the priestly class.

The Vedic hymns shine with images of nature:

Those who approached on their glorious deer . . . through fear of you, ye terrible ones, the forests even bend down, the earth shakes, and . . . even the mountain cloud, grown large, fears, and the ridge of heaven trembles . . . To thee the juice-wielding cow pours out all treasures.

Now for the greatness of the chariot of Vata. Its roar goes crashing and thundering. It moves touching the sky, and creating red sheens, or it goes scattering the dust of the earth. Afterwards there rise the gusts of Vata, they go toward him, like women to a feast. The god goes with them on the same chariot, he, the king of the whole of this world. When he moves on his paths along the sky, he rests not even a single day; the friend of the waters, the first-

born, the holy, where was he born, whence did he spring? The breath of the gods, the germ of the world, that go moves wherever he listeth; his roars indeed are heard, not his form—let us offer sacrifice to that Vata.

But behind the mythological visions of gods is an insight into the workings of the universe, the underlying oneness of all life that moves the multiplicity of forms and forces: "Truth is one, many are its names." Remarks indicating the oneness of all things are scattered throughout the *Vedas:*

One whole governs the moving and the stable, that which walks and flies, this variegated creation.

That which is one has developed into the all.

Much of the imagery in the **Vedas** is symbolic: Heaven and Earth represent parents, sun and moon are fosterers, bull and cow are impregnators, water and fire are cleansing and creative agents, tree, bird and swan are the cosmos or the human psyche. But this imagery is not always clear to the reader.

Often the hymns reflect the basic concerns of human survival such as in this hymn entitled "To Rudra":

O father of the Maruts . . . May I attain a hundred winters through the most blissful medicines which thou has given! Put away far from us all hatred, put away anguish, put away sickness in all directions! . . . Ward off all assaults of mischief. Let us not incense thee, O Rudra, by our worship, not by bad praise, O hero, and not by divided praise . . . O Rudra, where is thy softly stroking hand which cures and relieves? . . . O Maruts, those pure medicines of yours, most beneficent and delightful, O heroes . . . I crave from Rudra, as health and wealth.

One section of the **Vedas** concentrates in great detail on the rites pertaining to custom (such as marriages and funerals); a few discuss the reality of various demons and souls. There are also texts which say little about hymns or popular concerns and more about what seems like the well-being of the priests. These focus on extolling the virtue of alms-giving to the priests. This theme, however, hardly appears in the most important collection, the *Rigveda.*

Altogether a total of 10,580 verses appear in what is known as the **Vedas.** These are arranged in ten "song cycles" known as "mandalas." Although today the **Vedas** are not as popular as in other times in history, they have served as a rich compilation of the most ancient and rudimentary elements of the enormous collection of Indian religions we know of as "Hinduism."

THE KO JI KI AND THE NIHONGI

Sacred Scriptures of the Shinto

The *Ko ji ki* and the *Nihongi* are the two "Greater Scriptures" of Japan. Together they represent the most important myths and doctrines of Shintoism. Both are essentially collections of mythical episodes which explain the origins of natural forces and the imperial lineage. More than 1000 "Kami," or deities, as well as an equal number of human characters fill the texts, which, in format, resemble histories rather than religious works. Both works, smoothly blending history and myth, point to Japan's divine mission upon earth.

The text is often nothing more than a series of puzzling lists, inaccessible to the Western reader. However, each work is firmly rooted in a foundation of poetic allegory, even their nuances aren't immediately obvious.

Shinto is Japan's indigenous religion, having been embraced by Japanese sovereignty—and the people—for thousands of years. As a movement, it is distinguished by its devotion to deities of natural forces and by its doctrine that the Emperor of Japan is a descendent of the sun-goddess. These subjects, in fact, comprise the chief focus of the myths which appear in Shinto texts. In addition, it should be recognized that Shintoism in general places far greater emphasis on direct religious experience of divinity than do most Western sects, showing a deep sensitivity to the mystery of life, rather than analyzing theological principles.

Although Shintoism does not rely on a single literary work as the ultimate theocratic authority, the *Ko ji ki* and the *Nihongi* are certainly held in highest reverence, above the numerous "lesser scriptures." The *Ko ji ki* is the oldest of the two texts, and is considered canon by the Shinto. The words "ko ji ki" mean "Records of Ancient Matters," records which consists mostly of stories and genealogies of the ancient deities of the Japanese islands and their "descendants"—those who have peopled and ruled Japan through modern times. The *Ko ji ki* was written largely in the early part of the eighth century, although its contents sprang from an oral tradition that dates much earlier. The work of transcribing the *Ko ji ki*, states the epilogue, "was initiated in 682, when `Temmu Tenno, fortieth Sovereign,' issued an imperial decree:"

I learn that the annals of the Emperors and also the original words possessed by various families differ from the truth and have been added to by valueless inventions. Unless now these faults be corrected, before many years the meaning of this warp and woof of the country and prime foundation of the empire will be lost. I therefore now desire that the annals of the Emperors be taken and recorded and the ancient words examined and certified, inventions stricken out and the truth be ascertained, for handing down to future ages.

The *Nihongi*, meaning, "Written Chronicles of Japan," was also transcribed in the eighth century. But its happenings occurred centuries later than those of the *Ko ji ki*. It both supplements and amplifies the myths of the *Ko ji ki*—and adds a greater touch of humanity. It also touches upon the natural creation of the earth, human genealogy, hierarchy of the gods, and connection of the members of the human and immortal family. However, nearly all of these references are expressed through allegory (where the literary objects and characters stand for other moral or religious ideas and principles), in which vivid metaphoric pictures are conjured up by the language, the lilting rhythm, and the dramatic flow of events. Both this symbolic representation and the cyclical nature of the passages make for difficult reading for the Westerner, as typified by these mysterious lines from "The Beginning of the Sky and Earth":

Of old time the Sky and the Earth were not yet set apart the one from the other, nor were the female and male principles separated. All was a mass formless and egg-shaped, the extent whereof is not known, which held the life principle. Thereafter, the purer tenuous essence, ascending gradually, formed the Sky, the heavier portion sank and became the Earth. The lighter element merged readily, but the heavier was united with difficulty. Thus the Sky was formed first, the Earth next, and later Kami [humans] were produced in the space between them.

When the Sky and the Earth began, there was a something in the very midst of the emptiness whose shape cannot be described. At the first a thing like a white cloud appeared, which floated between Sky and Earth, and from it three Kami came into being in the High-Sky Plain. These three Kami, appearing earliest, were born without progenitors and later hid their bodies. They were:

MID-SKY-MASTER
HIGH-PRODUCER
DIVINE-PRODUCER
SKY-DIVINE-STANDER

A word should be said about the term "kami," since it carries such elite status in Shinto literature and practice. Although often translated as "god" or "gods," it may refer to many things—humans, beasts, birds, plants; seas and mountains; and storms and winds. An eighteenth-century Shinto scholar, Mootori Noringa, acknowledging the mysteriousness of the term, says that "All . . . things whatsoever which deserve to be dreaded and revered for the extraordinary and pre-eminent powers which they possess are called *kami*." And another, modern Shinto scholar, W.G. Aston, states, "The Japanese people themselves do not have a clear idea regarding the Kami . . . " Even though the Japanese word *kami* means "above" or "superior," its root (*ka*) is more an expression of wonderment or awe. Paradoxically, then, "kami" is an all-important yet vague, puzzling term, difficult—if not impossible—for one who has not been steeped in the ancient precepts of the indigenous and revered Japanese culture to grasp, either conceptually or intuitively. Thus, "the way of the kami"—whether referring to noble human rulers, traditional gods, guardian spirits, or natural forces—comprises a fundamental link between deity, the family, and the community.

The *Ko ji ki* text goes on to relate the allegorical creation of earth and man and the subsequent dealings of the kami in the daily lives of the people:

*Now while the soil of the young Earth which made the Lands drifted about as floating oil, like a jelly-fish sporting on the water-surface, or a cloud floating over the sea without root or attachment, a something **clear and bright like crystal** sprouted up, like a horn, like a reed shoot when it first emerges from the mud. This became transformed into Kamis of human shape, and there appeared, **springing out of the buds of the reed shoot,** two more Kami:*

PLEASANT-REED-SPROUT-PRINCE-ELDER
ETERNAL-SKY-STANDER

*These likewise were born without progenitors and later hid their bodies. **The Three Creator-Kami and these two are called the Sky-Kami.** Pleasant-Reed-Sprout-Prince-Elder was a divine man.*

The creation of the Sun-Goddess (from whom descended the lineage of the emperor) . . . One of the Kami, He-Who-Invites, returned from the netherworld to the upperworld. He had proclaimed "I have brought upon myself ill luck, and must purify my person of its filth," so he went to a small river mouth near Orance in Sun-Facing in the Island of Tsukushi, and on a plain covered with bush-clover, cleansed himself.

When he threw down his girdle and skirt there were born from them the Kami:

LONG-ROAD-SPACE
LOOSEN-PUT.

From his upper garment (or as some say from his foot-coverings) was born the Kami:

TROUBLE MASTER

***This Kami is the Kami of torture.** From his trousers, his hat, and his sandals were born the Kami:*

OPEN-MOUTH
OPEN-MOUTH-MASTER
ROAD-SPREAD-OUT

From his left bracelet there were born the two Kami:

SEA-HORIZON-DISTANT
WAVE-EDGE-SHORE-PRINCE

And from his right bracelet were born the three Kami:

SHORE-DISTANT
WAVE-EDGE-SHORE-PRINCE
INTERMEDIATE-SHORE-DIRECTION

When at length he was about to wash away the impurities of his body, he made a prayer, saying, "The male Kami has come to the bush-clover plain

of Orange to exorcise the filth of the Land-of-Night and make his body clean." Then he lifted his voice, saying, "The water in the upper current is swift and that in the lower current is sluggish." So he plunged into the middle current, and as he bathed there the following Kami were born from the filth he had acquired:

BODY-OF-EIGHT-EVILS
BODY-OF-GREAT-EVILS
DIVING-RECTIFYING-BODY
GREAT-RECTIFYING-BODY
FEMALE OF IZU

The last three were produced to root out the first two (which pair some account a single Kami). As he bathed in the water's bottom current were born the Kami:

OCEAN-BOTTOM-POSSESSOR
MALE-BOTTOM-POSSESSOR . . .

Both the myths of the *Ko ji ki* and *Nihongi* proceed in an elaborate fashion, describing the activities of colorfully-named deities such as the Emperor Divine-Lagoon-River-Ears, Sky-Southwest-Wind-Wondrous-Southwest-Wind, and Prince-Sky-Plenty-Earth-Plenty-High-As-Sky's-Sun-Fire-Ruddy-Plenty.

Following the birth of Young-Three-Hairs-Moor (Jimmu-Tenno), who is described as the first mortal emperor, the narrative describes the gradual conquest of the Japanese islands.

These stories have served a singular and tremendous function in Japanese society: namely, establishing the exclusive divine origin of the emperor and inhabitants of Japan. Additionally, however, they—even to this day—provide the religious fabric of Japanese culture.

In orthodox Shintoism, these texts have become the scriptural foundation of the religion itself. These excerpts, from a late 19th century instructional manual, describe the role of the *Ko ji ki* and the *Nihongi*:

Question: "In what manner was human life produced?"

Answer: "Their Augustness HE-WHO-INVITES and SHE-WHO-INVITES, in obedience to the divine will of the Sky Deity, first trods the path of spouses and produced deity-men, deigning to lay the foundations for all enterprises. Hence it was that all mankind breathe and have their being. For this reason the present writer's flesh and blood have been inherited from these deities and they are the first parents of the human race."

Both works implicitly and explicitly describe the Japanese as the original humans—direct descendants of a divine heritage. It had long been thought by the Shinto that this lineage was a factor that set the Japanese apart from other races. But in recent years, these texts have come to be much more widely regarded as an assortment of historically significant stories rather than a collection of absolute truths.

THE ANALECTS OF CONFUCIUS

China, under the Chou Dynasty (c. 771 BCE) was characterized by a prolonged state of violence and disunity. When its capital fell to barbaric rule, the Dynasty was forced to relocate to the east, resulting in the Dynasty's split into the "East Chou" and the "West Chou." This division fostered several competing philosophies that addressed the political concerns at hand, and advanced ideas which captured the minds of men such as Lao Tzu and Confucius, whose teachings comprise the dogma of Taoism and Confucianism.

Confucius and his disciples cultivated a world-view that was essentially humanistic. Taoism is less humanistic in that it stresses inactivity and passiveness; the universe will evolve with or without human interference. Further, the Taoist position maintains that what is seen is not reality: "The whole world recognizes the beautiful as the beautiful; yet this is only the ugly; the whole world recognizes the good as the good; yet this is only the bad. (taken from Lao Tzu's *Tao Te Ching*). In a word, Taoists assert that we mistake appearance for reality.

In contrast, Confucian thought regards appearance and reality to be closely related. In short, what one *sees* is *real*. In addition, since Confucianism is concerned with benevolence on both the individual and political level, undertakings that are passive or non-contentious are thought of as useless.

Central to Confucian ideas are *The Analects*, also known as the *lun yu*. Confucius (551-479 BCE) was an older contemporary of Lao Tzu. Confucianism grew out of a violent period in China, where warring factions divided the country. Yet the time of Confucius saw an abatement of this barbarous imperial rule.

One of Confucius' primary beliefs was that a man must think for himself. This notion was coupled with the concept of "chun tzu," a term which represents the ideal man whose character embodies benevolence and whose acts are in accordance with rightness. Like the *Tao Te Ching*, *Analects* heavily concerns itself with the art of politics, but further avouches that politics is only an extension of a society's individual morals.

Text Overview:

Confucius traveled to a number of different states within China, in an attempt to spread his ideals. However, he was largely unsuccessful. His teachings centered on moral character, primarily *Virtue (te)* and the *Way (tao)*. Virtue, which is in part a gift from Heaven, is what makes up a person's character; the Way represents the path of a particular person in question; thus, one individual's Way was separate and distinct from another's. According to Confucius:

I set my heart on the way, base myself on Virtue, lean upon benevolence for support and take my recreation in the arts.

Benevolence (*jen*, or good will), related to Virtue and pivotal to Confucian behavior, is dependent upon one's own efforts. The goal is to become as "good" an individual as possible, ignoring petty worries about success or failure. Confucius did not forecast success either in this world or the next, for as he "did not understand even life," how could he "understand death"? Hence, there is no assurance of an afterlife in *Analects*. Instead, benevolence is observed for its own sake.

The most elevated individual, according to Confucius, is the *"sage"* (shang jen). This rare, utmost benevolent man—indeed, a man who has advanced beyond benevolence—even causes Confucius to ask: "How dare I claim to be a sage or a benevolent man?" He was once asked: "If there were a man who gave extensively to the common people and brought help to the multitude, what would you think of him? Could he be called benevolent?" To which Confucius replied: "It is no longer a matter of benevolence with such a man. If you must describe him, 'sage' is, perhaps, the right word." Further, Confucius declared, "I have no hopes of becoming a sage," though he did acknowledge that such men exist.

Lower down on this benevolence scale is the *"good"* man (shan jen). Good men commonly labor in government, for they are responsible for doing good works:

How true is the saying that after a state has been ruled by good men it is possible to get the better of cruelty and do away with killing.

Below the good man is the *"complete"* man. Such a person "remembers what is right at the sight of profit and is ready to lay down his life in the face of danger." Such terms are used in *Analects* to describe the *gentleman* (chun tzu), or the benevolent man, who, according to Confucius, approaches the ideal moral character that is with in easy reach of all men (certainly only a few can become sages or governors, to work for the common good of the people, but all men can aspire to be gentlemen). Gentlemen include those in authority, as opposed to *"small"* men (hiao jen), those who are ruled. Gentlemen possess a highly cultivated moral character; small men do not. Benevolence, then, is the gentleman's most important quality:

If the gentleman forsakes jen (benevolence), in what way can he make a name for himself? The gentleman never deserts benevolence, not even for as long as it takes to eat a meal. If he hurries and stumbles, one may be sure that it is in benevolence that he does so.

The message of benevolence, then, is as follows: **Do not impose on others what you yourself do not desire.**

The method of benevolence is called *shu*, which is one aspect of the way of the Master. The other aspect is known as *chung*, or "doing one's best." It is through chung that a person puts into practice what is discerned by the method of shu. When asked of the way in which a subject should treat his ruler, for instance, Confucius replies:

The ruler should employ the services of his subjects in accordance with the rites. A subject should serve his ruler by doing his best.

The rites referred to also involve shu and chung, and direct the gentleman's behavior both personally and politically. It follows that one must do good in the personal and family realm just as he would in the political, and vice-versa:

While at home hold yourself in a respectful attitude; when serving in an official capacity be reverent; when dealing with others do your best. These are qualities that cannot be put aside, even if you go and live among the barbarians.

The culmination of this devout respectfulness and reverence is *love* for one's fellow man. The Confucian basis of morality is grounded on this natural, sincere love. And the love shared between father and son, Confucius felt, is the driving force of morality in society:

Being good as a son and obedient as a young man is, perhaps, the root of a man's character.

In other words, one merely takes the goodness discovered within the family and extends it to the common people. Thus, the gentleman achieves benevolence—"is generous and caring . . . and is just."

There are other virtues which the gentleman possesses. Among them are *wisdom* ("intelligence," or *chih*) and *courage* (*yung*):

The man of wisdom is never in two minds; the man of benevolence never worries; a man of courage is never afraid.

A man possessing wisdom can always distinguish between right and wrong. However, a man whose wisdom is blended with courage, rules over others. Confucius says, "I was not born with knowledge, but . . . I am quick to seek it." In short, according to *Analects*, to know is to "say you know when you know, and to say you do not know when you do not, that is knowledge." The effect of such honest self-appraisal would be that "where a gentleman is ignorant, one would expect him not to offer any opinion." However, Confucius warns that courage and wisdom can prove to be double-edged swords. Thus, *morality* is higher than they both:

For the gentleman it is morality that is supreme. Possessed of courage but devoid of morality, a gentleman will make trouble while a small man will be a brigand.

Another highly touted virtue is *hsin*, which, translated, denotes trustworthiness, or being true to one's word. Hsin includes promise-keeping and matching one's words with deeds, for "the gentleman is ashamed of his word out-stripping his deed," and "claims made immodestly are difficult to live up to." Therefore, the gentleman "puts his words into action before allowing his words to follow his action."

Two additional virtues put forth in *Analects* are *reverence* (*ching*) and *respectfulness* (*kung*). Ching is the awareness of one's huge responsibility to promote the welfare of the common people, and is connected with sacrifice. To follow kung is to do away with insult and humiliation. The gentleman is "respectful towards others and observant of the rites . . . of morality"; furthermore, he is "respectful when it comes to his [personal] demeanor." Consequently, if a person possesses kung, treating others with respect, it is

impossible for others to address him with disdain.

It is with these virtues that the gentleman/ruler/Emperor conducts the affairs of government, as mandated by the command of Heaven (*t'ien ming*). In fact, it is a major concern of Heaven that the welfare of the people be maintained; thus, the Emperor must rule in virtue and by the Decree of Heaven. If he should rule for his own sake, Heaven will withdraw the decree, and he will be deposed.

The Emperor is most humble in his high station:

[The Emperor] stands in awe of three things. He is in awe of the Decree of Heaven. He is in awe of great men. He is in awe of the words of the sages. The small man, being ignorant of the Decree of Heaven, does not stand in awe of it. He treats great men with insolence and the words of the sages with derision.

Hence, t'ien ming (Heaven's decree) is what a man *ought* to do—which may differ from what another man "ought" to do. *Ming* (fate, fortune), however, is concerned with Destiny, and the bringing about of what *will* come to pass. Whereas t'ien ming's "Heavenly decree" is understandable and must be obeyed by the gentleman, ming is a mystery best left alone. T'ien ming, for instance, may decree that someone be executed for committing a crime; it is decreed by law and Heaven that he must die, and the action "ought" to be carried out. Ming, on the other hand, would rule in instances such as an earthquake or flood; and, if something is destined to be, according to Confucius, it is futile try to change the natural course of events.

The ruler, then, should focus on those areas where he can make a difference: the morality and welfare of the common people (*min*). The ruler, in order to merit trust, must provide the people with "enough food, give them enough arms"; but, "when there is no trust, the common people will have nothing to stand on."

In further advising rulers, Confucius recommends:

In administering your government, what need is there for you to kill? Just desire the good yourself and the common people will be good. The virtue of the gentleman is like wind; the virtue of the small man is like grass. Let the wind blow over the grass and it is sure to bend.

Truly, it is this exceptional regard for the commoner—the peasant, the laborer, the farmer, the beggar—that constitutes a central thread of Confucius' *Analects*. Throughout, the importance of proper government cannot be overstated.

Though the teachings of Confucius are in some ways agnostic, and often pessimistic, his central, highly humanistic points are encouraging: Man thinks for himself and strives to promote benevolence in his family and government; the ruler, again in benevolence, follows the Decree of Heaven in guiding the common people, whom he loves as if they were his own family members; and, since benevolence fuels the goodness of society, it is Confucius' wish that all men, both great and small, will come to fathom and profit by this simple human quality.

THE TAO TE CHING

by
Lao Tzu
(441-479 BCE)

The *Tao Te Ching* is the main body of work in Taoist tradition. Known as the *Tao*, the text was transcribed during the Golden Age of Chinese philosophy, possibly around the fourth century BCE. Generally attributed to Lao Tzu (551-479 BCE), an older contemporary of Confucius, the Tao ("the Way" or "the Path") constitutes the path to *Ching*, or "virtue." The *Tao*, then, is a poetic treatise on the art of politics, government, and virtue.

Taoism grew out of a turbulent period of Chinese history known as the "warring states period," in which the country was divided into combative feudalists struggling for control and power. The *Tao Te Ching* emerged from this conflict as a way to establish needed change, and subsequently to achieve oneness, order and balance between the warring parties.

Balance, a central principle, is embodied in the Taoist symbol of the *yin* and *yang*, which represent the condition of absolute balance in the universe. Balance then, is the Way, or the Path, referred to as the tao (pronounced "dow"). The *tao* "is to the world as the river and the sea are to rivulets and streams." (XXXII) However, to describe the tao using specific terms would limit its function—and the *tao* has no limits.

> As a thing the tao is
> Shadowy, indistinct. [XXI]

One must study carefully to grasp the nature of the way:

> Yet within the tao is a substance.
> Dim and dark,
> Yet within the tao is an essence.
> This essence is quite genuine
> And within it is something that can be tested. [XXI]

Still, the tao is largely intangible, since "the great image has no shape. The way conceals itself in being nameless." [XLI] The point is, then, that the Way (*tao*) can be approached by adhering to a set of rules and prescriptions, but that fully to grasp it, one must internalize the concepts.

The Way has existed since before the creation of the universe, since before time began. The *tao* is something created from nothing.

> There is a thing confusedly formed,
> Born before heaven and earth.
> Silent and void
> It stands alone and does not change,
> Goes round and does not [become] weary.
> It is capable of being the mother of the world. [XXV]

Obviously, the *Tao Te Ching* states, that which came before the creation of the universe cannot be easily defined. It is too universal, too eternal to be represented by a mere name.

> I know not its name
> So I style it "the Way."
> I give it the makeshift name of "the great." [XXV]

The Way, then, is essential to the very structure of creation.

> Man models himself on earth,
> Earth on heaven,
> Heaven on the way,
> And the way on that which is naturally so. [XXV]

Integral to the universe's structure and balance are the two opposing forces—the named and the unnamed—which, together, constitute a harmonious whole, just like the yin and the yang. The Tao explains that since "the way that can be spoken of is not the constant way" [I], and "the name that can be named is not the constant name" [I], the named is the "creator," the mother of all life on earth, while the "nameless" is the way which is beyond the temporal world.

> The nameless was the beginning of heaven
>   and earth;
> The named was the mother of the myriad
>   creatures . . .
> These two are the same
> But diverge in name as they issue forth. [I]

The "nameless" and the "named"—also referred to as "nothing" and "something"—are held in perfect equilibrium, as are all the opposites required to make a whole. These balanced opposites provide the central dynamic of the *tao*, as the following passage explains:

> Thus Something and Nothing produce each
>   other;
> the difficult and the easy compliment each
>   other;
> the long and the short off-set each other;
> The high and the low incline towards each
>   other;
> Note and sound harmonize with each other;
> Before and after follow each other. [II]

"Balanced opposites" becomes a metaphor in the Tao Te Ching; every natural force has its opposites and contradictions, which, brought together, endow the world with balance and oneness. Use of the *tao* will not drain it of its power; after all, it has no limit. The *tao* is both empty and full.

It is empty without being exhausted:
The more it works the more comes out. [V]

Simply put, the *tao* simply *is*. It is strong, yet, because it has no substance, it is also weak.

Weakness is the means the way employs. [XL]

The *tao* is forceful, yet submissive. It provides structure to the universe, yet it is supple and easily manipulated, seeming paradoxes illustrated by the following passage:

A man is supple and weak when living, but hard and stiff when dead. Grass and trees are pliant and fragile when living, but dried and shrivelled when dead. Thus the hard and the strong are the comrades of death; the supple and the weak are the comrades of life. [LXXVI]

The vitality of the tao lies in its pliancy and receptiveness. It is not stiff or unyielding like iron; its strength is rather like water: though it is powerful enough to carve stone, yet it provides little resistance to the gentle caress.

At first it may be difficult to see the connection between Taoist philosophy and the turbulent era of Chinese history from which it sprang. However, the tao is closely linked to feudalism and sheds much-needed light on the world of politics, ethics, and government. For example, the notion of the weak thing manifesting itself as strong pertains to the way in which control and power flows amongst a people. The weak, afflicted serf, Lao Tzu writes, shall overcome, while the strong shall fall, just as "a tree that is strong shall suffer the axe." [LXXVI]

The strong and big takes the lower position,
The supple and weak takes the higher position. [LXXVI]

. . . The weak overcomes the strong,
And the submissive overcomes the hard,
Everyone in the world knows
yet no one can put this knowledge into practice. [LXXVIII]

Of course, as is the way of *yin* and *yang*, once the weak conquer the strong, weakness becomes strength, and will in turn be conquered as new weak forces arise in the future. This perpetual behavior of individuals as well as governments echoes another Taoist dynamic: the cyclical nature of all natural and human phenomena.

One who understands the meaning of the tao is known as a *sage* or *ruler*. A sage exhibits specific characteristics: The sage "embraces the One and is a model for the empire"; he is "well versed in the way"; and like the *tao* itself, a sage is "minutely subtle, mysteriously comprehending, and too profound to be known." Furthermore, the true sage is constantly evolving, changing, shifting.

Falling apart like thawing ice;
Thick like the uncarved block;
Vacant like a valley;
Murky like muddy water . . . [XV]

Further, the sage "desires not to be full. Because he is not full that he can be worn and yet newly made." [XV] The sage is also subtle yet powerful.

He does not show himself, and so is conspicuous;
He does not consider himself right, and so is illustrious;
He does not brag, and so has merit;
He does not boast, and so endures.
It is because he does not contend that no one in the
empire is in a position to contend with him. [XXII]

"Because he does nothing, he never ruins anything; and, because he does not lay hold of anything, he loses nothing." [LXIV] In short, the sage is made great because he never attempts to be so. He is the servant of all, and therefore, the ruler of all.

As a ruler, the sage is benevolent. He "has no mind of his own. He takes as his own the minds of the people." [XLIX] And, in "desiring to lead the people," the sage must "follow behind them." [LXVI]

In maintaining the government, the ruler neither trifles with his power nor interferes with the affairs of the state. "Governing a large state is like boiling a small fish," the *Tao* declares. Surely the state, like the fish, can be spoiled by too much handling.

The empire is a sacred vessel and nothing should be done to it.
Whoever does anything to it will ruin it; whoever lays hold of it will lose it. [XXIX]

Tampering with the empire frustrates its purposes. "It is always through not meddling that the empire is won. Should you meddle, then you are not equal to the task of winning the empire." [XLVIII] Rather, a sage will follow a course of "no action."

The sage keeps to the deed that consists in taking no action and practices the teaching that uses no words. [II]

The **Tao Te Ching** truly practices what it preaches, imparting instruction using the minimum of words and leaving the student to discover the *tao* on his own. Its verses mystify because attempting to explain them would muddle their meaning: the Way of the universe has no limit, and defining its nature implies that it has boundaries or form when in fact is has none. The Way is constantly changing, yet never changes. The **Tao Te Ching** simply reveals that change is an integral part of life. Change is the Way.

Chuang Tzu, along with the even more legendary Lao Tzu, is considered one of the chief philosophers of classical Taoism. His extant work, consisting of seven "inner chapters," is accepted by scholars as authentic. An additional 26 chapters attributed to Chuang may actually be the contributions of later, anonymous authors.

As a historical figure, Chuang Tzu is a mysterious, almost legendary element in the history of Chinese religion and philosophy. He is said to have lived in the Honan province of China around 400 B.C. He appears as an eccentric recluse with an obvious disdain for common social and political values. In one story Chuang is offered—and refuses—the position of prime minister of China. His writings explicitly reject the powerful Confucian dogma which was so influential during his time. Instead of a specific code or doctrine, Chuang recommends the *Tao* (the mystical, incomprehensible, universal source and nature of all existence) as the only true guide to living, moment by moment.

The 33 chapters of his writings—simply titled Chuang Tzu—are comprised of poems, philosophies, and stories which illustrate aspects of Taoist thought.

Great knowledge sees all in one.
Small knowledge breaks down into the many.

The *Tao* is all-pervading and prior to everything in the universe, Chuang Tzu asserts. The universe comes into existence in accordance with the *Tao* and manifests itself as "the many." Everything in the universe is begotten by the same source and is, therefore, equal. Any differences are relative, and are simply manifestations of the same original unified source.

Pleasure and rage
Sadness and joy
Hopes and regrets
Change and stability
Weakness and decision
Impatience and sloth:
All are sounds from the same flute,
All mushrooms from the same wet mould .

Since all qualities, ideas, sensations and emotions derive from the same source, they are, therefore, ultimately the same. Even the ideals of right and wrong do not exist in ultimate reality. "Right" is considered "right" only because of the existence of "wrong." "Up" and "down" arise together; "hot" and "cold" are simply *thought* of as such, relative to each other: a hot summer is cold, compared to a hot fire. And yet, the source of both fire and summer remains a mystery:

Day and night follow one another and come upon us

Without our seeing how they sprout!

But, Chuang Tzu continues, it is possible to come to the conclusion that there *must* be a source—which, he deduces, is the *Tao:*

If there were no "that"
There would be no "this."
If there were no "this"
There would be nothing for all these
winds to play on.
So far can we go.
But how shall we understand
What brings it about?

One may well suppose the True Governor
To be behind it all. That such a power
works
I can believe. I cannot see his form.
He acts, but has no form.

The *Tao,* then, is most mysterious, and yet we can and must recognize it as the source of all individual occurrences, objects, and thoughts.

The *Tao* encompasses all truth, apparent and unknowable alike. Rigid religious and philosophical systems—Confucianism in particular—miss the point entirely—as demonstrated by the tale of "Three Friends":

There were three friends discussing life.
One said: "Can men live together and know
nothing of it? Can they fly around in space and
forget to exist, world without end?"
The three friends looked at each other and
burst out laughing. They had no explanation.
Thus they were better friends than before.
Then one friend [Sung Hu] died.
Confucius sent a disciple to help the other two
chant his obsequies. The disciple found that one
friend had composed a song. While the other
played a lute, they sang together:

"Hey, Sung Hu!
Where'd you go?
Hey, Sung Hu!
Where'd you go?
You have gone
Where you really were.
And we are here—
Damn it! We are here!"

Then the disciple of Confucius burst in on
them and exclaimed: "May I inquire where you
found this in the rubrics for obsequies, this friv-
olous carolling in the presence of the departed?"
The two friends looked at each other and
laughed: "Poor fellow," they said, "he doesn't
know the new liturgy!"

The way of the *Tao* is Nature's way, constant and absolute. Because of Nature's way—the *Tao*—however, everything is also in constant change. And this constant change takes place completely within cycles. For example, every phenomenon in the universe first appears and then disappears. Nothing is forever, only everything is forever. This is also true of the cycle of human beings: We are born and we die.

By recognizing our essence, the eternally changing *Tao*, we can enjoy the freedom of non-attachment to the cycles of Nature—cycles such as life and death, pleasure and pain, affection and anger—which tend to tie us down to earthly "realities":

When Chuang Tzu's wife died, Hui Shih came to condole. As for Chuang Tzu, he was squatting with his knees out, drumming on a pot and singing. "When you have lived with someone," said Hui Shih, "and brought up children, and grown old together, to refuse to bewail her death would be bad enough, but to drum on a pot and sing —could there be anything more shameful?"

"Not so," Chuang Tzu replied. "When she first died do you suppose I was not able to feel the loss? . . . She has gone over to death. This is to be companion with spring and autumn, summer and winter, in the procession of the four seasons. When someone was about to lie down and sleep in the greatest of mansions, I with my sobbing knew no better than to bewail her . . . [Then] the thought came to me that I was being uncomprehending toward destiny, so I stopped."

From Chuang Tzu's perspective, the commonly accepted notions of knowledge are merely artificial constructions of the mind, with only relative meaning. The only true knowledge is the soul-deep knowledge and acceptance of the incomprehensible *Tao*.

The artificial constructions which men take to be knowledge, are actually the cause of much suffering, Chuang Tzu avers. Acting in accordance with this false knowledge, men blindly fight *against* what their minds tell them is bad and *for* what their minds claim is good. But these ideals of "good" and "bad" can never be achieved or acquired in a complete way. Only the *Tao* is complete; the perfect music comes from "a lute that has no strings."

When we wear out our minds, stubbornly clinging to one partial view of things, refusing to see a deeper agreement between this and its complementary opposite, we have what is called "three in the morning."

What is this "three in the morning?"

A monkey trainer went to his monkeys and told them: "As regards your chestnuts: you are going to have three measures in the morning and four in the afternoon."

At this they all became angry. So he said: "All right, in that case I will give you four in the morning and three in the afternoon." This time they were satisfied.

The two arrangements were the same in that the number of chestnuts did not change. But in one case the animals were displeased, and in the other they were satisfied. The keeper had been willing to change his personal arrangement in order to meet objective conditions. He lost nothing by it!

The truly wise man, considering both sides of the question without partiality, sees them both in the light of **Tao.**

This is called following two courses at once.

In letting go of intellectual judgments and prejudices, we are blessed to see the unity of all things. Ultimately, conflict will be seen as merely a mental projection; thus we will be liberated. This liberation is permanent and supreme; there is nothing to negate it. It is the way of Nature, the way of the *Tao*.

But this is not the normal experience of man:

Men are blocked, perplexed, lost in doubt.
Little fears eat away at their peace of
*   heart.*
Great fears swallow them whole.
Arrows shot at a target: hit and miss,
*   right and wrong.*
That is what men call judgement, deci
sion.
Their pronouncements are as final
As treaties between emperors.
O, they make their point!
Yet their arguments fall faster and feebler
Than dead leaves in autumn and winter.
Their talk flows out like piss,
Never to be recovered.
They stand at last, blocked, bound, and
gagged,
Choked up like old drain pipes.
The mind fails. It shall not see light again.

Only through transcending the dualistic thinking of the common man can one experience the peace of a sage. Hui Shih, though, did not understand this point and questioned Chuang Tzu and Chuang Tzu offered his rejoinders:

"Can a man really be without the essen
tial to man?"
"He can."
"If a man is without the essential to man,
how can we call him a man?"
"The Way gives him features, Heaven
gives him the shape; how can he be with
out the essential to man?"
"Judging `It's this, It's not' is what I
mean by the essential to man. What I mean by
being without the essential is that the man does
not inwardly wound his person by likes and dis
likes, that he constantly goes by the spontaneous
and does not add anything to the process of
life."

And so, Chuang Tzu affirms his understanding that everything is relative and the same; all distinctions—right and wrong, life and death, and up and down—are transitory and dependent upon each other for their relevant meaning. They have no real, independent existence. Only the mysterious, inexpressible, cyclical *Tao* is real. That is our true Nature, Chuang Tzu concludes, and we must each, individually, recognize this truth. For life without this recognition is miserable.

THE I CHING

(or Book of Changes)

The ancient Chinese *I Ching*, or *Book of Changes*, as it is known in the west, is said to explain all possible phenomena in the universe. Scholars consider it one of the first efforts made by the human mind to place itself within a cosmic schema. Formally attributed to the Chinese sage Fu Hsi (2953-2838 BCE), its origin stretches back to mythical antiquity. Most scholars now maintain that the older layers of the book, as we know them today, assumed their present form in the century before Confucius (circa 600 BCE).

Nearly all that is greatest and most significant in the five-plus thousand years of Chinese cultural history has either taken its inspiration from this book, or has exerted an influence on the interpretation of its text. While Eastern in origin, interest in it continues to spread throughout the Western world.

I, which means "change" in Chinese, comprises the essential theme of the book. First set down in the dawn of history as a book of oracles, the *I Ching* deepened in meaning when ethical values were attached to its oracular pronouncements. As such, it became considered a book of wisdom, eventually one of the Five Classics of Confucianism, and provided the common source for both Confucianist and Taoist philosophy. The *I Ching* was the main source of inspiration for great minds such as Lao-tse and Confucius; the latter is said to have spent the last years of his life studying the wisdom contained within its pages.

The *I Ching* has been described by Western scientists and philosophers as an early example of Chinese "parascience," meaning that it incorporated scientific principles but applied them to a broader sense of understanding. It considers change—rather than stability—as the root principle of virtually all things, tangible or spiritual. Contrary to traditional Western precepts that time and space are constant and unchanging, Eastern mystics perceived that nothing is absolute or changeless—a notion since validated by modern science.

Text Overview:

At the core of the *I Ching* are sixty-four different *hexagrams*. Each hexagram is comprised of six divided and/or undivided horizontal lines stacked upon each other like lines on a page. These hexagrams are universal symbols which represent microcosms of key phenomena within our universe. Each hexagram is inseparably related to the others and is given a name which reveals its unique characteristics.

The hexagrams are accompanied by a text known as *t'uan*, or judgment. This judgment is based on the observable nature of the hexagram—that is, the various arrangements of divided and undivided lines which ascertain the situation at that moment in time so that the proper action can be taken. Thus, the *I Ching* serves as a manual for predicting the future.

The word **I,** derived from an ancient pictogram depicting a round head, a sinuous body, and a number of legs, originally meant "lizard."

The lizard was believed to move about from one place to another and change from one moment to another. Again, this concept of changeableness is a central idea in the *I Ching*.

The sun and the moon—two fundamental forces which rule the world—also signify change in the *I Ching*. Both heavenly bodies move along ever-changing, but repeatable cycles—the moon waxes and wanes, the sun's light and position in the sky varies throughout the year bringing about the change in seasons. Also, since the sun governs the day and the moon governs the night, day and night are different, yet inseparable conditions. In the *I Ching*, the concepts of *yin* and *yang*—where light is symbolized by yang and darkness by yin—play a key role. Yin and yang symbolize the dynamic balance of opposites that exists in the world, and the constant interplay between these opposites. For example, some darkness is found in light and vice versa; similarly, every person is a mixture of both good and evil. And since the opposites found in the universe (light and dark, good and evil) constantly "interchange," yin (darkness) and yang (light) suggest that nothing is absolute.

"One yin and one yang [combined] are called the Way [Tao]." In short, yin and yang are the foundations for all change, and represent duality, or the paradoxical nature of all things.

For this reason, the hexagrams can be used to interpret the future, since the future constantly unfolds to change. While change is inevitable and often beyond our control, it does follow its own patterns. Therefore, if we can learn to understand these patterns, we can predict future changes.

Changes have three basic characteristics. The first characteristic of change is change via *unity* or *division;* anything can be changed when it is added to or taken from. The second is called *transformation,* which is the essence of life and death, birth and decay. And the third characteristic of change is *changelessness* (constancy)—change presupposes constancy, since the process of change itself is ever-constant. A running river, for example, is a metaphor for this third characteristic, in that the same river is constantly flowing, but different water flows by every moment; thus, the river is both changing and constant. Such is the nature of *yin* and *yang*.

The eight trigrams—pictures made with three lines—of the *pa kua* represent the fundamental ways that yin and yang can be combined to represent all possible situations of the universe. Three broken and/or unbroken lines are combined to make each picture, commonly representing interactions between opposites such as heaven and earth, mother and son, water and dryness, creativity and receptivity. When the trigrams are doubled—by arranging two trigrams vertically—they comprise hexagrams. Hexagrams are like atoms in that they comprise all matter and motions of the universe. Like atoms, they are microcosms of the universe: "The *I Ching* contains the measure of heaven and earth."

Each line of yin or yang comprises the crucial structure of each hexagram. A change in a single line from yin to yang, or vice versa, involves a change in the entire hexagram. Thus, by perceiving a change in a single line, the outcome of the entire hexagram can be predicted since processes usually move in a chain of events, or occurrences. And since hexagrams represent the universe (its shape, movement and ethereal nature), the future can be foreseen through a profound understanding of the symbols. When one learns to understand the way things proceed, and can recognize where one resides along that chain at any given moment, then one can predict what will follow. Change, therefore, is not meaningless but subject to universal law—Tao.

Besides change, two other themes prove fundamental to the *I Ching: ideas* and the *judgments*. The theory of ideas behind the *I Ching* considers the eight trigrams as images of states of change rather than as images of objects. That is, they are representational ideas. Both Lao-tse and Confucius considered every event in the visible world as the effect of an idea-image from the unseen world. This philosophical perspective maintains that everything which happens on earth is merely the reproduction, or echo, of an event that already occurred in a world beyond our sense perception. This perspective maintains that while humans live on the earthly plane, their lives are constantly effected by a higher plane. The *I Ching* enables one to perceive present events in a clearer perspective and, ultimately, from the present moment, view the entire chain of events forward into the future and back through the past. The *I Ching* explains itself this way: *The holy sages surveyed all the possible rules of change and movements under heaven. They contemplated the forms and phenomena, and made the representations of them, which were summarized in the symbols [hexagrams].*

Lastly, the judgments prove fundamental to the *I Ching* because they clothe the images in words; they bring a tangible understanding to the various concepts and outline proper action for the future. Based on the concept of change and relying on the assumption that linear images (trigrams and hexagrams) can accurately represent cosmic, unseen conditions, the judgments are the text that outline and discuss this phenomena in a way accessible to a person's psyche. If asking the oracle about whether a certain action should be taken (e.g., travel, work, relationships), the judgments—along with the line readings—can indicate whether a given action will bring good fortune or misfortune, praise or humiliation. The judgments allow readers to see and understand the "bigger picture" when it comes to cause and effect, and can thus help to free them from the tyranny of events—what some Eastern religions refer to as "Karma."

The Oracle:

Originally, the *I Ching* was a collection of linear signs to be used as oracles. In antiquity, oracles were everywhere in use; the oldest among them confined themselves to simple "yes" and "no" responses. This type of oracular pronouncement seems to be the basis for the *I Ching*—"yes" indicated by an unbroken line and "no" by a broken line. Over time, greater differentiation came to be desired, and double, then triple lines came into being, giving us the eight trigrams. These eight trigrams came to be conceived as images of all that happened in heaven and on earth. As well, these were considered to be in a state of continual transition, with one changing into another, and so on. In order to achieve a still greater multiplicity, these eight images were combined with one another to form the sixty-four hexagrams.

In addition to the law of change and to the images representing states of change, the judgments describe the proper course of action. Technically, when the judgments were added to the sixty-four symbols, the *I Ching* was born. Around approximately 1150 B.C.E., Chinese King Wen and his son, the Duke of Chou, brought about this modification. They endowed the hitherto mute hexagrams and lines, from which the future had to be divined as an individual matter in each case, with definite counsels for correct conduct. Thus the individual came to share in shaping fate. If one understands the movement of events and receives wise counsel in reference to personal actions concerning them, then a person can be more successful in his own life.

Inquiries about specifics in a person's life depend, to a large extent, upon how one's individual psyche interprets the hexagram and the accompanying text. The *I Ching* allows for individual interpretation and intuition. The *I Ching*, therefore, could be considered a mirror to an intuitive aspect of the unconscious mind—what the ancient Greeks and Romans called the *Daemon*, or kindred spirit. Hence, "All individuals are not equally fitted to consult the oracle," explained Carl Jung. "It requires a clear and tranquil mind, receptive to the cosmic influences hidden in the humble divining [oracle]."

While the *I Ching* presupposes that each moment is the product of cosmic influences which are expressed through all things, the reader does not need to necessarily believe in such things to benefit from the wisdom contained within. The *I Ching* can be used for meditative purposes by the agnostic as well. Either with the oracle or without it, the book can be consulted and meditated upon, appreciating the poetic beauty of its language and for the philosophical wisdom it provides.

A typical *I Ching* oracle might read:

Preponderance of the small. Success.
Perseverance furthers.
Small things may be done; great things should not be done . . .
It is not well to strive upward,
It is well to remain below . . .

Reminding us that all things change, the *I Ching* counsels that we must remember to be sensitive to these happenings, and know that they are inevitable. The *I Ching*, in its wisdom, recognizes that life is always in flux. If we can remember this fact, then we can respond wisely to each unique situation as it occurs.

THE EGYPTIAN BOOK OF THE DEAD

The Egyptian Book of the Dead, a collection of ancient Egyptian writings which refer to the afterlife, outlines how one can attain immortality within the Egyptian cosmology. Little can be said of the work's exact origins. According to Egyptian scholar Sir E.A. Wallis Budge, keeper of Egyptian and Assyrian Antiquities in the British Museum and author of the acclaimed *The Book of the Dead* (Routledge and Kegan Paul Ltd, London, 1960), "If the known facts be examined it is difficult not to arrive at the conclusion that many of the *beliefs* found in the *Book of the Dead* were either voluntarily borrowed from some nation without [and] introduced into Egypt . . . by some conquering immigrants who made their way into the country from Asia, either by way of the Red Sea or across the Arabian peninsula." This conclusion was made by interpreting the manner in which burials were made during this ancient period.

The oldest known method of burial in Egypt involved placing the bodies of the deceased on their left sides with their heads facing south. From these pre-dynastic times up to around 640 B.C.E.—which preceded the practice of mummification—preserved corpses were often dismembered in order to economize on space.

Since antiquity, the development of writing, along with a growing concern about immortality, helped catalogue and refine the religious beliefs contained in The Book of the Dead. These beliefs were formally drafted during the eighteenth-century dynasty (2000-1500 B.C.E.) Before that time, as far back as the first dynasty (3500-3000 B.C.E.), the prayers, words and ceremonies were recited by memory.

The creeds taught in *The Book of the Dead* are said to have come from the goddesses Isis and Nephthys, whose brother, the god-man, was king Osiris. After Osiris was killed and mutilated by his brother, Set, by way of instructions from the god Thoth, his sisters embalmed his body and covered it with amulets to protect it from all harm in the world beyond the grave. Isis and Nephthys, before interring the body, also recited a magical formulae, an intricate song/chant, endowing Osiris with everlasting life. In so doing, the sisters embraced and performed the most important ceremony in *The Book of the Dead,* the guide to immortality. As a result, Osiris was miraculously brought back to life. The central claim of the writings is that through closely following the prescribed rituals—by means of reciting magical names and words during the ceremonies—the departed dead will be protected from calamities of every kind.

The numerous individual chapters of *The Book of the Dead* are collectively titled the "Chapters of Coming Forth by Day."

These chapters have been meticulously composed, outlining all knowledge necessary to ensure salvation for the dead. Down through the myriad dynasties, the chapters were re-edited into various "Recensions" which, over the centuries, were then combined in three "entities." The Heliopolitan Recension, for example, used during the fifth and sixth dynasties, is found inscribed in hieroglyphs inside pyramids of this period. The Theban Recension was written on papyrus and painted on sarcophagi (coffins) from the 18th to the 22nd Dynasties. The beliefs and customs of succeeding generations contributed to the construction of these various revisions (Recensions), believed to be divine in origin.

Text Overview:

The life and example set by the legendary god-man Osiris is the key to the entire *Book of the Dead.* It was universally believed that Osiris was of divine origin, a man sent down to live on earth in a material body. Not much is known of his life, but following his death, Osiris' body "neither decayed nor rotted away." *The Book of the Dead* tells of the joy to be had (represented by the rejuvenation of the physical body) in the afterlife:

I shall live, I shall live. I shall grow, I shall grow. I shall wake up in peace; I shall not putrefy; my intestines shall not perish; I shall not suffer from every defect; mine eye shall not decay, the form of my visage shall not disappear; mine ear shall not become deaf; my head shall not be separated from my neck; my tongue shall not be carried away; my hair shall not be cut off; and no baleful injury shall come upon me. My body shall be [restored] and it shall neither fall into decay or be destroyed upon this earth.

The goddess Nut, guardian of heaven, was specifically given the task of bolstering and strengthening the body in the world beyond the grave:

Make ye me strong! The goddess Nut hath joined together the bones of my neck and back, even as they were in the time that is past . . .

Untold generations lived and died patterning themselves after Osiris, the "king of eternity, the lord of the everlasting, who passeth through millions of years in his existence." As it is written:

The dead rise up to see thee, Osiris, they breathe the air and they look upon thy face when the disk riseth on its horizon; their hearts are at peace inasmuch as they behold thee, O thou who art Eternity and Everlastingness.

Most of the facsimiles depicting Osiris' mummified image show him wearing a white crown and holding a snake-like staff, emblematic of sovereignty and dominion. At times, however, he is represented wearing ordinary vestment. This dual-garbed corpse implies that individual dead should be buried in whatever clothing would befit the activities they will enjoy in the afterworld. Provisions such as gifts and food were placed in the coffin to accompany and accommodate the needs of the deceased, as he journeyed to join his soul with Osiris, or the divine sun god Ra:

Ra receiveth thee, soul in heaven, body in earth . . . Thine essence is in heaven, thy body is in the earth . . . Thy soul is in heaven before Ra, thy double hath that which should be given unto it with the gods, thy spiritual body is glorious among the spirits of fire, and thy material body [the khat] is established in the underworld [grave].

Egyptians believed that, rising from the body's entombed remains, a spiritual body would emerge; like a butterfly surfacing from a cocoon, the dead body would metamorphose into a glorious being or essence, becoming like that of Osiris or Ra—a perfected form that would enable the person to drive away evil. Osiris would then reward the beautified, mummified dead by bestowing upon them his own spiritual form, the immortal body, called *sahu*.

Apart from the *sahu* was the *ka*, or "double," an abstract individuality possessing the attributes of the person to whom it belonged that could roam about at will: *May my soul come forth and walk hither and thither and whithersoever it pleaseth.* Only by way of a double could the dead partake of the food that had been prepared for the meandering journey across the river *tuot*, beyond which lay the kingdom of the dead.

The *ba*, or combined heart and soul, was connected to the *ka*; this essence of being often lived with either Ra or Osiris in heaven. The ba was said to assume both a material and an immaterial form, and was able to fly and bring air and food to the mummified body. The *ab*, or heart, was closely associated with the soul, embodying the source of good and evil in humankind. It was also believed to be the center of the spiritual feeling and thought. The *khaibit*, or shadow, also had an existence outside the body and could go wherever it pleased. In all ways, the dead not only hoped to be free from earth's chains—protected, again, through magical words, chants, and rites from *Rerek*, serpent of the underworld, and his evil followers—but also to become as Osiris, protected from all evil:

. . . Get thee back, thou crocodile-fiend Sui; thou shalt not advance to me, for I live by reason of the magical words which I have by me . . . O keep not captive my soul, O keep not ward over my shadow, but let a way be opened for my soul and for my shadow, and let them see the Great God in the shrine of the day of the judgement of souls, and let them recite the utterances of Osiris, whose habitations are hidden, to those who guard the members of Osiris, and who keep ward over the spirits, and who hold captive the shadows of the dead who would work evil against me.

The *khu*, or spiritual soul, seems to have been regarded as an ethereal being connected with the ba or heart-soul. Other bodies included *sekhem*, a person's power or vital force; *ren*, a person's "other," secret name, a key word that was to be preserved in the heavens and used as a password to enter in; and the *sahu*, the spiritual body which sprang from the material body. Each of these bodies awaited judgement in the Judgement Hall of Osiris. Soon after death, those who were condemned in judgement for having wrought evil works were devoured by the Eater of the Dead, and ceased to exist. Those not condemned, having performed "good acts," were spared being consumed and took their place next to Osiris and Ra, where they enjoyed everlasting life and happiness in conjunction with Ra and Osiris: *I am crowned king of the gods, I shall not die a second time in the Other World . . . [My wish is that] I may be as Osiris, greatly favored of the beautiful god, and beloved of the lord of the world.*

Another key component affecting the happiness of the dead were the magical formulae included in the funereal ceremonies. These formulae consisted, in part, of repeatedly chanting the names of specific gods and other supernatural beings. Every phrase spoken was followed by either a prayer—thereby bringing about a good effect— or a curse—a way to bring about harm to an insulted object. Good words were inscribed on amulets and wax human figures (representing persons the living wished to influence); these charms gave them power to carry out good acts on behalf of loved ones. Conversely, bad words were meant to bring evil down upon evil individuals. If a foe approached by ship, for instance, the right words and acts directed upon an amulet or wax person were said to sink the vessels and drown the enemy. On the other hand, if a person wished to dream of a certain goddess in order to converse with her, he or she must fashion a female wax figure embodiment and recite certain words in sequence, thus bringing the dream down from the heavens.

Most importantly, throughout the eternities these magical formulae were fundamental to ensuring that the soul of the departed would take its place beside Ra and Osiris, there to possess a life of happiness ever after.

The various renderings of **The Book of the Dead**—a figurative "songbook" to the Gods, an intricate appeal to immortals to bestow the blessings of immortality, and a praise to the all-powerful god-humans who protect all human souls—were the lifeblood of Egyptian worship. This life, to them, was a mere step toward the afterlife. And for the Egyptian living, it was an esteemed wish to live with the gods when death finally came:

May my name be proclaimed, and may it be found upon the board of the table of offerings . . . may there be made ready for me a seat in the boat of the Sun on the day when the god goeth forth; and may I be received into the presence of Osiris in the land of victory.

THE DHAMMAPADA: THE WORD OF BUDDHA

Sacred to Buddhists is the collection of verses called *The Dhammapada*—meaning the "path of truth, light and love"—written in the third century B.C.E. ("before common-era"—a term used by recent scholars to avoid continual reference to a "Christian" calendar). *The Dhammapada* exists as the word of Gotama Buddha (563-483 BCE). A prince who would be king, Gotama cast aside his life of privilege for one of nomadic contemplation. He changed his name to Buddha, meaning "to be awake, to know," when he experienced a revelation while meditating beneath a tree. What the Buddha experienced on that day was a "union of the finite with the infinite," where his spirit transcended the earthly realm into a new realm of being. This state, called "Nirvana," is the supreme objective of all Buddhists. In the words of the Buddha, "Few cross the river of time and are able to reach Nirvana. Most of them run up and down only on this side of the river."

Read individually, *The Dhammapada's* verses can inspire faith, purity, wisdom and virtue for all who seek truth, wish to enrich their lives, and find greater peace through proper living.

The Dhammapada outlines the foot-path that leads to Nirvana. The journey is incredibly long, for one must leave behind the seemingly endless circle of lifetimes (the result of reincarnation). This cycle, or wheel, is known as "Samsara," identified in the text as the "ever-returning life in death." In order to transcend Samsara, the Buddha prescribes an "eight-fold path" of enlightenment which must be trodden. The steps must be taken one at a time, for one level precedes the next on the path to Nirvana.

Stage 1

The first stage involves the attainment of the four great virtues of Buddhism: *Maitri, Karuna, Mudita,* and *Upeksha. Maitri* is the virtue of benevolence and goodwill. *Karuna* involves compassion, pity, and sorrow. *Mudita* is to have joy in the good of all. And *Upeksha* means forgiveness. The attainment of these four virtues prepares one for the second step, that of *Right Determination.*

Stage 2

We must learn to give up the world:
Leave the past behind; leave the future behind; leave the present behind. Thou art ready to go to the other shore. Never more shalt thou return to a life that ends in death.

Further, it is said:
Go beyond the stream, Brahmin [the enlightened one, one who has reached the highest stage], go with all your soul: leave desires behind. When you have crossed the stream of Samsara, you will reach the land of Nirvana.

Clearly, one must give up the cycle of earthly life in favor of a more enlightened state of being. However, simply leaving Samsara behind is not enough:
For whom "name and form" are not real, who never feels "this is mine," and who sorrows not for things that are not, he in truth can be called a monk.

Here it is understood that those names and forms found in Samsara are not real but are transient and everchanging, like a flowing river. Therefore, one who seeks enlightenment is willing to leave them— as well as personal possessions and human emotions—behind.

Stage 3

This stage involves *Right Words,* for "Better than a thousand useless words is one single word that gives peace." According to the Buddha:
Never speak harsh words, for once spoken they may return to you. Angry words are painful and there may be blows for blows. . . . let your words be self-controlled. Hurt not with words, but use your words well.

Further:
. . . if a man speaks but a few holy words, free from passion and hate and illusion . . . the life of this man is a life of holiness.

Stage 4

Stage four is *Right Action,* which involves holding to truth, avoiding anger, and helping others:
Speak the truth, yield not to anger, give what you can to him who asks: these three steps will lead you to the gods.

Right action means doing good:
If a man does something good, let him do it again and again. Let him find joy in his good work. Joyful is the accumulation of good work . . . Make haste and do what is good; keep your mind away from evil. If a man is slow in doing good, his mind finds pleasure in evil.

Right Action also includes self-control:
Good is control of the body, and good is the control of words; good is the control of the mind, and good is the control of our whole inner life. When a monk has achieved perfect self-control, he leaves all sorrows behind.

Stage 5

Stage five is *Right Livelihood,* known as the avoidance of ignorance, evil, violence, and earthly desires such as lust:
. . . He who lives not for pleasures, and whose soul is in self-harmony, who eats or fasts with moderation, and has faith and the power of virtue—this man is not moved by temptations, as a great rock is not shaken by the wind . . . Be therefore not bound to pleasure for the loss of

pleasure is pain. There are no fetters for the man who is beyond pleasure and pain.

The same concept applies to lust:

From lust arises sorrow and from lust arises fear. If a man is free from lust, he is free from fear and sorrow . . . [Hence], the man whose mind, filled with determination, is longing for the infinite Nirvana, and who is free from sensuous pleasures, is called uddhamsoto, "he who goes upstream," for against the current of passions and worldly life he is bound for the joy of the Infinite . . . Good men, at all times, surrender in truth all attachments. The holy spend not idle words on things of desire. When pleasure or pain comes to them, the wise feel above pleasure and pain.

Stage 6

Stage six, **Right Effort,** takes in not only performing actions which are good, truthful and virtuous, but also actively *seeking out* opportunities to do such good works. Of course, it is much easier *not* to act and fall into a state of apathy and idleness, swept along in the river's current. But according to Buddha, we must be proactive:

Better than a hundred years lived in idleness and in weakness is a single day lived with courage and powerful striving . . . If a man when young and strong does not arise and strive when he should arise and strive, and thus sinks into laziness and lack of determination, he will never find the path of wisdom.

In addition, **Right Effort** includes vanquishing evil and overcoming violence for the sake of good:

A man is not on the path of righteousness if he settles matters in a violent haste. A wise man calmly considers what is right and what is wrong, and faces different opinions with truth, non-violence and peace. This man is guarded by truth and is a guardian of truth. He is righteous and he is wise.

In general, one who has mastered **Right Effort** "in truth is a Samana [a monk, or Brahmin]."

Stage 7

Stage seven is **Right Remembrance,** or watchfulness. In the words of Buddha:

Watchfulness is the path of immortality: unwatchfulness is the path of death. Those who are watchful never die: Those who do not watch are already as dead. . . . Watchfulness is godlike, protectful and virtuous, since . . . by arising in faith and watchfulness, by self-possession and self-harmony, the wise man makes an island for his soul which many waters cannot overflow . . . Even the gods long to be like the Buddhas who are awake and watch, who find peace in contemplation and who, calm and steady, find joy in renunciation.

Thus, the Brahmin journeys forward on the path:

Watchful amongst the unwatchful, awake amongst those who sleep . . . like a swift horse runs his race, outrunning those who are slow . . . like a fire, burning all obstacles both great and small.

Stage 8

The final stage is called **Samandhi,** or union, and consists of four all-encompassing virtues: *Recollection, Meditation, Contemplation,* and *Union.* In preparation for higher realms of thought, *Recollection* requires focus and attention. *Meditation* includes higher intellectual thought, such as that found in philosophy and science. Beyond this realm is *Contemplation,* or silence of the mind. Contemplation cannot be reached through thought, poetry, art, or music. Indeed, all thoughts are left behind. Finally, the Brahmin, seeing *Union,* reaches the highest order of enlightenment, **Samandhi:**

. . . When beyond meditation and contemplation a Brahmin has reached the other shore, then he attains the supreme vision, and all his fetters are broken . . . Finally, after a great deal of effort and sacrifice, the wheel of myriad lifetimes is transcended; all suffering, ignorance and evil are cast aside, forsaken.

Upon arriving at the level of **Samandhi,** or **Nirvana,** one ceases to exist as an earthly, temporal individual entity. The bonds of time are finally obliterated; there is no self, no striving, no becoming. There is only pure Union and Being. One "whose vision is deep, who is wise, who has attained the highest end" is prepared to see the supreme Union in his surroundings, in everything, and is worthy to be called Brahmin: "This highest end is Samandhi, the oneness which is Nirvana."

A Brahmin who has reached the end "knows the going and the returning of beings—the birth and rebirth of life—and in joy has arrived at the end of his journey, and now he is awake and can see."

And so, *The Dhammapada's* "path of truth, light and love" is a spiritual guide for all who would be "virtuous, and righteous, and wise"; for he who "craves not for sons or power or wealth, who puts not his own success before the success of righteousness." The path requires many sacrifices; it is almost infinitely long. Like a great edifice which must grow one floor at a time, one must graduate step by step to each successive stage, or face living out entire lifetimes until one gains the mastery to approach the next stage. *The Dhammapada's* message is clear:

This is the path. There is no other that leads to vision. Go on this path, and you will confuse Mara, the devil of confusion . . . Live a life of inner heroism, the all-seer, the all-conqueror, the ever-pure, who has reached the end of the journey, who like Buddha is awake.

AN INTRODUCTION TO ZEN BUDDHISM

by D.T. Suzuki, Grove Press, New York, N.Y., 1964

In recent decades Zen Buddhism has received increased attention around the world. D.T. Suzuki was instrumental in the introduction of Zen to the West. His work, *An Introduction to Zen Buddhism,* is widely regarded as an excellent, ground-level script for those who are new to the subject, as well as those who are looking further into Zen.

Text Summary:

Zen is generally regarded as a religious development which flourished when Buddhism arrived in China and Japan from India. It is virtually impossible to neatly define or to limit it to one religious system. It can be said, however, that Zen's central aim involves a search for insight into the truth. Doko, a Buddhist philosopher (8th century A.D.) surrendered himself to a Zen master to find out the exact nature of truth. The dialogue went like this, with Doko first asking:

"With what frame of mind should one discipline oneself in the truth?"

Said the Zen master, "There is no mind to be framed, nor is there any truth in which to be disciplined."

"If there is . . . no mind to be framed and no truth in which to be disciplined, why do you have a daily gathering of monks who are studying Zen and disciplining themselves in the truth?"

The master replied: *"I have not an inch of space to spare, and where could I have a gathering of monks? I have no tongue, and how would it be possible for me to advise others to come to me?"*

The philosopher then exclaimed, *"How can you tell me a lie like that to my face?"*

"When I have no tongue to advise others, is it possible for me to tell a lie?"

Said Doko despairingly, "I cannot follow your reasoning."

"Neither do I understand myself," concluded the Zen master.

The origin of Zen is reputed to be the "Flower Sermon" of Gautama Buddha. On this occasion the Buddha held up a flower to a gathering of students, without saying a word. It is said that only one of his students understood.

Since that time students of Zen have developed techniques of meditation, debate and contemplation to gain insight into the object of Zen: the inexpressible truth, or void. What is sought is *satori,* an enlightened state of consciousness which transcends all change and duality of opposites. In satori one experiences a "general mental upheaval which destroys the old accumulation of intellect and lays down the foundation for a new life"; in essence, the mind, when allowed to experience the inner void, is the fountain or source of truth.

Although there are numerous techniques practiced by Zen students in search of satori, Zen masters have always insisted that satori can never be grasped by our minds. Indeed, it is beyond our minds. One is simply humbled by the mystery.

When Nangaken was approaching his teacher and was questioned "What is it that thus walks toward me?," he did not know what to answer. For eight long years he pondered the question, when one day it dawned upon him, and he exclaimed, "Even to say it is something does not hit the mark."

Likewise, when the Zen master Bodhidharma was asked who he was, he said, "I do not know." This was not because he wanted to avoid any verbal controversy, but just because he did not know what or who he was, save that he was what he was and could not be anything else.

Zen masters have constantly affirmed that the essential truth could not be spoken:

The Emperor Wu of the Liang dynasty requested [that] Fu Daishi discourse on a Buddhist sutra. The Daishi taking the chair sat solemnly in it but uttered not a word. The Emperor said, "I asked you to give a discourse, and why do you not begin to speak?"

Shih, one of the Emperor's attendants, said, "The Daishi has finished discoursing."

Later on, a Zen master commenting on the above says, "What an eloquent sermon it was!"

Zen thinkers have provided numerous and widely differing answers to the same questions. Why? Because the teachings of Zen are aimed at freeing the mind from "entanglements and attachments such as words, ideas, desires, etc., which are put up against us from the outside."

Some of the answers given to the question "Who or what is the Buddha?" are as follows:

"The dirt scraper all dried up."
"He is no Buddha."
"Three pounds of flax."
"Your name is Yecho."
"See the three-legged donkey go trotting along."
"The mouth is the gate of woe."

These are just a few of samples. Zen literature provides a seemingly strange collection of answers to this single question. Some of the answers appear at first to be irrelevant, or far from satisfying the requirements of what we would ordinarily consider to be a "logical" response.

But with these responses the Zen masters give their students the chance to break out of their ordinary, limited patterns of thinking, and to understand directly, intuitively.

Zen has no firm intellectual "truths." A monk, wondering where the truth might be found, asked his master:

Where is the abiding place for the mind?"

"The mind," answered the master, "abides where there is no abiding."

"What is meant by `there is no abiding'?"

"When the mind is not abiding in any particular object, we say that it abides where there is no abiding."

"What is meant by not abiding in any particular object?"

"It means not to be abiding in the dualism of good and evil, being and non-being, thought and matter; it means not to be abiding in emptiness or non-emptiness, neither in tranquility or in non-tranquility. Where there is no abiding place, this is truly the abiding place for the mind."

Zen, of course, should not be confused with either nonsense or nihilism. There is a purpose in all that Zen proposes:

A distinguished priest was once asked, "Do you ever make any effort to get disciplined in the truth?"

"Yes, I do."

"How do you exercise yourself?"

"When I am hungry I eat; when tired I sleep."

"This is what everybody does; can they be said to be exercising themselves in the same way as you do?"

"No."

"Why not?"

"Because when they eat they do not eat, but are thinking of various other things, thereby allowing themselves to be disturbed; when they sleep they do not sleep, but dream of a thousand and one things. This is why they are not like myself."

In Zen meditation, one seeks perfect quietude and silence within. However, meditation "does not point to mere idleness or inactivity":

The silence is not that of the desert shorn of vegetation, nor is it that of a corpse forever gone to sleep and decay. It is the silence of an "eternal abyss" in which all contrasts and conditions are buried; it is the silence of God who, deeply absorbed in contemplation of his works past, present, and future, sits calmly on his throne of absolute oneness and allness. It is the "silence of thunder" obtained in the midst of the flash and uproar of opposing currents.

Zen is an extremely practical way of life. It avoids metaphysical theorizing at all costs. There are numerous accounts of Zen masters "surprising" students into understanding:

Sekkyo asked one of his accomplished monks, "Can you take hold of empty space?"

"Yes, sir," he replied.

"Show me how you do it."

The monk stretched out his arm and clutched at empty space. Sekkyo said: "Is that the way? But after all you have not got anything."

"What then," asked the monk, "is your way?"

The master straightaway took hold of the monk's nose and gave it a hard pull, which made the latter exclaim "Oh, oh, how hard you pull at my nose! You are hurting me terribly!"

"That is the way to have good hold of empty space," said the master.

Perhaps the most well-known facet of Zen is its use of koans to help provoke an insight into satori. Some of the most famous koans include: "What is the sound of one hand clapping?" and "Are you breathing the breath, or is the breath breathing you?"

Koans, when approached with sincerity and with an open mind, tend to bewilder the rational mind and suspend it in a state free of normal belief structures. Nevertheless, these koans are not idle questions; they are meant to be worked out, usually through long hours of meditation.

The koan known as "Joshu's dog" is considered to be the consummate model:

A monk asked the master Joshu: "Has a dog a Buddha nature or not?"

Joshu replied "Mu!" (meaning "ney" or "nothing")

The number of koans is traditionally estimated at 1700. But even one may be "sufficient to open one's mind to the ultimate truth of Zen. A thorough enlightenment, however, is attained only through the most self-sacrificing application of the mind, supported by an inflexible faith in the finality of" the truth of the koan.

Zen monks are educated in meditation halls, called "zendos." The training of these monastic monks entails tough discipline, austerity, and stringent practicality. A monk may have a space of about 5 x 6 feet in the hall in which to sit, meditate and sleep; his possessions will be minimal. Work is considered a vital element in monastic life of a monk, and is part of a thousand-year-old tradition which began under the slogan "A day of no work is a day of no eating." A "perfect feeling of brotherhood prevails" among the monks as they sweep, clean, cook, gather fuel, and till the earth. "No work is considered beneath the dignity." The "sanctity of manual work" is guarded as part of the path of Zen.

In Zen, as in all Buddhism, the desire to possess is considered one of the worst of passions. There is no room for obsessions or preoccupations in Zen. Simplicity is in silent opposition to the extreme avarice of normal society—a society the monk leaves behind in his search for enlightenment.

THE TIBETAN BOOK OF THE DEAD

by Guru Rampoche according to Karma Lingpa,
translation with commentary by Francesca Freemantle & Chogyam Trungpa, 1975

The Tibetan Book of the Dead is a scripture of the "old tradition" of Tibetan Buddhism. The Tibetan variety of Buddhism is a form which developed distinctly from other branches, such as Zen (in China and Japan) and Hinayana (throughout much of Asia). Many of the practices found in Tibetan Buddhism involve meditation upon "deities"—often portrayed in vivid imagery—which represent aspects of the mind.

These particular practices have received increasing attention from the West, especially since the most famous Tibetan Buddhist, the Dalai Lama, won the Nobel Peace Prize in 1990.

The Tibetan Book of the Dead has been of particular interest to Westerners, and has resulted in several English translations. The work's primary concern regards the nature of the mind and its projections—beautiful or terrible, peaceful or wrathful—which inhabit the external world. It describes these projections as they appear immediately after death, with the purpose of teaching recognition of these terrifying and seductive forms, and, through recognition, attainment of the state of enlightenment.

Subtitled *The Great Liberation Through Hearing in the Bardo*, the text was composed in the eighth century by the Buddhist teacher Padmasambhava, who buried his writings as "hidden treasures" in the Gampo hills in Central Tibet. He then "gave the transmission of power to discover the texts to his twenty-five chief disciples." The "Bardo" texts were later discovered by Karma-Lingpa, "who was an incarnation of one of those disciples," and handed down through the ages to the present day.

Text Overview:

According to Chogyam Trungpa, one of the book's translators, *The Tibetan Book of the Dead* is quite unlike the *Egyptian Book of the Dead*, which presents myths and lore to describe the after-life experience. *The Tibetan Book*, rather than being "based on death as such" is concerned with "the fundamental principle of birth and death recurring constantly in *this* life. One could refer to this book as *The Tibetan Book of Life*."

The Tibetan term *bardo* means "gap." It refers not only to the "interval of suspension after we die" but also to experience in our everyday life, such as in our feelings of fear or uncertainty, those of "not being sure of our ground, not knowing quite what we have asked for or what we're getting into."

In Tibetan Buddhism, the basic cause of suffering is the belief that the ego or self is the center of existence. This belief is rooted in ignorance of the true nature of what is real—the "luminosity" or basic "ground in which the play of life takes place."

The experience of the ego-centered state of being is analyzed in terms of "six realms of existence we go through; the six realms of our psychological states." Each realm of the bardo is designed to purge some aspect of the ego.

In the period after death, different "deities" present themselves, typically according to the six realms of existence. These deities are categorized as either "peaceful" or "wrathful." But the deities, as well as other entities which appear after death, are *not* actual, external, existing beings. "... The essential point to remember is to recognize with certainty that whatever appears . . . is your own projection . . . " A "mind" projection is "a vision without any real nature of its own, like an illusion."

How do we know that these things actually happen to people who are dying? Has anyone come back from the grave and recounted their experience? No, but the impressions of death are "so strong that someone recently born (reincarnated) should have memories of the period between death and birth"; however, as we mature we are indoctrinated by our parents and society and we put ourselves into a different framework, so that the original deep impressions become faded [and] any occasional glimpse is "treated half-hearted or dismissed altogether."

But the descriptions in *The Book of the Dead* are not merely of "visions that appear after death"; they refer to experiences which can "be seen purely in terms of the living situation" and, certainly, within a "practical meditative situation." Visions of the wrathful and peaceful deities, in fact, are happening this very moment. If one is "open and realistic enough to look at it this way, then the actual experience of death and the bardo state will not be either purely a myth or an extraordinary shock."

The first bardo experience is *uncertainty* of whether or not one is actually going to die; "the possibility of stepping out from the real world into an unreal world." Then the "elements" of the body begin to dissolve and one loses contact with the physical world.

The next event is one of *luminosity*, the basic neutral background of all experience. Then, following four days of *unconsciousness*, there is an *awakening*, a sudden understanding that one is in the bardo state. There are vague perceptions of light and images in a way that differs completely from our worldly experiences.

Over the next five days the visions of the five buddhas (sages who have achieved a state of complete illumination and liberation) appear in succession as aspects of the principle of enlightenment.

Day 1: *The whole of space will shine with a blue light, and Blessed Vairocana will appear before you from the central Realm, All-pervading Circle. His body is white in colour, he sits on a lion throne, holding an eight-spoked wheel in his hand and embracing his consort the Queen of Vajra Space. The blue light of the skandha (psychological component of human personality) of consciousness in its basic puri-*

ty, the wisdom of the dharmadhatu (all encompassing space), luminous, clear, sharp and brilliant, will come towards you from the heart of Vairocana and his consort, and pierce you so that your eyes cannot bear it. At the same time . . . the soft white light of the gods will also come towards you and pierce you. At that time, under the influence of bad karma (actions), you will be terrified and escape from the wisdom of the dharmadhatu with its bright blue light, but you will feel an emotion of pleasure towards the soft white light of the gods. At that moment do not be frightened or bewildered by the luminous, brilliant, very sharp and clear blue light of supreme wisdom, for it is the light-ray of the buddha, which is called the wisdom of the dharmadhatu. Be drawn to it with faith and devotion, and supplicate it, thinking, "It is the light-ray of Blessed Vairocana's compassion, I take refuge in it." It is Blessed Vairocana coming to invite you in the dangerous pathway of the bardo; it is the light-ray of Vairocana's compassion . . . Do not take pleasure in the soft white light of the gods, do not be attracted to it or yearn for it. If you are attracted to it you will wander into the realm of the gods and circle among the six kinds of existence.

Day 2: On the second day; a white light, the purified element of water, will shine, and at the same time Blessed Vajrasattva-Aksobhya will appear before you from the blue eastern Realm of Complete Joy. His body is blue in colour, he holds a five-pointed vajra in his hand and sits on an elephant throne, embracing his consort Buddha-Locana. He is accompanied by the two male bodhisattvas (future buddhas who have vowed to help all sentient beings) Ksitigarbha and Maitreya and the two female bodhisattvas Lasya and Puspa, so that six buddha forms appear . . . The white light of the skandha of form in its basic purity, the mirror-like wisdom, dazzling white, luminous and clear, will come towards you from the heart of Vajrasattva and his consort and pierce you so that your eyes cannot bear to look at it. At the same time, together with the wisdom light, the soft smoky light will also come towards you and pierce you. At that time, under the influence of aggression, you will be terrified and escape from the brilliant white light, but you will feel an emotion of pleasure towards the soft smoky light of the hell-beings. At that moment do not be afraid of the sharp, brilliant, luminous and clear white light, but recognise it as wisdom. Be drawn to it with faith and longing, and supplicate it, thinking, "It is the light-ray of Blessed Vajrasattva's compassion, I take refuge in it." It is Blessed Vajrasattva coming to invite you in the terrors of the bardo; it is the light-ray hook of Vajrasattva's compassion, so feel longing for it . . . Do not take pleasure in the soft smoky light of the hell-beings. This is the inviting path of your neurotic veils, accumulated by violent aggression. If you are attracted to it you will fall down into hell, and sink into the muddy swamp of unbearable suffering from which there is never any escape.

The third, fourth, and fifth days follow the pattern of the first two. Each day, the buddha is accompanied by visions which, by way of invitations, instructions, and counsel, present the prospect of "liberation," first by virtue of longing for the compassion extended from the buddha, and second by choosing to observe the wisdom offered. By choosing wisdom over fear, liberation is truly realized:

Day 3: O son of noble family, listen without distraction. On the third day, a yellow light, the purified element of earth, will shine, and at the same time Blessed Ratnasambhava will appear before you from the yellow southern Realm . . . At the same time, together with the wisdom light, the soft blue light of human beings will also pierce your heart. . . . Do not be afraid of the yellow light, luminous and clear, sharp and bright, but recognise it as wisdom. Let your mind rest in it, relaxed, in a state of non-action, and be drawn to it with longing . . . and you will attain enlightenment. If you cannot recognise it as the natural radiance of your own mind, supplicate it with devotion, thinking, "It is the light-ray of Blessed Ratnasambhava's compassion, I take refuge in it" . . .

Day 4: . . . On the fourth day, a red light, the purified element of fire, will shine, and at the same time Blessed Amitabha will appear before you from the red western Realm, The Blissful . . . and you will attain enlightenment. . . . Do not be attracted to the soft yellow light of the hungry ghosts. That is the light-path of unconscious tendencies accumulated by your intense desire. If you are attracted to it you will fall into the realm of hungry ghosts, and experience unbearable misery from hunger and thirst.

Day 5: O son of noble family, listen without distraction. On the fifth day, a green light, the purified element of air, will shine, and at the same time Blessed Amoghaisiddhi, lord of the circle, will appear before you from the green northern Realm, Accumulated Actions . . . . . . So rest in the supreme state free from activity and care, in which there is no near or far, love or hate . . .

As noted, along with the appearance of each buddha come visions representing the realms of suffering. One must be very careful, in the bardo, not to be attracted by these temptations, since mere desire for them will lead one to misery. In any case, one must always be aware that everything seen is entirely a creation of the mind.

If a disciple has not attained liberation by day six, he continues through a procession of peaceful deities, then on to the wrathful deities. The wrathful deities, in a very literal sense, "irritate the hell out of existence." The ego-centered world-view is the root of hell; the wrathful deities simply do not tolerate egotistical manipulations, and thereby represent the death of ego.

Following the wrathful deities are the herukas and the gauris, more divisions of wrathful energy who, by piercing the ego, also offer the possibility of liberation and enlightenment.

The Tibetan Book of the Dead: The Great Liberation Through Hearing in the Bardo is to be used for study, meditation, and memorization. " . . . Its words and meaning should not be forgotten even if a hundred murderers were to appear and chase one . . . " To meet with it is great good fortune; "it is hard to meet with except for those who have cleared away their darkness and gathered merit. If one hears it, one is liberated simply by not disbelieving, therefore it should be greatly cherished . . . "

ZOROASTER

The Avestas: The Holy Books of Zoroastrianism

Zoroastrianism is an ancient religion which first developed in the northeastern region of what is now Iran. It was founded by Zoroaster (a Greek extraction of "Zarathustra") a prophet who lived around the sixth century BCE.

Although Zoroastrianism was largely replaced by the Muslim religion, it is still practiced in certain areas. In fact, the *Parsis* of India and small groups in Iran still may be found vigorously plying their religious liturgy.

Very little is known about Zoroaster, aside from a smattering of cryptic stories, such as the one the ancient Romans repeated: "Zoroaster was the only human being to laugh at birth." At age twenty he left home on a search for religious truth. After wandering from village to village and living alone for ten years, he had a vision. During the next ten years, he had six more revelations, in which he spoke with the chief angels and God himself. He was commanded to call the people together to worship God (Ahura Mazda) and to fight against Ahura Mazda's enemy, the Evil Spirit (Angra Mainyu). For the remainder of his life, Zoroaster went about gathering believers. At the time of his death in his mid-fifties, his teachings were beginning to have a strong influence in Persia.

Only a portion of Zoroaster's writings still exist, serving as the basis of Zoroastrian scripture. These writings constitute part of the "Avesta," a book written in a language (Gathic) spoken only in the Avesta region of the ancient Persian Empire. This language has posed formidable problems for interpretive scholars, and obscurities in translation continue to this day.

Text Overview:

The most essential components of the Avesta are the *prayer-hymns*, composed by Zoroaster and known as his "Gathas." The Gathas reveal Zoroaster's world-view in poetic form and give an account of his spiritual journey. Only five of these Gathas survive, yet this is sufficient for reconstructing Zoroaster's general religious perspectives and teachings.

Central to Zoroastrian doctrine is the belief that there are two classifications of deities: *Ahuras* and *Daevas*.

Ahuras—These are the positive, or "good" deities. But only one supremely good ahura, worthy of worship, is indicated. This ahura is known as Ahura Mazda, Ahura meaning "Lord" and Mazda meaning "wisdom." Ahura Mazda represents all positive attributes, but, curiously, is never portrayed as the only Ahura.

Daevas—These are the negative, or "evil" deities. They have only one will—to do evil. They are not true gods; they are the Evil Spirit, Angra Mainyu and the host of evil who sprang from his Evil Mind (Aka Manah). The classification of these deities forms the basis for the rest of Zoroaster's religion.

The world and everyone in it represent a battleground between good and evil. Followers of Zoroastrianism are called to fight on the side of the good, which, in the end, will win out; they are called to seek, obey, and worship Ahura Mazda, creator of all things, judge at the end of time, and neither honor or placate the daevas. Instead, they must relentlessly seek to defeat their diabolical aims.

Ahura Mazda's Bounteous Spirit, Spenta Mainyu, is His "son," who creates of life and the good in life. Because Ahura Mazda's spirit creates good, He has the primary attribute of goodness or righteousness, and all other secondary characteristics.

The divine qualities of Ahura Mazda are known collectively as *Amesa Spenta* ("Immortal Ones"). They participate as part of Ahura Mazda and are personified, almost as independent entities. They are:

1) Good Mind (*Vohu Manah*)
2) Truth (*Asha*)
3) Good Power of the Kingdom of God (*Khsanthra*)
4) Right-Mindedness or Devotion (*Armaiti*)
5) Wholeness or Perfection (*Haurvatat*)
6) Immortality (*Ameretat*)

By right aspiration and obedience, man may participate in the first four of these divine aspects. But the last two, Perfection and Immortality, cannot be won by man's efforts alone; they are gifts of God granted to those who seek to achieve the other qualities.

Embracing the quality of truth (*Asha*) is particularly important in Zoroaster's view:

Through the best Asha, through the highest Asha, may we obtain a vision of Thee, may we draw near unto Thee, and may we be in perfect union with Thee . . . I will esteem Asha above all as long as I am able. So do Thou guide me to Asha for whom I have ever yearned.

Again and again in the Gathas he invokes or speaks of Asha. In fact, Asha is mentioned in 176 of the 238 verses of the five Gathas. Solely through Asha one can achieve the supreme goal of human life:

Unto him, who moved by the call of the Holy Spirit and the Divine Mind, expresses

Asha in deed and word, will Ahura Mazda, bestow haurvatat (perfection) and ameretat (immortality)."

Of all the creatures God (Ahura Mazda) placed in the world, He created man alone to be His ally. Man possesses free will, and if he chooses rightly and accepts his divinely intended role, he will conform his mind to that of the characteristics of Good Mind, and will conform his will to that of Truth."

Zoroaster asked Ahura Mazda: "When the wise man . . . strives earnestly for the increase of Asha, would he then, by such action, become one with (or, be merged into) Thee, O Mazda Ahura?"

Ahura Mazda replies: "Whoso listens to and realizes Asha becomes the soul-healing Lord of Wisdom, O Ahura."

So there is a reward for conforming to divine characteristics. Specifically, humans can receive Perfection and Immortality:

Now, I shall speak of what the most virtuous one told me, that word which is to be heard as the best for men: "Those of you who shall give obedience and regard to this Lord of mine, they shall reach Perfection and Immortality. The Wise One is Lord through such actions stemming from good spirit."

Failure to follow the way of the divine characteristics leads man to suffering:

Now, I shall speak of the foremost doctrine of this existence that which the Wise Lord, the Knowing One, told me, "Those of you who shall not bring to realization each precept now exactly as I shall conceive and speak of it, for them shall there be woe at the end of existence."

God is the eternal enemy of Angra Mainyu, the Evil Spirit, at every level of the spiritual and earthly creation. If humans choose to respond in favor of Angra Mainyu, they will receive the opposite of the divine characteristics.

There are specific duties for all those who choose the good. If these duties are accepted and the war against evil is fought bravely, the world will be made perfect in a final judgement, bringing an end to time and eternally settling the battle between good and evil. Then, Zoroaster and his loyal followers will be entrusted with the perfecting of the world.

Prominent in Zoroaster's doctrines is the idea of the "Bridge of the Separator." He promises to help the pious over this bridge into the "House of Song," where God dwells forever with his own. This bridge is said, in later Zoroastrian teachings, to be broad for the righteous, but narrow as a razor for the wicked, who fall off it into hell.

Each individual will have to pass through a test of fire and molten metal. The good will pass unscathed, and may even be purified by the ordeal. Those who are evil, however, will be unmasked and seared unmercifully. Ahura Mazda, wielding the characteristics of Truth, Good Mind, and Devotion, will preside over this final judgement.

So understand these Laws ordained by Mazda, O ye mortals, regarding happiness and pain: Falsehood brings age-long suffering whilst Truth leads to a fuller, higher life; then, after these there shall be bliss.

For his followers, Zoroaster prescribes complete self-responsibility and adherence to the precepts of truth and the other divine characteristics. He looks forward to the "Great Crisis," the "day of reckoning when men's lives shall be finally weighed, and the followers of Asha shall have their reward." At that time, the followers of the "Druj" (the "lie") shall be banished to the "House of Druj":

Whoso cometh to the Righteous One, far from him shall be the future long aeon of misery, of darkness, ill food and crying woe. To such an existence, ye followers of Druj, shall your own Self bring you by your actions.

Good men will live forever in the grace of Ahura Mazda in his Kingdom of Righteousness, while evil men will face great doom, as a consequence of the choice they have made to follow evil.

Still, Ahura Mazda is a forgiving God:

When retribution descends upon the sinners, then unto them O Mazda, will thy Law be clearly revealed by . . . and unto them, O Ahura, shall teaching be given so that into the hands of Asha they will deliver up the false one.

When retribution destroys the past triumphs of the False ones, then they shall attain their innermost desire (namely, the innermost hidden longing for Ahura Mazda . . .); they shall attain the Blessed Abode of Vohu Manah, of Mazda and of Asha.

Thus, O Ahura Mazda, Zarathustra chooses for himself Thy Spirit which indeed is holiest. May Asha incarnate in us, filling our living being with Thy Life and Strength . . .

I shall try to turn Him hither to us by praises of reverence, for I have just now, knowingly through truth, seen the Wise One in a vision to be Lord of the word and deed stemming from good spirit . . .

I shall try to gratify Him for us with good thinking, Him who left our will to choose between the virtuous and the unvirtuous. May the Lord, Wise in His rule, place us in effectiveness, in order to prosper our cattle and our men in consequence of the good relationship of good thinking with truth.

Yes, praising, I shall always worship . . . Wise Lord, with truth and the very best thinking and with their rule through which one shall stand on the path of good power. I shall always obey you . . .

. . . Let wisdom come in the company of truth across the earth.

THE RUBAIYAT OF OMAR KHAYYAM

Here with a little bread, beneath the Bough,
A flask of wine, a book of verse—and thou,
Beside me singing in the wilderness—
Oh, wilderness were paradise enow!

Thus, in one of history's most famous quatrains, Iranian poet/philosopher Omar Khayyam simply recites his concept of paradise: a flask of wine, a piece of bread, a book of verse, and a lover beside him. Written 900 years ago and published in English in 1868, Khayyam's verses, composed so simply and naturally, are regarded as the "pattern of Persian poetry." Fortunately, the translations provided by the British poet Edward Fitzgerald—who at first refused to take credit for them, fearing the *Rubaiyat's* epicurean flavor would prove too spicy for his Victorian audience—are of the same quality.

In 1861 a bundle of pamphlets was placed on a second-hand bookstall in London for clearance at a penny apiece. The writings were titled *Rubaiyat of Omar Khayyam, the Astronomer-Poet of Persia, Translated into English Verse.* Not until Dante Gabriel Rossetti stumbled onto the poem did *Rubaiyat* (meaning a group of quatrains) begin its climb to popularity.

Born in the latter part of the 11th century, Omar Khayyam became an extremely strong, disciplined, and knowledgeable man. Proficient in science, astronomy and mathematics, he was one of eight learned men appointed by the Sultan to reform the calendar. Yet he neither flattered the kings nor bowed to the mullahs, who, in his view, pretended to be societal and religious leaders, but were in fact societal parasites. In his poetry, he boldly expressed his values and believes and therefore faced extreme opposition from the religionists of the time. Khayyam had, in effect, created his own religion. While the Muslim mullahs were causing the people to believe in such "ignorant" and "superstitious" as an afterlife, Khayyam invited them into the realm of knowledge and wisdom, which to him were the rudiments of religion.

Khayyam valued integrity, honesty, truth, wisdom and charity. In his poetry, however, he disputes that whatever we do will come back to us in this very world. Instead, we should achieve our paradise from within—and from the goblet: "So much concern for wealth, and so much regret of this world . . . The worry about this world is poison, and wine its antidote. Drinking the antidote you need not fear the poison." He warns only to be "aware" of all that we do, for the past can not be regained:

The Moving finger writes; and having writ,
Moves on: nor all your Piety nor Wit
Shall lure it back to cancel half a line
Nor all your tears wash out a word of it.

The poet's bitter outlook towards life remained constant. His was a worldly view, as opposed to the mystical view of the time. The only effective way to soothe the soul was through the senses. Especially in his younger years, he adored wine, the smell of flowers, and beautiful women:

Now, when it is the prime of my youth,
I drink wine for it is the time of my enjyment . . .

To enjoy every second of life was Khayyam's aim. Celebrate life, he preached, for tomorrow we shall die and come back no more. Stoically he mocks and seeks solutions for the religious and philosophical ideas that preach of a future life:

Ah, make the most of what we yet may spend,
Before we too into Dust descend,
Dust into Dust, and under dust to lie,
Sans wine, Sans song, Sans singer, and—Sans End!

By his philosophical and logical arguments, Omar Khayyam liberated many from what he considered repressive ideas. In place of religious ideals, he offered his own religion of logic. Although he was not able to alter entirely the society of his time, his literature greatly affected the next generations.

His beliefs are introduced by way of his magnificent poetry. In it, he invites us to think, talk and act freely, not to blindly accept the mullahs' moral blatherings about the Day of Judgment and being cast into fire. Rather, neither heaven nor hell even exist. Whatever does exist, is here, in this world—and it is only here that we will be punished or rewarded for our actions:

They tell me those who drink are doomed to Hell;
This is a common saying, but I can not believe it,
If all those in love and those who drink were to be in Hell,
Tomorrow you would see Paradise as empty as my hand.

With his scientific, logical, materialistic view, Khayyam considers human life—and death—as void and as senseless "as the birth and death of a fly":

There was a drop of water and it fell into the sea,
There was a particle of dust and it was united with The earth,
What is your coming and your going in the world?
A fly appeared and disappeared again.
This semblance of existence is all fancy and imagination,
Whoever is ignorant of this is not numbered among the enlightened.
Sit and drink a goblet of wine and be merry,
Freed from this fancy of impossible delusions.

To Khayyam, "borders of the pleasant green fields, rays of the sun that reflect a thousand shadows upon the goblet of purple wine, soothing melodies of the harp, beautiful cup bearers and fresh blooming flowers are the only realities of the life which is passing like a dreadful nightmare." No one has seen tomorrow; no one has ever returned from the grave. Therefore, let us enjoy life today:

Then to the lip of this poor earthen Urn
I lean'd, the secret well of life to learn:
And lip to lip it murmur'd—"While you live,

Drink!—for once dead, you never shall return."
As pitiful as we may feel, he advises us not to raise our hands to the sky in prayer, for the sky is as helpless as we:

And that inverted Bowl we call The Sky,
Whereunder crawling coop'd we live and die,
Lift not your hands to it for help—for it
As impotently rolls as you or I.

According to the astronomical notions of the time, Khayyam considers our lives subject to the laws of universal motion. Hence, he frequently complains of the "Universe," not of "God":

The spheres do not bestow upon us anything but grief
They bring us nothing that they do not take away again
The unborn, if they knew what we are getting
From the world
Would not come into it at all.

The desire of annihilation that Khayyam repeats in his poetry is similar to the Buddhist philosophy which compares this world to a dream:

Seek not for happiness, for the sum of life is a breath;
Each atom is part of some Kaikobad (king) or Jamshid (a legendary hero-seer)
The state of the world and the remaining part of your existence
Is a dream, a fancy, a deception, a breath.

His sympathy and passion for Persia's past great civilization—which he compared to "the cooing of the ringdove heard in moonlit nights on the ruins of Ctesiphon"—before the attack of the Arabs in the sixth century, was extreme. Persia's kings were exemplary, while the Arabs were both resented and regarded as a lesser race.

Oh to the threshold of yonder castle whose walls reached the spheres,
Kings have once bowed their brows.
Sitting on its battlement I now see,
A turtledove that keeps on calling "Koo? Koo? Koo? Koo?" (where? where?)

Khayyam did not believe in the God "imagined" by Semitic religions. As he grew older, however, he assumed a more serious and conciliatory attitude, and tried to find a logical explanation to these spiritual ideas. In the end, though, he concluded that his search was in vain:

Up from Earth's centre through the Seventh Gate,
I rose, and on the Throne of Saturn sate,
And many knots unravel'd by the road;
But not the Master-Knot of human fate.

As the middle east literary analyst Sadegh Hedayat states: "Khayyam believed that paradise and hell were in the interior of man":

The Firmament is a girdle of our worn-out life,
The Oxus is a vestige of our tear-drained eyes,
Hell is a spark of [the fire of] our useless regrets,
Paradise is a window [giving a glimpse] of our happy moments.

The beautiful flowers, the singing nightingales, the fresh breeze and the running rivers—these combined *are* paradise. Let us not exchange this real paradise for an imaginary one, he advised:

No one has seen Paradise or Hell, my heart
Nor has ever one returned from yonder world, my heart
Our hope and our fear are centered on a thing
Of which no one has beheld so much as a name or a vestige, my heart.

Do not, he cautioned, value this world too much:

Although to thine eyes the world appears adorned,
Value it not, for the wise value nothing.
Many like you have gone and many will come
Take from it thy share for thou will be taken from it.

Omar Khayyam, it seems, drank in order to forget. Life is nothing but pain, he reasoned, and this pain must be forgotten: "Life is one breath and let us forget that one breath too."

One of the most interesting groups of quatrains deals with the Potter and the Pots. Some of the Pots are "loquacious Vessels," and their thoughts reveal a skeptical attitude toward the mysteries of creation, life, and death. One vessel complains that surely the earth will not be molded into a figure and then broken or trampled back into earth again. A second pipes up that, as a "peevish boy" would not break a bowl from which he had drunk with pleasure, so the Potter will certainly not, in wrath, destroy what He has created. Then speaks a third Vessel:

After a momentary silence spake
Some Vessel of a more ungainly Make:
"They sneer at me for leaning all awry;
What! did the Hand then of the Potter shake?"
Then speaks Khayyam, represented by a fourth vessel:
... "Why," said another, "Some there are who tell
Of one who threatens he will toss to Hell
The luckless Pots he marr'd in making—Pish!
He's a Good Fellow, and 't will all be well."

Although, each of his many quatrains celebrate a different notion, all center, directly or indirectly, around one basic theme: *Life is short, unstable, and its fate so changing, that it is not worth paying so much attention to; put no confidence in tomorrow or the hereafter, but seize upon today with all its sensory pleasures.*

We can still imagine him entering into that very eternal world in which he did not believe, for in the eternal world of the Eastern mind, he exists and will always exist as a man who was brave enough to challenge what he considered the fearful ideas of a millennium ago and stand between his enemies and pray:

You know, my Friends, with what a brave Carouse
I made a Second Marriage in my house;
Divorced old barren Reason from my Bed,
And took the Daughter of the Vine to Spouse.

... Oh, that there was a resting-place!
Oh, that we might reach the end of this long path!
Oh, that there was a hope for us to rise again
After a hundred thousand years like grass springs from the bosom of the earth.

THE TALMUD

The *Talmud* is a collection of religious and civil Jewish laws combined with scholarly interpretations of their meaning. Considered the "textbook" for the training of rabbis (literally, "sages," "masters" or "teachers"), it represents a vast work that includes the lore, teachings, observances, and key messages of ancient rabbis during the first to sixth centuries of the Common Era (C.E.). Considered a supplement to the Old Testament—or *Torah*—the *Talmud* has been regarded by Rabbinic Jews as a sacred second revelation from God. Judaism considers the full-time study of the *Talmud* a most holy occupation.

Interlaced with the work's elaborate legal text is a veritable storehouse of wisdom—thousands of engaging parables, anecdotes, biographical vignettes and historical notes. In fact, many of the *Talmud's* maxims have become commonplace phrases, such as: "Give every man the benefit of the doubt"; "All's well that ends well"; "Why are we born into the world with clenched fists and leave it with outstretched fingers? . . . To remind us that we take nothing with us."

Historically, the *Talmud* concerns itself with approximately 1,000 years of Jewish religious and cultural tradition and appears in two related versions: (1) the work compiled by scholars in Palestine around 350-400 C.E., and (2) the work compiled by scholars in Babylonia near 500-600 C.E. Both versions answer questions about a Jew's relationship to God and the community.

The work is divided into two sections: the *Mishnah* and the *Gemara*. The *Mishnah* (meaning to "repeat" or "study") includes the written account of Jewish oral law. According to Jewish tradition, the *Mishnah* stems from the time of Moses (c. 1200 B.C.E.) and was memorized and handed down from generation to generation. Its contents were compiled and recorded from 70-200 C.E. The *Mishnah* consists of 63 subdivisions called *tractates* (expositions) which are divided into six main *orders*, each dealing with a different subject. The order *Nashim* (Women), for instance, addresses marriage, divorce, and other matters that pertain to male/female relationships. Other orders encompass such subjects as civil and criminal law, cleanliness, and religious feasts and celebrations.

The *Gemara* (meaning a "teaching" or "supplement") consists of extremely thorough explanations of passages from the *Mishnah*, and were often written in the form of debates, detailed narratives, and folk tales. Since the scholars who wrote the *Gemara* did not always agree in their interpretation of *Mishnah* passages, these historical customs and explanations do vary. Two versions of the *Gemara* (the *Palestinian Gemara* and the *Babylonian Gemara*) were written between 200 and 500 C.E.

Though the *Talmud's* "golden age" of thought and influence peaked during the centuries following the Roman defeat of the Jews in the year 70 C.E., its potency is still felt in the lives and communities of all Jews. The *Talmud's* purpose is to illustrate that *divine revelation is obtainable through reason and rational discourse.* Thus, it is through these activities that the rabbi/scholar is able to approach God, to become more God-like and holy, and to teach the people. As well, the interpretations and ideals promoted in the *Talmud* encompass the very fabric of Judaic life, and specify how Jews experience and describe mortality.

Text Overview:

The *Talmud* explains that God is the "Creator of Life, the Lord of history, the Lawgiver, and the Architect of human destinies." Like the Greek philosophers who preceded them, the rabbis preach the existence of a "first cause," a prime creator who is "Master of the universe." God has no tangible form and resides in no specific area in space. He is referred to in the *Talmud* as *Makom*, or "Place," meaning "The Holy One, praised be He, is the place of His universe, but His universe is not His place." This notion is illustrated by an anecdote wherein an Emperor says to a rabbi, "I desire to behold your God," to which the rabbi exclaims: "You admit you cannot look at the sun, which is only one of the ministering servants of the Holy One, praised be He; how much more beyond your power of vision is God Himself." Thus, the power and existence of God lie outside a human's capability to perceive:

The universe is pervaded by the might and power of God . . . He formed you and infused into you the breath of life. He stretched forth the heavens and laid the foundations of the earth . . . He causes the rain and the dew to descend, and causes the vegetation to sprout forth. He also forms the embryo in the mother's womb and enables it to emerge as a living being.

God also bestows upon each person certain attributes, among them an "evil impulse" or destructive self-interest, which is balanced by a desire toward goodness and self-denial. Thus, the "heart" in the command "Thou shalt love the Lord thy God with all thy heart," is comprised of these two balancing attributes. Each and every person, then, embraces both good and bad attributes.

Though each individual is a creation of God, not every person is truly ready to receive divine revelation from Him. The chosen few— the prophets—are instruments for disseminating revelation. It follows that the chosen nation is Israel: "[God selected Israel] because all the peoples repudiated the *Torah* [the Old Testament, or Pentateuch] and refused to receive it; but Israel agreed and chose the Holy One, blessed be He, and His Torah." This concept of providence, of being "chosen," has shaped the course of Israel to this day, as seen in the prolonged struggle with neighboring Arab nations over possession of the Holy Land.

Frequently, however, providence is not plainly seen, and it is the duty of *emunah*, or faith, to ensure that providence will work on behalf of an individual nation, as summarized by the phrase "The righteous shall live by his faith." The rabbis proclaim that God's providence should evoke a response of both love and fear (respect), which, in God's eyes, are one in the same: "Love does not coexist with fear, and fear does not coexist with love, except regarding the Omnipresent . . . Be not like servants who serve their master for the sake of receiving a reward, but . . . let the fear of heaven be upon you."

Faith is a central element of devotion, as is the Judaic moral code. Both are the subject of many Talmudic discussions. In one such discussion, the question is posed: "Lord, who shall sojourn in Your tabernacle? Who shall dwell on Your holy mountain?" The answer given is:

He who walks with integrity, and pursues righteousness, and speaks the truth in his heart, and who does not slander with his tongue, who commits no evil against a fellow-human, who does not bring shame to a neighbor, who despises a vile person, but honors those who revere the Lord.

Such are those who will be saved, those who demonstrate faith and obedience to the law.

According to the **Talmud,** on the Day of Judgment the following questions will be asked and must be answered by all: "Did you do your business honestly? Did you set aside time for the study of the Torah? Did you raise a family? Did you maintain our faith in the Messianic redemption? Did you pursue wisdom? Did you attain to the level of being able to reason inferentially from one proposition to another?" If the answer to these questions is yes, the judged will be considered a God-fearing man, "for the fear of God is the treasury in which all else is stored." If the judged "be not . . . a God-fearing man," all other virtues will not prove sufficient.

On the Day of Judgment, one additional question may be posed: "Do you perceive that all mankind are one, and that they are descended from one individual?" Indeed, the **Talmud** teaches that all humanity was derived from one single ancestor, and thus must be again united into one family. And "why did the Creator form all life from a single ancestor?" The answer is clear:

So that the families of mankind shall not lord one over the other with the claim of being sprung from superior stock . . . that all men, saints and sinners alike, may recognize their common kinship in the collective human family.

It follows from this statement, then, that "He who destroys one person has dealt a blow [to] the entire universe, and he who saves or sustains one person has sustained the whole world." In other words, all Talmudic law promotes the protection of human life, regardless of religious creed:

We are obligated to feed non-Jews residing among us even as we feed Jews; we are obligated to visit their sick even as we visit the Jewish sick; we are obligated to attend to the burial of their dead, even as we attend to the burial of Jewish dead.

These practices truly are regarded as "the ways of peace."

"Peace" can be found in and attributed to the way a society responds to individual citizens. Early Jews developed legal and political mechanisms, the most important of which is called halaka, which states: *All authority flows from the divine to the people.* Since rabbis receive inspiration on behalf of the people, the **Talmud**

orders the establishment of town councils to inform the community of God's will, to handle disputes, and make decisions. The deciding factor in all legal proceedings is public approval.

In the realm of public welfare, individual rights are equally as important as collective rights. Still, individual property and ownership are subject to considerations of public interest. The more affluent members of the community are expected to share with the poor; the indigent should be given an allowance of food and clothing, and transients should be given shelter. These amenities are to be culled from the imposition of a general tax to which all the residents of the community contribute. Such an attitude towards the underprivileged underscores the Jewish concept of spirituality and the development of character.

The **Talmud** also stresses the importance of doing one's best on behalf of God, since, as one Talmudic expression conveys, "Whatever the Lord does is best." The notion of serving others as a form of serving one's self is critically linked with serving God. The Talmud recounts the story of a rabbi who sought hospitality in a distant town, where he was refused shelter. That same night, robbers plundered the entire town. "He therefore said to the inhabitants, `Did I not tell you that whatever the Holy One, blessed be He, does is for the best?'" Thus the rabbis teach that one should always be charitable, perceptive, forbearing and forgiving, and avoid envy, hostility, jealousy or hypocrisy. One prayer reads:

May it be acceptable before thee, O God and God of my fathers, that no hatred against us may enter the heart of any man, that no hatred of any man enter our heart, that no envy of us enter the heart of any man, nor the envy of any man enter our heart.

And, more succinctly: "Who is deserving of honor? He who honors other people [and he who can] convert an enemy into a friend."

Through benevolence and *truth*—"The seal of God Himself"—the **Talmud** seeks to draw conflicting peoples together. "It is forbidden to mislead a fellow-creature, including a non-Jew," the **Talmud** reads; all mankind is called to live in harmony with one another:

Transgressions between man and God may be atoned on the Day of Atonement, but transgressions between man and man will not be atoned on the Day of Atonement until one has appeased his fellowman.

The **Talmud,** one of the most beautifully written and invigorating of all religious writings, aspires to increase a person's inner awareness of the divine. Seeking God's will draws one closer to God; reverence and obedience to Talmudic laws "ennoble the lives of men and women."

Undoubtedly, as is suggested throughout, the Benevolent ideals espoused in this work can apply equally to Jew and gentile, and can serve as a guideline to the advancement of an ideal community, which is both a *sacred* and *immortal* institution. The community is made sacred through service—yielding to the will of God. And the community is made immortal when families are raised unto God. Thus, the community becomes increasingly more sacred and immortal under the direction of the **Talmud.**

THE OLD TESTAMENT

Christians and Jews consider the Old Testament to be the foundational historical canon of religious worship; some of the earlier sections hold religious significance to Moslems as well. Said to include the entire history of the world, from its creation down to the last days, its prophetic—and often cryptic—utterances and chronicled events all point to one major occurrence: the coming of the Messiah.

The vast work is divided into four major sections: The creation, the story of Abraham, and the patriarchs in Canaan (Genesis and Job) make up the first section. The second (Exodus through Ruth) covers the period from Israel's bondage in Egypt, the exodus, all through the conquest of the Promised Land. The third section (I Samuel through Zephaniah) includes Israel's history as a united—then a divided—kingdom in the land of Canaan. And the final section (Ezekiel through Malachi) records the fall of the two major kingdoms, Israel and Judah, the Babylonian Captivity, and the release of the exiles to rebuild their country.

Text Overview:

I. In the Beginning

"In the beginning, God created heaven and earth." After forming Adam and Eve, he caused them to become living souls and placed them in the Garden of Eden, a paradise. He forbade them to eat fruit from the tree of knowledge of good and evil, on pain of death. They disobeyed, and were cast out of the garden. Thus, through this first transgression, sin and rebellion entered the world; Adam and Eve's fall from innocence was the beginning of humanity's estrangement from God.

After some 900 years, sin and iniquity became so widespread that God resolved to cleanse the earth of its inhabitants by sending a cataclysmic flood. God commanded the prophet Noah, who "found grace in the eyes of the Lord," to build an ark, in which he, his family, and male and female members of every species of animal were saved from drowning.

Following the flood, Noah's descendants flourished for a time, but eventually became so sinful and arrogant that they attempted to build a tower that would reach to heaven. Angry, God punished their folly by confusing their languages and scattering the people to different parts of the earth.

Out of the materially advanced but spiritually dead culture of the Near East, God chose Abraham as his prophet. God made a covenant with Abraham that his posterity would be a chosen people. Through Abraham, God promised that a Messiah would come to bless the whole world and redeem humanity from sin. Following God's injunction, Abraham traveled from Ur, in Mesopotamia, to Canaan, the Promised Land.

However, Abraham needed to learn certain lessons of faith and obedience. As a test of faith, God commanded Abraham to sacrifice his firstborn son Isaac on the altar. Just as Abraham was about to sacrifice his son, an angel from God intervened—Abraham's obedience and faith had been manifest.

Isaac's chief significance was that he fathered Jacob. Jacob tricked his father into giving him, not his older brother Esau, the birthright blessing reserved for the eldest son. In a vision, God promised Jacob that his posterity would "multiply as the stars of the heaven." Finally, Jacob reconciled with Esau, and his name, Jacob—which means "usurper" in Hebrew—was changed to Israel, meaning "prince of God," the title that God's "chosen people" would bear ever after.

II. On the March

Israel fathered twelve sons, each of which would someday lead one of Israel's twelve "tribes." The youngest, Joseph, was sold into slavery by his jealous older brothers. Eventually, Jacob's sons journeyed to Egypt to escape a severe famine in Canaan. Joseph, who had since risen to become a ruler of Egypt, second only to Pharaoh, forgave his brothers and provided for his family's needs.

Israel's family eventually settled in Goshen. After four hundred years in Egypt, the people had grown and prospered, becoming a mighty nation. Eventually, though, a Pharaoh took power who, fearing the Hebrews' vast numbers, enslaved them. By their suffering, the Israelites were taught to rely on God's mercy.

God selected Moses to lead the Israelites out of Egypt. Moses went to Pharaoh and demanded that the people be freed from bondage, but Pharaoh refused. Thus, God brought down ten successive plagues upon the Egyptians, the last of which killed all firstborn males throughout the land. This plague led to the institution of the Passover: the firstborn son of every believing Israelite family was spared death ("passed over" by the destroying angel) if the blood of a sacrificed lamb (symbolic of the coming Christ's sacrifice) was painted over the doorway. Death visited all who were not "under the blood."

Pharaoh, whose eldest son died in the plague, finally allowed the Israelites to leave. But his anger was again kindled, and he sent his army to slaughter the departing Israelites, who found themselves caught between the Red Sea and the Egyptian army. Miraculously, God parted the waters of the Red Sea, delivered them "dry-shod" through the channel, and destroyed Pharaoh's pursuing army. Despite this deliverance and many other blessing given them by God, the children of Israel often complained about their hardships.

They journeyed eastward to Mount Sinai, where God gave Moses Ten Commandments:

1. *Thou shalt have no other gods before me.*
2. *Thou shalt not make unto thee any graven image . . .*
3. *Thou shalt not take the name of the Lord thy God in vain . . .*
4. *Remember the sabbath day, to keep it holy . . .*
5. *Honour thy father and thy mother . . .*
6. *Thou shalt not kill.*

7. *Thou shalt not commit adultery.*
8. *Thou shalt not steal.*
9. *Thou shalt not bear false witness against thy neighbour.*
10. *Thou shalt not covet thy neighbour's [possessions]...*

These basic religious/societal laws became the core of doctrine for both the Jewish and Christian faiths, a foundation that endures up to the present day.

Because of unbelief, Israel became an itinerant, nomadic nation, and wandered in the wilderness thirty-eight more years, until all the faithless adult generation had perished. Moses, "whom the Lord knew face to face," also died before entering the Promised Land. Joshua, Moses' appointed successor, led the people across the Jordan River—again parting the waters—where they began to conquer, settle, and prosper in a land "flowing with milk and honey."

"In those days," however, "there was no king in Israel; everyone did what he thought best." (Judges 21:25) Lacking national unity, Israel was weak and in a state of perpetual anarchy.

III. In the Land

Responding to Israelite demands for a king, the prophet Samuel anointed Saul the first King of Israel. Although an effective military leader, Saul was unequipped to be Israel's spiritual leader. After disregarding God's command to "utterly to destroy" the Amalekites and their possessions, Samuel anointed David to replace Saul. David, as a young man, had first shown his favor with God by defeating the giant Philistine, Goliath, using only a sling.

David, eager to merge the northern and southern tribes, proclaimed centrally-located Jerusalem the political and religious capitol of a united Israel. Both a skilled statesman and an effective general, he defeated the Philistines and expanded the kingdom into a vast empire. While David's great sin—sending Uriah, one of his generals, to the front lines to die so that he could marry Bathsheba, Uriah's wife—did not cost him the throne, God promised David that the sword would bedevil his family forever. However, God also promised David that through his descendants, a Messiah would come to redeem Israel and the rest of the world from sin.

After a period of internal strife, David's son Solomon took the throne. Israel soon flourished in power, influence, wealth, and glory. Solomon, while not a military leader, was a wise political leader. He brought order to the nation and pursued an aggressive building program, including an elaborate temple and various fortifications. Funded by heavy taxes and built through forced labor, however, Solomon's great buildings alienated his own people, and eventually he fell into idolatry (the worship of idols or "heathen" gods). But despite the failings of their leaders, God continued to guide his people toward the fulfillment of the promise made to Abraham.

Through David and Solomon emerged some of the Old Testament's most powerful verse. David's twenty-third Psalm reads: *The Lord is my shepherd; I shall not want. He maketh me to lie down in green pastures: he leadeth me beside the still waters. He restoreth my soul . . . Yea, though I walk through the valley of the shadow of death, I will fear no evil: for thou art with me . . .*

Solomon's Proverbs are renowned for their insight and spiritual direction: *Trust in the Lord with all thine heart; and lean not unto thine own understanding. In all thy ways acknowledge him, and he shall direct thy paths.* (Prov. 3:5-6) *A soft answer turneth away wrath; but grievous words stir up anger.* (Prov. 15:1)

Over the ensuing centuries, Israel fell into various states of anarchy, and the kingdom was again divided, Israel to the north, Judah to the south. Babylonian attacks periodically brought both nations into captivity and destruction. These years also saw the prophetic ministries of Elijah, Elisha, Jehoshaphat, Micah, Hezekiah, Isaiah, Josiah, and the prophetess Huldah, each assisting the chosen king in his duties and trying to convince the people to keep the commandments and reject their idolatrous practices. Finally, the Babylonians conquered both of the principal kingdoms, leaving the nations mere shadows of their former glory.

IV. A Remnant Restored

The prophets Daniel and Ezekiel—who went into exile with Judah's last king, Jehoiakim—recorded the period of Israelite captivity. Those who were faithful to God during their captivity were blessed. God preserved three men who were cast into a fiery furnace for refusing to bow down and worship idols. A young man named Daniel likewise was cast into a den of lions for worshipping the Lord, and he was also saved. This Daniel, who grew to become both a statesman and a prophet, eventually rose from royal hostage to third in command in Babylon.

After seventy years in captivity, God raised up Cyrus, ruler of Persia, to conquer Babylon and to decree that Judah was to return to the land of Israel; the Jews began to rebuild their country. The first returning exiles reconstructed the temple, but it was a poor substitute for Solomon's glorious edifice. Seventy-five years later, Nehemiah rebuilt Jerusalem's walls, a feat accomplished despite the opposition of Samaria and Ammon.

The prophet Ezra finally led a group of Jews from Babylon to Jerusalem, where he reinforced the observance of the Torah (the "Pentateuch," or first five books of the Old Testament) and purified the temple rituals. Many Jews, though, never returned: some continued to reside in Persia, where they were saved from destruction by the courageous Jewish Queen Esther; others were scattered around the world. Still, Judaism continued to prosper, and most Hebrews continued to await the Holy Messiah's appearance. For, as the prophet Isaiah had foretold, the Messiah would come to deliver them from bondage, sin and death: "Surely he hath borne our griefs, and carried our sorrows . . . He was wounded for our transgressions . . . and with his stripes we are healed."

350

THE NEW TESTAMENT

(the King James edition)

For Christians and Christian religions, the New Testament embodies a central part of the *Bible*. Coupled with the Old Testament, today it is the doctrinal foundation for most of Christianity. The Old Testament is a compilation of Jewish secular and religious laws as well as prophecies concerning the coming of a "Messiah," the savior of the world. The New Testament comprises an account of the life and teachings of Jesus Christ, whom many consider to be the prophesied savior (the name "Christ," designates Jesus as savior). The New Testament also details events that occurred after Christ's death, profiling the gospel message dispersed by his *Apostles* (specially-called followers).

The New Testament is composed of separate "books," written by Jesus' followers. These writings, gathered together many centuries after the events actually took place, are separated into two sections: the *narratives* and the *epistles*.

The "narratives" consist of five books, historical accounts written by Matthew, Mark, Luke, and John; these relate the teachings and life of Christ from his birth through to his death by crucifixion. The Book of Acts—sometimes considered the second part of the Book of Luke—relates key experiences of the Apostles after Jesus' death and resurrection.

The "epistles" comprise a series of letters written by Jesus' Apostles to various Christian congregations around the Mediterranean. Included in this section is also the Book of Revelations, which contains prophecies concerning Christ's church and his eventual return.

The first four books in the New Testament (Matthew, Mark, Luke, and John) each cover the period of time from Christ's birth to his resurrection. The four accounts of his life, though similar in most details, differ somewhat in emphasis and purpose:

Matthew's gospel emphasizes how Jesus' life fulfills Old Testament prophecy, and includes many of Christ's discourses; Mark's gospel stresses Jesus' miraculous power, and presents a narrative of Jesus that is moving and full of action; Luke's account is characterized by an emphasis on Jesus' principles of forgiveness and love, and is the only gospel that underscores the role of women in Christ's ministry; and John's purpose seems to have been more to bear witness of Christ's divinity than to record places and events. The result is a portrait of Christ painted from many different angles, bringing to life the dynamic nature of this historic—and to many, divine—figure.

Text Overview:

The Narratives

Jesus was born in Bethlehem, Judea, to a virgin named Mary, who conceived through the power of God. Mary, and Jesus' earthly father, a carpenter named Joseph, raised Jesus in the Jewish faith. When he was only twelve years old, Mary and Joseph once found him preaching in a synagogue. Even at this early age, Jesus intimated that he was on a sacred mission.

But it wasn't until he was 30 that he started to minister full-time to the people. At that time, he

called twelve "Apostles" to help him in the ministry.

Jesus went about teaching and healing the people who believed in his divinity:

God anointed Jesus of Nazareth with the Holy Ghost and with power: who went about doing good, and healing all that were oppressed . . . for God was with him.

Jesus' message was one of good tidings and hope. He instructed thousands of people on hillsides, in the temples and synagogues, wherever any could gather together. He often taught using "parables," stories to illustrate his precepts. One parable invited his followers to find the "lost sheep," those who had strayed from the path of God:

And he spake this parable unto them, saying, What man among you, having an hundred sheep, if he lose one of them, doth not leave the ninety and nine in the wilderness, and go after that which is lost, until he find it? And when he hath found it, he layeth it on his shoulders, rejoicing. And when he cometh home, he calleth together his friends and neighbors, saying unto them, Rejoice with me: for I have found my sheep which was lost. I say unto you, that likewise joy shall be in heaven over one sinner that repenteth, more than over ninety and nine just persons, which need no repentance.

For the most part, Jesus' teachings were deceptively simple, often centering around the importance of loving both God and each other. He taught that when people love God, righteousness—and happiness—naturally follow. Such teachings formed the fundamentals of Christianity:

- *If ye love me, keep my commandments.* (John 14:15)

- Serve God, not self-interests: *No man can serve two masters.* (Matthew 6:24)

- *As I have loved you, love one another.* (John 13:34)

- Humility is a virtue: *Blessed are the meek: for they shall inherit the earth.* (Matthew 5:5)

- He taught the his disciples how to pray. *Our Father which art in heaven, Hallowed be thy name. Thy kingdom come. Thy will be done, as in heaven, so on earth. Give us this day our daily bread. And forgive us our sins; for we also forgive every one that is indebted to us. And lead us not into temptation; but deliver us from evil.* (Luke 11:2-4)

- Baptism is necessary for all: *Except a man be born of the water and the Spirit, he cannot enter into the kingdom of God.* (John 3:5)

- Set an example for good: *Let your light so shine before men, that they may see your good works, and glorify your father which is in heaven.* (Matthew 5:16)

- *. . . Thou shalt love the Lord thy God with all thy heart, and with all thy soul, and with all thy mind. This is the first and great commandment. And the second is like unto it, Thou shalt love thy neighbour as thyself. On these two commandments hang all the law and the prophets.* (Matthew 22:37-40)

Jesus performed many miracles during his ministry. On one occasion, he turned water into wine; on another, he fed thousands of people with just a few fish and loaves of bread; he healed those

351

who were crippled, strengthened the sick and infirm, and restored sight to the blind. On three different occasions, he brought the dead back to life. The Apostle John described Jesus coming to the grave of a friend who had been dead four days:

He cried with a loud voice, Lazarus, come forth. And he that was dead came forth. (John 11:43-44)

Through his miracles and spiritual counsel, Jesus gained many followers. However, not everyone was persuaded by his presence and accomplishments. Some Jewish leaders felt threatened by Jesus' power among the people, and, after suffering him for three years, determined to put an end to his ministry.

Jesus knew the end was near. Referring to Old Testament prophecy and relying on his own insight, he prepared his Apostles for what was to come, rehearsing to them how he would be crucified in fulfillment of his earthly mission.

Jesus, along with his Apostles, traveled to Jerusalem, where he continued to teach, preach and heal. Knowing he would soon be betrayed and slain, Jesus retired alone to a garden near the Mount of Olives, where, the Book of Luke says, he prayed, . . . *Father, if thou be willing, remove this cup from me: nevertheless not my will, but thine, be done.* Luke continues: "And being in an agony he prayed more earnestly: and his sweat was as it were great drops of blood falling down to the ground."

Ironically, it was one of his own Apostles, Judas Iscariot, who sold information about Christ's whereabouts to the Jewish leaders, who had him arrested. Jesus was first taken before Caiaphas, a Jewish high priest, who accused him of "blasphemy" for claiming he was the Son of God and sentenced him to death. But since Judea was an occupied land under Roman authority, Jesus was turned over to the Roman consulate, Pontius Pilate. During the interrogation, Pilate could not find Jesus guilty of breaking any Roman law. Not wishing to indict an innocent man, but aware of Jesus' unpopularity among the Jewish hierarchy, Pilate presented Christ, along with a murderer named Barabbas, to the Jews and offered to free one and crucify the other. Thinking they would rather crucify a known murderer, Pilate was dismayed when the crowd cried out that Jesus must be crucified. Anxious to keep the peace, however, Pilate gave in to their demands and ordered Christ's execution.

After being tortured by Roman soldiers, Jesus was forced to carry a wooden cross to the hill Golgatha (Calvary). There, his hands and feet were nailed to the cross, which was then propped up so everyone could witness the condemned man's death.

Jesus, after forgiving those who had murdered him, died. As the Jewish Sabbath was about to begin (Friday at dusk), his body was hurriedly laid to rest in a tomb.

On Sunday, the third day following the crucifixion, the followers of Christ went to the tomb to dress and prepare Jesus' body, according to Jewish rites. To their bewilderment, they found the tomb empty. Angels then appeared, announcing to Christ's disciples that Jesus had risen from the dead—he had been resurrected, his body and spirit reunited.

Over the next 40 days, Jesus revealed himself many times to his followers. He invited them to feel the marks of the wounds in his hands and feet so they would know it was really him, Jesus Christ.

Finally, Christ had completed his mission, as foretold by the Old Testament prophets. Before ascending into heaven, he announced that he would someday return, and instructed his Apostles to go and teach the world the things he had taught them.

The Book of Acts recounts many of the exploits of the Jesus' Apostles. Peter and John went about teaching Christ's gospel, and, like Jesus had done, also performed miracles. They were arrested many times. Yet, under the suspicious gaze of Jewish leaders, they continued to preach Christ's message.

As the Apostles went among the people, they were persecuted by angry unbelievers. Stephen, a disciple, was stoned to death as he taught. Most of the Apostles and many of the disciples were eventually caught and slain for their beliefs.

One of the great stories in the New Testament involves a man named Saul, who hated and persecuted the believers in Jesus the Christ. All that changed when the resurrected Christ appeared to Saul in a vision. Saul was converted to the Christian faith and changed his name to Paul. This Paul became one of the most active of the Apostles—who continued to be called after Christ's death—taking the Christian message to many foreign lands, including Rome itself. It is through Paul's letters to early Christian congregations that many of Jesus' teachings are preserved today.

The Epistles

The Apostles and other authorized disciples of Christ set up congregations in the cities they visited. These congregations required much spiritual and temporal assistance to survive the persecution heaped upon them. To help strengthen the followers and instruct them more fully in Christian doctrine, the Apostles sometimes wrote letters to the congregations, in which they encouraged Christ's people to be faithful and reminded them of his teachings. Some of these Apostolic admonitions include:

- *Whatsoever a man soweth, that shall he also reap.* (Gal 6:7)
- . . . *The love of money is the root of all evil.* (I Tim 6:10)
- *For as in Adam all die, even so in Christ shall all be made alive.* (I Corinthians 15:22)
- *Even so faith, if it hath not works, is dead, being alone.* (James 2:17)
- *If we say that we have no sin, we deceive ourselves, and the truth is not in us.* (1 John 1:8)
- *For I am not ashamed of the gospel of Christ: for it is the power of God unto salvation to everyone that believeth; to the Jew first, and also to the Greek.* (Romans 1:16)

The Apostle John—believed to be singularly blessed by Jesus to live until his return—wrote the Book of Revelations, which foretells the events of modern times. John also prophesied of Christ's "second coming" to the Earth. When Christ returns this second time, the New Testament says he will come with power and glory; as King, he will set up a kingdom to rule the Earth where the righteous will dwell.

THE GNOSTIC GOSPELS

The Nag Hammadi Library

In 1945, outside the town of Nag Hammadi in upper Egypt, an Arab peasant made a shocking archaeological discovery. Buried in an earthenware jar were ancient papyrus books with opening lines such as: "These are the secret words which the living Jesus spoke, and which Thomas wrote down."

The peasant did not understand the texts, and certainly did not comprehend their importance; in fact, his mother used some of them as kindling for her stove. But, as providence would have it, the documents made their way to the black market and eventually—after years of intriguing exchanges, plots, confirmations, smugglings, and political wrangling—they were exposed to public view.

The entire find, fifty-two texts in all, includes material which represents a radical challenge to orthodox Christianity. Dating from the years immediately following Jesus' death and inscribed by members of a Christian sect—the Gnostics—claiming to possess secret knowledge (*gnosis*) based on spiritual insights, the collection includes previously unknown gospels: the Gospel of Thomas, the Gospel of Philip, the Secret Book of James, the Apocalypse of Paul, the Letter of Peter to Philip, the Apocalypse of Peter, the Gospel of Truth, the Gospel to the Egyptians, and numerous other texts which suggest utterly new perspectives on Christianity.

There is little debate as to the dating of the manuscripts. Examination of the papyrus used to thicken the leather bindings, and of the Coptic script, indicate that they are at least 1500 years old. These manuscripts turned out to be translations of Greek texts (fragments of which were discovered some fifty years prior to the Nag Hammadi find.) The dates of these original Greek works is not so clear, but estimates for some of the gospels range between A.D. 50 and 180.

The emergence of these new texts has aroused intense controversy. In general, opinions have polarized into two camps: those who consider the works heretical, fraudulent and blasphemous; and a second group who accepts at least a portion of the works as historical accounts of the life and teachings of Jesus. Perhaps the debate lies in these radically different perspectives on traditional Christian belief. Adherents on both sides of the debate might point to the following account from the Gospel of Philip as an example of why they do not accept all of *The Gnostic Gospels* as certain truth:

... *The companion of the Savior is Mary Magdalene. But Christ loved her more than all the disciples, and used to kiss her often on her mouth. The rest of the disciples were offended* ...

They said to him, "Why do you love her more than all of us?" The Savior answered and said to them, "Why do I not love you as I love her?"

Other sayings in *The Gnostic Gospels* criticize important, commonly accepted Christian doctrines—including such staples as the "virgin birth" and Jesus' "bodily resurrection"—as naive misunderstandings.

Since at least A.D. 180, when Iraneus, the orthodox Bishop of Lyons, declared that there had been gospels, "Gnostic Gospels," which were "blasphemous," there has been an effort to eradicate the texts. This effort to conceal their existence apparently was so successful that, for hundreds of years prior to this century, no trace of them was found, despite the fact that they were, at one time, widely circulated throughout Rome, Greece and Asia Minor.

Now, once again, *The Gnostic Gospels* have been opened to widespread examination; and, once again, controversy regarding their authenticity has arisen.

Text Overview:

Resurrection

The Nag Hammadi texts put forth a unique perspective on the resurrection of the body—both Jesus' and mankind's. In the "Treatise on Resurrection," a gnostic teacher, Rhizinos, speaks of the resurrection as an experience of new perspective available to all during *this* life: "It is . . . the revealing of what truly exists . . . and a migration into newness." It is a means by which enlightenment is achieved, he adds. In fact, one can be "resurrected from the dead" in this very moment.

Rhizinos then makes the challenge: "Are you—the real you—mere corruption? (flesh) . . . Why do you not examine your own self, and see that you have arisen?"

The "Gospel of Philip" further corrects Christians who take the resurrection literally. Those who say they will die first and then rise are in error . . ." They must "receive the resurrection while they live."

Several of the Nag Hammadi texts recount *spiritual* visitations by Jesus to his disciples following his crucifixion and resurrection. One gospel, the "Apocrypha of John," states:

Immediately . . . the heavens were opened, and the whole creation which is under heaven shone, and the world was shaken. I was afraid, and I saw in the light a child . . . while I looked he became an old man. And he changed his form again, becoming like a servant . . . Then I saw . . . an image with multiple forms in the light . . . . As he marveled, the presence spoke: "John, John, why do you doubt, and why are you afraid? You are not unfamiliar with this form, are you? . . . Do not be afraid! I am the one who is with you always . . . I have come to teach you what is and what was, and what will come to be . . . "

The "Letter of Peter to Philip" describes a time when all the disciples were praying, and "a great light appeared, so that the mountain shone from the sight of him who had appeared. And a voice called out to them saying `Listen . . . I am Jesus Christ, who is with you forever.'"

In general, the authors of *The Gnostic Gospels* claim that Christ appeared to "a few of these disciples, who he recognized were capable of understanding such great mysteries," and taught them that his resurrection was a spiritual phenomena, not a physical event.

The gospels offer more criticisms of early Christian dogma. The "Testimony of Truth" chastises those who seek salvation through martyrdom:

> . . . They are empty martyrs, since they bear witness only to themselves . . . When they are "perfected" with a martyr's death, this is what they are thinking: "If we deliver ourselves over to death for the sake of the Name, we shall be saved." These matters are not settled in this way . . . They do not have the Word which gives life.

In the "Apocalypse of Peter" Christ criticizes the orthodoxy as those who do not take upon themselves his true spirit:

> They will cleave to the name of a dead man, thinking they will become pure. But they will become greatly defiled and they will fall into a name of error . . . and into a manifold dogma, and they will be ruled heretically. For some of them will blaspheme the truth and proclaim evil teaching. And they will say evil things against each other. . . . Many others, who oppose the truth and are messengers of error, will set up their error and their law against these pure thoughts of mine . . .

The "Apocalypse of Peter" also refutes the claim to authority of various church officials:

> Others . . . outside our number . . . call themselves bishops and also deacons, as if they had received their authority from God. They bend themselves under the judgment of the leaders. These people are waterless canals.

The "Tripartite Tractate" portrays the "gnostic" Christians as joining together often, as equals enjoying mutual love, as followers of Christ spontaneously helping one another. But the ordinary Christians are said to have "wanted to command one another, out-rivalling one another in their empty ambitions"; these are filled with "lust for power . . . each one imagining he is superior to the others."

The Gnostic Gospels sometimes depicts Jesus as a teacher who does not simply answer questions, but rather directs his disciples to look inward at their own souls to discover the answers, as in the "Gospel of Thomas":

They said to him, "Tell us who you are so that we may believe in you." He said to them, "You read the face of the sky and of the earth, but you have not recognized the one who is before you, and you do not know how to read this moment."

And when, in frustration, they asked him, "Who are you, that you should say these things to us?" Jesus, instead of answering, criticized their question: "You do not realize who I am from what I say to you."

As already noted, according to Thomas, when the disciples asked Jesus to show them where he was so that they might reach that place as well, he refused, focusing them instead back to themselves, to discover the truth hidden within.

The same theme follows in the "Dialogue of the Savior." As Jesus talks with his three chosen disciples, Matthew asks that he reveal to him the "place of life," which is, he says, the "pure light." Jesus answers, "Every one of you who has known himself has seen it." Here again he deflects the question, pointing the disciple toward his own self-discovery.

The Gnostic Gospels also seem to offer women a greater role in Christian worship than they are traditionally allowed. In "Pistis Sophia" (*Faith Wisdom*), the disciple Peter complains that Mary is dominating "the conversation with Jesus" and displacing the rightful priority of Peter and his brother apostles. He urges Jesus to silence her and is quickly rebuked. Later, however, Mary confesses to Jesus that she hardly dares speak to him freely because, in her words, "Peter makes me hesitate; I am afraid of him, because he hates the female race." Jesus replies that "whoever the spirit inspires is divinely ordained to speak, whether man or woman."

Another text, mysteriously titled "Thunder, Perfect Mind," submits a poem spoken in the voice of a feminine divine power:

For I am the first and the last.
I am the honored one and the scorned one.
I am the whore and the holy one.
I am the wife and the virgin . . .

I am the barren one,
and many are her sons . . .
I am the silence that is incomprehensible . . .
I am the utterance of my name.

The Nag Hammadi collection presents what some believe are original perspectives on Jesus of Nazareth and his teachings. Others doubt the authenticity of some—or all—of the texts.

For readers who would like to be treated to a safe and reliable introduction to *The Gnostic Gospels*, they might first try "The Gospel of Thomas," "The Gospel of Philip," or "The Secret Book of John."

THE CONFESSIONS OF ST. AUGUSTINE

by Aurelius Augustinus, Bishop of Hippo (A.D. 354-430)

The Confessions of St. Augustine is the classic and remarkably candid account of a deep, life-long, often anguished quest for knowledge and truth. Written in A.D. 397 shortly after Augustine was made bishop of the North African seaport village of Hippo, the work is considered by many to represent the first example of autobiography in the Western world. However, Confessions records a spiritual journey rather than a strictly factual "self-biography." Written in ten books, all addressed to God, Augustine recounts his progression from heathen to heretic to saint, as one of the greatest early Church patriarchs. We read, sometimes in painful detail, how Augustine, by degrees and often unwillingly, finds his way to Christ.

Most compelling is the extent to which Augustine allows his personality, interests, and emotions to reach through the text. It is as if he wants us, his readers, to be able to identify with the anguish, the torment, and the mental gyrations he went through in the period preceding his true conversion, perhaps to strengthen other Christians for the demands and trials which conversion inevitably requires.

Text Overview:

Augustine begins by invoking God's presence, praising His majesty and unchangeable nature, and expressing the desire to worship and follow Him. He then relates in detail his early life, his infancy and boyhood up to age fifteen.

Son of a pagan father and a devout Christian mother, Aurelius Augustinus was born in the northern African city of Tagaste (near what is now Constantine, Algeria). Though his mother, Saint Monica, had instructed him in the principles of the Christian faith, he largely ignored these teachings. At fifteen, wrote Augustine, he was more inclined to youthful pleasures and vices than he was to education: "I did not love Thee, and committed fornication against Thee; and those around me thus sinning cried, 'Well done! Well done!' . . . and for this I shed no tears."

Frankly confessing that he has abused the gifts God gave to him, Augustine concludes his first volume by expressing deep gratitude to God for sparing him in his youth, praising the endowments and blessings he has received form God, and dedicating the use of these gifts to God's purposes: "But all these are gifts of my God; I did not give them to myself; and they are good . . . and those things which Thou hast given me shall be developed and perfected." Stricken by disease at the end of his fifteenth year, he vowed to be baptized—if only God would restore his health. But like many repentant sinners, Augustine admits that after his recovery he forgot this desperate promise. " . . . I dared to grow wild again with various and shadowy loves; my form consumed away, and I became corrupt in Thine eyes, pleasing myself, and eager to please in the eyes of men."

Augustine's sixteenth year witnessed the rapid corruption of his morality. He totally abandoned his studies and indulged instead in "lustful pleasures." Happy in the company of his admiring and amenable friends, he also committed theft. While many of his sins were prompted by idleness, others he committed out of nothing more than sheer wantonness. But despite his willful, calculated iniquity, God's mercies preserved him from much harm during this period.

Between ages seventeen and nineteen, Augustine lived in Carthage, the venerable old North African trade capital, which had also become a center of Christianity. There, finally, he completed his formal studies. As his learning advanced, he became inflamed with the love of intellectual wisdom and the praise of others; he developed a distaste for the Scriptures, preferring the logical, philosophical tutoring of Neoplatonism over spiritual enlightenment. The Scriptures, he wrote, "appeared to me to be unworthy . . . for my inflated pride shunned their style, nor could the sharpness of my mind pierce their inner meaning." They were so simple and direct as to be understood by "little ones"—mere children; "but I scorned to be a little one . . . swollen with pride, I looked upon myself as a great one."

His pride, he asserts, caused him to fall into the "snares" and "heresies" of Manichaeism, a Christian-Gnostic religious sect that, among other things, preached disdain of the body in order to magnify worship and development of the soul, and taught that since God brought matter into existence—and since evil exists inherently in all material bodies—then God Himself must be the author of both all good and all evil. Augustine describes his mother's grief at his heresy, and her ardent prayers for his conversion. As a result of her faith, she received a vision from God and a visit from a bishop, both providing the comforting assurance that Augustine would eventually come to know and accept the true gospel.

From Augustine's nineteenth to his twenty-eighth years, which are covered in the fourth book, he followed the Manichaeans, all the time reveling in his love of knowledge, writing books on the liberal arts and Aristotle's categories, and converting others to the Manichaean heresy. In fact, he mourned the loss of one friend who was converted and baptized into the Christian faith.

In his thirtieth year, Augustine discovered what he saw as fallacies in Manichaean teachings on such subjects as the origin of evil and the nature of God—though he still lacked any clear concept of what the correct ideas might be. At this point he moved from Carthage to Rome, and then Milan, where he became a teacher of rhetoric. In Milan, he heard Bishop Ambrose preach, and was impressed both by Ambrose's rhetorical gift and by the content of his sermons. Soon, Augustine says, his growing alienation from the Manichaeans allowed him again to become a catechumen, or "inquirer"—and investigator of the Christian Church.

Augustine's leanings toward Christianity rapidly enlarged. He found that his Neoplatonist views differed only slightly from Christian teachings, although in spirit (logic vs. feelings) they were far apart. Following the injunctions embodied in Ambrose's lectures and sermons, he found more and more truth in orthodox Christian doctrines, and began to deliberate with himself on how to live a more moral, regulated life. In the meantime, his growing fear of God's judgment served to restrain, at least to some degree, his lustful, wanton desires.

Augustine's mother soon arrived in Milan. In concert with Bishop Ambrose, she persuaded Augustine again to study the Scriptures; having contracted what he considered a "spiritual disease," this prescription seemed appropriate. Augustine discovered that he had wrongly blamed the Catholic Church for teaching that God was bounded by space: "I was confounded and converted, and I rejoiced, O my God, that the one Church . . . did not [maintain] in her sound doctrine, any tenet that would confine Thee, the Creator of all, in space." This discovery removed an enormous obstacle to Augustine's conversion; he wrote that it was as though scales had fallen from his eyes in the manner of Saint Paul.

According to Augustine, God now began working more actively, preparing him to receive the gospel. "It was pleasing in Thy sight to reform my deformity, and by inward stings didst Thou disturb me, that I should be dissatisfied until Thou were made sure to my inward sight." For example, material conceptions of God and the origin of evil had continued to perplex him. But now, following an extensive study of "the sacred books," he was given a correct understanding of God's nature and the discernment that mankind's free will—not God—lies at the root of sin.

These understandings gave Augustine clearer notions about God, but still he fathomed little about Jesus Christ and His divinity. To him, Jesus was "a man of excellent wisdom, to whom no man could be equalled . . . But what mystery there was in `The Word was made flesh,' I could not even imagine." Again, Scripture answered Augustine's questions. From Platonic philosophy he began to comprehend the doctrine of the divinity of the word of God.

Then came the most memorable time of Augustine's life. First, his good friend Victorinus converted to Christianity, which awakened in him the desire to entirely devote himself to God. Another Christian friend, Simplicianus, told him about the conversion of others, and how their lives had been changed. Augustine's old habits, nevertheless, briefly overcame him. However, he was impressed by the history of St. Antony, the ascetic founder of Christian monasticism, and the conversion of still two other friends roused him to further prayer and study.

The turning point came one day as Augustine strolled in a garden. Feeling trapped by his vices and his many previous transgressions, he lamented, "Why is there not this hour an end to my uncleanness?" Suddenly, he heard a child's voice coming from a house bordering the garden. "Take up and read; take up and read," it repeated. Knowing of no children's games which included such a refrain, he picked up the volume of the apostles he had brought with him: "I grasped, opened, and in silence read that paragraph on which my eyes first fell—`Not in rioting and drunkenness, not in chambering and wantonness, not in strife and envying; but put ye on the Lord

Jesus Christ, and make no provision for the flesh, to fulfill the lusts thereof.'"

"No further would I read," Augustine wrote, "nor did I need; for instantly, as the sentence ended—by a light, as it were, of security into my heart—all gloom of doubt vanished away." Shortly after this, Augustine, his son Aeodatus (the issue of a youthful tryst; Augustine never married), and Augustine's friend Alypius, made ready to receive baptism.

Augustine determined to dedicate his life to God and gradually to forsake his profession of rhetoric. He corresponded extensively with Ambrose regarding his change of life, then returned to the country to prepare himself for baptism. In 387, Augustine, Aeodatus, and Alypius were baptized. Shortly afterward, Augustine's mother, Monica, now fifty-six, who had prayed long and fervently for his eventual conversion, died in Ostia on her way to Africa. Augustine praised her virtuous character and her concern and efforts on behalf of his soul.

When Augustine was about thirty-five, he returned to Tagaste, where he organized a community of monks. Then, while traveling to nearby Hippo, the Christian congregation there convinced him to stay. In 391 he was ordained a priest, and five years later was made bishop of Hippo, a post he held until his death some 34 years later. During the intervening years, Augustine wrote several books and essays defining his beliefs, which included: God exists in the soul of every living person; Individuals should direct their attention to God and not be distracted by the cares or pleasures of the world; People cannot change their sinful ways except by the grace of God, and only certain individuals are predestined to receive His grace; People can only receive His grace by belonging to the Church and receiving the sacraments, and though the Church's clergy is imperfect, God bypasses human weakness through the sacraments, thus blessing His children.

Having previously described his miserable life before baptism, Augustine now, in the last several volumes, confesses his remaining weaknesses and takes up the question, "Why write this confession?" The answer: "To examine and illustrate for others by what method God and the happy life could be achieved." After a lengthy exposition on the nature and power of memory, he asserts that humans, if they are to discover God, must move not only beyond living by impulse but beyond memory, beyond living—as we would probably put it today—by habit or convention. Even animals have the power of memory, Augustine argues; otherwise they could neither find nor recognize food. Humans, contrarily, must engage in an acts of will, of volition—acts that often defy convention as well as desire—if they are to come to God.

Finally, Augustine examines his own life of trials, a life that was once burdened under the triple weight of temptation—"the lust of the flesh, the lust of the eyes, and pride"—and suggests what Christian continence prescribes for each form of temptation. Lastly, Augustine praises Jesus Christ, the one mediator between God and humanity, and the only source of victory over human maladies and shortcomings.

THE IMITATION OF CHRIST

by
Thomas a Kempis
(1379/80 - 1471)

The Imitation of Christ, according to Matthew Arnold, is "the most exquisite document, after those of the New Testament, of all that the Christian spirit has ever inspired." A religious treatise of Roman Catholic persuasion, it was completed around A.D. 1427, and for more than five centuries has been acclaimed by men of many faiths as one of the greatest spiritual writings of all times. Through periods of peace and war, good times and bad, Imitation has provided many with inspiration and food for spiritual strength and consolation. Its intent is to point the way by which men will be able to follow Christ's teachings and, by so doing, imitate his life.

Constructed of four separate books— "Admonitions Useful for a Spiritual Life," "Admonitions Leading to the Inner Life," "The Inward Speaking of Christ to a Faithful Soul," and "Which Treats Especially of the Sacrament of the Altar"— the work proclaims the ancient tenets the Catholic church has always taught. The Imitation of Christ is one of the most widely-read Christian religious books, perhaps second only to the Bible.

Historical Overview:

Thomas a Kempis was an Augustinian monk whose order focused on Latin studies as well as the copying and illustration of manuscripts. Thomas was born Thomas Haemerken ("little hammer") to a blacksmith father and a schoolteacher mother living in the "Low Countries" of eastern Germany. He joined the Augustinians essentially as nothing more than a poor boy in search of an education. The religious world at the time was particularly confused. The foundations of the Catholic Church—and hence of Western civilization—seemed to be crumbling. Thomas' monastic order determined to live their lives as nearly as possible in imitation of the lives of the early Christians, their chief aim to deepen religious life as a cure for the widespread moral and ethical laxity of the times, and to promote sound learning. By the end of the eighteenth century, however, the Reformation had effectively swept the order's 80 units out of existence.

The Imitation of Christ was first translated from Latin into English by an unknown scholar in 1460. In 1530, Richard Whitford, a British monk, presented his translation, from which, in 1955, Harold C. Gardiner, a Jesuit, edited his modern ver-

sion. Whitford's fondness for the words "merry" and "glad" suggests that Thomas a Kempis was not gloomy or antisocial, as he is sometimes described. But in spite of Whitford's efforts, the book has often been called pessimistic, defeatist, and negative. Gardiner, in his updated version, quotes Scripture in more modern-day English: "Come to Me all you who labor and are heavily burdened, and I will refresh you."

Text Overview:

The central doctrine of Imitation is withdrawal into inner solitude. The book is not meant to represent the whole of the Catholic faith, but reflects Kempis' own point of view. Essentially, the work was written by a monk for monks, as an aid in managing the particular stresses of monastic life. On the surface it would appear that Thomas and the other monks of his order despised the human body. However, they merely meant to infer that, in comparison with the soul, the physical body is of little worth.

Thomas has been labeled anti-intellectual in that he stresses the vanity of worldly knowledge, though the order did sponsor many schools for poor boys. In fact, the most famous quote from Imitation is: "I had rather feel compunction of heart for my sins than only know the definition of compunction." In other passages, Thomas speaks of the legitimacy of inquiry and speculation, warning only that presumption and pride must be avoided in the intellectual search.

Book I, for the most part, discusses the reading of Scripture (there are more than 850 Scriptural passages either quoted or alluded to in Imitation) and how man—and monks—ought to act. Among the points addressed are:

- Learning from the ancient prophets: " . . . do not disdain the parables of the ancient Fathers, for they were not spoken without great cause."

- Obedience to truth: " . . . he is very well taught who forsakes his own will and follows the Will of God."

- Peace comes only to true, simple, humble people.

- All goodness is ascribed to God, none to man.

- Judge not: " . . . in judging others a man often labors in vain."

- Monastic monks ought to avoid the types of personal friendships that would exclude others, especially friendships which might hinder the charity that should exist among all.

- Subjugation of self and avoidance of temptation are musts: "As medicine for the body is administered too late when the sickness has been allowed to increase by long continuance, so it is with temptation. First, an unclean thought comes to the mind . . . then pleasure in it and various evil motions, and at the end follows a full consent; so little by little, the enemy gains full entrance, because he was not wisely resisted at the beginning. The slower a man is in resisting, the weaker he is to resist, and the enemy is daily stronger against him."

Book II treats such topics as inward conversion, knowledge of self, cultivating a pure conscience, and giving gratitude to God:

- The inner life consists of loving God above all things, having patience in adversity, and the ever-present distrust of one's own intelligence. Suffering constitutes the pathway to heaven; only thereby does a person earn God's grace: "When you come to such a degree of patience that tribulation is sweet to you, and . . . the love of God is savory and pleasant in your sight, then may you trust that it is well with you, and that you are in good estate; for you have found paradise on earth. But as long as it is irksome to you to suffer, and you seek to flee it . . . it is not well with you, and . . . you are not in the perfect way of patience."

Book III is essentially a prayer book that outlines specific litanies and meditations through which God can speak to the soul.

- "O my soul, take heed to what has been said before and shut the doors of your sensuality, which are your five senses, so that you may hear inwardly what our Lord Jesus speaks within your soul. Thus says your Beloved: I am your health, I am your peace, I am your life. Keep yourself in Me and you will find peace in Me."
- Through suffering we obtain the necessary spiritual freedom and purity of heart to be instructed, not only by the words of the ancient prophets, but directly by God.
- The effects of the love of God are to cause men do great things, to make burdens light, and to fill the soul with the desire for perfection. We ought to forsake self and follow Christ by bearing

His cross. All hope and trust are to be put in God alone.

- "It is sweet and pleasant to serve God, and to forsake the world."
- "Speak, Lord, for I, Your servant, am ready to hear You. I am Your servant: give me wisdom and understanding to know Your commandments. Bow my heart to follow Your holy teachings, that they may sink into my soul like dew into the grass."

Because of the ecclesiastical nature of the instructions contained in **Book IV,** it was not included in some early editions. This final primer focuses on the sacrament:

- A Catholic monk takes vows of poverty, chastity, and obedience, and thus accepts and promises a full forsaking of self. A priest should offer himself and all that he has to God, all the while gaining grace, subduing reason to faith, and praying for others.
- He who would receive the Sacrament, or Holy Communion, should prepare himself in all diligence, for in the sacrament he is made one with Christ. "This highest and most worthy Sacrament is the life of soul and body, the medicine of all spiritual sickness. By it all vices are cured, all passions are restrained, all temptations are overcome and diminished; by it grace is sent, virtue is increased, faith is made firm, hope is strengthened, charity is kindled and spread abroad."
- He who would administer the Holy Communion is instructed: "You are now made a priest and are consecrated to celebrate Mass. Take heed, therefore, to offer your sacrifice to God in due time faithfully and devoutly and to keep yourself without reproof. You have not made your burden more light, but you are now bound by a stricter bond of discipline and of higher perfection than you were before."

The language of the book is beautiful and resonates with Kempis' own deep convictions. Though the book's intentions are purely ecumenical, it's doctrines are purely Catholic. Kempis' focus on suffering, and the benefits that can be derived therefrom may be disturbing to both Catholics and non-Catholics. The God presented here also may seem to be a vague, distant, mysterious Personage, unapproachable by the finite human mind. In spite of this, the book should still be perceived for what it is: a series of meditations designed to enlighten the mind, edify the soul, and deepen spiritual awareness.

THE NINETY-FIVE THESES

by
Martin Luther
(1483 - 1546)

Martin Luther, the leader of the Protestant Reformation, was born at Eisleben, Prussian Saxony, in 1483. Raised during the height of the intellectual renaissance, he studied were the works of authors such as Augustine, Aquinas, Peter the Lombard, Aristotle, and Plato. Exposed to logical, philosophical, scientific reasoning at an early age, young Martin grew up with a great interest in theology, law, classic literature and languages.

After earning a bachelor of arts degree in 1502 from the prestigious University of Erfurt, and a master of arts degree three years later, he first studied law. But when a bolt of lightning struck him to the ground during a thunderstorm—reminiscent of St. Paul's vision on the road to Emmaus—Luther cried out to a local patron saint, "Saint Anne, help! I will become a monk!" Spared, he immediately gave up his legal studies to join an Augustinian monastery in Erfurt.

Luther's superior mental abilities enabled him to master Greek and Hebrew, and he committed most of the New Testament to memory. After being ordained a priest in 1507 and receiving his doctorate in 1512, his career as a university professor of philosophy at Wittenberg and Erfurt thrived.

A central concern of Luther's stemmed from the questions of God's grace and individual worthiness. The theological paradox of individual—as well as social—depravity obsessed Luther throughout his life. If man's natural condition is sinful, he reasoned, then each person must obtain forgiveness of sins from God through repentance. In Catholicism, confession—reciting one's sins to a priest—constituted the avenue by which each individual sought God's grace. Luther did not deem confession a suitable form of repentance, especially when it came in the form of *indulgences*—a pardon or exoneration from punishment necessary to absolve a sin.

Luther initially saw God as a wrathful God who might not grant grace as readily as many Christians supposed. Luther altered this opinion sometime between 1513 and 1519, in what is commonly known as the "tower experience." While the details of the "revelation" Luther received in the Augustian tower vary, most scholars agree that it was at this time that he came to believe that God is righteous, and therefore just. This position is the most fundamental in his mature theological thought. The other positions—that God's righteous grace can transform men's lives and that grace alone can be decisive in man's salvation—completed the foundation for what would become the Reformation.

The starting point of Luther's crusade as a reformer came with his posting the *Ninety-five Theses* on the church door at Wittenberg on October 31, 1517. Together, these constituted a passionate statement of what he considered the true nature of repentance as well as a protest against the selling of indulgences (the Church granting forgiveness in exchange for money). Luther deemed his act of civil and religious disobedience an acceptable means for seeking public discussion of these pertinent issues. In posting the *Theses*, Luther, perhaps naively, expected the support of his ecclesiastical superiors. He did not get it. After three years of controversy, during which time he refused to obey a summons to Rome, Luther published the three great documents that laid down the fundamental principles of the Reformation. In the "Address to the Christian Nobility of the German Nation," Luther attacked the "corruptions" of the Church and the abuses of its authority, and asserted the right of the layman to spiritual independence. In "Concerning Christian Liberty," he expounded the doctrine of justification by faith, and gave a complete presentation of his theological position. And in the "Babylonish Captivity of the Church," he criticized the sacramental system and recognized the Scriptures as the supreme authority in religion. In the midst of this activity came his formal excommunication and his renunciation of allegiance to the Pope.

In 1525, Luther, the former monk, married Katharine von Bora (1499-1552), a former nun. "I would not give up my beloved Katie for France and Venice," Luther declared, " . . . because God gave her to me and me to her . . . " They had several children, two of whom died in infancy. As he held one dying daughter in his arms, he sought to comfort her—and himself: "Dear daughter, you have another Father in heaven. You are going to go to Him."

After being banned by Holy Roman Emperor Charles V and imprisoned in the Castle Wartburg for his own protection, Luther commenced translating the New Testament from Latin to German. His complete translation of the Bible, issued in 1534, marked the establishment of the modern German literary awakening. The remainder of Luther's life was occupied with a vast amount of controversial intellectual activity. He died in Eisleben in 1546.

What started out as a mild and peaceful challenge to the selling of indulgences, inaugurated one of the greatest religious movements in history. Luther's *Ninety-five Theses* indirectly gave rise to Protestantism. In the nailing of the document to the door of the Wittenberg church, the dominance of the Catholic Church was for the first time contested with great force.

Text Overview:

Only about eight pages long, the *Theses'* major purpose was to stir debate. "Out of love and zeal for truth and the desire to bring it to light," it began, "the following theses will be publicly discussed at Wittenberg under the chairmanship of the Reverent Father Martin Luther, Master of Arts and Sacred Theology and regularly appointed Lecturer on these subjects at that place. He requests that those who cannot be present to debate orally with us will do so by letter."

As it turned out, no formal debate was ever held—not one person responded to the invitation. The contents of the *Theses*, however, was soon widely distributed by word of mouth and by its printers. In effect, a vigorous debate did ensue, lasting for a number of years.

The first theses deal with Luther's main premise: the act of repentance has been corrupted.

1. *When our Lord and Master Jesus Christ said, "Repent" (Matt. 4:17), he willed the entire life of believers to be one of repentance.*

2. *This word cannot be understood as referring to the sacrament of penance, that is, confession and satisfaction, as administered by the clergy.*

3. *Yet it does not mean solely inner repentance; such inner repentance is worthless unless it produces various outward mortifications of the flesh.*

The next several postulates condemn the use of canons (decrees of the Church which have the force of law) on the dead and dying. The Church had been occasionally imposing further penalties on those already thought to be in purgatory:

8. *The penitential canons are imposed only on the living, and, according to the canons themselves, nothing should be imposed on the dying.*

10. *Those priests act ignorantly and wickedly who, in the case of the dying, reserve canonical penalties for purgatory.*

Luther then proceeds to explain that the dying have no need for canonical absolution, and thus the Church should not profit from selling indulgences to either the dying or their living relatives:

13. *The dying are freed by death from all penalties, are already dead as far as the canon laws are concerned, and have a right to be released from them.*

20. *Therefore, the pope, when he uses the words "plenary remission of all penalties," does not actually mean "all penalties," but only those imposed by himself.*

21. *Thus those indulgent preachers are in error who say that a man is absolved from every penalty and saved by papal indulgences.*

In other words, people are no longer subject to papal decrees after they die, neither can the pope absolve a dead person's sins against Scripture. Up to that time, believers had been paying money to have their ancestors transported from Purgatory to Heaven. In the *Theses*, Luther declares that the pope cannot grant salvation to such souls:

27. *They preach only human doctrines who say that as soon as the money clinks in the money chest, the soul flies out of purgatory.*

28. *It is certain that when money clinks in the money chest, greed and avarice can be increased; but when the church intercedes, the result is in the hand of God alone.*

29. *Who knows whether all souls in purgatory wish to be redeemed, since we have exceptions in Saint Severinus and Saint Paschal, as related in a leg-*

end . . . (The legend, in effect, states that these two men wished to remain longer in purgatory so that they might have greater glory in heaven.)

The selling of indulgence letters (a certificate written by a papal agent granting the remittance of all or most of one's own or another's sins) is another action Luther finds objectionable:

32. *Those who believe that they can be certain of their salvation because they have indulgence letters will be eternally damned, together with their teachers.*

35. *They who teach that contrition is not necessary on the part of those who intend to buy souls out of purgatory, or to buy confessional privileges, preach unchristian doctrine.*

36. *Any truly repentant Christian has the right to full remission of penalty and guilt, even without indulgence letters.*

37. *Any true Christian, whether living or dead, participates in all the blessings of Christ and the church; and this is granted him by God, even without indulgence letters.*

At this point, Luther extols the performing of charitable acts over the purchasing of indulgences:

43. *Christians are taught that he who gives to the poor or lends to the needy does a better deed than he who buys indulgences.*

45. *Christians are to be taught that he who sees a needy man and passes him by, yet gives his money for indulgences, does not buy papal indulgences, but the wrath of God.*

46. *Christians are to be taught that, unless they have more than they need, they must reserve enough for their family needs and by no means squander it on indulgences.*

Finally, Luther preaches that true religion, godliness, and worship are preferred over all other teachings:

54. *Injury is done the Word of God when, in the same sermon, an equal or larger amount of time is devoted to indulgences than to the Word.*

62. *The true treasure of the church is the most holy gospel of the glory and grace of God . . .*

Luther ends his *Theses* by stating that Christ is the only source of salvation, and that all men should cast their hope upon Him. Lastly, there follows this "Protestation":

I, Martin Luther, Doctor, of the Order of Monks at Wittenberg, desire to testify publicly that certain propositions against pontifical indulgences, as they call them, have been put forth by me. . . . Yet there are, as I hear, some men of headlong and audacious spirit, who dare to pronounce me a heretic, as though the matter had been thoroughly looked into and studied.

. . . I implore all men, by the faith of Christ, either to point out to me a better way . . . or at least to submit their opinion to the judgment of God and of the Church. For I am neither so rash as to wish that my sole opinion should be preferred to that of all other men, nor so senseless as to be willing that the word of God should be made to give place to fables, devised by human reason.

INSTITUTES OF THE CHRISTIAN RELIGION

by
John Calvin
(1509 - 1564)

The doctrinal theology of John Calvin, one of the most notable Protestant reformers, transformed theology in his own day and continues to exert great influence, specifically in the modern Reformed and Presbyterian churches. Calvinists are noted for their fundamental Christian beliefs, specifically acknowledging absolute sovereignty of God in the lives of men and supremacy of the Bible.

Calvin was born in France in 1509. The theological, ecclesiastical, and political ideas he developed, the model church that he created and directed in the city of Geneva, and his interaction with political and intellectual leaders of diverse nations was a catalyst in the growth of Protestantism in Europe and North America. His *Institutes of the Christian Religion*, published in 1536, comprises a comprehensive and systematic manual of Protestant dogmatic theology and the most complete presentation of Calvin's principles.

Text Overview:

According to Calvin, *Institutes of the Christian Religion* is intended to be used as a religious handbook, a beacon to shed light on the Holy Scriptures. Further, *Institutes* is written

. . . to guide and instruct theological candidates in the reading of the Word of God, so that they may without hindrance proceed upon the right lines. I have therefore thought fit to summarize the whole body of religious doctrine and to reduce it to such order that whoever rightly studies it will not find it difficult to decide what he must especially seek in Scripture, and to what end he must judge of its contents.

. . . The pious reader will be spared trouble and annoyance if only he proceeds to read Scripture with a knowledge of this book as a necessary part of his equipment.

Since "no one can understand the smallest part of true and saving doctrine unless he be a student of Holy Scripture," Calvin teaches that studying the word of God is of utmost importance. Hence, "we must go to the Word, in which God is clearly and vividly mirrored for us in His Works, and where the works of God are appraised not by our perverse judgments but by the criterion of eternal truth."

Because we are men "who are born in darkness," the Word of God is not always immediately understood. We thus remain in our fallen condition, "ever more and more . . . hardened in blindness." Calvin, offering what he considered a true interpretation of the Holy Scriptures, presents his text as a pathway leading away from darkness.

Students must begin their study of the Bible with the understanding that God speaks to His children through His Word:

. . . Holy Scripture is for us a dead and ineffectual thing until we have come to realize that God speaks to us and manifests His will to us therein. That is what we should understand when Paul assures us that Holy Scripture is divinely inspired.

Truly, Calvin writes, the Bible is a prophetic, divinely inspired text, which is animated, or brought to life, by Christ. As soon as the text of the Bible is separated from Christ, however, it becomes a mere body of dead letters, a text without soul. In fact, Christ was the source of inspiration for all of the biblical prophets:

As truly as Christ tells us that no one has seen the Father save the Son and he to whomsoever the Son willeth to reveal Him, so certainly all those who have wished to come to the knowledge of God have always had to be guided by the same eternal wisdom. For how could they have understood or spoken of the secrets of God by their unaided reason unless they had been taught by Him to whom alone the mysteries of the Father are disclosed? Hence the holy men of long ago did not know God otherwise than by viewing Him in His Son as in a mirror. When I say that, I mean that God has never revealed Himself to men otherwise than through the Son; that is through the unique wisdom, light, and truth of the Son. From that wellspring Adam, Noah, Abraham, Isaac and Jacob and others have drawn all that they knew of divine things. And from it too all the prophets have derived whatever divine prophecies they have left behind them in their writings.

In order to fully recognize God and his divinity, individuals must first vigorously accept and live the teachings of the Bible; "God alone is an adequate witness to Himself and cannot be recognized except through his own testimony." This means that we may not find God "elsewhere than in His holy word, nor think of Him except in the terms which His word illuminates for us, nor speak of him except in so far as our words are taken from his word."

As Creator of the World, Calvin writes, God is not merely an animating force; rather, He cares for every living thing and guides everything toward its foreordained goal. In this manner, God is generous in His "Divine Providence." Yet, as a divine, perfect being, He also stands in wrathful, righteous judgement of men when they sin:

Marvelous are the judgements of God who punishes the godless, schools believers to patience, and mortifies their fleshly desires, purges through suffering the vices of the world, startles many people out of their indolence, destroys the pride of the impious, laughs to scorn the cunning of the prudent and brings to nought evil counsels. And on the other hand His incomparable mercy is evident when He helps the wretched, protects and assures the life of the innocent, and brings help when all appears to be lost . . . The life and death of men utterly depends upon the sole guiding providence of heaven.

Calvin's reference to the "sole guiding providence of heaven" brings out one of the fundamental tenets of Calvinism, that of *predestination*. Calvin holds that God, before the beginning of time, "predetermined" the course of history and those of His children who will be saved. These are the chosen and the "elect" of God. However, he strongly asserts, speculation about this "election" must be avoided since it is beyond our comprehension. This doctrine, far from being pessimistic or fatalistic, in Calvin's way of thinking merely assures us that our fate rests with God and that our "highest blessedness" can be found in recognizing and trusting in "God's providential designs." In return, God demands only that we strive to live a Christian life and "give the more diligence to make [one's] calling and election sure."

And if we are made pure, Calvin continues, this purity may indicate that indeed we are God's elect and have been chosen to dwell with Him:

Because God calls us and chooses us to the end that we should be pure and unspotted before His countenance, purity of life is not wrongly regarded as a sign of election and a proof whereby believers are not only made manifest to others as the children of God, but also are themselves confirmed in this faith, though they know that its sure foundation lies elsewhere.

Calvin disagrees with Augustine's assertion that man's primal sin is pride. Mankind's sin is, instead, *inattention to the word of God*. As a result of neglecting the scriptures, man becomes disobedient and full of disbelief. This unbelief brings about an alienation from God, and this rift between God and man leaves man "saturated in sin . . . a damned and corrupt race":

The Holy Spirit assures us in Holy Scripture that our understanding is so smitten with blindness, our heart in its motions so evil and corrupt, in fact our whole nature so depraved, that we can do nothing else but sin until He Himself creates in us a new will.

Fortunately for us, Calvin says, God can and does create "in us a new will," bidding His chosen children to become new creatures:

God desires that each one of us should be consecrated to Him, that we should renounce self-will, that we should be subject to Him and surrendered to His guidance; but before He requires that of us He bestows Himself upon us.

This point is of fundamental importance: since God, by His own voice, has invited us to walk in His way, it signifies that we have the possibility of salvation.

Because God bestows upon mankind this possibility of salvation, we are indebted to Him:

. . . All would have been hopelessly lost if the divine Majesty had not condescended to come down to us, seeing that we are not in a position to reach upwards to it.

This salvation takes place through God's mediator: Jesus Christ. Jesus Christ is the embodiment of God, "God revealed in the flesh." We are saved by faith, says Calvin, and this faith is manifest in the acceptance of God's freely given grace in the form of Christ. And when we accept Christ, He in turn will "receive" us as God's elect.

According to Calvin, in order to be received by Christ we must live the life of a Christian. This means that we should embrace the three basic tenets of Christianity:

1. *Imitation of Christ*. Our daily life should be molded by the idea that "We belong not to ourselves but to the Lord." Specifically, this means demonstrating a spirited discipleship of Christ and obedience to the subsequent two principles.

2. *Self-denial*. "Man becomes happy through self-denial . . . We are to renounce our own point of view, turn away from all covetous desires of the flesh, become as nothing that God may live in us and control us." We must, in effect, die to the world and "come even to despise the most precious thing in the world."

3. *Bearing the cross*. Bearing our own cross means to carry personal our trials and difficulties with cheerful acceptance, since "only those who gladly shoulder the burden can be said to carry it." The Christian man is always determined to sacrifice in the name of the Lord.

To be a true Christian, Calvin continues, we must also pour out our heart in the presence of God—that is, we must *pray*. When we pray, we release our thoughts and desires to God:

[Prayer is] a kind of conversation between men and God, by which they gain entrance into the heavenly sanctuary and personally address Him on the strength of His promises . . . with the result that in their distress they see that they have not vainly believed His word alone.

Being allied with the "true church" is an important goal of one seeking after Christ. The Roman Church, Calvin submits, is not the church of Christ "who makes His own flock recognizable by other tokens when he says: `My sheep hear my voice.'" The true church, however, rather than being a specific institution, only exists where the pure Word is preached. This was not the case with the Roman Church which, Calvin maintains, "completely lapsed from the adoration of God and the preaching of the Word."

God has, however, instituted an order of preaching to which He has given the gospel, Calvin finally suggests. And, "above all He has instituted the sacraments, of which we know in fact that they are efficacious means of grace—means of maintaining and consolidating our faith . . . It is certain that a church cannot be regarded as well ordered and governed if the holy meal instituted by our Lord is not often celebrated and well attended."

Thus, Calvin's view of true worship before Christ is characterized by Eucharistic fellowship, a sincere and abiding veneration of God and Christ, and a singular reliance on the Bible for obtaining God's word.

THE BOOK OF MORMON

Another Testament of Christ
as recorded by Joseph Smith, Jr.

Together with the Bible, *The Book of Mormon* is considered both an ancient historical record and sacred scripture by members of the Church of Jesus Christ of Latter-day Saints ("Mormons"). Mormons believe the account was originally engraved on thin plates of metal and written in an altered Hebraic dialect called "Reformed Egyptian." In that *The Book of Mormon* records its *own* history—that is, the writers write about *themselves* on a set of plates that are not now available to be examined—the authenticity of its claims cannot be corroborated.

The Book of Mormon professes to relate the spiritual and secular life of pre-Columbian American civilizations from approximately 2200 B.C. to A.D. 421. The 531-page volume is divided into fifteen sections called "books," nearly all of which bear the name of the author to which they have been attributed. *The Book of Mormon* is believed to be a compilation of various written histories condensed into a single text by one of the volume's last prophet-historians, Mormon. Not until the early nineteenth century was this record said to have been recovered in upstate New York, and translated "by the gift of God" by young Joseph Smith—a "modern-day prophet" who founded the Mormon religion. Translated today into many languages, the book's express purpose is to convince "the Jew and Gentile that Jesus is the CHRIST, the ETERNAL GOD, manifesting himself unto all nations . . ."

Text Overview:

Designated as "prophets," the ascribed contributors to *The Book of Mormon* varied in age and occupation; the common thread that connected them was religious devotion and their desire to record for future generations the religious history of their time.

For example, *The Book of Mormon* tells of Nephi, a righteous son of a Jewish prophet named Lehi. Lehi foretold the coming of the Messiah (the awaited, savior, deliverer and King of the Jews) and implored the people of Jerusalem to keep God's commandments (the biblical Ten Commandments and other Old Testament ordinances). However, the people refused to repent, and tried to kill Lehi. Warned in a vision that Jerusalem would soon be destroyed, Lehi led his own and several other families safely away from the city to prepare to journey to a "promised land" of which God had spoken. After leaving the city, Lehi's sons returned to Jerusalem to retrieve a religious record engraved on thin sheets of brass, Nephi was commanded to construct a ship to sail across the waters. The families met with great hardships, but, "led by the hand of God," eventually reached what is now the American continent.

There, the text states, Nephi crafted sheets made of gold and began recording the prophecies and instructions of his father—thereby commencing the first "book" (the First Book of Nephi) of *The Book of Mormon*—which were then "handed down from one generation to another."

In the book, Nephi affirms that all scripture testifies to Christ's divinity:

I do not write anything upon plates save it be that I think it be sacred . . . And I, Nephi, have written these things unto my people, that perhaps they might know concerning the doings of the Lord in other lands [and] that I might more fully persuade them to believe in the Lord their Redeemer I did read unto them that which was written by the prophet Isaiah; for I did liken all scriptures unto us, that it might be for our profit and learning.

Throughout his writings, Nephi supports the witness of the Old Testament prophets, records the words and teachings of Lehi, his father, and gives his own prophesies of the scattering and gathering of Israel, and the eventual coming of the Messiah.

Nephi exemplifies the driving force of faith so typical in the text's cryptic authors:

. . . I, Nephi, said unto my father; I will go and do the things which the Lord hath commanded, for I know that the Lord giveth no commandment unto the children of men, save he shall prepare a way for them that they may accomplish the things which he commandeth them.

The Book of Mormon explains that after their arrival in the New World, a rift developed between Lehi's sons: some followed the faithful Nephi, taking upon themselves the name "Nephites"; two of the sons rejected the faith of their father and called themselves "Lamanites," after the eldest brother, Laman. The text tells of many battles fought between these factions, and relates how over the centuries both the Nephite and Lamanite nations fluctuated between wickedness and righteousness.

The record gives mention of other individuals who prophesy of the coming of Christ. For example, in the land of Zarahemla, one King Benjamin, before his death, sought to deliver a final message to his people. A tower was constructed for him to speak from and the people gathered in tents to hear Benjamin's words. He first explained the conditions of Christ's redemption and defined mankind's dependency upon God. Moreover, the King entreated his people to be humble, charitable and kind, faithful, wise, prayerful and penitent:

. . . And behold, I tell you these things that ye may learn wisdom; that ye may learn that when ye are in the service of your fellow beings ye are only in the service of your God. And behold, ye have called me your king; and if I, whom ye call your king, do labor to serve you, then ought not ye to labor to serve one another?

Some one hundred years later, *The Book of Mormon* says, in another part of the land, a valiant prophet named Abinadi called the corrupt and sinful King Noah to repentance.

Fettered in chains, Abinadi was brought to the king's court, accused of treason, and burned to death. The executioner's hand was stayed, however, until Abinadi imparted to the court of priests his message of salvation through Christ.

Among the priests in Noah's court, the narrative continues, was a man named Alma who, upon hearing Abinadi, was converted. Alma managed to escape from the royal servants, repented of his sins, then went about teaching the words of Abinadi. Alma invited those who heard and believed in his words:

Behold, here are the waters of Mormon (for thus they were called) and now, as ye are desirous to come into the fold of God, and to be called his people, and are willing to bear one another's burdens, that they may be light; yea, and are willing to mourn with those that mourn; yea, and comfort those that stand in need of comfort, and to stand as witnesses of God at all times and in all things, and in all places that ye may be in, even until death, that ye may be redeemed of God, and be numbered with those of the first resurrection, that ye may have eternal life—Now I say unto you, if this be the desire of your hearts, what have you against being baptized in the name of the Lord, as a witness before him that ye have entered into a covenant with him, that ye will serve him and keep his commandments, that he may pour out his Spirit more abundantly upon you?

The Book of Mormon continues, reciting the words of prophets as well as the many trials and experiences of the followers of the church, both Nephite and Lamanite: Alma's son, a rebellious youth, is struck down and called to God's service by an angel; Alma "the Younger" and his colleagues become great missionaries, preaching God's word to many cities; wars continually flare up, with the righteous often spared by the hand of God; the righteous "saints" rise up in defense of their families and their freedom against a secret band of murderers who had taken a secret oath to destroy the church; a Lamanite prophet, Samuel, is protected from harm as he foretells of the imminent coming of Christ.

Nested at the heart of the text is a narrative about the resurrected Jesus appearing to the ancient American inhabitants. The prophet Nephi, a descendent of the earlier Nephi, is said to have written that Jesus descended from heaven, stood before the multitudes, and invited them to feel the wounds in his hands and feet:

And it came to pass that the multitude went forth, and thrust their hands into his side, and did feel the prints of the nails in his hands and in his feet; and this they did do, going forth one by one until they had all gone forth, and did see with their eyes and did feel with their hands, and did know of a surety and did bear record, that it was he, of whom it was written by the prophets, that should come. And when they had all gone forth and had witnessed for themselves, they did cry out with one accord, saying: Hosanna! Blessed be the name of the Most High God! And they did fall down at the feet of Jesus, and did worship him.

During Jesus' stay in the Americas, he appointed twelve disciples, bestowed upon them power and authority to baptize and manage the Church, established the ordinance of the sacrament—the partaking of bread and wine done in remembrance of his eternal sacrifice—and taught his gospel, as he had done in Israel:

. . . Watch and pray always lest ye enter into temptation; for Satan desireth to have you . . . Pray in your families unto the Father, always in my name, that your wives and your children may be blessed. . . . Ask and ye shall receive; knock, and it shall be opened unto you . . . And whoso believeth in me, and is baptized, the same shall be saved . . .

The Book of Mormon goes on to explain that the impact of Jesus' teachings resulted in the radical conversion of all Nephites and Lamanites. For a space of 200 years the people flourished in righteousness and peace. Gradually, however, pride and envy again prevailed.

Mormon, one of the last prophets said to have written, warned future readers that when these accounts were published to the world, it would be in fulfillment of prophecy: " . . . And when ye shall see these sayings coming forth among you . . . woe unto him that shall deny the revelations of the Lord, and that say the Lord no longer worketh by revelation, or by prophecy [or] that there can be no miracles wrought by Jesus Christ . . . "

As the complete annihilation of an increasingly wicked Nephite nation became apparent, the account reports that Mormon turned over the plates to his son Moroni, who finished the record:

. . . I am alone. My father hath been slain in battle, and all my kinsfolk, and I have not friends nor whither to go; and how long the Lord will suffer that I may live I know not. Behold, four hundred years have passed away since the coming of our Lord and Savior. And behold, the Lamanites have hunted my people, the Nephites, down from city to city, and from place to place, even until they are no more; and great has been their fall . . . "

In isolation, Moroni compiled histories of several other American civilizations, offered brief discourses, and proclaimed his belief in Christ. Then, before burying the plates, he predicted that they would eventually be taken from the ground and translated, to serve, along with the Bible, as a second witness of Christ.

The Book of Mormon's principal message, along with the plea to keep God's commandments, is that, through prayer, truth can be made known. In his conclusion, the solitary Moroni writes:

. . . And when ye shall receive these things, I would exhort you that ye would ask God, the Eternal Father, in the name of Christ, if these things are not true; and if ye shall ask with a sincere heart, with real intent, having faith in Christ, he will manifest the truth of it unto you, by the power of the Holy Ghost. And by the power of the Holy Ghost ye may know the truth of all things . . .

Yea, come unto Christ, and be perfected in him, and deny yourselves of all ungodliness . . . Then is His grace sufficient for you . . . Then are ye sanctified in Christ . . .

SYSTEMATIC THEOLOGY

by Paul Tillich

(1886 - 1965)

Paul Tillich was one of the most important theologians in all of Protestant history. Born in 1886 in Starzeddel, Germany, the son of a pastor and later superintendent of the Lutheran church, he attended several universities and received the degree of Doctor of Philosophy from the University of Breslau. He served as an army chaplain during the First World War and then began a teaching career.

In 1929 Tillich became professor of Philosophy at the University of Frankfurt, at which time he became involved in the Religious-Socialist movement. This preoccupation, along with his open antagonism toward National Socialism and Hitler's rise to power in 1933, led to his dismissal from his university chair and his forced exile from Germany.

Tillich moved to the United States and began teaching. At the age of 47 he learned and mastered English to such an extent that he could write and speak it creatively in the highly abstract idioms of philosophy and theology. He was openly received in the American academic community, and during his career he held prestigious positions at Harvard and the University of Chicago.

From the beginning Tillich was an activist in politics, social work, art, and culture in general. His theological work focused heavily on the sheltering of Christianity from the problems of culture. His fundamental beliefs were not based upon any special revelation in Christianity, but upon Christian faith as the clue to the eternal relation of God and man.

In the field of theology, Tillich is placed among the "liberal" tradition in that his theories do not attempt to advance traditional dogma. The direction of his theology is pragmatic to the extreme, calling both for cold analysis and an understanding of Christianity in terms of how it serves to promote an experience of God. Tillich's three-volume *Systematic Theology* best represents his comprehensive ideas, or theology, concerning how man can better come to know and experience God.

Text Overview:

Man was created to be guided by an "ultimate concern." This concern may be for "God," or for some finite object, being, idea, or goal, all of which have been created by God. In fact, every epoch, generation, people and nation is formed on the basis of its ultimate concern for and ultimate loyalty to some common object of love or devotion. For example, the ultimate concern guiding the American Revolution—the idea that galvanized and united the colonists—was, ideally, freedom and self-rule. This ultimate concern, being the basis for any culture, permeates every aspect of what is produced by any culture. It gives that culture its unique "style," especially in the fields of literature and art.

The job of the theologian is to "read" or decipher this style and then to interpret or clarify what it means. By reaching the goal of correct interpretation, the theologian determines the "faith" of each cultural situation. Once this faith is defined, a true theology, an "answering theology," may be forged.

Every attempt to understand human existence, declares Tillich, must begin in an immediate intuition of something ultimate in "value" and "being," something that transcends the distinction between *subject* (man) and *object* (God). Theology's goal, then, is to correlate—or link—man and God. The link exists in the tension between divine revelation and the questions generated by man in his concrete shell of reality.

Here, announces Tillich, is where the distinction between "philosophy" and "theology" becomes relevant. Philosophy is "that cognitive approach to reality in which reality as such is the object [again, God]." Hence, philosophy is aimed at investigating the object of reality, the "general structures" which make experience possible. In a sense, philosophy's aim is directed outward towards an "external reality."

In contrast, theology is aimed at the "ultimate concern" of man. Tillich writes: "The object of theology is what concerns us ultimately. Only those propositions are theological which deal with their object in so far as it can become a matter of ultimate concern for us . . . Our ultimate concern is that which determines our being or not-being. Only those statements are theological which deal with their object in so far as it can become a matter of being or not-being for us." So, in short, theology can be thought of as being directed more inward, toward the individual. Feelings, as well as thoughts, are deemed significant.

Theology often raises the same questions as philosophy does, but rather than being philosophically detached, religious inquiry demands some sort of action or involvement. While philosophy is interested solely in the "structure of being," theology is concerned with the ultimate meaning of being for each individual person.

Although there is a difference between these two fields of investigation, Tillich admits, both philosopher and theologian must operate from an ultimate concern—because they belong to a culture, nation, etc. that is founded on an ultimate concern. The theologian, however, must also work within the structure of being—because he needs to have experiences in order to interpret them. These two never contradict each other, for "no philosophy which is obedient to the universal logos [governing principle] can contradict the concrete logos, the Logos 'who became flesh' [Jesus Christ]." Theologically (not merely "philosophically"), Jesus Christ is the center around which all other thought revolves and from which all thought stems.

From where does theology spring? In general, Tillich explains, there are three sources of theological education:

1. **Scripture:** "The Bible . . . is the basic source of systematic theology because it is the original document about the events on which the

Christian church is founded." The Bible, however, is not the only source, for it could not have been either written or received without preparation in human religion and culture. But certainly the Bible is the basic document, for it contains original witness to the events upon which Christianity is based. Furthermore, "since there is no revelation unless there is someone who receives it as revelation, the act of reception is part of the event itself. The Bible is both original event and original document; it witnesses to that of which it is part."

2. **Church Tradition:** Church tradition is a source of theology because of the formulation of the biblical canon (accepted texts) through church history. The theologian, however, is free to use and critically examine church tradition without being bound to it. The "Protestant principle" should be the theologian's guide; it protests "against the identification of our ultimate concern with any creation of the church, including biblical writings in so far as their witness to what is really ultimate concern is also a conditioned expression of their own spirituality." In other words, the ultimate concern guiding man should not be religious doctrine or the teachings of a particular church, but the *object* of the church: God.

3. **Historical Religion and Culture:** The broadest source of systematic theology is what we garner from the history of religion and culture. The use of this source is unavoidable for the theologian; the language he uses, the culture in which he is educated, and the social and political climate in which his thought is formed, all influence every theological concept he may have.

Truth is existential, that is, based on existence or dealing primarily with what truly exists and what does not. Unearthing truth is a matter of "participation" and discovering the range of spiritual realities. *Experience by participation is the only way to know the truth*, Tillich affirms. Thus, experience is important for a developing theology. Specifically, the *mystical* experience is of primary concern for the theologian.

Revelation takes place in the mystical realm. But, regardless of how it is given or received, revelation is understood in terms of the cultural situation of each participant. That is, revelatory *answers* are formulated in accordance with the form of the question *asked*.

The essence of revelation transcends the normal subject-object (man-God) distinction of our normal experience. *Reason*, says Tillich, is not destroyed by revelation, but merely transcended; there occurs a "reintegration of reason."

The experience of revelation often comes as a "shock of being" in which the ordinary, limited mind is transcended, and one experiences the nature of salvation. Again, Tillich emphasizes that revelation does not exterminate reason, rather, "Final revelation . . . liberates reason from the conflict between absolutism and relativism by appearing in the form of a concrete absolute."

The power which overcomes the inherent conflicts of reason is *love*. "Love is absolute because it concerns everything concrete . . . " writes Tillich. "Love is always love; that is its static and absolute side. But love is always dependent on that which is loved, and [that is its relative side.]"

"God is being-itself," he continues. "He is not a being, but rather being itself. Even if he is called `the highest being' . . . when applied to God, superlatives become diminutives." Those individuals and groups who are able to become "transparent" to the *being-itself* are bearers of revelation. These are the types of people who are commonly referred to as "saints." A saint is one who is "transparent" to the ground of being, and this transparency reveals the divine; others "see" in and through the saint some aspect of the divine. Thus, the saint becomes a symbol or representative of divinity.

Symbols (words, any religious artifact—a cross, for example—a living priest or a deceased saint . . .) when used to refer to God or when used in any religious fashion, need not be true; they must merely be existentially effective—that is, they must evoke the awareness of the power of being. For example, the word "God" cannot encapsulate the "ground of being" to which it refers; the word cannot do justice to the concept. Symbols have their roots in the collective unconscious of believers, and only have value as long as they are so rooted. The value in the word "God," then, is that, for one who understands the word correctly, it can correctly refer to the *experience* of "God"—it can serve to direct one to the "ground of being."

The uniqueness of Christian revelation is that Jesus is the "final" revelation, the perfect revelation receiver. He was aware of the need for uninterrupted unity with the ground of being (God), and constant connected himself to this ground.

The Christ is only Christ because of his constant consciousness of God and because he was at first "denied equality" with God. But through his sacrifice on the Cross, "the Jesus who is Jesus [became the] Jesus who is the Christ." The primary purpose of theology, its writings and its symbols, is to elucidate the meaning and being of Christ in order to help man rise from his current state of existence into the "New Being" of Christ. As Tillich concludes:

The [current] state of existence is the state of estrangement. Man is estranged from the ground of his being, from other beings, and from himself. The transition from essence to existence [the Fall] results in personal guilt and universal tragedy.

Attempts to overcome estrangement within the power of one's estranged existence lead to hard toil and tragic failure . . . Only a New Being can produce a new action.

New Being [eventually conquers] the gap between essence and existence. For it is the Christ who brings the New Being, who saves men from the old being . . .

. . . In Jesus as the Christ, the eternal unity of God and man has become historical reality. In his being, the New Being is real, and the New Being is the re-established unity between God and man.

COMPACT

Classics®

Library #5: Western Philosophy...An Overview

Over two thousand years ago, Socrates said, "The unexamined life is not worth living." His Athenian disciples took him at his word, seeking to penetrate to the heart of truth by studying their world, the skies, and their own souls. When Plato, an ardent admirer of Socrates, took his stylus in hand to record and elaborate on the discourses and dialogues of his semi-literate master, Western civilization launched its quest.

That investigative journey has continued up until the present. On one hand, it has led us into fields of modern science—the various "whats" and "hows" of the world; on the other hand, it has compelled us to explore a less "solid" realm, the realm of *philosophy*—from the Greek "love of wisdom." Where science starts out with specific questions, philosophy searches beyond facts and theories to look for ultimate principles: the *big* "Hows," the *big* "Whats," and the *big* "Whys" of life and nature.

What is True? What is Good? What is Beautiful?... Can we even *begin* to answer these questions?

The quest continues with you. The following materials present an overview of current and historical philosophical adventures. These time-honored texts will introduce you to the methods, the problems, the language, the questions, and—hopefully—some of the answers that will help you reach your destination.

A BRIEF GUIDE TO PHILOSOPHY

The purpose of the following summaries is to expose readers to a sampling of the major philosophers of the Western World and to make the ideas of these master thinkers more accessible. Certainly there are many possible interpretations of their works—and many possible responses to them. It is not our purpose to evaluate either the content or the intentions of the works summarized here, but to leave readers with a more comprehensive understanding in order to form their own evaluations and judgments.

Condensing abstract philosophical concepts and interpreting them is a challenging enterprise. Complex ideas cannot always be reduced to simple statements, or even to a simple series of statements. Because the thinkers who develop these concepts are reaching under the surface of our common experience and understanding to search for unifying principles, their thoughts are often presented either in a sometimes highly technical jargon or in an innovative, figurative language that attempts to capture abstract ideas through imagery and metaphor.

The following material is offered as a brief historical guide to help you locate the writers whose work is summarized her as representatives of various philosophical movements in various periods of history.

❖ ◆ ❖

Classical Philosophy: In the Beginning

The seeds of Western philosophy were sown all across the scattered states of ancient Greece in Europe and Asia Minor. Many scholars were active in this early period, but none was so influential as Socrates, an Athenian living in the 4th century B.C. who wrote none of his philosophy down, but communicated his ideas by challenging his students in discourse. Plato is the most famous disciple of Socrates, and included Socrates as a character in many of his writings.

Aristotle, the heir to and rival of Platonic thought, was not a Greek himself, but a Macedonian. He traveled to Athens to study under Plato at the Academy, and later founded a school of his own, the Lyceum.

During the decline of the Greek empire and the rise of Rome, new ideas in philosophy emerged which emphasized patterns for living the best kind of life. Lucretius, a free-thinking **Epicurean** poet/philosopher, and the Roman Emperor Marcus Antonius, a more pious **Stoic,** contribute two divergent views of how humans should conduct their affairs in society and achieve piece of mind.

Early Modern Philosophy

One can say that "modern" philosophy began with Descartes in the mid-seventeenth century. It was during this period that philosophy made its decisive escape from medieval scholastic dependence on divine sanctions—on the resort to supernatural hope and authority for finding meaning, happiness and knowledge in this life. When Descartes said, "I think, therefore I am," he was re-inaugurating—and refining—the old Socratic ideal of doubting everything—of stripping the known world right down to the core of our most fundamental human experience (our self-awareness) and then reassembling it with our own human hands and minds. Issues raised during the modern period have occupied the minds of philosophers ever since; only since the mid-twentieth century has there been any significant change in approach and method.

Most metaphysical (basis-of-reality) systems in modern philosophy confront in one way or another two central issues: can one *prove* beyond a doubt that one has knowledge of the external world, and what is the nature of that knowledge? Different schools of philosophy emerged in response to this challenge. Descartes and Spinoza represent the **Rationalist** school, the view that *reasoning alone will lead to absolute* *knowledge.* **Empiricists,** on the other hand, (represented by Locke and Berkeley) believed that *knowledge is gained only through experience.* Immanuel Kant, a giant of the modern era, provided a synthesis of these two schools, taking into account the arguments of both. Kant was followed by Schopenhauer, who vehemently struck out against the prominent philosophy propounded by Hegel: **Idealism,** the view that *the external world is generated by the mind,* and is therefore not "real" in the absolute sense.

Due to the changing political and social climate throughout Europe—and, later, the Americas—the modern period has also been a fruitful time for the development of **political** and **economic** philosophy. Hobbes, Rousseau, Hayek, Mill, and Thoreau each present a different perspective on *the social nature of human beings, and on the rights we should—or should not—enjoy.* They are followed by other **social/economic** theorists, Adam Smith, Marx/Engels, and John Maynard Keynes.

Lastly, the nineteenth century saw the emergence of **Existentialism,** more of an approach to philosophic thinking than a distinctive school of thought. Soren Kierkegaard is traditionally seen as the founder of existentialism, a trend which emphasizes *issues of "being,"* and deliberates on the *questions of existence, death, choice, God and faith*—questions which also appeared in existentialist literature by Dostoevski and Tolstoy. Here, we also use Nietzsche to provide a view of existentialism somewhat different from that of Kierkegaard's.

Contemporary Thought

In the late nineteenth and early twentieth centuries, philosophy branched out in several new directions. **Pragmatism** (represented by Rorty and James) is an approach which *seeks out the most useful or explanatory theories* (what is true is essentially *works*), as opposed to theories held together by elegant rational systems of analytic proof.

The birth of **Logical Positivism** (or Symbolic Logic), vastly improved over the Aristotelian logical system, is attributed in large part to the British philosopher Bertrand Russell. This school introduced a new framework of discussion: positivism asserts that only issues which deal with our direct experience of the world have any real validity, and that questions about God—or about any overarching "Meaning" or "Purpose" or "Truth"—have no real *truth value;* they are literally meaningless.

The writings of Auguste Comte and later positivists spurred the development of analytic branches of philosophy, which make use of logical formulae to examine the truth value of statements. Ludwig Wittgenstein contributed early in his career to this school under the tutelage of Russell, but later developed a new philosophy of language which was highly critical of the analytic view. This **Deconstruction/Language** approach—which emerged mainly out of literary criticism—focuses on language and the assumptions to which it leads. Led by the renowned contemporary French philosopher Jacques Derrida, deconstructionism seeks a more accurate assessment of meaning by taking the spoken or written "text" apart, and examining the interrelated components.

The twentieth century has seen the further development of **Existentialism,** most prominently in the work of Sartre and Heidegger. Sartre is particularly credited with developing a school of existentialist thought, which touches on ideas having to do with *the existence of God and the notion of freedom as an imperative rather than a right.* (In Sartrian thought, it is not so much that humans *should* "have" freedom; it is more an issue of *freedom* "having" *us*—and holding us tight by the throat.)

Finally, John Rawls' work (as well as R.M. Hare's *The Language of Morals,* not included here) represents the emerging field of contemporary **Ethics**—the study of *the general nature of morals and moral choice*—a fascinating and growing concern in this age of indecision and moral questioning.

THE SOCRATIC DIALOGUES OF PLATO

by Plato

(c. 427 - 347 B.C.)

Plato wrote in the *dialogue* literary form, expressing his ideas in the form of conversations. This dialogue format is very effective for presenting philosophical arguments and criticisms. His 35 separate "dramas of ideas," or *Socratic Dialogues*, often depict several different characters, Socrates himself (Plato's esteemed teacher and mentor) dominating the action as the central figure.

In one of Plato's earliest dialogues, *Charmides*, he sets forth that Socrates' aim— and thus his own—is not to convert his hearers to his own beliefs, but to arouse each to think for himself. And Plato's *Dialogues* offer much for readers to think about: his topics include friendship, piety, history, virtuosity, art, kindness, misery, and just about any other topic that touches on the human condition. Many times in the dialogues, Socrates, professing ignorance, questions those who claim to know something, and proves in the end that they do not know it after all. Due to the quality of his dialogues, many scholars consider Plato to be the finest prose writer the world has produced.

Plato's early *Dialogues* include *The Apology, Crito,* and *Phaedo,* conversations which, together, make up an account of the last days and the death of Socrates.

Apology (Socrates' Defense)

In his "Defense" (*Apology*), Socrates has been brought before an Athenian court and charged with heresy: "Socrates is guilty of criminal meddling, in that he inquires into things below the earth and in the sky, and teaches others to follow his example." Also accused of believing in deities of his "own invention instead of the gods recognized by the state," Socrates attempted to explain how this false notoriety originated.

Chaerephon, a boyhood friend of Socrates, once inquired of a priestess if there was anyone wiser than Socrates. The priestess replied that there was no one. "After puzzling about it for some time," Socrates said, "I set myself at last with considerable reluctance to check the truth of it in the following way. I went to interview a man with a high reputation for wisdom, because I felt that here if anywhere I should succeed in disproving the oracle . . . " Socrates found that this man . . . "appeared to be wise [but] in fact he was not." He concluded:

It seems that I am wiser than he is to this small extent, that I do not think that I know what I do not know.

Socrates went about interviewing one person after another, and came up with the same result:

. . . The people with the greatest reputations were almost entirely deficient, while others who were supposed to be their inferiors were much better qualified in practical intelligence

After consulting all the politicians, Socrates tested the poets:

I decided that it was not wisdom that enabled them to write their poetry, but a kind of instance or inspiration, such as you find in seers and prophets who deliver all their sublime messages without knowing in the least what they mean.

Socrates next turned to the skilled craftsmen, who "understood things which I did not, and to that extent they were wiser than I was. But . . . these professional experts seemed to share the same failing which I had noticed in the poets. . . . They claimed a perfect understanding of every other subject, however important, and I felt that this error more than outweighed their positive wisdom."

The truth of the matter is, Socrates finally declared,

. . . Real wisdom is the property of God, and this oracle is his way of telling us that human wisdom has little or no value . . . as if he would say to us, "the wisest of your men is he who has realized, like Socrates, that in respect of wisdom he is really worthless."

Socrates thus became quite unpopular as he went about disproving anyone claiming to be wise. Further, he was accused by a man named Meletus of teaching the reality of new deities instead of that of the Gods recognized by the state. "Tell me honestly, Meletus," Socrates replied, "is that your opinion of me? Do I believe in no god?" Meletus replied, "No, none at all, not in the slightest degree." Socrates, after some discussion, finally answered:

. . . It is my belief that no greater good has ever befallen you in this city (Athens) than my service to my God. For I spend all my time going about trying to persuade you, young and old, to make your first and chief concern not for your bodies nor for your possessions, but for the highest welfare of your souls, proclaiming as I go, "Wealth does not bring goodness, but goodness brings wealth and every other blessing, both to the individual and to the state."

Finally, having explained why he had been charged with these crimes, Socrates argued against his death:

You will not easily find another liked me, gentlemen, and if you take my advice you will spare my life . . . Having said so much, I feel moved to prophesy to you who have given your vote against me, for I am now at that point where the gift of prophesy comes most readily to men—at the point of death. I tell you, my executioners, that as soon as I am dead, vengeance shall fall upon you with a punishment far more painful than your killing of me . . . If you expect to stop denunciation of your wrong way of life by putting people to death, there is something amiss with your reasoning. This way of escape is neither possible nor creditable. The best and easiest way is not to stop the mouths of others, but to make yourselves as good men as you can. This is my last message to you who voted for my condemnation.

Of his imminent execution, Socrates observed:

Death is one of two things. Either it is annihilation, and the dead have no consciousness of anything, or, as we are told, it is really a change— a migration of the soul from this place to another. Now if there is no consciousness but only a dreamless sleep, death must be a marvelous gain . . . If on the other hand death is a removal from here to some other place, and if what we are told is true, that all the dead are there, what greater blessing could there be than this, gentlemen?

Finally, Socrates closed his defense:

Now it is time that we were going, I to die and you to live, but which of us has the happier prospect is unknown to anyone but God.

Crito

The next dialogue, *Crito*, contains the account of Socrates' friends as they beseech the condemned philosopher to escape from his prison. Socrates answered by asking if it can ever be right to *defend* oneself against evil by *doing* evil, referring to the fact that if Socrates were to escape, his jailers would have to be bribed. "Look here, Socrates," Crito piped up. " . . . Your death means a double calamity for me. I shall not only lose a friend whom I can never possibly replace, but besides a great many people . . . will be sure to think that I let you down, because I could have saved you if I had been willing to spend the money. Most people will never believe that it was you who refused to leave this place although we tried our hardest to persuade you . . . Take my advice, and be reasonable." To this, Socrates answered:

I cannot abandon the principles which I used to hold in the past simply because this accident has happened to me; [I] regard the same principles now as before. So unless we can find better principles on this occasion, you can be quite sure that I shall not agree with you—not even if the power of the people conjures up fresh hordes of bogies to terrify our childish minds, by subjecting us to chains and executions and confiscations of our property. . . . One must not even do wrong when one is wronged, which most people regard as the natural course.

Socrates' unmistakable concern was not for himself, but for Athens; if he escaped, he would wrong that state which he held in esteem:

Do you imagine that a city can continue to exist and not be turned upside down, if the legal judgments which are pronounced in it have no force but are nullified and destroyed by private persons? . . . Shall we say, "Yes, I do intend to destroy the laws, because the state wronged me by passing a faulty judgment at my trial"? Is this to be our answer, or what?

In the end, Socrates' commitment to his country made him willingly face death. "Then give it up, Crito," urged Socrates, "and let us follow this course, since God points out the way."

Phaedo

Phaedo was named for one of Socrates' faithful pupils who was at his side on his execution day. Socrates claimed to suffer no regrets, and looked forward to his death as an opportunity to greet the great ones who came before him and to receive his reward for living a good life:

. . . Sometimes and for some people death is better than life . . . I have a firm hope that there is something in store for those who have died, and, as we have been told for many years, something much better for the good than for the wicked.

Socrates went on to explain his position on the afterlife, depicting death as simply the release of the soul from the body, which is a hindrance to the acquisition of knowledge:

So long as we keep to the body and our soul is contaminated with this imperfection, there is no chance of our ever attaining satisfactorily to our object, which we assert to be truth. In the first place, the body provides us with innumerable distractions in the pursuit of our necessary sustenance . . . Wars and revolutions and battles are due simply and solely to the body and its desires. All wars are undertaken for the acquisition of wealth, and the reason why we have to acquire wealth is the body, because we are slaves in its service.

It followed, therefore, that true "knowledge . . . is only possible after death, because it is only then that the soul will be separate and independent of the body . . . "

. . . It is natural for me to leave you and my earthly rulers without any feeling of grief or bitterness, since I believe that I shall find there, no less than here, good rulers and good friends.

This final exchange then turned to the subject of immortality. Knowledge, Socrates taught, must come from a time before earthly existence; knowledge is a rememberance of a former time:

. . . We acquired our knowledge before our birth, and lost it at the moment of birth; but afterward, by the exercise of our senses upon sensible objects, recover the knowledge which we had once before . . . and surely we should be right in calling this recollection.

This being true, Socrates then asked:

When do our souls acquire this knowledge? It cannot be after the beginning of our mortal life . . . then it must be before. Then our souls had a previous existence, before they took on this human shape. They were independent of our bodies, and they were possessed of intelligence.

Because humans can perceive of beauty and love, which are eternal characteristics, Socrates taught, within each individual there must be a spark of immortality.

Socrates' final day in mortality drew to a close, and his friends passed him the cup containing the poisonous hemlock. Without hesitation, Socrates drank it. Soon thereafter, he died. "Such was the end of our comrade," laments Phaedo, "who was we may fairly say, of all those whom we knew in our time, the bravest and also the wisest and most upright man."

ETHICS

by
Aristotle
(384-322 BCE)

Aristotle's influence on philosophy cannot be compared to any other figure. The rigorous, investigative, systematic, logical approach he brought to philosophical questions (in contrast to Plato's more lyrical, imaginative, mythical style) has shaped philosophy up to the present day.

At age seventeen, Aristotle was sent by his physician father from Macedonia to Athens to study under Plato at the *Academy*. Later, he returned to the Macedonian court as a tutor for the thirteen-year-old Alexander the Great. A philosopher, natural historian, and theorist, Aristotle soon founded his own school, the Lyceum in Athens. The death of Alexander in 323, however, brought a significant change in the political climate, and Aristotle was forced into exile, dying a year later at the age of sixty-two.

Text Overview:

Aristotle's *Ethics* attempts to unearth what actions and characteristics contribute to the "good" of men, and are therefore virtuous. Aristotle differentiates between the good of virtue and happiness and that of other sensations such as pleasure; the happiness of virtue is an end in itself, as opposed to pleasure, which depends on some conditional, outward cause or stimulus.

However, virtue must be manifested in the way one lives. In other words, it is not enough for one to *know;* one must *act* in the light of knowledge.

It was Aristotle's belief that "highest virtue" is available to very few. Men born into noble families are able to pursue more refined and virtuous qualities, such as wisdom and honor (hence the word "Aristocratic" has been used down through the centuries to denote nobility). Men of lower birth (and all women), Aristotle teaches, because of their nature, are not fit to strive for virtue, this "highest" or "best" good. However all people, according to Aristotle, seek the highest good *available to them.* Therefore, a slave can be a good slave by being faithful, docile and obedient, thereby obtaining the highest level of virtue available to him. However, the happiness of the slave is not as exalted as that of the well-born man, since the slave's virtue is of a lesser grade than that of the refined man.

In Book I of *Ethics*, Aristotle establishes "good" as that which is good *for its own sake:*

If . . . there is some end of the things we do, which we desire for its own sake, and if we do not choose everything for the sake of something else, clearly this must be the good and the chief good.

Aristotle then asks what sort of goods are good in themselves, and concludes:

The account of the good will have to appear identical in them all, as that of whiteness is identical in snow and in white lead. But of honor, wisdom, and pleasure, just in respect of their goodness, the

accounts are distinct and diverse.

Therefore, the "good" of seemingly similar things is not identical. Good "is not some common element answering to one idea . . . Even if there is some one good which is universally predicable of goods . . . clearly it could not be achieved by man." The chief good, then, "is clearly something final. Therefore, if there is only one final end, this will be what we are seeking, and if there are more than one, the most final of these will be what we are seeking." It follows that "we call that which is in itself worthy of pursuit more final than that which is worthy of pursuit for the sake of something else."

According to Aristotle, since the good of something is its purpose, or end, everything has a different good. For man, happiness is the purpose of existence, the good in itself. Yet, even in *happiness*, there are many degrees of good:

. . . Both the general run of men and people of superior refinement say that [good] is happiness, and identify living well and doing well with being happy; but with regard to what happiness is, [men] differ, and the many do not give the same account as the wise . . . To judge from the lives that men lead, most men, and men of the most vulgar type, seem to identify the good, or happiness, with pleasure; which is the reason why they love the life of enjoyment.

Aristotle vehemently argues against the popular view that happiness is locked up in "pleasure, honor and wealth." Unlike pleasure, true happiness is chosen "always for itself and never for the sake of something else." Happiness, then, is "something final and self-sufficient, and is the end of action."

Still, how one defines or identifies happiness varies from individual to individual, for "some identify happiness with virtue, some with practical wisdom, others with philosophical wisdom, accompanied or not with pleasure, or external property." Aristotle himself defines happiness as "a sort of good life and good action" which involves these activities, which he calls "best activities." In a few words, happiness is recognized as each individual's "best, noblest, and most pleasant thing in the world."

Aristotle maintains that happiness, being a "good," is "God-given": "[Happiness] comes as a result of virtue and some processes of virtue and training." By giving himself over to instruction (the "grace of God"), the virtuous man "will be happy throughout his life . . . for always he will be engaged in virtuous action and contemplation":

No happy man can become miserable; for he will never do the acts that are hateful and mean. . . . The man who is truly good and wise . . . bears all the changes of life becomingly and always makes the best of circumstances.

In book II Aristotle argues that "most people . . . incline towards [pleasure] and are slaves of their pleasures." For Aristotle, pleasure, while not necessarily a vice, was more of a "false good," because it must always be accompanied by activity:

Some things delight us when they are new, but later do so less, for the same reason; for at first the mind is in a state of stimulation and intensely active about them . . . but afterwards our activity is not of this kind, but has grown relaxed; for which reason the pleasure is also dulled.

Aristotle urges the man seeking after virtue to cease pursuing pleasures as ends of themselves. Instead, he praises virtuous action and a life of contemplation. Unlike pleasures, these activities are not dulled by time and do not depend on outside stimulation. They are permanent; and "the most valuable [behaviors] are the more durable."

Book III focuses upon "moral virtue acquired by practice." According to Aristotle, there are two types of virtue: *moral* virtue and *intellectual* virtue. Intellectual virtue "owes both its birth and its growth to teaching . . . " Moral virtue, on the other hand, "comes about as a result of habit." Both good and bad habits can be fashioned, just as "men will be good or bad builders as a result of building well or badly." Similarly, "by doing the acts that we do in our transactions with other men we become just or unjust." Thus, "we are made perfect by habit."

Aristotle recommends that an individual follow the middle path (the "Golden Mean") in regards to choosing action. In the application of virtue to a situation, he argues, there can always be too much or too little. For example, in battle, too much courage is heedless, while too little is cowardice.

Regarding the Golden Mean, in book IV Aristotle addresses the nature of wealth, which he defines as "all the things whose value is measured by money." To this definition Aristotle applies the concept of *liberality*, a middle ground "with regard to the giving and taking of wealth":

Those who practice liberality handle wealth in moderation. [Riches] will be used best by the man who has the virtue concerned with wealth; and this is the liberal man . . . The liberal are almost the most loved of all virtuous characters, since they are useful; and this depends on their giving.

Moreover, the liberal man will "give rightly . . . to the right people, the right amounts, and at the right time."

Not all people, however, strive toward liberality. Many succumb either to wastefulness or miserliness. Those who are wasteful "exceed in giving and not taking." Those who suffer from miserliness, on the other hand, "fall short in giving, and exceed in taking," exercising a common "sordid love of gain." However, unlike wastefulness, miserliness is incurable; wasteful men tend to change their ways after they squander all of their wealth, but miserly men carry a fatal disease. Thus, men should seek liberality, the common-ground mean between the two extremes.

Similarly, *pride* is a middle ground between vanity and excessive humility. " . . . He who thinks himself worthy of great things, being unworthy of them, is vain"; such people "are fools and ignorant of themselves." Conversely, "the man who thinks himself worthy of less that he is really worthy of is unduly humble . . . he robs himself of what he deserves." Hence, Aristotle recommends the middle ground of pride where a man "thinks himself worthy of great things." The proud man is one who lives up to his claims and is "a man of few deeds, but of great and noble ones":

Now the proud man, since he deserves most, must be good in the highest degree; for the better man always deserves more, and the best man most. Therefore the truly proud man must be good. And greatness in every virtue would seem to be characteristic of a proud man.

Aristotle concludes that "pride . . . seems to be a sort of crown of the virtues; for it makes [virtues] greater, and is not found without them. Therefore it is hard to be truly proud; for it is impossible without nobility and goodness of character."

A necessary part of living a happy and virtuous life is to enjoy lasting friendships; lesser men experience relationships that are far less ideal. Aristotle asserts that friendship is the glue which "holds states together . . . Without friends no one would choose to live, though he had all other goods; even rich men and those in possession of office and of dominating power are thought to need friends most of all."

Aristotle identifies various kinds of friendship. Friendship of utility is one of the lesser types, since "those who love for the sake of utility love for the sake of what is good for themselves, and those who love for the sake of pleasure do so for the sake of what is pleasant to themselves." This sort of unequal relationship is undesirable; "such friendships are easily dissolved . . . for if the one party is no longer pleasant or useful the other ceases to love him." It follows that "bad men will be friends for the sake of pleasure or utility, being in this respect like each other; but good men will be friends for their own sake, in virtue of their goodness. These, then, are friends without qualification . . . Loving seems to be the characteristic virtue of friends, so that it is only those in whom this is found in due measure that are lasting friends, and only their friendship that endures."

These characteristics between individuals should also be binding among nations and states, and between a ruler and his subjects. The good ruler "confers benefits on his subjects . . . he cares for them with a view to their well-being, as a shepherd does for his sheep." In a nation governed by tyrannical rule, however, "there is nothing common to ruler and ruled . . . since there is no justice . . . [Therefore], in democracies [friendship and justice] exist more fully; for where the citizens are equal they have much in common."

Abiding in such Golden Mean courses of action, the virtuous man achieves and enjoys the good life, flourishing in virtue, contemplation, happiness and love.

Perhaps the greatest problem with Aristotle's theories of human virtue and happiness is that not all people can achieve "great happiness," but only lower degrees of contentment. The contemporary reader will find fault in this assumption. This should, however, not nullify Aristotle's **Ethics**, but encourage a critical evaluation of the text, and of our own present-day society.

MEDITATIONS

by
Marcus Aurelius
(A.D. 121-180)

Marcus Aurelius, born in Rome in A.D.121, ruled as Roman Emperor from A.D. 161 to 180. His reign marked the last fruitful period of the Roman Empire. Following the murder of Marcus' son, the Emperor Commodus, the state began its decline, finally ending with the division of the realm into separate eastern and western empires in A.D. 285. Even then, foreign armies continuously besieged the empire from without, while prosperity and confidence wavered within.

Such was the state of the world when Marcus Aurelius wrote his *Meditations* ("Writings of Himself"). The text is not a theoretical work, but rather a diary of his personal reflections as a devoted practitioner of Stoicism, a system of philosophical and religious beliefs. *Stoicism*, which commenced around 300 B.C., was a ideological and ethical response to the breakup of the Hellenistic empire that had united under Alexander. During the time of Marcus, many educated Roman citizens turned to the teachings of the Stoics as a way to face the intensifying political chaos and disorder surrounding them.

In general, Stoics maintained that man should guide his life by reason, not by passion. Thus, *virtue*, according to the Stoics, was the "greatest good." The *Meditations*, considered among the most readable of all Stoic writings, contains Marcus' own rules for living and for accepting the difficulties of life.

Text Overview:

The Stoics believed that the universe is composed of two things: (1) finite matter (including the elements fire, water, earth and air), and (2) God, an active, moving "cause." God was said to act on matter through the medium of fire, the most fundamental of the four elements. Under the direction of God, fire periodically consumed the other elements, in what was known as "Cosmic Conflagration."

The cornerstone of Stoic belief is the idea that *rationality* ("Reason") is the ruling principle of the universe. This is manifested in humans through discourse, reasoning, and logic. Therefore, since Reason *is* nature, Reason is God. Reason is also equated with *Providence* ("God's Will," fate, destiny . . .). The principle of Reason presides over all the material elements, of which fire is the most dominant.

The Stoics believed that after forming the worlds, God sent his creations back through an unending cycle of constructions and fiery destructions in a purifying pattern of "cosmic (universal) conflagration." All things must return to the cleansing element of fire, since fire proceeded from God, who is the soul to the body of the world. Each new world, reborn from this purifying fire, resembles its predecessor in

every individual man; identical actions of the previous world take place in later ones. Thus, the Stoics believed, human freedom is swallowed up in Providence and Fate ("God's Will"). The only freedom that exists is "interior freedom," wherein man can alter his *judgment of* and *attitude towards* events—perceiving all events as God's Will and celebrating them as such.

Meditations makes a fundamental distinction between ambitions which are under human control and those which are not. In the second case, man must endure what he cannot alter, while cultivating a self-sufficient life of reason. *Meditations* holds that Reason, Fate, and Providence are all names for the same governing principle. Therefore, as previously noted, individual freedom is seen as a question of attitude rather than choice. That is, one cannot do *other* than that which one does; one does as one *must* do.

Stoics such as Chrysippus theorized that the *imperfection* of the individual contributes to the *perfection* of the whole. Good is balanced by evil. Furthermore, evil—and evil men—may later become good, and vice-versa—but only through divine Providence.

The Stoic "Cardinal Virtues" consisted of *Moral Insight, Courage, Self-control* and *Justice*. An individual who exhibits one of these qualities exhibits them all; one is either completely Virtuous or completely base. Thus, Pleasure, Sorrow, Desire, and Faith are seen as totally irrational and unnatural; the Stoic ethic is largely a fight against these affections. The Stoics also maintained that every man is a social being, and that all have a claim to goodwill, even slaves and enemies. This ethic is attained when individuals love others as they love themselves.

The *Meditations* consists of twelve books of aphorisms. Within these twelve books, Marcus Aurelius stresses four key areas of Stoic doctrine: the ethical obligations demanded of all men towards one another, living a life in accordance with reason and nature, the close affinity between God and man, and—the topic from which our present-day use of the term "stoicism" is most closely associated—the brevity of life and the stance that we must assume in the face of divine providence.

Mankind's Ethical Obligation

"Whenever anyone does you a wrong," Marcus wrote, "set yourself at once to consider what was the point of view, good or bad, that led him wrong. As soon as you perceive it you will be sorry for him, not surprised or angry. For your own view of good is either the same as his or something like in kind, and you will make allowance." (7,22) Like his Stoic teachers, Marcus realized that imperfections in men comprise a greater good. "It is man's gift to love even those who fall into blunders . . . " he taught. "This takes effect the moment we realize that men are our brothers, that sin is ignorance and unintentional, that in a while we shall both be dead, that, above all, no injury is done us, our inner self is not made worse than it was before." (7,22) Marcus held that whenever a man performs an act of kindness and furthers the common good, "he thereby fulfills the law of his being and comes by his own." (9,42)

Harmony With Reason/Nature

Marcus, like his Stoic predecessors, emphasized a life in harmony with Reason and Nature. Reason (*logos*)—more closely related to an innate "practical wisdom" than true analytical reasoning—means to love mankind and follow God. This is the "Law of the Universe": "All harmonizes with me which is in harmony with thee, O Universe. Nothing for me is too early nor too late which is in due season for thee . . . " The Universe is propelled by God's Will, Nature, or Reason; it acts "as nature wills it, and nothing is evil which nature wills." If one follows "reason" one is able to attain inner well-being regardless of one's external fortunes. Thus, by following our inborn capabilities, we are able to live in harmony with *nature*—namely, our *own* nature: "No man can hinder you from living according to the reason of your own nature; nothing will happen to you contrary to the Reason of Universal Nature." (6,58)

It is by following our inner dictates that we attain harmony. This turn inward is a fundamental aspect of Stoic thought; if the world is an uncertain, unstable place, look within for stability and comfort. With such a perspective, even tragic "loss is [reduced to] nothing else than change":

Nature has this work to do: to shift and to change, to remove from here and to carry there. All things are change, yet we need not fear anything new. All things are familiar and even the distribution of them also remains the same. (8,6)

Even though the elements of the universe continuously shift and change, these are accomplished through God's Will; hence, man is made happy by "doing what man's nature requires," and mankind's universe remains rational and one:

All parts of the Universe are interwoven with one another, and the bond is sacred. Nothing is unconnected with some other thing. For all things have been coordinated and combined to form the same universe. There is one Universe made up of everything, and one God who pervades everything, and one substance, one law, one common reason in all intelligent animals, and one truth; perchance there is one perfection for all beings of the same stock, who participate in the same reason. (7,9)

Mankind's Affinity to God

Marcus divided the "being" of a human into three parts: the body (soma), the soul (psyche) and the *mind* (nous). He believed that the mind contains within it the reason discussed above. This practical wisdom is the spark of divinity within us all; it is an emanation of God placed in us by God to serve as a guide.

Therefore, whoever disobeys the divine guide within himself, not only acts impiously towards God, but acts irrationally and violates the dictates of reason:

Live with the gods. . . . He lives with the gods whoever presents to them his soul accepting their dispensations and busied about the will of God, even that particle of Zeus which Zeus gives to every man for his controller and governor—to wit, his mind and reason. (5,27)

Life's Brevity

Throughout the **Meditations** Marcus stressed that life is short:

. . . Your life is short. You must make the most of the present with the aid of reason and justice. Be sober even in your relaxation. . . . Bear in mind that every man lives only in the present . . . all the rest of his life is either past or uncertain. Short then is the time which any man lives; and short too the longest posthumous fame, and even this is handed on by a succession of poor human beings, who will very soon die, and who know not even themselves, much less one who died long ago. (3,10)

Since, as Marcus explains, life is short, and everything—including actions, events, and thoughts—is preordained, man should accept "everything which happens, even though it seems disagreeable. . . . Willingly give yourself up to [fate], allowing her to spin your thread into whatever she pleases." In the face of divine providence, he adds, mankind is to "rest in these two ideas: first, that nothing will happen to me which is not in harmony with the nature of the universe; and second, that it is in my power never to act contrary to my god and divinity, for there is no man who can compel me to do this." (5,10)

Those who act according to the will of God are like tools which serve reason. The aim of man, then, should be to "pass your life in truth and justice, and show benevolence ever to liars and unjust men." (6,48) And during this short lifetime, "Do not act as if you would live ten thousand years. Death hangs over you. While you live, while it is in your power, be good." (4,17)

The basis of Stoic belief revolves around reason. And "to a rational being," Marcus declares, "the act that is according to Nature is according to Reason." (7,11) This world is merely a repeat of other worlds which rise and fall because of God's Will. Hence, both men and animals rise from and return to purifying fire according to God's Will, and everything is preordained by His Providence. Still, Reason is the fiber of all workings in the Universe, binding mankind in brotherhood, and dictating what is bad and what is good. Nothing happens which is contrary to Reason.

Marcus Aurelius died during a campaign against invading barbarians in A.D. 179. No doubt he accepted his fate with the assurance that his death fell perfectly into the plan of the Universe, and that he would return to the primeval fire of all things, into which all beings will eventually fall.

ON THE NATURE OF THINGS

by
Titus Lucretius Carus
(c. 99 - 55 B.C.)

Titus Lucretius Carus, a devoted student and follower of Epicurus and perhaps the most widely published vehicle for Epicurean thought, was born in Rome sometime between 99 an 95 B.C. The son of a ruling-class family, he lived during a time when eminent Greek teachers of the Epicurean sect were deeply influential among the governing class. Lucretius' *On the Nature of Things* has been compiled into five books, and although it is apparent that the general direction the writings on Epicurean philosophy takes is expository, it is also quite poetic and at times even whimsical. For this reason there are many who thought Lucretius to be unsound, as can be derived from the account of St. Jerome, written four centuries after the philosopher's death:

Titus Lucretius the poet is born. He was rendered insane by a love-philtre [potion] and after writing during intervals of lucidity, some books . . . he died by his own hand in the forty-third year of his life.

This matter cannot be validated, but historians have verified that love potions did occasionally produce madness, perhaps giving credence to St. Jerome's account. Other historians, however, consider this biographical sketch an attempt by critics of Epicurean thought to discredit Lucretius, and, by extension, Epicureanism. It should be noted that critics of Epicurean beliefs have often misunderstood this philosophic movement, considering it hedonistic. Actually, Epicurus proposed that greater happiness could come from pleasures of the mind, rather than those of the body.

In any case, Lucretius, Epicurus' disciple and a gifted poet, sought to explain his ideas to the "unbusied ears" of his readers, urging then not to "abandon [them] with disdain before they are understood. For I will assay to discourse to you on the most high system of heaven and the gods."

Since Lucretius' poetic and philosophic foundation is based on Epicurean thought, therefore a basic understanding of Epicureanism's founder proves invaluable to an understanding of Lucretius' work. Epicurus was born in Samos in 341 B.C. He went to Athens to do his military service in 323—a time when Aristotle was at his peak as the most powerful philosophical and political force in the world. With the free-thinking philosophies of Aristotle bringing an end to Stoic prominence, society's strict, moralistic structure was slowly crumbling.

After ten years of study, Epicurus presented himself as a teacher. His first school was in Mytiline, reputed to be a secluded and spacious home and garden set far away from the city, where the students met as friends with their mentor, who taught:

Of everything that wisdom lays in store for a lifetime of happiness, the possession of friendship is by far the most important.

Epicurus died at the age of 70 in 271 after a long and painful illness—a disease which certainly seemed to have influenced his philosophical outlook and passion for the value of all life. Lucretius paid him homage:

He was a god, yes, a god, this man who first discovered the way of life now called wisdom; the man who through his art enabled us to escape from such holocausts and such a dark night, and who set our lives on such a calm and luminous course.

Text Overview:
CANONS OF EPICUREAN THOUGHT

"Epicurus uses many colorful words," said Cicero, "but he rarely takes the trouble to be consistent." While Cicero's words may be true, and it has been noted by his own followers that Epicurus spoke much more than he wrote, Lucretius' works contain most of his fundamental convictions, or *canons*. The first of these is *Passion*, or, experiencing pleasure and pain. Epicurus held that human beings experience both pleasure and pain—as do dogs, turtles, trees, plants, and every other living thing; these all exist as passionate entities. Perhaps an example taken from the works of Lucretius can clarify this philosophy:

*But plain matter of fact clearly proves
that all things grow up in the air
and are fed out of the earth;
unless the season at the propitious
period send such abundant showers
that the trees reel beneath the soaking
storms of rain, and unless the sun
on its part foster them and supply heat;
corn and living trees could not grow.*

In other words, all things in nature respond to one another.

The second idea, or "canon," is *Sensation*. Similar to the first canon, sensation denotes being aware of the immediate evidence of the senses—seeing, hearing and feeling the world—and avoiding the temptation to reduce incoming sensory input to a system of reason, as the religious Stoics, philosophical Platoists, and other thinkers had. Rather, life's pleasures should be truly *experienced—sensed*.

The third canon is *Memory*, or as the Epicureans preferred, *Prenotion*. Prenotion is the idea that any question, if it is to be asked and understood, implies that we have, *in advance*, some notion of the thing involved. That is, contained within language itself is a basic understanding of the meaning of words. Therefore, if we can ask a question about a thing, then we are well on the way toward understanding the meaning of the thing. A person might ask, for instance, "Do horses exist?" Well, the average person has probably seen or heard of horses, so, yes, they exist. But to a person who has never seen a horse, horses don't exist; therefore, he or she possibly cannot even *inquire* about their existence. This concept extends even to the unseen forces around us:

All nature then, as it exists by itself

is founded on two things; there are
bodies and there is void in which
these bodies are placed and through
which they move about. In this way,
then, must the blasts of wind move on,
and when they, like a mighty
stream have borne down in any
direction, they pull things before
them, with repeated assaults,
sometimes catch them up in a
curling eddy and carry them away . . .

Resisting the Stoics' many rules of conduct and their belief that God's Will reigns supreme, Lucretius' Epicurean philosophy is based on free thinking. Far from advancing a hedonistic idealogy, the Epicureans maintained that there is no social "Golden Rule"; rather, each individual possesses his own sense of morality and ethics. The Epicureans simply wanted to sit with friends and discuss the world, living out their lives while enjoying all its native beauty. The world was too tied to traditional schools of thought, they insisted; too many of the popular thinkers of the day were consumed with ordering the world. Lucretius taught instead that beauty was inherent in the *disarray* of the world. Nature is not an ordered, rational science, but instead the exact opposite. Seeds are spread at random, not by some predetermined order. Plants grow without so-called "logic" or "reason." He taught his students to love the earth and observe the wonders of nature. "Survey the running water," is how he might address his student-friends, "how it erodes the river bank. The wind, to a lesser degree, also weathers the rocks and tree trunks. Observe the plants how they wither and die if deprived of water or sunlight—surely they have feelings. And watch how animals respond to danger. Humans must learn from these, nature's objects."

ATOMIC PHYSICS OF EPICUREAN THOUGHT

The Epicurean love of nature brings to mind two of its key philosophical concepts: the concept of *atoms* and the concept of *void*. The "atom"—while somewhat related to the notion of atoms in modern-day physics—to the Epicureans was never intended to take on a scientific meaning. Rather, the atoms of Epicurus are determined by their individual and separate function. For example, atoms that make up a human being are not the same type as those that comprise a plant or a dog. According to Epicurus, a person is composed of "me" atoms, while a plant is composed of "plant" atoms. Void, on the other hand, is basically all space that is not occupied by atoms:

If things came from nothing,
any kind might be born of any thing.
Men, for instance, might rise out of the sea . . .
Again wherever there is empty space
we call void, there body is not;
wherever again body maintains itself,
there empty void no longer exists.
. . . Clothes hung up on a shore
which waves break upon become
moist, and then get dry if spread out.
Yet it has not been seen
in which way the moisture of water
has sunk into them nor again in
what way this has been dispelled by heat.
The moisture therefore is dispersed

into small particles which the
eyes are quite unable to see.
. . . Nature therefore
works by unseen bodies.

It should be noted that lucretius and Epicurus did not develop the idea of atoms—Democritus is given credit for that. Instead, they expounded upon Democritus' theory by figuring chance into the movement of atoms.

RELIGION IN EPICUREAN THOUGHT

The followers of Epicureanism engendered many foes in the ancient world; this was primarily due to its preference to pre-Socratic philosophy and its disinterest in the more recent gods Zeus and Apollo of Hellenistic Greece and Rome. Epicurus espoused a return to an earlier Greek way of life, one espousing an unadorned belief and dependence on man and nature.

The Stoics, with their rigid, disciplined and hierarchial society, were disgusted by the Epicureans and wrongly accused them self-indulgence and laziness. Stinging insults soon catapulted from both sides.

In the final analysis, though, the Epicureans just wanted to be left alone. Though repeatedly invited to defend their positions at the famed Porch in Athens, Epicurus and his disciple Lucretius chose to remain, for the most part, in the solitude and silence of their gardens. *Simplicity* and personal responsibility were the watchwords:

This terror then and darkness
of mind must be dispelled not
by the rays of the sun and
glittering shafts of day,
but by the aspect and the law of nature;
the warp of whose design we shall
begin with this first principle:
nothing is ever gotten out of
nothing by divine power.
Fear . . . holds so in check all mortals,
because they see many operations
go on in earth and heaven,
the causes of which they can in no way under
stand,
believing them therefore to be done by power
divine . . .
both the elements out of which everything
can be produced and the manner in which al
l things are done
can be done without the hand of the gods.

Only the devoted poet Lucretius' works are left to herald Epicurean philosophy. To observe the world, to remain a passionate lover of good things, and to be at peace with what cannot be changed were its ancient tenets. To feel, to understand purely, to gain an empathy for all things—these entailed Lucretius' simple ambitions:

Nor does my mind fail to perceive
how hard it is to make clear in Latin verses
the dark discoveries of the Greeks.
But your worth and the looked-for
pleasure of sweet friendship
prompt me to undergo any labour
and lead me on to watch the clear nights . . .
seeking by what words and in what verse
I may be able in the end
to shed on your mind so clear a light
that you can thoroughly scan hidden things.

MEDITATIONS ON FIRST PHILOSOPHY

by
Rene Descartes
(1596-1650)

Rene Descartes' *Meditations* are central to the Western philosophical tradition for two reasons. First, they raise the question of what should be counted as knowledge: Can we trust the information we receive from our senses? Second, the *Meditations* posit a tradition of dualism between mind and body (spirit and matter), which, by nature, affirms Descartes, are different substances. *Matter* makes up the physical universe—the measurable "spatial" universe of which bodies form a part; while *mind,* or spirit—the thinking part of the universe—exists as a completely separate substance, outside of space. Mind has no shape or measurement. Although obviously the human mind must *somehow* communicate and interconnect with the body, it remains as an independent, immaterial entity. Cartesian dualism draws both on the philosophy of Plato and traditional Christian theology, developing the idea that we *possess* bodies instead of *being* bodies.

Text Overview:

Meditation One: Concerning Those Things That Can Be Called Into Doubt

Descartes begins the *Meditations* with the intention of finding a method by which one can arrive at certain knowledge—knowledge "beyond the shadow of a doubt." To establish knowledge, he avers, one must consent "earnestly and openly to the general destruction of former opinions . . . so as to begin again from the first foundations." And in this vigorous search, he finds that many assumptions which he once believed to be solid bastions of knowledge are not certain, and are little more than opinions.

Most of what we believe to be real is revealed to us through our senses. The senses, however, sometimes deceive. When we sleep, for example, we often dream and sense things as surely as when we are awake, yet they are not real. Sometimes in sleep, we even ask ourselves if we are dreaming, and feel convinced that we are awake. It seems doubtful that at a given moment, one can prove beyond question that one is not dreaming. Therefore, in devising a method for obtaining *certain* knowledge, the bodily senses do not provide a reliable guide.

Descartes' "Method of Doubt" now drives even deeper into preconceived notions of truth. He asks us to imagine the possibility that an evil genie is consistently deceiving us regarding all we see around us (like the enchanter in *Don Quixote,* transforming giants into windmills) Imagine further that the genie has also tricked us about what we believe to be indisputable analytic truths, such as the idea that a square is a four-sided figure, or two $2 + 2 = 4$. "I am forced to admit," says Descartes, "that there is nothing, among the things I once believed to be true, which it is not permissible to doubt."

Meditation Two: Concerning the Nature of the

Human Mind: That the Mind is More Known Than the Body

By the end of the first *Meditation,* almost all beliefs that are usually held to be categorically true have been called into doubt. Descartes can now begin building his theory of truth from the ground up. "I will suppose that all I see is false . . . Body, shape, extension, movement, and place are all figments of my imagination. What then will count as true? Perhaps only this one thing: that nothing is certain."

But then he notes that one citadel of certainty still remains standing: can it be possible for me to doubt my own existence? Even if I am dreaming, or being deceived by an all-powerful genie, it must be the case that some sort of "I" *has to* exist in order to *be* deceived in the first place—and that "I" must be, at its core, some sort of mind. In other words, Descartes could imagine himself existing without a body, but could not imagine himself existing without a mind. "[The genie] can never bring it about that I am nothing so long as I shall think I am something. . . . I am therefore precisely a thing that thinks; that is, a mind, or soul, or intellect, or reason." What I imagine may be false, concludes Descartes, but it is nevertheless *"I",* a mental entity, who does the imagining. **"I think, therefore I am."** And this concept—that we can be certain of our own existence in that we are thinking beings—constitutes the fulcrum for the lever of Descartes' entire philosophical system.

Meditation Three: Concerning God, That He Exists

Descartes next argues that he can clearly and distinctly perceive that an infinitely powerful and good God exists. First of all, what is the source of ideas and perceptions that fill our minds? Obviously they do not all *originate* in our minds. Not all thoughts originate in the mind. For example, the feeling of warmth from a fire is not something we "will" to happen, nor can the warmth be "willed" away when it grows uncomfortable. *Everything must have a cause, and a cause cannot be of a lesser reality than its effect,* Descartes reasons. "For if we posit that something is found in the idea that was not in its cause, then the idea would get it from nothing." Yet the warmth must come from somewhere.

And if we are sure that an idea or sensation did not come from within us (like the warmth of the fire was not created by us), then it follows that something else—"the cause of this idea"—must also exist outside of us. Furthermore, the *cause* of anything—including an idea—must be greater than its *effect.* And if this is true, then how could it be possible for us, as finite, imperfect humans to imagine something that is perfect and infinite? You cannot make a mountain out of a mud pie. Take, for instance, our frequent human feelings of guilt and sinfulness. How could we notice our own imperfections (and thus experience guilt) if we did not first have a conception of perfection? Hence, there must exist a being capable of perfection who is the cause of the idea of perfection within us—and this Being is God.

The whole force of the argument rests on the fact that I recognize that it is impossible that I should exist, being of such a nature as I am—namely, having the idea of God in me—unless God does in fact exist.

Finally, it is logically impossible that God could be an evil deceiver or an all-powerful genie. The *idea* of God's perfection is the necessary result of God's *actual* perfection; if God were evil, or deceptive, God would no longer be perfect. Thus, the idea of God's perfection can only be caused by God's real perfection—and a perfect God would not allow his creations to be deceived.

Meditation Four: *Concerning the True and the False*

The first three **Meditations** have shown that claims to knowledge cannot be based solely on sensory experience. Reason alone is able to yield certain truths, yet reason is itself subject to error. But how does this come about? Why would God (being perfect and thus unable to deceive) confer upon us a faculty that, even when used properly, can yield falsehood? If God made us capable of error, would that not be evidence of his imperfection?

Descartes answers that reason errs only when it is contaminated by wishful thinking. When we mistake vague ideas—or even hopes—for clear concepts, when we pretend that our finite powers of reason are infinite, then we are betraying reason itself. Human, finite reason must struggle in order to triumph. If we were to clearly and immediately know the true and the good over the false and evil without putting forth the effort to discover for ourselves these opposites and their meanings, we would be denied *free will*, the God-given power to choose. In fact, free will hinges on our "imperfections," on our ability to fall into error and learn from our mistakes.

Meditation Five: *Concerning the Essence of Material Things, and Again Concerning God, That He Exists*

At this stage Descartes is sure of the reality of his own mind and of the fact that God exists, but he has yet to establish certainty regarding the world external to him. To establish the existence of material entities, he again appeals to his idea of God: God is not a deceiver and hence would not present the senses with a false world. "I then conclude that everything I clearly and distinctly perceive is necessarily true." The viability of all sciences—or of any attempt to presume truth from evidences in the external world—depends, then, upon this certain knowledge of God.

Meditation Six: *Concerning the Existence of Material Things, and the Real Distinction of the Mind from the Body*

Descartes concludes that material objects can and do exist since, through mathematical representations ("a *square* box," for instance, or "a

circular path"), their spatial properties can be clearly and distinctly perceived. But can the *senses* be trusted to accurately convey the material world to our mind?

At this point Descartes briefly recapitulates the development of his argument so far: He has called into doubt all information delivered by the senses: his body with all its parts; appetites such as hunger and thirst; sensations such as pain and pleasure; and qualities of external objects such as size and color. He has demonstrated that existence is proved by the functions of the mind, not by the evidences of the body. He has also pointed out that we feel many sensations independent of own will, such as heat from a fire. It now follows that there must be something which is the *cause* of these sensations. We *clearly and distinctly* experience these sensations as emanating from our own bodies; thus, since God is not a deceiver, our bodies must exist. And through the body, in turn, we clearly and distinctly sense things which emanate from outside the body. Again, since God is not a deceiver, it follows that other material things besides our own bodies must also exist.

The human body—like all animal bodies—functions on the basis of *instinct*; by nature, not by intellect. These instincts guide action but do not provide *knowledge* about the outside world. The mind must be on guard against deceptions from the body in order to correct them. Bodily sensations alone can provide no certain basis for knowledge, whereas the reality of the mind—that is, the *self* as a "thinking" soul, a single, complete entity—can rest on the solid foundation of self-knowledge.

Thus, Descartes' proof of his own existence endures as an undisputed cornerstone of knowledge. Not even the most extreme philosophical skepticism and doubting is capable of undermining the origin of knowledge: the self.

The Cartesian statement "I think, therefore I am" is much more than an obvious statement of fact; it is an important philosophical premise with many implications for the status of knowledge. How much can we truly know—or how little?

The premises put forward by Descartes in his **Meditations** have remained to this day topics of debate. But whatever the merits of his philosophical system may or may not ultimately prove to be, Descartes' ideas established a milestone in the history of Western thought: First, by calling into question the nature of knowledge and trying to establish some degree of genuine certainty, he gave us new insights into the whole concept of knowledge. Second, by boldly claiming that the mind was qualitatively distinct from the body—a claim that still generates controversy—Descartes advanced some provocative and original arguments. And third, Descartes introduced a new method of inquiry ("systematic doubt") into the philosophical arena. It is these contributions that have made Descartes one of the most influential philosophers of the modern era.

ETHICS

Benedict (Baruch) Spinoza
(1632 - 1677)

Benedict Spinoza, a descendent of Portuguese Jews who fled persecution in Spain, was born in Amsterdam, Holland, in 1632.

Even at an early age, he was a lover of philosophy, studying the Old Testament and the Talmud in depth, as well as the writings of Descartes and various mystical and Cabalistic authors.

As a young man, Spinoza began to question the strict formalism of his religious upbringing, openly straying from the dogmatic beliefs presented in his synagogue. Not long after, he declared an open revolt which not even his parents' threats of disinheritance could stifle.

In 1656, at the age of twenty-four, Spinoza was called before the elders of the synagogue on charges of heresy. They asked him if it were true that he had said that God might have a body, in the corporal sense. Had he, in fact, said that angels might actually be the product of hallucinations? Had he suggested that the soul of man might be similar in nature to that of an animal? Was it true that he had pronounced that the Old Testament spoke nothing of the immortality of man? Although he was offered a considerable annuity if he would consent to at least outward support of his synagogue and his faith, Spinoza rejected the Hebrew religion and was formally cut off.

Essentially banished from Amsterdam—and once nearly assassinated—Spinoza left his family and most of his friends to live a humble, mostly reclusive life of contemplation and study. He prized independence and intellectual pursuits so highly that he preferred to make a living grinding lenses rather than accept a university professorship or financial aid.

Spinoza's publications were met with such sanctioned condemnation that, during his lifetime, he received no widespread recognition, and his major work, *Ethics*, was not published until after his death. Today Spinoza is regarded as one of the greatest, most influential of philosophers.

Inspired by a love of Descartes' theory that the universe is divided into "mind" and "matter," Spinoza saw, as Descartes did not, that if mind and matter are separate substances, they cannot interact. Thus, Spinoza attempted to construct a unified and complete system of the knowledge of God, the universe, and man in accordance with geometric science. Hence, as an expression of that goal, his famous statement: "I will therefore write about human beings as though I were concerned with lines and planes and solids."

Spinoza espouses a rational view of religion, rooted in a "natural vision." Hence he has often been favored among individuals who have a distaste for traditional religious beliefs.

Text Overview:

The human intellect, Spinoza taught, can be clearly examined and improved, producing a greater understanding of God. In its correct state, human reason is self-sufficient, its own guide, and its own judge; rational thought should not only be sought in philosophical concerns but also in ethical matters.

Spinoza shunned dogma; he did not subscribe to any particular faith, and was even quite open to the possibility of his own views being incomplete. However, he was certain that, given time and effort, his mind could work out a comprehensive explanation of what constituted true religious belief.

The five parts, or books, of *Ethics* each deal with a particular subject:

I. God

II. The nature and order of the mind

III. The emotions

IV. Human bondage

V. Human freedom.

The first, *God*, is by far the most detailed; the last states and clarifies the purpose of his work.

I. God

Since, for Spinoza, everything must exist and be conceived *in* and *through* "God," an understanding of the universe ("universal reality") can only be established upon reference *to* God. For this reason, and by virtue of the fact that man's understanding of ethics and morality is rooted in a belief in God, *Ethics* begins with a discussion of God's true nature. Nothing can be understood apart from its relation to God, and all understanding involves the location of isolated events and their causes within the infinite, broad picture of God.

But "God," Spinoza argues, is not the "great being" many religions make "him" out to be. In fact, God is "substance," or "that which exists by itself and is conceived by itself." God is substance, both mind and matter.

There is a distinction between that which is entirely *independent* (eternal, is "self-caused," or does not require anything else to account for its existence), and that which is *dependent* (brought into existence by another force or being). The infinite substance (God, mind and matter) is independent, *eternal*. Everything else is dependent.

Apart from the term "substance," two other key expressions are central to Spinoza's ideology:

(1) *Attribute:* "That which the intellect perceives as constituting the essence of substance." Attribute is a property of, or quality belonging to, substance. A lemon, for instance, possesses the attributes of being both sour and yellow. Being infinite, however, God possesses many attributes, most of which are incomprehensible to man. *Mind* (thought) and *matter* (things) are the only two Godly attributes humans can comprehend.

(2) *Mode:* Mode consists of "the modifications of substance, or that which exists in, and is conceived through, something other than itself." Modifications, including individual human beings and physical objects, cannot exist without God (substance). Since we human beings are a part of God (since we consist of mind and matter), it is through God that we and all finite things have "being." Man, therefore, is "diminished God."

Spinoza held that substance (God) is beyond being limited by attributes; rather, it has "infinite attributes." He refutes the position held by some that "God, like a man, consists of body and mind, and is susceptible of passions," because God is, by nature, infinite:

All who have in anywise reflected on the divine nature deny that God has a body. Of this they find excellent proof in the fact that we understand by body a definite quantity, so long, so broad, so deep, bounded by a certain shape, and it is the height of absurdity to predicate such a thing of God, a being absolutely infinite.

Part I of *Ethics* contains Spinoza's famous "proof" that there can only be one substance that is absolutely infinite, and thus only one that can be its own cause. The main elements of this proof consist of four points:

1. *Either nothing exists or else an absolutely infinite substance exists.*
2. *Something does exist.*
3. *The presence of such an infinite substance includes everything else as part of itself and precludes the possibility of another, equal substance.*
4. *Such a substance cannot be divided, nor can the existence of a second such substance even be conceived, since every possible attribute conceivable is already included in the substance.*

This fourth point leads to Spinoza's most famous doctrine:

Whatever is, is in God, and without God nothing can be, or can be conceived.

Clearly, Spinoza's references to God are not references to an individual, divine agent, but to that which he believes *fundamentally, eternally* exists. Spinoza's argument that substance is the one and only thing that can be said to exist is an example of philosophical "Monism" (a group of theories which claim only one thing—or one type thing— actually exists).

Only God is absolutely free. Man does not have independent free will. Our *will* is simply the disposition of our *reason* to recognize and accept a true idea. Our will is really only "a necessary or constrained cause" in the perfection of God.

II. Nature and Order of the Mind

In Book II Spinoza explores the nature, origin and layout of the mind as one of the infinite number of things springing from God. To understand humankind's "ethics" (moral choice and reasoning), the human mind must be appreciated. Most importantly, a distinction must be seen between a mere "idea," and an *"adequate"* or *"true"* idea. The material world is an extension of God and is, as such, perfect. And every material thing has an idea paralleling it.

Ideas are true insofar as they are connected to God. As mentioned earlier, nothing can be understood apart from God. When they are abstracted and viewed *away* from their natural place within the infinite spectrum of God, they wallow in confusion. Although human intellect and reason generally does tend toward abstraction, the human mind innately has "an adequate knowledge of the eternal and infinite essence of God." This position is radically different from most theological doctrines, which assert that the mind is incapable of comprehending God.

III. Emotions

Book III centers on the emotions, and begins to deal directly with the subject of ethics. Here Spinoza asserts that "the passions of hatred, anger, envy, and so on . . . follow from the necessity and efficacy of nature; they answer to certain definite causes, through which they are understood . . . " Thus, passions can be analyzed just as the mind is analyzed.

The law of existence is that everything should do its best to persevere in its unique mode of being—that is, as God has deigned. However, Spinoza's original take on God's nature permits him to believe that humans *can*, through exertion, intuitively sense God's eternal underlying structure. In fact, this effort is the essence or duty of every living thing. Spinoza held that people's highest happiness was achieved by coming to understand and appreciate the truth that they are a tiny part of an all-inclusive God. When humans are able to progress and pass through to a higher state of being, they experience "joy." On the other hand, they feel "sorrow" when, due to passivity, they consign themselves to a lower state.

IV. Human Bondage

Good and evil are defined in Book IV in terms of what is useful to us and what stands in the way of our obtaining something which is useful. *Desire*, Spinoza concludes, is what directs us to *act*, to put forth effort, with the end result being an increase of *virtue* (personal power).

Because our day by day emotions can only be subdued by *stronger* emotions, our ability to resist the negative pressures we encounter—and thus avoid sorrow—depends on our strength to fend off the lessening emotions surrounding us. This implies a constant battle. But, if we develop the highest virtue of the mind—that is, *to know God*—then our ideas will become more "adequate" and our desire and power for action will increase. Consequently, we will liberate ourselves from bondage, which leads to the final, most portentous element and purpose of *Ethics:* Human Freedom.

V. Human Freedom

Book V maps out the way to freedom. Here Spinoza states that, by achieving adequate, truthful ideas (i.e., ideas which authentically represent their subject), we become adequate ourselves; we *can* modify our own characters, experiencing as a byproduct, real joy. This is true human freedom— *freedom from the bondage of our passions.*

Spinoza also states that "blessedness is not the reward of virtue; but virtue itself." Through this blessed state of virtue we are given power to traverse the extremely difficult path of increasing our understanding of God, until the time we reach the final goal of complete understanding. This is the highest aspiration of the human spirit and the chief interest of the wise.

Spinoza concludes:

. . . [The wise man] surpasses the ignorant man . . . for the ignorant man is not only distracted in various ways by external causes without ever gaining the true acquiescence of his spirit, but moreover lives, as it were, unaware of himself, of God, and of things . . . Whereas the wise man, in so far as he is regarded as such, is scarcely at all disturbed in spirit, but, being conscious of himself, and of God, and of things, by a certain eternal necessity, never ceases to be, but always possesses true acquiescence of his spirit.

Though attaining the station of "wise man" is difficult to achieve, "all things excellent are as difficult as they are rare."

AN ESSAY CONCERNING HUMAN UNDERSTANDING

John Locke
(1632-1704)

Published in 1690, John Locke's treatise *An Essay Concerning Human Understanding* describes his theory of how the mind functions. In particular, Locke is arguing against Descartes' reformulation of the classic Platonic doctrine of *innate ideas*—the belief that some essential concepts, like our ideas of roundness and squareness, for example, or of God or justice or time and space and number, are already imprinted within the mind at birth. There are no such principles, declares Locke sweepingly. The human mind at birth is a blank tablet—a *tabula rasa*—and we can know *nothing*—nor even *think* anything—until this tablet has been inked with *sensation* (feeling) and engraved by *reflection* (thinking)—the two components that make up our *experience*.

Locke's essay, the first significant presentation of an empirical theory of knowledge to penetrate British philosophical thought. This thrust towards empiricism (or experiment-ism) was inspired by the dazzling experiments and discourses of contemporary scientists like Sir Isaac Newton and Robert Boyle, with whom Locke was acquainted. His claim that all real knowledge is derived from experience has continued to impact philosophy to this day, especially in America and Great Britain.

In a nutshell, Locke maintains that *sensory stimulation* is the beginning of both knowledge and thought. For example, our idea of an apple is formed by our experience with such sensations as redness, juiciness, roundness, and sweetness. He then continues through the rest of the essay to use "this historical, plain method" in constructing a whole theory of knowledge from what he sees as the basic "sensational" building blocks of experience to more and more elaborate levels of thinking and apprehending.

Principal Ideas of Human Understanding

Locke first sets forth certain principles when looking into the methods by which knowledge and understanding are gained:

- At birth the mind is a blank tablet (*tabula rasa*); we cannot possess any knowledge or thought *prior* to experience:

  Let us then suppose the mind to be, as we say, white paper, void of all characters, without any ideas; how comes it to be furnished? Whence comes it by that vast store, which the busy and boundless fancy of man has painted on it with an almost endless variety? Whence has it all the materials of reason and knowl-edge? To this I answer, in one word, from EXPERIENCE: in that all our knowledge is founded, and from that it ultimately derives itself.

- All knowledge derives from a combination of *sensation* and *reflection*. First of all we *feel* and *perceive* the world (sensation), and then we *think* (reflect) about our perceptions and feelings.

- Complex *ideas* are formed as the mind combines simple ideas generated from experience.

- There are three modes of being in the universe: Everything that exists, exists as either *mind, body,* or *God*. And all objects (or "bodies") possess both primary and secondary properties.

  - *Primary properties,* such as length, shape and weight, exist within the bodies themselves, even when no one is observing them, and can be mathematically measured.

  - *Secondary properties,* such as sound and color, do not actually inhere in "bodies"—or anywhere else in the external world, they can only come to life within the mind of the observer. But secondary qualities *do* exist as *powers,* or potentials, within all bodies; "yellowness is not actually in gold," explains Locke, "but is a *power* in gold to produce that idea in us by our eyes."

The Origin of Ideas

The model of the mind that Locke presents is analogous to an industrial operation. The raw materials used in this operation consist of our individual *sensations*—our perceptions and feelings. The mind then processes these sensations to give them meaning through associations. For example, the smell of perfume takes on an enhanced meaning when that smell is identified with a particular person or situation. Other sensations also take on more and more meaning from a growing web of associations. Finally, our *reflection* on these sensations and combined associations produces the finished product—an *experience* consisting of some "practical knowledge" necessary to properly conduct our lives. "Our business here is not to know all things," he writes, "but those which concern our conduct." This practical knowledge, he asserts, can only be obtained through an honest discovery of the "bounds" or limits of human understanding: "When we know our own strength, we shall the better know what to undertake with hopes of success..."

Simple and Complex Ideas

Locke posits that all ideas can be placed into one of two categories: *simple* or *complex*. Simple ideas come from "simple," indivisible, individual sensations—such as the smell of a rose. The smell lingers as a sensation in the mind, much like a footprint in the sand, available for immediate recall. Then, when one simultaneously experiences the simple sensations of the taste, smell, size and shape of an apple, for instance, the mind compounds these simple ideas into the complex idea of "apple." Thus, from the single, simple ideas produced by specific sensations, all complex or compounded notions can be constructed and accounted for.

Complex ideas all fall under one of three headings: **modes** (concepts that cannot exist independently, such as "gratitude," "happiness," and "walking"), **bodies and substances** ("particular things subsisting by themselves," such as "hand," "book," and "rose"), and **relations** (the results of comparing one idea to another, bringing "mode" and "substance" together to form a completed, complex idea).

Abstract (or "General") Ideas

Having laid the foundation for explaining abstract reasoning, Locke next explores the *abstract ideas* of space, duration, number, the infinite, pleasure and pain, substance, relation, and cause and effect. By separating the particular details from all things that exist, we can finally abridge or "abstract" them to form *general* ideas ("generalities"). The first triangle you see on a school chalkboard, for example, might be a right isosceles triangle with a base of seven inches. At first, these specific descriptions and measurements may form your whole idea of "trianglehood." However, after repeated experience with triangles, the mind "abstracts" the *general* idea of "triangle" by ignoring the particular characteristics of *specific* triangles, and you no longer automatically assume that *all* triangles have a base of seven inches. Instead, you assimilate the abstract idea of a three-sided shape and classify all shapes that meet this criterion as "triangles."

The Nature of Knowledge

Knowledge, then, according to Locke, is "the perception of the connection of and agreement, or disagreement and repugnancy, of any of our ideas . . . Truth, [then, is] the joining or separating of signs [words or concepts], as the things signified by them do agree or disagree one with another." This means that, ultimately, all our knowledge is based on the direct, intuitive association of simple ideas. We have never experienced "white" in the same place and time as we have experienced "black"—so we know that white is different from black. Likewise, thunder, in our experience, has always followed lightning, so we know that lightning "causes" thunder, just as we know—again through experience—the "laws" that water freezes as 32 degrees Fahrenheit and that moving objects continue traveling in a straight line until they are slowed or deflected by an intervening force.

What we really do *not* know (and cannot know), however, is just what it means to "cause" something or to function as a "law" of nature. Whatever mysterious or magical transactions may take place between a magnet and the metal it attracts, they ultimately lie beyond our experience; we may be able to record just exactly *how* each subatomic particle responds to the magnetic force, but we will never be able to say precisely *why* it responds or what a "force" actually *does* to compel motion.

All we can ultimately say is that in our experience *fire burns wood.* The possibility always remains that tomorrow the wood chips in the stove will *not* ignite, or that next April when the temperature rises, the ice in the pond will *not* melt. It is never safe to make "always" statements (or even "never" statements like this one) about the external world. But there are two areas where we can have fruitful and universal knowledge, asserts Locke: in the realm of logic and mathematics, where we ourselves assign limits and definitions; and in ethical systems—where, just as in mathematics, *we* make the rules, and then go on to discover how they apply. In ethical situations, just as in mathematical or logical situations, we can define for ourselves through perception and reflection how principles interconnect and "agree" with each other.

Ethical Applications

Locke's ideas are obviously a long way from Plato's otherworldly forms. They are robust, earthy, and dynamic, and they should be applied to advance the human condition.

According to Locke, a good life is one dedicated to the increase of human pleasure—that is, the pursuit of happiness. "God Almighty Himself is under the necessity of being happy," he avers, "and the more any intelligent being is so, the nearer is its approach to infinite perfection and happiness." Thus Locke posits his criterion for ethical action—his "pleasure principle": Which act in a given situation will produce the greatest pleasure? As individuals each follow their unique paths to long-term pleasure, allowing the same liberty to others, they draw closer to God.

THREE DIALOGUES BETWEEN HYLAS AND PHILONOUS

by
George Berkeley
(1685-1753)

George Berkeley [pronounced "Barkley"] was respected as an educator and an Anglican Bishop. Nevertheless, he was censured and passed over for a professorship at Glasgow University, largely due to his immaterialist postulates, which, in his day, were disparaged as an endorsement for "tar-water"—an eighteenth-century version of snake oil.

In his *Three Dialogues*, Berkeley presents eighteenth-century empiricism (rationalism) in its most extreme form. Berkeley outlines his notions using a series of Socratic-style philosophical conversations between the "materialist" Hylas and his friendly "immaterialist" adversary, Philonous. Philonous supplies Berkeley's position that the only thing which truly exists is God's mind and imagination. Ideas are the source of knowledge, he states; ideas, perceptions, thoughts these alone are real. Matter, on the other hand, does not exist in the same sense; it is a mere function of the mind, a deception.

For three successive mornings, Hylas and Philonous meet in the garden of a university to debate.

The First Dialogue

"Can anything be more fantastical, more repugnant to common sense or a more manifest piece of skepticism than to believe there is no such thing as matter?" begins Hylas with certainty. Philonous responds that indeed there is, namely, *assuming* matter exists, and he offers to prove his views beyond doubt. Eager to see Philonous attempt to escape a philosophical knot of his own making, Hylas agrees to engage in a philosophical debate which he expects will demonstrate the truth and superiority of his claim: that matter exists.

Hylas first asks how it is possible to deny the existence of physical "things" (matter) when their existence was "sensibly" (through the senses) proven beyond reproach. Philonous quickly responds that the senses do not actually give humans *knowledge* of things, but only of "sensible *qualities*." For example, humans do not "perceive by sight anything besides light and colors and figures; or by hearing anything but sounds; by the palate, anything besides tastes; by the smell, besides odors; or by the touch, more than tangible qualities." Thus, Philonous concludes, "sensible *things* . . . are nothing else but so many sensible *qualities*," and are therefore not the things themselves.

Forced to admit that information obtained from the senses does not *prove* the existence of matter, Hylas next attempts to show that sensations such as hot or cold are qualities *possessed* by things or objects, which are thereby apprehended by the senses. But Philonous shows that sensations (the apprehension of "sensible qualities") are relative, experienced somewhat differently by each individual and in each location in time and space. A snake, for instance, can sense vibrations that a human cannot; conversely, a human can distinguish sounds and colors that a snake cannot, but that does not render either of these perspectives "true" or "false." Hylas concedes, "I frankly own, Philonous, that it is in vain to stand out any longer. Colors, sounds, tastes . . . have certainly no existence without the mind."

Hylas then suggests that size and shape are inherent qualities which exist in things *apart from their conception in each individual's* mind. Philonous counters this assertion, describing the relativity of "sensible qualities" once again: to a mite, a man is an immense danger, something to avoid; but to a man, the mite is "nothing." That is, largeness is relative to the observer.

Unwilling to admit defeat, Hylas then appeals to the idea of a "substratum" of real "things" underlying "sensible qualities" i.e., the sensations humans experience that objects actually exist are not themselves objects, but are *caused* by the objects which produce sensations when they interact with minds. This claim allows Philonous to inaugurate his final assault by showing Hylas that a "substratum" could only be conceived of in terms of "sensible qualities," and further that any "ideas" of "things" were creations of memory operating upon "sensible qualities" and not representations of actual "things." That is to say, our *sensations* "of things" are very real, but the things we assume they are *sensations of*, are not. To solidify his claim, Philonous demonstrates that it is impossible for anything to exist outside of the mind. Hylas professes, however, to have indeed conceived of a tree outside of his mind. Philonous retorts that the act of conceiving a tree *outside* of the mind took place *in* Hylas' mind, not in the "eternal" world. Therefore, both the "idea" of a tree and the perception of a "real" tree equally exist *within* Hylas' mind. Hylas finally yields to Philonous' argument (perhaps due to fatigue or to a sense of his own inadequacy): " . . . I plainly see that all I can do is to frame ideas in my own mind. I may indeed conceive in my own thoughts the idea of a tree . . . but that is all."

"So, I have gained my point . . . " Philonous concludes. However, reluctant to surrender completely, Hylas requests that they meet the following day for further dialogue.

The Second Dialogue

The next day, Hylas immediately objects to the previous day's argument against the existence of matter. Philonous responds by making his most convincing attack on materialism. He begins by showing how a belief in "real things" outside or apart from human experience is unfounded. Humans can only *know* what they *experience*. Therefore, *experience* is all that can be known. He proceeds with a brilliant and powerful description of the world as perceived through sense, and asks: "Is not the whole system immense, beautiful, glorious beyond expression and beyond thought! What treatment, then, do these philosophers deserve who would deprive these noble and delightful scenes of all reality? How should those principles be entertained that lead us to think all the visible beauty of the creation a false imaginary glare?"

At this point, Hylas points out that Philonous seems to have put himself in the same position, since his theory posits the existence of only "sensible qualities," thus his view seems contrary to all available evidence. Building from the final point of their first dialogue, that nothing exists outside the mind, Philonous concedes that ideas not yet experienced by an individual must exist somehow, in *some* mind, because no "sensible world" (external world) exists. Therefore, "an infinite omnipresent Spirit, who contains and supports" the apparently "sensible world" surrounding humans, must exist. Such a Spirit is God.

One cannot create an idea, except from another idea; there are no never-before-asked questions. That is to say, no idea has ever been conceived, since ever seemingly "new" ideas are mere combinations of old ones. Philonous argues that the existence of an omnipotent, all-knowing God, in whose mind every idea that *could* exist exists already, renders matter superfluous. In fact, by the simple act of God imagining something, it exists! As a result, Philonous contends, any appeal to matter attempts to diminish God's perfection, which is an "absurdity."

At this, Hylas is entirely flustered. He replies, "I acknowledge you have proved that matter is impossible . . . " Trying to fathom the skeptical abyss his earlier materialism had created—and in which he still finds himself—Hylas requests that Philonous meet again with him the next day, and show him the way out. Philonous agrees.

The Third Dialogue

Hylas commences the day with skeptical ruminations, bemoaning his conclusion that now he can know nothing with certainty. "How often must I tell you that I know not the real nature of any one thing in the universe?" he cries. "You amaze me," Philonous replies, adding, "Wood, stones, fire, water, flesh, iron, and like are things that I know. And, I should not have known them but that I perceived them by my senses . . . Away then with all that skepticism, all those ridiculous philosophical doubts." Materialism has been shown to be an empty charade—ideas most "fantastical, repugnant, and skeptical." Stunned, Hylas wonders how this could possibly be the truth. Because all things actually exist as ideas in the mind of God, Philonous answers, humans *call* sense perceptions "real."

However, Hylas still has one conceivable objection: how can Philonous simultaneously accept the account of a physical creation in Genesis and reject the actuality of a physical world? Philonous' response to this dilemma is to claim that Genesis—indeed all writing—merely records sensory perceptions. Further, he demonstrates how "other minds" could perceive the same thing differently, or the same; two minds think differently depending on what imagination each is given from God at that moment. The human mind—which, to a lesser degree, *can* make choices—is subject to God's larger, unquestionable, perfect imagination. In fact, God's imagination is *everything;* everything exists and evolves through His imagination. Even we—as God's creation, just like Adam and Eve—exist only through His all-encompassing imagination.

Hylas rejoices: "I have been a long time distrusting my senses: methought I saw things by a dim light and through false glasses. Now the glasses are removed and a new light breaks in upon my understanding. I am clearly convinced that I see things in their native forms and am no longer in pain about their *unknown natures* or *absolute existence*." Philonous, gazing at a fountain, sums up his argument for immaterialism: like the rising waters of the fountain, denying materialism at first may appear to be taking a deceptive flight of fancy; but, just as the running water returns to the pool below from which it was taken, it is an ever-filling sea of truth. "You see, Hylas . . . the same principles, which at first view, lead to skepticism, pursued to a certain point, bring men back to common sense."

Considered a classic work by philosophers, *Three Dialogues* clearly portrays the philosophical desire to discover precisely what is real and what is illusion. Hylas, however, is a "straw man," a deliberately weak opponent who never forcefully argues *for* materialism, but, like most people, simply assumes it is true. Hylas' naivete allows Philonous to lay out the tenets of his theory without serious opposition, which is standard to Socratic form. One cannot say that Philonous *proves* his point beyond a doubt, but that he has worked out a viable critique to the common assumptions about the world.

Berkeley's question—"What is real?"—remains valid. Modern-day scientists continually push back the parameters of knowledge, farther and farther, to expose new realities that were once thought to be impossible, such as quantum mechanics or the existence of subatomic particles. Moreover, Berkeley's notions have enjoyed somewhat of a renaissance in "New Age" debates over what is "real."

CRITIQUE OF PURE REASON

by
Immanuel Kant
(1724 - 1804)

Immanuel Kant published his *Critique of Pure Reason* in Germany in 1781. He described the achievement of his metaphysical work as a "Copernican revolution" in the field of epistemology (the study of knowledge . . . its nature, scope, reliability, and source.) This treatise has long been revered—even in its complexity—as the work of genius; Kant has often been typified as the most gifted philosopher who ever lived.

Since publication, *Critique* has been widely considered one of the greatest classics of Western philosophy. The text, however, is notorious for its difficulty due to its long, dense passages and unusually obscure concepts. Indeed, interpreting a typical paragraph, especially for a modern-day reader, is often akin to trying to decipher an unknown foreign language. Kant's own colleagues—trained philosophers who studied the text in the original German—complained about its perplexing vagueness and ambiguity. For this reason, it is usually examined through secondary sources.

In the *Critique,* Kant attempts to blend two divergent theories of knowledge. The first theory, "empiricism," holds that sense-experience is the only legitimate source of our concepts about the world. The second theory, "rationalism," insists that important truths concerning the physical and metaphysical (abstract, speculative) world can only be known by pure reason.

Text Summary:

Kant's *Critique* begins by questioning why metaphysics (the study of universal truth, absolute reality, the possibility of God, etc.) failed to progress as a science, while at the same time mathematics and the natural sciences were flourishing. In response to this question, Kant asserts that a science of metaphysics would require the "orderly establishment of principles, clear determination of concepts, insistence upon strictness of proof, and avoidance of venturesome, non-consecutive steps in our inferences." Metaphysics can be a science only if there are metaphysical truths which are not . . .

a) synthetic truths, derived merely through the senses (sight, sound, touch, taste or smell): "I *see* that square has a circle in it."

OR

b) analytic truths, which are true simply by definition: "All squares have four sides," or "All bachelors are unmarried males."

Analytic statements are true independently of observation or sense-experience. As Kant points out, analytic statements involve cases where the predicate is contained in the very concept of the subject. So, for example, an unmarried male is precisely what a bachelor *is,* and requires no verification via our senses. The statement "*All* bachelors are tall," in contrast, is

a synthetic one, since "tallness" is not part of the definition of a bachelor.

There must be true statements which are neither synthetic nor analytic, Kant argues. He theorizes, in other words, that there must be a distinct category of statements which are not simply synthetic nor simply analytic. In effect, Kant discovered a kind of "hybrid" statement called the *synthetic a priori,* which previous philosophers had ruled out. Such statements are *a priori* in the sense that they are *necessary,* i.e. they state things that must be true and are not merely contingent. In addition, such statements are also synthetic since they reflect truths about the empirical world; they amplify our knowledge of the world and do not merely tell us what we know via definition. These "synthetic *a priori* statements" are true, then, *independent of sense experience* (logically "prior to"), and yet are *not determined by definition* alone. That is, they are not facts based solely on sense-experience nor are they simply definitions of things. All mathematical assertions are regarded as "synthetic a priori" statements, as is the framework of Newtonian science.

Are such metaphysical truths possible? They are possible only *if* it can be shown that within human knowledge there are *a priori* concepts which originate exclusively in our *understanding* as opposed to experience. This may be possible: although "there can be no doubt that all our knowledge begins with experience . . . it does *not* follow that it all arises out of experience."

For example, space and time are concepts that we seem to instinctually understand. If space and time are true examples of *a priori* knowledge, they must form the basis for human knowledge; the concepts of space and time, then, form the patterns of perception in which all our other perceptions come clothed.

Kant further reasons that space and time *must* be *a priori* notions because our perceptions of the external world depend on their existence. We perceive objects as separate and distant from us in space, "and we absorb (apprehend) our perceptions in succession, through time." We cannot conceive of objects or events separately from space and time. Thus, space and time must exist as *a priori* "forms of intuition" which cannot be differentiated from the "contents" of sense experience.

In a sense, we project space and time onto all the objects of experience. So, contrary to what Newton had thought, space and time are not entities independent of us. Rather, they are "built-in structures" that our mind imposes on the world.

Human knowledge is dependent upon "forms of intuition" which *precede* sense-experience. Furthermore, Kant establishes that the contents of sense-experience are organized into twelve categories of judgment within human understanding. These can be thought of as twelve essential categories of structures of the mind that organize our experience and make reality coherent. Put simply, without these categories of judgment, we could not explain things and make sense of the world. For example, human understanding interprets sense-experience through the concept of "causality," as in the case of "if . . . then" judgmental statements. Our minds impose these judgments upon sense-experience in the act of interpretation. Another "category of understanding" is "property," the predicate in a subject-predicate sentence. That is, the quality of "belonging to," in the sense that a table "has" a particular kind of color, is imposed on experience by the human mind.

The *a priori* condition of space and time and the categories of judgment constitute the basis for human understanding. But what role do they play in metaphysical speculation? In short, is *knowledge* pertaining to metaphysics possible in the same sense that knowledge about physics or biology is possible? Kant ultimately believes that this is an impossibility, since *a priori* conditions and categories of understanding can be applied only to sense-experience. Metaphysics claims to deal with, not things as they *appear*, but with things as they *are in themselves*, or as they would be understood by an omniscient intellect. And *pure reason*, the faculty which would construct such absolute judgments, inevitably is weak in establishing and documenting "provable" knowledge.

In theory, there are only three ways to "prove" the actuality of God; such proof must proceed by one of the following ways:

• Originate from some definite experience, then climb by causal links up to the highest cause.

• Generate from experience in general.

• Be acquired from concepts alone.

All three methods, however, rely upon *inference.* But inferences gained from experience or from concepts fall short as *proof* in themselves, since the "forms of intuition" and "categories of understanding" which are the basis for human knowledge cannot go beyond what we receive through our senses. And, in fact, one of Kant's central aims in the *Critique* is to actually demonstrate the "limits of reason in order to make room for faith." Kant attempts to demonstrate this, in part, through *antinomies,* which are seemingly unresolvable paradoxes that appear to be both true and false at the same time. For instance, one of Kant's antinomies states that the universe must necessarily have a beginning. This is an antinomy, Kant claims, because its antithesis seems equally true: the universe cannot have a beginning in time. Both statements seem to be true. But, of course, they cannot be; it would be a contradiction. And this is Kant's way of showing how reason is limited in its power to explain—that ultimately we must rely on faith, especially in our speculations about God. "The attempt to establish the

existence of a supreme being by means . . . of argument," Kant concludes, "is merely so much labor and effort lost."

Descartes' famous so-called "ontological proof" of the existence of God (to confirm the *existence* of God from the *concept* of God) is a case in point. Simply put, this argument states that since we have the *idea* of God's perfection, God must exist; an existent being is more perfect than a mere imagined one. The problem with this argument lies in the fact that, because the *concept* of a supreme being is "a mere idea, it is incapable, by itself alone, of enlarging our knowledge in regard to what exists." Since what exists is either analytic or synthetic, and neither of these forms of thought grant certain knowledge or proof of an absolute Being, the argument is not sufficiently proven.

In the final analysis, we cannot formulate proofs of God or an absolute Being; none will answer our intricate metaphysical speculations. On the other hand, Kant also maintains that "as reason is incompetent to arrive at affirmative assertions in this field (metaphysics), it is equally unable, indeed even less able, to establish any negative conclusion in regard to these questions. For from what source will the freethinker derive his professed knowledge that there is, for example, no supreme being? This proposition is . . . beyond the limits of all human insight." That is, although reason is incapable of verifying God's existence, it is further unable to *disprove* any speculative metaphysical theory.

Additionally, although metaphysical speculation is limited and cannot be supported by knowledge, it does have practical value. It *can* serve, for instance, to encourage scientists to seek unity in nature and, in the course of doing so, discover new connections in nature.

The *Critique of Pure Reason,* which Kant himself described as "dry, obscure, contrary to all ordinary ideas, and on top of that wordy," still managed to establish revolutionary concepts which are considered by many to be the last great leap in the field of metaphysics.

The remarkable conclusion of *Critique* grants immense significance and homage to the act of pure reasoning, encouraging metaphysical speculation as a fruitful activity in and of itself. Accordingly, although Kant denies that truth can be achieved exclusively by reason, he nevertheless remains in partial agreement with the rationalist school of thought.

On the other hand, Kant champions the empiricist school's refusal to accept true knowledge beyond the realm of sense-experience, but asserts that our knowledge of sense-experience is rooted in concepts which originate *prior* to experience i.e., *a priori* concepts. In this fashion he was able to propose a radical synthesis of the two predominant strains of epistemological thought of his day.

And finally, Kant attempted to demonstrate that the "mind" is not just a passive receptacle imposed upon by external reality. Rather, the mind is *active,* and contributes something to our experience.

LOGIC
by G.W.F. Hegel

Hegel was a key member of the German idealist movement launched in the late eighteenth and nineteenth century. This movement in general held that what would normally be considered in philosophy to be the "external world," has its intelligible basis in the mind.

Clearly developing his philosophy from the foundation laid by Immanuel Kant, Hegel maintained that the categories and forms with which we interpret experience are the basis for all of our knowledge. But Hegel took his ideas even further, proposing that interpretations (thoughts, perspectives, ways of conceiving ideas) are as real as experience itself. Hence, his famous statement: "What is actual is rational, what is rational is actual."

Hegel's most renowned contribution to philosophy is his "dialectical" logic. This form of argumentation is often described in the terms "thesis-antithesis-synthesis" (although Hegel did not actually use these terms).

Dialectical logic has had enormous social impact; it set the pattern for important subsequent intellectual developments, including the economic theories of Karl Marx, and Charles Darwin's theories of biological evolution.

Hegel's text, *Logic*, published in 1817, consists of the first part of his "Encyclopaedia of the Philosophical Sciences," considered by many to be the most lucid introduction to Hegel's mature system of thought. Unfortunately, the esteemed philosopher was a much better lecturer than writer, and so his work is often almost indecipherable.

Text Overview:

"Philosophy misses advantages of the other sciences," declares Hegel. It cannot, like them, assume the existence of objects solely because they appear to us though our senses. Nor can it assume that its method of thinking is one which is already accepted.

Philosophy, however, must allow some prior knowledge of its objects, because this is a bare necessity for any intellectual investigation. But, as this investigation progresses, we discover that thought soon requires certain knowledge of the existence and qualities of its objects. Consequently, our "prior knowledge" of these objects is called in question, and soon found to be inadequate: " . . . We can assume nothing and assert nothing dogmatically; nor can we accept the assertions and assumptions of others." And yet, "we must make a beginning; and a beginning . . . is an assumption."

Assumptions, or ideas, form the basis for the only kind of knowledge we have; we know only ideas, and furthermore we know them only through other ideas. Therefore, reality must be seen, for all intelligible purposes, as composed solely of ideas.

"Logic," in this text, does not refer to the study of methods or forms which the mind discovers and must submit to (as in classical, Aristotelian terms). Rather, the term *logic* refers to "the science of the pure Idea." It is the "self-developing totality" of the laws and terms of the mind.

Logic can be evaluated in three distinct stages:

(1) The *abstract* stage, or that of the understanding—included in the "Doctrine of Being."

(2) The *dialectical* stage, or that of negative reason—included in the "Doctrine of Essence."

(3) The *speculative* stage, or that of positive reason—included in the "Doctrine of Notion or Idea."

In the abstract stage, according to the "Doctrine of Being," the individual considers an element of his thought as *existing independently*, "abstracted" into a "being." These units, usually called "impressions," are regarded by the understanding as devoid of relations, and standing alone.

Thus we find *Being* identified with what persists amid all change, with *matter*, susceptible of innumerable determinations—or even, unreflectingly, with a single existence, any chance object of the senses or of the mind. But every additional and more concrete characterization causes *Being* to lose that integrity and simplicity it has in the beginning. Only in, and by virtue of, this mere generality is it *Nothing*, something inexpressible, whereof the distinction from *Nothing* is a mere intention or meaning.

All that is wanted is to realize that these beginnings are nothing but these empty abstractions, one as empty as the other.

The reflection which finds a profounder connotation for Being and Nothing is nothing but logical thought, through which such connotation is evolved, not, however, in an accidental, but a necessary way.

But, Hegel asserts, in order to have anything to say about an impression, the individual must first *compare* it with something. This requires advancement to the second, dialectical stage, where the elements of thought are defined *by what they are not.*

The terms in Essence are always mere pairs of correlatives, and not yet absolutely reflected in themselves: hence in essence the actual unity of the notion is not realized, but only postulate by reflection. Essence—which is Being coming into mediation with itself through the negativity of itself—is self-relatedness, only in so far as it is relation to an Other—this Other however coming to view at first not as something which is, but as postulated and hypothesized. Being has not vanished: but, firstly, Essence, as simple self-relation, is Being, and secondly as regards its one-sided characteristic of immediacy, Being is deposed to a mere negative, to a seeming or reflected light—Essence accordingly is Being thus reflecting light into itself.

The Absolute is the Essence. This is the same definition as the previous one that the Absolute is Being, in so far as Being likewise is simple self-relation. But it is at the same time higher, because Essence is Being that has gone into itself: that is to say, the simple self-relation (in Being) is expressly put as negation of the negative, as immanent self-mediation.

Unfortunately when the Absolute is defined to be the Essence, the negativity which this implies is often taken only to mean the withdrawal of all determinate predicates. This negative action of withdrawal or abstraction thus falls outside of the Essence—which is thus left as a mere result apart from its premisses— the caput mortuum of abstraction. But as this negativity, instead of being external to Being, is its own dialectic, the truth of the latter, viz. Essence, will be Being as retired within itself— immanent Being. That reflection, or light thrown into itself, constitutes the distinction between Essence and immediate Being, and is the peculiar characteristic of Essence itself.

At this point in the process of logical analysis, an element of thought possesses a *being*, and is limited by what it is *not*. This leads to the next stage, the speculative stage.

In the speculative stage, elements of thought are given definite existence in-and-of themselves. Being is now understood, not in a physical sense, but in terms of a notion or idea.

The Notion is the principle of freedom, the power of substance self-realized. It is a systematic whole, in which each of its constituent functions is the very total which the notion is, and is put as indissolubly one with it. Thus in its self-identity it has original and complete determinateness . . . The notion, in short, is what contains all the earlier categories of thought merged

in it . . . It certainly is a form, but an infinite and creative form, which includes, but at the same time releases from itself, the fullness of all content . . . It involves Being and Essence, and the total wealth of these two spheres with them, merged in the unity of thought.

This breakdown of logic into distinct stages of abstraction, dialectics, and speculation, also describes the evolution of thought itself. *Thought* begins as an indeterminate "being." This being is merely an impression, not yet an idea. In order to reach its essential existence as an idea, this being must first be removed from its immediate moment in the bare present: it must be *defined.* And definition is only achieved *after* thought establishes what it is *not.*

This progression of logic is what is referred to as "dialectical" logic. It always consists of three stages (commonly referred to by modern philosophers as "thesis-antithesis-synthesis") by which a concept is transformed from its original, barely-conceived state (thesis) into a more refined rendering (synthesis). This transformation is made possible through the "contradictory" interaction of two "opposites" (the thesis and its antithesis). For example:

Thesis: *All* dogs are ugly.
Antithesis: But *some* dogs are pretty.
Synthesis: *Some* dogs are ugly.

Dialectical logic has often been referred to as the "logic of change," a thought process that attempts to explain change and make it more rational. Prior to Hegel's codification of dialectical logic, there was no system of thought in Western philosophy which directly addressed the underpinnings of change-oriented thought. Logic, prior to this time, tended to be entirely static, timeless.

It is interesting to observe that Hegel's systematization of the "logic of change" roughly coincided with a period of tremendous change in Western culture. The industrial revolution, and the emergence of capitalism and socialism, for example, dawned in this era; all of these advancements depended heavily upon a conceptualization of the world as changeable, dynamic, unfixed.

Hegel undoubtedly reflected what he himself referred to as the "Spirit of the Age," and his greatest contribution was to discern and formulate the type of thinking which revolutionized his time. And, fortunately for us, there were those around who were able to cut through the thickets of Hegel's abstruse verbiage, simplify and extend his theories, and apply what they had learned from his body of work.

LEVIATHAN

The Matter, Form, and Power of a Commonwealth, Ecclesiastical and Civil
by Thomas Hobbes
(1588 - 1679)

Thomas Hobbes was born in Westport, England in 1588. At the time of his birth, England was gripped by the fear of the approaching Spanish Armada. In fact, fear—embodied by Hobbes' mother's terror at the prospects of both giving birth and surviving an imminent invasion—marked Hobbes' work. "Fear and I were born twins," he often stated.

Hobbes studied at Oxford, after which he became the private instructor of Lord William Cavendish. This association allowed him to travel extensively and meet many influential people in Europe, including Galileo, with whom he shared an interest in mathematics and physics. Later, Hobbes worked for a time as a secretary for Francis Bacon.

Leviathan, Hobbes' most famous work, outlines his ideas concerning political theory. In this work, he denies that people are naturally social beings, arguing instead that they are moved only by their own self-interests. Hobbes advocates what he called a "natural religion," based on his theory that man is naturally "unmoral." He also perpetuated the idea that God, Jesus Christ, and the Holy Ghost are three separate persons, an idea for which he was nearly executed by the Anglican clergy. His friends, the Cavendishes, protected him, however, and Hobbes died peacefully at the Cavendish estate in 1679.

Text Overview:

Hobbes, aroused by Galileo's laws of physics, asserted that only matter exists and that everything that happens can be predicted in accordance with exact, scientific laws. Everything—every object, person, or group of people—constitutes a "body," and each body is governed by laws of motion that dictate its behavior.

With *Leviathan*, Hobbes attempts to illustrate how groups of people also create "bodies"—societies, communities, and governments—designed to protect themselves from one another, and that these bodies are best governed by a *sovereign* (a king or absolute ruler). In that individuals are innately selfish, a "commonwealth" or *leviathan* (literally, "sea monster," and used as a metaphor for a large, monstrous governmental body administered by a benevolent yet all-powerful monarch) is the best, most just form of government. Only through the power wielded by a protective monarch can the rights and growth of a Commonwealth's citizens be defended.

Divided into four parts, *Leviathan* first describes the nature of man, then the nature of a Commonwealth, and then the nature of a "Christian" Commonwealth. Finally, Hobbes offers his theory concerning what he calls the "Kingdom of Darkness."

Part I: Of Man

The human mind is wondrous indeed, Hobbes begins; whereas man's senses are limited to worldly perceptions, his *imagination* is limitless. Given an object plainly visible to the eye, for instance, "after [it] is removed or the eyes are shut, we still retain an image of the thing seen, though more obscure than the original. This is imagination . . ."

Since the fading mental image is represented in memory, memory and imagination are the same—merely considered from different points of view. Hobbes calls the culmination of memories "experience," which forms the foundation of an individual's thoughts and insight.

Thoughts and insight, in turn, govern man's mental discourse, whereupon "mental discourse is transferred into verbal discourse," which, Hobbes says, "is man's most noble invention. Men did not construct speech because they are rational animals, [rather] men became rational beings because they invented speech." True knowledge, then, comes from the interactive speech we term "discussion."

From knowledge comes man's *power*, which is whatever means he has to attain some "higher good." If a man has significant means to do good, he has much power; if he has limited means for doing good, his power is also limited. Power is thus derived from man's knowledge, of which, argues Hobbes, all men are equally capable of attaining.

However, says Hobbes, though men are *intellectually* created equal and possess equal capacity, such cannot be said of their *morals;* men differ greatly in ethical matters. And this condition of intellectual equality and moral inequality often brings about divisions in a citizenry—divisions that eventually lead to civil war. "If two men desire a single thing which cannot be obtained by both of them, envy and hostility will be the result."

This "warring" social scenario can only be avoided if a higher power is watching over the citizenry. In civil states where there is no supreme power—a *republic*, for instance—perpetual war is the standard. This perpetual war is not necessarily marked by unending combat, but by an unending *threat* of combat—spawning fear, selfishness, competitiveness, hatred—"much like foul weather is marked as much by the threat of showers as by the showers themselves."

Though over the centuries mankind has developed a great capacity for war, Hobbes points out that mankind has also cultivated a great capacity for peace. "The Right of Nature is each man's freedom to protect his own life . . . The Fundamental Law of nature is to seek peace and follow it." In other words, the right to self-protection is unalienable; it cannot be given up. Self-protection is the only law that no one—not even a sovereign—has the right to supersede. From this comes Hobbes' Second Law: " . . . Man should lay down his right to all things and be contented with as much liberty for himself as he would allow for his fellow man." These rights can be laid aside either through renunciation, or, preferably, through transferring them to another person—a sovereign.

Part II: Of a Commonwealth

The individual citizen is the essential unit of a Commonwealth. However, the individual, standing alone or in a small group, is weak. Hence, a greater "body," the larger, stronger Commonwealth, was forged for the protection of its people. And, Hobbes writes, "in this artificial giant, sovereignty is the soul giving life to the whole body. . . . The wealth of its members is its strength; the safety of the citizens is its business . . . "

A Commonwealth exists for one reason only: the security of its citizens. This security cannot come from nature, for mankind only has the capacity for either war or peace. Neither can security come from an association of a small number of people—a small number cannot protect itself from a larger number. And security cannot even come from a large association, unless that association is governed by a great, continuous power—a sovereign. "Where there is no supreme power, there is no law; where no law, no justice," and such a society sinks into despair and chaos. Without an all-powerful sovereign to rule them, people's lives would be "poor, nasty, brutish, and short."

A Commonwealth is established by society conferring all its strength and power upon "one man . . . one single will [or one assembly] . . . to the end that he [the sovereign] may use the strength and means of [all the citizenry] as he shall think expedient, for their peace and common defense . . . " This citizenry, Hobbes concludes, this "multitude so united is the great Leviathan…" This Commonwealth is established "for the achievement of a peaceful life amongst themselves and protection against enemies." From a *Commonwealth*, then—a common granting of privileges to one individual or group—derives the rights and faculties of a *Sovereignty*. A sovereign's powers are absolute, and he cannot be accused of injustice since "every subject . . . is the author of all the actions and judgments of the Sovereign . . . Among other things, the Sovereign has dominion over the private property of the citizens; he also is the Supreme Judge in all controversies . . . decides which doctrines are conducive to peace and which are contrary to it. He leads in wars and negotiates in peace. He can reward and punish, and he is authorized to establish the proper place of men in society." Anyone who opposes such absolute power must be reminded that "human life can never be without some inconvenience and that the calamities of a civil war are far more unpleasant than restrictions imposed by laws. Furthermore . . . most of the time their troubles originate from their own restiveness and disobedience."

A Commonwealth's best chance for success arises when it takes the form of a monarchy. A king's *wealth, power,* and *glory* are a direct reflection of the wealth, power, and glory of the public. Thus, in a monarchy, private interests are the same as public interests; every citizen is obliged to obey the doctrines set forth by the monarch. A citizen who disobeys the king's decrees presupposes that his rights supersede the rights of society, and the king must then take action to guarantee the rights of society. Still, a citizen is only required to obey as long as the sovereign is able to protect that citizen. When a monarch loses that power, cit-izens are not required to obey. That is to say, the Right of Nature—self-protection, the guarding of one's life—cannot be given up, even to a sovereign. Therefore, a citizen's obligation to obey will never require him to give up his life. If, in time of war, the citizen is captured and must subject himself to another authority, he may do so, since his life depends on making such a covenant. This releases that citizen from his duty to obey his earlier sovereign.

Commonwealths are not always permanent structures. They can grow in security and prosperity, or they can perish through violence from within or from faults in government. In fact, the gravest defect a ruler can display is a *lack* of absolute power. In such a case of being ruled by a weak ruler, Hobbes maintains, private citizens are allowed to "judge what is good or evil for them and are allowed to rely on the dictates of their own conscience"; in other words, for reasons of self-preservation, an individual may legitimately choose to dissent. A Commonwealth *as a whole*, however, can never prosper for long when many of its citizens act of their own conscience; Civil Law is the dictate of a public conscience, not a private interest.

Part III: Of a Christian Commonwealth

A Christian Commonwealth, Hobbes explains, is one that subjects itself to the words of the prophets. The scriptures outline those principles which should be exercised for the spiritual salvation of all.

The main problem inherent in a Christian Commonwealth is "the question of obedience whenever there is a conflict between the commandments of God and men." Spiritual principles and temporal principles are not always compatible. This problem is resolved if citizens can distinguish between the religious, spiritual doctrines that are truly necessary, and those that are unimportant in matters of salvation. Obedience to the Law of God is all that is necessary to enter into the Kingdom of God; however, in a kingdom of men, civil law must be obeyed. And the sovereign, in turn, "though he be an infidel," will not persecute his Christian subjects if he knows they are subject to his will.

Thus, Hobbes favors a Christian Commonwealth over any other form of rule. A Christian monarch will rule with benevolence and mercy, and will, at the peril of his life, defend and assist his citizens.

Part IV: Of the Kingdom of Darkness

Finally, Hobbes, invoking as yet his most fervent petition, urges his readers to accept Christ, the true Light of the World. In order to accept Christ with all "heart, might, mind and strength," one must vigilantly avoid the Kingdom of Darkness, which would destroy the soul of man.

There are four causes of spiritual darkness, which, Hobbes insists, if not eschewed, will lead a man to the Kingdom of Darkness: "ignorance of the scriptures, acceptance of heathen demons and idols, Greek philosophy, and the mingling of heathen tenets with uncertain traditions." Christ only brings salvation to the earth, he declares. And for those who do not believe in Christ, "the darkest corner of Satan's kingdom is reserved."

THE SOCIAL CONTRACT

by
Jean-Jacques Rousseau
(1712-1778)

Man is born free; and everywhere he is in chains. One thinks himself the master of others, and still remains a greater slave than they. With these words Jean-Jacques Rousseau begins one of the most influential political essays ever written. More than a simple political essay, *The Social Contract* explores the lofty dilemma of how man loses his identity and freedom through the very act which confers it upon him: creating a state.

Rousseau is usually misunderstood as a romantic because of his earliest works which included the ideas of "noble savagery" and a belief that man should be in a natural state, living as so—called savages did. He even praised Caliph Omar for having burnt the library at Alexandria. Voltaire, in a famous reply to Rousseau upon receiving a copy of one of his earlier works, responded: "I have received your new book against the human race, and thank you for it. Never was such cleverness used in the design of making us all stupid. One longs, in reading your book, to walk on all fours."

However, by 1760, the year *The Social Contract* was published, Rousseau's thought had changed. There is no mention of noble savagery, or of a return to the forest. This work also differed in that it was tightly reasoned and coherent; elements often missing from his earlier books. It pleads with its readers to recognize the necessary tragedy of society, to submit to the power of the state and to our own political obligations. It is in this context that we should read the famous opening lines of *The Social Contract*. Rousseau is not calling for anarchy but is rather inquiring how the "chains" can be legitimized, for his views by this time had evolved to see civil society as necessary and that which makes a *stupid and dull-witted animal* into an intelligent being. Therefore, if we assume that there is such a thing as political obligation, what does it rest upon and how do we legitimize it?

Text Overview:

"The social order [hierarchy]," submits Rousseau, "is a sacred right which is the basis of all other rights." But, he continues, this right does not come from nature, it is created by man. Rousseau frames the problem as follows:

To find a form of association which will defend and protect with the whole common force the person and goods of each associate, and in which each, while uniting himself with all, may still obey himself alone, and remain as free as before.

In his investigation into the nature of our political obligations, Rousseau lists *force* and *slavery* as possible foundations of the social order. He concludes, however, (contrary to Hobbes) that it does not come from force, because whomever is most powerful will ultimately be conquered by one or many. Thus, "as soon as it is possible to disobey with impunity, disobedience is legitimate; and, the strongest being always in the right, the only thing that matters is to act so as to become the strongest." Force, then, is not the foundation of the social order, but merely a mechanism within it.

If not force, could slavery—the willing negation of an individual's liberty in exchange for life—be the foundation of the social order? No, answers Rousseau:

To say that a man gives himself gratuitously, is to say what is absurd and inconceivable; such an act is null and illegitimate, from the mere fact that he who does it is out of his mind. To say the same of a whole people is to suppose a people of madmen; and madness creates no right.

Clearly, slavery is not the foundation of the social order.

Having eliminated force and slavery, says Rousseau, only *consent* remains as a possible foundation for political obligation. Rousseau maintains that some point in time men had to have gathered together and decided—whether actually or implicitly—that, "each of us puts his person and all his power in common under the supreme direction of the general will, and, in our corporate capacity, we receive each member as an indivisible part of the whole. This is the social contract." Such a contract does not require submission to a king or an elected body, but rather submission to the *general will*.

At the point in time that any group agrees to the social contract, several things occur. Most importantly, an entity is formed, which "is called by its members *State*, when passive, *Sovereign*, when active, and *Power* when compared with others like itself." This *state* exists apart from all the individuals within it, but is absolutely dependent upon the individuals for its existence.

The second event that takes place at the execution of the contract is that the individuals involved in it become known collectively as a *people*, individually as *citizens*, who share in the sovereign authority, and *subjects* under the laws of the State. And the third and final event is the selection of a system of government.

The Sovereign is, in a sense, a being. A being given life, power, and authority by the citizenry to rule over them:

The Sovereign, being formed wholly of the individuals who compose it, neither has nor can have any interest contrary to theirs; and consequently the sovereign power need give no guaran-

tee to its subjects, because it is impossible for the body to wish to hurt all its members . . . The Sovereign, merely by virtue of what it is, is always what it should be.

It is imperative to bear in mind that the sovereign is not an individual, or a monarchy or any form of government, but only a concept or principle. Thus, a true "Sovereign" must be attentive to *its* subjects. Because of the moral obligation placed upon it, there are severe restrictions placed upon the Sovereign, namely, that it cannot abrogate the rights of citizens, that it cannot commit itself to slavery, and that it cannot will itself non-existent. Being made-up of the citizenry it is impossible for the Sovereign to run contrary to their interests, and always it functions as it should. Additionally, through its creation by the social contract, the Sovereign acquires the right to use force to compel citizens to conform to the conditions of the social contract, even though their individual needs or desires may conflict with the general (majority) will. Consequently, the Sovereign has, by virtue of its service to the people, all power, and the individual gives up some personal freedoms in order to live under the social contract:

Although, in this state, he [the individual] deprives himself of some advantages which he got from nature, he gains in return others so great, his faculties are so stimulated and developed, his ideas so extended, his feelings so ennobled, and his whole soul so uplifted, that, did not the abuse of this new condition often degrade him below that which he left, he would be bound to bless continually the happy moment which took him from it for ever, and instead of a stupid and unimaginative animal, made him an intelligent being and a man.

However, the social contract itself is not the ultimate cause of man's distress because, "instead of an uncertain and precarious way of living they have got one that is better and more secure; instead of natural independence they have got liberty, instead of the power to harm others, [they have] security for themselves, and instead of their strength, which others might overcome, [they own] a right which social union makes invincible."

That which is responsible for man's suffering in society is too much government, Rousseau believes. Government, in this sense of the word, is an intermediary between the Sovereign and its subjects. Theoretically beholden to the Sovereign, which cannot do anything contrary to the will of the subjects who comprise it, the government is run by individuals who, as dictated by human nature, cannot possibly place the interests of the state above their own individual interests. Thus, government, not the Sovereign, ends up running the state. Individual will[s] begins to replace the general will; internal alliances are slowly formed—and the citizenry suffers.

These abuses occur in two of the three types of government. In democracy, where every person takes part equally in the matters of state this issue is null and void for, "there never has been a real democracy, and there never will be. It is against the natural order for the many to govern and the few to be governed. It is unimaginable that the people should remain continually assembled to devote their time to public affairs, and it is clear that they cannot set up commissions for that purpose without the form of administration being changed."

This change is to *aristocracy*, the most prevalent form of government. Aristocracy is where a small group governs over a large. Aristocracies, in their purest sense, constitute the best form of government:

In a word, it is the best and most natural arrangement that the wisest should govern the many, when it is assured that they will govern for its profit, and not for their own. There is no need to multiply instruments, or get twenty thousand men to do what a hundred picked men can do even better.

Thus, even though the poor must be contented with their lot, aristocracy works as long as it is based upon merit and not heredity. Unfortunately this is not usually the case; whether good or bad, says Rousseau, an aristocracy is *always* unequal. And the citizenry suffers under the repression and tyranny heaped upon it.

The United States, Rousseau reasons, is an obvious form of aristocracy, since the few make laws for the many.

The type of government which persecutes the citizenry most is *monarchy*. In this system citizens are reduced to nothing but the means of support for the regent:

The best kings desire to be in a position to be wicked, if they please, without forfeiting their mastery: political sermonizers may tell them to their hearts' content that, the people's strength being their own, their first interest is that the people should be prosperous, numerous, and formidable; they are well aware that this is untrue. Their first personal interest is that the people should be weak, wretched, and unable to resist them.

Rousseau espouses the social contract as a means of putting a state's citizenry in the position of power. The social contract empowers the individual to have a say in his government, ensuring that democratic, Sovereign rule prevails over the less desireable aristocratic or monarchic governmental forms.

However, because of the utter corruptibility of government, Rousseau concludes, it is destined to always decline and be replaced; in other words, government's natural course is to evolve through a series of revolutions. As a new state is created, the government eventually supersedes the Sovereign, the government then declines and a new revolution ensues creating yet another new state—as the cycle starts all over again. Ultimately, man cannot change this course of events—but his very social nature requires him to try.

THE ROAD TO SERFDOM

by
Friedrich A. Hayek
(1899 - 1992)

By 1944, many nations throughout the world began to adopt the controlled-economy of a central planning authority. *The Road to Serfdom* was for Austria's Professor Friedrich Hayek a passionate "wake-up call" to humankind. He sensed the increasing presence of socialism, which in his opinion threatened the future of individual freedom. Writing this "political book" was Hayek's fulfillment of a personal call to duty. Having full knowledge that *The Road to Serfdom* would not please many people, and that it might render his more academic works questionable, he nevertheless took on the controversy and published his wake-up call to the world.

In its time, *The Road to Serfdom* was perceived as a rather charming piece of literature attacking the Socialist "modern movement for planning," particularly in Hayek's portrayal of a directed economy replacing the free market, competitive system. There, people unite in a common hostility toward competition, but can agree on little else. When competition is eliminated, the consumer is at the mercy of organized, independent monopolies, which require State regulation (and ultimately, autocratic control) to keep them in line. Hayek felt that monopolies were not direct products of capitalism, but rather "fostered by deliberate policy...attained through collusive agreement and promoted by public policies."

"...A policy of freedom for the individual," he concluded, "is the only truly progressive policy."

Text Overview:

The close of World War II was the "present state of the world" when Hayek launched his critique on Communism. He believed that, in many cases, individual liberty had been abandoned for an easier route of central planning and control, or, in his words, "the road to serfdom."

Hayek saw liberal Western intellectuals as adopting the same attitudes and philosophical beliefs as socialist and communist governments. He perceived little difference between Nazi Germany's "National Socialists" and Josef Stalin's government in Soviet Russia; what alarmed Hayek the most was that Western democracies--most ruled by a liberal society with an already socialist face--were falling into the same historical process which preceded these cases of totalitarian rule.

Apathy: The State of the World

"Growing impatience with the slow advance of liberal policy," Hayek suggests, has caused people to re-evaluate the costs of preserving a liberal democracy. Today, declared Hayek, people apathetically take for granted the improvements achieved through democracy as though they had been "acquired once and for all." Hayek lamented the sad contradiction that "[we are] fighting for freedom to shape our [lives] according to our own ideas," and yet we are simply not willing to take the necessary steps to preserve such freedom. A spirit of apathy has blanketed the earth, he announced.

Even if America was to win the war (which at the time was still questionable), Hayek felt that totalitarianism (absolute, unopposed rule by one governmental faction) would still threaten democracy. While collective forces directed the masses toward their collective goals, individualism was at the risk of being forgotten. The world, Hayek asserted, must find its way back to the road which fosters individual freedom, justice, and prosperity by upholding those very same ideals for which a war was being fought.

The Lure of Socialism

Hayek argued that a population never consciously chooses socialism, but is led into it through a program of governmental propagandizing. A former Fabian Socialist, Hayek does defend "misguided socialists of all parties" who naively followed a pathway to socialism. And, Hayek believed, the inevitable progressive result of socialism would be something worse: totalitarian, a corrupt form of government which ultimately destroys the individual spirit of political and economic liberty. "Socialism can be put into practice only by methods of which most socialists disapprove."

Historically, "the old socialist parties were inhibited by their democratic ideals and...did not possess the ruthlessness required for the performance of their chosen task." Any socialist may be totally sincere in his belief that greater freedom is the result of socialism's practice. His mistake, however, is in prescribing this ideology to all people, whereby they became "responsible for luring more and more liberals along the socialist road..."

Dangerous Ideas

Economic, political, and social problems, as well as a "pedigree" of *dangerous ideas*, Hayek says, all commenced with the emergence of well-meaning "social planners" wanting to boost economic activity. "If in the long run we are the makers of our own fate," he wrote, "in the short run we are the captives of the ideas we have created. Only if we recognize the danger in time can we hope to avert it. ...The intellectual history of the last sixty or eighty years is indeed a perfect illustration of the truth that in social evolution nothing is inevitable, but thinking makes it so." Essentially, it is important to think one's ideology out, thoroughly and carefully, and know the full implications of what one believes.

Ominous Disguises

Hayek perceived political rhetoric, such as "democratic socialism," "progressive movement," and the "freedom party," to be dangerous and manipulative; these were all part of the propaganda war of socialism. He was convinced that "the unforeseen but inevitable consequences of socialist planning create a state of affairs in which, if the policy is to be pursued, totalitarian forces will get the upper hand." Hayek argued that the idea of complete centralization [government control] is appalling to most people due to the fantastic amount of work involved as well as the "horror inspired by the idea of everything being directed from a single center." Nevertheless, Hayek claimed, we were moving toward such a state-run society.

No Middle Way

The appeal of a centralized government results from the prevalent belief that it "must be possible to find some middle way" between a totalitarian government and a free market system. There seemed to be at first a very rational basis for this notion that some "judicious mixture of the two methods" would combine the beliefs of both systems. *Planning* would be substituted for *competition* in a middle way approach. However, Hayek pointed out, this would eliminate individual choice, both for consumers and producers, thereby stifling a liberal democratic economy.

Why Socialism Won't Work

Hayek cited two principal reasons why an effective economic system cannot be "planned." First, no individual or group could possibly consider or anticipate all of the circumstantial variables likely to occur, and therefore the stated goals could never be achieved as planned. Secondly, economic planning requires a restriction of individual choices in a manner inconsistent with the individualism which characterizes modern Western liberalism. Therefore, a middle-way approach is ideologically problematic.

In order for a planned economy to benefit a population, the State would have to become involved in almost every aspect of daily life, including the designation of occupations and working conditions. In order to control all variables, as would be needed for accurate planning, State intervention would become so extensive that it would undermine the original goal of increasing liberty. For Hayek, State regulations would eventually become coercive, the worst-case scenario exemplified by Germany under the dictatorship of Hitler.

The Rule of Law

Hayek contrasts a "totalitarian" rule with the "rule of law." "The difference between the two kinds of rules is the same as that between laying down a Rule of the Road, as in the Highway Code, and ordering people where to go; or, better still, between providing signposts and commanding people which road to take." The rule of law is designed to protect the freedoms of the individual, to provide a framework in which an individual can make personal choices.

The rule of law is "fixed and announced beforehand"; like signposts or highway signs, it assists "the individual in freed pursuit of personal ends and desires." Under the rule of law, the State would confine itself to establishing rules for general situations, making it possible for the individual "to foresee with fair certainty how the authority [would] use its coercive powers in given circumstances and to plan one's individual affairs on the basis of this knowledge." So long as one knows the rules of the game, "the powers of government [would] not be used deliberately to frustrate his efforts." If State actions can be predicted, individuals can formulate their plans within the established boundaries. In order for government's actions to be predicable, however, they must be determined by general rules, and not individual circumstances.

The Preservation of Competition

Hayek's response to a call for a socialized, centralized economy was not, however, of a "dogmatic laissez faire attitude." Instead, he suggested limited government involvement, as opposed to absolutely free competition. While pleading that British readers should remember their roots of economic freedom (Adam Smith, Locke, Hume, Burke and Milton), Hayek argued that social systems require a "carefully thought-out legal framework" to provide political freedom and economic prosperity. Economically, liberals traditionally advocated full utilization of "competition as a means of coordinating human efforts." The legal system should therefore be "designed both to preserve competition and make it operate as beneficially as possible."

Hayek's Solution

The natural laws of competition will surely be disrupted if the principles of economic and individual freedom become engulfed in a planned economy. The rule of law must apply, along with limited government involvement to assure the safety of productive competition. The rule of law, assisted by the principle of voluntary cooperation, will help guide society along productive lines, while allowing for the freedom of individual choice and decision-making.

Totalitarian government can be avoided by taking conscious steps to preserve individual liberty. The followers of socialism are stumbling along a dark path--and inviting the whole world to stumble along with them. Their words are soft; the socialist planners are promising "freedom." We must not heed their call, Hayek warns. Wouldn't it be a tragedy, he asks in conclusion, "if it should prove that what was promised to us as the Road to Freedom was in fact the High Road to Servitude?"

ON LIBERTY

by
John Stuart Mill
(1806-1873)

On Liberty is a systematic attempt to grapple with the central problem in modern democracy: the tension between majority rule and the protection of minority and individual rights.

As a British Utilitarian philosopher writing in the mid nineteenth century, Mill argued that individuals should not be required to sacrifice their own happiness for the benefit of society.

I. Introduction

The subject of this essay is civil or social liberty: "the nature and limits of the power which can be legitimately exercised by society over the individual."

In previous eras, Mill says, the struggle between liberty and authority was a contest between the classes of people who composed the citizenry and another class who controlled the government. "By liberty was meant protection against the tyranny of political rulers." A time came, however, "when men ceased to think it a necessity of nature that their governors should be an independent power opposed in interest to themselves." Espousal of the new social contract theory [that individuals willingly forego absolute freedom for the benefits of living in a society] proposed by Locke, Hobbes, and other writers, had instituted the periodic election of rulers by the ruled. "What was now wanted was that the rulers should be identified with the people, that their interest and will should be the interest and will of the nation . . . The will of the people . . . means the will of the most numerous or the most active part of the people—the majority, or those who succeed in making themselves accepted as the majority."

Thus it follows that democratic self-government "is not the government of each by himself, but of each by all the rest." Hence, the issue of limiting the government's power over individuals does not disappear when "the people" elect the government from among themselves; if anything, it becomes more acute.

"There is a limit to the legitimate interference of collective opinion with individual independence," continues Mill. "All that makes existence valuable to anyone depends on the enforcement of restraints upon the actions of other people." It is easy enough to gain agreement on this principle. What exactly these restraints should be, however, "is the principal question in human affairs." All people naturally feel happiest living in a society which enforces rules that give *them* rights. However, the assumption of almost every individual and every culture that *everyone else* ought to live as *they* do, makes the formulation of such rules difficult in a pluralistic society.

This essay champions one very simple principle: "The only purpose for which power can be rightfully exercised over any member of a civilized community, against his will, is to prevent harm to others . . . Over himself, [however], over his own body and mind, the individual is sovereign." Mill offers one caveat: This notion of near absolute liberty only applies to "human beings in the maturity of their faculties": children and the "mentally deficient" are excepted.

Three components are crucial to individual liberty: (1) freedom of thought and expression, (2) freedom to plan one's own life pursuits, and (3) freedom to unite in groups for any purpose not involving harm to others. Governments and majorities have historically encroached on all three of these liberties.

II. On the Liberty of Thought and Discussion

Encroachments on free expression are always illegitimate, even when sanctioned by the government or the people. "If the opinion is right, they are deprived of the opportunity of exchanging error for truth; if wrong, they lose what is almost as great a benefit, the clearer perception and livelier impression of truth produced by its collision with error." (Mill's endorsement of social open-mindedness is known as the "Public Discourse Theory.")

No person, nation, or age has ever possessed opinions which were free from error; we are all fallible. One must leave open the possibility of one's opinions—even one's deepest convictions—being disputed. Human affairs can progress only through the ability to see and rectify mistakes in the light of discussion and experience. Wisdom can only be gained through exposure to as wide an array of opinions as possible. *The strongest foundation for any belief is a standing invitation to prove it unfounded.* Therefore, social tolerance and a free press are indispensable to a free society.

Legal persecution and social stigmatizing of non-majority beliefs persist, however, even in our own time. Social intolerance is often enough to prevent the expression and circulation of an idea. A position is not fully understood or acceptable until it is considered superior to the strongest, most genuine expression of the *opposite* case.

Most political arguments contain at least *partial* truths. Dialogue between these viewpoints makes possible the creation of a third, stronger position, as in the case of opposed political parties in a legislative body. "Not the violent conflict between parts of the truth, but the quiet suppression of half of it, is the formidable evil . . . The fatal tendency of mankind to leave off thinking about a thing when it is no longer doubtful is the cause of half of their errors."

III. Individuality As One of the Elements of Well-Being

For the same reasons that different opinions should be protected, there should also be different "experiments of living" [what we today would term "lifestyles"]. Here, Mill espouses another premise: Action must be more restrained than opinion. However, even the expression of opinion must be curtailed if it causes harm to others. But so long as the individual alone bears the costs of his opinions, he should be free to live according to his personal beliefs.

"If it were felt that the free development of individuality is one of the leading essentials of well-being . . . there would be no danger that liberty should be undervalued, and the adjustment of the boundaries between it and social control would present no extraordinary difficulty." But individuality and spontaneity are not valued as ends in themselves; people continue to believe that the way of the majority is and should be good enough for all. "Society has now fairly got the better of individuality; and the danger which threatens human nature is not the excess, but the deficiency, of personal impulses and preferences."

"Human nature is not a machine to be built after a model, and set to do exactly the work prescribed for it, but a tree . . . [sprouting] on all sides, according to the tendency of the inward forces which make it a living thing." Once again, freedom of one's own exposure to a variety of ideas and situations are the two necessary conditions for human progress. Though the "quality" of human experiences differs (the pleasures of thinking, understanding, enjoying the arts, for example, are higher and more noble than those of eating, sleeping or sex; it is better to be a "Socrates dissatisfied than a fool . . . satisfied"), humans are responsible to cultivate their own potentials through making personal choices. The love of liberty can be antagonistic to the dictates of custom. But anything that denies individuality is, by definition, despotism.

IV. Limits to the Authority of Society over the Individual

Where does one draw the line between individual liberty and legitimate social authority? "To individuality should belong the part of life in which it is chiefly the individual that is interested; to society, the part which chiefly interests society." Therefore, society is justified in establishing two constraints upon individuals: (1) The prohibition against injuring the interests or rights of another, and (2) The stipulation that each person must bear his share of the labors and sacrifices necessary to defend the society and its members from injury.

Many, says Mill, refuse to admit a distinction between those actions which affect only the individual and those which concern society. "How [it may be asked] can any part of the conduct of a member of society be a matter of indifference to the other members?" If an individual, for example, willfully damages his own mental or physical abilities, he fails society in three ways: he places a burden on others for his care, he becomes unable to fulfill his societal obliga-

tions, and he corrupts by example. But it is only when a person directly fails to fulfill specific social obligations (the payment of debt or caring for his family), answers Mill, that legal or social sanctions become legitimate. And these sanctions are to be exacted not as "punishment" for sin or extravagance, but rather as reparations for breach of duty. "Whenever, in short, there is a definite [measurable] damage, or a definite risk of damage, either to an individual or to the public, the case is taken out of the province of liberty and placed in that of morality or law." However, as long as the action (or omission) neither violates a specific duty nor harms any person but the perpetrator himself, "the inconvenience is one which society can afford to bear, for the sake of the greater good of human freedom."

Finally, says Mill, we cannot forget the strongest argument against social interference in the lives of individuals: *the position of the majority may be wrong*. People often feel they are being injured simply because of their strong distaste for the life-choices of others and therefore feel justified in sanctioning the offensive action, as seen in the prohibition of alcohol and attacks on certain religious customs. However, such cases call for discussion and persuasion in preference to legal or social coercion.

V. Applications

In what areas, then, *should* a society sacrifice individual freedom to governmental constraints? The results of competition, for example, should not be considered injurious, because freedom of trade contributes to the good of all people.

Two undisputed functions of government are the prevention and punishment of crime. However, the *preventive* function can also serve as a powerful tool for the *oppression* of liberty. Almost any action (dancing, playing chess in a park . . .) could be construed as *potentially* fostering delinquency. Therefore, only when criminality (by definition, "harm to others") is the *only* possible outcome of an action should the action be legitimately constrained.

Finally, the State is obliged to retain vigilant watch over situations where one person has assumed legal control over others. In the most prevalent cases of Mill's time—where husbands legally controlled wives, and parents controlled children—the State actually exercised few constraints. The despotic power of husbands over wives should have been addressed by giving women all the rights of men. In the case of children, fathers and mothers should have been legally compelled to see that they are protected, fed, clothed and educated.

If anything, Mill's contention that "the individual is the locus of value" resounds even louder today than in the mid-nineteenth century when *On Liberty* was written. Contemporary arguments over recreational drugs, abortion, pornography, gun control, homosexuality, and the right to die make Mill's treatise vital reading for anyone who wants to join thoughtfully in the modern debate over social constraint and personal liberty.

CIVIL DISOBEDIENCE

Henry David Thoreau
(1817 - 1862)

An essential tenet of Henry David Thoreau's *Civil Disobedience* entails breaking a law for the *sake* of that law. Thoreau spoke out firmly in favor of individuals acting freely, according to the dictates of their own ideas of right and wrong, without governmental interference.

In the late 1830's, Abraham Lincoln observed that "whenever vicious persons were permitted . . . to burn churches . . . shoot editors, and hang unpleasant or obnoxious persons . . . with impunity, the . . . government can not last." Thoreau was no doubt aware of these words, but he nonetheless made his own words known, and was briefly jailed for his beliefs. The author believed that any control by the government was objectionable, no matter the issue on which that control was exercised.

Thoreau, in his famous 1848 essay *On Civil Disobedience*, began his discourse with the motto, "That government is best which governs least." Even further, Thoreau maintained, "That government is best which governs not at all." He cited inexpedience, or imprudence, as a flaw of governments, and warned against any need of a standing army, which is "only an arm of the standing government . . . Witness the present Mexican war, the work of comparatively few individuals using the standing government as its tool; for, in the outset, the people would not have consented to this measure." Thoreau observed the American government and reported, "what is it but a tradition, though a recent one, endeavoring to transmit itself unimpaired to posterity, but each instant losing some of its integrity?" Governments in general, he said,

. . . *show thus how successfully men can be imposed on, even impose on themselves, for their own advantage . . . It does not keep the country free. It does not settle the West. It does not educate. The character inherent in the American people has done all that has been accomplished; and it would have done somewhat more, if the government had not sometimes got in the way. For government is an expedient by which men would fain succeed in letting one another alone; and, as has been said, when it is most expedient, the governed are most let alone by it.*

"But," Thoreau adds, "to speak practically and as a citizen, unlike those who call themselves no-government men, I ask for, not *at once* no government, but at once a better government. Let every man make known what kind of government would command his respect, and that will be one step toward obtaining it."

Thoreau described "a better government" as one that freely answered to no one, not even the majority. He asked: "Can there be a government in which majorities do not virtually decide right or wrong, but conscience?—in which majorities decide only those questions to which the rule of expediency is applicable?" Thoreau asked, "Must the citizen ever for a moment, or in the least degree, resign his conscience to the legislator? Why has every man a conscience, then? I think that we should be men first, and subjects afterward."

Those who are state soldiers Thoreau termed "wooden men," who serve the state "not as men . . . but as machines, with their bodies." Still others are subjects of the mind: " . . . most legislators, politicians, lawyers, ministers and officeholders . . . serve the state chiefly with their heads; and, as they rarely make any moral distinctions, they are as likely to serve the Devil, without *intending* it, as God." The exceptions are the very few heroes, patriots, martyrs, and reformers who "serve the state with their consciences also, and so necessarily resist it for the most part; and they are commonly treated as enemies by it." Therefore, "he who gives himself entirely to his fellowmen appears to them useless and selfish; but he who gives himself partially to them is pronounced a benefactor and philanthropist." With this notion in mind, Thoreau asked:

How does it become a man to behave toward the American government today? I answer, that he cannot without disgrace be associated with it. I cannot for an instant recognize that political organization as my government which is the slave's government also . . . All men recognize the right of revolution, that is, the right to refuse allegiance to, and to resist, the government, when its tyranny or its inefficiency are great and unendurable.

Thoreau recognized that most people of his day did not recognize this problem.

. . . *when a sixth of the population of a nation which has undertaken to be the refuge of liberty are slaves, and a whole country is unjustly overrun and conquered by a foreign army, and subjected to military law, I think that is not too soon for honest men to rebel and revolutionize. What makes this duty the more urgent is the fact that the country so overrun is not our own, but ours is the invading country.*

Thoreau went on to remind citizens of their duty:

There are thousands who are in opinion opposed to slavery and to the [Mexican] war, who yet in effect do nothing to put an end to them . . . They hesitate, and they regret, and sometimes they petition; but they do nothing in earnest and with effect. They will wait, well disposed, for others to remedy the evil . . . At most, they give only a cheap vote, and a feeble countenance and God-speed, to the right, as it goes by them.

Thoreau concludes that "all voting is a sort of gaming . . . It is only expressing to men feebly your desire that it should prevail . . . A wise man will not leave the right to the mercy of chance, nor wish it to prevail through the power of the majority."

On the subject of obedience to law, Thoreau makes it clear that people should refuse to submit to any law they believe is unjust:

Unjust laws exist: shall we be content to obey them, or shall we endeavor to amend them, and obey them until we have succeeded, or shall we transgress them at once? Men generally, under such a government as this, think that they ought to wait until they have persuaded the majority to alter them. They think that, if they should resist, the remedy would be worse than the evil. But it is the fault of the government itself that the remedy is worse than the evil. It makes it worse.

This then, is a cause for civil disobedience. "If the injustice is part of the necessary friction of the machine of government," Thoreau says, "let it go, . . . : perchance it will wear smooth—certainly the machine will wear out . . . .but if it is of such a nature that it requires you to be an injustice to another, then, I say *break the law*. Let your life be a counter friction to stop the machine." This passive resistance theory is at the heart of *Civil Disobedience.*

Having defined his theory of when a law should rightly be disobeyed, Thoreau focuses his attention on tax-gatherers "If a thousand men were not to pay their tax-bills this year, that would not be a violent and bloody measure, as it would be to pay them, and enable the State to commit violence and shed innocent blood. This is, in fact, the definition of a peaceable revolution, if any such is possible."

For six years, Thoreau paid no poll-taxes, although he admitted: "I have never declined paying the highway tax, because I am desirous of being a good neighbor as I am of being a bad subject; and, as for supporting schools, I am doing my part to edu-

cate my fellow countrymen now".

For failing to pay his taxes, Thoreau was jailed for one night. This led to his rejoinder, "Under a government which imprisons any unjustly, the true place for a just man is also a prison."

Finally, Thoreau is prompted to proclaim: "I, Henry Thoreau, do not wish to be regarded as a member of any incorporated society which I have not joined. I simply wish to refuse allegiance to the State, to withdraw and stand aloof from it effectually . . . In fact, I quietly declare war with the State, after my fashion, though I will still make what use and get what advantage of her I can, as is usual in such cases."

Thoreau was insistent that he "did not wish to quarrel with any man or nation"; he simply wanted change, though he did not expect it from statesmen and legislators who "speak of moving society, but have no resting place without it."

He declared: "There will never be a really free and enlightened State until the State comes to recognize the individual as a higher and independent power, from which all its own power and authority are derived, and treats him accordingly."

THE SICKNESS UNTO DEATH

by
Soren Kierkegaard
(1813 - 1855)

Danish philosopher Soren Kierkegaard has occasionally been called "the Melancholy Dane," "the Danish Socrates," and "the Father of Modern Existentialism."

Kierkegaard was raised in a stern Christian environment in which he reacted against orthodox religions and official philosophies. Although he considered himself a Christian, on his deathbed he refused last rites from a representative of the Lutheran church, the state's religious organization.

The Sickness unto Death (published in 1848, and, curiously, penned under the pseudonym "Anti-Climacus" with Kierkegaard listing himself as editor) reflects Kierkegaard's intellectual and spiritual maturity. Subtitled "A Christian Psychological Exposition," this work represents his investigation into the corruption of human nature—commonly known as "sin." Kierkegaard, however, maintaining a "psychological" viewpoint, chose to employ the term "despair" instead.

For Kierkegaard, man can only achieve a truly authentic existence by becoming a true Christian. He sees "Christianity" as the only cure for the disease which afflicts the soul of every man and woman: despair.

Kierkegaard, it should be noted, was another of the philosophers for whom clear, simple writing did not come naturally. Hence, the notorious opening paragraph of *The Sickness unto Death:*

Man is spirit. But what is spirit? Spirit is the self. But what is the self? The self is a relation which relates itself to its own self, or it is that in the relation which accounts for it that the relation relates itself to its own self; the self is not the relation but consists in the fact that the relation relates to its own self. Man is a synthesis of the infinite and the finite, of the temporal and the eternal, of freedom and necessity, in short it is a synthesis. A synthesis is a relation between two factors. So regarded, man is not yet a self.

Text Overview:

Kierkegaard starts out by explaining that Christianity views death not as the last event for a person, but rather as merely a small event within the all-encompassing eternal life. The "natural man" shudders at death, though it is actually not dreadful. Man is ignorant of what is really horrible and therefore does not shudder at the truly dreadful.

Only Christians know what is meant by "the sickness unto death." Acquiring a courage not possessed by the natural man, religious men face with fortitude the fear of this truly dreadful "sickness."

The true sickness unto death consists of despair (sin). And despair is a sickness in the self. The specific despair that is examined in the text is despair at "willing to be oneself." It is man's will to "tear his self away from the Power which constituted it." The "torment of despair," in fact, is precisely not being "able to die."

According to Kierkegaard, man is a spirit,

and when we speak of spirit, we actually mean "self." Kierkegaard asserts that the self is a composite of man's spirit and a higher power, and that the nature of the spirit rests in the relationship between the self and that power.

Therefore, man doesn't have the power to abolish despair alone. In trying to do so, he is actually conveying himself higher and higher into a "rising fever" of despair:

. . . The dying of despair transforms itself constantly into a living [entity] . . . The despairing man cannot die; no more than 'the dagger can slay thoughts' can despair consume the eternal thing, the self, which is the ground of despair, "whose worm dieth not, and whose fire is not quenched."

Sensing despair is both an advantage and a drawback. It is man's advantage over animals—distinguishing him far more than his erect posture—for it indicates his loftiness of spirit. An understanding of his sinfulness is also the Christian's advantage over the "natural man," since he can be healed of this sickness. Yet despair is also the most miserable misfortune. Man possesses the ability to ascend, as well as the ability to fall.

The origin of despair is God's permission to let man be aware of the relationship between himself and God's power. When man realizes the nature of the relationship, that God is power and man is merely spirit, he despairs.

Despair must be actualized each moment from possibility, it is constantly in the present, and consequently the despairer is responsible for each instant of his despair.

Literally, "sickness unto death" means a serious illness—the end of which is death.

. . . This sickness in the self is the sickness unto death. The despairing man is mortally ill. In an entirely different sense than can appropriately be said of any disease, we may say that the sickness has attacked the noblest part; and yet the man cannot die. Death is not the last phase of the sickness, but death is continually the last. To be delivered from the sickness of death is an impossibility, for the sickness and its torment—and death—consist in not being able to die. This is the situation of despair . . .

For Christians, as opposed to the natural man, there is no corporeal sickness unto death, since death itself is a transition into life.

In the most strict sense of the word, "despair" is the opposite of bodily death, for it means not to be *able* to die. It is *spiritual* death, or death of the self. Yet it does not mean "hope of life," either. Sickness unto death implies total hopelessness, since it involves the *absence* of hope of something better, that can be achieved through the traditional Christian notion of death, such as eternal life in the presence of God.

Despair is a self-consumption in which the despairer is not able to do what he wishes: namely, to consume himself. This is the torment of the despairer. Seemingly, he is despairing of something outside himself; actually, he is despairing of himself. He can neither get rid of himself nor possess himself.

What the despairer really yearns for is to break away from the Power which constitutes it. This Power, however, is stronger than he, and it compels him to be the self he does not want to be.

This sickness of "sin," is universal. Just as there is perhaps not a single human being who enjoys perfect bodily health, there is not a single individual outside of Christianity who is not in despair—unless he is a *true* Christian.

The common view is that most men are not wallowing in despair; despair is considered a rare phenomenon. But, in fact, the exact opposite is true: the person who is not in despair is a rare exception. The common view overlooks the important reality that one form of despair is not to be aware of it. In other words, we sin simply by ignoring our sins. In a word, most people never become aware of themselves in a spiritual sense, "for their sensuous nature is generally predominant over their intellectuality," and, because of this, the majority of men live in despair.

The "self" is a synthesis of the finite and the infinite. At each moment of its existence, the self is in the process of becoming whole. If it does not become whole, it remains in despair. The process by which the self fulfills the task of becoming itself, consists in moving away from oneself infinitely by the process of becoming aware of one's spirituality, then in returning to oneself infinitely by seeing through natural eyes.

But, in addition to the factors of the infinite and the finite in the determination of the self, are the factors of "possibility" and "necessity." A self without either possibility or necessity is in despair: "The despair of possibility is due to the lack of necessity" and "the despair of necessity is due to lack of possibility."

There is also the "despair which is not conscious that it is despair." Despair is negativity, while lack of awareness of it develops "additional aggravation." Unawareness not only prevents the removal of despair, but may even be the most dangerous form of despair; the person, through his unconsciousness of it, has lost his chance of finding out about his state, and thus he is trapped in the jaws of despair.

"Historical paganism and paganism within Christendom" are of this unconscious type of despair, since any human existence which is not conscious of itself as a spirit—which is not "grounded transparently in God but obscurely reposes" in some abstract concepts or in a consideration of its own inexplicable being—is filled with despair. Paganism within Christendom is even worse than historical paganism because it amounts to renunciation of Christianity.

For a man to become conscious of his despair, a "true conception of what despair is" must be acquired. This added degree of consciousness in turn can intensify despair until attitudes and behaviors can be changed in conformity to truth. On the other hand, if he remains consciously entrenched in sin, his despair is heightened even more:

In the same degree that a man has a truer conception of despair while still remaining in it, and in

the same degree that he is more conscious of being in despair, in that same degree his despair is more intense. He who, with the consciousness that suicide is despair, and to that extent with the true conception of what despair is, then commits suicide—that man has a more intense despair than the man who commits suicide without having the true conception that suicide is despair.

"Despair is sin." And sin is despair before God. The borderline between despair and sin could be termed a "poet-existence." The poet, finding himself in the presence of God, would gladly be himself; he feels love for God, and God is his only comfort in his torment. Yet, since he loves his torment (sins), he will not let go of the torment.

Sin committed in the presence of God infinitely increases the degree of its malice. Sin, Kierkegaard asserts, is not wildness of the flesh, but is the spirit's consent to it; sin is conscious disobedience and is therefore of a spiritual character.

The opposite of sin is faith. The faithful man will follow God's teachings, strictly adhere to them, be aware of his own imperfections (despair) and faithfully rely on his own will and God's grace to remove them from him.

Socrates defined sin as ignorance. But sin lies not in the intellect but in the will. Socrates' definition, says Kierkegaard, misses the essential meaning of sin; his Greek intellectualism was too aesthetic to grasp the concept that a person could *know* what was right and yet *do* what was wrong. Therein, Kierkegaard adds, lies the guilt of many modern Christians and the irony of their behavior: that they understand what is right, but do not act accordingly.

In addition to the aforementioned types of sins, there are many others:

- The sin of remaining in sin.
- "The sin of despairing over one's sin . . . " since there is nothing more miserable than a devil who despairs and thereby rejects repentance and grace.
- "The sin of despairing of the forgiveness of Sin."
- "The sin of abandoning Christianity . . . of declaring it a falsehood," which is the peak of sin.

One cannot always drag oneself out of despair; but one can *always* receive succor from God. Sadly, however, those who are most need of God's assistance, suffering to the extreme in their sins, are those who most resist:

The situation is this. A sufferer has one or more ways in which he would be glad to be helped. If he is helped thus, he is willing to be helped. But when in a deeper sense it becomes seriousness with this thing of needing help, especially from a higher or from the highest source—this humiliation of having to accept help unconditionally and in any way, the humiliation of becoming nothing in the hand of the Helper for whom all things are possible . . . —ah, there are doubtless many sufferings, even protracted and agonizing sufferings, at which the self does not wince to this extent, and which therefore at bottom it prefers to retain and to be itself.

BEYOND GOOD AND EVIL: PRELUDE TO A PHILOSOPHY OF THE FUTURE

by Friedrich Nietzsche (1844-1900)

Published in 1886, Nietzsche's *Beyond Good and Evil* is an exposition of his arguments concerning the nature and function of truth, the problems of morality, and the importance of the strong will. At times, these arguments scathingly criticize the very foundations of Western thought and morality, held since the time of Plato.

Nietzsche's assertion that excellence in human beings is achieved through harnessing one's own *Will to Power* is a central theme throughout the work. The will to power is a way of achieving power over the self by acting on one's natural desires, impulses, and beliefs. The will to power affirms life through action; it is the motivation to live a life unencumbered by the rules of others.

Nietzsche condemns the practice of philosophies of judging the objects of analysis to be either "true" or "false," "right" or "wrong." This type of judgement is based on the assumption that absolute truth and morality *do* exist in the world, which Nietzsche denies. Thus, will to power represents the strength to deny the existence of universal truth and allow the individual to flourish.

Truth

Philosophers have long assumed the existence of opposite values: truth vs. error, good vs. evil, selflessness vs. selfishness. Philosophers have found reasons to doubt most everything, but they have not yet doubted the existence of opposites. But what proof is there that opposite values *are* real?

"Truth" exists only as we "will" it to exist. "For all the value that the true, the truthful, the selfless may deserve, it would still be possible that a higher and more fundamental value for life might have to be ascribed to deception, selfishness, and lust." To recognize *deception* as a condition of life equal to truth, means resisting traditional values of stability and absolute truth in a dangerous way.

The basis for evaluating a philosophy for living should not be whether it is true or false, but the strength of the *will* behind it . . , "to what extent is it life-promoting, life-preserving, species-preserving, perhaps even species-cultivating?" These are the desireable criteria for living which Nietzsche prescribes. Positing a universal good and a fixed truth (what is "true" holds for all people), as Plato did, is to deny the individual perspective, the basic condition of all life. For Nietzsche, such "fixed" philosophy has been the most damaging dogmatism in European civilization.

The desire to posit philosophical "truths" is not fundamentally a desire for knowledge, but for obtaining *mastery*. "Every philosophy also conceals a philosophy; every opinion is also a hideout, every word also a mask." Logic and science attempt to create order in the world by simplifying it. The desire for knowledge therefore leads, paradoxically, to falsification; to describe the multiplicity of the world in terms of singularity (prescribed language, mathematics and logics) is merely an attempt to unite and stabilize its randomness and change—to dominate.

While such domination makes life predictable, it is also a negation of the true essence of life. The desire to *control* one's fate demands that one have knowledge about the world. Thus, people create "truths" out of insecurity, ignoring the real, unpredictable nature of the world.

Philosophers continually adopt popular prejudices, then exaggerate them, failing to recognize that all knowledge is an interpretation, not an explanation, of the world. There are no "immediate certainties" such as in Descartes' assertion "I think, therefore I am." Even the word "I" pushes us to assume that the existence of an ego and its role as a cause are self-evident. The word "I" assumes simplicity of the self. Even basic concepts like cause and effect are interpretations, not concrete facts. It is too easy to be seduced by assumptions. *Nothing* is self-evident; everything that exists for us exists only as an act of will, an interpretation.

"It is no more than a moral prejudice that truth is worth more than mere appearance; it is even the worst proved assumption there is in the world." Why do we believe there are only certain things about the world which are true, and what is it that makes us think we have knowledge of them? Nietzsche seeks to destroy the dichotomy between truth and falsity by claiming that *all* truths are created. The difference between truths discovered by the individual and truths created by society is that of choosing to will over oneself, or blindly following the dictates of others. That a "doctrine for living" should result in a certain amount of control or societal approval does not make it correct; indeed, such a doctrine is harmful in the highest degree. "Supposing that this also is only interpretation—and you will be eager enough to make that objection?—well, so much the better."

Morality

Like universal truths, universal morality destroys the life of the individual. Moral judgements do not affirm, but deny the importance of the will, and are therefore "a bit of tyranny against nature." Moral codes are recipes for dominating the individual's unique inclinations. Nietzsche describes the morals of Christianity as a "religious neurosis": the controlling of weak individuals by prescribing a doctrine which teaches meekness and humility as ideal behaviors.

The urge to transcend this world and the temporal life is yet another result of weakness. "Sick religions," such as Christianity, are pervaded by a fear that there is no ultimate meaning, unity, goal, or purpose in life. Therefore, the promise of an eternal hereafter is to quell the fears of the weak, to give them a goal, and a sense of security that the universe is a place where good is rewarded.

The world is what it *is*, claims Nietzsche, not what we choose to describe it as being. The fear of meaninglessness leads those who are weak in spirit—weak in will—to cling to religion as the source of significance or value, thereby pacifying their fears. Religion inverts "love of the earthly and of dominion over the earth into hatred of the earth and the earthly." The temporal world is only given value because of something *outside* it—God, "truth," the divine plan, the after-life. Hence, the temporal world is debased, when in fact it should be celebrated, enjoyed without God. "Christianity," Nietzsche claims, "is Platonism for the people."

Master Mentality and Slave Mentality

Two fundamental types of mentality spring from the social conditions in which people exist: the *rulers* and the *ruled*. The ruling group determines for society what is good, and thereby defines what the society values. Hence, a noble person experiences himself as the most virtuous and powerful since he rules by his own moral beliefs—as he wills.

The slave mentality describes most common individuals. Slaves perform out of a sense of moral obedience—they passively obey. Yet, simultaneously, slaves despise their masters because they covet the power and influence their masters wield. From this unconscious desire arises the impulse to "level": to democratize, making everyone equal either in the eyes of God or the law. The slave mentality thus describes "Evil" as individual power and strength, while "Good" is seen as that which is nonthreatening: equality, humility, modesty, compassion, and charity. This is the morality of herd animals. But for Nietzsche, masters are equally as weak as slaves, for they derive their strength only from *power over others*. True power is power over the individual self, the power to impose one's will on the world, not in acts of tyranny, but in self affirmation. Christian morality is a slave mentality that placates the weak and serves the interests of the manipulative. The very notion of "sin" (that "Thou shalt not . . . ") contradicts the will to power: to become, create, act, and flourish.

What the slave considers "evil" is that which elevates the individual above the group. However, the desire that all people be equal, both socially and spiritually, is a corruption of reality. A favored group that uses its will and creative drive will naturally flourish more fully.

The Will to Power

"The most high-spirited, alive, and world-affirming human being who has not only come to terms and learned to get along with whatever was and is, but who wants to have what was and is repeated to all eternity," this is the *will to power*. "The great epochs of our

life come when we gain the courage to rechristen our evil as what is best in us." In short, life must be affirmed by going beyond the values of good and evil. Liberation of the will requires overcoming previously held "eternal values," and the possibility of embracing deception, lust, selfishness and evil as being equally desirable as truth, chastity, and goodness.

Free Spirits

"In all desire to know there is a drop of cruelty." To be a true philosopher, a "free spirit," is to insist on profundity, multiplicity and thoroughness. This "extravagant honesty" is somehow cruel, something which inevitably results in the denigration of the free spirit by the common people. To be a "free spirit" is to sacrifice comfort and security for the higher goal of knowledge.

Philosophers

Most philosophers of the past have served as mere "philosophical laborers," studying values which have long been assumed to be truths. Genuine philosophers, on the other hand, are commanders and legislators. They *create* values. Their "knowing" is creating; their thirst for their own truth *is* the will to power. "A philosopher has nothing less than a right to `bad character,' as the being who has so far always been fooled best on earth; he has a duty to suspicion today, to squint maliciously out of every abyss of suspicion."

As moral theory, Nietzsche's philosophy is revolutionary. He is frequently placed alongside Marx and Freud as one of the three greatest influences on contemporary social theory. He has particularly had strong sway on the contemporary French philosophers Michel Foucault and Jacques Derrida. For these reasons, an understanding of Nietzsche is central to any perception of recent (and controversial) theories on the nature and function of language, knowledge, truth and value.

Nietzsche's prose is both beautiful and clever. His brief aphorisms and unrestrained critiques of Socrates, Plato, Hobbes, Hume, Locke, Descartes, and Kant are revealing and passionate. However, Nietzsche calls into question so many of the values which are accepted by Western civilization that his philosophy is often subject to intense criticism.

Outside of philosophy proper, his scathing critiques of Christianity (such as his infamous proclamation that "God is dead") and political democracy have won him many enemies. For contemporary readers, Nietzsche's extended tirades against women and his elitism can prove to be somewhat of a turn-off. The question of whether his misogyny can be separated from the "substance" of his philosophy is still open to debate. We need not forgive his elitist attitudes, but must place them in the context of the work. Finally, the praise for the quality of the will of the Jewish people that is found in this book should serve to debunk the Nazi's blatant misinterpretation of Nietzsche's philosophy to justify anti-Semitic notions and actions.

THE WEALTH OF NATIONS

by
Adam Smith
(1723 - 1790)

Adam Smith spent over a decade in the research and writing of his classic treatise, *An Inquiry Into the Nature and Causes of the Wealth of Nations,* the first complete work on political economy. The book addresses such issues as the relationship between individual freedom and social order and the mechanisms governing economics. Responding to governmental systems of economic control (such as the tariffs and other limitations the British government had imposed on free trade in his time), Smith was in close accord with sentiments of the age. Born in Kirkcaldy, Scotland, he studied at the University of Glasgow and Oxford, becoming a full professor at Glasgow. He later moved to France, where he began writing Wealth of Nations, and, upon returning to England, devoted the next ten years to the work. His theme of economic liberty (emancipation of economic interests from the tyranny of custom, tradition and religion) became the standard doctrine of *laissez-faire* economics (an economy without governmental restraints, regulated solely by self-interest and competition).

In **Wealth of Nations,** published in 1776, Smith presents a unified social theory, a blueprint for a free market economy where individuals could accumulate wealth according to their own desires. Although his day's mercantilists (those subscribing to an ideology of the accumulation of national wealth in gold via trade) were powerfully attracted to Smith's message conveying the necessity of free trade among nations, this was only one element in the emerging picture of a capitalist economy. Self-interested pursuit of profit is sanctioned as an activity that, when unregulated, becomes productive and beneficial for the entire populace in that it works for the general, overall good. Smith advocates a policy of free trade among all nations and endeavors to separate economic interests from governmental control. *The Wealth of Nations* represents the first comprehensive description of the economic system known today as "capitalism."

Text Overview:

Nature of Wealth

Smith's concern is with national as well as individual prosperity; he therefore first inquires as to the *nature* and *causes* of wealth. Wealth is redefined from the mercantilist concept of gold and silver to the "necessaries and conveniences" of life. According to Smith, wealth consists of all the goods and services that all people consume (a radical notion for the time.)

Labor is the "source of value." The wealth of a nation is dependent on one of two things: either upon the products of its labor, or what is purchased with its output. And a *division of labor* is the easiest route toward increasing the productive power of labor.

Smith example of an eighteenth-century pin factory illustrates the point, where "the important business of making a pin is . . . divided into about eighteen distinct operations." As a result of such a labor-divided system, workers are able to become more skillful and efficient at their individual tasks. "It is the great multiplication of the productions of all the different arts, in consequence of the division of labour," Smith explains, "which occasions, in a well-governed society, that universal opulence which extends itself to the lowest ranks of the people." Even at the lowest ranks, it is human nature to have "the propensity to truck, barter, and exchange one thing for another." In other words, people have a natural inclination to pursue their own self-interests in commerce and trade—an apparent hindrance to human progress and social order. However, individualism in truth actually leads to order and progress. In order to make money, people produce things that others are willing to buy. When buyers and sellers meet in the marketplace, a pattern of production and *voluntary cooperation* results, and overall social harmony is enhanced.

Voluntary cooperation, which brings about the maximum benefits for all, is a result of the inherent self-interest of human beings. Voluntary cooperation occurs when "we address ourselves, not to their humanity but to their self-love, and never talk to them of our own necessities but their advantages." Thus, self-interest, the motivating force in a free market system, unintentionally promotes the *common interest*, wherein each individual helps others achieve their own ends, "as if by an *invisible-hand.*"

Use vs. Exchange Value

Smith writes of the difference between *use* value and *exchange value:* "The things which have the greatest value in use have frequently little or no value in exchange; and on the contrary, those which have the greatest value in exchange have frequently little or no value in use. Nothing is more useful than water: but it will purchase scarce anything; scarce anything can be had in exchange for it. A diamond, on the contrary, has scarce any value in use; but a very great quantity of other goods may frequently be had in exchange for it." So, for the producer of goods, "use value" was unimportant. His only interest was in exchanging the product of his labor for the things he needed for sustenance.

Capital is explained by referring to the correlation between productive and unproductive labor. "Productive" labor adds to the value of something, whereas "unproductive" labor does not. For instance, the product/labor of a manufacturer increases the value of the material used in its production; a menial servant's labor, on the other hand, does not increase the employer's value because there is no product. Crises result when government spending diverts resources to unproductive labor. "Great nations are never impoverished by private, though they sometimes are by public prodigality and misconduct." Therefore, when money is spent, it should be spent on something of value. The ideal is a "progressive state, while the society is advancing to the further acquisition." Essentially, accumulation of wealth is crucial to social prosperity and the elimination of poverty.

Cooperation naturally occurs between people engaged in trade. At the stage of production, cooperation is an essential component of the division of labor; at the time of exchange, it assures a balance in the distribution of income. The factory owner makes a profit (the difference between the selling price and the costs of production i.e. materials, labor, and rent), whereupon these profits would be used to further expand production. This expansion would in turn create more jobs and thus the national income—wealth of nations—would grow.

Production and distribution are further unified by the *principle of natural liberty*, which expresses in the idea of a *natural price* a "central price, to which the prices of all commodities are continually gravitating." Pricing quickly arrives at an equilibrium, where "the quantity brought to market is just sufficient to supply the effectual demand and no more."

Perfect liberty ensues when the natural price—"or the price of free competition"—is exactly equal to the total costs of wages, profits and rents expended in the production process. *Supply and demand* principles were introduced when Smith asserted that the market price (actual selling price) increased when the quantity of a commodity brought to market fell short of demand. But, while a market price can endure above the natural price, it "can seldom continue long below its natural price."

As prices plummet, the value of whatever is being sold *exceeds* what the market will pay. Thus, sellers "immediately withdraw either so much land, or so much labour, or so much stock, from being employed about it, that the quantity brought to market would soon be no more than sufficient to supply the effectual demand. Its market price, therefore, would soon rise to the natural price."

Class Structure
In Smith's day, capitalist relations resulted in the formation of a class structure in which the distribution of income depended upon the appropriation of *land, labor, and capital*. "In this state of things, the whole product of labour does not always belong to the labourer. He must in most cases share it with the owner of the stock which employs him." With the buying up of private property, "the landlords, like all other men, love to reap where they never sowed, and demand a rent even for its natural produce."

Smith could see the class gulf widening, with the accumulation of capital serving as an added profit-making vehicle for the capitalist.

This was acceptable to Smith, however, in light of the proper social purpose of capital, which is to maintain production: "To maintain and augment the stock which may be reserved for immediate consumption, is the sole end and purpose both of fixed and circulating capitals. It is this stock which feeds, clothes, and lodges the people. Their riches or poverty depends upon the abundant or sparing supplies which those two capitals can afford to the stock reserved for immediate consumption." Unrestrained accumulation, "free trade," and a "self-regulating economy," according to Smith, is therefore in the best interest of society; so long as expenditures are made for "productive labor," for replacing capital goods, or for producing a capitalist surplus, a "hands off" policy of *economic liberalism* is preferred.

Principle of Free Competition
Competition is the salient force in a freely adjusting market. Unimpeded by governmental regulations, competition assures the accumulation process. A decline in competition is signaled by an increase in profits and a resulting decrease in accumulation. Without the restraints of government, the simple system of natural liberty regulates commercial activity. Individuals, so long as they do not violate the laws of justice, are perfectly free to pursue their own best interests. The validity of such interests cannot be judged by government, since they are known best by the individual.

Minimal government involvement is needed in a system dependent upon individual decisions and self-interest. Smith writes that the State should be dismissed from the "duty of superintending the industry of private people . . . " There are, of course, limited governmental functions essential to maintaining the system of voluntary cooperation. These include: an exact administration of justice, protection of individuals and their private property, provisions for the national defense, supply of public works, and support for education to those lacking sufficient means. Institutional funding (taxes) should be derived from either state or personal revenue, the sources of which are rents, profits and wages. This, Smith argues, constitutes an equitable, certain, convenient and economical system of taxation, hence facilitating revenue collection.

Synthesizing the important economic theories of his day, Adam Smith, "father of modern economics," presents an outline capitalism and the workings of a free market. Since his time, nations have experienced the devastating effects of monopoly, as well as the workers' demise during the Industrial Revolution. Smith had no historical framework for anticipating these events, nor the problems of over-accumulation. Although his ideas have had a highly significant effect on the evolution of economic thought, he—like every other economist that, to date, has followed—was yet unable to provide a satisfactory guide for a fair and just distribution of income.

THE COMMUNIST MANIFESTO

by
Karl Marx
(1818-1883)

The *Communist Manifesto*, first published in 1848, comprises a statement of the basic tenets of mid-nineteenth century communism. The particular forms of communism (Stalinism, Maoism, etc.) implemented in the former Soviet Union, China and elsewhere, along with the general hostility toward communism in the West, have resulted in a somewhat distorted understanding of communism as first envisioned by Karl Marx (1818 - 1883). The importance of returning to the original document is therefore essential for a clear understanding of Marx's ideology.

The Manifesto was commissioned by the Congress of the Communist League to serve as their party platform. Friedrich Engels (1820-1895), a friend and collaborator of Marx, contributed many of the ideas and earlier drafts from which Marx worked, and is therefore often named as co-author. As a propaganda pamphlet, the Manifesto differs substantially in terms of both style and substance from the bulk of Marx and Engels' writings on social and economic theory. Hence, it is important to keep in mind that these writings—which counter some of the common conceptions about Marxism while reaffirming others—is not a sole paradigm of Marx's thought, though it is arguably the most influential of his works.

Text Overview:

"There is a spectre haunting Europe—the spectre of Communism." Parties of opposition are most often accused of being communistic. Given this, members of oppositional parties must accept two things. First, acknowledge communism as a power. Second, "Communists should openly, in the face of the whole world, publish their views, their aims, their tendencies, and meet this nursery tale of the Spectre of Communism with a Manifesto of the party itself."

Part I: Bourgeois and Proletarians

All of recorded history can be viewed in terms a series of class struggles. In the modern age, this struggle takes place between the *bourgeoisie* and the *proletariat*. "By bourgeoisie is meant the class of modern Capitalists, owners of the means of social production and employers of wage labor." The bourgeois property owners, due to their possession of material wealth, stand in power over the working-class proletarians. The proletariat is "the class of modern wage laborers who, having no means of production of their own, are reduced to selling their labor power in order to live."

- **The Bourgeoisie.** The establishment of colonies around the world brought about the growth and change of European commerce and industry. The feudal system of guild-monopoly (an organized community of self-employed artisans and craftspeople) was replaced by a manufacturing system in which the middle-classes employed workers, creating a *division of labor* (breaking down the manufacturing process into a number of specialized jobs for the means of mass production). Following the growth of markets in Europe and around the world, manufacturing became mechanized and steam-powered, speeding the replacement of the "petit bourgeois" (small shop owners) by modern factory owners and laborers. This large-scale, mechanized mode of production we call "Modern Industry."

As modern means of production evolved, new social structures arose.

The bourgeoisie has since put an end to all previous forms of social relations. So-called "natural" relations—such as the feudal system of lord and serf—have been torn asunder, leaving only "naked self-interest," the callousness of "cash payment," or as Engels aptly puts it: "social relations have been reduced to a cold cash nexus." Personal worth is now measured in terms of exchange value. "In one word, for exploitation, veiled by religious and political illusions, it has substituted naked, shameless, direct, brutal exploitation," euphemistically termed "free competition" or "free trade."

Periodic commercial crises (recession, depressions), most commonly brought on by over-production, regularly threaten the existence of bourgeois society. This over-production (an excess of products above any demand for them) reduces the value of bourgeois property, and hence threatens the existence of the bourgeoisie itself. To survive, either productive forces must be destroyed en masse to reduce the quantity of products or new markets must be found on which to dump the excess. This elimination of excessive production capacity revives—temporarily—the products' exchange value, the source of the wealth of the bourgeoisie.

- **The Proletariat.** In a capitalist mode of production, laborers become "a commodity, like every other article of commerce, and are consequently exposed to all the vicissitudes of competition, to all the fluctuations of the market." With the rise of machinery, work becomes more simple and monotonous—in short, unskilled—and hence workers are easily replaced. The more mechanization, the less complex the work, and, in accordance with the laws of the market, the less its value. Working men are replaced by women and children, who can do the work just as well and more cheaply. At the same time, the lower middle-class (the "petty bourgeois": small tradespeople, shopkeepers, craftsmen, farmers) are driven into the proletariat as their means of subsistence become out-dated by Modern Industry.

The increasingly impoverished status under which the proletariat exists calls into question the ability of the bourgeois to rule. In other words, the bourgeois perpetuates and advances the very conditions which will result in its downfall: increasing capital accumulation in the form of increasing industrialization, which simultaneously concentrates masses of workers and worsens their conditions, laying the groundwork for political identification and revolutionary action. Initially, resistance is scattered. But with the development of urban industry, proletarians become concentrated in great numbers, and hence their strength grows. The technological advancement of industry allows for increasing communication and trade unions begin to unite to create a national class struggle. The proletariat becomes a class, and hence a political party.

If the proletariat is to become the ruling class, the structures that support bourgeois rule must be abolished. "Law, morality, religion, are to him so many bourgeois prejudices, behind which lurk in ambush as many bourgeois interests . . . They have nothing of their own to secure and fortify; their mission is to destroy all previous securities for, and insurances of, private property."

Part II: Proletarians and Communists

"The immediate aim of the communists is the same as that of all other proletarian parties: formation of the proletariat into a class, overthrow of bourgeois supremacy, conquest of political power by the proletariat." You say, Marx claims, that we are abolishing private property, freedom, individuality, family, education, nation, etc. To the extent that you mean bourgeois property, bourgeois freedom, bourgeois individuality—you are right. You must realize, he continues, that the bourgeois way is not the only real, "natural" way, as evidenced by any cursory examination of the historical variability of these concepts. Those aspects of religion, morality, philosophy and law that have remained constant have done so only because of the constancy of class antagonisms and the exploitation of one by another. But you take them as the only form of culture, law, society, etc. So when we state our desire to abolish them, you mistake this for the abolition of all culture, all law, all society, all property.

The abolition of private property: this is the summation of the communist position. What distinguishes the communist position is the abolition of *bourgeois* property, not property in general. "Hard-won, self-acquired, self-earned property" is perfectly legitimate. But bourgeois property is won through exploiting workers—by taking the profits of their labor from them without fully compensating them for the value their labor added to the raw materials upon which they worked. "You are horrified at our intending to do away with private property. But in your existing society, private property is already done away with for nine-tenths of the population; its existence for the few is solely due to its non-existence in the hands of the nine-tenths."

"Communism deprives no man of the power to appropriate the products of society: all that it does is to deprive him of the power to subjugate the labor of others by means of such appropriation." This will be accomplished in the following stages:

1. The proletariat will raise itself to the position of the ruling class.

2. Using its political supremacy, the proletariat will wrest all capital from the bourgeoisie. All instruments of production will be centralized in the hands of the proletariat-controlled State.

3. This will ultimately lead to the complete revolutionizing of the modes of production. Inequities in wealth and education will be eliminated.

4. Once class distinctions have disappeared, the public power of the proletariat will lose its political character, for political power "is merely the organized power of one class for suppressing another." Having swept away the conditions for class antagonisms, and the existence of classes generally, the proletariat will have abolished its own supremacy as a class. "We shall have an association, in which the free development of each is the condition for the free development of all."

Part III: Socialist and Communist Literature

Many forms of socialism exist which are not truly revolutionary, but reactionary, backward looking:

• "Feudal Socialism." With the rise of the bourgeoisie, the aristocracy lost its position of supremacy. In order to arouse sympathy, they attacked the bourgeois in the interests of the exploited working class. "But the people, so often as it joined them, saw on their hindquarters the old feudal coats of arms, and deserted with loud and irreverent laughter." Ultimately, the aristocrats are reactionary, not revolutionary, because their complaint is that the bourgeoisie has uprooted society's old order.

• "Petty Bourgeois Socialism." Small shop-owners and farmers have oscillated between being bourgeois and proletariat, but the increase of modern industry and "competition" pushes them evermore into the proletariat. Thus, this class often takes on a socialist tint. However, its socialism is not revolutionary, but reactionary as well; its ultimate goal is the restoration of the guild monopolies and patriarchal relations in agriculture. Its interests are not those of the proletariat.

• "Bourgeois Socialism." This is a construct of "reform socialism," desirous of redressing social grievances and raising the standard of living among the proletariat. This system, however, retains the basic scheme of bourgeois exploitation and, in fact, furthers it by easing the severity of the inequalities that lead to proletariat uprisings.

• "Critical-Utopian Socialism and Communism." This group is critical in orientation; it clearly points to the conditions under which exploitation occurs and attacks every principle of the existing society. It is utopian in that it hopes to achieve, through peaceful means, the transformation to an ideal society. This group becomes trapped in its ideal and rejects revolutionary action. Ultimately, they oppose political action on the part of the proletariat, fearing it will not result in their ideal. And, in the end, fantasy replaces history.

"The proletariat alone is a really revolutionary class."

Part IV: Position of the Communists in Relation to the Various Existing Opposition Parties

In short . . . Communists everywhere support every revolutionary movement against the existing social and political order of things . . . They openly declare that their ends can be attained only by the forcible overthrow of all existing social conditions. Let the ruling classes tremble at a Communist revolution. The proletarians have nothing to lose but their chains. They have a world to win.

Working men of all countries, unite!

THE GENERAL THEORY OF EMPLOYMENT, INTEREST, AND MONEY

by John Maynard Keynes

"To understand my state of mind . . . you have to know that I believe myself to be writing a book on economic theory which will largely revolutionize—not, I suppose at once, but in the course of the next ten years—the way the world thinks about economic problems . . . I can't expect you or anyone else to believe this at the present stage. But for myself I don't merely hope what I say—in my own mind, I'm quite sure."

These words, in the mouth of almost any economist, would, for good reason, seem bombastic. But when John Maynard Keynes made this statement in 1935 he was simply predicting with confidence what he expected, and later proved, to be true. He proposed, and proved, that traditional "supply side" economics does not always function and cannot account for all economic activity. Instead, he theorized on the influence of "demand side" economics, and revolutionized economic theory, especially in the role governments should play during periods of economic depression.

When Keynes' master work, *The General Theory of Employment, Interest, and Money* came out in 1936, it changed the course of Western economy. The book was a bombshell.

John Maynard Keynes, a British economist with a Cambridge education who also held an important post in British government, was regarded as a multi-talented man of genius whose originality was needed to produce a new perspective within modern economics. Outside of his formal work as an economist, he led an active social life, rubbing shoulders with the intellectual elite of his time—Virginia Woolf, George Bernard Shaw, Clive Bell, as well as other famous authors, poets, composers, actors and artists. The author Robert Heilbroner once described him as "a man incapable of doing only one thing at a time." While he was constructing *The General Theory* in his head, he was building a theater in Cambridge with his pocketbook. It was a typical Keynesian venture. Starting at a loss, the theater was in the black in two years, and its artistic success was immense. Keynes was everywhere at the same time: financial backer, ticket taker (at least on one occasion when the clerk failed to show), husband of the leading lady . . . even concessionaire. He attached a restaurant to the theater and closely watched its receipts, graphing them against different types of entertainment to ascertain how food consumption varied with the state of one's humor. He collected and displayed modern art before it was fashionable to do so. He became Director of the Bank of England. He spoke freely with Roosevelt and Churchill, Bernard Shaw, and Pablo Picasso. And he once claimed that he had but one regret in his life—he wished he had "drunk more champagne."

Keynes obviously was far from the stereotypical economist, and when *The General Theory* was published, it ushered in a whole new attitude in economics.

But Keynes' most important work was

hardly written for the masses. The preface of the treatise begins with this warning. "This book is chiefly addressed to my fellow economists. I hope that it will be intelligible to others. But its main purpose is to deal with difficult questions of theory . . . " Then, with content as forbidding as "Let Z be the aggregate supply price of the output from employing N men, the relationship between Z and N being written $Z = o(N)$, which can be called the Aggregate Supply Function," it quickly becomes clear that the text is not for casual reading. It has been described as "an endless desert of economics, algebra, and abstraction, with trackless wastes of differential calculus, and only an oasis here and there of delightfully refreshing prose." Fortunately for us, there have been economists to interpret Keynes' theory and to apply his revolutionary perspectives to our own social and economic situations.

When *The General Theory* appeared, the Great Depression was at its peak, and Western leaders were desperately searching for solutions to revitalize and stabilize the financial systems of their countries.

Text Overview:

There is, Keynes asserts, no safety mechanism to assure that an economy will rebound from depression; despite the conclusions of previous economists, the economy is not like a moving see-saw which will always right itself. Rather, it is like an elevator which could be rising, lowering, or simply standing still at the bottom of a shaft.

Previously, it was held that, caught up in a depression, a citizenry would focus on saving its income, thereby driving interest rates down. With lower interest rates, businesses would be encouraged to once again invest in economic growth. But this reasoning was built upon the assumption that there would be a "flood of savings at the bottom of the trough." Keynes shows how this assumption is false.

What actually tends to happen when a country's economy seriously declines is that its citizens' income contracts and the possibility of saving diminishes. A community simply cannot save as much when it is struggling as when it is prosperous.

Now, the overall effect of such a decline of savings is quite dramatic. It puts the economy in paralysis—a frozen state of economic balance amidst a suffering society. This can be understood through the following line of reasoning: the essential characteristic of a depression is a drop in investments. Since, in a depression, there is not a surplus of savings, interest rates cannot be driven down. Investment will not be encouraged, since the risks increase and the amount of return on investment dips. Consequently, an economy in a depression may very well stay that way—in depression.

Keynes therefore illustrates the ruthless, speculative nature of economies. During a depression, a totally reasonable, accepted theory may be contradicted, unveiling itself as a hoax.

Masses of people can be crying for goods, while the economy refuses to produce. Rather than the result of some kind of cold, immoral attitude on the part of anyone in the business or political community, an economy can only respond to demands which are backed up financially.

This is, in fact, a rather strange situation, like a tragedy in which there is no villain. Society cannot be blamed for saving rather than consuming, since that is a prudent, proven way to manage one's affairs. And, likewise, people involved in business cannot be criticized for refusing to invest if perilous or unfavorable conditions exist. The problem is more mechanical or mathematical than moral.

Meanwhile, a rising segment of unemployed needy simply do not have the ability to make a sparse economy respond since they do not have the resources necessary to generate economic change.

The catastrophe facing America and the whole Western world during its "great depression," says Keynes, boils down to a lack of sufficient investment on the part of business. Thus, he concludes, if business is not able to expand to fill the void, the government must involve itself in order to stimulate the economy.

Investment typically follows a pattern: an initial enthusiasm toward exploiting new opportunities, followed by a period of caution since overexpanding could possibly check growth, and finally a period of inactivity comes about when the market becomes saturated. When this happens, a government must step in to curb the downward trend.

Ideally, government influence would stimulate investment directly, but even the more simple procedure of stimulating *consumption* would prove effectual. "If the Treasury were to fill old bottles with bank notes," Keynes speculates, "bury them at suitable depths in disused coal mines, which are then filled up to the surface with town rubbish, and leave it to private enterprise on well-tried principles of laissez-faire to dig the notes up again . . . there need be no more unemployment, and . . . the real income of the community would probably become a good deal larger than it is. It would, indeed, be more sensible to build houses and the like; but if there are practical difficulties in the way of doing this, the above would be better than nothing."

This is not to say that private enterprise should be pushed out of the market by government. However, it is one of government's roles to provide a "guiding influence on the propensity to consume." Government should only invest enough to awaken the economy, encouraging it to return back towards sufficient growth. Beyond this, "no obvious case is made out for a system of State Socialism which would embrace most of the economic life of the community. It is not the ownership of the instruments of production which it is important for the state to assume." In short, the State should function as a "catalyst" to repair the economy without actually dominating it.

The schools of modern capitalist economic theory center around two major strains of large-scale economic thought. The first is referred to as "classical"; the second is usually termed "Keynesian." It is obvious, therefore, that John Maynard Keynes' work (chiefly his *General Theory*) had a profound effect on how we understand our economic system. Keynes' theory, in fact, has been responsible for the implementation of many major policy shifts in the West, and his ideas sway governmental and private behavior to this day.

Keynes' ideology was largely constructed in response to the classical viewpoint, so his points may be best understood when contrasted with the classical theory. These can be summarized as follows:

1. In the classical perspective the output of an economy is determined by the *level of employment*. Keynes, in contrast, insists that the *demand for goods* is a more important factor.

2. The classical model states that a government's proper role is to concern itself only with the money supply, and to otherwise leave the economy to regulate itself. Keynes believes instead that, when necessary, government should actively involve itself, influencing the demand for goods when there is high unemployment.

3. The classical model claims that *interest rates* are what determine how much people save and—because investment money is drawn from savings—how much is invested. Keynes, on the other hand, argues that it is people's *income level* that determines how much they put into savings and investments.

4. The classical school holds that the *price levels for goods* in an economy are set by the volume of money flowing in the economy. For Keynes, the *costs of producing goods* sets the price.

In the classical perspective—often referred to as "supply-side" economics—the most influential factor on an economy's growth is the quantity of supplies (i.e., how much producers are selling on the market). It is stated that "supply creates its own demand," meaning that producers pay out incomes in order to produce their product and, by so doing, give people money to either spend or invest. Very few people, they argue, will take their earnings and put them in a tin box under the bed; they will either spend them or invest them.

Keynes, on the other hand, is the preeminent "demand-side" economist. He believes that *demand* for goods must be added as an important factor in the economic equation, since demand is a primary force determining whether or not goods are produced.

To this day these two factions represent the major coalitions of economic thought. For example, in the United States in the 1980s we saw the implementation of "Reaganomics," an economic policy largely in line with supply-side economic theory. Many believe that what the middle and late nineties bring to the American and World economies will depend heavily on whether or not a "Keynesian" perspective is brought to the fore.

ON THE PRINCIPLE OF POPULATION

by
Thomas Robert Malthus
(1766 - 1834)

It has been said, that the great question is now at issue, whether man shall henceforth start forwards with accelerated velocity towards illimitable, and hitherto unconceived improvement; or be condemned to a perpetual oscillation between happiness and misery, and after every effort remain still at an immeasurable distance from their wished-for goal.

Against the backdrop of the closing of the eighteenth century—with its gigantic revolutions in science, philosophy, politics, and individual empowerment—Thomas Malthus questions whether the *utopianists* (those who believe in an achievable ideal world) would turn out to be right or whether a revised *status quo* (the "oscillation between happiness and misery") would rule. "It is to be much lamented," he states, "that the writers on each side of this momentous question still keep far aloof from each other." The supporters of the "present order of things" view utopianists as "designing knaves" or "mad-headed enthusiasts," while the utopianists view one who clings to the establishment "as a character who prostitutes his understanding to his interest." In Malthus' time, both sides argued that humanity was becoming an "ostrich," even though men did not show that their necks had been "gradually elongating; that the lips have grown harder and more prominent; that the legs and feet are daily altering their shape; and that the hair is beginning to change into stubs of feathers." Thus, Malthus maintains, only complete and defensible ideas must be allowed into the argument, not "ostriches." His essay *On the Principle of Population* produces such ideas.

Text Overview:

Malthus begins:

I think I may fairly make two postulata.
First, That food is necessary to the existence of man.
Secondly, That the passion between the sexes is necessary,
and will remain nearly in its present state.

These laws have been in force since the beginning of time, and there is no reason to suppose, nor any evidence to indicate that they ever will change. "Assuming, then, my postulata as granted," Malthus continues, "I say, that the power of population is indefinitely greater than the power in the earth to produce subsistence for man." This is based upon the facts that population increases in a *geometric* ratio (population doubles), while subsistence only increases in an *arithmetic* ratio (adds to itself). Seeing as how "food is necessary to the life of man, the effects of these two unequal powers must be kept

equal." Therefore, both reason and nature have devised strong and constant checks against large population increases; and these checks will necessarily affect the great majority of mankind.

A society which has no regulations controlling early marriage has never existed, neither among "the lower classes, from a fear of not providing well for their families; or among the higher classes, from a fear of lowering their condition in life." In other words, population always has at least one check against outgrowing its food supply. But if a society were founded on more equality and virtue with abundant means of subsistence, Malthus supposes, prohibitions on early marriage would lessen and "the increase of the human species would evidently be much greater than any increase than that which has hitherto been known." Evidence of this is to be found in America, where "the population has been found to double itself in twenty-five years." Thus, when unchecked, population increases in a geometric ratio every 25 years.

By taking any area of land—England, for example—it can be demonstrated that limits are quickly reached in the means of subsistence. In the first twenty-five years a doubling of production as well as population may be possible. However, that ratio of increase could not possibly continue both because of limits on arable land and because of the scale of operations necessary to ensure production.

Malthus provides an illustration of the geometric and arithmetic ratios: "It may be fairly said . . . that the means of subsistence increases in arithmetical ratio . . . Taking the population of the world at any number, a thousand millions, for instance, the human species would increase in the ratio of - 1, 2, 4, 8, 16, 32, 64, 128, 256, 512, etc., and subsistence as - 1, 2, 3, 4, 5, 6, 7, 8, 9, 10, etc. In two centuries and a quarter the population would [outnumber available food] 512 to 10."

Instinct (the human sex drive, or the natural desire to have children) would seem to propel this population increase forward, but *reason*—that is, concerns for familial support—has for centuries interrupted reproduction. Nonetheless, instinct is strong enough to ensure an increase in population *prior* to an increase in the means of subsistence. As a result, "the food which before supported seven millions must now be divided among seven millions and a half, or eight millions. The poor consequently must live much worse . . . " As population outstrips resources, the number of laborers soon exceeds the available work, thus wages fall and inflation rises. At this point population increases are abated—but only until cheap labor production increases, which allows population to rise once again. This oscillation holds all societies in a constant state of flux, and allows ruthless landowners and the upper classes to endlessly exploit laborers and the poor. Because of this, individuals in higher stations *avoid* early marriage, as it might affect their social life; laborers *delay* marriage, due to a fear of poverty—to stay one step ahead of squalor. This check on population is preventive, in that it stops population before it begins; by marrying later, there are fewer years of child-producing potential, thus, fewer children.

Far more dangerous and sinister, however, than the rational, preventive check on population growth, declares Malthus, is the *positive* or *natural* check against overpopulation, a check that operates on populations on the rise, and almost exclusively among the world's lower classes: *famine*. Infant and childhood mortality decimates these classes, he continues, "indeed it seems difficult to suppose that a labourer's wife, who has six children, and who is sometimes in absolute want of bread, should be able always to give them the food and attention necessary to support life."

Famines are due to increases in population above the production capacity of the land. Further, anywhere "the lower classes of people are in the habit of living almost upon the smallest possible quantity of food, and are glad to get any putrid offals that European labourers would rather starve than eat," is always teetering on the edge of wide-scale famine. The root cause of this problem is a "real" increase in population with no corresponding real increase in the means of subsistence, which means that the same amount of food must be divided among more people. Thus, with lowered intake of food, the health and well-being of the overall population is lowered and the standard of living utterly destroyed. Once enough people die of malnutrition or starvation or enough are not born (through couples marrying later) to re-balance population with subsistence, the cycle beings all over again.

Apparently, then, the principle of population growth has destined mankind to live forever in misery and vice. But, Malthus interrupts, there are possible alternatives, based in each human being's capacity to make sensible choices: " . . . Reason and conviction wears much more the promise of permanence, than any change effected and maintained by force. The unlimited exercise of private judgment is a doctrine inexpressibly grand and captivating, and has a vast superiority over those systems where every individual is in a manner the slave of the public. The substitution of benevolence as the master-spring . . . of society, instead of self-love, is . . . devoutly to be wished . . . But, alas! that moment can never arrive. The whole is

little better than a dream, a beautiful phantom of the imagination. These `gorgeous palaces' of happiness and immortality, these `solemn temples' of truth and virtue will dissolve, `like the baseless fabric of a vision', when we awaken to real life, and contemplate the true and genuine situation of man on earth." In other words, Malthus contends that it would be nice if people realized that they were cyclically breeding themselves into famine and would, therefore, restrain themselves—having fewer children, who would consequently live much more comfortable lives. Human nature, however, will prevent this.

Suppose for a moment, Malthus asks, that utopia were truly possible: that property was shared equally, that no limits were placed on marriage, and that food were plentiful. As population began to increase, as it necessarily must due to the lack of checks against it, the per capita amount of available food would decrease, property ownership would develop, tyrannical leaders would arise, and individuals' reproduction would again be controlled—probably through the tragic effects of famine. At this point in the utopian system, "the spirit of benevolence, cherished and invigorated by plenty, is repressed by the chilling breath of want . . . The temptations to evil are too strong for human nature to resist," and "mankind is once again plunged into misery, class, and reality . . . "

This scenario, asserts Malthus, is the irrefutable history of mankind; and mankind's tragic future will follow this same pattern to the end: (1) "The increase of population is necessarily limited by the means of subsistence," (2) " . . . population does invariably increase when the means of subsistence increase," and (3)" . . . the power of population is repressed, and the actual population kept equal to the means of subsistence by misery and vice."

Malthus' *Essay on the Principle of Population* is one of the single-most important philosophical works of the modern age. His theory formed the basis for the work of Darwin, Wallace, Nietzsche, Freud, Adam Smith, Durkheim, and many others. The key to Malthus' theories was his identification of *environmental pressure* as central to man's (or any organism's) individual and collective development.

A dark work that leaves little hope for the future without proper recognition of the past, Malthus' words are still relevant. Speaking of himself in his original preface to the work, Malthus gives no doubt that his views have been offered sincerely: "The view which he has given of life has a melancholy hue; but he feels conscious, that he has drawn these dark tints, from a conviction that they are really in the picture."

THE VARIETIES OF RELIGIOUS EXPERIENCE

A Study in Human Nature
by William James
(1842-1910)

William James was born in New York City in 1842. He was strongly influenced by his Swedish-born theologian father, who sensitized young William toward religion.

William completed an M.D. at Harvard in 1870, and remained there until his death in 1910, teaching anatomy and physiology, psychology, and philosophy. His writings progressed from psychology to philosophy and finished in the subject he considered to be at the root of psychology: metaphysics (the philosophical investigation into first causes and the nature of ultimate reality).

The Varieties of Religious Experience, published in 1902, is one of James' earlier works, and is a masterpiece in the field of psychological interpretation. Its subject, the religious impulse, had never before been examined with the open-minded, scientific approach James employed.

The book consists of lectures delivered by James in Edinburgh, Scotland, and provides a valuable overview of a question faced by most people: the question of transcendental belief.

Text Overview:

"What are the religious propensities and . . . what is their philosophic significance?" James asks. There is world of difference between these two questions. The first pertains to the nature, history, constitution, and origin of religion, and requires a *descriptive* answer, "an existential judgement." The second question demands an *evaluation, a spiritual judgement"* which validates the significance of religious inclinations.

The Varieties of Religious Experience focuses almost entirely on answering the first; it does not promote any spiritual judgement concerning the value (or significance) of the religious experiences examined. This method, according to James, is the natural approach of a psychologist toward religious experience:

There can be no doubt that as a matter of fact a religious life, exclusively pursued, does tend to make the person exceptional and eccentric. I speak now not of your ordinary religious believer, who follows conventional observances of his country, whether it be Buddhist, Christian, or Mohammedan. His religion has been made for him by others, communicated to him by tradition, determined to fixed forms by imitation, and retained by habit. It would profit us little to study this second-hand religious life. We must search rather for the original experiences which were the pattern-setters to all this mass of suggested feeling and imitated conduct. These experiences we can only find in individuals for whom religion

exists not as dull habit, but as an acute fever . . .

However, these rare individuals, who James chooses to study over the mere religious follower, tend to exhibit characteristics which seem to be symptoms of nervous instability. And perhaps more than any other type of "genius," he warns, religious geniuses have been subject to abnormal psychical visitations.

Speaking of these zealous founders and propagators of religion, James says:

Invariably they have been creatures of exalted emotional sensibility. Often they have led a discordant inner life, and had melancholy during a part of their career. They have known no measure, been liable to obsessions and fixed ideas; and frequently they have fallen into trances, heard voices, seen visions, and presented all sort of peculiarities which are ordinarily classed as pathological.

Though these characteristics may seem pathological in nature, he adds, we must be willing to view them in the larger context of the religious life of the person, and to try to assess their state without prejudice.

The investigation into religious experience can focus on the thought component as well as on feelings. However:

Individuality is founded in feeling; and the recesses of feeling, the darker, blinder strata of character, are the only places in the world in which we catch real fact in the making, and directly perceive how events happen, and how work is actually done. Compared with this world of living, individualized feelings, the world of generalized objects which the intellect contemplates is without solidity or life.

In surveying the field of religion, there is great diversity among theories and concepts. But, while the ideas and symbols of religion serve specific purposes, they "may be perfections and improvements, and even some day all be united into one harmonious system." Therefore, the symbolic contents of a religion should not be viewed "as organs with an indispensable function, necessary for the religious life to go on."

James quotes Canadian psychiatrist Dr. R.M. Bucke, who agrees that feelings deeply felt are as real and important as thoughts deeply reflected. The religious experience, says Bucke, is permeated by "a state of moral exaltation, an indescribable feeling of elevation, elation and joyousness, and a quickening of the moral sense which is fully as striking [as] is the enhanced intellectual power."

Normally, personal reflection is applied to religious experience, combining to produce firm belief. "This explains the passionate loyalty of religious persons everywhere to the minutest details of their so widely differing creeds."

The religious life generally includes the following beliefs:

1. *That the visible world is part of a more spiritual universe from which it draws its chief significance.*

2. *That union or harmonious relation with that higher universe is our true end.*

3. *That prayer or inner communion with the spirit thereof—be that spirit "God" or "law"—is a process wherein work is really done, and spiritual energy flows in and produces effects, psychological or material, within the phenomenal world.*

Profound religious experiences can further result in the following psychological conditions:

4. *A new zest which adds itself like a gift to life, and takes the form either of lyrical enchantment or of appeal to earnestness and heroism.*

5. *An assurance of safety and temper of peace, and, in relation to others, a preponderance of loving affections.*

Although the "warring gods and formulas of the various religions" do not always agree one with another, there is "a certain uniform deliverance in which religions all appear to meet." It consists of two parts:

1. *The uneasiness—reduced to its simplest terms, is a sense that there is something wrong about us as we naturally stand.*

2. *The solution—is a sense that we are saved from the wrongness by making proper connection with the higher powers.*

"In those more developed minds which alone we are studying," James infers, "the wrongness takes a moral character, and the salvation takes a mystical tinge."

Analyzing religious experience can clarify the basis of religious beliefs:

For our ancestors, dreams, hallucinations, revelations, and cock-and-bull stories were inextricably mixed with facts. Up to a comparatively recent date such distinctions as those between what has been verified and what is only conjectured, between the impersonal and the personal aspects of existence, were hardly suspected or conceived.

Whatever you imagined in a lively manner, whatever you thought fit to be true, you affirmed confidently; and whatever you affirmed, your comrades believed. Truth was what had not yet been contradicted . . .

But although rational, scientific thinking contributes to the understanding, intellectual analysis should *not* be considered the final authority by which we can verify the truth of the religious experience. There is also feeling:

That unsharable feeling which each of us has of the pinch of his individual destiny as he privately feels it rolling out on fortune's wheel may be disparaged for its egoism, may be sneered at as unscientific, but it is the one thing that fills up the measure of our concrete actuality, and any would-be existent that should lack such a feeling, or its analogue, would be a piece of reality only half made up.

It is ridiculous for the scientific community to claim that feelings and personal elements of experience must be ignored, since personal experience *is*, in a sense, reality. "The axis of reality runs solely through the egoistic places—they are strung upon it like so many beads." In fact, a description of the world which does not include feelings would be an empty picture, void of the most fundamental element of human experience. And although an individual's religion may be "egoistic," it would remain "infinitely less hollow and abstract, as far as it goes, than a science which prides itself on taking no account of anything private at all."

Therefore, asserts James, "it does not follow, because our ancestors made so many errors of fact and mixed them with their religion, that we should therefore leave off being religious at all." Indeed, investigations of religion *must* include feeling, if they seek to arrive at a greater understanding:

When I read in a religious paper words like these: "Perhaps the best thing we can say of God is that his is the Inevitable Inference," I recognize the tendency to let religion evaporate in intellectual terms. Would martyrs have sung in flames for a mere inference, however inevitable it may be? . . . . . . The intellect, everywhere invasive, shows everywhere its shallowing effect.

If the religious impulse is in fact a natural phenomenon, as James suggests, what is needed is not abstract metaphysics, but a pragmatic approach which will include the religious impulse as part of its explanation. It is reasonable to believe that there are facts beyond those studied by the physical scientist. A pragmatic approach to a theory of religious experience would involve more than just a context in which the materialistic world could be seen religiously. It would view the world as having a "natural constitution different at some point from that which a materialistic world would have. It must be such that different events can be expected in it, different conducts must be required."

This pragmatic view of religion seems always to have had a position in the minds of common men. "It is only the transcendentalist metaphysicians that think that, without adding any concrete details to Nature, or subtracting any, but by simply calling it the expression of absolute spirit, you make it more divine just as it stands." The pragmatic approach allows phenomena to be understood on their own terms, apart from science or metaphysics, granting religion "body as well as soul."

PHILOSOPHY AND THE MIRROR OF NATURE

by Richard Rorty, Princeton University Press, Princeton, N.J. 1980

One could argue that since the 17th century, philosophy has increasingly developed into an "attempt to underwrite or debunk claims to knowledge made by science, morality, art or religion." Often, philosophy acts as a self-appointed judge, deciding the validity of claims to knowledge made by other disciplines. Most philosophers view knowledge as an accurate representation of what is outside the mind—the external world—and view epistemology, the study of knowledge, as the attempt "to understand the way in which the mind is able to construct such representations."

"The aim of this book," Richard Rorty states, "is to undermine the reader's confidence in 'the mind' as something about which one should have a 'philosophical' view, in 'knowledge' as something about which there ought to be a 'theory' and which has 'foundations,' and in 'philosophy' as it has been conceived since Kant." His analysis of these concepts seek to dispel misconceptions and assumptions which have previously dictated their roles in philosophy, and to achieve a practical approach by which *mind, knowledge,* and *philosophy* can be better understood.

Mind

"Discussions in the philosophy of mind usually start off by assuming that everybody has always known how to divide the world into the mental and the physical—that this distinction is common-sensical and intuitive." Historically, however, the mind-body distinction has had many different, sometimes muddled, interpretations. The Greeks, for example, believed sensations of pain were physical in nature. Descartes, in contrast, deemed pain to be a mental phenomenon. The distinction, then, between mind and body depends on how any person or culture *decides* what is considered mind and what is considered body; and this demarcation requires a "familiarity with a language-game."

When seen from this perspective, the important question to ask is not "How do we distinguish mind from body?" but "Why has this been taken as an important problem?" The answer to the second question lies in our notion of the mind as a "knowing entity." Faced with the task of distinguishing humans from other animals, Greek philosophers concluded that merely "the ability to know" was an insufficient distinction. It is the ability to gain *universal* knowledge, not simply the knowledge of particulars, that sets humans apart from animals. For example, we know that two parallel mountain ranges will never meet because of the universal principle that two parallel lines never meet—not because we traversed the length of each range.

This separation of types of knowing—the understanding of a universal principle and the its application to various circumstances—was posited in terms of the distinction between the "eye of the body" (walking the mountain ranges) and the "Eye of the Mind" (applying the universal principle). This Eye of the Mind is what truly separates humans from other animals.

Knowledge

Conceiving of knowledge as analogous to the senses in general and to the sense of sight in particular, has profoundly influenced the history of Western thought. The analogy between the senses and sight led to an understanding of knowledge as the "Mirror of Nature," the mirror being either the ideas in our minds or the language with which we express those ideas. This metaphor describes knowledge as a representation, or reflection, of the world. The primary criterion by which to judge knowledge, therefore, is the accuracy of its representation—the clarity of the mirror.

The two primary schools of thought in modern epistemology, while strongly opposed, both accept this underlying metaphor. Lockian epistemology (fathered by John Locke) sees the mind as a *tabula rasa,* a blank slate or tablet upon which objects make impressions. Having an *impression* of the object is the nearest one can come to having *knowledge* of that object.

Immanuel Kant developed the second, more influential epistemology. He argued that the mind played a far more active role because it contributed the object of knowledge through the exercise of certain "faculties" (e.g., the comprehension of space and time). Since these faculties are intrinsic structures of the human mind, they make possible the claim that different perceivers can come to know the same things about an object of knowledge (representation). Lockian and Kantian epistemology disagree on the nature of mind, but agree on the "mirror of nature" metaphor of knowledge, and thus the criterion of accuracy.

Most epistemology focuses on the perceived—the object—for an accurate explanation of how the mind and the world are related. Rorty, however, says we should focus instead on the criteria by which we establish that an object, or representation, is a piece of knowledge. If we think of *certainty* (the goal of knowledge) "as a matter of victory in argument rather than of relation to an object known," we will look to perceptions other than our own by which we know the object. "Our certainty will be a matter of conversation between persons, rather than a matter of interaction with nonhuman reality . . . We should look for an airtight case rather than an unshakable foundation."

Rorty's position reflects a *pragmatic* view of truth: what matters is not so much trying to establish what is true within that vague thing we call "reality," but what is taken to be true within a particular community. This leads to an emphasis on reasons and arguments rather than objects. In other words, the model for "knowing" becomes a *conversation* between knowers rather than a *confrontation* with the object. Knowledge, in Rorty's model, is based on human interaction.

The crucial premise of this argument is that we understand knowledge when we understand the social justification of belief, and thus have no need to view it as accuracy of representation. Once conversation replaces confrontation, the notion of the mind as Mirror of Nature can be discarded. Then the notion of philosophy as the discipline which looks for privileged representations among those constituting the Mirror of Nature becomes unintelligible.

Claiming that "knowledge" is relative can potentially lead to chaos. However, in Rorty's model, determination of what counts as truth remains a very orderly affair; it is simply ordered by societal processes rather than by absolute facts. Rorty rejects the assumption that there are some representations (objects of knowledge) which have a privileged relationship with reality. Truth is not a matter of accuracy, he claims, but of perception. While "relativism" of this type is not synonymous with "anything goes," it does herald the death of philosophy as the guardian of truth, of knowledge and the Mirror of Nature.

Philosophy

"The desire for a theory of knowledge is a desire for constraint—a desire to find `foundations' to which one might cling, frameworks beyond which one must not stray, objects which impose themselves, representations which cannot be gainsaid."

Epistemology operates on the assumption that all contributions to a given topic are commensurable, that is, "able to be brought under a set of rules which tell us how rational agreement can be reached." Further, says Rorty, "the dominating notion of epistemology is that to be rational, to be fully human, to do what we ought, we need to be able to find agreement with other human beings." This agreement, of course, would accurately reflect the world. "The assumption that an epistemology can be constructed is the assumption that such common ground exists . . . To suggest that there is *no* such common ground endangers rationality. To question the need for commensuration seems the first step toward a return to a war of all against all." The ideal of philosophers as the guardians of knowledge is eliminated, if there is no real knowledge to be had.

If this is the case, how does philosophy fit into society's framework? Philosophers can play one of two roles: The first is that of "intermediary between disciplines," a person or "interpreter" who brings together thinkers from various disciplines in order to mediate their theoretical differences of opinion through conversation. The second is that of "cultural overseer."

"The first role is appropriate to hermeneutics [using interpretation to break down the barriers of constraint and confrontation about meaning], the second to epistemology." Hermeneutics allows each discipline to interact with all the others, to participate in an ongoing conversation, where no unifying ground is presumed, but the hope of agreement—or at least fruitful disagreement—lasts as long as the conversation persists. "Epistemology sees the hope of agreement as token of the existence of common ground which, perhaps unbeknownst to the speakers, unites them in a common rationality. For hermeneutics, to be rational is to refrain from epistemology—from thinking that there is a special set of terms in which all contributions to the conversation should be put." Hermeneutics is interpretation—the attempt to move from your discourse to another's in order to achieve some form of understanding.

It is difficult to imagine philosophy as not concerned with absolute knowledge. But hermeneutics *presumes* an inability to find a common ground of what constitutes knowledge, and is therefore not "another way of knowing" but "another way of coping," or "perceiving." For hermeneutics, the goal of thinking is not knowledge, but "edification"—the project of finding "new, better, more interesting, more fruitful ways of speaking."

How is this more desirable than epistemology? The desire to be the Mirror of Nature is the desire to be *such a perfect mirror* as to *no longer be a mirror at all.* "The notion of a human being whose mind is such an unclouded mirror, and who *knows* this, is, as Sartre says, the image of God." Such a being would never confront another with anything alien, anything which requires a choice of action, evaluation or description. Rather, such choices would be made unnecessary by complete and total understanding.

The Mirror of Nature is an fabrication, an attempt to escape our humanity. Culture would `freeze over, everything forever fixed, and thus human beings would be cease to be human. "The cultural role of the edifying philosopher is to help us avoid the self-deception which comes from believing that we know ourselves by knowing a set of objective facts."

Philosophy, then, must keep the conversation going and affirm and preserve what makes us human. "To see keeping a conversation going as a sufficient aim of philosophy, to see wisdom as consisting in the ability to sustain a conversation, is to see human beings as generators of new descriptions rather than beings one hopes to be able to describe accurately."

OUR KNOWLEDGE OF THE EXTERNAL WORLD

Bertrand Russell

(1872-1970)

From the age of eleven Bertrand Russell maintained a passionate interest in and talent for mathematics, combined with a belief that science must be the source of all human progress. With youthful ambition, he wished to be *a benefactor of mankind*.

As the young man matured, he found himself "increasingly attracted to philosophy, not, as is often the case, by the hope of ethical or theological comfort, but by the wish to discover whether we possess anything that can be called knowledge." He recorded in his diary that it seemed to him that, with the exception of "consciousness," no fact was indubitable.

Russell soon concluded that mathematics—and the certain, precise knowledge it yields—might serve as a pattern for philosophical inquiry. But, at the age of eighteen, upon reading popular essays for the validity of arithmetic and geometry, he became dissatisfied with the arguments which purported to establish the foundations of mathematics, and decided to investigate those foundations for himself.

For more than twenty years Russell expanded his research into mathematics, during which time, along with Alfred North Whitehead, he published a seminal work titled *Principia Mathematica* (1903). Although this treatise failed to resolve Russell's immediate philosophical inquiries, it later spawned a radically new system of thought, becoming a foundation upon which Russell's mind became capable of descending to the most profound depths and soaring to the abstract heights of human thought.

Following the completion of *Principia Mathematica*, Russell, a gentle, sensitive though outspoken—man, took up several different humanitarian endeavors. Shocked by the violence and cruelty of World War I, he worked tirelessly to sway public opinion toward peace. During this time he set aside abstract pursuits, concluding that little could be achieved by "writing for specialists." Instead he set himself to writing practical—though controversial—social, psychological, philosophical, and political commentaries. He participated strongly in the campaign for women's suffrage and took many opportunities to point out what he felt to be "ridiculous inconsistencies" in the positions of "traditional moralists" and preachers. He was also well-known for his potent attacks on Christianity, and religious faith in general:

We may define faith as a firm belief in something for which there is no evidence. When there is evidence, no one speaks of faith. We do not speak of faith that two and two are four or that the earth is round. We only speak of faith when we wish to substitute emotion for evidence . . . We were told that faith could remove mountains, but no one believed it; we are now told that the atomic bomb can remove mountains, and everyone believes it.

He displayed a similar attitude toward traditional philosophy. To him, "Science is what you know, philosophy is what you don't know."

Our Knowledge of the External World, published in 1914, is one of the masterpieces of Russell's work as a philosopher. Its significance lies in the fact that it offers new insights into philosophical methodology. In this book, Russell took then-recent developments in mathematics and applied them to philosophical problems. This new approach resulted in the formation of a sizeable new school of philosophic thought: the "analytic" school.

Text Overview:

Russell's theories in *Our Knowledge* are, in part, a reaction to the grand metaphysical system of Hegel, which dominated philosophy in the late nineteenth century. In this respect, he continues with the empiricist tradition of Locke, Hume and Mill. However, at the same time Russell belongs to the class of philosophers who were also mathematicians, such as Pythagoras, Plato and Descartes. Like these thinkers, he was impressed by the clarity and precision of mathematics and wished to make mathematical procedure the model for other areas of knowledge. Russell's argument was that philosophy was essentially *logic,* and that logic and mathematics were indistinguishable. Therefore, philosophy could be absorbed into mathematics.

. . . Every philosophical problem, when it is subjected to the necessary analysis and purification, is found either to be not really philosophical at all, or else to be . . . logical.

The aim, then, of Russell's "logical analysis" is to show that all genuine knowledge is comprised both of logic and mathematics. There can be no "other realities" or metaphysical realms that transcend what is given in experience. When a thing is "known," based on evidence from the external world, then that knowledge is not merely speculative, but is true knowledge.

The method of logical analysis, or the *analytic method* ("analytic" referring to the process of breaking concepts down into smaller pieces for easier analysis), resolves the philosophical problem concerning our understanding of the external world by breaking down our knowledge into fundamental parts. In the old Hegelian system, the doctrine of *internal relations* held that "to know anything is to know everything." Hegel perpetuated this idea because he believed that all things—both in the physical universe and in the realm of ideas and mathematics—are related to each other. Take for example the statement, "The cat is on the mat." In Hegel's system, you can not know everything about the single entity "cat" unless you also know about the "mat" which it is lying on. Similarly, you cannot fully know about the "mat" unless you know where it is located, its size . . . and this web of interrelationships continues on and on. In the Hegelian system, to know one thing you must know everything, because all things are inseparably connected to their surroundings.

Russell, in contrast, by denying Hegel's doctrine of internal relations, makes way for his *analytic* method. Essentially, Russell's view is that our knowledge can be separated into "atomic facts" (isolated ideas, opinions, perceptions, etc.), and that our common-sense, experiential views of the world are correct (what we see and hear are true perceptions). Contrary to Hegel's view, Russell argues that we *can* claim singular bits of knowledge about the world, independent of other knowledge. With regard to "the cat on the mat" example, in Russell's philosophical system you can *know* something about the single entity "cat" without having to give an account of everything related to it. Similarly, you may gain an *indirect* knowledge of something: you can "know" a truth without directly experiencing it. You can come to know the meaning of the word "Renaissance," for instance, without actually living through the Renaissance; that is, you understand the term or concept without any direct sense-experience.

In *Our Knowledge of the External World* Russell also attempts to answer the question regarding the *problem of other minds*. He holds that an individual's "private world" is composed of all of the data within his or her perspective. If we also admit the existence of other minds, however, we can then add these other perspectives to our own, expanding our view of the "real" world and our knowledge of perceived objects. In other words, rather than assuming that a thing exists in itself, we can know it through a compilation of various perspectives. In this manner we can achieve knowledge which is based entirely upon evidence from the external world, and thus is not speculative.

This new, simple way of viewing knowledge was highly radical. As Russell put it: "It represents . . . the same kind of advance as was introduced into physics by Galileo: the substitution of piecemeal, detailed, and verifiable results for large untested generalities recommended only by a certain appeal to imagination."

Russell also turns his attention to the famous paradoxes of the Greek philosopher Zeno. Zeno advanced several arguments, all based on his theory of the infinite divisibility of space and time—arguments which went so far as to demonstrate the impossibility of motion. For example, Zeno postulated that if you shoot an arrow and follow its trajectory, the arrow will first cover half the distance of its target, then three fourths the distance, then seven eighths—and so on into an infinite regress of smaller and smaller fractions; but the arrow never can actually reach the target. Russell is able to apply his logical analytic method to such paradoxes to bring about apparent resolutions.

According to Russell, Zeno's error came from applying the geometrical definition of a *"point"* as a non-dimensional coordinate. If a point has no dimensions, then it occupies no space, and an infinite number of points can be located along any line. This means that, logically, the trajectory of the arrow would have to cover an infinite number of points—which would, of course, take an infinite amount of time.

But, argues Russell, geometry and logic are not the actual "stuff" of reality; they are formal constructs that help us to describe and sort out the "stuff" that is supplied to us through our senses. And in the sensory world, we do not perceive "points," but *"point-events"*—actual *happenings*, which occur *one by one*. The arrow hitting its target is very decidedly one of these *point-events*.

Russell honors logic and mathematics too much to leave the solution here; he also looks for a way to accommodate logic to sensory reality. The problem with "time and space" paradoxes, he says, involves a confusion in terminology, which obscures the difference between *infinite* and *finite* numbers. These two categories *must* be understood as different. Infinite numbers, first of all, are *not* increased by adding 1 to them (infinity + 1 still equals infinity), whereas finite numbers *are* increased ($617,249 + 1 = 617,250$). Because of this difference, the infinite quantity of even numbers (2, 4, 6 . . .) can be said to equal the quantity of all numbers combined (the total of both even and odd). Therefore, in the case of infinite numbers, it *is* possible for *part* of a category of events (such as a series of points across a measured distance) to equal the *whole* category of events (such as an infinitely divisible distance).

For Russell, there is no paradox—only a semantic misinterpretation. Thus, the logic inherent in mathematics provides the methodological basis for Russell's philosophical reasoning.

Russell was devoted to the application of scientific investigation, and was adamantly opposed to blind—or speculative—belief. He once commented that "Aristotle could have avoided the mistake of thinking that women have fewer teeth than men by the simple device of asking Mrs. Aristotle to open her mouth." But, paradoxically, Russell also maintained that there certainly was value in speculative pursuits, claiming that "there is much pleasure to be gained from useless knowledge."

In 1950, Bertrand Russell received the Nobel Prize for literature for his writings (he published over 40 books in his lifetime) and for his role "as a defender of humanity and freedom of thought." Russell was a man who attempted to lift the everyday human world into the more subtle realms of philosophy—and vice versa. He was also keenly aware that many of the values held by society were in opposition to his own highly liberal beliefs.

Still, in spite of his weighty ideas and often radical social views, Russell possessed a healthy sense of perspective. Not wishing others to take him too seriously—and perhaps also wishing to remind himself of his own position in the "big picture"—he once said, "One of the symptoms of an approaching nervous breakdown is the belief that one's work is terribly important."

PHILOSOPHICAL INVESTIGATIONS

by Ludwig Wittgenstein, Macmillan, New York, N.Y., 1953

Philosophical Investigations was first published in 1953, two years after Wittgenstein's death in 1951. Completed four years previously, the work represents Wittgenstein's mature, systematic philosophy of language, which focuses specifically on how ambiguous use of language propagates obstacles in philosophical discourse.

Ludwig Wittgenstein was born in Austria in 1889. He studied engineering in Berlin and then at the University of Manchester in England, where his attention shifted from aeronautical engineering to mathematics, and eventually to philosophy.

With the support of Bertrand Russell, Wittgenstein earned a doctoral degree from Cambridge University. He became a professor at Cambridge in 1937, holding the chair previously occupied by the prominent philosopher G.E. Moore. There Wittgenstein assembled his *Investigations*.

Interestingly, the text proposes an ideological position which opposes the stance Wittgenstein took in his earlier work, *The Tractatus Logico-Philosophicus*. There, Wittgenstein had defended the denotation theory of language—a theory which sought to clarify philosophical problems by devising an "ideal" language in which each simple object or property would be represented by a fixed, unambiguous symbol. In *Philosophical Investigations*, however, this theory is rejected; it is incorrect to conceive of words as simply representing a single reality in language.

Text Overview:

Words—and the language in which they are used—can best be described as tools: "Think of the tools in a toolbox: a hammer, pliers, a saw, a screwdriver, a rule, a glue-pot, glue, nails and screws . . . The functions of words are as diverse as the function of these objects."

Words can be employed in a variety of ways—not simply to denote specific objects. To understand the meaning of a word is to understand how it is *used*—in fact, "the meaning *is* the use." Therefore, an accurate description of what a word means would not involve pointing out an individual thing to which it is applied, because words do not function as name tags for the objects of experience. Instead, one would describe the meaning of a word by describing the *context* in which it is used.

Understanding the uses of words is like understanding the rules of a game. If a player does not follow the rules, confusion results. Likewise, when someone does not use language in accordance with its rules, they will fail to be understood.

In philosophy, a multitude of problems arises when philosophers employ terms in non-ordinary ways. However, it is not always readily apparent that a word is being wrongly employed. By *looking to the language*, philosophical problems can be solved, or more accurately, *dissolved*. Because they arise out of subtle misuses in the language, the problems of philosophy are not real problems, but verbal muddles.

For example, if we use the word *see* in the ordinary way, we will never be inclined to make the statement "all we can *see* are sense data . . . we will never see tables and chairs and other physical objects." And yet, this statement has often been made in the field of philosophy. Much confusion has been generated in philosophy because of such misapplication of terms.

Take Descartes' compelling question, "How can I *know* I am not dreaming?" Although the question seems valid, since it is possible to dream that one is awake, it appears that the word `knowledge' is being used in an odd way. What kind of knowledge could one possibly have, in addition to what one *already knows*, to prove that one is awake? To satisfy the question as Descartes asks it, one must produce indubitable proof that one is not dreaming. But, as Wittgenstein points out, knowledge is not qualified by indubitable proof, thus always holding the possibility of being wrong. However, this does not make knowledge any less valid. "For `I know' seems to describe a state of affairs which guarantees what is known, guarantees it as fact. One always forgets the expression, `I thought I knew.'" What is the use of a philosophical investigation, if philosophy has been shown to be pursuing imaginary problems? It is to understand how words have been previously employed in philosophical language, and to clarify how philosophical problems arise "when language goes on holiday"—that is, when language is applied in an inaccurate manner.

The "whole process of using words," Wittgenstein asserts, can be seen as a game, a "language-game." The term—"language-game"—emphasizes "the fact that the speaking of language is part of an activity, or of a form of life." The conventions of language are far more complex than simple denotation. Various language games are governed by different rules, but these rules are not absolute, for they may change over time, or from culture to culture.

For example, giving orders, describing and reporting events, making up stories, translating, and irony are language games which may find completely different meanings for the same words, all of which are understandable. If a person who has just won the lottery is asked how she is doing, she may answer "Terrific!"—an accurate account of her state of mind. However, a person who has had a perfectly awful day might also answer "Terrific" to the same question, meaning "I'm perfectly awful." One doesn't suppose the second person is lying, but using the word *terrific* sarcastically. This is what is meant by "the multiplicity of the tools in language and the ways they are used."

Meaning, furthermore, is not the same as, or even analogous to, *thinking of* something: "Nothing is more wrong-headed than calling meaning a mental activity!" That is to say, knowing the meaning of the word "dog" is not to have a mental image of "dog" summoned by the word itself.

Words do not have a single or "objectifiable" meaning. "Look and see whether there is anything common to all [of the different meanings a word can have], and the result of this examination is: we see a complicated network of similarities overlapping and crisscrossing; sometimes overall similarities, sometimes similarities of detail. . . . These phenomena have no one thing in common which makes us use the same word for all—but they are related to one another in many different ways. And it is because of this relationship, or these relationships, that we call them all [the same]."

Because terms do not carry exactly the same meaning every time, but rather make sense in terms of similarities, or "family resemblances," the meaning of a word can only be found by examining the context in which it is actually *used*. So we must bear in mind that the meaning of a word exists only in its use, and does, therefore, vary with each original usage. We forever "need to call to mind the differences between the language games."

To understand a word is much like understanding an act which makes no sense at all, until we notice what the act *does*, what the act is *for*, what the *purpose* of it is—what *meaning* it takes.

In a chess match, for example, it would be considered strange to ask what a move stands for or represents. And yet the move *does* have meaning, and this meaning is its *function* as a move in the game of chess. The meaning exists in the *context* of the game: the rules, the board, the various other pieces—not in "standing for" anything.

Defining words in terms of a single use does not seem to resolve difficulties in meaning, since even if one decides on a single definition, complications tend to arise. The uses of words are multiple, but not arbitrary; therefore, *misuse* is a serious matter. And this is precisely where philosophical problems spring from. To use one of Wittgenstein's examples: "I say `I describe my state of mind' and `I describe my room . . . '"—these are two very different uses of the word *describe*. One refers to an activity concerned with a purely internal psychological condition, the other to an activity concerned with external sensations.

"Essence is expressed by grammar." To understand the nature of something is to acquire the technique of using the language within the context which the "something" appears. So, in one sense, there is no need to try to say what the "essential nature" of something is—as so much of the philosophy has sought to do in the past. The problems philosophy deals with are essentially dissolved through linguistic analysis, since they emerge out of linguistic misunderstanding.

Does the conclusion that there is no intrinsic meaning to language imply that there is no nature to objects? Is it that there are only contexts—nothing more? "Not at all," Wittgenstein answers. "It is not a *something,* but not a *nothing* either! The conclusion was only that a nothing would serve just as well as a something about which nothing can be said. We have only rejected the grammar which tries to force itself on us here."

The key to dealing with philosophical problems is not so much to *solve* them, as it is to *dissolve* them by finding the grammatical errors which produce them. What we need is to "command a clear view of the use of our words . . . Our grammar is lacking in this sort of perspicuity. A perspicuous representation produces just that understanding which consists in `seeing connexions'."

This type of understanding has the effect of dismantling all in philosophy "that is great and important." But for Wittgenstein this is not such a terrible thing. In fact, with this method one is really destroying "nothing but a house of cards."

The purpose of philosophy should not be to produce static answers to questions, but *rather to clear up the muddled language which generates philosophical difficulties,* "for the clarity that we are aiming at is indeed *complete* clarity. But this simply means that the philosophical problems should completely disappear."

Philosophical Investigations is not so much a presentation of a philosophical viewpoint or belief system, but a discourse on a method for eliminating philosophical problems. Wittgenstein's style is sometimes elusive, cryptic, and has been subject to various interpretations since the Investigations was published. This has contributed to Wittgenstein's reputation as somewhat of a cult figure; he is also referred to as the greatest philosopher of this century. Certainly Wittgenstein has been influential, affecting the field of philosophy from logic to poststructuralism. Perhaps most importantly, Wittgenstein's work revolutionized the way philosophers *think about what they do,* insisting that philosophy be a self-conscious activity. For philosophy must take place within the language which it analyzes—not as an objective observer, but as a participant.

STRUCTURE, SIGN, AND PLAY IN THE DISCOURSE OF THE HUMAN SCIENCES

by
Jacques Derrida
(1930 -   )

French philosopher Jacques Derrida has been highly influential in forming the "post-structuralist" school of thought. Post-structuralism, which involves analysis known as "deconstruction," rejects the assumption that there exist universal, intrinsic structures of meaning in the human mind, and therefore, in literature, science, psychology, philosophy—in short, any human intellectual activity. These imagined structures take the form of seemingly "real" opposing forces such as true/false, inside/outside, mind/body, nature/culture, reason/emotion, light/dark, and male/female. Derrida attempted to show that these oppositions are *not* universal—not *discovered*, but *created* by man in an effort to organize his world. Oppositions, in other words, are societal constructs.

The basis for Derrida's theories is the operation of language and its relation to objects and ideas. Derrida's conclusion alters the way a reader interacts with a text—be it a short story or a philosophical tract—because it *redefines* how language is related to meaning.

In this essay, delivered to a conference on structuralism in 1966, Derrida introduces North American academics to his radical ideas.

Structure

The concept of "structure" is at the core of Western *episteme* (system of knowledge). Any structure, according to structuralist theory, has at its center an organizing principle. This principle governs the structure; it is both within and outside, both a part of the structure and at the same time its governing element. The legal system, for instance, with its laws, lawyers, judges, police force, prisons, and criminals, is centered on the principle of "justice." Though "justice" itself is difficult to define independently, without it a "justice system" would be meaningless, even absurd. "The center is at the center of the totality," Derrida states, "and yet, since the center does not belong to the totality (is not a member of the totality), the totality *has its center elsewhere* (is outside of the totality)." The concept of "justice" is at the center of our legal system, but, paradoxically, it is believed to exist independently of any individual legal system. Thus, the legal "structure" has a center—justice—that is not *at* the center.

As the example of justice and the legal system suggests, "the concept of centered structure—although it represents coherence itself," is contradictory. The history of the concept of structure is a series or chainwork of substitutions of center for center; one basic theory replaces another as a definition of the center. For example, "piety" was at the center

of philosophy during the Middle Ages, but now the center has shifted to logic, or pragmatism. The history of Western thought, indeed the history of our intellectual development, is the history of the succession of "names" (words that define the center). These names always seek to describe a presence: form, origin, purpose, energy, being, truth, essence, God, man, etc. They attempt to organize the parts of understanding into a purposeful whole.

The concept of structure was challenged when the laws it obeyed were questioned. For example, if justice governs the legal system, does that imply that nothing governs justice? To believe justice or any other principle to be universal, is an assumption. Deconstruction seeks to demonstrate that apparently universal principles can actually be broken down into a series of lesser concepts; these concepts, however, are no more basic than the principle which they comprise. "From then on it was probably necessary to begin to think that there was no center . . . that the center had no natural locus, that it was not a fixed locus but a function," a place-holder, sign, or symbol that could be replaced by another place-holder, sign or symbol—such as logic replacing piety as the center of philosophy. However, in truth, neither piety nor logic is the "real" center of philosophy. There is no real center, according to Derrida. Humans simply "made" logic the center, because it explained their world better than did piety.

These replaceable signs which act as a center are formed by language. A sign is composed of two elements: the *signifier* and the *signified*. The signifier is the physical manifestation, either a word, symbol, or spoken sound. The signified is the meaning linked with that signifier. However, the meaning of a sign cannot be explained merely by saying the word. For example, "justice" (a signifier) does not inform us of the *meaning* of justice; the concept of justice remains elusive. We look for the meaning in a dictionary—where "real meanings" of words are thought to be found—but find that the definition consists of more words (signifiers). We are trapped in a type of "infinite loop," in a never-ending chain of signifiers defined in terms of other signifiers! Signifiers work, not because they can be linked to particular signifieds, but because one signifier is different from another. For instance, the signifier "cat" possesses meaning in three ways: (1) because we know it is not "bat," "rat," or "car"; (2) because it is used in certain situations and not others (in "Did you put the cat out?" but *not* in "Pour me a cup of cat—and hold the sugar.)"; and (3) because other concepts or objects (litter box, mouse, purring . . .) are related to it in certain ways.

Just as intellectual structures lack as "real" center, language lacks a "transcendental signified," a real meaning or concept that provides a foundation for language. Essentially, the meanings language seems to point towards are only real in so far as we *give* them meaning. Americans, for example, call the large automobile that hauls cargo a "truck," the British call it a "lorry"—different signifiers, but the same signified. There is no *real* meaning for either "truck" or "lorry."

At this point, "Structure" does not refer to some independently existing concept; the concept possesses meaning only in the context of an entire discourse or language. Hence, an inquiry into the nature of structure has *decentered* the concept, and forced us to see "center" as a function, endlessly signified by a chain of signifiers which supposedly "refer" to it, but never coming to rest at absolute meaning. Derrida cites Claude Levi-Strauss' concept of *nature vs. culture* to demonstrate this paradox.

Levi-Strauss, considered by many the creator of cultural anthropology, was a strong proponent of deconstruction, one of its central themes being "nature versus culture." Levi-Strauss defined these terms as follows: "That belongs to nature which is *universal* and spontaneous, not depending on any particular culture or on any particular norm. That belongs to culture, on the other hand, which depends on a system of *norms* regulating society and is therefore capable of *varying* from one social structure to another."

In his classic work *The Elementary Structures of Kinship*, however, Levi-Strauss encountered what he called a "scandal," a paradox that destroyed this nature/culture opposition. This scandal was the universal presence of *incest-prohibition*, the cultural taboo against sexual relations between close kin. Incest-prohibition appeared to be universal, a natural, globally accepted fact. On the other hand, it was also a system of societal norms and interdicts, and thus was also "cultural" in nature. Structuralists considered this a paradox; post-structuralists, however, recognize that the perceived "scandalous paradox" exists only in Levi-Strauss' opposing definitions of nature and culture.

This example reveals that language bears within it the potential for its own critique, the possibility of contradicting its own definitions. Such a critique could be avoided in either of two ways. First, "once the limit of the nature/culture opposition makes itself felt, one might want to question systematically and rigorously the history of these concepts." Second, one can continue to use the concepts in the course of research while acknowledging their limits, treating them as tools, and denying them any ultimate truthvalue.

Levi-Strauss adopted the second option, distinguishing between the *methods* the instruments used and the *truths*, or conclusions, drawn. He characterized his method as *bricolage*, the use and adaptation of whatever instruments one has at hand. This led him in *The Raw and the Cooked* to abandon any reference to a center, or an ultimate reference. He held, for example, that his analysis of myth was itself also a myth, not an underlying, overarching, or originary discourse. The implication of this approach is inevitable: no discourse can claim privilege over another (e.g., literary criticism over the piece of literature it analyzes) since all discourses are embodied in language.

Another problem with language is that one cannot describe a totality (like the legal system or philosophy) because there is always an unbounded "freeplay" as a result of the insubstantiality of the concept of center. Language, though a finite system, is a field of infinite substitutions because there *is* no absolute center, no transcendental signified, no foundation in "reality."

Symbols—that is, words—stand in for the "missing" center ("logic," "justice" . . .), but they can take on any value required for the system to be universal. They are, in essence, "empty" terms because they lack, as we have seen, fixed meaning. Confronted with the question, "Why did the tree fall on the house *today?*" one might answer by using a term such as "destiny," "fate," or "God's will." The number of possible answers illustrates the inability of a particular concept to explain any event. "Destiny," "fate," or "God's will" are therefore *supplements* because they each may stand for the nonexistent center of the concept which explains why the tree fell *today*. The simple fact that we may easily substitute one of the answers for another illustrates freeplay. Signifiers, then, are the result of an absence (a new concept, or a previously unknown species of frog, for instance) which must be either supplemented (finding a term we may use as the "center" of the concept) or eliminated (naming the new species of frog).

Language is always a system of freeplay, a disruption of the illusion of the simple presence of meaning. Yet its use—the chain of signifiers (like in defining the concept of "justice") attempting to get at the illusive, nonexistent foundation—is always driven by the nostalgic desire to return to simple meaning.

But what does this theory mean for nonacademics, asks Derrida. The philosopher Friedreich Nietzsche perceived the absence of ultimate meanings as a source of joy, because it implied for people a freedom not constrained by truth, center, or definite purpose. However, a world not limited by purpose, to Nietzsche, did not suggest a purposeless world. Indeed, it suggested a world where people were free to define their *own* meaning, to decide for themselves what their purpose would be, to discover their own truth. They would be free, that is, from having purpose, truth, or meaning *imposed* upon them. Such a world, perhaps, would be a liberating, empowering world, devoid of the confining chains of structure.

EXISTENTIALISM AND HUMAN EMOTIONS

by
Jean-Paul Sartre
(1905 - 1980)

"What counts is total involvement; some one particular action or set of circumstances is not total involvement."

This foundational belief of Sartre's (and major tenet of existentialism—a view of the individual as being unique or alone in an indifferent and even hostile environment) made him the most visible philosopher of the twentieth century. Whether working in the French Resistance during World War II, battling for abortion rights in the '50s, denouncing the French war in Algeria, boating with Castro, or declining the Nobel Prize in the '60s, Sartre was always a "man of action." Many times his activism and philosophy were derided as empty, irresponsible, licentious, incoherent, or evil. Undaunted, however, by these incessant attacks, he pushed his philosophy forward, writing numerous works of drama and fiction to illustrate his philosophy (*No Exit*, *The Flies*, *The Ways of Freedom*, etc.), many of which are still very popular in certain philosophical and literary circles.

Though Sartre's philosophy of existentialism is rejected by most Anglo-American philosophers, in the rest of the world it is embraced as legitimate modern-age theory. His influence was and is wide among artists and intellectuals the world over, as evidenced by the harsh criticism levied against him still now, over a decade after his death. Sartre was controversial largely due to his bold claims about *responsibility*. Essentially, he felt that we are individually and totally responsible for *all* of our actions. We have total freedom to make choices, he said, and we each define ourselves via these choices. Those individuals who denied this, he declared, were simply in "bad faith" (a key term Sartre uses to describe those who escape responsibility).

In *Existentialism and Human Emotions*, Sartre combines several essays to show that existentialism, far from being an evil, could actually serve to unlock human potential and make modern life more bearable. Nonetheless, its frank, up-front material was not written for the faint of heart.

The definitive biography of Sartre is subtitled *Hated Conscience of His Century*. This description is apt. In a public letter declining the Nobel Prize, Sartre stated that accepting the prize would require him to reject the concept of "freedom" the Nobel committee had so majestically cited in its award. Sartre gave his succinct answer to the committee: "Freedom means nothing if one has no shoes, my fellow men have no shoes."

Text Overview:

"I should like on this occasion to defend existentialism against some charges which have been brought against it," Sartre begins. It is said that existentialism encourages "quietism," in that it holds that solutions to the world's problems are impossible. It is also said that existentialism dwells on "human degradation . . . the sordid, shady, and slimy, and neglects the gracious and beautiful." Further, existentialism is charged with denying hope and human solidarity; by rejecting God, man leaves his life meaningless and arbitrary. "I shall try," Sartre announces, " . . . to answer these different charges."

" . . . What can be said from the very beginning is that by existentialism we mean a doctrine which makes human life possible and, in addition, declares that every truth and every action implies a human setting and a human subjectivity."

He continues: "As is generally known, the basic charge against us [existentialists] is that we put the emphasis on the dark side of human life." But, this is not so; the same people who brand existentialism as pessimism also believe in the "wisdom of the ages," that is, in not resisting authority, following the status quo, promoting violent repression, and blame it all on, and justify it on the basis of, the natural state of "humanity." These are the people, he claims, who accuse existentialism of being too gloomy. "And to such an extent that I wonder whether they are complaining about it, not for its pessimism, but much rather its optimism. Can it be that what really scares them in the doctrine I shall try to present here is that it leaves to man a possibility of choice?"

Existentialists declare that "*existence precedes essence, or if you prefer, that subjectivity must be the starting point.*" This is the leading idea of existentialism. Consider the book in your hand, he asks his reader. It was made by an individual whose "inspiration came from a concept." Then, specific operations were carried out to produce the book according to a plan. Thus, in the case of the book, *essence* (a concept or plan) preceded *existence* (the actual book). And since the existence of the book was determined by a concept or plan *prior* to it, it can only be a book. Its "essence" is that of a book and it cannot "decide" to be something other than what it is. So, then, not only does a book's essence precede existence, it is also fixed.

In the case of man, the exact opposite is true. Although, traditionally, man has been conceived of as coming into existence out of the essence of God's mind, existentialism denies the existence of God, and, accordingly, the notion that human essence (due to God) comes *prior* to human existence. Therefore, existence precedes essence. "What is meant here by saying *existence precedes essence*? It means that, first of all, man exists, turns up, appears on the scene, and, only afterwards, defines himself." That is, man is not a determinate thing; rather, he must face the universal task of determining and defining himself. "If man, as the existentialist conceives him, is indefinable, it is because at first he is nothing . . . " This brings us to existentialism's first principle, also called subjectivity: *"Man is nothing else but what he makes of himself."*

Subjectivity means that a person chooses what he will be, and then goes out and attempts to create that self. Also, in a lesser sense, by example, he chooses for all men. "In fact, in creating the man that we want to be, there is not a single one of our acts which does not at the same time create an image of man as we think he ought be." This places a great amount of responsibility on each individual.

" . . . Our responsibility is much greater than we might have supposed, because it involves all mankind," he explains. "If I am a workingman and choose to join a Christian trade-union rather than be a communist, and if by being a member I want to show that the best thing for man is resignation, that the kingdom of man is not of this world, I am not only involving my own case—I want to be resigned for everyone."

Because of this premise of subjectivity, or choice, all individuals are forced to feel three overwhelming emotions: *anguish* (duty to others), *forlornness* (total individual responsibility), and *despair* (the realization that one cannot change the world in which he is forced to exist).

Anguish, in the "Sartrean" sense of the word, means that "the man who involves himself and who realizes that he is not only the person he chooses to be, but also a lawmaker who is, at the same time, choosing all mankind as well as himself, cannot help escape the feeling of his total and deep responsibility." In effect, says Sartre, every act in which an individual involves himself is actually an act which directs humanity, which brings on an inevitable feeling of dutiful anguish.

Forlornness connotes facing not only the fact that God does not exist, but also everything that this fact entails. But these two beliefs, Sartre contends, do not make things easier to understand: "The existentialist . . . thinks it very distressing that God does not exist, because all possibility of finding values in a heaven of ideas disap-

pears along with him . . . Indeed, everything is permissible if God does not exist, and as a result man is forlorn, because neither within him nor without does he find anything to cling to. He can't start making excuses for himself."

This condition of being totally responsible for one's own actions, truly frees man: there are no excuses for past actions, nor justification for future ones. This is precisely the reason for forlornness. Consider, for example, the case of the young man who, in the throes of World War II, had to choose between leaving his elderly mother to join allied forces in England, or staying with his mother and joining the French resistance. In this case, no one could tell the young man what to do; there was no divine power whispering in his ear what path he should follow; there were no absolute values to guide him. He was utterly alone—forlorn, totally responsible. But he was also utterly *free*—free to choose.

Despair, the third choice-induced emotion, is the feeling brought on by the realization that only one's individual actions— not collective ones—make up ones life; thus, Sartre points out, while it is impossible to "change the world," it is still necessary to live in it. "To be sure, this may seem a harsh thought to someone whose life hasn't been a success. But, on the other hand it prompts people to understand that reality alone is what counts, that dreams, expectations, and hopes warrant no more than to define a man as a disappointed dream, as miscarried hopes, as vain expectations."

Though every human being is responsible for his effect on others—and even though only his *own* existence is real to him, and, ultimately, he is his *own* judge—still, in a nihilistic (meaningless, unknowable, baseless) universe, nihilism reigns, and "all human activities are equivalent, all destined [to go down in] defeat."

An espousal of these controversial concepts—the hostile nature of the world, subjectivity (free choice), anguish (duty), forlornness (individual responsibility), and despair (fatalism)—has caused existentialism to be labelled a philosophy of pessimism. However, Sartre counters, "at our core we are toughly optimistic." To him existentialism *is* idealistic and hopeful, in that it endows man with freedom. Man is the sole author of his ethics, Sartre concludes, the sculptor of his image. And by accepting existentialism's tenets, each individual is capable of attaining true personal freedom: "What the existentialist says is that the coward makes himself cowardly, that the hero makes himself heroic. There's always a possibility for the coward not to be cowardly . . . and for the hero to stop being heroic. What counts is total involvement."

A THEORY OF JUSTICE

by John Rawls, Belknap Press of Harvard University, Cambridge, Massachusetts, 1971

In *A Theory of Justice,* John Rawls presents his famous defense for philosophic liberalism, a thesis which proposes a definition of justice as the "appropriate distribution of the benefits and burdens of social cooperation ("justice as fairness"). Rawls' notion that *true* justice *is* "fairness" is referred to as the "original position." This original position advocates that social decisions should be equitable for all and founded on the cornerstone of true justice. For Rawls, "justice as fairness" is procedural; its aim is to establish the means by which differing individuals can get along.

Rawls is a champion of "liberality." The term "liberal" in this case denotes a belief that choice should be left to the individual, that the State should not interfere with individual rights, and that the individual takes precedence over the society in which he lives. Like many advocates of liberal theory, Rawls relies upon the concept of a "social contract" to support his primary principle, "justice as fairness," and to introduce two subsequent corollaries: protected individual rights and egalitarian public institutions.

Briefly stated, the social contract is an agreement (either real or hypothetical) among moral agents to set aside differences and establish procedures for fair cooperation. The social contract is used to establish "principles that free and rational persons . . . would accept in an initial position of equality."

Since individuals' aims are different, a mutually acceptable agreement cannot favor any one set of disputed ends. The conception of "justice as fairness" proposes a neutral framework allowing individuals to get along harmoniously. "Among individuals with disparate aims and purposes," Rawls reasons, "a shared conception of justice establishes the bonds of civic friendship."

Many contract theorists preceded Rawls, the most notable being the eighteenth-century French philosopher, Jean Jacques Rousseau. Parallels are also often drawn between Rawls and Immanuel Kant, the eighteenth-century German philosopher, whose categorical imperatives include criteria for unanimity, autonomy and equal respect. (Kant claimed that human beings should never be treated as a mere means to an end.) Likewise, Rawls' social contract requires unanimous agreement between equally valued and independent agents. Rawls admits Kantian roots, writing, "the original position may be viewed . . . as a procedural interpretation of Kant's conception of autonomy and the categorical imperative."

While Rawls borrows ideas from many philosophers, his formulation of the social contract and political liberalism remains groundbreaking work in social thought. Indeed *A Theory of Justice* has inspired one of the most vigorous debates in contemporary social philosophy, with "Rawlsian" liberalism defending a position somewhere between views from both the political right and political left. This debate continues today, with Rawls publishing a further clarification of his theories as recently as 1993 (*Political Liberalism,* Columbia University, New York).

The Original Position

The Rawlsian social contract (the "original position") is an agreement seeking a neutral framework toward disputed personal conceptions of the good. The "original position" is not an actual event, but a "purely hypothetical situation characterized so as to lead to a certain conception of justice." The primary Rawlsian principle, "justice as fairness," is the conception which *results from* the "original position."

The "original position" is a unique device which allows individuals to get along collectively while still being free to pursue personal ends. It is "a working agreement on the fundamental question of political justice" which can then "regulate all further agreements and the forms of government that can be established." The "original position" establishes principles by which society's "primary goods ("rights and liberties, powers and opportunities") are equally distributed.

So that legal principles (laws) favor no particular person or group, each agent within the "original position" must possess equal bargaining power. To achieve this, agents are placed behind a figurative "veil of ignorance," which suspends knowledge of their particular circumstances. "No one knows his situation in society nor his natural assets," Rawls says, referring to this veil of ignorance, "and therefore no one is in a position to tailor principles to his advantage." Thus, a government, school, or company official cannot, theoretically, pass laws or give out scholarships or offer a bonuses that would benefit him or any particular class of individuals to the detriment of another person or class of individuals. The distribution of "goods" (any opportunity or object that could be distributed) must be made equally, without bias, as if the giver were "blind"—blind to the recipient's background, ethnicity, religion, etc. This metaphoric veil would ensure that only considerations of reason—rather than prejudice—would be allowed within the social contract.

Rather than being based on *bargaining power,* contractual principles are based upon what is *reasonable* for each and every party to accept. Although the parties do not know their exact situations, they know it is "not reasonable . . . to expect more than an equal share and . . . not rational for them to accept less."

To ensure consensus, the "original position" seeks agreement only on shared ends, and purposely excludes disputed matters (such as which of several religions is correct). Since agents do not know their circumstances, they choose principles which are mutually and maximally beneficial, principles that "protect their liberties, widen their opportunities, and enlarge their means for promoting their aims, whatever these are."

This consensus process leads to the neutral principle of "justice as fairness." Since the agents select principles which not only "protect their basic rights but [which also] insure themselves against the worst eventualities," freedoms are zealously defended regarding private ends while equality is promoted in public matters. To facilitate agreement, the "original position" includes two other principles derived from "justice as fairness": the strict protection of individual liberties (hence the term "liberalism") and redistributive public policies (such as affirmative action and welfare).

The Priority of Individual Rights

The social contract advances indisputable governmental power but does not intrude into private matters. To ensure minimal agreement, disputed conceptions of the good are excluded from the "original position" and the freedom to pursue those goods are left alone.

By keeping disputed conceptions of the good outside the social contract, principles are chosen which allow disparate persons to live together. Given the variety of individual concerns within society, the freedom to pursue personal ends is often cited as liberalism's fundamental appeal. Liberties such as the freedom of religion, speech, assembly and due process exist to protect the individual's right to pursue personal aims even when contrary to majority opinion. "Each person possesses an inviability founded on justice which even the welfare of society as a whole cannot over-ride."

The "original position" establishes a maximum of liberties, ensuring the greatest ability to pursue individual aims in the many possible circumstances an agent may actually inhabit. However, to guarantee an equal protection of rights, some personal behaviors may be prohibited (such as today's legal right of nonsmokers not to breath a smoker's second-hand smoke in a public place, or demanding adherence to traffic rules while driving on the highway). Restrictions are placed upon certain freedoms to ensure that each agent's similar freedoms are fully protected. "Each person is to have an equal right to the most extensive basic liberties compatible with a similar liberty for others." While actions which unequally infringe upon another's protected liberties (such as slavery, murder or libel) are disallowed, the merit of unaffected and competing aims is not to be determined.

Excluding disputed personal aims does not suppose that individuals are unconcerned about these matters, rather it allows them to get along given that they are, in fact, so deeply concerned but often cannot agree. The formulation of "justice as fairness" is "prudential [and] allows the groups in the overlapping consensus to pursue their own good subject to certain constraints which each thinks to be for its [own] advantage given existing circumstances."

The emphasis liberalism places on protected freedoms leads to a sharp division between the consensual principles of the "original position" (the public sphere) from the competing ends of actual individuals (the private sphere). A strict division is required between those things which properly fall within the public sphere and those which do not. The importance liberals place on separation of church and state, says Rawls, is a prime example of protecting individual liberties through maintaining a strict religious neutrality in the public sphere.

The Difference Principle

While consensus protects personal liberties, it likewise demands that public institutions be devoid of favoritism, unless such bias benefits everyone. "Justice as fairness requires that all primary social goods be distributed equally unless an unequal distribution would be to everyone's advantage."

Since bargaining agents would not accept an unequal share of social goods, bias within the public sphere must always work to rectify any disparity of those goods. This bias toward aiding the "worst off" individuals in the public sphere (termed the "difference principle") ensures that widely divergent agents can reach agreement even when bargaining from the position of society's "worst off." "The division of advantages should be such as to draw forth the willing cooperation . . . of those less well situated."

Rawls' "difference principle," which guards against institutions being structured to favor the powerful, allows only those inequities which enable advantage to flow toward the worst off. While an entirely neutral framework is preferred, given the already unequal distribution of social benefits the best alternative is to encourage a more equitable redistribution of goods. "The higher expectations of those better situated are just if and only if they work as part of a scheme which improves the expectations of the least advantaged."

To ensure unanimity, today's utopian, more ideal institutions must be structured with a built-in bias toward the disadvantaged. Any other bias cannot be allowed, since it would jeopardize the neutral arrangement. The "original position" represents a minimal agreement about the fair structure of social cooperation. Any disputed aims must be kept without this "kernel of overlapping consent," just as any included aims must actively promote the equal distribution of primary goods.

In *A Theory of Justice*, Rawls forcefully espouses a social contract (the "original position") to establish a neutral framework for making social decisions that are equitable for all ("justice as fairness"). Neutrality (fairness) results in both the protection of diverse personal freedoms and egalitarianism.

Today, liberalism's influence is evident in the constitutions of most modern nations. Global concern for human rights, equal justice, and fair elections emphasize the strength liberal theory retains in contemporary politics and world opinion. Still, critics of liberalism abound. While few criticize liberalism's goal of maintaining individual rights and fair procedure, many allege that its theoretic assumptions and devices (such as the social contract) are difficult and problematic.

Many recent philosophic attacks have been focused on liberalism's concept of the individual as isolated and independent. Both communitarians on the right and feminists on the left (in spite of their many real differences) maintain that actual persons are far too complex and deeply embedded within communities to divide their public and private concerns. Regardless of these many critiques and their possible merits, liberal theory remains a powerful force in contemporary social thought, with *A Theory of Justice* standing formidably in the center of the controversy.

Personal Notes:

COMPACT

Classics®

LIBRARY #6: Reaching & Understanding

Want to expand your world view, rouse yourself to action, touch heart-strings or soul-strings, or just make life a little easier? The books featured in this library do just that: they deliver and deal with today's most meaningful issues and vital topics.

Included here are selections on personal finance, business, health, happiness, understanding yourself and others, and enhancing your personal relationships. Some of the works are forceful often controversial; others offer helpful principles and techniques; and still others consist of personal-outlook summaries. Confirm what you always suspected in John Gray's *Men Are From Mars, Women Are From Venus*; treat yourself to Anne Lindbergh's *Gift From the Sea*; build your understanding of self with Thomas Harris' *I'm OK, You're OK*; and examination a variety perspectives, from Susan Faludi's *Backlash* to Rush Limbaugh's *The Way Things Ought to Be*.

Here's to reaching your potential and to understanding yourself and others!

PRINCIPLE-CENTERED LEADERSHIP

by Stephen R. Covey, Summit Books, New York, N.Y., 1991

In this work, the author of the best-selling *Seven Habits of Highly Effective People* differentiates between "ineffective" and "effective" people. Ineffective individuals, in any professional or personal endeavor, are those who manage their time according to their own priorities, whereas *highly effective* people lead their lives according to principles and values that are universally valid. The ability to "lead" is amplified by applying these principles to problem solving, which results in improvements in quality of experience, in productivity, and in social harmony.

CHARACTERISTICS OF PRINCIPLE-CENTERED LEADERS

"From study and observation and from my own strivings, I have isolated eight discernible characteristics of people who are principle-centered leaders," Covey writes. "These traits not only characterize effective leaders, they also serve as signs of progress for all of us."

Principle-centered leaders possess the following characteristics:

1. They are continually learning

Principle-centered people keep learning. They experience life; they read, take classes, ask questions and listen to others. They continually expand their skills—and discover that the more they know, the more they don't know. Almost all of this learning and growth is self-directed; to them, learning is thoroughly enjoyable.

Principle-centered people have discovered that one of the most important precepts of self-growth is that they can only grow through self-trust: "You will develop your abilities faster by learning to make and keep promises or commitments," says Covey. "Start by making a small promise to yourself; continue fulfilling that promise until you have a sense that you have a little more control over yourself. Now take the next level of challenge. Make yourself a promise and keep it until you have established control at that level. Now move to the next level; make the promise, keep it. As you do this, your sense of personal worth will increase; your sense of self-mastery will grow, as will your confidence that you can master the next level."

It is important to be serious and intent when making promises, because failing to keep promises weakens resolve and self-esteem.

2. They are service-oriented

Those who are striving to be principle-centered see what they do in life as a *mission*, not as a career. Every morning they "yoke up" for service to their fellow human beings: "See yourself each morning yoking up, putting on the harness of service in your various stewardships. See yourself taking the straps and connecting them around your shoulders as you prepare to do the work assigned to you that day. See yourself allowing someone else to adjust the yoke or harness. See yourself yoked up to another person at your side— a co-worker or spouse—and learning to pull together with that person."

Throughout the book Covey emphasizes this principle of service, or "yoking up." He has observed that the attempt to become principle-centered *without* being service-oriented is not only a meaningless attempt, but it simply will not succeed. Leadership is a hollow role without accepting the burden to care for—and at times to carry—others.

3. They radiate positive energy

Principle-centered people are cheerful, pleasant, optimistic and upbeat. They are enthusiastic, hopeful and believing. They literally radiate positive energy. The author explains: "This positive energy is like an energy field or an aura that surrounds them and that similarly charges or changes weaker, negative energy fields around them. They also attract and magnify smaller positive energy fields. When they come into contact with strong, negative energy sources, they tend either to neutralize or to sidestep this negative energy. Sometimes they will simply leave it, walking away from its poisonous orbit. Wisdom gives them a sense of how strong it is and a sense of humor and of timing in dealing with it . . . Be aware of the effect of your own energy and understand how you radiate and direct it. And in the middle of confusion or contention or negative energy, strive to be a peacemaker, a harmonizer, to undo or reverse destructive energy. You will discover what a self-fulfilling prophecy positive energy is when combined with the next characteristic."

4. They believe in other people

Principle-centered people don't feel imbued with power when they discover the weaknesses in others. Neither do they overreact to negative behaviors or criticism. They realize that all people have strengths and weaknesses, and rather than focusing on weaknesses and flaws, they find the unseen potential in all people—including themselves. They are grateful for their blessings and willingly forgive and forget the wrongs done to them, avoiding the tendency to label or prejudge others. They understand that in the acorn lies the mighty oak.

Covey illustrates these points: "Once my wife and I felt uneasy about the labels we and other had attached to one of our sons, even though these labels were justified by his behavior. By visualizing his potential, we gradually came to see him differently. When we believed in the unseen potential, the old labels vanished naturally, and we stopped trying to change him overnight. We simply knew that his talent and potential would come in its own time. And it did, to the astonishment, frankly, of others, including other family members. We were not surprised because we knew who he was."

Covey stresses that in order to engender an environment conducive to growth, people must learn to believe in the unseen potential of themselves and of others. Self-centered people believe

433

that the key to growth lies in *themselves* and in doing things *to* other people: "This works only temporarily," Covey point out. "If you believe it's `in' them, not `in' you, you relax, accept, affirm, and let it happen. Either way it is a self-fulfilling prophecy."

5. They lead balanced lives

Those governed by principles read the best literature and keep up on current events. They socialize with many friends; they have a few confidants. Intellectually active and maintaining a wide variety of interests, they observe and learn from everything and everyone around them. Physically active as well—in ways appropriate to their age and health—they enjoy life. Their sense of humor is also nimble, in a healthy way. They are particularly able to laugh at themselves rather than at others. Extremely self-honest, they view themselves quite realistically, and positively. They're not religious zealots, workaholics, political fanatics or pleasure addicts. They refrain from condemning themselves or others for mistakes, nor do they brood over the past—or the future.

"They can feel their own worth," continues Covey, "which is manifest by their courage and integrity and by the absence of a need to brag, to drop names, to borrow strength from possessions or credentials or titles or past achievements. They are open in their communication, simple, direct, nonmanipulative. They also have a sense of what is appropriate, and they would sooner err on the side of understatement than on the side of exaggeration . . . They are not extremists—they do not make everything all or nothing. They do not divide everything into two parts, seeing everything as good or bad, as either/or. They think in terms of continuums, priorities, hierarchies. They have the power to discriminate, to sense the similarities and differences in each situation. This does not mean they see everything in terms of situational ethics. They fully recognize absolutes and courageously condemn the bad and champion the good . . ."

6. They see life as an adventure

Principle-centered individuals have no need to categorize and label everyone and everything around them. Instead they live an extended adventure; they see old faces and environs freshly and are always gazing past the horizon, never really sure what they will find, but always eager to explore and make their contribution: "Their security lies in their initiative, resourcefulness, creativity, willpower, courage, stamina, and native intelligence rather than in the safety, protection, and abundance of their home camps, or their comfort zones . . . They rediscover people each time they meet them . . . They ask questions and get involved," Covey notes. "They are completely present when they listen. They learn from them. They don't label them from past successes or failures . . . They are not overawed by top government figures or celebrities. They resist becoming any person's disciple. They are basically unflappable and capable of adapting virtually to anything that comes along. One of their fixed principles is flexibility. They truly lead the abundant life."

7. They are synergistic

Synergy is a state in which the interplay *between* parts produces more intense, imaginative energy than the parts *alone* can produce. Principle-centered people are synergistic; they are catalysts for change and will contribute in almost any situation. They are excellent team players because they are adept at balancing their strengths and weaknesses with those of others around them. Effective delegation comes naturally for them because they are not intimidated by others who are better at some things than themselves.

Covey sees other advantages for practicing principle-centered synergy: "When principle-centered people negotiate and communicate with others in seemingly adversarial situations, they learn to separate the people from the problem. They focus on the other person's interests and concerns rather than fight over positions. Gradually others discover their sincerity and become part of a creative problem-solving process. Together they arrive at synergistic solutions, which are usually much better than any of the original proposals, as opposed to compromise solutions wherein both parties give and take a little."

8. They exercise for self-renewal

Principle-centered people regularly exercise the four dimensions of being: the physical, the mental, the emotional and the spiritual.

• They participate in a periodic, balanced exercise program which stresses cardiovascular fitness and endurance. Thus, they provide their bodies and brains with the conditioning necessary for fulfilling lifestyles.

• They exercise their minds by reading, writing, creative problem solving, visualizing—all with a sense of play rather than obligation.

• "Emotionally they make an effort to be patient, to listen to others with genuine empathy, to show unconditional love, and to accept responsibility for their own lives and decisions and reactions."

• And "spiritually they focus on prayer, scripture study, meditation, and fasting."

"I'm convinced," says Covey, "that if a person will spend one hour a day on these basic exercises, he or she will improve the quality, productivity, and satisfaction of every other hour of the day, including the depth and restfulness of sleep." He goes on to challenge his readers to think of the interplay of the four dimensions of being, metaphorically, as a saw used to fashion lives: "No other single hour of your day will return as much as the hour you invest in sharpening the saw—that is, in exercising these four dimensions of the human personality. If you will do this daily, you will soon experience the impact for good on your life . . . Some of these activities may be done in the normal course of the day; others will need to be scheduled into the day. They take some time, but in the long run they save us a great deal of time. We must never get too busy sawing to take time to sharpen the saw."

THE ART OF WAR

by Sun Tzu (translation by Samuel B. Griffith), Oxford University Press, New York, N.Y., 1963

The Art of War is, in essence, a step-by-step guide to the process of waging war. Early on, this work was considered a mere how-to guide for planning a military conquest. In modern times, it has become a reference work for administrators and managers (comments which, in this summary, are set off in brackets).

Not only do Sun Tzu's philosophies apply to war strategies and preparations, but they are equally adaptable to the adversarial world of business and commerce. Sun Tzu was a philosopher before he was a general. In fact, *The Art of War* was written *before* Sun Tzu was called upon to lead armies for the Emperor.

Sun Tzu addresses the relevance of his work by saying:

The art of war is of vital importance to the state. It is a matter of life and death, a road either to safety or to ruin. Hence under no circumstances can it be neglected.

From here, Sun Tzu outlines the 10 elements of approach to a conflict. Each point is crucial to achieving "total victory."

1. **Laying Plans:** *The general who wins a battle makes many calculations in his temple before the battle is fought. The general who loses a battle makes but few . . .* [Thorough planning is central to the success of any undertaking, large or small.]

2. **Waging War:** The key to waging a successful campaign is to prepare well, so that victory can be obtained quickly. A long siege will impoverish the people. This does not mean one should act in haste, but with cleverness. And Tzu asserts, "cleverness has never been associated with long delays . . . " [Modern business leaders understand the value of careful planning and timely action.]

3. **The Sheathed Sword:** *To fight and conquer in all your battles is not supreme excellence. Supreme excellence consists in breaking the enemy's resistance without fighting.*

A leader who is truly skillful can subdue the enemy and his troops without bloodshed. He will capture cities without laying siege to them. His gathered forces alone dispute the mastery of the empire, and thus, his triumph is complete without losing a man. [In the business world, a company's good reputation is often the essential element in the success of its new product or service.]

There are three ways a government [or a business] can bring misfortune upon its "army."

• When it gives an order the army cannot obey.
• When the army is governed without knowledge of the conditions that affect the army.
• When army officers are employed indiscriminately.

[Today, we might restate these rules as follows:

* Do not ask an employee to act unethically.

* Managers should not lose touch with their employees.

* Cultivate and reward leadership skills and innovation, and place employees according to merit and talent.]

4. **Tactics:** Tactics are governed by an army's ability to put itself beyond the possibility of defeat, and then wait for an opportunity to defeat the enemy. The ability to defend lies in the hands of the army; the ability to defeat lies in the hands of the enemy.

It is not enough to *know* how to conquer. One must be able to *do* it—and do it with ease. By committing few mistakes and exploiting the mistakes of the enemy, the victory is achieved before the battle is fought. Winning comes from fighting after seeking victory; defeat comes from fighting before seeking victory. [To put this in modern parlance, a good idea must also be practical; a goal must be achievable.]

5. **Energy:** *Energy may be likened to the bending of a crossbow; decision, to the releasing of the trigger.* Heightened energy is the result of combining one or more elements. There are only eight musical tones, but the combinations of those notes make more melodies than can be heard. And though there are only two methods of attack, yet the combinations make possible an endless number of maneuvers. [And business leaders know that a good plan, to be effective, must be set into motion at the right time.]

Energy is pent up in the momentum of the army. This energy is released when a decision is made of how to pursue. And indecision can ruin the best-laid plans. *The quality of decision is like the well-timed swoop of a falcon that enables it to strike and destroy its victim. Therefore, the good fighter will be terrible in his onset, and prompt in his decision.*

6. **Weak Points and Strong:** Knowledge of the weak points and the strong points is a science that can be used so that "the impact of your army may be like a grindstone dashed against an egg."

Whoever is first in the field of battle has the leisure of resting until the enemy arrives. The enemy, rushing to the engagement, then arrives exhausted. [IBM, because it made the first computer, was able to dominate the early market.]

The enemy that is resting must be harassed; the enemy that is camped must be forced to move. The enemy must be forced to defend an unexpected position. [Likewise, IBM "rested" too long on its reputation, in time losing its dominance to younger, hungrier, more energetic companies.]

Certainty of attack lies in assailing that which is undefended. Strike from a superior position. Attempt to discover your enemy's disposition, while keeping your own invisible. The point of attack must be shrouded in secrecy so that the enemy cannot prepare a defense. [Even today, entrepreneurs know the value of secrecy of market research.]

So in war, the way is to avoid what is strong and attack at what is weak. Water shapes its course according to the nature of the ground over which it flows; the soldier works out his victory in relation to the foe whom he is facing. [So, before you build a better mousetrap, make certain people need or want a better mousetrap, and that no one is make a better one than yours.]

7. **Maneuvering:** Success in movement comes from discipline. The ability to move an army is advantageous, but moving an undisciplined multitude is dangerous. Likewise, moving an army through unknown terrain is akin to making an alliance with a neighbor before knowing his design. Knowing the terrain allows the army to take advantage of natural positions among mountains, forests, pitfalls and precipices.

A Chinese general, Tu Mu, told the story of Wu Ch'i, who was fighting against the Ch'in state. Before the battle, one of Wu Ch'i's soldiers went secretly into the enemy's camp and captured two of their officers. When the soldier returned, Wu Ch'i had the man executed. One of Wu Ch'i's commanders observed that the man had been a good soldier and should not have been executed. But Wu Ch'i replied, "I fully believe he was a good soldier. But he was executed because he didn't follow orders."

8. **Terrain:** Ground that is easily traversed is *accessible* ground. It is important to note that if one's army can traverse the land easily, so can one's enemy.

Terrain that is easily abandoned but hard to reoccupy is *entangling*. From this position, an enemy who is unprepared is easily defeated. But if one is forced to retreat, disaster will ensue.

The ground that cannot be gained by either side making the first move is *temporizing* ground. The enemy may attempt to bait one's army, but it is critical not to snatch at the bait. In fact, it is better to retreat, thereby enticing the enemy onto more temporizing ground. [As smart executives will testify, sometimes it is better to let the competition make the mistakes.]

Narrow passages are easily defended when they are fully garrisoned. They are also easily attacked when they are not. So, in order to attack from a superior position, one must occupy the *precipitous heights* before the enemy, making an assault before he has achieved equal or greater height.

9. **The Use Of Spies:** Spies are essential to victory. Armies may fight for years, only to be victorious or defeated in the course of one day. *This being so, to remain in ignorance of the enemy's condition, simply because one grudges the outlay of a hundred ounces of silver . . . is the height of inhumanity.*

One who is not willing to obtain information pertaining to his enemy's condition will not be a master of victory. Foreknowledge is what allows the good general to strike and conquer, and it is obtained from men, not from divination, or inductive calculation.

There are five kinds of spies, each with their own strengths.

- *Local spies* are recruited in the enemy's own district. They are won over with kindness, then employed as spies.

- *Internal spies* are made from enemy officials who have been demoted or have fallen into disfavor. They are bought with bribes— and with reassurance that they have been wronged.

- A *converted spy,* detached from the services of the enemy by means of bribes and liberal promises, may prove an invaluable asset.

- One's own spies must sometimes be deceived so that when they are taken captive, they give false reports that cause the enemy to take false action. These are termed *doomed spies;* they are invariably put to death when the deception is uncovered.

- Finally, *surviving spies,* the ordinary class, are those that simply bring back information from the enemy.

10. **Nine Situations:** Battles take place on nine types of ground, all of which require a different course of action.

Dispersive ground is the territory nearest the homes of the army, where a soldier's inclination is to scatter toward home when the fighting is fierce. It is best to fight on the enemy's dispersive ground.

When the army has succeeded in penetrating the enemy's territory, but not at a great distance from his own, is called *facile ground.* And ground that is advantageous for neither side is ground that is *contentious.*

When both sides can move freely, the armies are fighting on *open ground.* When *intersecting highways* (critical to the movement of armies and supplies) form the lifeline of three or more contiguous states, the army that occupies that ground commands most of the empire.

An army that has penetrated deep into enemy territory is on *serious ground;* while *difficult ground* is characterized by mountains, rugged hills and marshes.

Land that reaches through canyons and tortuous paths—places where a small number of the enemy can defeat a large body—is considered *hemmed-in ground.*

Lastly, ground on which the only means of survival rests in destroying the enemy is termed *desperate ground.*

On dispersive ground, fight not. On facile ground, halt not. On open ground, do not block the enemy's way. On ground of intersecting highways, join hands with your allies. On serious ground, gather in plunder. In difficult ground, keep steadily on the march. On hemmed in ground, resort to stratagem.

On desperate ground, fight.

HOW TO RUN A SUCCESSFUL MEETING IN HALF THE TIME

by Milo O. Frank, Simon and Schuster, New York, N.Y., 1989

After many years of experience as a successful consultant, Milo Frank has discovered that people often schedule meetings that are superfluous. Those that aren't, he finds, usually take about twice as much time as is needed. By offering practical tips on how to determine when a meeting should be called as well as how to conduct one, *How to Run a Meeting in Half the Time* details how to get the most out of any meeting in the shortest amount of time.

TO MEET OR NOT TO MEET

When should you call a meeting?

According to Frank, the only time you should call a meeting is when a face-to-face consultation is the best or only way to achieve your objectives. Oftentimes, Frank points out, you can achieve your goals—and save a lot of time and money—with a few simple phone calls.

Begin by determining your objective.

A meeting without a clear-cut objective is like a trip nowhere: it can go on forever. Frank asserts that very few people in management positions—"from middle managers to top executives"—understand "the objectives of the meetings they call or are asked to attend." To save time, the author suggests that every meeting needs to have a "single clear-cut objective." To help you uncover your objective, Frank has designed a series of questions you can ask yourself: (1) Why am I holding/attending the meeting? (2) Why/how am I going to participate in the meeting? (3) What do I want to achieve after the meeting is over?

Should meetings be held on a regular basis?

Frank submits that meetings should be held on a regular basis only if each one has a specific purpose that cannot be fulfilled in any other way. "Meetings held on a routine basis—weekly, bimonthly, monthly—are generally tedious and wasteful. Often you are forced to find or create situations in order to have something to talk about." Instead, it is much better to meet only when there is a specific purpose.

What damage can an unnecessary meeting do?

An unnecessary meeting can destroy any chance of achieving your objectives. Frank cites the following example from his own experience:

A business manager friend of mine found an excellent investment opportunity at a marina near Los Angeles. He talked to a number of his clients about the investment, and I was included. We liked the deal and gave him authority to proceed. During his negotiations the price was upped. We told the business manager to go ahead anyway, but his junior partners wanted a meeting with all of us to discuss the problem. We said on the phone, "Don't waste time, just close the deal." But no, we had to have a meeting. Weeks passed before everyone was available. At the meeting we all agreed to go forward, just as we had agreed in our phone conversations. Nothing new was accomplished. However, because of the passage of time, the sellers had found another buyer who, incidentally, paid more than we would have. They closed the deal with him, and within one year the value of the property had doubled.

WHEN YOU CALL A MEETING

Who should participate in the meeting?

Frank argues that the only people who should take part in a meeting are those who can contribute to reaching the meeting's objective(s). Unnecessary participants waste everyone's time. However, you need to recognize every participant's objectives and interests. That is, you shouldn't exclude a potential participant just because his interests/objectives are contrary to the meeting's objective(s). In fact, including a person who has opposing ideas can produce cohesion in a group as well as diffuse resistance others may feel.

To help you decide whom to include, Frank suggests asking yourself some questions:

1. Whom am I obligated to invite?
2. Who can give me what I want?
3. Who is in favor of my objective?
4. Who might oppose my objective?
5. Who is on the fence?
6. Who can cause trouble if not invited?

Frank reminds his readers that the length of any meeting is directly proportional to the number of people attending. "Here's where the psychology of group dynamics comes into play," he writes. "Small groups invite candor, intimacy, and real results. When the group is larger than about ten people, the theatrics begin as opposing parties try to impress their colleagues, playing more for effect than for results."

How should you prepare for the meeting?

The best way to prepare for a meeting, says Frank, is to formulate a well-thought-out agenda that will function as a blueprint. The agenda—which can be written as a memo—will serve not only to announce the meeting, but, more importantly, will provide a vehicle through which you can reach your objectives. "A written memo or agenda is the best means of giving and securing information and . . . will focus you as well as the recipients on the objective of the meeting and the means to achieve it." Pre-set agendas also act as the meeting guide, and as a reminder of what was discussed. To truly save time, however, an agenda must be kept brief—*no longer than one page.* If additional materials like charts and graphs are needed, these "should be included on separate pages."

What should a good memo/agenda include?

A well-formulated memo/agenda "should state the objective of the meeting, the issues to be discussed, the time the meeting will begin *and* end, the place, the participants involved, and what is expected of them in the way of preparation before the meeting."

Should you mix meetings with meals?

According to Frank, socializing is a powerful means to achieving your business objectives. "I have arranged social evenings," confesses Frank, "where the word *business* was not even mentioned." Having broken the ice at the social meeting, a business meeting can then be scheduled to get right to the matters at hand.

WHEN YOU ATTEND A MEETING

When should you attend a meeting that may be a waste of time?

Attend a meeting only if it provides an opportunity to further business objectives. Some so-called wasted gatherings can be considered "career training." Find a way to make that meeting valuable, and work to extract that value. Perhaps the only thing that will come of the meeting will be the association with others in a business setting—potential future associates. Only if you see each meeting as a business opportunity can you expect to attain your objectives.

What preparations might you make to enhance the success of your meeting?

Frank suggests that before the start of each meeting, you develop a "brief message" to help you define your objectives. After you have formulated your message, you can "then find or create an opportunity in the meeting to get that message across." These sorts of concise messages or statements oftentimes "command understanding and respect"; they "can win in a busy meeting where a 'dissertation' would be cut off or relegated to another time and place."

Is there a specific form to be used for your concise message?

"Every message should include a 'grabber' opening, a main idea, and a demand on the audience," Frank writes. The *grabber*, besides being a way to "grab" everyone's attention, can be an effective means of communicating an objective. For example, a manager working for a chemical waste management company was once invited to a meeting of young people who claimed his corporation caused environmental damage. Although not invited as an active participant, the manager did not want to become a target for adversarial, confrontational questions. He decided to use the meeting as an opportunity to disarm his company's adversaries. Thus, he prepared the following brief message, which included a grabber and a main idea:

The Sunday New York Times, one of our greatest newspapers, costs 75,000 trees. The Sunday Chicago Tribune costs 16,500 trees. We had better take pictures of our Main Idea: forests so our grandchildren will know what a tree looked like. Or better still, recycle and save the trees, and then their children can even climb them. My company is a leading proponent of recycling.

He then concluded with a demand on his audience:

We want you to get involved. You can write or call me and we can talk about how what we do benefits us all.

How do you prepare for a meeting where there is opposition to your objective?

When there is opposition to your ideas, Frank suggests that you first determine your opponent's objectives and strategies, and then, before the meeting begins, ask yourself:

- *What does my opponent want, and why?*
- *Who else is on my opponent's side?*
- *Who are my allies?*
- *What are the strongest points in favor of my opponent's objective?*
- *What are the strongest points against it?*
- *What are the strongest points I can make that will accomplish my objective?"*

The answers to such questions will help you determine your chances of success, and also what you specifically need to do to make success more likely.

AT THE MEETING

What is the best way to overcome the pressure of a meeting?

"Meetings are pressure situations." They can expose you to both "time pressure" and "peer pressure"—certainly, everyone wants to perform well around his or her colleagues and boss. To reduce these pressures, plan in advance what to say and how you are going to say it. Frank advises that you not read a prepared message aloud and that you not memorize it. Instead, keep in mind those *topics* you need to cover and be aware of how you are going to present them, perhaps rehearsing a little beforehand.

Be prepared to use someone else's question for your own purpose: to get your message across.

Frank explains how he pushes meetings along *and* presents his message at the same time:

I am a participant in a meeting and I do not have the floor. If I get the chance, I want to say, "Most meetings are twice as long as they should be." . . . I have gotten my message across. But what if someone asks me, "What did you have for breakfast?" . . . I think and answer, "Fresh fruit, cereal, sourdough toast, jam, and coffee. A big breakfast. And I usually need it because most of the meetings I attend are twice as long as they should be, so I'm prepared if we're late for lunch."

I was asked about breakfast and I told the questioner how long most meetings are. I answered his question in the process. That is the technique of making any question bridge to your prepared message.

The name of the game . . .

"I cannot emphasize enough," says Frank, "that using someone else's question or statement to get a prepared, short message across is absolutely the best method of achieving your objective in any meeting." When you use someone else's question or answer to communicate your own message, *you* become the leader, controlling the meeting while you speak. Moreover, if the topic you introduce continues to be discussed, then your influence and leverage in the meeting grows even stronger. *This*, Frank asserts, is the name of the game: To make meetings conform to your own objectives.

Frank concludes his book by listing *four elements* that will make a meeting twice as successful in half the time.

1. *Time constraints.* Time constraints keep all participants aware that their message needs to count.

2. *Advance preparation.* If you prepare in advance a brief, formal, written *memo/agenda*, the participants in the meeting know what is expected of them.

3. *Proper presentation.* Allow time for proper presentation, giving every participant an opportunity to share his or her views within an allotted time period.

4. *Control.* If you are leading the meeting, try to regulate each person's participation in a firm but polite manner, and see to it that priorities are set and adhered to.

Frank's many practical suggestions for carrying out effective meetings in the shortest time possible is helpful reading for anyone who regularly attends or conducts meetings.

SMART TALK

The Art of Savvy Business Conversation
by Roberta Roesch, AMACOM Publishing, New York, N.Y., 1989

Good communication skills are essential both to the beginning manager and to the person who is already in upper-management. In any business situation, saying the right thing in the right manner can advance your career—while saying the wrong thing can ruin it.

Roberta Roesch's *Smart Talk* contains clear suggestions on how to develop the verbal skills necessary for business. And though the strategies presented are specifically illustrated for use in the business world, many can also be applied in home and personal situations. "Through real life stories and typical corporate dialogues," Roesch says, "you'll learn what to say, how to say it, and when and where to speak. You'll find out how to increase your visibility and display your upper-management potential."

What's Your Verbal IQ?

A department manager killed her chances for advancement because she spent too much supervisory time rambling on about irrelevant subjects. In essence, she communicated to her manager that she was unable to make a point and that she was a talker rather than a doer.

"A high verbal IQ is the packaged result of your ability to speak effectively, with verbal fluency and flexibility. It's based on your being in control of your words—and the way you deliver them—as you face common situations in the business world."

A high verbal IQ builds self-esteem and heightens your image, increasing your potential for business success. *Smart Talk* tips for projecting a high verbal IQ include:

* Prepare for every encounter
* Refrain from talking too much
* Remember the hierarchy
* Concentrate on solutions

Listen To Your Voice

A junior account executive in an advertising firm was not promoted—not because her supervisor felt she was not qualified, but because her soft, high-pitched whine kept people from taking her seriously. Supervisory duties in the senior position required someone who could give a stronger, more assertive impression.

"The way you sound to others can strengthen your visibility, showcase your upper-management potential, and have tremendous impact on your business success." A "high-quality voice" indicates you are in control; a poor-quality, high-pitched voice connotes nervousness; mumbling suggests insecurity. Some tips for improving the way you sound are:

* Pay attention to tone
* Monitor volume
* Articulate words and phrases
* Monitor pace

Choose Your Words Carefully

"A large part of getting your verbal messages across depends on selecting words and phrases that help, rather than handicap, your efforts to obtain the responses you want." The well-chosen word or phrase enhances your professional image. Some "winning words" are listed below, according to the effect you want to leave with your listener.

Words that tranquilize—"It's my impression that . . . " "Let's talk this over so we can . . . "

Words that convey urgency—"I'll do it immediately." "I can see this matter is very important."

Words to avoid include pointless phrases such as, *sort of* and *I guess*, and abrasive statements such as, *You don't understand* and *I know I'm right*.

Wait For Your Cue

A magazine fiction editor hired an assistant, Jane, and presented her with some heavy typing duties. Jane hated typing—she had only taken the job because she thought it would help her become an editor—and, thinking her judgement was better, she failed to listen carefully as her boss dictated letters and manuscripts. Of course, soon she was fired.

"Because one of the primary needs of people in business is to be heard, how skilled you are at listening can have a tremendous effect on your upper-management potential." Good listening is not only vital to business success, but to personal, social and educational success alike.

Making Business Requests

"Will you please make time to work on this agenda today?"

Employees are generally more receptive when they feel respected. Managers agree that, when making a request, a respectful and pleasant tone rather than a demanding one gets results. "People's different behavioral makeups influence the way they respond when you make a business request. You need to tailor your method to each individual."

One way to ensure that requests—and demands—will be carried out is to use a "team approach"; sponsoring a mutually respectful relationship makes people more receptive. Another way is to offer sincere praise. Increased self-esteem improves performance.

Presentations and Meetings

"The purpose of this meeting is to talk about our expansion program." When calling a meeting, first and foremost remember to state its purpose, clearly and concisely.

Important pre-meeting strategies include:

* Know your subject thoroughly
* Know what needs to be said and why
* Establish a credible point of view early on

During any presentation or meeting, it is imperative to use upbeat, winning words. "Managers are quick to point out that the opportunity to move ahead is built into most presentations because when higher authorities see a middle manager projecting a positive verbal image, they're more likely to view that person as a candidate for advancement." Presenters will also do well to:

* Prepare an attention-getting opener
* Concentrate on problem-solving
* Get people involved

A question-and-answer session at the end of a presentation is a good way to elicit involvement and feedback, and allows you a prime opportunity to reinforce your message.

Telephone Tactics

"Is this a good time to call you?" Such statements are important when making a call; showing courtesy, then getting right to your reason for calling show that you respect the other's time. "In the final analysis, no matter what kind of call you're handling, your interested and respectful attitude can combine with a clear, straightforward approach to add up to a high telephone verbal IQ that presents you at your corporate best."

Some calls are routine, requiring only the usual telephone etiquette. Some, however, will be "crisis calls," which may require the more careful use of certain tactics:

- Collect your thoughts beforehand
- Identify yourself
- Ask if it's a good time to discuss your topic
- Take notes of your conversation
- Never put him or her on hold

When *receiving* unexpected "crisis calls," here are some useful phrases to help you stall for time to think: *"I want to give this my full attention, so I'll check into it and get back to you,"* or *"I've got someone in the office now. Can I get right back to you?"*

Giving Effective Performance Appraisals

"It's critical that we agree on objectives." Ensure that communication is clear, that the other person understands what you expect of him, and how he is to meet the objectives that have been outlined. But then how do you proceed? "Since managers at all levels lack the expertise for giving performance appraisals, another way to stand out in a corporation is to develop good verbal skills for evaluating your employees' performance and for encouraging them to improve their performance." A manager who is effective in evaluating employee performance (1) gives generous praise, (2) gives greatest attention to those key people who perform well, and (3) is prepared to handle objections and excuses. Effective performance appraisals are crucial because they are the valves that open the lines of communication between managers and staff.

Offering Criticism

"Now that you know, I'm sure it won't happen again." Supportiveness quells defensiveness. Appropriate criticism "can be the genesis of a healthy relationship as well as a way of providing constructive and considerate help." Ways to offer effective criticism include:

- Know *why* you need to criticize
- Weigh the *consequences* before you criticize
- Choose the right place and time
- Ease into the criticism
- Substantiate the criticism by using specific positive and negative examples

Walter, a hotel manager, thought Bill was one of the smartest young assistants he had ever had, but Bill had the habit of interrupting people with irrelevant comments. Walter first chose to compliment Bill's fine performance, then bring up the disturbing habit.

Conflicts and Confrontations

"Perhaps we can find a solution that will satisfy both of us."

In any negotiation, it is important that your "adversary" maintain the impression that you and she are on equal ground.

Another imperative is to maintain a calm atmosphere. "The managers who keep their cool under fire and speak up effectively are the men and women who earn the respect of others and eventually realize their career potential."

Because personality traits differ widely—especially in the corporate world—there is no single right way to resolve a conflict or respond to a confrontation, but following certain rules can help minimize conflicts:

- Give explanations rather than excuses
- Plan ahead how you will phrase your ideas and needs
- Be willing to compromise

Firings and Terminations

"Sooner or later, most managers have to terminate employees, so it's important to learn how to do it; how to deliver the verbal message as humanely and effectively as possible."

"Unfortunately, this is the end of our working relationship," may be the best choice of words when you feel you need to be more to the point.

Employees, however, have the right to be given suggestions and warnings about their performance long *before* a firing is warranted. The first warning should be oral; the second, written. In the end, if dismissal is the only choice, carefully select an opportune time and place. Most importantly, use an approach that does not crush the person's self-respect:

- Stick to facts instead of launching off on feelings
- Keep your remarks work-related
- Ensure that the person has heard and understood everything you have said

Unwelcome Talk

When in the middle of a discussion someone brings up a concept that is completely unrelated to the business at hand, the best response is: *"I believe that's a personal [or an extraneous] matter and not relevant here."*

If, on the other hand, you are confronted with a question that seems strange or awkward, try to find out why the person is asking it. A boss might query an employee about a personal matter—possibly in an innocent attempt to establish a relationship. Other questions that seem personal at first, may actually be in the interest of business. "Sometimes it's difficult to answer questions that straddle the line between personal and business matters, especially if you're anxious to postpone the answer," the author admits. "But if the question is business-related, you can't put off answering it forever. You need to offer a straightforward reply, or a strategy that will buy you more time, if the situation warrants it."

Skillful communication is one of the most important tickets to business success. *Smart Talk* is a reference book that provides the "how to's" of verbal agility. Its strategies could be used by anyone who wants to enhance his image by becoming a better communicator.

THE EFFECTIVE EXECUTIVE

by Peter F. Drucker, Harper and Row Publishing, New York, N.Y., 1967

. . . I have tried to study systematically what effective executives do that the rest of us . . . do not do, and what they do not do that the rest of us tend to do . . . The most important thing to report is that I have found that effectiveness can be learned—but also that it must be learned. It does not come by itself.

Drucker's *The Effective Executive* searches for answers to the question: What makes an executive most effective?

To learn how to be effective executives, we need to understand two basic concepts. *Efficiency* is defined as doing things in the right *way; effectiveness* is doing the right *things* in the right way.

In the past, most employees were "manual" workers managed by a few "executives," and the key issue was "worker efficiency." Today, most workers are "knowledge" workers—people whose contributions derive from their intellect and "effectiveness" has become the key issue.

To be "effective"—do the right things the right way—means executives must:

- Know where their time goes.
- Gear their efforts to results and not to effort.
- Build on strengths.
- Force themselves to set priorities and stay with them.
- Make effective decisions.

Know Thy Time

Time is a scarce and irreplaceable resource. Knowing where your time goes is the first step to controlling it. Effective executives should not focus on *planning* their time, rather, they need to *manage* it effectively. Accordingly, they first determine how their time is actually used. Second, time wasters must be eliminated and discretionary time must be consolidated into the largest possible blocks. For example, one company chairman estimated that he spent one-third of his time with senior management, one-third with important customers and one-third on community activities. After keeping a log of his time, he discovered that very little was invested in *any* of these activities.

The next step is to decide which activities could just as well be done by someone else. Effective delegation does not mean getting others to do our work, but that we stop doing other people's work. One executive found that he was so swamped with social functions that he never ate meals at home. He discovered that a two-thirds of these events not only could but *should* be attended by someone else—leaving him large blocks of time to be used as he saw fit.

Managers also need to be concerned with time-loss that results from poor management and deficient organization. One hospital administrator spent much of his time helping doctors find beds for their patients because he had better information at hand on recent discharges than did the admitting office. Turning over the admit-ting and discharge data to Admitting—where it belonged in the first place—freed his time.

The third step of time management is consolidating discretionary time, scheduling "time pieces" into single, categorized blocks to be handled as separate tasks.

What Can I Contribute?

The effective executive . . . looks up from his work and outward toward goals. He asks: "What can I contribute that will significantly affect the performance and the results of the institution that I serve?" His stress is on responsibility. The focus on contribution is the key to effectiveness.

When executives are more concerned with effort than with results, with authority than with responsibility, they make themselves ineffectual. Focusing on *contributions*, however, has three impacts: 1) creates direct results, 2) builds or reaffirms values, and 3) develops people.

The securities department in a bank performed only routine functions such as stock transfers and recordkeeping. A new manager realized that his work brought him into contact with senior financial executives, and he remolded his department into an efficient marketing organization for the bank's other services.

Focusing on contributions also fosters personnel development, better communications, and teamwork. Spotlighting contributions turns an executive's weakness—dependence on others—into a strength. It creates a team of enthused individuals, working together, centered on producing results.

Making Strength Productive

The effective executive builds on people's strengths. Unfortunately, however, business leaders have a tendency to organize around weaknesses. During the Civil War, President Lincoln was criticized for placing hard-drinking Ulysses S. Grant at the head of the Union forces. Lincoln suggested sending a barrel of whiskey to his other generals as well, for Grant possessed the strength he needed at the time: the ability to win battles. The general's weaknesses were of secondary concern, if he performed his primary function, winning.

Thus, when designing or filling a position, keep in mind four ideas:

- Jobs that look good on paper may be unrealistic. Redesign them.
- Start with what the person can do, rather than what the job requires.
- Make each job demanding and big.
- To bring out strengths, you may have to tolerate some weaknesses.

" . . . It must be an unbreakable rule to promote the man who, by test of performance, is best qualified for the job to be filled." Ignore all arguments to the contrary such as, "he is too young," or "he has no field experience."

We also need to build on a superior's strengths, since a superior's poor performance reflects on the whole department or company. The correct approach is not to "brown nose," but to capitalize on a superior's strong points and work around weaknesses.

The task of an executive is not to change human beings . . . the task is to multiply the performance capacity of the whole by putting to use whatever strength, whatever health, whatever aspiration there is in individuals.

First Things First

Effective executives are able to concentrate on the task at hand; they do first things first and one thing at a time. In fifteen years, one focused chief executive of a pharmaceutical firm turned a small corner business into a giant international corporation. For the first five years, he concentrated on establishing a first-class research program. The second five years he worked to establish international business contacts, particularly in countries that were expanding medical coverage. And the last five years were spent studying and developing domestic markets. During each step, he practiced the same singular focus that he preached.

Setting priorities is easy; anyone can do it. Effective executives set and *stick to* their priorities, regardless of the pressures of the moment. Successful companies abandon those projects that are no longer bringing in results—often doing away with programs *before* they begin to decline.

The important rules for identifying priorities are dictated by courage:

- Aim for the future rather than the past.
- Concentrate on the opportunities, not the problems.
- Choose your own direction; ignore the bandwagon.
- Aim for something that will make a difference, not for the safe and easy way.

The Elements of Decision Making

Effective executives fix their attention on a few major decisions rather than a lot of little ones. For example, in the 1920s, the Bell System's Theodore Vail made four key decisions that boosted the health of Bell's private telephone service. He decided that: 1) Their business was service; 2) A monopoly needs effective regulation; 3) Good business needs effective research and development; and 4) Big business needs good capital markets.

Vail's example highlights the attributes of effective decision-making:

Understand the problem. Is the problem specific or general in nature? Am I applying the "right" solution to the "wrong" problem? The auto industry, for instance, fought for years to make roads safer, when studies showed that most accidents were caused by "problem drivers." Recently, automobile manufacturers have begun to make *cars* safer—their real area of concern and control all along—regardless of the quality of the road or driver.

Understand the limits. What are my objectives? What conditions do I *have* to satisfy? The clearer the goals, the more likely a decision will accomplish what was intended. Of course, boundaries are not etched in stone; indeed, they can be changed more easily once they are properly defined. Franklin Roosevelt, for example, campaigned on the promise of "economic recovery." But a bank collapse just before his inauguration forced him to redefine his objectives. The point is not to make the achievement of complex goals contingent on *everything going as planned.* If you do, you are destined to fail; the probability of "something" going wrong is extremely high.

Convert the decision into action. What action do we need to take? Who needs to know about this decision, and who will implement it? Once a decision is made, proper channeling of the new information is vital. One company decided to stop producing a particular machine. Faced with a last-minute rush of orders for the machine, the clerk who ordered construction materials, not yet having been advised of the decision to discontinue the product, boosted the long-term inventory according to the usual formula—a mistake that cost the company millions of dollars.

Devise a feedback loop to measure results against expectations. Decisions must be reexamined and revitalized continually. Feedback is the way to do it. When Eisenhower became president, he encountered problems getting accurate feedback. As a general, he had learned that the only reliable way to find out what was going on was to visit the battlefield and have a look around. And as president he learned to do the same.

Effective Decisions

Often, decisions force executives to choose between two relatively equivalent options. Measuring and evaluating alternatives is often the best work an executive can do. In fact, most effective decisions are made after combining factual information with "the clash and conflict of divergent opinions," and then letting the stew simmer. Opinions need to be tested and facts weighed.

Once, when General Motors' board of directors unanimously agreed on a decision, Chairman Alfred Sloan asked each of the members to return the next day after doing a bit of rethinking. As it turned out, new ideas emerged that led to a much better decision.

Finally, one of the most valid alternatives in any decision is often, "Do nothing." Not every situation requires action.

Drucker argues that an executive's principal task is to *learn to be effective.* Learning how to make better use of time, striving to focus on results, building on strengths, and making "right" decisions makes the average executive an *effective* executive.

WHAT THEY STILL DON'T TEACH YOU AT HARVARD BUSINESS SCHOOL

by Mark H. McCormack, Bantam Books, New York, N.Y., 1989

A no-nonsense guide to success for all business people, this follow-up to the former business best-seller *What They Don't Teach You at Harvard Business School* offers new ideas and strategies that you won't learn on any campus. These ideas come from McCormack's years of astute observation in the business arena.

The book first presents the **Ten Commandments of Street Smarts:**

1. *Never **underestimate** the importance of money:* "I have always been grateful to my mother for cleverly letting me know that it was really all right to be concerned about money. It is, after all the way most businesspeople keep score."

2. *Never **overestimate** the importance of money:* "Cash is by no means the only currency in business. There is much to be said for a job well done, the respect of others, or the thrill of building something from nothing. Pursue these goals . . . and let the profits follow."

3. *You can never have too many friends in business:* "Loyal friends who derive as much pleasure from your success as you do are the best leverage in business. Given the choice, people always prefer to do business with a friend, even if they sometimes can make a better deal elsewhere."

4. *Don't be afraid to say "I don't know":* "If you don't know something, say so. There's no shame in not knowing everything. In fact, there is a subtle form of flattery and ego-stroking at work when you plead ignorance and ask the other person to educate you. If you're going to bluff, do so out of strength, not ignorance. I will very often say I don't know even when I do know—to find out how much the other person really knows."

5. *Speak less:* "You cannot blunder or put your foot in your mouth if you are not speaking. More important, while you're busy talking, you are probably not reading the constantly shifting rhythms of your audience and your situation. Flapping gums dull your two most important senses—your eyes and ears."

6. *Keep your promises, the big ones and the little ones:* "Few things in this world impress me as much as someone who does what he says he will do. Likewise, few things depress me more than someone who doesn't keep his word."

7. *Every transaction has a life of its own:* "Some [transactions] need tender loving care, some need to be hurried along. Once you figure that out, be adaptable. Go into a negotiation with as few preconceptions as possible. Whether you get less or more than you really wanted, it will always be more than you started with."

8. *Commit yourself to quality from day one:* "Concentrate on each task, whether trivial or crucial, as if it's the only thing that matters (it usually is). It is better to do nothing at all than to do something badly."

9. *Be nice to people:* "Be nice to people . . . not because you'll meet them on the way down (as the cliché goes), but because it's the most pleasant route to the top.

10. *Don't hog the credit:* "Share [credit] with your colleagues. If you have to tell the world how smart

you are, you probably aren't."

What Makes a SuperSalesperson?

* **Knock on old doors**

"I'm a firm believer in the 80/20 rule: 80 percent of your business is derived from 20 percent of your customers. That's because a customer you've sold and satisfied once is more likely to buy from you again. You see this in corporate life so often—giant defense contractors as well as upstart advertising agencies sustain the bulk of their payroll with three or four important clients—that it amazes me when people don't realize their old customers are their best prospects."

* **Make your obsession their obsession**

"One thing I've learned in sports marketing is that it's a lot easier to sell participation in a sporting event to someone who shares my enthusiasm for sports. Yet even with people marginally interested in sports I keep trying—on the off chance that with careful exposure my obsession can be infectious."

* **Choose little ponds to catch big fishes**

Here, the idea is to find uncharted territory and dive right in. If the territory seems unlikely, think about it carefully; you may be overlooking a small gold mine. To use a golf analogy, you can win a golf tournament more convincingly if you play against a weak field. Of course, in golf this sort of easy victory is not very gratifying, but I guarantee that in business it is."

* **Bring something new to each party**

"A lot of salespeople are great at first impressions. They dress right, have a sense of humor, use all the right catch phrases and buzzwords. They even have something to sell. But on the second meeting, if they're back with the same patter the customer may sense that they lack substance—and walk away."

* **Backpedal aggressively**

"There's nothing more refreshing than a salesperson who honestly says, 'This is probably not right for you. Let's defer it for another time.' . . . The best salespeople know that aggressive backpedaling in many cases is more important for long term success than pushing forward full throttle to close a sale." As you apply this technique, not only will customers trust you more but they'll be more receptive when you ask if there's anything more you can do for them.

* **Remove objections gently**

"SuperSalespeople remove objections without the customer's noticing—often by learning to live with the objections or by letting the customer remove them himself . . . I don't know how many times I've heard a customer object to a proposal for reasons that I know are illogical or factually incorrect. Demolishing the customer's position might be the easiest thing in the world for me to do. But why bother? Customers don't buy because you're one point up in a debating contest—and they certainly don't buy when they're angry or humiliated."

* **Follow up after the sale**

"One of the best salespeople I ever met could sell anybody anything. He had wit, charm, substance, practicality, and a British accent. He genuinely knew what customers wanted. Unfortunately, he had no follow-up and rarely delivered what he sold. After closing a sale, he would zip out of town and you'd never hear from him again."

To McCormack, the fundamentals of negotiating are five-fold: silence, patience, sensitivity, curiosity and showing up.

1. Bite your tongue

"I've been telling myself this for so long that you'd think it would be automatic. But it's not. There is nothing more excruciating—and more important—than a protracted silence in a tense negotiating session. I still have to remind myself not to be the one who breaks that silence, no matter how awkward it seems."

2. Wait a minute. Or longer

"I never cease to marvel at how the simple passing of time can alter a situation. And so I wait—for people to cool off, for problems to solve themselves, for bad deals to self-destruct, or for a better idea to come along. Waiting is tough to do. A dynamic executive is trained to act decisively. Yet in many crises, doing nothing is the most constructive thing you can do. Whenever I don't believe this, I remember that the bulk of our successes have somehow involved the exercise of patience and the overwhelming majority of our failures the lack of it."

3. Be sensitive to the other person's point of view

Here McCormack repeats his former advice: "Being sensitive to other people's feelings always pays off; it has an uncanny way of (1) alerting you to their business needs, (2) sharpening your sense of timing, and (3) getting you out of awkward situations. All things being equal, courtesy can be most persuasive."

4. Look for insights in unexpected places

"Over the years I've learned as much about people outside the office as inside. That's one reason it's nice to dine out or play golf or tennis with `adversaries' or potential clients. People are easier to read in these fringe periods when their guard is down." But bear in mind that others will also "let their guard down" in the most mundane of situations: standing in line for lunch, pouring a cup of coffee . . . so keep your eyes open at all times.

5. Show up in person

Show up—in the flesh, in all your glory. "Nothing is more flattering to the other guy or more revealing about your opinion of him. It's the difference between visiting a friend in the hospital and sending a get-well card."

Lastly, McCormack offers some bits of advice directed at any person remotely involved in business:

When in Doubt, Delay

"Business people are encouraged to react quickly and decisively to situations. But this need to appear decisive sometimes gets in the way of sound decision-making. Not every point in a negotiation needs to be resolved on the spot. Sticky side issues have a way of gumming up the works. Sometimes it's wiser to step back, risk appearing indecisive, and hope the matter will fade away due to lack of interest." Better yet, if you can create a team-work mentality to begin with, then there is nothing wrong with needing to find the answer to a question or two.

One Thing That Must Happen in Every Negotiation

There comes a point in every negotiation where you must look the other person in the eyes and commit to something! You can ask them for their order, you can tell them (in a tactful way) that they are full of baloney, or you can just set a time and a place for your next meeting. "Fail to commit to something in every meeting or negotiation and you have doomed yourself to an endless cycle of frustration. Unless you have a valid strategic reason for procrastinating, you are wasting your time and theirs."

Three Reasons to Walk Away from a Sale (and One Reason to Stay)

"Walking away from a transaction that `doesn't feel right' is an undervalued achievement in business. Companies don't encourage it; employees don't pursue it. After all, there are no commissions for avoiding a bad deal . . . Nevertheless, it is a discipline that, with 20/20 hindsight, I have learned to appreciate. I don't know how many times in the past 25 years I wish we had had the wisdom to walk away from a deal."

There are several legitimate reasons for walking away: The first rule is to *back down when you can't deliver.* "There's nothing worse in the beginning of a relationship than to lead the buyer on, to promise something that you know you can't deliver . . . At any point in a business relationship, but especially in the beginning, you're always better off *understating* your ability to deliver and *overdelivering* on what you stated. If you can't do that, walk away."

A second time to walk away is when *price and one other ingredient somehow don't add up.* "Price alone doesn't usually kill a sale. It's price and one other ingredient . . . For example, I've often found that if the price isn't right, I might still want to make a sale to establish a long-term relationship. But if the price isn't right and there's no chance of a long-term relationship, I'll walk away (or at least not make a concession)."

A third reason for walking is when *someone demands that you abandon your principles.* "Believe it or not, people will respect your principles. They will admire you for adhering to them rather than trying to slide around them to make a sale. Quite often, they'll see the light, follow you out the door, and agree to do things your way."

The time not to walk away is when you've already invested a lot of time and money. " . . . I'm a great believer in knocking on old doors—because a customer who bought from you once will probably buy from you again. That logic applies just as well to prospects who *almost bought.* Having invested months in courting a customer, regardless of the outcome, you have left certain seeds in their mind—so that going back to them in a few months is infinitely better than making a cold call on someone new."

THE GAME OF WORK

How to Enjoy Work As Much As Play
by Charles A. Coonradt, Deseret Book, Salt Lake City, Utah, 1984

"Why is it that, in recreation, people will pay for the privilege of working harder than they will work when they are paid?" Similarly, what makes people endure terrible conditions during play, while, if forced to undergo the same conditions at work, they will quit their jobs or go home early? Let's say the air conditioner goes out in your office. Will you stay when the temperature reaches 85 degrees? Ninety? After hearing several complaints, the boss might say, "Okay, let's knock off early . . . " Then, as the workers leave the office, you're likely to hear, "What do you think, golf or tennis?"—they're leaving a hot office to go *play* on in even hotter conditions. What makes the difference between the two activities?

In *The Game of Work*, Charles A. Coonradt says that most people see "recreation" as pleasurable because it involves *clearly defined goals* and an opportunity for *autonomy*. Work can be more enjoyable too, he says, if goals are clearly defined and we feel like we are productive and contributing.

GOALS

Coonradt's premise is simple—and powerful: *In the absence of clearly defined goals, we are forced to concentrate on activity and ultimately become enslaved by it.*

In athletics, the goal is to "win"; winning is the driving force. Likewise, work should be driven by goals. Coonradt outlines ten attributes of goals which he feels can contribute to personal and business success:

1. Goals should be written.
2. Goals must be your own.
3. Goals must be positive.
4. Goals must be measurable and specific.
5. Goals are best stated in inflation-proof terms.
6. Goals must be stated in the most visible terms available.
7. Goals must contain a deadline.
8. Goals must allow for personality changes.
9. Goals must contain an interrelated statement of benefits.
10. Goals must be realistic and obtainable.

In sports, observers can very quickly determine who is winning—they only need to look at the scoreboard. The corporate environment, Coonradt claims, needs to have a similar scoreboard so workers immediately know how well they are doing in relation to the overall goal. However, in most organizations, there is no "scoreboard" of any type.

SCOREKEEPING

There are three basic styles of management: *company-observation, judgment,* and *measurement.* Managing by measurement allows for scorekeeping, while managing by judgment or observation does not.

For example, a boss who manages in the observation style walks by the salesroom and observes her salespeople laughing and having a good time. Her response, generally negative, might be, "Listen, if you guys would get to work we might actually sell something around here." Or, if she manages in the judgmental style, she might respond with something like, "Kids today just don't work as hard as I did when I was their age." But what if the salespeople were celebrating the biggest sale of the month? This manager's observations and judgments would then consist of nothing more than faulty generalizations, and she would only be focusing on the nonproductive aspects of worker behavior.

Managing by measurement, on the other hand, measures the productivity of workers as compared to a clearly defined goal. The system is more exact, and it allows for enjoyment—because participants are given a way to *win.*

There are three basic kinds of workers, or "players," according to Coonradt:

1. *Those who know they are winning.*
2. *Those who know they are losing.*
3. *Those who don't know the score.*

How many of *your* employees (friends, children, spouses . . .) know if they are winning or not? How many truly know the score?

Coonradt contends that knowing the score is contingent on receiving feedback. In other words, *When performance is measured—and measurements are reported to the worker—performance improves.* A boss who gives frequent feedback to workers about their performance as it relates to goals (whether it be via memos, verbal acknowledgement, or some less formal "pat-on-the-back" type method), and who gives them positive assistance in achieving those goals, will propel everyone to higher levels of excellence.

No football coach would hand his quarterback a list of plays before a game and tell him to execute them in the exact order listed. Instead, plays are called based on "feedback" received from the previous set of plays. If the receivers can't get open, the team likely won't try to execute a long pass. Each play is conceived individually, based on the situation and on constant feedback.

In football, the quarterback often has the option either to pass or to run. Similarly, *choice* (autonomy) is what drives America. Life—as well as the workplace—is a never-ending succession of "have-tos" and "want-tos." When we recreate or enjoy hobbies, we are doing those things we *like* to do—"want-tos"; seldom do you hear someone say, "Well, I have to play tennis today." On the other hand, we tend to avoid the "have-tos."

Choice endows us with two magical gifts: *freedom* and *creativity.* In our society, the more *important* someone is, the more choices he or she is allowed to make. Thus, when employees are not trusted to make choices, they don't *feel* very important—and probably won't do their best.

All too often, people are only *told what to do.* Workers, in addition to being entrusted with the freedom and responsibility to make decisions, need to know the *reasoning* behind what they are being asked to do. If they understand the underlying reasoning, they will be better prepared to achieve the expected results. Thus they have the opportunity to make a difference in the success of the company.

Finally, employees need to be allowed to use the methods they are comfortable with in bringing their chosen—or expected—goals to fruition.

Fields of Play

As in the sports world, businesses need their figurative "fields of play"—criteria which establish policy, vacations, benefits, etc. Clearly defined "fields,"—*boundaries* or rules of play—help to avoid uncertainty about what is expected from employees. When there is uncertainty, workers find that their performance is restricted, since they never know exactly where they stand.

Visualize in your mind a football field, complete with sidelines and end zones. In playing to "win," you're trying to move the ball across the goal line at the far end of the "field of play"; your goal is to reach "paydirt," an infinitely large end zone with unlimited growth potential.

A player can operate from various positions on Coonradt's field. On the left side of the field sits the "terminal out of bounds," representing those things that will get you immediately fired. To the right (the "operational out of bounds") are those things you are not allowed to do while working (e.g., wearing inappropriate clothing); you might not be fired if you venture into this out-of-bounds area, but you might be avoided, reproached (sent home to change). Whenever you're sitting on a sideline, you're really not in the game; you're on the bench, and will probably remain there if you don't do something about it.

In the course of playing the game, employees and employers alike need to adjust their strategies and outline which expectations/performance levels constitute achievement of the goal of *winning*. They need to come out of their "safety zone" to perform, knowing they can call on their "coach" whenever they want.

Coonradt recommends several tools a coach (manager) can use to help his team win: a "Field of Play Development Agenda" defines what is expected in terms of commitments from both players and coaches; a "Field of Play Review Sessions Agenda" can help the coach form lists of immediate and long-term goals, prioritized in 30-day segments; a "Field of Play Monthly Plan" initiates goals, with deadline dates specified month by month; and, lastly, a "Field of Play Coach's Expectations" clarifies the coach's expectations. These agendas and plans should be monitored and refined often in regularly scheduled meetings. After the "game plan" has been clearly spelled out (a "scoreboard" has been provided), the coach then can relax—and become a conscientious counselor, one who supports the performer with frequent positive and specific feedback.

Another valuable tool for discovering your "return on investment" as a manager, says the author, is by figuring your *"results to resources ratio"* (RRR). Basically, it entails listing your "Resources" on one side of a blank sheet and your "Results" on the other. By weighing the two lists, you should be able to ascertain how much you're getting from your organization as a whole. According to Coonradt, these employer/employee

agreements and analysis tools, coupled with habitual, honest, positive feedback and the opportunity for players to contribute ideas, will result in a winning *team*.

COACHING WINNERS TO GREATNESS

What is *motivation*? How do we motivate ourselves? And how do we motivate our most prized employees? "If you split the word in half, the first word you have is `motive.'" Then, Coonradt points out, by adding one letter to the last half of the word you get "action." *Motivation is a motive for action—a reason to do something.*

If you offered an employee $1,000 to call you "Mr. ___" rather than by your first name, Coonradt suggests, you would get instant results. In this case, the *motive* outweighs the *action*. If, on the other hand, you flip him a quarter and ask him to run ten miles with a 50-pound pack strapped to his back, very likely the *action* will outweigh the *motive*—the employee will look at you as if you're crazy.

Employers should get involved with their employees, Coonradt urges. They should tie the goals of their people to the goals of the business. "To win at work, you create a methodology where people and the business are closely linked together with common or compatible goals." However, employers must be prepared to recognize and deal with the following, instinctive employee responses:

WIIFM - *What's in it for me?* This is something all employees have on their minds when coming to work for you.

WSI - *Why should I?* This question does not connote defiance; in effect, it means, "Help me out . . . Let me understand more . . . Tell me again . . . Motivate me."

MMFI - *Make me feel important.* Assembly-line workers at a piano factory need to understand that they are not merely putting keys on a piano but are creating an instrument that will bring joy into many people's lives.

Different strokes for different folks. By promising food, clothing, and homes to a small band of communists, China's Mao Tse-Tung seized control of all of China. Mao understood how the people thought. Coonradt's correlation is obvious: Employers should get to know their people—their spouse's name, their children's names, their interests away from work, etc. They should make employees feel important, and be aware of what is important to them.

The principles outlined in *The Game of Work* have "increased the profitability of nearly every type of business imaginable. The principles are timeless." Coonradt asserts. "They work as well in business as they do in athletics and recreation." Once managers are sold on scorekeeping, then help their workers' personal goals become consistent with company goals, they will be winners. Once employee rules are clearly defined and employees know day to day whether they are winning or losing, their productivity will expand. Both managers and employees will come to enjoy *work* as much as they enjoy *play*.

ZIG ZIGLAR'S SECRETS OF CLOSING THE SALE

by Zig Ziglar, Fleming H. Revell Company, New York, N.Y., 1984

Using many entertaining stories and examples, one of America's master salesmen—and most proficient persuaders—reveals his secrets and techniques for "closing" a sale.

The Psychology of Closing

"This is not a book on psychology," Ziglar begins, "but I can absolutely guarantee you that you're going to have to know some psychology (or common sense) if you're going to be a truly professional salesperson." The underlying logic of the book is contained in the author's conviction that *"you can get everything in life you want if you will just help enough other people get what they want."*

When a prospective customer says no, Ziglar points out, the odds are at least a hundred to one that you will not get him to change his mind. After all, people just hate to admit they were wrong the first time. When the prospect initially says no, you need to get him or her to reevaluate and make another decision based on *new* information. The prospect may still not change his mind, "but he will be delighted to make a new decision based on *new* information."

A buyer of real estate, for example, might say, "Why didn't you tell me the property was outside the city limits and I won't have to pay city taxes?"—a sure sign that he or she is reevaluating the desirability of the property, and thus reevaluating his or her decision. The wise salesperson will then follow Ziglar's advice: " . . . *Try for the close as soon as you have established value or aroused desire for ownership, but before you give all the information."*

Using Your Voice

According to Ziglar, voice inflection may be the single most underdeveloped skill you need to cultivate in a professional sales career. He suggests that you develop your voice by tape-recording a single sentence until you can—by mere inflection—arrive at eight distinct, separate meanings. For example:

(1) "I did not say he stole the money." That's a simple factual statement; you are denying that you made the accusation.

(2) "I did not say he stole the money," implies that the accusation was made, but by someone else.

(3) "I **DID NOT** say he stole the money," is a vigorous denial that you accused him.

(4) "I did not **SAAYY** he stole the money," hints that you might have *implied* it, but you didn't *say* it.

(5) "I did not say **HE** stole the money," suggests that someone other than the accused stole the money.

(6) "I did not say he **STOLE** the money." Here you hint that the accused might have only "borrowed" the money.

(7) "I did not say he stole **THE** money," implies that he might have stolen *some* but not **THE** money.

and

(8) "I did not say he stole the **MONEY**," intimates that he might have stolen *something* but certainly not the money.

Once the groundwork is laid, then you can begin to develop on tape an effective sales presentation. Ziglar recommends that you save the first recording. You will see, he promises, "a definite improvement in the recording—and more importantly, in the sales results."

The Heart of Your Sales Career

"Selling is essentially a transference of feeling," Ziglar says. "If I (the salesman) can make you (the prospect) feel about my product the way I feel about my product, you are going to buy my product, if there is any way in the world you can come up with the money."

However, Ziglar warns, "in order to transfer a feeling, you've got to have that feeling." Personal commitment to the product, then, is of the utmost importance: few people can persuade another person to buy a product when they don't believe in it themselves. Indeed, if possible, you should own the product yourself, and use it. If you *can* afford the product but haven't bought it, then you probably shouldn't try to sell it: your own lack of enthusiasm is likely to be apparent.

Enthusiasm for the product goes hand-in-hand with positive thinking. Although positive thinking won't make you a superman, it will help you do everything better. Ziglar writes: "I don't . . . believe I could take out your appendix and have you live. But this I know: if you and I were isolated on a desert island a thousand miles from everybody and you were to suffer an attack of appendicitis, I personally believe you would prefer I approach you with a winning attitude! . . . [I might say] I have an extremely sharp knife with me and some powerful medicine that will kill all the infection . . . Personally I believe that despite my lack of training I can get your appendix out of there, and I just flat believe you're going to make it!'" Such a positive approach, Ziglar points out, would be far more appealing than "looking you in the eye and saying, `Man, you're gonna die!'"

A positive approach is critical to increasing sales. If you feel positive about your product, your company, your supervisor, your city, and your family, and are able to talk enthusiastically about it wherever you go, then you are going to be a much more effective salesperson.

In my travels I see people in every walk of life selling every conceivable product, from ten-cent whatnots to multimillion-dollar computers. Regardless of the company, industry, or section of the country, some are doing extremely well, some are doing fairly well, and some are going broke. The business is there for all but, everything else being equal, the salesperson with a good self-image and positive mental attitude will get more than his share of business, and the salesperson suffering from `stinkin thinkin' will get a much smaller share.

The Sales Professional

Ziglar asks, "Do you respond or react?" *Responding*, he indicates, is "positive," while *reacting* is not. If you "respond" to a doctor's prescription, for instance, that's a good sign; if you're "reacting" to it, that's not! In sales, you want customers to *respond* to your presentation or product, not merely "react" to it.

Ziglar concedes that not everything you encounter in the world of selling—or the world in general—is going to be positive. For instance, probably 99 percent of all salespeople have been stood up for a sales appointment. The way you *handle* the rejection, however, makes all the difference between failure and success.

My brother, Judge Ziglar, who broke the national sales record at that time for the Saladmaster Corporation in 1964 by selling over $104,000 worth of cookware, had a most unique **response** *to broken appointments . . . On occasion, when he arrived at the appointed time, no one would be at home. Instead of* **reacting** *with dismay, despair, frustration, or anger, Judge* **responded** *by saying, "Oh, boy! That's a sure sale!"*

The next day at precisely the appointed hour for the day before, he would again appear at the door. When the host or hostess came to the door, Judge would immediately start with an apology. "I'm so sorry I missed you yesterday. I did everything in my power to see you, but it just wasn't possible." (He was being 100 percent honest. He had done everything in his power to see them. He had been there at the appointed time.)

Judge points out that you would be astonished at the number of grown people who would let him take the blame for their discourtesy. At that point, as he expressed it, he knew the sale was his. Here's why. If they did not have the courage to face him and say no at the appointed time, then they were not psychologically equipped to deal with a highly motivated, enthusiastic, well-trained professional salesman like him. By **responding** *with that attitude, it's not difficult to understand why he broke the record.*

The Nuts and Bolts of Selling

Objections, Ziglar maintains, are the keys to closing the sale. When prospects object to something, they are in effect demonstrating interest in the product.

I can state with considerable confidence that in most cases involving significant purchases, if you do not encounter objections from the prospect when you make your presentation, you do not have a prospect. When your prospect raises an objection you ought to grin internally and think to yourself, **Oh, boy! I've got a live one today!** *Just remember if all the benefits and values of your product were obvious to the prospect, the salesman (that's you) would not be necessary. Also remember that if* everybody instantly bought your product, commission rates would drop dramatically.

It is valuable to know that, while an objection may seem frivolous to you, it may be important to the prospect, especially if he or she raises it a second time. If the sale is to be made, it is critical for the salesperson to address these concerns with respect and honesty, and without intimidation or "high pressure."

. . . Some salesmen can be so persuasive and charming they can "hypnotize" their prospects into buying products, goods, or services which are not needed or are grossly overpriced. However, no salesman is so hypnotic in his presentation that he can **keep** *the prospect hypnotized and feeling good about the purchase until the product is delivered and paid for.*

Ziglar suggests that the best time to answer an objection is before it occurs.

If you are consistently getting the same objections after your presentation, it is a sure sign your presentation is in trouble. You need to analyze the presentation so you will be able to handle **most** *objections in the body of the presentation. This approach enables you to answer the objection before it occurs, which means you are selling on the offense instead of defensively reacting. This is far more positive and effective.*

Ziglar also urges salespeople to avoid taking objections to their products personally. If you can stay calm, he says, your chances of making a sale are greatly enhanced. Too many salespeople, Ziglar adds, take the attitude that a sale is a "win" for them and a "loss" for the prospect. When the salesperson forgets that he or she is there to *solve* a problem for the prospect or provide a *service*, then the presentation may as well be over.

Prospects Want to Say Yes

Ziglar believes that "prospects do not want to say no, because no is final and the prospect is just as eager to have his problem solved as you are to help him solve it." He also believes that "objections thrive on opposition but basically they die with agreement." It is vital, then, to avoid sounding like a lecturer when dealing with a prospect. If you can remember to answer objections with *questions*, then you will increase your chances of uncovering the prospect's motive for buying.

Summing up, Ziglar underscores the part played by emotions in a salesperson closing a sale:

. . . Just remember, the prospect . . . buys the future enjoyment of what you're selling, regardless of the product. . . . He doesn't buy the house on the lot, he buys the shade of the trees in the yard; the warmth of the fireplace in the cold winter months; the convenience of the telephone in the bathroom. He buys the coolness of the evening on the lake, the exhilaration of the downhill skiing experience with his family, the joy of his motorboat on the lake, the luxury of the dip in the heated pool. Again, all of these are intangibles made possible by the tangible property which he's buying.

THE TEN COMMANDMENTS OF BUSINESS & HOW TO BREAK THEM

by Bill Fromm, G.P. Putnam Sons, New York, N.Y., 1991

Bill Fromm's book lists ten very traditional rules for conducting business today—and then explains why, for the most part, the wisdom of the ages (at least when it comes to actually conducting business) is bunk.

"No one ever sits back and asks what these rules are there for," contends Fromm. "They're etched so firmly in our minds that we don't see a need to reconsider why we're following them . . . There is only one way to make a mark in business. And, it's not by following the rules. It's by breaking them."

So, what are these generally accepted commandments, and why should they be broken?

THE FIRST COMMANDMENT: THY CUSTOMER IS KING

One of the first things any novice learns when he goes into the workplace is that the customer rules. But once he finds himself sitting manager's desk, this edict changes: "For managers—be they chief executive officers of Fortune 500 companies or managers of small departments—THE CUSTOMER IS NOT KING. If you want your people to deliver outstanding customer service, then you need to treat them as if they were more important than the customers."

Of course, satisfied customers are critical to a company's success. But, as a manager, "you must make that transition in your thinking which places your people's interests ahead of all others. *Tell* your employees that the customer is king, but *show* them that they're royalty as far as you're concerned . . . If you want to improve customer service, improve the way you treat your people. As their feeling of importance increases, the way they treat the customer will improve correspondingly."

THE SECOND COMMANDMENT: THY GOAL SHALL TO BE TO MAKE A PROFIT

You don't have to be a Harvard graduate to know that the goal of any business is to make a profit. Survival in a competitive marketplace depends on making money. "Sounds painfully obvious, right? . . . Wrong. The goal of business is not to make a profit. Even if the only reason you work is to get filthy rich, the goal of your business cannot be to make profits. Not if you ever hope to make any. Profits cannot be viewed as the principal *goal* of a successful business, but rather as the *result* of operating a successful business.

And speaking of profits, many companies don't even know if they *are* making money. They "believe that financial statements will disclose how well their company is competing in the marketplace. It simply isn't true . . . The only accurate measurement of how successfully a company is competing . . . is the trend line of its *share of market* . . . And, sadly, most companies don't know what their market share is."

Over twenty years ago, Fromm's ad agency did some work for a sizeable company that manufactured replacement mufflers and tail pipes. The managers of this company thought they were making a lot of money; "I thought they were doing terribly. They were looking at their profits and sales increases, and they were happy with what they

saw. I was looking at the trend line of their share of market, and I was worried because at the same time that they were making more money than they'd ever made before, they were losing their piece of the pie . . . The reason is that during the mid-1960s, automobile manufacturers started making cars with dual exhaust systems. By the time those cars came into the replacement market, there were two mufflers and two tail pipes to replace, rather than one. The marketplace virtually doubled overnight. Even though the company had a significant sales increase each year, it was actually losing business to the competition."

THE THIRD COMMANDMENT: RANK HATH ITS PRIVILEGES

"If you've ever been in the military, you know that R.H.I.P. is an acronym for Rank Has Its Privileges. That means that officers enter doors first, get into cars last, and get to the front of the mess line, among other things. The military has a pecking order, and it seems to work—for the military. But a private in the army can't decide to quit his job and go to work for another army because he doesn't like his commanding officer . . . A manager *does* have to worry about those possibilities . . . "

" . . . When you separate 'officers' from 'enlisted men' in your organization, you end up with not one, but two, teams. And two teams don't work as one; they compete . . . The one thing an organization doesn't need is an 'us and them' attitude among the employees."

When he first came to work there, the meeting rooms in Fromm's agency were always a mess. Whenever a meeting adjourned, the senior people would glide out as quickly as possible to avoid responsibility for the mess. "These days," says Fromm, " . . . responsibility for straightening up . . . falls to the most SENIOR person in the room. When I'm in a meeting, I'm responsible for cleaning up . . . Funny thing: the minute I start to empty an ashtray or pick up an empty Coke can, I have a lot of help from the other people who were in the meeting. Without my saying a word, the room gets cleaned up faster than you can imagine."

THE FOURTH COMMANDMENT: THOU SHALT SCORN NEPOTISM

"Almost any book on management will tell you that business and family don't mix. When a company becomes nothing more than a family dynasty, the employees will feel resentment. Furthermore, hiring friends and family frequently backfires into an incurable case of office politics. Work is work. And home is home. And it should stay that way.

"This commonly held sentiment causes managers to go to great lengths to resist a family atmosphere at work . . . But the truth is that you can't shut off your emotion like a faucet when you get to the office. A formal business environment is cold and unnatural . . . People need to feel a sense of belonging at work."

THE FIFTH COMMANDMENT: THOU SHALT KNOW WHAT THOU SELLETH

Fromm offers an interesting example to show that, while it's always important to know and improve your *product*, the really crucial factor in long-term success is to know what *services* your business is providing to its customers. " . . . At the turn of the century, the railroads practically owned the transportation industry in this country . . . [However], the railroads never understood what business they were in. They thought they were selling transportation by train. But what the customers were buying was an efficient way to move people and cargo. If the railroads had really known what business they were in, they'd probably own the airlines today.

"The landscape of American business is littered with companies that didn't know the business they were in," Fromm continues. "They focused on what they were trying to sell rather than what the customer was buying."

THE SIXTH COMMANDMENT: THOU SHALT PUT IT IN WRITING AND PRODUCE IT IN TRIPLICATE

"Whether you already manage thousands of people or you aspire to manage a few, you've got to have good communication skills to be successful. To a lot of business people, good communication simply means writing concise memos, producing professional reports, and documenting everything that happens. Or, in other words, keeping the paper flowing around the office.

"I call that mentality CYA, meaning `Cover Your Ass.' It describes people who feel like they have to document everything. They need evidence and excuses, so they can pass the blame if and when catastrophe strikes. In that type of environment, people must provide a record of every action, statement, and idea."

This is not to say that documentation is unnecessary. Certainly, every business must keep some records for reference and clarification. "But," declares Fromm, "that's where the utility of paper ends. As a means of communicating between yourself and others, writing stinks. Putting paper between you and other people makes communication impersonal. It also makes the message less effective. The most effective form of office communication is, and always will be, a good old-fashioned face-to-face talk."

THE SEVENTH COMMANDMENT: THOU SHALT COVET NEW CUSTOMERS

"We in advertising meet a lot of people who want to see their businesses grow. They come to an advertising agency because they believe that advertising is the best way to do that. They want to attract hordes of new customers. That's understandable . . . [But] it's a lot more profitable to increase your business with current customers . . . Here's why. If you increase your business by 20 percent with an old customer, you'll still have only one account receivable. Your salesman can handle this increase in business with the same sales call. Your freight costs will probably be less than shipping to a new customer. In every respect, this 20-percent increase in business from your existing customer will be more profitable than a similarly sized new account. McDonald's figured this out a long time ago. That's why they ask you if you also want fries or pies."

THE EIGHTH COMMANDMENT: THOU SHALT HAVE RULES

One day a woman came to work at Fromm's advertising agency dressed in cutoff shorts and tennis shoes with no socks. This caused quite a stir. The employee's manager came to warn Mr. Fromm about the woman's appearance and, as others had in the past, to recommend that a dress code be adopted. "I explained to him that 95 percent of our staff came to work looking just fine—without a dress code," Fromm relates. "How would these people feel if we suddenly started treating them like children, just because one person didn't use good judgment? Instead of imposing a dress code, I arranged a meeting with the woman and suggested that she try a slightly less informal look in the future. It was a little embarrassing for both of us, but it worked."

But what if it hadn't worked? "I still wouldn't have imposed a dress code. I would probably have tried a more serious talk with the woman . . . I would have explained why we don't have rules and how that doesn't mean that I want people showing up in beach attire . . . I'd have also asked her if there was something else bothering her. Something that was happening at the office or at home that was upsetting her. Was she happy with her job? That's how you solve a problem—not with rules . . . I never want to work with a person with whom I can't sit down and talk."

THE NINTH COMMANDMENT: THOU SHALT NOT MIX BUSINESS AND PLEASURE

"One of the biggest problems with American business can be summed up in four words: thank God it's Friday. T.G.I.F. Americans work for the weekend. They work because they have to or because they want to make enough money to afford the luxuries in life. From the moment the alarm goes off on Monday morning, many people are already counting the hours to the weekend, the next vacation, or the next job. Few people admit to working because they want to.

"I love my weekends as much as the next person, but I also love my weeks. My work is fun. And it's my belief that work should be fun for everybody. It doesn't make sense to spend five-sevenths of the week doing something you hate so that you can spend the other two-sevenths enjoying yourself . . . When people truly enjoy their work, they're not only happier, but they also perform much better."

THE TENTH COMMANDMENT: THOU SHALT LABOR FOR THY BOSS

You don't work for your boss; you work for *you!* "Everyone is really self-employed. Regardless of the title you have on your business card, ultimately you are responsible for yourself and to yourself. What does all of this really mean? . . . It means that . . . the person that drives you has to be you."

Fromm's bottom-line rule is: "Don't wait for someone else to demand the best of you. Demand it of yourself."

Filled with secrets for improving employee morale, elevating customer service, and increasing profits, *The Ten Commandments of Business* emphasizes having fun along the way. Behind it all, Fromm exemplifies and features this simple, basic, overriding "Eleventh Commandment": *Always question the rules, and be willing to break them if they don't work.*

THE DO'S AND TABOO'S OF INTERNATIONAL TRADE

by Roger Axtell, John Wiley & Sons, New York, N.Y., 1989

"If you believe we can live and work and prosper entirely within our own nation and our own marketplace then you also believe the world is flat," states Roger Axtell in his *The Do's and Taboo's of International Trade*. Global interdependence has made international trade an economic necessity for nearly all nations. The United States, as the largest of the free market economies, is not exempt. "Largest" does not necessarily mean "strongest." Although this country remains one of the world's leading exporters, we are also *the* leading importer, meaning that we buy more from foreign markets than we sell to them. No business can survive—let alone prosper—if it operates this way; neither can a nation.

In order to ensure individual corporate growth and the growth of the national economy as a whole, American businesses must become much more involved in international commerce.

The book begins with one probing question "Why haven't more American businesses become involved in international trade?" This is a very good question, considering the huge profits that can be made in foreign markets. Studies have shown that companies engaging in international trade grow faster than companies limited to the domestic market. In fact, the U. S. government actively encourages foreign commerce, specifically in the area of exporting. Axtell concludes that the true reason American businesses haven't become more involved in world trade is *fear*. And this display of timidity, he says, is "as disturbing as it is un-American." *The Do's and Taboo's* attempts to eliminate this fear and to promote bold expansion into international marketplaces.

Exporting, importing, joint ventures, licensing, direct overseas investment, and *countertrade* are all different modes of international trade. The book gives clear and thorough descriptions of how to proceed in each of these areas, but the main focus is exporting—the most common way to break into the international arena.

As he guides the reader through each step of the international trade process, Axtell emphasizes two important facts:

1. International trade is not easy in the beginning, but it pays off tremendously.
2. Any business, large or small, can enter the international market.

How and Where to Begin

"*The best single piece of advice to the new-to-export researcher is: Run, don't walk to the nearest Department of Commerce [DoC] district office.*" The Department of Commerce oversees both the *International Trade Administration* and the *United States and Foreign Commercial Service*—two agencies that can provide potential exporters with invaluable information. Some companies complain that they are immediately "hit by a deluge of paper." But remember, says Axtell, the "DoC

is like a large haystack full of information and, with their help, you are searching for your particular needle."

The U.S. government should be "first base and starting lineup for assistance," but the private sector also offers important resources to the prospective exporter. World trade centers, local trade associations, private trading firms, export management companies, market research services and private consultants are all sources of information—and places to gain meaningful contacts.

The First Overseas Trip

"*If there is one cardinal rule that all experienced international managers agree upon it is this: There is no substitute for getting out into the marketplace.*" Visit your target market to ferret out the customs, needs, and objectives of your contacts. Your objectives for the first trip should be: to examine customary—and successful—business practices in order to decide what type of distribution to use; to establish contacts; to find out if products will need to be modified for differing needs or appeal; and to acquire a feeling for the culture.

"*Successful business in other countries is difficult without an appreciation and awareness of culture and business protocol.*" Protocol for greetings, exchanging business cards, dining out, gift-giving, entertaining, meeting and dealing with women, etc. may differ radically from culture to culture, and an understanding of these differences is crucial. "An open mind and a willingness to adapt are two qualities that will pay handsome rewards."

The Law and Exporting

"Laws governing exports and international trade are frighteningly complex, vary significantly from country to country and are constantly changing." But with a little research, almost any legal question can be resolved—including tax issues.

Since entry into trade is usually initiated by shipping goods to a distributor the most important document in international business is the *distributor agreement*. A properly worded agreement can eliminate many initial difficulties that otherwise might leave you floundering. DoC trade specialists can also help you obtain information on patents, trademarks, and product liability—all important issues for exporters.

Pricing

"*It is absolutely essential to bear in mind that because of distances, duties, and special middlemen, your costs will necessarily increase before they reach the marketplace.*" A pricing structure should therefore include certain "unfamiliar" costs added to the "familiar" ones. Unfamiliar costs might include import duties, taxes, and disparate currency exchange rates.

Export Financing and Payments

"Two predominant questions are: Where can I get help financing this new venture, and after I begin receiving orders, what payment and credit practices should I use to assure I am paid in full and in a timely fashion?" Again, first consult the DoC for details about export financing. Your second trip should be to the international department of a commercial bank; and a third meeting should take place with the agency in your state government that deals with international commerce.

Collecting payment for your exported goods can be a complex process. Since distance, communication barriers and legal differences all contribute to the web of potential problems, certain methods of payment are recommended over others. Typically, there are five basic methods of payment. In order of preference (least risk) they are:

1. *Cash in advance*
2. *A letter of credit*
3. *Documentary drafts for collection*
4. *Open account*
5. *Consignment sales*

Shipping

"For aspiring international careerists the most popular single seminar, night course, workshop, or college course offered is the one on export shipping and documentation." International shipping is a specialty. Shipping specialists are known as "international freight forwarders." Freight forwarders can expedite the entire shipping process through their expertise on all its facets—documentation, credit transactions, insurance, packaging, bonding, labeling, import duties, etc.

Managing the Distributor

"Managing overseas distributors is a new challenge because there are new elements: different languages, different business methods, and different attitudes . . . Your distributor represents an extension of your company in his assigned market. If he succeeds, you succeed." Distributors should be knowledgeable about market conditions, as well as the particular factors that impact exporting and importing.

Communication

"Communication in international business is both a skill and an art requiring special, new sensitivities." Fortunately for American entrepreneurs, English is the language of international business; still, it is a "dynamic language and that makes it difficult for the foreigner who has tried to learn English only to discover that it is a moving target." When dealing with foreign business contacts, avoid miscommunication:

* Use short sentences
* Speak slowly and clearly
* Use visual aids to put across difficult points
* Paraphrase or repeat important instructions—several times, if necessary
* Avoid using idioms, colloquialisms or slang

This last point is crucial; common American expressions and informal British expressions, in actual meaning, often end up miles apart. For example, an American might innocently say "I made a presentation to the board today and bombed, and then when I got home I found a notice from my bank that I had a large overdraft." But in Britain to "bomb" means to succeed, and a bank "overdraft" is a line of credit.

Because of differences in language and culture, foreign advertising also is orchestrated in a different key. In China, for instance, *Pepsi Cola's* slogan "Pepsi Comes Alive" translated to "Pepsi Brings Your Ancestors Back From the Grave." Such problems can be avoided by close acquaintance and interaction—as well as many open channels for feedback—with the culture of the target market.

Dealing with the Japanese Mystique

"In our desire to unmask the Japanese, to resolve the mystique, Americans seem to have overlooked the obvious: The Japanese work harder." The Japanese are not only an industrious people, but a polite, protocol-oriented culture. Some rules for dealing with the Japanese are:

* Seek the highest possible pattern of politeness
* When making introductions, always use the person's title
* Bring a good supply of business cards
* Give gifts
* Show patience and good will

Countertrade

Countertrade is an exchange method usually used in markets where hard currencies are scarce. " . . . A complex business, risky but often loaded with deep profit margins for the negotiators," it is widely practiced in the international economy, a trend that seems to be growing each year—a fact that makes it "nearly impossible to ignore."

Boeing and Pepsi Trading Company are two corporations that have benefitted from international countertrade: Boeing and Saudi Arabia recently exchanged ten 747 aircraft for a billion dollars' worth of oil; Pepsi even more recently sent *Pepsi Cola* products to Russia in exchange for Stolichnaya vodka.

Axtell's book includes an appendix which lists addresses and phone numbers of DoC district offices, plus the names of the trade specialists attached to the state's district office. Other lists include the names of DoC desk officers located in the country in which you might do business and contacts for various trade associations and chambers of commerce.

"Economic interdependence is a reality," and those companies who are considering stepping into international trade would do well to consult the information and agencies specializing in such matters. *The Do's and Taboo's of International Trade* may be a wise first step in the journey.

BARBARIANS TO BUREAUCRATS

Corporate Life Cycle Strategies: Lessons from the Rise and Fall of Civilizations
by Lawrence M. Miller, Clarkson N. Potter, Inc. New York, N.Y., 1989

Lawrence Miller believes that all human institutions, from small businesses to civilizations, like the human beings who create them—and all other living organisms—progress through distinct stages of a life cycle, each stage demanding different skills and emphasizing different aspects of leadership and character. From Barbarians to Bureaucrats explores these stages, and defines what sorts of skills and leaders are important to each stage.

STAGE I THE PROPHET: INSPIRATION AND INNOVATION

Reasonable men adapt themselves to their environment; unreasonable men try to adapt their environment to themselves. Thus all progress is the result of the efforts of unreasonable men.

-George Bernard Shaw

The evolution of civilizations and corporations follows a common path. Both spring from the vision and faith of individuals, or small groups of individuals. *The role of the Prophet—both in business and in the advancement of civilization—is to provide the key ideas for the future.* "Ideas are the seed of material creation. Ideas are the foundation of great corporations. Ideas are what power all social and religious revolutions. And in promoting their ideas over the established order, Prophets—those social, intellectual, religious, or entrepreneurial visionaries who bring new ideas to birth—all possess personalities that set them apart from the crowd.

You may be a Prophet if among other things:

- Your ideas are long-range and visionary.
- You are willing to make great sacrifices in time and energy to see your ideas realized.
- You tend to withdraw for long periods to work through your ideas.
- Others see you as a bit "different."

The Prophet phase of any organization begins with the inception of an idea. In this stage of its life cycle the company is made up of few, if any—employees, and realizes little if any revenue. If the organization is to survive and flourish, the Prophet's vision must be sound. But often, even with unequalled vision, the Prophet will lack the necessary traits to move his/her organization or civilization into the future.

STAGE II THE BARBARIAN: CRISIS AND CONQUEST

Every successful enterprise requires three men—a dreamer, a businessman, and a son-of-a-bitch.

-Peter MacArthur, 1904

A "sense of crisis" and a "need to conquer" characterize the Barbarian and his or her organization. "The personality of the Barbarian is well suited to single-minded, even fierce, dedication to a mission. His actions are based as much on his emotional commitment to his goals as to any rational plan . . . Others respond to his force with their own excitement."

Barbarian Lee Iacocca is a good example of

the type of leader organizations need when they are, proverbially, up against the wall. Maybe their organization is young and weak; or maybe it has become rich, slow and dumb. Regardless, Iacocca describes the typical Barbarian response to any crisis—in his case, to entering the foundering Chrysler Corporation: "All through the company, people were scared and despondent . . . I had never seen anything like it! . . . I had to fire 33 out of the 35 vice presidents. . . . I had to [find] guys with experience who could move fast."

The Barbarian phase is a time of rapid growth—or a time of resurrection from near-disaster. Because Barbarian leadership is so dynamic and result-oriented, one should expect these companies to be filled with great mental and emotional highs and lows. Every employee is likely to understand the mission and be extremely dedicated to it; each will feel part of a team whose sole purpose is to serve the customer. Anybody who feels over worked in these organizations will either overcome that feeling or be out the door.

You may be a Barbarian if among other things:

- Your mission is clear and urgent. Survival is the priority.
- You are in charge and very comfortable making decisions.
- Others accuse you of being authoritarian and not consulting them on decisions
- You are very action-oriented and have little patience with planning and administration.

STAGE III THE BUILDER AND EXPLORER: SPECIALIZATION AND EXPANSION

The time in an organization's life when it begins to specialize and expand, both horizontally and vertically, is dominated by the Builder and the Explorer. Before, the organization was consumed with survival; now it is concerned with doing things in a better way. Centralized decision making, as it existed under Barbarian leadership, no longer makes sense. "Delegation, and the development of consensus or group decision making, is now the only method of creating effective decisions that integrate the knowledge of various specialized experts."

The Builder is charged with knowing the product or service and getting it delivered to the customer. The Builder shares some traits with the Barbarian: a "leadership-by-example" attitude, a commitment to the company's mission, a vision of where her still small production operation could be . . . When the Builder is promoted to management, however, she enters a world where decisions are based on group consensus—a world that requires coordinated efforts between different groups with differing goals and outlooks. Success requires her to change her thinking and evolve with the organization.

The Explorer evolves in a world where communication and persuasion are keys to growth and reward. "The Explorer has no more fondness for administrative systems than the Builder. His 'real work' is being out with the customer, getting him to buy. That is what it is all about! The Explorer has been highly successful at this. He has been repeatedly rewarded, not for sitting around in meetings in the home office, but for being out on the road, making the sale."

You may be a Builder if among other things:

- You enjoy the "real work" of your company, making the product or the delivery of the service.
- You enjoy measuring the results of your work.
- You like to make decisions quickly, take action, and see the results.
- You don't waste a lot of time dreaming about the future.

You may be an Explorer if among other things:

- You are a convincing and enthusiastic communicator.
- You sometimes feel that you work for your customer, and others in your own company often seem to be obstacles to your goal of serving your customers.
- You love to keep score; you are competitive by nature.
- You believe your company should place a higher priority on expansion.
- You feel that your company gets bogged down in paperwork.

STAGE IV THE ADMINISTRATOR: SYSTEMS, STRUCTURE AND SECURITY

Whenever an individual or a business decides that success has been attained, progress stops.
-Thomas Watson, Sr.

" . . . During the period of the Builder and Explorer, in which specialization of functions and organizations develop, the need for administration is on the rise. Initially, administration serves the needs of those producing and selling, building and exploring. But gradually the tide turns, and . . . those producing and selling increasingly come to serve those administering. And it is the turning of this tide that signals the entry into the Administrative stage." The problem is that as the organization grows it must maintain order, and this can often be adverse to the interests of those who make the company move, the Builders and Explorers. The *Administrator* is more concerned with holding ground in an orderly way. In the beginning, administrative procedures are helpful to the organization; for that matter, they are irreplaceable members of the mature company as well. However, as administration comes to *dominate* an organization, creativity, risk-taking and progress are stifled.

You may be an Administrator if among other things:

- You have risen in the corporation's staff organizations.
- You consider yourself expert at the procedures, processes, and systems of management.
- Order, consistency, and smooth operations are high priorities for you.
- You devote more time to checking on what has happened, as reflected in financial reports, for example, than you spend focused on future growth in products, service, or customers.

STAGE V THE BUREAUCRAT: THE TIGHT GRIP OF CONTROL

The distinguishing characteristic of the Bureaucratic *stage is the loss of social cohesion, unity and purpose.* The different layers within an organization are increasingly divorced from each other and come to view those outside their layer with suspicion and distrust.

Bureaucrats the world over have the characteristic of not being willing to take chances. This is not always bad; we don't need, for instance, an entrepreneurial, risk-taking military establishment. The problem is that as organizations and governments grow, administration can be become very risk-averse, which in turn quashes creativity, experimentation and innovation. As the outside world becomes less appealing, more resources and attention are paid to internal issues, further eroding the commercial viability of the organization. Small, cutthroat companies (or nations for that matter) often outgunned and just barely viable, can offer deadly competition to these large, well established but selfconsumed organizations.

You may be a Bureaucrat if among other things:

- You spend most of your time in meetings reviewing what has already happened or should have happened.
- You cannot remember when you last participated in the development of a new product or service . . . and you don't think that's your job.
- You are more concerned with how you and your company are viewed by Wall Street analysts than by your customers.
- You believe tighter control will solve many of your organization's problems.
- You spend more time with central staff managers than with line sales and production managers.

THE SYNERGIST PRESCRIPTION

Civilizations and organizations grow, and they decay. The challenge is to break the natural cycle of rise and fall by finding ways to coordinate human and organizational energies to retain vitality and innovation. For this, we need *Synergistic* leaders. *A Synergist is a leader "who has escaped his or her own conditioned tendencies toward one style and has incorporated the different styles of leadership that are needed as the corporation goes through its life cycle.* The best-managed, most stable companies are Synergistic. They are a balance and blend of the characteristics of the Prophet, Barbarian, Builder, Explorer, and Administrator. But most important, the Synergist is one who can create social unity."

The keys of Synergistic leadership are global, process-oriented thinking rather than local, outcome-oriented thinking. Successful coordination and innovation among and within specialized work groups in these organizations are a most distinguishing characteristic.

"The growth of the global economic system, with its increasing size, complexity, and interdependence, requires integration and synergy. We are entering a period of one world civilization." Pushing forward in a spirit of creative vitality, teamwork, and purpose, the Synergist, like a musical conductor, can gradually persuade the whole world to play to the same beat.

HOW TO GET YOUR POINT ACROSS IN 30 SECONDS—OR LESS

by Milo O. Frank, Simon and Schuster, New York, N.Y., 1986

Communicating effectively, persuasively, and concisely can be easily learned. How to Get Your Point Across in 30 Seconds—or Less *will show you how to get your listener's attention, keep his interest, tell a wonderful story, ask for and get what you want—all in 30 seconds. You will be able to get your point across to your business associates, your family, your friends, and all the people you deal with from the secretary to the accountant to the president of the company. Follow the simple steps outlined in this book. Use the easy techniques. You'll save time and accomplish more than you ever thought possible. And you'll have fun doing it.*

You have just read a 30-second message, a concise bulletin that effectively gets its point across. Those who want to be better communicators, Milo O. Frank asserts, have to be able to create such a message. Frank's book aims to teach techniques to help anyone develop this skill.

Frank has spent his entire business career in the communications field. As a long time writer, director and producer, he has spent a lifetime teaching practical communication skills to business people and politicians alike.

Obviously, all business communications cannot be kept to only 30 seconds. Building a rapport with your listener is also important, and every situation is unique. But, when the time comes to make your point, *make it in 30 seconds—or less.* It doesn't matter if you have five minutes or five hours to talk to your listener—you should express the heart of the matter within 30 seconds. The rest of your time should be spent in preparation and follow-through.

The right 30-second message will, in the final analysis, enable you to get your point across and keep it where it belongs—in the mind of your listener. Wherever and whenever attention is required, 30 seconds works.

When you have learned how to prepare your 30-second message, you will be able to:

- Focus your thinking and communication.
- Keep conversations on track.
- Prepare any type of message more rapidly.
- Be more logical and concise.
- Facilitate listening.
- Get better results in both your business and personal life.

How To Get Your Point Across in 30 Seconds—or Less is composed of three main parts. The first part, titled "The Three Principles of Effective Communication," explains how to *organize* an effective message. The second part, "The Three Techniques of Effective Communication" specifies how to *deliver* an effective message. And the third and last part describes precise steps you can take to add impact to what you have to say.

THE THREE PRINCIPLES OF EFFECTIVE COMMUNICATION

The first component of an effective 30-second message—the passive, pre-planned part of your communication—consists of the three principles necessary for effective communication: *know your objective, know your listener,* and *know your approach.*

To communicate effectively, you must first **know your objective.** "The objective is the goal, the destination, the purpose, the end in view, the target . . . It is what you want to achieve. It is why you're there." Knowing your objective improves communication, because you focus your mind on what is really important.

Frank says he's learned through experience that even the most powerful leaders in business, industry and government don't always know what their objective is, and they sometimes select a target that does not best serve their interests or requirements. To find your objective, ask: *"Why am I going there?" "What do I want to achieve?" "Why do I want to have this conversation or communication?"* . . . "The operative word [here]," Frank explains, "is almost always *why*. Once your objective is clear—once you know why—you can begin to prepare your message."

Sometimes, though, it is poor strategy to state your objective outright; it might be best to keep your objective *hidden.* For example, during the World War II's *D-Day* invasion, the Allies concealed their true objective from the Germans. They wanted Hitler to think they were going to land somewhere other than on the beaches of Normandy—and they succeeded, gaining a great advantage through the element of surprise.

Frank also offers an example from when he was casting for "Playhouse 90," one of the all time great live theatrical shows on television. While he certainly wanted to hire the best actors available, the salaries they were demanding always exceeded what the budget could handle. So, Frank developed a new routine called "guest star" billing, advertising the potential career benefits of appearing on the show. Before long, big-time actors flocked to his studio; Frank, through his hidden objective, thus, by showing how his opportunity could benefit them, he managed to hire actors for less money than he dreamed possible.

The second principle of an effective 30-second message, **know your listener,** will help you reach your objective. Truly knowing your listener, however, hinges on you being able to contact the person who can help you to reach it. In other words, "go to the person who can get it done."

At the same time, be aware of what your listener *wants to hear.* Identify with your listener; know as many facts as possible about that person. Ask: "What does he want from me? What one thing more than any other will get a favorable reaction from him?"

The third principle in your 30-second message, **know your approach,** is crucial to success. Once you have decided *what* you want and *who* can best give it to you, then simply decide *how* you can best reach your objective. Remember to stick to just *one* objective, just one approach. "The right approach," says Frank, "is the single thought or sentence that will best lead to your objective."

The number of possible "right" approaches is only limited by your imagination and creativity. As an aid in finding the right approach, ask yourself a few questions:

- What is the single best statement that will lead to my objective?
- Will this relate to the needs and interests of my listener?
- What is the basis of my game plan?
- What is the heart of what I will say?

The three principles of the 30-second message, then, can be summed up in the questions: *What is it that you want?; Who can give it to you?; and How do you plan to get there?*

THE THREE TECHNIQUES OF EFFECTIVE COMMUNICATION

The second part of your 30-second message is the actual message itself. The effectiveness of your message pivots on the three techniques of effective communication—the *three K's* of your message. Your "hook" is designed to **"Katch"** your listener; the "subject" will **"Keep'em"** interested; and the "closing" will **"Konvince'em"** to work with you.

1. *"Katch'em" with your hook.* "A hook is a statement or an object used specifically to get attention . . . It is to allure, entice, captivate, or catch your listener." Newspapers use headlines as hooks to charm readers into picking up and buying their paper.

To find your most forceful hook, ask: "What is the most unusual, interesting, exciting, dramatic, or humorous part of my subject?" Visual effects and props can effectively "hook" your listener. Frank suggests acquiring the habit of keeping a "hook book," a personal-reference note pad in which you can jot down and preserve those personal experiences and anecdotes that might serve as hooks.

2. *"Keep'em" with your subject.* "The subject of your 30-second message must explain, reinforce, and prove the point you are there to make." In order to do this, the subject must contain all or any part of that famous formula: What? Who? Where? When? Why? and How? Make sure that your subject reinforces and explains your objective, and that it relates to your listener.

3. *"Konvince'em" with your closing.* To determine how you should close your message, simply ask yourself, "What do I want from my listener?" You can close in two basic ways: a *demand for action* or a *demand for reaction.*

A demand for action comes as a specific request you make of the listener, something that must be done by a specific time: "We would appreciate it if everyone would write down three ways we can cut costs by our meeting next Tuesday." A demand for a reaction, on the other hand, is an indirect close that uses the *power of suggestion or example* to ask for the desired action. Three common demands for reaction are

"Buy Now," "Come in Today," and "Take advantage of this once-in-a-lifetime offer." Instead of asking for a specific action now, i.e. "Buy this Magic Mixer Blender today for only $39.95" (which is a demand for action), the request is stated in more subtle terms.

ADDING IMPACT

The finishing touches of a 30-second message include a number of measures you can take to add impact. "To be truly effective your 30-second message should be more than a hook, a few words, and a close. It should paint a picture that your listener will remember."

Painting a picture that is both vivid and real involves four components:

- **Imagery** - Make sure your listener *sees* as well as *hears* what you are saying. "Descriptive words help the listener visualize what you're about."

- **Clarity** - Choose words and images appropriate to your listener's level of understanding.

- **Personalizing** - Use personal stories or examples to illustrate key points. If your listener can identify with your story, your message will be that much more effective.

- **Emotional Appeal** - The most effective messages are those that reach the listener's heart.

The *way* in which something is said is far more important than *what* is said, Frank reminds us. Good first impressions demand a positive delivery, style, and image. Smile, both before and after your message. Learn to integrate your movements, gestures and posture to fit into and add impact to your message. Good communicators learn to control their facial expressions, body language, and voice in ways that add force to their message. What you wear also sends powerful signals.

When you speak in public—whether delivering your 30-second message to one or to one thousand listeners—following some basic rules will increase your chances of success:

- Don't read or memorize a speech; instead use an outline on 3 x 5 cards.

- Rehearse your speech and strive for spontaneity, variety, and naturalness in both your words and movements.

- Establish your credibility and credentials by sharing personal anecdotes.

- Write your own introduction.

- And, most importantly, *know when to stop.*

The genuine value of the 30-second message lies in its versatility; it can be used anytime, anywhere. It is an essential tool of communication. It can serve as the perfect solution to any communication situation—in a one-on-one business situation, on the phone, with answering machines, in meetings, or in presenting a dinner toast. The 30-second message can be effectively exercised in memos, letters of recommendation and thank-you notes. And when you master it, the 30-second message becomes almost second nature, equipping you with a whole new mindset and transforming the way you think and deal with others every day.

GIFT FROM THE SEA

by Anne Morrow Lindbergh, Vintage Books Ed., New York, N.Y. 1965

I began these pages for myself, in order to think out my own particular pattern of living, my own individual balance of life, work and human relationships . . . . In varying settings and under different forms, I discovered that many women, and men, too, were grappling with essentially the same questions as I...

In this book, Anne Morrow Lindbergh describes her own questions, philosophies and thoughts about life as she spends several solitary weeks on an isolated island. Passing her days at the beach, Lindbergh's mind soon returns to the "primeval rhythms of the seashore." In contemplation, she studies five different shells that have been tossed on the shore as a "gift from the sea." Each shell seems to contain a message for those seeking simplicity, wholeness, and a growing awareness—as painful as it may sometimes be—in everyday living.

CHANNELED WHELK

Like the hermit crab who once borrowed this spiral-shaped shell for his home and then, when it became an encumbrance, ran away, "I too . . . have shed the shell of my life for these two weeks," she muses. And now she turns the shell of her life in her hands, comparing it to the shell of the channeled whelk. This little dull-gold snail shell "is simple; it is bare; it is beautiful . . . its architecture is perfect, down to the finest detail . . . My shell is not like this, I think. How untidy it has become! Blurred with moss, knobby with barnacles, its shape is hardly recognizable any more . . . What is the shape of my life?"

The reality is that the modern American woman's life does not foster simplicity." It is a life filled with distractions. Faced with "ever-widening circles of contact and communication," women struggle to juggle community, family, workplace and personal obligations. "We run a tight rope daily, balancing a pile of books on the head. Baby-carriage, parasol, kitchen chair, still under control. Steady now!"

It is not only the American woman who suffers under this burden of multiplicity. The American man, and indeed all of modern civilization, is in danger of losing life's precious simplicity. And yet, the problem is essentially woman's, "for to be a woman is to have interests and duties, raying out in all directions from the central mother-core, like spokes from the hub of a wheel." With the necessity of being open to all points of the wheel—husband, children, friends, and community—a woman must continually fight the forces that pull her off center. How can she remain strong and balanced, amid such dividing powers?

The chambered whelk may offer beginnings of an answer. Encrustations can be stripped from our outward life too until "each whorl . . . each criss-cross vein" in our essential human design "is as clearly defined as on the day of creation." On the beach, there is no need for many material possessions. The question to ask is "how little, not how much, can I get along with?" Few clothes, open windows—the ideal of a simplified life. "Washable slipcovers, faded and old—I hardly see them; I don't worry about the impression they make on other people. I am shedding pride. As little furniture as possible; I shall not need much. I shall ask into my shell only those friends with whom I can be completely honest. I find I am shedding hypocrisy in human relationships. What a rest that will be! . . . I have shed my mask."

Simplification of the outward life is not enough. This is only a technique, a road to grace. *"The final answer, I know, is always inside. But the outside can give a clue, can help one to find the inside answer."* And it can also serve as a reminder that "one is free, like the hermit crab, to change one's shell."

MOON SHELL

The perfect, ever widening spiral of this opaque, milky and faintly pinkish shell, is centered in a "tiny, dark core . . . the pupil of the eye . . . an island, set in ever-widening circles of waves, alone, self-contained, serene." Islands in time, moments of solitude, like this vacation, give individuals the time and temperament to find peace and wholeness. Cut off from past and future by a continual present, we better learn to respect others and discover each person's unique gifts.

But modern society does not teach the value of solitude. "How one hates to think of oneself as alone. How one avoids it. An early wallflower panic still clings to the word." We employ the constant chatter of radio and television to fill the void of silence. Then, when the outer music and noise die down, "there is no inner music to take its place."

Solitude, however, is the means by which women—and men—are replenished. In the midst of daily pressures and activities and constant giving, solitude and stillness offer the harried soul much needed spiritual food. To be alone during part of a year, some portion of each week, and for some prime minutes each day instills the energy necessary to nourish self and others. Giving, then, becomes more purposeful. "Moon shell . . . you will say to me `solitude' . . . You will remind me that I must try to be alone . . . each day, even for an hour or a few minutes in order to keep my core, my center, my island quality." Like the axis of a revolving wheel, a woman of strength is one who is still, immovable in the midst of the circle of events around her.

DOUBLE-SUNRISE

A perfect double-sunrise shell is rare, both halves exactly matched in shape and pattern, connected by a delicate hinge. Pure relationships are like this delicate, butterfly-shaped shell: Two people listening to each other, meeting one another, creating one world between them; free of ties or claims, reality rests in the simple trust and understanding.

In the beginning, all relationships are this way. " . . . Then how swiftly, how inevitably the perfect unity is invaded; the relationship changes; it becomes complicated, encumbered by its contact with the world." As men and women take on specialized roles at home and work, they long for the beautiful, original pattern of their love. "But can the pure relationship of the sunrise shell be refound once it has become obscured?" Lindbergh says that it can—by reserving time alone with a loved one. Such one-and-only moments, alone *together*, can restore the essence of a relationship.

The double-sunrise shell expresses the first form, the core of all relationships. Once this fragile beauty is created, it may flee or return according to circumstance. The sunrise shell paves the way for new and complex patterns in a loving relationship's tapestry.

OYSTER BED

An oyster bed is not rare, nor is it simple. Its conglomeration of oyster shells is cluttered with moss and barnacles; it contains the movement and irregularity of something growing.

The life of the oyster bed is similar to the middle years of marriage. "Its form is not primarily beautiful but functional . . . It is untidy, spread out in all directions . . . firmly imbedded on its rock." During wedded life's middle years, the bonds of love in marriage expand to many loyalties and interdependencies. While romantic love—represented by the double-sunrise shell—is fastened by only one hinge, the oyster bed stage of marriage is made up of many bonds, an enduring web of relationships that two people have built together over the years.

But what do you do when the oysters' grasp loosens and breaks away? What happens when "the tide of life recedes" and the house, little by little, begins to empty? As children grow up and marry, and family obligations and the struggle to make a living are no longer the central concerns, "married couples are apt to find themselves in middle age, high and dry in an outmoded shell, in a fortress which has outlived its function."

Lindbergh suggests that this stage is a period for shedding the shells of ambition, possessions, and accumulations. By eliminating some of the material burdens of life, "one might be free to fulfill the neglected side of one's self . . . Middle age can be looked upon as a period of second flowering . . . " "Shedding" can lead to unimaginable personal growth: "One might be free for growth of mind, heart, and talent; free at last for spiritual growth; free of the clamping sunrise shell. Beautiful as it was, it was still a closed world one had to outgrow. And the time may come when—comfortable and adaptable as it is—one may outgrow even the oyster shell."

ARGONAUTA, or PAPER NAUTILUS

(a flat, wrinkled, "free-spirited" creature)

The "free-spirited" Argonauta is never fastened to its shell; a temporary dwelling is used as a cradle for its young. When the eggs are hatched and the young swim away, the flat, wrinkled mother argonaut leaves her shell and heads into the open sea, beginning anew.

Why is it that middle aged men and women face their own "open sea" with dread and embarrassment? Society often frowns upon the realities of growing old, considering age as a sign of weakness rather than strength. This perception, however, is misguided. With fewer bonds or pressing responsibilities, the years of middle-age can be a time for renewal and personal development. At this phase of life, the neglected sides of the personality can be greatly expanded. Relationships can grow more meaningful as two fully developed individuals contribute their separate selves to strive for joint objectives.

In these now free and mature relationships, "Both partners are lost in a common sea of the universal which absorbs and yet frees, separates and yet unites." The Argonaut phase of life allows an individual to discard his or her shell completely, and seek the "golden fleece," enjoying the adventure of the chartless seas of social and personal growth.

Yet a woman must also become self-sufficient. "This is the essence of `coming of age'—to learn how to stand alone. She must learn not to depend on another, not to feel she must prove her strength by competing with another." By becoming whole and happy with herself, a woman's ability to love freely is given wings.

LESSONS FROM THE SEA

As Anne Lindbergh leaves the beach to return to her Connecticut home, she takes with her a few shells—"they are more beautiful if they are few"—and a most important lesson: "Simply the memory that each cycle of the tide is valid; each cycle of the wave is valid; each cycle of a relationship is valid . . . [My shells] are only there to remind me that the sea recedes and returns eternally."

Though aware that her "holiday vision" will fade, she hopes that the shells, these small tokens of her experience, will remind her to see with "island eyes." In every-day living, such a vision will recall to mind the importance of simplicity, solitude, trust, love, growth, acceptance and adaptation.

How to adopt these qualities in a bustling world is the challenge. On the beach, and indeed in all nature, are clues. By discovering these "gifts," Lindbergh promises "some of the joy in the now, some of the peace in the here, some of the love in the me and thee which go to make up the kingdom of heaven on earth."

The waves echo behind me. Patience—Faith— Openness, is what the sea has to teach. Simplicity— Solitude—Intermittency . . . But there are other beaches to explore. There are more shells to find. This is only the beginning.

A KICK IN THE SEAT OF THE PANTS

Using Your Explorer, Artist, Judge & Warrior To Be More Creative
by Roger von Oech (illustrated by George Willett), Harper & Row, New York, N.Y., 1986

When was the last time you had a creative idea? This morning? Last month? Last year? Sometimes, says Roger von Oech, you need A kick in the seat of the pants to get your thinking going. This fun, imaginative workbook, a follow-up to von Oech's book *A Whack in the Side of the Head*, does just that: It takes you on a guided tour through the creative process and offers a wealth of immediate and lighthearted advice. Students, caregivers, executives, gardeners, or anyone working to come up with ways to make things better can use the practical and original ideas presented. Included in the book are many illustrations, such as a picture of a shoe for the reader to cut out, color, and hang in a spot where it will remind him or her that a good swift kick in the pants may just be what the doctor ordered.

At the end of each chapter, von Oech presents a sort of "toolbox" of ideas, or "pantkickers" designed either to get us going or to move us on to the next level of creativity. Each idea is introduced by a command, followed by an explanation of what we can *do* to carry out the command.

Virtually every profession and activity can occasionally, if not frequently, benefit from a creative idea. Von Oech suggests that when you're *searching for new information*, become an **Explorer;** when you're *turning your resources into new ideas*, become an **Artist;** when you're *evaluating the merits of an idea*, become a **Judge;** and when you're *carrying your idea into action*, become a **Warrior.**

Your Role as *Explorer*

When it's time to seek out new information, the beginnings of a great, one-of-a-kind idea, von Oech recommends you adopt the mind-set of an EXPLORER. "Get off the beaten path," he says, "poke around in outside areas, and pay attention to unusual patterns [or uncommon materials]."

Von Oech lists several reasons why you might *not* go exploring: you're stuck in the daily routines of living; you don't want to run the risk of getting lost; or perhaps you have become overly specialized, focusing only on narrow subjects. To perform effectively, your Explorer-self needs to maintain flexibility, courage, and openness.

Use the Explorer mode of thinking to answer such questions as: "How do you keep a fish from smelling?" Answers might include: " . . . Cook it as soon as you catch it, freeze it, wrap it in paper, keep a cat around, burn incense, leave it in the water, or cut its nose off." The Explorer goes out looking for new pathways.

As a "pantkicker," von Oech offers THE EXPLORER'S COMPASS as a guide to being a successful Explorer:

Be curious. *Adopt an "insight outlook."*
Create a map for yourself. *Have an idea of what you're looking for.*
Leave your own turf. *Look in outside fields, disciplines and industries*
Too much is not enough. *Look for lots of ideas.*
Don't be afraid to be led astray. *You'll find what you weren't looking for.*
Break up your routine. *Use obstacles to get out of*
ruts.
Shift your focus. *Pay attention to a variety of information.*
Don't overlook the obvious. *What's right in front of you?*
Get out your magnifying glass. *Big things come in small packages.*
What does it all really mean? *Stand back and look at the big picture.*
Slay a dragon. *Look for ideas in a place you've been avoiding.*
Remember where you've been. *Trigger the ideas you already have.*
Stake your claim to the new territory. *Write your ideas down when you find them.*

Your *Artist* Role

EVERY CHILD IS AN ARTIST. THE PROBLEM IS HOW
TO REMAIN AN ARTIST AFTER HE GROWS UP.

- Picasso

"When you need to create a new idea," the author suggests, "let the Artist in you come out. Ask `what-if' questions and look for hidden analogies. Break the rules and look at things backwards. Add something and take something away. Ultimately, you'll come up with an original idea." Your Artist is an imaginative, playful self, whose job it is to take the materials the Explorer has collected "and transform them into original, new ideas." The greatest danger your Artist-self faces is "becoming a prisoner of familiarity." The more often you see or do anything in the same way, the more difficult it is to think about it in any other way.

"Suppose you're designing a solar cell," von Oech prompts. "Posing the problem as an attempt to raise efficiency to 30% would lead your thinking in one direction, while asking how to reduce inefficiency to 70% would lead your thinking to a very different destination. Similarly, the shift in focus from `cure' to `prevention' in stating medical goals has changed the field of medicine." As an Artist, it is vital to continually look to gain new perspectives on things which may be old and familiar.

THE ARTIST'S PALETTE is von Oech's way of helping us see the Artist's viewpoint:
Take your concept and "do" something to it. What patterns can you change? How can you alter the way you think about it?
Adapt. *What different contexts can you put your concept in? What historical contexts? What futuristic ones? . . .*
Imagine. *What unusual "what-if" questions can you make up involving your concept? . . .*
Reverse. *Look at your concept backwards. How does it look upside down? Or inside out?*
Connect. *What can you combine with your concept? How does your concept fit in with the rest of your knowledge?*
Compare. *Make a metaphor for your concept. What similarities does it share with music? Medicine? Warfare? . . .*

Eliminate. What rules can you break? What's obsolete? What's taboo? . . .

Parody. Make fun of your concept . . . How silly can you be? How outrageous? . . .

Incubate. What ideas are you working on that it would pay you to pause for a little bit?

Your *Judge* Role

IF YOU SPEND TOO MUCH TIME WARMING UP, YOU'LL

MISS THE RACE. IF YOU DON'T WARM UP AT ALL, YOU

MAY NOT FINISH THE RACE.

- Grant Heidrich

Von Oech counsels that "when it's time to decide if your idea is worth implementing, see yourself as a Judge. Ask what's wrong and if the timing's right . . . Question your assumptions, and make a decision. Your Judge is your evaluative role. His job is to examine what the Artist has created and then decide whether to implement it, modify it, or discard it. There's an art to being a Judge. You have to be critical enough to insure that you give the Warrior an idea worth fighting for and you have to open up enough so as not to stifle your Artist."

The author shares three reasons why people get stuck in the Judge role more than any other: "a lot of crap, hype and pretense is in the world to cut through, it is easier to criticize than to explore, transform, or act, and it's the least risky role."

"Here's a chance for you to play Sherlock Holmes," he continues. "You walk into a room and you find John and Mary lying dead on the floor. There's broken glass and water all around them. Your job is to figure out how they died . . . Was it murder? Were they poisoned or shot to death? Perhaps they were stabbed with broken glass? . . . These explanations are plausible, given the information with which you were provided and assuming that John and Mary are people. But your Judge can examine the problem and suppose they are *not* people. If you assume that they're fish, then you might come to a different judgment. Maybe the cat came in and knocked the fish bowl off the table." A good Judge can look at a problem or situation objectively, while still searching for the best solution.

Von Oech's JUDGE'S SCALES may help you decide how to proceed:

Objective: What is the idea trying to do?

Positives: What's interesting and worth building on?

Negatives: What are the idea's drawbacks?

Probability: What are its chances of success?

Downside: If it fails, what can be salvaged?

Ripeness: Is the timing right for this idea?

Bias: What assumptions are you making?

Currency: Are these assumptions still valid?

Blind Spot: What assumptions are you making that you're not even aware of?

Arrogance: Have you been successful with similar ideas in the past? If so, could this success prevent you from seeing pitfalls in the idea?

Humor: What would the fool say about the idea?

Verdict: What's your decision?

Your All-Important *Warrior* Role

WHETHER YOU THINK YOU CAN OR CAN'T, YOU'RE RIGHT.

- Henry Ford

"When you carry your idea into action, be a Warrior," von Oech urges. "Put a fire in your belly, eliminate your excuses, and do what's necessary to reach your objective. Your Warrior is your `doer'! . . . It is the Warrior who completes the loop and gives feedback to the other roles about what works, what doesn't and what has possibilities. The two greatest enemies of action are fear and lack of confidence. Your most important weapon to combat these is in your head—your belief that you can make it happen."

Von Oech relates the story of an engineer's attempts to quit smoking. Every time he would stop, it seems, he would become constipated. After a week of constipation, he'd use it as an excuse to resume smoking. This cycle went on for months. Finally, he took charge and *destroyed* his excuse. "He went to the grocery store and bought a twenty-five pound bag of prunes and then quit smoking again. Then every time he desired a cigarette, he popped a prune. Within several weeks, he had solved both of his problems.

The warrior part of him led him to bat, and hit and win, in an important game of his life."

THE WARRIOR'S BATTLE CRY prompts us to not quit at the Explorer, Artist, or Judge roles, but to forge on—to *do* something:

Be bold. What qualities do you have that will enable you to implement your idea?

Put together your plan. What's your strategy to reach your objective?

Put a fire in your belly. What motivates you to reach your goal?

Put a lion in your heart. What are you willing to sacrifice? What are the consequences of failure?

Get going. What excuses may prevent you from getting started?

Capitalize on your resources. Who are the five people who can help you realize your idea?

Sharpen your sword. What skills can you develop to implement your idea?

Know what you're selling. What is your idea's "product of the product?"

Strengthen your shield. What type of criticism do you expect to receive? How can you deflect it?

Follow through. What obstacles might get in the way? How will you get around them?

Use your energy wisely. What are some needless battles you can avoid?

Get up when you get knocked down. How persistent are you?

Savor your victories and learn from your defeats. What did you accomplish? What did you learn?

THE ONLY TRULY HAPPY PEOPLE ARE CHILDREN

AND THE CREATIVE MINORITY.

- Jean Caldwell

Von Oech insists that each of us is equipped with these creative roles—but sometimes we need a kick in the seat of the pants to get us going, to help us reach our natural potential. "If you choose to be involved in projects that stretch you creatively, that force you to explore, manipulate, evaluate, and act in challenging ways, then ultimately you will be the beneficiary. And that's the biggest kick of all!"

ALL I REALLY NEED TO KNOW I LEARNED IN KINDERGARTEN

by Robert Fulghum, Villard Books, New York, N.Y., 1990

A friend of Robert Fulghum's once gave him a "Storyteller's License" containing the following creed:

I believe that imagination is stronger than knowledge.
That myth is more potent than history.
That dreams are more powerful than facts.
That hope always triumphs over experience.
That laughter is the only cure for grief.
And I believe that love is stronger than death.

In addition to being a storyteller, Robert Fulghum describes himself as an elementary philosopher who likes to think about the simple things in life and then theorize about them. In *All I Really Need to Know I Learned in Kindergarten,* he offers his insight into those "small things" in life that have big meanings.

Having worked as a cowboy, a salesman, an artist, a minister, a bartender and a teacher, Fulghum's observations often embrace unique perspectives. His book's format abandons formal structure and continuity—at times resembling the medley of thoughts a kindergartner might possess. Some chapters resemble poetry, some relate anecdotes or diary entries, and still others indulge in stream-of-consciousness writing. Whatever the technique, Fulghum approaches each topic from a refreshingly simple angle. The overall message is clear: *Childlike joy of life need not be lost.*

Fulghum invites his readers to share in the freedom that comes naturally to children; to "let go" of the adult rules and restraints that bind and constrict. Life is a journey, he says, one meant to be enjoyed.

On Rules

Share everything.
Play fair.
Don't hit people.
Put things back where you found them.
Clean up your own mess.
Don't take things that aren't yours.
Say you're sorry when you hurt somebody.
Wash your hands before you eat.
Flush.
Warm cookies and cold milk are good for you.
Live a balanced life—learn some and think some and draw and paint and sing and dance and play and work every day some.
Take a nap every afternoon.
When you go out into the world, watch out for traffic, hold hands, and stick together.
Be aware of wonder. Remember the little seed in the Styrofoam cup: The roots go down and the plant goes up and nobody really knows how or why, but we are all like that.
Goldfish and hamsters and white mice and even the little seed in the Styrofoam cup—they all die. So do we.
And then remember the Dick-and-Jane books and the first word you learned—the biggest word of all— LOOK.

On Spiders, Crayons, and Places

Fulghum urges us to not only learn from the rules of kindergarten but to also learn from the world of nature. Take spiders for example: spiders have crawled around on the earth for millions of years. They know how to cope with anything. They're determined creatures; they just choose where they want to go and then move toward their target. They don't worry about anything getting in their way, but if something *does* block their path, they deal with it when it happens. We would do well to act with the mixture of tenacity and flexibility that spiders use every day.

Tenacity can get you where you're going, but imagination can help you enjoy the ride. "Crayolas plus imagination (the ability to create images)—these make for happiness if you are a child," Fulghum says. Children have done more, learned more, and felt more with crayons than with any other object. What would life be like, Fulghum speculates, if someone invented a happy Crayola bomb? "People would smile and get a little funny look on their faces and cover the world with imagination," he responds. This kind of bomb is the one the world *really* needs.

Imagination can create new worlds for us, but we also need something solid and real, something to anchor us to our memories and our roots. Visiting an old, familiar place can provide stability in a very unstable world. "There are places we all come from: deep-rooty-common places that make us who we are," Fulghum explains. Sometimes we ignore these places and treat them lightly, but the sights and smells and sounds and feelings of early childhood still create memories in our minds and give us identity. After all, each of us has a need to belong somewhere.

On Yard Work, Neighbors, and Betting

Fulghum believes the most important thing we can do in life is enjoy the experience. If we spend our time worrying over insignificant things, life's happiness will likely pass us by. For example, one of Fulghum's neighbors spends all his summers raking the yard and his winters shoveling snow. The neighbor's yard always looks neat and tidy, but he never has time to sit back and *enjoy* it. Fulghum's yard sometimes appears unkempt, but he spends many hours walking through the grass, collecting colorful leaves, picking flowers, or leaving footprints in the snow. He takes the time to enjoy what he has—without worrying that it's not perfect. His theory is that we each will "become what the leaves and snow become, and go where the leaves and snow go—whether we rake or shovel or not." In other words, in some respects we should regain a more healthy, carefree, childlike outlook.

Another of Fulghum's neighbors is a great believer in betting on life—but also in doing *his* part to see that his bets pan out. This neighbor's wall is covered with hundreds of neatly mounted maxims:

*Always trust your fellow man. And always cut
the cards.
Always trust God. And always build your
house on high ground.
Always love thy neighbor. And always pick a
good neighborhood to live in.
The race is not always to the swift, nor the bat
tle to the strong, but you better bet that way.
Place your bet somewhere between turning-the-other-
cheek and enough-is-enough-already . . .
About winning: It isn't important. What really
counts is how you play the game.
About losing: It isn't important, What really counts
is how you play the game.
About playing the game: Play to win!*

On Holidays

At one point, Fulghum uses freeverse to
reflect on what he really would like to receive
for Christmas. In a way, the last line may be seen
as the over-arching theme of his book:

> *I want to be five years old again for an hour.
> I want to laugh a lot and cry a lot.
> I want to be picked up and rocked to sleep in
> someone's arms, and carried up to bed just
> one more time.
> I know what I really want for Christmas.
> I want my childhood back.*

Fulghum, however, sees Christmas not
only as a time for wishing, but also a time for
giving. A gift doesn't have to be fancy, he says;
what really counts is giving your best. One year
he bought his wife a cuckoo clock for Christmas.
He assembled the clock, then tested it to make
sure it worked. The bird came out and cuckooed
three times—then promptly died. But Fulghum
gave the clock to his wife anyway, advising:
"Assemble the best that is in within you, and
give it away."

Fulghum stresses the importance of giving. Every Valentine's Day each of Fulghum's
children makes a "gummy lump"—a decorated
Valentine's box. The box is a symbol of the children's love for their father and his love for them.
All of us have our own special gummy lump,
Fulghum says, something that is a unique gift
from the heart. It may not be a Valentine's box,
but whatever the gift is, it has been carefully
prepared and is a thing of value and beauty.

On Letting Go

One day a deaf boy appeared at the
Fulghums' door with a note asking if he could
rake up the leaves in the front yard for a dollar.
At first, Fulghum wasn't sure he *wanted* his
leaves raked, but he finally agreed to the boy's
proposal—upping the payment to three dollars.
"The leaves let go, the seeds let go," Fulghum
philosophizes, "and I must let go sometimes,
too, and cast my lot with another of nature's
imperfect but tenacious survivors." No, none of
us can actually bring back our childhood, but we
can, like the previously-mentioned spider, savor
love, life and happiness wherever we find it.

On Others

Fulghum believes that, as humans, we are
all linked together by a common bond. The rela-

tionships we construct with each other have a
profound impact on our lives, sometimes in
ways we don't even acknowledge. Over the
years, Fulghum's barber has become an important fixture in his life. "Without realizing it," this
barber/philosopher asserts, "we fill important
places in each other's lives . . . And of course,
we fill that role ourselves." We never know
which people are watching us and how much
they may be learning from us, and we are all
much more important than we might think.

Each person is important in different
ways. If every human being walking the planet
were to line up side by side, we would discover
that we are all unique. At the same time, as living, breathing souls with comparable needs,
wishes and feelings, we humans are also very
much alike. Why must we know that we are
both *like* everyone else and *different* at the same
time? It is because we all need to feel both
accepted *and* special.

When children play the game of hide-n-
seek, there is usually one too-well-hidden child
who does not get "found." Fulghum compares
this scenario to the story of a man he once knew
who died of cancer. The man did not tell anyone
that he had the disease, and after his death,
many of his friends marveled at how brave he
was, suffering the pain alone, not wanting to
bother anyone with his illness. The dead man's
family, however, was angry and rejected; apparently he had not needed them, nor trusted them;
they were hurt that he did not say goodbye. This
man hid too well. Much to the harm of his family, he did not want to be found.

Those who do "find" each other must love
with fidelity and sacrifice, Fulghum says.
Charles Boyer was an actor whose wife developed cancer of the liver. Night and day for six
months he stayed by her bedside. Two days
after she died, he went out and took his own life;
he just couldn't live without her. Fulghum proposes that this type of love, however, may stem
from selfishness; *devotion*—complete, true love—
is very unselfish.

Another important component of love is
liberation. Fulghum's neighbors across the
street bought themselves a tandem bike. Now,
the husband thinks he is stronger and has a better sense of direction than his wife—and the
wife lets him believe this. The husband gets
what he thinks he wants—and what does the
wife get in return? Liberation. "Liberation finally
amounts to being free from things we don't like
in order to be enslaved by things we approve
of."

Every person counts; every person has
something valuable to give; life is pleasant and
exhilarating in its perfect, child-like simplicity—
if you allow it to be. As Fulghum's "Exchange
Principle" states:

> *Every person passing through this life will
> unknowingly leave something and take something
> away. Most of this something cannot be seen or heard
> or numbered. It does not count in the census. But
> nothing counts without it.*

MAN'S SEARCH FOR MEANING

by Viktor E. Frankl, Simon & Schuster, New York, N.Y. 1984

He who has a why to live can bear almost any how.

Throughout **Man's Search for Meaning**, psychiatrist Victor Frankl makes frequent reference to these words of nineteenth-century German philosopher Friedrich Nietzsche. For Dr. Frankl and his fellow World War II Jewish prisoners, the "how" to be lived through was a Nazi Death Camp. Those who survived, Frankl observed, were usually among those who could call upon a "why"—a purpose outside themselves, a meaning which transcended their individual existence—for the strength to carry on.

Frankl himself is a quietly miraculous example of this dictum: somehow he was able to transform an experience of almost unimaginable suffering into an epiphany. He learned, he says, "that life holds a potential meaning under any conditions, even the most miserable ones . . . . I therefore felt responsible for writing down what I had gone through . . . "

The first part of this book is Frankl's first-hand account of both the brutalities and the spiritual growth he experienced in the infamous concentration camp, Auschwitz. He then goes on in the second section to describe his theory of psychological treatment—"logotherapy"—which grew from that experience.

EXPERIENCES IN A CONCENTRATION CAMP

Frankl balances his identity as a former inmate with his role as a psychiatrist: *To attempt a methodical presentation of the subject is very difficult, as psychology requires a certain scientific detachment. But does a man who makes his observations while he himself is a prisoner possess the necessary detachment? Such detachment is granted to the outsider, but he is too far removed to make any statements of real value.*

Torn from home and family, Frankl and his young wife, along with fifteen hundred others, were loaded onto a train so crowded that some had to lie atop their luggage. For several days and nights they traveled with no indication of their destination or their fate. When the train finally slowed to approach a station, Frankl heard a passenger yell, "There is a sign, Auschwitz!"

Everyone's heart missed a beat . . . Auschwitz—the very name stood for all that was horrible: gas chambers, crematoriums, massacres. Slowly, almost hesitatingly, the train moved on as if it wanted to spare its passengers the dreadful realization as long as possible: Auschwitz!

When Frankl and his fellow prisoners deboarded, the men were first separated from the women, and then herded by blows from room to room, to be stripped of their clothes, their possessions, even their wedding rings. A manuscript containing his "life's work" was taken from Frankl. His head was shaved.

"While we were waiting for the shower," he writes, "our nakedness was brought home to us: we really had nothing now except our bare bodies . . . all we possessed, literally, was our naked existence."

Frankl points out that the common conception of prison camp life, which is mingled with sentiment and pity, is misleading. Within the prisoners there was a fight for existence, an unrelenting struggle for life and for their daily bread.

The prisoners were in shock. Their reactions to the events around them was a grim lesson in the adaptability of human mind. A surreal sense of humor overtook them—they laughed in relief as the showers into which they were herded sprayed "real water." With a detached and "cold" curiosity they considered their circumstances and their potential fate.

As they settled into camp life, the prisoners often surprised themselves by the atrocities they survived: standing naked and wet in the freezing cold; sneaking muddy shoes into their tents just to have a pillow; malnourishment, almost to the point of starvation; frequent beatings; cruelty, not only from guards, but also from among their fellow prisoners. Amidst the daily agony, Frankl came to believe that "If there is a meaning in life at all, then there must be a meaning in suffering. Suffering is an ineradicable part of life, even as fate and death. Without suffering and death human life cannot be complete." And, in fact, despite their hellish existence, some prisoners did find their spiritual life somehow deepening. The intensification of this "inner life" provided a refuge from their desolate circumstances.

Not knowing whether she was even still alive, Frankl clung nonetheless to the image of his wife, and "conversed" with her frequently. One grey morning while he was at work in a trench, he writes, *I was struggling to find the reason for my sufferings, my slow dying. In a last violent protest against the hopelessness of imminent death, I sensed my spirit piercing through the enveloping gloom. I felt it transcend that hopeless, meaningless world, and from somewhere I heard a victorious "Yes" in answer to my question of the existence of an ultimate purpose . . . . I stood hacking at the icy ground. The guard passed by, insulting me, and once again I communed with my beloved. More and more I felt that she was present, that she was with me; I had the feeling that I was able to touch her, able to stretch out my hand and grasp hers. The feeling was very strong: she was there.*

In addition to this "presence" of his wife ("worked"—and eventually died—in another section of the camp), Frankl was also sustained by the vision to share with others what he was learning. He speaks of vividly imagining himself in a comfortable room, lecturing about his experience to an attentive group. While those who could not look beyond the fences of the camp and see an end to their "provisional existence" often gave themselves up to death, Frankl and others committed to live for some purpose beyond themselves. One prisoner, about to kill himself because he "had nothing more to expect from life," finally became convinced that life was still expecting something from *him*. Specifically, he had yet to raise his child, "whom he adored and who was waiting for him in a foreign country." For another suicidal prisoner, it was the anticipated completion of his scientific work which gave him a reason to go on—the "why" for his existence strengthening him to bear almost any "how."

LOGOTHERAPY IN A NUTSHELL

As the title *Man's Search for Meaning* suggests, Frankl's theory of psychotherapy emphasizes the importance of "Logos" (a Greek word for "meaning") in the lives of patients. Throughout his description of logotherapy, Frankl highlights how he has parted ways with the more traditional psychology based on Freudian theory and practice.

Frankl contends that we are not driven by base and primitive psychological defenses or reactions. Instead, "striving to find a meaning in . . . life is [our] primary motivational force . . . " Thus, rather than focusing on a patient's childhood or other past events, logotherapy is primarily concerned with what *meaning* the future holds for the patient.

The typical approach to therapy—with its endless probing for hidden inner conflicts—is viewed by Frankl as misguided: *Unmasking . . . should stop as soon as one is confronted with what is authentic and genuine in man, e.g., man's desire for a life that is as meaningful as possible. If it does not stop then, the only thing that the "unmasking psychologist" really unmasks is his own "hidden motive"—namely, his unconscious need to debase what is genuine, what is genuinely human, in man.*

Where other psychologists may advise us to reduce conflict and stress in our lives, Frankl holds that what we actually need is "not a tensionless state but rather the striving and struggling for a worthwhile goal, a freely chosen task." Indeed, he contends that "mental health is based on a certain degree of tension, the tension between what one has already achieved and what one still ought to accomplish . . . the gap between what one is and what one should become."

The Existential Vacuum

Boredom is the primary "presenting symptom" of a life that lacks meaning. More and more patients—with more and more leisure time—are visiting psychiatrists complaining of boredom, rather than distress. A prime example of this is the phenomenon of "Sunday neurosis"—that sense of depression which so often afflicts people when the rush of the busy week is over, and the are left to face the "void within." Not a few cases of suicide can be traced back to this underlying existential vacuum.

Seeking Meaning

Logotherapy is implemented by helping the patient find meaning in his or her own life:

* What is the Meaning of Life?

"One should not search for an abstract meaning of life." An individual must find a *specific* vocation or mission, a concrete assignment which demands fulfillment. "Therein he cannot be replaced, nor can his life be repeated. Thus, everyone's task is as unique as his specific opportunity to implement it."

* What is the Meaning of Love?

When we love, we become more aware of our potential and more able to actualize that potential. In logotherapy, love is not reduced to a "mere side-effect of sex; rather, sex is a way of expressing the experience of that ultimate togetherness which is called love."

* What is the Meaning of Suffering?

An elderly physician once sought the help of Frankl. For two years he had grieved over the death of his dearly loved wife. Frankl's approach was to ask him what would have happened if he had died first. "Oh," the man replied, "how she would have suffered." Then Frankl pointed out: "Such a suffering has been spared her . . . at the price that you now have to survive and mourn her." When confronted with a situation that cannot be changed, logotherapy challenges us to "change ourselves." When we alter our own view and find—or create—meaning in our suffering, in a sense we have changed the situation. "Suffering ceases to be suffering at the moment it finds a meaning."

Balancing the book's earlier focus on Auschwitz, however, is Frankl's emphatic insistence that suffering is in no way *necessary* to achieve a meaningful life. In fact, "To suffer unnecessarily is masochistic rather than heroic."

Psychiatry Rehumanized

Frankl espouses a vision of a less mechanistic, more humanized psychiatry; one which recognizes both man's ability and responsibility to choose. In the living laboratory of the concentration camps "we watched . . . some of our comrades behave like swine while others behaved like saints. Man has both potentialities within himself; which one is actualized depends on decisions . . . not on conditions." A life well-lived is a life filled with meaning, a life discovered even in the worst of conditions.

Frankl concludes: *You may be prone to blame me for invoking [heroic] examples that are the exception to the rule . . . . It is true that they form a minority. And yet I see therein the very challenge to join the minority. For the world is in a bad state, but everything will become still worse unless each of us does his best.*

HOW TO BE ORGANIZED IN SPITE OF YOURSELF

by Sunny Schlenger and Roberta Roesch, Penguin/Signet Books, New York, N.Y., 1990

In spite of a rash of books on being organized, many of us are still not as organized as we would like to be. Most of us resist change; we just want to be better at being ourselves. This book accepts that premise as its starting point.

Each of us can be classified into one of two broad categories: we are either *time controllers* or *space controllers*. Basic organizing rules can be adapted to each type. The descriptions, quizzes and advice in *How to Be Organized* can help you discover your individual style and then help you tailor traditional time and space management techniques to your individual lifestyle, making your life easier and more organized.

Schlenger and Roesch first review the basic rules of time management, then they adapt them to fit individual needs:

(1) Decide what you really want to accomplish.

(2) Turn your wants into Specific, Measurable, Attainable, Realistic, Timely (**SMART**) goals.

(3) Break your goals down into small, easy-to-take steps. Keep a time log for a few days to help you identify time-wasting activities that keep you from achieving your goals. Place each activity under one of four categories: **Important/pressing; Important/not pressing; Unimportant/ pressing;** or **Unimportant/not pressing.**

Once you split your activities into these categories, it becomes easier to prepare a daily activity list that is focused on the most important tasks.

Each individual functions under a unique set of factors that constitute his or her *organizational style*. A person's *organizational style* is composed of individual interests, needs, energy level, and aptitude. These factors determine whether the individual is a time controller or a space controller.

Time Controllers

There are five types of time controllers: *Hoppers, Perfectionists, Allergic to Detail, Fence Sitters,* and *Cliff Hangers.*

Hoppers

"Hoppers" who represent the most widespread organizational style--like to have many irons in the fire and, easily distracted, move from one task to another, leaving many unfinished. Most Hoppers are not as effective as they could be.

However, Hoppers enjoy variety and change of pace; they also often desire immediate gratification. If they can overcome the inherent problems, for some hopping may be an effective style, enabling them to complete several projects at once, make good use of different energy levels, and keep themselves active and alert.

If you're a Hopper and your style is hurting you, it may help to set mini-goals for yourself, such as committing to spend one hour on a job before proceeding to the next one. Set up a master task list and check off tasks as you do them, a habit that gives you immediate feedback and rewards along the way.

Perfectionists

"Perfectionists" believe that they should be able to do everything--and do it well. Though Perfectionist are proficient at setting goals, focusing on them, and striving for excellence, they get so involved with details that they often don't complete tasks on schedule. They have compulsively high standards and have a hard time distinguishing high standards from superhuman ones. They also become easily discouraged; what might be an average performance to them is perfectly acceptable to others.

Perfectionists should constantly test their assumption of what is truly important, then learn to say no more often to low-priority activities. Delegating some of their tasks and lowering their standards when carrying out less critical tasks also might help.

Allergic to Detail

Some people are so involved in going after the "big picture," that they forget the details. Such a person would rather make a plan than carry it out.

"Allergic to Detail" people perform great when dealing with the overall issues. However, sometimes essential details slip by them. Often, they are simply too impatient to handle followup. They can organize around this problem by making sure their to-do list includes who has the responsibility for the details, even when it is not them. Such personality types also like to move quickly and resist routine. Understanding this aspect of one's personality, one can be most effective by learning to delegate details to others. Simple check lists allow for the easy handling of needful items.

People allergic to detail must also learn to say that all-important word--"Stop"--several times a day. By taking time for details, even if only to assign them to others, they can take more control of their lives and be happier with the results.

Fence Sitters

"Fence sitters" have trouble making choices. They put off decisions or seek ideal solutions. Their problems usually result from failing to make commitments to what they really want. Accordingly, Fence Sitters must learn to evaluate their needs, and make firm decisions.

Fence Sitters are sometimes afraid of making the wrong choice, so they make no choice at all. For example, Dana wants to host a party for her colleagues to celebrate a promotion, but, having never done it before, she is afraid. Thus, weeks go by--until she feels it's too late.

Another type of Fence Sitter includes those who doesn't know how to start moving. These silent sufferers first needs to narrow down, in writing, their possible alternatives, then rank each one against set objectives. If they still feel compelled to obtain more information, they should limit the amount required, create firm deadlines for themselves, check their gut feelings, and then get off the fence.

Cliff Hangers

Some people always delay a decision or task until the last minute, needing outside pressure to force them to get it done. They are always in a last-minute rush and get bored when things are going too well. Typically, "Cliff Hangers" estimate time inaccurately, such as budgeting a two-week block for a two-month assignment.

To solve this problem, Cliff Hangers should create a to-do list with two dates: a "should be done by," and an "absolute deadline." By focusing on the first date, they give themselves some room for unforeseen obstacles that might arise.

Similarly, Cliff Hangers, rather than always thriving on stress to impel them along, need to become realistically aware of how long thing actually take, and then plan accordingly. Some people enjoy stress--except at the rare time when it works *against* them. If these people will just move up all vital deadlines by a week or so, then they will have a reasonable margin of error to work with.

Space Controllers

When you are immersed in a great many activities, it's almost impossible to have a mess-free existence. A so-called "mess" in itself needn't be a problem, however--if everything in your mess has a specific place. You'll save time and money, and be more productive, when you are not always looking for things.

There are five types of space controllers: *Everything Outs, Nothing Outs, Right Anglers, Pack Rats,* and *Total Slobs.*

Everything Outs

"Everything Out" folks prefer having every item they own out on their desk or table where they can see them. After all, they'll probably just have to take them back out tomorrow, so why put them away today?

These people might suffer a lack of storage space or a major paper processing problem. One cure might be to create specific piles of paper, with categories such as: "to read," "to do," "to file," "incoming," "outgoing," and "trash."

Many office products are now available to help the Everything Out. A bulletin board or white board creates a place for messages so they don't get buried. Clear stacking trays keep things in sight, and organized. Computer filing systems can save a ton--literally--of paperwork.

Nothing Outs

"Nothing Outs" demand order. To them, a clear desk means a clear mind. Just putting things away to them becomes a significant accomplishment.

Cramped quarters is a major contributor to the Nothing Out style. Dennis' pint-size, extremely sterile office, for instance, was created following a few simple rules: no plants, no pic-tures, every paper saved, but hidden. Peggy, on the other hand, also has a small office, but saves only important papers. Flowers on top of her single file cabinet and decorations on the walls transformed it into a very pleasant working space.

Nothing Outs must regularly and ruthlessly clean out their files. Daily planners, roll-top desks, closable stacking files, and computers are all new products useful for this style of worker.

Right Anglers

Neatness is more important to a Right Angler, yet clutter doesn't bother them as long as it is arranged properly. A need to feel in control, compulsively straightening things, and valuing form over substance are the hallmarks of the Right Angler.

Right Anglers need to understand that unorthodox management systems are okay, as long as their systems are workable. They also need to be merciless about discarding junk. Since they don't like to start anything they can't finish in one sitting, they need to re-organize tasks into smaller, more easily completed jobs.

Pack Rats

If you save everything because it might come in handy someday, then you're a "Pack Rat." Pack Rats feel sentimental about possessions, commonly regard items as "treasures," or they might simply be unable to decide what to keep and what to throw away.

In order to overcome Pack Rat tendencies, decide, for example, which publications are most useful, then cancel the rest. Throw or give away unneeded items. Pack Rats also gain from setting for themselves a rule that for everything they buy, something they already have has to be thrown away.

Total Slobs

Where Pack Rats intentionally save things, "Total Slobs" accumulate stuff by *inattention.* They hate to organize, and often lose things. Sometimes slobs are a product of their parents' training--or lack of it; in other instances they are absent-minded, rebellious or depressed.

Of all the groups discussed, Total Slobs must change fundamental values before much can be accomplished to organize their lives. After probing the causes of their behavior and capturing a vision of how much better and happier they could live by incorporating some order in their lives, Total Slobs can make gradual changes. Rather than throwing clothes anywhere, they might start by always dropping them in the same chair; or they could simply move the clothes hamper closer to where they undress.

You can be organized in spite of yourself, as Schlenger and Roesch's book says. The standards you set are up to you. Regardless of the standards, however, anyone can keep on track if they know what they want, know how to get there, know what they can and cannot control, know when to relax and be kind to themselves, and know when to push on toward their goals.

THE DANCE OF ANGER

A Woman's Guide to Changing the Patterns of Intimate Relationships
by Harriet Goldhor Lerner, Ph.D., Harper & Row, New York, N.Y., 1985

Harriet Lerner writes that for many years women have been discouraged not only from expressing anger, but even from acknowledging it. While men are labeled heroes for fighting and dying for what they believe in, women are condemned for waging a humane and bloodless war for their own rights. Society has taught women to fear and deny anger, to vent it ineffectively, or to turn it inward—in effect, to "dance" around it rather than to confront it.

In *The Dance of Anger*, Lerner invites women to use the motivating power and energy of anger in a positive way—in the service of dignity and growth. Through anger, women can "gain a clearer and stronger 'I,' and, with it, the capacity for a more intimate and gratifying 'we'." By responding to the dictates of their inner selves, women no longer have to choose between having a *relationship* or having a *self*; it is now possible to have both.

Lerner states that women have been taught two ways to manage anger: to be either a "nice-lady" or a "bitchy woman." "Nice ladies" avoid anger and conflict at all costs, begetting a self-defeating and self-perpetuating cycle that squanders huge amounts of energy in the process of protecting others and preserving the harmony of relationships. On the other hand, "bitchy women" act like nags. Both types of women voice anger without clarity, direction, or control; thus, society writes them off, refusing to take them seriously.

Both categories of women, however, are prone to "overfunction" in a relationship, whereas men tend to "underfunction." Yet, ironically, women who overfunction in terms of housework, childcare and expressing emotions, tend to underfunction when it comes to dealing with men. In contrast, men usually distance themselves from stress in relationships; men may even be rewarded for such distancing because they relinquish their strong roles: "The weaker sex must protect the stronger sex from recognizing the strength of the weaker sex," Lerner gibes, "lest the stronger sex feel weakened by the strength of the weaker sex."

Underfunctioners, Lerner notes, possess distinguishing characteristics:

* They tend towards disorganization.
* They become less competent under stress.
* They develop physical or emotional symptoms under stress.
* They are often labeled as "sick" or "irresponsible."

Overfunctioners, on the other hand, possess other attributes:

* They "know" what is best for themselves and for others.
* They quickly offer advice and rescue others under stress.
* They may be labeled as "reliable" or "together."
* They have difficulty sharing their own vulnerabilities.

According to Lerner, most relationships suffer from a "seesaw" effect, and it is normally the woman who remains, figuratively, on the ground. In such a relationship, if one person decides to re-balance the seesaw, the other person may suddenly feel threatened and attempt to revert to old patterns. For a long-term relationship to be a success, the seesaw must be balanced.

Thus, a woman's attempts to assert herself in a relationship can create a great deal of opposition from her male counterpart. Anxious to retain the status quo, a man may successively use various verbal ploys:

(1) "You are wrong," followed by much argumentative support.

(2) "Change back and we will accept you again."

(3) "If you don't change back, these are the consequences . . ."

Clearly, these countermoves represent an increasing impatience to regain the relationship's stability.

Circular Dances in Couples

Lerner says that if one method of managing anger does not work, we try another. Even rats in a maze vary their behavior when they keep hitting a dead end. This fact notwithstanding, behavioral habits die hard. Since the very quality that a partner may suddenly detest in the other can be what initially attracted him or her, the behavior of each serves to maintain and provoke that of the other. This process institutes a circular dance which only stops when behavior changes; each partner, however, is trying to change the other, when, in actuality, each should be trying to change him or herself.

Lerner gives the example of the "blaming game." One person characterizes the other as the one who "started it," thereby escaping personal responsibility. In reality, however, arguments (dances) are "circular," for the behavior of one person justifies and provokes that of the other. The real issue, then, becomes not "who started it," but rather, "How do we break out of it?" with both partners changing their *own* dance steps, not the other's.

"Emotional Pursuer-Emotional Distancer" is another old dance. *Emotional Pursuers* (usually women) seek to reduce anxiety by sharing feelings and maintaining close emotional contact, while *Emotional Distancers* (usually men) attempt to reduce anxiety by intellectualizing and withdrawing. The result is that one expresses dependence, the other expresses autonomy. Yet, when a pursuer begins to energize his or her own life without distancing the other person, the circle has been broken; as a result, the relationship becomes more balanced.

A third dance is "Overinvolved Mother-Underinvolved Father." If a father is physically and emotionally detached from the family, the woman may try to fill the empty space by becoming overly-engrossed in her children's lives. When the father tries to change, the mother may criticize him, causing him again to become detached—thus perpetuating the cycle of unbalanced involvement. In this scenario, then, the overinvolved mother needs to focus on improving her own personal life—and allow her underinvolved husband to develop closer ties with the children.

Using Anger As A Guide

"Anger is a tool for change," Lerner stresses, "when it challenges us to become more of an expert on ourselves and less of an expert on others." Thus, learning to use anger effectively and positively requires letting go—particularly at the most difficult times. Many of us have tried to control another person's health, for example, perhaps becoming exasperated when that person refuses to take prescribed medication, lose weight, or seek needed medical attention. Women especially are prone to play out this role of emotional reactor. However, it is important to allow others to assume the primary responsibility for their own health. Expressions of concern are appropriate, of course, once one's own needs are fulfilled.

In order to break old patterns and develop a healthy sense of identity, anger must be translated into clear, non-accusing statements about the self. Women especially must anticipate negative reactions to their new assertiveness.

Up and Down the Generations

People inherit their strengths and weaknesses from preceding generations. Lerner suggests that "if we do not know about our family history, we are more likely to repeat past patterns or mindlessly rebel against them, without much clarity about who we are, how we are similar or different from other family members, and how we might best proceed in our own lives."

Each of us is responsible for our own behavior. Still, the degree of "fusion" in a family is high and there is often little distinction between the separate "I's" within the "we" of family. As a result, individual family members may project guilt for another family member's failure—or perceived failure—onto themselves.

Women, in particular, are often discouraged from taking responsibility for their own lives, and encouraged to adopt the guilt of others. Hence, "guilt and self-blame are a `women's problem' of epidemic proportions"; when someone "knocks us down, *we're* the ones who apologize." In such situations, women can transform their anger into useable information by following a three-step course:

1. *Observe*. Notice the sequences of interactions that lead to anger.
2. *Clarify the Pattern*. Gather objective facts about who does what, when, and in what order.
3. *Gather Data*. Learn how your family generally interacts, taking into account such facts as birth order and individual likes/dislikes. Ascertaining one's own unique role in a family helps to create a sense of separateness in each member.

Women in relationships customarily assume that they alone are responsible for fixing whatever is wrong. Yet, Lerner maintains that "when we do not put our primary energy into solving our own problems, we take on other people's problems as our own," thereby stunting relationships. Once this pattern is established, it's perpetuated, year to year, generation to generation.

Lerner declares that women who find themselves in such situations must *stop trying to be helpful*, and consider that they may not even have the answers to their own problems, let alone someone else's. "Stepping back," however, does *not* mean "withdrawing emotionally"; sometimes people can be most helpful by sharing their own deficiencies.

As parents, women also tend to overfunction when dealing with their children. Society has fostered in mothers the idea that every ounce of their children's behavior is a direct result of their influence. Realistically, mothers cannot force children to behave as mothers would like. However, they can be firm and clear about what behaviors they will and will not accept.

Mothers frequently feel the urge to "rescue" their children—to scratch when they itch—a tendency that frequently spawns underdeveloped children. "When we learn to stay in our own skin," Lerner says, "and avoid assuming an overfunctioning or `fix it' position, children . . . demonstrate a remarkable capacity to manage their own feelings, find solutions to their problems, and ask for help when they want it."

Thinking In Threes

In the battle to reduce anxiety, we often unconsciously pull a third person into our relationships, Lerner points out, because we hope to reduce emotional intensity. This universal pattern is referred to as a "triangle"—and triangles can be dangerous in many ways. Ideally, if we are angry at Sue, we will confront Sue rather than complaining to Sally.

Lerner suggests that in examining our relationships it is useful to analyze the families we were born into, perhaps by creating historical family diagrams. Such outlines should cover at least three generations and include birth dates, death dates, marriages, divorces, serious illnesses, and records of the highest levels of formal education achieved by members of the extended family. This information could clarify patterns in our own relationships: "If we do not observe and understand how our triangles operate, our anger can keep us stuck in the past, rather than serving as an incentive and guide to form more productive relationship patterns for the future."

There is a veritable flood of advice on how we should overcome our anger: "Jog, meditate, ventilate, bite your tongue, silently count to ten . . . " However, if we don't learn to *exercise* our anger to achieve a clearer definition of ourselves and our relationships, we are destined to perpetuate the destructive patterns which cause us to be angry.

Lerner's *The Dance Of Anger* stresses the importance of women connecting not only with their immediate families, but also with the "family" of womankind. She further urges women to question the old roles and rules prescribed by society: "If we do not challenge and change the societal institutions that keep women in a subordinate and de-selfed position outside the home, what goes on inside the home will continue to be problematic."

HOW TO GET OFF THE FAST TRACK

and live a life money can't buy
by M.M. Kirsch, Harper Paperbacks, New York, N.Y., 1991

M.M. Kirsch and her husband decided that the time had come to live a fulfilling lifestyle and step off the fast track. Their decision became a marvelous experiment. In ten years, they decided, they would have at least the same standard of living and be doing the things that made them happy. This involved a good deal of hard work and a very good plan—as is always the case for a Maverick, or one who successfully gets off the fast track. Along the way they encountered many people conducting the same experiment, and many who had already succeeded. The knowledge they gleaned through this process led the author to tell their stories to others.

Who Gets Off The Fast Track And Why

For many, the fast track means financial security, the freedom to travel, a nice car, a big house, and the ability to spend money and not worry about having it in their "golden years." For others, the fast track means having the opportunity to be the best you can possibly be in a demanding, highly rewarding career—simply to be counted among the best. For most, the fast track provides strong feelings of self-worth and an invigorating sense of accomplishment.

"For others, however, the fast track leads down a road without purpose. Their goals bring them financial success but not peace of mind. How did they become so misdirected?" Kirsch asks. Whose idea of the "successful lifestyle" and "successful career" did they accept? Did they become professionals—stockbrokers, systems analysts, attorneys, doctors, accountants, advertising directors, executives—and work 70-hour weeks simply to earn a lot of money? Are they seeking security, fulfillment, accomplishment? Do their high-dollar, high-status careers also offer them an opportunity to develop personal skills and talents? "Are they a true reflection of the person?"

Who are some of those who have decided that fast-track living is not for them? And perhaps more important, what did they choose in exchange for life in the fast lane?

- *A banker and her husband, a former car salesman, quit their careers to start an international cycle-touring company.*
- *A successful Manhattan leather-goods manufacturer liquidates, moves upstate, and becomes a goat farmer producing French-style goat cheese.*
- *A Wall Street stockbroker walks away from a six-figure salary so he can manage a short-of-cash riding stable in Tucson.*
- *A successful New York City businesswoman decides she wants out, buys property in New Mexico, and opens a bed-and-breakfast inn.*
- *A graphic designer and his wife, both filmmakers, forfeit lucrative businesses in San Francisco and move to a remote rural area in California. They start a business handcrafting beautiful books using nineteenth-century methods.*

There are a variety of reasons that people leave the fast track. Some hope to find more meaningful work; others hope to tighten the bonds of family; and still others merely want to get away from it all and live in a place where everybody knows your name you don't need to lock the door.

"Do you wonder if there is a better life for you off the fast track? Are you wasting natural talents and skills because you have chosen a career that offers greater financial rewards? Do you feel that living in the country would improve the quality of your life? Are you eager to continue your education? Do you need more time for personal enlightenment? Is your work in balance with your family and personal needs? Do you long for a sense of accomplishment in your work?"

If you answered "yes" to any of these questions, maybe, in some fashion, at least, you need to get off the fast track.

Do You Have What It Takes To Get Out?

Three key ingredients enable fast trackers to get out successfully: First, they have a realistic view of themselves and are fully aware of their talents, skills and interests. Secondly, they have a clearly defined idea of what they want from life; their sense of happiness and achievement exists independently form social influences. Most importantly, however, "Getting off the fast track is an adventure reserved for the individual with a vision that comes from the heart. It is an adventure reserved for pioneer stock—the enterprising, the stalwart, the brave, the confident, the optimistic, and most important, the maverick. *Webster's New Collegiate Dictionary* defines a maverick as 'an individual who refuses to conform with his group.'"

Successful ex-fast trackers had a number of common characteristics, among them:

- Fierce independence and self-sufficiency.
- Boundless initiative, energy and vitality.
- A keen sense of humor.
- Enthusiastic and persistent; not intimidated by a first, tenth, or hundredth failure.
- Trustworthy.
- Willing to take risks and be responsible for results.
- Willing to sacrifice.
- Spends time doing things considered enjoyable.
- Highly organized.
- Patient, listens, and able to learn from others.
- Creative and imaginative.
- Respectful of inner values.

Any person contemplating withdrawing from the fast track must distinguish between wanting to get *away* from something and wanting to *find* something better. If you are trying to escape a very specific set of circumstances, getting off the fast track may land you in a different but equally disagreeable set of circumstances. "Consider the individual eager to escape the noise and pollution of the city. She relocates to a rural environment only to discover that summer mosquitoes and humidity, and winter ice and sub-zero temperatures, are worse than what she left behind. Another example is the fast-tracker who hates the competitive atmosphere at his company. He relocates to a smaller city and discovers that office politics are even more magnified in a closer-knit community."

If you are unsure about getting off the fast track or think that you could solve a lot of your problems in a more conventional way than quitting your job and moving away, leaving behind all that you have gained, then you need to *take time out* to decide. Joseph Campbell offers this advice: "You must have a room, or a certain hour or so a day, where you don't know what was in the newspapers that morning, you don't know who your friends are, you don't know what you owe anybody, you don't know what anybody owes to you. This is a place where you can simply experience and bring forth what you are and what you might be." In short, Kirsch cites many ways to make your *present* lifestyle more meaningful (focusing exercises, finding a place of "creative incubation," setting meaningful goals, enlarging your interests and sense of "fun" . . .) without taking drastic measures or sacrificing your standard of living.

By working towards a more intimate knowledge of yourself you will discover what is unique about you. You will discover what is most important to you and the talents, skills and attitudes that make you who you are. "You may discover that the life you are leading now *can* make you happy, and that your motivations for wanting to escape have been spurred by superficial problems or shortcomings that can be dealt with more pragmatically."

In Search Of The Good Life

The ex-fast tracker often finds herself in search of many of the things traditionally associated with "the good life." Idealists have long argued that "the good life" should raise one's aspirations beyond materialism. Happiness and fulfillment, they insisted, came from "living a life of simplicity that allowed the individual time to wonder at and appreciate the simple joys in life. To live the good life was to be able to control one's life and one's destiny, and not be at the mercy of the marketplace." The good life meant plain living and high moral aspirations centered on family, civic, and spiritual ideals. It was achieved through hard work, self-discipline, commitment, perseverance despite adversity, and a respect for leisure and solitude.

What these visionaries—and ex-fast trackers, in general—see as "the good life" includes: taking time to appreciate the simple things in life and trying to live more simply; appreciating what you have rather than longing for more, and appreciating who you are rather than trying to be who you are not; devoting more time and energy to relationships with friends and family; and pursuing virtuous and socially constructive activity. Most of all, the good life means doing those things you most long to do.

Doing That Which You Long To Do

"Many ex-FTers have come to understand that how you spend your working day is how you spend your life. To separate life from work is to sacrifice one or the other. They felt the sting of that sacrifice and found it intolerable, for the quality of one's work ultimately equals the quality of one's life. This knowledge of what Buddhists call `right livelihood,' coupled with a strong sense of purpose and direction in life, is an essential aspect of knowing who you are and what you want." *Chop Wood, Carry Water,* describes the Buddhist concept of right livelihood:

The Buddha, in his wisdom, made "right livelihood" . . . one of the steps to enlightenment . . . Responsible work is an embodiment of love, and love is the only discipline that will serve in shaping the personality, the only discipline that makes the mind whole and constant for a lifetime of effort. There hovers about a true vocation that paradox of all significant self-knowledge—our capacity to find ourselves by losing ourselves. We lose ourselves in our love of the task before us, and in that moment we learn an identity that lives both within and beyond us.

Recently, many have discovered that success is not defined by material success but by personal satisfaction and the achievement that comes with doing something you truly love. "Less and less is being written about today's money-makers as people become more intrigued with those `eccentrics' who are doing what they always wanted to do without regard to how much money they make." We have grown less intrigued by the high-salaried professional by the craftsperson who revives "the lost art of blacksmithing; the farmer who raises pesticide-free produce; the factory worker who buys out management, takes a pay cut, and works to produce better quality goods; the teacher who devotes extra time to students."

What do all of these people have in common? They work at jobs they love and take great pride in them. They work at jobs that come naturally to them. They work hard, using talents and skills that perhaps are unique to them.

Many fast trackers don't have the freedom to choose what they do for a living because they live in fear of losing their livelihood. Ex-fast trackers may make less money than their fast track counterpart, but remain independent of anybody else's notion of value. Many fast trackers live in slavery to their possessions, cannot change their lives at a whim, and are not as open to experimentation and exploration. "Successful ex-FTers talk about working at jobs that allow them to express their creativity, their joy, and their fullness as human beings."

If you find yourself longing for more personal freedom (and, if necessary, can stand to take a cut in pay) then perhaps this is the best indication that getting off the fast track is something you should consider. This is not a decision to make lightly; far from making life easier, getting off the fast track generally involves putting forth great effort to succeed in some way that is uniquely fulfilling to you.

A GUIDE TO CONFIDENT LIVING

by Norman Vincent Peale, Norman Vincent Peale, 1976

The secrets of happiness lie within you, and in *A Guide to Confident Living,* Dr. Norman Vincent Peale demonstrates how you can *think* your way to success and happiness. Step by step, Dr. Peale teaches and demonstrates proven, uplifting techniques to achieve lasting fulfillment.

A New-Old Way To Free Your Powers

Dr. Peale tells the story of a young and highly skilled physician who sometimes gives the most curious prescription to people afflicted with a sense of fear, inferiority, and general burnout: *Go to church once a week for the next three months.* In a church, the doctor explains, there is a mood and atmosphere with a healing power effective in curing the above mentioned problems.

"He further asserts that he does not particularly care whether the patient listens to the sermon. Church-going is of value if a person merely sits quietly, yielding himself to the mood and atmosphere of the church." This doctor reports that his patients have benefited from this unusual prescription.

Don't Keep Your Troubles To Yourself

It can be commendable, even inspiring when people keep their troubles to themselves. Most of us have known people who have had to suffer pain for years and who have done so with admirable spirit and a determination not to be a burden to others. "On the other hand, some people seem to develop into whiners and complainers . . . victims of self-pity, thinking constantly about themselves. They do not keep their troubles to themselves and they should learn to do so. They want everybody else to keep their troubles for them, and people do not like to be the repositories of other people's troubles. Ella Wheeler Wilcox well says:

Laugh, and the world laughs with you;
Weep, and you weep alone."

But the practice of keeping your troubles to yourself can be dangerous. There is a sense in which the human personality must have release from itself. People cannot forever bottle up within themselves the guilt, problems, and adversity which have affected them. To use a common expression, it is advisable to get some things "off your chest." It is significant that the word "chest" is used in this idiom, since "the heart has been traditionally considered the center of emotional life."

Inner release, explains Dr. Peale, is something every human being needs. It is dangerous to carry problems around too long or they will hurt you. Find someone who is skilled in listening to and solving problems of the heart—a minister, priest, rabbi, psychologist, or just a wise and understanding friend. Often, merely the act of sharing a burden with another human being will provide immediate relief.

How To Get Rid Of An Inferiority Complex

There is tremendous power within every one of us. Socrates urged us to "know thyself"—and knowing ourselves includes knowing and appreciating our innermost spiritual powers. When you know yourself, it is difficult to be defeated by a false sense of inferiority. "Quite possibly you often do feel defeated. Depression settles over you, bringing the disheartening feeling that there isn't much use in fighting on. Probably everybody is tempted to sink into this dull and gloomy attitude occasionally, but not everybody yields to it. Those who accept the idea that they are defeated usually *are* beaten; for, as a famous psychologist says, 'There is a deep tendency in human nature to become like that which you imagine yourself to be.' Believe you are defeated, believe it long enough, and it is likely to become a fact."

People who achieve lasting happiness and success are those who, feeling themselves sinking into depression, refuse to think they are defeated. They refuse to think that situations and circumstances—or their enemies—have put them there. They know that thinking they *are* defeated, or *might be* defeated, is the surest way to *be* defeated. They also know that the consistent practice of thinking positively—thinking of ultimate victory—is the key to success.

How To Achieve A Calm Center For Your Life

The main ingredient in tension is *mental disorganization.* The mind refuses to make decisions about many different things and as a result always carries around numerous burdens, never really resolving any of them. "The mind in this situation reacts somewhat like the body in shivering. One shivers when passing suddenly from a warm to a cold area; the body attempts to accommodate itself quickly to the sudden change in body temperature. It has been estimated that as much energy is expended in a half-minute of shivering as in several hours of work. This results in depletion of vigor. In a similar way, shivering in the mind depletes its force when one fails to practice the fundamental principle of mental organization."

To unload our excess mental baggage—unresolved decisions—and use our energy for enjoying the finer things in life, Dr. Peale suggests the following: "Get the calm selective ability to take up one thing at a time and concentrate upon it. Deal finally with it, if possible, before passing to the next matter. When you organize your mind, a sense of power will come to you, and you will soon wonder at the ease with which you can handle responsibilities. Your capacity for work will increase; so will your pleasure in what you are doing. Strain and tension will subside."

How To Think Your Way To Success

The power to think is one of our greatest powers and we need to cultivate practical techniques to improve our thinking and so improve our lives. It is by changing our thinking that we change our world.

People become what, habitually, in their conscious and subconscious mind—or in their heart—*they think*. The wisest of all books says, "As [a man] thinketh in his heart, so is he." And two of the world's wisest thinkers said: "Our life is what our thoughts make of it."

- Marcus Aurelius

and

"A man is what he thinks about all day long."

- Ralph Waldo Emerson.

Surely a person thinks about many things in the course of a day. Beneath all of these thoughts, however, is one basic or primary thought. Through this fundamental thought, all other thoughts are filtered and take their color and content.

For example, some people allow fear to become their primary thought. Fear usually begins as a thin trickle of worry across the mind. Repeated over many days, it becomes habitual until it cuts a deep channel across the consciousness. As a result, *every* thought—about family, business, health, or the world—is colored by dark thoughts of fear, stained by the tarnish of anxiety and insecurity. Fear, in all its forms, dominates their thinking.

To counteract this condition we must develop the only type of thinking that can defeat fear: FAITH. Faith will change our dim image of the world to a brighter, more glorious hues of gold and silver.

How do we develop faith? " . . . Affirm the positive thought. Faith, too, begins as a thin trickle across the mind. Repeated, it becomes habitual. It cuts deeply into the consciousness until finally . . . you have two basic channels of thought—one of fear, and one of faith. But fear can never defeat faith." the more we operate by faith, the less we operate by fear. Gradually, deepening faith supplants fear; it displaces it so completely that the "fears channel" finally dries up. "The faith thought overflows and becomes the deep, flowing, primary thought of the mind. Then every thought about your business, about your family, about the world is touched by the thought of faith and comes up bright, resplendent, optimistic and positive."

As a result of cultivating this positive train of thought, you will find that your optimism, your *faith*, will touch everything and everybody in your life. You will come to believe more deeply in yourself and your fellow human beings.

Prayer - The Most Powerful Form Of Energy

Dr. Peale underscores certain commonsense spiritual principles, long tested in the "laboratory of human experience." The principle of seeking divine guidance—of simple trust, of faith—has repeatedly proven itself to be of great value in living a happy, successful life.

"Whatever your problem, no matter how difficult, you can release spiritual power sufficient to solve your problem. The secret is—*pray* and *believe*. Even though it may be hard to believe, do it nevertheless. Simply believe that Almighty God will give His power to you. Pray and mentally yield yourself to God's power. Do this by affirming that you have not sufficient power within yourself and that, therefore, you are willing to put yourself completely in contact with spiritual force. The basic secret of the Christian religion is not effort or will power, important as they are. The secret of Christianity is faith. The only struggle it urges you to exert is the effort to believe. The art is to learn to have faith. When you have done so you become a channel through which divine power flows. It flows through *you*. You then have all the strength you need to meet any situation involving you."

Dr. Peale suggests a few rules to follow when praying. Again, these are guides for praying that have proven most effective in the laboratory of human experience:

1. Set aside a few minutes to be alone in a quiet place. Relax mind, body and spirit by thinking about God in a way that is most natural for you.

2. Do not try to use formal language; talk to God in the most natural way.

3. Talk to God as you go about the business of your day whenever you have a few minutes to spare. This will remind you of God's presence and guidance all day long.

4. Affirm the fact that God is with you at all times and helping you—do not merely beseech God for assistance but be assured of it.

5. Pray with the thought that you prayers will reach out to touch all of your loved ones with blessings.

6. Especially when praying, think positive thoughts.

7. Ask for what you want but remain willing to accept God's will. Seek God's will in your prayer.

8. Put everything in God's hands and pray for the strength to do your best.

9. Say prayers for people who do not like you or who have wronged you. This will help both them and you.

10. Every day say a prayer for this country, this world and for lasting peace.

Again Dr. Peale emphasizes the importance of changing your thinking: "Change your thoughts and you change everything." Again and again in life, what you think has much more to do with success and happiness than any set of circumstances. "A man's world is not primarily made of the circumstances that surround him . . . You are not what you think you are, but what you *think*, you are."

THE SKY'S THE LIMIT

by Dr. Wayne Dyer, Pocket Books, New York, N.Y., 1980

Dr. Dyer's *The Sky's the Limit* focuses on the *why* and the *how* of human achievement. The book endeavors to teach us how to transcend our everyday normal selves to become the *extraordinary* people that we all can be.

THE NEZ PERSON AND THE NO-LIMIT PERSON

Dr. Dyer describes a *NEZ (No Erroneous Zones)* person as someone who has successfully eliminated self-defeating thinking and behavior. After reaching the NEZ state, one is then ready to become a *No-Limit person:*

Each person on this planet is inherently . . . capable of attaining "dizzying heights" of happiness and fulfillment. The main barrier to most people's doing so seems to be fear, fear that the heights will make them dizzy instead of rooting their feet more firmly to the ground, which is actually what happens—as you will see.

Dyer's definition of the "No-Limit Person" is derived from Dr. Abraham Maslow's theory of "self actualization," which represents "the very highest levels of being or evolution available to humanity." Dyer explains that "Maslow wanted to look at humanity from a different perspective. He believed in studying the great achievers and learning from their examples, rather than confining psychology to the study of sickness and low achievement, and ending up viewing humanity solely from the point of view of what can go wrong with the human psyche. Maslow believed in humanity's greatness. So do I."

This approach diverges from that of mainstream psychology—and medicine in general—which is concerned with moving people from sickness to "normality"; thus, the possibilities of *super*-health and *super*-achievement are often overlooked. In contrast, Dyer specifically emphasizes techniques that he has found useful in promoting lasting happiness and success.

NEZ TO NO-LIMITS: You're Allowed To Be Perfect

"You know the ocean is perfect," says Dyer. "So are flowers, the sky, your pet cat, and everything else in nature. They are as perfect as they can be even if they are always changing..." Humans are perfect, too, Dyer says. Just like an ever-changing, perfect sky, "you can grow, change, and be different in a thousand ways, and still be a perfect creature."

Dyer continues: "The essence of your perfection is in your own ability to look at yourself, accept what you see as perfect in the present moment, and then be able to grow into something quite different, *but still perfect*. It is ironic that we always think of animals as perfect, and yet we deny that same quality to ourselves."

So, why do people feel *imperfect?* "Somehow we got it all screwed up," Dyer asserts. "We have convinced ourselves that the real

purpose of life is to try to outdo everyone else and to chase endlessly after goals that always elude us . . . We all are so busy chasing after external objects of one kind or another that we have no time left for enjoying our lives."

If we wish to end these futile pursuits and become No-Limit people, we must first carefully evaluate how we spend the precious days of our lives. If we are constantly engaged in the pursuit of "points"—the money and position and retirement nest-egg that we use to evaluate success in our culture—we have no time left to enjoy living or experience the perfection that exists within us *right now.*

Focusing on the future instead of enjoying the present is commonplace in our society; Dyer refers to this tendency as *futurizing*. While he does not propose marching blindly into the future and simply forgetting about earning a living, he does believe that if we cannot derive satisfaction from the "doing," we will be unable to detect whether or not an undertaking was successful.

In order for us to transcend "futurizing," we need to keep in mind this truth: *Now is the only time you ever really have.* We don't have the luxury of second chances; if we constantly fear the future or regret the past, we are in danger of living "*in absentia*—absent, even alienated from the only time in which [we] can ever `really be living'*." Thus, Dyer recommends that whenever we find ourselves reminiscing about the "good old days" or lamenting the failures of the past, we must "let go"—and surrender the past in order to take on new challenges and opportunities. There is always something to be learned from the past, Dyer acknowledges, but when we dwell on it, ironically, we *don't* learn from it.

Similarly, while we must plan for the future, we cannot let the future—which is actually little more than a big guessing game—take precedence over our enjoyment of the present. If we are aware of the perfection all around us and are working *right now* to add to that perfection, countless opportunities will present themselves to us. The key is to do *something*, and do it *perfectly*, right now; after all, in one respect or another, as human beings we are already perfect. The process of finding and building perfection "involves only giving up the self-defeating attitudes and behaviors that have kept you from enjoying your present moments *for a few of those moments every day.* The entire process of getting into the present begins with giving up the past and the future in favor of the now, for as many of your life experiences as you possibly can."

The art of being *totally engaged* in the act of living right now, however, is seldom seen or practiced in our culture; we do not even have a single word or phrase to describe this experience. Other cultures, however, are more aware of the importance of this concept. In Zen, this experience is referred to as *mu*, which literally means nothing or zero. But *mu*, or *muga*, connotes far more than a state of nothingness; it is a state of total and pleasurable involvement in the here and now—in the task at hand.

LIVING NOW

There are three components necessary to living in the "now." They are *survival, normality, and engagement.*

Survival: Forced Back To Now

"As it turns out, *the capacity for survival of the human race seems to depend on the ability of some individuals to live totally in the present moment when their lives are threatened,"* Dyer notes.

He cites Terrence des Pres, author of *The Survivor: An Anatomy of Life in the Death Camps,* who tells about existence in the Nazi concentration camps of World War II. While our everyday problems may be very real to us, we rarely, if ever, are subjected to the extreme mental and physical torture that the survivors of these camps had to endure. In reference to those courageous souls—many of whom literally forced themselves to survive—Dyer quotes des Pres:

Only a radical and defiant return to elemental life could keep them going in a dark, dead universe; minute by minute, day by day, month by month, year by year. Time ceased (menstrual cycles stopped); place lost significance; the mind closed down in self-defense.

It seems that we all possess innate abilities to sustain our own lives; our natural, spontaneous reaction is to negotiate situations one day, one minute, or one second at a time. Indeed, we cling to the present for survival's sake. A survivor of the Holocaust, according to des Pres, "lived from moment to moment in a state of elemental struggle, focusing upon whatever infinitesimally small item of existence was before him: a helping hand when someone fell, the gift of a coat from someone who had two, a fish head, a bowl of bean soup, a morning fleck of sunlight upon a spear of grass glimpsed during roll call, a bowel movement, the fag end of a cigarette, a minute's rest at the side of the road. These were not fancy consolations, nor were they some sort of Survivors' Zen. They were milliseconds of sanity in a long madness. They were points of light in a long darkness."

Those who, for whatever reason, were unable to live completely in the moment were unable to keep their spirits alive; more often than not, they died.

Normality: Living Now Sometimes

Children seem uniquely able to live in the present.

A small child can follow a bug for ten minutes, oblivious to anything but the fascinating shape, color and movements of that bug. When he is tired of chasing the bug, he may move on to playing a teasing game with a playmate, and then to throwing stones at a tree. Whatever he does, he is com- pletely lost in the present.

Children's "fascination for being in the present is possible for all of us," Dr. Dyer point out, "because each of us has both a child and a survivor deep within us . . . "

"We have all experienced what we call `magic moments' in our adult lives," Dyer points out, "moments we remember as being ecstatic, blissful, rapturous, glorious, perfect; states of total involvement in the present." These memorable moments or periods in our lives frequently involve "peak" events: childbirths, athletic achievements, creative undertakings. "Artists have told me of painting for hours with the single-minded fascination of being totally lost in their work. Others with well-established creative outlets tell how they can spend twelve hours at a sewing machine working on a new article of clothing, or in writing a poem or a book."

Likewise, we all have experienced times when we have been so involved in a task that we are amazed how quickly the day has passed. The key word here is *involvement.* When totally involved in some pleasurable, creative experience that is neither too stressful nor too monotonous, we are at our absolute best as human beings. But "while all of us have experienced `living now sometimes' most of us have had these experiences all too rarely in our adult lives," Dyer says. "The transition from NEZ to No-Limit living means (a) cultivating the art of living now to the point where we can enter the Muga state *whenever we choose,* and (b) entering it more and more often, for longer and longer periods."

Engagement

Finally, to live fully in the present, we must be *engaged.* Dyer defines this as the "final stage of present-moment living":

The French existentialists had a word for it: engage. It means to be engaged in something that has such deep meaning for you that the more deeply you allow yourself to dedicate yourself to it, the more creative you allow yourself to be in the pursuit of it, the more of your inner resources you muster in `working on it,' the more you are living now.

Thus, it is important to occupy ourselves with *living now*—whatever our vocations, strengths, or so-called limitations may be. If we are unfulfilled by our vocations or friendships, it is essential to find "meaning and engagement" in avocations (hobbies, or volunteer work), a new, more accepting group of friends, or in building up latent talents. Regardless of how it's done, we need to find purpose, joy, and satisfaction in how we choose to spend our time. "The No-Limit person is capable of engaging totally in virtually *everything* he or she may do," Dyer reminds us, "from getting shoes repaired to landing on the moon."

Cultivating the art of living in the present is the most rewarding "lifestyle" a person can lead. Dr. Dyer challenges his readers to become engaged in living; the sky's the limit to the person who *believes* and *does.*

PEOPLE OF THE LIE

The Hope for Healing Human Evil
by M. Scott Peck, M.D., Simon and Schuster, New York, N.Y., 1983

This is a dangerous book . . . We cannot begin to hope to heal human evil until we are able to look at it directly. It is not a pleasant sight.

M. Scott Peck is best known for his best-selling *The Road Less Traveled*. A thoughtful, religious man, and an experienced psychiatrist, in *People of the Lie* Peck undertakes a scientific study of the reality of evil in the world. While he does not attempt to solve the problem of evil, he tries to create an awareness of the existence of evil as well as an understanding of the problems that all-too-commonly overrun our lives.

People of the Lie is intended to shine the light of scientific inquiry on the subject of human evil—defined, most simply, as characteristics such as *deception, selfishness, laziness, passivity, callousness,* and *lack of compassion.* Only by examining these evils openly, objectively—and carefully—can we hope to begin to address and eliminate the crises, both big and small, that rule over our world today.

To address the problem of evil we must first look to ourselves, for we can never hope to heal and confront the deceptions in others until we are honest with ourselves. It is important to realize that there is no single, successful approach to understanding the ancient problem of evil. To delegate the problem of evil solely to the religious or philosophical realm denies us the advantage of the *scientific* model, as "science seeks, as far as it might, to penetrate the mystery of the world."

Psychiatrists and psychologists have much to learn from those in religion who seek to understand the human soul. The reverse is also true. When the subject of investigation is "evil," we must use every resource available to understand it. Some of us, perhaps most, prefer to think of the manifestations of evil as rare—those few instances of extreme cruelty or sadism. On the contrary, evil is quite prevalent, much more common than we would like to acknowledge. And because of the fact that evil pervades almost every facet of everyday existence, we must seek, even at personal risk, a greater understanding of the phenomenon.

"The problem of evil is a very big mystery indeed. It does not submit itself easily to reductionism. We shall, however, find that some questions about human evil can be reduced to a size manageable for proper scientific investigation. Nonetheless, the pieces of the puzzle are so interlocking, it is both difficult and distorting to pry them apart. Moreover, the size of the puzzle is so grand, we cannot truly hope to obtain more than glimmerings of the big picture. In common with any early attempt at scientific exploration, we shall end up with more questions than answers."

Despite the prevalence of evil in the world today, it can be difficult to spot. A number of case studies illustrate how the evil in a person can be obscured, often hidden from the evil person himself. Evil grows stronger in the dark, away from the illuminating light of psychiatry. It is therefore rare for the psychiatrist to have a patient who is totally evil. More often, therapists are called upon to treat the *victims* of evil individuals.

The Case of Bobby

Bobby was hospitalized for depression some months after his older brother committed suicide. On the surface, Bobby's problem seemed obvious; who wouldn't be depressed in these circumstances? His parents, apparently worried, however took few measures to rescue Bobby—until his depression led him into criminal behavior. Only then did they seek professional help.

Early in Bobby's treatment, the therapist made a startling discovery. Just a month earlier Bobby's parents had given him a gun for Christmas. But the gift wasn't just any gun; it was the very weapon Bobby's brother had used to kill himself. When Bobby's parents were confronted with this troubling fact, they displayed a high degree of naivete, ignorance, and unconsciousness. These traits, according to Peck, exemplify the essence of evil. That is, they failed to display a compassionate understanding of Bobby's situation. How could they give their depressed son the very symbol of his brother's tragic death? "We couldn't afford to get him a new gun," they rationalized. "I don't know why you're picking on us. We gave him the best present we could. Money doesn't grow on trees, you know. We're just ordinary working people. We could have sold the gun and made money. But we didn't. We kept it so we could give Bobby a good present."

The therapist then asked, "Did you think how that present might seem to Bobby?"

"No, we didn't think about that," the parents answered. "We're not educated people like you. We haven't been to college and learned all kinds of fancy ways of thinking. We're just simple working people. We can't be expected to think of all these things."

Perhaps the most disturbing attribute of evil is a lack of awareness and sensitivity for other's feelings. Some people seem to manifest the total inability to comprehend how their actions might harm others.

The Traits of Evil

Whether treating the victim of evil or, in those rare instances, the evil person himself, it is mandatory to the healing process that the evil first be recognized, then acknowledged, and, finally, confronted. Evil individuals share certain traits with those who suffer from psychological problems, but who are not evil. Often the therapist must rely on his own feelings to guide him in uncovering evil.

"The feeling that a healthy person often experiences in a relationship with an evil one is revulsion. The feeling of revulsion may be almost instant if the evil encountered is blatant. If the evil is more subtle, the revulsion may develop only gradually as the relationship with the evil one deepens."

Feelings of revulsion can be extremely useful to a therapist, sort of "a diagnostic tool par excellence" that can signify more truly than anything else the presence of evil in a human being. "Yet, like a sharp scalpel, it is a tool that must be used with the greatest care."

People who are evil also use lies to confuse those who are not. " . . . The evil are `the people of the lie,' deceiving others as they also build layer upon layer of self-deception."

"People of the lie," it should be pointed out, display certain characteristics that correspond with recognized psychiatric disorders. "People of the lie" invalidate and deny responsibility for their actions—and the consequences such actions may have on others, as all people with personality disorders do. They may also, Peck says, exhibit these characteristics:

(a) *consistent destructive, scapegoating behavior, which may often be quite subtle.*

(b) *excessive, albeit, usually covert, intolerance to criticism and other forms of narcissistic injury.*

(c) *pronounced concern with a public image and self-image of respectability, contributing to a stability of life-style but also to pretentiousness and denial of hateful feelings or vengeful motives.*

(d) *intellectual deviousness, with an increased likelihood of a mild schizophrenic-like disturbance of thinking at times of stress.*

Evil people love and look out only for themselves. Not only do they lie to others, but most especially they lie to themselves, taking narcissism (self-love) to its ugliest extreme. They are unable to see the world through the eyes of others. Like the mother who forces her daughter to dye her black hair blond, evil people can appreciate only their *own* cravings, ambitions, and yearnings. Such a mother is unable to distinguish her daughter's personal desires; indeed she is incapable of seeing the daughter as a separate entity at all. Evil people, in their narcissism, often attempt to consume all those around them into their evil games and intentions. For this reason, working with the evil can be dangerous for everyone, especially the therapist.

The Case of Mylai

Given the inclination and aptitude of evil people to subject those around them to their own desires, we should perhaps expect evil committed by groups of people to be rather common. The disturbing fact is, evil in individuals *can* easily be translated to groups of people, particularly when aided by structures and forces which work to encourage narcissism within the group.

On the morning of March 16, 1968, in a hamlet in South Vietnam, a group of American soldiers attacked and brutally murdered between five and six hundred unarmed villagers—women, children, and old men. "The atrocities that took place in Mylai were not particularly unique to the Vietnam war." They were made possible by a military structure that fused individual identities into a single group identity, "while simultaneously perpetuating extreme group narcissism." With individual responsibility suspended, a kind of collective mentality takes command. Yet in the case of the Mylai Massacre, as it became known, the men of Task Force Barker neither assumed nor were assigned any individual or collective accountability for what occurred that March morning. As part of a military structure, they were only following orders, just as their leaders were following orders from other higher-ups—who, in turn, were "just following orders." And so we climb the ladder of culpability until we find a country at war which is blindly following leaders who only claim to be enacting decisions made by American citizens. The problem with "collective accountability," then, is that " . . . responsibility becomes diffused within groups—so much so that in larger groups it may become nonexistent."

We live today in a society brimming with groups, institutions, and corporations. It is therefore most imperative that we turn—and turn urgently—back to the individual, "for the `group mind' is ultimately determined by the minds of the individuals who make up the group . . . [and] it is in the solitary mind and soul of the individual that the battle between good and evil is waged and ultimately won or lost."

Peck concludes, "the effort to prevent group evil—including war—must therefore be directed toward the individual. It is, of course, a process of education. And that education can be conducted most easily within the traditional existing framework of our schools. This book is written in the hope that someday in our secular as well as religious schools all children will be carefully taught the nature of evil and the principles of its prevention . . . Children will, in my dream, be taught that laziness and narcissism are at the very root of all human evil, and why this is so. They will learn that each individual is of sacred importance."

As Peck points out, in the final analysis evil people are to be pitied—and loved. If the children of the world come to understand this, when they look upon "people of the lie" they will say to themselves, "There but for the grace of God go I," and will always treat others with love.

I'M OK, YOU'RE OK

by Thomas A. Harris, M.D., Avon Books, New York, N.Y., 1969

More than seven million copies of Harris' best-selling book have been sold, primarily due to the down-to-earth insights it offers into our personal behavior and relationships with others.

In the 1950s, Dr. Wilder Penfield, a neurosurgeon from McGill University, conducted a series of experiments in which he touched a portion of the human brain with a weak electrical probe. He found that by stimulating a particular point in the brain, he could trigger specific memories. Different points triggered different memories, but touching the same point in the same person always triggered the same memory.

Penfield found that the patient recalled not only the details of a certain incident, but the exact same *feelings* previously experienced as well—an actual *renewal* or detailed *reliving* of the feelings, not just a remembrance. Much like a tape recorder, he concluded, our minds "save" experiences for later recall.

For Thomas Harris, author of *I'm OK, You're OK*, the research of Penfield and others showed that no experience is unimportant. A person's experiences—recorded memories—shape how he interprets himself and the world around him. Harris uses this notion as the basis for his psychological study.

Transactional Analysis

The basic unit of psychological study, Harris says, ought to be the stimulus-response "transaction." A transaction occurs when one person affects someone else—provides the "stimulus"—and the second person follows through with some type of "response." These transactions are complicated, however, by the fact that each of us is a multiple-natured individual—our characteristics and personality can change from minute to minute. Depending on the situation and our need for control, we vacillate back and forth between three "states of being": the Parent, the Child and the Adult. We can assume any of these states, moment to moment, throughout our lives.

The *Parent* is defined by the huge collection of external event "recordings" we encode in the first few years of life. A large part of the Parent is formed by the rules, laws and admonitions we heard while growing up, particularly from our own parents. Included are the thousands of verbal and non-verbal "no's" and "don'ts" we received, as well as our mother's "coos of pleasure" when she saw our first smile and our father's instructions on how to tie our shoelaces. The Parent is also shaped by the spectrum of input from other sources—notably television. These early recordings are made without any judgement or editing, becoming encoded as "truth" in our brain. Recordings that are consistent with each other reinforce our self-image and sense of identity; they give us the "how to do it" and "how things are" data base that lets us start to move away from our parents (small p) and function independently. Conversely, recordings that are inconsistent—such as unresolved conflicts between our parents—inevitably frighten us, and our inner Parent is weakened as we try to repress or even block out the conflicting

data. All together, these early-childhood messages form the "*taught* concept of life."

The *Child* is a different person altogether. While we are recording *external* events in the Parent mode, we are simultaneously recording what is happening *internally*—our desires, perceptions, and feelings. Since a child's vocabulary is limited at these early ages, most of what we recorded then were unverbalized feelings, feelings which make up the "Natural Child" mode. This Natural Child is the source of our creativity, our curiosity, spontaneity and spirituality—in a sense, the Child is the center of our "true" being. However, the Natural Child has an inseparable twin—the "Not OK" Child—who is molded by predominantly negative feelings. "Not OK" is the mode in which we accept the civilizing demands of our inner Parent and actual parents. In order to grow, and even survive, we must learn to curb our urges and emotions, to "behave," to stay out of the street, to stay "on task." Too much curbing leads to repression. Taken together, the Not-OK and the Natural Child give us the "felt concept of life."

The *Adult* possesses a whole different outlook. At about ten months of age, we begin to move around and develop self-awareness and thought. Increasingly, we test parental admonitions against experience. This testing process eventually forms the Adult, a "data-processing computer" that makes decisions after consulting three sources: the Parent, the Child, and, hopefully, the *past* Adult. We can never and should not seek to erase the Parent recording. However, our Adult self can learn to judge whether the Parent recording is valid and appropriate to our present circumstances, and turn it off when necessary. In the same way, our Adult can process our Child data to learn which feelings are okay to express right now. The Adult gives us the "thought concept of life."

The Four Life Positions

From the experiences (recordings) we receive to form these three states of being (Parent, Child, and Adult), we gradually adopt one of four attitudes toward ourselves and others. Unlike the states of being, attitudes do not change easily, if at all; they make up our basic personalities.

1. **I'm Not OK, You're OK:** This is the universal mode of the first year of childhood. We all begin life going from wet to hungry to unhappy, and all these unpleasant situations are made right by *others'* positive responses, or *strokes*. However, the necessary correction and guidance by parents in early childhood often serve to reinforce the feeling that the child is *not* OK while parents and society *are*. "Not OK" is the inescapable attitude of childhood, and it is to this position that we often return throughout life in times of stress or difficulty. When things go bad, some become immediately depressed—their failings must mean they're not OK. "Not OK" can remain as our permanent attitude throughout life unless experiences in our second year lead us to adopt one

of the other three modes of response.

2. **I'm Not OK, You're Not OK:** By the end of the first year of life, as we learn to feed ourselves and to crawl or walk, the automatic "stroking" from our parents declines. If our parents are cold or dictatorial, the stroking may cease entirely, while punishment becomes harsher. If we continue in this state, we conclude, "I'm not OK, you're not OK either." Locked into a cycle of hating others and hating self, our Adult stops developing. A person living in this mode can turn suicidal—even "getting through" life seems too arduous.

3. **I'm OK, You're Not OK:** A child who is brutalized—or completely deprived of strokes—may eventually take this third attitude—termed the "criminal position," since so many serious criminals seem characterized by it. It is easy to see why an abused child might think that others are not OK, but how he comes to feel that he *is* OK is less clear. Having survived abuse, he now considers himself a survivor, a fighter, even a winner. However, since he does not perceive others as OK, he feels he has a right to control, manipulate, and abuse them. In some cases, he takes his perceptions so far as to coolly justify murder. Once a child is caught in this stage, it is difficult for him to change his behavior. Since true strokes can be had only from OK people—and, in his perspective, not even a caring friend or therapist is OK—the "I,m OK, you're not" person is caught in a cycle of narcissistic anger and negativity.

4. **I'm OK, You're OK:** The first three positions are outgrowths of unconscious choices made in early childhood. But it is only possible to advance to the higher "I'm OK, you're OK" position through *conscious* choice. Of course, this healthier position is easier to achieve when early experiences have reinforced the value of the child's trust (you're OK) and self-esteem (I'm OK.) The "I'm OK, You're OK" person relates respectfully and responsively to others and to himself. Because his Adult is fully developed and operational, he can truly enjoy and nurture the Natural Child within himself. He can listen thoughtfully to his "Parent tapes," selecting those that enlarge his Child's capacity to feel and create, and reach his potential.

So, we have three states of being governed by one over-riding attitude, or personality. This combination determines how we respond to stimulus, how we perform in psychological transactions with other people. Transactions between two people, says Harris, can be classified into three types. *Complementary* transactions occur when a person responds in "parallel movement" to the same type of "tapes" he hears. For example, two ladies waiting for a bus, complaining that "The bus is late again . . . Yes, it is always late," are talking Parent-to-Parent—a complementary transaction. They are, in essence, reinforcing each other's pre-packaged judgements. On the late bus, a passenger and a bus driver who sit discussing a scheduled stop are completing an Adult-to-Adult transaction. Complementary transactions also take place when the Parent mode in one person talks to the Child mode in another person, and that Child

responds—from the same mode in which she was addressed— back to that Parent.

Crossed transactions result when the response doesn't match the initial stimulus. Usually, when a transaction is crossed, communication ends. For example, when a patient makes the Adult comment, "I would like to work in a hospital like this," and the nurse comes back with the Parent-like response, "You can't even solve your own problems," the conversation is over almost before it began.

Duplex transactions carry double messages. The question, "Where did you hide my socks this time?" could either denote Adult teasing or Parental criticism. The response—Child to Parent, Parent to Parent, Adult to Parent . . . —depends on how the communication was understood.

Transactions can also be carried out in six different situations, or levels of communication:

- *Withdrawal*—the mind doesn't take part in what is happening around it; there is no interaction at all with others.

- *Ritual*—a social situation in which both parties politely agree, as in a cocktail party ("I'm a rotten golfer." "Me, too."). There is little commitment, and, therefore, little fulfillment.

- *Activities*—these interactions are satisfying but have no need for intimate involvement with another person. They include time set aside to deal with external realities, such as shoveling snow, reading a book, etc.

- *Pastimes*—typical small-talk or social probing to uncover information about others in a non-threatening way ("So, what's your major?").

- *Games*—transactions with ulterior motives, such as when people complain that they never get invited to go anywhere, yet they have an excuse to reject every invitation they do receive; rather than seeking solutions, they seek pity and reinforcement that says "I'm not OK."

- *Intimacy*—transactions in which two people totally accept each other: "I'm OK, you're OK." *Adults* are in charge, which makes giving and accepting love both possible and desirable.

"Many marital problems—and problems with adolescents," suggests Harris, "can be resolved by attending to what is going on in the relationship's transactions. Individuals who are taught about P-A-C (Parent-Adult-Child)—even children who have been severely damaged by abuse—tend to conduct their own analysis and make their own changes. If we pay attention to what we are saying and doing, we can learn to let our *Adult* `re-value' the lessons of Parenthood and the feelings of Childhood in light of our greater understanding. We can learn that we are, indeed, `OK.'"

Is there an underlying, objective morality that has a claim on all humans? Harris believes that there is, and that morality is based on knowing that people are *important*. This is the Adult approach to the worth of persons:

I am a person. You are a person. Without you, I am not a person . . . If I devalue you, I devalue myself. . . . We are responsible to and for one another, and this responsibility is the ultimate claim imposed on all men alike.

THE ART OF LOVING

by Erich Fromm, Harper and Row, New York, N.Y., 1956

. . . Love is not a sentiment which can be easily indulged in by anyone, regardless of the level of maturity . . . Satisfaction in individual love cannot be attained without the capacity to love one's neighbor, without true humility, courage, faith and discipline.

Erich Fromm's *The Art of Loving* examines love and its mastery from various perspectives. Fromm asserts that while most of us consider love to be of paramount importance, we feel that we have little to learn about it, largely because we think of love as something we "fall into." We don't understand, Fromm continues, the difference between the first rush of "falling" in love and the work required to "stand" in love.

The Theory of Love

Isolated from the moment of birth, we try to compensate for our alienation in a number of ways. Early peoples, for instance, used metaphysical trances, drugs, or communal sex to reduce their sense of isolation. Nowadays, we often try to find unity through conformity. This desire for conformity, however—which diminishes even traditional differences of gender—has caused us to lose our uniqueness.

At best, our attempts to overcome alienation have been only partly successful. As Fromm stresses, "The full answer lies in the achievement of interpersonal fusion, of fusion with another person, in love." He adds that the need for interpersonal fusion—creation of a sense of "family"—is our strongest driving force, and that real love is active, not passive: it entails giving.

While we sometimes think of giving in terms of "giving up" something, Fromm views giving as an expression of joy and potency—of "strength," "wealth," and "power." Our joy, interests, understanding, and even sadness are all aspects of meaningful giving. In giving, we enliven another and ourselves. Thus, the power of love is that it *engenders* love.

To be able to give in this way, however, requires other important elements of love: namely, *caring, concern,* and *responsibility.* According to Fromm, "Love is the active concern for the life and growth of that which we love." And taken together, care and concern signify responsibility. To the Biblical question "Am I my brother's keeper?" the responsible person answers with an emphatic "Yes." He or she then responds to others' needs, not merely out of a sense of duty, but as a voluntary act.

Responsibility, however, might otherwise lead to domination if it were not for *respect:* the ability to allow another "to grow and unfold for his own sake, and in his own ways, and not for the purpose of serving me." To respect someone, we must know them. Thus, *knowledge* is also essential to love. For instance, if we are insightful we may know that anger is merely a symptom of fear. Because we understand fear, we can overlook the anger within a person and love the person instead.

Knowledge plays another role in love, exemplified by our desire to know ourselves. Yet, paradoxically, we can't know ourselves without knowing others. Knowledge of others, however, cannot be acquired through study; it can only be found through union with another. Only psychological union, the joining of two souls—as opposed to physical union—will promote our knowledge of ourselves and mitigate our alienation. To exhibit care, concern, responsibility, respect, and knowledge, we must be mature: able to produce according to our own powers.

Love Between Parent and Child

Most of us first learned the meaning of love as children in our mother's arms. There we discovered unconditional love—the kind that doesn't need to be "earned." Later, we became aware of our father's love, a more conditional kind of love in which we learned that doing certain things somehow made us *more* lovable. Thus, ideally, our mother's love gave us security while our father's love taught us to survive in society. As mature people, then, we incorporate both kinds of love—developing both a "motherly conscience" and a "fatherly conscience." Together, these two consciences form the basis for a healthy and mature love.

Objects of Love

Because, according to Fromm, love is "an attitude, an orientation of character," we cannot love "only one other person" and be "indifferent to the rest . . . " To do so, Fromm argues, is an case not of love, but rather of "symbiotic attachment." Hence, when we assert that we fall in love only with "the right person," we are like those who say they will be great landscape artists as soon as they find the right sunset. If we truly love, we must be capable of *brotherly love.* Loving one's flesh and blood is no achievement. It is only when we begin to love others beyond our family that we demonstrate genuine love. Neither should we reserve our love for those who are most like us. Fromm writes: "Only in the love of those who do not serve a purpose love begins to unfold."

In addition to loving others, Fromm

states, we must also love life itself—a capacity that our mother's love instills, and which may be analogous to love of oneself. "Self-love," although it often connotes selfishness, involves just the opposite: we cannot love others unless we love ourselves. "If it is a virtue to love my neighbor as a human being, it must be a virtue—and not a vice—to love myself, since I am a human being, too."

"Love thy neighbor as *thyself*," the Bible reads. But far more than being a religious truth, this phrase is also a psychological truth. Selfishness, then, in Fromm's view, is not the result of *too much* self-love, but *too little*.

Springing from the same source is love of God, which Fromm interprets as a desire to end separateness. Although modern western religions are dominated by the male image of God, Fromm sees in them a strong inclination towards motherly love— a concept in which salvation is achieved through *belief* rather than *actions*. Eastern religions, on the other hand, assert that God can not be understood intellectually, but only through action that unites our lives and wills with His. Clearly, our love of God grows through several stages before we reach a point "where man has incorporated the principles of love and justice into himself, where he has become one with God."

Love and Its Disintegration

In our modern civilization, where *things* have increasingly been given higher value than *people*, love has been traditionally viewed in two ways: (1) as sex, and (2) as teamwork. Freud, for instance, taught that love results from sexual intimacy. In this view, neuroses are the result of repressed sexual feelings. Other psychoanalysts subsequently declared that love results from teamwork, from "two people pooling their common interests and standing together against a hostile and alienated world." Both views—or partial views—have contributed to the disintegration of love.

Similarly, as a society, our love of God has crumbled. Although it seems to many that we are undergoing a resurgence of religious zeal, what we have been experiencing is a regression to a concept of God as a father or mother who gives us what we want—and who we can ignore the rest of the time.

In short, Fromm says, "there is only one proof of the presence of love: the depth of the relationship, and the strength and the aliveness in each person concerned; this is the fruit by which love is recognized."

The Practice of Love

Since love is an art and not a science, it can best be learned by practice rather than by theory. Yet, Fromm argues, we can-

not prescribe a set of exercises, a do-it-yourself course in love. The best we can do is provide some general guidelines.

According to Fromm, the major elements in mastering any art include *discipline, concentration, patience* and *priority*. Discipline, for instance, builds the strength of will to accomplish our goal—in this case, learning the art of loving. Concentration teaches us how to be alone with ourselves and how to eliminate harmful or trivial things that clutter our lives. Patience supplements our learning and practice, because no skill is acquired quickly. Finally, giving our new art high priority enables us to master love.

The delicate art of love, however, encompasses some additional requirements. We must, for instance, rid ourselves of narcissism, of total involvement with ourselves. We must also practice *humility, objectivity,* and, perhaps most importantly, *faith*. We must develop faith in ourselves and in others, which demands a rational acceptance both of weaknesses and of strengths. When we exercise faith, we *educate* others; when we lack faith, we *manipulate* others.

In addition to faith, we must also possess courage, the willingness to take a risk, even to experience pain and disappointment. The practice of faith and courage, Fromm continues, begins by taking small steps. Moreover, we must notice where and when we begin to lose faith and to recognize our cowardly acts of rationalization. "To love," Fromm says, "means to commit oneself without guarantee, to give oneself completely in the hope that our love will produce love in the loved person."

Some critics have argued that Fromm's theory of love is not compatible with modern society. The fact, however, that love—in the sense that Fromm defines it—is frequently lacking in our society does not mean that it is incompatible. Rather, it may mean that we need to work harder to master this most basic of all human needs, love.

In the nearly forty years since *The Art of Loving* was published, the problems that Fromm described seem to have worsened. If anything, we appear to be more confused about issues of sexuality, intimacy, and love; we seem to be more intent on "looking out for number one." But the fact that we have lost ground isn't surprising, Fromm points out, when we see the diminishment of faith and courage in our society and the encouragement of cynicism. His theory of love, however, might help us to better understand that our search for unconditional love is unrealistic. Instead, he concludes, we should perhaps turn our efforts to the practice of giving love.

MEN ARE FROM MARS, WOMEN ARE FROM VENUS

by John Gray, Ph.D., Harper Collins Publishers, New York, N.Y., 1992

John Gray's *Men Are From Mars, Women Are From Venus* is a manual designed to promote loving relationships in the 1990s by focusing on gender *differences*. Dr. Gray asserts that men and women communicate, think, feel, perceive, react, respond and love differently than men—almost as if men and women come from different planets. Gray does not detail *why* men and women are different, but simply asks us to accept that they are different and use that information to improve our relationships.

Begin by imagining that men once lived on Mars and women on Venus. After discovering each other, the two genders unitedly journeyed to a more hospitable planet, Earth. Everything went along beautifully for a time—until the day when the Earth inhabitants *forgot* that they really were different! This is the exact situation in which we now find ourselves.

Mr. Fix-it and the Home Improvement Committee

Earth women (Venusians) complain that Earth men (Martians) don't listen to them. Instead, the Martians slap on their "Mr. Fix it caps" and start proposing solutions.

It seems Martians define themselves in terms of achieving results. Accordingly, they place high value on personal power, competency, and achievement. A Martian may ask for help, but only if the task is something he is unable to accomplish on his own. Thus, when a Martian hears someone discussing a problem, he sees it as an invitation to give advice. When the advice is ignored, he feels personally rejected.

Because a Martian wants to solve his own problems, offering *him* unsolicited advice on anything is tantamount to saying that he is incompetent—a touchy accusation indeed. Venusians, on the other hand, tend to value themselves based on their feelings and the quality of their relationships. A Venusian takes pride in considering the needs and feelings of others, and she is very intuitive in sensing those needs. So, when she offers helpful advice, it is a sign of great love, not an attempt to point out something significantly wrong with her male counterpart. She can't understand why her suggestions offend her success-oriented Martian: " . . . When a woman offers unsolicited advice or tries to `help' a man, she has no idea of how critical and unloving she may sound . . . " Conversely, when a man tries to help a woman solve a problem, instead of just listening to her, he is devaluing her feelings and saying that she and her ideas are unimportant.

The fundamental methods and attributes of neither Martians or Venusians are "wrong." What often *is* wrong, however, is their approach. Rather than offering advice, if a man will try to just sit back and listen when a woman is upset, the relationship will improve. Likewise, if a woman will refrain from stepping in until a man "asks" for assistance, they will both be happier.

Men Go to Their Caves and Women Talk

Apparently, Martians cope with stress by, figuratively, retreating into their caves—mulling over the day, distracting themselves with newspapers or sports or cars—in an effort to relax. As a result, they often fail to give Venusians needed support and attention. In contrast, when Venusians are stressed, they want to discuss their emotions. Simply talking about their feelings makes them feel less overwhelmed.

When women and men understand their respective "planetary" differences, they can work out their problems. For example, after work each partner could first savor a quiet period of solitude, followed by a period of open discussion. Thus, both partners get to benefit from their distinctive coping skills.

How to Motivate the Opposite Sex

Men and women alike are motivated by *love*. The difference is that Martians typically feel loved when they are *needed*, while Venusians feel loved when they are *cared for*.

Early in a relationship, a man overcomes his fears of commitment when a woman sends him the message that she needs him. Later on, though, the woman might forget to keep sending this message. Hence, Gray says, "to become motivated again he needs to feel appreciated, trusted, and accepted. Not to be needed is slow death for a man."

For a Venusian, love is caring. When she is worried, confused, exhausted, or devoid of hope, she needs to feel that she is not alone, that she is loved and cherished. The man often doesn't realize this, his Martian instincts have programmed him to leave her alone, or to try to solve her problem.

Speaking Different Languages

Martian and Venusian languages are comprised of the same words—but those words have different, often confusing meanings. When, for example, a woman says, "We never go out," the Martian interprets the message as a complaint that they, literally, *never* go out, when the Venusian actually means that she is tired and would like to go out to unwind. If a man understands the *real* message, he won't feel hassled or attacked. Rather, he can say, "I can tell you need a break. Let's go get some dinner . . . " A woman, too, can aid this process by frequently exercising the four magic words: "It's not your fault."

The biggest communication complaint Venusians have with Martians is directed at what they do *not* say. When a Martian is silent, a Venusian feels rejected and asks, "What's wrong?" Of course, he replies, "Nothing." What he *means*, though, is, "I have a small problem, but I am working it out, okay. No advice is needed." When the Venusian doesn't understand the hidden message, she rushes in with her therapy—exactly the wrong approach. A woman can, however, shorten a man's time in his "cave" by allowing him to withdraw and spending her time with something else. A man can aid this process by explaining, "I will be back." These are the four magic words a woman needs to hear.

Discovering Our Different Emotional Needs

Gray insists that men and women manifest different needs. Women tend to need greater caring, understanding, respect, devotion, validation and reassurance. Men, meanwhile, need to receive greater trust, acceptance, appreciation, admiration, approval and encouragement.

We can best get what *we* need, Gray continues, by giving our partner what he or she needs. The power of these needs is their reciprocity—if a Martian expresses caring, he knows he will receive trust in return; if a Venusian extends trust, caring will flow back to her.

How to Avoid Arguments

If we remember that we come from two different planets and then learn to master appropriate communication skills, Gray says, we can avoid arguments. After all, we argue for only one reason: we do not feel loved. And not feeling loved leads to crankiness and accusations.

Invalidation is the primary way that men unknowingly incite arguments. " . . . Arguments escalate when a man begins to invalidate a woman's feelings (by trying to solve the problem) and she responds to him disapprovingly." The most common way women innocently start arguments is by failing to be direct when they express their feelings. "How could you be so late?" they might ask, when what they really mean is, "I was worried that something had happened to you."

Scoring Points with the Opposite Sex

Martians are predisposed to focus on a few *big things;* Venusians consider *small things* to be important. A man thinks he scores big with a woman because he has a good job and can provide a comfortable standard of living. To her, however, the job and its benefits are negligible—especially if he neglects her.

Gray submits that a woman is equipped with a "love tank," that, like a car's gas tank, needs continual refilling. Fortunately, it is easy to fill—if the man is willing to do a few small things each day, like listening completely for a few minutes, or giving hugs.

Men, it seems, give big scores for big love messages. For example, a woman can score big every time she doesn't make a big deal out of one of her Martian's mistake. She also can make points by giving him extra support, admiration and trust, particularly when they aren't deserved.

How to Communicate Difficult Feelings

When we are angry or disappointed, we have a hard time communicating in a loving way. Negative feelings overwhelm us, and we want to lash out at our unthinking, uncaring, unappreciative partner. In these circumstances, both Martians and Venusians should consider writing their partner a "Love Letter."

Love letters have a way of melting negative feelings. To do this, you must first communicate the anger, sadness, fear, or regret that you

feel, followed by your expression of love. Finally, a "P.S." is a way to state directly what it is you need from your partner and how you would like him or her to respond in the future: "I need you to listen to me rather than solve my problems," or "I would appreciate an apology." Such honest statements are invaluable in eliciting further support. Whether you choose to share the letter with your partner or not, the simple process of venting your negative feelings has led to positive declarations of regret and love.

How to Ask for Support and Get It

Sometimes you have to *ask* for love and support in order to get it—and women, Gray asserts, seem to have the most difficulty asking: "Women make the mistake of thinking they don't have to ask for support. Because they intuitively feel the needs of others and give whatever they can, they mistakenly expect men to do the same." If a woman needs more support from a man, she must learn to ask in three stages:

1. Ask *"correctly":* Acknowledge first what he is already giving. Asking correctly also involves good timing, speaking in a non-demanding tone, being brief, being direct ("Would you bring in the groceries?" instead of "The groceries are in the car."), and employing phrases using "would" and "will" rather than "could" or "can." "Would" connotes a request; "could" looms as either a demand or a criticism of past behavior.

2. *Practice* asking for support, even if you expect the answer to be no. If he is reading the newspaper, ask him to go to the store. If he says no, just respond with, "Okay." This practice gives you confidence in meeting his resistance in future requests.

3. Ask *assertively:* maintain silence after you make the request, regardless of his response. Men have a tendency to grumble at such times. Grumbling, however, should *not* be seen as a sign of unwillingness, but an indication that he is thinking about the request. If a woman remains silent, the grumbles—and sometimes even the "no's"—will turn to "yes's." Moreover, if she then shows appreciation, she will help "program" him to offer support on his own.

"Men are like rubber bands," Gray adds—they'll frequently pull away for a time, but they will relax and return. Likewise, "women are like ocean waves"—they're sometimes caught in a low tide, but, unquestionably, they will rise and crest again.

Building and maintaining relationships is not easy. And neither is the process of learning and maintaining new skills. We learn, we forget . . . To remember again, we constantly need to relearn and re-practice. Finally, we just need to keep trying. So, Gray reminds us, "next time you are frustrated with the opposite sex, remember men are from Mars, women are from Venus. Even if you don't remember anything else from this book, remembering that we are supposed to be different will help you to be more loving."

BACKLASH

The Undeclared War Against American Women
by Susan Faludi, Crown, New York, N.Y., 1991

Susan Faludi's book is an insightful, extensively researched and a thought-provoking commentary on modern-day society's response to women. With painstaking detail Ms. Faludi documents what she sees as powerful forces to deny American women the freedom and equality they have struggled for centuries to attain.

Quite likely, this book will inspire strong feelings in readers: for those who agree with the writer's arguments, her claims may provoke anger, despair, fierce determination, or gladness that these issues are being addressed; for those opposed, her words may engender a different form of anger, defensiveness, derisiveness, or scorn. Regardless of one's political leanings or feminist sentiments, however, Ms. Faludi's work should make all Americans stop and re-evaluate the ways we empower and disempower each other.

Text Overview:

The history of American women has been one of struggle as they have courageously sought to free themselves from the burdens of social and political inequality. But following each successful struggle, says Ms. Faludi, women have faced a vicious, often unrelenting *backlash* against their hard-won advances. The intellectual force of each backlash invariably lies in the twisted argument that it is women's very progress *toward* equality—*not* the unequal status they are still battling to overcome—which lies at the root of their dissatisfaction. In a sleight of hand reversal worthy of the best snake oil salesman, women are being convinced that their increased freedom, the small gains they have made, are, in truth, the *cause* of their unhappiness.

During the history of the United States, there have been four distinct periods in which women struggled for greater equality. Each women's rights battle met with a powerful counterassault, a backlash in popular culture, in the media, in the courtroom, and in medicine.

The Backlashes of Yesterday

Even before Abraham Lincoln fought the Civil War and emancipated African American slaves, Susan B. Anthony and Elizabeth Cady Stanton had inaugurated the first American women's movement, which pressed for equal rights in education, voting, and property ownership. But by the late 19th century, religious and political leaders were acting in unison to revoke women's rights: fair divorce laws and property rights were repealed, and, for the first time in the country's history, laws were passed making abortion illegal.

The suffrage movement of the early 20th century succeeded in winning back some of these lost rights. But in 1920—the same year that saw women win the right to vote—the establishment of the Miss America Beauty Pageant introduced another backlash cycle. While allowing women their new license to vote, the new backlash leaders told them, in effect, to be pretty, to be quiet, and to stay in their place—in the home or among the ranks of beauty-pageant contestants. Women were not welcome in professional circles.

Then in the 1940s, as men went off to war, women answered the nation's call to duty and stepped into the workplace in larger numbers than ever before. The end of the war, however, ended women's advancement in the workplace, as women were subtly forced out of their higher-paying wartime jobs to make way for the returning soldiers. "When the United Nations issued a statement supporting equal rights for women in 1948, the United States government was the only one of the twenty-two nations that wouldn't sign it."

Riding on the wave of the Civil Rights movement of the 1960s, the fourth and most recent women's movement experienced remarkable progress in the workplace, the home, the legislature and the courtroom. But the end of the 1970s coincided with the beginning of the Reagan/Bush era—and a fourth period of backlash.

The Backlash of Today

In the last decade we have seen women's salaries drop back to the real-money level of the 1950s. Subsidies for child-care and prenatal programs have been slashed. Divorce laws, altered during the 1970s to reflect some semblance of fairness for both parties, have been declared discriminatory and returned to their pre-1970s status.

The New Right, enjoying its greatest support since the 1920s, has escalated its very vocal and public campaign against women with charges that career women destroy the family unit and feminism threatens to rip apart America's social fabric. At the same time, during the 1980s, career women—left without legal protection—found themselves once again fired for becoming pregnant, denied equal pay, denied promotions, and facing increased hostility and harassment from their male colleagues. Violence against all women escalated, reaching epidemic proportions.

The Reagan/Bush Administration, despite token efforts to the contrary, worked actively to restrict women from participating in the political and legislative process. Turning to women such as Phyllis Schlafly and Beverly LaHaye to lead the revolution against women's rights, the New Right defended its actions with claims that women themselves were seeing the error of their ways and returning to the home to nest.

In reality, women throughout the 1980s entered the workforce in record numbers, inspite of decreases in salary and increases in incidents of discrimination and harrassment. Poll after poll taken during the 1980's backlash documented women's strong, vocal—and majority—support for the feminist movement.

The medical profession contributed to the recent backlash by sanctioning more unnecessary surgeries on women, and by "approving" dangerous and untested cosmetic products. The male-dominated medical profession also turned its back on young women who suffer from mood and eating disorders.

Every conceivable social tool became a weapon of the backlash. One of the most disturbing tactics was—and remains—the attempt to eliminate women's freedom to choose what happens to their bodies. The *Roe v. Wade* abortion decision (1973) was attacked in the courts, in state legislatures, and in the doorways of women's health clinics. Often employing violent strategies, anti-abortion activists—claiming to be protecting the rights of the fetus— attempted to deny women access to safe and legal abortions. By denying them the right to decide when and if to bear children, some activists expressly hoped to make independent women easier to control.

The Media in Today's Backlash

Perhaps the worst offenders in both past and current backlashes has been the media. *The press first introduced the backlash to a national audience—and made it palatable. Journalism replaced the `pro-family' diatribes of fundamentalist preachers with sympathetic and even progressive-sounding rhetoric. It cosmeticized the scowling face of antifeminism while blackening the feminist eye. In the process, it popularized the backlash beyond the New Right's wildest dreams. . . . Carried by tides it rarely fathomed, [the press] acted as a force that swept the general public, powerfully shaping the way people would think and talk about the feminist legacy and the ailments it supposedly inflicted on women.*

Through undocumented, poorly researched and misleading "trend" stories, the media continue to fuel the fires of backlash, heralding gloom and doom for all women who attempt to resist the submissive roles determined for them by their opponents. These trend stories—"articles that claimed to divine sweeping shifts in female social behavior while providing little in the way of evidence to support their generalizations"—did enormous damage.

Week after week, women were bombarded with newspaper and magazine articles—and a multitude of books—heralding the doom of strong, independent, successful women. For example, due to a "man shortage," the media claimed that single, college-educated women faced dismal odds of marrying. This in turn mutated into the allegation that these "failed women" inevitably would suffer from psychotic depressions at their situation.

The press perpetuated these myths of domesticized feminine bliss by constantly repeating statistics from one erroneous study after another, even when their research collided time and time again with reality. While journalists published the grim numbers depicting women's poor chances of marrying—and their dark prospects if they did *not* marry—they overlooked studies and polls that showed that young college-educated *men* were finding singlehood a much more bleak and dangerous state than their female counterparts. Men, not women, the studies repeatedly showed, were far more likely to develop physical and mental illnesses if they did not marry, or if they divorced and failed to remarry soon afterward. Women, on the contrary, were often found happier *after* a divorce, regardless of who had initiated the break-up. With the typical tactics of backlash, facts were turned, twisted, and delivered in reverse in an attempt to push women into self-doubt and unhappiness.

The print media were soon joined by television and movie producers who offered replicated features with misleading images of miserable, often psychopathic career women and ecstatic, obedient housewives. Perhaps the best-known and most disturbing of these "trend" movies was *Fatal Attraction*, in which Glenn Close's character is eventually killed by the housewife for having an affair with a very willing Michael Douglas. The clear message for every female viewer: Marry, raise a family, and keep your husband satisfied, or misery will follow you every day of your life.

The current backlash will "never mold America into the backward-looking, dad-hailing, nuclear family fantasy it promotes," Faludi insists. *But it could implant that image in many women's minds and set up a nagging, even tormenting dissonance. If women were miserable in the '80s—and no doubt many were, more so as the backlash deepened—it was not for the reason most widely offered. In the end feminism and the freedom that came with it had little part in making women unhappy. It was rather that women's desire for equality, an impulse that refused to disappear throughout the decade, kept clashing with the backlash's agenda, spurring women to batter against the walls of self-doubt and recrimination that the backlash helped to build.*

In essence, . . . *the backlash decade produced one long, painful, and unremitting campaign to thwart women's progress. And yet, for all the forces the backlash mustered—the blistering denunciations from the New Right, the legal setbacks of the Reagan years, the powerful resistance of corporate America, the self-perpetuating myth machinery of the media and Hollywood, the `neotraditional' marketing drive of Madison Avenue— women never really surrendered.*

THE WAY THINGS OUGHT TO BE

by Rush Limbaugh, Pocket Books, New York, N.Y., 1992

Rush Limbaugh has gone from his start as a local "top 40's" DJ to fame as one of America's most successful—and controversial—national talk-show hosts. He has been able to do this by recognizing that first and foremost his job is to entertain. While Limbaugh quickly acknowledges his very real sense of mission as a spokesman for conservative causes (from issues dealing with middle-class rights to the Biblical account of the creation), his satire, sarcasm, and overstated examples are purposefully geared to invite responses at the extremes of passion—either outright adoration or foot-stomping outrage. Many of his critics take him too literally. "Lighten up," he advises them. "We should all laugh more at ourselves . . . "

Viewed in the context of entertainment, this book is a marvelous success. For those who can't see beyond the literal words, it becomes either an encyclopedia of conservatism or the ultimate in political un-correctness—depending on your political persuasions.

(In order to maintain Limbaugh's inimitable flavor as he tells us "the way things ought to be," we have retained the original first-person narrative style here, with exact quotes placed in italics.)

Going National

I had a successful talk show in Sacramento. When I was approached about taking my show national, I felt I was ready to accept a new challenge. Ed McLaughlin was able to put together a package that included a two-hour "local" show in New York and a two-hour national show. The New York show was a difficult challenge, because they were used to, and wanted, argumentative radio, and that is not my style. When the national show proved to be a success, the New York local show was dropped and the national show was expanded to three hours.

I have been asked many times what makes my show a success. I was initially a little afraid to think about that, afraid I might try too hard to capitalize on those ingredients and forget to just be me. But as I think about it now, I believe there were probably two ingredients to my success, 1) The recognition that I was there to entertain, and 2) The amazing popularity of the conservative viewpoint.

So there it was, this unique blend of humor, irreverence, and the discussion of events with a conservative slant. Nowhere else in the media today will you find all of these ingredients in one presentation. I would love to tell you that this was the result of a brilliantly conceived and flawlessly executed strategy, but it wasn't. It was just me being myself. I like to have fun, I like being irreverent, and I am dead serious about the things I feel passionately about.

This style can be difficult for local stations who aren't used to it. When a station in South Bend, Indiana got a flurry of calls insisting that I be taken off the air, I responded on my show by asking people to call in and let the station know that the protesters were not really in the majority. They got calls from all over the Midwest supporting my show.

The show is devoted exclusively to what I think. I took the risk of formatting the show this way, so I insist on maintaining the elements that have made it popular. On the other hand, I do not believe I should use my show for activism. I don't demonstrate my influence in politics by adopting campaigns and hyping them. I do believe though that my views have some influence, because they represent the conservative views of millions of people who for decades have been either grossly underestimated, blamed, or ignored by the liberals.

Demonstrating Absurdity by Being Absurd

Every Friday, I urge my audience to enjoy themselves over the weekend, knowing that on Monday I will tell them what has happened *and* what to think about it. This upsets the liberals because *they* are used to being able to tell people what to think.

My "Updates" are a perfect example of absurdity. I once confessed to my audience that I had discovered that a Slim Whitman peace song I had been playing contained a Satanist message when played backwards. Many of the audience never did get the joke, even when we repeated it later with the confession that it was all tongue in cheek. My comments about uglo-Americans and taxing the poor have also raised public ire. Please realize that the biggest part of these messages was dead serious, but the absurd suggestions I made should have raised red flags right in front of the point I was aiming at—you should not believe everything you hear or read simply because it confirms your preconceived notions.

Abortion: Our Next Civil War

It's hard to argue about abortion because views are so deeply entrenched. I do want to state my views on abortion. I am pro-life because 1) I believe that life begins at conception and therefore, abortion is murder; 2) I believe that abortion cheapens human life. We are now deciding who lives and who dies on the basis of whether it is convenient . . . That's dangerous. We have had 30 million legal abortions and most of those are a result of a lack of responsibility. *Our society would be better off if we exercised responsibility, rather than using abortion as a selfish way of escaping from what is, in truth, careless and reckless behavior.*

Pro-choice people really don't want choice, they want power. If they really want choice, why do they object so strongly when someone who wants an abortion is talked out of it? Isn't that a choice? Don't you have to have more than one option in order to have a choice? Trying to find a way to make a point with the pro-choice folks, I started a part of my program where I would "abort" callers I didn't like with a vacuum noise and a scream sound. I did this for two weeks and received thousands of protests. Then I pointed out on my show that I had really harmed nobody. *Where is the outrage against those who do it for real just down the street from where they live? . . .*

In Defense of the Eighties

Because the prosperous Eighties was a decade that showed the success of conservative economics, the period had to be attacked by liberals. These liberals have ceaselessly maligned the decade and its principal benefactor, Ronald Reagan. Because the evidence doesn't support their case, the liberals make their point by calling the Eighties the decade of greed. *For the left to condemn . . . across-the-board improvements by labeling them as greed is tantamount to saying that they are opposed to prosperity for the poor and middle classes if the wealthy also happen to benefit.*

The evidence shows that charitable giving increased by 57.7% in the Eighties. Growth in manufacturing tripled. More new jobs were created in the higher-skills areas. It is not true that the poor got poorer and the rich got richer under Reagan. From 1983 to 1989, the poorest fifth of the population saw their income increase by twelve percent. So did the richest fifth. The Reagan tax cuts actually produced more revenue than the earlier higher rates did, because people were more productive.

There is nothing wrong or greedy with wanting to earn more money. Liberals want more money, too, but they want it from the government rather than from working for it. Don't let liberals make you feel guilty about having money and wanting to keep more of it for yourself and your family. *You have a real job; they just beg for a living.*

The Imperial Congress

The banking scandal in the U.S. House of Representatives is proof positive that something is terribly wrong with our government. According to the General Accounting Office, 355 members of Congress wrote 20,000 bad checks in a three-year period. Ninety-nine members of Congress bounced checks at least twice, checks worth a total of at least eleven million dollars. Fifty-five members of Congress were consistently overdrawn.

There are lots of people serving time in jail in this country for what some members of Congress did with their House checking accounts. Yet, instead of attacking the problem, the liberal Congress and the media rationalized the situation, laughed it off—and then attacked me when I spoke out against it.

Before the New Deal, most of our representatives served only four to six years in Congress, then returned home to live under the laws they had passed. Now we have professional legislators who stay in Congress forever and are forever immune to many of the laws that afflict the rest of us. Term limitation would solve some of these problems, but Congress will never act to limit its own power.

Animals Have No Rights

Animal rights activists are upset with me because I question their basic premise that animals are more important than humans. They often won't admit that this is their position, but their actions make it clear. Animals have no rights. To have rights you have to understand and agree with and obey social contracts, which no animal can do. This is not to say that animals should be abused; they shouldn't. But their protection comes from human concern, not from any God-given or Constitutional rights. Animals raised for food or for fur, ought to be used for those purposes. Needless slaughter of wild animals is something different and ought to be dealt with firmly.

Feminism and the Culture War

Feminism is one of those issues where name-calling has replaced meaningful debate. Feminism has also changed over time. It began as a drive for equal opportunity, equal pay. Now the movement is . . . *driven by women who are angry . . . with their particular lot in life. Many of the women who have risen to leadership ranks in the movement are man haters . . . They are at war with traditional American values and fundamental institutions such as marriage and the American family.*

I suspect that my views are not in disagreement with the majority of American women; my disagreement is with some of the leaders of the movement, who espouse two key rights: abortion rights and lesbian rights.

Who Needs The Media

The problems of The Media lie in the areas of accountability, responsibility and attitude. The Media demand regulation of big business to control dishonesty, yet they are incredulous at the proposal that they also should be regulated. They seem to assume that they can regulate themselves. Well, we all know how that works for any other group, and the media have blatantly shown us that they are no exception.

The Media pretend that they aren't engaged in a business, but have a calling as the sacred guarantors of the First Amendment. They have adopted a religious zeal about themselves that places them above normal rules and law. Fortunately, the public has not accepted that premise. *The Media is now considered just another part of the arrogant, condescending, elite, and out-of-touch political structure which has ignored the people and their concerns and interests.*

The Last Word

We are winning! I know it doesn't look like it, but we are. The Left is getting louder and louder because they know it too. They have run out of our money to fund all their programs, so they are fighting over what is left. The citizens have learned not to trust Washington.

So take heart, dear reader. Don't get down. Remember how I handle them. I laugh at their outrageous statements and I ridicule their latest lunacies. So should you. Laugh and move on. They are the past. We conservatives are the future.

FUTURE SHOCK

by Alvin Toffler, Random House Publishers, New York, N.Y., 1970

Many people have trouble coping with change—particularly when it comes too fast. Since changes in our rapidly advancing society are both common and sudden, many of us are experiencing great stress. Alvin Toffler's phrase "future shock" has become a classic byword to describe this inner turmoil.

The Death of Permanence

For many centuries, societies changed slowly, if they changed at all. Today, points out Toffler, this is no longer true; variation and upheaval are facts of life. Cities, communities, families, businesses, religious organizations, informational needs, and, especially, technology, have all adopted an affinity to change. Not only is technology advancing more rapidly than ever before, the time required for technology to be applied and for those applications to spread through society had been drastically reduced. How can we learn to cope with the multitude of events that compress our lives into a dream-like state punctuated by lightning-quick flashes? "To survive . . . the individual must become infinitely more adaptable and capable than ever before. He must search out new ways to anchor himself . . . "

Each culture has established its own pace—and events proceed at a rate acceptable to that culture. Meals may last from a few minutes to an hour or more; an education may be either nonexistent, or highly structured into multi-hour sessions, with homework to boot; a romantic relationship in one culture may last a night—in another setting, forever. When the cultural pace and these "durational expectancies" are not met, it brings on stress and dissatisfaction—at least until we learn to reorient our personal timetables and expectations to match the quickening pace.

Transience

Transience—the new "temporariness" in everyday life—is evident in the high rate of turnover that pervades our roles and our many and varied relationships. Transience refers to rapidity of change—change that pushes not-so-distant-past ideas and values into irrelevancy.

At one time, man, in an effort to survive in the marketplace, built products to last. Now, with more advanced technology, it is often cheaper to buy a new—and better—toaster, or calculator, or TV set. At one time, we bought dwellings, cars and furniture; now we rent and trade these items. Things rapidly wear out or become obsolete as fads pass, tastes shift, or a better music box comes along.

We live in a throw-away, one-time-use society, which, in turn, spawns a throw-away mentality. Even our buildings are constantly being torn down and rebuilt. Soon we come to expect relationships as well as "things" to be characterized by short durations. As more and more of us move to cities, the neighborhood ties we develop tend to be more shallow. Job changes are more frequent, so, likewise, work relations are

more distant and fleeting. Even today's heroes—real, perceived and imaginary—are becoming transitory. The upshot is that even though we meet many more people during our lifetime than our parents or grandparents did, we do not usually know or commit to friends, or even family members, with the depth and permanence of earlier generations.

Our connection to places has also deteriorated. We travel more in one year than perhaps our parents did in a lifetime. We commute to work and jet away on vacations. Just decades ago, homes were lifetime dwellings. Now we move regularly, many of us changing residences every year or two. Some people seem to thrive on this mobility, this new freedom. Others are stressed by it. For both groups, however, less attachment and loyalty to places diminishes, along with attachment to people and things.

Nor do our business organizations have the same stability they once had. It seems our jobs are continually changing—even when we don't change jobs! Mergers, acquisitions, reorganizations, downsizing, reorienting, renewing—these affect the nature of our positions. And as the concept of "team assembly" for specific projects becomes more and more popular—and traditional, multi-level bureaucracies grow extinct—more and more jobs are *designed* to be short-lived, project-team-type set ups.

The acceleration in information flow brings on a certain measure of stress. In earlier cultures, most information was derived naturally, in a loose, unstructured form; nowadays, our burgeoning information pool offers ideas and comparisons at the touch of a button. Books, television images, radio, music, newspapers, art, even the words we use are changing rapidly. As the world and its "truths" shift in transforming images right before our eyes, our mental models of what the world is like must also undergo a metamorphosis:

. . . by speeding up change in the outer world, we compel the individual to relearn his environment at every moment. New discoveries . . . force a faster and faster pace of daily life. They demand a new level of adaptability. And they set the stage for that potentially devastating social illness—future shock.

Novelty

If transience is the first key to our increasingly troubled lives, then the second key is novelty. Not only are changes *occurring*, they are moving in staggering new directions with potentially devastating implications: cities under the sea or in space; genetic manipulations; robots, cyborgs and artificial intelligence; organ transplants and artificial organs . . .

Under the stresses of future shock, the family—already in a state of flux—may well adopt extremely novel future forms: more single-male-parent families, homosexual families, group families, corporate families, and communes. We may even see babies "selectively engineered" for certain genetic characteristics, then bought off a "store" shelf—to be reared by "professional parents." (ital) As we hurtle into tomorrow, millions of ordinary men and women will face emotion-packed options so unfamiliar, so untested, that past experience will offer little clue to wisdom.

Diversity

Some forecasters suggest that the citizens of the future will suffer a lack of choice. An analysis of trends, however, indicates the opposite: if anything, says Toffler, we will suffer from *too many* choices, or "overchoice"—too many kinds of foods, cleansers and choices in entertainment. Industrialization and mass production once encouraged standardization and a leveling of choice, in direct contrast to the new "super-industrial society." "As technology becomes more sophisticated, the cost of introducing variations declines."

This trend toward diversity is already creating problems in the current educational system, which typically offers standardized packets of learning. Students are increasingly demanding variety in education; with the common use of the personal computer, schools are just beginning to decentralize; and the movement of higher education is away from traditional majors and credits.

Much of the media, Toffler notes, has already become fragmented in the effort to provide diversity: a network of small theaters has replaced a single, large theater; the variety of books, magazines, movies and radio stations (and now, television channels) has grown enormously.

The pressures of these changes are splintering us into enclaves, tribes and subcults, groups of individuals who share a few common goals or desires. There are surfing clubs, dance clubs, and clubs for lovers of rodeo riding and book reading; there's a cult for every belief and musical group; and proud, self-labeled groups espousing a certain sexual preference are exploding in number and solidarity. This fragmentation helps explain why our cities seem to have become ungovernable—they are *not* at all one city any longer—one community with a common center of interests and cultural bonds—but many separate "communities" and enclaves.

The Limits of Adaptability

Clearly "change carries a psychological price tag. And the more radical the change, the steeper the price." Psychologists and sociologists have found strong links between the frequency of change and poor health. Even death rates have increased as a result of the stresses of future shock. And future shock can deeply scar the mind as well, triggering depression and many other pathological symptoms. And as future shock disorients individuals, society is disoriented too. When we perceive the world as "going crazy," in other words, we may be right.

Strategies for Survival

To face *future* future shock, "we need neither blind acceptance nor blind resistance [to change], but an array of creative strategies for shaping, deflecting, accelerating or decelerating change . . . " The problem, says Toffler, is not to *deny* change, but to *manage* it by constructing permanent, personal "stability zones."

Stability zones are those areas of our lives that remain permanent, thus providing us with a stable platform from which to weather the onslaught of the future. A stable marriage can reduce the shock of a job shake-up; daily or weekly routines can soothe our minds and bodies and preserve a feeling of stability.

We can not predict the future, but we can anticipate it and plan for it. Planning strategies to handle the inevitable—retirement, the death of a parent, the departure of children from the nest—helps soften the impact when the event indeed occurs.

Other group coping strategies can provide strength and support. "Situational groups" [support groups] have sprung up all over, where grieving, phobic, divorced, addicted, or afflicted individuals can join together for help and support with others in similar circumstances.

Professional therapy, including counseling by clergy and lay experts, are other sources of "crisis support." Many clinics—the outgrowths of rape and abuse crisis centers and "halfway houses"—have expanded their services to include advice for those who suffer from temporary bouts with depression or other emotional stress.

One creative idea to diminish the effects of future shock is the development of "enclaves of the past—communities in which turnover, novelty and choice are deliberately limited"; where individuals can escape "overstimulation" for days, weeks, or even years, if necessary.

To counteract future shock, says Toffler, we also need to rethink education. We need more diversity in classes. Moreover, we need to teach children how to learn, how to relate, and how to choose and how to cope for a whole lifetime of change. We need to teach them to anticipate the future.

Growth in technology, one of the triggers of future shock, cannot be slowed. So, what we need is to give workers more control over the development and implementation of the technology they will utilize. And, as in other areas, we need to take advantage of "social indicators" and "transience indices" to monitor and anticipate the non-obvious, negative social and cultural impacts of particular technologies:

. . . the time is late, [and] technology must be tamed if the accelerative thrust is to be brought under control. And the accelerative thrust must be brought under control if future shock is to be avoided.

Future Shock analyzes in detail the potential stressful effects of fast-paced and varied change. Ironically, the solution to such problems itself *involves* change; change is both the villain and the potential hero. Anticipating change, recognizing the inevitable—and then, where we can, changing the direction of change itself—are the key ingredients to coping and retaining our moral freedom in an ever-changing world.

THE RELAXATION RESPONSE

by Herbert Benson, M.D., Morrow Publishing, New York, N.Y., 1975

. . . The present world is a difficult one. Grief, calamity, and evil cause inner bitterness . . . Evil influences strike . . . they injure the mind and reduce its intelligence and they also injure the muscles and the flesh.

These words, timely as they may sound, were actually written by a Chinese physician 4,600 years ago. Since that time, our lives have become much more complex, but technological growth has done little to help us cope with the pressures that come with modern living.

In modern times, people often lack job security, bear heavy burdens of personal obligation, strain to adjust to the seemingly constant shifting of social norms, and endure the daily commute and noise and fumes of city life. Stress *defines* modern life.

In his nationally acclaimed best-seller *The Relaxation Response*, Dr. Herbert Benson tells modern victims of stress how they *can* cope, and live more full, enjoyable lives.

The Fight-or-Flight Response

Not only does stress have a negative psychological impact, it has an enormous effect on our physiology. One major physiological impact of long-term stress is the chronic state of arousal known as the *fight-or-flight response*. When we experience events which arouse our emotions, our bodies respond with involuntary increases in blood pressure, accelerated heart rate, rapid breathing, and increased blood flow to the muscles. These reactions are the same mechanisms which ensure the survival of animals in the wild. An enraged dog, threatened by a rival, snarls; muscles tensed and ready for conflict; a gazelle runs for its life to escape its attacker. These survival reactions are possible because of the automatic physiological preparations made by the body's nervous system. In times of danger, the autonomic nervous system switches from the "conserve" (parasympathetic) mode to the "survival" (sympathetic) mode. The fight-or-flight instinct—for that is what it truly is—has been repressed in today's "civilized" society, but it still resides deep within each human being.

The Hidden Epidemic

The increased energy and responsiveness brought on by the instinctive fight-or-flight response provides humans with resources for coping with emergencies. While this heightened arousal may be advantageous in urgent situations of physical danger, repeated activation of this response in situations where no outlet for the adrenaline "charge" is possible or desirable can be hazardous. Dr. Benson believes that chronic arousal of the fight-or-flight response leads to permanent high blood pressure.

The prevalence of hypertension (the medical term for high blood pressure) in today's busy populace is staggering. Currently, 15 to 33 percent of American adults suffer from hypertension, and the percentage is increasing steadily. Hypertension often develops slowly and without apparent symptoms—until it manifests itself in the form of a heart attack or stroke. Furthermore, hypertension is striking victims at a younger age. A few years ago, it was considered rare for a young adult to experience such problems; today, it is common.

The Causes of Hypertension

There are several causes of hypertension. Traditional medical explanations have focused on physiological factors such as diet, exercise, and genetic predisposition. A factor frequently left out of the equation, however, is stress. Although doctors have long recognized the potential link between stress and high blood pressure, only recently has the relationship between stress and hypertension been analyzed systematically. Not surprisingly, a connection has been found between fluctuating stress factors in an individual's life—including the "good" stress that comes with a job promotion, for example, as well as the "bad" stress of a divorce or job loss—and hypertension.

Combating Stress

Now that scientific research has confirmed that stress does in fact play a part in inducing—and complicating—heart problems as well as other physical illnesses, the question is, what can be done? After years of research, Dr. Benson has concluded that the body may actually be its own best healer. We come equipped, he says, with natural, built-in resources designed to neutralize the effects of stress.

Just as the body has a way of arousing the nervous system at the approach of danger, Dr. Benson has found that "there is another response which leads to quieting of the same nervous system. Indeed, there is evidence that hypertensive subjects can lower their blood pressure by regularly eliciting this other response." It is "this other response" that he calls the *Relaxation Response*.

Ancient and Modern Techniques

A number of techniques, both ancient and modern, are known to deactivate the "sympathetic" (survival mode) nervous system and thereby unlock the body's natural restorative abilities. Yoga, Zen, meditation, prayer, autogenic training, exercise, and other related mental routines are now known to produce measurable positive physiological effects on the human body. Some of the measured benefits are decreased oxygen consumption, lower respiration and heart rates, an increase in the "alpha-wave" brain activity that is linked to enhanced feelings of well-being, and decreased muscle tension and blood pressure.

Practicing the Relaxation Response

"The Relaxation Response," says Dr. Benson, "is a natural gift that anyone can turn on and use. Unlike the fight-or-flight response, which is . . . elicited without conscious effort, the Relaxation Response can be evoked only if time is set aside and a conscious effort is made."

The point is that we must deliberately develop techniques in order to trigger the relaxation response. In his study of practices such as prayer, Yoga, Zen meditation, and relaxation training, Dr. Benson has identified the four principal steps for eliciting the Relaxation Response:

1. **Find a Quiet Environment.** Choose a place with as few distractions as possible. Some people prefer a room in their home, some a chapel or other place of worship, still others a peaceful outdoor location.

2. **Choose an Object to Dwell On.** To keep your mind from wandering, focus on a single word, gaze at some object, or concentrate on the rhythm of your breathing. The anonymous fourteenth-century author of a book on Christian mysticism, *The Cloud of Unknowing*, recommends that you let your mind dwell on a word such as "God" or "love":

Clasp this word tightly in your heart so that it never leaves it no matter what may happen. This word shall be your shield and your spear . . . With this word you shall strike down thoughts of every kind and drive them beneath the cloud of forgetting.

3. **Maintain a Passive Attitude.** This is perhaps the most important element in the Relaxation Response. Relaxation must be allowed; it cannot be forced. Of course distracting thoughts will inevitably enter your mind. When they do, simply allow them to leave again by returning your attention to the object on which you are dwelling. Do not worry about how well you are doing; just "let it happen." This passive approach is central to St. Teresa's description of engrossing, submissive prayer:

May the Lord teach this manner of prayer to those who do not know it, for I confess, myself, that I never knew what it was to pray with satisfaction until he instructed me in this method.

4. **Select a Comfortable Position.** Make yourself comfortable, but not so comfortable that you fall asleep. Practitioners of a Taoist technique of inner breathing let down their hair, remove their shoes and loosen their clothing, then stretch out on the floor and concentrate on slow, deliberate breathing. You may prefer a sitting position if you are likely to doze off while lying down.

A Useful Technique

Depending on your preference, the specific technique you choose for eliciting the Relaxation Response can be religious or non-religious. At the Beth Israel Hospital in Boston, Dr. Benson teaches his patients a form of Transcendental Meditation:

(1) Sit quietly in a comfortable position.

(2) Close your eyes.

(3) Deeply relax all your muscles, beginning with your feet and progressing up to your face. Keep them relaxed.

(4) Breathe through your nose. Become aware of your breathing. each time you finish breathing out, repeat the word, "ONE," silently to yourself. For example, breathing easily and naturally, breathe IN . . . OUT, and think "ONE"; IN . . . OUT, "ONE"; etc.

(5) Follow this routine for 10 to 20 minutes. You may open your eyes to check the time, but do not use an alarm clock or oven timer. When you finish, sit quietly for several minutes, at first with your eyes closed, and later with your eyes open.

(6) "Do not worry about whether you are successful in achieving a deep level of relaxation. Maintain a passive attitude and permit relaxation to occur at its own pace. When worrisome thoughts confront your mind, do not dwell upon them; return to repeating `ONE.'"

With practice, the response should come with very little effort. Repeat the technique once or twice daily, but not within two hours after any meal, since the digestive processes seem to interfere with the Relaxation Response.

Dr. Benson claims that regular attempts to elicit the Relaxation Response—ten to twenty minutes, once or twice a day—have been found to reduce blood pressure in many hypertensive patients. In addition to the medical benefits of the Relaxation Response, those who practice it also report decreased anxiety and a greater overall sense of well-being. If we use the excuse that we are "too busy" or "too tired" to take advantage of the potential benefits of the Relaxation Response, we deny our body the chance to heal itself, our mind the chance to slow down, and our soul the chance to "find" itself.

The Relaxation Response should become an integral part of our daily lives, Dr. Benson insists. Instead of a coffee break, he suggests taking a "Relaxation Response Break." The increased health and energy and the decreased stress that the Relaxation Response provide will not only enhance our inner peace, but will also allow us to cultivate better relations with others and expand our ability to work and play.

FIT FOR LIFE

by Harvey and Marilyn Diamond, Warner Books, Inc., New York, N.Y., 1985

The authors of *Fit For Life* encourage their readers to stop "living to eat" and to begin "eating to live." While their approach contains a few rather controversial proposals, most of their recommendations seem logical. In its two sections, the book first discusses the principles of "Natural Hygiene," and concludes with recipes and shopping lists that correspond with these principles.

Sixty-two percent of Americans are overweight; conventional "dieting," however, is not the answer. Since diets are temporary, the results of diets are also temporary: dieting reconditions our bodies with new foods, but once we go off the diet our bodies, habits, routines and attitudes all revert back to former patterns.

Fit For Life is designed to help make permanent changes in eating habits that the time of eating and the combination of foods, according to the Diamonds, affect body weight. The Fit for Life program utilizes the concepts of natural hygiene to provide proper food combinations: "The basic foundation of *natural hygiene* is that the body is always striving for health and that it achieves this by continuously cleansing itself of deleterious waste material." In fact, a basic Fit for Life tenet is that the body can cleanse, heal, and maintain *itself*.

Natural Hygiene

Daily, we eat, absorb, and eliminate food. We will have more energy and be more successful in managing weight if we learn to appropriate, assimilate, and eliminate food according to natural body cycles. Elimination is the most important of these processes. "Safe and permanent weight reduction," the authors assert, "is directly related to the amount of vital energy you have at your disposal and to the efficient use of this energy to eliminate waste . . . from your body." And eating fruit, especially in the morning hours, is at the heart of an energized, efficient diet.

The following "Energy Ladder" chart outlines the optimum times you may partake of certain foods in order to obtain the maximum level of energy during the elimination process.

A.M. (morning to noon)
Fresh fruits and juices.
P.M. (noon to evening)
Fresh vegetable juices and salads, steamed vegetables, raw nuts and seeds, grains, breads, potatoes, and legumes.
Evening
Meat, chicken, fish, dairy.

If we cannot efficiently eliminate waste from our bodies, we lose energy. This adverse effect—called toxemia, or metabolic imbalance—exhibits itself in two ways, one less threatening, one a more serious hazard. First, toxic cells are often eliminated from the body through the body's natural metabolic processes. As long as the toxic material is eliminated at the same rate as it is produced, little damage occurs.

However, when toxemia originates from eating food byproducts— food which is usually altered from its natural state by barbecuing, steaming, stewing and boiling—the toxic residues will frequently prevent it from assimilating and digesting properly. It is critical that we understand how to cleanse our body of toxic waste in order to feel healthy and maintain weight.

Three general principles can abet this cleansing process:

1. *The Principle of High-Water-Content Food*

Since our bodies, by weight, are 70 percent water, the foods and liquids we consume should, on average, contain at least 70% water. Water transports nutrients and eliminates toxic waste. Drinking large quantities of water is not the solution, however, since drinking water does not have the enzymes necessary for transporting and eliminating that fruit and vegetable juices have. All the nutrition required by the body can be found in fruits and vegetables: "All three of our body cycles function with the greatest ease when supplied with [fruit and vegetable] water on a regular basis."

Unfortunately, the most prevalent foods in most American diets tend to be clogging foods, which we have been conditioned to find most flavorful. If we truly want to have more energy and stay in shape, however, we must eat food that is "alive"—foods having high-water content. "No practice will expedite the elimination cycle more than the regular consumption of an adequate amount of high-water-content food."

2. *The Principle of Proper Food Combining*

"Nothing streamlines the appropriation cycle more than adhering to the principles of proper food combining," the Diamonds stress. The body needs high energy to eliminate toxic waste; we *assist* the body in the elimination cycle by supplying it with a sufficient amount of energy on a regular basis.

Certain combinations of food may be digested more efficiently than others. For example, the body is incapable of assimilating more than one "concentrated" food— one having little water content—at a time. Certain combinations of foods are more compatible than others. The body is capable of modifying food that contains a natural protein-starch combination, such as beans and rice. "Proper food combining does not prevent you from eating the foods you like," the authors note, "you just shouldn't eat them all at the same time." This point is essential especially to successful weight management.

3. *The Principle of Correct Fruit Consumption*

"Fruit requires less energy to be digested than any other food." Fruit supplies the body with vitamins without depleting energy during the digestion process. With its high-water content, fruit makes a natural detoxifying agent for the body. Fruit, however, should *not* be eaten with—or followed by—any other type of food. What are the "rules" for eating fruit?:

1) Only consume fruit that is fresh. Processed or canned fruit is lower in nutritional value.

2) After eating fruit, wait at least twenty minutes before eating anything else. This allows adequate time for the fruit to leave the stomach on its mission to detoxify the body. The reverse is also true: don't eat any fruit soon after eating another food. The qualities of fruit and how the body reacts to it give support to this reasoning. The following chart illustrates the correct time frames for eating fruit:

HOW LONG TO WAIT AFTER EATING OTHER FOOD BEFORE AGAIN EATING FRUIT

FOOD	TIME TO WAIT
Salad or raw vegetables	2 hours
Properly combined meal, without flesh	3 hours
Properly combined meal, with flesh	4 hours
Any improperly combined meal	8 hours

In other words, a properly combined meal is based on the following principle: "THE HUMAN BODY IS NOT DESIGNED TO DIGEST MORE THAN ONE CONCENTRATED FOOD [a non-fruit or non-vegetable food] IN THE STOMACH AT THE SAME TIME." In general, meals should be ordered so that the body's natural cycles can be regulated. Here's how it's done:

Before noon, eat only fresh fruits. This will initiate the three-cycle process:

Cycle I: Elimination—Waste products from fruit move quickly through the body taking other toxins with them—providing a cleansing effect. Because in the morning the body's toxic load is greatest, eating fruit then helps regulate the body without adding toxicity.

Cycle II: Appropriation—Digestion takes more exertion than any other function of the body. When less energy is used to break down a meal, more energy is retained for other body functions.

Cycle III: Assimilation—A properly combined meal will exit the stomach just three hours after being consumed. When the last meal of the day is taken early in the evening, it is possible to go to bed on an empty stomach. A stomach that is empty at bedtime will, of course, be empty in the morning. Then, when fruit is eaten for the breakfast meal, weight loss will be accelerated and enhanced.

Protein

Of all the food elements, protein is the most difficult to assimilate and eliminate. First, protein cannot be digested in its natural state; before the body can begin to store protein calories, the protein must be broken down by enzymes into amino acids. Since meat is a primary source of protein, three points should be considered when ingesting it: (1) Seek a meat source that provides chemically-free, high quality products, (2) Eat meat no more than once a day, and (3) Properly combine meat with other foods during a meal, but never combine it with another protein.

Dairy Products

Any dairy product is considered a concentrated food (low in water content) and should not be eaten along with another concentrated food. Some people are concerned about meeting the proper intake of calcium, but it is important to note that fruit contains all the calcium the body needs.

Exercise and Attitude

As essential as a sound diet, a program of consistent exercise helps to insure lasting health. Accordingly, a twenty-minute-a-day aerobic activity is necessary to maintain the correct caloric balance of intake and expenditure.

No fitness program can be successful, however, if the participant does not engage the mind as well as the body in the pursuit of health. Health originates first as a desire to be healthy, a desire that is expressed through sensible eating habits and daily exercise.

Fit for Life Goal

The Fit For Life program stresses total body detoxification. While temporary discomfort may be experienced at the onset of the cleansing process—due to the body's reaction to a sudden increase of energy as toxins are flushed out—the benefits far outweigh any adverse effects. By adhering to the principles of *Fit For Life*, your body will be thinner, exude more energy, and feel more alive.

ANATOMY OF AN ILLNESS AS PERCEIVED BY THE PATIENT

by Norman Cousins, Bantam Books, Inc., New York, N.Y., 1981

In August 1964, Norman Cousins contract ed an undiagnosed infection severe enough to require hospitalization. Finally diagnosed with *ankylosing spondylitis*, a serious collagen deterioration of the connective tissue in the spine, Cousins was given a one-in-five-hundred chance for full recovery.

Cousins quickly became discontent with his treatment at the hospital. He found little regard for patients' sleep requirements, no coordination of lab work to avoid reduplicated blood extractions and other testing procedures, a lack of basic sanitation, and common use of powerful drugs as a patient-management technique rather than a clinical procedure. What's more, the nutritional content of the hospital food was alarmingly deficient. Cousins felt his recovery depended too heavily on the regimens of doctors, nurses, and hospitals—and decided to take responsibility for his own care and treatment.

Dr. Hitzig, Cousins' doctor and long-time friend, allowed him to dictate his own medical therapy. These patient-care alterations proved not only instrumental in bringing about Cousins' own recovery and inspiring other patients to take greater responsibility for their own care, but soon came to impact the medical community as a whole.

THE HEALING POWER OF NATURE

Living a long life is an underlying theme in *Anatomy of an Illness*. While Cousins concedes that a genetic predisposition to longevity is important, he is convinced that the *will to live* is even more crucial. It in this vital will (made up of a combination of biological and psychological mechanisms) that mobilizes the body's natural adaptiveness to resist disease. And even in the off-chance that disease wins the short-term battle, and we *do* become ill, our body can still work to heal itself spontaneously, and eventually win the war; in the long run, our immune system can become more resilient than ever. Ancient physicians called this dynamic the *vis medicatrix naturae*—"the healing power of nature."

Other authorities have testified to the phenomenon of the body fighting off illness on its own. William Osler of John Hopkins Hospital, whom Cousins calls "the greatest clinician of the Anglo Saxon world," believed that cures to organic illnesses were brought about by the patient's *faith* in the treatment used, combined with good nursing care. Osler suggested that an atmosphere of optimism and good cheer was central to the healing process, and used the phrase "faith healing" when referring to John Hopkins' recovery rates, because positive psychological influences caused patients to *heal themselves*.

Dr. William Henry Welch, "the main architect of scientific medicine in the U.S.," further endorses the premise of faith healing. According to Welch, *faith*—both in the medical treatment being offered and in the doctor—is the key to spontaneous recovery from organic illness.

MORE ON MENTAL ATTITUDE

The body's defense against infection depends in large part on the "mechanisms of humoral and cellular immunity," which are greatly influenced by our mental state. Hypnosis is one way to boost "psychologic immunity." In the Mantoux test, a doctor introduces tuberculin under a patient's skin and awaits the expected vascular response. In most cases, it was found that hypnotic suggestion allowed test subjects to counteract the early stages of tuberculosis, a procedure that immunologists refer to as "cell-mediated immunity."

There is now good reason to believe that the mind can have an effect on all diseases that involve immunological reactions. Emotional states produce the secretion of hormones, like those of the adrenal glands and the thyroid. These hormones trigger the brain's release of endorphins—natural tranquilizers and pain blockers altering our perception of the disease.

As the concept of self-healing develops within the medical community, patients are encouraged to participate more actively and fully in their own medical care and well being. Responsibility and decisions about administering medications are shared by physician and patient. The patient's active role is to synchronize the healing efforts of mind and body in order to produce the natural defense mechanisms that will overcome the disease.

In Cousins' case, he took *full* control over his illness, and deduced that he was suffering from adrenal exhaustion, which tended to lower his resistance. Consulting books on the subject and finding that a potential cause of adrenal exhaustion is emotional tension (frustration or suppressed rage), Cousins pondered how *positive* emotions might affect his illness. Reasoning that engineering a more positive outlook at least couldn't hurt, he formulated a plan of action to help heal himself.

First of all, he felt uncomfortable with the medications he was being given: twenty-six aspirin tablets and twelve phenylbutazone tablets daily. The aspirin, he realized, reduced retention of vitamin C in his blood, and the phenylbutazone taxed his adrenal glands. However, if he quit taking the drugs altogether, he was warned that his spinal column and other joints would probably cause more pain than he could deal with.

Cousins then made a monumental decision: he chose to focus upon his attitude. He could easily put up with the pain, he reasoned—*if* it meant that he was getting better. First he went off sleeping pills and pain relievers entirely. Then, in an effort to halt the breakdown of connective tissue in his body, Cousins quit taking the other prescribed drugs and turned to treatments of increasingly higher dosages of intravenous vitamin C to combat collagen breakdown. According to Cousins, vitamin C restores homeostasis to the blood, is essential for the synthesis of collagen, and serves as a liver metabo-lite which detoxifies the blood. Cousins' health made an immediate and remarkable turn for the better.

When Cousins shared the results with Dr. Hitzig, the doctor became excited by this novel approach and sought to apply it to other patients. He had never heard of using such high doses of vitamin C to fight infection. In partnership with his patient, Hitzig's first order of business—in a move to enhance body chemistry—was to find ways to heighten *positive outlook* and *affirmative emotions*. They discovered, for example, that ten minutes of "genuine belly laughter"—offered by way of comical videos and TV programs—was good for two hours of pain-free sleep. Another startling side-effect was laughter's apparent magic in fighting infection, as reflected by Cousin's blood tests. Hence, in order to relieve the hospital of complaints and potential liability, Cousins checked himself into a motel room—where he could laugh as long and hard as he wanted. Recovery progressed steadily until he could move freely. He was well.

Cousins affirms that humor is indeed a "miracle" treatment. Immanuel Kant stated in his *Critique of Pure Reason* that laughter produces a "feeling of health through the furtherance of the vital bodily processes . . . "; William Osler termed laughter the "music of life"; and Cousins follows up with a philosophical analogy of his own, comparing laughter to "jogging internally without having to go outdoors." In physiological terms, laughter produces pain-blocking endor-phins that positively alter the outcome of an ill-ness. It is generally agreed upon that positive emotions are life-giving experiences strongly connected with healing and well-being.

Cousins drew two conclusions from his personal experience. First, "the will to live is . . . a physiologic reality with therapeutic character-istics." Second, doctors must combine tradition-al, "medically acceptable" methods with meth-ods that encourage and help mobilize patients' natural body-and-mind resources against illness. Cousins also argues that patients must be active-ly *involved* in their treatment. "The capacity of the human mind and body to regenerate should never be underestimated. *It is a natural drive which represents the ultimate exercise in human free-dom."*

THE PLACEBO EFFECT

The question as to whether, in Cousins' case, the vitamin C acted as a placebo, raises a good point. Placebos, usually made up of a milk-sugar combination, have been used for years to test the effects of various drugs; they have also been found, in many instances, to be more effec-tive in relieving pain than morphine. Some researchers theorize that placebos somehow acti-vate the cerebral cortex, which in turn triggers the endocrine system and adrenal glands.

The placebo holds high status in today's medical community because it so often *acts* like a powerful medication. Thus, "the placebo becomes the emissary between the will to live and the body." It can actually be more powerful than the drug it replaces. Up to 90% of the patients who reach out for medical help are suf-fering from disorders that the body itself can heal. So, when a placebo is prescribed, the patient feels comfortable; she has both a pre-scription and a caring doctor. The doctor also is confident that the placebo will improve the patient's condition. "The human body is its own best apothecary because the most successful pre-scriptions are those filled by the body itself."

Granted, says Cousins, placebos are not the total answer in most cases. Even when they are administered, other treatments are also usu-ally called for, and much depends on the illness and the patient's relationship with the doctor.

YOUR UNDERLYING CONDITION

Americans are inclined to take a pill at the first onset of pain or sickness. In fact, however, 90% of our pain is due to such illness-producers as stress, diet and boredom. Instead of changing the underlying problem, we immediately call the doctor or take a couple of aspirin, Cousins asserts. Doctors and patients alike, he continues, would do well to tolerate a "threshold" variety of pain—which, as a "warning system," is actually helpful in correctly diagnosing problems—and educate themselves about what is really happen-ing inside and outside the body. If stress is the cause of a headache, for instance, then we ought to deal with the stress, not the ache, and avoid aspirin's minimal short-term side effects as well as its potentially long-term damage. In Cousin's case, aspirin intensified his *underlying* arthritic condition, accelerating the deterioration of his connective tissue.

HOLISTIC MEDICINE

Holistic medicine attempts to eliminate the underlying causes of illness rather than merely treating symptoms, to bring into thera-peutic focus the combined effects of all human factors: work, nutrition, family, personality, emotions, and environment. How does a partic-ular individual react to his occupation? How has the health of another been diminished by her anorexic behaviors? Before prescribing powerful antibiotics and steroids to treat physical ail-ments, the good they do has to be carefully weighed against the harm they might cause.

There are two basic principles of healing in a holistic setting. First, the *trust* the patient places in the physician (the physician's *presence*) and second, the *laying on of hands.* "Both pres-ence and touch help establish a reassuring con-nection with the patient." Holistic practitioners generally become personally involved with their patients, integrating such treatments as *human touch and warmth* into their medical repertoires. The end result is an, *involved, mind-body* attack on the illness.

The human mind has the capacity to disci-pline the body, Cousins insists. Once a patient *knows* his or her own body—and accepts *respon-sibility* for it—this engenders a confidence in the healing process, rousing the mind and body to work in harmony to meet the challenges of recovery from disease or disability.

GROW RICH SLOWLY

The *Merrill Lynch* Guide to Retirement Planning
by Don Underwood and Paul B. Brown, Viking Press, New York, N.Y., 1993

In their book *Grow Rich Slowly*, Don Underwood and Paul B. Brown contend that the only way for America to maintain its "entrepreneurial drive" is to "rediscover the old habits of saving and investing that made us the most affluent nation and the leading economic power on earth." The authors—using a combination of accessible quotes, examples, and graphs—go on to outline various strategies for building wealth, saving and investing which they believe will not only help us attain "a financially secure retirement," but will also "keep America on top in an increasingly competitive global economy."

The 4-S Savings Formula

There are no tricks when it comes to planning your retirement, say Underwood and Brown. Americans simply must save. To help you think more clearly about savings strategies, the authors present what they call the "4-S Savings Formula." In essence, the formula shows how to:

1. Save More
2. Save Systematically
3. Save Tax-Advantaged
4. Save Smarter

Save More

The odds are high that you are not saving enough, that a "Savings Gap" exists between what you are putting away today and what you will need tomorrow. It's never too late to start saving, either, because your future is at stake.

People save for a variety of reasons: to enjoy a financially secure retirement, to put children through college, to leave a substantial estate . . . No matter what your goals are, the point is that you need to give yourself *real* reasons, if you're going to save more, that is.

The authors cite the examples of John and Lori Peters. John, a mid-level manager at the IRS, and Lori, a secretary, have a combined income of $78,000 a year. They share what John describes as a "low-key life-style." Although they are sensible with their money, John and Lori nonetheless worry that their retirement savings won't be sufficient to allow them to do the kind of things that they enjoy doing now—like "going to a concert or the movies."

The authors believe, however, that the Peters have made a good start. Aware that their retirement days are not far off, they have begun to set aside $1500 a month (or 23% of their gross monthly income) to invest in a variety of retirement plans. Moreover, by increasing their house payments by $100 each month, the Peters will be able to pay off the remaining $30,000 of their mortgage six years early.

Save Systematically

Retirement plans are "like noses—[they] come in all sizes and shapes." Whether you fashion a retirement plan that is "huge," "elegant," or "barely there," like a nose, "it is better to have a pension plan than not." And it's even better if you have a *disciplined* plan; a haphazard savings plan will be insufficient if you want a comfortable, worry-free retirement.

Among the numerous retirement plans available today, Underwood and Brown point in particular to the advantages of the *401(k)*. Introduced in the late 1980s, the plan has quickly become a favorite with large and small companies alike. Employers like the plan because it "limits their costs" by fixing the amount of their "retirement contributions." Thus, unlike plans which require employers "to keep paying out benefits" as long as their retired employees live, the 401(k) enables employers to know in advance exactly how much their contributions will be.

The authors also find that employees are attracted to the plan, though in their case because of its flexibility and portability. For instance, in contrast to traditional company pension plans, the *401(k)* allows employees to direct the growth of their retirement funds by determining the amount of money they wish to contribute—an amount which, in many cases, is then supplemented by employers. Perhaps even more significant in today's job market, the authors suggest, is the fact that contributions to the *401(k)* plan are portable. That is, once employees are "vested" in the plan, they can transfer their retirement contributions from job to job.

Save Tax-Advantaged

Underwood and Brown list several tax advantages employees enjoy with the *401(k)* plan. For instance, with the exception of Social Security taxes, both federal and state taxes on contributions to the *401(k)* can be deferred until retirement benefits are drawn. Thus, the *401(k)* plan can substantially reduce taxable income.

Similarly, any interest, dividends, or capital gains earned from contributions to the fund can also be deferred from federal and state taxes. The authors refer to a hypothetical employee who contributes $2000 a year to a *401(k)*. In this scenario, the employer contributes nothing. Assuming the fund earns 10% interest (compounded annually), the authors calculate that in the space of 30 years the *401(k)* would grow to

$361,887. The employee's contribution to the fund would be $60,000, and the tax-deferred interest he would enjoy would amount to $301,887.

Most employers, the authors note, do make contributions to their employees' retirement funds, typically matching every dollar the employee contributes (up to 6% of the gross salary) with 50 cents of their own. What's more, employer contributions are tax-deferred as well.

Save Smarter

Chances are you already know more about retirement planning than you give yourself credit for. However, say the authors, most of us could raise our "investment sights a notch or two."

One of the ways you can learn to "save smarter" is to consider hiring an investment counsellor. One executive mentioned in the book attributes his business success to the fact that "I always hire people smarter than me." When it comes to planning your retirement, Underwood and Brown suggest you do the same: hire people who know more than you do about savings and investments to help you devise a smarter retirement plan.

Profiling Yourself

The book cautions not to lose sight of your own comfort level when you consult a professional for financial advice. An expert "can serve as a guide," but you are the one who has to live with the investments.

To help clarify various investment criteria, the authors identify six basic types of investors.

1. Conservative, focused on preserving capital. This type of investor is most concerned with preserving capital. He does not feel comfortable exposing his investments to risks. The authors observe that this kind of investor tends to keep his money in cash (or cash equivalents), highly rated corporate and government bonds, and even a few stocks.

   However, this strategy involves a frequently overlooked risk: it "works only if inflation doesn't outstrip . . . earnings."

2. Conservative, concentrating on current income. This investor is "willing to absorb a modest amount of risk" to establish a "*secure* income stream." Her portfolio usually includes "blue chip stocks—shares of big companies . . . with a long history of paying dividends to their shareholders." Even though blue chips have growth potential, she is more concerned with "the dividend these stocks pay."

3. Conservative, oriented toward growth. This person, though concerned with the principal, accepts the fact that growth stocks are volatile. Consequently, he divides his portfolio between growth stocks and fixed income investments.

   Investing in growth stocks may simply mean that, rather than cashing out, he uses dividend checks to buy more stock and reinvests any interest in money market funds. The fixed income side of his portfolio will likely comprise government securities, high-grade corporate and municipal bonds, and "perhaps some zero coupons."

4. Nonconservative, oriented toward growth tomorrow. This investor is one who is less concerned with earnings today. Instead, she invests in growth stocks that promise "above-average capital gains over a three-to-five-year period." She accepts market volatility, and three quarters of her investment portfolio is made up of stocks. Moreover, the stocks are not simply of the blue chip variety; she also buys stock in "small capitalization companies"—those that often outperform larger companies but whose market value is less than $500 million. The risk here, the authors point out, is that small cap stocks can fall as fast and far as they rise.

5. Nonconservative, oriented toward capital appreciation. This investor looks for capital appreciation. He wants to outperform the market by moving his capital between "asset classes—stocks, bonds, cash—on a regular basis . . . " Perhaps two-thirds of his portfolio will consist of stocks. A higher percentage of his investments will include not only small cap stocks, but speculative issues as well.

6. Aggressive. Finally, there is the aggressive investor, whose motto is "No risk, no reward." A "long-term" investment to her means one in which her capital is tied up for no more than a year or two. Investments with broader "time horizons," she believes, fail because they don't "take *immediate* advantage of the changes [in the marketplace]."

   For instance, if the aggressive investor sees that interest rates are about to fall, she'll move assets from cash to bonds. Similarly, if she sees that bonds are performing poorly, she'll move her capital to "investments with far greater growth opportunities." In short, she is "comfortable with volatility" and is willing to assume large risks.

   In *Grow Rich Slowly*, Underwood and Brown present common-sense, strategic approaches to planning a smarter retirement. Although their emphasis is retirement planning, the basic concepts and suggestions are applicable to anyone, whether they are "big-time" players or those who merely want to dabble on the sidelines.

THE PORTABLE MBA

The Best Wisdom From the Top University Programs
by Eliza G.C. Collins and Mary Anne Devanna, John Wiley & Sons, Inc., 1990

The Portable MBA is designed to teach people how to think like an MBA. This book outlines how to manage people optimally through the use of a consistent behavioral model, as well as how to manage departments to maximize productivity. It also details the most effective use of information technolgy.

I.THE FOUNDATIONS OF MANAGEMENT

The R factors

The key skills covered by a good MBA program relate to managing people. Individual and organizational behavior are so complex that it helps to have a conceptual model from which to work. "R factors"—so-called because each factor begins with the letter R—provide just such a model.

SITUATIONAL R FACTORS

Situational R factors arise in response to organizational pressures. They include *roles, relationships, rewards and rites*. Organizational *roles* are defined by a set of expectations about an individual's behavior. Organizational roles consist of a required set of tasks and responsibilities that are not always spelled out in a job description. The formal roles tell the workers what is expected in exchange for a salary; informal roles carry "unofficial" expectations that, nonetheless, strongly influence behavior. "Whether a role is formal and written, or emerges from informal interaction with others," these factors influence workers' attitudes and behavior.

Most organizational tasks are performed in *relationship with others*. Among the most powerful organizational relationships are the groups that form either as project teams or social entities. Group *norms*, like individual roles, govern expectations about such things as how much to produce, how to interact with management, how to treat others, and even how to dress. "When a member does not conform to a group's norms, increased interaction is addressed to that person in an attempt to bring him or her into line; if that fails, the group gradually ignores the person."

Rewards help govern and encourage performance. "It is not exactly startling news that people tend to do what they are rewarded for, although organizations sometimes have difficulty implementing that truth." Although no single reward system works for everyone and different organizations utilize vastly different reward systems, the best systems are those that take as many abilities and preferences into account as possible while maintaining optimal performance in pursuit of organizational goals.

The *rites* of an organization are its routines, rituals—the way it does things. Should one simply follow orders, or should you challenge an illogical or unfair idea or decision? Is leadership rigidly hierarchical, or is management's role downplayed? Do Friday afternoon beer-busts serve to reinforce informal connections, or do co-workers rarely socialize?

INDIVIDUAL R FACTORS

Individual R factors relate primarily to an individual's personality. They include *recall, reach, reasoning, repetition and reconciliation-of-self.*

Recall of one's past experiences strongly influences how one acts in an organizational situation. Experience provides the skills that people use in their jobs and in navigating the workplace social environment.

Reach refers to a person's goals, values and beliefs. Goals—both realistic and unrealistic—motivate people to perform. All organizational behavior is goal-driven.

In contrast to goals, values are beliefs about what is important in life; much more fundamental than goals, they often take the form of ultimately "unobtainable" goals. "Because values are global, they can easily conflict with one's specific goals. This clash creates tensions within the person; how the tensions are resolved helps to shape the person and may result in alteration of either the goals or values."

Beliefs, on the other hand, make it possible for us to function by providing a set of guidelines within which we experiment and learn. "In general, people act on their beliefs as if they were true." If Kim, a manager, believes, for example, that all the other managers in the division would walk over their own mother to get ahead, Kim is likely to be on guard when dealing with them. Indeed, she may take any opportunity to disparage them as a defensive tactic against their "aggressiveness." Kim then fulfils her own prophecy. They become increasingly hostile in response to their own perception that Kim is a vicious competitor. Hence, Kim's suspicions are validated.

Many aspects of behavior are habitual. Habits develop over time in response to the successes elicited by the behaviors either now or in the past. Some habits are harmless, some simply interesting, some annoying. "Based on early experiences, managers develop favored ways of dealing with sticky situations which they automatically repeat in vaguely similar situations . . . even when the behavior is essentially ineffective."

Though they can act as seperate elements, Individual R factors also interact with one another. Together, they make up a person's self-concept (*reconciliation-of-self*). "The goals, values, and beliefs arising from experience converge to form a view of self that in turn shapes behavior. Once such a self-concept is formed, people strive to maintain that concept by engaging in behavior consistent with it." Thus, an ambitious person would be willing to confront a boss perceived as an obstacle to career advancement, while an inexperienced and powerless person likely will tolerate managerial ineptness. The most useful thing to remember about *reconciliation-of-self* is that when viewed from within, behavior almost always makes sense at the time.

QUANTITATIVE TOOLS

Success and failure of a business inevitably comes down to numbers. "Numbers are the fundamental language of business. . . . The bottom line on the income statement is a number. Efficiency on the production line is expressed numerically . . . Executives and managers stand to gain significantly from knowing that many of their real-world problems can be solved with tools that work with numbers, the tools of quantitative methods." Some of these quantitative methods and applications include:

1) Statistical estimation and quality control

2) Regression analysis as a tool for explaining statistical associations

3) Statistical forecasting

4) Decision analysis

5) Operations research

II. THE FUNCTIONS OF A BUSINESS

THE ROLE OF ACCOUNTING IN BUSINESS

There are two functions of accounting: *control* and *planning.* The *control* function is intended "to make those placed in authority and given the responsibility over resources accountable to the people they serve." Accounting and auditing ar the tools to measure and improve control. "Accounting provides the scorecard, and auditing is designed to ensure that the scorecard is correct."

Planning helps determine how much inventory to purchase, when to make the purchase, how much to invest and where, and deals with such matters as consolidation and divestiture. The analysis of financial statements (balance sheets, income statements, cash flow statements, and auditors' reports) is particularly important. These documents supply useful guidelines for reaching financial decisions. Hard figures also aid in making accurate analyses and in determining both liquidity and profitability. (The book offers various "tests" that can be used to derive decision-making numbers—specifically "percentage of sales" and "return on investment"—that will bring about more sound business decisions.)

BECOMING A MARKET-DRIVEN COMPANY

"Marketing" relates to a plethora of business functions: production, finance, research, advertising, etc., all key components of any company. "Marketing's essential responsibility is to create customers—just as production creates products." The marketing executive must use an assortment of tools to create an effective marketing strategy. These tools are known as "the marketing mix"—the manager's blueprint for action.

A difference exists between a *market-driven* company and a *marketing* company. The first tries to provide what the buyer wants; the second tries to sell what it already makes. In marketing, the goal is to sell a product or service; it's that simple. In a *market-driven* company, however, "everyone shares a common mission: The customer comes first," which means that all company activities are customer-driven. In such companies, "the mission is clear and shared by all."

THE STRATEGIC USE OF INFORMATION TECHNOLOGY

"The current and potential impact of information technology on the economy is driven home by the observation that in 1983 . . . the information processing industry revenues were a staggering $200 billion, which made it the second largest industry in the United States after oil . . . " Inevitably, the impact of information technology on all business operations will increase substantially.

There is a critical link between (1) the information available to a company, (2) the information it is able to gather and use, and (3) its ability to succeed in an information-driven economy.

THE ROLE OF BUSINESS IN A DEMOCRATIC SOCIETY

Society has long thought of business enterprises as instruments for *creating wealth,* "but only recently have they come to be thought of as having the equally important social function of *distributing wealth.*" Companies distribute wealth in many ways, primarily by paying wages, salaries and dividends. Work alone creates wealth; all other ways of distributing wealth consume it.

"Participation implies democracy." One of the most important changes taking place in business is employee participation in the corporate decision-making process.

The essence of democracy is the absence of an ultimate authority. Democracy requires that anyone who has authority over others be subject to their collective authority, a principle called the "circularity of power." This requirement is met by a *circular organizational structure,* one in which each person in a position of authority belongs to a "management board." Each management board consists of at least a manager, the manager's immediate supervisor, and the manager's immediate subordinates. This opens each manager to input both from above *and* below. The net benefit to the organization is two-fold: a reduction in miscommunication, and an increase in the flow of useful information.

ONE UP ON WALL STREET

by Peter Lynch, Simon and Schuster, New York, N.Y., 1989

This acclaimed personal investment guide, written by one of America's top money managers, offers some unique and effective strategies for using what you already know about finance to make money in the stock market.

PART I: PREPARING TO INVEST

While completing a college internship, Peter Lynch made what to him was a startling discovery: traditional business-school teachings aren't of much use when it comes to picking a good stock—in fact, some of them "could only help you fail."

"Wall Street thinks just as the [ancient] Greeks did . . . [Philosophers] used to sit around for days and debate how many teeth a horse has. They thought they could figure it out by just sitting there, instead of checking the horse. A lot of investors sit around and debate whether a stock is going up, as if the financial muse will give them the answer, instead of checking the company." Yet " . . . it's very hard to support the popular academic theory that the market is irrational when you know somebody who just made a twentyfold profit in Kentucky Fried Chicken, and . . . who explained in advance why the stock was going to rise."

Lynch goes out of his way to underscore again and again that there is nothing "mystical" about selecting which stock to invest in. Good stock is "good" only because the particular company offers a good product, is well-managed, and is doing good business. The list of companies meeting these simple criteria is endless: *Subaru, Toys "R" Us, 7-Eleven, Circle K . . .* Equally endless is the list of companies that may have had an excellent product or service, yet were poorly managed or simply didn't have the foresight to plan for the future. Along with their profit margins, their stock prices—very predictably—soon dropped out of sight.

The real joy in buying stocks is in consistently picking "tenbaggers"—underappreciated and/or undervalued stocks that increase ten times or more in value, not over a period of twenty years, but in five years or less. Lynch points out that this is not an unusual occurrence and that as a small investor you have definite advantages over the conventional professional—if along the way you apply some research and common sense. "With every spectacular stock I've managed to ferret out," he avers, "the virtues seemed so obvious that if 100 professionals had been free to add it to their portfolios, I'm convinced that 99 would have done so. But," Lynch adds, " . . . there are simply too many obstacles between them and the tenbaggers."

Under the current system, a stock isn't truly attractive until a number of large institutions have recognized its suitability, and an equal number of respected Wall Street analysts (the same researchers who track the individual industries) have put it on the "recommended" list. With so many experts waiting for other experts to make the first move, it's amazing that anything ever gets bought. "Every year . . . thousands of experts study overbought indicators, oversold indicators, head-and-shoulder patterns, put call ratios . . . foreign investment, the movement of the constellations through the heavens, and the moss on oak trees, and they can't predict markets with any useful consistency, any more than the gizzard squeezers

could tell the Roman emperors when the Huns would attack."

Lynch uses prominent examples to point out how relatively few brokers are truly aware of the nuts and bolts of picking good stocks:

* *Dunkin' Donuts,* between 1977 and 1986, was a 25-bagger (in other words, during that time its stock value rose a whopping 2500%). But even today only two major firms follow *Dunkin's* ups and downs—and neither of these analysts showed the slightest interest at all five years ago.

" . . . Contrast [this and numerous other examples]," Lynch dares his reader, "with the fifty-six brokerage analysts who normally cover *IBM* or the forty-four who cover *Exxon.*" In fact there's an unwritten rule on Wall Street: "You'll never lose your job losing your client's money in IBM." The thinking goes that " . . . if IBM goes bad and you bought it, the clients and the bosses will ask: 'What's wrong with that damn IBM lately?' But if La Quinta Motor Inns goes bad, they'll ask: 'What's wrong with you?'"

As a private investor, however, you are not obliged to answer to a boss; and you are not forced to spend 25% of your time answering to a corporate investor. "If no company seems attractive on the fundamentals, you can . . . wait for a better opportunity . . . Most important, you can find terrific opportunities in the neighborhood or at the workplace, months or even years before the news has reached the analysts and the fund managers they advise . . . "

Historically, stockmarket investments have been much more profitable than any other investment vehicle. "Since 1927, common stocks have recorded gains of 9.8 percent a year on average, as compared to 5 percent for corporate bonds, 4.4 percent for government bonds, and 3.4 percent for Treasury bills . . . The real return on Treasury bills, known as the most conservative and sensible of all places to put money, has been nil. That's right. Zippo."

Lynch admits that any investment carries with it some risk, and that some are more risky than others. But—even in Las Vegas and at the track—there are those who consistently win:

Once the unsettling act of the risk in money is accepted, we can begin to separate gambling from investing not by the type of activity (buying bonds, buying stocks, betting on the horses, etc.) but by the skill, dedication, and enterprise of the participant. To a veteran handicapper with the discipline to stick to a system, betting on horses offers a relatively secure long-term return, which to him has been as reliable as owning a mutual fund or shares in General Electric. Meanwhile, to the rash and impetuous stockpicker who chases hot tips and rushes in and out of his equities, an "investment" in stocks is no more reliable than throwing away paychecks on the horse with the prettiest mane, or the jockey with the purple silks . . .

PART II: PICKING WINNERS

The best place to begin looking for the tenbagger is close to home—if not in the backyard then down at the shopping mall, and especially wherever you happen to work. With most of the tenbaggers already mentioned . . . the first signs of success were apparent at hundreds of locations across the country . . . The customers in central Ohio where Kentucky Fried Chicken first opened ... the mob down at Pic 'N' Save ... all had a chance to say, "This is great; I wonder about the stock," long before Wall Street got its original clue ... You don't necessarily have to know anything about a company for its stock to go up. But the important point is that (1) the oil experts, on average, are in a better position than doctors to decide when to buy or to sell [oil stock]; and (2) the doctors, on average, know better than oil experts when to invest in a successful drug. The person with the edge is always in a position to out-guess the person without an edge ...

By whatever means a potentially good stock has just come to your attention—"whether via the office, the shopping mall, something you ate ... "—now what?

Now hold on for a minute, says Lynch. The mere existence of a great new product or service is *not* necessarily a signal to buy. "Just because Dunkin' Donuts is always crowded or Reynolds Metals has more aluminum orders than it can handle doesn't mean you ought to own the stock. Not yet. What you've got so far is simply a lead to a story that has to be developed."

Thus, Lynch unfolds his **Thirteen Characteristics of the Perfect Company:**

1. It sounds dull—or, even better, ridiculous

"*Pep Boys—Manny, Moe, and Jack* is the most promising name I've ever heard. It's better than dull, it's ridiculous ... What Wall Street analyst or portfolio manager in his right mind would recommend a stock called *Pep Boys—Manny, Moe, and Jack*—unless of course the Street already realizes how profitable it is, and by then it's up tenfold already."

2. It does something dull

"I get even more excited when a company with a boring name also does something boring. *Crown, Cork, and Seal* makes cans and bottle caps. What could be duller than that? You won't see an interview with [its] CEO in **Time** magazine alongside an interview with Lee Iacocca, but that's a plus. There's nothing boring about what's happened to the shares of *Crown, Cork, and Seal*."

3. It does something disagreeable

"Better than boring alone is a stock that's boring and disgusting at the same time ... Take Safety-Kleen. Safety-Kleen goes around to all the gas stations and provides them with a machine that washes greasy auto parts. This saves auto mechanics the time and trouble of scrubbing the parts by hand in a pail of gasoline, and gas stations gladly pay for the service."

4. It's a spinoff

"Large parent companies do not want to spin off divisions and then see those spinoffs get into trouble, because that would bring embarrassing publicity that would reflect back on the parents. Therefore, the spinoffs normally have strong balance sheets and are well-prepared to succeed as independent entities."

5. The institutions don't own it, and the analysts don't follow it

"If you find a stock with little or no institutional ownership, you've found a potential winner. Find a company that no analyst has ever visited, or that no analyst would admit to knowing about, and you've got a double winner."

6. The rumors abound: It's involved with toxic waste and/or the Mafia

"It's hard to think of a more perfect industry than waste management ... That's why I got very excited one day when the solid waste executives showed up in my office. They had come to town for a solid waste convention complete with booths and slides—imagine how attractive that must have been. Anyway, instead of the usual blue cotton button-down shirts that I see day after day, they were wearing polo shirts that said `Solid Waste.' ... These are the kind of executives you dream about ... As you already know if you were fortunate enough to have bought some, *Waste Management, Inc.* is up about a hundredfold."

7. There's something depressing about it

"In this category my favorite all-time pick is *Service Corporation International* (SCI), which also has a boring name ... Now, if there's anything Wall Street would rather ignore besides toxic waste, it's mortality. And SCI does burials."

8. It's a no-growth industry

"Many people prefer to invest in a high-growth industry, where there's a lot of sound and fury. Not me. I prefer to invest in a low-growth industry like plastic knives and forks ... In a no-growth industry ... there's no problem with competition. ... SCI already owns 5 percent of the nation's funeral homes, and there's nothing stopping them from owning 10 percent or 15 percent."

9. It's got a niche

"I'd much rather own a local rock pit than own *Twentieth Century-Fox*, because a movie company competes with other movie companies, and the rock pit has a niche. *Twentieth Century-Fox* understood that when it bought up Pebble Beach, and the rock pit with it."

10. People have to keep buying it

"I'd rather invest in a company that makes drugs, soft drinks, razor blades, or cigarettes than in a company that makes toys. In the toy industry somebody can make a wonderful doll that every child has to have, but every child gets only one each."

11. It's a user of technology

"Instead of investing in computer companies that struggle to survive in an endless price war, why not invest in a company that benefits from the price war—such as *Automatic Data Processing?* As computers get cheaper, *Automatic Data* can do its job cheaper and thus increase its own profits."

12. The insiders are buying

"There's no better tip-off to the probable success of a stock than that people in the company are putting their own money into it."

13. The company is buying back shares

"Buying back shares is the simplest and best way a company can reward its investors. If a company has faith in its own future, then why shouldn't it invest in itself, just as the shareholders do?"

Lynch discusses many more criteria and methods to use in determining stocks that might make worthwhile investments. "All you have to do is put as much effort into picking your stocks as you do into buying your groceries."

COMPACT
Classics®

LIBRARY #7: More Quotes & Anecdotes

Quotes & Anecdotes
(Character, Integrity, Virtue and Vice, Spirituality)

An ethical man is a Christian holding four aces.
-*Mark Twain*

What is moral is what you feel good after.
-*Ernest Hemingway*

I am responsible for what I did, not guilty.
-*Larry Gitlin*

Morality is suspecting other people of not being legally married.
-*George Bernard Shaw*

Morality is the theory that every human act must be either right or wrong, and ninety-nine percent of them are wrong.
-*H.L. Mencken*

When choosing between two evils, I always like to try the one I've never tried before.
-*Mae West*

How easy it is to be virtuous when we have no inclination to be otherwise.
-*Dolf Wyllarde*

What is morality in any given time or place? It is what the majority then and there happen to like—and immorality is what they dislike.
-*Alfred North Whitehead*

First secure an independent income, then practice virtue.
-*Greek Proverb*

I would much rather be the man who bought the Brooklyn Bridge than the man who sold it.
-*Will Rogers*

If facts do not conform to theory, they must be disposed of.
-*N. R. F. Maier*

Walk groundly, talk profoundly, drink roundly, sleep soundly.
-*William Hazlitt*

I would not like to be a political leader in Russia. They never know when they're being taped.
-*Richard Nixon*

An ambassador is an honest man sent abroad to lie for his country.
-*Henry Wotton*

Nothing which is morally wrong can ever be politically right.
-*Anonymous*

Character is destiny.
-*Heraclitus*

Dignity does not consist in possessing honors, but in deserving them.
-*Aristotle*

It is better to deserve honors and not have them than to have them and not deserve them.
-*Mark Twain*

A man should endeavor to be as pliant as a reed, yet as hard as cedar-wood.
-*The Talmud*

Everyone is the son of his own works.
-*Cervantes*

Clear conscience never fears midnight knocking.
-*Chinese Proverb*

A man without ethics is a wild beast loosed upon this world.
-*Manly P. Hall*

Give the investigators an hors d'oeuvre and maybe they won't come back for the main course.
-*Richard M. Nixon*

Reputation is what men and women think of us; character is what God and angels know of us.
-*Thomas Paine*

Talent is nurtured in solitude; character is formed in the stormy billows of the world.
-*Goethe*

Man consists of two parts: essence and personality. Essence in man is what is his own. Personality in man is what is "not his own." "Not his own" means what has come from outside, what he has learned, or reflects, all traces of exterior impressions left in the memory and in the sensations, all words and movements that have been learned, all feelings created by imitation.
-*Gurdjieff*

Many individuals have, like uncut diamonds, shining qualities beneath a rough exterior.
-*Juvenal*

Life every man holds dear; but the dear man holds honor far more precious—dearer than life.
-*Shakespeare*

The discipline of desire is the background of character.
-*John Locke*

Honor is like an island, rugged and without shores; we can never re-enter it once we are on the outside.
-*Nicholas Boileau*

It is in men, as in soils, where sometimes there is a vein of gold which the owner knows not.

-Jonathan Swift

The integrity of men is to be measured by their conduct, not by their professions.

-Junius

Action, looks, words, steps, form the alphabet by which you may spell character.

-Lavater

A man never shows his own character so plainly as by his manner of portraying another's

-Richter

Our own heart, and not other men's opinion, form our true honor.

-Samuel Coleridge

Reputation is only a . . . candle, of wavering and uncertain flame, and easily blown out, but it is the light by which the world looks for and finds merit.

-James Lowell

If you create an act, you create a habit. If you create a habit, you create a character. If you create a character, you create a destiny.

-Andre Maurois

He that always gives way to others will end in having no principles of his own.

-Aesop

Men of principle are always bold, but those who are bold are not always men of principle.

-Confucius

What are our natural principles except our accustomed principles? And in children, those that they have received from the custom of their fathers, as the chase in animals. A different custom will give other natural principles.

-Blaise Pascal

Every honest man will suppose honest acts to flow from honest principles, and the rogues may rail without intermission.

-Thomas Jefferson

Important principles may and must be flexible.

-Abraham Lincoln

In law, a man is guilty when he violates the rights of another. In ethics he is guilty if he only thinks of doing so.

-Immanuel Kant

I have but one system of ethics for men and for nations—to be grateful, to be faithful to all engagements and under all circumstances, to be open and generous, promoting in the long run even the interests of both.

-Thomas Jefferson

The aim of ethics is to render scientific—i.e. true and as far as possible systematic—the apparent cognitions that most men have of the rightness or reasonableness of conduct be considered as right in itself, or as the means to some end conceived as ultimately reasonable.

-Henry Sidgwick

Ethical systems are roughly distinguishable according as they take for their cardinal ideas 1) the character of the agent; 2) the nature of the motive; 3) the quality of his deeds; and 4) the results.

-Herbert Spencer

Character, in great and little things, means carrying through what you feel able to do.

-Goethe

Honor is the inner garment of the Soul, the first thing put on by it with the flesh, and the last it layeth down at its separation from it.

-Akhenaton

We are usually mistaken in esteeming men too much; rarely in esteeming them too little.

-Stanislaus Leszynski

Sometimes we may learn more from a man's errors than from his virtues.

-Henry W. Longfellow

Ethics is the art of living well and happily.

-Henry More

Integrity without knowledge is weak and useless, and knowledge without integrity is dangerous and dreadful.

-Samuel Johnson

Honest men fear neither the light nor the dark.

-Thomas Fuller

I do not remember in my whole life I ever willfully misrepresented anything to anybody at any time. I have never knowingly had connection with a fraudulent scheme.

-J. Pierpont Morgan

The natural man has a difficult time getting along in this world. Half the people think he is a scoundrel because he is not a hypocrite.

-E. W. Howe

Mine honor is my life; both grow in one;
Take honor from me and my life is done.

-William Shakespeare

An ill deed cannot bring honor.

-George Herbert

Whoever would not die to preserve his honor would be infamous.

-Blaise Pascal

The louder he talked of his honor, the faster we counted our spoons.
-Ralph W. Emerson

Be honorable yourself if you wish to associate with honorable people.
-Welsh Proverb

A little integrity is better than any career.
-Ralph W. Emerson

Men are generally more pleased with a widespread than with a great reputation.
-Pliny the Younger

The blaze of a reputation cannot be blown out, but it often dies in the socket.
-Samuel Johnson

I am accounted by some people a good man. How cheap that character is acquired! Pay your debts, don't borrow money, nor twist your kitten's neck off, nor disturb a congregation, etc. your business is done, I know things of myself, which would make every friend I have fly from me as a plague patient.
-Charles Lamb

To enjoy and give enjoyment, without injury to yourself or others: this is true morality.
-Nicolas Chamfort

The notion of morals implies some sentiment common to all mankind, which recommends the same object to general approbation, and makes every man, or most men, agree in the same opinion or decision concerning it.
-David Hume

One should not destroy an insect, one should not quarrel with a dog, without a reason sufficient to vindicate one through all the courts of morality.
-William Shenstone

Morality is simply the attitude we adopt toward people whom we personally dislike.
-Oscar Wilde

Morality turns on whether the pleasure precedes or follows the pain. Thus it is immoral to get drunk because the headache comes after the drinking, but if the headache came first, and the drunkenness afterwards, it would be moral to get drunk.
-Samuel Butler

All moral laws are merely statements that certain kinds of actions will have good effects.
-G. E. Moore

It is not surprising that lambs should bear a grudge against birds of prey, but that is no reason for blaming birds of prey for pouncing on lambs.
-F. Nietzche

Righteousness exalteth a nation.
-The Bible, Proverbs 14:34

Our ideas of right and wrong are simple ideas, and must therefore be ascribed to some power of immediate perception in the human mind. He that doubts this need only try to give definitions of them which shall amount to more than synonymous expressions.
-Richard Price

One man in the right will finally get to be a majority.
-R. G. Ingersoll

If it be right to me, it is right.
-Max Stirner

The principles which men profess on any controverted subject are usually a very incomplete exponent of the opinions they really hold.
-John S. Mill

He who governs himself according to what he calls his principles may be punished either by one party or the other for those very principles. He who proceeds without principle, as chance, timidity, or self-preservation directs, will not perhaps fare better; but he will be less blamed.
-St. John de Crèvecoeur

I have never lived on principles. When I have had to act, I never first asked myself on what principles I was going to act, but I went at it and did what I thought fit. I have often reproached myself for my want of principle.
-Otto von Bismarck

I believe long habits of virtue have a sensible effect on the countenance.
-Benjamin Franklin

We seldom speak of the virtue which we have, but much oftener of that which we lack.
-Oliver Goldsmith

To be proud of virtue is to poison yourself with the antidote.
-Benjamin Franklin

A man has virtues enough if he deserves pardon for his faults on account of them.
-G. C. Lichtenberg

The lion and the calf shall lie down together, but the calf won't get much sleep.
-Woody Allen

The only complete love is for God. The goal is to love everyone equally, but it doesn't necessarily work out that way.
-George Harrison

I don't see myself as a preacher on television at all . . . I see myself as a doctor in an emergency ward, and those people who are flipping their dials are in pain and dying . . . I heal through offering what America needs on TV—a philosophy of self-esteem that will make us great once more.

-Dr. Robert Schuller

Americans are so tense and keyed up that it is impossible even to put them to sleep with a sermon.

-Norman Vincent Peale

The Christian life is not a way *out* but a way *through* life.

-Rev. Billy Graham

Had I gone my own way and not gotten to know God or accepted Him as a part of my life, I think that I would have been a very belligerent individual, full of hate and bitterness.

-Anita Bryant

In our era, the road to holiness necessarily passes through the world of action.

-Dag Hammarskjöld

The difference between the pessimist and the cynic is that the pessimist carries on the losing battle against life in his own soul, while the cynic tries to wage the battle in someone else's soul.

-Fulton J. Sheen

A real Christian is a person who can give his pet parrot to the town gossip.

-Rev. Billy Graham

When you break the big laws, you do not get liberty; you do not even get anarchy. You get the small laws.

-G. K. Chesterson

Civilization begins with order, grows with liberty, and dies with chaos.

-Will Durant

Wealth consists not in having great possessions, but in having few wants.

-Epicurus

Every man is rich or poor according to the proportion between his desires and his enjoyments.

-Samuel Johnson

It is far more easy to acquire fortune like a knave than to expend it like a gentleman.

-Colton

In this world, it is not what we take up, but what we give up, that makes us rich.

-Beecher

Arrogance is a mixture of impertinence, disobedience, indiscipline, rudeness, harshness and a self-assertive nature.

-Sivananda

We rise in glory as we sink in pride.

-Young

Pride is increased by ignorance; those assume the most who know the least.

-Gay

He that falls in love with himself will have no rivals.

-Benjamin Franklin

Small things make base men proud.

-William Shakespeare

Let another praise you, and not your own mouth; a stranger, and not your own lips.

-Proverbs

Power corrupts the few, while weakness corrupts the many.

-Eric Hoffer

The measure of a man is what he does with power.

-Pittacus

There are two perfect men: one dead, and the other unborn.

-Chinese Proverb

When a wise man is advised of his errors, he will reflect on and improve his conduct. When his misconduct is pointed out, a foolish man will not only disregard the advice but rather repeat the same error.

-Buddha

Those who wish to appear wise among fools, among the wise seem foolish.

-Quintilian

Every good act is charity. A man's true wealth hereafter is the good that he does in this world to his fellows.

-Mohammed

Kindness is a language which the deaf can hear and the blind can read.

-Mark Twain

Wherever there is a human being there is an opportunity for a kindness.

-Seneca

Confidence in the goodness of another is good proof of one's own goodness.

-Montaigne

I have found men more kind than I expected, and less just.

-Samuel Johnson

No good book, or good thing of any sort, shows its best face at first.

-Thomas Carlyle

PEOPLE

Quotes & Anecdotes
(Human Nature, Man and Animal, Humanity, The Essence of Life)

In spite of everything, I still believe that people are really good at heart.
-Anne Frank

Once the king of Denmark was asked by the Nazis to establish anti-Jewish legislation. He refused, saying, "But you see, there isn't any Jewish problem here. We do not consider ourselves inferior to them."
-Christian X, King of Denmark

The closest to perfection a person ever comes is when he fills out a job application form.
-Stanley J. Randall

The more I see of man, the more I like dogs.
Mme. de Staël

I think, somehow, we learn who we really are and then live with that decision.
-Eleanor Roosevelt

Society is always taken by surprise at any new example of common sense.
-Ralph Waldo Emerson

It is impossible in a democratic comity to think of a single measure for the improvement of social well-being which is not subject to subversion by ill-conceived minority or even majority pressures.
-John Kenneth Galbraith

In Genesis it says that it is not good for man to be alone, but sometimes it's a great relief.
-John Barrymore

O God, make the bad people good, and the good people nice.
-Anonymous

Sir George Mellish was one of the great jurists of England. As a member of the committee appointed to draw up resolutions of congratulations to the Queen, he discovered that his colleagues had begun one resolution with the words, "Being conscious as we are of our own defects . . ."

"No, no," said Judge Mellish, "that will never do. We must not lie to her Majesty. Change it to, 'Being conscious as we are of one another's defects . . .'"

Most people are about as happy as they make up their minds to be.
-Abraham Lincoln

If we could trace our descendants, we should find all slaves to come from princes, and all princes from slaves.
-Seneca

When two people meet, there are really six people present. There is each man as he

sees himself, each man as the other person sees him, and each man as he really is
-William James

Every man has three characters—that which he exhibits, that which he has, and that which he thinks he has.
-Alphonse Karr

If you cannot get rid of the family skeleton, you may as well make it dance.
-George Bernard Shaw

We usually see only the things we are looking for—so much so that we sometimes see them where they are not.
-Eric Hoffer

No two men are alike, and both of them are happy for it.
-Morris Mandel

How a person masters his fate is more important than what his fate is.
-Wilhelm von Humboldt

It's human nature to keep doing something as long as it's pleasurable and you can succeed at it—which is why the world population continues to double every 40 years.
-Peter Lynch

There's men all over . . . blaming on his boots the faults of his feet.
-Samuel Beckett, Waiting for Godot

It's easy to make a buck. It's a lot tougher to make a difference.
-Tom Brokaw

We are all mortal until the first kiss and the second glass of wine.
-Eduardo Galeano

It is not the mountain we conquer but ourselves.
-Sir Edmund Hillary

I don't love humanity. I don't hate them either. I just don't know them personally.
-Alan Arkin

People are too good for this world.
-Kurt Vonnegut, Jr.

Although the world is very full of suffering, it is also full of the overcoming of it.
-Helen Keller

The poor may inherit the earth, but it will appear that the rich . . . will inherit the church.
-Rev. James A. Pike

People have to make themselves predictable, because otherwise the machines get angry and kill them.
-Gregory Bateson

It should be possible to explain the laws of physics to a barmaid.

-Albert Einstein

Humanity is acquiring the right technology for all the wrong reasons.

-R. Buckminster Fuller

Man has lost the capacity to foresee and to forestall, and he will end up destroying the earth.

-Albert Schweitzer

Society does not understand nature.

-R. B. Fuller

We can destroy ourselves by cynicism and disillusion, just as effectively as by bombs.

-Kenneth Clark

To have arrived on this earth as the product of a biological accident, only to depart through human arrogance, would be the ultimate irony.

-Richard Leakey

We should now give some real thought to the possibility of reforming our technology in the direction of smallness, simplicity, and nonviolence.

-E. F. Schumacher

Civilization can be defined at once by the basic questions it asks and by those it does not ask.

-André Malraux

What I want is some assurance before I die that the human race will be allowed to continue.

-Bertrand Russell

Life is bliss; no person need suffer anymore.

-Maharishi Mahesh Yogi

Every soul speaks the same language. Know that language of love which swells within the human temple.

-Maharaj Ji

Those who say life is worth living at any cost have already written for themselves an epitaph of infamy, for there is no cause and no person they will not betray to stay alive.

-Sidney Hook

It does not do to leave a dragon out of your calculations, if you live near him.

-J. R. R. Tolkien

It is better to be a live jackal than a dead lion—for jackals, not men.

-Sidney Hook

The game is not about becoming somebody, it's about becoming nobody.

-Baba Dam Rass

It is easier to love humanity as a whole than to love one's neighbor.

-Eric Hoffer

Hell is—other people.

-Jean-Paul Sartre

From family to nation, every human group is a society of island universes.

-Aldous Huxley

The faces of men, while sheep in credulity, are wolves for conformity.

-Carl Van Doren

We must have respect for both our plumbers and our philosophers or neither our pipes or our theories will hold water.

-John W. Gardner

One man's taboo is another man's charisma.

-Herman Kahn

Charisma means looking like everyone else.

-Marshall MacLuhan

Man is unique among animals in his practiced ability to know things that are not so.

-Philip Slater

When wisdom and sagacity rise, there are great hypocrites.

-R. D. Laing

Passionate hatred can give meaning and purpose to an empty life.

-Eric Hoffer

Sport is a product of human culture. America seems to need football at this stage of our social development. When you get ninety million people watching a single game on television, it . . . shows you that people need something to identify with.

-Joe Paterno

All men's gains are the fruit of venturing.

-Herodotus

The way of heaven is to diminish the prosperous and augment the needy. The superior man gains without boasting.

-I Ching

. . . Our days upon earth are a shadow.

-Bildad the Shuhite, The Bible, Job 8:9

Life is easy to live for a man who is without shame, bold after the fashion of a crow, a mischief-maker, an insulting, arrogant, and dissolute fellow.

But life is hard to live for a modest man, who is free from attachment, unassuming, spotless, and of clear vision.

-The Dhammapada

If you live according to nature, you never will be poor; if according to the world's caprice, you will never be rich.

-Seneca

We are always beginning to live, but are never living.

-Manilius

All that is alive tends toward color, individuality, specificity, effectiveness, and opacity.

All that is done in life inclines toward knowledge, abstraction, generality, transfiguration, and transparency.

-Goethe

At birth we come
At death we go
Bearing nothing.

-Chinese Proverb

Whosoever knows others is clever.
Whosoever knows himself is wise.
Whosoever conquers others has force.
Whosoever conquers himself is strong.
Whosoever asserts himself has will-power.
Whosoever is contented is rich.
Whosoever does not lose his place has duration.
Whosoever does not perish in death lives.

-Lao-Tzu

Man is a microcosm, or little world, as possessing in miniature all the qualities found on a great scale in the Universe; by his reason and intelligence partaking of the Divine nature; and by his faculty of changing aliments into other substances, of growing, and reproducing himself, partaking of elementary Nature.

-Pythagoras

No one has lived a short life who has performed his duties with unblemished character.

-Cicero

A well-written life is almost as rare as a well-spent one.

-Thomas Carlyle

Life is what we make it, and the world is what we make it. The eyes of the cheerful and of the melancholy man are fixed upon the same creation; but very different are the aspects which it bears to them.

-Albert Pike

A good man doubles the length of his existence; to have lived so as to look back with pleasure on our past existence is to live twice.

-Martial

The good life is the healthful life, the merry life. Life is health, joy, laughter.

-Jean Bodin

Every man's life is a fairy tale, written by God's fingers.

-Hans Christian Andersen

Human affairs are like a chess game: only those who do not take it seriously can be called good players.

-Hung Tzu'cheng

We should live as though our life would be both long and short.

-Bias

It is impossible to live pleasurably without living prudently, honorably, and justly; or to live prudently, honorably, and justly, without living pleasurably.

-Epicurus

Enter by the narrow gate; for the gate is wide and the way is easy, that leads to destruction, and those who enter by it are many. For the gate is narrow and the way is hard, that leads to life, and those who find it are few.

-Jesus Christ

This span of life was lent for lofty duties, not for selfishness; not to be wiled away for aimless dreams, but to improve ourselves, and serve mankind.

-Aubrey De Vere

The great use of life is to spend it for something that will outlast it.

-William James

In spite of chain-smoking Pall Malls since I was fourteen, I think my wind is still good enough for me to go chasing after happiness.

-Kurt Vonnegut, Jr.

We have to face the fact that one day humanity will disappear. There is no escaping that fact. The question is, when?

-Richard Leakey

It's a very selfish decade. It's all me. People who experienced profound disappointment trying to change the system are juggling and growing vegetables and concentrating on brightening their corner of the world.

-Tom Hayden

I take a tremendous amount of vitamins, which includes a giant Swiss pill each morning, and six protein-rich pony pills—what's good for a horse is good for people.

-Diana Vreeland

The body is a test tube. You have to put in exactly the right ingredients to get the best reaction out of it.

-Jack Youngblood

Men of the future—perhaps very soon—can live as fishes!

-Jacques Cousteau

As for man . . . he doesn't even consider himself an animal—which, considering the way he considers them, is probably, all things considered, the only considerate thing about him.

-Cleveland Amory

If it weren't for people, life wouldn't be quite so interesting.

On the other hand, if it weren't for life, people wouldn't be quite so interesting, either.

-Dave Allhargen

Some people say man is the most dangerous animal on the planet. Obviously those people have never met an angry cat.

-Lillian Johnson

Very few animals sing in the shower, but those that do can be assured of a strong voice and a sweet smell.

-K. Kirkhauer

Life is an error-making and an error-correcting process, and nature in marking man's papers will grade him for wisdom as measured both by survival and by the quality of life of those who survive.

-Jonas Salk

Unfortunately, unlike bones, behavior does not become fossilized.

-Richard Leakey

The ordinary affairs of men proceed if they do not always progress.

-Eric Sevareid

The danger of the past was that men became slaves. The danger of the future is that men may become robots.

-Erich Fromm

All things are already complete in us. There is no greater delight than to be conscious of right within us. If one strives to treat others as he would be treated by them, he shall not fail to come near the perfect life.

-Mencius

Excellence when concealed, differs but little from buried worthlessness.

-Horace

Those who attain to any excellence commonly spend life in some one single pursuit, for excellence is not often gained upon easier terms.

-Samuel Johnson

To feel much for others and little for ourselves; to restrain our selfishness and exercise our benevolent affections, constitute the perfection of human nature.

-Adam Smith

The seed of God is in us. Given an intelligent and hard-working farmer, it will thrive and grow up to God, whose seed it is; and accordingly its fruits will be God-natured. Pear seeds grow into pear trees, nut seeds into nut trees, and a God seed into God.

-Meister Eckhart

Everybody who lives, dies. But not everybody who dies has lived.

-Dhaggi Ramanashi

There is beauty in everybody. You are born with it. It's just a matter of what you do with it, and if you lose it, it's like losing your soul.

-Francesco Scavullo

Most of God's children are, in fact, barely presentable. The most common error made in matters of appearance is the belief that one should disdain the superficial and let the true beauty of one's soul shine through. If there are places on your body where this is a possibility, you are not attractive—you are leaking.

-Fran Lebowitz

Fashionable men and women don't just put on fashionable clothes . . . The truly fashionable are beyond fashion.

-Cecil Beaton

Those who take the long view of man's experience will find that from time to time there were other societies no less honest and courageous than ours in facing all the ugliness, cruelty, and indifference the mirror reveals, but with the greater honesty still to hold the brighter, nobler view of man and with the greater courage to pursue the vision.

-Archibald Cox

MEN AND WOMEN

Quotes & Anecdotes

(Feminism, Chauvinism, Marriage, Male/Female Interaction)

I once asked a Burmese why women, after centuries of following their men, now walk ahead of them. He explained, "There are many unexploded landmines since the war."

-*Robert Mueller*

Every once in awhile, nature stops experimenting and creates a man.

-*Anonymous*

I don't mind living in a man's world, as long as I can be a woman in it.

-*Marilyn Monroe*

Until Eve arrived, this was a man's world.

-*Anonymous*

Whether women are better than men, I cannot say. But I can say they are certainly no worse.

-*Golda Meir*

I go for two kinds of men—the kind with muscles, and the kind without.

-*Mae West*

Once made equal to man, woman becomes his superior.

-*Socrates*

Life isn't fair to us men.
When we are born, our mothers get the compliments and the flowers.
When we are married, our brides get the presents and the publicity.
When we die, our widows get the life insurance and winters in Florida.
What do women want to be liberated from?

-*Anonymous*
(but allegedly written by a man)

I'm a practicing heterosexual . . . but bisexuality immediately doubles your chances for a date on Saturday night.

-*Woody Allen*

Men always fall for frigid women because they put on the best show.

-*Funny Brice*

Marriage has many pains, but celibacy has no pleasures.

-*Samuel Johnson*

A man may be a fool and not know it, but not if he is married.

-*H.L. Mencken*

Judge not a man by his clothes, but by his wife's clothes.

-*Thomas R. Dewar*

Most hierarchies were established by men who now monopolize the upper levels, thus depriving women of their rightful share of opportunities to achieve incompetence.

-*Laurence J. Peter*

We won't marry the boy with a camel,
Nor even the one with two donkeys.
We're going to marry the boy
That comes to take us away in a Mercedes.

-*African Folk Song*

It seems obvious from the start that I should use my womanness as an asset rather than a liability.

-*Estée Lauder*

While most people agree that second thoughts are always better, most women would also agree that Adam was God's first thought and Eve was His second.

-*Anonymous*

God created man, and finding him not sufficiently alone, gave him a female companion so that he might feel his solitude more acutely.

-*Paul Valèry*

Marriage is the only adventure open to the timid.

-*Voltaire*

A science career for women is now almost as acceptable as being a cheerleader.

-*Myra Barker*

Despite my thirty years of research into the feminine soul, I have not yet been able to answer . . . the great question that has never been answered: what does a woman want?

-*Sigmund Freud*

No man is as anti-feminist as a really feminine woman.

-*Frank O'Connor*

A woman once attempted to draw Sir John Mahaffy into a feminist argument saying, "You are a man. I am a woman. What is the essential difference between us?"

"Madam," he replied, "I can't conceive."

There is no female mind. The brain is not an organ of sex. As well speak of a female liver.

-*Charlotte Perkins Gilman*

Thanks to feminism, women can now acquire status in two ways: through marriage or their own achievements. Cure cancer or marry the man who does, either way society will applaud . . . It doesn't work that way for men. Wives shed no glory on their husbands. Having tea with Nancy Reagan is an honor. Having tea with Dennis Thatcher is a joke.

-*Katha Pollitt*

Boys will be boys these days and apparently, so will girls.

-Jane Howard

Most women would rather cuddle a baby than a typewriter or a machine.

-Phyllis Schlafly

I don't believe man is woman's natural enemy. Perhaps his lawyer is.

-Shana Alexander

It is a cliché of our time that women spent half a century fighting for "rights," and the next half wondering whether they wanted them after all.

-Betty Friedan

A suburban mother's role is to deliver children obstetrically once, and by car forever after.

-Peter de Vries

All human life on the planet is born of woman.

-Adrienne Rich

The woman is the fiber of the nation. She is the producer of life. A nation is only as good as its women.

-Muhammad Ali

A great philosopher once said—I think it was Henry Kissinger—nobody will ever win the battle of the sexes. There's just too much fraternizing with the enemy.

-Robert Orben

If there hadn't been women we'd still be squatting in a cave eating raw meat, because we made civilization in order to impress our girlfriends.

-Orson Welles

I do nothing that a man of unlimited funds, superb physical endurance, and maximum scientific knowledge could not do.

-Batman

[James Bond] smoked like Peter Lorre and drank like Humphrey Bogart and ate like Sydney Greenstreet and used up girls like Errol Flynn and then went out to a steam bath and came out looking like Clark Gable. It was all so reassuring that we never stopped to think that all these people are dead.

-Harry Reasoner

There's nothing so similar to one poodle dog as another poodle dog, and that goes for women, too.

-Pablo Picasso

Early to rise and early to bed makes a male healthy and wealthy and dead.

-James Thurber

The difference between men and boys is the price of their toys.

-Liberace

When I was young, I used to have successes with women because I was young. Now I have successes with women because I am old. Middle age was the hardest part.

-Arthur Rubinstein

There are three things men can do with women: love them, suffer for them, or turn them into literature.

-Stephen Stills

Girls have an unfair advantage over men: if they can't get what they want by being smart, they can get it by being dumb.

-Yul Brynner

The most important thing a man can know is that, as he approaches his own door, someone on the other side is listening for the sound of his footsteps.

-Clark Gable

Never loan "Shylock money" to a woman, because you can't beat her up to collect.

-Mafia motto

In the forties, to get a girl you had to be a GI or a jock. In the fifties, to get a girl you had to be Jewish. In the sixties, to get a girl you had to be black. In the seventies, to get a girl you had to be a girl.

-Mort Sahl

The basic and essential human is the woman.

-Orson Welles

There are men I could spend eternity with, but not this life.

-Kathleen Norris

The most exciting attractions are between two opposites that never meet.

-Andy Warhol

I have never hated a man enough to give his diamonds back.

-Zsa Zsa Gabor

In any relationship in which two people become one, the end result is two half people.

-Wayne Dyer

Friendship is the hardest thing in the world to explain. It's not something you learn in school. But if you haven't learned the meaning of friendship, you really haven't learned anything.

-Muhammad Ali

A successful marriage is not a gift; it is an achievement.

-Ann Landers

Immature love says I love you because I need you. Mature love says I need you because I love you.

-Erich Fromm

Marriage is like pantyhose. It all depends on what you put into it.

-Phyllis Schlafly

The difference between divorce and legal separation is that a legal separation gives a husband time to hide his money.

-Johnny Carson

There is one thing more exasperating than a wife who can cook and won't, and that's the wife who can't cook and will.

-Robert Frost

My wife's jealousy is getting ridiculous. The other day she looked at my calendar and demanded to know who May was.

-Rodney Dangerfield

As usual, there's a great woman behind every idiot.

-John Lennon

Why does a woman work ten years to change a man's habits and then complain that he's not the man she married?

-Barbra Streisand

An archaeologist is the best husband any woman can have: the older she gets the more interested he is in her.

-Agatha Christie

No man is a hero to his wife's psychiatrist.

-Eric Berne

In love the paradox occurs that two beings become one and yet remain two.

-Erich Fromm

We found that living together was getting in the way of our relationship. It doesn't mean that we don't dig each other. It just means we can't live together.

-David Harris

We sleep in separate rooms, we have dinner apart, we take separate vacations—we're doing everything we can to keep our marriage together.

-Rodney Dangerfield

Marriage is like a three speed gearbox. affection, friendship, love. It is not advisable to crash your gears and go right through to love straightaway. you need to ease your way through. The basis of love is respect, and that needs to be learned from affection and friendship.

-Peter Ustinov

Friendship is everything. Friendship is more than talent. It is more than government. It is almost the equal of family.

-From The Godfather

I am a marvelous housekeeper. Every time I leave a man, I keep his house.

-Zsa Zsa Gabor

Sometimes I wonder if men and women really suit each other. Perhaps they should live next door and just visit now and then.

-Katharine Hepburn

I have learned only two things are necessary to keep one's wife happy. First, let her think she is having her own way. Second, let her have it.

-Antony Armstrong-Jones

Marriage isn't an up or down issue. It's a side-by-side one.

-Prince Charles

Love is the best, most insidious, most effective instrument of social repression.

-Rainer Werner Fassbinder

Male domination has had some very unfortunate effects. It made the most intimate of human relations, that of marriage, one of master and slave, instead of between equal partners.

-Bertrand Russell

Mummy is the head of state, and I am boss in the house.

-Prince Bernhard

A strong man doesn't have to be dominant toward a woman. He doesn't match his strength against a woman weak with love for him. He matches against the world.

-Marilyn Monroe

Marrying a man is like buying something you've been admiring for a long time in a shop window. You may love it when you get home, but it doesn't always go with everything else in the house.

-Jean Kerr

When I wake up in the morning, I think of me first and then my wife and then my children. I'd like to meet the guy that can honestly admit he does differently.

-Jerry Lewis

Marriage essentially is a contract, and there are so many loopholes in it that Wilbur Mills and the entire Ways and Means committee at their height couldn't figure it out.

-Warren Beatty

I never loved another person the way I loved myself.

-Mae West

The housewife is interested in serious things. It gives her something to tell her husband when he comes home.

-Mike Douglas

Even though a girl may loathe cooking, she should make an effort to cater to her husband's likes and dislikes and to make meals appetizing and interesting.

-Elizabeth Post

No one ever filed for divorce on a full stomach.

-Mamma Leone

It all comes down to who does the dishes.
-Norman Mailer

I am a woman meant for a man, but I never found a man who could compete.
-Bette Davis

They're not going to get married or anything. They're only nine.
-Lillian Carter, on Amy's first boyfriend

To catch a husband is an art; to hold him is a job.
-Simone de Beauvoir

I hate to be a failure. I hate and regret the failure of my marriages. I would gladly give all my millions for just one lasting marital success.
-John Paul Getty

She is an extremely beautiful woman, lavishly endowed by nature with but a few flaws in the masterpiece: she has an insipid double chin, her legs are too short, and she has a slight pot-belly. She has a wonderful bosom, though.
-Richard Burton, on Elizabeth Taylor

I prefer the word "homemaker" because "housewife" always implies that there may be a wife someplace else.
-Bella Abzug

When you get married you forget about kissing other women.
-Pat Boone

Sensual pleasures have the fleeting brilliance of a comet; a happy marriage has the tranquility of a lovely sunset.
-Ann Landers

For some reason, it seems that the bride generally has to make more effort to achieve a successful marriage than the bridegroom.
-Elizabeth Post

Throughout history, females have picked providers for males. Males pick anything.
-Margaret Mead

A man's home may seem to be his castle on the outside; inside, it is more often his nursery.
-Clare Booth Luce

Every bride has to learn it's not her wedding but her mother's.
-Luci Johnson Nugent

A man's job, basically, is to tame this world; a wife's job is to control herself—and, indirectly, her husband.
-Ruth Stafford Peale

The ultimate betrayal is not a wandering wife, but a wandering wife who tells her lover that her husband doesn't make as much as everyone thinks.
-Harry Golden

The story of love is hello and goodbye . . . until we meet again.
-Jimi Hendrix

Trouble is a part of your life, and if you don't share it, you don't give the person who loves you a chance to love you enough.
-Dinah Shore

Sex appeal is fifty percent what you've got and fifty percent what people think you've got.
-Sophia Loren

Plain women know more about men than beautiful women.
-Katharine Hepburn

If I hadn't had them, I would have had some made.
-Dolly Parton

Women who insist upon having the same options as men would do well to consider the option of being the strong, silent type.
-Fran Lebowitz

Men resent women because women bear kids, and seem to have this magic link with immortality that men lack. But they should stay home for a day with a kid; they'd change their minds.
-Tuesday Weld

Ever since Eve gave Adam the apple, there has been a misunderstanding between the sexes about gifts.
-Nan Robertson

You see an awful lot of smart guys with dumb women, but you hardly ever see a smart woman with a dumb guy.
-Erica Jong

To a smart girl men are no problem— they're the answer.
-Zsa Zsa Gabor

Love is like a friendship caught on fire. In the beginning a flame, very pretty, often hot and fierce but still only light and flickering. As love grows older, our hearts mature and our love becomes as coals, deep-burning and unquenchable.
-Bruce Lee

Put together, narcissistic people can provide considerable misery for each other—and an interesting evening for others.
-Theodore Isaac Rubin

Falling madly in love with someone is not necessarily the starting point to getting married.
-Prince Charles

A woman without a man is like a fish without a bicycle.
-Gloria Steinham

Why can't a woman be more like a man?
-Henry Higgins, in George Bernard Shaw's "Pygmalion"

CHILDREN

Quotes & Anecdotes
(Youth, Parenting, Generation Gaps)

The child is the father of the man.
-*William Wordsworth*

Children aren't happy with nothing to ignore
And that's what parents were created for.
-*Ogden Nash*

Many children, many cares; no children, no felicity.
-*Bovee*

When a father gives to his son, both laugh; When a son gives to his father, both cry.
-*Jewish Proverb*

It is a wise father that knows his own child.
-*Shakespeare*

Men are what their mothers made them.
-*Ralph Waldo Emerson*

What gift has Providence bestowed on man that is so dear to him as his children?
-*Cicero*

Children are poor men's riches.
-*John Ray*

When I was a boy of fourteen, my father was so ignorant I could hardly stand to have the old man around. But when I got to be twenty-one, I was astonished at how much he had learned in seven years.
-*Mark Twain*

My mother loved children. She would have given anything if I had been one.
-*Groucho Marx*

Heredity is what a man believes in until his son begins to behave like a delinquent.
-*Presbyterian Life*

You know children are growing up when they start asking questions that have answers.
-*John J. Plomp*

A three-year-old is a being that gets almost as much fun out of a fifty-six-dollar set of swings as it does out of finding a small green worm.
-*Bill Vaughn*

The secret to dealing successfully with a child is not to be its parent.
-*Mell Lazarus*

I must have been an insufferable child. All children are.
-*George Bernard Shaw*

When asked why he did not become a father, Thales answered, "Because I am fond of children."
-*Diogenes Laertius*

Give me the children until they are seven and anyone may have them after.
-*St. Francis Xavier*

Children are our most valuable natural resource.
-*Herbert Hoover*

Every child should have an occasional pat on the back as long as it is applied low enough and hard enough.
-*Bishop Fulton J. Sheen*

Children need love, especially when they do not deserve it.
-*Harold S. Hulbert*

It's hard for the modern generation to understand Thoreau who lived by a pond but didn't own water skis or a snorkel.
-*Bill Vaughan*

Only the young die good.
-*Oliver Herford*

And another lot of young people will appear, and consider us completely outdated, and they will write ballads to express their loathing of us, and there is no reason why this should ever end.
-*Alfred Jarry*

If youth is a defect, it is one that we outgrow too soon.
Robert Lowell

Blessed are the young, for they shall inherit the national debt.
-*Herbert Hoover*

Never have children, only grandchildren.
-*Gore Vidal*

An elderly man said, "Thank God for my sons. My first is a doctor, the second a lawyer, the third a chemist, the fourth an artist, and the fifth a writer."

He was asked, "Well, what do you do?"

He replied, "I have a dry goods store. Not a big one, but I manage to support them all."
-*Gordon Dakins*

Familiarity breeds contempt—and children.
-*Mark Twain*

One of the mysteries of life is how the boy who wasn't good enough to marry the daughter can be the father of the smartest grandchild in the world.
-*Anonymous*

Youth is such a wonderful thing. What a crime to waste it on children.
-*George Bernard Shaw*

© 1993, Compact Classics, Inc.

Oh to be only half as wonderful as my child thought I was when he was small, and only half as stupid as my teenager now thinks I am.

-Rebecca Richards

If you can't hold children in your arms, please hold them in your hearts.

-Mother Clara Hale

There's nothing like having grandchildren to restore your faith in heredity.

-Doug Larson

Don't trust anyone over thirty.

-Mario Savio

Youth has become a class.

-Roger Vadim

Adolescence is that period in a kid's life when his or her parents become more difficult.

-Ryan O'Neal

I'm convinced that every boy, in his heart, would rather steal second base than an automobile.

-Justice Tom C. Clark

Childhood is where competition is a baseball game and responsibility is a paper route.

-Erma Bombeck

The only thing that impresses me most about America is the way parents obey their children.

-The Duke of Windsor

Parents are the bones on which children cut their teeth.

-Peter Ustinov

Kids are wonderful, but I like mine barbecued.

-Bob Hope

The hardest part of raising children is teaching them to ride bicycles . . . A shaky child on a bicycle for the first time needs both support and freedom. The realization that this is what the child will always need can hit hard.

-Sloan Wilson

The easiest way to convince my kids that they don't really need something is to get it for them.

-Joan Collins

There is no such thing as a kid who needs fixing . . . They're born with everything. And what most people do is squash it and take it away from them.

-Robert Blake

When I was kidnapped my parents snapped into action; they rented out my room.

-Woody Allen

Teenage children are totally intolerant of midlife parents for having much the same romantic fantasies they have.

-Gail Sheehy

They take their tactics from Castro and their money from Daddy.

-Spiro T. Agnew

The trouble with teenagers is that if you ask them the number that comes after nine, they tell you it's Operator.

-Jackie Mason

What's done to children, they will do to society.

-Karl Menninger

We can only know as adults what we can only feel as children.

-Leslie Fiedler

If the very old will remember, the very young will listen.

-Chief Dan George

Your children need your presence more than your presents.

-Jesse Jackson

The good still die young. Eternal youth— that's what you need. Nothing improves with age.

-Lauren Bacall

The correct way to raise a kid in America would be half by authority and half by explanation.

-Herman Kahn

Do not weep for them, America. Your children, far braver than you, were a moment in the conscience of a man.

-Mark Lane

Children wish fathers looked but with their eyes; fathers that children with their judgment looked; and either may be wrong.

-William Shakespeare

It is of no consequence of what parents a man is born, so he be a man of merit.

-Horace

Some men by ancestry are only the shadow of a mighty name.

-Lucan

Those who depend on the merits of their ancestors may be said to search in the roots of a tree for those fruits which the branches ought to produce.

-Isaac Barrow

Train up a child in the way he should go; and when he is old he will not depart from it.

-The Bible, Proverbs 22:6

The utmost reverence due to a child.

-Juvenal

A child tells in the street what its father and mother say at home.

-*The Talmud*

A child is a man in a small letter, yet the best copy of Adam before he tasted of Eve or the apple.

-*John Earle*

Better a snotty child than his nose wiped off.

-*George Herbert*

Teach your child to hold his tongue; he'll learn fast enough to speak.

-*Benjamin Franklin*

Lacking all sense of right and wrong, a child can do nothing which is morally evil, or which merits either punishment or reproof.

-*J. J. Rousseau*

What power is there in the smile of a child, in its play, in its crying—in short, in its mere existence. Are you able to resist its demands? Or do you hold out to it, as a mother, your breast, or, as a father, whatever it needs of your belongings?

-*Max Stirner*

Respect the child. Be not too much his parent. Trespass not on his solitude.

-*Ralph Waldo Emerson*

Give a little love to a child, and you get a great deal back.

-*John Ruskin*

There is only one pretty child in the world, and every mother has it.

-*Chinese Proverb*

Beat your child once a day. If you don't know why, your child does.

-*Chinese Proverb*

A child learns to talk quicker than to keep silent.

-*Norwegian Proverb*

Give to a pig when it grunts and a child when it cries, and you will have a fine pig and a bad child.

-*Danish Proverb*

He that is childless has no light in his eyes.

-*Persian Proverb*

Soldier, robber, priest, atheist, courtesan, virgin, I care not what you are, if you have not brought children into the world . . . your life has been as vain and as harmless as mine has been.

-*George Moore*

Heaven lies about us in our infancy.

-*William Wordsworth*

What art can paint or gild any object in afterlife with the glow which nature gives to the first baubles of childhood! St. Peter's cannot have the magical power over us that the red and gold covers of our first picture book possessed.

-*Ralph W. Emerson*

It is a great honor to you that are married that God, designing to multiply souls, which may bless and praise Him to all eternity, makes you cooperate with Him in so noble a work, by the production of bodies into which He infuses immortal souls, like heavenly drops, as he creates them.

-*St. Francis de Sales*

Children suck the mother when they are young and the father when they are old.

-*English Proverb*

If parents carry it lovingly towards their children, mixing their mercies with loving rebukes, and their loving rebukes with fatherly and motherly compassions, they are more likely to save their children than by being churlish and severe towards them.

-*John Bunyan*

Children have neither a past nor a future. Thus they enjoy the present—which seldom happens to us.

-*Jean de la Bruyère*

Men are generally more careful of the breed of their horses and dogs than of their children.

-*William Penn*

I must whip my children for going into bad company instead of railing at bad company for ensnaring my children.

-*Richard Steele*

I am determined my children shall be brought up in their father's religion, if they can find out what it is.

-*Charles Lamb*

If you wish to study men you must not neglect to mix with the society of children.

-*Jesse Torrey*

Of all people children are the most imaginative. They abandon themselves without reserve to every illusion. No man, whatever his sensibility may be, is ever affected by Hamlet or Lear as a little girl is affected by the story of poor Red Riding Hood.

-*J. B. MacAuley*

Children need models more than they need critics.

-*Joseph Joubert*

Children have wide ears and long tongues.

-*H. G. Bohn*

He that has no children knows not what is love.

-*H. G. Bohn*

It is one of my rules in life not to believe a man who may happen to tell me that he feels no interest in children.

-Charles Dickens

If a man leaves children behind him, it is as if he did not die.

-Moroccan Proverb

He is unworthy of life that gives no life to another.

-Latin Proverb

The hen who, from chilly air,
With pious wing protects her care,
And every fowl that flies at large,
Instructs me in a parent's charge.

-John Gay

Kids are like money. The more you got, the more you want.

-Bill Priest

If children were allowed to run the country, we'd have soda flowing out of the drinking fountains, bridges built with Tinkertoys, styrofoam airliners, and bad countries would have to play by themselves.

-Walter Wandheim

Children don't ask for things they don't want. They just don't want them after they get them.

-Howard Stevens

If I could live my childhood over again, I probably wouldn't.

-John Smith

Childhood is a state of mind that some people never grow out of. Unfortunately, we usually elect those people.

-Andrew Van Leeuwen

My kids are always telling me to get a life. But if I had to live their lives, I'd be dead.

-Calvin Smoot

There's no trick to getting a kid to like you. Just feed him cookies and let him stay up past his bed time.

-J. F. Niel

God created dogs and kids to remind us not to take things too seriously.

-Frank Fletcher

Some people say if it weren't for their children, their house would always be clean. At my house, if it weren't for the children, the house never would have been clean.

-William Calhoun

I would rather be kissed by my three-year-old daughter than by the entire [Sports Illustrated] Swimsuit Issue.

-Rod Grafton

PATRIOTISM

Quotes & Anecdotes
(Loyalty, Love of Country)

If I have to lay an egg for my country, I'll do it.
-Bob Hope

True patriotism doesn't exclude an understanding of the patriotism of others.
-Queen Elizabeth II

Loyalty must arise spontaneously from the hearts of people who love their country and respect their government.
-Justice Hugo L. Black

Patriotism is your conviction that this country is superior to all other countries because you were born in it.
-George Bernard Shaw

If anyone attempts to haul down the American flag, shoot him on the spot.
-John A. Dix

A real patriot is the fellow who gets a parking ticket and rejoices that the system works.
-Bill Vaughan

Next to the love of God, the love of country is the best preventative of crime. He who is proud of his country will be particularly cautious not to do anything which is calculated to disgrace it.
-George Borrow

Whatever insults my state, insults me.
-Preston Brooks

White is for purity, red for valor, blue for justice.
-Charles Sumner

The first requisite of a good citizen in this Republic of ours is that he shall be able and willing to pull his weight.
-Theodore Roosevelt

Patriotism is nothing more than a feeling of welfare and the dread of seeing it disturbed.
-Stanislaus Leszcynski (King of Poland, 1763)

I, for one, do not call the sod under my feet my country. But language, religion, laws, government, blood—identity of these makes men of one country.
-Samuel Coleridge

There is no such thing as a little country. The greatness of a people is no more determined by their number than the greatness of a man is determined by his height.
-Victor Hugo

A small country and few people may be equivalent in wealth and strength to a far greater people and territory.
-William Petty

Methinks I see in my mind a noble and puissant nation rousing herself like a strong man after sleep, and shaking her invincible locks; methinks I see her as an eagle mewing her mighty youth and kindling her undazzled eyes at the full midday beam.
-John Milton, Aeropagitica

A Frenchman once tried to flatter Lord Palmerston, former prime minister of England, saying, "If I were not a Frenchman, I would wish to be an Englishman."

Lord Palmerston was not impressed. He replied, "If I were not an Englishman, I would wish to be an Englishman."

During the Occupation, King Christian X of Denmark once noticed a Nazi flag flying over a public building in Copenhagen. He called the German commander and demanded that he remove the flag. The commander refused. The king then said, "Then a soldier will go and take it down."

The commander, taken aback, replied, "But he will be shot."

"I think not," the king retorted. "For I shall be the soldier."

Within an hour, the flag was removed.

So to be patriots as not to forget we are gentlemen.
-From Thoughts on the Cause of the Present Discontents

In the days to come as through all time that is past, man will lord it over his fellow, and earth will be stained red from veins of young and old. That sweet and sounding name of "patria" becomes an illusion and a curse.
-By The Ionian Sea

Such is the patriot's boast, wher'er we roam,
His first, best country, ever is, at home.
-Oliver Goldsmith

Patriotism is the last refuge of a scoundrel.
-Samuel Johnson

What scoundrels we would be if we did for ourselves what we are ready to do for [our country].
-Camillo di Cavour

Treason is in the air around us everywhere. It goes by the name of patriotism.
-Thomas Corwin

Patriotism depends as much on mutual suffering as on mutual success, and it is by that experience of all fortunes and all feelings that a great national character is created.
-Benjamin Disraeli

Patriotism is . . . to most men a moral necessity. It meets and satisfies that desire for a strong, disinterested enthusiasm in life which is deeply implanted in our nature.
-W. E. Leckey

Standing as I do in view of God and eternity, I realize that patriotism is not enough. I must have no hatred or bitterness toward anyone. They have all been very kind to me here.
-Edith Cavell, the night before her execution

You'll never have a quiet world until you knock the patriotism out of the human race.
-George Bernard Shaw

Patriotism may be defined as a sense of partisan solidarity in respect of prestige.
-Thorstein Veblen

Patriotism is easy to understand in America. It means looking out for yourself by looking out for your country.
-Calvin Coolidge

The country of every man is that one where he lives best.
-Aristophanes

Love of country is more potent than reason itself.
-Ovid

Nothing is sweeter than one's own country.
-St. John Chrysostom

Had I a dozen sons—each in my love alike . . . I had rather have eleven die nobly for their country than one voluptuously surfeit out of action.
-William Shakespeare

I do love my country's good with a respect more tender, more holy and profound, than mine own life.
-William Shakespeare

Our country is wherever we are well off.
-John Milton

What a pity is it that we can die but once to serve our country.
-Joseph Addison

We must love our country, even though it treats us with injustice.
-Voltaire

I am sure that I can save my country, and that nobody else can.
-William Pitt

Who loves his country cannot hate mankind.
-Charles Churchill

The proper means of increasing love we bear our native country is to reside some time in a foreign one.
-William Shenstone

To make us love our country, our country ought to be lovely.
-Demund Burke

My country is the world, and my religion is to do good.
-Thomas Paine

O dream of joy! Is this indeed
The lighthouse top I see?
Is this the hill, is this the kirk?
Is this mine own countree?
-Samuel T. Coleridge, The Ancient Mariner

Breathes there the man with soul so dead
Who never to himself hath said,
This is my own, my native land!
-Walter Scott

The more I see of other countries, the more I love my own.
-Anna Louise de Staël

My affections are first for my own country, and then, generally, for all mankind.
-Thomas Jefferson

He who loves not his country can love nothing.
-Lord Byron

Let our object be our country, our whole country, and nothing but our country.
-Daniel Webster

Our country is the world—our countrymen are mankind.
-W. L. Garrison

O God—if there be a God—save my country—if my country is worth saving.
-Ascribed to "an old soldier"

You belong to your country as you belong to your own mother.
-E. E. Hale

It is no shame to a man that he should be as nice about his country as about his sweetheart.
-J. R. Lowell

Our country, right or wrong. When right to be kept right. When wrong, to be put right.
-Carl Shurz

"My country, right or wrong," is like saying "My mother, drunk or sober."
-G. K. Chesterson

He serves his party best who serves the country best.

-Rutherford B. Hayes

He loves his country best who strives to make it best.

-R. G. Ingersoll

How can a man be said to have a country when he has no right to a square inch of soil?

Henry George

It is sweet to serve one's country by deeds, and it is not absurd to serve her by words.

-Sallust

Any relation to the land, the habit of tilling it, or mining it, or even hunting on it, generates the feeling of patriotism.

-Ralph W. Emerson

How dear to all good hearts is their fatherland.

-Voltaire

A fatherland is an association on the same soil of the living and the dead, with those yet to be born.

-Joseph de Maistre

A loyal American is one who gets mad when an alien cusses the institutions he cusses.

-Huntington Herald

I should like to be able to love my country and to love justice.

-Albert Camus

Do not . . . regard the critics as questionable patriots. What were Washington and Jefferson and Adams but profound critics of the colonial status quo?

-Adlai Stevenson

The Athenian democracy suffered much from that narrowness of patriotism which is the ruin of all nations.

-H. G. Wells

As soon as any man says of the affairs of state, "What does it matter to me?" the state may be given up as lost.

-Jean Jacques Rousseau

If I added to the pride of America, I am happy.

-Carl Sandburg

If a man is fortunate he will, before he dies, gather up as much as he can of his civilized heritage and transmit it to his children.

-Will Durant

Naturally the common people don't want war . . . Voice or no voice, the people can always be brought to the bidding of the leaders . . . All you have to do is tell them they are being attacked and denounce the pacifists for lack of patriotism.

-Hermann Goering

There are three virtues: duty, loyalty, patriotism.

-Gordon Liddy

No other factor in history, not even religion, has produced so many wars as has the clash of national egotisms sanctified by the name of patriotism.

-Preserved Smith

If man commits suicide, it will be . . . because they will obey the cliches of state sovereignty and national honor.

-Erich Fromm

Patriotism is as fierce as a fever, as pitiless as the grave, blind as a stone, and irrational as a headless hen.

-Ambrose Bierce

One of the great attractions of patriotism— it fulfills our worst wishes. In the person of our nation we are able, vicariously, to bully and cheat. Bully and cheat, what's more, with a feeling that we are profoundly virtuous.

-Aldous Huxley

The standardization of mass-production carries with it a tendency to standardize a mass-mind . . . The worst defect of patriotism is its tendency to foster and impose . . . and to stifle liberty.

-J. A. Hobson

Many studies have discovered a close link between prejudice and "patriotism" . . . Extreme bigots are almost always super-patriots.

-Gordon W. Allport

. . . Schools are out to teach patriotism; newspapers are out to stir up excitement; and politicians are out to get reelected. None of the three, therefore, can do anything whatever toward saving the human race from reciprocal suicide.

-Bertrand Russell

What is good for the country is good for General Motors, and what's good for General Motors is good for the country.

-Charles E. Wilson

With malice toward none, with charity for all . . . let us finish the work we are in, to bind up the nation's wounds.

-Abraham Lincoln

Abandon your animosities and make your sons Americans.

-Robert E. Lee

In the great fulfillment we must have a citizenship less concerned about what the government can do for it and more anxious about what it can do for the nation.

-Warren G. Harding

Patriotism, to be truly American, begins with the human allegiance.
-Norman Cousins

Human sovereignty transcends national sovereignty.
-Lester B. Pearson

Love for one's country which is not part of one's love for humanity is not love, but idolatrous worship.
-Erich Fromm

Patriotism is the virtue of the vicious.
-Oscar Wilde

For us, patriotism is the same as the love of humanity.
-Mohandas Gandhi

To me, it seems a dreadful indignity to have a soul controlled by geography.
-George Santayana

It is the love of country that has lighted and that keeps glowing the holy fire of patriotism.
-J. Horace McFarland

Patriotism is a praiseworthy competition with one's ancestors.
-Tacitus

Whoever serves his country well has no need of ancestors.
-Voltaire

Schools have always inculcated patriotism, but the terms of allegiances are often narrowly conceived. The fact that loyalty to the nation requires loyalty to all subgroups within the nation is seldom pointed out.
-Gordon W. Allport

Too often a sense of loyalty depends on admiration, and if we can't admire it is difficult to be loyal.
-Aimee Buchanan

Loyalty is one thing a leader cannot do without.
-A. P. Gouthy

The strongest bulwark of authority is uniformity; the least divergence from it is the greatest crime.
-Emma Goldman

There is only the finest of lines that separates patriotism from bigotry.
-Ted Wallace

Patriotism, the love of one's country, is a virtue that must not be stamped out. But at the same time, it must not be fueled so that it becomes a raging inferno of hatred.
-D. Smythe

Everybody thinks his own country is the greatest in the world, even as he is risking his life to get out of it.
-Pascual Ramirez

Everybody says America isn't the world's policeman. But guess who gets called when somebody needs a cop.
-Colin Powell

Just because I would die for your right to worship the way you want doesn't mean you should kill me for worshipping the way I want.
-Stanley Eichel, on arresting a Muslim American terrorist

You want to know who the patriots in this country are? They're the ones who don't speak English, who don't have a job, who sometimes live in the streets, but who will tell you that their life here is infinitely better than where they came from.
-Paul Linery

A starving Haitian who has paid every cent he had, even mortgaged his family's future, just to set foot on American soil is a greater patriot than the millionaire who lives in Scarsdale and complains that the government is taxing him out of his twenty-room Victorian.
-Kevin B. Todd

We are all patriots. We all have causes. It's just that some of our causes are better for the country, and some of our causes are better for ourselves. But we are all still patriots.
-Patricia Adams

POLITICS

Quotes & Anecdotes
(Governments, Public Officials and S.O.B.'s, Democracies and Other Nefarious Institutions)

Princes and governments are by far the most dangerous elements of society.

-Niccolo Macchiavelli

Forgive your enemies, but never forget their names.

-John F. Kennedy

Politicians and roosters crow about what they intend to do. The roosters deliver what is promised.

-Anonymous

Political success is the ability, whenever the inevitable occurs, to get credit for it.

-Laurence Peter

It is not a government's obligation to provide services, but to see that they are provided.

-Mario Cuomo

If it looks like a duck, quacks like a duck, and walks like a duck, it is probably a horse.

-Theodoro Valencia

Man's capacity for justice makes democracy possible, but his inclination to injustice makes democracy necessary.

-Reinhold Niebuhr

Get all the fools on your side and you can be elected to anything.

Frank Dune

I know that when things don't go well, they like to blame the president, and that is one of the things presidents are paid for.

-John F. Kennedy

A politician thinks of the next election—a statesman of the next generation.

-James Clarke

During the 1968 Democratic convention in Chicago, then-Mayor Richard Daley said, "The police are here not to create disorder. They are here to preserve disorder."

While seeking Democratic nomination in 1958, John F. Kennedy once said in a speech to Washington's Gridiron Club, "I have just received the following wire from my generous Daddy: 'Dear Jack—Don't buy a single vote more than is necessary. I'll be damned if I am going to pay for a landslide.'"

Bad officials are the ones elected by good citizens who do not vote.

-George Nathan

Democrats can't get elected unless things get worse, and things won't get worse unless they get elected.

-Jeane Kirkpatrick

Senator George H. Moses once complained to Calvin Coolidge that a man being considered for a Republican senatorial nomination was an "out and out S.O.B."

Coolidge agreed, saying, "That may be. But there's a lot of those in the country and I think they are entitled to representation in the Senate."

-Calvin Coolidge

In politics one frequently hears it said that so-and-so may be an S.O.B., but he is *our* S.O.B. and therefore deserving of our support.

-George Allen

The man with the best job in the country is the vice-president. All he has to do is get up every morning and say, "How is the president?"

-Will Rogers

Former secretary of state, Dean Acheson, was asked about his future plans. "I will undoubtedly have to seek what is happily known as gainful employment," he replied, "which I am glad to say does not describe holding public office."

While I'd rather be right than president, at any time I am ready for both.

-Norman Thomas

Nothing is more foreign to us Christians than politics.

-Tertullian

The members who composed [a typical Democratic National Convention] were, seven-eighths of them, the meanest kind of bawling and blowing office-holders, office-seekers, pimps, malignants, conspirators, murderers, fancy-men, custom-house clerks, contractors, kept-editors, spaniels well trained to carry and fetch, jobbers, infidels, disunionists, terrorists, mail-riflers, slave catchers, pushers of slavery, creatures of the President, creatures of would-be Presidents, spies, bribers, compromisers, lobbyers, sponges, ruined sports, expelled gamblers, policy-backers, monte-dealers, duellists, carriers of concealed weapons, deaf men, pimpled men, scarred inside with vile disease, gaudy outside with gold chains made from the people's money and harlot's money twisted together; crawling, serpentine men, the lousy combinings and born freedom-sellers of the earth.

-Walt Whitman

In politics it is difficult sometimes to decide whether the politicians are humorless hypocrites or hypocritical humorists; whether in fooling the people they also fool themselves, which means that both the politicians and the people are stupid; or whether the politicians are smarter than the people and know exactly what they are doing. Probably the truth is the politicians are smarter, but not much smarter, and that both are without any humor whatsoever.

-Frank Kent

Politics is such a torment that I would advise everyone I love not to mix with it.

-Thomas Jefferson

Columnist Ann Landers was once approached at a social function by a pompous senator who said, "So, you're Ann Landers. Say something funny."

Without hesitating, she replied, "So, you're a politician. Tell me a lie."

A politician [is] one that would circumvent God.

-Shakespeare

Great politicians owe their reputations, if not to pure chance, then to circumstances at least which they themselves could not foresee.

-Otto Von Bismarck

If I had engaged in politics, O men of Athens, I should have perished long ago, and done no good either to you or to myself.

-Socrates

I hold [politics] to be subject to laws as fixed as matter itself, and to be as fit a subject for the application of the highest intellectual power.

-John Calhoun

Politics are now nothing more than a means of rising in the world.

-Samuel Johnson

A statesman makes the occasion, but the occasion makes the politician.

-George Hilliard

Politicians are like the bones of horse's foreshoulder—not a straight one in it.

-Wendell Phillips

If you want to understand democracy, spend less time in the library studying Plato and more time in the buses with people.

-Simeon Strunsky

Popular government is still a theory because no one has yet found a government that is popular.

-Anonymous

Only a company that is rich and safe can afford to be a democracy, for a democracy is the most expensive and nefarious kind of government on earth.

-H.L. Mencken

Nobody believes a rumor here in Washington until it's officially denied.

-Edward Cheyfitz

Public office is the last refuge of the incompetent.

-Boies Penrose

He knows nothing; he thinks he knows everything—that clearly points to a political career.

-George Bernard Shaw

Nothing is so admirable in politics as a short memory.

-John Galbraith

The short memories of American voters is what keeps our politicians in office.

-Will Rogers

Voters quickly forget what a man says.

-Richard Nixon

The middle of the road is all of the usable surface. The extremes, right and left, are in the gutters.

-Dwight D. Eisenhower

To rule is easy, to govern, difficult.

-Johann von Goethe

Applause, mingled with boos and hisses, is about all that the average voter is able or willing to contribute to public life.

-Elmer Davis

Politicians should read science fiction, not westerns and detective stories.

-Arthur C. Clarke

Next time a man tells you talk is cheap, ask him if knows how much a session of congress costs.

-Anonymous

I'm thinking of entering politics . . . I'd love to do it. But I haven't got the right wife.

-Mick Jagger

It is simply untrue that all our institutions are evil, that all adults are unsympathetic, that all politicians are mere opportunists, that all aspects of university life are corrupt. Having discovered an illness, it's not terribly useful to prescribe death as a cure.

-George McGovern

A silent majority and government by the people are incompatible.

-Tom Hayden

Now and then, an innocent man is sent to the legislature.

-Kin Hubbard

Our local congressman admits his opponent resembles Abraham Lincoln—if you can imagine a short, fat, dishonest Abraham Lincoln.
-Bill Vaughan

An elected official is one who gets 51 percent of the vote cast by 40 percent of the 60 percent of voters who registered.
-Dan Bennett

Government is too big and important to be left to the politicians.
-Chester Bowles

Since a politician never believes what he says, he is always astonished when others do.
-Charles de Gaulle

This country has come to feel the same when Congress is in session as when the baby gets hold of a hammer.
-Will Rogers

In politics, experiments mean revolutions.
-Benjamin Disraeli

The government is the only known vessel that leaks from the top.
-James Reston

Do you ever get the feeling that the only reason we have elections is to find out if the polls were right?
-Robert Orben

What is politics but persuading the public to vote for this and support that and endure these for the promise of those?
-Gilbert Highet

Politics is the gentle art of getting votes from the poor and campaign funds from the rich, by promising to protect each from the other.
-Oscar Ameringer

Political ability is the ability to foretell what is going to happen tomorrow, next week, next month and next year. And to have the ability afterward to explain why it didn't happen.
-Winston Churchill

Some problems are so complex that it takes high intelligence just to be undecided about them.
-Anonymous

That a man before whom the two paths of literature and politics lie open, and who might hope for eminence in either, should choose politics, and quit literature, seems to me madness.
-T.B. MacCaulay

. . . Whoever could make two ears of corn, or two blades of grass, to grow upon a spot of ground where only one grew before, would deserve better of mankind, and do

more essential service to his country, than the whole race of politicians put together.
-Jonathan Swift, Gulliver's Travels

Timid and disinterested politicians think much more about the security of their seats than about the security of their country.
-T.B. MacCaulay

When a man assumes a public trust, he should consider himself as public property.
-Thomas Jefferson

There is nothing in the world like a persuasive speech to fuddle the mental apparatus.
-Mark Twain

Politicians say they're beefing up the economy. Most don't know beef from pork.
-Harold Lowman

One person with a belief is a social power equal to 99 who have only interests.
-John Stuart Mill

Washington appears to be filled with two kinds of politicians—those trying to get an investigation started, and those trying to get one stopped.
-Earl Wilson

I know you will vote for me until I die. And even after I'm dead I think some of you will write my name in.
-Adam Clayton Powell

The mark of a good politician is the ability to stop at two drinks.
-Charles Colson

The difference between the men and the boys in politics is, and always has been, that the boys want to be something, while the men want to do something.
-Eric Severeid

All of us in the Senate live in an iron lung—the iron lung of politics—and it is no easy task to emerge from that rarefied atmosphere in order to breathe the same fresh air our constituents breathe.
-John F. Kennedy

I admit I may have dozed through some of the sessions. But I haven't had a good rest since the campaign.
-S. I. Hayakawa

Influence is like a savings account. The less you use it, the more you've got.
-Andrew Young

Sometimes it is said that a man cannot be trusted with the government of himself. Can he, then, be trusted with the government of others?
-Walter Cronkite

We made no progress at all . . . and we didn't intend to. That's the function of a national committee.
-Ronald Reagan

The only summit meeting that can succeed is one that does not take place.
-Barry Goldwater

Where else could it happen but in a country like this? To let a foreigner make peace for them, to accept a man like me—I even have a foreign accent.
-Henry Kissinger

How can anyone govern a nation that has two hundred and forty-six different kinds of cheese?
-Charles de Gaulle

I don't think politics is a workable system any more . . . They gotta invent something better.
-David Crosby

Life somehow finds a way of transcending politics.
-Norman Cousins

There are only two kinds of politics . . . the politics of fear and the politics of trust. One says: You are encircled by monstrous dangers . . . The other says: The world is a baffling and hazardous place, but it can be shaped to the will of men.
-Edmund Muskie

Being in politics is like being a football coach. You have to be smart enough to understand the game and dumb enough to think it's important.
-Eugene McCarthy

I have often been accused of putting my foot in my mouth, but I will never put my hand in your pockets.
-Spiro T. Agnew

Sometimes people mistake the way I talk for what I am thinking.
-Idi Amin

I don't know what sort of president he'd make. He talks and talks and talks. He'd make a helluva wife.
-Groucho Marx

Now when I bore people at a party they think it's *their* fault.
-Henry Kissinger

I would not be truthful if I said I was fully qualified for the office. I do not play the piano, I seldom play golf, and I never play touch football.
-Barry Goldwater

These presidential ninnies should stick to throwing out baseballs and leave the important matters to serious people.
-Gore Vidal

Vote for the man who promises least; he'll be the least disappointing.
-Bernard Baruch

If you want to talk to somebody who's not busy, call the vice president. I get plenty of time to talk to anybody about anything.
-Walter Mondale

Pessimism in our time is infinitely more respectable than optimism . . . The man who foresees catastrophe has a gift of insight which insures that he will become a radio commentator, or editor of *Time*, or go to congress.
-John Galbraith

We debated this bill now for nine days. I heard the world was created in seven.
-Robert C. Byrd

If you want to make peace, you don't talk to your friends. You talk to your enemies.
-Moshe Dayan

Nothing great will ever be achieved without great men, and men are great only if they are determined to be so.
-Charles de Gaulle

It's possible to dazzle a crowd if you really work at it. But that is no qualification for leadership. Hitler was a master of crowds.
-George McGovern

A diplomat is a man who always remembers a woman's birthday, but never remembers her age.
-Robert Frost

It is perhaps common in the world for individuals and nations to suffer for their noble qualities more than for their ignoble ones. For nobility is an occasion for pride, the most treacherous of sentiments.
-Daniel Moynihan

Diplomacy is the art of the possible, and we have to keep readjusting our concept of what is possible.
-Alfred L. Atherton

Government is only as good as the men in it.
-Drew Pearson

Governments tend not to solve problems, only rearrange them.
-Ronald Reagan

Instinct is no guide to political conduct.
-Henry Kissinger

FREEDOM

Quotes & Anecdotes
(Liberty, Rights, Definitions)

The price of liberty is eternal vigilance.
-John Stuart Mill

The shepherd drives the wolf from the sheep's throat, for which the sheep thanks the shepherd as his liberator while the wolf denounces him for the same act as the destroyer of liberty.
-Abraham Lincoln

Liberty has restraints but not frontiers.
-Lloyd George

No man was ever endowed with a right without being at the same time saddled with a responsibility.
-Gerald W. Johnson

The basic test of freedom is perhaps less in what we are free to do than in what we are free *not* to do.
-Eric Hoffer

The secret of Happiness is Freedom, and the secret of Freedom, courage.
-Thucydides

Democracy arose from men's thinking that if they are equal in any respect, they are equal absolutely.
-Aristotle

A country cannot subsist well without liberty, nor liberty without virtue.
-Rousseau

Liberty, according to my metaphysics . . . is a self determining power in an intellectual agent. It implies thought and choice and power.
-John Adams

Enslave the liberty of but one human being and the liberties of the world are put in peril.
-William Garrison

The only freedom which deserves the name is that of pursuing our own good, in our own way, so long as we do not attempt to deprive others of theirs, or impede their efforts to obtain it.
-John Stuart Mill

Liberty is not merely a privilege to be conferred; it is a habit to be acquired.
-Lloyd George

When people are free to do what they please, they usually imitate each other.
-Eric Hoffer

Democracy is a process, not a static condition. It is becoming, rather than being. It can easily be lost, but never is fully won. Its essence is eternal struggle.
-Anonymous

Governing sense, mind and intellect, intent on liberation, free from desire, fear and anger, the sage is forever free.
-Bhagavad Gita

Liberty is one of the most precious gifts which heaven has bestowed on man; with it we cannot compare the treasures which the earth contains or the sea conceals; for liberty, as for honor, we can and ought to risk our lives; and, on the other hand, captivity is the greatest evil that can befall man.
-Cervantes

The natural progress of things is for liberty to yield and government to gain ground.
-Thomas Jefferson

Freedom exists only where people take care of the government.
-Woodrow Wilson

Democracy is the worst system devised by the wit of man, except for all the others.
-Winston Churchill

The Constitution . . . speaks of liberty and prohibits the deprivation of liberty without due process of law. In prohibiting that deprivation the Constitution does not recognize an absolute and uncontrollable liberty.
-Charles Evan Hughes

Whereas each man claims his freedom as a matter of right, the freedom he accords to other men is a matter of toleration.
-Walter Lippmann

A nation may lose its liberties in a day and not miss them for a century.
-Baron de Montesquieu

Our responsibility: every opportunity, an obligation; every possession, a duty.
-John D. Rockefeller, Jr.

Man must cease attributing his problems to his environment, and learn again to exercise his will—his personal responsibility—in the realm of faith and morals.
-Albert Schweitzer

Freedom comes from human beings, rather than from laws and institutions.
-Clarence Darrow

To enjoy freedom we have to control ourselves.
-Virginia Woolf

It is a great and dangerous error to suppose that all people are equally entitled to liberty.
-John C. Calhoun

At no time is freedom of speech more precious than when a man hits his thumb with a hammer.

-Marshall Lumsden

Freedom is the one purport, wisely aimed at, or unwisely, of all man's struggles, toiling and suffering on this earth.

-Thomas Carlyle

You can only protect your liberties in this world by protecting the other man's freedom. You can only be free if I am free.

-Clarence Darrow

No man is wholly free. He is a slave to wealth, or to fortune, or the laws, or the people restrain him from acting according to his will alone.

-Euripides

They tried their best to find a place where I was isolated. But all the resources of a superpower cannot isolate a man who hears the voice of freedom, a voice I heard from the very chamber of my soul.

-Anatoly B. Shcharansky

What light is to the eyes—what air is to the lungs—what love is to the heart, liberty is to the soul of man.

-Robert G. Ingersoll

Freedom is the open window through which pours the sunlight of the human spirit and human dignity.

-Herbert Hoover

Those who would give up essential liberty to purchase a little temporary safety deserve neither liberty nor safety.

-Benjamin Franklin

Those who expect to reap the blessings of freedom must, like men, undergo the fatigue of supporting it.

-Thomas Paine

The wish to be independent of all men, and not to be under obligation to any one, is the sure sign of a soul without tenderness.

-Joubert

Not free from what, but free for what?

-Frederick Nietzsche

Liberty means responsibility. That is why most men dread it.

-George Bernard Shaw

If a nation values anything more than freedom, it will lose its freedom; and the irony of it is that if it is comfort or money that it values more, it will lose that, too.

-Somerset Maugham

The death of democracy is not likely to be an assassination from ambush. It will be a slow extinction from apathy, indifference, and undernourishment.

-Robert Hutchins

Man is condemned to be free; because once thrown into the world, he is responsible for everything he does.

-Jean-Paul Sartre

Freedom is the sure possession of those alone who have the courage to defend it.

-Pericles

Men well-governed should seek after no other liberty, for there can be no greater liberty than a good government.

-Walter Raleigh

Let us not be unmindful that liberty is power, that the nation blessed with the largest portion of liberty must in proportion to its numbers be the most powerful nation upon earth.

-John Adams

Whoever will be free must make himself free. Freedom is no fairy gift to fall into a man's lap. What is freedom? To have the will to be responsible for one's self.

-Max Stirner

If the fires of freedom and civil liberties burn low in other lands, they must be made brighter in our own . . . If in other lands the eternal truths of the past are threatened by intolerance, we must provide a safe place for their perpetuation.

-Franklin D. Roosevelt

Such being the happiness of the times, that you may think as you wish, and speak as you think.

-Tacitus

If a man does not keep pace with his companions, perhaps it is because he hears a different drummer. Let him step to the music which he hears, however measured or far away.

-Henry David Thoreau

It is by the goodness of God that in our country we have those three unspeakably precious things: freedom of speech, freedom of conscience, and the prudence never to practice either.

-Mark Twain

Liberty doesn't work as well in practice as it does in speeches.

-Will Rogers

Wherever public spirit prevails, liberty is secure.

-Noah Webster

Liberty is being free from the things we don't like in order to be slaves of the things we do like.

-Ernest Benn

Men rattle their chains to show that they are free.

-Anonymous

The spirit of liberty . . . is the spirit which is not too sure it is always right.
-*Learned Hand*

The tree of liberty must be refreshed from time to time with the blood of patriots and tyrants. It is its natural manure.
-*Thomas Jefferson*

A free society is one where it is safe to be unpopular.
-*Adlai Stevenson*

What citizen of a free country would listen to any offers of good and skillful administration in return for the abdication of freedom?
-*John Stuart Mill*

Better to be a free bird than a captive king.
-*Danish Proverb*

Better to die on your feet than live on your knees.
-*Aztec Camera*

Who are a free people? Not those over whom government is reasonably exercised, but those who live under a government so constitutionally checked and controlled that proper provision is made against its being otherwise exercised.
-*John Dickson*

. . . There have existed in every age and every country, two distinct orders of men—the lovers of freedom and the devoted advocates of power.
-*Robert Hayne*

I would rather sit on a pumpkin, and have it all to myself, than to be crowded on a velvet cushion. I would rather ride on earth in an ox-cart with a free circulation than go to Heaven in the fancy car of an excursion train and breathe malaria all the way.
-*Henry David Thoreau*

America wasn't founded so that we could all be better. America was founded so we could all be anything we damn well pleased.
-*P. J. O'Rourke*

Freedom is the last, best hope of earth.
-*Abraham Lincoln*

We must not mistake noise for weight, anger for argument, militance for virtue, passion for sense, or gripes for principles.
-*Leo Rosten*

If you want a symbolic gesture, don't burn the flag, wash it.
-*Norman Thomas*

You can kill a man, but you can't kill an idea.
-*Medgar Evers*

Free at last, free at last. Thank God Almighty, I'm free at last.
-*Inscription on Dr. Martin Luther King's headstone*

Revolution is the festival of the oppressed.
-*Germaine Greer*

It's a sad and stupid thing to have to proclaim yourself a revolutionary just to be a decent person.
-*David Harris*

Who of us knows for sure a revolutionary when he sees one, even if it is himself?
-*Hortense Calisher*

Freedom is truly a short blanket that if it covers one part of the body, leaves some other part out in the cold.
-*Guido Piovene*

We are so large that we can neither afford to depend on the world, nor can the world afford to keep us dependent. That is the logic of our freedom, our self-reliance.
-*Rajiv Gandhi*

The soul of a journey is liberty, perfect liberty. We go on a journey to be free of all impediments; to leave ourselves behind, much more than to get rid of others.
-*William Hazlitt*

Freedom is not something that anybody can be given, freedom is something people take.
-*James Baldwin*

To want to be free is to be free.
-*Ludwig Borne*

The Bill of Rights is a born rebel. It reeks with sedition. In every clause it shakes its fist in the face of constitutional authority . . . It is the one guarantee of human freedom to the American people.
-*Frank I. Cobb*

America's greatness has been the greatness of a free people who shared certain moral commitments. Freedom without moral commitment is aimless and promptly self-destructive.
-*John Gardner*

Freedom is money in the bank: the more you have, the richer you are.
-*Anonymous*

Freedom is an indivisible word. If we want to enjoy it, and fight for it, we must be prepared to extend it to everyone, whether they are rich or poor, whether they agree with us or not, no matter what their race or the color of their skin.
-*Wendell L. Wilkie*

No man is wholly free. He is a slave to wealth, or to fortune, or to the laws, or the people restrain him from acting according to his will alone.

-Euripides

There is a road to freedom. Its milestones are Obedience, Endeavor, Honesty, Order, Cleanliness, Sobriety, Truthfulness, Sacrifice, and Love of the Fatherland.

-Adolf Hitler

We look forward to a world founded upon four essential human freedoms. The first is freedom of speech and expression—everywhere in the world. The second is freedom of every person to worship God in his own way—everywhere in the world. The third is freedom from want . . . The fourth is freedom from fear.

-Franklin Delano Roosevelt

Freedom is getting up happy and looking forward to the day ahead. Freedom is knowing that you can cope with and enjoy this day, and very likely, tomorrow, and the next day.

-Anonymous

There is no denying that the winds of freedom are blowing, east and west. They are brisk and bracing winds, sweeping out the old and, I believe, ushering in a new era of freedom, an era in which democracy is once again recognized as the new idea.

-Ronald Reagan

Freedom is relative. Anywhere there is an obligation, there is a lack of freedom. It's just that some people's obligations are less obligatory than other's.

-Bill Sneed

There is no want for liberty among those who do not know what freedom is.

-Johann Schubert

People always ask me why the truth will make them free. I say, if you find yourself on the edge of a cliff, you understand the truth about gravity, and the truth about falling, and the truth about rocks. All of this truth keeps you from stepping over the edge. This makes you free.

-Rev. Shalimar Reese

A dog chained to a stake in the yard is not free, but his captivity keeps your children free.

-Carl Wiggington

As long as we are slaves to instinct, to our base desires, and to those habits that would ensnare us in their encircling webs, we are not free.

-Hung T'zu-chen

. . . She danced among the revelers, tossing petals as she skipped . . . wearing no shoes or socks, her hair pulled back, her eyes sparkling in delight . . . she defied convention, and was free.

-From Cliff House Nights

The rope is about a quarter of an inch thick, but can lift a Volkswagen. Some people like to climb without it. Personally, I understand the risks and prefer to use the rope.

-Matthias Helmrich

Freedom is a mighty sword. In one hand it defends, in another, it strikes down.

-A. Papadakis

More people have been enslaved for the cause of freedom than for the cause of religion.

-Carel Mobley

There was that guy who wanted to buy an island somewhere and start his own country. He wanted to make his own rules, saying this was his pursuit of liberty. But wasn't he just running away? And how can you say you are free if you are running? No, liberty is learning to live with the rules you've been given, asserting your rights as they exist without saying you can only live by your own laws.

-Michael Moon

Freedom can't replace the right to dignity, and dignity cannot replace freedom.

-Dylan Overstreet

Anarchy is not freedom, nor is freedom anarchy. Prisons ensure freedom as much as laws and government documents.

-Judge Thomas A. Wilder

Many people have died for freedom, but not as many have lived for it.

-General Alvin Barker

Freedom is being able to get up at one in the morning, walk down to Seven-Eleven, buy a pint of B and J's Chocolate-Chip Cookie Dough ice cream, take it home, and watch Hawaii Five-O reruns.

-Steve Conklin

MEDIA

Quotes & Anecdotes
(Newspapers and Journalists, Advertising, and Southern California)

If newspapers are useful for overthrowing tyrants, it is only to establish a tyranny of their own.

-James Fenimore Cooper

An ounce of image is worth a pound of performance.

-Laurence Peter

Getting an award from TV is like getting kissed by someone with bad breath.

-Mason Williams

Newspaper editors are men who separate the wheat from the chaff, and then print the chaff.

-Adlai Stevenson

Animation is not the art of drawings-that-move, but of movements that are drawn.

-Norman McLaren

TV is chewing gum for the eyes.

-Frank Lloyd Wright

I find television very educational. Everytime someone turns it on, I go in the other room and read a book.

-Groucho Marx

Do you realize if it weren't for Edison, we'd be watching TV by candlelight?

-Al Boliska

[Television] can teach, it can illuminate. Yes, and it can even inspire. But it can do so only to the extent that humans are determined to use it to these ends. Otherwise, it is merely lights and wires in a box.

-Edward R. Murrow

If you read a lot of books you're considered well-read. But if you watch a lot of TV, you're not considered well-viewed.

-Lily Tomlin

There must be a better way to earn a living than this.

-Jack Paar, as he walked off the "Tonight" show.

I hate television. I hate it as much as peanuts. But I can't stop eating peanuts.

-Orson Welles

TV is addictive. It's a drug.

-Marshall MacLuhan

There is a young and impressionable mind out there that is very hungry for information . . . It has latched on to an electronic tube as its main source of nourishment.

-Joan Ganz Cooney, creator of "Sesame Street"

Television is a gold goose that lays scrambled eggs; and it is futile and probably fatal to beat it for not laying caviar.

-Lee Loevinger

Television is a superficial medium made so by the short attention span of a peripatetic audience.

-Richard Salant

Tell 'em not to make the mistakes Hollywood made . . . Don't start making shows better after the people have stopped coming.

-Samuel Goldwyn, on television

It's time we questioned such power in the hands of a small and unelected elite. The great networks have dominated America's airwaves for decades. The people are entitled to a full accounting of their stewardship.

-Spiro T. Agnew

How many marches and demonstrations would we have if the marchers did not know that the ever faithful TV cameras would be there to record their antics?

-Spiro T. Agnew

I don't want to be quoted, and don't quote me that I don't want to be quoted.

-Winston Burdett

Woe is me . . . because less than 3 percent of you people read books! Because less than 15 percent of you read newspapers! Because the only truth you know is what you get over this tube.

-Peter Finch

The one function that TV news performs very well is that when there is no news we give it to you with the same emphasis as if there were news.

-David Brinkley

If there were any medium that should not be concerned with censorship, it should be TV. You have a dial.

-Burt Reynolds

What passes for a culture in my head is really a bunch of commercials.

-Kurt Vonnegut, Jr.

Television is going to be the test of the modern world . . . and in this new opportunity to see beyond the range of our vision we shall discover either a new and unbearable disturbance of the general peace or a saving radiance in the sky. We shall stand or fall by television—of that I am quite sure.

-E. B. White

The price of freedom of religion or of speech or of the press is that we must put up with, and even pay for, a good deal of rubbish.

-Robert Jackson

Along with responsible newspapers, we must have responsible readers.

-Arthur Sulzberger

The American reading his Sunday paper in a state of lazy collapse is perhaps the most perfect symbol of the triumph of quantity over quality . . . Whole forests are ground into a pulp daily to minister to our triviality.

-Irving Babbitt

The day of the printed word is far from ended. Swift as is the delivery of the radio bulletin, graphic as is television's eyewitness picture, the task of adding meaning and clarity remains urgent. People cannot and need not absorb meaning at the speed of light.

-Erwin Canham

Journalism consists in saying "Lord Jones Dead" to people who never knew Lord Jones was alive.

-G.K. Chesterton

The old nobility would have survived if they had known enough to become masters of printing materials.

-Napoleon Bonaparte

Self-government will be the more secure if the editorial page recovers the vigor and stature it had before the businessman took over from the editor as top man in journalism.

-Herbert Brucker

A superior man understands what is right. An inferior man understands what will sell.

-Confucius

Few people at the beginning of the nineteenth century needed an adman to tell them what they wanted.

-John Galbraith

If it wasn't for [advertising], most people wouldn't even know what color their hair should be.

-Cornell C. Cornell

The advertising industry is one of our most basic forms of communication and, allegedly, of information. Yet, obviously, much of this ostensible information is not purveyed to inform but to manipulate and to achieve a result—to make somebody think he needs something that very possibly he doesn't need, or to make him think one version of something is better than another version when the grounds for such a belief don't really exist.

-Marvin E. Frankel

Of course advertising is information. How did everybody learn about airbags and antilock brakes? From a technical bulletin? They learned about them from advertising.

-William Cleartree

Few people have the ability or the inclination to do the research necessary to make an informed decision about purchasing a product or service. For this reason advertising is not just important, it is a critical element in the dissemination of public knowledge.

-D. Thurman Gracie

Advertising may be described as the science of arresting the human intelligence long enough to get money from it.

-Stephen Leacock

Advertising relies on two factors—that people will receive a message, and that they will have the capacity to intelligently respond to that message.

-John-Jacob Wainright

Advertising has done more to cause the social unrest of the twentieth century than any other single factor.

-Clare Barnes, Jr.

It is easier for people to criticize advertising than it is for them to admit their identities are firmly rooted in the images it portrays.

-Anson B. Brougham

Advertising is not the reduction of a product to mere features and benefits. It is the explanation of how your life will be unfulfilled unless you get up, get in your car, drive to the store, and purchase this product without delay.

-Earl Rothman

The real news is bad news.

-Marshall MacLuhan

All advertising is good news.

-Marshall MacLuhan

Instead of just recording reality, photographs have become the norm for the way things appear to us, thereby changing the very idea of reality and of realism.

-Susan Sontag

And then there is the art of altering the photos themselves. Given today's technology, you may see a picture of George and Saddam lunching together at Gino's when we know that George wouldn't be caught dead at Gino's.

-Steve Lakes

Oh, why do all you American journalists ask the same question? What factory do you come out of?

-Yevgeny Yevtushenko, to Barbara Walters

While the right to talk may be the beginning of freedom, the necessity of listening is what makes the right important.

-Walter Lippmann

There is no news, there's only media.

-Susan Halas

The challenge is to preserve the truth of that person without distorting what he says.

-Studs Terkel

If the reader buys it, it's moral.

-Steve Dunleavy—New York Post

I don't have any fixed ideas on what's right and wrong. If I did, I would probably be writing editorials in newspapers.

-James Earl Ray

We've uncovered some embarrassing ancestors in the not-too-distant past. Some horse thieves, and some people who killed on Saturday nights. One of my relatives, unfortunately, was even in the newspaper business.

-Jimmy Carter, on being presented a copy of his family tree

The plain fact is that a celebrity is anyone *People* writes about.

-Nora Ephron

Rock journalism is people who can't write interviewing people who can't talk for people who can't read.

-Frank Zappa

Mr. Hume: I've read your review of my daughter Margaret's concert last night and I've come to the conclusion that you're an eight-ulcer man on four-ulcer pay. And after reading such poppycock, it's obvious that you're off the beam and that at least four of your ulcers are working overtime. I hope to meet you and when I do, you're going to need a new nose, plenty of beefsteak for black eyes, and perhaps a jockstrap below.

-Harry S Truman, in response to a bad review of his daughter's singing

A communications professor was expounding on the advent of new technologies that would allow people to conduct virtually all their business from the convenience of their own home. "Once this system is in place, can you think of any reason to leave your house?" he asked.

One student raised his hand. "Fresh air," he replied.

-Mark Danielson

Right now, cable television companies are scurrying to provide more and more viewing choices for their customers . . . But our studies have shown that people will only watch five or six channels consistently, and the most frequently watched channels are over-the-air signals they can get for free.

-Dr. Paul Worthy

Today's media are at a crossroads. Some factions are pushing for digital delivery systems to high-definition receivers. Some would rather relay their signals from satellites to small antennae mounted on the television itself. Still others would like to see microwave transmission replace the spectrums normally used for broadcast. But the fact is, people don't really care how they get their programming. Just as long as they get it, and it doesn't cost too much, they're happy.

-Dr. Paul Worthy

Comparing fiber-optic cable to copper wire is like comparing a nineteenth-century wagon trail to a six-lane freeway. Not only does fiber-optic cable carry vastly increased amounts of information, it allows that information to travel at vastly increased velocities.

-Frederick Williams

Virtual reality, as the name suggests, is simply the creation of an entirely artificial environment whose sole purpose is to precisely imitate a real environment.

-Gillian Koenig

We have indeed become an arrogant species with our claims that we can create worlds with computers. I doubt the Good Lord used a computer to create this world.

-Edward Minson

I am curious to know why we would spend millions of dollars to create a computer-generated meadow complete with grass and bubbling brooks when all we have to do is step outside to interact with a rendering of that meadow that is more complete and satisfying than mere mortals could ever achieve with their piddling machines.

-Bill Dryer

I tape, therefore I am.

-Studs Terkel

Our major obligation is not to mistake slogans for solutions.

-Edward R. Murrow

This is the age of the journalist, more than the age of the artist, the teacher, the pastor. It is the age of non-fiction because imagination cannot keep up with the fantastic daily realities.

-Eric Severeid

An editor once put this notice in his newspaper: "If you find an error, please understand it was put there on purpose. We try to publish something for everyone, and some people are always looking for something to criticize."

-Anonymous

I always turn to the sports pages first, which records people's accomplishments. The front page has nothing but man's failures.

-Earl Warren

To the press alone, checkered as it is with abuses, the world is indebted for all the triumphs which have been gained by reason and humanity over error and oppression.

-Thomas Jefferson

The newspaper is the natural enemy of the book as the whore is of the decent woman.

-Edmond and Charles de Goncourt

The press is free to do battle against secrecy and deception in government. But the press cannot expect from the constitution any guarantee that it will succeed.

-Potter Stewart

Most American television stations reproduce all night long what only a Roman could have seen in the Coliseum during the reign of Nero.

-George Faludy

The medium is the message because it is the medium that shapes and controls the search and form of human associations and action.
-Marshall MacLuhan

We are drowning our youngsters in violence, cynicism, and sadism piped into the living room and even the nursery. The grandchildren of the kids who used to weep because the Little Match Girl froze to death now feel cheated if she isn't slugged, raped and thrown into a Bessemer converter.
-Jenkin Lloyd Jones

News is the first rough draft of history.
-Ben Bradlee

I don't even watch the news. I figure, if it's important, someone will call me.
-Merlin Fish

A free press is one that prints a dictator's speech but doesn't have to.
-Anonymous

If you stay in Beverly Hills too long, you become a Mercedes.
-Robert Redford

Always stay in your own movie.
-Ken Kesey

[In Hollywood] the drinking is tremendous . . . At four o'clock, everybody becomes a big martini.
-Blair Sabol

People have forgotten how to tell a story. Stories don't have a middle or an end any more. They usually have a beginning that never stops beginning.
-Steven Spielberg

I'm a Hollywood writer; so I put on a sports jacket and take off my brain.
-Ben Hecht

When in doubt, make a Western.
-John Ford

Cartoons are the art form of the movie industry I learn most from . . . Life now is a cartoon. We are cartoons.
-Richard Pryor

One movie studio is the best toy a boy ever had.
-Orson Welles

I often feel I'll just opt out of this rat race and buy another hunk of Utah.
-Robert Redford

Photography is truth. And cinema is truth twenty-four times a second.
-Jean-Luc Godard

I'm not a writer. I'm just someone who writes plays and scripts for a single purpose—to serve as skeletons awaiting flesh and sinew.
-Ingmar Bergman

My movies were the kind they show in prisons and airplanes, because nobody can leave.
-Burt Reynolds

Actors don't retire. They just get offered fewer roles.
-David Niven

I can get a better grasp of what is going on in the world from one good Washington dinner party than from all the background information NBC piles on my desk.
-Barbara Walters

Hitler said that he always knew you could buy the press. What he didn't know was you could get them cheap.
-Mort Sahl

Some newspapers are fit only to line the bottom of birdcages.
-Spiro T. Agnew

I won't buy a magazine that will publish what I write.
-Goodman Ace

If truth is less shapely than fiction, still it is more honest.
-Geoffrey Wolff

Reporters are puppets. They simply respond to the pull of the most powerful strings.
-Lyndon B. Johnson

Censorship, like charity, should begin at home; but unlike charity, it should end there.
-Clare Boothe Luce

A good reporter remains a skeptic all his life.
-Jack Smith

The interview is an intimate conversation between journalist and politician wherein the journalist seeks to take advantage of the garrulity of the politician and politician of the credulity of the journalist.
-Emery Kelen

The press conference is a politician's way of being informative without actually saying anything.
-Emery Kelen

What we think we know is that young sells better than old, pretty sells better than ugly, sports figures don't do very well, TV sells better than music, music does better than the movies, and anything does better than politics.
-Richard Stolley

I don't believe in that "no comment" business. I always have a comment.
-Martha Mitchell

Change is the biggest story in the world today, and we are not covering it adequately.
-James Reston

And that's the way it is . . . and most of the time we hope it isn't.
-Walter Cronkite

OPPORTUNITY

Quotes & Anecdotes
(Change, Chance, Choice)

Anything great that has ever happened is merely an opportunity that someone had the foresight to take advantage of.
-Carlos Waddicks

In the mid-1980s, Toyota launched a new luxury car under the Lexus nameplate. The introduction was a milestone for Japanese automakers entering the highly-competitive luxury car market, and thus the event was surrounded with an unbridled media frenzy. Within just a few months of its debut, however, the Lexus car had to be recalled to correct a design flaw. Many observers felt that this would be disastrous for Lexus. But the young company proved the "experts" dead wrong. They began by issuing a polite, apologetic letter to everyone who had bought a new Lexus. Then, they explained that someone would pick up their new Lexus and leave them a loaner while the Lexus dealer was taking care of the problem. Their repaired car would be delivered within 24 hours, freshly detailed and fueled. A year later, a survey revealed that more than 99 percent of all Lexus owners expressed satisfaction with their purchase, and said they would buy another Lexus, based solely on the way the initial recall problem had been handled. Lexus proved that there is no problem that does not manifest itself without a corresponding opportunity.
-Advertising Today Magazine

For many of the problems that arise in everyday interpersonal communication, the root is in the view we take of failure. Failure for most people represents our inability to control something: the situation, another person, even ourselves. But a better way to look at failure is as an opportunity for self-discovery. What can we learn about ourselves? What can we learn about others? The essence of the self-discovery paradigm is recognizing opportunities.
-Rich Grant

Carpe diem (seize the day).
-Latin saying

The right man is the one who seizes the moment.
-J. W. Goethe

When a freshly-graduated student comes to me for a job, I don't ask him what he knows. I don't ask him what his grades were. I don't care what clubs or organizations he belonged to. I simply give him a hypothetical set of circumstances and ask

how he would respond. Those that find the problems but not the opportunities, I send on their way with my best wishes. Those that see the opportunities but not the problems, I send right behind the first. But those who recognize the problems, and the opportunities that arise because of them, I offer them a position on the spot.
-Garland Worthington

Opportunity is not a roaming wanderer that blesses households at random. It seeks only those individuals that are well-prepared to meet it.
-Reed Thomas

Opportunity is nothing more than a kid on the corner with a lemonade stand.
-Paul R. Johnson

Living on the Vineyard and driving a German automobile are merely the results of an opportunity well exercised.
-G. T. Graham

Everything changes, nothing remains without change.
-Buddha

In all things, there is a law of cycles.
-Tacitus

We must obey the great law of change. It is the most powerful law of nature.
-Burke

We are negative in our relationships with that which is of a higher potential than we are; and we are positive in our relationships with that which has a lower potential. This is a relationship which is in a perpetual state of flux, and which varies at every separate point at which we make our innumerable contacts with our environment.
-Kabbalah

There is nothing permanent except change.
-Heraclitus

The seen is the changing, the unseen is the unchanging.
-Plato

As the blessings of health and fortune have a beginning, so they must also find an end. Everything rises but to fall, and increases but to decay.
-Sallust

The end of all motion is its beginning; for it terminates at no other end save its own beginning from which it begins to be moved and to which it tends ever to return, in order to cease and rest in it.
-Joannes Scotus Erigena

Still ending, and beginning still.
-Cowper

In this world of change, nothing which comes, stays, and nothing which goes is lost.
-Anne Swetchine

Change is inevitable . . . change is constant.
-Benjamin Disraeli

The atom, being for all practical purposes the stable unit of the physical plane, is a constantly changing vortex of reactions.
-Kabbalah

The universe is moved by a power which cycles endlessly from day to day. Such greatness endures for all time. As in heaven, so on earth.
-I Ching

As when rivers flowing towards the ocean find there final peace, their name and form disappear, and people speak only of the ocean, even so the different forms of the seer of all flows towards the Spirit and find there final peace, their name and form disappear and people speak only of Spirit.
-Upanishads

In human life there is constant change of fortune; and it is unreasonable to expect an exception from the common fate. Life itself decays, and all things are daily changing.
-Plutarch

The customs and fashions of men change like leaves on the bough, some of which go and others come.
-Dante

It is not strange that even our loves should change with our fortunes.
-William Shakespeare

There is such a thing as a general revolution which changes the taste of men as it changes the fortunes of the world.
-La Rochefoucauld

The world goes up and the world goes down,
And the sunshine follows the rain;
And yesterday's sneer and yesterday's frown
Can never come over again.
-Charles Kingsley

All things must change to something new, to something strange.
-Henry Wadsworth Longfellow

It is the greatest mistake to think that man is always one and the same. A man is never the same for long. He is continually changing. He seldom remains the same even for half an hour.
-Gurdjieff

To change and change for the better are two different things.
-German Proverb

The way of the Creative works through change and transformation, so that each thing receives its true nature and destiny and comes into permanent accord with the Great Harmony: this is what furthers and what perseveres.
-I Ching

Today is not yesterday: we ourselves change; how can our Works and thoughts, if they are always to be the fittest, continue always the same? Change, indeed is painful; yet ever needful: and if Memory has its force and worth, so also has Hope.
-Thomas Carlyle

To live is to change, and to be perfect is to have changed often.
-John Henry Newman

Keep what you have; the known evil is best.
-Plautus

Change is certain. Peace is followed by disturbances; departure of evil men by their return. Such recurrences should not constitute occasions for sadness but realities for awareness, so that one may be happy in the interim.
-I Ching

Men must be prepared for every event of life, for there is nothing that is durable.
-Menander

No sensible man ever imputes inconsistency to another for changing his mind.
-Cicero

Observe constantly that all things take place by change, and accustom thyself to consider that the nature of the Universe loves nothing so much as to change the things which are, and to make new things like them.
-Marcus Aurelius

Perfection is immutable. But for things imperfect, change is the way to perfect them.
-Owen Feltham

Weep not that the world changes—did it keep a stable changeless state, it were cause indeed to weep.
-William Cullen Bryant

Slumber not in the tents of your fathers. The world is advancing.
-Giuseppe Mazzini

To act and act wisely when the time for action comes, to wait and wait patiently when it is time for repose, put man in accord with the rising and falling tides [of affairs], so that with nature and law at his back, and truth and beneficence as his beacon light, he may accomplish wonders. Ignorance of this law results in periods of unreasoning enthusiasm on the one hand, and depression on the other. Man thus becomes the victim of the tides when he should be their Master.

-H. P. Blavatsky

Force never moves in a straight line, but always in a curve vast as the universe, and therefore eventually returns whence it issued forth, but upon a higher arc, for the universe has progressed since it started.

-Kabbalah

The wheel of fortune turns round incessantly, and who can say to himself, "I shall today be uppermost."

-Confucius

Fate is the endless chain of causation, whereby things are; the reason or formula by which the world goes on.

-Zeno

It is fortune, not wisdom, that rules a man's life.

-Cicero

It is not in the stars to hold our destiny but in ourselves; we are underlings.

-William Shakespeare

Luck is tenacity of purpose.

-Elbert Hubbard

Throw a lucky man into the sea, and he will come up with a fish in his mouth.

-Arabian Proverb

A man's felicity consists not in the outward and visible blessing of fortune, but in the inward and unseen perfections and riches of the mind.

-Ancharsis

Birth goes with death. Fortune goes with misfortune. Bad things follow good things. Men should realize these. Foolish people dread misfortune and strive after good fortune, but those who seek Enlightenment must transcend both of them and be free of worldly attachments.

-Buddha

The fates lead the willing, and drag the unwilling.

-Seneca

Fortune gives too much to many, enough to none.

-Martial

It is wrong to think that misfortunes come from the east or from the west; they originate within one's own mind. Therefore, it is foolish to guard against misfortunes from the external world and leave the inner mind uncontrolled.

-Buddha

No man has perpetual good fortune.

-Plautus

Men are seldom blessed with good fortune and good sense at the same time.

-Livy

A lucky man is rarer than a white cow.

-Juvenal

Everything that exists is in a manner the seed of that which will be.

-Marcus Aurelius

He who owes least to fortune is in the strongest position.

-Machiavelli

Men at some time are masters of their fates.

-William Shakespeare

Everyone is the architect of his own fortune.

-Mathurin Regnier

He that waits upon fortune, is never sure of a dinner.

-Benjamin Franklin

Human life is more governed by fortune than by reason.

-David Hume

Man supposes that he directs his life and governs his actions, when his existence is irretrievably under the control of destiny.

-Goethe

There is no such thing as chance; and what seems to us merest accident springs from the deepest source of destiny.

-Schiller

Chance happens to all, but to turn chance to account is the gift of the few.

-Bluwer-Lytton

Fortune truly helps those who are of good judgment.

-Euripides

Whatever the universal nature assigns to any man at any time is for the good of that man at that time.

-Marcus Aurelius

The way of fortune is like the Milky Way in the sky; which is a number of small stars, not seen sunder, but giving light together: so it is a number of little and scarce discerned virtues, or rather faculties and customs, that make men fortunate.

-Francis Bacon

Chance corrects us of many faults that reason would not know how to correct.

-La Rochefoucauld

To be thrown upon one's own resources is to be cast into the very lap of fortune, for our faculties then undergo a development and display an energy of which they were previously unsusceptible.

-Benjamin Franklin

The best fortune that can fall to a man is that which corrects his defects and makes up for his failings.

-J. W. Goethe

See that prosperity elate not thine heart above measure; neither depress thy mind unto the depths, because fortune beareth hard against thee. Her smiles are not stable, therefore build not thy confidence upon them; her frowns endureth not forever, therefore let hope teach thee patience.

-Akhenaton

Great progress and success can be realized. But spring does not last forever, and the favorable trend will reverse itself in due time. The wise man foresees evil and handles its threat accordingly.

-I Ching

People naturally fear misfortune and long for good fortune, but if the distinction is carefully studied, misfortune often turns out to good fortune and good fortune to be misfortune. The wise man learns to meet the changing circumstances of life with an equitable spirit, being neither elated by success nor depressed by failure.

-Buddha

Chance never helps those who do not help themselves.

-Sophocles

Persevere: It is fitting, for a better fate awaits the afflicted.

-Vergil

If matters go badly now, they will not always be so.

-Horace

Chance is always powerful. Let your hook always be cast; in the pool where you least expect it, there will be a fish.

-Ovid

Depend not on fortune, but on conduct.

-Publilius Syrus

We are sure to get the better of fortune if we do but grapple with her.

-Seneca

If fortune favors you, do not be elated;
If she frowns, do not despond.

-Ausonius

If a man looks sharply and attentively, he shall see fortune: for though she be blind, yet she is not invisible.

-Francis Bacon

When fates impose, that men must needs abide;
It boots not to resist both wind and tide.

-William Shakespeare

We should manage our fortune as we do our health—enjoy it when good, be patient when it is bad, and never apply violent remedies except in an extreme necessity.

-La Rochefoucauld

It is a madness to make fortune the mistress of events, because in herself she is nothing, but is ruled by prudence.

-Dryden

Industry, perseverance, and frugality make fortune yield.

-Benjamin Franklin

Chance generally favors the prudent.

-Joubert

Wherever the fates lead us let us follow.

-Virgil

Fortune knocks at every man's door once in a life, but in a good many cases the man is in a neighboring saloon and does not hear her.

-Mark Twain

That which is not allotted, the hand cannot reach, and what is allotted, will find you wherever you go.

-Saadi

The less we deserve good fortune, the more we hope for it.

-Moliere

Destiny has two ways of crushing us—by refusing our wishes and by fulfilling them.

-Henri Frederic Amiel

Fortune is like the market, where, many times, if you can stay a little, the price will fall.

-Francis Bacon

A strict belief in fate is the worst of slavery, imposing upon our necks an everlasting lord and tyrant, whom we are to stand in awe of night and day.

-Epicurus

When fortune favors a man too much, she makes him a fool.

-Publilius Syrus

Whatever fortune has raised to a height, she has raised only to cast it down.

-Seneca

Although men flatter themselves with their great actions, they are not so often the result of a great design as of chance.

-La Rochefoucauld

We do not know what is really good or bad fortune.

-Rousseau

EDUCATION/EXPERIENCE

A school should not be a preparation for life. A school should be life.

-Elbert Hubbard

Education is what survives when what has been learnt has been forgotten.

-B. F. Skinner

Sixty years ago, I knew everything; now I know nothing; education is a progressive discovery of our own ignorance.

-Will Durant

To be caught up in the world of thought—that is being educated.

-Edith Hamilton

The man who has ceased to learn ought not to be allowed to wander around loose in these dangerous days.

-M. M. Coady

What we want is to see the child in pursuit of knowledge, and not knowledge in pursuit of the child.

-George Bernard Shaw

Experience is not what happens to a man. It is what a man does with what happens to him.

-Aldous Huxley

It is impossible for a man to learn what he thinks he already knows.

-Epictetus

He that studies only men, will get the body of knowledge without the soul; and he that studies only books, the soul without the body. He that to what he sees, adds observation, and to what he reads, reflection, is on the right road to knowledge, provided that in scrutinizing the hearts of others, he neglects not his own.

-Colton

It is only when we forget all our learning that we begin to know.

-Henry David Thoreau

The chief object of education is not to learn things but to unlearn things.

-G. K. Chesterson

Lessons are not given, they are taken.

-Cesare Pavese

The great teacher who skillfully waits to be questioned may be compared to a bell when it is struck. Struck with a small hammer, it gives a small sound; struck with a great one, it gives a great sound. But let it be struck leisurely and properly, and it gives out all the sound of which it is capable.

-Confucius

Iron sharpens iron; scholar, the scholar.

-The Talmud

The most effective kind of education is that a child should play amongst lovely things.

-Plato

We have need of very little learning to have a good mind.

-Montaigne

Crafty men condemn studies, simple men admire them, and wise men use them.

-Francis Bacon

You cannot teach a man anything; you can only help him to find it within himself.

-Galileo

The supreme end of education is expert discernment in all things—the power to tell the good from the bad, the genuine from the counterfeit, and to prefer the good and the genuine to the bad and the counterfeit.

-Samuel Johnson

The aim of education should be to teach us rather how to think, than what to think—rather to improve our minds, so as to enable us to think for ourselves, than to load the memory with the thoughts of other men.

-James Beattie

A college education shows a man how little other people know.

-Haliburton

Seeing much, suffering much, and studying much are the three pillars of learning.

-Benjamin Disraeli

The advantage of a classical education is that it enables you to despise the wealth which it prevents you from achieving.

-Russell Green

Why should society feel responsible only for the education of children, and not for the education of all adults of every age?

-Erich Fromm

The best education in the world is that got by struggling to get a living.

-Wendell Phillips

There are three schoolmasters for everybody that will employ them—the senses, intelligent companions, and books.

-Henry Ward Beecher

Reading and writing, arithmetic and grammar do not constitute education, any more than a knife, fork and spoon constitute a dinner.

-Lubbock

Education does not consist merely in studying languages and learning a number of facts. It is something very different from, and higher than, mere instruction. Instruction stores up for future use, but education sows seed which will bear fruit, some thirty, sixty, some one hundred fold.
-Lubbock

To live a single day and hear a good teaching is better than to live a hundred years without knowing such teaching.
-Buddha

Only the educated are free.
-Epictetus

Learning makes a man fit company for himself.
-Young

There is an unspeakable pleasure attending the life of a voluntary student.
-Goldsmith

Education is the cheap defense of nations.
-Burke

The true teacher defends his pupils against his own personal influence.
-Amos Alcott

The teacher is like the candle which lights others in consuming itself.
-Giovanni Ruffini

Education is leading human souls to what is best, and making what is best out of them; and these two objects are always attainable together and by the same means; the training which makes men happiest in themselves also makes them most serviceable to others.
-John Ruskin

Learning is weightless . . . A treasure you always carry easily.
-Chinese Proverb

All wish to be learned, but no one is willing to pay the price.
-Juvenal

To be proud of learning, is the greatest ignorance.
-Jeremy Taylor

It is a thousand times better to have common sense without education than to have education without common sense.
-Robert G. Ingersoll

. . . The advantage lieth not in possessing good things, but in the knowing the use of them.
-Akhenaton

If I am walking with two other men, each of them will serve as my teacher. I will pick out the good points of the one and imitate them, and the bad points of the other and correct them in myself.
-Confucius

What we have to learn to do, we learn by doing.
-Aristotle

Wear your learning like your watch, in a private pocket; and do not pull it out and strike it merely to show that you have one.
-G. K. Chesterfield

There is no easy method of learning difficult things. The method is to close the door, give out that you are not at home, and work.
-De Maistre

Never regard study as a duty but as an enviable opportunity to learn to know the liberating influence of beauty in the realm of the spirit for your own personal joy and to the profit of the community to which your later works belong.
-Albert Einstein

The one real object of education is to have a man in the condition of continually asking questions.
-Bishop Mandell Creighton

The primary purpose of liberal education is to make one's mind a pleasant place in which to spend one's leisure.
-Sydney J. Harris

Aristotle was once asked how much educated men were superior to the uneducated. Aristotle answered, "As much as the living are to the dead."
-Diogenes Laertius

I call a complete and generous education that which fits a man to perform justly, skillfully, and magnanimously all the offices, both private and public, of peace and war.
-John Milton

Today, educational levels are replacing class structures as the significant vertical stratification of society . . . Possibly—and this may be the hardest task of the next fifty years—we may even discover how to preserve and enhance the self respect of those who fall far behind in the education race.
-Max Ways

At the desk where I sit, I have learned one great truth. The answer for all our national problems—the answer for all the problems of the world—comes to a single word. That word is "education."
-Lyndon B. Johnson

The main thing needed to make men happy is intelligence . . . and it can be fostered by education.
-Bertrand Russell

The ultimate victory of tomorrow is democracy and through democracy with education, for no people in all the world can be kept eternally ignorant or eternally enslaved.

-Franklin D. Roosevelt

Education makes people easy to lead, but difficult to drive; easy to govern, but impossible to enslave.

-Henry Peter

The traditional educational theory is to the effect that the way to bring up children is to keep them innocent, in other words, believing in biological, political, and socioeconomic fairy tales, as long as possible . . . That students should be given the best possible maps of the territories of experience in order that they may be prepared for life, is not as popular as might be assumed.

-S. I. Hayakawa

The logic of all this seems to be that it is alright for young people in a democracy to learn all about civilization or social theory that is not dangerous, but that they should remain entirely ignorant of any civilization or social theory that might be dangerous on the ground that what you don't know can't hurt you . . . a complete denial of the democratic principle that the general diffusion of knowledge and learning through the community is essential to the preservation of free government.

-Carl Becker

Education can train, but not create, intelligence.

-Edward McChesney Sait

The purpose of all higher education is to make men aware of what was and what is; to incite them to probe into what may be. It seeks to teach them to understand, to evaluate, to communicate.

-Otto Kleppner

I prefer the company of peasants because they have not been educated sufficiently to reason incorrectly.

-Michel de Montaigne

If I had learned education I would not have had time to learn anything else.

-Cornelius Vanderbilt

All of us learn to write in the second grade . . . most of us go on to greater things.

-Bobby Knight

We must open the doors of opportunity. But we must also equip our people to walk through those doors.

-Lyndon B. Johnson

Good teaching is one-fourth preparation and three-fourths theater.

-Gail Godwin

What school, college, or lecture bring to men depends on what men bring to carry it home in.

-Ralph Waldo Emerson

Books have to be read. It is the only way of discovering what they contain. A few savage tribes eat them, but reading is the only method of assimilation revealed to the West.

-E.M. Forster

If you think education is expensive, try ignorance.

-Derek Bok

A college education seldom hurts a man if he's willing to learn a little something after he graduates.

-Anonymous

Charles Eliot, former president of Harvard University once commented, "It is true, as you say, that Harvard has become a storehouse of knowledge. But I scarcely deserve credit for that. It is simply that the freshmen bring so much and the seniors take away so little."

Experience is a good school. But the fees are high.

-Heinrich Heine

A recent graduate handed his diploma to his father and said, "I finished law school to please you and Mom. Now I'm going to be a fireman like I've been saying to you since I was six."

-Gene Brown

Go to school. I tell you to go to school. I'm well known and I made a lot of money and I lost a lot of money. I'd be better off if I had gone to school longer, and so will you.

-Joe Louis

Experience enables you to recognize a mistake when you make it again.

-Franklin P. Jones

If history repeats itself, and the unexpected always happens, how incapable must man be of learning from experience.

-George Bernard Shaw

A proverb is a short sentence based on long experience.

-Miguel de Cervantes

He who has burned his mouth blows his soup.

-German Proverb

People should be free to find or make for themselves the kinds of educational experiences they want their children to have.

-John Holt

It is easy enough to praise men for the courage of their convictions. I wish I could teach the sad young of this mealy generation the courage of their confusions.
-John Ciardi

Let the learner direct his own learning.
-John Holt

We all learn by experience, but some of us have to go to summer school.
-Peter De Vries

The task of the modern educator is not to cut down jungles but to irrigate deserts.
-C. S. Lewis

Sometimes it's necessary to go a long distance out of the way in order to come back a short distance correctly.
-Edward Albee

There's no road back to childhood, but what fool would care to go?
-Nicholas Dandolos

If you don't run your own life, someone else will.
-John Atkinson

Avoid the temptation to put too much stock in that well-worn adage about how it's all right to be a radical in your youth if you're conservative in your old age. The people who pronounce that one, it turns out, are old conservatives. The old radicals have a different way of looking at it.
- Kirkpatrick Sale

It is the malady of our age that the young are so busy teaching us that they have no time left to learn.
-Eric Hoffer

A university is what a college becomes when the faculty loses interest in students.
-John Ciardi

Colleges are like old-age homes; except for the fact that more people die in colleges.
-Bob Dylan

When a subject becomes totally obsolete we make it a required course.
-Peter Drucker

In universities they don't tell you that the greater part of the law is learning to tolerate fools.
-Doris Lessing

We are people of this generation, bred in at least modest comfort, housed now in universities, looking uncomfortably to the world we inherit.
-Tom Hayden

By its most dominant voices, its most unforgettable faces, and its chief acts of bravery does a generation recognize itself and history mark it.
-Eric Severeid

It is far better to err on the side of daring than on the side of caution.
-Alvin Toffler

Today's fact becomes tomorrow's misinformation.
-Alvin Toffler

It took twenty of us working twenty hours a day, six days a week for an entire year, to accomplish what one [college] student now can do in one afternoon.
-John Kemeny, architect of the A-bomb, speaking about the pocket calculator

Fact and fancy look alike across the years that link the past with the present.
-Helen Keller

There is no yesterday, so what's left is today.
-Bob Dylan

The entire movement to acquire antiques was born out of sheer respect for things that lasted longer than fifteen minutes.
-Erma Bombeck

It has been said that there is no fool like an old fool—except a young fool. But the young fool has first to grow up to be an old fool to realize what a damn fool he was when he was a young fool.
-Harold MacMillan

Tomorrow is the most important thing in life. It comes to us at midnight very clean; it's perfect when it arrives and puts itself in our hands. It hopes we've learned something from yesterday.
-John Wayne

I must be getting absent-minded. Whenever I complain that things aren't what they used to be, I always forget to include myself.
-George Burns

What youth is afraid of is that in old age the strength to protest will be gone, but the terror of life will remain.
-Harry Reasoner

MIND AND ATTITUDE

Quotes & Anecdotes
(Intelligence and Intellectuals, Geniuses and Logic)

Millions say the apple fell, but Newton was the one to ask why.
                                                    -Bernard M. Baruch

Let us train our minds to desire what the situation demands.
                                                    -Seneca

Faced with a choice between changing one's mind and proving that there is no need to do so, almost everyone gets busy on the proof.
                                                    -John Galbraith

If you keep your mind sufficiently open, people will throw a lot of rubbish into it.
                                                    -William A. Orton

It requires a very unusual mind to make an analysis of the obvious.
                                                    -Alfred North Whitehead

The mind is its own place, and in itself can make a heaven of Hell, a hell of Heaven.
                                                    -John Milton

At a certain age, people's minds close up; they live on their intellectual fat.
                                                    -William Lyon Phelps

The growth of the human mind is still high adventure, in many ways the highest adventure on earth.
                                                    -Norman Cousins

Genius is the power of lighting one's own fire.
                                                    -John Foster

Doing easily what others find difficult is talent; doing what is impossible for talent is genius.
                                                    -Henri Amiel

Inventing is a combination of brains and materials. The more brains you use, the less material you need.
                                                    -Charles Kettering

An intellectual is a man who takes more words than necessary to tell more than he knows.
                                                    -Dwight D. Eisenhower

If an animal does something, we call it instinct; if we do the same thing for the same reason, we call it intelligence.
                                                    -Will Cuppy

It would take only one generation of forgetfulness to put us back intellectually several thousand years.
                                                    -Dean Tollefson

If the Aborigine drafted an IQ test, all of western civilization would presumably flunk it.
                                                    -Stanley Garn

I do not feel obliged to believe that the same God who has endowed us with sense, reason, and intellect has intended us to forego their use.
                                                    -Galileo

The difference between intelligence and education is this: intelligence will make you a good living.
                                                    -Charles F. Kettering

Everyone is a genius at least once a year; a real genius has his original ideas closer together.
                                                    -Georg Lichtenberg

Your attitude determines your altitude.
                                                    -Stephen R. Covey

If everybody contemplates the infinite instead of fixing the drains, many of us will die of cholera.
                                                    -John Rich

Those who desire to rise as high as our human condition allows, must renounce intellectual pride . . . the omnipotence of clear thinking . . . belief in the absolute power of logic.
                                                    -Alexis Carrel

The weather for catching fish is that weather, and no other, in which fish are caught.
                                                    -W. H. Blake

Walter Shandy attributed most of his son's misfortunes to the fact that at a highly critical moment his wife had asked him if he had wound the clock, a question so irrelevant that he despaired of the child's ever being able to pursue a logical train of thought.
                                                    -Laurence Sterne

There is no genius free from some tincture of madness.
                                                    -Seneca

The first and last thing required of genius is the love of truth.
                                                    -J. W. Goethe

Genius unexerted is no more genius than a bushel of acorns is a forest of oaks.
                                                    -Henry Ward Beecher

Men of genius are often dull and inert in society, as a blazing meteor when it descends to earth is only a stone.
                                                    -Henry Wadsworth Longfellow

Sometimes men come by the name of genius in the same way that certain insects come by the name of centipede—not because they have a hundred feet, but because most people can't count above fourteen.

-Georg Lichtenberg

If we can advance propositions both true and new, these are our own by right of discovery; and if we can repeat what is old, more briefly and brightly than others, this also becomes our own, by right of conquest.

-Colton

The mind is restless, turbulent, obstinate, and very strong. To subdue it is more difficult than controlling the wind, but it is possible by constant practice and attachment. He who strives by right means is assured of success.

-Bhagavad Gita

A drop of water has the tastes of the water of the seven seas: there is no need to experience all the ways of worldly life. The reflections of the moon on one thousand rivers are from the same moon: the mind must be full of light.

-Hung Tzu-ch'eng

Leisure and solitude are the best effect of riches, because they are the mother of thought. Both are avoided by most rich men, who seek company and business, which are signs of being weary of themselves.

-William Temple

The reflections on a day well-spent furnish us with joys more pleasing than ten thousand triumphs.

-Thomas a Kempis

Conversation enriches the understanding, but solitude is the school of the genius.

-Gibbon

The contemplation of truth and beauty is the proper object for which we were created, which calls forth the most intense desires of the soul, and of which it never tires.

-William Hazlitt

I used to spend whole days without food and whole nights without sleep in order to meditate. But I made no progress. Study, I found, was better.

-Confucius

The life that is unexamined is not worth living.

-Plato

Hardly one man in ten knows himself.

-Plautus

Contemplate thy powers, contemplate thy wants and thy connections; so shalt thou discover the duties of life, and be directed in all thy ways.

-Akhenaton

Let no sleep fall upon thy eyes till thou hast thrice reviewed the transactions of the past day. Where have I turned aside from rectitude? What have I been doing? What have I left undone, which I ought to have done? Begin thus from the first act, and proceed; and in conclusion, at the ill which thou hast done, be troubled, and rejoice for the good.

-Pythagoras

The point of the teachings is to control your own mind. Restrain your mind from greed, and you will keep your body right, your mind pure, and your words faithful. Always be thinking of the transiency of your life, you will be able to desist from greed and anger and will be able to avoid all evils.

-Buddha

The superior man will watch over himself when he is alone. He examines his heart that there may be nothing wrong there, and that he may have no cause of dissatisfaction with himself.

-Confucius

We should every night call ourselves to an account: What infirmity have I mastered today? What passions opposed? What temptation resisted? What virtue acquired? Our vices will abate of themselves if they be brought every day to the shrift.

-Seneca

Forget not on every occasion to ask thyself, is this not one of the unnecessary things?

-Marcus Aurelius

Make it thy business to know thyself, which is the most difficult lesson in the world.

-Miguel de Cervantes

There is one art of which man should be master, the art of reflection.

-Samuel Coleridge

Make no violent effort to control the mind, but rather allow it to run along for a while, and exhaust its efforts. It will take advantage of the opportunity and will jump around like an unchained monkey at first, until it gradually slows down and looks to you for orders. It may take some time to tame the mind, but each time you try it will come round to you in a shorter time.

-Sivananda

I study myself more than any other subject; it is my metaphysic, and my physic.

-Montaigne

I've developed a new philosophy—I only dread one day at a time.

-Charles Schulz's Charlie Brown

One out of four people in this country is mentally imbalanced. Think of your three closest friends—if they seem okay, then you're the one.

-Ann Landers

You are perfect exactly the way you are.

-Werner Erhard

Sometimes I feel like a figment of my own imagination.

-Lily Tomlin

I'm complicated, sentimental, lovable, honest, loyal, decent, generous, likeable, and lonely. My personality is not split; it's shredded.

-Jack Paar

All of us are crazy in one way or another.

-Theodore Isaac Rubin

Any breakdown is a breakthrough.

-Marshall MacLuhan

Insanity—a perfectly rational adjustment to an insane world.

-R. D Laing

When you look directly at an insane man, all you see is a reflection of your own knowledge that he's insane, which is not to see him at all. To see him you must see what he saw.

-Robert Pirsig

We cannot unthink unless we are insane.

-Arthur Koestler

Insanity is a matter of degree.

-Aldous Huxley

At least my neurosis is creative. It could have been writer's block.

-Woody Allen

Creativity is neither the product of neurosis nor simple talent, but an intense courageous encounter with the Gods.

-Rollo May

There's no heavier burden than a great potential.

-Linus

You don't have to try, you just have to be.

-David Viscott

One cannot be deeply responsive to the world without being saddened very often.

-Erich Fromm

Stress is the spice of life . . . Complete freedom from stress is death.

-Hans Seleye

I have called the major crisis of adolescence the identity crisis; it occurs in that period of the life-cycle when each youth must forge for himself some central perspective and direction, some working unity, out of the effective remnants of his childhood and the hopes of his anticipated adulthood.

-Erik Erikson

Looking back, my life seems like one long obstacle race, with me as its chief obstacle.

-Jack Paar

Self-pity in its early stage is as snug as a feather mattress. Only when it hardens does it become uncomfortable.

-Maya Angelou

Only the insecure strive for security.

-Wayne Dyer

If life is to be sustained, hope must remain, even where confidence is wounded, trust impaired.

-Erik Erikson

To be is to be vulnerable.

-Norman O. Brown

Our strength is often composed of the weakness we're damned if we're going to show.

-Mignon McLaughlin

I'm cheerful. I'm not happy, but I'm cheerful. There's a big difference . . . A happy woman has no cares at all; a cheerful woman has cares and learns to ignore that.

-Beverly Sills

Facts do not cease to exist because they are ignored.

-Aldous Huxley

Anybody who goes to see a psychiatrist ought to have his head examined.

-Samuel Goldwyn

Everyone carries around his own monsters.

-Richard Pryor

Words of comfort, skillfully administered, are the oldest therapy known to man.

-Louis Nizer

The essence of greatness is the ability to choose personal fulfillment in the circumstances where others choose madness.

-Wayne Dyer

He won't get to the root of his problem, because the root of his problem is himself.

-Carrol O'Connor, as Archie Bunker

Trouble is the common denominator of living. It is the great equalizer.

-Ann Landers

Toleration . . . is the greatest gift of the mind; it requires the same effort of the brain that it takes to balance oneself on a bicycle.

-Helen Keller

Let us not look back in anger or forward in fear, but around in awareness.

-James Thurber

There is no importance in anything save the emotions.

-William Carlos Williams

The pain of leaving those you've grown to love is only the prelude to an understanding of yourself and others.

-Shirley MacLaine

When the satisfaction or the security of another person becomes as significant to one as one's own satisfaction or security, then the state of love exists . . . Under no other circumstances is a state of love present, regardless of the popular usage of the word.

-Harry Stack Sullivan

The two greatest influences in my life have been my parents and asthma.

-Stanley Siegel

When you make a world tolerable for yourself, you make a world tolerable for others.

-Anaïs Nin

In life, you throw a ball. You hope it will reach a wall and bounce back so you can throw it again. You hope your friends will provide that wall.

-Pablo Picasso

You can make more friends in two months by becoming interested in other people than you can in two years by trying to get other people interested in you.

-Dale Carnegie

Pleasure is not happiness. It has no more importance than a shadow following a man.

-Muhammad Ali

The ultimate mystery is one's own self.

-Sammy Davis, Jr.

Any time friends have to be careful of what they say to friends, friendship is taking on another dimension.

-Duke Ellington

To have no friends at all is the worst state of man. To have only one good friend is enough.

-David Viscott

The best cure for hypochondria is to forget about your own body and get interested in someone else's.

-Goodman Ace

The best book for two people to read to improve their love life together is the chronicle of each other's feelings about themselves.

-David Viscott

Great minds struggle to cure diseases so that people may live longer, but only madmen ask why. One lives longer in order that he may live longer. There is no other purpose.

-Robert Pirsig

The purely abstract theorist runs the risk that, as with modern decor, the furniture of his mind will be sparse, bare, and uncomfortable.

-Robert Merton

It's co-existence or no existence.

-Bertrand Russell

In three words I can sum up everything I've learned about life. It goes on.

-Robert Frost

HUMOR/WIT

Quotes & Anecdotes
(Bits and Pieces, Retorts, Observations, Proverbs and Profundities)

When a man sits with a pretty girl for an hour, it seems like a minute. But let him sit on a hot stove for a minute—and it's longer than any hour. That's relativity.

-Albert Einstein

A man's legs should be long enough to reach the ground.

-Abraham Lincoln

You can get much farther with a kind word and a gun than you can with a kind word alone.

-Al Capone

There is a fine line between fishing and standing on the shore like an idiot.

-Stephen Wright

There is a difference between philosophy and a bumper sticker.

-Charles Schulz

Philosophy is a walk on a slippery rock.

-Edie Brickell

Heredity is an omnibus in which all our ancestors ride, and every now and then, one of them puts his head out and embarrasses us.

-Oliver Wendell Holmes

If your neighbor does you harm, show your desire to be a friend by buying his child a drum.

-Herbert V. Prochnow

Money isn't everything. After all, there are checks, charge accounts, and credit cards.

-Anonymous

I suppose it is much more comfortable to be mad and not know it than to be sane and have one's doubts.

-G. B. Burgin

There's something fishy going on here and it's not the chicken.

-From Always

There's more to life than increasing its speed.

-Mahatma Gandhi

Will Rogers was once invited by William Randolph Hearst to spend the weekend at his ranch in San Simeon. Hearst, known for his penchant of surrounding himself with the stars, made a big show of introducing Rogers to all his friends. A few days later, Hearst received a bill from Rogers for several thousand dollars, to be paid for professional services. Hearst called Rogers and exclaimed, "I didn't engage you as an entertainer, I invited you as my guest." Rogers replied, "When people invite me as a guest, they invite Mrs. Rogers, too. When they ask me to come alone, I go as a professional entertainer."

Rabbi Stephen S. Wise was attending a formal dinner, when a snooty lady told him that she was a member of the Daughters of the American Revolution and that her ancestors had witnessed the signing of the Declaration of Independence. Dr. Wise replied, "This is very well. But my ancestors witnessed the signing of the Ten Commandments."

As the story goes, Lady Astor once said to Winston Churchill, "If I were your wife, I would put poison in your coffee." Churchill replied, "If your were my wife, I would drink it."

When Jack Benny was invited to visit the White House, he was stopped by a guard who asked what was in the violin case he was carrying. "A machine gun," Benny said, keeping a straight face. The guard, mimicking Benny's expression, said, "Oh, okay. I was afraid for a moment that it was your violin."

It's going to be fun to watch and see how long the meek can keep the earth after they inherit it.

-Kin Hubbard

Most of the time I don't have much fun. The rest of the time I don't have any fun at all.

-Woody Allen

The witty man merely says what you would have said if you had thought of it.

-Anonymous

If lawyers are disbarred and clergymen defrocked, doesn't it follow that electricians can be delighted; musicians denoted; cowboys deranged; models deposed; tree surgeons debarked; and dry cleaners depressed?

-Virginia Ostman

To provoke laughter without joining in it greatly heightens the effect.

-Balzac

Courage is walking naked through a cannibal village.

-Leonard Louis Levinson

I never wanted to see anybody die, but there are a few obituary notices I have read with pleasure.

-Clarence Darrow

I'm not afraid to die, I just don't want to be there when it happens.

-Woody Allen

If you don't go to other men's funerals, they won't go to yours.

-Clarence Day

Behind every great man is a woman with nothing to wear.

-L. Grant Glickman

May you live all the days of your life.

-Jonathan Swift

My whole life is a movie. It's just that there are no dissolves. I have to live every agonizing moment of it. My life needs editing.

-Mort Sahl

The rich man and his daughter are soon parted.

-Kin Hubbard

It doesn't matter if you're rich or poor, as long as you've got money.

-Joe E. Lewis

It is more profitable for your Congressman to support the tobacco industry than your life.

-Jackie Mason

I never think of the future. It comes soon enough.

-Albert Einstein

We still say ESP is spinach and stands for Essentially Silly People.

-Cleveland Amory

Bachelors' wives and old maids' children are always perfect.

-Nicolas Chamfort

Very few people can afford to be poor.

-George Bernard Shaw

The difference between my quotations and those of the next man is that I leave out the inverted commas.

-George Moore

I quote others only the better to express myself.

-Michel de Montaigne

I often quote myself. It adds spice to my conversation.

-George Bernard Shaw

Anyone who has begun to think, places some portion of the world in jeopardy.

-John Dewey

Do not take life too seriously. You will never get out of it alive.

-Elbert Hubbard

If it were not for space, all matter would be jammed together in one lump and that lump wouldn't take up any room.

-Irene Peter

Put three grains inside a vast cathedral, and the cathedral will be more closely packed with sand than space is packed with stars.

-Sir James Jeans

I want to thank everybody who made this day necessary.

-Yogi Berra

You can't think and hit at the same time.

-Yogi Berra

Have you ever noticed what golf spells backwards?

-Al Boliska

The only reason I ever played golf in the first place was so I could afford to hunt and fish.

-Sam Snead

If you watch a game, it's fun. If you play it, it's recreation. If you work at it, it's golf.

-Bob Hope

One man's remorse is another man's reminiscence.

-Gerald Horton Bath

Whoever named it necking was a poor judge of anatomy.

-Groucho Marx

High heels were invented by a woman who had been kissed on the forehead.

-Christopher Morley

Walking isn't a lost art—one must, by some means, get to the garage.

-Evan Esar

In our life, we travel many roads. Some are giant superhighways that carry us from destination to destination, and some are mere paths in the dust. And if you're driving a Lamborghini, it doesn't really matter what road you're on.

-Jeremy North

No call alligator "long mouth" till you pass him.

-Jamaican Proverb

Have the courage to live. Anyone can die.

-Robert Cody

Love thy neighbor as thyself, but choose your neighborhood.

-Louise Beal

Do not use a hatchet to remove a fly from your friend's forehead.

-Chinese Proverb

If Patrick Henry thought that taxation without representation was bad, he should see how bad it is *with* representation.

-The Old Farmer's Almanac

Why does a slight tax increase cost you two hundred dollars and a substantial tax cut save you thirty cents?

-Peg Bracken

We don't know what we want, but we are ready to bite somebody to get it.

-Will Rogers

Never play cards with a man called *Doc*. never eat in a place called *Mom's*. Never sleep with a woman whose troubles are worse than your own.
-Nelson Algren

If you can tell the difference between good advice and bad advice, you don't need advice.
-Anonymous

We should forgive our enemies, but only after they have been hanged first.
-Heinrich Heine

A light supper, a good night's sleep, and a fine morning have often made a hero of the same man who by indigestion, a restless night, and a rainy morning, would have proved a coward.
-Earl of Chesterfield

My method is basically the same as Masters and Johnson, only they charge thousands of dollars and it's called therapy. I charge fifty dollars and it's called prostitution.
-Xaviera Hollander

If your parents didn't have any children, there's a good chance that you won't have any.
-Clarence Day

In a museum in Havana there are two skulls of Christopher Columbus, "one when he was a boy and one when he was a man."
-Mark Twain

A nose that can see is worth two that sniff.
-Eugene Ionesco

It is a far, far better thing to have a firm anchor in nonsense than to put out on the troubled seas of thought.
-John Galbraith

You know you're getting old when the candles cost more than the cake.
-Bob Hope

No man is a failure who is enjoying life.
-William Feather

A pessimist is one who thinks all women are bad. An optimist is one who hopes they are.
-Chauncey Depew

Ade's Law—Anybody can win—unless there happens to be a second entry.
-George Ade

Berra's Law—You can observe a lot just by watching.
-Yogi Berra

Levenson's Law—No matter how well a toupee blends in back, it always looks like hell in the front.
-Sam Levenson

Runyon's Law—The race is not always to the swift, nor the battle to the strong, but that's the way to bet.
-Damon Runyon

A magazine once asked J. Paul Getty to submit a short article explaining the secret to success. He returned the following: "Some people find oil. Others don't."

It is impossible to keep a straight face in the presence of one or more kittens.
-Cynthia E. Varnado

There are some girls who are turned on by my body and some others who are turned off. But for the majority I just use it as a conversation piece. Like someone walking a cheetah down Forty-Second Street would have a natural conversation piece.
-Arnold Schwarzenegger

I don't believe in an afterlife, although I am bringing a change of underwear.
-Woody Allen

Why does man kill? He kills for food. And not only food: frequently there must be a beverage.
-Woody Allen

He's so snobbish he has an unlisted zip-code.
-Earl Wilson

Happiness is having a scratch for every itch.
-Ogden Nash

If my mind ever listened to what my mouth said, I'd have a lot of accounting to do.
-Steve Allen

The truth is where the truth is, and it's sometimes in the candy store.
-Bob Dylan

The jean. The jean is the destruction. It is the dictator. It is destroying creativity. The jean must be stopped.
-Pierre Cardin

Blue jeans? They should be worn by farm girls milking cows.
-Yves St. Laurent

Eat plenty of garlic. This guarantees you twelve hours of sleep—alone—every night, and there's nothing like rest to give you shining orbs.
-Chris Chase

I'm tired of all this nonsense about beauty being only skin-deep. That's deep enough. What do you want—an adorable pancreas?
-Jean Kerr

Cheese—milk's leap toward immortality.
-Clifton Fadiman

You're never too old to become younger.
-Mae West

In Palm Beach, you do not ever get divorced during the season.
-*Charlotte Curtis*

There's more to me than just hair.
-*Farrah Fawcett*

Hollywood's a place where they'll pay you a thousand dollars for a kiss, and fifty cents for your soul.
-*Marilyn Monroe*

If God meant us to eat sugar he wouldn't have invented dentists.
-*Ralph Nader*

Nature does have manure and she does have roots as well as blossoms, and you can't hate the manure and blame the roots for not being blossoms.
-*R. Buckminster Fuller*

The perils of duck hunting are great, especially for the duck.
-*Walter Cronkite*

No one would have been invited to dinner as often as Jesus was unless he were interesting and had a sense of humor.
-*Charles Schulz*

Being a comedian is like being a con man. You have to make 'em like you before you can fool 'em.
-*Flip Wilson*

Laughter is a response to a gestalt formation where two previously incompatible or dissimilar ideas suddenly form into a new piece out of understanding—the energy released during that reaction comes out in laughter.
-*Del Close*

Nothing is quite as funny as the unintended humor of reality.
-*Steve Allen*

Success to me is having ten honeydew melons and eating only the top half of each one.
-*Barbra Streisand*

There's no deodorant like success.
-*Elizabeth Taylor*

Reality is something you rise above.
-*Liza Minelli*

I've never been out of this country, but I've been to California. Does that count?
-*Bob Bergland*

We take a handful of sand from the endless landscape of awareness around us and call that handful of sand the world.
-*Robert Pirsig*

I can hold a note as long as the Chase National Bank.
-*Ethel Merman*

A man who lives in Connecticut and works in New York commonly spends an hour and a half getting to work; he drives from five minutes to a half an hour to get to the station; rides from fifty minutes to an hour and twenty minutes on the train; once in New York, he taxis or walks or subways an additional distance before he checks in, frequently already worn out and disgruntled, for what in our civilization is laughingly called a day's work.
-*Harry Reasoner*

If at first you don't succeed, try, try again. Then quit. No use being a damn fool about it.
-*W. C. Fields*

By the time you're eighty years old, you've learned everything. You only have to remember it.
-*George Burns*

How can I die? I'm booked.
-*George Burns*

In the end, everything is a gag.
-*Charlie Chaplin*

CREATIVITY

Quotes & Anecdotes
(Nature, Applications and Insights)

In the beginning God created the Heaven and the earth. And the earth was without form, and void; and darkness was upon the face of the deep. And the Spirit of God moved upon the face of the waters. And God said, Let there be light: and there was light.

-The Bible, Genesis 1:1-3

Now I really make the little idea from clay, and I hold it in my hand. I can turn it, look at it from underneath, see it from one view, hold it against the sky, imagine it any size I like, and really be in control almost like God creating something.

-Henry Moore

When I am . . . completely by myself, entirely alone . . . or during the night when I cannot sleep, it is on such occasions that my ideas flow best and most abundantly. Whence and how these come I know not nor can I force them . . . Nor do I hear in my imagination the parts successively, but I hear them at the same time all together.

-W. A. Mozart

Somebody once asked the great composer Anton Bruckner, "How, when, and where did you think of the divine motif of your Ninth Symphony?" "Well, it was like this," Bruckner replied. "I walked up the Kahlenberg, and when it got hot and I got hungry, I sat down by a little brook and unpacked my Swiss cheese. And just as I opened the greasy paper, that darn tune pops into my head!"

All the really good ideas I ever had came to me while I was milking a cow.

-Grant Wood

I put a piece of paper under my pillow, and when I could not sleep I wrote in the dark.

-Henry David Thoreau

The best time for planning a book is while you're doing the dishes.

-Agatha Christie

It is the function of creative men to perceive the relations between thoughts, or things, or forms of expression that may seem utterly different, and to be able to combine them into some new forms—the power to connect the seemingly unconnected.

-William Plomer

Creativity is so delicate a flower that praise tends to make it bloom, while discouragement often nips it in the bud. Any of us will put out more and better ideas if our efforts are appreciated.

-Alex F. Osborn

For after the object is removed or the eyes shut, we still retain an image of the things seen, though more obscure than when we see it . . . Imagination, therefore, is nothing but decaying sense.

-Thomas Hobbes

Nature never breaks her own laws.

-Leonardo da Vinci

Nature imitates herself. A grain thrown into good ground brings forth fruit; a principle thrown into a good mind brings forth fruit. Everything is created and conducted by the same Master: the root, the branch, the fruits—the principles, the consequences.

-Blaise Pascal

Creativity cannot be commanded, only obeyed.

-Carel Mobley

Creativity is a muse of the most demanding sort. When it whispers in your ear, you sit down and write what it says to write. If you ignore it, there is a good chance it won't come back.

-Gale Petersen

An idea is a feat of association.

-Robert Frost

Creative individuals are no more dispensable than are analysts or researchers. While the latter invariably take credit for landing a man on the moon, it was a creative person that thought of going there in the first place.

-Hal Halverson

Someone once asked a well-known playwright why he chose his profession. "When I was a kid, I was the best liar on the block," he replied.

-From Off-Broadway

A student at an Oklahoma university, Ricky walked into the wrestling coach's office one day to ask for a try-out. The coach was impressed with the young man's rock-hard physique and the ice-cold determination in his eyes. But still he hesitated. Though Ricky was a fine physical specimen, the coach couldn't help noticing that where his hands should have been, Ricky only had stumps—the result of a birth defect. Finally, he asked Ricky how he had developed his upper body without being able to hold a weight bar. "I imagine it," Rick replied. "I spend two hours a day imagining I am working out, going through the motions with my arms." The coach let Ricky try out, and wasn't surprised when he pinned four of his best wrestlers.

-Richard Griffin

Creativity comes from awakening and directing men's higher natures, which originate in the primal depths of the universe and are appointed by Heaven.

-I Ching

Imagination is the eye of the soul.

-Joseph Joubert

Genius is essentially creative; it bears the stamp of the individual who possesses it.

-Germaine de Stael

Originality is simply a pair of fresh eyes.

-Thomas Higginson

It is the great triumph of genius to make the common appear novel.

-J. W. Goethe

Genius does what it must, talent does what it can.

-Bulwer-Lytton

To do a great work a man must be very idle as well as very industrious.

-Samuel Butler

Everything has been thought of before, but the problem is to think of it again.

-J. W. Goethe

Imagination disposes of everything; it creates beauty, justice, and happiness, which is everything in this world.

-Blaise Pascal

Imagination rules the world.

-Napoleon Bonaparte

All good things which exist are the fruits of originality.

-John Stuart Mill

Imagination is more important than knowledge.

-Albert Einstein

There is happiness which comes from creative effort. The joy of dreaming, creating, building, whether in painting a picture, writing an epic, singing a song, composing a symphony, devising a new invention, creating a vast industry. Work is the great redeemer. It has therapeutic value. It brings happiness.

-Henry Miller

If people knew how I work to gain my mastery, it wouldn't seem wonderful at all.

-Michelangelo

Originality is nothing but judicious imitation.

-Voltaire

He who has imagination without learning has wings but no feet.

-Joseph Joubert

The imagination is of so delicate a texture that even words wound it.

-William Hazlitt

In every work of genius we recognize our own rejected thoughts; they come back to us with a certain alienated majesty.

-Ralph Waldo Emerson

The human body is the magazine of inventions, the patent office, where are the models from which every hint is taken. All the tools and engines on earth are only extensions of its limbs and senses.

-Ralph Waldo Emerson

The lunatic, the lover and the poet
Are of imagination all compact.

-William Shakespeare

If we can advance propositions both true and new, these are our own by right of discovery; and if we can repeat what is old, more briefly and brightly than others, this also becomes our own, by right of conquest.

-Colton

Originality does not consist in saying what no one has ever said before, but in saying exactly what you think yourself.

-James Stephens

When I am finishing a picture I hold a God-made object up to it—a rock, a flower, the branch of a tree or my hand—as a kind of final test. If the painting stands up beside a thing man cannot make, the painting is authentic. If there's a clash between the two, it is bad art.

-Marc Chagall

The courage to imagine the otherwise is our greatest resource, adding color and suspense to all our life.

-Daniel J. Boorstin

Parents can plant magic in a child's mind through certain words spoken with some thrilling quality of voice, some uplift of the heart and spirit.

-Robert MacNeil

If a man had as many ideas during the day as he does when he has insomnia, he'd make a fortune.

-Griff Niblack

Not everybody has a creative bent. Some of us just have a bent.

-Samuel Trollier

Every beginning is a consequence—every beginning ends some thing.

-Paul Valèry

One must not lose desires. They are mighty stimulants to creativeness, to love, and to long life.

-Alexander A. Bogomoletz

Contrary to some opinions, creativity is not enhanced by mind-altering chemicals.

-Alan Sandomir

Research is to see what everybody else has seen, and to think what nobody else has thought.

-Albert Szent-Györgyi

The nature of artistic attainment is psychologically inaccessible to us.

-Sigmund Freud

Had I been present at the Creation, I would have given some useful hints for the better ordering of the universe.

-Alphonso the Learned

Heaven and earth, center and circumference were made in the same instant of time, and clouds full of water, and man was created by the Trinity on the 26th of October, 4004 B.C. at 9 o'clock in the morning.

-John Lightfoot

It is easier to suppose that the universe has existed from all eternity than to conceive a Being beyond its limits capable of creating it.

-Percy Bysshe Shelley

There is no great genius without a touch of dementia.

-Seneca

Great geniuses have their empire, their renown, their greatness, their victory, and their lustre, and have no need of material grandeurs with which they have no relation. They are not seen with the eyes, but with the mind; that is enough.

-Blaise Pascal

The great despise men of genius who have nothing but genius; men of genius despise the great who have nothing but greatness; the upright pity all who have either greatness or genius without virtue.

-Jean de la Bruyère

Time, place, and action may with pains be wrought;
But genius must be born, and never can be taught.

-John Dryden

A fine genius, in his own country, is like gold in the mine.

-Benjamin Franklin

I have always thought geniuses much inferior to the plain sense of a cookmaid, who can make a good pudding and keep the kitchen in order.

-Mary Montagu

The animal kingdom costs nature no more effort than the vegetable, and the most splendid genius no more than a blade of wheat.

-J. O. de la Mettrie

Genius is patience.

-George de Buffon

Talent finds its models, methods, and ends in society, exists for exhibition, and goes to the soul only for power to work. Genius is its own end, and draws its means and the style of its architecture from within.

-Ralph Waldo Emerson

To do what is impossible to talent is the mark of a genius.

-H. F. Amiel

Every man hath his proper gift of God, one after this manner, and another after that.

-The Bible, 1st Corinthians 5:7

No one respects a talent that is concealed.

-Desiderius Erasmus

There are some bad qualities which make great talents.

-La Rochefoucauld

Let us not overstrain our talents, for if we do we shall do nothing with grace; a clown, whatever he may do, will never pass for a gentleman.

-Jean de la Fontaine

Talent is a gift which God has given us secretly, and which we reveal without perceiving it.

-C. L. de Montesquieu

By different methods different men excel,
But where is he who can do all things well?

-Charles Churchill

If every man stuck to his talent, the cows would be well tended.

-J. P. de Florian

What is talent? Reason manifested gloriously.

M. J. de Chénier

Imagination is a sort of faint perception.

-Aristotle

Nature has implanted in our souls an inextinguishable love of everything great and exalted, of everything which appears beyond our comprehension. Whence it comes to pass, that even the whole world is not sufficient for the depth and rapidity of the human imagination, which often sallies forth beyond the limits of all that surrounds us.

-Longinus

Such tricks hath strong imagination,
That if it would be but apprehend some joy,
It comprehends some bringer of that joy;
Or in the night, imagining some fear,
How easy is a bush supposed a bear!

-William Shakespeare

This is a gift that I have, a foolish extravagant spirit, full of forms, figures, shapes, objects, ideas, apprehensions, motions, revolutions, these are begot in the ventricle of memory, nourished in the womb . . . and delivered upon the mellowing of occasion.

-William Shakespeare

Wit in the poet is no other than the faculty of imagination, which, like a nimble spaniel, beats over and ranges through the field of memory till it springs the quarry it hunted after.

-John Dryden

Imagination is the deceptive part in man, the mistress of error and falsehood, and so much the more deceitful as she is not always so . . . But being most frequently false, she gives no mark of her quality, marking with the same character the true and the false.

-Blaise Pascal

A man of polite imagination is let into a great many pleasures that the vulgar are not capable of receiving. He can converse with a picture, and find an agreeable companion in a statue. He meets with a secret refreshment in a description, and often feels a greater satisfaction in the prospect of fields and meadows than another does in the possession.

-Joseph Addison

Were it not for imagination, a man would be as happy in the arms of a chambermaid as of a duchess.

-*Samuel Johnson*

There is nothing more fearful than imagination without taste.

-*J. W. Goethe*

I am certain of nothing but the holiness of the heart's affections, and the truth of imagination. What the imagination seizes as beauty must be truth—whether it existed before or not . . . The imagination may be compared to Adam's dream—he awoke and found it truth.

-*John Keats*

The great instrument of moral good is the imagination.

-*Percy Bysshe Shelley*

The virtue of the imagination is its reaching, its intuition and intensity of gaze (not by reasoning, but by its authoritative opening and revealing power), a more essential truth than is seen at the surface of things.

-*John Ruskin*

Imagination is the result of heredity. It is simply concentrated race-experience.

-*Oscar Wilde*

Dreams are made up mainly of matters that have been in the dreamer's thought during the day.

-*Herodotus*

Your old men shall dream dreams, your young men shall see visions.

-*The Bible, Joel 2:28*

In sleep, every dog dreams of food, and I, a fisherman, dream of fish.

-*Theocritus*

Dreams lift up fools.

-*The Bible, Ecclesiastes 34:1*

After midnight, dreams are true.

-*Horace*

I have had a dream, past the wit of man to say what dream it was.

-*William Shakespeare*

Dreams are the true interpreters of our inclinations; but there is art required to sort and understand them.

-*Michel de Montaigne*

Dreams go by contraries.

-*English Proverb*

Dreams are excursions into the limbo of things, a semi-deliverance from the human prison.

-*H. F. Amiel*

The creative conscious is always seeking to be fed; it derives nourishment from the everyday experience.

-*Paula Sheehy*

No one asserts that creativity is the source of life, but most will claim that they are unique expressions of divine imagination.

-*Miles P. Callahan*

There are those for whom creativity is a nuisance to be dealt with through reason and truth, and there are others for whom creativity is a bracing wind that refreshes the mind and invigorates the soul.

-*Thomas Redding*

I went into the garage to change the oil in Mom's car and the fancy struck me to make an adjustment here and a calibration there. Next thing I knew, Mom had the fastest station wagon on the block and I was on my way to Indianapolis.

-*Vic Manwaring, formula-car mechanic*

Suddenly waking one night, I looked at the clock and saw that it was nearly two o'clock. I listened to make sure a prowler wasn't in the house and as I lay there in the darkness, I realized the prowler was in my mind and was merely looking for a way out. So I started up the computer and began to write. I stopped eight months later, having completed my first novel.

-*Theodoro Plano*

Ideas are like persistent salesmen. If you send them away without buying from them, they often come back later and restate their case—sometimes just when you need it.

-*K. Komatsu*

Cloe and I were having a knock-down, drag-out fight when she threw a bottle of ketchup at me. Later, I scooped the ketchup into a bowl and, just before I threw it away, I had the thought to burn it in the kiln. It worked beautifully; my next three pieces had a hint of blood in them that will always remind me of Cloe.

-*Writer Jeremy Herrick*

Intense creativity does not come from a visionary outlook, but a visionary inlook.

-*G. Harding Wilder*

Creativity is seeing.

-*Fred Sallinger*

Insanity is merely creativity with no outlet.

-*Dr. John Roget*

A blank page presents endless opportunities.

-*Ned Williams*

Creativity is applied inspiration.

-*Lance Johnson*

This is no longer the age of the guru. The genius that creates must eventually give way to the innovator that figures out how to make it profitable, how to make it fly.

-*T. Larson*

I cannot study the incredibly detailed and poetic description that modern physics gives us of the construction of elementary particles (of which all matter is composed) without being convinced that this did not happen by chance but by virtue of a truly noble plan.

-*Warren Weaver*

MUSIC

Quotes & Anecdotes
(Musicians, Composers, Song and Dance)

I know that the twelve notes in each octave and the varieties of rhythm offer me opportunities that all of human genius will never exhaust.
-Igor Stravinsky

I adore [music] . . . When I am alone with my notes, my heart pounds and the tears stream from my eyes, and my emotion and my joys are too much to bear.
-Giuseppe Verdi

Music and woman I cannot but give way to, whatever my business is.
-Samuel Pepys

I have my own particular sorrows, loves, delights; and you have yours. But sorrow, gladness, yearning, hope, love, belong to all of us, in all times and in all places. Music is the only means whereby we feel these emotions in their universality.
-H. A. Overstreet

Without music life would be a mistake.
-Friedrich Nietzsche

Music owes as much to Bach as religion to its founder.
-Robert Schumann

Bach almost persuades me to be a Christian.
-Roger Fry

Mozart is the human incarnation of the divine force of creation.
-Johann von Goethe

Never did Mozart write for eternity, and it is for precisely that reason that much of what he wrote is for eternity.
-Albert Einstein

I cannot write poetically, for I am no poet. I cannot artfully arrange my phrases so as to give light and shade. Neither am I a painter; nor can I even express my thoughts by gesture and pantomime, for I am no dancer. But I can do so in sounds. I am a musician.
-W. A. Mozart

I write music as a sow piddles.
-W. A. Mozart

Music is nothing else but wild sounds civilized into time and tune.
-Thomas Fuller

Music should strike fire from the heart of a man, and bring tears from the eyes of a woman.
-Ludwig van Beethoven

Where painting is weakest, namely, in the expression of the highest moral and spiritual ideas, there music is sublimely divine.
-Harriet Beecher Stowe

There is music wherever there is harmony, order, or proportion.
-Thomas Browne

Music resembles poetry:
In each are nameless phrases which no methods teach
And which a master-hand alone can reach.
-Alexander Pope

Music—the one incorporeal entrance into the higher world of knowledge which comprehends mankind but which mankind cannot comprehend.
-Ludwig van Beethoven

All the intelligence and talent in the world can't make a singer. The voice is a wild thing. It can't be bred in captivity.
-Willa Cather

When thunder comes it relieves the tension and promotes positive action. Music can do the same by making people enthusiastic and united together. When used to promote good it brings them closer to heaven.
-I Ching

Music produces a kind of pleasure which human nature cannot do without.
-Confucius

Music is the art of the prophets, the only art that can calm the agitations of the soul.
-Martin Luther

He who sings frightens away his ills.
-Miguel de Cervantes

Music is the only sensual gratification which mankind may indulge in to excess without injury to their moral or religious feelings.
-Joseph Addison

I always loved music; whoso has the skill in this art is of a good temperament, fitted for all things. We must teach music in schools; a schoolmaster ought to have skill in music, or I would not regard him; neither should we ordain young men as preachers unless they have been well exercised in music.
-Martin Luther

There are certain pleasures which only fill the outward senses, and there are others also which pertain only to the mind or reason, but music is a delectation so put in the midst that both by the sweetness of the sounds it moveth the senses, and by the artificiousness of the number and proportions it delighteth reason itself.
-John Northbrooke

Music hath charms to soothe a savage breast,
To soften rocks, or bend a knotted oak.
-William Congreve

Generally, music feedeth the disposition of spirit which it findeth.
-Francis Bacon

Music is a higher revelation than philosophy.
-Ludwig van Beethoven

I love Wagner; but the music I prefer is that of a cat hung up by its tail outside a window, and trying to stick the panes of glass with its claws.
-Charles Baudelaire

Wagner's music is better than it sounds.
-Mark Twain

Life can't be all bad when for ten dollars you can buy all the Beethoven sonatas and listen to them for ten years.
-William F. Buckley, Jr.

Bach opens a vista to the universe. After experiencing him, people feel there is meaning to life after all.
-Helmut Walcha

Music washes away from the soul the dust of everyday life.
-Berthold Auerbach

There is no feeling, except the extremes of fear and grief, that does not find relief in music.
-George Eliot

After silence, that which comes closest to expressing the inexpressible is music.
-Aldous Huxley

All the sounds of the earth are like music.
-Oscar Hammerstein

Tones that sound, and roar and storm about me until I have set them down in notes.
-Ludwig van Beethoven

Music, once admitted to the soul, becomes a sort of spirit and never dies; it wanders perturbedly through the halls and galleries of the memory, and is often heard again, distinct and living as when it first displaced the wavelets of the air.
-Bulwer-Lytton

Much of the effect of music, I am satisfied, is owing to the association of ideas. Scotch reels, though brisk, make me melancholy, whereas the airs in "The Beggar's Opera," many of which are very soft, never fail to render me gay, because they are associated with the warm sensations and high spirits of London.
-Samuel Johnson

Music is the moonlight in the gloomy night of life.
-Jean Paul Richter

A violinist of some reknown had recently completed a tour which had been well received by the public and the critics alike. The reviews described his interpretations as brilliant and moving, but wondered if a large part of the violinist's success was a result of the magnificent Stradivarius violin which he played. The controversy grew until everywhere he went, the violinist was met with lukewarm crowds and tepid reviews. One night, he stepped onto the stage and played a wonderful solo. The last notes faded in the silent hall, after which a few people clapped, mostly out of courtesy. He started to play again. This time, he poured his heart and soul into the piece, even causing a few tears to fall in the audience. After the second piece, a few more people clapped, but the applause soon died as the restless crowd awaited his next solo. A third time, the violinist played. This time, he drew on every ounce of talent he had, pulling celestial tones from his instrument and setting them free into the concert hall. When he was finished, the audience broke into a thunderous applause that echoed for several minutes. One by one, they stood in ovation to the great violinist. When the applause finally died, the musician broke the violin over his knee. As the shocked audience held its breath, the violinist called off stage, "Now, bring me my Stradivarius."

If I were to begin life again, I would devote it to music. It is the only cheap and unpunished rapture upon the earth.
-Sydney Smith

Music is another planet.
-Alphonse Daudet

Music is an incitement to love.
-Latin Proverb

Where there is music there can be no harm.
-Spanish Proverb

The voice is the flower of beauty
-Zeno

There's no more rock and roll. It's an imitation. I never did do rock and roll. The Beatles weren't rock and roll, nor the Rolling Stones. Rock and roll ended with Little Anthony and the Imperials.
-Bob Dylan

Rock 'n roll is music by the inept for the untutored.
-An anonymous L.A. recording executive

Half the battle is selling music, not singing. It's the image, not what you sing.
-Rod Stewart

The softer you sing the louder you're heard.
-Donovan

It was noise, such as the world has rarely heard—absolute cacophony, metallic, brash, the sound of our age . . . It hurtled from all sides, from some four hundred amplifiers and was as near total noise as anything I have so far experienced.

-*James Michener, describing rock music*

The typical rock fan isn't smart enough to know when he's being dumped on.

-*Frank Zappa*

Music is the major form of communication. It's the commonest vibration, the people's news broadcast.

-*Richie Havens*

Music can measure how broad our horizons are. My mind wants to see infinity.

-*Stevie Wonder*

Rock and roll music is still very much a raunchy, too physical, and unrefined music. Those who approach it as something more delicate, artful, or fashionable do so at great risk and danger, because they probably miss it altogether. Rock and roll is not polite. It is rude.

-*Jann Wenner*

A good rock 'n roll show on any given day could probably outdraw the president.

-*Paul Kantner*

All my concerts had no sounds in them: they were completely silent . . . People had to make their own music in their minds.

-*Yoko Ono*

Everybody else is talking about how hard life is, and here I am singing about how good it is to be alive.

-*John Denver*

Music is the timeless experience of constant change.

-*Jerry Garcia*

Every man, when at work, even alone, has a song, however rude, to soften his labor.

-*Quintillian*

I never heard the old song of Percy and Douglas that I found not my heart moved more than with a trumpet.

-*Philip Sidney*

Soft words, with nothing in them, make a song.

-*Edmund Waller*

Let me make the songs of a nation, and I care not who makes its laws.

-*Andrew Fletcher*

What will a child learn sooner than a song?

-*Alexander Pope*

Why should the Devil have all the good tunes?

-*Rowland Hill*

All deep things are song. It seems somehow the very central essence of us, song; as if all the rest were but wrappings and hulls.

-*Thomas Carlyle*

I would rather be remembered by a song than by a victory.

-*Alexander Smith*

There are German songs which can make a stranger to the language cry.

-*Mark Twain*

If she can strike a low G or F like a death rattle and a high F like the shriek of a little dog when you step on its tail, the house will resound with acclamations.

-*Hector Berlioz*

A sound so fine, there's nothing lives Twixt it and silence.

-*J. S. Knowles*

In a fiddler's house all are dancers.

-*Thomas Fuller*

Dancing is a necessary accomplishment, although of short use; for the French rule is wise, that no lady dances after marriage. This is founded in solid physical reasons.

-*Thomas Jefferson*

How imitably graceful children are in general—before they learn to dance.

-*Samuel Coleridge*

I always have a picture in my mind when I am composing, and I follow its outlines.

-*Ludwig van Beethoven*

The composer is almost the only creative artist who must depend upon a host of intermediate agents to present his work—some intelligent, some stupid; some friendly, some hostile; some energetic, some indolent; but all capable, from first to last, of either augmenting the brilliance of his work, or of disfiguring it, misrepresenting it, or even destroying it altogether.

-*Hector Berlioz*

The great pianists have nothing to show save technique and affectation.

-*Ludwig van Beethoven*

Don't be ashamed if you can't play the piano. Be proud of it.

-*E. W. Howe*

I never see a latter-day pianist on his travels but I am reminded of a comedian with his rouge-pot, grease-paints, wigs, arms and costumes.

-*James Huneker*

He who plays the piano keeps sane.

-*Italian Proverb*

Tis wonderful how soon a piano gets into a log-hut on the frontier.

-*Ralph Waldo Emerson*

The organ, to my eyes and ears, is the king of instruments.

-W. A. Mozart

Tis God gives skill,
But not without men's hands; he could not make Antonio Stradivari's violins
Without Antonio.

-Marian Evans

I heard that stupendous violinist, Signor Nicholao, whom I never heard mortal man exceed on that instrument. He has a stroke so sweet, and made it speak like the voice of a man, and when he pleased, like a concert of several instruments.

-John Evelyn

I tell you before God and on my word as an honest man that your son is the greatest composer I have ever heard of.

-Joseph Haydn, to Leopold Mozart

O Mozart, immortal Mozart, what countless images of a brighter and better world thou hast stamped upon our soul.

-Franz Schubert

The best, most beautiful, and most perfect way that we have of expressing a sweet concord of mind to each other is by music. When I would form, in my mind, ideas of a society in the highest degree happy, I think of them as expressing their love, their joy, and the inward concord, and harmony, and spiritual beauty of their souls, by sweetly singing to each other.

-Jonathan Edwards

Indefinitiveness is an element of true music—I mean of true musical expression. Give to it any undue decision—imbue it with any very determinate tone—and you deprive it, at once, of its ethereal, its ideal, its intrinsic and essential character. You dispel its luxury of dream. You dissolve the atmosphere of the mystic upon which it floats. You exhaust it of its breath of fairy.

-Edgar A. Poe

If musical sounds affect us more powerfully than the sounds of nature, the reason is that nature confines itself to expressing feelings, whereas music suggests them to us.

-Henry Bergson

Hell is full of musical amateurs. Music is the brandy of the damned.

-George Bernard Shaw

Music arouses in us various emotions, but not the more terrible ones of horror, fear, rage, etc. It awakens rather the gentler feelings of tenderness and love, which readily passes into devotion . . . It likewise stirs up in us the sense of triumph and the glorious ardor for war.

-Charles Darwin

Who is there that, in logical words, can express the effect music has on us? A kind of inarticulate unfathomable speech, which leads us to the edge of the Infinite and lets us for moments gaze into that.

-Thomas Carlyle

Some cry up Haydn, some Mozart,
Just as the whim bites. For my part,
I do not care a farthing candle
For either of them, or for Handel.

-Charles Lamb

An ear for music is a very different thing from a taste for music. I have no ear whatever; I could not sing an air to save my life; but I have the intensest delight in music, and can detect good from bad.

-Samuel Coleridge

Music rots when it gets too far from the dance.

-Ezra Pound

Music is, first of all, motion; after that, emotion. I like movement, rhythmical variety, polyphonic life.

-James Huneker

It is easier to understand a nation by listening to its music than by learning its language.

-Anonymous

As the music is, so are the people of the country.

-Turkish Proverb

The power of music is in association. Music is, in effect, a sixth sense.

-George Herbert

All objects have a resonant frequency at which a tone will amplify the natural motion of the molecules within the object. On glass, this can have the subtle impact of allowing a nail to pass through without leaving a mark, or the more powerful impact of shattering the glass altogether.

-Max Gerstein

There is something about the ocean and its incessant movement that appeals to the inner rhythm of the soul.

-Marabel Baker

Music is the backdrop of life. It has been used to incite wars, to incite intimacy, to enhance performance, to decrease stress, to accompany all human activity . . . even to propel submarines.

-J. F. Niel

ART

What is art? Nature concentrated.
-*Honore de Balzac*

Modern art is what happens when painters stop looking at girls and persuade themselves that they have a better idea.
-*Joan Ciardi*

A rich American was visiting Picasso's studio. He paused in front of a painting that puzzled him. "What does this picture represent?" cho asked.

"Two-hundred thousand dollars," Picasso replied.

If I had gone into politics, I would have been president. If I had entered the church, I would have become pope. But I went into painting, and I became Picasso.
-*Pablo Picasso*

Every child is an artist. The problem is how to remain an artist once he grows up.
-*Pablo Picasso*

Appreciation of works of art requires organized effort and systematic study. Art appreciation can no more be absorbed by aimless wandering in galleries than can surgery be learned by casual visits to a hospital.
-*Dr. Albert C. Barnes*

I paint things as they are. I don't comment I record.
-*Henri de Toulouse-Lautrec*

I see little of more importance to the future of our country and of civilization than full recognition of the place of the artist. If art is to nourish the roots of our culture, society must set the artist free to follow his vision wherever it takes him.
-*John F. Kennedy*

Art is not a thing; it is a way.
-*Elbert Hubbard*

He bores me. He ought to have stuck to his flying machines.
-*Renoir, speaking of da Vinci*

The connoisseur of art must be able to appreciate what is simply beautiful, but the common run of people are satisfied with ornament.
-*Johann W. von Goethe*

A nation in which a congressman can seriously ask, "Do you think the artist is a special person?" is a nation living in cultural jeopardy.
-*James Thurber*

[An artist] is either a revolutionist or a plagiarist.
-*Paul Gauguin*

I shut my eyes in order to see.
-*Paul Gauguin*

The aim of art is to represent not the outward appearance of things, but their inward significance.
-*Aristotle*

A man paints with his brains, not with his hands.
-*Michelangelo*

The artist is a perceptual window.
-*Jack Chambers*

When one is painting one does not think
-*Raphael Sanzio*

All great art is by its very essence in conflict with the society with which it coexists. It expresses the truth about existence regardless of whether this truth serves or hinders the survival purpose of a given society. All great art is revolutionary because it touches upon the reality of man and questions the reality of the various transitory forms of human society.
-*Erich Fromm*

Only work which is the product of inner compulsion can have spiritual meaning.
-*Walter Gropius*

Without art, the crudeness of reality would make the world unbearable.
-*George Bernard Shaw*

To paint a fine picture is far more important than to sell it.
-*Edward Alden Jewell*

After watching one of his paintings sell for more than $100,000 at an auction, Degas commented, "I feel as the horse must feel when the beautiful cup is given to the jockey."

Artists can color the sky red because they know it's blue. Those of us who aren't artists must color things the way they really are or people might think we're stupid.
Jules Feiffer

Painting is silent poetry, and poetry is painting that speaks.
-*Simonides*

Art, as far as it is able, follows nature, as a pupil imitates his master; thus your art must be, as it were, God's grandchild.
-*Dante*

The true work of art is but a shadow of the divine perfection.

-*Michelangelo*

Now nature is not at variance with art, nor art with nature, they being both servants of his providence: art is the perfection of nature; were the world now as it was the sixth day, there were not yet a chaos; nature hath made one world and art another. In brief, all things are artificial; for nature is the art of God.

-*Thomas Browne*

The highest problem of any art is to cause by appearance the illusion of a higher reality.

-*Johann von Goethe*

Light is the first consideration of painters. There is no object so foul that intense light will not make it beautiful.

-*Ralph Waldo Emerson*

The object of art is to crystallize emotion into thought, and then fix it in form.

-*Francois Delsarte*

Art is more Godlike than science. Science discovers; art creates.

-*John Olpie*

Art is like a border of flowers along the course of civilization.

-*Lincoln Steffens*

Ah! Would that we could at once paint with the eyes! In the long way, from the eye, through the arm to the pencil, how much is lost!

-*Gotthold Lessing*

Nature I love, and next to Nature, Art.

-*Walter Savage Landor*

A painting in a museum hears more ridiculous opinions than anything else in the world.

-*Edmond de Goncourt*

Art, like morality, consists in drawing the line somewhere.

-*G. K. Chesterton*

It is only an auctioneer who can equally and impartially admire all schools of Art.

-*Oscar Wilde*

An artist never really finishes his work; he merely abandons it.

-*Paul Valery*

A great artist is always before his time or behind it.

-*George Moore*

One reassuring thing about modern art is that things can't be as bad as they are painted.

-*M. Walthall Jackson*

For the mystic, what is how. For the craftsman, how is what. For the artist, what and how are one.

-*William McElcheran*

A subject that is beautiful in itself gives no suggestion to the artist. It lacks imperfection.

-*Oscar Wilde*

He paints as a bird sings.

-*Paul Signac, speaking of Monet*

Art alone supplies an enjoyment which requires no appreciable effort, which costs no sacrifice, and which we need not repay with repentance..

-*J. Schiller*

The mother of the practical arts is need; that of the fine arts is luxury. The father of the former is intelligence and of the latter genius, which is itself a kind of luxury.

-*Arthur Schopenhauer*

The world is a king, and, like a king, desires flattery in return for favor; but true art is selfish and perverse—it will not submit to the mold of flattery.

-*Ludwig van Beethoven*

Art is long, and time is fleeting.

-*Henry Wadsworth Longfellow*

Our arts are happy hits. We are like . . . a traveler, surprised by a mountain echo, whose trivial word returns to him in romantic thunders.

-*Ralph Waldo Emerson*

You must treat a work of art like a great man: stand before it and wait patiently til it designs to speak.

-*Arthur Schopenhauer*

The first universal characteristic of all great art is tenderness, as the second is truth.

-*John Ruskin*

No one can explain how the notes of a Mozart melody, or the folds of a piece of Titian's drapery, produce their essential effects. If you do not feel it, no one can by reasoning make you feel it.

-*John Ruskin*

A work of art is a corner of creation seen through a temperament.

-*Émile Zola*

It is a gratification to me to know that I am ignorant of art.

-*Mark Twain*

Art is not an end in itself, but a means of addressing humanity.

-*M. P. Mussorgsky*

Art is not nature. Art is nature digested. Art is a sublime excrement.

-*George Moore*

When art is understood by everybody, it will cease to be art.
-Arsène Houssaye

No kind of good art exists unless it grows out of the ideas of the average man.
-G. K. Chesterson

There are but two boons in life: the love of art and the art of love.
-Anonymous

Only the artist, or the free scholar, carries his happiness within him.
Ludwig van Beethoven

The artist has a twofold relation to nature: he is at once her master and her slave. He is her slave, inasmuch as he must work with earthly things, in order to be understood; but he is her master, inasmuch as he subjects these earthly means to his higher intentions, and renders them subservient.
-Johann von Goethe

One who has some artistical ability may know how to do a thing, and even show how to do it, and yet fail in doing it after all; but the artist and the man of some artistic ability must not be confounded. He only is the former who can carry his most shadowy precepts into successful application.
-Edgar Allan Poe

He is the greatest artist who has embodied, in the sum of his works, the greatest number of the greatest ideas.
-John Ruskin

In even a mediocre artist one sometimes finds a remarkable man.
-Friedrich Nietzsche

The artist shows what he is going to do the moment he puts pen to paper, or brush to canvas. He improves on his first attempts, that is all.
-George Moore

A true artist takes no notice whatever of the public. The public are to him nonexistent.
-Oscar Wilde

An artist is a dreamer consenting to dream of the actual world.
-George Santayana

The true artist will let his wife starve, his children go barefoot, his mother drudge for his living at seventy, sooner than work at anything but his art.
-George Bernard Shaw

An artist's first obligation is to reflect himself in his work.
-Anonymous

To be a first-rate painter you mustn't be pious, but rather a little wicked and entirely a man of the world.
-John Ruskin

Godfrey Kneller was once approached by his tailor who asked the artist to take his son as a pupil. Kneller replied, "Only God Almighty makes painters."

Zeuxis was so excellent in painting that it was easier for any man to view his pictures than to imitate them; who . . . painted grapes so lively that birds did fly to eat them.
-Francis Meres

The painter who draws by practice and judgment of the eye without the use of reason is like the mirror which reproduces within itself all the objects which are set opposite to it without knowledge of the same.
-Leonardo da Vinci

What vanity is painting, which attracts admiration by its resemblance to things which in the original we do not admire.
-Blaise Pascal

There are three things I have always loved and never understood: painting, music and women.
-Bernard de Fontenelle

I have generally found that persons who had studied painting least were the best judges of it.
-William Hogarth

Painting is the intermediate somewhat between a thought and a thing.
-Samuel Coleridge

It does not matter how badly you paint, so long as you don't paint badly like other people.
-George Moore

Painting—the art of protecting flat surfaces from the weather and exposing them to the critic.
-Ambrose Bierce

Sculpture is not the mere cutting of the form of any thing in stone; it is the cutting of the effect of it.
-John Ruskin

[Pop art is] the use of commercial art as subject matter in painting.
-Roy Lictenstein

The purpose of art is always, ultimately, to give pleasure—though our sensibilities may take time to catch up with the forms of pleasure that art in a given time may offer.
-Susan Sontag

Pop art is the inedible raised to the unspeakable.
-Leonard Baskin

Having the critics praise you is like having the hangman say you have a pretty neck.
-Eli Wallach

An artist is born kneeling; he fights to stand. A critic, by nature of the judgment seat, is born sitting.

-Hortense Calisher

The worst thing that can happen to an actor is to be hailed as a genius the first time he walks on stage.

-Joahn Wood

If society were different, we might be content just to do something well. But no one is pleased to simply do what they do. What's important for us is always what doesn't exist.

-Jasper Johns

My total conscious search in life has been for a new seeing, a new image, a new insight. This search not only includes the object, but the in-between place.

-Louise Nevelson

Architecture should be dedicated to keeping the outside out and the inside in.

-Leonard Baskin

Good architecture lets nature in.

-I. M. Pei

A doctor can bury his mistakes, but an architect can only advise his client to plant vines.

-Frank Lloyd Wright

Painting is an indoor art. You don't put a Rembrandt on the lawn.

-Henry Moore

I am not interested in the relationships of color or anything else . . . I am interested only in expressing the basic human emotions—tragedy, ecstasy, doom.

-Mark Rothko

Strong and convincing art has never arisen from theories.

-Mary Wigman

A picture lives by companionship. It dies by the same token. It is therefore risky to send it out into the world. How often it must be permanently impaired by the eyes of the unfeeling.

-Mark Rothko

We all know that art is not truth. Art is a lie that makes us realize truth.

-Pablo Picasso

Abstract art is uniquely modern . . . It is a fundamentally romantic response to modern life—rebellious, individualistic, unconventional, sensitive, irritable.

-Robert Motherwell

Abstract Art: A product of the untalented, sold by the unprincipled to the utterly bewildered.

-Al Capp

Take an object. Do something to it. Do something else to it.

-Jasper Johns, on creating art

In art, spontaneity must always be calculated.

-Ned Rorem

I like painting on a square because you don't have to decide whether it should be longer-longer or shorter-shorter or longer-shorter; it's just a square.

-Andy Worhol

The more minimal the art, the more maximum the explanation.

-Hilton Kramer

Everybody wants to understand painting. Why is there no attempt to understand the song of the birds? Why does one love a night, a flower, everything that surrounds a man, without trying to understand it all?

-Pablo Picasso

I do not try to dance better than anyone else. I only try to dance better than myself.

-Mikhail Baryshnikov

It is very peaceful to be able to live for your work alone. The self-denial, the sacrifices that our work demands are all compensated for by that lovely serenity of giving yourself up to dance.

-Edward Villella

The artist doesn't see things as they are, he sees things as he is.

-Robert Beverly Hale

One has a nose. The nose scents and it chooses. An artist is simply a kind of pig snouting truffles.

-Igor Stravinsky

When in doubt, sing loud.

-Robert Merrill

LITERATURE

Quotes & Anecdotes
(Words, Writers, Writing, and Wit)

Posterity—what you write for after being turned down by publishers.
-George Ade

A great book should leave you with many experiences and slightly exhausted at the end. You live several lives while reading it.
-William Styron

Masterpieces are no more than the shipwrecked flotsam of great minds.
-Marcel Proust

If I had to give young writers advice, I'd say don't listen to writers talking about writing.
-Lillian Hellman

Writing is the hardest way of earning a living, with the possible exception of wrestling alligators.
-Olin Miller

What no wife of a writer can ever understand is that a writer is working while he's staring out the window.
-Burton Rascoe

Sometimes I think it sounds like I walked out of the room and left the typewriter running.
-Gene Fowler

A writer's mind seems to be situated partly in the solar plexus and partly in the head.
-Ethel Wilson

It took me fifteen years to discover I had no talent for writing, but I couldn't give it up because by that time I was too famous.
-Robert Benchley

Literature is an occupation in which you have to keep proving your talent to people who have none.
-Jules Renard

The tools I need for my trade are tobacco, food, and a little whiskey.
-William Faulkner

I write at high-speed because boredom is bad for my health. It upsets my stomach more than anything else. I also avoid green vegetables. They're grossly overrated.
-Noel Coward

An essayist is a lucky person who has found a way to discourse without being interrupted.
-Charles Poore

No passion in the world is equal to the passion to alter someone else's draft.
-H. G. Wells

The profession of book-writing makes horse racing seem like a solid, stable business.
-John Steinbeck

In composing, as a general rule, run your pen through every other word you have written; you have no idea what vigor it will give your style.
-Sydney Smith

Read over your compositions, and when you meet a passage that you think is particularly fine, strike it out.
-Samuel Johnson

Whenever you feel the impulse to perpetrate a piece of exceptionally fine writing, obey it . . . and delete it before sending your manuscript to the press.
-Sir Arthur Quiller-Couch

I never can understand how two men can write a book together; to me that's like three people getting together to have a baby.
-Evelyn Waugh

No one can write decently who is distrustful of the reader's intelligence, or whose attitude is patronizing.
-E. B. White

The only sensible ends of literature are, first, the pleasurable toil of writing; second, the gratification of one's family and friends; and lastly, the solid cash.
-Nathaniel Hawthorne

My purpose is to entertain myself first and other people secondly.
-John D. MacDonald

I never write *metropolis* for seven cents because I can get the same price for *city*. I never write *policeman* because I can get the same money for *cop*.
-Mark Twain

I would say that music is the easiest means in which to express . . . But since words are my talent, I must try to express clumsily in words what the pure music would have done better.
-William Faulkner

Words are the best medium of exchange of thoughts and ideas between people.
-William Ross

At the beginning there was the Word—at the end just the Cliché.
-Stanislaw J. Lec

I had always assumed that cliché was a suburb of Paris, until I discovered it to be a street in Oxford.

-Philip Guedalla

A reporter covering a breaking story was told to send six-hundred words. The reporter, concerned that he might not be able to adequately cover the story, said, "It can't be told in less than twelve hundred."

His editor replied, "The story of the creation of the world was told in six-hundred. Try it."

During WWII the Civil Defense authorities had posters which read "Illumination must be extinguished when premises are vacated."When President Franklin Roosevelt saw the signs, he exclaimed, "Damn, why can't they say 'Put out the lights when you leave?'"

Originality is not seen in single words or even sentences. Originality is the sum total of a man's thinking or his writing.

-Isaac B. Singer

A powerful agent is the right word. Whenever we come upon one of those intensely right words, in a book or a newspaper, the resulting effect is physical as well as spiritual.

-Mark Twain

The difference between the right word and *almost* the right word is the difference between lightning and lightning bug.

-Mark Twain

Words are but pictures of our thoughts.

-John Dryden

Books are children of the brain.

-Jonathan Swift

The last thing that we discover in writing a book is to know what to put at the beginning.

-Blaise Pascal

It is with books as with men: a very small number play a great part, the rest are lost in the multitude.

-Voltaire

The only end of writing is to enable the readers better to enjoy life or better to endure it.

-Samuel Johnson

Words are both better and worse than thoughts; they express them, and add to them; they give them power for good or evil; they start them on an endless flight, for instruction and comfort and blessing, or for injury and sorrow and ruin.

-Tryon Edwards

Words are often seen hunting for an idea, but ideas are never seen hunting for words.

-Josh Billings

Words are potent weapons for all causes, good or bad.

-Manly P. Hall

Knowledge is the foundation and source of good writing.

-Horace

The desire to write grows with writing.

-Erasmus

Syllables govern the world.

-John Selden

Oaths are but words, and words are but wind.

-Samuel Butler

The world is satisfied with words. Few appreciate the things beneath.

-Blaise Pascal

Proper words in proper places, make the true definition of style.

-Jonathan Swift

Ideas in the mind are the transcript of the world; words are the transcript of ideas; and writing and printing are the transcript of words.

-Joseph Addison

Words are the only things that last forever.

-William Hazlitt

The great art of writing is the art of making people real to themselves with words.

-Logan Smith

Great literature is simply language charged with meaning to the utmost possible degree.

-Ezra Pound

We see then how far the monuments of wit and learning are more durable than the monuments of power, or of the hands. For have not some books continued twenty-five hundred years or more, without the loss of a syllable or letter; during which time infinite palaces, temples, castles, and cities have been decayed and demolished?

-Francis Bacon

The chief glory of every people arises from its authors.

-Samuel Johnson

The writings of the wise are the only riches our posterity cannot squander.

-Walter Savage Landor

The writer that does the most [is the one] who gives his reader the most knowledge, and takes from him the least time.

-Colton

That is a good book which is opened with expectation and closed with profit.

-Amos B. Alcott

In the highest civilization, the book is still the highest delight.
-*Ralph Waldo Emerson*

Literature is an avenue to glory, ever open for those ingenious men who are deprived of honors or of wealth.
-*Benjamin Disraeli*

But for all their inadequacy and their radical ugliness to the facts to which they refer, words remain the most reliable and accurate of our symbols. Whenever we want to have a precise report of facts or ideas, we must resort to words.
-*Aldous Huxley*

Words are used to express meaning; when you understand the meaning, you can forget about the words.
-*Chuang-tzu*

The difference between journalism and literature is that journalism is unreadable and literature is not read.
-*Oscar Wilde*

Let your literary compositions be kept from the public eye for nine years at least.
-*Horace*

Ye who write, choose a subject suited to your abilities.
-*Horace*

A good writer does not write as people write, but as he writes.
-*Montesquieu*

Make the same use of a book that the bee does of a flower: she steals sweets from it, but does not injure it.
-*Colton*

The writer must earn money in order to be able to live and to write, but he must by no means live and write for the purpose of making money.
-*Karl Marx*

The paper burns, but the words fly away.
-*Ben Joseph Akiba*

Books are ships which pass through the vast sea of time.
-*Francis Bacon*

Whatsoever things were written aforetime were written for our learning.
-*The Bible, Romans 15:4*

Literature is a kind of intellectual light which, like the light of the sun, may sometimes enable us to see what we do not like.
-*Samuel Johnson*

Delicacy—a sad, false delicacy—robs literature of the best two things among its belongings: family-circle narrative and obscene stories.
-*Mark Twain*

Literature always anticipates life. It does not copy it, but molds it to its purpose.
-*Oscar Wilde*

Great literature is the creation, for the most part, of disreputable characters, many of whom looked rather seedy, some of whom were drunken blackguards, a few of whom were swindlers or perpetual borrowers, rowdies, gamblers or slaves to a drug.
-*Alexander Harvey*

Hell hath no fury like a hustler with a literary agent.
-*Frank Sinatra*

The relationship of an agent to a publisher is that of a knife to a throat.
-*Marvin Josephson*

We have people earning $250,000 a book thinking they're failures.
-*Joni Evans, Simon & Schuster*

The dubious privilege of a freelance writer is he's given the freedom to starve anywhere.
-*S. J. Perelman*

Write out of love, write out of instinct; write out of reason. But always for money.
-*Louis Untermeyer*

They'd publish my parking tickets.
-*Sylvester Stallone, on books by superstars*

A writer is someone who always sells. An author is one who writes a book that makes a big splash.
-*Mickey Spillane*

The rules seem to be these: If you have written a successful novel, everyone invites you to write short stories. If you have written some good short stories, everyone wants you to write a novel. But nobody wants anything until you have already proved yourself by being published somewhere else.
-*James Michener*

Nothing stinks like a pile of unpublished writing.
-*Sylvia Plath*

Having been unpopular in high school is not just cause for book publication.
-*Fran Lebowitz*

If you can't be funny, be interesting.
-*Harold Ross*

A bad book is as much a labor to write as a good one; it comes as sincerely from the author's soul.
-*Aldous Huxley*

Good writing is true writing. If a man is making a story up it will be true in proportion to the amount of knowledge of life that he has had and how conscientious he is; so that when he makes something up it is as it would truly be.

-Ernest Hemingway

Life is the only sentence which doesn't end with a period.

-Lois Gould

Wrestling with illusion is part of writing. Invent illusion, and you murder it.

-Bernard Malamud

Writing is a suspension of life in order to re-create life.

-John McPhee

The complete novelist would come into the world with a catalog of qualities something like this. He would own the concentration of a Trappist monk, the organizational ability of a Prussian field marshal, the insight into human relations of a Viennese psychiatrist, the discipline of a man who prints the Lord's Prayer on the head of a pin, the exquisite sense of timing of an Olympic gymnast, and by the way, a natural instinct and flair for exceptional use of language.

-Leon Uris

A writer is not someone who expresses his thoughts, his passion, or his imagination in sentences, but someone who thinks sentences. A Sentence-Thinker.

-Roland Barthes

I do not write for a select minority . . . nor for that adulated platonic entity known as "The Masses." Both abstractions, so dear to the demagogue, I disbelieve in. I write for myself and my friends and I write to ease the passing of time.

-Jorge Luis Borges

It is the function of art to renew our perception. What we are familiar with we cease to see. The writer shakes up the familiar scene, and as if by magic, we see a new meaning in it.

-Anaïs Nin

I do borrow from other writers, *shamelessly!* I can only say in my defense, like the woman brought before the judge on a charge of kleptomania, "I do steal; but, Your Honor, only from the very best stores."

-Thornton Wilder

A successful book cannot afford to be more than 10 percent new.

-Marshall MacLuhan

The wastepaper basket is a writer's best friend.

-Isaac B. Singer

I am the beneficiary of a lucky break in the genetic sweepstakes.

-Isaac Asimov

Unlike God, the novelist does not start with nothing and make something of it. He starts with himself as nothing and makes something of the nothing with the things at hand.

-Walker Percy

Fiction is our only continuous history of our struggle to be illustrious.

-John Cheever

A style is a writer's passport to posterity.

-Leon Edel

One reason the human race has such a low opinion of itself is that it gets so much of its wisdom from writers.

-Wilfrid Sheed

If you're looking for messages, try Western Union.

-Ernest Hemingway

For most people, fiction is history; fiction is history without tables, graphs, dates, imports, edicts, evidence, laws; history without hiatus—intelligible, simple, smooth.

-William Gass

I've made characters live, so that people talk about them at cocktail parties, and that, to me, is what counts.

-Jaqueline Susan

You can lie to your wife or your boss, but you cannot lie to your typewriter. Sooner or later you must reveal your true self in your pages.

-Leon Uris

The writer . . . is a person who talks to himself, or better, who talks *in* himself.

-Malcolm Cowley

You never have to change anything you got up in the middle of the night to write.

-Saul Bellow

Asking a working writer what he thinks about critics is like asking a lamppost what it feels about dogs.

-John Osborne

Reading reviews of your own book is . . . a no-win game. If the review is flattering, one tends to feel vain and uneasy. If it is bad, one tends to feel exposed, found out. Neither feeling does you any good.

-Walker Percy

Every time I open a book, I risk my life . . . Every work of imagination offers another view of life, an invitation to spend a few days inside someone else's emotions.

-Anatole Broyard

The child in me is delighted. The adult in me is skeptical.

-Saul Bellow, upon receiving the 1976 Nobel Prize for Literature

COMPACT

Classics®

LIBRARY #8: More Trivia To Learn By

Trivia to Learn By

• What was the movement in painting that swept across France during the 1860s as a reaction against romanticism, and heavily influenced Edgar Degas, Claude Monet and Pierre Auguste Renoir in their repudiation of *imitative* art?

Impressionism

• Name the artistic movements that match each of these descriptions:

- Naturalistic art; implying a desire to depict things accurately and objectively.

Realism

- American scenic painting of the 1930s and early '40s in which the artist concentrated on the realistic depiction of specific scenes and ethnic and cultural types from the Midwest through the Deep South.

Regionalism

- The revolutionary intellectual and artistic movement beginning in 14th-century Italy whose name literally means "rebirth."

Renaissance

- A late 18th-/early 19th-century movement built upon the view that artists should paint from individual experience, from their own explored intuition and instinct — rather than following societal norms. Painters of this movement — French artist Giorgione da Castle is one example — eschewed imitation and focused on creating "ideal" and sometimes sentimentalized scenes and portraits.

Romanticism

• Which 16th-century Flemish painter of panoramic landscapes and detailed peasant scenes created such works as "The Tower of Babel" and "The Triumph of Death"—a grim painting that portrays an army of skeletons slaughtering a village of peasants?

Pieter Brueghel the Elder

• What geometric shape is used most often when artists set up a standard composition?

A triangle

• Name the artist who matches the list of clues — including birth and death dates; nationality, dominant artistic style or school, and the name of one famous work — given below:

- 1832-1883; French forerunner of impressionism; "Olympia"

Edouard Manet

- 1840-1926; French impressionist; "Water Lillies"

Claude Monet

- 1853-1890; Dutch impressionist; "The Starry Night"

Vincent van Gogh

- 1863-1944; Norwegian expressionist; "The Scream"

Edvard Munch

- 1881-1973; Spanish expressionist; "Guernica"

Pablo Picasso

- 1861-1909; American Western painter of landscapes; "Howl of the Weather"

Frederic Remington

- 1904-1989; Spanish surrealist; "Persistence of Memory"

Salvador Dali

- 1928-1987; United States pop artist; "Green Coca-Cola Bottles"

Andy Warhol

- 1834-1903; American realist; "The Artist's Mother"

James Abbott McNeill Whistler

• What is the artistic term that denotes a halo or radiant glow around the heads of glorified beings (saints, angels, etc.) in paintings with religious themes?

Aureole

• What is the title that describes artists whose works are unconventional and experimental?

Avant-garde

• Fill in the blanks with the words that fit these definitions:

- A _____ is an accurate painting of buildings grouped in arbitrary, imaginary arrangements.

Capriccio

- A painting done on wax is a _____.

Cerograph

- A _____ is created by ripping away sections of pictures (or other works) and applying them in layers so the exposed underlayer contributes to the finished work. — De coupage

- _____ art denotes the actual use of natural objects (i.e., dirt, rocks, leaves, weeds, etc.) in an arrangement to help create a painting or collage. — Earth

- The carving, stamping, molding, or pushing of a surface that raises or sinks the design in projection or retraction is called _____. — Embossing

- Wall paintings that depict curtains or drapes are called _____ drapery. — Mock

- Wall or cave paintings are formally known as _____. — Murals

- In painting, red, yellow and blue represent the _____ colors. — Primary

- What are the three "secondary" colors? — Orange, green and violet

- A portrait or statue depicting exaggerated facial expressions and anatomy is a _____. — Caricature

• What 20th-century avant-garde artist worked in a New York studio dubbed "The Factory"? — Andy Warhol

• What 19th-century French impressionist was virtually blind, and lived most of his life in seclusion until his death in 1917? — Edgar Degas

• What Flemish artist, largely undiscovered until after his death in 1569, was said to first look at mountains then "spit them out again on canvas"? — Pieter Brueghel the Elder

• What 17th-century Dutch painter, often proclaimed the "master of light and shade," painted no less than 64 self portraits? — Rembrandt Harmenszoon van Rijn

• Name the art form adopted by the early Greeks (1,000 to 700 B.C.)that implied angular lines and shapes? — Geometric art

• From the definitions below, identify the art term which best corresponds:

- A thin, transparent layer of water-color ink applied in broad strokes. — A wash

- Art or literature that is primarily intended to arouse sexual emotions. — Erotic Art

- Colors such as yellow, ocher, terra verte, umber and Venetian red that are specifically derived from metal oxides. — Earth colors

- The involuntary mixing by the eye and brain of juxtaposed colors seen from a distance creating, for example, the effect of the color orange when red and yellow dots are interspersed. — Optical mix

- A thin skin or film that forms when oil paints dry. — Pellicle

- A work of art openly created in the style of another artist—or even several artists—and not considered as fake or plagiarized. — Pastiche

- An illusionistic painting on a ceiling or wall which gives the impression that the interior is open and abyssal. — Quadratura

• On a color wheel, what color complements each of these colors?

- Black — White
- Blue — Orange
- Yellow — Violet
- Red — Green

• What is the term for a print that is "stamped" from the face of a wooden block, parts of which have been carved away to form a design? — Woodcut

- Give the artist's technique or equipment that matches each of the following descriptions:

- The tray or surface on which colors are set out and mixed before being applied to canvas.	Palette
- A stick of colored drawing material made of dry pigment and chalk bound with gum tragacanth or wax.	Crayon
- A sticky liquid from trees that makes up the staple medium of water colors, pastels and tempura paints.	Gum
- A drawing material made from calcium carbonate or other soft stone.	Chalk
- The tip of an ink-dipped or fountain pen.	Nib

- What is the term for a transparent layer of paint applied over another surface or color so that passing light is reflected back by the under-surface? — Glaze

- In 1891, what post-impressionist French painter fled his homeland for a career in Tahiti, complaining that France was "artificial and conventional"? — Paul Gauguin

- What Spanish painter, who died in 1973, became the only artist to have his work displayed in the Louvre while he was still alive? — Pablo Picasso

- What is the complete name of the Louvre museum? — The Grand Gallery of the Louvre

- What is by far the most looked-at painting in the Louvre? — The Mona Lisa

- What signature did Vincent van Gogh always put on his drawings? — Vincent

- With which hand is God bestowing life upon Adam in Michelangelo's Sistine Chapel ceiling? — His right hand

- How many human figures appear in Leonardo da Vinci's "The Last Supper," and how are they placed to achieve a triangular motif? — 13; Christ is the work's triangular focal point, and the remaining 12 Apostles are arranged in groups of 3

- What are "cherubim" and "seraphim" in religious paintings? — Orders of angels

- What is "Venus de Milo" missing, and who is said to have sculpted her? — Arms; Alexandros of Antioch

- The New England countryside was a favorite subject of this modern-day American painter, who switched to painting at the age of seventy-six only after arthritis made it hard for her to embroider. — Grandma Moses

- What was Grandma Moses' real name? — Anna Mary Robertson Moses

- An outline image in one solid, flat color, appearing as a shadow, is also known as a _____ . — Silhouette

- Answer these questions dealing with architecture and shapes:

- The Sidney Opera House in Australia, built by John Utzon, has walls that resemble what type of mollusk shell?	A nautilus
- The minaret of the Great Mosque of Samanra, Iraq has the same shape as the Thanksgiving Chapel in Dallas, Texas. What shape do these two landmarks have?	A spiral
- It is forbidden for aircraft to fly above what exquisite palatial mausoleum in India, built between 1632-1654?	The Taj Mahal
- The Salisbury Cathedral in England was built in a cruciform plan. What shape does the cathedral resemble?	A cross

- Some buildings are built in shapes resembling natural organisms while other buildings and landmarks serve as symbols. What does each of these buildings symbolize:

- The 630-foot stainless-steel Gateway Arch in St. Louis, Missouri.	The gateway to the American West
- The Porcelain Tower temple in Nanking, China.	Spiritual aspiration

- The metal grids of the Eiffel Tower in Paris, France.	France's 19th-century industrial achievements
• Which 20th-century American architect attracted the eye of architect Louis Sullivan after designing the Larkin Company Administration Building in New York? Other buildings designed by this gifted architect include the Kaufman residence, "Falling Water," in which a mountain stream runs through the house.	Frank Lloyd Wright
• A 1948 painting by Andrew Wyeth shows a girl dressed in pink lying in a field of grass and looking towards a farmhouse. According to one interpretation, which has almost achieved legendary status, this girl was a cripple who had crawled down the hill from the house and now lacked the strength to return. What is the title of the painting?	"Christina's World"
• Louis I. Kahn designed a six-arch art museum in Ft. Worth, Texas in 1972. What is the name of this museum?	Kimbell Art Museum
• Fill in the blanks of the architectural terms:	
- The space in an interior formed by supporting structural members of walls or ceilings is called a _____.	Bay
- A row of windows above the row of arches in a church or cathedral is a _____.	Clerestory
- A panel recessed into the surface of a ceiling or dome is a _____.	Coffer
- The section of a church containing the altar where sacramental rites are performed is known as the _____.	Choir
- A tall, narrow window which comes to an acute point at the top is called a _____.	Lancet
- A window or painting of a semi-circular shape is called a _____.	Lunette
- A large, single block of stone carved into a pillar statue or a column is a _____.	Monolith
- A row of arches on columns or an arched, covered gallery, (especially in a cathedral) is an _____.	Arcade
- An arched ceiling or roof constructed of masonry is called a _____.	Vault (or vaulting)
• What is referred to as the "Mother of Arts"?	Architecture
• In the book of Genesis, what did 80,000 men cut and use to build the great Temple of Solomon?	Cedars of Lebanon
• Pop art encompasses many different fields—including sculpture, architecture, and even comic book illustrations. Here are a few pop art questions surrounding the world of comics:	
- What kind of animals are Babar and his family?	Elephants
- What kind of animal is Walt Kelly's "Pogo," and where does Pogo live?	He is an opossum from the Okefenokee Swamp
- What facial features are missing from the "Little Orphan Annie" characters?	The iris and pupils are missing from their eyes
- What two comic strips are the only syndicated strips in America to show the characters aging with time?	For Better or For Worse" and "Gasoline Alley"
- Flattop, Pruneface, The Brow, and Mumbles are all enemies of which great comic detective?	Dick Tracy
• Graffiti is any type of unauthorized painting on walls or other public surfaces. Some argue that it's vandalism; others consider it viable art. At any rate, what is the singular form of the collective plural "graffiti"?	"Graffito"
• From what Egyptian writing material does the word *paper* come?	Papyrus
• What are the Pyramids at Ghizeh, Egypt made from? What tracking star does the entrance to the Great Pyramid of Cheops face?	Limestone; the North Star

- A Gothic waterspout sculpted in the form of an open-mouthed demon or dragon is called a what?

Gargoyle

- Name the famous building that matches each of these descriptions:

- The tall white obelisk designed by Robert Mills.

The Washington Monument

- The black, shiny, reflective wall in Washington D.C., designed by Maya Lin, bounded by two-inch-tall tapered sides and gradually ascending to 10 feet tall in the middle, and engraved with the names of thousands of soldiers.

The Viet Nam War Memorial

- A renowned residence in Bear Run, Pennsylvania made from concrete, rock, and a waterfall and designed in 1936 by Frank Lloyd Wright.

Falling Water

- A dome in Florence, Italy which was begun in 1294 and consecrated in 1436, it is the city's oldest surviving building and its artist, Filippo Brunelleschi, is buried inside.

Dome of the Cathedral of Santa Maria Delfiore

- One of the major landmarks in London, completed in 1709 and designed by Christopher Wren, its dome was used as a model to design the dome of the U. S. Capitol Building in Washington D.C.

St. Paul's Cathedral

- Name the architects who designed these famous landmarks. Each one was begun and completed in the years shown next to its listing:

- Johnson Wax Building; Racine, Wisconsin (1936-1944)

Frank Lloyd Wright

- Central Park; New York, New York (1858-1880)

Frederick Law Olmsted

- Monticello; Charlottesville, Virginia (1768-1809)

Thomas Jefferson

- Hearst Castle; San Simeon, California (1919-1939)

Julia Morgan

- National Treasury Building; Washington D.C. (1836-1869)

Robert Mills

- Wainwright Building; St. Louis, Missouri (1886-1890)

Louis H. Sullivan and Dankmar Adler

- U.S. Capitol; Washington D.C. (1806)

Benjamin Henry Latrobe

- What Chicago building, completed in 1974, is the tallest skyscraper in the world? How many stories high is it?

The Sears Tower; 110 stories (1,454 feet)

- What Barcelona, Spain cathedral, designed by Anton Gaudi, begun in 1883 and still unfinished today, was considered by critics as "one of the most hideous buildings in the world . . . never to be finished," yet praised by architect Walter Gropius as possessing "marvels of technical perfection"?

Church of Sagrada Familia

- During the age of cathedrals (between 1000 and 1400 A.D.), by what name were architects known?

Masons

- Egyptians believed that the first architect, builder of the earliest Egyptian pyramids, ascended to heaven as a god. What is his name?

Imhotep

- Which German architect, who lived between 1883 and 1969, was known as the greatest teacher of architecture in the modern age? (Hints: he had a reputation of being able to "breathe soul into the dead product of a machine," and he designed the Pan Am building in New York.)

Walter Gropius

- Sculptures have a way of capturing the psyche of the culture that produces them. Name the sculptors who designed the works described here:

- A polished bronze shaft standing 4 feet tall, completed in 1925 and titled "Bird in Space."

Constantin Brancusi

- A bronze sculpture called "The Thinker," finished in 1880 and originally conceived as a figure set apart to brood contemplatively over a larger work entitled "Gates of Hell," based on Dante's "Divine Comedy."

Auguste Rodin

• Which country boasts the biggest bronze statue ever made—a 13th-century rendition of "The Great Buddha"?	Japan
• What are the cracks called that form in the glaze of pottery due to improperly blended cement or to the unequal shrinking of the pot after firing?	Crazing
• What is so unique about the *Mona Lisa*'s smile, and what makes the background of the painting so unusual?	It was the first portrait to show a smile; the foreground figure separates two different landscapes that don't mesh together
• What 1495 Leonardo da Vinci painting was the first to demonstrate both central focal points and perspective?	"The Last Supper"
• The art of the Renaissance was expressed in the 15th-century "rebirth" of what earlier aesthetic and spiritual values?	The art marked a return to the classical visions of ancient Greece and Rome
• Michelangelo's sculpture of "David" is stylistically different from any of its predecessors. How?	David is posing and not in action
• One of the most contemporary art forms is photography. Complete each of the following sentences with the correct missing photographic term:	
- The photograph of a moving subject standing out in striking clarity against a blurry back ground is called an _____ shot.	Action
- A base of metallic oxide or hydroxide—the opposite of an acid-base is an _____-base.	Alkali
- In motion pictures, giving apparent movement to drawings or inanimate objects by slightly varying their positions with a series of rapid frame changes is called _____.	Animation
- The difference in tone, composition and elements of a picture or subject and background is known as _____.	Contrast
- The clarity of details, shapes, tones and colors in an image is called _____.	Definition
- The "double image" condition that often occurs when an electronic flash is used with a fairly bright secondary light is known as _____.	Ghosting
- An early 1890s motion picture viewing machine, using the rapid, riffling of flip-book pictures used to produce movement was called a _____.	Mutoscope
• What American camera company's motto in the 1960s was, "You push the button, we do the rest"?	Eastman-Kodak
• What American photographer, born in 1902, remained strongly associated with the visionary sense of the wilderness and the importance of wilderness preservation until his death in 1984?	Ansel Adams
• What English inventor, who assumed the presidency of the Photographic Society of London in 1892 as its first true authority, invented negative intensification using copper bromide and silver nitrate?	Sir William de Wiveleslie Abney
• In 1826, who recorded the earliest, still-existing permanent image in a photograph?	Joseph Nicephore Niepce
• In what year was the first actual photographic film, made of light-sensitive silver compounds, introduced to the public?	1939
• What is a three-dimensional photograph called?	A holograph
• What camera, developed by Oscar Barnack, was introduced to the public in 1924, becoming a major factor in the popularization and growth of the 35mm camera? (Hint: this name is well known to anyone who uses a camera.)	Leica Camera
• What is the graphic reproduction whose name literally means "stone writing," and is based on the principle that oil and water repel each other?	Petroglyph

MUSIC
Trivia to Learn By

• What 1957 musical, based on a Shakespeare play and scored by Leonard Bernstein and Stephen Sondheim, was not labeled an opera but an operetta, since the final scenes were not sung?

"West Side Story" (based on "Romeo and Juliet")

• What "nighttime" composition is written with the intent of being sung or played under a lover's window?

A Serenade

• What Al Capp comic strip about a hillbilly town came to life in this 1956 musical?

"Li'l Abner"

• How old was Stevie Wonder when he made his debut on Dick Clark's American Bandstand? What was his first single called?

13; "Fingertips"

• Which English rock vocalist sang the title role on the recorded soundtrack of "Jesus Christ Superstar"?

Deep Purple's Ian Gillan

• What was the first production to win Best Musical at the Tony Awards? (Hint: It was in 1949.)

"Kiss Me Kate"

• Name the man who wrote and composed the musicals "Jesus Christ Superstar," "Evita," "Cats" and "Phantom of the Opera."

Andrew Lloyd Webber

• What is a "librettist"?

One who writes the spoken dialogue for musicals

• What American folk singer and composer wrote more than 1,000 songs, among them "This Land Is Your Land" and "Bound for Glory"? Also, name this artist's famous folk-singing son.

Woody Guthrie; Arlo Guthrie

• Which best-selling Stephen King thriller recently became a Broadway musical?

"Carrie"

• Who first said, "If you want to understand a nation, listen to its music?"

Chinese philosopher Confucius (c. 6th century B.C.)

• Who invented the modern "Do, Re, Mi . . . "scale, and is considered by some to be the inventor of formal musical text?

Guido d'Arezzo, an early Catholic Monk

• What pear-shaped plucking instrument is believed to be the forerunner of the modern mandolin?

The lute

• Give three or more instruments that fit in the classifications below (only the principal instruments in each class are listed as answers):

- Woodwind instruments (woodwinds).

Clarinet, bass clarinet, flute, piccolo, bassoon, saxophone (soprano, alto and tenor . . .), oboe, and English horn

- Brasses (another sub-class of wind instruments).

Trumpet, bugle, trombone, French horn, sousaphone, baritone horn, and flugelhorn

- Stringed instruments.

Violin, viola, cello, bass, harp, guitar, banjo, mandolin, and lute

- Percussion instruments.

Kettledrum, snare drum, bass drum, bongo drums, vibraphone, triangle, cymbals, chimes, gong, sleigh bells, as well as a number of other ringers, clickers, bangers and scratchers

- Keyboard and electronic instruments.

Piano, harpsichord, pipe organ; electric guitars and basses, electric pianos, electronic organs, and synthesizers

• What instrument does jazz artist Chuck Mangione play?	The flugelhorn
• Which classical romantic composer, having gone completely deaf by his mid-thirties, couldn't hear the audience's standing ovation after he finished conducting his last symphony?	Beethoven
• Sesame Street's Kermit the Frog made it to Billboard's Top 40 when he sang what song?	"Rainbow Connection"
• Which modern composer's western-flavored works include "Appalachian Spring," "Billy the Kid" and "Rodeo"?	Aaron Copeland
• Name the German-born composer who used the solar system as his inspiration for a symphony ("The Planets"—including "Mars, Bringer of War" and "Saturn, Bringer of Old Age").	Gustav Holst
• What Tchaikovsky ballet features two short movements titled "Tea" and "Coffee"?	The Nutcracker
• True or false?The music composed by Mozart in the 18th century is still performed today exactly the way he intended it to be played.	False.Music pitch has jumped a full 1/2 note since 1791.If Mozart—with his ear for perfect pitch—were to hear a G-minor scale today, he would consider it G-sharp minor.
• Who was the reclusive widow who, over a 13-year period, supported Tchaikovsky both financially and emotionally, sending him a combined total of over 1,100 letters? Also, what was notably strange about their relationship?	Madame Naezhda von Meck; she never actually spoke with Tchaikovsky face to face
• What famous symphony led Richard Wagner to decide to become a composer?	Beethoven's "Ninth Symphony"
• Name the modern avant-garde composer who authored a whole piece consisting of a pianist sitting at the piano in silence without touching a note for 4 minutes and 33 seconds.	John Cage in his piece 4′33″
• Elvis Presley's hit "It's Now or Never" was based on which well-known Italian operetta piece?	"O Sole Mio"
• In what studio did Elvis Presley cut his very first record in 1953? What were the two minor-hit songs it included?	Sun Recording Studio, Memphis; "That's When Your Heart Aches" and "My Happiness"
• Who originally recorded "My Happiness"?	The Ink Spots (1942)
• In what month and year did Elvis die?How old was he?	August, 1977; 42
• After Elvis' controversial 1956 appearance on the Milton Berle Show, Ed Sullivan said he wouldn't touch Elvis with a 10-foot-long pole.Under what conditions did Sullivan finally agree to have "Elvis the Pelvis" appear on his show?	Elvis was to be shown on television from the waist up only
• Who sang about the privilege of crying at her own party in 1963?	Leslie Gore, in "It's My Party" (and I'll cry if I want to)
• Who wrote "The Twist"?	Hank Ballard (Chubby Checker only recorded it)
• Which country-western singer gave up his fatal airplane seat to Buddy Holly, on a flight that also carried the Big Bopper, Richie Valens, and several other country and rock musicians to their deaths in 1959?	Waylon Jennings
• How old was Paul Anka when his single "Diana" became a hit in the U.S.and Great Britain?	15
• Provide the "real" name that corresponds to each famous nickname:	
- "The Boss"	Bruce Springsteen
- "The Lizard King"	Jim Morrison
- "Slow Hand"	Eric Clapton

- "Motor City Madman"	Ted Nugent
- "Red Rocker"	Sammy Hagar
- "Bocephus"	Hank Williams Jr.
- "The Cute One"	Paul McCartney
- "The Toxic Twins"	Joe Perry and Steven Tyler of Aerosmith
- "The Man In Black"	Johnny Cash
- "Father of Soul"	Sam Cooke
- "Old Blue Eyes"	Frank Sinatra
• What was the real cause behind the girls' "swooning" at Frank Sinatra's early shows?	Money (Sinatra's publicity crew paid girls to swoon and faint during his performances)
• Name some prominent members of the Hollywood "Rat Pack."	Frank Sinatra, Sammy Davis Jr., Dean Martin, and Liza Minelli
• What is recording artist Englebert Humperdink's real name?	Arnold George Dorsey
• What singer has the distinction of once having over 100 records on Billboard Magazine's *Top 40* weekly listing?	Elvis Presley
• Give the correct musical term corresponding to each definition below.	
- Sharps and flats and naturals not included in a key signature.	"Accidentals"
- A unit of musical time containing an indicated number of beats.	"Measure"
- The sign seen at the beginning of a staff that fixes the position of notes on the lines and spaces of the staff.	"Clef"
- An interval of eight notes.	"Octave"
- An organ stop (also, another word for a bassoon).	"Fagotto"
- A combination of three or more tones played at the same time.	"Chord"
- The quality of a sound which is determined by its wavelength frequency.	"Pitch"
- To pluck, bow or strike, as on a guitar, violin, etc.	"Excite"
• What famous 1966 theme hit—written by Van Morrison—was subsequently recorded by both The Doors and Jimi Hendrix?	"Gloria"
• Jimi Hendrix, Janis Joplin and Jim Morrison all died at what tender age?	27
• Who was the New York artist who designed The Rolling Stones' zipper-laden "Sticky Fingers" album cover and the banana album cover for The Velvet Underground?	Andy Warhol
• How many "nervous breakdowns" did the Rolling Stones sing about?	Nineteen
• Jimi Hendrix was the stage name for who?	Johnny Allen Hendrix
• Ahmet Rodan, Moon Unit, and Dweezil are the children of what famous father?	Frank Zappa
• What lead singer from which 1960's band claimed to have an IQ of 150 and worshipped enigmatic thinkers Nietzsche and Kafka?	Jim Morrison of The Doors
• In the 1970s, Don Kirshner gave the group Kansas its big break. What 1960s *parody* band did he earlier help create?	The Monkees
• Linda Ronstadt's back-up band from the mid 1970s went on to become what supergroup?	The Eagles

- The original 1976 blockbuster recording debut of the band Boston was made where?

In guitarist Tom Scholz's basement

- In 1979, Fats Domino's "Ain't That A Shame" became a hit—thanks to what band?

Cheap Trick

- Beatles trivia:
  - How many songs did The Beatles record from 1962 to 1966?

102

  - Who was the oldest Beatle?

Ringo Starr

  - Where did The Beatles give their first American concert?

The Coliseum Sports Arena in Washington

  - What American Television show presented the first film clip of The Beatles?

The Jack Parr Show

  - Which American television M.C. first hosted the band on his live variety show?

Ed Sullivan on "Toast of the Town"

  - Who was considered the "5th Beatle," a man who tragically took his own life in Aug. 1967?

Brian Epstein, the band's manager

  - What was the title of the group's first hit single, released in 1962?

"Love Me Do"

  - Who was originally scripted to sing "Love Me Do," but, because of voice problems in the studio, turned it over to an obviously nervous Paul McCartney?

John Lennon (careful listening betrays Paul's shaky voice)

  - In 1970, The Beatles released their last single. What was it?

"Let It Be"

  - What was the first single put out by The Beatles—a Capitol Records hit—to be released in the U.S.?

"I Want To Hold Your Hand"

  - Did the group once release a short movie called "Sgt.Pepper's Lonely Hearts Club Band"?

No, there *was* a Sgt. Pepper movie, but the Bee Gees, Peter Frampton and Aerosmith were its star attractions

  - During The Beatles' career, the band released three full-length feature movies. What are they?

"A Hard Day's Night," "Yellow Submarine" and "Let It Be"

  - When the White Album's "Revolution Number Nine" is played backwards, what phrase allegedly can be heard?

"Turn me on, dead man" repeated over and over

  - When was John Lennon murdered, and by whom?

December 8, 1980, by Mark Chapman

  - What stringed instrument from India did John Lennon introduce to young Americans in the 1960s?

The sitar

- What group in 1971 sold out New York's Shea Stadium faster than The Beatles did in 1965?

Grand Funk Railroad

- Which 1972 Grand Funk Railroad album was packaged in the shape and layout of a huge silver coin?

E Pluribus Funk

- How many Tony Awards did "My Fair Lady" win in 1957? What were they?

Five: Best Musical, Best Actor, Best Composer, Best Librettist, and Best Director

- Who is considered the "Grandfather of Soul"?

James Brown

- In what year was the first Kingston Trio formed? What were the names of the trio's original members?

1957; Dave Guard, Bob Shane, and Nick Reynolds

- What is a "sideman"?

A player in a jazz or dance band, as differentiated from the leader, or "frontman"

- Provide the meanings to these other jazz expressions:
  - "Vamp"

An accompanimental or transitional chord used during solos

- "Weak notes"	Rhythmically unstressed notes
- "Shout"	Singing or playing in a forceful manner
- "Stomp"	A heavy or strongly marked beat, or a characteristic "blues" beat
- "Rip"	Playing on the harmonic overtones
- "Noodling"	Playing isolated fast passages or runs during a song
- "Growl"	A raspy, rough effect produced with wind instruments
- "Ghost notes"	Implied notes that are not played
- "Fluff"	A mistake or goof up; missed notes
- "Dicty"	Elegant or high-class
- "Book"	The repertoire of a band
- "Bombs"	Strong, off-beat accents used by drummers
- "Accelerando"	Speeding up the tempo
• In 1958, Berry Gordy Jr.launched Motown Records.What was the first group he signed?	Smokey Robinson and The Miracles
• Who were the three original Supremes?	Diana Ross, Florence Ballard and Mary Wilson
• Who discovered the Jackson 5 and produced their first album?What was the first hit single released from this talented family band?	Diana Ross; "I Want You Back"
• Kenny Rogers' number one country hit "Lady" was written by which Motown star?	Lionel Richie
• Who is country star Loretta Lynn's famous singing sister?	Crystal Gayle
• What did the Devil offer Johnny in exchange for his soul in Charlie Daniels' "The Devil Went Down To Georgia"?	A golden fiddle
• What popular country western singer was initially—and relentlessly—accused of making it big by impersonating Elvis?	Conway Twitty
• The 1980s megagroup Journey consisted of various members from what popular Latin jazz-rock group?	Santana
• For whom did Roy Orbison write the 1964 hit "Oh, Pretty Woman?"	For his wife, Claudette
• Robert Allen Zimmerman is the original name of what legendary singer/poet, whose songs have been recorded by The Byrds, Jimi Hendrix, and Peter, Paul and Mary?	Bob Dylan
• Simon and Garfunkle recorded their first hit single under different names.What names did they use—and what was the name of their 1957 single?	Tom and Jerry; "Hey, Schoolgirl"
• Identify each of these six well-known musical groups from their original names.	
- The Four Lovers	The Four Seasons
- Moondogs	The Beatles
- The Herd	Buffalo Springfield
- Pud	The Doobie Brothers
TW4	Styx
- Earth	Black Sabbath

- Which classical composers wrote these piano pieces?
  - "The Minute Waltz" — Fredric Chopin
  - "Moonlight Sonata" — Ludwig van Beethoven
  - "Slavonic Dances" — Antonin Dvorak
  - "Ma Mere L'oye" — Maurice Ravel
- What opera character—whose name is also the opera's title—descends into hell during the final act? — Don Giovanni
- Identify each of these opera title characters from their closing scenes:
  - She throws herself from a prison roof. — Tosca
  - Attempting to carry out murderous designs on a duke, he kills his own daughter instead. — Rigoletto
  - He discovers the lost, sleeping Norse Goddess Brunnhilde, wakes her with a kiss, and falls in love with her. — Siegfried
  - After she kisses the severed head of her lover, her father, Herod, commands that she be crushed to death by the shields of the surrounding guards. — Salome
- Name the musical production which introduced each of these songs:
  - "Sunrise, Sunset" — Fiddler On The Roof
  - "A Puzzlement" — The King And I
  - "Pore Judd is Dead" — Oklahoma!
  - "Put On A Happy Face" — Bye, Bye Birdie
  - "One" (singular sensation . . .) — A Chorus Line
  - "Dancing" — Hello, Dolly
- Who made hits out of these songs?
  - "Wind Beneath My Wings" — Bette Midler
  - "Bandstand Boogie" — Barry Manilow
  - "Go Away Little Girl" — The Osmonds
  - "Who's Lovin' You" — The Jackson 5
  - "Over My Head" — Fleetwood Mac
  - "Spinning Wheel" — Blood Sweat and Tears
  - "Joy To the World" — Three Dog Night
  - "Walks Like A Lady" — Journey
  - "Babe" — Styx
  - "People Are Strange" — The Doors
- Where did The Doors get their name? — From Aldous Huxley's "Doors of Perception"—an essay on expanding the limits of consciousness—and William Blake's "There are things that are known and that are unknown; and in between are the doors."
- The Doors' keyboardist, Ray Manzarek, once played in a band with his two brothers Rick and Jim.Name the band. — Rick and The Ravens
- How many albums did The Doors record after singer Jim Morrison's death?What are the titles of these albums? — Two; Other Voices, and Full Circle
- Who wrote the original 1966 *Batman* theme?Who performed it? — Nelson Riddle; The Marketts
- Who wrote the new 1989 *Batman* movie theme?What singer recorded the song? — Danny Elfman; Prince
- The Rolling Stones' hit "I Can't Get No Satisfaction" was performed as a single by which revolutionary, new-wave band in 1980? — Devo

• What was singer David Bowie's name at birth?	David Jones
• Which female singer tore up a picture of the Pope on national television during a 1992 *Saturday Night Live* appearance, resulting in a wave of criticism aimed toward her?	Sinead O'Connor
• The 1970s rock band Supertramp hit it big in the U.S. with "The Logical Song," "Take The Long Way Home" and "Goodbye, Stranger." These songs came from an album whose cover featured a Manhattan skyline made from dishes and the Statue of Liberty posing as a waitress. What is the name this album?	"Breakfast In America"
• What famous comedienne appeared on the Led Zeppelin II album cover?	Lucille Ball
• What happened to the inside sleeve of Led Zeppelin's "In Through The Out Door" album cover when it got wet?	It changed colors
• What band did Ted Nugent head during the late 1960s and early 1970s?	The Amboy Dukes
• Name the three-man Texas boogie band that made an appearance in Steven Spielberg's "Back To The Future III."	ZZ Top
• What song title and artist(s) correspond to the lyrics below?	
- `Stop children, what's that sound . . . '	"For What It's Worth"; Buffalo Springfield
- `It's not far down to paradise; at least it's not for me . . . '	"Sailing"; Christopher Cross
- `I remember all my life raining down as cold as ice . . . '	"Mandy"; Barry Manilow
- `Rollin,' rollin,' rollin' on the river . . . '	"Proud Mary"; Credence Clearwater Revival
- `Hello, is there anybody in there . . . '	"Comfortably Numb"; Pink Floyd
- `Time it was and what a time it was, it was . . . '	"Bookends"; Simon and Garfunkle
- `There's a lady who's sure all that glitters is gold . . . '	"Stairway to Heaven"; Led Zeppelin
- `Mother Mary comes to me, speaking words of wisdom . . . '	"Let It Be"; The Beatles
- `Someone help me, help me, help me, please . . . '	"Puppy Love"; The Osmonds
- `Ridin' around in my automobile . . . '	"No Particular Place To Go", Chuck Berry
• Name the Troggs' biggest hit ever, released in 1966.	"Wild Thing"
• Name the Irish band that paid tribute to Martin Luther King with the hit "Pride (In The Name of Love)" during the late 1980s.	U2
• What band wrote a rock version of Mussogorsky's "Pictures At An Exhibition"?	Emerson, Lake and Palmer
• What was Bruce Springsteen's back-up band called?	The E Street Band
• What does the term "Bee Gees" stand for?	"Brothers Gibb"
• Female singers Deborah Harry of Blondie and Terry Bozzio of Missing Persons both once worked as part of a million-dollar-magazine enterprise. Who was their big boss?	Hugh Hefner (They were both Playboy Bunnies)
• What rock band was spotlighted in the *Guiness Book of World Records* for being the loudest musical group in the world?	The Who
• Keyboard whiz Thomas Dolby made his worldwide debut on what rock album?	Foreigner 4
• What 1971 Don McLean song ran more than 10 minutes long when played in its entirety?	"American Pie"

• What instrument looks and plays almost like a piano, but uses a "pluck" to vibrate its cords and make music rather than striking the cords with a hammer?	The harpsichord
• What was Janis Joplin's last album titled?	"Pearl"
• What does the word "fine" mean when it appears on sheet music?	End

LITERATURE

Trivia to Learn By

• What book in the Bible, filled with the imagery of erotic love, is omitted as a non-canonical work by some Christian denominations, and is regarded by others as a metaphor for the relationship between Christ ("the Bridegroom") and his church ("The Bride")?

The Songs of Solomon

• What work, prepared in Greece by Appolonious the Sophist during the reign of Augustus from 27 B.C. to A.D. 14, is said to be the world's first real dictionary?

"Homeric Words"

• What is the standard term used to designate word lists, books or repertoires—including cookbooks, glossaries, text books, and , especially, dictionaries?

A Lexicon, from the Greek *lexi* for "word"

• Who authored the following works?

- *Rip Van Winkle* — Washington Irving
- *Where the Red Fern Grows* — Wilson Rawls
- *The Russians* — Hendrick Smith
- *Alaska, Poland,* and *Hawaii* (three separate books) — James Michener
- *Birth of a Tragedy* — Friedrich Nietzsche
- *The Fountainhead* — Ayn Rand
- *Kidnapped* — Robert Louis Stevenson
- *King Rat* — James Clavell
- *Where the Wild Things Are* — Maurice Sendak
- *Watership Down* — Richard Adams

• What complex—the female counterpart of the Oedipus Complex—is present when a daughter has an obsessive attachment to her father?

Electra complex

• When a person makes a "play on words" based on the like sound of two or more words with different meanings, he has made a _____.

Pun

• In 1918, what work by Ernest Poole received a Pulitzer Prize for fiction? By Sara Teasdale for poetry?

His Family; "Love Song"

• How many Pulitzer Prizes for drama did playwright Tennessee Williams, author of "The Rose Tattoo," win? In what years and for what works were they awarded?

Two; for "A Streetcar Named Desire" in 1948, and for "Cat On A Hot Tin Roof" in 1955

• Name the first major literary organization of African-American writers, a group that congregated in Harlem immediately after World War I.

The Harlem Renaissance

• In every Greek tragedy, a fatal error, a character flaw, a mistaken judgment, or some misstep causes the fortune of a hero to reverse. What is this error called?

A hamartia

• Why did Rumpelstiltskin claim that he was entitled to the first-born child of a princess?

He had been promised the princess's first-born in return for saving her life by spinning straw into gold.

• In 1972, Studs Terkel published a best seller about America's occupational force. The subtitle was "People Talk About What They Do All Day and What How They Feel About What They Do." What was the title of this book?

Working

• What is a seven-line stanza called?

A heptastich

• Name the authors of these well known books— all of them once banned at some time or place:

- *The Catcher in the Rye* — J.D. Salinger
- *Of Mice and Men* — John Steinbeck
- *The Big Sky* — Mary Calhoun
- *Still Life With Fruit* — Doris Bett
- *Shane* — Jack Shaefer

- *If Beale Street Could Talk*	James Baldwin
- *Children of the Corn*	Stephen King

• Salman Rushdie, a Muslim writer, published a book in 1989 which, according to many Muslims, attacked the Islamic faith, and a death warrant was placed on his head. What was the book's title? — *The Satanic Verses*

• What title was given to a group of 18th-century poets including Thomas Parnell and Edward Young, who wrote lengthy poems on death and immortality? — The Graveyard School

• August Strindberg, in 1901, and W.H. Auden, in 1933, both wove famous works around the theme of the legendary dance which depicts the character of Death leading a line of mesmerized followers, dancing hand in hand, to their graves. What is the name of this grim and ghostly dance? — "Dance Macabre"

• What is the Greek phrase meaning "I have found it," which has gained panache as the legendary exclamation of Archimedes when he leaped from his Ancient Greek bath tub with his famous formula for buoyancy — based on the principle that a floating body displaces its own lost weight in fluid? — "Eureka!"

• Fagin and the Artful Dodger are characters in which novel by what author? — *Oliver Twist*, by Charles Dickens

• Although he was neither, what Shakespearian character was described as a fat old knight-friend of young Prince Hal, and a self-conceived brave womanizer? — Falstaff

• What did the narrator dine on and drink of when he entered the "pleasure dome" of the lost Xanadu that was decreed by Kubla Khan? — Honeydew and the Milk of Paradise

• What D.H. Lawrence book was banned because of its explicit, earthy depiction of sexual acts between a married woman and her estate's gamekeeper? — *Lady Chatterley's Lover*

• Bigwig, Cowslip, Hazel, and Fiver all star in the book _____. What type of creatures are they? — Watership Down; rabbits

• In this nineteenth-century work *Pensées d'Aout*, Charles Augustin Sainte-Beuve wrote about a place or state of mind in which idealists or theorists can become isolated from the surrounding reality. Since then, the image he used has become an idiomatic metaphor to represent a place where intellectual and artistic matters are held exclusive of the mundane. What is this place? — An Ivory Tower

• How old is Alice in Lewis Carroll's *Alice's Adventures in Wonderland*? — Seven years old

• Charles Lutwidge Dodgson, aka. Lewis Carroll, was employed in what profession when he published Alice's Adventures in Wonderland in 1865? — He was a teacher of mathematics at Christ Church, Oxford, England

• The Old Testament prophet Moses suffered a speech impediment (perhaps a lisp or a stutter). How was it that he was able to communicate with the Children of Israel and preach? — Through his brother Aaron

• Name the Greek heroine who was sure her dead brother's soul would be damned unless she gave him a proper burial. — Antigone

• The Ant and the Grasshopper, the Fox and the Crow, and the Dog in the Manger are characters dreamed up by what ancient slave? — Aesop

• Dr. Victor Frankenstein, Mary Shelly's protagonist, created a "man" who eventually became a monster. What name did the doctor give to his creation? — Adam, after the first man created by God

• Identify the literary area of interest of each of these nine goddess daughters of Zeus and Mnemosyne:

- Calliope	Epic poetry
- Clio	History
- Erato	Lyric and erotic poetry
- Euterpe	Music

- Melpomene	Tragedy
- Polyhymnia	Sacred choral poetry
- Terpsichore	Choral works, dance and song
- Thalia	Comedy
- Urania	Astronomy

• See how well you can fill in the blanks for these literary terms, names and phrases:

- _____ _____ is a Latin term that, traditionally, labeled a work as a masterpiece, but today is often used with connotations of irony and sarcasm. — **Magnum Opus — (literally "great work")**

- A short, narrative poem or song is often referred to as a ____. — **Lay**

- A figurative, metaphorical phrase used in Old Germanic languages as a synonym for a simple noun (e.g. "swan road" for "river") is a _____. — **Kenning**

- The _____ _____ was the name of a group of writers in and about New York City during the early 1800s including Washington Irving, Samuel Woodworth, James Fenimore Cooper and Joseph Rodman Drake, were lampooned in Edgar Allen Poe's *The Literati of New York City*. — **The Knickerbocker Group**

- The era 1832 and 1870, when the Romantic style of writing and thought was yielding to a steady stream of realist writers—Charles Dickens, Robert Browning, Matthew Arnold, etc.—was known as the _____ _____ _____. — **Early Victorian Age**

- A comic opera made up of music and songs but also some spoken dialogue is called an _____. — **Operetta**

- A song of praise or joy, originally a ballad sung by a Greek chorus in honor of Apollo, is a _____. — **Paen**

• An _____ is a self-contradictory series of words (the ear-splitting silence; an honest thief; cruel kindness) in grammatical sequence. — **Oxymoron**

• The change of a character's fortune or a literary turn of events (i.e., a fall from grace in a tragedy or a raging success in a comedy) is known as a _____. — **Peripateia**

• Tomas, Sabina, Franz, and Tereza are all characters in Milan Kundera's 1984 novel exploring "lightness and weight" and "soul and body." Name the novel, the country, and the year in which most of the action takes place. — ***The Unbearable Lightness of Being;* Prague, Czechoslovakia; 1968**

• Permission granted by the Roman Catholic church to publish a book was once called "Nihil Obstat." What is the English translation of this Latin phrase? — **"Nothing Obstructs"**

• Name the "Old Sea Dog" who visits young Jim Hawkins and his sick mother in the first chapter of Robert Louis Stevenson's *Treasure Island*. What other notable, one-legged buccaneer enters the scene later on? — **Captain William "Billy" Bones; Long John Silver**

• What is the second title of Shakespeare's "Twelfth Night"? — **"What You Will"**

• Name the missing of this list of Seven Deadly Sins that Dante wrote about in *The Divine Comedy*. (Hint: Its Latin title might be "concupiscence.") Pride, envy, wrath, sloth, avarice, gluttony and _____. — **lust**

• Prudence, justice, fortitude, temperance, faith, hope and love on the other hand are referred to as the Seven Cardinal _____ in *The Divine Comedy*. — **Virtues**

• What Shakespearian character, often assuming the name Robin Goodfellow, serves as Oberon's mischievous page? In what play does he make his most famous appearance? — **Puck; "A Midsummer Night's Dream"**

- After reading each definition, name these other literary characters and the plays or stories they star in:

- Because she had seduced her servant Jean at a party while his fiancee, Christine, slept, she decides to kill herself with a razor. Who is she?	Miss Julie, from Henrik Ibsen's play *Miss Julie*
- A New England salesman, husband to Linda and father of two boys, Biff and Happy, who, while allegedly working, is caught with a prostitute by Biff.	Willy Loman, from Arthur Miller's *Death of a Salesman*
- A little boy tells his mom he'll eat her up and is sent to his room, where he imagines sailing to a far-away land inhabited by wild beasts.	Max, in Maurice Sendak's story *Where the Wild Things Are*
- He is a member of the Outer Ring of the Party, employed at the Ministry of Truth writing "Newspeak." He hates Big Brother, but, through mind games, is eventually made to love him.	Winston Smith, in George Orwell's novel *1984*
- A hapless Cuban fisherman fights off shovelnose sharks so he can bring an 18-foot marlin back to Havana, only to find that the sharks have picked the carcass clean. Who is he?	Santiago, from Ernest Hemingway's novel *The Old Man and the Sea*
- This young boy refuses to grow up and "adopts" a young girl of about his own age as his mother. Who is he?	Peter Pan, from the James Barrie novel *Peter Pan*
- A man yearns to eat some pies, but after accosting a pie seller, he realizes he doesn't have any money.	Simple Simon, from *Mother Goose Nursery Rhymes*

- Complaining that there was no real "young adult" literature, she published her first book featuring "Socs" and "Greasers" in 1968 at the age of 16. Name this author, born and raised in Tulsa, Oklahoma. — S.E. Hinton

- Name the authors who produced each of these young adult works:

- *Are You There God? It's Me Margaret* (1970)	Judy Blume
- *Blinded By The Light* (1978)	Robin F. Brancato
- *The Lion, The Witch and The Wardrobe* (1950)	C.S. Lewis
- *Rumble Fish* (1975)	S.E. Hinton
- *A Wrinkle In Time* (1962)	Madeleine L'Engle
- *Moreta, Dragon Lady of Pern* (1983)	Anne McCaffrey
- *The Black Pearl* (1967)	Scott O'Dell
- *The Dolphin Crossing* (1967)	Jill Paton Walsh
- *The Gift for Sarah Barker* (1981)	Jane Yolen
- *The Pigman* (1968)	Paul Zindel

- After this "unorthodox" and "idiosyncratic" poet died in 1886, her sister Lavina discovered a box containing hundreds of her works, which were eventually published with the help of the editor who had rejected the poet's first four poems. Who was this poet? — Emily Dickinson

- Name the villain or villains who imperils the life of each hero or heroine below:

- Pinocchio	Monstro the Whale or Stromboli the Puppetmaster
- Peter Pan	Captain James T. Hook
- *The Hobbit's* Bilbo Baggins	Smaug the Dragon, and Gollum, a sly lake-dweller
- Antigone	King Creon

- In Leslie Charteris' story series, Englishman Simon Templar assumes his secret identity as Scotland Yard's enigmatic and suave detective known as _____ _____ each time he is needed to fight international crime. — The Saint

• A penchant for vodka martinis (shaken, not stirred) . . . a degree from the University of Geneva after he was expelled from Eton . . . a history of one tragic marriage which ended when his bride was killed on their honeymoon . . . are all attributes of what famous literary spy?	James Bond
• What was the name of Dr. Doolittle's pet duck?	Dab Dab
• How many blackbirds were baked in the pie that was set before the king?	24 (four-and-twenty)
• Who allegedly wrote *The Hardy Boys* mysteries? Who authored the *Nancy Drew* mystery series?	Franklin W. Dixon; Carolyn Keene
• What Arthur Hailey novel describes the hysteria that follows a commercial airline disaster?	Airport
• Name Honolulu's most famous Chinese detective. (He broke the case of Dr. Fu Manchu)	Charlie Chan
• What is the meaning of the Russian newspaper title *Pravda*? What is the English translation for the title, "Mainichi Shimbun," the name of the Japanese daily?	"Truth"; "Everyday Newspaper"
• Identify the Indian Brave who lived on the edge of the river Gitchee Gumee in Henry Wadsworth Longfellow's epic poem.	Hiawatha
• Why did A.A. Milne create Winnie the Pooh?	To please his son, the "real-life" Christopher Robin
• What was the claim to fame of the fictional character Phileas T. Fogg?	He traveled around the world in 80 days
• When Boris Pasternak received literature's 1958 Nobel Prize for Dr. Zhivago, what did he do?	He turned it down (It was later discovered that the Soviet government had coerced him into rejecting the prize as punishment for criticizing Communist ideals)
• In the Biblical book of Exodus, the first four commandments teach, in general, what? The remaining six pertain to what?	Love of God; love of others
• "Do unto others as you would have others do unto you," is one of many variations of a precept know by what name?	The Golden Rule
• What story by Mark Twain was the first of its kind to link child abuse with runaways?	The Adventures of Huckleberry Finn
• What is the name of the escaped slave who accompanied Huck Finn on a raft down the Mississippi River?	Jim
• Name the two children cared for by nanny Mary Poppins.	Jane and Michael Banks
• In what year and in what newspaper did the comic strip "Mutt and Jeff" first appear?	In 1908; the New York Times
• Who is L'il Abner's heartthrob?	Daisy Mae
• Where did Charlie Brown go to adopt his dog Snoopy?	The Daisy Hill Puppy Farm
• Give the written works that open with the following famous first lines:	
- "It was the best of times, it was the worst of times . . ."	Charles Dickens' *A Tale Of Two Cities*
- "'Twas the night before Christmas . . ."	Clement Clarke Moore's "A Visit From St. Nicholas"
- "At a certain village in La Mancha, which I shall not name . . ."	Cervantes' *Don Quixote*
- "If music be the food of love, play on . . ."	Shakespeare's "Twelfth Night"
- "It was a dark and stormy night . . ."	L'Engle's *A Wrinkle In Time*
- "Once upon a midnight dreary . . ."	Poe's poem, "The Raven"
- "In 1815, M. Charles Francois-Bienvenu Myriel was bishop . . ."	Victor Hugo's Les Miserables
- "The great fish moved silently through the night water . . ."	Peter Benchley's *Jaws*

- "Who is John Galt?"	Ayn Rand's *Atlas Shrugged*
• Mary Dodge wrote about a Dutch boy named Hans Brinker. What was it that Hans wanted most in his life, aside from the recovery of his amnesia-stricken father?	A pair of silver skates
• What motto do the Three Musketeers live by?	"All for one and one for all"
• Sherlock Holmes was an admitted _____ junkie who played a stringed instrument called the _____.	Cocaine; violin
• Who was married to Anne Hathaway?	William Shakespeare
• What Catholic saint used a shamrock to illustrate the composition of the Holy Trinity?	St. Patrick
• What is Ian Flemming's master-spy James Bond's secret cover (in other words, where does he work when he's not out spying, killing and loving)?	He's an employee of Universal Import and Export
• What is the name of Sunday comic serial character Prince Valiant's wife?	Queen Aleta
• Upon receiving his superhero powers from ancient Greek gods Zeus, Mercury and Achilles, the young boy Billy Batson assumes what secret identity?	Superhero Captain Marvel
• Hans Christian Anderson's "Ugly Duckling," though he didn't know it at first, was really a _____.	Swan
• In "Hi, Diddle Diddle," who ran away with spoon?	The dish
• What is the significance of the title of Ray Bradbury's novel Fahrenheit 451?	It's the temperature at which paper bursts into flames — and books are made from paper
• The initials "T.S." in poet T.S. Eliot's name stand for what?	Thomas Stearns
• The Saturday Evening Post often featured covers painted by whom?	Norman Rockwell
• According to J.P. Chartier, where do you arrive after you go "over the river and through the woods"?	At Grandmother's house
• What is the name of the lioness celebrated by Joy Adamson in *Born Free*?	Elsa
• Ostensibly, why was the Guiness Book of World Records written?	To settle arguments in English pubs
• What tasty edibles did the evil witch in C. S. Lewis' The Lion, The Witch and The Wardrobe use to seduce children into becoming her servants?	Turkish delights
• In Aesop's well known fable, what fruits did the fox try in vain to reach, before finally concluding they must be sour anyway?	Grapes
• Joel Chandler Harris penned stories about a briar patch, a fox, and a rabbit, as supposedly told by whom during the pre Civil War era in the South?	Uncle Remus
• What did the three little kittens lose?	Their mittens
• The yearly Hugo Award is bequeathed for the best literary work in which category?	Science fiction
• Who was the famous rodent created by Beatrix Potter?	Peter Rabbit
• In what country do we find the town Hamelin, for which the Pied Piper became an exterminator of rats?	Germany?
• What did Georgie Porgie do to make the little girls cry?	He kissed them
• What best-selling Stephen King novel uses fantasy instead of his trademark horror and supernatural elements to relate a story of regicide?	*The Eyes of the Dragon*
• In J.R.R. Tolkien's *The Lord of The Rings*, in what thicket of wood do you find goblins and elves?	Mirkwood
• What was the original title Christina Crawford's book *Mommie Dearest* that recalls the alleged abuse she suffered at the hands of her mother, Joan Crawford?	*The Hype*
• What is the name of "Daddy" Warbucks' Indian servant in *Little Orphan Annie*?	Punjab

- For what reason might the dormouse who attended the Mad Hatter's tea party in Alice's Adventure in Wonderland been so drowsy?

Dormice are nocturnal – the party was held during the day

- Name the two top-selling magazines in America.

TV Guide; Reader's Digest

- What grew in a row in Mistress Mary's garden?

Pretty maids

- Name the nursery rhyme character who coincides with each of the following descriptions:

  - He called for his pipe and bowl

  Old King Cole

  - She whipped her children soundly and sent them to bed

  The old woman who lived in a shoe

  - She ate curds and whey

  Little Miss Muffet

  - He ran upstairs and downstairs in his nightgown

  Wee Willie Winkie

  - He went fishing for a whale in his mother's pail

  Simple Simon

  -He stole a pig and away he ran

  Tom, the piper's son

  - His daddy wraps him in a rabbit skin?

  Baby Bunting

  - He's the one who had a tremendous fall off a wall

  Humpty Dumpty

  - It ran down the clock when the clock struck one

  A mouse

  - She cut the tails of the three blind mice

  The farmer's wife

- What is the Latin for Julius Caesar's "I came, I saw, I conquered . . . "?

"Veni, vidi, vici . . . "

- Tennessee Williams, author of the Pulitzer Prize-winning dramas "Cat On A Hot Tin Roof" and "A Streetcar Named Desire," was christened under what name?

Thomas Lanier Williams

- What popular magazine featuring articles pertaining to American life was first issued in November, 1936? What men's entertainment magazine first came out in December of 1953?

Life; Playboy

- Who was the first female movie star to ever appear on the cover of Life magazine?

Jean Harlow

- What does Dr. Seuss' cat always wear?

A hat

- Rip Van Winkle fell asleep for 20 years while hiking in what mountain range?

The Catskills

- Name the talking mouse created by E.B. White, who went searching for a bird friend victimized by the family cat, and, later, rode a motorcycle?

Stuart Little

- What did the three Stygian Witches pass around to get a better look at Perseus, a mortal son of Zeus, when he asked them for help in finding Medusa, the snake-haired Gorgon?

A single eyeball

- What entryway does the three-headed dog, Cerberus—the hound defeated by Perseus—guard?

Hades

- In "Pygmalion," Dr. Henry Higgins teaches Eliza Doolittle how to speak proper English by putting what objects into her mouth?

Marbles

- Name the characters who uttered these lines and the poems or stories in which they were pronounced:

  - "Get thee to a nunnery . . . "

  Hamlet, in Shakespeare's "Hamlet"

  - "A stately pleasure dome . . . "

  The poet-narrator in Coleridges dream vision "Kubla Khan"

  - "Call me Ishmael . . . "

  The crewman from "The Pequod" who narrates *Moby Dick*

  - "The moon is down . . . "

  Fleance in "MacBeth"

  - "Pieces of eight! Pieces of eight!"

  The parrot Captain Flint, in *Treasure Island*

  - "After all, tomorrow is just another day . . . "

  Scarlet O'Hara, in *Gone With the Wind*

- "All animals are equal but some animals are more equal than others . . . "

The leader-pigs, Napoleon and Snowball in *Animal Farm*

WORDS & PHRASES

Trivia to Learn By

- This English word comes from a Latin word, *eradere*, meaning to "scratch out." The ancient Romans used wax tablets for writing and had to "scratch out" mistakes.
  — Erase

- This word originally meant "to trample" in English, but in another sense, derived from the French word for "leaf," it can also mean a thin sheet of aluminum or other metal.
  — Foil

- If your mother's brother's only brother-in-law is asleep on your couch, who is asleep on your couch?
  — Your father

- What is the term used to describe words such as "gurgle," "pow" and "buzz," that actually sound like the noises they depict?
  — Onomatopoeia

- What words fit the descriptions given below?
  - You will find this German "garden" in the introductory class of an American school.
    — Kindergarten
  - In Malaysia and Southeast Asia, this "man of the forest" is an orange-haired jungle-dweller.
    — Orangutan
  - The name of this three-step dance comes from a German word meaning "roll about."
    — Waltz
  - This Australian marsupial actually doesn't have a name. The English name is derived from an Aboriginal term meaning "I don't know."
    — Kangaroo
  - This English word that names a circus character is related to a Swedish word meaning "clumsy."
    — Clown (klunn or kunni)
  - This flower obtained its name from the Middle English term for "eye of the day" and is derived from the Anglo-Saxon "daegeseage."
    — Daisy
  - This liquid takes its name from the Hindu verb meaning to massage or knead (the hair).
    — Shampoo
  - Taken straight from French, this word comes from the verb "garer," meaning to protect or guard. Now in America it refers to a "protector" of certain possessions—particularly, all the mementos and clutter that used to be stored in the attic.
    — Garage

- Give the common saying or cliche that corresponds to each of these rewordings:
  - Effortlessly arrive, effortlessly depart.
    — "Easy come, easy go"
  - As sound as a violin
    — "Fit as a fiddle"
  - All objects beneath a bright, burning "daystar"
    — "Everything under the sun"
  - The path taken by a disintegrating chocolate chip or sugar snack (including an Oreo)
    — "The way the cookie crumbles"
  - Leave dreaming mongrels in peace
    — "Let sleeping dogs lie"
  - Pause and inhale the aura of the blooms
    — "Stop and smell the roses"
  - Grab the male bovine by its protruding boneline projections
    — "Take the bull by the horns"
  - Distant from view, no longer in the brain
    — "Out of sight, out of mind"
  - Prior to jumping, examine the situation
    — "Look before you leap"
  - Draw the "Ovis Aries" across a person's sight organs
    — "Pull the wool over one's eyes"
  - Either the arrival of Satan's home or the threat of floods
    — "Come hell or high water"
  - Beside a void
    — "Next to nothing"
  - Everything scrubbed and cleaned to new heights
    — "All washed up"
  - Refrain from assessing text based on its outer layer
    — "Don't judge a book by its cover"

© 1993, Compact Classics, Inc.

- Rendered visionless by the bright glare	"Blinded by the light"
• A soothsayer is one who can presumably foretell events. What does the archaic Old English word *sooth* literally mean?	"Truth" or "reality"

• Homonyms are words that lead a double life; under the cloak of the same sound and spelling they often carry very different origins and meanings. Find the "cloakword"—the homonym—that covers each set of dual-origin definitions listed below:

- From an Old English word for "bread," or from a German word that means "to wander."	Loaf
- From a Latin word that means "measure or model," and the Scandinavian word for fungus.	Mold
- A signal, and a pool stick.	Cue
- The meaning derives from the middle English word for a tooth or notch on a gear or wheel, and a subordinate member of an organization.	Cog
- From a word meaning to strike with a beak in old German, or, in old French, a measure for grain.	Peck
- From an Old English word meaning "to feed on growing grass" and from a French verb meaning "to glance off a surface."	Graze
- To be in a horizontal position, or to prevaricate truth.	Lie
- From an Old English name for a bird of prey, and a German verb meaning to sell or peddle on the street.	Hawk
- A verb meaning to bend, lie down, or rest on something, or an adjective meaning thin.	Lean

• Give the words ending in *-ism* that match these definitions:

- The belief in one god.	Monotheism
- The belief of those who wish to keep the status quo and avoid radical change.	Conservativism
- An earthquake or disruption of magnetic fields.	Seismism
- Stereotyping of social roles based on gender.	Sexism
- The doctrine that nothing exists or can be known; skepticism on a grand scale.	Nihilism
- The denial of the existence of god.	Atheism
- Habitual tooth grinding, especially during sleep.	Bruxism
- The belief in a plurality of gods.	Polytheism
- Appropriating the ideals or literary works of another.	Plagiarism

• Occupational slang, professional buzzwords, doublespeak, and abbreviations are all forms of what?	Jargon

• From the following definitions, identify each of these *pot* expressions:

- Whatever food happens to be available for a meal, especially when offered to a guest.	Potluck
- A gun blast fired at a target within easy range or without taking careful aim, or, by extension, a criticism made without careful thought and aimed at an easy target.	Potshot
- A hole in a road surface.	Pothole
- A protruding stomach.	Potbelly
- Potassium carbonate or potassium hydroxide.	Potash
- A thick vegetable soup or stew including meat.	Pottage
- Beef that is browned and then cooked until tender in a covered pot.	Pot roast

- What is the Scottish term for "times gone by" that literally refers to the "old long since"? (Hint: think of New Year's Eve.) — "Auld Lang Syne"

- Idioms are special expressions that don't follow the usual grammatical or semantical conventions of a language. Using the key words in parentheses as clues, supply the idiomatic English phrases that match the "definitions" below:

  - Lose one's temper (*fly*) — "Fly off the handle"
  - Sing on pitch (*carry*) — "Carry a tune"
  - Recover your self control (*together*) — "Pull yourself together"
  - Hold nothing back (*stops*) — "Pull out all the stops"
  - Taking dangerous risks (*fire*) — "Playing with fire"
  - Go to bed (*hit*) — "Hit the sack" or "Hit the hay"
  - Capture one's attention (*eye*) — "Catch one's eye"
  - Play the piano (*tickle*) — "Tickle the ivories"
  - Don't be impatient (*horses*) — "Hold your horses"
  - Makes me crazy (*wall*) — "Drives me up the wall" or "Climbing the wall"
  - Fully satisfies (*spot*) — "Hits the spot"
  - Caught in a predicament (*pickle*) — "In a pickle"

- A common English slang term descends from the Old English "guiser" which referred to a man in disguise, or odd, eccentric fellow and is now used to designate an "old coot." What is this word? — Geezer

- When Americans use "hari-kari" as a synonym for "suicide," they are actually modifying the Japanese words "hara kiri," which means what? — "Cutting of the belly"

- Another Japanese word, *kamikaze* also became synonymous with suicide when World War II kamikaze pilots were sent out to give their lives in the cause of their motherland by guiding their aircraft into head-on collisions with ships or other targets. What is the literal meaning of the word *kamikaze*? — "Divine wind"

- A number of colorful foreign words have been directly adopted into English. Identify each of the common expressions of "foreign English" described below:

  - Yiddish for food correctly prepared in accordance with Jewish dietary laws. — Kosher
  - A French word meaning a step-like formation of troops or a hierarchical arrangement. — Echelon
  - French term for a cube of toasted bread. — Crouton
  - The Japanese name for the art of paper-folding, also used to refer to any decorative object made of folded paper. — Origami
  - Hebrew for "praise the Lord." — Hallelujah
  - French term for a type of knitting with a large, hooked needle. — Crochet
  - A Hawaiian word used in greetings and farewells. — Aloha
  - An Italian name for a secret organization. — Mafia
  - The Japanese name for a dwarf tree or shrub. — Bonsai
  - The French description for any menu dish served flaming or singed. — Flambe'
  - German for "Health to you," used in response to a sneeze. — Gesundheit
  - Italian term used in greeting or farewell (in English, usually reserved to say goodbye) — Ciao

- French term for "first prize."	Grand prix (literally Grand Prize)
- Hawaiian for a wreath of flowers to be worn around the neck.	Lei
- The French designation for "miss" or "young lady."	Mademoiselle
• Give the modern-day equivalent to the following outdated expressions:	
- "Water closet"	Toilet
- "With child"	Pregnant
- "Inexpressibles"	Trousers or underwear
- "Happy hunting grounds"	Heaven
- "Spittoon"	Cuspidor
• Originally the word "harem" (from *harim*, meaning "forbidden") was used not to describe the women of a Moslem household, but what?	The house or apartments set aside for the women
• This off-shoot of the English language dialect can be heard primarily in the South-Sea islands and part of the Orient. The name of this language also sounds like a bird. What is it?	Pidgin English
• Eak-say At-whay means "say what" in what kind of "language"?	Pig Latin
• Here's another quiz on homonyms. For each entry below, identify the single word that fits both definitions:	
- A slow-burning stick used to light fireworks, or a socially disenfranchised person with green hair.	Punk
- To hand out money, or a snail's home.	Shell
- To caress or taste with the tongue, or to beat with a switch.	Lick
- To move your hand or foot against some surface in time with a musical beat, or else a faucet.	Tap
- To kill or extinguish, or else a finely ground tobacco powder.	Snuff
- To rouse from a sleep, or a gathering to pay tribute to the dead before a funeral.	Wake
• What does the Anglo-Saxon word "were" mean in the word werewolf?	Man
• Give the familiar Yiddish word from the definitions below:	
- A clumsy person	Klutz
- To drag or transport laboriously	Schlep
- Junk or low quality goods	Schlock
- An unpleasant thing or person	Schmuck
- A luckless person or victim	Schlimazl or Schlemiel
- To watch or be an onlooker — as at a card game — and offer unsolicited comment	Kibitz
• During the upheavals of industrialization, wooden shoes were often thrown into European factory machines to hinder production and soon the French word for shoe or boot spawned a derivative that has been directly adopted into English to denote any act of deliberate subversion. Identify both the root word and its derivative.	Sabot; Sabotage
• An organism that lives and feeds off another without contributing anything to the relationship is called a _____.	Parasite
• A bizarre and unserviceable gift is often referred to as a _____ elephant.	White
• Give the approximate definitions for each of these English slang expressions:	
- Cool	Good, great, fine

- Gross	Sickening
- Rank	Smelly or dumb
- Geek	A strange person
- Nerd	A brainy, social misfit
- Ditched	Got rid of

• After a theatrical performance, a male star is praised by the audience using the word bravo, a female star by the word _____, and both by the word _____. — Brava; bravee

• In the song "Yankee Doodle," what does the word "maca roni" really mean? — A coxcomb or jesters cap

• When a member of Congress stands on the floor jabbering about anything to pass time or prevent the voting on of a bill, that person is what? — Filibustering

• The literary equivalent to the mathematical expression of 3.14 is what? — Pi

• Supply the common nicknames or given names that double as matchwords for the definitions below:

- Wealthy	Rich
- To touch lightly	Pat
- A Christmas song	Carol
- An indicator, or a visible trace left behind	Mark
- Informal for *microphone*	Mike
- An aesthetically pleasing work	Art
- The docked tail of a horse	Bob
- Paper money	Bill
- A covered stack of hay	*Rick*
- A bathroom or toilet	John

• A point formed by hair growing down the middle of the forehead is called a what? — A widow's peak

• What is a projecting piece of hair that refuses to lie flat called? — A cowlick

• The Old English word that depicts the familiar of the modern-day "you" is what? — Thou

• Give the English equivalents to these Latin phrases, used commonly, without translation, in written and spoken English:

- Ad Hoc	For this situation; for a specific purpose only
- Villa	Country estate or large residence
- Via	Way or road
- Bona Fide	In good faith; genuine, authentic
- Triennium	A three-year period
- Thesaurus	Treasure; treasure house (a book of synonyms)
- De Facto	In actuality
- Ergo	Hence
- Quasi	Seemingly; partly, almost, somewhat
- Nexus	A joint or a bond; partnership.

• One who is acquainted with and appreciative of all the nuances of an art or pleasure is a _____. — Connoisseur

• Give the actual meaning of each descriptive phrase below:

- "Hot under the collar"	Angry
- "Turning over a new leaf"	Making a complete change

- "Full of hot air"	Exaggerates the facts
- "Catch the gold ring"	Get lucky
- "Knuckle under"	Bend to pressure
- "A wet blanket"	A spoil sport or boring a companion
- To "toot one's horn"	To brag
- "Put in the loop"	Include a newcomer
- "Have the world on a string"	To be very content or prosperous
- "Yellow as a lemon"	Scared

• What is the term for a mask that covers half the face, like that used in "Phantom of the Opera"? — A loup (from the French for *wolf*)

• An electrician might call the light switch on your wall a what? — A toggle switch

• The outlet in a wall that an electric plug sticks into is known as a what? — A receptacle

• The part of a telephone you talk into is called a what? What is the listening piece called? — A transmitter; a receiver

• Give the correct and not-so-famous name for each of these body parts:

- The bony ridge on top of your nose. — Bridge

- The row of heavy side-whiskers connected to a mustache worn with a clean-shaven chin. — Burnsides (sideburns only denotes the side-whiskers without the mustache)

- A lock of hair that grows on or falls across the forehead. — Forelock

- The fleshy, cartilaginous bump on your ear between your face and the ear opening. — Tragus

- The dividing wall inside your nose that separates the nostrils. — Septum

- The small, fleshy flap hanging down in the back of your throat. — Uvula

- The corner at either side of your eye where the upper and lower eyelids meet. — Canthus

- The strip of skin at the base of each fingernail and toenail. — Cuticle

- The official name for the belly button. — Navel or umbilicus

- The back of the neck. — Nape or scruff

• What is formed from the initial letters of the words in a name, title or series of words? — An acronym

• What is RADAR an acronym for? — Radio detecting and ranging

- SCUBA? — Self-contained underwater breathing apparatus

- NATO? — North Atlantic Treaty Organization

- MADD? — Mothers Against Drunk Driving

- MASH? — Mobile Army Surgical Hospital

- UNICEF? — United Nations International Children's Emergency Fund

- ITERPOL? — International Criminal Police Organization

- SWAT? — Special Weapons And Tactics

- OPEC? — Organization of Petroleum Exporting Countries

- What fields of study do the following -ologies—all taken from Greek roots—refer to in English?

- Pathology	Diseases - from the Greek *pathos* meaning *suffering* or an *experience*
- Geology - from *geo* meaning *earth*	Rocks and landforms
- Embryology	Embryos and their development - from *embryos*, meaning swelling or growth
- Ophthalmology	The eye and vision - from *opthalmos*, meaning eyeball
- Paleontology	Ancient life, esp. fossil remains - from *palaci* meaning *early*, and *ancient* and *onto*, meaning *existence*
- Entomology	Insects
- Ornithology	Birds - from *oronos* (bird)
- Ichthyology	Fish - from *icthys* (fish)
- Ichnology	Fossil footprints - from *ichnos* (footprints)
- Bibliology	Books - from *biblions* (book)

- This Greek word means "circle of animals" and refers to a special astral calendar that is sometimes consulted to see if two people are compatible. What is the word?   Zodiac

- The Greek goddess of victory had an American missile named after her as well as a popular line of sportswear. What is this god's name?   Nike

- What is the unit used to measure the speed of an aircraft once it surpasses the speed of sound?   Mach

- What is the term for a transient explosive sound caused by the shock wave preceding an aircraft traveling at supersonic speed?   A sonic boom

- Compound words are words formed from two or more smaller words. Identify the common compound word from the italicized clues that matches each of these descriptions:

- to warm up with, you may find these clues both *pungent* and *sugary*.	Bittersweet
- Here's a *cardboard container* combined with a *Mercedes Benz*.	Boxcar
- And to follow up in style here is a *soaring, yellow breadspread*.	Butterfly
- Here's a *foundation* for your *orb*.	Baseball
- Is it getting any harder? Well, here's an *enlightening ray* from a *satellite* to guide you.	Moonbeam
- Little *Theodore* was really a *grizzly*.	Teddybear
- By now you may find yourself in the *heart* of *darkness*.	Midnight
- So turn around and contemplate an *angry little city*.	Crosstown
- If you want to *observe* the world, climb to a *pinnacle*.	Watchtower
- Up here, you can *scratch* the back of the *atmosphere*.	Skyscraper
- A *shaky dance* completes the picture with a *tool for cutting wood*.	Jigsaw
- Always *retain* your sense of *purpose*.	Keepsake

- *Charles* is in the *ascendant*.	Upchuck
- An *astute split* will only increase tension.	Wisecrack
- When the *world shakes*.	Earthquake
- A *child delivery* in a *24-hour period*.	Birthday
- *Above everything,* keep plugging through these questions.	Overall
- This clue will undoubtedly *render* you *speechless*.	Dumbfound
- You may want to climb behind your *breeze guard* to get warm.	Windbreaker or Windshield
- When the *thin ice gnaws and gnashes* you have _____.	Frostbite
- Now that you have honorably finished this quiz, *go forth* on your *successful* designated way.	Farewell

SCIENCE

Trivia to Learn By

• Which planet takes the shortest amount of time to rotate on its axis? Which planet's day most closely approximates the length of Earth's?

Jupiter (10 Hours); Mars (24 hours and 37 minutes)

• On a 25-mile bike ride, the bike's front wheel will actually travel farther than the back wheel. Why?

The front wheel moves back and forth at various angles as the bike is steered; the back wheel follows, assuming a straighter path

• Name the technological innovation that matches each description:

- A small computer that is used to sort and edit text.

Word processor

- An internal combustion engine that produces power on every fourth stroke in an intake-, compression-, combustion-, and exhaust-stroke cycle. (During which of the four strokes is the power generated?)

Four-stroke engine; compression is the crucial "power stroke"

- A "wave machine" that finds the position and speed of flying objects by bouncing radio waves off them and detecting the reflected waves.

Radar

- Computer-controlled technology that allows the user to explore imaginary environments which exist only as computer drawings.

Virtual reality

• The five jaws of a sea urchin, which allow it to chew through tough seaweed, were described by Aristotle as "lantern teeth." What is the modern scientific name of these teeth?

Lack Jaws

• Name the 15th-century mathematician, physicist and astronomer who is said to have set the Renaissance's scientific revolution in motion, pulling modern science out of the magicians' hat of speculative natural philosophy.

Galileo Galilei

• The theory articulated by Galileo that says two different-sized objects fall at the same speed is known by what name?

"The Law of the Fall"

• In 1992, the world's first poisonous bird was discovered in New Guinea. Name it.

The hooded pitohui

• English medical student William Harvey is famous for discovering a vital physiological function in 1622, 20 years after leaving the Padua School of Anatomy. What is this function?

The circulation of blood by the heart

• Any respectable 15th-century surgeon went by the title _____.

"Barber"

• Which Polish astronomer, in 1543 located the sun as the center of the solar system?

Nicolaus Copernicus

• Which two planets, depending on their proximity to the sun, are known interchangeably as "the evening star" and "the morning star"?

Mercury and Venus

• Io, Europa, Ganymede, and Callisto are the names of four what?

Jupiter's 13 moons

• Identify the first U.S. satellite, launched January 31, 1958.

Explorer I

• Name the first U.S. woman astronaut. (Her first mission took place in the STS7 Space Shuttle launch of June 18, 1983).

Sally Ride

• English physicist James Chadwick, in studying the structure of atoms, discovered a nuclear particle that has the same mass as the proton, but is electrically neutral. What is this particle called?

A neutron

• The process of two opposite bits of matter combining and canceling each other, leaving no matter at all, is called _____ annihilation.

Mutual

• When light, traveling in a straight line, hits a glass of water or a prism, it bends. The light is said to have been _____.

Refracted

• What is the speed of sound at sea level? What is the speed of light?

1,090 feet per second (or 750 miles per hour); 186,282.3959 miles per second

• What Italian physicist first attempted to measure the speed of light — by standing on a hill and signalling his assistant on an opposite hill by uncovering a lantern, then trying to time the response from his assistant's lantern?	Galileo Galilei
• How much energy does it take to raise the temperature of one gram of water one degree celsius?	One calorie
• Scottish musical instrument maker James Watt was the first to perfect what type of engine?	The steam engine
• The Latin word "molecule" literally means what?	"Small mass"
• What is one major difference in the cellular makeup of animals and plants?	A cork covering, or cell wall, surrounds each of a plant's cell (animal cells don't have this covering)
• Cells working in tandem constitute an organ. Organs working together constitute a _____.	System
• When a baby develops teeth, which teeth usually grow in first: cuspids, molars or incisors?	Incisors
• The framework around which the human body is formed is called the _____.	Skeleton
• Name the parts or features of the human body that coincide with these descriptions:	
- The thigh bone	Femur
- The stringy matter that bears and moves the skeleton, and gives the body its shape.	Muscles
- The ducts that drain body tissues, returning intracellular fluid to the circulatory system.	The lymphatic ducts
- The organs that draw air into the body through the nose and mouth by a muscle under the rib cage in order to gather oxygen to be absorbed into the bloodstream.	The lungs
- The organ in which food is first broken down physically and chemically so nutritional elements can be absorbed by the body.	The stomach
- The system that includes kidneys, ureters, the bladder, and the urethra.	The urinary system
- An outgrowth of the top of the spinal chord that controls actions and thought.	The brain
- Small patches of melanin pigment in the epidermis that darken in response to sunlight.	Freckles
- The extremities of the lungs which allow air to come in close contact with blood in capillaries so that nitrogen-, oxygen-, and carbon dioxide-exchange can take place.	Alveoli, or air sacs
- The "little brain" that monitors information from muscles, tendons, joints and the inner ear, and coordinates muscle movement on instruction from the larger brain.	Cerebellum
• Name the tiny, simple organisms that live off cells, which they attack for both their nutritional and reproductive needs, and usually bring on disease.	Viruses
• Over-production of the antibody IgE—which binds to the surface of mast cells and increases the production of histamines, prostaglandins and leukotrienes—is known as an _____ reaction.	Allergic
• Fill in the blanks below with the correct chemistry-related terms:	
- The melting of metals by using high amounts of energy. For example, converting iron oxide to metallic iron by heating is called _____.	Smelting
- Gold is represented in the periodic table of elements with the letters _____; iron is shown as _____.	Au; Fe

- The most malleable or shapeable metal is _____.	Gold
- _____ fibers are utilized extensively as reinforcing agents for lightweight, high-strength plastics in tennis rackets and other sports equipment.	Carbon
- The principal lead-bearing ore is _____.	Galena
- The aqueous solution commonly used for preserving biological specimens is called _____.	Formaldehyde
- Around 8,000 B.C., _____ was first used by late stone-age man. Its name derives from the Latin word "cuprium," and its chemical symbol is Cu.	Copper
- The mixture of nitroglycerin (glyceryl trinitrate) with stabilizing wood pulp is known as _____.	Dynamite
- The result of melting tin with antimony, copper, and lead is a product called _____. Combining just tin with copper produces _____.	Pewter; Bronze
- The glow of a blank sign is produced when positive ions strike an electrode which in turn gives off secondary electrons enclosed in a glass tube.	Neon
- A Geiger counter detects _____ in rocks.	Nuclear radioactivity

• Now for some biology fill-in-the-blanks:

- A complex compound found in blood whose molecules consist of proteins coordinated with a central iron atom is known as _____.	Hemoglobin
- Xylem vessels, consisting of long, spliced narrow cells, govern _____ _____ in a plant.	Water circulation
- The loss of water through the stoma or small respiratory opening on a leaf is called _____.	Transpiration
- The microscopic bodies most concerned with cell respiration — also labeled as cell "powerhouses" or "energy releasers" — are officially known as _____.	Mitochondria
- The hereditary disorder which manifests itself in an absence of pigments in the body and usually yields non-colored, white hair, red eyes and pink skin is known as _____.	Albinism
- The phylum classification *mycota* is the Latin name for common _____, the simplest of plant forms. (These plants are unable photosynthesize and must survive by absorbing soluble materials through a host plant.)	Fungi
- The infamous carnivorous venus fly-trap is obliged to devour insects because of the surrounding soil's lack of what chemical?	Nitrogen
- The _____ is the world's largest flower. (Measuring up to 35 inches across and giving off a scent that smells like rotting meat, it is found only in the Malayoian Forest.)	Rafflesia

• Flowers and other plants, like animals, are composed of various organs. Give the correct plant part that matches the following definitions:

- It contains and surrounds the female egg-cell of a flowering plant, and, after fertilization, develops into a seed.	The ovule
- The stalk of an ovule.	The funicle
- A protective layer of dead cells on the outside of a stem or root.	Cork
- A fruit such as a plum, peach or cherry in which the seed is first surrounded by a stone or pit, and then a fleshy layer.	A drupe
- Any part of a plant capable of being dispersed and growing on its own.	A diaspore

- The vertical slits or divisions under the cap of a toad-stool or common mushroom.	Gills
- A large underground bud composed of leaf bases which are swollen with food reserves.	A bulb
- A leaf stalk.	A petiole
- A specialized, dust-like reproductive cell which can give rise to a new plant.	A spore

• Snails, abalone, sea slugs, octopi, and squids are all a species of the boneless bodied family known as _____.

Mollusks

• The phrase "birds of _____" is used to describe carnivorous raptors such as eagles, hawks, falcons and buzzards.

Prey

• The long, ivory tusks in adult walruses are actually overgrown teeth. What kind of teeth are they?

Canines

• Name the part of an animal's anatomy that matches the following descriptions:

- Composed of the protein keratin, they evolved from a knob or follicle in the scales of the reptilian ancestors of birds; they are used in flight and to control body temperature.	Feathers
- Porcupines raise and shake these thick protruding hairs as a defence warning.	Quills
- These brush-like plates suspended from a whale's palate are used to filter krill from sea water.	Baleen
- These muscular "pre-stomachs" break prior to diegestion, sometimes with the aid of swallowed stones.	The gizzard
- This rigid support system lies outside the muscular structure in arthropods like lobsters, spiders and bumblebees.	The exoskeleton

• Discoveries:

- Joseph Priestley, the discoverer of oxygen, found that the heavy latex of India gum extracted from certain trees could erase or rub out pencil marks. What name did he apply to this thick elastic matter?	Rubber

• What fastening material was born from the inspiration of inventor George DeMestral after he returned home from a walk in the 1950s and noticed his jacket covered with cockleburs?

Velcro

• When the earth, sun, and moon are in "quadrature" (at right angles to one another, with the earth at the apex), the gravitational forces generating the oceans' tides are at their weakest. What is this least powerful, lowest range tide called?

Neap tide

• What form of birth control, introduced in the 1960s, is said to have been responsible, at least in part, for the sexual revolution, the emancipation of women, and the secularization or division of thought of the Catholic church in the Western world?

"The Pill"

• Radio and light waves are more abundant and used in more ways than most people recognize. Give the correct wave type described below:

- The waves used in medicine to photograph bones and body tissues.	X-rays
- The waves given off by sunlamps to tan your body.	Ultraviolet rays
- The waves that transfer heat and are discharged by anything hot.	Infrared rays
- The waves used to "jiggle" molecules and cook food in ovens.	Microwaves
- The waves that carry sound- and picture-signals for radio and TV.	Radio waves

• Certain psychological phobias, or "irrational" fears, are quite common; others are very rare. Name the fear that each of these phobias targets:

- Xenophobia	Fear of foreigners

- Hydrophobia	Fear of water
- Claustrophobia	Fear of being confined in small, enclosed spaces
- Gynephobia	Fear of women
- Basophobia	Fear of walking or standing
- Autophobia	Fear of oneself
- Panophobia	Fear of everything
- Monophobia	Fear of being alone
- Phobophobia	Fear of fear
- Androphobia	Fear of men
- Arachniphobia	Fear of spiders
- Phonophobia	Fear of noise
- Hippophobia	Fear of horses

• Without inventors, the world of science—and life itself—would still be in the dark ages. Identify the inventor of the following materials or devices.

- Dynamite	Alfred Nobel (Sweden, 1866)
- The stock ticker	Thomas Edison (U.S., 1869)
- The lighting rod	Benjamin Franklin (U.S., 1752)
- Friction lighting matches	John Walker (England, 1827)
- The magnetic telegraph	Samuel Morse (U.S., 1837)
- Vulcanized rubber for carriage tires	Robert Goodyear (U.S., 1839)
- The cotton gin	Eli Whitney (U.S., 1793)
- The revolving pistol (revolver)	Samuel Colt (U.S., 1836)
- The pendulum	Galileo Galilei (Italy, 1583)
- The gas-flame burner	Robert Wilhelm Bunsen (Germany, 1855)
- The airship (blimp or dirigible)	Count Ferdinand von Zeppelin (Germany, 1900)

• As we gaze at the stars on a clear night, they seem to flash or twinkle. What causes this? — Uneven heat distribution in the earth's atmosphere

• What force can either propel a car into motion or stop it? — Friction

• The pull of gravity of a gyroscope enables it to circle around the tip of a pencil without falling off. What is this effect called? — Precession

• In the zero-gravity, conditions of space, when suddenly "weightless" people and objects float, they are actually doing what? — Freefalling

• Fill in the blanks for these two environmental statements:

- Oil, coal, and natural gas are all _____ fuels. — Fossil

- The presence of heavy carbon dioxide particles in the earth's atmosphere, letting the sun's heat in but not out, is responsible for the _____ _____. — Greenhouse Effect

• When individuals suffer from "hyperopia," they are _____ sighted. — Far

• Aristotle taught that all things are made up of combinations of four great elements. Name these Aristotelian elements. — Earth, air, fire, and water

• _____ is the universal solvent. — Water

• Fill in the blanks for these general scientific statements:

- Mixing the flavors coffee and _____ produces mocha. — Chocolate

- _____ is so named because of its 100 feet. — Centipede

- A _____ is a type of medium-density matter that always takes the shape of its container. — Liquid

- When a magnet is rubbed over a piece of iron numerous times, the iron becomes _____. — Magnetized (it becomes a weak magnet, too)

- _____ is the chemical that gives plants their green color.	Chlorophyll
- _____ is the study of trait inheritance in living things.	Genetics
• The energy given off by a moving object is known as what? Stored energy, the energy "lurking" in a raised weight before it falls, for example, is called what?	Kinetic energy; potential energy
• Why would a massive contingent of marching soldiers be commanded to stagger their steps when crossing a bridge?	If they stepped in time, the resulting vibration could shake the bridge to pieces
• What atmospheric phenomenon occurs when a rocket breaks— or slows down to meet—the sound barrier?	A sonic boom
• What spiraling, molecule of nucleic acid did Francis Crick and James Watson unravel in 1944?	DNA (Deoxyribonucleic Acid)
• Name the largest mammal to have ever lived.	The blue whale
• An observer would say that birds fly in a "flock" and that cows graze in a "herd." What would a group of these animals be known as?	
- Bears	Sleuth
- Lions	Pride
- Ants	Formicary or colony
- Crows	Murder
- Wolves	Pack
- Bees	Swarm
- Fish	School
• Name the largest living lizard— a reptile that grows up to ten feet long and is found on several scattered Indonesian islands.	The komodo dragon
• What famous inventor said, "Genius is one percent inspiration and 99 percent perspiration"?	Thomas Edison
• What are the tiny blood vessels that connect veins to arteries?	Capillaries
• What "point" is met when heat turns a solid into a liquid?	The melting point
• What name is given to heat that is used to turn a liquid into a gas or a solid into a liquid rather than to raise temperature?	Latent heat
• Glass is not as solid as one might think—it flows. The seemingly solid substance of glass is actually a supercooled _____.	Liquid
• What natural substance makes up the major ingredient of glass?	Sand (silicon)
• A "mixture" is a combination of elements that can be easily separated; a "compound" is made of two or more elements that can't be easily separated. What must occur in order to create a compound out of a mixture?	A chemical reaction (usually attained by applying heat) that bonds molecules
• Give the chemical element corresponding to each of these symbols:	
- Hg	Mercury
- He	Helium
- C	Carbon
- O	Oxygen
- K	Potassium
- Na	Sodium
- N	Nitrogen
- S	Sulfur
- H	Hydrogen
- Pb	Lead
- Ag	Silver
• Which early 19th-century English physicist was the first to prove that the eye focuses on objects at various distances by changing the shape of its lens?	Thomas Young

• What vaccine was developed in 1955 while Dwight D. Eisenhower was President of the United States?	The polio vaccine
• Fill in the blanks:	
- A device used to change alternating electrical current into direct current is called a _____.	Rectifier
- The white, crystalline, magnesium sulfate powder often used as a laxative is known as _____ salts.	Epsom
- An _____ is a compound formed when inorganic or organic acids react with alcohols.	Ester
- A gently sloping strip of land along the margin of a body of water and washed by waves or tides is a _____.	Beach
- A free-moving manned vehicle for deep-sea exploration is called a _____.	Bathyscaphe
- A protein that catalyzes (chemically alters) a chemical reaction within a living organism is known as an _____.	Enzyme
- A molecule of linked amino acids is a _____.	Protein
- The study of ancient ruins and artifacts is called _____.	Archaeology
• How about some archaeology fill-in-the-blanks?	
- The famous boy-king of Egypt, whose tomb has become a world famous repository of archaeological treasures, went by the name _____.	Tutankhamen
- In 1709, a peasant digging a well above the Roman city Herculaneum brought up fragments of sculptured marble statues. When examined closely, the life-size "statues" were actually found to be body casts of people entombed in lava and ash. The peasant had unearthed victims of the eruption of Mt.Vesuvius in 79 A.D.in the buried city of _____.	Pompeii
• What was the name given to the fossil of a human woman—a bipedal, ape-like hominid who lived some four million years ago—discovered by Donald Johanson in November 1974?	"Lucy"
• Now for some animal descriptions and questions:	
- With the largest eye-to-body ratio of any animal, and with 100 times more light detectors in its huge eyes than there are in the human eye. This undersea animal devotes over half of its large brain to eyesight — so it can "jet" itself toward its prey. What is it?	The giant squid
- Other than at a zoo, why won't you ever see polar bears and penguins living in proximity?	Penguins live near the South Pole; Polar bears toward the North
- What fish, once believed to be extinct, was caught in a net off the coast of South Africa in 1938, and now is known as "the living fossil"?	The coelacanth
- What animal lives in a lodge—and never stops growing?	The beaver
- What fish has bones made of cartilage?	The shark
- Its saliva contains an anticoagulant; a heat-sensitive "nose-leaf" guides it to where the blood is nearest the surface of its victims.What is it?	A vampire bat
- One of its tusks spirals out through its mouth into a 7- or 8-foot-long spear, the tusk is used to cut through the ice so the creature can breathe. What is it?	The narwhal, a close relation to the whale
- It "walks" sideways on its ribs, levering itself with horny shields that grip the ground; "heat sensors" help it locate prey in the dark. What is it?	A snake
• What disease is known as the "white plague"?	Tuberculosis
• Where in the human body does the balance mechanism originate? What is this mechanism called?	The ear; It is known as the vestibular apparatus

- What number is written out as the digit 1, followed by one hundred zeros? — Googol

- Name the dinosaurs that correspond to the following nicknames:
    - "Terrible King Lizard" — Tyrannosaurus Rex
    - "Three-horned Face" — Triceratops
    - "Duck-billed Lizard" — Trachadon
    - "The Plated Lizard" — Stegosaurus
    - "Thunder Lizard" — Brontosaurus

- What small New Zealand lizard is said to be a survivor of the dinosaur age? — The tuatara

GEOGRAPHY
Trivia to Learn By

• If you were standing directly on Antarctica's South Pole facing north, which direction would you travel if you took one step backward?

North; from the South Pole, *all* directions are north

• Name the Greek librarian and astronomer who, in 200 B.C., was among the first to theorize that the earth might possibly be a sphere?

Eratosthenes

• The imaginary lines of latitude on the earth's surface run parallel and, therefore, are the same distance apart. How far apart are they in actual miles?

About 69 miles

• Earth's 360 longitudinal lines don't run parallel; instead, they meet at the poles and are the greatest distance apart at the equator. How many miles apart are they when they pass through the equator?

Also about 69 miles apart

• Only one state in the United States has never had a foreign flag fly over it. Which state is this that was never claimed by a foreign country?

Idaho

• Where is the only place on earth that a person can stand and see both the Atlantic and Pacific Oceans?

Mt. Irazu in Costa Rica, Central America (it stands 11,000 feet above sea level)

• After Canada and Mexico, what country is closest to the United States?

Russia (at the Bering Strait across from Alaska)

• What are the only three South American countries located along the Equator?

Brazil, Ecuador and Columbia

• What are the largest landforms on earth called, and how many of these landmasses are found on the earth?

Continents; seven

These next questions are for mountain buffs:

• What do geologists refer to as the "Ring of Fire"?

The outer edges of the Pacific Ocean from Japan to South America; they form a major "hot rim" of volcanic activity

• Where is the highest mountain in the Alps found? What is its name, and how tall is it?

On the border of France and Italy, Mont Blanc stands at 15,771 feet above sea level

• In 1889, Henry Morton Stanley was the first European to reach the range of mountains that run along the Uganda-Zaire border of Central Africa.What is the range called?

Mountains of the Moon

• The Arlberg, the Brenner, the Saint Bernard, and the Simplon are all names of what geographical features?

Mountain passes in the Swiss Alps

• In which country are the Smokey Mountains found?

The United States

• Give the countries or locales that feature these mountain ranges:

- The Urals

Russia

- The Grampians

Scotland

- The Pennines

England

- The Pindus Range

Greece

- The Carpathians

Romania

- The Grand Tetons

The United States

- The Massif Central

France

• Rivers are even "stronger" than the highest mountains. What river, for example, cut and shaped the famous Grand Canyon in Arizona?

The Colorado

• A river in West Africa that flows from the mountains of Guinea toward the Sahara Desert and then turns south to join the sea in Eastern Nigeria is known as the "Strong Brown God." What is this river's name?

The Niger River

- What dams are found on these rivers?
  - Tennessee — Pickwick
  - Columbia — Grand Coulee
  - Missouri — Fort Peck
  - Colorado — Hoover
  - Sacramento — Shasta
- Rivers either dry up or eventually flow to an ocean or sea. These questions deal with rivers, seas and oceans:
  - What is the world's largest sea, which lies on the northern border of Iran and spanning 143,550 square miles? — The Caspian Sea
- Reaching 5,315 feet deep and found in Siberia, what is the world's deepest lake? — Lake Baikal (Baykal)
- Lake Eyre, the Dead Sea, the Salton Sea, and the Caspian Sea all possess what common feature besides water. What is it? — They are all below sea level
- Of all the North American Great Lakes, which is the largest? — Lake Superior, covering 31,800 square miles
- What river gave India its name? — The Indus
- Only one town in the United States bears the official name of Beach. In what state is the town of Beach found? — North Dakota
- What's so special about the Pacific Ocean's Mariana Trench? — It is the deepest known spot (36,201 feet deep) in any ocean
- Where was Captain Bligh's ship "The Bounty" bound with its cargo of breadfruit trees to in the novel and true-life saga Mutiny on the Bounty? — Jamaica
- Name the body of water into which these rivers flow:
  - The Mississippi — The Gulf of Mexico (in the Atlantic Ocean)
  - The Vistual — The Baltic Sea
  - The Columbia — The Pacific Ocean
  - The Indus — The Bay of Bengal (in the Indian Ocean)
  - The Colorado — The Gulf of California (a finger of the Pacific Ocean)
  - The Tigris — The Arabian (or Persian) Gulf (a finger of the Indian Ocean)
  - The Jordan — The Dead Sea
  - The Zaire — The Atlantic Ocean
  - The Saskatchewan — Hudson Bay (in the North Atlantic Ocean)
  - The Nile — The Mediterranean Sea
- Most islands are surrounded by some body of water, with the obvious exception of a desert oasis, which is usually surrounded by sand. What group of islands, consisting of Pinta, Pinzon, Santa Cruz and Isabella, were made famous by Charles Darwin's expedition on the *Beagle?* — The Galapagos Islands
- What straits separate the following countries:
  - Cuba and Haiti — Windward Passage
  - Luzon and Taiwan — The Luzon Strait
  - Ireland and Wales — The Saint George Channel
  - France and Great Britain — The English Channel (or Strait of Dover)
  - Korea and Japan — The Korean Strait
  - Spain and Morocco — The Strait of Gibraltar
  - Sri Lanka and India — The Palk Strait

• What is the only inhabited island continent? It was first settled by Europeans as a penal colony.	Australia
• In A.D. 986, Norseman Eric the Red discovered the largest island in the Atlantic Ocean, measuring 840,000 square miles. What island is this?	Greenland
• If you lived near the Indian Ocean, what would you call a hurricane? What if you lived in East Asia?	A cyclone; a typhoon
• In the spring, when cool, dry air from Canada collides with warm, wet air from the Gulf of Mexico, what is generally formed in Oklahoma, Kansas and Arkansas? What do they call this storm in Iowa?	A tornado; a cyclone
• 1990's "Operation Desert Storm" was fought in what two middle Eastern countries?	Kuwait and Iraq
• In 1487, a delegation of Aztecs from throughout Mexico, gathered at Tenochtitlan for a massive four-day ceremony to dedicate their great temple by ritualistically killing somewhere between 10,600 and 80,400 people. What name is Tenochtitlan known as today?	Mexico City
• An ethnic and literary term meaning "noble" was twisted by the Nazis and others into a racist term designating "superior beings." The "noble" people referred to did in fact once exist but not as a racial entity. They consisted of an assortment of Indo-European speaking Asiatic tribes who invaded and settled the Iranian plateau and the Indian subcontinent during the second millennium B.C. What was the name of these people?	Aryans
• Give the country or countries usually associated with these major ethnic groups:	
- Quebecois	Canada
- Kurds	Iraq
- Basques	Spain, France
- Ukrainians	Russia
• If it weren't for explorers, much of earth's vastness, as we know it today, would still be unidentified. In 1524, what Italian navigator was supposedly the first European to visit the site of New York City?	Giovanni Da Verrazano
• What explorers "discovered" these other sites:	
- The Bering Strait in 1728	Vitus Bering
- Antarctica in 1842	Sir James Clark Ross
- Angel Falls, Venezuela in 1935	Jimmy Angel
- Old Faithful Geyser in Yellowstone Park, Wyoming, in 1870	General Henry D. Washburn
• What well-known type of porcelain is named after the Asian Country that was famous for producing it?	China
• What five Asian countries are landlocked (i.e., do not border on water?)	Afghanistan, Mongolia, Nepal, Bhutan and Laos
• Thailand once went by what name?	Siam
• What Asian country is the only country in the world to have a Hindu monarchy?	Nepal
• In what Asian British colony can you find Causeway Bay, Repulse Bay, Aberdeen, Happy Valley, and Victoria Peak?	Hong Kong
• In an authentic Chinese meal, what is the last course that allows the roast duck entre to "swim" toward its digestion?	Soup
• What Thai city is also known as "The Venice of Asia"?	Bangkok
• What Russian city, built on a network of canals, is called "The Venice of the Baltic"? What is the former name of this city?	St.Petersburg (Petrograd); Leningrad
• The cities of Karachi, Rawalpindi, and Islambad were all once capitals of which Middle Eastern country?	Pakistan
• Out of China's 57 ethnic groups, which one comprises 94 percent of the total Chinese population?	The Han

- What large, tubular variety of grass inspired the design of the Chinese junk (a type of flat-bottomed sailing vessel), with its series of independent, waterproof compartments? — Bamboo
- What Asian country supports half the world's silk distribution? — China
- What Middle Eastern country has the world's largest petroleum reserves? — Saudi Arabia
- Give the base currency used in the following countries:
  - Japan — Yen
  - Austria — Schilling
  - Holland — Guilders
  - Russia — Rubles
  - Hong Kong — Dollars
  - Mexico — Pesos
  - Belgium — Francs
  - China — Yuan
  - Zambia — Qwachas (Kwachas)
  - Portugal — Escudos
  - South Africa — Rands
- Stonehenge, the famous arrangement of upright megalithic stones set in concentric circles and probably used anciently for astronomical observations, is located on a notable plain in Wiltshire, England? What is the name of this plain, and who were the builders of Stonehenge? — Salisbury Plain; its builders remain a mystery
- In what famous 18th-century Scottish textile center was the popular paisley design developed? — Paisley, Scotland
- Bosnia, Herzegovina, and Montenegro were once part of what former European country? — Yugoslavia
- How do bullfights in Spain differ from bullfights in Portugal? — In Spain the bull is killed
- On the lid of a Haagen Das ice cream container, there is a Scandinavian map demarcating the cities Oslo and Copenhagen. Where is this ice cream actually manufactured? — Teaneck, New Jersey
- On what river can you find Cambridge, England? — On the Cam
- Stephen Foster's song "Swanee River" speaks of a river that flows out of the Okefenokee Swamp and makes its way through which two U.S. states before being deposited in what body of water? — It flows through Georgia and Florida on its way to the Gulf of Mexico
- What are the English equivalents of these European country names?
  - Sverige — Sweden
  - Norge — Norway
  - Ellas — Greece
  - Polska — Poland
  - Magyar — Hungary
  - Suisse — Switzerland
  - Espana — Spain
  - Deutschland — Germany
  - Suomi — Finland
  - Eire — Ireland
- What does the Russian word "kremlin" mean? — Castle
- What is the "buffer" state that separates Russia from China? — Mongolia
- Identify the South American countries in which these dances originated:
  - The Tango — Argentina
  - The Samba — Brazil
  - The Joropo — Venezuela

- What South American country, lying just south of Panama, is famous for its exports of cut flowers, pop-up books and clothing? What other, less desirable products are also exported from this country? — Colombia; marijuana and cocaine

- Amerindians, as well as the descendants of African, British, East Indian, Portuguese and Chinese settlers and slaves all reside in one of the smallest South American countries, known as the "land of the six peoples." Name the country. — Guyana

- From what country do brazil nuts generally come? — Bolivia

- Which two South American countries are landlocked (do not border either ocean)? — Paraguay and Bolivia

- What famous U.S. Secretary of Treasury was born on the Caribbean Island of Nevis in 1757? — Alexander Hamilton

- What eastern U.S. State is named after a Greek Island? — Rhode Island (after the Island of Rhodes)

- What is the largest island in the Mediterranean Sea? — Sicily

- What famous U.S. island, ironically and affectionately known as "The Rock", once served as a maximum security prison? In what bay does it lie? — Alcatraz; San Francisco Bay

- The Pacific Ocean is nearly twice the size of what other major body of water? — The Atlantic Ocean

- What does "Baton Rouge" mean in French? — Red Stick

- Give the states that go by the following nicknames:
    - The Lone Star State — Texas
    - The Sunshine State — Florida
    - The Beehive State — Utah
    - The Show Me State — Missouri
    - The Big Bend State or The Volunteer State — Tennessee
    - The Silver State — Nevada
    - The Sooner State — Oklahoma
    - The Empire State — New York
    - The Beaver State — Oregon
    - The Garden State — New Jersey

- In what city was the first U.S. zoo built in 1876? — Philadelphia, Pennsylvania

- Which city boasts the longest subway system in the U.S.? What city has the longest "underground railroad" in the world? — New York; London

- What U.S. state capital claims over 30 Buddhist Temples? — Honolulu

- What transcontinental railroad has 97 stops within its 5,799-mile route, and served as the setting for a best-selling Agatha Christie mystery novel? — The Trans-Siberian Railway or "Orient Express"

- The word *orient* refers to the "East"; what corresponding word refers to the "West"? — *Occident*

- Where can you find the subway system *Metropolitana*? — Rome, Italy

- In the United States, state capitals aren't necessarily the largest cities in their states. Give the capital and state that corresponds with each of these "larger cities":
    - Los Angeles — Sacramento, California
    - New York City — Albany, New York
    - Detroit — Lansing, Michigan
    - Miami — Tallahassee, Florida
    - Seattle — Olympia, Washington
    - Wichita — Topeka, Kansas
    - Chicago — Springfield, Illinois
    - Portland — Salem, Oregon
    - New Orleans — Baton Rouge, Louisiana
    - Pittsburgh — Harrisburg, Pennsylvania

- Many names for common goods, foods, entertainments and countless other items contain an adjective depicting a special nation or locale associated with the item, such as Roman numerals and Japanese beatles. Fill in the adjectival form of a nation or region to complete the list below:

- _____ jumping beans	Mexican
- _____ horn	French
- _____ bacon	Canadian
- _____ cheese	Swiss or American
- _____ measles	German
- _____ delight	Turkish
- _____ rug	Oriental
- _____ flu	Asian
- _____ bank account	Swiss

- A gigantic scar left on the earth's crust, measuring 177 meters (580 feet) deep and 1,250 meters (4,100 feet) wide and probably formed by a meteorite, was discovered in Arizona in 1891 near Canyon Diablo. What name was given to this remarkable landmark? — Barringer Meteorite Crater

- In what Western U.S. state can you find the Petrified Forest, a forest of ancient logs that have been turned to stone through mineralization? — Arizona

- Countries are often equated with their national dishes. However, often a country's "native" food originated somewhere else. Name the country that created the following dishes:

- Swiss Steak	The United States
- Chop Suey	The United States
- Russian Dressing	The United States
- Hamburger in a bun	The United States

- What country or region did each of these cooking herbs and spices come from?

- Bay leaves	The Mediterranean
- Basil	India
- Vanilla	Tropical America
- Ginger	India and China
- Allspice	The Caribbean
- Chives	China
- Cloves	Southeast Asia
- Caraway Seeds	Turkey
- Cinnamon	Southeast Asia
- Paprika	Tropical America
- Cumin	The Nile Valley

- What mountain range makes up "the backbone" of Italy? — The Apennines

- Kicking Horse Pass is found in what North American mountain range? — The Rockies

- What Himalayan mountain is considered by local inhabitants as the "Goddess Mother of the Earth"? — Mt. Everest

- What island chain is home to Volcano National Park? — The Hawaiian Islands

- In which U.S. state would you find the gigantic, eroded volcanic ash monument known as "Devil's Tower"? — Wyoming

HISTORY

Trivia to Learn By

• When the American colonists began discussing rebellion against the British crown, those who favored liberation by force were known as "patriots." What were the colonists called who were horrified by the thought of armed rebellion?

"Loyalists"

• Those who opposed ratification of the U.S. Constitution in 1787-1788 were called what?

Antifederalists

• Why did so many late 18th Century colonists in British North America feel that the British had no right to tax them?

"No taxation without representation" - they had no representatives in Parliament

• Who did Mia Farrow call "Charlie Brown" because he furrowed his brow like the cartoon character?

Her one time husband, Frank Sinatra

• Which U.S. President lifted his shirt to show the world the long diagonal scar from his kidney stone and gall bladder operation?(Hint:he also pulled the ears of his pet beagle).

Lyndon B. Johnson

• In 1952, the movie "Bwana Devil" featured an innovation that made the audience feel as though they had landed inside the picture. What was this visual effect called?

3-D (for *three dimensional viewing*)

• On July 29, 1981, one of the most expensive and most witnessed weddings in the world attracted over 700 million TV viewers around the world. Whose wedding was it, and in what church did it take place?

Prince Charles and Lady Diana Spencer's; at St. Paul's Cathedral in London

• Flight engineer Judith A. Resnik, who two years earlier had been the second U.S. woman in space, and high-school teacher Christa McAuliffe were both killed in what January 1986 space disaster?

The explosion of the space shuttle *Challenger*

• In the Bible, baby Moses was set adrift in what river?

The Nile

• One of the oldest inhabited areas in the Middle East is the region known as Mesopotamia. What does "Mesopotamia" mean?

"The land between two rivers"

• In Mesopotamia around 2600 B.C., what was the regular tradition observed by the royal servants after their masters died?

Suicide, so they could continue their service in the next life

• To keep out the hordes of nomads invading China around 221 B.C., Zheng, the "First August Lord" of China began building what?

China's Great Wall

• Which Roman scholar, known as "The Censor," campaigned against Greek influence in Roman life?(Clue: He died in 149 B.C. at the age of 85?

Cato

• What was Chinese philosopher Confucius' real name?

Kung Fu Tzi

• One of Central Europe's most notorious mass murderers during the 1400s, Count Vlad IV was also known as _____, which means "devil."

Dracula

• Which 18th-century Japanese emperor opened Japan to Western influence after nearly 700 years?

Meiji

• After the death of Vladimir Lenin, what former leader of the Bolshevik Revolution in Russia lost control of the country to Joseph Stalin?

Leon Trotsky

• Dr. John Styth Pemberton concocted a cocaine-laced drink which he dubbed "French Wine of Coca." Finally, in 1889, he decided on a catchier name. What was that name? (Hint:The cocaine was later replaced by caffeine.)

Coca-Cola

• What was the name of Orville and Wilbur Wright's first air plane?

"Flyer I"

• On December 4, 1908, who became the first African-American to win the World Heavyweight Boxing title in Sydney, Australia?

Jack Johnson

• What Italian Fascist chief dubbed himself "Il Duce" (The Leader) in Rome in November, 1921?

Benito Mussolini

• What major gangster-style execution took place in Chicago on February 14, 1929, in which seven members of George "Bugsy" Moran's gang were massacred?

The St. Valentine's Day Massacre

- Name the dance crazes that correspond to the descriptions below:

- A Colonial dance involving high hand holding, a three-step strut and bowing.	The Minuet
- In this dance, one starts out in a sitting position with knees bent, hips back, and arms extended to the front, and then bounces in time with the music (1960s).	The Watusi
- In this dance the foot shuffles and kicks as the arms jerk back towards the chest as if pulling a horse's reins. (Hint:It is usually performed while imitating personalities, places or things, 1960.)	The Hully Gully
- This millie-girl flapper dance was dubbed "immoral" by the Catholic Church in 1926.	The Charleston
- A 1970s dance craze characterized by swivelling hips and pulsating lights, and inaugurated by the movie "Saturday Night Fever."	Disco
- A 1990s dance where dancers stop motion on the beat in frozen, glamourous poses.	Voguing/Posing

- What early to mid-19th-century American movement sought to achieve the immediate emancipation of all slaves? — The Abolitionist Movement

- What invasion was sponsored by the United States Government and futiley carried out by some 2,000 exiled Cubans on Cuba's Playa Giron on April 17, 1961? — Bay of Pigs

- The first Ten amendments to the U.S. Constitution are known as what? — The Bill of Rights

- What May 17, 1954 Supreme Court case ended the federal sanction of racial segregation? — Brown vs.The Board of Education of Topeka

- "Old Blood and Guts" was the nickname of what U.S. World War II general? — George S. Patton, Jr.

- What Japanese city was the target of the second American atomic bomb strike in 1945? — Nagasaki

- Name the European country that took no part in either World War I or World War II. — Switzerland

- What U.S. President was the first to survive being shot while in office? — Ronald Reagan

- What U.S. fort flew the flag that inspired Francis Scott Key to pen "The Star-Spangled Banner"? — Fort McHenry in Baltimore, Maryland

- What is the minimum age a U.S. presidential candidate must have attained in order to run for office? — 35

- What Czechoslovakian city was named "Rome of the North" in 1350 by Roman emperor Charles IV? — Prague

- What English king led the Third Christian Crusade in 1189-1192? (Hint:he failed to take Jerusalem but, after nearly bankrupting England, he did bring Cyprus under control.) — Richard I

- After twenty years of heretic hunting during the Roman Inquisition of the 1200s, what new strategy was authorized to coerce confessions of heresy? — Physical torture

- What was the name of the box used by the Hebrews to carry the tablets of the Ten Commandments during their wilderness wanderings? — The Ark of the Covenant

- What British monarch was dubbed "the Virgin Queen" in 1588? — Elizabeth I

- What measuring device, based on the principle that air expands when heated, was invented by Galileo Galilei in 1592? — The thermometer

- The expressed belief that Anglo-Saxon Americans were on a mission to expand their civilization and institutions across North America in the 1840s was known as what? — Manifest Destiny

- What 1966 Supreme Court case decision mandated that a verbal statement must be read to arrestees, informing them of their "right to remain silent"? — Miranda vs. Arizona

- Give the answer that corresponds to the given information about disasters around the world:
  - May 6, 1937: a German airship explodes over New Jersey while attempting to land.

    The Hindenburg disaster
  - August 6, 1945: the Japanese city of Hiroshima is devastated and lies in ruins.

    The first atomic bomb strike against an enemy nation
  - April 19, 1906: a disaster triggers numerous fires in San Francisco. Martial law, looters, and curfew limits follow.

    The San Francisco Earthquake
  - The year 1650: a sickness kills over 1 million people, ravaging Europe.

    Bubonic plague epidemic
  - August 28, 1883: In Java, a volcano erupts and kills over 30,000 people.

    The Krakatoa eruption
- To what two countries did the United States assign the label "yellow peril" during the 1890s?

  China and Japan
- Who was the first African-American U.S. Supreme Court Justice, a man who died in 1993?

  Thurgood Marshall
- How much money was George Willie fined for illegally scaling the World Trade Center in May 1977?

  One cent for each floor, bringing the total to $1.10
- On October 29, 1929 the Great Depression began. By what term is this date usually referred to?

  Black Tuesday
- Concerning Native American history:
  - In 1763, British Captain Simeon Ecuyer, serving in the American Colonies in defense of Fort Pitt (now Pittsburgh, Pa.), ordered blankets to be passed out to hostile Indians attacking the fort. Why?

    The blankets were infested with the small pox virus, to which the Indians had virtually no resistance. The strategy worked: the "enemy" was mercilessly decimated and the attack was thwarted
  - Ninety-five percent of the Native American population was wiped out during the 1800s. What was the major cause of this destruction?

    The transmition of European diseases
  - What do Kansas, Potomac, Delaware, Erie, Michigan, Illinois and Tulsa all have in common?

    They are all names of Native American origin
  - What does Okefenokee mean?

    "Land of trembling earth"
  - Name the five "civilized tribes" of the southeast.

    Choctaw, Creek, Cherokee, Seminole and Chickasaw
  - In 1838, 60,000 Cherokees, accompanied by an army escort, began a long march from their homes in the Southeast to reservations in Oklahoma. This "walk" claimed 4,000 Cherokee lives. What did the indians call this forced march?

    "The Trail of Tears"
  - During the Colonial era, the most advanced political body among Native American tribes was known as what? Which tribes did it include?

    The League of Iroquois; The Seneca, Oneida, Onondaga and Mohawk tribes, among others
- The year was 1992. What significant event occurred involving Illinois politician Carol Moseley Braun?

  She became the first African-American woman to be elected to the U.S. Senate
- What tropical disaster desolated Southeast Florida and Louisiana in August of 1992, leaving, in Florida alone, 90,000 homes destroyed and 86,000 people unemployed?

  Hurricane Andrew
- What country did the United Nations vote to expel from its membership on September 22, 1992?

  Yugoslavia
- What Jewish leader, after fighting for the Zionist Ideal for 55 years, negotiated a treaty of detente with Egypt in 1978? What was the name of the Egyptian leader who signed the treaty, and what honor were both given for their courageous act?

  Menachem Begin; President Anwar Sadat; the Nobel Peace Prize
- Although Egypt's President Sadat won widespread admiration for his peace making initiatives with Israel, he was severely criticized by other Arab leaders for negotiating independently, and was assassinated on Oct. 6, 1981. What was the nationality of his slayers?

  Egyptian (they were religious militants who opposed Sadat's politics)

- Who was the German counterpart of "Tokyo Rose," Japan's radio voice to American troops during World War II? **Axis Sally**

- Give the name of the U.S. President, presidential candidate, or First Lady that corresponds to each of these descriptions:

  - An Independent candidate in the 1980 campaign, he ruined the chances for Jimmy Carter's re-election, leaving Ronald Reagan as the victor. **John Anderson**

  - A Texas billionaire who entered the 1992 Presidential campaign. He later dropped out, then reentered the race. **H. Ross Perot**

  - As president, he pardoned both Tokyo Rose and Richard Nixon. **Gerald R. Ford**

  - He was elected to office twice, serving two separate terms (1885-1889 and 1893-1897). **Grover Cleveland**

  - He was not a member of any political party. **George Washington**

  - He was the first President to resign from office. **Richard Nixon**

  - While her husband was President, she was variously known as "The Presidentress," "Mrs. President" and "Lady Washington" **Martha Washington**

  - She became known as the "first woman president" when she assumed many of her husband's duties after he was incapacitated by a stroke. **Edith Galt Wilson, wife of Woodrow Wilson**

- What is the maximum number of years a president can now, by law, serve as President of the United States? What is the exception to this law? **Eight years is the maximum; however, when a Vice President becomes President after the elected President's death, he or she can later be elected to two full terms**

- What does it mean for the individual fate of each soldier when an Islamic leader calls for a Holy War, or *Jihad*? **Any Muslim who dies in battle will automatically be saved by Allah**

- In 1851, what did Elias Howe, Walter Hunt, and Isaac Merritt Singer all invent simultaneously, each in a different part of the United States? **The sewing machine**

- Who is famous for helping other black slaves escape the American South via "The Underground Railroad"? **Harriet Tubman**

- What Quaker abolitionist, often known as the "president of the Underground Railroad," helped over 3,000 blacks escape the South during the mid-1800s? **Levi Coffin**

- What was the name of the abolitionist newspaper, started by Frederick Douglass in 1847, that advised leaders in the North about the problems of freed African-American slaves? *The North Star*

- Identify these African-American slaves and former slaves:

  - In 1737, he and his son became the first African-American landowners in America, when 120 acres of farm land were conveyed to them in exchange for "seven thousand pounds of tobacco." **Robert Bannaky and his six-year-old son, Benjamin**

  - A well-know scholar, mathematician and astronomer, he published his own almanac in 1791 and sent it to President Thomas Jefferson along with a respectful letter appealing for equal rights for blacks. **The same Benjamin Bannaky, having taken the last name "Banneker"**

  - Believing himself to be an instrument of divine justice, he led seventy five slaves in a bloody and successful siege on a Virginia armory killing more than 50 whites before being captured and executed. **Nat Turner; the revolt was the so-called Southampton Insurrection, the most substantial U.S. slave revolt on record**

- Who led 13 whites and 5 blacks on an attack of the arsenal at Harper's Ferry in 1859, winning him posthumous fame as a hero and a martyr after he was captured and hanged? (Hint: a song commemorating his deeds and "soul" soon swept the North and is still well-known today.) **John Brown; The song is "John Brown's Body"**

- What African-American freedom fighters spoke or wrote these words?

- "I pity the poor in bondage who have none to help them. That is why I am here. It is my sympathy with the oppressed and wronged who are as good as you and as precious in the sight of God. If it is necessary that I lose my life in the cause of justice, I say, let it be done." (1859)	John Brown
- "Liberty must cut the throat of slavery or have its own throat cut by slavery . . . Let the slaves and free colored people be called into service and formed into a liberating army to march into the South and raise the banner of Emancipation among the slaves." (1861)	Frederick Douglass
- "Remember that ours is not a war for robbery nor to satisfy our passions. It is a struggle for freedom. Ours must be deeds, not words." (1831)	Nat Turner
- "Sir, I freely and cheerfully acknowledge that I am of the African race, and in that color which is natural to them of the deepest dye. With profound gratitude to the Supreme Ruler I now confess to you that I am not under that state of inhuman captivity to which too many of my brethren are doomed, I have tasted the blessings of free and unequaled liberty." (1791)	Benjamin Banneker

- Two Frenchmen, Jacques Balmart and Michael-Gabriel Paccard, conquered the highest peak in Europe in 1786. Name the mountain. — Mont Blanc

- When Japan ousted him from the Philippines in 1942, what U.S. General left with the prophetic words, "I shall return"? — Douglas MacArthur

- What brand name sunglasses shaded General Douglas MacArthur's eyes from the sun? — Ray Ban

- Born in 1906, he was known as China's "Last Boy Emperor"? — Xuantong "Henry" Puyi

- After the English Parliament severed ties with the Roman Church in 1534, who officially became head of the Church of England? — King Henry VIII

- Who finally pushed King Henry VIII to leave the Catholic Church and form the Church of England after Pope Element VIII refused to annul his first marriage to Catherine of Aragon. — Anne Boleyn

- The *Baby Ruth* candy bar was named after the infant daughter of what U.S. President? — Grover Cleveland

- In 1977, the Coca-Cola Company (and its twenty-two bottling plants) was forced out of what country after refusing to reveal its secret formula? — India

- What famous waterway opened its "locks" on August 15, 1914? — The Panama Canal

- On September 16, 1630, the town of Shawmut, Massachusetts changed its name to what? — Boston

- What worldwide charity organization was established by William Booth in London on July 5, 1865? — The Salvation Army

- What English ruler won the nickname of "Good Queen Bess"? — Elizabeth I

- Who was the first U.S. President to televise a news conference? — Dwight D. Eisenhower

- How long did it take to erect the Berlin Wall in August 1961? — It was built overnight

- What was the profession of John Wilkes Booth, the man who shot President Abraham Lincoln? — Stage actor

- Who is the founding minister of the "Moral Majority"? — The Reverend Jerry Falwell

- What worldwide service organization did British Colonel Robert Baden-Powell form in 1907? — The Boy Scouts

- What was so significant about U.S. President Jimmy Carter's birth? — He was the first President born in a hospital

- German flying ace Manfred von Richthofen is also known by what noble nickname? — The Red Baron

- What British king lost the American Colonies to the Revolutionary War? — George III

- Give the historical figures corresponding to these given nicknames:
  - "The Maid of Orleans"   Joan of Arc
  - "The Cowboy President"   Theodore "Teddy" Roosevelt
  - "Tania"   Patricia Hearst
  - "The Birdman of Alcatraz"   Robert F. Stroud
  - "Billy the Kid"   William Bonney
  - "The Lone Eagle"   Charles A. Lindbergh
  - "Silver Fox"   Former First Lady Barbara Bush

  - "The Mad Monk"   Rasputin
  - "The Iron Lady"   Former English Prime Minister Margaret Thatcher

  - "Stonewall"   Confederate General Thomas Jackson

- What do the call letters in radio station WLS Chicago stand for? The call letters RCA?   World's Largest Store; Radio Corporation of America

- "Four score and seven years ago . . . " began what November 19, 1863 speech?   Abraham Lincoln's Gettysburg Address

- What name was seaman/pirate Edward Teach known as in 1718?   Blackbeard

- What term was used to signify the hostile, political contest conducted without direct military confrontation between the U.S. and the former Soviet Union?   Cold War

- This 11th-century fortress in London has functioned since as a palace, a mint, a prison, and an observatory. Name it.   London Tower

- What 1852 American novel by Harriet Beecher Stowe did much to galvanize Northern public opinion against slavery? What was the second part of its full "parenthetical" title?   *Uncle Tom's Cabin; Life Among the Lowly*

- What organization received the only Nobel Peace Prize awarded during World War I?   The International Red Cross

- According to Karl Marx, religion becomes the _____ of the people?   opiate

- What fellow German philosopher helped Karl Marx pen the *Communist Manifesto?*   Friedrich Engels

- Who is the African-American woman often credited with launching the Human Rights Movement of the 1960s when she refused to give up her bus seat to a white man in 1955?   Rosa Parks

- What was the name of the group who tossed 340 cases of tea from three British trade vessels into Boston Harbor as part of a tax protest on December 16, 1773?   The Sons of Liberty

- Where did the Clantons, McLowerys and Earps shoot it out on October 26, 1881?   The O.K. Corral

- The first Constitution of the United States, from 1781 until an official constitution went into effect in 1788, was known by what name?   The Articles of Confederation

- Which U.S. Constitutional Amendment inaugurated the prohibition of liquor in 1918? Which Amendment ended it in 1933?   The 18th Amendment; the 21st Amendment

- What 17th-century mountainman/trapper-turned Congressman became an idol for kids in 1955, boosting coonskin caps sales?   Davy Crockett

- Answer these questions pertaining to John F. Kennedy:
  - What was JFK's religious affiliation?   Roman Catholic; he was the first non-protestant to occupy the White House

  - Whose murder was the first-ever actually televised nationally? Who squeezed the trigger, and what was his last name at birth?   Lee Harvey Oswald's; Jack Ruby (Rubenstein)

  - Who was the New Orleans District Attorney obsessed with proving the existence of a conspiracy in JFK's assassination?   James Garrison

- What U.S.sponsored 1961 invasion triggered a chain of events that helped lead to the showdown over Russian missiles in Cuba?	The Bay of Pigs
- What blonde movie star was said to have been romantically linked to John F. Kennedy and his brother Robert?	Marilyn Monroe
- Who served as President Kennedy's Attorney General?	His brother Robert
- Which Kennedy brother was the only one to die during World War II?	Joseph P. Kennedy, Jr.
- What New-Orleans businessman went to trial on charges of conspiring to kill President Kennedy?	Clay Shaw; he was acquitted
- What number was painted on the side of Kennedy's naval PT boat?	109
- Who assassinated Robert Kennedy?	Sirhan Sirhan; he shot Kennedy during the Senator's 1968 Presidential bid
- Who lit the Eternal Flame at President Kennedy's tomb in Virginia in 1963? In what cemetery does the "eternal flame" still burn?	His widow, Jacqueline Bouvier Kennedy, Arlington National Cemetery
• Who led the revolt of Roman slaves and gladiators in 73 B.C.?	Spartacus the Thracian
• On May 4, 1970, a National Guardsmen fired into a crowd of students protesting the Vietnam War, killing four and wounding nine others. On what university campus did this tragedy take place?	Kent State, in Ohio
• What white supremacist organization takes its name from the Greek term for "Circle" or "Band"? It is also known as "Knights of the Great Forest"?	Ku Klux Klan
• What was Amelia Earhart attempting to do when she disappeared in 1937?	Fly around the world
• What terrorist group, led by Donald DeFreeze, kidnapped Patricia Hearst in 1974 and forced her to participate in several crimes?	Symbionese Liberation Army
• What employment did Patricia Hearst claim when she was booked? Name the U.S. President who pardoned her?	Urban Terrorist; Jimmy Carter
• Fill in each blank with correct war or type of war:	
- January 8, 1967, President Lyndon B. Johnson declared war against _____.	Poverty
- Florence Nightingale tended wounded troops who fought in the _____ War.	Crimean
- The longest war the United States was ever involved in was the _____ War.	Vietnam
- Nancy Reagan's "Just Say No" was the slogan in the 1980s war against _____.	Drugs
- The "Mother of all Wars" was the _____ War.	Persian Gulf (the term was coined by Saddam Hussein)
- The "War Between the States" was the _____ War.	U.S. Civil
- The 38th parallel divided two countries during the _____ War.	Korean (North and South Korea)
- When Mexico refused to accept the United States' annexation of Texas in 1845, the U.S. launched the _____ War.	Mexican
- Prior to World War II is/was also known as the _____ War.	Great
- How long did the "Hundred Years' War" actually last?	115 years
- The "War to End All Wars" was known as _____.	World War II

- What peace treaty ended World War I?
- The Battleship Missouri was the site of what Sept. 3, 1945 event?
- Whose kidnapping/murder was dubbed the "Crime of the Century" in the 1930s?
- What was the name of the 1960s radical group that included Abby Hoffman, Jerry Rubin, and Tom Hayden?
- Give the acronymic nickname for Members of the "Youth International Party."
- How many voyages had the Titanic completed when it struck an iceberg and sunk, taking some 1,500 people to their deaths on April 15, 1912?
- In 1957, what household item gave birth to the idea for the Frisbee Flying Disc?
- Before Christianity replaced it as the official religion in Western Europe in A.D. 391, what was the accepted religion of the region?
- The 19th-century factories that employed youth-workers, often under dangerous and unhealthy conditions, went by what name?
- What insect did John the Baptist eat while he was preaching as a "voice in the wilderness"?
- Before two-term limitations were imposed on the U.S. Presidency, how many four-year terms was Franklin Delano Roosevelt elected to?
- What religious holiday was Abraham Lincoln assassinated on?

- Who was serving as President of the U.S. Congress when the Declaration of Independence was signed in 1776?

The Treaty of Versailles

The Japanese surrender to the United States

Charles Lindbergh, Jr.'s

The Chicago Seven

Yippies

The ship was on its maiden voyage

A pie pan

Paganism

Sweatshops

Locusts

Four

Good Friday—the Friday before Easter

John Hancock

QUOTES

Trivia to Learn By

- What self-proclaimed philosopher came up with these two thought gems?
  "If you come to a fork in the road, take it."
  "You can observe a lot by watching."

  Baseball player Yogi Berra

- "To see life; to see the world; to eye-witness great events; to watch the faces of the poor and the gestures of the proud . . ." Publisher Henry R. Luce called this the mission of what classic American magazine?

  Life Magazine

- What quote, a classic consciousness-raiser that may have helped change history, first appeared on the cover of the October 1966 issue of Esquire magazine and was featured in the issue's account of battle action in Vietnam?

  "Oh, my god—we hit a little girl"

- Who said, "You're no John Kennedy," during the 1988 vice presidential debate? At whom was the quote directed?

  Sen. Lloyd Bensen made this observation to Sen. Dan Quayle

- What famous inventor said, "Results! Why, man I have gotten a lot of results. I know several thousand things that won't work"?

  Thomas Edison

- What great humanitarian said, "A man is ethical only when life, as such, is sacred to him, that of plants and animals as well as that of his fellow man, and when he devotes himself helpfully to all life that is in need of help"?

  Albert Schweitzer

- Fill in the blanks to complete these great commentaries on human nature and humankind:

  - One of the best temporary cures for pride and affectation is _____; a man who wants to vomit never puts on airs. (Josh Billings)

    Seasickness

  - A life spent in _____ _____ is not only more honorable but more useful than a life spent in doing nothing. (George Bernard Shaw)

    Making mistakes

  - "Moral indignation is _____ with a halo." (H.G. Wells)

    Jealousy

  - "Nothing in life is to be _____. It is only to be understood." (Marie Curie)

    Feared

  - "What is _____ in a country will be cultivated there." (Plato)

    Honored

  - "Fame creates its own standards. A guy who twitches his lips is just another guy with a lip twitch—unless he's _____ _____." (Sammy Davis, Jr.)

    Humphrey Bogart

  - "A man is _____ in proportion to the things he can afford to let alone." (Henry David Thoreau)

    Rich

  - "You grow up the day you have the very first _____—at yourself." (Ethel Barrymore)

    Laugh

  - "When a man has pity on all living creatures, then only is he _____." (Buddha)

    Noble

- "Do or do not. There is no try," was uttered by one of the greatest science fiction mentors of all time. Name this mighty warrior trainer of the Knights of Jedi.

  Yoda

- When Franklin D. Roosevelt noted during World War II that "All we have to fear is fear itself," he was actually paraphrasing an earlier adage: "Nothing is so much to be feared as fear." This maxim was originally penned in 1841 by what nature-loving philosopher?

  Henry David Thoreau

- Name the historical figure who coined each of these other versions of these "fearsome" sentiments.

  - "That thing I fear most is fear." (1580)

    Michel Eyquem de Montaigne

  - "Nothing is terrible except fear itself." (1623)

    Francis Bacon

  - "The only thing I am afraid of is fear." (1831)

    Duke of Wellington ("The Iron Duke")

- What famous comedian and movie director acclaimed for films such as "Hannah and Her Sisters" and "Take the Money and Run" said, "Eighty percent of success is showing up"? — Woody Allen

- What modern Spanish artist said, "God is really only another artist. He invented the giraffe, the elephant, the ant. He has no real style. He just goes on trying other things" ? — Pablo Picasso

- What comedian said, "My wife and I were happy for 20 years—then we met"? — Rodney Dangerfield

- What 1960s folk/rock singer said, "He who is not busy being born is busy dying"? — Bob Dylan

- According to Mark Twain, why doesn't the world owe you a living? — "It was here first."

- If death were a restaurant host or hostess, what would it say to you—according to Robin Williams? — "Your table is ready."

- For each adage, fill in both blanks with the same word:
  - "_____ thy business or it will _____ thee." (Benjamin Franklin) — Drive
  - "Ask not what your _____ can do for you, but ask what you can do for your _____." (John F. Kennedy) — Country
  - "I am ready to meet my _____, but whether my _____ is prepared for the great ordeal of meeting me is another matter." (Winston Churchill) — Maker
  - "Put all your eggs in one _____ and WATCH that _____." (Mark Twain) — Basket
  - "The _____ always happens that you really believe in! And the belief in a _____ makes it happen." (Frank Lloyd Wright) — Thing
  - "_____ walking and _____ smiling." (Ukeleleist Tiny Tim) — Keep
  - "If you trap the moment before it's _____, the tears of repentance you'll certainly wipe. But if you let the _____ moment go, you can never wipe off the tears of woe." (William Blake) — Ripe
  - "The superior man _____ always of virtue; the common man _____ of comfort." (Confucius) — Thinks
  - "First we _____ habits, then they _____ us." (Dr. Robert Gilbert) — Form
  - "In the last analysis, our only _____ is the _____ to discipline ourselves." (Bernard Baruch) — Freedom
  - "_____ for things we did can be tempered by time; it is _____ for the things we did not do that is inconsolable." (Sydney J. Harris) — Regret

- Below are some U.S. Presidential and vice presidential quotes. Give the person who said:
  - "Khadafi, you can run but you cannot hide." — Ronald Reagan, just after launching a strike against Libya in 1986
  - "I tried pot once. I didn't like it and I didn't inhale." — Arkansas Gov. Bill Clinton in the 1992 presidential race
  - "Slow down, take a breath—inhale." — Vice President Dan Quayle in the 1992 Vice presidential debates
  - "Friends this is political garbage." — 1988 Presidential candidate Massachusetts Governor Michael Dukakis after reading a pamphlet by Reagan supporters about convicted killer Willie Horton in Massachusetts

- "I like a little rebellion now and then."

Thomas Jefferson when he learned about the Shay's farmer rebellion in 1786

- Fill in the blanks for the quotes listed below:
    - Publilius Syrus: "I have often regretted my speech, never my _____." — **Silence**
    - John Wesley: "Though I am always in haste, I am never in a _____." — **Hurry**
    - Alfred, Lord Tennyson: "'tis better to have loved and _____ than never to have loved at all." — **Lost**
    - Samuel Goldwyn: "I don't want any `yes-men' around me. I want everybody to tell me the truth even if it costs them their _____." — **Jobs**
    - Richard Nixon: "Don't try to take on a new _____, it doesn't work." — **Personality**
    - Lewis Grizzard: "Life is like a dogsled team. If you ain't the lead dog, the _____ never changes." — **Scenery**
    - Ralph Waldo Emerson: "All life is an _____." — **Experiment**
- What famed pediatrician advised parents to "Love 'em; feed 'em; leave 'em alone"? — **Dr. Benjamin Spock**
- Give the actor or actress famous for the following lines:
    - "Well, you look about like an angel. I'd guess sort of a fallen angel, aren't you? What happened to your wings?" — **Jimmy Stewart ("It's a Wonderful Life" 1946)**
    - "May the force be with you, Luke." — **Sir Alec Guinness ("Star Wars" 1977)**
    - "I'm afraid of nothing except being bored." — **Greta Garbo ("Cammile" 1936)**
    - "Insanity runs in my family. It practically gallops." — **Cary Grant ("Arsenic and Old Lace" 1944)**
    - "A free man dies, he loses the pleasure of life; a slave loses pain. Death is the only freedom a slave knows. That's why he's not afraid of it. That's why we'll win." — **Kirk Douglas ("Spartacus" 1960)**
    - "Remember, no bastard ever won a war by dying for his country. He won it by making the other poor, dumb bastard die for his country." — **George C. Scott ("Patton" 1970)**
    - "Oh, no. It wasn't the airplanes. It was beauty killed the beast." — **Robert Armstrong ("King Kong" 1933)**
    - "Hello, gorgeous." — **Barbara Streisand ("Funny Girl" 1968)**
    - "Rosebud!" — **Orson Welles ("Citizen Kane" 1941)**
    - "Louis, I think this is the beginning of a beautiful friendship." — **Humphrey Bogart ("Casablanca" 1942)**
- What general said, "I know only two tunes: one of them is `Yankee Doodle,' and the other isn't"? — **Ulysses S. Grant**
- And who quipped, "Wagner's music is better than it sounds"? — **Mark Twain**
- Fill in the blanks:
    - "At the precise moment you take off your shoe in a shoe store, your _____ _____ will pop out of your sock to see what's going on." (Allen Ginsburg) — **Big toe**
    - "____ is a friend to silence." (Mother Teresa) — **God**
    - "Anybody who keeps a chip on his shoulder isn't _____ much wood." (Ronald Reagan) — **Chopping**
    - "God will not look you over for medals, degrees or diplomas, but for _____." (Elbert Hubbard) — **Scars**
    - "Plastic surgery is a science that can do anything with a human _____ except keep it out of other people's business." (Robert Redford) — **Nose**

- "After silence, that which comes nearest to expressing the inexpressible is _____." (Aldous Huxley)	Music
- "The darkest hour in any man's life is when he sits down to plan how to get _____ without earning it." (Horace Greeley)	Money
- "You can get _____ in life you want if you help enough other people get what they want." (Zig Ziglar)	Everything
- "_____ should merely indicate where smiles have been." (Mark Twain)	Wrinkles
- "_____ is the only drink for a wise man." (Henry David Thoreau)	Water
- "You can't say that civilization don't advance. For every war they _____ you in a new way." (Will Rogers)	Kill

• What does "Two all beef patties, special sauce, lettuce, cheese, pickles, onions on a sesame seed bun" describe?	A McDonald's Big Mac
• What is the Girl Scout motto?	"Be Prepared" (same as the Boy Scouts')
• "He ain't heavy. He's my brother" is the motto for what well-known refuge?	Father Edward J. Flanagan's Boy Town near Omaha, Nebraska

• Who made these words famous?

- "That's another fine mess you've gotten us into."	Oliver Hardy
- "You blockhead."	Charles M. Schultz' Lucy van Pelt
- "I am not an animal. I am a human being."	John Merrick—the Elephant Man
- "You look maaaaarvalous."	Billy Crystal
- "Eat my shorts."	Bart Simpson

• Sports personalities have given us many great lines, some quite profound. Who spoke these lines?

- "You can't think and hit at the same time."	Yogi Berra
- "You don't save a pitcher for tomorrow. Tomorrow it may rain."	Leo Durocher
- "The only reason I ever played golf in the first place was so I could afford to hunt and fish."	Sam Snead
- "You gotta be a man to play baseball for a living, but you gotta have a lot of little boy in you, too."	Roy Campanella
- "Pro football is like nuclear warfare. There are no winners, only survivors."	Frank Gifford
- "If people don't want to come out to the park, nobody's going to stop them."	Yogi Berra

• Name the product or organization whose catchlines are or were:

- "The real thing"	Coca-Cola
- "Be all that you can be"	The U.S. Army
- "Just do it"	Nike athletic shoes
- "You're in good hands with the good hands people"	Allstate Insurance
- "Put a tiger in your tank"	Exxon petroleum
- "Built to stay tough"	Chevy Trucks
- "The few, the proud"	The U.S. Marine Corps
- "Follow the leader"	Honda motorcycles
- "Is it live or is it . . . ?"	Memorex audio tapes
- "You asked for it. You got it"	Toyota automobiles
- "Two, two, two mints in one"	Certs breath mints
- "Reach out and touch someone"	Bell Systems telephone company

- "When it rains, it pours"	Morton Salt
- "The King of Beers"	Budweiser
- "They're grrrrrreat!"	Kellogg's Sugar Frosted Flakes
- "Brush your breath"	Dentyne chewing gum
- "No more tears"	Johnson and Johnson baby products
- "Don't leave home without it"	American Express charge card
- "Plop-plop, fizz-fizz"	Alka Seltzer
- "Get a piece of the rock"	Prudential Insurance
- "Does she . . . or doesn't she?"	Miss Clairol hair color
- "Have it your way"	Burger King
- "It's fun to put snap, crackle and pop into your morning"	Kellogg's Rice Crispies

- Who always signed off, "Goodnight, Mrs. Calabash, wherever you are"? — Jimmy Durante

- "Whether women are better than men I cannot say—but I can say they are certainly no worse," was spoken by whom? The author of this quote was one-time leader of what country? — Golda Meir ; Israel

- Fill in the blanks for these quotations on women and the women's movement:

- "Once made equal to man, woman becomes his _____." (Socrates)	Superior
- "When an individual is kept in a situation of inferiority, the fact is that ____ does become inferior." (Simone de Beauvoir)	the individual
- "A woman has to be _____ as good as a man to go _____ as far." (Fannie Hurst)	Twice; half
- "Well, it's hard for a _____ _____ to believe that woman doesn't have equal rights." (Dwight D. Eisenhower)	Mere man
- "Women should remain at _____, sit _____, keep _____, and bear and bring up _____." (Martin Luther)	Home; still; house; children
- "Resolved, that the women of this nation in _____ [a date], have greater cause for discontent, rebellion and revolution than the men of _____ [another date]." (Susan B. Anthony)	1876; 1776

- What amusement park claims to be "the happiest place on earth"? — Disneyland / Disneyworld

- Ringling Brothers and Barnum and Bailey Circus' slogan is what? — "The Greatest Show on Earth"

- What patriot shouted, "The British are coming! The British are coming"? — Paul Revere

- What literary figure said, "Off with her head"? — The Queen of Spades (*Alice's Adventures in Wonderland*)

- What animated movie character sang, "Someday my prince will come"? — Snow White

- When Jesus hung on the cross, he pronounced a blessing of forgiveness on his executioners. What were the words he used? — "Forgive them Father, for they know not what they do."

- "For some good advice on how to live ask someone who knows he's dying" was said by which advice columnist? — Abigail van Buren

- "The way to see by faith is to shut the eye of _____" was coined by Benjamin Franklin. — Reason

- What Chinese philosopher said, "With only plain rice to eat, with only water to drink, and with only an arm for a pillow, I am still content"? — Confucius

- Which Shakespearean characters said these lines?
    - "Out, damned spot! out I say."
    - "I die, Horatio."
    - "If we shadows have offended
      Think but this, and all is mended—"
    - "Killing myself, I die upon a kiss."
    - "I dreamt a dream tonight."
    - "In praising Antony, I have dispraised Caesar."
    - "Upon that I kiss your hand, and I call you my Queen."
    - "I am very glad of it: —I'll plague him; I'll torture him."
    - "He receives comfort like cold porridge"
    - "Heaven truly knows that thou art false as hell."

Lady Macbeth
Hamlet
Puck (in "A Midsummer Night's Dream")
Othello
Romeo
Cleopatra
King Henry VIII

Shylock, in "The Merchant of Venice"
Sebastian, in "The Tempest"
Othello
Edgar Allen Poe

- What famous mystery/horror writer wrote, "Lo! 'tis a gala night within the lonesome latter years"?
- In what movies did these lines appear?
    - "I've grown accustomed to her face."
    - "I don't know nothin' 'bout birthin' babies!"
    - "Where does he get those wonderful toys?"
    - "If she was president, she'd be Babe-raham Lincoln."
    - "We are not alone."

    - "So let it be written—so let it be done."
    - "Go ahead, make my day."
    - "There's no place like home."
    - "I'm late for a very important date!"
    - "Oh, God! Look Mother, blood!"
    - "Let's make him an offer he can't refuse."
    - "Phone home."
    - "Seize the day!"from the Latin phrase "carpe diem"
    - "Tell me about the rabbits, George."
    - "Pardon me, is this the way to Europe, France?"
    - "Toga! Toga!"
    - "Let's consume mass quantities."
    - "Evacuate? In our moment of triumph!"

"My Fair Lady"
"Gone With the Wind"
"Batman the Movie" (1989)
"Wayne's World"
"Close Encounters of the Third Kind"
"The Ten Commandments"
"Sudden Impact"
"The Wizard of Oz"
"Alice in Wonderland"
"Psycho"
"The Godfather"
"E.T.— the Extra-terrestrial"
"Dead Poets Society"
"Of Mice and Men"
"Gentlemen Prefer Blondes"
"Animal House"
"Coneheads"
"Star Wars"

- What musicians said these lines?
    - "I write [music] as a sow piddles."
    - "I'll play it first and tell you what it is later."
    - "I haven't understood a bar of music in my life, but I have felt it."
    - "Listen, kid, take my advice, never hate a song that has sold a half-million copies!"

Mozart
Miles Davis
Igor Stravinsky

Irving Berlin to Cole Porter

- — - — - — - — - — - — -FOLD— - — - — - — - — - — -

Place
First-Class
Postage
Here

Compact Classics, Inc.
P.O. Box 526145
Salt Lake City, Utah 84152-6145

WE WOULD LIKE TO HEAR FROM YOU

❑ I am a new customer. Please put me on your mailing list.

Name_____

Address _____

City_____ State_____ Zip _____

Phone (   )_____

❑ I have a comment or idea.

Your ideas and suggestions will make a difference. In fact, we'll pay you $10.00 if you're the first to suggest a popular book or topic used in a future edition.

Below, please give us your suggestions or briefly describe favorite books or topics you'd like to see included in up-coming Compact Classics.

Comment:_____

_____

_____

_____

❑ I would like to order.

ORDER FORM

Complete Satisfaction Guaranteed! 30-Day Money Back Guarantee

Method of Payment:

Name _____

Address_____

City_____ State_____ Zip_____

Phone (   ) _____

Check One (To avoid delay, payment must accompany order)
❑ Check enclosed payable to Compact Classics
❑ Money Order (enclosed) Sorry, no C.O.D.'s or Cash
❑ VISA   ❑ MasterCard   ❑ Discover

Acct# _____ Exp. Dt. _____

Signature _____

Mail this form today, or for faster service call: TOLL-FREE 1-800-755-9777, 8 AM-6 PM (MST) Mon. - Fri.

Cover Selection	Qty.	Price	Total
The Great American Bathroom Book Vol. I ISBN 1-880184-04-4		$19.95	
The Great American Bathroom Book Vol. II ISBN 1-880184-10-9		$19.95	
Compact Classics Library Edition Vol. I ISBN 1-880184-01-X		$19.95	
Compact Classics Library Edition Vol. II ISBN 1-880184-11-7		$19.95	
Leather Library Edition Vol. I ISBN 1-880184-06-0		$49.95	
Planner Edition		$39.95	
Also available in many fine bookstores.	Shipping & handling (Utah residents add 6.25% sales tax)	$3.00	$3.00
		TOTAL	